Almanac of
American Military History

Almanac of American Military History

Volume II
1831–1913

Spencer C. Tucker

ABC-CLIO

Santa Barbara, California • Denver, Colorado • Oxford, England

Copyright 2013 by ABC-CLIO, LLC

Library of Congress Cataloging-in-Publication Data

Tucker, Spencer, 1937-
  Almanac of American military history. / Spencer C. Tucker.
      p.   cm.
  Includes bibliographical references and index.
  ISBN 978-1-59884-530-3 (hbk. : alk. paper) — ISBN 978-1-59884-531-0 (ebook)
 1. United States—History, Military.   I. Title.
  E181.T93   2013
  355.00973—dc23   2012034656

ISBN: 978-1-59884-530-3
EISBN: 978-1-59884-531-0

17 16 15 14 13   1 2 3 4 5

This book is also available on the World Wide Web as an eBook.
Visit www.abc-clio.com for details.

ABC-CLIO, LLC
130 Cremona Drive, P.O. Box 1911
Santa Barbara, California 93116-1911

This book is printed on acid-free paper ∞
Manufactured in the United States of America

CONTENTS

Volume I

Volume II

MOVING WEST
Conflict with Native Americans, the Mexican-American War, and Manifest Destiny, 1831–1849

BROTHER FIGHTING BROTHER
The American Civil War and the Era of Reconstruction, 1850–1877

EXPANSION AT HOME AND ABROAD
The Later Indian Wars, the Spanish-American War, and the Philippine-American War, 1878–1913

Volume III

THE WAR TO END ALL WARS
World War I and its Aftermath, 1914–1930

MOVING WEST

Conflict with Native Americans, the Mexican-American War, and Manifest Destiny, 1831–1849

OVERVIEW

Texan defenders are overrun by the Mexican Army at the Alamo in San Antonio on March 6, 1836, during the Texas Revolution. (Library of Congress)

In 1820, Connecticut-born entrepreneur Moses Austin traveled to San Antonio de Béxar to present to Spanish authorities his plan to bring North American colonists into Spanish-held Texas. Austin pledged to Antonio Mario Martínez, the governor of Coahuila y Texas, that Texan colonists would learn the Spanish language, convert to Catholicism, serve as a buffer between Mexico and raiding Comanches, and, after 10 years, sever all economic ties with the United States and trade exclusively within the Spanish Empire. Although he had misgivings, Martínez accepted Austin's offer. Moses Austin then returned to Missouri to recruit the 300 families stipulated in the treaty with Spain, but he died soon thereafter. His son, Steven Fuller Austin, now took up his father's agenda and assumed his father's role as *empresario*.

Austin chose as the site for the settlement the rich bottomlands of the Colorado and Brazos Rivers, east of San Antonio. There he and his colonists planned to expand the slave-based plantation economy of the lower South. Although Austin had no trouble finding recruits for his colony, the plan was dealt a near fatal blow when on September 27, 1821, Spanish Royalist colonel Agustín de Iturbide marched into Mexico City at the head of a rebellious army, overthrew the Spanish viceroy, and established Mexican independence. Undeterred, however, Austin made contact with the new government in Mexico City, which duly ratified his father's contract.

By the end of 1824, 300 families had settled the Austin colony, content under the federal Mexican Constitution of 1824, which bore much resemblance to that of the United States. By the end of 1835, 41 *empresarios* had received land grants from the Mexican government that permitted 13,500 families to settle in Texas, bringing the Anglo-American population of the Mexican province to a total of approximately 30,000, in addition to their 5,000 African American slaves. At the same time, an estimated 3,470 Hispanics lived north of the Rio Grande.

Two circumstances doomed the harmonious relationship between the Republic of Mexico and its colonists in Texas. First, a steady stream of North Americans entered Texas illegally, exacerbating Mexican fears of American expansionism. For this reason, the central government passed a series of measures that imposed more rigorous tax collection, blocked the further importation of slaves, occupied Texas with military garrisons, and culminated with the Decree of April 6, 1830, which prohibited any further immigration of North Americans into Texas. Second, the government of the Republic of Mexico was highly unstable, and consequently it could not devote its full attention to affairs in Texas. On January 3, 1833, General Antonio López de Santa Anna led an army into Mexico City, and three months later he was elected president of the republic. His administration was forced to confront the growing tensions in Texas.

Indeed, the laws designed to assert Mexican control over Texas had led to armed resistance in 1832, with skirmishes at Anahuac. Then, the Turtle Bayou Resolutions of June 13, 1832, clearly expressed the colonists' resentment of the Mexican government's policies and seeming abandonment of the principles set forth in the 1824 constitution. In April 1833, a convention of Anglo-American colonists drafted a petition calling for the recognition of Texas as a separate state within the Mexican federation rather than as a province of Coahuila, as it was then configured. Against his better judgment, Austin delivered this petition to authorities in Mexico City, where, after experiencing a series of disappointments, he drafted a letter encouraging the colonists to establish a separate state government, with or without the approval of the Mexican government. This letter was intercepted, and Austin was placed under arrest; he spent the next year in prison. Not only did this experience compel the moderate Austin into a less conciliatory stance regarding the Mexican central government, but it also stirred up a great deal of the anti-Mexican sentiment among Anglo colonies.

By 1835, moreover, a minority of Mexican legislators, capitalizing on fears that federalism had only promoted social chaos, had begun to restructure the Mexican government, vesting all power in a central authority and largely stripping the states of their powers. Several of Mexico's states were quick to respond to this abrogation of the Constitution of 1824 with military resistance. Resistance to the new centralist government was especially strong in Zacatecas, Tamaulipas, and Yucatán. To stamp out the flames of rebellion, in May 1835 Santa Anna led his army into Zacatecas, routed the state's militia, and sacked the state capital.

Then, following the clash at Anahuac in July 1835 between Mexican soldiers and Texan militiaman, Santa Anna ordered the garrisons in Texas to be reinforced. The Anglo-Texan community responded with a call to arms. On October 2, 1835, a column of Mexican lancers sent by General of Brigade Martín Perfecto Cos to take possession of a small cannon at the village of Gonzalez clashed with a group of Texan militiamen fighting under a banner inscribed with the words "Come and Take It." Although the skirmish itself was nearly bloodless, the action can be viewed as the beginning of the Texas Revolution.

From the nucleus of the Gonzalez Militia grew the Army of the People, as settlers from all of Texan colonies rushed to join in what they viewed as a fight against Mexican tyranny. Under the command of Stephen F. Austin, this "army"—in fact, little more than a rabble in arms—set out for San Antonio and a battle with Mexican forces there under the command of General Cos. Austin's small force arrived at San Antonio on October 9 to begin a lengthy and ill-coordinated siege. Despite several minor tactical victories, including a fight at Mission Concepción on October 20 in which volunteers under James Bowie and James Walker Fannin drove back a strong Mexican sortie, and the so-called Grass Fight, which interdicted the forage supply of the Mexican cavalry, as autumn phased into winter the Army of the People began to grow demoralized.

On the verge of collapse from lack of leadership—Austin was in Washington heading a delegation seeking assistance from the United States—as well as internal disputes, the army rallied for an assault on the Mexican garrison on the morning of December 5, 1835. After five days of hand-to-hand combat in the streets of the villa in which the insurrectionists were greatly assisted by the arrival of two companies of volunteers from Louisiana, the New Orleans Greys, the Mexican troops withdrew into the walls of the former Franciscan mission known as the Alamo. There on December 9, General Cos surrendered with the understanding that he would withdraw his troops beyond the Rio Grande and that they would make no further resistance to the reestablishment of the federal constitution of 1824.

While the siege of San Antonio de Béxar was under way, delegates from the Anglo colonies met at San Felipe de Austin to create a government. This convention authorized the creation of a regular army under the command of Sam Houston, issued a Declaration of Causes stating that the rebellion in Texas had been precipitated by the abrogation of the Constitution of 1824, and sent a commission, headed by Steven F. Austin, to Washington to seek support for the Texan cause. The delegates further appointed Henry Smith of Brazoria as governor and constituted themselves a legislative body known as the General Counsel.

Following their success at San Antonio, the loosely organized Texas government planned an expedition against Matamoros. Outside of San Antonio, the largest contingent of Texan volunteers was located at Goliad on the San Antonio River about 100 miles downstream. From there Frank W. Johnson and Dr. James Grant launched an expedition toward the Rio Grande, only to be intercepted and routed by a Mexican counteroffensive under General of Brigade José Urrea. Urrea's strike force was one of two columns that Santa Anna had sent into Texas in reaction to Cos's surrender of San Antonio. The other, under Santa Anna's personal command, crossed the Rio Grande late in January 1836, marching for San Antonio. Santa Anna's army reached San Antonio de Béxar on February 23 and began its siege of the Alamo. The garrison, initially a mere 150 men, was divided between Texas regulars under Lieutenant Colonel William Barrett Travis and volunteers under James Bowie. Travis's call for reinforcements was heeded by only 18 volunteers, who fought their way into the fortress from Gonzales. After a 13-day siege, Santa Anna's 3,000-man army stormed the Alamo at dawn on March 6, 1836, overwhelming the garrison and leaving no male survivors.

At the same time Urrea's column, having crushed the Texans at San Patricio on February 26 and at Agua Dulce Creek on March 2, marched toward the mission La Bahía at Goliad, which the rebel garrison under James Walker Fannin had renamed Fort Defiance. Fannin, realizing himself to be outnumbered, vacillated, determining first to hold the fort and then to fall back, first on Travis's position at the Alamo and then on Sam Houston's nucleus of an army at Victoria. Fannin delayed doing either for too long, however, and was pinned down by Mexican cavalry near Coleto Creek. Urrea's infantry and artillery arrived, and Fannin was forced to surrender. His 300 troops were marched back to Goliad, where on March 27, 1836, they were shot to death under Santa Anna's orders.

By then, a second congress, known as the Convention of 1836, had met at Washington-on-the-Brazos. There on March 2, while the Alamo was under siege and on the very day that Fannin surrendered to Urrea, the delegates signed a declaration of independence from Mexico. Ironically, the defenders of the Alamo died fighting under the Mexican flag, never knowing that Texas was then an independent republic.

With the destruction of Travis's command at the Alamo and Fannin's at Goliad, the republic showed no sign of being able to outlive its birth. Only Sam Houston and a handful of men at Gonzalez remained in arms against Santa Anna's army, and on learning of the fall of the Alamo, Houston began a rapid retreat across eastern Texas toward Louisiana. In a mass evacuation known as the Runaway Scrape, almost all of the Anglo-Texan colonists fled their homes for the safety of the United States.

Confident that Texas resistance had collapsed, Santa Anna, with a 1,000-man vanguard, moved rapidly in pursuit of Houston's fleeing force, sure of destroying it. But as Houston approached the Sabine River, he was steadily reinforced by a stream of volunteers from the United States, and on April 21, 1836, with an army of some 900 men, he surprised and overran Santa Anna's camp on the San Jacinto River. Shouting the battle cries "Remember the Alamo!" and "Remember Goliad!" the Texan army killed more than 630 Mexican soldiers and captured 730 others in a bloody 18-minute battle. Houston's casualties were only 9 killed and 30 wounded.

Santa Anna, captured by the victorious Texan forces, was offered the option of signing the Treaty of Velasco, which would give Texas its independence and national territory extending all the way to the Rio Grande, or face immediate execution by hanging. Santa Anna chose the former. He sent orders to his subordinate commanders to immediately evacuate Texas, while he himself was put aboard ship and sent to Washington, D.C., where he met with President Andrew Jackson.

Not surprisingly, the Mexican Congress failed to ratify the Treaty of Velasco and continued to regard

Texas as part of the Mexican national territory. Thus, for a 10-year period the Republic of Mexico and the breakaway Republic of Texas carried on a desultory border war of raid and counterraid, with neither side able to win a decisive victory over the other.

Hoping to make good its claim to all territory on the left bank of the Rio Grande, the 321-man Santa Fe Expedition, led by Colonel Hugh McCloud, marched out of Austin in June 1841 and ventured as far west as present-day Tucumcari, New Mexico, only to be surrounded by Mexican forces and captured on September 17, 1841. The brutal treatment of the Santa Fe prisoners gave Anglo-Texans further reason to seek vengeance against their Mexican neighbors.

Hoping to at least remind its breakaway province that Mexico still claimed sovereignty over Texas, 400 Mexican soldiers under Colonel Rafael Vásquez crossed the Rio Grande and marched into San Antonio on March 5, 1842. After occupying the town for only three days, however, the column returned to Mexico before Texas authorities could gather a force to resist it. Later that same year on September 10, a second Mexican incursion of 1,082 troops, led by General Adrian Woll, again briefly retook San Antonio. A hastily organized Texan counteroffensive clashed with Woll's column at Salado Creek, just outside of San Antonio, on September 18. Both sides claimed victory, but Woll withdrew his force below the Rio Grande.

Seeking to secure its territory from further Mexican incursions and regain lost national honor, the Republic of Texas prepared a counterstrike. The Houston administration authorized Alexander Somervell to organize a 700-man force to be known as the Southwestern Army of Operations, with the objective of invading northern Mexico. Somervell's command departed San Antonio late in November 1842 and then on December 8 captured Laredo. Demoralization and insubordination, however, caused the army to stall at that point, whereupon Somervell ordered the men to demobilize and return to their homes. Some 300 of them, however, refused to give up the campaign and, selecting William S. Fisher as their commander, crossed the Rio Grande on December 23 and occupied Mier. There on Christmas Day they were surrounded by Mexican regulars under General Pedro de Ampudia, and after a 24-hour siege Fisher surrendered his command. The prisoners were marched to Salado, where at the command of acting president Nicolás Bravo every 10th man—those who drew black beans rather than white ones from an earthen jar—was executed by firing squad. Those who survived the decimation were marched to the state of Veracruz, where they experienced confinement at the notorious Perote Prison.

In addition to its ongoing war with Mexico, Texas was increasingly beset by Comanche war parties raiding its western frontier. Beginning with the attack on Parker's Fort on May 19, 1836, and culminating with the Council House Fight on March 19, 1840, and the Great Comanche Raid and the decisive Battle of Plum Creek on August 12, 1840, Indian warfare absorbed much of Texas's resources and slowed the republic's westward expansion.

Perhaps the sole positive aspect of Texas's war with Mexico occurred at sea. The Navy of the Republic of Texas dominated the Gulf of Mexico for 10 years and gave considerable assistance to the rebels in Yucatán. In the Battle of Campeche off the coast of Yucatán (April 30, 1843), Commodore Edwin Ward Moore, commanding the Texan sloop of war *Austin* and brig *Wharton,* defeated two of the most advanced warships of the time, the Mexican steamship-of-war *Guadalupe* and the equally formidable *Moctezuma.* The Texas Navy died an ignominious death, however, when President Sam Houston ordered its ships sold at auction because the republic could not afford their upkeep.

With finances of their nation in a perilous state and with the constant threat of reannexation by Mexico, the prospect of becoming a state in the American union was entirely pleasing to a majority of Texans. Sam Houston, as the first president of the Republic of Texas, sought annexation, but because Texas would have entered the Union as a slave state, its entry was for 10 years blocked by abolitionist elements in the U.S. Congress. And not all Texans wanted to become part of the United States. Maribeau B. Lamar, for example, the republic's second president, fought to maintain Texas sovereignty.

After a decade of diplomatic proposals from Texas and rebuffs by the American congress, at last President John Tyler, a Tennessee planter and slave owner, finessed an agreement that admitted Texas to the Union. The U.S. Senate signed the annexation agreement on February 27, 1845, and the House of Representatives followed suit the next day. The state's admission was formalized in Austin, Texas, on February 19, 1846.

Not surprisingly, Mexico viewed this acquisition by the United States of what it still considered to be its own territory as a blatant land grab. Mindful that war with Mexico might be the result of Texas annexation, in mid-1845 President Polk ordered Brigadier General Zachary Taylor to Fort Jesup, Louisiana, to take command there of the regiments of the regular U.S. Army, to be known as the Army of Observation. As the possibility of war with Mexico increased, on July 25, 1845, Polk ordered Taylor's 3,400-man force to Corpus Christi, Texas, on the Nueces River, provocatively close to the disputed zone between the Nueces and the Rio Grande.

An attempt at finding a diplomatic solution to the U.S.-Mexican border dispute failed in December 1845 when Mexican authorities refused to treat with Polk's emissary, John Slidell. Exerting further pressure on the Mexican government to recognize Texas's annexation, on January 13, 1846, Polk ordered Taylor's command (renamed the Army of Occupation when it entered Texas) to the Rio Grande. The army arrived at the site of the present-day city of Brownsville, Texas, on March 28 and began construction of a fortification that it called Fort Texas (later Fort Brown).

Mexican authorities, viewing this U.S. movement into an area that it still believed to be part of the state of Coahuila, responded by sending General of Division (Major General) Pedro de Ampudia at the head of the Army of the North to Matamoros, opposite Fort Texas. Ampudia was shortly thereafter replaced by General Mariano Arista. A period of uneasy watchfulness was shattered on April 25 when a sizable Mexican force under Colonel Anastasio Torrejón overwhelmed a squadron of U.S. dragoons commanded by Captain Seth Thornton north of the Rio Grande. This incident proved to be the immediate catalyst for the U.S. war declaration the following month.

Taylor's primary problem was one of logistics, and on May 1, 1846, he marched the largest part of his command out of Fort Texas to establish a line of communication and supply with Point Isabel at the mouth of the Rio Grande. Seeking to take advantage of Taylor's exposed position, Arista's army crossed the Rio Grande and on May 8, 1846, attacked the American army—then marching back to Fort Texas—at Palo Alto. There the Mexican army, although greater in numbers, was defeated, largely by superior American artillery. The following day, May 9, the opposing forces clashed again, this time with Arista's army fighting a defensive battle. The result was another U.S. victory. At this point, the demoralized Army of the North withdrew to Matamoros, where Arista was relieved of command by General Ampudia, and Taylor's men continued their march to the relief of Fort Texas, which had been under siege since May 1.

Although Washington had not yet received word of the fighting at Palo Alto and Resaca de la Palma, on May 11, 1846, President Polk called a joint session of Congress and, based on the attack on Thornton's dragoons, called for a declaration of war against Mexico, claiming that "American blood has been shed on American soil." Although Congressman Abraham Lincoln of Illinois and a few other Whigs raised their voices in protest, war was declared on May 13 and remained generally popular in the South and West, where the belief in America's Manifest Destiny was especially strong and where the desire for new farmlands, especially land where slavery could be practiced, made northern Mexico a tempting target for takeover. Southern hopes of a southwestern empire for slavery were somewhat diminished by the introduction of the Wilmot Proviso, a rider to the house appropriations bill that funded the war that stipulated that no territory taken from Mexico would ever be a home to slavery. The proviso easily passed in the House of Representatives, and although it failed to gain a majority in the Senate, it served as a dire warning to the South that its labor system and indeed its whole way of life were in peril.

Following the twin Mexican defeats at Palo Alto and Resaca de la Palma, Ampudia shifted the conduct of the war from an offensive strategy to one of defense deep in his home territory, behind the forbidding deserts of northern Mexico that he hoped would exhaust any U.S. column that sought to pursue his army. The Army of the North therefore abandoned Matamoros and fell back 175 miles to the fortress city of Monterrey. Taylor's army followed, occupying Matamoros during May 17–18. Then, led by patrols of Texas Rangers that scouted out water sources and forage for the army's draft animals, the Americans marched out of Matamoros on September and began their trek toward Monterrey.

With the war now well under way, the Polk administration was faced with two major tasks. The first of these was raising an army. The regular U.S. Army in 1846 numbered only 7,500 officers and men. The soldiers were by and large well disciplined and ably led, largely by a cadre of fine junior officers recently graduated from the U.S. Military Academy at West Point. Their numbers, however, were obviously much too small to win a war with Mexico. To augment his force of regulars, Polk called upon the states to raise regiments of volunteers to be mustered into U.S. service. Support for the war in the South and West made recruitment there an easy job, but in the Northeast, particularly in New England, where the war was much less popular, volunteers were scarce.

While generally enthusiastic and eager for adventure, volunteers proved to be highly resistant to military discipline and liable to committing atrocities against Mexican civilians. Their officers, elected by the men or appointed by state governors, were of uneven quality, varying from very good—John A. Quitman and Alexander Doniphan—to abominable, such as Gideon J. Pillow, the president's former law partner commissioned a major general solely on his loyalty to the Democratic Party. In all, the administration raised 73,532 volunteers for the war.

Polk's second task lay in devising a strategy for the war. When his initial hope that Mexico would give up the fight and cede not only Texas but also California and what is now the American Southwest to the United States after the North Americans won a battle or two on the Rio Grande proved illusory, the president realized that a longer and more complex war was at hand. With the help of Secretary of War Randolph B. Marcy and Major General Winfield Scott, the Polk administration initially devised a two-part strategy, first sending Taylor into Mexico to occupy the republic's northern provinces as bargaining chips at the negotiating table. Concurrently, Polk authorized the formation of a second smaller army—the Army of the West—to march down the Santa Fe Trail, capture the important trading center of Santa Fe, and then to march overland to California to assist in the conquest of that greatly desired province. The U.S. Navy, operating in the Pacific, would aid in this mission by capturing such Alta California ports as San Diego, Los Angeles, and Monterey.

Taylor, having arrived at Walnut Springs, three miles north of Monterrey, on September 19, planned to use three of his four divisions, those of Brigadier General John A. Quitman, Brigadier General David Emanuel Twiggs, and Major General William Butler, to smash the city's defenses from the north and east. At the same time, Taylor would send his fourth division, that of Brigadier General William Jennings Worth, on a sweeping flanking maneuver around to the west of the city to interdict the highway to Mexico City and serve as the anvil against which he planned to hammer the Mexican Army. On September 20, Taylor threw the three divisions against Arista's forces but was able to make no headway against the heavily fortified city. On its eastern outskirts, Mexican engineers had made a formidable fortress of buildings; all of Taylor's attempts to breach this line were costly failures.

Worth, however, had better luck. Arriving at the rear of the city, he stormed and captured two major fortresses—the Bishop's Palace atop Independence Hill and El Soldado on Federation Hill—and then entered Monterrey, clearing the western half of the city in hand-to-hand fighting. Taylor, however, unaware of his subordinate's success and mindful of his own heavy losses, requested a truce. Arista, realizing as Taylor did not that he was surrounded and in danger of annihilation, was happy to negotiate an armistice under the terms of which he evacuated the city on September 24 but moved out with his entire army with all of its arms, baggage, and equipment. The terms of the capitulation also stipulated that the two armies would observe a two-month truce.

Taylor was pleased with the terms of this agreement, but the Polk administration immediately abrogated the truce, reminding Taylor in a scathing letter that his job was not to make treaties but rather to "kill the enemy." The president was genuinely anxious to carry the war through to a successful conclusion, because the American people were beginning to lose their enthusiasm for the conflict. He was also concerned about Taylor's rising political star. "Old Rough and Ready," as Taylor had come to be known by his adoring public, was the hero of Palo Alto, Resaca de la Palma, and now Monterrey, and he was a Whig. Polk was hooked on the horns of a political dilemma. He could scarcely fire his most successful and popular general, but to give him the opportunity to achieve further military glory was certain to sweep Taylor into the White House in the election of 1848. The president therefore attempted a difficult middle course by ordering Taylor to discontinue his invasion of Mexico and stand on the defensive at Monterrey. While this order made some strategic sense—the hundreds of miles of barren desert terrain between Monterrey and Mexico City would have been almost impossible for a horse- and mule-drawn army to traverse—it infuriated the sensitive Taylor, who although largely apolitical to that point was beginning to harbor strong presidential ambitions. Taylor therefore in defiance of the War Department's instructions moved south out of Monterrey and on November 16, 1846, occupied Saltillo.

While Taylor was waging his campaign in northern Mexico, the second front was opening in California and the Southwest. Even before the war had begun, the Polk administration had sent brevet Captain John C. Frémont to California with a group of soldiers in civilian clothing on an ostensible scientific expedition. Politely but firmly California authorities expelled Frémont, who then drifted north toward the Oregon Territory to await developments. On May 9, 1846, the same day that Taylor was fighting Arista at Resaca de la Palma, Frémont returned to California, intent upon fomenting rebellion among the American settlers in the Mexican state.

On July 4, 1846, Frémont declared California independent from Mexico and helped instigate the so-called Bear Flag Republic. In support of this insurrection, Commodore John Drake Sloat, in command of the Pacific Squadron, seized Monterey, California, on July 7, and on August 12 his replacement, Commodore Robert Field Stockton, occupied Los Angeles.

To further the administration's ambition to annex the Mexican state of Alta California, on June 5, 1846, Colonel Stephen Watts Kearny marched out of Fort Leavenworth, Kansas, at the head of the Army of the West. This patchwork army of 1,700 men was to seize Santa Fe and then assist in the conquest of the Pacific coast. Manuel Armijo, the governor of New Mexico, attempted to rally the citizens of his province to the defense of its capital, but his numbers were insufficient and ill-trained and dispersed as Kearny approached. The Army of the West therefore bloodlessly occupied Santa Fe on August 18, 1846. When a second regiment of Missouri mounted volunteers arrived at Santa Fe some weeks afterward, commanded by Colonel Sterling Price, Kearny, with his dragoons, departed the city on September 25, 1846, undertaking a grueling march of 850 miles across the Sonoran Desert for San Diego. En route he encountered veteran scout Christopher "Kit" Carson, eastbound as a courier bearing dispatches to the effect that Frémont and the navy had already pacified California. Assuming therefore that his men would not be needed, Kearny turned back all but 121 of his 300 dragoons.

Unbeknownst to Kearny, however, the Californios had revolted against American rule at Los Angeles on September 22–23, 1846, and had regained control of much of the region for Mexico. The situation in California was thus much different than Kearny expected when on December 6, 1846, his exhausted dragoons encountered a force of Ranchero cavalry at San Pasqual, a few miles north of San Diego. Although his forces were near the point of starvation after the desert crossing and his ammunition was wet from a recent rainfall, on Carson's advice Kearny decided to disburse the enemy horsemen. Although Kearny's men were initially successful, the Mexicans, under command of Don Andrés Pico, turned and counterattacked when they saw that American horses were failing, and the Mexican lancers were able to ride down the American horsemen, whose guns would not fire. Kearny himself was severely wounded, and his 60 surviving dragoons were forced to take a defensive position on Mule Hill, holding out until Carson and Edward Fitzgerald "Ned" Beale were able to reach San Diego and return with a relief column from Stockton's flotilla. The Battle of San Pasqual is considered the only significant engagement of the Mexican-American War that the United States lost.

Kearny, who arrived at San Diego on December 12, took command of all U.S. forces on the West Coast and on January 8, 1847, defeated the Mexican insurgents at the Battle of San Gabriel. On January 10, 1846, Commodore Stockton reoccupied Los Angeles, effectively bringing to an end resistance to the American occupation of California.

Kearny had left the 1st Missouri Mounted Volunteers, under Colonel Alexander Doniphan, at Santa Fe to suppress Indian raids and to keep in check any New Mexican unrest resulting from the American occupation. With the arrival of Price's regiment and the appearance that the province was thoroughly pacified, Doniphan's regiment rode out of Val Verde on December 12, 1846, heading south down the Rio Grande to invade Chihuahua.

Before departing for California, Kearny appointed Charles Bent as territorial governor of New Mexico. Although the situation there appeared calm, many New Mexicans and Native Americans in fact resented the U.S. takeover of their territory and feared that Mexican land titles would not be recognized by the new government. On the morning of January 19, 1847, insurrectionists, led by Pablo Montoya and Tomás Romero, revolted in Taos. A group under Romero broke into the home of Governor Bent and wounded and scalped him in the presence of his family. When the assailants left, Bent sought assistance but was discovered and murdered. Also killed and scalped that day were three other local officials. On the following day, a force of some 500 Mexicans and Indians killed from 6 to 8 men at Arroyo Hondo and 7 American traders at Mora.

Price moved swiftly against the rebels. During February 3–5, his men surrounded some 1,500 Mexicans and Indians in Taos and, after breaching the adobe walls with cannon fire, stormed the pueblo, killing an estimated 150 rebels and capturing 400 others. A second column of U.S. troops defeated and dispersed the rebel force at Mora. Ultimately 15 men were found guilty of murder and treason and sentenced to death; 6 of them were hanged in Taos Plaza on April 9. On April 25 another 5 were executed. Altogether, some 28 people were executed for having taken part in the revolt. Tomás Romero was murdered in his cell before trial, while Montoya was among those tried, sentenced to death, and hanged. Some sporadic fighting continued in the ensuing months, but the rebellion was crushed.

By the time of the Taos Revolt, Doniphan's regiment was in Mexico. On Christmas Day the Missourians defeated Colonel Antonio Ponce's 2,000-man force at the Battle of El Brazito and two days later occupied El Paso. After a month of rest and refitting there, Doniphan again moved south, defeating General of Brigade José A. Heredia's force of nearly 4,000 regulars and militiamen, supported by 16 guns, at the Battle of Río Sacramento on February 28, 1847, and occupying Chihuahua on March 1. From there, Doniphan's Thousand, as they came to be known, moved east across northern Mexico, absolutely unopposed. On May 22 they connected with Taylor's army at Saltillo and from there moved on to the port of Brazos Santiago, where they were taken aboard transports and sailed to New Orleans. From there they steamed up the Mississippi River to St. Louis and ultimately to Saint Joseph, the point of their departure. The men of the First Missouri Mounted Rifles had traveled 3,600 miles overland and 2,000 by water and fought two significant battles but otherwise had faced little serious resistance. Doniphan's March was of little strategic significance, but it did capture the imagination of the American people and demonstrated that if American raiders were unable to hold the territory they traversed, neither did they incite local people to attempt to expel them.

Yet another large-scale incursion into northern Mexico was led by Brigadier General John E. Wool, who led 900 American soldiers out of San Antonio on September 25, 1846, the same day that Kearny departed New Mexico for California, bound for Chihuahua. Wool occupied Monclova without opposition on October 29, 1846, and on December 5 occupied the city of Parras, and from there he joined Taylor's army at Saltillo. Like Doniphan's March, Wool's was of little strategic value but gave further evidence of the fact that the common Mexican people had little interest in the war.

General Santa Anna, who had been exiled to Cuba in 1845 in the wake of his failed fifth presidential administration, was eager to return to power in Mexico. He thus concluded a deal with the Polk administration in which Santa Anna promised to end the war and deliver a favorable boundary resolution to the United States in return for passage to Veracruz and a payment of $30 million. Santa Anna returned to Mexico on August 16, 1846. He then reneged on his agreement to befriend the Polk administration and vowed to drive the Yankee invaders from his country. President Polk, saddled with an increasingly unpopular war, had discovered that the occupation of Mexican territory was not driving the enemy to the negotiating table, and perhaps worse, his most successful general was of the wrong political party. He therefore engineered a change in strategy, determining to strike at the enemy's capital and thus force Mexico to terms. Bypassing Taylor, Polk appointed Major General Winfield Scott to command the new expedition. Scott had been denied a field command at the beginning of the war because he, like Taylor, was a Whig, a potential presidential candidate, and a bitter political foe of the commander in chief. Nevertheless, most likely realizing that of all his generals only Scott had the necessary military skills to successfully carry out such an operation, on November 18, 1846, the president appointed Scott to the command of a new American army. Its task was to undertake an amphibious landing on Mexico's Gulf coast, capture the vital port city of Veracruz, and then march inland to Mexico City.

Scott had been given an army without troops and on January 3, 1846, was forced to remove from Taylor's command almost all of the regular regiments of the American army. This stripping of his army of its best units stirred Taylor to great resentment of the president and of his fellow general, a resentment that would have lasting repercussions when Taylor became president in 1848.

Stung by the evisceration of his army and the lack of respect, on February 5, 1847, Taylor, in defiance of Polk's orders to remain at Monterrey, moved his diminished army to an advanced position at Agua Nueva. Santa Anna, aware that Scott's invasion was imminent, rightly perceived that he and the Mexican Army were about to be caught between two American forces. Faced with the choice of meeting Scott's landing force on the beaches below Veracruz or attacking Taylor in his advanced position at Agua Nueva, the Mexican general chose the latter, hoping to destroy Taylor's weakened army and then march north into Texas.

Santa Anna put this bold and daring plan into action, raising a new army and marching north, catching Taylor virtually by surprise. Only astute reconnaissance by a company of Texas Rangers warned him of the enemy's presence in time to fall back to a strong defensive position at Buena Vista on February 21. The two-day Battle of Buena Vista (February 22–23, 1847) was closely contested and came near to being a decisive Mexican victory. Superior American artillery and the stand of the First Mississippi Rifles under Colonel Jefferson Davis broke the spirited Mexican attacks, however, and with both armies largely shattered, Santa Anna withdrew to Mexico City. There he declared a victory and recruited a new army with which to face Scott.

Santa Anna, however, did not have time to fully raise, equip, and organize an army before Scott arrived. Santa Anna was certain nevertheless that the walls of Veracruz and the seemingly impregnable fortress of San Juan de Ulúa, with their combined garrison of 4,390 men, could hold the American army on the beach long enough for him to march to the rescue or that the dreaded yellow fever (*vómito negro*), so prevalent in the Mexican low country, would destroy the American army without a fight. Thus, on March 9, 1847, Scott's armies splashed ashore just below Veracruz unopposed. With remarkable speed, Scott's West Point–trained engineers erected heavy batteries around Veracruz and began a systematic siege and bombardment. Within three days the walls were breached, and on March 29, 1847, the Mexicans surrendered the city.

With equal rapidity, Scott prepared his army to move to the Mexican interior, out of reach of the yellow fever mosquitoes. On April 8 he began to move inland using the port of Veracruz as his base. Ever hopeful that each American success would bring peace, on April 15 Polk appointed Nicholas Trist of the State Department as commissioner plenipotentiary and sent him to negotiate a peace with Santa Anna. The Mexican general, however, was not prepared to discuss peace, instead moving his new army into a superb defensive position at Cerro Gordo, the only route that Scott could take into the highlands and on to the Mexican capital. Santa Anna's position appeared impregnable, but engineer Captain Robert E. Lee, in a daring reconnaissance, discovered a path around his flank, and Scott was able to move his regulars into position on the enemy left and rear. Utterly surprised by an attack from that quarter, the Mexican army scattered, and its general barely escaped from the field, leaving behind his personal carriage, the army's payroll, and one of his several wooden legs.

Scott moved quickly inland, and on April 22 his vanguard, led by Brigadier General William J. Worth, occupied Perote and then on May 15 occupied Puebla, the second-largest city in Mexico. There, however, the invasion ground to a halt when 4,000 of Scott's volunteers, their enlistment periods up, insisted upon being allowed to return home. The army therefore remained halted at Puebla until August, waiting for replacement troops to arrive from the United States. The energetic Santa Anna took full advantage of this delay and raised yet another army for the defense of his capital.

At last, with his army reinforced by new recruits, Scott again began his advance. Santa Anna had used time wisely, surrounding Mexico City with a chain of powerful fortifications, but once again Scott's remarkable young engineers performed heroic reconnaissance missions to locate a soft spot in the enemy line. On August 20, having found a trail across an apparently impassable lava bed called El Pedregal, Scott engaged the Northern Division, under the command of General of Division Gabriel Valencia, at the Battle of Contreras and engaged the Army of the Center, led by General of Division Manuel Rincón, at Churubusco. Both of these actions were decisive U.S. victories, breaching Santa Anna's defenses and leaving open the way to Mexico City, then only five miles distant.

The Americans, however, hoped for a negotiated settlement rather than a continuation of the bloody and increasingly unpopular war; Scott also feared that Mexican congressmen would scatter if Mexico City were captured, making the negotiation and ratification of a treaty almost impossible. Therefore, on August 24 he and Santa Anna agreed upon an armistice, ostensibly to provide an opportunity for Trist and the Mexican commissioners to meet and discuss a conclusion to the war. Neither side was to reinforce its army or to construct defensive works while the armistice was in effect. Almost immediately, however, Santa Anna broke the terms of the agreement, repulsing American supply trains and strengthening the capital's defenses. Therefore, on September 6, Scott terminated the Tacubaya Armistice and prepared again for offensive operations.

Acting on a flawed piece of intelligence that had located a cannon foundry at El Molino del Rey, Scott decided to make his next strike there. He left tactical control of the battle, however, to William J. Worth, who failed to carry out proper reconnaissance before launching his troops in a frontal assault on the breast-high walls of the mill. Although the American army carried the position with the bayonet, routing its defenders, the Battle of Molino Del Rey, fought on September 8, 1847, was the single most costly battle of the war for the United States.

At however high a cost, control of Molino del Rey brought Scott's army one step closer to the final assault on Mexico City. Only the key fortress of Chapultepec Castle remained between them and the gates of the city. Formerly the home of the Spanish viceroy, this castle was now the Mexican national military academy, and alongside the regular Mexican soldiers, the cadets, ever after known as Los Niños Héroes, defended their school. After an intense artillery bombardment, Scott's infantry surged forward on September 13, 1847; scaled the walls; and overran the citadel. With no further organized resistance outside its walls, U.S. soldiers quickly secured the capital's gates and began a street-by-street and house-by-house battle for control of the city. Scott entered the capital early on the morning of September 14; his troops had assumed full control of Mexico City following a two-day riot led by members of Mexico City's underclass. That same day, September 16, Santa Anna, who had fled with the remains of his army in the early morning hours of September 14, relinquished the presidency but continued a brief and sporadic campaign against Scott's attenuated supply line.

Meanwhile, Trist's apparent lack of progress toward a peace settlement angered the president, and on October 8 Polk ordered his recall. Not until November 16, however, did Trist receive word of his dismissal, and in view of the fact that the capital had fallen since Polk had issued his recall and negotiations with Mexican officials were well under way, Trist decided to defy the president's order and remain in Mexico. After months of negotiations, on February 2, 1848, Trist and the Mexican commissioners signed the Treaty of Guadalupe Hidalgo. It stipulated, in brief, that the present-day states of California, Utah, New Mexico, Nevada, most of Arizona, and parts of Colorado and Wyoming—a total of 525,000 square miles—would be ceded to the United States. In return Mexico would receive $15 million in restitution, and all debts owed to American citizens by the Republic of Mexico—some $3.25 million—would be paid by the U.S. Treasury. On March 10, 1848, the treaty was ratified by the U.S. Senate; on March 25 the Mexicans ratified it. On June 12, Americans troops evacuated Mexico City.

While the American conquest of California and the Southwest represented a huge and potentially highly valuable land acquisition, this growth did not come without tremendous cost. Gold discovered at Sutter's Mill, California, in 1848—ironically, almost simultaneously with the signing of the Treaty of Guadalupe Hidalgo—brought to the United States fabulous wealth. It also brought to the political forefront the question of whether or not slavery should be allowed in the newly acquired territories. Gold fever drew tens of thousands of settlers to California, and they of course soon demanded statehood. The question of whether the state, as well as the other territories taken from Mexico, would enter the Union as slave or free became the most burning issue of the next decade of American political debate.

The Compromise of 1850, which brought California into the Union as a free state but left the remaining territories free to choose their status under the concept of popular sovereignty, settled this vexing question but only temporarily. The rancor and animosity engendered between the two sides of this debate was instrumental in driving a sharp wedge between the North and the South, leading inevitably to Southern secession and civil war by 1861. As the American philosopher Ralph Waldo Emerson had rightly predicted, "Mexico will poison us."

THOMAS W. CUTRER

MOVING WEST

Conflict with Native Americans, the Mexican-American War, and Manifest Destiny, 1831–1849

TIMELINE

June 30, 1831

First movement of troops by rail. Rioting at Sykes Mill (present-day Sykesville), Maryland, by railroad workers striking for back pay leads to the dispatch there of some 100 men of the 1st Maryland Light Division, commanded by Major General George H. Steuart. The militiamen travel to Sykes Mill on the Baltimore & Ohio Railroad, the first movement of troops by rail in the nation's history. Some 50 strikers are arrested.

August 21–23, 1831

Nat Turner's Rebellion. In Southampton County, Virginia, African American slave and preacher Nat Turner believes that God has called on him to lead a revolt against whites and "slay them with their own weapons." Fifty-seven whites, including men, women, and children, are slain. Virginia militiamen quickly end the rebellion, with Turner and some 60 of his followers scattered. Turner is not captured until October 30. Tried and found guilty, he is hanged on November 11 in Jerusalem (present-day Courtland), Virginia.

In all, the State of Virginia executes 56 blacks for the rebellion. Hysteria grips the South, and hundreds of innocent African Americans are killed or imprisoned. The rights of free blacks are also sharply curtailed. The revolt also discourages discussion of ending slavery, on the assumption that this will only encourage similar revolts.

November 1831

Beginning of the Trail of Tears. Secretary of War Lewis Cass appoints Alabamian George S. Gaines to manage the removal of the Choctaws, the first tribe to be relocated to Indian Territory (present-day Oklahoma) under the Indian Removal Act of 1830. Gaines decides to move the Choctaws in three phases, starting in November 1831 and ending in 1833. Conditions are difficult, and food is scarce. When the first Choctaws reach Little Rock, a Choctaw chief (believed to be Thomas Harkins or Nitikechi) describes the removal as a "trail of tears and death." This term is applied to subsequent Indian removals as well.

Nearly 17,000 Choctaws make the trek, and between 2,500 and 6,000 perish along the way. Those Choctaws choosing to remain in newly formed Mississippi are subject to legal action, harassment, and even death.

February 6, 1832

Battle of Kuala Batu. The U.S. Navy frigate *Potomac* (52 guns), commanded by Captain John Downes, has been sent to Kuala Batu on the western Sumatra coast to seek redress for the plundering of the U.S. merchantman *Friendship* and the murder of 3 members of its crew. The *Potomac* arrives off Kuala Batu at dawn on this day and lands 282 sailors and marines in four parties under marine first lieutenant Alvin Edson and navy lieutenants Irvin Shubrick, Henry Hoff, and Jonathan Ingersoll. After two hours of fighting, the landing party captures all 4 shore forts defending Kuala Batu (Quallah Battoo), which is then burned. Some 150 Sumatrans are killed; U.S. casualties are 2 dead and 11 wounded.

 **Railroads**

The first practical application of the steam engine to land transportation came in the locomotive designed by Richard Trevithick in England in 1801, but George Stephenson built the first true railway, between Stockton and Darlington, also in England, in 1825. The first U.S. rail line was constructed in 1828.

Prussia was the first nation to grasp the importance of the railroad in war. German writers were quick to point out how rail lines could help their nation in case of war against powerful neighbors. The railroad enabled Prussia and later Germany to use railroads in interior lines by which forces could be mobilized and shifted rapidly.

In 1846 the Prussians conducted the first major troop movement by rail, while the American Civil War saw the first such movement by rail in war, when Confederate forces were transported from the Shenandoah Valley to fight in the First Battle of Bull Run (Manassas) (July 21, 1861), but the much more developed rail net in the North was an important factor in the Union victory in the war. Railroads proved critical in enabling Prussia to win a rapid victory over Austria in 1866. Railroads were also an important factor in the later stages of the American Indian Wars in the West after the Civil War. Armored trains and railroad artillery appeared in the American Civil War and in the Boer War of 1899–1902.

At the beginning of World War I, France may have survived militarily because of its well-developed rail net that enabled rapid shifting of major units to meet the German foot-bound invasion of northeastern France in August 1914. Russia's ambitious program for a strategic railroad net would have rendered obsolete Germany's Schlieffen Plan for waging a near-simultaneous war against France and Russia and was certainly a factor in Germany's decision to declare war in 1914. Germany could not have been able to win a two-front war five years later.

During World War I, railroads moved the bulk of the vast numbers of men and quantities of munitions and supplies to the front. Railroad artillery allowed rapid deployment of the heaviest guns, and railroad cars also served as mobile command posts. The inability of the Russian rail system to meet both civilian and military needs led to food riots in the cities and ultimately to revolution in March 1917.

Rail lines were also of immense importance in World War II, although modern aircraft rendered them much more vulnerable to attack. Disruption of the movement of the enemy's supplies by rail became a primary concern of both sides in the war, as in the bombing and resistance activities prior to the Allied landings in Normandy in June 1944, and the rapid restoration of the French rail system thereafter was a top priority for the Western Allies.

During the Cold War, railroads were to be the primary means by which the Soviet Union would deploy its massive armored forces from Russia and Ukraine into Eastern Europe and to the inter-German border. The key challenge for the Soviets was the fact that their railroads used broader-gauge tracks than the railroads of their opponents and the rest of the world. This meant that all rail traffic transiting between east and west had to go through large transloading zones at the Soviet border. North Atlantic Treaty Organization (NATO) intelligence officers made extensive studies of the Soviet and Warsaw Pact rail networks, and officers developed extensive targeting lists against such critical choke points as tunnels, bridges, switching centers, and especially the transloading zones.

Railroads continue to be a major factor in military planning for the movement of troops, equipment, and supplies.

SPENCER C. TUCKER

Further Reading
Bishop, Denis, and W. J. K. Davies. *Railways and War before 1918*. London: Blandford, 1972.
Bishop, Denis, and W. J. K. Davies. *Railways and War since 1917*. London: Blandford, 1974.
Westwood, John N. *Railways at War*. San Diego, CA: Howell-North Books, 1981.

April 5, 1832
Congress establishes a separate Ordnance Department in the army, directed by Colonel George Bomford.

April 1832
Beginning of the Black Hawk War. This last Native American War in the Old Northwest is led by Black Hawk (Makataimesh-Ekiakiak), a strong opponent of white settlement and a British ally during the War of 1812. Forced across the Mississippi River by Illinois militia in 1831, in April 1832 Black Hawk returns with some 500 mounted Sauk and Fox warriors and 500 women and children in hopes of regaining traditional lands. Some 1,600 militiamen march against him.

May 14, 1832
Black Hawk War (continued): Battle of Stillman's Run. On May 14, 1832, some 300 militia under Major Isaiah Stillman, suspecting a ruse, seize and kill several of Black Hawk's emissaries who have approached them under a flag of truce. In response, Black Hawk attacks the militia camp with only 40 warriors, killing 12 militiamen and scattering the rest. This ends any immediate possibility of peace.

June 16, 1832
Black Hawk War (continued). Angered by Brigadier General Henry Atkinson's lack of progress, U.S. president Andrew Jackson orders Major General Winfield Scott to assume command in Illinois. At the beginning of July, some 1,000 reinforcements arrive under Scott, although more than 200 of them die in an outbreak of cholera. Additional Illinois militia are also called up.

July 21, 1832
Black Hawk War (continued): Battle of Wisconsin Heights. Although Black Hawk's warriors kill more than 200 white settlers following the Battle of Stillman's Run, Black Hawk knows that he cannot win and attempts to withdraw with his people to the Mississippi. Near present-day Madison, Wisconsin, on July 21 they run into army regulars under Brigadier General James D. Henry. In the Battle of Wisconsin Heights, Black Hawk's warriors manage to delay the troops sufficiently to allow most of the natives to escape across the Wisconsin River. Some 40–70 warriors are killed, for only 1 American killed and 8 wounded.

August 1–2, 1832
Black Hawk War (continued): Battle of Bad Axe. Army and militia troops under Brigadier General Henry Atkinson pursue Black Hawk, his warriors, and their families across the Wisconsin River in hopes of catching them before they can cross the Mississippi into Iowa. On August 1–2 near the juncture of the Mississippi and Bad Axe Rivers, Black Hawk is forced to fight. The Battle of Bad Axe River (sometimes called the Bad Axe Massacre) pits fewer than 500 Indians, including women and children, against 400 U.S. Army regulars and 900 militia.

Depiction of fleeing bands of Sauk and Fox Indians caught and attacked by U.S. Army troops and militia in the Battle of Bad Axe during August 1–2, 1832, the final engagement of the Black Hawk War. (North Wind Picture Archives)

Approaching the Mississippi on August 1, 1832, the Indians have two options. They can attempt to cross, or they can continue along the riverbank until they reach the safety of other area Indian tribes, particularly the Winnebagos. Black Hawk favors the latter course, but many of his followers begin building rafts and start to cross the river. This takes time, and while a number get across the river, most are trapped by the arrival of the steamboat *Warrior*, pressed into service by the U.S. government.

Realizing that the situation is hopeless, Black Hawk waves a piece of white cloth in an attempt to surrender, but either he is not seen, the effort is misunderstood, or it is simply ignored by those in the *Warrior*, who open fire. Twenty-three Native Americans, including one woman, are killed by the time the shooting ends.

Battle of Bad Axe (Bad Axe Massacre)		
Date	August 1–2, 1832	
Location	Near the juncture of the Mississippi and Bad Axe Rivers	
Opponents (*winner)	*United States	Sauk and Fox Native Americans
Commander	Brigadier General Henry Atkinson	Chief Black Hawk
#	1,300 men (400 U.S. Army, 900 militia)	500 Native Americans (including women and children)
Casualties	5 killed, 19 wounded	Some 150 warriors and a like number of women and children killed; 75 captured

The second day of fighting, August 2, turns into a massacre as the soldiers kill those trying to cross the river. In the two days of fighting, some 150 warriors and an equal number of women and children are slain; reportedly the soldiers scalp many of the dead. An additional 75 Native Americans are captured. The army and militia lose only 5 killed and 19 wounded. Those natives who escape across the river find only temporary reprieve; many are subsequently killed by Sioux warriors acting in conjunction with the army. The Sioux bring in 22 prisoners and 68 scalps in the weeks after the battle.

The Bad Axe Massacre is the last major action of the war. Black Hawk is among the some 150 of his original band who escape.

September 21, 1832

Black Hawk War (continued): Treaty of Fort Armstrong. Black Hawk surrenders on August 27, 1832. He is held hostage to ensure compliance with the terms of the Treaty of Fort Armstrong of September 21, 1832, which is signed by Chief Keokuk, friendly to the United States. Under its terms the Fox and Sauk Indians are forced to cede their lands west of the Mississippi River, approximately one-fifth of present-day Iowa.

March 2, 1833

In order to meet the need for mounted troops, Congress passes an act creating the United States Regiment of Dragoons. Organized at Jefferson Barracks, Missouri, it becomes the 1st Regiment of Dragoons when the 2nd Dragoons is raised in 1836. With the beginning of the Civil War, on August 3, 1861, the 1st Regiment of Dragoons becomes the 1st Regiment of Cavalry. Dragoons typically employ horses to ride to battle but generally fight dismounted.

March 20, 1833

Captain David Geisinger of the U.S. Navy sloop *Peacock* (22 guns) concludes a treaty of commerce with the Kingdom of Siam.

June 17, 1833

The U.S. Navy's first dry dock opens at the Charlestown Navy Yard in Boston, Massachusetts, receiving the ship of the line *Delaware* (92 guns).

June–December 1835

Background to the Second Seminole War. Since the acquisition of Florida from Spain in 1819, demands grow for removal of the Seminole Indians from Florida Territory to the West to make their lands available for white settlement. The Seminoles are pressured into signing several treaties calling for their relocation on western lands. Many Seminoles, however, resist.

On June 19, 1835, violence occurs at Hickory Sink when white settlers beat Seminoles accused of stealing a cow, which the Seminoles claim is theirs. Other Seminoles arrive, and in the ensuing clash three whites are wounded; one Seminole is killed and another wounded. In August, Seminoles kill one of the whites they hold responsible for the beatings earlier. By September, many Seminoles have rallied to Osceola, leader of those opposing removal. Meanwhile, U.S. Army brigadier general Duncan L. Clinch orders Seminole leaders to begin assembling their people for removal. By December 1835, hundreds of Seminoles have collected at several U.S. Army forts and are soon removed west of the Mississippi River.

September 1835

Background to the Texas War of Independence. Many factors pull Texas, a province of northern Mexico, away from the rest of Mexico. In 1831 the Mexican

Osceola (ca. 1804–1838)

Native leader in the Second Seminole War (1835–1842). Born near the Tallapoosa River in present-day Alabama circa 1804, Osceola was the son of a mixed-blood Creek mother. His father was probably Scottish trader William Powell, so Osceola in his youth was called Billy Powell, although he later asserted that he had been born before his mother's relationship with Powell and that his father was Creek. Following the Creek War (1813–1814), Osceola and his mother moved to Spanish Florida and settled in a Seminole town at Peas Creek. There Osceola's hunting and leadership skills gained him prominence.

When Major General Andrew Jackson invaded Florida in 1818, Osceola and his mother were captured but soon released. They eventually moved to a Seminole reservation in central Florida, where Osceola worked for the U.S. government in the 1820s, policing the Seminole boundaries against intruders.

In 1834, the Seminoles became divided over acquiescence to the Treaty of Payne's Landing, in which many members of the tribe accepted removal to the west. Osceola's denunciation of the treaty earned him a leadership position among the Seminoles who opposed removal. Wiley Thompson, U.S. agent to the Seminoles, tried to convince Osceola to sign the treaty on April 22, 1835, but Osceola refused. Some accounts say that he thrust a knife into the document in an act of defiance. Fearing Osceola's influence, Thompson had him arrested. After five days' imprisonment, Osceola consented to sign the treaty and was released. However, he immediately fled to the swamps and began preparing for war.

Osceola and his followers began their campaign by killing Charley Emathla, a chief who had favored removal, and attacking his supporters. On December 28, 1835, Osceola attacked Fort King, killing Thompson and an army officer. The same day, the Seminoles ambushed an army baggage train and killed all but 3 of 110 soldiers. At the Withlacoochee River on December 31, Osceola turned on a force of 600 regulars and militia sent to attack him. Catching them as they crossed the river, Osceola mauled 250 men on one side while the remainder watched. Osceola was, however, wounded in the battle.

Osceola's offensive ignited the Second Seminole War (1835–1842). U.S. officials and Florida governor Richard K. Call recognized Osceola's importance as leader of Seminole resistance and targeted him for death or capture. Eventually 8,000 troops were in the field pursuing Osceola, but for two years the Seminole leader evaded them while launching hit-and-run raids against vulnerable U.S. detachments and posts. In one such operation in June 1837, Osceola freed several hundred Seminoles held in a detention compound.

Throughout the campaign, army officers had made overtures to the Seminoles, urging them to meet and negotiate peace. Osceola accepted Brigadier General Joseph M. Hernandez's offer of a parley on October 22, 1837. On the orders of his superior, Major General Thomas S. Jesup, Hernandez violated the truce and arrested Osceola and 80–100 of his followers.

Osceola was imprisoned in St. Augustine until December 31, 1837, when he was transferred to Fort Moultrie in Charleston, South Carolina. He became ill but refused treatment because he distrusted the fort's doctor, Frederick Weedon, who was the brother-in-law of Wiley Thompson. Osceola died in Charleston on January 31, 1838.

JIM PIECUCH

Further Reading

Bland, Celia. *Osceola: Seminole Rebel.* New York: Chelsea House, 1994.
Oppenheim, Joanne. *Osceola: Seminole Warrior.* Mahwah, NJ: Troll Associates, 1979.

government outlaws slavery, although exceptions are granted for Texas. The Mexican government is in constant turmoil, and there are disagreements about tariffs, representation, immigration, and army garrisons. Matters come to a head in 1835 when Mexican president General Antonio López de Santa Anna abolishes the federal Constitution of 1824 and proclaims a new unitary constitution that will sweep away states' rights. This causes widespread unrest, and revolts occur in Yucatán, Zacatecas, and Coahuila and in Texas.

Throughout 1835 there are altercations in Texas, and Santa Anna decides to send additional troops and punish the Texans, as he has done with the citizens of Zacatecas.

October 2, 1835

Texas War of Independence: Battle of Gonzales. With unrest spreading in Texas, commander of Mexican troops at San Antonio de Béxar (present-day San Antonio) Colonel Domingo de Ugartechea believes it prudent to retrieve a cannon given by the Mexican government to Texas militia to help protect Gonzales from raiding Comanche Indians. His request for its return refused, Ugartechea dispatches Lieutenant Francisco Castañeda and 100 dragoons to Gonzales to retrieve it. Gonzales is located near the confluence of the San Marcos and Guadalupe Rivers. Ugartechea instructs Castañeda to use force only if necessary. He is to arrest the alcade, Andrew Ponton, and any others who resist and bring them back to San Antonio de Béxar as prisoners.

Castañeda and his dragoons arrive in the vicinity of Gonzales on September 29, but the colonists ask him to wait until Ponton returns while at the same time dispatching appeals to nearby settler communities for assistance. With all boats having been removed, Castañeda is unable to cross the swollen Guadalupe River, although the Texans do permit 1 soldier to swim across with messages as they take up position on the opposite bank. During the next two days some 150 Texans gather at Gonzales under a banner picturing a single star, a cannon, and the words "come and take it."

Although Castañeda's men have made no hostile move, the colonists believe that he is awaiting reinforcements or about to move to a location where he can easily ford the river. They decide to take the initiative. Early on October 2 Colonel John Henry Moore and some 40 Texan militiamen with the cannon surprise the Mexican force in bivouac. Fighting begins at dawn, and in the ensuing exchange of fire 1 Texan is wounded. There is also 1 Mexican casualty. This engagement, known as the Lexington of Texas, is widely regarded as the first battle of the Texas War of Independence (1835–1836). News of the clash quickly spreads as Castañeda falls back to San Antonio.

October 9, 1835

Texas War of Independence (continued): Skirmish at Goliad. A force of 50 Texans led by Captain James Collingsworth advance from Victoria against the strategically important town of Goliad, located on the San Antonio River between San Antonio de Béxar (present-day San Antonio) and the Gulf coast port of Copano. Goliad's well-fortified presidio is held by some 30 Mexican troops under Captain Francisco Salazar.

In the late evening of October 9, the Texans enter the presidio by means of the adjoining church and

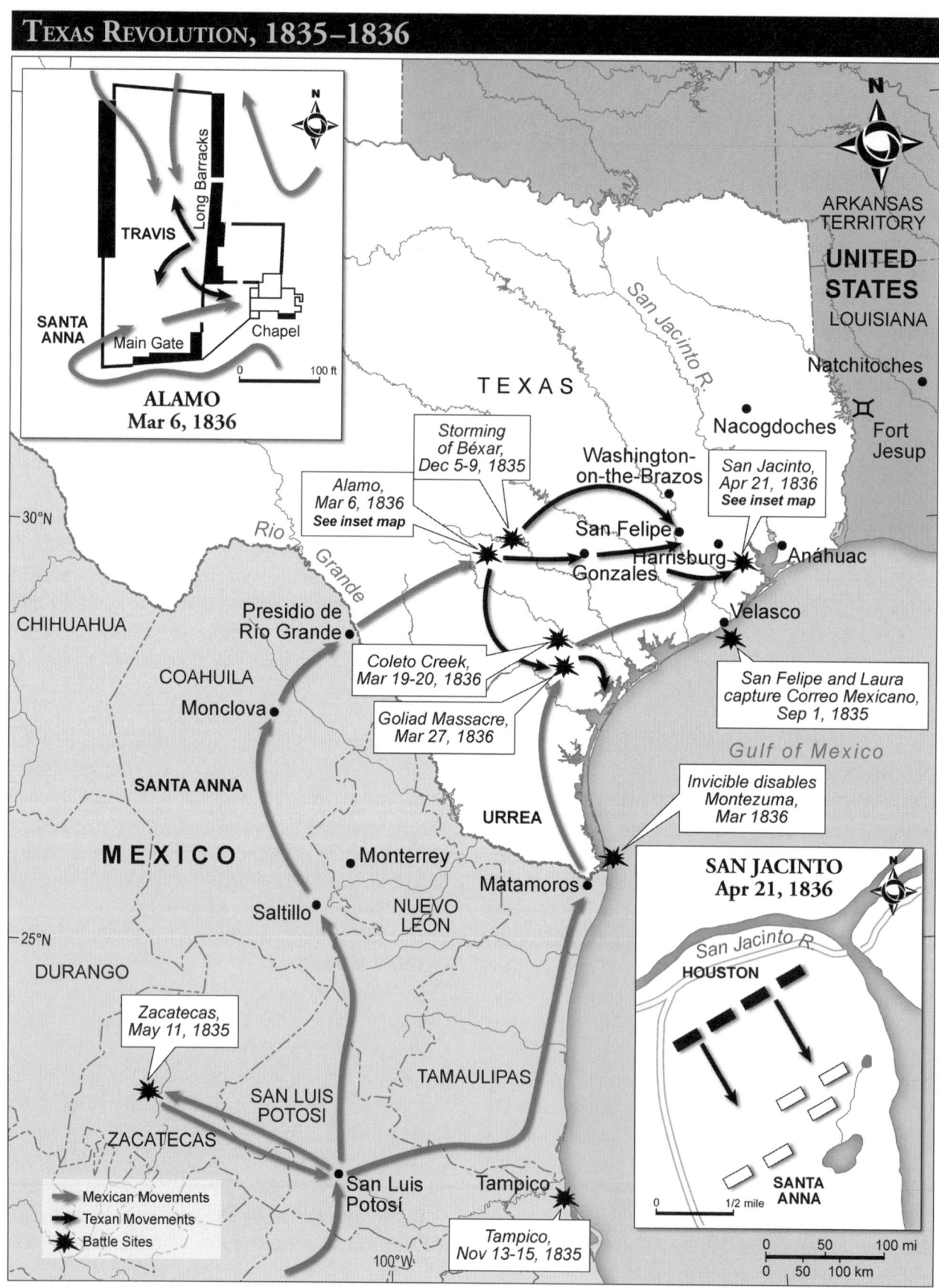

Texas Revolution, 1835–1836

ALAMO
Mar 6, 1836

- Long Barracks
- TRAVIS
- SANTA ANNA
- Main Gate
- Chapel
- 0   100 ft

ARKANSAS TERRITORY

UNITED STATES

LOUISIANA

T E X A S

Natchitoches

Nacogdoches

Fort Jesup

Storming of Béxar, Dec 5-9, 1835

Washington-on-the-Brazos

San Jacinto, Apr 21, 1836 See inset map

Alamo, Mar 6, 1836 See inset map

San Felipe

San Jacinto R.

Rio Grande

30°N

Gonzales

Harrisburg

Anáhuac

CHIHUAHUA

Presidio de Río Grande

Coleto Creek, Mar 19-20, 1836

Velasco

COAHUILA

Monclova

Goliad Massacre, Mar 27, 1836

San Felipe and Laura capture Correo Mexicano, Sep 1, 1835

SANTA ANNA

Gulf of Mexico

URREA

Invicible disables Montezuma, Mar 1836

M E X I C O

Monterrey

Matamoros

SAN JACINTO
Apr 21, 1836

25°N

Saltillo

NUEVO LEÓN

San Jacinto R.

HOUSTON

DURANGO

Zacatecas, May 11, 1835

SAN LUIS POTOSÍ

TAMAULIPAS

ZACATECAS

San Luis Potosí

Tampico

SANTA ANNA

0   1/2 mile

Mexican Movements
Texan Movements
Battle Sites

100°W

Tampico, Nov 13-15, 1835

0   50   100 mi
0   50   100 km

quickly overwhelm its garrison. Casualties are light on both sides. In addition to capturing this important fortress, the Texans gain a strategic location and secure substantial supplies, recently delivered there for forthcoming Mexican military operations in Texas. These prove invaluable to the Texans in the forthcoming Siege of Béxar.

October 28, 1835

Texas War of Independence (continued): Battle of Concepción. Following the skirmish at Gonzales on October 2, 1835, Texas forces under Stephen F. Austin grow to some 400 men as they advance on the Mexican garrison at San Antonio de Béxar (present-day San Antonio). There Mexican general Martín Perfecto de Cos, recently arrived with reinforcements, commands some 750 men. Cos fortifies the plazas in San Antonio and the Alamo mission (San Antonio de Valero) across the San Antonio River.

On October 27 Austin orders James Bowie and James W. Fannin Jr. to lead 90 men from San Francisco de la Espada Mission, occupied by the Texans the day before, in a reconnaissance of the Mexican positions. Reaching Nuestra Señora de la Purísima Concepción de Acuña Mission two miles south of San Antonio, Bowie and Fannin decide to camp there for the night rather than return to the main army, as Austin had ordered.

Cos seizes the opportunity and sends out before dawn on October 28 Colonel Domingo de Ugartechea with 275 men (200 of them cavalry) and two cannon. The Mexican cavalry drives in the Texan pickets, but the Texans repel three Mexican charges and kill or wound most of the attackers before they themselves counterattack and capture one of the Mexican guns. The Mexican cavalry then covers the withdrawal of the remaining Mexican infantry.

Austin and the rest of the Texan army hurry to the battlefield on the sound of the firing but arrive too late to do anything other than harry the Mexican withdrawal. Mexican losses are 14 killed and 39 wounded (some mortally), as opposed to Texan casualties of 1 killed and 1 wounded. This battle marks the opening of the siege of San Antonio de Béxar.

October 28–December 11, 1835

Texas War of Independence (continued): Siege of San Antonio de Béxar. Following the Battle of Concepción on October 28, the 400-man Texan army commanded by Stephen F. Austin lays siege to San Antonio de Béxar (present-day San Antonio), held by Mexican general Martín Perfecto de Cos and some 750 men. Cos has already fortified both the town plazas west of the San Antonio River and the Alamo, a former mission to its east.

The Texans establish camps. With reinforcements, they have some 600 men. Although Austin wants to assault the town, most of his officers believe that it is too well fortified to attack, and some of the volunteers then go home for winter clothes and equipment. Volunteers from eastern Texas offset these departures, but both armies suffer from the winter weather and limited supplies.

Texan and Mexican cavalry occasionally skirmish as the Texans attempt to capture Mexican supplies. The arrival of some 100 volunteers from the United States in mid-November leads Austin to plan an assault. His officers again opposed, it is called off. Austin then departs to raise support and volunteers in the United States, and on November 25 former Indian fighter Edward Burleson assumes command.

On November 26 when some 100 Mexican cavalry are reported approaching San Antonio with a pack train, Jim Bowie leads out 60 mounted volunteers to attack it. A skirmish occurs near Alazán Creek west of the town. Attacks and counterattacks occur in what is known as the Grass Fight because the captured Mexican supply animals carry fodder for horses rather than the rumored silver in pay for Mexican soldiers. The Mexican cavalry withdraws back into San Antonio.

When a Mexican officer surrenders with news of the poor state of morale in San Antonio de Béxar, Texan officers Benjamin R. Milam and William Gordon Cooke gather more than 300 volunteers for an attack. Burleson and some 400 men protect the Texan camp and supplies, forcing Cos to divide his 570 men between the town and the Alamo.

The Texan attack opens before dawn on December 5 with artillery fire on the Alamo. The main Texan attacking force then enters the town from the north and captures several houses, but Mexican musket and artillery fire prevent them from taking the plaza. The Texans spend the next day fortifying and linking up their positions. On December 7 they expand their perimeter, although Milam is killed by a Mexican sniper. On December 8 Colonel Domingo de Ugartechea, who had left the town earlier to guide in reinforcements, returns with more than 600 men, but only 170 of these are trained soldiers. Cos sends his cavalry against the Texan camp, but it is too well defended, and they are forced to withdraw.

With some of his cavalry having deserted, Cos asks Burleson for terms on the morning of December 9. The surrender is finalized on December 11. Burleson secures most of the Mexican weapons and military equipment, but he does not have the resources to care for so many prisoners and thus allows Cos and his men to retire southward.

The siege claims some 20 Texan dead and a like number wounded; Mexican losses are some 150, but an equal number have deserted. With San Antonio and most all Texas under their control, most of the volunteers return home in the mistaken belief that the war is over.

November 3, 1835

Texas War of Independence (continued). Elected Texan representatives, known as the Consultation, meeting at San Felipe, vote to oppose Mexican president General Antonio López de Santa Anna as loyal citizens of Mexico. The delegates demand the restoration of Mexico's federal Constitution of 1824, and they call on all Mexicans to oppose Santa Anna's dictatorial rule. The Consultation serves as the provisional government of Mexican Texas from November 1835 through March 1836.

November 4, 1835

Texas War of Independence (continued): Battle of Lipantitlán. Having departed Goliad with some 30 men on October 30, Ira J. Westover heads for Fort Lipantitlán in northwestern Nueces County. The fort had been erected on a campground of the Lipan Apache Indians on the west bank of the Nueces River about three miles upstream from the old town of San Patricio on the east side of the river. En route to the fort, additional volunteers join Westover, bringing his strength to about 60–70 men.

On November 3, Westover secures the surrender of the 21-man Mexican garrison at Fort Lipantitlán, on condition that the men are paroled. The Texans also take possession of the fort's two cannon. The next day Westover quits the fort and establishes an excellent defensive position across the Nueces. It is attacked by 90 Mexicans commanded by Captain Nicolás Rodríguez.

In a battle lasting about half an hour, the Texans kill 28 Mexicans, themselves suffering only 1 wounded. Rather than risk another Mexican attack while they attempt to move the captured cannon taken in the fort, the Texans elect to dump the two guns into the Nueces.

December 17, 1835

Marines are landed from the U.S. Navy frigate *Brandywine* (54 guns) to protect the U.S. embassy at Lima, Peru. They are withdrawn on January 24, 1836.

December 28, 1835

Second Seminole War: Dade Massacre. The Second Seminole War (1835–1842) is the longest and most expensive of all Native American wars in the United States; it begins with the Dade Massacre (Dade's Massacre). On December 23, 1835, Major Francis L. Dade departs Fort Brooke (Tampa Bay) in Florida Territory with 107 men to reinforce Fort King in central Florida, garrisoned only by a single company and vulnerable to being overrun. The troops are shadowed by the Seminoles for five days.

On December 28 a few miles north of the Little Withlacoochee River, some 160 hostile Seminoles and allied African Americans ambush Dade's column. The attackers are led by Chief Micanopy of the Alachuas, his nephew Wildcat, Abraham Jumper, and Alligator (Halpatter Tustenuggee). Despite Dade's 6-pounder gun, the column is destroyed. Only 3 men survive: 1 is hunted down and killed the next day, and 2 badly wounded soldiers make it back to Fort Brooke, 1 of whom dies several days later. Reportedly the Seminoles lose 3 men killed and 5 wounded.

That same afternoon, Chief Osceola leads 40 warriors in an ambush outside of Fort King, killing 7 soldiers there before retiring southward to join Micanopy.

December 31, 1835

Second Seminole War (continued): Battle of the Withlacoochee River. In Florida Territory on December 29, 1835, Brigadier General Duncan L. Clinch leads a second larger column into hostile Seminole territory with the plan to attack a Seminole camp across the Withlacoochee River at what is now Lake Tsala Apopoka. Clinch has 250 U.S. Army troops under Lieutenant Colonel Alexander C. W. Fanning and 500 volunteers under Florida Militia brigadier general Richard K. Call. Crossing the Withlacoochee River on December 31, Clinch's column is attacked by some 230 Seminole warriors and 30 allied African Americans, all led by Chief Osceola. Osceola is wounded in the ensuing fighting, but Clinch is forced to withdraw back across the river, having suffered 5 dead and 59 wounded.

At the same time, hostile Seminole bands raid Florida Atlantic coast sugar plantations, destroying many. A number of the slaves on these plantations join the Seminoles.

January 7, 1836

Texas War of Independence (continued): President of Mexico Antonio López de Santa Anna reaches Saltillo in the state of Coahuila in northern Mexico, there to gather a larger military force to invade and reconquer breakaway Texas. Within three weeks he heads northward with some 6,000 men, including some 4,500 infantry, 1,120 cavalry, 190 artillerymen, and 185 sappers.

January 19, 1836

Second Seminole War (continued): U.S. Navy support. The navy dispatches the sloop *Vandalia* (20 guns) from Pensacola to Fort Brooke (Tampa Bay). Also this same day, the navy sends 57 marines to Fort Brooke from Key West. Throughout the conflict, navy and U.S. Coast Guard ships help ferry men and supplies to forts and installations along the Florida coasts. With the U.S. Army now numbering fewer than 7,000 men manning a total of 53 posts, the U.S. government must also rely heavily on state and territory militias and self-organized militia units.

January 21, 1836

Second Seminole War (continued). Major General Winfield Scott is ordered to assume command of U.S. troops in Florida Territory. Also on this date, Commodore Alexander J. Dallas, commanding the U.S. Navy West India Squadron, is directed to institute a blockade of the Florida coast. The settlers claim that the Seminoles are receiving arms from Cuba and the Bahamas. Although no gun-running activities are ever uncovered, the blockade remains in effect throughout the war.

February 23–March 6, 1836

Texas War of Independence (continued): Siege of the Alamo. Mexican president General Antonio López de Santa Anna and 3,000–4,000 troops lay siege to the former Spanish mission of the Alamo in San Antonio de Béxar (present-day San Antonio). The first half of the Mexican Army arrives at the Alamo on February 23, 1836, sooner than had been expected.

Although the vastly outnumbered 187 defenders led by Jim Bowie and William Barret Travis repulse several assaults, superior Mexican Army numbers and artillery eventually prevail. The Alamo is taken on March 6, and all the defenders are slain. The Mexicans suffer some 400–600 killed or wounded. The

Siege of the Alamo		
Date	February 23–March 6, 1836	
Location	San Antonio, Texas	
Opponents (*winner)	*Mexico	Republic of Texas
Commander	Mexican president General Antonio López de Santa Anna	Jim Bowie; William B. Travis
#	3,000–4,000 men	187 men
Casualties	400–600 killed or wounded	All defenders slain

David Crockett, (1786–1836)

Soldier, frontiersman, politician, and frontier folk hero. David ("Davy") Crockett was born into a poor frontier family on August 17, 1786, in Greene County in eastern Tennessee. He only rarely attended school and was hired out by his father in 1798 to help on a cattle drive to Virginia. Crockett ran away when his employer tried to keep him against his will and then made his way back to Tennessee but soon was off again on his own.

Crockett married in 1806 and moved to middle Tennessee in 1811, settling in Franklin County, near the border with the Mississippi Territory. Crockett proved to be a poor farmer, but he was an excellent hunter. In 1813 he joined the Tennessee Militia fighting in the Creek War (1813–1814). He participated in the campaign under Major General Andrew Jackson against the Creek Red Stick faction. Crockett apparently served primarily as a scout and guard for the horse herds. After his first enlistment expired, he returned home. In the late summer of 1814, Crockett again enlisted and spent the autumn of 1814 at Pensacola.

Following the war, Crockett was elected a lieutenant in the 32nd Militia Regiment of Franklin County. His wife died that summer, and Crockett married a widow with two children the following year. In 1817 they moved to Lawrence County, Tennessee, where Crockett was appointed justice of the peace. He apparently used stories about his exploits in the war against the Creeks to enhance his reputation. He was elected colonel of the 57th Militia Regiment in 1818, and in 1821 he was elected to the state legislature, where he established himself as a supporter of settlers' rights on public lands. He won reelection in 1823 but was defeated in 1825.

In 1827 Crockett was elected to the U.S. House of Representatives after having campaigned as an honest country boy. He soon became a noted member of the House, thanks to his backwoods persona. Strangers called him "Davy," a name appropriate to that image.

Crockett's support for settlers' rights, for the Bank of the United States, and against Native American removal brought him into conflict with President Andrew Jackson. The anti-Jackson faction, later to become the Whig Party, took interest in Crockett as a potential national candidate. He was reelected to the House in 1829 but was defeated in 1831. With Whigs' support, Crockett won reelection in 1833.

In 1833 a book of frontier stories appeared titled *Sketches and Eccentricities of Colonel David Crockett of West Tennessee*. Supposedly written by Crockett, it was in fact ghosted by an anonymous Whig but was enormously popular, making Crockett into a folk hero among Eastern readers. Although Crockett probably supplied many of the stories, he was apparently embarrassed by the extent to which the truth was bent. He then wrote, with help, his own autobiography, titled *A Narrative of the Life of David Crockett of the State of Tennessee*. Published in 1834, the book could be viewed as a campaign biography for a future run for the presidency. Crockett spent a month traveling through the Northeast to promote the book and to make himself known to voters. In his autobiography, Crockett again portrayed himself as a simple frontiersman, honest and straightforward, who stood up for the common man.

His opposition to Jackson ultimately led to Crockett's political demise, and he was defeated in the election of August 1835. On November 1, 1835, he and a small party left for Texas to seek their fortunes. In early February 1836 he arrived in San Antonio, where he joined the garrison of the Alamo. He died there on March 6, 1836, during the Battle of the Alamo when Mexican forces under General Antonio López de Santa Anna attacked the fort. Crockett's frontiersman reputation has long survived him; he remains a part of American legend to this day.

TIM WATTS

Further Reading

Hollman, Robert E. *Davy Crockett.* Dallas, TX: Durban House Publishing, 2005.
Remini, Robert V. *Andrew Jackson and His Indian Wars.* New York: Viking, 2001.

execution of the Alamo defenders provides the Texan battle cry "Remember the Alamo!"

February 27, 1836

Second Seminole War (continued): Renewed fighting along the Withlacoochee River. Brigadier General Edmund P. Gaines, a longtime rival of new U.S. commander in Florida Major General Winfield Scott, departs New Orleans for Florida with some 1,100 regulars and volunteers, arriving at Fort Brooke (Tampa Bay) in Florida Territory on February 9. Believing that Scott had sent supplies to Fort King, on February 13 Gaines marches inland with 1,000 men and one 6-pounder gun to reinforce Brigadier General Duncan L. Clinch in central Florida. Reaching the site of the Dade ambush, his men bury the remains of the dead. Gaines then pushes on to Fort King, arriving there on February 22, only to find that the supplies are not there.

Gaines departs Fort King on February 26, but the next day his men are attacked while attempting to cross the Withlacoochee River, sustaining 4 dead (including Lieutenant James Izard, mortally wounded) and 38 wounded. Gaines then constructs a defensive works known as Camp Izard, which comes under Seminole siege. Gaines sends an appeal to Clinch for assistance, hoping that the Seminoles at Fort Izard can be crushed between the two army forces. Soon Gaines's force is in dire straits, the men reduced to eating their horses and mules.

Clinch disobeys Scott's order that he remain at Fort Drane and instead marches to Gaines's assistance (Scott's order authorizing the move arrives only after his departure), rescuing Gaines and his men on March 6. Gaines then returns to New Orleans, and Clinch assumes command of his men.

March 2, 1836

Texas War of Independence (continued): Texas declares its independence. On February 28, 1836, 41 Texas delegates arrive at Washington-on-the-Brazos. The convention convenes the next day, and on March 2 a five-man committee headed by George Childress submits a draft declaration of independence, which is approved the same day without debate. General Sam Houston leads the Republic of Texas military forces.

March 2, 1836

Texas War of Independence (continued). At Aqua Dulce Creek a Mexican Army cavalry patrol surprises and wipes out a foraging party of 23 Americans and 3 Mexicans led by Dr. James Grant. Only 6 escape (5 of these join James W. Fannin Jr. at Goliad, only to die in the Goliad Massacre of March 27), and 6 are captured and taken to Matamoros as prisoners; all the others are killed in the engagement.

March 11, 1836

Texas War of Independence (continued): Texan retreat from Gonzales. Learning that the Alamo has fallen and that Mexican general Ramírez y Sesma is approaching with 700 troops, Texas Army commander General Samuel Houston decamps from Gonzales and withdraws eastward with his 375 men. He orders Texan commander at Goliad James W. Fannin Jr. to withdraw his garrison.

Samuel Houston (1793–1863)

Soldier, frontiersman, and politician who led Texan forces during the struggle for independence from Mexico and subsequently became president of the Texan Republic. Samuel ("Sam") Houston was born on March 2, 1793, in Rockbridge County, Virginia, but moved to Tennessee as a boy. A rebellious youth, Houston left the family farm at age 16 and lived with the Cherokees. He remained with them for two years before he returned and established a school for frontier children.

Following the outbreak of the War of 1812, in 1813 Houston enlisted in the army as a private, but his leadership skills were quickly recognized, and he was commissioned an ensign four months later. During the war he served with Major General Andrew Jackson in the campaign against the Creeks, including the Battle of Horseshoe Bend, when Houston was wounded three times. His heroism and leadership caught the attention of Jackson, who subsequently helped Houston at several points during his career.

Houston remained in the army after the war and was promoted to second lieutenant. In 1817 he was assigned to participate in the removal of the Cherokees from their lands to the Oklahoma Territory. In 1818 Houston resigned from the army after he was given an official reprimand by Secretary of War John C. Calhoun for appearing before the secretary in Cherokee garb.

Houston then studied law, passed the bar, and established a practice in Lebanon, Tennessee. On Jackson's recommendation, Houston was appointed a colonel and then was elected major general of the state militia. Houston also became active in politics and was elected first as attorney general for Nashville and then to the U.S. House of Representatives in 1823. In Congress, Houston worked to support Jackson's candidacy for the presidency following the election of 1824. In 1827 Houston left the House and became the governor of Tennessee. Although he was reelected in 1829, Houston left politics and Tennessee after a brief failed marriage.

Once again Houston lived among the Cherokees, this time in Oklahoma. During this three-year period, Houston met and married a woman of mixed Cherokee and European ancestry. The couple established a trading post on the Neosho River. In 1832 Jackson, then president, dispatched Houston to Texas to negotiate with tribes in the region.

Houston became involved in regional politics in Texas and emerged as one of the foremost proponents of independence from Mexico. He attended the San Felipe Convention in 1833 that drew up a constitution for the territory and a petition to the Mexican government requesting that the area be made a state. In 1835 he was appointed commander of the Army of Texas with the rank of major general. The following year Houston was a delegate when the Texas assembly declared independence. Although the Mexican forces initially enjoyed military success against the rebellious Texans, Houston was able to win a major victory at the Battle of San Jacinto on April 21, 1836. During the engagement, Houston was wounded and had his horse shot out from under him. The day after the battle, the Mexican commander General Antonio López de Santa Anna was captured. The battle confirmed Texan independence, although Mexico officially refused to accept the loss of Texas until after the Mexican-American War.

Houston's popularity led to him being elected as president of Texas in 1836. He worked hard to convince the United States to annex Texas as a new state and to improve relations between white settlers and Native Americans. After his first term as president ended in 1838, Houston served in the Texas

House of Representatives, but he was reelected president in 1841. After Texas joined the Union in 1845, Houston served two terms in the U.S. Senate, where he supported the Mexican-American War.

In the Senate, Houston supported efforts to compromise on the issue of slavery and became well known as a staunch Unionist Democrat. His support for the Union and his efforts on behalf of Native Americans eroded his popularity in Texas. He ran unsuccessfully for governor of Texas in 1857 and left the Senate in 1859. He again ran for governor that same year and won in his second attempt. Once in office, Houston favored the use of force to establish a protectorate over Mexico and other areas of Central America as a way to divert attention from the growing sectional strife in the Union.

Following the election of Abraham Lincoln in 1860, Houston called a special session of the Texas legislature to debate secession. He opposed secession, but the convention voted overwhelmingly to leave the Union. Houston oversaw the initial steps to sever ties with the Union but refused to take the oath of allegiance to the Confederacy. On March 16, 1861, the legislature removed him from office. Houston and his family moved to Huntsville, Texas, where he died on July 26, 1863.

JACK COVARRUBIAS AND TOM LANSFORD

Further Reading

Braider, Donald. *Solitary Star: A Biography of Sam Houston.* New York: Putnam, 1974.
Bruhl, Marshall de. *Sword of San Jacinto: A Life of Sam Houston.* New York: Random House, 1993.
Campbell, Randolph B. *Sam Houston and the American Southwest.* New York: Addison-Wesley, 1993.
Day, Donald, and Harry Herbert Ullom, eds. *The Autobiography of Sam Houston.* Norman: University of Oklahoma Press, 1954.
Williams, John Holt. *Sam Houston: A Biography of the Father of Texas.* New York: Simon and Schuster, 1993.

Houston's troops are accompanied by a larger number of refugees. The flight of Texans from their homes ahead of the advancing Mexican Army, beginning in February 1836, is known as the Runaway Scrape.

March 12–15, 1836

Texas War of Independence: Battle of Refugio. Commander of Texas forces at Goliad James W. Fannin Jr., aware that Mexican general José de Urrea y Elías Gonzales is advancing north from Matamoros with 1,400 men, delays implementing an order from Texas Army commander General Samuel Houston to evacuate to Guadalupe Victoria, 28 miles distant. On March 10, 1836, Fannin sends Amon B. King and 28 men to the village of Refugio to aid evacuation of families there to Goliad. Meanwhile, Carlos de la Garza and some 80 rancheros, serving as scouts and advance cavalry for Urrea's army, raid Refugio. On March 12 before leaving Refugio, King seeks to punish Garza and his rancheros, but he underestimates their strength and is himself obliged to retreat with the families back to the Nuestra Señora del Refugio Mission, where he takes refuge and sends an appeal to Fannin for assistance.

In what proves to be a disastrous move, Fannin sends Lieutenant Colonel William Ward and some 120 men to assist King. On March 13 they rescue King, his men, and the settlers, but King and Ward then argue over who should command and how to proceed, with the result that King and some of the men embark on a punitive mission against the rancheros, allowing Urrea's main body to surround the remainder under Ward at the mission.

When King attempts to return to the mission, he encounters Urrea's army and is forced to make a stand in woods along the Mission River. Although Ward's men at the mission withstand assaults during March 14, they are short of food, water, and ammunition.

Ward is able to communicates this to Fannin, who orders him to withdraw to Victoria, where they are to rendezvous. After leaving some volunteers with the Texan wounded and the families, Ward departs with the remainder of his men on the night of March 14 and moves toward Copano through woods and swamps, avoiding Mexican cavalry. King's company also attempts to escape during the night of March 14 but is overtaken and captured the next day, then marched back to the mission, now occupied by Urrea's forces. On March 16 those who had remained at the mission from Ward's battalion, together with King and all of his company, are executed except for two Germans, another individual, and the local families who are saved thanks to the intercession of German-born Mexican lieutenant colonel Juan José Holzinger.

Ward and his men reach Victoria, but finding it occupied by Urrea's troops, they continue on to Dimitt's Landing, where they surrender. Except for some who are detailed to build boats, the rest are marched back to La Bahía, where they are executed in the Goliad Massacre (see March 27, 1836).

Though the battle of Refugio is one of the lesser-known engagements of the Texas War of Independence, it has significant consequences, for in splitting his forces and delaying his departure from Goliad, Fannin brings about the Battle of Coleto Creek while also reducing by 150 the number of men he will have there, helping to ensure his defeat.

March 19–20, 1836

Texas War of Independence (continued): Battle of Coleto Creek. Mexican general José de Urrea y Elías Gonzales advances north in Texas from Matamoros with 1,400 men, making his way north along the coast to allow the Mexican Navy to land supplies. James W. Fannin Jr. commands 500 Texans at Goliad's La Bahía presidio (Fort Defiance, as Fannin calls it) in southeastern Texas. Having spent considerable time fortifying that post, Fannin is reluctant to give it up. His men are confident and anxious to confront the Mexicans. Yet with the fall of the Alamo on March 6, 1836, Texan general Sam Houston orders Fannin to withdraw from Goliad to Guadalupe Victoria, 28 miles distant, "as soon as practical on receipt of this order." Fannin knows that the Gulf coast port of Copano has already been lost, reducing the significance of his own position, yet he is slow to obey Houston's order.

Fannin weakens his own force and delays his departure by sending some 150 men to Refugio to assist in the evacuation of families to Goliad (see March 12–15, 1836). This includes wagons and teams that he himself needs in an evacuation of Goliad. He also delays his own departure because he is hoping to receive oxen and wagons from Guadalupe Victoria, but the chief reason is his insistence on hearing from the dispatched contingents before he himself moves with the main body. Urrea has captured Fannin's couriers and is aware of the Texan's plans, while Fannin is largely ignorant of Mexican strength and movements.

On March 17, Fannin learns of the defeat at Refugio, yet no movement occurs until early on March 19. Fannin insists on taking with him 9 cannon and some 1,000 muskets, slowing the march considerably and allowing Urrea the opportunity to close. Fannin has also failed to take sufficient water and has food for only several meals.

Urrea's cavalry has already reached Goliad when Fannin quits that place. Urrea is preparing to lay siege to the Presidio La Bahía, but learning from his scouts of Fannin's withdrawal, Urrea detaches men to garrison the presidio and sets out with some 360 troops in pursuit of the Texans, two hours ahead.

Urrea catches up with Fannin at about 1:30 p.m. on March 19 while the Texans are crossing a stretch of open prairie. Urrea orders his cavalry to halt the Texans before they can reach protective timber about a mile away or Coleto Creek, two miles distant. The resulting engagement, one of the most important battles of the Texas War of Independence, is known as the Battle of Coleto Creek, the Battle of the Prairie, and the Battle of Oak Grove Creek.

Fannin deploys his men in a moving hollow square. When the Texans are about a mile from the creek and in a low area trying to reach higher ground 400–500 yards distant, the ammunition wagon breaks down. When Fannin calls a council of war to consider taking what ammunition they can carry while trying to reach the timber, Urrea attacks.

Although Urrea's cavalry and infantry are unable to penetrate the Texan formation, by nightfall they have killed 10 Texans and wounded another 60, 40 of them seriously. Fannin is among the wounded. Fannin's men are also running out of ammunition, and they have no water. Still, spirits are high, for the men believe that they will soon be reinforced from Guadalupe Victoria.

The battle resumes the next morning, March 20, when Urrea, who has brought up reinforcements during the night and now has 700–1,000 men, commences artillery fire from higher ground at close range. His situation now hopeless, Fannin treats with Urrea. What transpires is still debated, but Fannin asks for terms that will have the Texans surrendering as prisoners of war "according to the practices of civilized nations," to be paroled and returned to the United States. Urrea rejects these and offers written terms, with the Texans becoming prisoners of war "at the disposal of the Supreme Mexican Government." Urrea maintains that no prisoner of war "at the disposal" of Mexico has ever been executed. He also promises to recommend to Mexican president General Antonio López de Santa Anna that these terms be honored and expresses confidence that Fannin's men would be paroled and repatriated to the United States within eight days. Fannin accepts.

The Battle of Coleto Creek not only removes a large Texan fighting force from the field but also ensures Mexican military control of the port of Copano and the coastal region south of the Brazos River. However, it also instills in the Mexicans a sense of overconfidence that will cost them later.

March 25, 1836

Second Seminole War (continued): Beginning of Scott's offensive. On this date commander of U.S. forces in Florida Territory Major General Winfield Scott launches a three-pronged offensive with more than 5,000 men against the Seminoles. Three columns are to converge simultaneously on the main Seminole villages along the Withlacoochee River.

Scott accompanies the right column from Fort Drane, commanded by Brigadier General Duncan L. Clinch. Brigadier General Abraham Eustis leads the left column and is to proceed southwest from Volusia, a town on the St. Johns River. Colonel William Lindsey leads the center column of Alabama and Florida militia, moving north from Fort Brooke.

Scott has little success. Eustis and Lindsey are to have their forces ready on March 25 so that Clinch can drive the Seminoles into them. Proceeding from St. Augustine to his starting position at Volusia, Eustis burns Pilaklikaha, also known as Abraham's Town for its Black Seminole leader Abraham, and all three columns are delayed. Clinch and Lindsey are not in place until March 28, while Eustis is not ready until March 30. Clinch crosses the Withlacoochee River on March 29 but finds the Seminole villages deserted. The Seminoles refuse to be drawn into conventional battle, and Scott's men withdraw; only a few Seminoles are killed or captured. Out of supplies, all three of Scott's columns proceed to Fort Brooke.

March 27, 1836

Texas War of Independence (continued). Goliad Massacre. Mexican general José Urrea's flying column had forced the surrender of some 300 Texans under Colonel James Fannin near Coleto Creek (see March 19–20, 1836). While Urrea continues on to Victoria with the bulk of his force, the Texan prisoners are returned to Goliad. They are joined there by other prisoners, bringing to more than 350 the number of men held at Goliad. Although the Texans assume that they will be treated honorably, Mexican president General Antonio López de Santa Anna bypasses Urrea and orders Colonel José Nicolás de la Portilla, commanding at Goliad, to implement the congressional decree of December 30, 1835, which calls for captured armed rebels to be executed as pirates.

On March 27, 1836, Palm Sunday, the Texan prisoners including Fannin are summarily executed. In all, about 342 Texans are executed. More than 20 men escape, carrying news of the massacre.

The Goliad Massacre hardens opinion against Mexico in the United States and gives the Texans another point in their rallying cry, now "Remember the Alamo! Remember Goliad!"

April 18, 1836

Texas War of Independence (continued): Houston arrives near Harrisburg. After a two-and-a-half-day forced march to Harrisburg with the bulk of the Texas field forces, Texas Army commander General Samuel Houston learns that Mexican forces under President Antonio López de Santa Anna y Pérez de Lebrón have divided. Santa Anna had arrived at Harrisburg with some 700 men on April 15 and burned that place. Houston's army is quite close to this part of the Mexican Army. On April 19 Houston's men cross to the Harrisburg side of Buffalo Bayou and the next day take up position along the San Jacinto River to await the Mexicans' arrival.

April 20–24, 1836

Second Seminole War (continued): Siege of Fort Drane. In April 1836 the Seminoles attack a number of forts in Florida Territory. They strike Camp Cooper in the Cove of the Withlacoochee, Fort Alabama on the Hillsborough River north of Fort Brooke, and Fort Barnwell near Volusia. Then on April 20, 1836, the Seminoles mount a major night attack on Fort Drane. Their assault fails, and the fort is relieved on April 24.

April 21, 1836

Texas War of Independence (continued): Battle of San Jacinto. At dawn on April 20, 1836, Texas Army forces under General Sam Houston continue down Buffalo Bayou. At Lynch's Ferry they capture a boat carrying supplies to Mexican forces under Mexican president General Antonio López de Santa Anna. They then withdraw about one mile on the Harrisburg road and encamp in some timber on rising ground. That afternoon some Texas cavalry clash with the Mexican infantry, almost bringing on a general engagement. Two Texans are wounded, one mortally.

Santa Anna makes camp about three-quarters of a mile from the Texans, and both sides prepare for battle the next day. The Texans are eager for battle, but at about 9:00 a.m. Houston learns that Mexican general Martín Perfecto de Cos has crossed Vince's Bridge and reinforced Santa Anna with 540 men, nearly doubling the latter's strength to some 1,360 men. Houston orders the bridge destroyed to prevent further Mexican reinforcement, but its destruction means that neither side will be able to retreat toward Harrisburg.

Shortly before noon, Houston calls a council of war. While some want an immediate assault on the Mexican position, a majority favor waiting for a Mexican attack. Houston withholds his own views at the council but then formulates an attack plan. He forms up his forces and attacks at about 3:30 p.m. while the Mexicans are taking their afternoon siesta. Inexplicably, no Mexican pickets are posted, although initial Texan movements are screened by the rising ground and woods. The Texans then rush the Mexican lines with the cry "Remember the Alamo! Remember Goliad!"

The battle is over in only 18 minutes. With 910 men, Houston has routed the larger Mexican force of 1,200 men in what turns out to be the concluding military event of the Texas War of Independence. The Texans lose 9 killed or mortally wounded; 30 others receive lesser wounds, among them Houston with an ankle shattered by a musket ball. The Mexicans suffer 630 killed and 730 taken prisoner, including 208 wounded. The Texans also capture a large number of muskets and other small arms, ammunition, provisions, horses and mules, and $12,000 in silver.

Battle of San Jacinto		
Date	April 21, 1836	
Location	Near present-day La Porte, Texas	
Opponents (*winner)	*Republic of Texas	Mexico
Commander	General Sam Houston	President and General Antonio López de Santa Anna
#	910 men, 2 guns	1,360 men, 1 gun
Casualties	9 men killed or mortally wounded; 30 wounded	630 killed, 730 captured (including 208 wounded); large quantity of arms and ammunition

Santa Anna is not among those initially captured, and the next day search parties are sent out to find him. He is discovered hiding in the grass. Clad as a common soldier, he is not recognized until one of the Mexican prisoners is heard addressing him as "el presidente." Santa Anna now agrees to recognize the independence of Texas. Although this action is repudiated by the Mexican government, Texas independence is a recognized fact.

April 27, 1836

Second Seminole War (continued). Marching to the relief of Fort Alabama, on this date 600 Alabama militiamen under Colonel William Chisholm are ambushed by Seminoles at Thonotosasa Creek in Florida Territory. The militiamen suffer 5 killed and 24 wounded. Fort Alabama is abandoned at the end of the month, as is Fort King in late May.

May 21, 1836

Second Seminole War (continued): Scott transferred. In Washington, Secretary of War William Cass, displeased with Major General Winfield Scott's lack of success against the Seminoles in Florida Territory, orders him to Georgia to take charge of the removal of the Creek Indians to the West. Florida territorial governor Richard K. Call takes command in Scott's absence.

Fort King is abandoned in late May. In June soldiers are rescued from a blockhouse on the Withlacoochee River, where they had been besieged for 48 days. Serious illnesses among the troops that summer force the abandonment of Fort Drane in July and Fort Defiance at the end of August.

May 23, 1836

Creek War. Although Creek Native Americans had been forced from Georgia and many Lower Creeks had moved to Indian Territory (present-day Oklahoma), some 20,000 Muscogee Creeks remain in Alabama. That state moves to abolish tribal governments and extend state laws over the Creeks. The Creeks appeal to President Andrew Jackson for protection, but no assistance is forthcoming, and in the Treaty of Cusseta of March 24, 1832, the Creek lands are divided into individual allotments, which the Creeks can then sell and use the money to move west or remain in Alabama and submit to state law. Land speculators and squatters soon defraud the Creeks of their rightful allotments, and violence breaks out in the so-called Creek War of 1836.

On May 23, President Jackson orders U.S. Marine Corps commandant Colonel Archibald Henderson to send all available men to aid in suppressing the Creeks. Henderson personally leads two battalions of marines, more than half of the corps, to Alabama and Georgia. On the conclusion of the Creek War that summer, the marines continue on to Florida to join the war against the Seminoles.

June 10–28, 1836

Creek War (continued): Campaign against the Creeks. In Georgia while still serving as the army's quartermaster general, Brigadier General Thomas S. Jesup takes the offensive against hostile Creeks and captures their main camp. Major General Winfield Scott, who had been preparing his own offensive, is angry that Jesup twice disobeyed orders to stop. Scott is about to begin proceedings against Jesup when he is himself ordered to Washington. There Scott finds himself before a court of inquiry concerning his dealings with Brigadier General Edmund P. Gaines. The inquiry ends with Scott being cleared of any wrongdoing and Gaines censured.

July 2, 1836

Creek War (continued): Removal of the Creeks. At Fort Mitchell, Georgia, the forced relocation of the Creek Indians to Indian Territory (present-day Oklahoma) begins.

July 4, 1836

The U.S. government recognizes the Republic of Texas, an action that greatly angers the Mexican government.

July 12, 1836

Charles H. Haswell, who designed the steam engines for the U.S. Navy steamship *Fulton II*, becomes the first engineer commissioned in the U.S. Navy.

Archibald Henderson (1783–1859)

U.S. Marine Corps commandant, often referred to as the "Grand Old Man of the Marine Corps," having served for nearly 53 years. Archibald Henderson was born near the village of Dumfries, Virginia, on January 21, 1783. After working in his father's ironworks for a time, he secured a commission as a second lieutenant in the U.S. Marine Corps on June 4, 1806. He was promoted to first lieutenant on March 6, 1807, and to captain on April 1, 1811.

Henderson commanded the marine detachment in the frigate *President* during 1811–1812 and was assigned to the Charleston Navy Yard at the beginning of the War of 1812 during 1812–1813. In June 1814 he took command of the marine detachment in the frigate *Constitution,* and he took part in the engagement with and capture of the British frigate *Cyane* and sloop *Levant.* In 1816 he was breveted major, to date from August 1814.

From September 16, 1818, to March 2, 1819, Henderson was acting U.S. Marine Corps commandant. On October 17, 1820, following the cashiering of Lieutenant Colonel–Commandant Anthony Gale, Lieutenant Colonel Henderson was appointed the fifth commandant of the U.S. Marine Corps. He served in this position for almost 39 years, the longest tenure in that position in history. On July 1, 1834, he was promoted to colonel commandant.

As commandant, Henderson not only restored the reputation of the U.S. Marine Corps but also is generally credited with preserving the corps, thwarting an attempt by President Andrew Jackson in 1829 to combine it with the army. Instead, in 1834 Congress passed the Act for the Better Organization of the Marine Corps, ensuring that the U.S. Marine Corps would remain part of the Navy Department. Henderson proved to be an able administrator who established the rigid, Spartan training regimen for which the marines became famous, and he secured better facilities for the men. He also made standard the carrying of the Mameluke pattern sword by marine officers. He was also able to expand the role of the U.S. Marine Corps beyond mere ship service and naval yard security. Taking advantage of the Indian Wars, he developed select marine battalions that could serve in the field in conjunction with the army.

Indeed, Henderson took to the field himself while commandant. In 1836 Jackson ordered Henderson to send marines to assist in fighting during the Creek War. Henderson personally led two battalions of marines, more than half of the corps, in fighting in Alabama and Georgia. On the conclusion of the Creek War that summer, the marines transferred to Florida, where they fought in the Second Seminole War (1835–1842). Henderson was breveted brigadier general on January 27, 1837, for his role in the fighting.

Henderson lobbied unceasingly for an expansion in the size of the U.S. Marine Corps, but he achieved this as a consequence of the Mexican-American War, although the battalion he organized to take part in amphibious operations with the navy did not arrive in Mexico until three months after the fall of Veracruz. (Some 180 marines from the ships of the Home Squadron did take part in the landings, however.) Attached to Major General John A. Quitman's division, the marine battalion gained laurels in the assault of Chapultepec Castle on September 13, 1847.

Henderson was a strong advocate for the marines acquiring their own artillery units, and he secured authorization for artillery training in 1857. This helped ensure the future role of the U.S. Marine Corps in amphibious warfare. In June 1857 Henderson played an important role in suppressing rioters supporting the No-Nothing Party in Washington, D.C. Henderson died suddenly in Washington, D.C., on January 6, 1859.

Spencer C. Tucker

Further Reading

Dawson, Joseph G. "With Fidelity and Effectiveness: Archibald Henderson's Lasting Legacy to the U.S. Marine Corps." *Journal of Military History* 62(4) (October 1998): 727–753.

Millett, Allan R. *Semper Fidelis: The History of the United States Marine Corps.* New York: Macmillan, 1980.

July 19, 1836

Second Seminole War (continued): At Micanopy in Florida Territory, Seminole chief Osceola leads an ambush of a supply train of 22 wagons escorted by U.S. Army infantry and dragoons. Although a relief column arrives and the natives are driven off, the troops lose five dead and six wounded.

August 21–24, 1836

Second Seminole War (continued): Engagement near Fort Defiance. In Florida Territory, Dragoons and artillerymen commanded by Major Benjamin F. Pierce surprise and attack a Seminole encampment near Fort Defiance on the edge of the Alachua prairie. The soldiers are forced back after having suffered 1 dead and 16 wounded. Three days later Fort Defiance is abandoned.

September 29–Late November 1836

Second Seminole War (continued): Call's campaign. Richard K. Call, appointed Florida territorial governor on March 16, 1836, in June receives authorization from Secretary of War Lewis Cass to begin offensive operations against the Seminoles. After lengthy delays, on September 29, 1836, Call crosses the Suwannee River with some U.S. Army regulars, local militiamen, and 1,500 Tennessee volunteers to attack the principal Seminole area of the Cove of the Withlacoochee. He is subsequently joined by 200 regulars and 750 Creek Indians under Colonel John F. Lane.

Call reaches the now abandoned Fort Drane, then proceeds on to the Withlacoochee, where he arrives on October 13. With the river up because of recent flooding and the men not having brought axes, there is no way to cross the river. Call then proceeds west along the river, but a steamer with supplies sinks in the lower part of the river. Out of food, Call must return to Fort Drane.

In mid-November, Call mounts a second offensive. This time his men cross the Withlacoochee but find the Seminole villages deserted. His men then proceed south, up both banks of the Withlacoochee. On November 17 and 18, they defeat the Seminoles in two large skirmishes, killing 15 for 3 of their own dead.

On November 21 Call's force approaches Wahoo Swamp, where a major battle occurs as some 600 Seminole warriors and African Americans seek to protect their nearby families. The Seminoles withdraw across a stream. Major David Moniac, a mixed-blood Creek and the first Native American to graduate from the U.S. Military Academy, West Point, is shot and killed while trying to determine the depth of the steam. Uncertain of the depth of the water and again short of supplies, Call retires toward Volusia after having suffering 55 casualties. His two months of campaigning have accomplished little, and on December 9 he is replaced by U.S. Army brevet major general Thomas Jesup.

January 10–27, 1837

Second Seminole War (continued): Jesup's Campaign. New commander of U.S. forces fighting the Seminoles U.S. Army brevet Major General Thomas S. Jesup institutes new tactics. Instead of sending large columns into hostile territory in the futile hope of drawing the Seminoles into pitched battle, he attempts to wear down his opponent. This requires a large force, and Jesup eventually has 9,000 men available, about half of them militiamen and volunteers. Sailors, marines, and Revenue Service personnel also assist operations.

January 28, 1837

Second Seminole War (continued): Battle of the Hatchee-Lustee River. In the Great Cyprus Swamp, U.S. Marine Corps commandant Colonel Archibald Henderson, commanding one of the army's two brigades in Florida, which includes his marines, engages the Seminoles in the largest battle fought by the marines during the war. Six marines are killed or mortally wounded, but his men capture 30–40 Seminoles and Black Seminoles, mainly women and children, along with some 100 packhorses and 1,400 head of cattle. This battle leads a number of Seminole chiefs to request a meeting with U.S. Army commander in Florida Territory Major General Thomas S. Jesup.

March 6, 1837

Second Seminole War (continued): Treaty of Fort Dade. Following a meeting with U.S. commander in Florida Territory Major General Thomas S. Jesup, a number of chiefs, including Micanopy, sign a truce and agree to assemble their people at Fort Brooke for relocation to the Indian Territory (Oklahoma) on condition that they be accompanied by their allies and "their Negroes, their 'bona fide' property."

It appears as if the war is over, but neither side trusts the other. Slave catchers claim blacks who had sought refuge with the Seminoles, while other whites seek to have Seminoles arrested for crimes. On their part, many of the Seminole warriors seem chiefly interested in securing promised supplies and fail to bring in their women and children. Also, two principal Seminole chiefs, Osceola and Sam Jones (also known as Abriaca and Opoica), have not surrendered and oppose relocation.

June 2, 1837

Second Seminole War (continued): Osceola's raid on Fort Brooke. On the night of June 2, 1837, Chiefs Osceola and Sam Jones (also known as Abriaca and Opoica) lead a daring raid on the poorly guarded holding camp at Fort Brooke (Tampa) in Florida Territory, releasing the 700 Seminoles who are awaiting deportation. The war now resumes, with numerous small engagements, sieges, and ambushes.

October 21, 1837

Second Seminole War (continued): Capture of Osceola. Commander of U.S. forces in Florida Major General Thomas S. Jesup no longer trusts the Seminole leaders. He keeps pressure on the Seminoles by dispatching small units into the field in regular operations against them. In September, army and militia units capture two groups of Seminoles, one including King Philip and the other with Yuchi Billy. Both are principal Seminole chiefs. Jesup arranges for King Philip to send a message to his son Coacoochee (Wildcat) for a meeting with Jesup. When Coacoochee arrives under a flag of truce, Jesup has him arrested.

In October, Osceola, the greatest of the Seminole leaders, and Coa Hadjo, another chief, request a meeting with Jesup. It is set for Fort Payton south of St. Augustine. When the two chiefs arrive on October 21, 1837, also under a flag of truce, they too are seized and imprisoned at Fort Marion in St. Augustine. Osceola's capture by deceit causes a considerable uproar in the United States and condemnation of both Jesup and the Martin Van Buren administration. In December, Osceola and other Seminole prisoners are relocated to Fort Moultrie, South Carolina, where Osceola dies of malaria on January 30, 1838, and is buried with military honors.

Not all of the Seminoles remain captured. While Osceola was being held at Fort Marion, 20 others, including Coacoochee (Wildcat) and John Cavallo, a Black Seminole leader, escape through a narrow window.

December 13, 1837

The *Fulton II* is commissioned at New York. The U.S. Navy's first seagoing steamer, it is employed to test the efficiency of steam power, which many in the navy oppose.

December 25, 1837

Second Seminole War (continued): Battle of Lake Okeechobee. Major General Thomas S. Jesup, commander of U.S. forces against the Seminoles in Florida, assembles a large force that includes volunteers from as far away as Missouri and Pennsylvania and plans a massive drive from northern Florida to push the Seminoles farther south. U.S. Army brigadier general Joseph Marion Hernández will proceed down the east coast, Brigadier General Abraham Eustis will move southward up the St. Johns River, and Colonel Zachary Taylor will lead a column from Fort Brooke into the middle of Florida Territory and then turn southward between the Kissimmee and Peace Rivers. Other troops are to clear additional parts of the state, while a joint army-navy force of 200 men patrols the Florida east coast.

Taylor's unit sees the major action. On December 19, 1837, Taylor departs Fort Gardiner on the upper Kissimmee River with some 1,000 men (mostly regulars but some volunteers and Native American allies), driving toward Lake Okeechobee. In the first several days, some 90 Seminoles surrender. Taylor halts briefly to build Fort Basinger, where he leaves his sick along with sufficient men to guard the captured Seminoles. Then on Christmas Day, Taylor and about 800 men engage some 400 Seminoles led by Wildcat (Coacoochee), Sam Jones (also known as Abriaca and Opoica), and Alligator (Halpatter Tustenuggee) in a pitched battle on the north shores of Lake Okeechobee. The Seminoles are well positioned in a hammock surrounded by saw grass.

In this largest battle of the Second Seminole War, Taylor sends his men forward in two lines, with the Missouri volunteers leading. Their commander Colonel Richard Gentry, 3 other officers, and more than 20 enlisted personnel are killed before the militiamen break and retire. They are followed by 200 men of the 6th Infantry Regiment, who lose 4 officers and sustain nearly 40 percent casualties before they too retire. Taylor then sends in men of the 4th Infantry Regiment, along with the remnants of the militia and the 6th Infantry Regiment. They finally scatter the Seminoles in a bayonet charge.

Although celebrated as a great American victory, Taylor has lost 26 killed and 112 wounded. The

Battle of Lake Okeechobee		
Date	December 25, 1837	
Location	Lake Okeechobee, Florida	
Opponents (*winner)	*United States	Seminoles
Commander	Colonel Zachary Taylor	Wildcat, Sam Jones, and Alligator
#	Some 800 men (mostly regulars but some volunteers and Native American allies)	Some 400 warriors
Casualties	26 killed, 112 wounded	11 killed, 25 wounded

Seminoles suffer only some 11 killed and 25 wounded, and the remainder escape across the lake. The Battle of Lake Okeechobee is inconclusive, for the surviving Seminoles and their African American allies merely withdraw into the swamps. Guerrilla warfare continues.

December 29, 1837

Caroline Incident. Scottish-born Canadian journalist and former mayor of Toronto William Lyon Mackenzie, fleeing after a failed attempt at rebellion to establish a republic in Upper Canada, on December 14, 1837, takes refuge on Navy Island on the Canadian side of the Niagara River. American supporters furnish him and some 400 of his followers with money, arms, and supplies via the small steamboat *Caroline*.

On December 29 Canadian loyalist Colonel Sir Allan MacNab and ex–Royal Navy captain Andrew Drew lead some 50 militiamen in boats across the boundary into the United States, killing 1 member of the *Caroline*'s crew, wounding others, and seizing the steamer.

Setting the *Caroline* on fire, the Canadians cast it adrift to go over Niagara Falls. The *Caroline* Affair brings violent anti-British protests in the United States. President Martin Van Buren on January 5, 1838, warns Americans not to engage in hostile acts against Great Britain. He also calls out the militia and posts it on the frontier, and he dispatches Major

General Winfield Scott to command U.S. forces there and prevent any local initiatives. At the same time, professional officers replace MacNab and Drew on the Canadian side. Although tensions remain high for a time, Mackenzie and his followers abandon Navy Island on January 12, 1838, whereupon Canadian militiamen occupy it two days later.

January 8–9, 1838

Patriot raid on Amherstburg. Despite efforts by U.S. and Michigan authorities to prevent such activities, cross-border raids into Canada continue by Canadian revolutionaries and sympathetic Americans, known as Patriots. The Patriot aim is to seize Upper Canada and establish a republican form of government. Having stolen a large quantity of muskets, on January 8, 1838, some 200 Patriots, led by Irish-born self-proclaimed brigadier general Edward Theller, sail from Gibraltar, near Detroit, in the schooner *Anne* and the sloop *George Strong*, then occupy Bois Blanc Island opposite Amherstburg in Upper Canada (Ontario).

Canadian militia Lieutenant Colonel John Prince masses militia on the Canadian shoreline. These include a colony of ex-American slaves from Windsor, led by the Reverend Josiah Henson (said to be the inspiration for Harriet Beecher Stowe's novel, *Uncle Tom's Cabin*).

On January 9, Theller proceeds in his two ships to near Fort Malden in Canada and opens fire on both it and Amherstburg, exchanging shots with the militia ashore. That evening the *Anne* with a crew of 21 men runs aground and is captured by the British, who find 1 dead and 8 wounded aboard (Theller among the latter). Now leaderless, the remaining revolutionaries retire to Sugar Island on the American side of Lake Erie. The Canadians capture 2 cannon, some 300 muskets, a quantity of gunpowder, and supplies.

January 15, 1838

Second Seminole War (continued): First Battle of the Loxahatchee River. As Major General Thomas S. Jesup's other forces proceed down the peninsula on the east side of Lake Okeechobee, U.S. troops along the Caloosahatche River prevent Seminoles from moving north on the west side of the lake. At the same time a combined army-navy force is operating along the eastern coast, and on January 15, 1838, U.S. Navy lieutenant Levin Powell and 80 men in small boats, directed by a captured Seminole woman, move up the southwest fork of the Loxahatchee (Lockahatchee) River against a Seminole camp at present-day Jupiter, Florida. They see smoke rising from the Seminole camp when they are suddenly attacked and almost completely surrounded by a much larger Seminole force. Powell's men are able to fight their way out but at a cost of 4 dead and 22 wounded.

January 24, 1838

Second Seminole War (continued): Second Battle of the Loxahatchee River. Informed of the fighting along the Loxahatchee (Lockahatchee) River, Major General Thomas S. Jesup, commander of U.S. forces against the Seminoles, and his main column of some 1,500 men head southeast to engage these Seminoles. On January 24, Jesup's men are proceeding east of Lake Okeechobee when they encounter some 300 Seminoles. The Indians fire on Jesup's advance guard of dragoons, leading them into a cypress swamp while they themselves take up position in a hammock. Cannon and rocket fire drive the Seminoles from the hammock and across the Loxahatchee at a shallow point ("Indian Crossing"), where they make another stand. Jesup takes personal command. Dismounting and drawing a pistol, he calls on the Tennessee volunteers to follow him but is soon slightly wounded. The battle ends when Colonel William Harncy and his dragoons cross the river at another point and outflank the Seminoles. Jesup's force suffers 7 dead and 31 wounded; Seminole losses are fewer. This is the last standup battle of the Second Seminole War. The Seminoles simply disperse and head south into the swampy area now known as the Everglades.

February 8–March 21, 1838

Second Seminole War (continued). With fighting having died down, on February 8 Seminole chiefs Tuskegee and Halleck Hadjo inform U.S. commander in Florida Major General Thomas S. Jesup that they will stop fighting if they are allowed to remain in the area south of Lake Okeechobee. Jesup

 ## Pistols, Early Types

As a consequence of the introduction of gunpowder into Europe, in the late 14th and early 15th centuries a wide variety of individual hand gonnes appeared. Most were larger and evolved into the musket, but some were small enough to be classified as pistols. The true pistol came about with the introduction of the wheel-lock, which made possible firing the weapon with one hand. The name "pistol," which was in common use in England in the 1540s, may have evolved from the term *pistolese,* a dagger made in Pistola in northern Italy that in France and England was known as a *pistolet.*

Wheel-lock pistols were certainly in use by the 1540s. In the wheel-lock, pressing the trigger caused a cover over the pan containing the powder to slide forward. At the same time, iron pyrites known as the spanner, clamped into a cock or dog-head, brushed against a rough-edged wheel as the latter turned, creating sparks that ignited the exposed priming powder.

The snap-lock was the next improvement. Appearing in English pistols by 1580, the snap-lock employed flint and steel for the first time. Pulling the trigger opened the pan cover, while at the same time the cock swung forward, scraping the flint against the face of a piece of upright steel, driving it forward and causing sparks to fall in the exposed pan below.

The final step in the evolution of early pistols was the flintlock. Its firing device was simply a refinement of the snap-lock, in which the steel and pan cover were of one piece. The flintlock was a simpler and more reliable and effective flintlock than its predecessors. It was also safer and far easier to load.

To load the flintlock, the individual would rotate a cock holding a piece of flint to half cock so that the sear fell into a safety notch on the tumblers. The individual would pour a set amount of gunpowder down the weapon's muzzle, then ram a round ball (usually of lead) after it, seating the ball against the powder charge at the bottom of the breech with a ramrod that was usually stored on the underside of the barrel. The ball was wrapped in a cloth wad to ensure a tight fit between ball and barrel in order to hold the ball next to the powder. A small amount of fine-grain powder was then placed in the flash pan, and its lid or frizzen was closed. The pistol was now considered primed and loaded.

To fire the flintlock, the cock was rotated farther to release the safety lock. Pulling the trigger released the cock with the flint, which sprung forward. The flint struck the steel frizzen on the priming pan lid, opening it and exposing the priming powder to the sparks caused by the flint striking the frizzen. The resulting flash from the burning powder passed through the vent or touchhole in the barrel leading to the main powder charge. It then ignited, and the gases sent the ball down the barrel.

The ballistic dynamics imparted by windage (the difference in the diameter of the bore and the diameter of the ball), which caused the ball to in effect bound down the bore, meant that the effective range of the flintlock pistol was extremely limited. In general, one could depend on hitting one's target out to 10 15 yards at the very most, depending on the length of the pistol's barrel. Beyond 20 yards, the early flintlock pistol's main use was firing into a line or massed grouping of enemy combatants. Moreover, given the use of open gun powder, early flintlock pistol operations in wet weather proved problematic and unreliable. However, the flintlock firing system remained the most prominent small-arms design for many years. Alexander John Forsyth, a Scottish minister, invented a rudimentary percussion cap system in 1807 that eventually replaced the flintlock weapon.

(continued)

(Continued)

The first pistols were used by the military and civilians for personal defense, for hunting from horseback, and above all as a cavalry weapon. The Thirty Years' War (1618–1648) in Europe saw a great increase in pistol production. Pistols were especially favored for the close-in fighting at which cavalry actions occurred and in which accuracy was not an overriding factor. Pistols were also far easier to withdraw from saddle holsters and fire than were muskets. Often cavalrymen carried them in pairs.

Pistols were also popular aboard ship for boarding an enemy vessel or to repel boarders from one's own vessel. Pistols intended for naval use often were designed with a belt hook, an iron clip on the left-hand side of the stock.

Pistols came to be the favored individual firearm for officers and were often used in duels, commonplace to settle so-called affairs of honor among gentlemen of the time. The second half of the 18th century saw the production in England of precisely manufactured dueling pistols.

Pistols appeared in a bewildering array of sizes and styles. They generally ranged in bore size of from .45-caliber to .62-caliber. Some early pistols were as much as .80-caliber. Barrel length, at first as long as 20–25 inches, was reduced in the course of the 17th century to 15–18 inches. It continued to decrease in the course of the 18th century. Those pistols with the shortest barrels were known as pocket pistols. They had barrel lengths of up to 5 inches and an overall length of only 7–9 inches. The English light dragoons pistol that appeared around 1759 had a 9-inch barrel. The heavy dragoons pistol had a 12-inch barrel. Most pistols were single-shot firing, but multiple-shot pistols were also manufactured. Coachmen utilized blunderbuss pistols with large bores and flared muzzles for close-in defensive work.

Most pistols were muzzle-loaders, but the small size of pistols made breech-loaders possible, and from circa 1640–1850 there were turn-off pistols in which the barrel simply screwed off. The pistol was then loaded and the barrel screwed back in place.

Spencer C. Tucker

Further Reading

Blair, Claude, ed. *Pollard's History of Firearms.* New York: Macmillan, 1985.
Kinard, Jeff. *Pistols: An Illustrated History of Their Impact.* Santa Barbara, CA: ABC-CLIO, 2003.

favors this, knowing how difficult it will be to ferret out remaining Seminoles from the Everglades and believing that this task will be easier when more whites have settled in Florida. Jesup, however, has to secure the approval of Secretary of War Joel Poinsett. Awaiting his decision, Seminoles led by Tuskegee and Halleck Hadjo establish a camp near that of the American troops, and considerable fraternization occurs. Poinsett rejects the proposal, however. Jesup then summons the two Seminole chiefs for a meeting in his camp. They refuse.

Unwilling to let 500 Seminoles escape, Jesup sends his troops and captures the Seminoles with but little resistance.

February 23–25, 1838

Patriot raid on Fighting Island. There is considerable popular American support for the Canadian revolutionaries known as the Patriots and their American sympathizers who seek to establish a republic in Canada. Despite U.S. efforts to prevent this, the Patriots continue cross-border forays from the United States into Canada. Charles Duncombe, one of the leaders of the failed 1837 revolt in Upper Canada, now in Detroit, encourages another Patriot attempt. On February 23, 1838, Patriots in the seized steamer *Little Erie* depart Detroit and occupy Fighting Island, the largest Canadian island in the Detroit River below Sandwich in Upper Canada (Ontario). They are joined by some other Patriots who have departed Cleveland, Ohio, under self-proclaimed major general Donald McLeod, a former British Army sergeant. In all, the Patriots number perhaps 150 men. They also have one 6-pounder gun.

Forewarned by U.S. major general Hugh Brady at Detroit, British major Henry Dive Townshend departs Fort Malden (Amherstburg) with two companies of British regulars, 400 militiamen, and one gun. Attacking across the ice at daybreak on February 25, they capture the island but do not cross the border, which Brady ordered marked with red flags on the ice. (He also had ordered his troops to fire on the British should they indeed cross the border.)

U.S. forces briefly detain a few of the fleeing Patriots but soon release them. The British claim that there are no deaths on either side, but other reports put British losses at 5 dead and 15 wounded and Patriot casualties at 5 wounded, some seriously.

May 15, 1838

Second Seminole War (continued): Taylor assumes command. In the spring of 1839, with the War Department having failed to accept his recommendations, Major General Thomas S. Jesup asks to be relieved of command in Florida. During the 18 months that he has held command, more than 2,000 Seminoles have been captured and another 300 killed. Jesup returns to his post as quartermaster general of the army.

On May 15, 1838, Brevet Brigadier General Zachary Taylor assumes command of the 2,300 men in Florida. He concentrates on trying to keep the Seminoles out of northern Florida so that settlers might return to their homes. Although there are some Seminole raids in northern Florida, for the most part they concentrate on harvesting their crops and gathering supplies for the winter.

In October 1838 Taylor supervises the removal of the last Seminoles from their former stronghold along the Apalachicola River. Seminole raids in the Tallahassee area lead him to shift forces from southern Florida to improve security in northern Florida. There is little military activity during the winter, although Taylor continues to send small numbers of Seminoles west. At the same time he supervises the erection of more than 50 new posts and some 850 miles of wagon roads.

August 19, 1838–July 6, 1842

Wilkes Expedition. Officially known as the U.S. Exploring Expedition and the first large operation of this type undertaken by the navy, Lieutenant Charles Wilkes has command. It departs Norfolk, Virginia, on August 19, 1838, in the sloops *Vincennes* (flagship,

The U.S. Navy sloop *Vincennes* in the Antarctic. The *Vincennes* was the flagship of the Antarctic-exploring mission led by Lieutenant Charles Wilkes during 1838–1842. (National Oceanic and Atmospheric Administration)

10 guns) and *Peacock* (22 guns), the converted pilot boats and tenders *Sea Gull* and *Flying Fish,* and the storeship *Relief.* The expedition includes nine scientists. Wilkes is to survey various parts of the Pacific and explore the South Pole region. The voyages of the expedition extend over nearly four years, until July 6, 1842, covering some 85,000 miles, charting 280 islands, collecting thousands of specimens, and discovering the continent of Antarctica.

November 12, 1838

Hunter invasion of Prescott, Upper Canada. Americans seeking to overthrow the Canadian government and replace it with a republic, perhaps joining it to the United States, commandeer the paddle-wheel steamer *United States* and depart Sackets Harbor, New York, on November 12, 1838, towing the schooners *Charlotte of Oswego* and *Charlotte of Toronto.* The three ships carry 400 Americans led by self-proclaimed general John Ward Birge in an invasion of Ontario. The men are known as Hunters for the "Hunters' Lodges" formed the previous summer to advance such an attempt.

Early on the morning of November 12, the ships approach Prescott, Upper Canada (Ontario), on the St. Lawrence River but sheer off when discovered and Canadian sentries open fire. Some 200 Hunters disembark about a mile downriver at Windmill Point, but the arrival of the British steamer *Experiment* prevents other Hunters from reinforcing their compatriots by crossing the river from Ogdensburg on the opposite bank.

The Hunters are soon besieged by Canadian militia and British regulars. On the evening of November 21, 161 survivors surrender. Thirty others have been killed by artillery and small-arms fire. Eleven are subsequently tried and executed, and many others are sentenced to be transported to the Australian penal colony of Van Diemen's Land.

December 4, 1838

Battle of Windsor. After the Fighting Island battle (see February 23–25, 1838), U.S. and Canadian troops patrol their respective sides of the border, and there is little activity in the Detroit-Windsor area by the Patriots, the Canadian revolutionaries and their American supporters seeking to establish a republic in Canada. Skirmishes do occur along the St. Lawrence River and at Short Hills, with Patriot losses.

Patriot activity at Detroit begins anew with the onset of winter, however. Patriots in both the United States and Canada had planned an invasion across the Detroit River for the beginning of December, but reinforcements from Detroit fail to arrive, and British authorities learn of the plan and deploy troops and artillery along that section of the border. Some 300 Ohio and Pennsylvania Patriots now join several hundred locals and Canadians at Detroit.

Early on the morning of December 4, 1838, the Patriots cross the Detroit River into Canada in the commandeered steamboat *Champlain.* After attacking and burning a military barracks, they capture the town of Windsor, Upper Canada (Ontario). Shortly thereafter, Colonel John Prince, commander of troops at Fort Malden, leads 130 militiamen in defeating the invaders. Prince orders the immediate execution of 5 captured Patriots, causing considerable outrage in both Canada and the United States. The remaining captives are tried at London, Ontario. Six are executed, and 18 are transported to Tasmania.

The fighting at Windsor marks the end of military action in the rebellions in Upper and Lower Canada during 1837–1838.

December 1838

Trail of Tears (continued): Removal of the Cherokees. President Martin Van Buren authorizes Major General Winfield Scott and some 7,000 regular troops, volunteers, and Georgia, Alabama, North Carolina, and Tennessee militia to collect some 13,000 Cherokees in camps at the U.S. Indian Agency near Cleveland, Tennessee, in preparation for sending them to Indian Territory (present-day Oklahoma) in the West. On May 8, 1838, Scott orders his men to show consideration toward the Indians they are removing, but one Georgia participant later writes that "I fought through the War Between the States and have seen many men shot, but the Cherokee Removal was the cruelest work I ever knew."

The Cherokee removal begins in December 1838, with many of the Cherokees not even having moccasins for the 1,200-mile trek, which brings the deaths of some 4,000 Cherokees.

January 1–2, 1839

Second Battle of Kuala Batu. In retaliation for the murder of the captain of the American merchant ship *Eclipse,* Commodore George C. Read, commanding the U.S. Far Eastern Squadron, attacks the Sumatran village of Kuala Batu (Quallah Battoo). The U.S. Navy had earlier attacked Kuala Batu (see February 6, 1832) for similar reasons. Supported by fire from the frigate *Columbia* (54 guns) and the sloop *John Adams* (24 guns), Commander Thomas W. Wyman leads 360 men ashore to capture five forts and most of the village. Following payment of an indemnity by the Sumatrans and a pledge to reform, the ships depart.

February 12, 1839

Aroostook War. This war (also spelled Aroostock and known as the Pork and Beans War, the Coon-Canuck War, the Lumberjacks' War, and the Northeastern Boundary Dispute) is an armed confrontation in the winter of 1838–1839 between Americans and Canadians over lumbering in the disputed international border area between New Brunswick and Maine. The border here has been in dispute since 1783, and the Treaty of Ghent ending the War of 1812 did not address the issue.

After Maine became a state in 1820, its government disregarded British claims by issuing land grants to settlers along the Aroostook River. In 1827 the U.S. and British governments had submitted the matter to arbitration by King William I of the Netherlands. While Britain accepted his compromise decision, the U.S. Senate in June 1832 rejected the treaty in a vote of 21 to 20.

During the winter of 1838–1839, Canadian lumberjacks from New Brunswick enter the disputed Aroostook region of northern Maine and begin logging. On January 24, 1839, the Maine legislature authorizes newly elected governor John Fairfield to send land agent Rufus McIntyre and some volunteer militia to the lumber camps and assert Maine's authority. Departing Bangor on February 8, they begin seizing the loggers' equipment. But McIntyre

and his assistants are taken prisoner by Canadians on the night of February 12. His arrest and transportation to Woodstock, New Brunswick, and the refusal of the Canadians to leave the disputed area touch off the so-called Aroostook War.

Both sides now send militia to the disputed area. The Nova Scotia legislature makes preparations for war, while the U.S. Congress authorizes the creation of a force of 50,000 men and votes $10 million for a possible emergency. Some three dozen Americans and two dozen Canadians are killed in the ensuing violence. To restore order and prevent a wider war, President Martin Van Buren sends Major General Winfield Scott to the area.

A wider war is averted when Scott arranges a truce on March 25, 1839, following talks with lieutenant governor of New Brunswick John Harvey. (During the War of 1812 Scott had been for a time a prisoner of British forces under the control of Harvey, and the two men greatly respect one another.) Both sides agree to withdraw troops from the disputed region and submit the matter to a boundary commission for adjudication. The issue is resolved in the 1842 Webster-Ashburton Treaty, which awards some 7,000 square miles of the disputed area to the United States and 5,000 square miles to Canada.

February 15, 1839

Second Seminole War (continued). Secretary of War Joel Poinsett approves Brevet Brigadier General Zachary Taylor's pacification plan. Taylor would divide the disaffected area into districts 20 miles square and connected by wagon roads, with each district having its own stockade and garrison of 20 men, half of whom would be mounted, to comb the area on alternate days. The War Department is unwilling to provide the resources to implement this, however.

April 5, 1839

Second Seminole War (continued): Establishment of the Florida Expedition. Convinced that the blockade of the Florida coasts is not preventing the Seminoles from securing weapons through Cuban and Bahamian arms dealers, the army purchases the schooners *Wave* and *Otsego* and a number of barges to supplement

Revenue Service cutters operating off the coast. The additional vessels are manned by naval personnel. The side-wheel steamer *Poinsett* is later added. On April 5, 1839, this command is unified as the Florida Expedition under Commander Isaac Mayo.

April 26, 1839

Wilkes Expedition (continued). The tender *Sea Gull*, commanded by Midshipman J. W. E. Reid, with a crew of 16, separates from the tender *Flying Fish* during the passage from Tierra del Fuego to Valparaiso and disappears without a trace.

May 19, 1839

Second Seminole War (continued): Peace agreement. With public sentiment in the United States shifting against the war and in favor of letting the remaining Seminoles stay in Florida Territory, President Martin Van Buren dispatches Major Alexander Macomb, commanding general of the army, to negotiate a peace treaty. Although the Seminoles, remembering broken past treaties and the seizure of their negotiators under a flag of truce in violation of accepted rules of war, are slow to respond to this overture, Chief Sam Jones sends Chitto Tustennuggee to meet with McComb at Fort King. On May 19, 1839, Macomb announces an agreement, whereby the Seminoles will cease fighting in exchange for a reservation along the Kissimmee River in southern Florida.

July 23, 1839

Second Seminole War (continued): Seminole attack on the Caloosahatchee Trading Post. The peace agreement reached at Fort King in May appears to be working, with only scattered killings by isolated Seminole bands or renegade whites. A trading post is established on the Caloosahatchee River and Seminoles who frequent it appear to be friendly. On July 23, 1839, however, some 150 hostile Seminoles attack the post and its 23-man garrison, commanded by Lieutenant Colonel William S. Harney. Harney and a few of his men reach the river and get to safety in boats, but most of his command are killed, along with some civilians. Responsibility for the attack is not established, but many believe that it rests with Chief

Sam Jones, who had negotiated the peace treaty. In any case, the war resumes.

November 11, 1839

The Virginia Military Institute is founded on the site of the state arsenal at Lexington; it is the nation's oldest state-supported military college.

December 2, 1839

Second Seminole War (continued): Creation of the Mosquito Fleet. The U.S. Navy is taking a more active role in the war (see April 5, 1839). On December 2, 1839, U.S. Navy lieutenant John T. McLaughlin assumes command of the Florida Expedition from Commander Isaac Mayo. McLaughlin utilizes the joint army-navy force of small schooners, barges, boats, and even canoes to patrol the coast, rivers, and streams and to operate in the Everglades. McLaughlin's force becomes known as the Mosquito Fleet.

January 19, 1840

Wilkes Expedition (continued): U.S. Navy lieutenant Charles Wilkes, in the sloop *Vincennes* (10 guns) and commanding the U.S. Exploring Expedition, discovers the coast of Antarctica. This is one day before a French expedition 400 miles to the west makes the same discovery.

May 6, 1840

Second Seminole War (continued): Armistead assumes command. Brevet Brigadier General Zachary Taylor's undermanned blockhouse and patrol system is unable to prevent the resumption of small-scale Seminole raids and ambushes. In May a frustrated Taylor, who has commanded in Florida Territory longer than anyone else in the war, asks to be relieved. His replacement, Brigadier General Walter K. Armistead, can call on 3,400 regulars and 1,500 militiamen. He immediately takes the offensive, dispatching up to 100 soldiers at a time to hunt down the Seminoles. He also campaigns in the summer months and initiates the destruction of Seminole dwellings, crops, livestock, and supplies.

Armistead gives the militia and volunteers responsibility for security north of Fort King, while he and his regulars seek to hunt down the Seminoles in southern Florida. Some reinforcements are sent to Florida, and at Fort Bankhead on Key Biscayne, Lieutenant Colonel William S. Harney institutes a program to train the troops how to fight in swamp and jungle conditions.

July 26, 1840

Wilkes Expedition (continued). At Malolo in the Fiji Islands, Lieutenant Charles Wilkes, commander of the U.S. Exploring Expedition, leads a landing party to destroy the towns of Sualib and Arro in retaliation for the murder by Fijians of two of the expedition's officers.

August 6–7, 1840

Great Comanche Raid of 1840: Battle of Victoria. War chief Buffalo Hump leads a sizable raid by Comanche Indians from the Edwards Plateau in western Texas against white settlements in southeastern Texas, attacking the town of Victoria, only 30 miles from the Gulf coast. Victoria's inhabitants mount a stout defense, and although the Indians are able to loot several stores, they fail to achieve their goal of burning the town. The Indians depart and attack settlements on nearby Peach Creek, killing the inhabitants and looting and burning buildings.

August 7, 1840

Second Seminole War (continued): Attack on Indian Key. A small island in the upper Florida Keys, Indian Key is a wrecking port for area shipwrecks. Despite sightings of Native Americans in the area, some 70 residents remain. They have a militia company and six cannon, and a navy installation is located at nearby Tea Table Key.

Early on August 7, some 135 "Spanish Indians," led by Chief Chakaika, traverse 30 miles of open water in canoes to attack Indian Key. They are spotted and the alarm is given, but the invaders are too numerous. While most of the residents manage to escape to a schooner off the island and reach Tea Table Key, 13 are killed.

Most of the naval personnel are away from Tea Table Key. Only five able-bodied personnel are there under Midshipman Francis K. Murray. They and seven sick patients load two 4-pounder cannon on two barges and row to Indian Key, opening fire on the Indian canoes in an effort to strand the raiders until the squadron returns, but both guns recoil overboard on the third shot, and the Indians return fire with a captured 6-pounder, causing Murray to retire. The Indians loot and burn buildings at Indian Key before withdrawing.

August 8, 1840

Great Comanche Raid of 1840 (continued): Attack on Linnville, Texas. Following their unsuccessful attack on Victoria of the day before, Comanche raiders under Buffalo Hump attack Linnville, then the second-largest Texas port. The Indians kill a number of inhabitants, carry off a woman, and loot stores of a large quantity of goods. Linnville never recovers and is subsequently abandoned; most of its residents move to the new settlement at Port Lavaca.

August 12, 1840

Great Comanche Raid of 1840 (continued): Battle of Plum Creek. Emboldened by his success at Linnville, Texas, on August 8, 1840, Comanche leader Buffalo Hump imprudently turns north and heads for home in western Texas with a large quantity of plunder and a considerable number of stolen horses, moving through the more populous white settlement areas. At Good's Crossing of Plum Creek near present-day Lockhart, some 27 miles south of Austin, Texas, they are intercepted by some 200 Texas Rangers and militia led by Edward Burleson, Matthew Caldwell, John Moore, and "Bigfoot" Wallace.

The Battle of Plum Creek is actually more of a running fight over a span of some 15 miles than a pitched battle. Although most of the Comanches escape with a great many of the stolen horses and much of their plunder, the Texans report that some 80 Comanches are killed (only 12 bodies are recovered). Buffalo Hump continues raids against white settlements until 1856, when he agrees to lead his followers onto the Brazos River Reservation.

December 3–24, 1840

Second Seminole War (continued): Successful army expedition into the Everglades. On December 3, 1840, Lieutenant Colonel William S. Harney departs

Fort Dallas on the Miami River with 90 men on an operation into the Everglades. Traveling in 16 canoes borrowed from the Mosquito Fleet and led by a black who had been held captive for a time by the Seminoles, they capture and hang some Seminoles, then locate the camp of Chakaika and the "Spanish Indians" who had raided Indian Key earlier (see August 7, 1840). Disguised as Seminoles, the soldiers are able to achieve surprise. Chakaika is among those killed. Harney and his men return to Fort Dallas, having sustained one killed but killing four Indians in action and hanging five others.

By the spring of 1841, U.S. Army commander in Florida Brigadier General Walter K. Armistead has sent 450 Seminoles west. He estimates that there are not more than 300 Seminole warriors left in Florida Territory.

February 25, 1841

Wilkes Expedition (continued). The sloop *Peacock* (22 guns), one of the ships in the U.S. Exploring Expedition commanded by U.S. Navy lieutenant Charles Wilkes, lands 70 sailors and marines, who burn three villages on Upolu in the Solomon Islands in retaliation for the murder of an American merchant seaman.

April 9, 1841

Wilkes Expedition (continued). Lieutenant William L. Hudson, commanding the sloop *Peacock* (22 guns), one of the ships in the U.S. Exploring Expedition under Lieutenant Charles Wilkes, sends ashore on Drummond Island in the Gilbert Islands an 80-man landing party. It disperses a force of some 800 native warriors and burns two villages in an unsuccessful attempt to rescue a seaman kidnapped in one of the ship's landing parties earlier.

May 31, 1841

Second Seminole War (continued): Worth assumes command. Colonel William J. Worth takes command of U.S. forces in Florida Territory. With the war very unpopular in the United States and government funding curtailed, Worth changes tactics. He consolidates smaller units and introduces aggressive larger-scale operations designed to destroy Seminole crops and habitations, driving the remaining Seminoles out of the Cove of the Withlacoochee and clearing most of northern Florida.

On May 1, 1841, Lieutenant William Tecumseh Sherman escorts Seminole chief Coacoochee to meet with Major Thomas Childs at Fort Pierce. Following talks, Coacoochee agrees to the transportation of his people west, but Childs is convinced that the chief will not honor the agreement; he asks for and receives permission to seize Coacoochee and 15 of his followers on June 4.

Worth now bribes Coacoochee, who sends out letters to other Seminole leaders urging them to move west. A total of 211 Seminoles surrender in consequence, including most of Coacoochee's own band. In August, Chief Hospetarke agrees to a meeting at Camp Ogden, and he and 127 of his band are taken prisoner. As the number of Seminoles in Florida is continually reduced, it is easier for those who are left to hide, especially in the southwestern swamps.

June 19–October 5, 1841

Texan Santa Fe Expedition. Republic of Texas president Mirabeau B. Lamar seeks to secure for Texas part of the trade over the Santa Fe Trail and, at best, to gain jurisdiction over the Santa Fe area. He promises Texas merchants transportation and protection for their goods to Santa Fe. Hugh McLeod commands the five companies of infantry and one company of artillery to accompany 21 ox-drawn wagons carrying supplies and merchant goods valued at $200,000. Including the merchants and teamsters, the expedition numbers 321 men.

Known as the Santa Fe Pioneers, they set out from Kenney's Fort 20 miles north of Austin, cross the Brazos River, and proceed northwest. In August at present-day Wichita Falls, they mistake the Wichita for the Red River and follow it for two weeks until they realize their mistake and locate the Red River. Harassed by Indians and suffering from insufficient provisions and a scarcity of water, in present northwestern Motley County McLeod sends out horsemen to locate the New Mexican settlements while he waits with the wagons and rest of the men at the foot of the Llano Estacado (Staked Plains).

William Tecumseh Sherman (1820–1891)

U.S. Army general. Born in Lancaster, Ohio, on February 8, 1820, William Tecumseh Sherman graduated from the U.S. Military Academy, West Point, in 1840 and was commissioned a second lieutenant of artillery. He fought in the Second Seminole War in Florida and was promoted to first lieutenant in November 1841. During the Mexican-American War, Sherman was a staff officer under Colonel Stephen Watts Kearny in California, winning a brevet promotion to captain.

Resigning his commission in 1853, Sherman became the agent for a St. Louis–based banking firm, but the bank failed in 1857. He briefly practiced law in Kansas and was then superintendent of the Alexandria Military Academy (later Louisiana State University) during 1859–1861. Sherman had great affection for the South, but when Louisiana seceded from the Union, he resigned and moved to St. Louis.

Sherman reentered the U.S. Army as colonel of the 13th Infantry Regiment in May 1861, then commanded a brigade in the First Battle of Bull Run (Manassas) on July 21, 1861. Commissioned a brigadier general of volunteers that August, he was ordered to the Western theater to help hold Kentucky for the Union. There his eccentric behavior prompted questions about his sanity. Temporarily relieved of his duties, he returned in Major General Henry W. Halleck's Department of the Missouri in February 1862, where Sherman assumed command of the Cairo Military District, Brigadier General Ulysses S. Grant's former post.

Assuming command of a division in Grant's Army of the Tennessee, Sherman distinguished himself in the Battle of Shiloh on April 6–7, 1862, where he was slightly wounded. Promoted to major general of volunteers in May, he developed a close friendship with Grant and by that summer was Grant's principal subordinate. Sherman participated in Halleck's Corinth Campaign during May–June 1862 and the effort to take Vicksburg, where Sherman was rebuffed in fighting north of the city at Chickasaw Bayou on December 29, 1862. Sherman then led XV Corps and took part in the capture of Arkansas Post on January 11, 1863. He aided Grant in the capture of Vicksburg on July 4, 1863, for which Sherman was promoted to regular army brigadier general in July.

When Grant took charge in the Western theater, he assigned Sherman command of the Army of the Tennessee in October 1863. Sherman then led the Union left wing in the Battle of Chattanooga on November 23–25. When Grant became Union Army general-in-chief, Sherman took command of the Military Division of the Mississippi in March 1864.

With his Armies of the Cumberland, the Tennessee, and the Ohio, Sherman launched a campaign against General Joseph E. Johnston's Confederate Army of Tennessee in May 1864, driving toward Atlanta. Sherman made steady, if slow, progress against the able delaying tactics of Johnston, who was however replaced by General John Bell Hood. Sherman also won battles with the offensive-minded Hood, occupying the major rail center of Atlanta on September 2. For this accomplishment, Sherman was promoted to regular army major general.

Destroying such military stocks as would not be of use to him and detaching part of his force to deal with Hood in Tennessee, Sherman began his March to the Sea on November 16, 1864. He was very much a modern general in the sense that he practiced total war. He believed that destroying property

(continued)

(Continued)

would likely bring the war to a speedier conclusion. Sherman encouraged his armies to forage liberally off the land, cutting a wide swath of destruction through Georgia. Reaching the coast, his forces occupied Savannah on December 21, 1864.

Turning northward, Sherman began a drive through the Carolinas on February 1, 1865, taking Columbia, South Carolina, on February 17. Sherman then accepted the surrender of the last Confederate field army under General Johnston near Durham Station, North Carolina, on April 26.

In June 1865 Sherman took command of the Division of the Missouri. When Grant was promoted to general in July 1866, Sherman was advanced to lieutenant general, and when Grant became president in March 1869, Sherman moved up to become commanding general of the army as a full general. During his years in command, the army successfully ended the wars with Native Americans in the West.

As commanding general, Sherman took a deep interest in professionalism and in military education, establishing the School of Application for Infantry and Cavalry (today the Command and General Staff College) in 1881. He also encouraged the publication of military journals. Sherman stepped down as commanding general on November 1, 1883. He retired on February 8, 1884, and lived in New York City. His two volumes of memoirs, *The Memoirs of General William T. Sherman,* are, like the man who wrote them, plain-spoken and direct. Refusing to run for president on the Republican ticket, Sherman died in New York City on February 14, 1891.

Spencer C. Tucker

Further Reading

Kenneth, Lee. *Sherman: A Soldier's Life.* New York: HarperCollins, 2001.
Marszalek, John F. *Sherman: A Soldier's Passion for Order.* New York: Free Press, 1993.

On September 12 the Texan advance party encounters Mexican traders and sends a guide back to lead the remainder to the settlements. The Texans expected to be welcomed, but Spanish governor Manuel Armijo of New Mexico sends out troops to look for the Texans. Captain William G. Lewis, one of the advance party to reach the settlements, turns traitor and persuades his comrades to lay down their arms on September 17. The New Mexican authorities again use Lewis to secure the surrender of the main force on October 5. Having crossed the Llano Estacado, the men are encamped at Laguna Colorada near present-day Tucumcari, New Mexico. Not a shot has been fired.

The Texans are marched to Mexico City and subjected to many indignities both en route and after their imprisonment. They become the subject of heated diplomatic exchanges between the United States and Mexico before most are released in April 1842. Although a failure, the expedition stimulates renewed interest in Texas within both the United States and Mexico and forms the basis for Texas's claim to western territory.

July 18, 1841

Wilkes Expedition (continued): Loss of the *Peacock*. The U.S. Navy sloop *Peacock* (22 guns), commanded by Lieutenant William H. Hudson and part of the U.S. Exploring Expedition (known as the Wilkes Expedition), grounds on a bar in the Columbia River, Oregon Territory, and is lost. All crew members survive, thanks to a canoe rescue spearheaded by John Dean, an African American servant of the ship's purser, and a number of Chinook Indians.

March 5, 1842

Vásquez raid into the Republic of Texas and occupation of San Antonio. On this date Mexican brigadier general Ráfael Vásquez arrives at San Antonio de Béxar (present-day San Antonio) with some 700 men and demands its surrender. The Texans evacuate without a fight. Vásquez raises the Mexican flag and declares Mexican laws in force. Two days later, however, Vásquez and his men depart, returning to Mexico.

Texan volunteers gather in San Antonio for a retaliatory raid into Mexico. The release and repatriation of the Texan Santa Fe Expedition prisoners (see June 19–October 5, 1841), however, causes Republic of Texas president Sam Houston to withdraw government sanctions.

April 15, 1842

The Stevens Battery. In the midst of a war scare with Britain over the boundary between Maine and New Brunswick, a government contract is signed with Robert Stevens of Hoboken, New Jersey, for construction of what would have been the world's first steam-powered ironclad warship, but it is never completed.

June 29, 1842

U.S. Navy lieutenant Matthew Fontaine Maury, unable to serve at sea because of a leg injury, is appointed superintendent of the Depot of Charts and Instruments. He will assemble the data laying the foundations for modern oceanography.

July 7, 1842

Rosillo's raid into southern Texas and the Battle of Fort Lipantitlán. Mexican Army colonel Antonio Canales Rosillo leads 700 men in an invasion of southern Texas. The Mexicans attack Fort Lipantitlán, located at a campground of the Lipan Apache Indians on the west bank of the Nueces River three miles upstream from the old town of San Patricio. James Davis, adjutant general of the Texas Army, and 192 Texans hold the fort. They manage to hold off the Mexicans, who then withdraw.

August 9, 1842

Webster-Ashburton Treaty. In Washington, D.C., U.S. secretary of state Daniel Webster concludes a treaty with special British minister Alexander Baring, first Lord Ashburton. It addresses such issues as boundary disputes between the United States and British North America and cooperation in suppressing the African slave trade.

The controversial northeast boundary provisions of the Treaty of 1783 are scrapped, and the Maine–New Brunswick boundary is set along its present line. The United States thus receives some 7,000 of the 12,000 square miles of disputed territory, or somewhat less than had been awarded under the mediation of King Albert I of the Netherlands in 1831 and accepted by Britain but rejected by the U.S. Senate in June 1832. Claims by Maine and Massachusetts are in part satisfied by the award of $150,000 from the U.S. government to each. This compromise enables the British to retain a military route between New Brunswick and Quebec. The frontiers of Vermont and New York and westward to the Lake of the Woods are adjusted about a half mile north of the 45th Parallel. This enables the United States to retain military works under way at the northern head of Lake Champlain. The United States also obtains the right to navigation on the St. John River, important to the Maine economy. The British also agree, without reciprocal concession, to a line between Lake Superior and Lake of the Woods that gives the United States control of the Mesabi iron deposits.

The treaty also provides for establishment of a U.S. African squadron to suppress the slave trade. This effort had been severely handicapped by the U.S. failure to maintain such a squadron and Washington's insistence that Royal Navy warships not search vessels flying the U.S. flag. As a consequence, the slave trade is largely carried on in American-built ships flying the Stars and Stripes. Spanish, Portuguese, and Brazilian ships sail from Cuba or Brazil with false papers and an American who can pose as its captain should the ship be stopped by the Royal Navy. The slave trade is very lucrative; one estimate holds that by 1847 as many as 100,000 slaves a year are being shipped to the New World.

Stevens Battery

The United States had an opportunity to lead the world in ironclad warships when, during the war scare with Britain over the border between New Brunswick and Maine and other matters, Robert L. Stevens of Hoboken, New Jersey, proposed to the Department of the Navy in August 1841 building a steam warship driven by screw propellers and with iron plates to protect it from enemy fire. Stevens and his brother Edwin Augustus Stevens experimented with laminated iron plate 4.5 inches thick and discovered that it could, at 30 yards, withstand shot from an 8-inch 64-pounder gun. Stevens also experimented with elongated shell.

The Board of Naval Commissioners approved the Stevens proposal in January 1942, and on April 14, 1842, Congress made the world's first governmental appropriation for a seagoing ironclad vessel, authorizing a contract with Stevens for a revolutionary war steamer that preceded the French *Gloire* by 15 years. Stevens wanted his steamer to be shot- and shell-proof, faster than any other ship afloat, and capable of firing shot and elongated shell that would explode after penetration. But the Stevens Battery, as the project was known, never was completed.

The original design was for a ship 250 feet in length, 40 feet in beam, and displacing 1,500 tons. It was to be armed by six large-caliber muzzle-loading guns in open casemates but loaded from below the main deck by crews in armored casemates. The ship's engines were to be capable of 900 horsepower, driving the ship at an estimated speed of 18 knots. The ship was to be a semisubmersible, able to submerge to its gunwales, making it less a target for enemy gunners.

While the ship was under construction, John Ericsson arrived in the United States with a heavy wrought-iron 12-inch gun, and its projectiles could smash through 4.5 inches of wrought iron. This forced the Stevens brothers to increase the thickness of their armor to 6.75 inches. The ship had to be enlarged to take the extra weight, one reason why it was never finished.

Ultimately more than $700,000 was expended on the project. During the American Civil War there was talk of finishing the battery, but the cost was estimated at $812,000, and in the 1870s the Stevens Battery was sold for scrap.

SPENCER C. TUCKER

Further Reading

Small, Stephen C. "The Ship That Couldn't Be Built." *Naval History* 22(5) (October 2008): 58–63.
Tucker, Spencer C. "The Stevens Battery." *American Neptune* 51(1) (Winter 1991): 12–21.

London had repeatedly pressed the United States to give up its ban on Royal Navy searches or to send a sufficient number of vessels to the African coast to investigate suspected slavers flying the American flag. The Webster-Ashburton Treaty provides for maintenance of joint British and American squadrons off Africa. Each is to mount at least 80 guns. They will operate independently but are to coordinate their actions to maximize effectiveness. In 1843 Congress provides funding for a much larger Africa squadron.

August 14, 1842

Second Seminole War (continued): End of the war. Early in 1842, U.S. Army colonel William Worth, commander of U.S. forces in Florida Territory, recommends that the remaining Seminoles be left alone,

Matthew Fontaine Maury (1806–1873)

U.S. and Confederate Navy officer and oceanographer. Born on January 14, 1806, in Spotsylvania County, Virginia, Matthew Fontaine Maury was raised in Tennessee and there attended Harpeth Academy. He secured a warrant as a midshipman in the U.S. Navy on February 20, 1825, and completed three long cruises during the course of the next nine years. Promoted to passed midshipman on June 4, 1831, and to lieutenant on June 10, 1836, Maury had a keen interest in navigation and published a treatise on the subject in 1836. Writing under various pseudonyms, he had also pushed for naval reform, especially in the education of midshipmen through establishment of a naval academy.

In 1839 Maury's promising career at sea was cut short when he injured his leg and was left crippled for life. In June 1842 he became superintendent of the Depot of Charts and Instruments in Washington, D.C., and in 1844 he was also made director of the Naval Observatory. In these posts Maury made major contributions in meteorology and oceanography. After examining thousands of ships' logs and securing assistance from many ship captains, he published two highly acclaimed books: *Winds and Current Chart of the North Atlantic* (1847) and *The Physical Geography of the Sea* (1855). His pioneering research in oceanography helped reduce sailing time on long voyages and led to an international conference in Brussels in 1853 on the subject of marine navigation. Maury's work was so important that he might be called the father of oceanography; indeed, he was known as the "Pathfinder of the Seas." Among other projects, Maury called for the laying of a transatlantic cable.

In 1855 the Naval Efficiency Board, which had been created to remove the logjam in promotion by culling dead wood from the service, placed Maury on the reserve list (September 14). He immediately protested, blaming Stephen Mallory of Florida, chairman of the Senate Committee on Naval Affairs and later Confederate secretary of the navy, a champion of the process. Maury's supporters helped him win reinstatement on the active list as a commander, with date of rank of September 14, 1855.

With the beginning of the American Civil War (1861–1865), Maury resigned from the U.S. Navy on April 26, 1861. Joining the Confederacy, he was attached to the Office of Orders and Detail at Richmond. He clashed frequently with Mallory over naval policy, principally over the type of navy for the South. Maury favored a larger number of small gunboats mounting two to four guns each, whereas Mallory wanted fewer powerful ironclads. The success of the ironclad CSS *Virginia* reversed support in the Confederate Congress for Maury's proposal.

Maury worked hard to develop defenses for the James River, chiefly in the form of electrically detonated mines, but late in 1862, largely because of his international reputation, Mallory sent Maury to Europe to purchase ships and naval supplies for the Confederacy. Maury finished out the war in Great Britain.

After the war, Maury settled first in Mexico and then in England. He returned to the United States in 1868 to become professor of meteorology at the Virginia Military Institute in Lexington, Virginia. He died there on February 4, 1873.

SPENCER C. TUCKER

Further Reading
Lewis, Charles L. *Matthew Fontaine Maury: The Pathfinder of the Seas.* Annapolis, MD: Naval Institute Press, 1927.
Stanton, William. "Matthew Fontaine Maury: Navy Science for the World." In *Captains of the Old Steam Navy: Makers of the American Naval Tradition, 1840–1880,* edited by James C. Bradford, 46–63. Annapolis, MD: Naval Institute Press, 1986.
Whipple, A. B. C. *Stranded Navy Man Who Charted the World's Seas.* Washington, DC: Smithsonian Institution Press, 1984.

William Jenkins Worth (1794–1849)

U.S. army general. William Jenkins Worth was born in Hudson, New York, on March 1, 1794. He worked briefly as a clerk before the start of the War of 1812, when he joined the army as a private. He was commissioned a first lieutenant in the 23rd Infantry Regiment on March 19, 1813, and served as an aide to Brigadier General Winfield Scott, who was both a mentor and a friend for the next 30 years. Worth's service in the conflict won him brevets to both captain and major.

Beginning in 1820, Worth served for a year as commandant of cadets at the U.S. Military Academy, West Point, where he had a reputation as something of a martinet. In 1835 Worth was promoted to colonel and assigned to command the 8th Infantry Regiment. During the Second Seminole War (1835–1842), he distinguished himself as commander of the 8th Infantry Regiment, serving under Major General Zachary Taylor. By 1841 Worth had charge of U.S. forces in the war. His strategy of carrying the war to the Seminoles by the destruction of their crops and dwellings and campaigning in the hot summer months, even at high cost to his own men in sickness and disease, helped bring the war to a victorious conclusion. His accomplishment brought a brevet to brigadier general.

In 1845 Worth was assigned to Taylor's Army of Occupation in southern Texas on the Mexican border. There he became engaged in a feud with Colonel David E. Twiggs. Worth claimed that he should be Taylor's second-in-command based on the fact that he was senior in rank because of his brevet promotion. When President James K. Polk ruled in favor of Twiggs, Worth angrily resigned his commission and departed for Washington to plead his case. Learning of the outbreak of hostilities between Mexico and the United States in May 1846, Worth withdrew his resignation and returned to service, although he missed the first battles of the war.

As a brigadier general, Worth commanded a division in Taylor's army and assumed the position of his second-in-command. Worth distinguished himself in fighting for the city of Monterrey, Mexico, carrying out a flanking maneuver with 2,000 men, capturing the high ground overlooking Monterrey, and then driving into the city. Monterrey fell on September 24, 1846. Lauded in press dispatches, Worth was breveted major general. Following the departure of the Mexican forces, Worth was appointed military governor of Monterrey and quickly established order. He also captured the city of Saltillo without a fight on November 17.

In January 1847 Worth was transferred to Major General Winfield Scott's forces preparing for the invasion of Veracruz and march on Mexico City. Worth helped Scott plan the campaign and on March 9, 1847, led the first division ashore at Collado Beach south of the city. Following three weeks of American shelling, Veracruz surrendered on March 29, 1847. Worth, however, was critical of Scott for the time it took to take Veracruz, although the assault favored by Worth would have claimed more American lives. Scott appointed Worth military governor, and Worth quickly established order in Veracruz.

When the march to Mexico City began, Worth was angered that his division was third in the column and that it was to act as a reserve unit, while his rival Twiggs commanded the vanguard. This was most probably the beginning of what would become a bitter rift between Worth and his former close friend Scott. The relationship between the two men worsened following the Battle of Cerro Gordo on April 18, 1847, when Worth believed that he had been slighted in Scott's after-action report. On May 15 Worth secured Puebla in advance of Scott's army but under controversial terms, which Scott subsequently countermanded. Worth demanded a court of inquiry, which found in favor of Scott and called on the latter to reprimand Worth, although Scott circulated the reprimand only among senior officers.

On August 20, 1847, Worth's division bore most of the fighting at Churubusco and then sustained heavy casualties in the bloodbath of the Battle of El Molino del Rey on September 8. Worth blamed Scott for not allowing him to alter the plan of attack. Worth's division also played a key role in the final assault on and capture of Mexico City. In recognition of his achievements, Congress voted Worth a ceremonial sword.

The feud between Scott and Worth did not end with the war. Major General Gideon Pillow penned an after-action report on the battle for Mexico City that highlighted his role and downplayed that of Scott. Also, an anonymous letter appeared in the press praising Worth, not Scott, as responsible for the successful plan to approach Mexico City from the south. Scott issued a general order reminding his officers that it was a violation of military orders to publish accounts of military operations and condemned "scandalous letters" and "false credit" given certain officers. Believing this to be directed at him, Worth appealed to President Polk, accusing Scott of conduct "unbecoming an officer and a gentleman." Scott overreacted by ordering the arrest of both Pillow and Worth for having broken the chain of command.

Polk, no friend of Scott, met with his cabinet and ordered Scott to release the prisoners and to convene a court of inquiry to meet in Mexico to deal with their charges. He also relieved Scott from command. Meanwhile, Scott and Worth had arranged an uneasy truce so that when the court met in March 1848, it had only to resolve the controversy with Pillow. Restored to command, Worth oversaw the final withdrawal of U.S. troops from Mexico City on June 12, 1848.

Worth then commanded the Department of Texas. He died in San Antonio, Texas, on May 7, 1849. The city of Fort Worth, Texas, is named for him.

ROBERT W. MALICK AND SPENCER C. TUCKER

Further Reading

Bauer, K. Jack. *The Mexican War 1846–1848.* New York: Macmillan, 1974.

Wallace, Edward S. *General William Jenkins Worth: Monterrey's Forgotten Hero.* Dallas, TX: Southern Methodist University Press, 1953.

Wheelan, Joseph. *Invading Mexico: America's Continental Dream and the Mexican War, 1846–1848.* New York: Carroll and Graf, 2007.

providing they agree to settle in southern Florida. In August 1842, Worth meets with the Seminole chiefs still in Florida and offers each warrior a rifle, money, and a year's worth of rations if they will agree to move west. Some agree, but most hope to move to southwestern Florida. Having been authorized by the government to leave the remaining Seminoles alone in that area and to declare the war at an end on a date of his choosing, Worth does so on August 14, 1842. Worth is breveted brigadier general for having brought the war to a close.

Some violence continues, with attacks by Seminoles on white settlers as far north as Tallahassee, but by April 1843 there is only one army regiment, the 8th, in Florida. That November, Worth estimates that only 300 Seminoles remain. The seven-year Second Seminole War has cost the U.S. Army 1,466 dead—all but 328 from disease—and 290 wounded.

No more than 6,000 Seminoles have been sent to Indian Territory (Oklahoma).

August 30, 1842

Woll's invasion of southern Texas. Hopes for peace between the Republic of Texas and Mexico are shattered when Mexican general Adrián Woll, having received orders to invade Texas with his 2nd Division and capture San Antonio de Béxar (present-day San Antonio), crosses the Rio Grande at Presidio by August 30. With some 1,000 infantry, 500 cavalry, and two artillery pieces, Woll enters San Antonio on September 11.

August 31, 1842

The U.S. Navy establishes the Bureau System. Congress abolishes the Board of Navy Commissioners and creates five bureaus: Construction and Repair, Yards and Docks, Provisions and Clothing, Ordnance and Hydrography, and Medicine and Surgery.

September 18, 1842

Woll's invasion of southern Texas (continued): Battle of Salado Creek. In response to Mexican general Adrián Woll's invasion of southern Texas and capture of San Antonio de Béxar (present-day San Antonio) on September 11, some 200 Texas volunteers from such lower Colorado River settlements as Gonzales and Seguin assemble on the east bank of Salado Creek, seven miles from San Antonio. Captain Mathew Caldwell has command. They are joined there by 14 rangers under Captain John C. Hays from San Antonio. The Texans establish an excellent defensive position in woods at the creek.

Although heavily outnumbered, Caldwell is anxious to engage the Mexicans. With only 38 horsemen available, he sends them under Hays at sunrise on September 18 to San Antonio in hopes of luring Woll into battle at his established defensive position on Salado Creek. The decoy force arrives about a mile from the city at 9:00 a.m. Most men dismount and prepare an ambush position. Hays and 7 others ride to San Antonio close to the Alamo, taunting the Mexican cavalry there to come out and fight.

Hays had hoped to be pursued by a maximum of 40–50 Mexicans. Instead, virtually all of Woll's 500 cavalrymen, accompanied by some of the Mexican residents of San Antonio, chase after the decoy force. Woll personally leads the pursuit.

Hays reaches the ambush position and orders the men there to mount and fall back. All 38 Texans then swiftly withdraw across the prairie toward Caldwell's position, closely pursued by the Mexicans.

Following several hours of skirmishing with artillery and small-arms fire, the Mexicans attack the Texan position at Salado Creek, but they are easily turned back by accurate Texan rifle fire. With nightfall, Woll retires. The Mexicans have suffered 60 killed and many more wounded; Texas losses are reported as 1 killed and 9–12 wounded.

Heavy rain delays a Texas pursuit for a day, and Woll evacuates San Antonio de Béxar on the night of September 20. Caldwell pursues, overtaking Woll on September 22 while he is crossing the Hondo River. Hays, riding with his company in advance of the bulk of the Texans, surprises Woll's rear guard and captures his two artillery pieces. Realizing that Hays is unsupported by infantry, Woll counterattacks and retakes the guns. Caldwell then comes up with the remainder of the force. Although urged by some of his men to attack, Caldwell demurs, and early on September 23 Woll gets across the Hondo and marches toward the Rio Grande. The Texans break off their pursuit.

Woll returns to Coahuila. The Mexican government trumpets the campaign as a great success, promoting him to general of division and awarding him its Cross of Honor. In February 1843 Woll receives command of the Mexican Army of the North.

September 18, 1842

Woll's invasion of southern Texas (continued): Dawson Massacre. Responding to Mexican general Adrián Woll's invasion of southern Texas, Texas captain Nicholas M. Dawson raises a company of 53 men at La Grange. Dawson is moving toward Captain Mathew Caldwell's position at Salado Creek near San Antonio de Béxar when his men are intercepted by several hundred irregular Mexican cavalry supported by two fieldpieces. After a spirited but futile resistance in which half of their number fall victim to Mexican artillery fire, Dawson's men begin to surrender. Once they are disarmed, the Mexicans again open fire on them in what is called the Dawson Massacre. Two of Dawson's men escape, but 15 others are marched off to Perote Prison in Mexico. Of the latter, only 9 survive to return to Texas.

October 2, 1842

The U.S. Navy sloop *Concord* (rated at 24 guns), captained by Commander William Boerum, runs aground and is destroyed at the mouth of the Loango River in Mozambique. Three members of its crew drown, including Boerum.

October 20, 1842

Mistaken U.S. seizure of Monterey. Commander of the U.S. Pacific Squadron Commodore Thomas ap Catesby Jones is at Callao, Peru, when he learns from newspapers of a strong note by the Mexican government to President John Tyler. Assuming that war is inevitable, Jones sails with the frigate *United States* (52 guns) and the sloop *Cyane* (20 guns), arriving at Monterey, California, on October 19, 1842. He forces the Mexican governor there to surrender the city the next day. Learning on October 21 from other papers that war has not been declared, Jones promptly returns Monterey to Mexican control and sails away. The affair produces considerable acrimony in U.S.-Mexican relations.

November 25–December 19, 1842

Somervell Expedition. Following the three raids by Mexican forces into southern Texas in 1842, in September two regiments of Texas militia are ordered to reinforce San Antonio de Béxar (present-day San Antonio). Under political pressure from Texans demanding retaliation, on October 3, 1842, President Sam Houston calls on Alexander Somervell to organize a counterinvasion of northern Mexico if there are sufficient numbers of militia and volunteers as well as supplies and equipment to allow success. Volunteers

arrive in San Antonio eager to punish Mexico and secure glory and plunder.

Somervell's expeditionary force of some 700 men departs San Antonio on November 25 and captures Laredo on December 8. Two days later 186 Texans return home, leaving Somervell only about 500 men. The Texans capture Guerrero, but on December 19 Somervell, fearing disaster if he continues, orders a halt to the incursion and instructs his men to return home by way of Gonzales. Only 189 men obey; another 308, commanded by William S. Fisher, continue on in what is known as the Mier Expedition.

December 1, 1842

Somers mutiny. The U.S. Navy brig *Somers* (12 guns), commanded by martinet Commander Alexander S. Mackenzie, is returning from Africa when Purser's Steward James Wales reports to Mackenzie that 19-year-old Midshipman Philip Spencer had asked him to join a mutiny. On November 26 Mackenzie orders Spencer, son of Secretary of War John C. Spencer, placed in irons, followed the next day by his suspected accomplices Seaman Elisha Small and Boatswain's Mate Samuel Cromwell. Incriminating correspondence is found in Spencer's possession that he and others planned to seize the ship, throw the officers overboard, and employ the *Somers* as a pirate vessel. Spencer admits his role.

With the mood reportedly having turned threatening among the remaining crew members, who are largely impressionable teenage apprentices in what is basically a school ship, Mackenzie does not wait until the *Somers* returns to the United States but instead orders his officers and midshipmen to conduct a full investigation. They unanimously conclude, despite scanty evidence, that the prisoners are indeed guilty of planning a mutiny and that the danger is such that they should be put to death. Mackenzie concurs, and the sentence is carried out on December 1, 1842. The three are hanged.

Mackenzie's precipitous decision remains controversial and creates a great national scandal on the brig's return to the United States in mid-December, largely because of the prominence of Spencer's father.

Mackenzie himself is brought before a court of inquiry and then a court-martial but is found innocent after two months of proceedings. The *Somers* mutiny also generates considerable debate concerning the training and education of midshipmen and helps bring the creation of the U.S. Naval School (later known as the Naval Academy) at Annapolis in 1845. It remains the only recorded mutiny aboard ship in the history of the U.S. Navy.

December 20, 1842

Mier Expedition. The Mier Expedition is an offshoot of the Somervell Expedition (see November 25–December 19, 1842), mounted in retaliation for three Mexican raids into southern Texas earlier that year. Although the Texans had captured Laredo and Guerrero, Texan leader Alexander Somervell rightly feared disaster and on December 19 ordered the remaining 500 men to return home; 308 vow to continue with the expectation of crossing the Rio Grande and securing cattle and horses. Their motivations are plunder, revenge, and military glory.

Those remaining move down the Rio Grande, camp, and elect William S. Fisher as their commander. Thomas J. Green leads 40 men downstream in four vessels captured near Guerrero. Texas Rangers under Ben McCulloch, known as McCulloch's Spy Company, scout along the west bank of the Rio Grande, while the main body of men under Fisher proceeds down the east side. On December 22 the Texans reach a point on the east bank of the river opposite Mier, and McCulloch's men reconnoiter. They learn that the Mexicans are assembling in force along the river and advise Fisher against crossing. Indeed, McCulloch's advice is to abandon the expedition altogether, but Fisher ignores it. John R. Baker assumes command of the Spy Company.

Leaving a camp guard of 45 men, Fisher and the remainder cross the river on December 23 and occupy Mier without opposition. Fisher demands that the townspeople furnish his men with supplies. This is accomplished by late afternoon. There is no means to transport the supplies, but the alcalde promises their delivery to the Texan camp the next day. This does not occur. On December 24 also, 1 of the Texans crosses the river to look for horses and is captured by Mexican cavalry. His journal reveals the size and organization of the Texan force.

On December 25 Fisher learns from a captured Mexican that Mexican general Pedro de Ampudia had arrived at Mier and had prevented delivery of the supplies. The Texans now decide to go to Mier to retrieve them. Fisher leaves 42 men under Oliver Buckman to guard the camp, and 261 Texans again cross the Rio Grande, attack Mier, and engage Mexican forces there until the late afternoon of December 26, when outnumbered almost 10 to 1 and running out of ammunition they surrender. Mexican losses are reportedly 600 killed and 200 wounded and 31 Texans killed or wounded. Warned by 2 Texan escapees from Mier, the Texans at the camp, with the exception of 2 men, escape capture and return to Texas.

The Texans later claim that they had surrendered as prisoners of war, but terms of capitulation are not signed until after the Texans have laid down their arms, and these state only that they are to be treated with "consideration." Texas president Sam Houston's subsequent statement that the men had acted without authority of the Texas government further weakens their claim to be treated as prisoners of war. The captured Texans are sentenced to execution, but on December 27 Ampudia has the decree reversed. The able-bodied prisoners are marched to Matamoros, where they are held until ordered to Mexico City.

En route to the Mexican capital at Salado on February 11, 1843, the men escape, but 176 of them are rounded up and returned to Salado; only 3 manage to reach Texas. Mexican president Antonio López de Santa Anna orders that those who had fled be executed, but Governor Francisco Mexía of the state of Coahuila refuses to obey the order, and foreign diplomats in Mexico City are able to get the decree modified. The government then orders that every 10th man be executed. In the so-called Black Bean Episode, 17 men are chosen for execution by drawing black beans from a pot of otherwise white beans. The unlucky individuals are blindfolded and shot. Most of the remaining prisoners are then marched into Mexico City, where during the summer of 1843 they perform hard labor. In September they are transferred to Perote Prison east of Mexico City. There many die, a few escape, and several others are released because of foreign intervention. Santa Anna releases the last of the prisoners on September 16, 1844.

March 15, 1843

Loss of the *Grampus*. The U.S. Navy schooner *Grampus* (10 guns), commanded by Lieutenant Albert E. Downes, is last spoken to off St. Augustine, Florida, on this date. It is presumed lost in a gale off Charleston, South Carolina, with all hands.

April 30, 1843

Battle of Campeche. Off the coast of Yucatán, Commodore Edwin Ward Moore, commanding the Texas sloop of war *Austin* and the brig *Wharton*, engages two of the most advanced warships of the day, the Mexican steamers *Guadalupe* and *Moctezuma*. In an indecisive encounter, the Texans suffer 7 killed and 24 wounded; the Mexicans lose 30 killed and 55 wounded.

April 1843

Creation of the U.S. Navy Africa Squadron. Under terms of the Webster-Ashburton Treaty (see August 9, 1842), Secretary of the Navy Abel Parker Upshur establishes the Africa Squadron. Although technically coordinating with the British West Africa Squadron, in practice the Americans operate independently. Commodore Matthew C. Perry is the first commander of the squadron, which is based at Cape Verde in the central Atlantic some 340 miles off the African coast. His ships have between them fewer than the 80 guns required by treaty. Perry's orders are to protect American commerce and suppress the slave trade carried out by Americans or under the U.S. flag. His orders also state that Washington does not recognize the right of any other nation (i.e., Britain) to board or detain vessels belonging to American citizens.

August 26, 1843

Destruction of the *Missouri* (10 guns). On August 25, 1843, the new steam frigate *Missouri* arrives at Gibraltar, the first U.S. Navy steam-powered warship

Matthew Calbraith Perry (1794–1858)

U.S. Navy officer and diplomat. Born in South Kingston, Rhode Island, on April 10, 1794, Matthew Calbraith Perry was the son of American Revolutionary War and Quasi-War captain Christopher R. Perry. Matthew followed his older brother, Oliver Hazard Perry, to sea, securing a midshipman's warrant on January 16, 1809. Matthew sailed with his older brother in the schooner *Revenge* during 1809–1811, then served in the frigate *President* under Commodore John Rodgers in 1810–1812, taking part in the engagement with HMS *Little Belt* on May 17, 1811. Early in the War of 1812, Matthew Perry then was transferred to the frigate *United States* under Commodore Stephen Decatur during 1813–1815. Perry was promoted to lieutenant on July 24, 1813, but spent the balance of the conflict blockaded at New London, Connecticut. After the war, he commanded the brig *Chippewa* in Commodore William Bainbridge's squadron during the brief naval war with Algiers in 1815.

During the next 30 years, Perry fulfilled numerous and far-ranging naval and diplomatic activities. He was promoted to commander on March 21, 1826, and to captain on February 9, 1837. Perry hunted slave ships off the African coast in the corvette *Cyane* during 1819–1820, then chased down pirates in the West Indies. He commanded the schooner *Shark* during 1821–1824 and assisted in the founding of

(continued)

(Continued)

Liberia. He was the first lieutenant in the ship of the line *North Carolina* in the Mediterranean Squadron during 1824–1828, then commanded the Boston Navy Yard.

Perry commanded the sloop *Concord* during 1830–1833 and then the Brooklyn Navy Yard during 1833–1842, during which time he established his reputation as a naval reformer. He was active in the education movement for seamen and also established the first U.S. naval testing laboratory. Perry outfitted the U.S. Exploring Expedition led by Charles Wilkes. However, Perry's biggest contribution to the service was his forceful advocacy of steam power. He helped design the steamer *Fulton II* in 1837, then commanded it during 1838–1840. He subsequently supervised construction of the steam frigates *Mississippi* in 1841 and *Missouri* in 1842. Perry then took command of the African Squadron, where he had a conspicuous role in suppressing the slave trade during 1843–1845.

Perry's only command experience in war came during the Mexican-American War of 1846–1848. Originally posted to Commodore David Conner's Gulf Squadron as second-in-command, Perry captained the frigate *Mississippi*. He then captured the port of Frontera, demonstrated against Tabasco, and participated in the Tampico expedition. Perry then returned in the *Mississippi* to the Norfolk Navy Yard for repairs and thus missed the actual Veracruz landing on March 9, 1847, but returned with orders relieving Conner of command of the squadron on March 20. Perry then supported the siege of Veracruz on March 22–29 and operated up the Tuxpan River on April 18–22 and the Tabasco River on June 14–22, where he was the first ashore and led a land operation against Tabasco on June 16. After the war he was general superintendent of mail steamers during 1848–1852.

Having wrested the Pacific coast from Mexico, the United States looked for markets in Asia. A major stumbling block was Japan, which had sealed itself off from the outside world for nearly two and a half centuries. President Millard Fillmore authorized Perry to open diplomatic relations with that country, and Commodore Perry's squadron of four ships arrived at Japan on July 8, 1853. Perry parleyed with reluctant local officials and promised to return the following year. When he did so with an even larger force in February 1854, the Tokugawa shogunate reluctantly signed the Treaty of Kanagawa on March 31, 1854, which established an American consulate and opened two ports. However, that government's inability to control the influx of foreigners into Japan contributed to its overthrow by the Meiji emperor in 1868.

Perry returned to the United States in January 1855 and concluded his seafaring career. After several years with the Naval Efficiency Board and having prepared his three-volume *Narrative of the Expedition of an American Squadron to the China Seas and Japan,* he died in New York City on March 4, 1858. Known as "Old Bruin," Perry was one of the most important officers in the history of the U.S. Navy.

JOHN C. FREDRIKSEN AND SPENCER C. TUCKER

Further Reading

Barrows, Edward M. *The Great Commodore: The Exploits of Matthew Calbraith Perry.* Indianapolis: Bobbs-Merrill, 1935.

Morison, Samuel E. *"Old Bruin": Commodore Matthew C. Perry, 1794–1858.* Boston: Little, Brown, 1967.

Pineau, Roger, ed. *The Japan Expedition, 1852–1854: The Personal Journal of Commodore Matthew C. Perry.* Washington, DC: Smithsonian Institution Press, 1968.

Schroeder, John. *Matthew Calbraith Perry: Antebellum Sailor and Diplomat.* Annapolis, MD: Naval Institute Press, 2001.

to cross the Atlantic. The next night a fire breaks out in one of the ship's storerooms, and the *Missouri* blows up and is destroyed. Its crew is saved.

September 9, 1843

The U.S. Navy screw sloop *Princeton* is commissioned. Commanded by Captain Robert F. Stockton, it is the first screw propeller warship in any navy and the first American warship with its machinery all below the waterline.

December 15, 1843

Little Berebee Incident. Commodore Matthew C. Perry, commander of the U.S. Navy Africa Squadron, lands with 200 sailors and marines at Little Berebee on the Ivory Coast to seek redress for the murder here of the crew of the U.S. merchant ship *Mary Carver* two years earlier. Talks with native leader Ben Krako end in a fight in which Krako is mortally wounded and taken prisoner. The Americans then torch Little Berebee.

 ## USS *Princeton*

The U.S. Navy steam sloop *Princeton* was the world's first warship designed and built as a screw steamer. In Britain, U.S. Navy captain Robert Stockton witnessed the trials of John Ericsson's screw propeller. Stockton was instrumental in getting Ericsson to come to the United States and in lobbying for a prototype warship to combine the innovations of a new heavy armament and screw propeller.

Congress authorized construction of the 672-ton steam sloop *Princeton,* which was named for Stockton's hometown. Work began in 1841, and the ship was launched in 1843. Ericsson set down the hull lines and general dimensions, while naval constructor John Lenthall drew the detailed working plans. Ericsson also designed the engine and the six-blade screw propeller. Stockton oversaw the construction and designed the ship's sail rig.

The 673-ton second-rate (warship classification) steam sloop *Princeton* was 164' in deck length with a beam of 30'6". It displaced 1,046 tons, and the engine could drive it at 7 knots. The ship had a complement of 166 men.

The most technologically advanced warship of its time, the *Princeton* was the first screw propeller warship in any navy, the first warship with machinery entirely below the waterline, and the first to burn anthracite coal and use fan blowers for its furnace fires. The *Princeton's* armament consisted of two large 12-inch wrought-iron guns and two 42-pounder carronades. On a demonstration cruise down the Potomac River on February 28, 1844, one of these guns, the Peacemaker, designed by Stockton and built in the United States, blew up, killing eight people, including two cabinet members.

Stockton continued in command of the *Princeton,* which served in the Home Squadron. The ship performed extensively and well in the Gulf Coast Squadron during the Mexican-American War (1846–1848) and helped establish the value of steamers, especially in blockade duty. After undergoing a refit, it served in the Mediterranean until July 1849. On its return, the *Princeton* was found too rotten for repair and was broken up at the Boston Navy Yard.

SPENCER C. TUCKER

Further Reading

Silverstone, Paul H. *The Sailing Navy, 1775–1854*. Annapolis, MD: Naval Institute Press, 2001.
Tucker, Spencer C. "U.S. Navy Steam Sloop *Princeton*." *American Neptune* 49(2) (Spring 1989): 96–113.

February 28, 1844

Peacemaker explosion. The U.S. steam sloop *Princeton*, commanded by Captain Robert F. Stockton, mounts two 12-inch wrought-iron guns: the Oregon (designed by John Ericsson and manufactured in England) and the Peacemaker (ordered by Stockton and built in the United States). During a demonstration cruise down the Potomac, Stockton orders the Peacemaker fired. The gun blows up, killing Secretary of the Navy Thomas W. Gilmer, Secretary of State Abel P. Upshur, and six others. President John Tyler, who is below at the time of the incident, is uninjured.

The explosion brings renewed investigation into manufacturing techniques for heavy ordnance and results in a restriction on powder charges, which remains in effect into the Civil War and probably affects the outcome of the battle between the ironclads USS *Monitor* and CSS *Virginia*.

April 13, 1844

Colt's "torpedo." Inventor Samuel Colt employs his "Submarine Battery," an electrically operated underwater mine (then known as a torpedo), to blow up from shore the old schooner *Brunette* (renamed the *Styx* for its final cruise) in the Eastern Branch or Anacostia River near the Washington Navy Yard.

April 15, 1844

U.S. Home Squadron concentrates in Mexican waters. Fearful of a preemptive Mexican invasion of

 **Torpedo**

The success of stationary mines in the Crimean War (1854–1856) but primarily in the American Civil War (1861–1865), where mines were known as torpedoes, for the torpedo fish that gives a shock to its prey, led to efforts to develop a self-propelled mine. The first modern automotive mine, or torpedo, was developed by Captain Johannes Luppis of the Austro-Hungarian Navy in 1865 and perfected two years later by the Scottish engineer Robert Whitehead, who managed an engine works in Fiume.

The Luppis-Whitehead torpedo was a long cylinder, streamlined for movement through the water. It had an 18-pound dynamite warhead and was powered by an engine that ran on compressed air. The torpedo moved just below the surface at a speed of six to eight knots and had an effective range of only several hundred yards. Its secret was a balance chamber that enabled the torpedo to keep a constant depth beneath the surface. The Austrian government, strapped financially by the 1866 war against Prussia and Italy, declined to buy the exclusive rights to the invention.

Whitehead then traveled to Britain to demonstrate the weapon, and in 1870 the Admiralty was sufficiently impressed that it purchased the rights to it. Two years later Whitehead opened a torpedo factory in England. The British concentrated on a 16-inch 1,000-yard-range version driven by contra-rotating screws at a speed of 7 knots, or 300 yards at 12 knots.

The torpedo was first employed in combat in 1877 when the British frigate *Shah* attacked the Peruvian monitor *Huascar*. The *Shah* launched its torpedo within 600 yards, but the *Huascar* easily changed direction and escaped.

Whitehead made improvements in his torpedo, further streamlining it and fitting it with fins to stabilize its movement toward the target. He also increased the explosive charge threefold by replacing gunpowder with guncotton. A three-cylinder gas-powered engine dramatically improved torpedo speed to 18 knots, making it more difficult for a targeted vessel to escape. The addition of a gyroscope, adapted for torpedo use by the Austrian Ludwig Obry, made the torpedo more accurate. Range also increased so that by 1877, torpedoes could reach 800 yards.

Disappointment over the performance of torpedoes in the Russo-Japanese War (1904–1905) led to a new propellant to replace compressed air. During 1904–1905 both the Whitehead factory at Fiume and the Armstrong Whitworth works at Elswick in Britain came up with heaters to produce hot gas. This had a dramatic effect on both speed and range. A typical 18-inch torpedo driven by compressed air could range out about 800 yards at a speed of 30 knots. The new hot gas torpedo of the same size could travel more than 2,000 yards at 34 knots or 4,400 yards at 28 knots. By 1909, the British Mk VII 18-inch (actually 17.7-inch) torpedo reached 3,500 yards at 45 knots or 5,000 yards at 35 knots. Torpedoes also grew in size. The German 500-millimeter (19.7-inch) Type G of 1906 could reach 6,000 yards at 36 knots, and its charge of 440 pounds was double that of an 18-inch weapon. The British Mk II 21-inch torpedo of 1910 carried a 400-pound charge some 5,000 yards at 35 knots.

The first successful torpedo attack in warfare occurred during the Russo-Turkish War of 1877–1878. On January 26, 1878, off Batum on the Black Sea, the Russian torpedo boat *Constantine* fired two torpedoes at a range of some 80 yards to sink the Turkish patrol boat *Intikbah* in Batum Harbor. Torpedoes had a more spectacular result during the Indochina Black Flag/Tonkin Wars (1882–1885). On August 23, 1884, at the Chinese naval base at Fuzhou (Foo Chow), French torpedo boats Nos. *45* and *46* sank the Chinese flagship cruiser and damaged a second vessel. Torpedoes found their natural delivery system in the submarine, and during World War I they wreaked havoc on both warships and merchant ships.

Torpedoes increased in both size and speed. In 1908 a torpedo 21-inches in diameter appeared. This soon became the standard size. The British Weymouth Mark II torpedo of 1914 weighed 2,794 pounds, could travel at 29 knots, and had a range of 10,000 yards. To pierce torpedo nets, swung out by ships when they were stationary, some torpedoes were equipped with net-cutting devices. Propellers underwent improvement, and the air-blast gyroscope improved stability at long ranges.

The finest torpedo early in World War II was the Japanese Long Lance. U.S. submarine operations early in the Pacific theater were in fact severely crippled by faulty torpedoes that lacked an effective pistol mechanism and thus often failed to explode on striking their target or that dove too deep. One U.S. submarine, the *Tang,* was actually sunk by its own torpedo, which circled around to strike the submarine itself and then exploded. Only after several years were these problems effectively solved, but at war's end Germany and the United States possessed the most technologically advanced torpedoes in the world, with the former having the best antiship torpedo and the latter having the world's only antisubmarine torpedo, designated the Mark 24 mine to hide its true nature. Employed mostly by submarines, torpedoes also figured in many ship actions during the war, notably those off Guadalcanal as utilized in destroyers, cruisers, and specially designed small, fast torpedo boats. Torpedoes were responsible for more than 30 percent of World War II warship losses and 70 percent of merchant shipping losses.

Torpedo improvements in World War II included the magnetic pistol, which set off the explosive charge when the torpedo was under a ship; electric drive; acoustic torpedoes that honed in on sound; and a

(continued)

(Continued)

system developed by the Germans whereby the torpedo would circle after its initial straight run in order to improve the chances of hitting a ship in a convoy.

Torpedo developments in the early Cold War period included smaller, lighter weight models for aircraft use, although the standard heavy torpedo was still 21 inches in diameter. The U.S. Mary 44 torpedo was powered by a seawater battery and had active sonar to seek out its target. Most torpedoes employ acoustic homing. Active acoustic torpedoes generate sound and then hone in on the echoes, while passive acoustic types are attracted by sound. Torpedoes have also been developed specifically to operate against other submarines.

Modern torpedoes utilize a variety of drive mechanisms, including electric motors and gas turbines. Some, such as the Russian VA-111 Shkval, utilize supercavitation to produce speeds of more than 200 knots. The U.S. Mark 48 heavy torpedo is 21 inches in diameter and 19 feet in length. It weighs 3,695 pounds, with a warhead of 650 pounds. It has wire guidance and passive and active sonar homing and is detonated by a proximity fuse, and its swash-plate piston engine gives it a speed of some 55 knots and a range of more than 23 miles.

SPENCER C. TUCKER

Further Reading

Gray, Edwyn. *The Devil's Device: Robert Whitehead and the History of the Torpedo.* Rev. and updated ed. Annapolis, MD: Naval Institute Press, 1991.

Jenkins, E. H. *A History of the French Navy: From Its Beginnings to the Present Day.* Annapolis, MD: Naval Institute Press, 1973.

the Republic of Texas before it can be annexed by the United States, Secretary of the Navy John Y. Mason orders Commodore David Conner to concentrate his Home Squadron in Mexican waters and to warn the commander of any Mexican invasion force that once Texas annexation is consummated, such an action would be considered cause for war with the United States. On June 6 the Senate rejects the treaty, and Conner's ships are withdrawn.

April 22, 1844

War Department reorganization. In Washington, D.C., the army is reorganized into Eastern and Western Divisions, headed by Major Generals John E. Wool and Edmund P. Gaines, respectively. Each division is further divided into nine departments, each headed by a brigadier general. Major General Winfield Scott continues as the army's general-in-chief.

July 3, 1844

Treaty of Wanghia between the United States and China. In the Treaty of Wanghia signed in the Kun Iam Temple by U.S. diplomat Caleb Cushing, dispatched to China by President John Tyler, China is forced to grant to the United States the same commercial status enjoyed by the British. This includes extraterritoriality for U.S. citizens and most-favored nation status.

September 29, 1844

USS *Michigan* is commissioned, the first U.S. Navy iron-hulled warship.

March 1, 1845

Annexation of Texas. Following protracted negotiations, the Republic of Texas is, at its request, formally annexed to the United States. There is considerable opposition to this step in the northern United States

David Conner (1792–1856)

U.S. naval officer. David Conner was born in Harrisburg, Pennsylvania, in 1792 and entered the navy as a midshipman on January 16, 1809. He was assigned to the frigate *President*. In 1811 Conner transferred to the sloop of war *Hornet* and served in it throughout the War of 1812 except for a brief period early in the war, when he was a prisoner of war of the British.

Conner won promotion to lieutenant on July 24, 1813. He participated in the engagement with the British sloop of war *Peacock* on February 24, 1813, in which he was reportedly the last man to leave the sinking British ship, and the capture by the *Hornet* of the British brig-sloop *Penguin* on March 23, 1815, an encounter where he suffered a severe hip wound. Congress awarded him a medal for his gallantry.

Thereafter Conner served in the Pacific, ashore at the Philadelphia Navy Yard, and in command of the schooner *Dolphin*. Advanced to commander on March 23, 1825, he commanded in succession the sloops of war *Erie* and *John Adams*. Conner was promoted to captain on March 3, 1835. During 1841–1842 he served on the Board of Navy Commissioners. He was then the first chief of the new Bureau of Construction, Equipment, and Repair.

Late in 1843 Conner assumed command of the Home Squadron, consisting of all U.S. Navy vessels in the Gulf of Mexico and the Caribbean. Conner's position was the most important naval command of the war. His ships not only had to maintain the lines of communication and supply to the United States but also had to carry out a blockade of the Mexican coasts. Conner was also expected in the event of hostilities to seize Mexican ships, secure Mexican ports, and cooperate with and support U.S. forces ashore.

With war with Mexico looming, Conner concentrated his ships off the Mexican port of Veracruz, but he did not believe that Mexico would resort to hostilities. In 1846 Conner's ships instituted a highly effective blockade of the Mexican Gulf coast. Despite a shortage of suitable vessels for such operations, Conner attempted an operation up the Alvarado River to seize Mexican ships that had taken refuge at Tlacotalpan. Lacking sufficient shallow-draft vessels, his attempts in July, August, and October were unsuccessful. On November 14, 1846, however, Conner took Tampico with a view to using it for future operations against Mexico City. This operation also provided valuable experience for the subsequent operation against Veracruz. Because of the shallow coastal waters and his lack of small steamers, Conner was cautious in the employment of his larger ships, which was the correct approach but one that nonetheless frustrated President James K. Polk.

Conner's greatest success in the war was the conduct of the U.S. landing at Veracruz, the largest amphibious landing in U.S. history to that point. On March 9, 1847, Conner's ships put ashore in surfboats 10,000 men and supplies of Major General Winfield Scott's invasion force. Thereafter Conner oversaw substantial assistance by his ships and men in the siege operations leading to the capture of Veracruz on March 29.

Conner had been in poor health for some time and had held his command for 15 months beyond a normal tour. Consequently, Secretary of the Navy John Young Mason secured President Polk's permission

(continued)

(Continued)

to relieve Conner. On March 21 Conner's second-in-command, Commodore Matthew C. Perry, took charge of the Home Squadron. Although it was done for health reasons, the timing of his relief robbed Conner of much recognition for his Veracruz accomplishment. Eventually recovering his health, Conner assumed command of the Philadelphia Naval Yard. He died in Philadelphia on March 20, 1856.

SPENCER C. TUCKER

Further Reading

Bauer, K. Jack. *Surfboats and Horse Marine: U.S. Naval Operations in the Mexican War.* Annapolis, MD: U.S. Naval Institute, 1969.

Conner, Philip Syng Physick. *The Home Squadron under Commodore Conner in the War with Mexico.* N.p.: N.p., 1896.

because Texas permits slavery. With a vote of 35 to 16 for approval, the treaty formalizing the annexation fails to win the required two-thirds majority in the U.S. Senate, however. With the support of president-elect James Polk, the annexation bill is then resubmitted as a joint resolution. It passes the Senate by only a narrow margin (27 to 25). President John Tyler signs the resolution on March 1, 1845.

March 20, 1845

Background to the Mexican-American War. Following the annexation of Texas, Secretary of the Navy John Y. Mason orders Commodore David Conner to concentrate his Home Squadron in Mexican waters. It consists of the frigate *Potomac* (50 guns), the sloop *Falmouth* (10 guns), and the brigs *Lawrence* (10 guns) and *Somers* (10 guns).

March 31, 1845

Background to the Mexican-American War (continued). Mexico breaks relations with the United States over the U.S. annexation of Texas, fueling speculation that war is imminent.

April 23–27, 1845

Creation of the Army of Observation. Brigadier General Zachary Taylor is appointed commander of the 1st Military District, headquartered at Fort Jesup, Louisiana. Taylor receives secret orders to form an "Army of Observation," then march it to the Sabine River border with the Republic of Texas.

June 15, 1845

Background to the Mexican-American War (continued): U.S. troops ordered into Texas. James K. Polk had campaigned for the presidency on a platform of Manifest Destiny—that is, the destiny of the United States to expand west to the Pacific and south at least as far as the Rio Grande. The Mexican government threatened war if the United States annexed Texas but has not done so. Still, relations are badly strained when Polk takes office on March 4, 1845. He further angers Mexicans by trying to buy California. When the offer is rejected, Polk baits Mexico into war over the southern border of Texas, with the real prize being California.

On June 15, 1845, after Texas has formally accepted annexation, Polk orders Brigadier General Zachary Taylor and his Army of Observation from Fort Jesup, Louisiana, into Texas to protect the new U.S. state from possible Mexican attack.

July 26, 1845

Background to the Mexican-American War (continued): Taylor arrives in Texas with his Army of Occupation. In accordance with President James K. Polk's order, Taylor's men begin to leave New Orleans for Corpus Christi in late July, the infantry

 ## John Ellis Wool (1784–1869)

U.S. Army general. John Ellis Wool was born at Newburgh, New York, on February 29, 1784. His parents both died when he was young, and he then lived with his grandfather near Troy, New York. Wool had little formal education before being apprenticed to an innkeeper and working in a store in Troy. He joined the New York Militia in 1807 and then read for the law.

In June 1811, Wool secured a militia commission as an ensign. As the nation moved toward war with Britain, in April 1812 Wool helped raise a company of the newly created 13th U.S. Infantry Regiment and secured a commission as its captain. Dispatched to the Niagara Frontier with little training that September, Wool's regiment took part in the Battle of Queenston Heights in Upper Canada in October, won by the British. Wool was in the first wave across the Niagara River. He was wounded in the thigh but managed to rally his men and capture a British battery before he was evacuated. On his recovery, Wool returned to duty on the Niagara Frontier and was promoted to major and assigned to the newly created 29th Infantry Regiment in April 1813. He saw action in the Battle of Châteauguay in October 1813, a British victory. He then returned with his regiment to Plattsburg, New York, where in the summer of 1814 with fewer than 300 men he helped retard the advance of the 10,000-man British invasion force from Lower Canada. He took part in the subsequent Battle of Plattsburg in September. For his role in that battle, Wool was breveted lieutenant colonel.

Wool remained in the U.S. Army after the war. In June 1815 he transferred to the 6th Infantry Regiment. He was promoted to colonel in April 1816 and assumed the post of inspector general of the army. Breveted brigadier general in 1826, he was ordered to Europe in 1832 to study fortifications. During 1836–1837 he assisted Brigadier General Winfield Scott in the relocation of the Cherokee Nation from the Southeast to Indian Territory (Oklahoma). In 1838 during the Patriot War in Canada, Wool helped halt gunrunning along the northern U.S. border. In June 1841 he was advanced to permanent brigadier general and took command of the Eastern Department.

In the first six weeks of the Mexican-American War, Wool oversaw the mustering in and training of 10 volunteer regiments (12,000 men) in the Ohio River Valley region. Assigned to Major General Zachary Taylor's command in northern Mexico in July, the next month Wool led 3,400 men from Camp Crockett in San Antonio, Texas, to Chihuahua, Mexico. Receiving an urgent request from Major General William Worth to join him and help meet 15,000 Mexican troops marching north under General Antonio López de Santa Anna, Wool then led his men to Rancho Agua Nueva south of Saltillo and there joined Taylor's army. Wool was second-in-command of American forces in the Battle of Buena Vista during February 22–23, 1847. For his role in that battle he was breveted major general and received a sword from Congress.

From March to November 1847, Wool commanded the Saltillo District. When Taylor left Mexico in November, Wool assumed command of U.S. forces in northern Mexico. Although forced to improvise from lack of instructions, Wool performed effectively, improving security and restoring commerce, opening schools, establishing local Mexican police, and beginning tax collection. He held this command until the end of the war.

(continued)

(Continued)

Wool commanded in succession the Department of the East (1848–1853), the Division of the Pacific (1854–1857), and the Department of the East (1857–1861). Still on duty at the beginning of the American Civil War at age 77, Wool commanded the Department of Virginia. Wool managed to keep Union control over Fort Monroe and subsequently directed the Union occupation of Portsmouth and Norfolk. That action brought promotion to major general the same month. In June 1862, Wool took command of the Middle Department. The next month he assumed command of VIII Corps, but he returned to administrative duties as commander of the Department of the East in January 1863, in which capacity he helped put down the New York City draft riots in July 1863. He retired from the army in August 1863, at age 79, ending 51 years of military service. Wool died in Troy, New York, on November 10, 1869.

SPENCER C. TUCKER

Further Reading

Bauer, K. Jack. *The Mexican War: 1846–1848.* New York: Macmillan, 1974.

Hinton, Harwood P. "The Military Career of John Ellis Wool, 1812–1863." Unpublished doctoral dissertation, University of Wisconsin, 1960.

Lavender, David. *Climax at Buena Vista: The American Campaigns in Northeastern Mexico.* New York: Lippincott, 1966.

Malcomson, Robert. *A Very Brilliant Affair: The Battle of Queenston Heights, 1812.* Toronto: Robin Brass Studio, 2003.

by ship and dragoons by land. Taylor himself arrives in Aransas Bay with 1,500 men of the 3rd Infantry Regiment on July 26 aboard the steamship *Alabama*. He establishes a base at Fort Marcy near Corpus Christi and the mouth of the Nueces River, traditionally regarded by Mexicans as the southern border of Texas. Now dubbed the Army of Occupation, Taylor's force grows by mid-October to some 3,500 men, representing about half the strength of the regular U.S. Army.

October 10, 1845

Establishment of the U.S. Naval Academy. Strongly influenced by the mutiny on the brig *Somers* (see December 1, 1842) regarding the training and education of midshipmen, Secretary of the Navy George Bancroft persuades the army on August 15, 1845, to give up its 10-acre Fort Severn at Annapolis, Maryland, avoiding the expense of a new building and enabling Bancroft to act without congressional spending and there establish the Naval School.

It opens on October 10 with 50 midshipmen and 7 professors. Captain Franklin Buchanan is the first superintendent. The curriculum includes mathematics and navigation, gunnery and steam power, chemistry, English, natural philosophy, and French. In 1850 the Naval School became the United States Naval Academy. A new curriculum then goes into effect requiring midshipmen to study at the academy for four years and to train aboard ships each summer.

October 30, 1845

Background to the Mexican-American War (continued): U.S. Pacific Squadron reinforced. Captain Robert F. Stockton sails from Hampton Roads, Virginia, in the frigate *Congress* (50 guns) to become second-in-command of the U.S. Pacific Squadron, commanded by Commodore John D. Sloat and consisting of the frigate *Savannah* (54 guns); the sloops *Cyane* (22 guns), *Levant* (22 guns), *Portsmouth* (22 guns), and *Warren* (20 guns); the schooner *Shark* (12 guns); and the storeship *Erie* (4 guns).

USS *Michigan*

The *Michigan* was the first iron-hulled warship in the U.S. Navy and also the navy's first prefabricated ship. The ship was built in Pittsburgh and then shipped to Erie, Pennsylvania, for assembly. Designed as a steam paddle-frigate of exceptional speed and power, the *Michigan* was intended to redress the balance of naval power on the Northwest frontier following tensions between the United States and Great Britain. Launched in December 1843 at Erie and commissioned on September 29, 1844, the *Michigan* was fitted for service on the upper Great Lakes. It was 582 tons burden, 167'6" in length, and 27' in beam. It was capable of 14 knots and was pierced to mount up to 18 32-pounders and 8-inch guns.

By the autumn of 1844 following delivery to the navy, the *Michigan* was armed with two 8-inch and four 32-pounder guns. This far exceeded naval limitations set forth by the informal Rush-Bagot Agreement that limited both size and armament of naval vessels on the Great Lakes following the War of 1812. However, the ship was seen as a necessity to counter British naval strength. As fate would have it, the *Michigan* sailed into the peaceful atmosphere brought on by the Webster-Ashburton Treaty of August 9, 1842.

The *Michigan* thus began its 89-year patrol of the Great Lakes shorn of all of its heavy weaponry except one 8-inch pivot gun. This demonstrated peaceful intent if not exact compliance with the Rush-Bagot Agreement. Throughout the ship's long career, it was involved in many pivotal events, including the death of James Strang and the destruction of his Mormon sect on Beaver Island.

During the American Civil War, there were several Confederate efforts to seize the *Michigan* and use it to destroy U.S. merchant shipping on the Great Lakes before destroying it, although none of these were successful.

The *Michigan* was later involved in the suppression of mining strikes in Michigan, the 1866 Fenian invasion of Canada, and the rescue of ships in distress on the Great Lakes. Renamed the *Wolverine* in 1905, the ship remained in service until May 1912. It was scrapped in 1949, despite attempts by preservationists to save it.

BRADLEY A. RODGERS AND SPENCER C. TUCKER

Further Reading
Rodgers, Bradley A. *Guardian of the Great Lakes: The U.S. Paddle Frigate Michigan.* Ann Arbor, MI: University of Michigan Press, 1996.
U.S. Navy Department, Naval History Division. *Civil War Naval Chronology, 1861–1865.* Washington, DC: U.S. Government Printing Office, 1971.

November 29, 1845
Background to the Mexican-American War (continued). U.S. diplomat John C. Slidell arrives at Veracruz aboard the U.S. sloop *St. Mary's* (22 guns) hoping to reopen talks with the Mexican government. He seeks to secure recognition of the Rio Grande as the southern boundary of Texas and to purchase New Mexico and California for the United States.

December 14, 1845–January 2, 1846
Background to the Mexican-American War (continued): Revolt against the Mexican government.

Franklin Buchanan (1800–1874)

U.S. Navy and Confederate States of America naval officer. Born in Baltimore, Maryland, on September 17, 1800, Franklin Buchanan joined the navy as a midshipman in January 1815. In the course of routine sea and shore assignments, he was promoted to lieutenant in 1825 and to commander in 1841. His first independent command was the sloop *Vincennes* in 1842.

In 1844, U.S. Navy secretary George Bancroft asked Buchanan to draft proposals for a naval academy to be built at Annapolis, and during 1845–1846 Buchanan served as the new academy's first superintendent. His emphasis on discipline and academics endowed the nascent academy with its traditions of excellence.

With the beginning of war with Mexico in 1846, Buchanan petitioned for a combat assignment and received command of the sloop *Germantown* during 1847–1848. He twice led landing parties to capture Mexican shore installations. Buchanan commanded the steam frigate *Susquehanna* during Commodore Matthew Perry's expedition to Japan in 1853–1854. Promoted to captain in 1855, in 1859 Buchanan was assigned to command the Washington Navy Yard until the American Civil War.

Buchanan had married into a powerful slave-holding Eastern Shore family and soon adopted its proslavery views. Believing that his home state of Maryland would soon secede from the Union, Buchanan tendered his resignation from the U.S. Navy on April 22, 1861. When he realized that Maryland would remain in the Union, he asked U.S. Navy secretary Gideon Welles to withdraw his resignation. Welles refused and dismissed Buchanan from the service. In July, Buchanan joined the Confederate Navy as a captain. He then served as chief of the Confederate Bureau of Orders and Detail until February 1862.

Buchanan actively sought a combat command, and on February 24, 1862, he assumed command of Confederate naval defenses in the James River. His flagship was the new Confederate ship the *Virginia* (the ex–U.S. Navy steam frigate *Merrimac,* scuttled in the loss of the Norfolk Navy Yard, raised, and rebuilt as an ironclad).

As soon as the *Virginia* was ready and without any preliminary trials, on March 8, 1862, Buchanan sortied and engaged and sank the U.S. Navy sloop *Cumberland,* utilizing his own ship's ram, and then shelled the U.S. Navy frigate *Congress* into a wreck that blew up that night. In the course of transferring the crew of the *Congress,* Buchanan exposed himself recklessly on the deck of the *Virginia,* firing a musket at Union troops ashore. In the exchange of fire he was seriously wounded in the thigh. As a result, Buchanan missed the battle with the U.S. ironclad *Monitor* the following day.

Following his recovery, in August 1862 Buchanan received promotion to rear admiral and received command of the naval defenses of Mobile Bay. His small squadron, centered on the powerful ironclad *Tennessee,* met defeat by Union rear admiral David Farragut's squadron in the August 5, 1864, Battle of Mobile Bay. In the latter part of the fighting, Buchanan engaged the entire Union squadron with the *Tennessee* alone. Buchanan was again wounded, in the leg, and forced to surrender his ship. He remained a prisoner until he was exchanged in March 1865. He returned to Mobile just as the war ended.

After the war, Buchanan returned to his home in Maryland. He was president of Maryland Agricultural College (now the University of Maryland) and then secretary of the Life Association of America in Mobile. He retired altogether in 1871 and died at his home, the Rest, in Talbot County on May 11, 1874. A consummate professional and a staunch disciplinarian with a strong sense of right and wrong, Buchanan was an aggressive, determined, and even rash commander.

SPENCER C. TUCKER

Further Reading

Davis, William C. *Duel between the First Ironclads.* New York: Barnes and Noble, 1981.

Friend, Jack. *West Wind, Flood Tide: The Battle of Mobile Bay.* Annapolis, MD: Naval Institute Press, 2004.

Symonds, Craig L. *Confederate Admiral: The Life and Wars of Franklin Buchanan.* Annapolis, MD: Naval Institute Press, 1999.

Mexican general Mariano Arrillaga y Paredes, commander of Mexican forces at San Luis Potosí, begins a revolt against the central government of President José Joaquín Herrera. Paredes and his coconspirators hope to establish a monarchist regime in Mexico. President Herrera provides the pretext for the revolt when he appears willing to enter negotiations with American emissary John Slidell over the cession of Mexican territory. Charging that Herrera is preparing to abandon Texas, Paredes begins his rebellion on December 14, 1845. He overthrows Herrera on January 2, 1846, and takes office as interim president on January 4.

Once in power, Paredes vacillates regarding both establishment of a monarchy and war with the United States. He allows both monarchists and republicans to believe that he sympathizes with them while at the same time insisting that only Congress has the power to decide the Mexican political system. Well aware that the Mexican Army is in no condition to wage war, Paredes keeps Slidell at arm's length while making no overtly hostile moves in the direction of the United States.

January 13, 1846

Background to the Mexican-American War (continued): Polk orders Taylor to the Rio Grande. A day after U.S. president James K. Polk receives word that the Mexican government has refused to treat with U.S. minister John Slidell, on January 13, 1846, Secretary of War William L. Marcy, acting at the behest of President James K. Polk, orders Brigadier General Zachary Taylor to move his Army of Occupation in Texas from the Nueces River to "positions on or near the left bank" of the Rio Grande. This is in effect an act of war, since the Nueces River has been the southern boundary of Texas for a century, and the Republic of Texas had never exercised authority beyond it.

January 15, 1846

Background to the Mexican-American War (continued): Frémont in California. On June 1, 1845, U.S. Army brevet captain of engineers John C. Frémont, already having gained fame as an explorer (the "Pathfinder") and son-in-law of influential Missouri senator Thomas Hart Benton, a close adviser of President James K. Polk, sets out with 55 men from St. Louis, with Christopher "Kit" Carson as guide, on a third exploring expedition. The stated goal of the expedition is to "map the source of the Arkansas River" on the east side of the Rocky Mountains. Although no written documents exist to prove this, it seems clear that the plan is to prime a revolt in sparsely populated Alta (Upper) California against Mexico, for on reaching the Arkansas, Frémont suddenly proceeds to California.

Arriving in the Sacramento Valley in January 1846, Frémont meets with leaders of the American settlers as well as U.S. consul in Monterey Thomas O. Larken and stirs up sentiment for revolt, promising that in the event of war with Mexico his small force will provide the settlers protection. After securing

John Drake Sloat (1781–1867)

U.S. Navy officer. John Drake Sloat was born on July 26, 1781, in Goshen (Sloatsburg), New York; his father, John, a captain in the Continental Army during the American Revolutionary War, was killed in action two months before Sloat's birth. Sloat received a warrant as a midshipman in the U.S. Navy on February 12, 1800. He served under Commodore Thomas Truxtun in the frigate *Constellation* during the Quasi-War with France (1798–1800) and participated in the engagements with the French frigates *L'Insurgente* and *Vengeance*. Then without orders, Sloat secured a leave of absence to serve in merchant ships during 1801–1811, rising to command of a ship in 1811.

On January 10, 1812, Sloat returned to naval duty as a sailing master aboard the frigate *United States* under Captain Stephen Decatur and went to sea in that ship at the beginning of the War of 1812. During the October 1812 action with the Royal Navy frigate *Macedonian,* Sloat was wounded and later cited for gallantry, resulting in his promotion to lieutenant on July 24, 1813.

Following the War of 1812, Sloat served as first lieutenant in the ship of the line *Franklin* and then in the frigate *Congress*. His first command was the schooner *Grampus*. Sloat participated in antipiracy operations in the Caribbean in 1825 and then in antislavery operations off West Africa.

Sloat was promoted to commander on March 21, 1826, and to captain on February 9, 1837. From 1840 to 1844 he commanded the Portsmouth Navy Yard in New Hampshire. He was then assigned as commander of the Pacific Squadron.

Anticipating hostilities with Mexico, in early 1846 Secretary of the Navy George Bancroft ordered Commodore Sloat to proceed to California should war break out but in the meantime to avoid anything that might be construed as "an act of aggression." In the event of war, Sloat was to take San Francisco and then choose other ports to seize or blockade as well as to protect American property and citizens.

On May 31 Sloat, then at Mazatlán, received news that war had begun, but he waited to sail to California until June 7, when he received confirmation from Mexico City that Mexico and the United States were indeed at war. Bancroft was furious at the delay and in mid-August fired off letters relieving Sloat of command.

The Pacific Squadron arrived off Monterey, California, on July 2, 1846. There Sloat delayed until July 7, finally issuing a general order to his squadron to seize California and hold it for the United States. That same day Sloat's marines seized Monterey, and on July 9 the squadron took San Francisco. Men of the squadron also occupied nearby San José.

On July 29, by now in failing health, Sloat relinquished command of the squadron to Commodore Robert Field Stockton, who had arrived two weeks before in the frigate *Congress* and was pressing Sloat for more dramatic action. Sloat then returned to Washington, D.C., and held assignments ashore. Sloat was placed on the reserved list on September 27, 1855, after the Naval Efficiency Board recommended the removal of more than 200 officers from active duty. He was placed on the retired list on December 21, 1861. He was promoted on the retired list to commodore in 1862 and to rear admiral on July 25, 1866. Sloat died in Staten Island, New York, on November 28, 1867.

CLAUDE BERUBE

Further Reading

Bauer, J. Jack. "George Bancroft." In *American Secretaries of the Navy*, Vol. 1, *1775–1913*, edited by Paolo E. Coletta, 217–229. Annapolis, MD: Naval Institute Press, 1980.

Harlow, Neal. *California Conquered: War and Peace on the Pacific, 1846–1850*. Berkeley: University of California Press, 1982.

Reynolds, Clark G. *Famous American Admirals*. Annapolis, MD: Naval Institute Press, 2002.

permission from Mexican authorities, Frémont moves south toward Monterey.

March 5, 1846

Background to the Mexican-American War (continued): Frémont ordered from Monterey. Having secured permission from Mexican authorities to resupply his 55-man "exploring mission" at Monterey, Brevet Captain John C. Frémont and his men are about 25 miles from the city when he is peremptorily ordered to leave California. Instead Frémont entrenches at Gavilán Peak northeast of Salinas. There the Americans are besieged by 350 Mexican troops under General José María Castro. After several days, Frémont decamps at night and heads north to Oregon.

March 8, 1846

Background to the Mexican-American War (continued): Taylor begins his move to the Rio Grande. On February 3, 1846, U.S. Army brigadier general Zachary Taylor receives President James K. Polk's order of January 13, 1846, to proceed to the Rio Grande. Taylor does not begin his advance until March 8, however.

March 28, 1846

Background to the Mexican-American War (continued): U.S. troops arrive at the Rio Grande. On March 24 Brigadier General Zachary Taylor's Army of Occupation arrives at Point Santa Isabel. U.S. supply ships are waiting there. The American vanguard also enters nearby El Frontón; its 280-man Mexican garrison torches the town and departs when the U.S. troops arrive.

On March 28, Taylor's men take up position on the left (north) bank of the Rio Grande. Taylor's position is opposite the Mexican city of Matamoros, where the Mexicans have about 2,200 men under Colonel Francisco Meja. Taylor rejects Meja's demands that he withdraw, and during the next month both sides fortify. Taylor establishes Camp Texas, while the Mexicans build Fort Paredes. Although incidents occur between U.S. and Mexican troops, Taylor's orders are to refrain from any aggressive act until a state of war, either by declaration or by events. At the same time, Taylor issues a proclamation in Spanish to the Mexican people living on the left bank of the Rio Grande stating that their rights of property, person, and religion will be fully respected.

March 30, 1846

Background to the Mexican-American War (continued): Slidell leaves Mexico. Rebuffed by the Mexican government in his efforts to secure recognition of the U.S. annexation of Texas with a border at the Rio Grande and to purchase California and New Mexico, U.S. diplomat John Slidell departs from Veracruz in the U.S. steam frigate *Mississippi* (10 guns).

April 4, 1846

Background to the Mexican-American War (continued). Mexican general and former president Mariano Arista is tasked with organizing an "Army of the North" to counter American forces under Brigadier General Zachary Taylor north of the Rio Grande.

April 11, 1846

Background to the Mexican-American War (continued): Mexican reinforcements reach Matamoros. On this date the vanguard of Mexican general Mariano Arista's Army of the North, consisting of some 1,500

John Charles Frémont (1813–1890)

U.S. Army officer, politician, and explorer who played an important role in promoting settlement of the American West. John Charles Frémont was born John Charles Fremon in Savannah, Georgia, on January 21, 1813, the illegitimate son of a Virginia socialite and an impecunious French refugee. In 1837 Frémont entered the U.S. Army's Corps of Topographical Engineers. He soon became an enthusiastic supporter of Missouri senator Thomas Hart Benton and Benton's vision for westward expansion. Frémont provoked Benton's fury by eloping with the senator's daughter, Jessie, but was soon back in Benton's favor, with the senator acting as a patron for Frémont's army career.

Frémont participated in and later led exploratory expeditions into the western territories of the United States and sometimes into Canada and Mexico. In the late 1830s these explorations led him into what later became Iowa, and in the early 1840s he led more dramatic explorations along the Oregon Trail and into the Sierra Nevada. Guided by renowned mountain man Christopher Houston "Kit" Carson, Frémont made a number of geographic discoveries in the West and won the nickname "the Pathfinder." His explorations and the publicity surrounding them helped encourage American migration into western areas of the country, much to Benton's satisfaction.

When the Mexican-American War began in 1846, Frémont was leading another exploratory expedition in the western mountains. That May after a band of Modoc Native Americans attacked his party, Frémont attacked a Klamath fishing settlement in Oregon, ending in the virtual massacre of the Native Americans there. Frémont himself was nearly killed in the engagement. Some weeks later without authorization, he led his band into California just prior to the official outbreak of hostilities and, with the aid of recent American settlers in the region, successfully established the independent Bear Flag Republic, which soon became part of the United States. By that time, however, Frémont had become embroiled in a dispute with his U.S. Army superior in California, Colonel Stephen W. Kearny. Court-martialed and convicted of insubordination, Frémont was subsequently pardoned by President James K. Polk but nonetheless resigned his commission.

As a civilian, in 1848 Frémont led another western expedition. Without Carson and other key guides, Frémont lost his way in the snows of the mountains. Several members of the party died, and Frémont and the others narrowly escaped. Frémont then became a U.S. senator from California, serving from 1850 to 1851. Meanwhile, gold discovered on his land in California made him wealthy.

In 1856 Frémont became the first presidential candidate of the newly organized Republican Party. He made a respectable showing in the general election, although he failed to carry his own state of California and lost the electoral vote to Democratic candidate James Buchanan. Taking advantage of Frémont's popularity, new president Abraham Lincoln on May 14, 1861, appointed him one of just four major generals at the start of the American Civil War. Urged by Frémont's supporters, Lincoln gave him command of the strategically important Western Department, a decision the president would soon regret. Frémont reportedly spent several hundred thousand dollars to augment the defenses of the department's headquarters city of St. Louis but allowed his field commanders to engage the Confederates while poorly armed. Humiliating Union defeats at Springfield and Lexington, Missouri, caused Lincoln much angst. Then on August 30, 1861, Frémont unilaterally issued his "emancipation proclamation," essentially declaring all slaves in the state owned by secessionists freed. In the meantime, he had imposed martial law in Missouri.

Lincoln was aghast at Frémont's unauthorized move and immediately rescinded the order. By mid-September, Lincoln had also relieved Frémont of his command. On his part, Frémont believed his proclamation to be a clever war measure; Lincoln saw it as unnecessarily alienating the border states and turning the conflict into an antislavery crusade, which he was not yet willing to do.

Following a brief hiatus, Frémont took command of the new Mountain Department in March 1862. He performed poorly, and his forces were outmaneuvered by those of Confederate major general Thomas J. (Stonewall) Jackson during Jackson's Shenandoah Valley Campaign (May–June 1862). After Lincoln appointed Major General John Pope as his superior, Frémont resigned his commission and left military service. Frémont is generally acknowledged to have been one of the Union's most inept commanders.

After the war, President Rutherford Hayes appointed Frémont governor of the Arizona Territory, where he served from 1878 to 1881. He died in New York City on July 13, 1890.

ETHAN RAFUSE

Further Reading

Chaffin, Tom. *Pathfinder: John Charles Frémont and the Course of American Empire.* New York: Hill and Wang, 2002.
Warner, Ezra J. *Generals in Blue: Lives of the Union Commanders.* Baton Rouge: Louisiana State University Press, 2006.

infantry and 1,000 cavalry all under General Pedro de Ampudia, reaches the town of Matamoros on the Rio Grande. The next day, April 12, Ampudia demands that Taylor return with his troops to the Nueces within 24 hours, declaring that otherwise "arms and arms alone must decide the question." Taylor refuses and requests that U.S. warships blockade the mouth of the Rio Grande, cutting off Mexican forces at Matamoros from seaborne resupply.

April 17, 1846

Background to the Mexican-American War (continued). At the mouth of the Rio Grande, the U.S. brig *Lawrence* (10 guns) and the Texas schooner *Santa Anna* turn back the schooners *Equity* and *Floridian* carrying supplies for the Mexican forces at Matamoros. Learning of this five days later, Mexican general Pedro de Ampudia lodges a formal protest.

April 23, 1846

Background to the Mexican-American War (continued). Mexican president Mariano Arrillaga y Paredes declares before the Mexican Congress that "from this day defensive war begins."

April 25, 1846

Mexican-American War: Start of the war. Both sides have built up manpower resources along the Rio Grande and are spoiling for a fight. With American commander Brigadier General Zachary Taylor refusing to withdraw his men back to the Nueces River, Mexican minister of war José María Torrel y Mendivil orders Army of the North commander General Mariano Arista at Matamoros to take action. Arista orders General Anastasio Torrejón with some 1,600 cavalry to cross the Rio Grande a few miles upstream from American Fort Taylor (better known as Fort Texas).

On April 25, 1846, at Carricitos Ranch about 28 miles from the main U.S. encampment, the Mexican cavalry overwhelms a reconnaissance force of 63 men of the 2nd Dragoons under Captain Seth Thornton. Eleven Americans are killed, and 5 are wounded; the remainder are captured. On April 26 Taylor sends a report to Washington that "hostilities may now be considered as commenced."

April 28, 1846

Mexican-American War (continued). Captain Samuel Walker, having recruited a volunteer company of 77 scouts, which he calls the Mounted Texas Rangers, is ambushed near Point Isabel, Texas, by Mexican irregulars while on his way to join U.S. forces under Brigadier General Zachary Taylor. Walker's force suffers six killed and four taken prisoner.

April 30–31, 1846

Mexican-American War (continued). Mexican general Mariano Arista crosses the Rio Grande with his 5,700-man Army of the North to engage U.S. brigadier general Zachary Taylor's Army of Occupation. Fearing that he is about to be flanked, Taylor leaves Major Jacob Brown and some 436 men at Fort Taylor (better known as Fort Texas) and withdraws with his remaining 2,300 men and 300 wagons northeastward to Point Santa Isabel, where he strengthens Fort Polk.

May 3–9, 1846

Mexican-American War (continued): Siege of Fort Texas. During May 3–9 Mexican artillery opens fire across the Rio Grande on Fort Taylor (better known as Fort Texas). Mexican forces under General Mariano Arista, having crossed the river, lay siege to this outpost. Major Jacob Brown commands the fort. He has 436 men, centered on his 7th Infantry Regiment, and eight guns. Brown rejects calls to surrender but is mortally wounded by a shell during the course of an inspection. The siege is raised on May 9. Despite the Mexicans having fired some 3,500 shot and shells at the fort, only 2 of the defenders are killed; 10 others are slightly wounded. The Mexicans lose 2 killed and 2 wounded. The fort is renamed in Brown's honor and becomes present-day Brownsville, Texas.

May 8, 1846

Mexican-American War (continued): Battle of Palo Alto. After marching to Point Isabel to strengthen the defenses of Fort Polk, on the afternoon of May 7 U.S. brigadier general Zachary Taylor starts back to Fort Taylor (better known as Fort Texas) with about 2,300 men and 400 wagons to relieve the siege there by Mexican forces. After camping overnight midway between Point Isabel and Fort Texas, at Palo Alto Taylor encounters some 3,200 Mexican troops under General Mariano Arista drawn up in a 1.5-mile-long line blocking the road.

Against greater Mexican numbers and superiority in cavalry, U.S. forces enjoy the advantage in artillery, especially heavy 18-pounder guns intended for Fort Texas. The Mexican powder is weak, adversely affecting accuracy of fire, and the Mexicans have only solid shot and no explosive shells. Highly mobile American

Samuel Ringgold (ca. 1800–1846)

U.S. Army officer. Samuel Ringgold was born in Washington, D.C., sometime between 1796 and 1801. He graduated from the U.S. Military Academy, West Point, in 1818 and was commissioned in the artillery. He was then ordered to Europe to study British and French artillery tactics. He was promoted to first lieutenant in 1823 and to captain in 1826. Ringgold was breveted major in 1838 for his conduct during the Second Seminole War (1835–1842) in Florida.

Ringgold developed the tactics of the so-called flying artillery of the U.S. Army. His Company C of the 3rd Artillery Regiment was the first of four light artillery companies organized in the army. Basing his tactics on those of the British, Ringgold trained his company to be extremely mobile, capable of moving throughout a battlefield rapidly but also able to fire at a fast rate. In 1843 the army issued Ringgold's revision of *Instructions for Field Artillery, Horse and Foot,* which had been based on French tactics. The revised *Instructions* reflected Ringgold's preference for British over French tactics. In 1846 he was promoted to major in acknowledgment of his work in reorganizing the artillery.

Major Ringgold was able to test the flying artillery concept while in command of an artillery battery in Brigadier General Zachary Taylor's Army of Observation. The light 6-pounder bronze howitzers of Ringgold's battery were mounted on large-wheel caissons and could be easily moved about by horses. Many long-serving army officers, including Taylor, expressed skepticism concerning the guns, however. They believed that larger, less mobile 18-pounder siege guns and 12-pounder howitzers were better suited for infantry support.

On May 8, 1846, U.S. forces under Taylor clashed with those commanded by Mexican general Mariano Arista in the Battle of Palo Alto, the first major engagement of the war. Arista's men had been besieging Fort Texas, and Taylor led some 2,200 men, supported by 18-pounder siege guns and 12- and 6-pounder howitzers, to relieve the fort. Taylor's artillery included two light batteries, commanded by Ringgold and Captain James Duncan. Anticipating an American relief force, Arista detached most of his army from the siege and moved northward to intercept Taylor. Estimates of Arista's force vary, but he probably commanded about 3,300 men.

Ringgold's battery provided support to Taylor's right flank, while Duncan assisted the American left. Following an hour-long artillery duel involving the larger American guns, Arista ordered his men to assault the American lines. Two of Ringgold's 6-pounders supported the 5th Infantry Regiment, which had formed a battle square to repel Mexican cavalry accompanied by two cannon. The American gunners quickly moved into position and commenced firing on the Mexican guns, silencing them before they had an opportunity to fire and then turning their attention to the Mexican cavalry. The speed with which Ringgold's crews could fire, reload, and fire wreaked havoc among the Mexican cavalrymen, who withdrew.

While surveying the battlefield on horseback to move his guns, Ringgold was badly wounded by a Mexican cannonball. Horse and rider collapsed together. Ringgold died from his wounds two days later on May 10, 1846, at Point Isabel, Texas, the first U.S. Army officer killed in the war. Although both sides camped on the battlefield that night, the Mexicans then withdrew, and the Americans claimed victory.

Brigadier General Taylor later credited Ringgold for the victory at Palo Alto. The Americans suffered 5 deaths that day, including Ringgold, while Mexican casualties amounted to some 102 men killed, 26 missing, and 129 wounded. Ringgold's masterful application of flying artillery tactics in the battle proved beyond any doubt the efficacy of the light, mobile guns.

TERRY M. MAYS AND SPENCER C. TUCKER

Further Reading

Birkhimer, William F. *Historical Sketch of the Organization, Administration, Material, and Tactics of the Artillery, United States Army.* Washington, DC: James J. Chapman, 1984.

Dillon, Lester. *American Artillery in the Mexican War, 1846–1847.* Austin, TX: Presidial, 1975.

Haecker, Charles M., and Jeffrey G. Mauck. *On the Prairie of Palo Alto: Historical Archaeology of the U.S.-Mexican War Battlefield.* College Station: Texas A&M University Press, 1997.

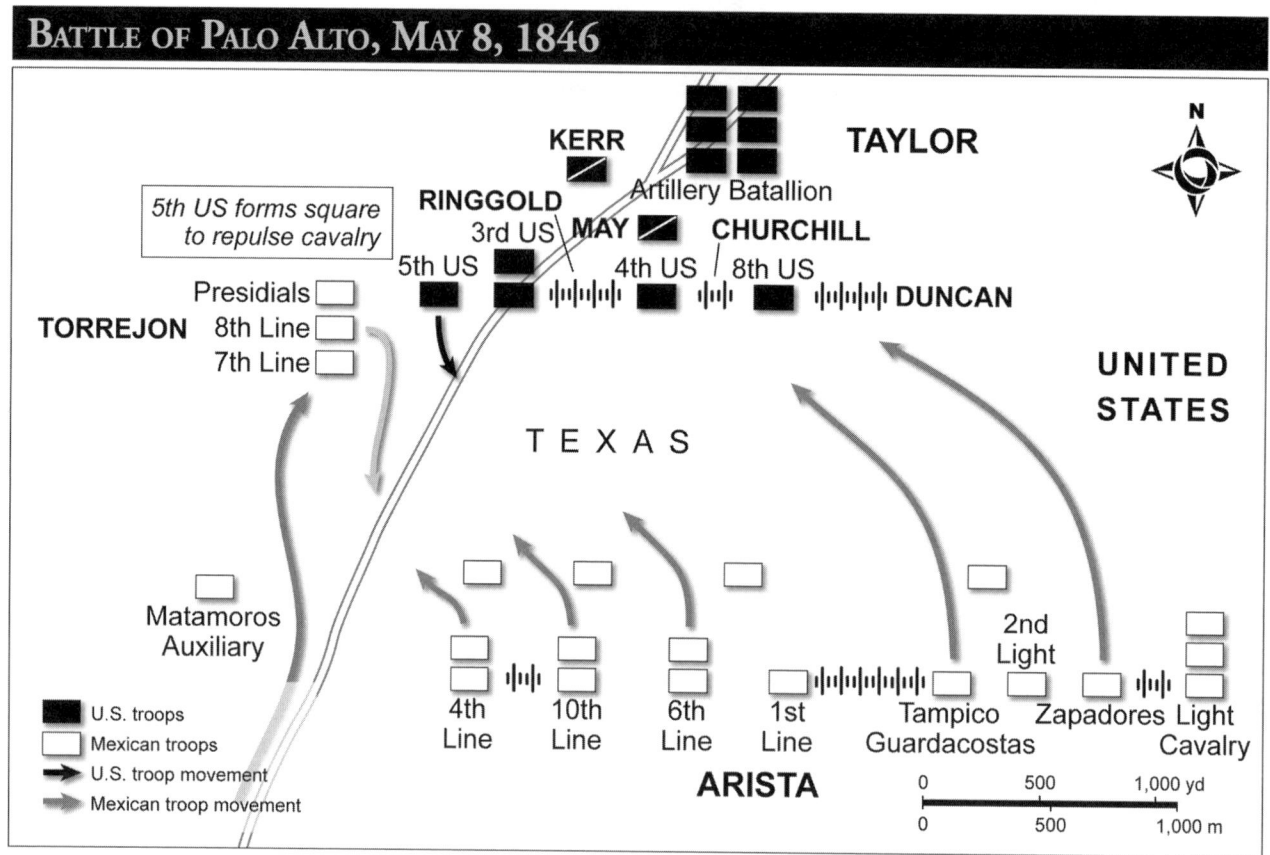

BATTLE OF PALO ALTO, MAY 8, 1846

horse-drawn artillery provides effective fire against the static Mexican positions. Major Samuel Ringgold, who had developed the flying artillery tactics, skillfully handles his guns, breaking a Mexican cavalry charge before it can develop.

The four-hour battle, largely an artillery cannonade, ends in a U.S. victory. U.S. losses are 9 killed (including Ringgold), 44 wounded, and 2 missing; the Mexicans lose 102 killed, 129 wounded, and 26 missing. After spending much of the night burying their dead, Mexican forces withdraw early the next morning to Resaca de la Palma.

May 9, 1846

Mexican-American War (continued): Battle of Resaca de la Palma. Despite being outnumbered by Mexican forces under General Mariano Arista, U.S. commander Brigadier General Zachary Taylor with 1,700 men pursues the withdrawing Mexicans. In midafternoon

he encounters Arista's 4,000 men occupying an excellent natural defensive position at Resaca de la Palma six miles south of Palo Alto. Arista has positioned his men in a dry riverbed with dense chaparral.

With the Mexicans again in a long-drawn-out line, Taylor decides in favor of an attack down the road against the Mexican center. Although the ensuing battle is fragmented because of the heavy undergrowth, the Americans finally drive the Mexicans from their positions. Two Mexican counterattacks are beaten back. The Mexicans then flee, abandoning 474 muskets and carbines, 8 guns, and substantial baggage. U.S. losses are 33 killed and 89 wounded. Official Mexican figures are 154 killed, 205 wounded, and 156 missing. Many of the latter drown trying the cross the Rio Grande. Taylor claims to have buried 200 Mexican dead. That same evening, Taylor raises the Mexican siege of Fort Taylor (better known as Fort Texas and now renamed Fort Brown).

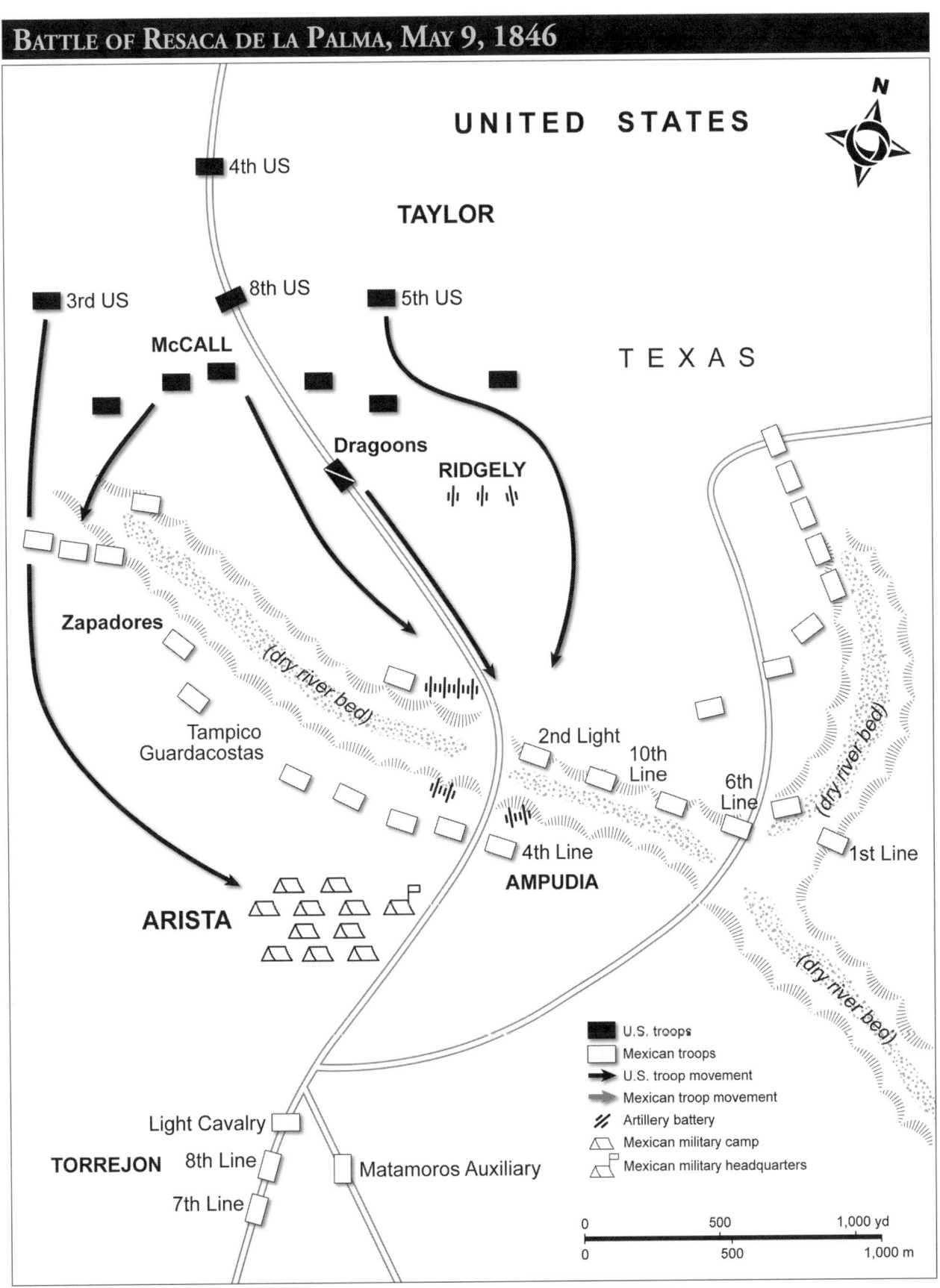

BATTLE OF RESACA DE LA PALMA, MAY 9, 1846

UNITED STATES

TAYLOR

4th US

3rd US

8th US

5th US

McCALL

T E X A S

Dragoons

RIDGELY

Zapadores

(dry river bed)

Tampico
Guardacostas

2nd Light

10th
Line

6th
Line

(dry river bed)

1st Line

4th Line

AMPUDIA

ARISTA

(dry river bed)

U.S. troops
Mexican troops
U.S. troop movement
Mexican troop movement
Artillery battery
Mexican military camp
Mexican military headquarters

Light Cavalry

TORREJON   8th Line

Matamoros Auxiliary

7th Line

| 0 | 500 | 1,000 yd |
| 0 | 500 | 1,000 m |

May 10, 1846

Frémont's attack on a Klamath Indian village in Oregon. Following a May 9, 1846, Modoc Indian attack on his 55-man "exploring expedition" that had been forced to withdraw from California into Oregon, Captain John C. Frémont retaliates the next day by attacking a peaceful Klamath Indian fishing village at the junction of the Williamson River and Klamath Lake. Frémont's men completely destroy the village and reportedly kill more than 20 of its inhabitants, including women and children.

May 13, 1846

Mexican-American War (continued): U.S. declaration of war. On May 11 President James K. Polk sends a message to Congress detailing the "wrongs" committed by Mexico against the United States and announcing that "Mexico has passed the boundary of the United States, has invaded our territory and shed American blood upon American soil." Polk asks for a declaration of war. It is passed overwhelmingly by the two houses of Congress: 173 to 14 in the House of Representatives on May 11 and 40 to 2 in the Senate on May 12. Polk signs the declaration on May 13, and the United States is officially at war. Congress appropriates $10 million and calls for 50,000 volunteers to supplement the small U.S. regular army.

Many Mexican leaders are optimistic about the outcome, and some European observers believe that the 32,000-man European-trained Mexican Army will be more than a match for the 7,365-man U.S. Army. To fight the war, the United States relies primarily on volunteers, with most serving 6- and 12-month enlistments. Ultimately the United States will field 31,000 regulars and marines and some 104,000 volunteers. The Mexican Army is never more than 36,000 men. Mexico has little navy to speak of, while the United States has 70 warships. The U.S. industrial base is also far stronger than that of Mexico, and the U.S. population is more than twice that of Mexico (17 million to 7 million).

There are three principal theaters of war: California, northern Mexico, and central Mexico. The U.S. Navy also plays a vital role, blockading the Mexican coasts and preventing military supplies from reaching Mexico while maintaining lines of communication and supply for the U.S. Army.

May 14, 1846

Mexican-American War (continued). Commodore David Conner, commanding the U.S. Navy Home Squadron, proclaims a blockade of the Mexican Gulf coast ports of Matamoros, Tampico, Alvarado, and Veracruz.

May 16, 1846

Mexican-American War (continued). Eleven cutters of the U.S. Revenue Cutter Service are detailed to support U.S. Army and U.S. Navy operations.

May 18, 1846

Mexican-American War (continued): U.S. troops occupy Matamoros. After regrouping his forces at Fort Brown, U.S. commander Brigadier General Zachary Taylor pushes across the Rio Grande on May 17, 1846. Mexican general Mariano Arista evacuates Matamoros that same day, and Taylor's men occupy it the next day. Taylor delays in Matamoros for three months, awaiting supplies and training the arriving volunteer reinforcements.

May 18, 1846

Mexican-American War (continued). The Mexican Navy steamers *Montezuma* (10 guns) and *Guadalupe* (6 guns)—the two most powerful ships in the small Mexican Navy—escape the American blockade and steam for Cuba, where they are repossessed by their British builders for lack of payment.

June 8, 1846

Mexican-American War (continued). The sloop *St. Mary's* (22 guns), captained by Commander John L. Saunders, shells the Mexican port of Tampico.

June 10–14, 1846

Mexican-American War (continued): American capture of Sonoma. In June 1846 a number of Californios, unhappy with rule by the central government of Mexico, join U.S. settlers to organize a rebellion to overthrow the Mexican government in Sonoma,

California. On June 10, 1846, Ezekila Merritt and a half dozen other American settlers seize 150 horses destined for the Mexican Army. On June 14, 33 heavily armed settlers at Sonoma arrest General Mariano Guadalupe, Mexican commander in northern California, securing 8 guns, 250 muskets, and 250 horses. The rebels subsequently receive assistance from U.S. Army captain John C. Frémont, who returns to California from Oregon with his 55-man exploring expedition.

June 15, 1846

Oregon Treaty. This treaty between the United States and Britain settles the long-standing boundary dispute between Canada and the United States over the northern border of Oregon Territory, which had led to the U.S. slogan of "Fifty-four forty, or fight!" Although in a December 1845 speech President James K. Polk had claimed the whole of Oregon for the United States, he is anxious to secure harmonious relations with Britain during the war with Mexico. Britain's repeal of the Corn Laws is another incentive.

The border is set at an extension of the existing 49th Parallel line to the middle of the channel between Vancouver Island and the mainland and then southward through the Strait of Juan de Fuca to the Pacific.

June 26, 1846

Mexican-American War (continued). U.S. Army colonel Stephen W. Kearny, who is promoted to brigadier general several days later, departs Fort Leavenworth, Kansas, with 1,700 infantry and cavalry. Kearny's force, grandiosely titled the Army of the West, is centered on 300 regulars of the 1st Dragoons and 860 men of the 1st Missouri Mounted Volunteers. His first objective is Bent's Fort on the Santa Fe Trail.

July 1, 1846

Mexican-American War (continued). Having returned from Oregon, U.S. Army captain John C. Frémont leads his 55 men across San Francisco Bay to spike the 10-gun unoccupied San Joaquin Battery on its south shore.

July 4, 1846

Mexican-American War (continued): Bear Flag Republic proclaimed. On this date a group of American settlers in California proclaim themselves independent from Mexico, calling their new state the Bear Flag Republic for a flag with a single star, a grizzly bear, and the words "California Republic." U.S. Army captain John C. Frémont is appointed to head the "California Army." He proceeds to Monterey to join U.S. naval forces under Commodore John D. Sloat.

July 6–August 18, 1846

Mexican-American War (continued): Taylor's army at Camargo. Zachary Taylor, promoted to major general at the end of June 1846, receives orders from the War Department to advance from Matamoros on Monterrey with his now renamed Army of the Rio Grande in hopes that capture of this important northern Mexico city will prompt the Mexican government to enter into peace negotiations. Taylor, however, opts to first seize Camargo on the San Juan River, a tributary of the Rio Grande, and establish it as a supply base before proceeding south.

Taylor begins establishment of a camp at Camargo on July 6. He himself proceeds there on August 4. Conditions are appalling, with very hot weather and poor sanitary practices by the volunteer troops, ultimately bringing some 1,500 deaths. Nonetheless, Taylor remains there, building up supplies, receiving reinforcements, and trying to instill some order in the volunteers. With an influx of large numbers of volunteers, Taylor's Army of the Rio Grande ultimately numbers some 12,000 men.

July 7, 1846

Mexican-American War (continued): U.S. forces take possession of Monterey. Learning of the start of hostilities, Commodore John D. Sloat, commanding the U.S. Pacific Squadron, arrives at Monterey in the frigate *Savannah* (54 guns) on July 3, joining there the 22-gun sloops *Cyane* and *Levant* at Monterey. Sloat calls on Mexican authorities to surrender. With no effective means to resist, Mexican commander at Monterey Captain Mariano Silva withdraws, and Sloat sends ashore 85 marines and more than 140

Stephen Watts Kearny (1794–1848)

U.S. Army officer. Stephen Watts Kearny was born on August 30, 1794, in Newark, New Jersey, 1 of 15 children. His father was a prosperous merchant, but much of his wealth was confiscated as a result of his support of the Crown during the American Revolution. Kearny attended school in Newark and was admitted to Columbia College in 1811.

The War of 1812 cut Kearny's college career short, as he joined the army in March 1812. He demonstrated great bravery in the Battle of Queenston Heights on October 13, 1812. Captured, he was subsequently released in a prisoner exchange with the British. Beginning in 1819, he served almost exclusively on the western frontier and rose rapidly through the ranks. In 1820 Kearny made an exploratory march through the upper Midwest, during which he kept a detailed diary. He achieved literary celebrity posthumously when the journal was published in book form 88 years later.

During the late 1820s and early 1830s, Kearny was responsible for establishing numerous forts throughout the Midwest, including Jefferson Barracks, Fort Des Moines, and what would later be called Fort Kearny in present-day Nebraska. In 1825 he made an expedition to the edge of Yellowstone, and in 1828 he assumed command of Fort Crawford in present-day Wisconsin. He was promoted to major in 1829, and in 1833 he was made lieutenant colonel of the 1st Dragoons. In 1836 he was transferred to Fort Leavenworth, Kansas, and promoted to colonel. Throughout his travels and expeditions, he made detailed notes of his dealings with Native Americans. By the early 1840s, Kearny had ordered small military units under his command to escort white settlers and travelers along the Oregon Trail. Kearny's decision became de facto government policy for many years.

At the beginning of the Mexican-American War, Kearny received command of the so-called Army of the West. In June 1846 he led a force of 1,660 men from Fort Leavenworth and headed west. Their goal was to assist in the conquest of California. Kearny's force took Santa Fe, New Mexico, on August 18, 1846, without resistance. President James K. Polk advanced Kearny to brigadier general and ordered him to proceed to California to augment U.S. forces there. Leaving most of his force behind to garrison New Mexico, Kearny set out on September 25 with some 300 men. On October 6 he encountered Lieutenant Christopher "Kit" Carson, who informed Kearny, incorrectly, that California had already been conquered. As a result of this misinformation, Kearny sent two-thirds of his men back to Santa Fe and continued on with only 121 men.

Shortly after his arrival in California, on December 6, 1846, Kearny attacked a force of Californios (Spanish-speaking inhabitants of California) northeast of San Diego, but the Californios inflicted heavy losses on Kearny's men in the ensuing Battle of San Pascual. Kearny himself was badly wounded.

His escape route blocked, Kearny sent word to San Diego for help. A relief column was quickly dispatched, so Kearny and his men were able to continue on to San Diego. There he joined forces with new Pacific Squadron commander Commodore Robert F. Stockton, and they proceeded to Los Angeles, winning two victories on the way: the Battle of San Gabriel on January 8 and the Battle of La Mesa on January 9. On January 13, 1847, the Mexican governor surrendered California.

There now immediately arose the question of who was in charge of California: Lieutenant Colonel John C. Frémont, of the U.S. Mounted Rifles, had accepted the surrender and claimed that Stockton had named him California's military governor. Kearny, however, who outranked Frémont, sent word to

Washington, D.C., about the impasse. Washington backed Kearny, and Frémont was subsequently tried and convicted of insubordination. Kearny served as military governor for three months before turning over authority to Colonel Richard Barnes Mason.

In 1847 Kearny became civil governor of Veracruz, Mexico, and for a time governor of Mexico City. In September 1848 Kearny received a brevet to major general. While in Veracruz, however, he caught a fever—most likely malaria—and, after returning to St. Louis, died there on October 31, 1848.

CRAIG CHOISSER

Further Reading
Clarke, Dwight D. *Stephen Watts Kearny: Soldier of the West.* Norman: University of Oklahoma Press, 1961.
Von Sachsen Altenberg, Hans, and Laura Gabiger. *Winning the West: Stephen Watts Kearny's Letter Book, 1846–1847.* Boonville, MO: Pekitanoui Publications, 1998.

sailors and seizes Monterey on July 7. Sloat declares California annexed to the United States.

July 7, 1846
Mexican-American War (continued). In Havana, Cuba, U.S. Navy commander Alexander Slidell Mackenzie meets with former Mexican general and president Antonio López de Santa Anna regarding possible peace between the United States and Mexico. Santa Anna, who is in exile, gives the impression that if he returns to power he will sign the sort of treaty that President James K. Polk desires. Santa Anna is subsequently allowed to pass through American lines.

July 9, 1846
Mexican-American War (continued): Occupation of San Francisco. U.S. Navy commander John D. Montgomery arrives off San Francisco in the sloop *Portsmouth* (22 guns) and sends 70 men ashore at Clark's Point to occupy San Francisco and secure its harbor for the United States. There is no resistance, as American settlers have already seized power from the Mexican authorities, and Captain John C. Frémont has spiked its guns (see July 1, 1846).

July 9, 1846
Mexican-American War (continued): Bear Flag Republic dissolved. When news of the U.S. seizures of Monterey and San Francisco reaches Sonoma and Sutter's Fort this afternoon, American settler leaders formally dissolve the Bear Flag Republic and declare their allegiance to the United States.

July 11, 1846
Mexican-American War (continued). The Royal Navy sloop *Juno* (26 guns) enters San Francisco Bay. U.S. commander John D. Montgomery of the sloop *Portsmouth* (22 guns) prepares for a possible clash, fearful that Rear Admiral Sir George Seymour and his British Pacific Squadron might seek to take advantage of the turmoil to claim the excellent harbor here. The *Juno* departs without incident six days later, however.

July 15, 1846
Mexican-American War (continued). Captain Robert F. Stockton arrives at Monterey in the frigate *Congress* (50 guns).

July 16, 1846
Mexican-American War (continued). U.S. Army captain John C. Frémont, commanding some 160 men made up of the men he had brought with him to California and a majority of settler volunteers, on this date occupies the abandoned Mexican base of San Juan Bautista, securing there 9 guns, 200 old muskets, and ammunition.

July 19–23, 1846

Mexican-American War (continued). On July 19, 1846, U.S. Army captain John C. Frémont arrives in Monterey. He meets there with U.S. Pacific Squadron commander Commodore John D. Sloat. On July 23 Sloat names newly arrived U.S. Navy captain Robert F. Stockton commander of U.S. operations ashore. Stockton then organizes the California Battalion under Frémont, breveted lieutenant colonel.

July 20, 1846

Commodore James Biddle with the ship of the line *Columbus* (86 guns) and the sloop *Vincennes* (20 guns) anchors in Edo (Tokyo) Bay but is rebuffed in his effort to open diplomatic relations between the United States and Japan.

July 27–August 5, 1846

Mexican-American War (continued): Mexican president Paredes overthrown. On July 7, 1846, Mexican president Mariano Arrillaga y Paredes heads north from Mexico City to assume command of Mexico's armies in the field, leaving his vice president, General Nicolás Bravo, in charge in the capital. An effort to unseat the Paredes government is under way, and the plotters intercept and arrest Paredes as he travels north, overthrowing his government by August 5. José Mariano Salas becomes acting president.

July 27, 1846

Mexican-American War (continued). Commodore W. Bradford Shubrick is named commander of the U.S. Pacific Squadron.

July 28, 1846

Mexican-American War (continued). U.S. Commodore David Conner is forced to call off a naval assault on the Gulf coast port of Alvarado when the frigate *Cumberland* (52 guns) runs aground on Chopas Reef.

July 29, 1846

Mexican-American War (continued). Ailing U.S. Navy commodore John D. Sloat transfers command of the Pacific Squadron to Commodore Robert F. Stockton, who had been pressing him for more dramatic action. Sloat sails for the East Coast in the sloop *Levant* (22 guns).

July 29, 1846

Mexican-American War (continued). Lieutenant Stephen D. Rowan leads a landing party ashore from the sloop *Cyane* (22 guns) and seizes control of San Diego.

July 31, 1846

Mexican-American War (continued): Kearny dispatches Cooke to Santa Fe. Having departed from Fort Leavenworth, Kansas, on June 26, 1846, with his 1,700-man Army of the West, U.S. Army brigadier general Stephen W. Kearny arrives at Bent's Fort in southern Colorado 650 miles distant on July 31. There on August 2, Kearny sends Captain Philip St. George Cooke ahead to New Mexico under a flag of truce, hoping to secure the peaceful surrender of New Mexico. Cooke first goes to Las Vegas and then on to Santa Fe, where he arrives on August 12. Cooke and his party meet with Mexican governor Manuel Armijo, but Armijo announces that he will oppose the U.S. invasion.

August 4, 1846

Mexican-American War (continued). Commodore Robert F. Stockton arrives off Santa Barbara in the frigate *Congress* (50 guns) and sends ashore a landing party of 17 men under Midshipman William Mitchell to garrison it.

August 7, 1846

Mexican-American War (continued): Assault on Alvarado. Early in the war, the U.S. Navy easily accomplishes its primary task of securing control of the seas. When additional ships become available, Home Squadron commander Commodore David Conner is able to undertake operations to seize key Mexican ports. On August 7, 1846, Conner attacks the Gulf coast port of Alvarado with the steamer *Mississippi* (10 guns), frigate *Potomac* (50 guns), the screw sloop *Princeton* (13 guns), and the 1-gun schooners *Bonita*, *Petrel*, and *Reefer*. Conner is forced to call off the assault because of foul weather and the drafts of the U.S. warships being too deep.

August 13, 1846

Mexican-American War (continued). U.S. forces occupy Los Angeles. On August 6, 1846, Commodore Robert F. Stockton sends ashore at San Pedro 360 men from the frigate *Congress* (50 guns) under U.S. Marine Corps lieutenant Jacob Zeilin. A week later they occupy Los Angeles, its 100-man Mexican garrison having evacuated the town.

Shortly after the U.S. Navy sailors and U.S. Marine Corps troops arrive in Los Angeles, Brevet Lieutenant Colonel John C. Frémont arrives overland there from the opposite direction. On August 14, the remnants of Mexican general José María Castro's forces surrender, along with 10 guns. A joint force of marines and Frémont's men then pursue and capture at San Luis Obispo former governor Juan B. Alvarado and other Mexican officials.

August 14, 1846

Mexican-American War (continued): Loss of the *Truxtun*. Commodore David Conner, commander of the U.S. Home Squadron off the Gulf coast, orders the U.S. Navy brig *Truxtun* (10 guns), commanded by Lieutenant Edward W. Carpender, to blockade the port of Tampico. On August 14 the *Truxtun* runs aground on Tuxpan Reef in a heavy gale while approaching Tuxpan to take on provisions. Efforts to free the ship prove unsuccessful, and Mexican general Antonio Rosas, commanding at Tuxpan, demands that Carpender surrender.

For two days Carpender refuses. Utilizing his ship's boats, he seizes a small Mexican vessel and dispatches it to the American base at Antón Lizardo to request assistance, but he is forced to surrender before the screw sloop *Princeton* can arrive on the afternoon of August 20. Commander Frederick Engle, captain of the *Princeton*, discovering that the Mexicans have already stripped the *Truxtun* of most of what is valuable, takes off what remains and then fires the ship, destroying it to the waterline. In October the *Truxton*'s crew is exchanged for Mexican

general Rafael de la Vega and other officers taken prisoner during the Battle of Resaca de la Palma on May 9, 1846.

August 16, 1846

Mexican-American War (continued). Former Mexican president and general Antonio López de Santa Anna returns to the Mexican port of Veracruz in the British mail packet *Arab* and is permitted to pass through the blockade because he has led Washington to believe that he will help conclude a peace favorable to the United States.

August 18, 1846

Mexican-American War (continued): U.S. capture of Santa Fe. Mexican governor of New Mexico Manuel Armijo rejects Brigadier General Stephen W. Kearny's call for his surrender carried to Armijo by Captain Philip St. George Cooke. Indeed, Armijo issues a call to arms that elicits an enthusiastic response from the Mexican citizens. In the meantime Cooke, U.S. consul Manuel Alvarez, and merchants James Magoffin and Henry Connelly all meet with Armijo and urge him not to fight.

On August 18, Kearny and his 1,700-man Army of the West arrive at Los Vegas. There is no Mexican opposition, and Kearny continues westward. Meanwhile, on August 14 Armijo had ordered the Mexican volunteers to Apache Canyon east of Santa Fe to defend the New Mexican capital, but when he arrives there himself on August 16 he decides that it is useless and orders the defenders home. On August 18 Kearny and his troops take possession of Santa Fe, and Kearny establishes there a provisional government. Armijo and his men retire toward Albuquerque.

August 19, 1846

Mexican-American War (continued): Taylor quits Camargo. Major General Zachary Taylor leaves behind at Camargo some 4,700 volunteer troops while advancing for Mier and Cerralvon (state of Nuevo León) with 3,200 regulars and 3,000 of his best volunteer troops.

September 2, 1846

Mexican-American War (continued): Du Pont's raid on San Blas. U.S. Navy commander Samuel F. Du Pont, captain of the sloop *Cyane* (22 guns), proclaims a blockade of the Mexican Pacific coast. At San Blas he seizes a Mexican sloop, the *Solita*, and sends ashore a landing party that spikes 14 cannon.

September 2, 1846

Mexican-American War (continued). U.S. Navy commodore Robert Stockton names Lieutenant Colonel John C. Frémont military governor of California and instructs him to continue to recruit men for the California Battalion. Christopher "Kit" Carson, the noted scout who had come to California with Frémont, is ordered east with dispatches for Washington informing the James Polk administration of California developments.

September 7, 1846

Mexican-American War (continued): Raid on Mazatlán. On this date the sloop *Warren* (22 guns), captained by Commander Joseph B. Hull, arrives off the Mexican Pacific port of Mazatlán. Hull sends in 70 men under Lieutenant William Radford in four boats. They cut out the Mexican brig *Malek Ahdel* (12 guns), which is subsequently taken into the U.S. Navy. The next day, the *Warren* captures the inbound brig *Carmelita* off Mazatlán.

September 12, 1846

Mexican-American War (continued): Taylor's march on Monterrey. On this date, the vanguard of Major General Zachary Taylor's Army of the Rio Grande quits Cerralvo and begins to march on the key northern Mexico city of Monterrey in the state of Nuevo León. The remainder of the army follows during the next three days. Taylor neglects to bring heavy siege guns.

September 14, 1846

Mexican-American War (continued). At La Paz, Baja California, the U.S. Navy sloop *Cyane* (20 guns) under Commander Samuel F. Du Pont seizes three brigantines, five schooners, and one sloop.

September 14, 1846

Mexican-American War (continued). In Mexico City, former Mexican president and general Antonio López de Santa Anna is named commander in chief of the Mexican Army. Ignoring his pledge to the James Polk administration concerning a peace agreement with the United States, Santa Anna prepares to take the field against the invading American troops. In December the Mexican Senate names Santa Anna president of Mexico.

September 18, 1846

Mexican-American War (continued). Mexican president and general Antonio López de Santa Anna leaves Mexico City to travel north to San Luis Potosí to begin assembling forces with which to confront the U.S. army in northern Mexico under Major General Zachary Taylor.

September 21–24, 1846

Mexican-American War (continued): Battle of Monterrey. On September 19, 1846, Major General Zachary Taylor's 6,640-man Army of the Rio Grande arrives at Bosque de San Domingo (which the Americans call Walnut Springs) three miles from Monterrey, the principal city of northern Mexico on the Santa Catarina River. Taylor has not brought heavy siege guns with him and plans to circle around the city and cut the Mexican supply lines.

Mexican general Mariano Arista, commander of the Army of the North, recognizing that Monterrey

Battle of Monterrey		
Date	September 21–24, 1846	
Location	Monterrey, northern Mexico	
Opponents (*winner)	*United States	Mexico
Commander	Major General Zachary Taylor	General Pedro de Ampudia
#	6,640 men	Some 7,000 men (4,000 regulars, 3,000 militia)
Casualties	120 killed, 368 wounded, and 43 missing	430 killed or wounded

Brigadier General Zachary Taylor, commander of the U.S. Army of the Rio Grande and astride a white horse, at the Battle of Monterrey, September 21–24, 1846. (Library of Congress)

would be the next American objective, had ordered there a battalion of engineers and sappers to fortify key positions and to place artillery to protect the city approaches. About 1,000 yards from the city on the road north, they fortify the ruins of an unfinished cathedral. It becomes known as the Ciudadela (Citadel). To the east, they fortify a stone tannery (La Tenería) and establish a fort known as El Rincón del Diablo (Devil's Corner). West of the city they place artillery on the hills on either side of the road to Saltillo. The hill to the north is known as Loma Independencia (Independence Hill), while that to the south is Loma Federación (Federation Hill). The lower part of Independence Hill is also protected by the abandoned Obispado (Bishop's Palace). The key defensive positions are too far separated to be mutually supporting, however.

In early August, General Pedro de Ampudia assumes command in Monterrey. Unhappy with Arista, Mexican Army commander in chief General Antonio López de Santa Anna had ordered Ampudia to resume his former command of the Army of the North. In 1846 Monterrey occupies an area of about a mile long and a half mile wide. Its streets are narrow and easily barricaded, and many of its buildings are of stone and will make excellent defensive positions. To defend the city of about 10,000 people, Ampudia has some 7,000 men (4,000 regulars and 3,000 militia) and 42 guns.

Taylor plans to send 2,000 men under Brigadier General William J. Worth in from the west to cut the road to Saltillo and prevent Mexican reinforcements from reaching Monterrey and then to seize the fortified heights that provide a commanding view of the

Case Shot

Artillery round intended for extremely short-range actions against personnel, known to have been in use in the 17th century. Case shot (also known as canister or canister shot) took its name from a container with many smaller projectiles that was fired from an artillery piece. In its earliest form, the case was made of wood or canvas, which was then filled with many pieces of small trash metal, musket balls, or even stones. Later case shot was made up a cylindrical tin case containing iron balls packed in wooden shavings or sawdust. The iron balls weighed from as little as two ounces each to as much as one pound in the case of a 32-pounder gun. The thin case split in the bore of the gun and then broke open entirely on clearing the muzzle, producing an effect much like a shotgun.

Case shot was employed in artillery both on land and at sea. On land it was primarily used against enemy troops in the open but not at ranges beyond 500 yards. At sea, case shot could be used against light boats but was used primarily to clear the decks of an enemy vessel. Case shot found modern expression in the antipersonnel (APERS) artillery rounds used in the Vietnam War. Also called "Beehive," the APERS round also was fired directly at enemy troops at close ranges. Each round contained thousands of tiny finned fléchettes, each no larger than a small nail.

Case shot is not to be confused with grapeshot, which employed larger-sized balls packed around a central sabot and held in place in the bore by canvas and cord. Grapeshot was effective at longer ranges than canister and was especially effective at breaking up cavalry charges.

Spencer C. Tucker

Further Reading

Hogg, Ian, and John Batchelor. *Naval Gun.* Poole, Dorset, UK: Blandford, 1978.

Peterson, Harold L. *Round Shot and Rammers.* Harrisburg, PA: Stackpole, 1969.

Tucker, Spencer C. *Arming the Fleet: U.S. Naval Ordnance in the Muzzle-Loading Era.* Annapolis, MD: Naval Institute Press, 1989.

area. While this is in progress, Taylor plans to draw off Mexican forces by a diversion to the east.

Worth's troops set out on September 20 and spend that night close to their objective. The Mexicans detect this move but do little to counter it. Following a cold night with rain, the battle begins early on September 21 when Mexican lancers under Lieutenant Colonel Juan Nájera attack the Texas cavalrymen of Worth's force under Colonel John C. Hayes. Following two abortive charges, the Mexicans are driven off by artillery fire after having sustained some 100 casualties (Nájera is among those killed). The Texans suffer only 1 dead and 7 wounded.

Worth's men then cut the Saltillo Road. Crossing the Santa Catarina River under heavy fire, Captain Charles F. Smith leads regulars and Texans against the western face of Federation Hill. The Americans capture its guns and turn them against Independence Hill.

Meanwhile, Taylor permits fighting on the eastern side of the city to grow from a diversion into a full-scale attack, mistakenly committing forces piecemeal and without artillery support. The first unit engaged is Brigadier General David E. Twiggs's regular army division (without Twiggs, who is ill). Encountering stiff Mexican resistance and flanking fire, it is soon pinned down. Taylor then orders in Major General

BATTLE OF MONTERREY, SEPTEMBER 21–24, 1846

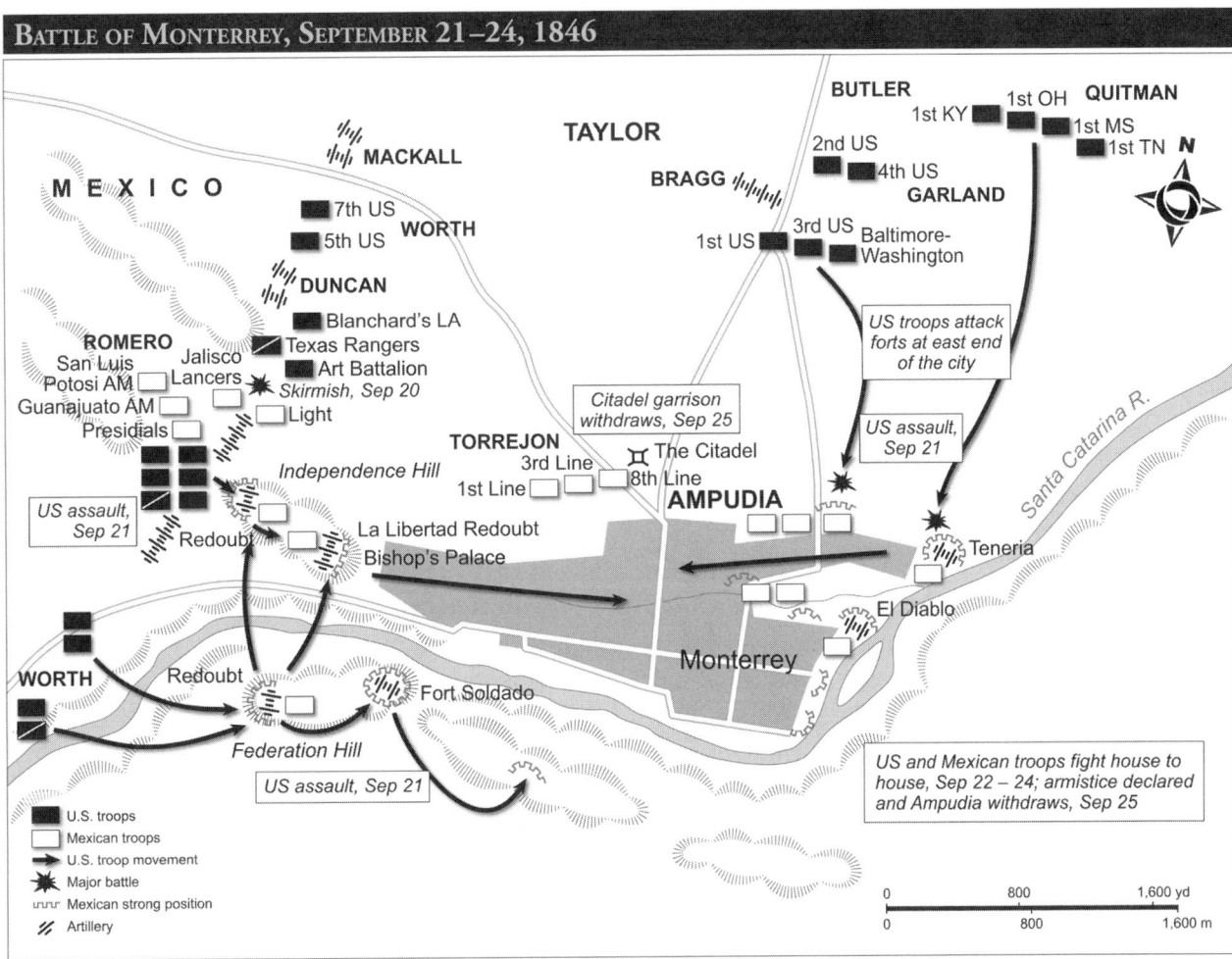

MEXICO

MACKALL

TAYLOR

BUTLER
1st KY · 1st OH · QUITMAN
2nd US · 1st MS
4th US · 1st TN
BRAGG
GARLAND
1st US · 3rd US · Baltimore-Washington

7th US
5th US
WORTH
DUNCAN
Blanchard's LA
Texas Rangers
Art Battalion
Skirmish, Sep 20
Light

ROMERO
San Luis Potosi AM · Jalisco Lancers
Guanajuato AM
Presidials

Citadel garrison withdraws, Sep 25

US troops attack forts at east end of the city

US assault, Sep 21

Santa Catarina R.

Independence Hill

TORREJON
3rd Line · The Citadel
1st Line · 8th Line
AMPUDIA

Teneria

US assault, Sep 21

Redoubt

La Libertad Redoubt
Bishop's Palace

El Diablo

Monterrey

WORTH
Redoubt
Fort Soldado

Federation Hill

US assault, Sep 21

US and Mexican troops fight house to house, Sep 22 – 24; armistice declared and Ampudia withdraws, Sep 25

- ■ U.S. troops
- □ Mexican troops
- → U.S. troop movement
- ✳ Major battle
- ⌇ Mexican strong position
- ⧄ Artillery

0 — 800 — 1,600 yd
0 — 800 — 1,600 m

William O. Butler's volunteer division. The Americans capture La Tenería and fight their way into the city but come under heavy fire in the narrow streets from rooftops and houses. Taylor then withdraws his eastern forces for the night. In all, American troops engaged here suffer some 400 casualties. That night it is again cold, with heavy rain.

The next day, September 22, all the fighting occurs on the city's west side involving Worth's men, where Ampudia shifts his resources. Worth orders his men up at 2:00 a.m., sending Lieutenant Colonel Thomas Childs and 500 regulars and Texans up the steep face of Independence Hill an hour later. In hand-to-hand fighting just before dawn, the Americans force the Mexicans to withdraw from the summit. A Mexican counterattack that afternoon fails, and

other American soldiers manage to get a dismantled 12-pounder howitzer to the top of the hill. They use it to fire on the Bishop's Palace below and drive the Mexican defenders from that place. That night, Ampudia withdraws from most of the outer defenses, concentrating his men in the city's Grand Plaza and the Ciudadela.

On the morning of September 23, Taylor's troops on the east side of Monterrey occupy the abandoned Mexican outposts, including El Rincón del Diablo. That afternoon Taylor orders his troops there to withdraw to the edge of town, a strange decision that he never explains.

At the same time, Worth moves into Monterrey from the west. Employing grape and canister fire to clear the narrow streets, he slowly works his way block by block and house by house toward the city plaza. Texas Rangers lead the way in intense fighting. By midafternoon, the Americans have almost reached the city center. Taylor rejects a plea from Nuevo León governor Don Manuel M. Llano for a truce to allow women and children to depart, and that night Worth's guns shell the city center.

At 3:00 a.m. on September 24, Ampudia, increasingly concerned that American artillery fire will touch off the large supply of ammunition stored at the cathedral, requests the "honors of war" that will allow his men to depart with colors flying and all their arms and equipment. Taylor rejects that request but does agree to a personal meeting that afternoon. With his own forces low on supplies and ammunition and facing strongly entrenched Mexican forces, Taylor agrees to a commission of three men from each side to discuss capitulation terms.

The conferees agree that Ampudia will surrender Monterrey and its arms and munitions but that Mexican troops will be allowed to withdraw with their personal weapons and a single six-gun artillery battery with ammunition. The Citadel will be surrendered immediately, and Monterrey is to be evacuated within a week, the Mexicans retiring to a line some 40 miles beyond the city beyond which both sides will not advance for eight weeks or until either government gives notice that it has disavowed the armistice.

On September 25 the American flag is raised over Monterrey, and U.S. troops take possession of the city. Mexican casualties in the battle total 430 killed or wounded; American losses are 120 killed, 368 wounded, and 43 missing.

Taylor's acceptance of the armistice proves controversial, and President James K. Polk sees the terms as far too generous. The armistice, however, avoids heavy U.S. losses that would have undoubtedly occurred in securing the city. Taylor also believes that American magnanimity will help bring about a quicker end to the war, given the recent change in the Mexican government.

Taylor's army remains at Monterrey for the next six weeks, resting and refitting. Polk is alarmed at growing popular support for Taylor, who he believes might stand for the Whig Party nomination for president

in 1848. Polk will subsequently siphon off much of Taylor's force to join Major General Winfield Scott's forces for an invasion of central Mexico at Veracruz.

September 23, 1846

Mexican-American War (continued): Mexican Revolt. At Los Angeles at dawn on September 23, 20 Californio (Californians of Mexican descent) guerrillas attack U.S. Marine Corps lieutenant Archibald H. Gillespie's 48-man garrison. This leads to a general uprising by Californios under paroled Mexican captain José María Flores against occupying American forces, with the Californios laying siege to the small American forces holding San Diego, Santa Barbara, and Los Angeles. In the absence of other authority, Flores becomes acting Mexican governor.

On September 24 Flores and 150 men trap Gillespie's small force atop Fort Hill, forcing his surrender by September 29. According to its terms, the Americans are to depart with their arms from San Pedro in the merchantman *Vandalia* by October 4.

September 23, 1846

Mexican-American War (continued): Wool departs San Antonio. In June 1846, U.S. Army brigadier general John E. Wool had been ordered to San Antonio, Texas, and instructed to assemble there a force of regulars and volunteers to be known as the Division of the Center. Wool is to support U.S. forces in northern Mexico under Major General Zachary Taylor.

On September 23, 1846, Wool quits San Antonio with 1,300 men and heads for Presidio del Rio Grande (present-day Eagle Pass, Texas). He is followed a month later by another 1,200 men under Colonel Sylvester Churchill. Wool's ultimate objective is Chihuahua and seizure of the lower trade route linking New Mexico and the Mexican interior.

September 25, 1846

Mexican-American War (continued). In Santa Fe, New Mexico, Brigadier General Stephen W. Kearny detaches Colonel Alexander W. Doniphan and his 1st Missouri Mounted Volunteer Regiment from the Army of the West and charges them with controlling New Mexico. Kearny then departs with 300 men of the 1st Dragoon Regiment of regulars to march to California.

Early October–Late November 1846

Mexican-American War (continued): Doniphan's New Mexico Indian Campaign. Reinforced at Santa Fe (New Mexico) by 1,200 men of Colonel Sterling Price's 2nd Missouri Mounted Infantry Regiment as well as Lieutenant Colonel Philip St. George Cooke's 500-man Mormon Battalion, Colonel Alexander W. Doniphan, commander of the 1st Missouri Mounted Volunteer Regiment and acting U.S. governor of New Mexico, undertakes a seven-week campaign against the Utah and Navajo Indians who have been attacking outlying Mexican settlements in the province.

October 1–4, 1846

Mexican-American War (continued). On October 1, 1846, the U.S. Navy sloop *Cyane* (20 guns), under Commander Samuel F. Du Pont, captures the Mexican schooners *Libertad* and *Fortuna* at Loreta, Baja California. The next day there the *Cyane* takes the schooner *Rosita,* and on October 4, the *Cyane* captures the sloops *Chapita* and *Alerto* at Mulejé.

October 6, 1846

Mexican-American War (continued): Kearny encounters Carson. Near Socorro (New Mexico), U.S. Army brigadier general Stephen W. Kearny and his 300 dragoons meet scout Christopher "Kit" Carson and 8 other scouts traveling to Washington, D.C. with news of the American conquest of California. Believing that California is now secure for the United States, Kearny detaches some 200 men from his 1st Dragoon Regiment to return to Santa Fe, while he continues west with the remainder.

October 7, 1846

Mexican-American War (continued): The *Cyane* off Guaymas. The U.S. Navy sloop *Cyane* (20 guns), captained by Commander Samuel F. Du Pont, arrives off Guaymas on the Gulf of California. When Mexican commander Colonel Antonio Campuzano refuses Du Pont's demand to hand over ships in the harbor, Du Pont shells the port. Two gunboats, the *Anáhuac*

U.S. Marine Corps first lieutenant Archibald Gillespie carried secret documents from President James K. Polk to U.S. officials in California before the start of the Mexican-American War and during the war commanded the U.S. garrison at Los Angeles. (U.S. Marine Corps Art Collection)

and *Sonorense,* are set afire, possibly by their crews, and destroyed. Du Pont sends in boats from the *Cyane* under Lieutenant George W. Harrison to cut out the Mexican brig *Condor.* Found in poor repair, it is scuttled.

October 7–8, 1846

Mexican-American War (continued): U.S. forces march on Los Angeles. U.S. Navy captain William Mervine of the frigate *Savannah* (54 guns) lands 225 sailors and marines at San Pedro to march against and retake Los Angeles. They camp at Rancho Dominguez (present-day North Long Beach) and on October 8 encounter 80 Californios (Californians of Latin American descent) and 10 Mexican soldiers with a 4-pounder gun, all under José Antonio Carrillo. Despite three attempts, the Americans cannot get past the blocking force and are forced to withdraw to their ship. Ten Americans are wounded in the skirmish, 4 mortally.

October 15, 1846

Mexican-American War (continued): Renewed U.S. Navy assault on Alvarado. U.S. Navy Home Squadron commander Commodore David Conner again attempts to take the Mexican port of Alvarado, three miles upriver from the Gulf of Mexico, astride the Rio Papaloapán, where three Mexican Navy gunboats have taken refuge. With the attempt of August 7 having failed because of the deep drafts of the U.S. warships, Conner secures two shallow-draft Revenue Service cutters. Meanwhile, Mexican forces reinforce and improve Alvarado's defenses.

Conner arrives off the mouth of the Papaloapán with two large steamers, two small steamers, and five schooner gunboats. Early this day, the steamer *Mississippi* (10 guns) shells the outer forts while other warships attempt to cross the sandbar. The *Mississippi's* fire proves nearly useless, however, because the ship's deep draft will not allow it to close within effective range. Rough surf further complicates the mission.

That afternoon with the surf having subsided, Conner orders a second advance up the river. He commands in the *Vixen* (3 guns), with two schooner-gunboats in tow, while the side-wheeler Revenue Service cutter *McLane* (6 guns) tows three schooner-gunboats.

The *Mississippi* remains behind, providing gunfire support. Although the column safely passes over the bar, the *McLane* runs aground before the U.S. warships can reach the main port, and Conner calls off the expedition.

The captain of the *McLane* manages to refloat his vessel, and the Americans return to the Gulf and then to Antón Lizardo. The Americans sustain only a few men slightly wounded; there are no known Mexican losses. Alvarado remains in Mexican hands until the spring of 1847.

October 23–27, 1846

Mexican-American War (continued): Tabasco River Expedition. Following the failure of the navy's second operation against Alvarado, Commodore Matthew C. Perry, who arrived as second-in-command of the Home Squadron in late September 1846, suggests a raid up the Tabasco River in the Yucatán Peninsula to capture or destroy Mexican ships, ordnance, and military supplies there.

Home Squadron commander Commodore David Conner concurs and provides the large steamer *Mississippi* (10 guns), the small steamers *McLane* (6 guns) and *Vixen* (3 guns), the schooners *Reefer* and *Bonita* (1 gun each), the former Mexican schooner *Nonata* (4 guns), and the Revenue Service cutter *Forward* (6 guns). They are augmented by a landing force of 253 marines and seamen drawn from the frigates *Cumberland* (52 guns) and *Raritan* (54 guns), commanded by Captain French Forrest. The expedition's ultimate goal is Tabasco, some 72 miles upriver.

The ships depart their anchorages along the Gulf coast on October 16, 1846. A heavy storm separates the *Reefer* and causes it to miss the operation, but the remaining ships arrive off the mouth of the Tabasco on October 22. To protect the port of Frontera at the mouth of the Tabasco, the Mexicans have largely relied on the very shallow water of the bar. Perry's men spend the remainder of October 22 preparing to cross the bar, and Perry shifts his flag to the smaller *Vixen* from the large *Mississippi,* which remains behind with the *McLane.*

On October 23 the *Vixen* tows the *Forward* and *Bonita* across the bar. The *McLane* follows, towing

U.S. forces come ashore during the Tabasco River Expedition, commanded by Commodore Matthew C. Perry during October 23–27, 1846. This painting is by a participant, U.S. Navy lieutenant Henry A. Walke, later a rear admiral. (Library of Congress)

the *Nonata* and the boats with Forrest's landing party. The *McLane* soon grounds but casts off the *Nonata* and the boats, and the *Nonata* proceeds upriver under sail. The *Vixen* arrives at Frontera in midafternoon. One Mexican schooner, the *Amado,* flees upriver; the schooner *Laura Virginia* and the steamers *Petrita* and *Tabasqueña* are quickly captured.

After detaching a few men under Lieutenant Joseph C. Walsh to garrison Frontera, supported by the ships across the bar, Perry sets out upriver in the remaining ships for Tabasco before the Mexicans can augment its defenses. Shortly after departing Frontera they encounter the *Bonita,* which had captured the *Amado.* The *Petrita,* carrying the landing party, leads the progression upriver. It is followed by the *Vixen,* towing the *Forward* and *Bonita.*

Steaming all night, the expeditionary force arrives at Tabasco on the morning of October 25. The town is poorly defended. Provincial governor Lieutenant Colonel Juan Bautista Traconis has fewer than 300 men: one regular company of infantry and cavalry, two dozen artillerymen, and a militia battalion. Tabasco's only fortification is Fort Acachapan, two miles downstream from the town near a sharp bend in the river. It mounts four 24-pounders, but its garrison flees on the Americans' approach, and a landing party spikes its guns.

By 1:00 p.m. on October 25 the American ships are anchored at Tabasco. Traconis rejects Perry's surrender demand. The Americans then fire a few shots over the town, and the Mexican garrison decamps. That afternoon Perry sends in the landing party to

Shrapnel

Shrapnel, or spherical case shot, was invented in 1784 by Lieutenant (later Lieutenant General) Henry Shrapnel (1761–1842) of the British Royal Artillery. Shrapnel came up with the idea in order to extend the range of highly effective case or canister shot against enemy troops.

During the Spanish siege of Gibraltar (1779–1783), the British successfully fired 5.5-inch mortar shells from their 24-pounder long guns, but in 1784 Shrapnel improved on this by inventing what he called "spherical case shot." The new artillery ammunition was later known simply by its designer's name. Spherical case or shrapnel consisted of a thin-walled hollow round shell filled with a small bursting charge and small iron or lead shot. A time fuse set off the charge in the air, scattering the shot and pieces of the shell casing among opposing troops. The bursting charge was only a small one, allowing the scattered balls and burst casing to continue on the same trajectory as before the explosion (a greater charge would increase the velocity but scattered the balls more widely and reduced their effectiveness). Explosive shell had for some time been utilized in high-trajectory fire mortars but had not before been widely projected in horizontal fire by guns.

Shrapnel shells had thinner walls than other shells and had to be carefully cast. Their weight empty was about half of that for solid shot of the same caliber, but their loaded weight made them comparable to solid shot.

The British first fired shrapnel during the Napoleonic Wars in 1804 in the siege of Surinam and continued to use it thereafter. Early shrapnel had a wooden plug and a paper fuse, but in the 1850s it incorporated the more precise Bormann fuse. Shrapnel was widely used in the American Civil War both on land and in naval actions, most often in the 12-pounder Napoleon and Dahlgren boat howitzers. Shrapnel soon became a staple round in the world's artillery establishments. Britain alone produced 72 million shrapnel shells during World War I.

By the end of the 19th century, shrapnel rounds had evolved to a similar size and shape as the other cylindo-conoidal shells fired by breech-loading artillery. The operating principle was still similar to the original spherical case. The thin-walled projectile was packed with small steel balls and an expelling charge. The expelling charge, however, did not rupture the projectile. Rather, it blew the fuse off the front end and expelled the shrapnel balls forward. Thus, the shrapnel round was something like a huge flying shotgun shell. Because of the imprecise burning times of the black powder time fuses of the era, the adjustment of the proper height of burst was very difficult. Also, shrapnel was only effective against troops in the open. As trench warfare set in during World War I and field fortifications became more robust, shrapnel became virtually worthless. Meanwhile, advances in both explosives and metallurgy during World War I finally produced high-explosive (HE) shells that had both significant blast and fragmentation effects. After World War I shrapnel completely disappeared, replaced entirely by HE shells. Today, the fragmentation produced by an HE round is popularly but incorrectly called shrapnel.

SPENCER C. TUCKER AND DAVID T. ZABECKI

Further Reading

Bull, Stephen. *Encyclopedia of Military Technology and Innovation.* Westport, CT: Greenwood, 2004.

Ripley, Warren. *Artillery and Ammunition of the Civil War.* New York: Van Nostrand Reinhold, 1970.

Tucker, Spencer C. *Arming the Fleet: U.S. Navy Ordnance in the Muzzle-Loading Era.* Annapolis, MD: Naval Institute Press, 1989.

take possession. In the meantime, the Americans have seized the schooners *Tobasco* and *Alvarado*, the brigs *Yunaute* and *Rentville*, and the sloops *Desada* and *Campeche*.

Traconis does not permit civilians to leave Tabasco, and that night his men reenter the town and take up positions there. Perry lacks the manpower to assault Tabasco and hold it. He had decided not to subject the civilians to hostile fire but instead to return to Frontera with his prizes, when at dawn on October 26 the Mexicans open fire on his ships. Perry answers with shrapnel. At 7:00 a.m. a white flag appears, and Perry agrees to an appeal by the merchants not to fire on the town unless his ships are fired upon. But at 10:00, when Mexican forces ashore open up on the prize *Desada,* which has grounded, and then on the other ships of the squadron, Perry orders a bombardment. After about a half hour, the Mexican shore fire stops, and Perry orders his own ships to cease fire and to prepare to return to Frontera. In the fighting the Americans sustain six casualties (Lieutenant Charles Morris and a sailor killed, two men drowned, and two wounded); the Mexicans lose five soldiers and four civilians killed.

Perry's small force departs on October 26, arriving at Frontera the next morning. The *Petrita* and *Laura Virginia* (renamed the *Morris* in honor of Lieutenant Morris) are taken into American service; others of the prizes would also have been added but are lost to a storm at the end of November.

October 31, 1846

Mexican-American War (continued). Commodore Robert F. Stockton, having arrived at San Diego in the frigate *Congress* (50 guns) the day before, sends reinforcements ashore to aid the beleaguered American garrison commanded by Lieutenant George Minor.

November 14, 1846

Mexican-American War (continued). Conner's capture of Tampico. The weakly defended Mexican Gulf coast port of Tampico, principal town of the state of Tamaulipas, lies five miles up the Pánuco River. During November 11 and 12, U.S. Navy commodore David Conner, commander of the Home Squadron,

sends the frigates *Potomac* (50 guns) and *Raritan* (54 guns) from the U.S. base at Antón Lazardo to cruise between Lobos and the mainland. The next day he sails with the screw sloop *Princeton* (flagship, 13 guns); the side-wheel steamers *Mississippi* (10 guns) and *Vixen* (3 guns); the schooner *Spitfire* (11 guns); the 1-gun schooners *Bonita, Petrel,* and *Reefer;* and the former Mexican schooner *Nonata* (4 guns). While the frigate *Cumberland* (52 guns) remains at Antón Lazardo, Conner embarks from it some 100 men and a number of its boats in the *Mississippi.*

The expeditionary force reaches the mouth of the Pánuco at dawn on November 14. With the *Potomac* and *Raritan* not having arrived, Conner forms two divisions. The first division, under himself, consists of the *Spitfire, Petrel,* and *Reefer* and the boats from the *Cumberland, Mississippi,* and *Princeton.* The second division is commanded by Commodore Matthew C. Perry and consists of the *Vixen, Bonita,* and *Nonata* and boats from the sloop *St. Mary's* (22 guns) and the brig *Porpoise* (11 guns). The ships' boats carry about 300 men.

Conner crosses the bar late that same morning and pushes upstream. After extended and fruitless talks with a civilian truce party at Tampico, Conner declares that no formal surrender of the town is necessary, sends in a temporary occupying force, and seizes without opposition the Mexican schooner gunboats *Union, Pueblana,* and *Mahonese;* the Mexican merchant schooner *Ormigo;* and the Spanish schooner *Isabella.* That same day, Conner dispatches Commodore Perry in the *Mississippi* to American Gulf ports on a quest to secure a permanent garrison for the city. Perry returns on November 23 with some 500 men plus a field battery from Point Isabel, Texas.

Conner remains at Tampico until December 13. After learning that there are insufficient roads from Tampico to Mexico's interior, Tampico is abandoned in favor of Veracruz as the main landing point for the overland campaign against Mexico City.

November 15, 1846

The sloop *Boston* (20 guns), under Commander George F. Pearson, is proceeding to Mexico to join the naval blockade there when it wrecks in a sudden squall at Eleuthera Island in the Bahamas. All crew members are saved.

November 16, 1846

Mexican-American War (continued). Near San Luis Obispo, some 100 Californios (Californians of Latin American heritage) under Manuel Castro attack and scatter a number of American settler volunteers marching to Monterey to assist the 400 Americans there.

November 16, 1846

Mexican-American War (continued): Taylor's capture of Saltillo. Having decided that his Army of the Rio Grande will be better positioned by occupying the high ground to the southeast, on November 13, 1846, Major General Zachary Taylor pushes southwest from Monterrey and, without a shot being fired, takes the undefended Mexican town of Saltillo, the last major urban area occupied by U.S. forces in northeastern Mexico. Taylor subsequently leaves 1,400 men there under Major General William J. Worth and relocates most of his men and his headquarters to Monterrey.

Shortly thereafter Brigadier General John E. Wool informs Taylor that he believes that the Mexicans are preparing to launch a major offensive against American forces in northern Mexico. Wool suggests that he shift his own division to Parras to be within supporting distance of Taylor, who authorizes this movement.

November 16–21, 1846

Mexican-American War (continued). Two days after the capture of Tampico, on November 16, 1846, Commodore David Conner, commander of the U.S. Navy Home Squadron, orders Commander Josiah Tattnall to proceed 25 miles up the Pánuco River to

Josiah Tattnall (1795–1871)

U.S. Navy officer. Born on the family plantation of Bonaventure near Savannah, Georgia, on November 9, 1795, Josiah Tattnall was the son of a Georgia senator and governor. Orphaned in 1805, Tattnall was sent to England to live with his paternal grandfather for schooling. Tattnall entered the U.S. Navy on a midshipman's warrant on January 1, 1812, and was assigned to the frigate *Constellation*. Although his ship was blockaded in Hampton Roads during the War of 1812, Tattnall saw action in the Battle of Craney Island in June 1813. Assigned to the Washington Navy Yard, he took part in the Battle of Bladensburg in August 1814 and in the Algerine War in the sloop *Epervier*.

Promoted to lieutenant on April 1, 1818, Tattnall served in the frigate *Macedonian* in the Pacific during 1818–1820. During 1822–1823 he participated in antipiracy operations in the West Indies. He then served in the frigate *Constitution* in the Mediterranean. In April 1831 Lieutenant Tattnall assumed command of the schooner *Grampus* in the Gulf of Mexico.

Tattnall was ashore for almost four years awaiting orders until returned to active duty in 1836, when he served three years at the Boston Navy Yard. He was promoted to commander on February 25, 1838.

Following service in the Mediterranean and African Squadrons, in 1846 during the Mexican-American War Tattnall was assigned command of the converted steamer *Spitfire*. In this ship he participated in various operations, including the capture of Tampico on November 14, 1846. During November 16–17, Tattnall led an expedition up the Pánuco River in the boats of the *Spitfire* and the steamer *Vixen* and took several small Mexican prizes. On November 19, he arrived at Pánuco with the *Spitfire* and the schooner *Vixen* and destroyed cannon removed there from Tampico.

Tattnall played an important role in the U.S. landing at Veracruz when on March 10, 1847, he mounted a diversionary attack by the *Spitfire* against the Castle of San Juan de Ulloa on Gallega Reef to the north of the city in order to distract the Mexicans. On March 22 and 23 Tattnall had charge of the steamers *Spitfire* and *Vixen* and the schooners *Bonita, Falcon, Petrel,* and *Tampico* in a bombardment of Veracruz itself. On the second day, he brought his ships in at only 600 yards from Mexican Fort Santiago. In a subsequent expedition up the Tuxpan River, on April 17 Tattnall and three of his officers in the *Spitfire* were wounded by a Mexican musket volley from the shore.

Following the war, Tattnall returned to duty at the Boston Navy Yard. He was promoted to captain on February 5, 1850, and in March he took command of the side-wheeler *Saranac*. During 1851–1854 he commanded the Pensacola Navy Yard, and during 1854–1855 he was flag captain of the ship of the line *Independence* in the Pacific Squadron.

During 1858–1860, Tattnall commanded the East India Squadron with his flag in the screw steamer *San Jacinto*. On June 25, 1859, during the Second Opium War he violated his orders and American neutrality by assisting the British. Several eyewitnesses reported Tattnall as declaring that "blood is thicker than water," and one has him also saying that "he'd be damned if he'd stand by and see white men butchered before his eyes." The Americans lost one man killed. Tattnall might have been court-martialed had it not been for highly favorable coverage in the U.S. press and in the usually anti-American British newspapers but also primarily because of strong British government praise conveyed to Washington.

In 1860 Tattnall transported the first Japanese diplomatic mission to the United States. He next commanded the Sackets Harbor Naval Station. Although personally averse to secession, Tattnall resigned his commission on February 21, 1861. A week later he was commissioned the senior officer in the Georgia Navy. On March 26, Tattnall was also commissioned a captain in the Confederate Navy.

Tattnall commanded the few Southern naval units available in the defense of Port Royal, South Carolina, until it was secured by the U.S. Navy on November 7, 1861. In March 1862, he succeeded the wounded Franklin Buchanan as commander of the James River Squadron with his flag in the Confederate ironclad *Virginia*. Tattnall's efforts to do battle with USS *Monitor* met rebuff when the latter remained under the guns of Fort Monroe.

Learning of the loss of the Norfolk Navy Yard on May 9 and unable to lighten the *Virginia* sufficiently to get it up the James, Tattnall ordered the Confederate ironclad destroyed on May 11, 1862. A subsequent court-martial cleared him in this action. On May 15, Tattnall resumed command of the naval forces of Georgia until March 1863, when he concentrated on the defense of Savannah. With the fall of that city to Union forces imminent, he ordered destruction of the remaining Confederate ships. Tattnall was subsequently taken prisoner at Augusta.

Paroled in May 1865, Tattnall lived in Nova Scotia for four years until he returned to Savannah as inspector of the port. He died there on June 14, 1871.

SPENCER C. TUCKER

Further Reading

Jones, Charles C. *The Life and Services of Commodore Josiah Tattnall.* Savannah, GA: Morning News Stream Printing House, 1887.

Tucker, Spencer C. *Blue and Gray Navies: The Civil War Afloat.* Annapolis, MD: Naval Institute Press, 2006.

Pánuco and there destroy cannon and military stores. Tattnall sets out with the schooners *Spitfire* (flagship, 11 guns) and *Petrel* (1 gun) and a landing party of 20 marines and 12 sailors. Receiving the surrender of the town, Tattnall and his men dig up and destroy 9 18-pounders, dump a quantity of shot into the river, and destroy some equipment. The Americans also carry off a 24-pounder and some military equipment. Tattnall returns to Tampico on November 21.

November 23, 1846

Mexican-American War (continued): Scott assumes command of an expeditionary force against Veracruz. Following the U.S. victory in the Battle of Monterrey (see September 21–24, 1846), there is a strategic debate in Washington. President James K. Polk favors an advance on Mexico City from the north by troops under Major General Zachary Taylor. Commanding general of the army Major General Winfield Scott, however, prefers an amphibious landing at Mexico City's port of Veracruz, then a march overland 260 miles to the capital. Polk is already unhappy with Taylor for his handling of the Battle of Monterrey when Taylor rejects the suggestion that he can move 300 miles across desert to San Luis Potosí and then another 200 miles to Mexico City. Taylor's counterproposal is an advance from Veracruz, much as Scott has recommended.

Polk, a Democrat, for political reasons does not wish to name as commander either Taylor or Scott, both Whigs. Taylor has infuriated Polk for the Armistice of Monterrey, but the general has become quite popular at home, and Polk fears that Taylor might run against him for the presidency. Polk reluctantly names Scott to command the expedition, authorizing him to take units for the expeditionary force from Taylor, who will thereby be restricted to defensive operations. This decision results in Taylor becoming a lifelong enemy of Scott.

Scott departs Washington for New York City on November 23, 1846, sailing from that place on November 30 and arriving in New Orleans on December 19. Scott sets the invasion date for February 1847.

November 26, 1846

Mexican-American War (continued): Destruction of the *Criolla*. Taking advantage of the fact that most of the American squadron is off station at Tampico with only the brig *Somers* (12 guns) maintaining the American blockade at Veracruz, the captain of the Mexican schooner *Criolla* sails there. With the *Criolla* at anchor under the guns of the San Juan de Ulúa island fortress, on this date Lieutenant Raphael Semmes, commanding the *Somers*, sends in a boat with eight volunteers led by Lieutenant James L. Parker to cut out the *Criolla*.

Raphael Semmes (1809–1877)

U.S. Navy and Confederate Navy officer and, as captain of the *Alabama*, one of the most successful commerce raiders in history. Born on September 27, 1809, in Charles County, Maryland, Raphael Semmes was raised by relatives in Georgetown, District of Columbia, following the death of his parents. In 1826 he won appointment as a midshipman in the U.S. Navy. Promotion was then slow, and in leaves of absence ashore Semmes took up the study of law, a profession he followed when not at sea.

From 1837 until the Mexican-American War, Semmes spent most of his time on survey work along the southern coast and in the Gulf of Mexico. Early in the Mexican-American War he commanded the brig *Somers*. It sank in a sudden squall in December 1846 and half the crew was lost, but a court-martial found Semmes blameless. In March 1847 he took part in the capture of Veracruz; later he participated in the expedition against Tuxpan and, accompanying land forces to Mexico City, was cited for bravery. In 1852 he published *Service Afloat and Ashore during the Mexican War.* Promoted to commander in 1855, the next year he joined the Lighthouse Board.

Semmes had moved his permanent residence to Alabama and, following that state's secession and creation of the Confederate States of America, in February 1861 he resigned his U.S. Navy commission and the next month entered the Confederate Navy as a commander. Sent into the North, he purchased military and naval supplies and equipment. In mid-April Semmes secured command at New Orleans of the *Sumter,* the first Confederate commerce raider. Between June 1861 and January 1862 he took 18 Union prizes. His ship in poor repair and blockaded by Union warships, Semmes abandoned it at Gibraltar.

In August 1862 the Confederate Congress advanced Semmes to captain, and he took command of a new ship nearing completion in England, which he commissioned as the *Alabama.* For nearly two years the *Alabama* ravaged Union shipping. Through July 1864 it took 66 prizes and sank a Union warship, the *Hatteras.* In all, Semmes took 84 Union merchantmen.

Semmes finally put into Cherbourg, France, with the *Alabama* for repairs. On June 19, 1864, he sortied to engage the Union steam sloop *Kearsarge.* In the ensuing battle the *Kearsarge* sank the *Alabama,* but Semmes escaped on an English yacht.

Returning to the South, Semmes was promoted to rear admiral in February 1865 and given command of the James River Squadron of three ironclad rams and seven wooden steamers. When Confederate forces abandoned Richmond on April 2, Semmes destroyed his vessels. The men of the squadron then formed into a naval brigade under Semmes as a brigadier general. Semmes was the only officer North or South to serve as a flag officer in both the army and the navy. He surrendered his unit at Greensboro, North Carolina.

After the war, Semmes was briefly arrested. He was then a probate judge, professor, newspaper editor, and lecturer before resuming the practice of law. In 1869 he published *Memoirs of Service Afloat.* Semmes died at his home in Point Clear, Alabama, on August 30, 1877.

SPENCER C. TUCKER

Further Reading

Semmes, Raphael. *Memoirs of Service Afloat, during the War between the States.* 1869; reprint, Secaucus, NJ: Blue and Grey, 1987.
Taylor, John M. *Confederate Raider: Raphael Semmes of the Alabama.* Washington, DC: Brassey's, 1994.
Tucker, Spencer C. *Raphael Semmes and the Alabama.* Abilene, TX: McWhiney Foundation Press, 1996.

The boarding party easily takes the ship and its crew shortly before midnight, but the noise alerts a sentinel at San Juan de Ulúa, who asks what is transpiring. Parker replies in excellent Spanish that the men had become drunk and he is placing them in irons. But when the Americans are ready to sail the schooner out to the *Somers,* there is no wind, and Parker is forced to burn the schooner. The Americans escape to the *Somers* under a hail of fire from San Juan de Ulúa, bringing with them seven Mexican prisoners. Unfortunately, it is later learned that the *Criolla* was a spy ship, which had sailed to Veracruz with the blessing of U.S. Home Squadron commander Commodore David Conner.

November–December 1846

Mexican-American War (continued). With no end in sight to the war, the War Department issues a second call for state volunteers. These men are needed to replace the 12-month units that will leave Mexico at the expiration of their enlistments.

December 6, 1846

Mexican-American War (continued). In Mexico City on this date, the Mexican Senate narrowly votes 11 to 9 to confirm general and former president Antonio López de Santa Anna as the new president of Mexico.

December 6, 1846

Mexican-American War (continued): Battle of San Pascual. Brigadier General Stephen W. Kearny arrives in California with only 121 men, having marched more than 2,000 miles from Fort Leavenworth, Kansas, since May. Kearny's men join 40 U.S. marines and sailors with a 4-pounder gun under Lieutenant Archibald Gillespie.

On December 5 while trying to intercept Gillespie, Mexican major Andrés Pico and some 100 Californios (Californians of Latin American extraction) take shelter from the wet weather in the Native American village of San Pascual. That night the Americans learn that the Californios are nearby. Uncertain of the Californios' position, half of the 179 Americans charge the village just prior to dawn on December 6. The worn-out American horses are strung out over some distance. The Californios exchange gunfire with the Americans outside the village, then turn and ride away. Their fresher horses outdistance the pursuing Americans for about three-quarters of a mile, stringing out the Americans even more. The Californios then turn and attack with their lances. The Americans do not use their guns, probably because of damp powder caused

 ## Lance

The lance was a long pole-arm cavalry weapon, most identified in the popular mind with medieval Europe. Dating from ancient times and ranging in length from 9 to 14 feet, the lance was the cavalry version of the pole-arm spear or pike carried by the infantry. Next to the sword, the lance was the most important cavalry weapon. Lances were of wood, usually ash, and had a small metal tip to penetrate armor. The advent of the stirrup greatly facilitated its use. A horseman held the lance pointing forward under his arm but stationary in the charge, utilizing the momentum of the horse for shock power. Most often, lances were used to unseat other knights.

Lances continued in use even into the 20th century. They are especially identified in the popular mind with the jousting of medieval Europe, but all the major continental powers of the Napoleonic Era had lance-equipped units. Because early North America was so heavily forested, lances were little used in the colonial period. They were, however, adopted by Native Americans of the Great Plains after the arrival of the horse. The lance continued in service for such a long time because of the difficulty of reloading early firearms while on horseback.

SPENCER C. TUCKER

Further Reading

Davenant, Charles. *An Essay upon Ways and Means of Supplying the War.* London: Printed for Jacob Tonson, 1695.
Starkey, Armstrong. *European and Native American Warfare, 1675–1815.* Norman: University of Oklahoma Press, 1998.

by days of rain, and their sabers are no match for the Californio lances.

After about 30 minutes, the Californios capture a mountain howitzer when the mules transporting it bolt into their line. The Americans then fire the other howitzer, which temporarily disperses the Californios. In the fighting, 19 Americans are killed and 17 are wounded, the latter including both Gillespie and Kearny. The Californios suffer only 11 wounded and 1 captured. The Battle of San Pascual is the bloodiest engagement in the California theater of the war.

The next day, December 7, as Kearny's men approach Rancho San Bernardo, they are attacked by a large body of Californios. Kearny withdraws his men to a nearby hill and there slaughters his mules, their carcasses serving as makeshift breastworks. That night Kearny sends scout Christopher "Kit" Carson, U.S. Navy lieutenant Edward F. Beale, and a Native American scout from the surrounded position on foot 30 miles to San Diego to request assistance from Pacific Squadron commodore Robert F. Stockton. Stockton dispatches more than 200 sailors and marines. Before the relief column arrives on December 11, however, Pico's force is recalled. Kearny and his men arrive at San Diego on December 12.

December 8, 1846

Mexican-American War (continued): Loss of the *Somers*. On this date, the U.S. Navy brig *Somers* (12 guns), commanded by Lieutenant Raphael Semmes, is chasing a blockade-runner off Tampico when the *Somers* is caught in a sudden squall and thrown on its beam ends. The crew is unable to right the ship, and it capsizes in only 10 minutes. Thirty-two members of its crew of 76 drown. Seven are captured by the Mexicans, while the remainder, including Semmes, are rescued by boats from British, French, and Spanish warships stationed at Sacrificios. A subsequent court of inquiry acquits Semmes of any blame and even commends him on his seamanship.

December 14, 1846

Mexican-American War (continued): Capture of San Luis Obispo. On this dark, rainy night while marching from San Juan Bautista against the Californios (Californians of Latin American heritage) at Los Angeles, Brevet Lieutenant Colonel John C. Frémont and his California Battalion capture San Luis Obispo, taking prisoner local Mexican commander Jesús Pico and 35 members of his garrison.

December 14, 1846

Mexican-American War (continued): Commencement of Doniphan's March. Colonel Alexander W. Doniphan's 1st Regiment of Missouri Mounted Volunteers had accompanied Brigadier General Stephen W. Kearny from Fort Leavenworth, Kansas, to Santa Fe, New Mexico. Doniphan, a lawyer in civilian life, sets up a governmental structure for the new U.S. territory, and his men pacify much of New Mexico. On the arrival of reinforcements and a new commander, on December 14 Doniphan departs Santa Fe with some 800 men of his regiment for El Paso del Norte (present-day Ciudad Juárez, Mexico), 250 miles distant, to reinforce Brigadier General John E. Wool in the state of Chihuahua.

December 18–21, 1846

Mexican-American War (continued): Threat of Mexican attack. In mid-December 1846, Major General Zachary Taylor, commander of the U.S. Army of the Rio Grande, sends Brigadier General David E. Twiggs's division southeast toward Ciudad Victoria (Tamaulipas state). Meanwhile, Brigadier General William J. Worth, commanding the division of Taylor's army occupying the town of Saltillo, receives word of the advance of Mexican troops under General Antonio López de Santa Anna from San Luis Potosí and requests Taylor to send reinforcements. Taylor immediately retraces his steps back to Monterrey, ordering Brigadier General John A. Quitman to continue to Victoria with an all-U.S. volunteers force.

Worth is reinforced at Saltillo on December 19 by a force from Monterrey under Major General William O. Butler and on December 21 by Brigadier General John E. Wool's Division of the Center from Parras. Realizing that U.S. forces are concentrating against him, Santa Anna cancels his plan to attack.

December 21, 1846

Mexican-American War (continued): Capture of El Carmen. In order to sever clandestine trade through the port of Yucatán, U.S. Navy commodore Matthew C. Perry sails from Antón Lizardo on December 18 with the steamers *Mississippi* (flagship, 10 guns) and *Vixen* (3 guns) and the 1-gun schooners *Bonita* and *Petrel*. Perry arrives off El Carmen on December 20 and, transferring to the *Vixen,* proceeds across the bar with it and the *Bonita* and *Petrel*. On December 21, El Carmen surrenders unconditionally. After taking off military stores, Perry leaves the *Vixen* and *Petrel* there and departs with the two other ships on December 22.

December 25, 1846

Mexican-American War (continued): Doniphan's March (continued): Battle of Brazito. On December 25 some 9 miles south of present-day Las Cruces, New Mexico, at the confluence of the Brazito River and the Rio Grande, U.S. colonel Alexander W. Doniphan's 1st Regiment of Missouri Mounted Volunteers is caught by surprise by some 1,200 Mexican soldiers led by Colonel Antonio Ponce de León.

Although heavily outnumbered, Doniphan skillfully halts a series of Mexican charges. The Battle of Brazito costs the Mexicans about 50 killed and 150 wounded; the Americans suffer only 7 wounded. Two days later Doniphan occupies El Paso del Norte (present-day Ciudad Juárez, Mexico), with no resistance.

December 27, 1846

Mexican-American War (continued). Major General Winfield Scott, charged with command of the U.S. expedition against Veracruz, arrives at Brazos Santiago at the mouth of the Rio Grande. Scott orders 2,500 of Taylor's men to embark there and 5,500 more to embark at the captured Mexican port of Tampico. Scott has already settled on the island of Lobos midway between Tampico and Veracruz as the assembly site for the invasion. Although the troops are ready by the end of January, a shortage of transports delays their embarkation for more than a month. When the latter is completed, Taylor's force will consist largely of untrained and unreliable volunteers.

December 29, 1846

Mexican-American War (continued). U.S. volunteer forces under Brigadier General John A. Quitman approach Victoria (Tamaulipas state), causing 1,500 Mexican cavalrymen there to abandon it without a fight. On January 4, 1847, Major General Zachary Taylor, commander of the U.S. Army of the Rio Grande, arrives at Victoria with the bulk of his army.

January 2, 1847

Mexican-American War (continued): Clash near Santa Clara Mission. On December 29, 1846, U.S. Marine Corps captain Ward Marston departs San Francisco with 100 men and a fieldpiece to quell an insurrection by Californios (Californians of Latin American extraction). On January 2, 1847, about seven miles from the Santa Clara Mission, the Americans encounter some 120 Californios led by Francisco Sánchez. A brief skirmish ensues, during which the Californios are dispersed, having sustained 4 killed and 5 wounded; American losses are 2 wounded.

January 5–6, 1847

Mexican-American War (continued). On each of these two days, Brevet Lieutenant Colonel John C. Frémont with 400 men and six fieldpieces meets and disperses Californio (Californians of Latin American heritage) horsemen at San Buenaventura Mission (Ventura, California).

January 8, 1847

Mexican-American War (continued): Battle of San Gabriel. On December 28, 1846, Brigadier General Stephen W. Kearny and Commodore Robert F. Stockton depart San Diego with 607 men: dismounted U.S. Army dragoons, members of the California Battalion, and seamen and marines. They plan to march 140 miles northwest and recapture Los Angeles from the Mexicans.

The Americans do not encounter any resistance until the evening of January 7, when they discover 450 Mexicans and Californios (Californians of Latin American heritage) with several artillery pieces under Captain José María Flores at La Jabonería Ford on the San Gabriel River. The next morning the Americans

 ## Explosive Shell and the Shell Gun

The introduction of a bursting projectile and a gun specifically designed to project it had tremendous impact on warship design and naval warfare. Solid shot had been the mainstay at sea for centuries. Shot was used to hole a vessel, damage and destroy spars and masts, and create crew casualties. But wooden warships with their thick oak sides could absorb a tremendous number of hits. Even if it penetrated, shot tended to leave regular rounded holes easily plugged by a ship's carpenter, especially as the wooden fibers tended to close after shot had passed through. In any case, it took a great many such holes to sink a large wooden warship. Occasionally ships were lost by a magazine explosion, but most captured vessels were disabled through damage to masts, spars, and rigging or from heavy personnel casualties that enabled them to be taken by boarding.

The antipersonnel effects of shot occurred when it exited the wood and produced showers of splinters. The effects of this were greatest when the force of the shot was only slightly more than that required to pass through the wood. But far too often, shot failed to penetrate the wooden side of a ship at all.

Shell was designed not to penetrate. It moved at a slow velocity in order to lodge in the side of a ship and there explode, causing an irregular hole that would be difficult to patch and, in many cases, large enough that it might even sink the vessel. Shot had greater range, but shell was much more destructive.

With improvements in both shells and fusing (crews firing early shells dreaded them because on occasion the shells exploded prematurely, bursting the gun), special guns were developed to fire shell. The French took the lead because they had less to lose and more to gain than the British from the introduction of an entirely new system (the British had by far the world's largest navy). In trials conducted in the 1820s, French colonel (later general) Henri Paixhans proved the effectiveness of explosive shell against wooden ships.

Shell guns had the great advantage of being lighter than shot guns, as shell was fired with smaller charges. This meant that the weight of metal that a warship fired in broadside might actually be increased at the same time that the weight of its ordnance was reduced. In 1837 the French introduced the Paixhans 80-pounder shell gun as a part of every ship's regular battery. It weighed as much as a 36-pounder shot gun. A frigate armed with a few of the new guns could easily defeat a much larger ship of the line.

In the 1840s shells and shell guns came into general use in the world's navies. In the United States, Lieutenant John Dahlgren developed his own ordnance system for the U.S. Navy. In effect, explosive shell projected by special shell guns rendered wooden ships obsolete and led to the introduction of the ironclad warship. The irony is that with the appearance of the ironclad ship during the American Civil War, Dahlgren's shell guns fired solid shot rather than explosive shell against Confederate ironclads.

SPENCER C. TUCKER

Further Reading

Hogg, Ian, and John Batchelor. *Naval Gun*. Poole, Dorset, UK: Blandford, 1975.
Lambert, Andrew, ed. *Steam, Steel & Shellfire: The Steam Warship, 1815–1905*. Annapolis, MD: Naval Institute Press, 1992.
Tucker, Spencer C. *Arming the Fleet: U.S. Navy Ordnance in the Muzzle-Loading Era*. Annapolis, MD: Naval Institute Press, 1989.

attempt to flank the defenders by crossing at Bartolo Ford, but Flores detects this and shifts horsemen there. The Americans form a hollow square and push across the ford, scattering the defenders with artillery fire. In the fighting each side sustains 2 killed and 9 wounded.

January 9, 1847

Mexican-American War (continued): Battle of La Mesa. Following the Battle of San Gabriel (see January 8, 1847), Brigadier General Stephen W. Kearny and Commodore Robert F. Stockton continue their advance on Los Angeles. In the Battle of La Mesa near present-day Pasadena, the Americans again form a hollow square and defeat the outnumbered and out-gunned Mexicans and Californios, commanded by Captain José María Flores. One American is killed, and five are wounded; one Californio is also killed, and an unknown number are wounded.

Stockton and Kearny cross the Los Angeles River late on January 9 but wait until the next day to enter Los Angeles and retake it from the Californios. For 20 American casualties, Kearny and Stockton have captured the last Mexican stronghold in California.

January 11, 1847

Mexican-American War (continued). Late this evening, Brevet Lieutenant Colonel John C. Frémont with 400 men and six fieldpieces encounters the remaining 100 Californio (Californians of Latin American heritage) horsemen of Captain José María Flores, who had been defending Los Angeles. Frémont persuades them to surrender the next day.

January 13, 1847

Mexican-American War (continued). The Capitulation (Treaty) of Cahuenga is signed by Brevet Lieutenant Colonel John C. Frémont and Mexican major Andrés Pico in what is now North Hollywood, Los Angeles. The treaty formally ends organized resistance to U.S. rule in California.

January 13, 1847

Mexican-American War (continued). In the village of Villagrán between Monterrey and Ciudad Victoria,

U.S. Army lieutenant John A. Richey is killed while attempting to buy provisions. Richey had been carrying to Major General Zachary Taylor, commander of U.S. forces in northern Mexico, one of two sets of Major General Winfield Scott's plans for the invasion of Veracruz. The papers are sent on to Mexican Army commander General Antonio López de Santa Anna at San Luis Potosí.

January 16, 1847

Mexican-American War (continued). U.S. Army brigadier general Stephen W. Kearny produces orders from the War Department naming him governor of California. U.S. Navy commodore Robert F. Stockton, however, believes that he still has authority in California and insists that his appointee, Brevet Lieutenant Colonel John C. Frémont, retain the position of governor.

January 19–February 9, 1847

Mexican-American War (continued): Taos Revolt. On the morning of January 19, 1847, an uprising of Mexican nationals and allied Pueblo Native Americans occurs in the town of Don Fernando de Taos (present-day Taos, New Mexico). The revolt, in planning for some time, is led by Mexican national Pablo Montoya and Taos Indian Tomás Romero (Tomasito). At Governor George Bent's residence, Tomasito and a number of Indians shoot Bent with arrows, killing and scalping him in the presence of his wife and children. At least three other government officials are also killed and scalped.

Later that same day, some 500 Mexicans and Native Americans attack Simeon Turley's mill in Arroyo Hondo, outside of Taos. One of the employees escapes to Santa Fe to inform U.S. forces there of events. Of 8–10 men left defending the mill, only 2 survive. Other insurgents kill 7 American traders in the village of Mora.

On January 24, U.S. captain Jesse I. Morin leads a small force to defeat insurgents at Mora. Colonel Sterling Price departs Santa Fe for Taos with some 300 U.S. troops and 65 volunteers. En route, Price defeats some 1,500 Mexicans and Indians at Santa Cruz de la Cañada and Empudo Pass, killing 36 for

U.S. artillery fires on the church at Don Fernando de Taos, New Mexico, on February 4, 1847. The projectiles had little effect on the church's thick adobe walls, but an infantry assault by Colonel Sterling Price's Missouri troops forced the rebels to flee and brought an end to the three-week-long Taos Revolt. (Hulton Archive/Getty Images)

U.S. losses of 3 killed and 6 wounded. Shortly thereafter Price is reinforced, bringing his strength up to 479 men. The rebels retreat to Don Fernando de Taos, where they seek refuge in its church.

The siege of the church at Don Fernando de Taos is the final action of the Taos Revolt. On February 3 U.S. forces shell the church, but the light artillery fire has little effect on its thick adobe walls. On February 4, however, Price's men mount an assault, and the rebels flee into the surrounding mountains. Two days later, the remaining insurgents surrender. Some 150 rebels are killed and 400 are captured, while Price loses 7 soldiers killed and 45 wounded.

Price imposes martial law in Taos and sets up a court to try the imprisoned rebels. Following a two-week trial, the jury returns a verdict of guilty of treason and murder against 15 men and sentences them

to death. In all, 28 individuals are executed for the revolt. Tomás Romero is murdered in his cell before trial, while Montoya is among those tried, sentenced to death, and hanged. There is no further organized opposition to U.S. rule in New Mexico.

January 24, 1847

Mexican-American War (continued). U.S. major general of volunteers Robert Patterson reaches Tampico, Mexico, with 4,500 men for the planned assault on Veracruz.

January 25, 1847

Mexican-American War (continued). Some 50–60 miles south of Saltillo, a large formation of Mexican cavalry surprises and captures a 50-man U.S. patrol under Majors John P. Gaines and Solon Borland.

Another U.S. patrol of 30 men under Captain William J. Healy, sent out to discover the fate of the first patrol, is also taken prisoner.

January 28, 1847

Mexican-American War (continued): Santa Anna decides to attack U.S. forces in northern Mexico. Thanks to captured U.S. strategic plans (see January 13, 1847), at San Luis Potosí Mexican Army commander General Antonio López de Santa Anna is well aware of the greatly diminished strength of U.S. forces in northern Mexico and decides to capitalize on this. The Mexican vanguard sets out on January 28, followed by additional forces over the next three days. In all, Santa Anna has more than 20,000 men.

February 1, 1847

Mexican-American War (continued): Doniphan's March (continued). Colonel Alexander W. Doniphan and his 1st Regiment of Missouri Mounted Volunteers depart El Paso del Norte (present-day Ciudad Juárez, Mexico) for Chihuahua, Mexico, but are dogged by Apache Indians seeking to make off with horses and supplies.

February 11, 1847

Mexican-American War (continued). With the conflict lasting longer than many thought it would, the U.S. Congress passes the Ten Regiment Bill to raise troops required for the war. These units will be part of the regular establishment but are to be disbanded once the war is over.

February 17, 1847

Mexican-American War (continued): Mexican forces arrive at Encarnación. General Francisco Pachero's division of Mexican Army commander General Antonio López de Santa Anna's forces arrives at Encarnación. It is followed shortly thereafter by the remainder of the army. Only 14,000 troops with 17 guns of the 20,000 men who had set out from San Luis Potosí complete the grueling three-week 300-mile march, however. Many desert, while others simply fall by the wayside from a variety of causes. Santa Anna now prepares, however, to attack U.S. major general Zachary Taylor's encampment, located nearby at Agua Nueva (Coahuila).

February 20–22, 1847

Mexican-American War (continued): Taylor's withdrawal. On February 20, 1847, a 400-man U.S. Army cavalry reconnaissance unit commanded by Lieutenant Colonel Charles A. May detects Mexican general José Vicente Miñón's 1,600-man cavalry brigade, the advance of General Antonio López de Santa Anna's army approaching Hediona Ranch. Riding throughout the night, the Americans are able to get word to Major General Zachary Taylor, commander of U.S. forces in northern Mexico, at Aqua Nueva. More detailed information on the composition of Santa Anna's army comes in at midday with the arrival at Aqua Nueva of Major Benjamin McCulloch of the Texas Rangers, who had been able to penetrate the Mexican camp at Encarnación in disguise.

Taylor considers making a stand where he is but is persuaded by Brigadier General John E. Wool to fall back to La Angostura, a narrow pass on the Buena Vista Hacienda six miles south of Saltillo. Taking up position here will prevent Santa Anna from turning the American flank with his far more numerous forces. Leaving behind the 1st Arkansas Cavalry Regiment under Colonel Archibald Yell to break camp at Aqua Nueva, Taylor retires to Buena Vista Hacienda with the rest of his army. Mexican forces arrive at Aqua Nueva shortly after midnight on February 22 and chase Yell's men and some other smaller American units north.

February 21, 1847

Mexican-American War (continued): Scott arrives at Lobos. Having departed Brazos de Santiago on February 15, Major General Winfield Scott, commander of the U.S. expeditionary force against Veracruz, arrives at the coastal island of Lobos, midway between Tampico and Veracruz, there to learn that only five of his volunteer regiments are in place. When the bulk of his regular troops arrive from Brazos de Santiago and Tampico at Lobos a week later, Scott still has fewer than 9,000 of his anticipated 14,000 men. Worse, he has less than half the number of the surfboats required for the landing operation, and he is short of ordnance and other military equipment.

 **February 22–23, 1847**

Mexican-American War (continued): Battle of Buena Vista. Major General Winfield Scott's preparations to invade Veracruz have left Major General Zachary Taylor with only some 4,800 men—the vast majority of them volunteers—to defend northern Mexico. Forewarned of the approach of some 16,000 Mexican troops under General Antonio López de Santa Anna, Taylor takes the advice of Brigadier General John E. Wood to occupy an excellent defensive position on high ground at La Angostura, a narrow pass on the Buena Vista Hacienda six miles south of Saltillo. Mountains help prevent Santa Anna from turning the American flank with his far more numerous forces, and the terrain also helps offset Santa Anna's 6,000 cavalry. Overall, the Mexicans outnumber the Americans 3 to 1. Of Taylor's 4,800 men, only about

Battle of Buena Vista		
Date	February 22–23, 1847	
Location	Puerto de la Angostura, Coahuila, Mexico	
Opponents (*winner)	*United States	Mexico
Commander	Major General Zachary Taylor	General Antonio López de Santa Anna
#	Some 4,800 men	16,000 men
Casualties	267 killed, 456 wounded, and 23 missing	500 dead, 1,000 wounded; 300 men and 2 guns captured

500 are seasoned veterans, divided between dragoons and artillerymen. The remainder are volunteers. Taylor has 18 guns. Santa Anna has 17 guns, but the American artillerymen are far better trained.

At 11:00 a.m. on February 22 under a flag of truce, Santa Anna sends a surrender demand, which Taylor promptly rejects. The battle commences around

Braxton Bragg (1817–1876)

U.S. Army officer and Confederate Army general. Braxton Bragg was born on March 22, 1817, in Warrenton, North Carolina. After attending local schools, he graduated 5th in his class of 50 from the U.S. Military Academy, West Point, in 1833. Commissioned a second lieutenant in the 3rd Artillery Regiment, Bragg was ordered to Florida to participate in the removal of the Seminoles. His health failed as a result of the conditions and stress, and he spent most of 1838 recovering. He also gained a reputation as a rigid commander and for being quarrelsome and critical of faults among superiors and subordinates alike. Lacking tact in delicate situations, he made his dissatisfaction known publicly.

In 1845, Bragg was assigned to Brigadier General Zachary Taylor's Army of Occupation in Texas. During the 1846–1848 Mexican-American War, Bragg distinguished himself by his ability to mold raw recruits into disciplined fighting men as well as for his administrative skill, and he was breveted for bravery in battle. He was also hated by his men, some of whom reportedly tried to kill him. Bragg especially distinguished himself as an artillery battery commander in the Battle of Buena Vista (February 23, 1847). Among officers on the field that day was Colonel Jefferson Davis. Following the war, Bragg became dissatisfied with the lack of progress in his military career, resigned his commission as a lieutenant colonel in 1855, and purchased a sugar plantation in Louisiana.

(continued)

(Continued)

When Louisiana seceded from the Union in 1861, Bragg became the head of its army. He was appointed a brigadier general in the Confederate Army in March 1861 and was sent to confront Fort Pickens. Bragg quickly turned his inexperienced volunteers into disciplined soldiers. Following the fall of Forts Donelson and Henry in Tennessee in February 1862, Bragg, acting on Davis's orders, led his men from Florida to join the main Confederate Army in the Western theater.

As a major general, Bragg distinguished himself in the Battle of Shiloh on April 6–7, 1862, where he commanded a corps under General Albert Sidney Johnston. Bragg retained the corps command during the Battle of Corinth (October 3–4). In June 1862, President Davis appointed him a full general and named him to command the Army of Tennessee.

Bragg performed well in Tennessee in the late summer of 1862 and mounted an invasion of Kentucky in connection with forces under Major General Edmund Kirby Smith, but Bragg was forced to withdraw following the Battle of Perryville (October 8). On December 31, 1862, and January 2, 1863, Bragg attacked Union major general William S. Rosecrans's Army of the Cumberland in the Battle of Stones River and was defeated. Rosecrans then maneuvered Bragg out of Chattanooga, but Bragg counterattacked, caught Rosecrans off guard, and defeated him in the Battle of Chickamauga (September 19–20). Bragg followed up the victory by virtually besieging Rosecrans in Chattanooga. Meanwhile, discontent among some of Bragg's subordinates grew intense, and several of his generals urged President Davis to relieve him, without success. Davis traveled to Chattanooga to assess the situation in person but determined that the complaints were the work of malcontents and decided to retain Bragg.

Bragg suffered a major defeat at the hands of U.S. major general Ulysses S. Grant in the Battle of Chattanooga (November 23–25, 1862). Bragg resigned his command under pressure on November 29. Davis then brought Bragg to Richmond as his military adviser. In this position, Bragg improved conscription and the supply system and reduced corruption. Sent to Fort Fisher near Wilmington, North Carolina, in October 1864 to defend the Confederacy's last Atlantic seaport, Bragg was unsuccessful. Fort Fisher fell in January 1865, although Bragg managed to extricate most of his force and win a small battle at Kinston (March 8–10, 1865). Bragg ended his military career as a subordinate to General Joseph E. Johnston in the Army of Tennessee, who unsuccessfully tried to block William T. Sherman's march through North Carolina. Bragg's last action was the Battle of Bentonville (March 19–21, 1865).

Following the war, Bragg, having lost his plantation, worked as superintendent of the waterworks in New Orleans and then later worked in an insurance firm. In 1874 he accepted a position as the chief engineer for the Gulf, Colorado, and Santa Fe Railroad. Bragg died in Galveston, Texas, on September 27, 1876.

Tim Watts and Spencer C. Tucker

Further Reading

Connelly, Thomas Lawrence. *Autumn of Glory: The Army of Tennessee, 1862–1865*. Baton Rouge: Louisiana State University Press, 1971.

McWhiney, Grady. *Braxton Bragg and Confederate Defeat*. New York: Columbia University Press, 1969.

Woodworth, Steven E. *Jefferson Davis and His Generals: The Failure of Confederate Command in the West*. Lawrence: University Press of Kansas, 1990.

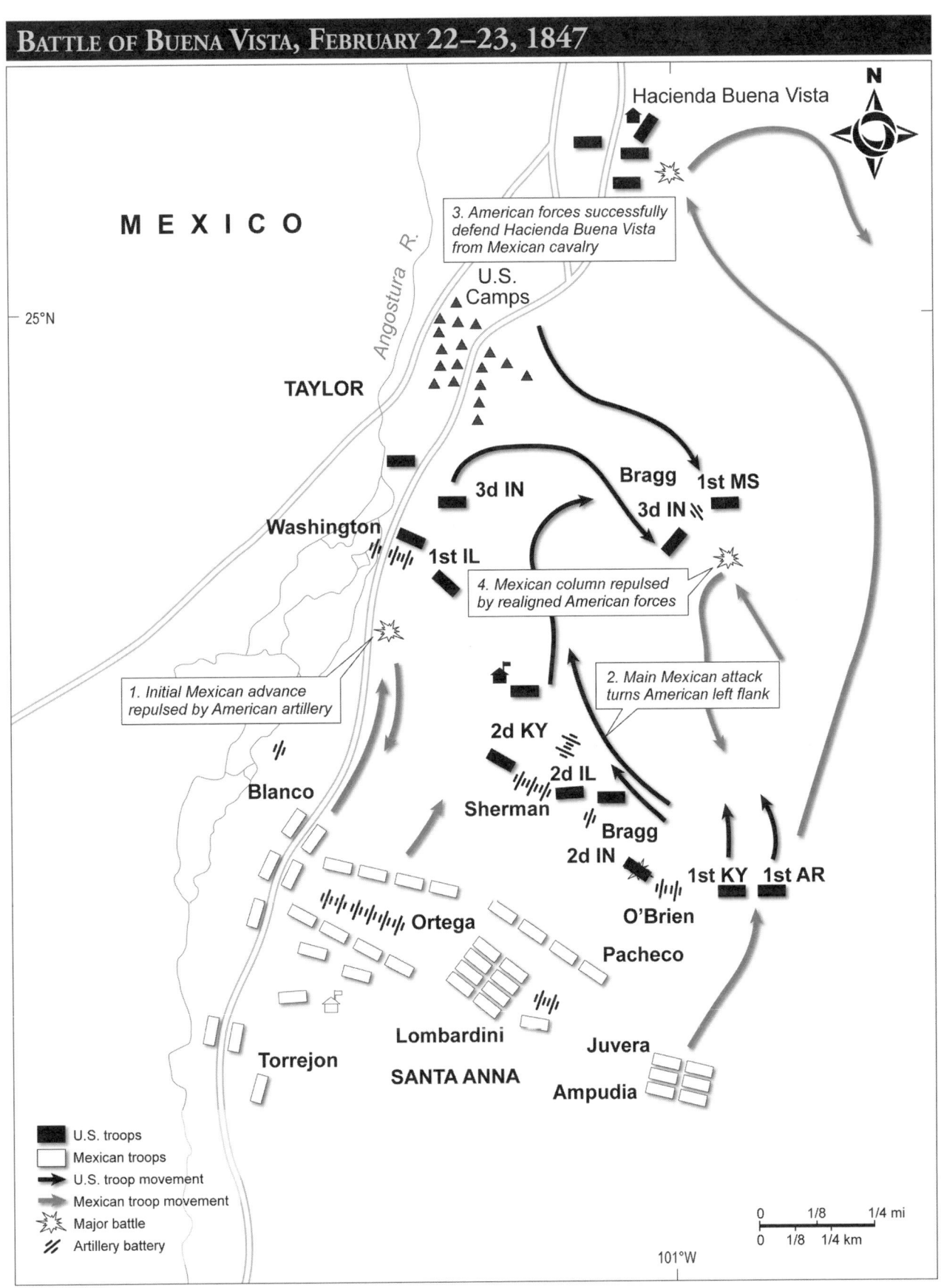

BATTLE OF BUENA VISTA, FEBRUARY 22–23, 1847

MEXICO

Hacienda Buena Vista

3. American forces successfully defend Hacienda Buena Vista from Mexican cavalry

Angostura R.

U.S. Camps

25°N

TAYLOR

Bragg
1st MS
3d IN

3d IN

Washington

1st IL

4. Mexican column repulsed by realigned American forces

1. Initial Mexican advance repulsed by American artillery

2. Main Mexican attack turns American left flank

Blanco

2d KY

2d IL

Sherman

Bragg

2d IN

1st KY   1st AR

O'Brien

Ortega

Pacheco

Lombardini

Juvera

Torrejon

SANTA ANNA

Ampudia

■ U.S. troops
□ Mexican troops
➤ U.S. troop movement
➤ Mexican troop movement
✴ Major battle
⫽ Artillery battery

0   1/8   1/4 mi
0   1/8   1/4 km

101°W

noon when Santa Anna sends infantry and cavalry to occupy high ground east of the plateau. Taylor promptly shifts units in that direction to prevent the Mexican flanking effort. During the first day of fighting, Santa Anna's cavalry drive in Taylor's outlying forces, with the Americans withdrawing at nightfall. Although the Mexicans have fought well, they are exhausted from their long march.

The main fighting occurs the next day, February 23. The Americans occupy excellent defensive positions, and Santa Anna's attacks are both piecemeal and poorly coordinated, nullifying his significant numerical advantage. As in the past the American horse-drawn guns rapidly move about to plug gaps in the line and halt Mexican breakthroughs. Colonel Jefferson Davis's 1st Mississippi Volunteer Regiment plays a pivotal role, defeating a Mexican cavalry charge, as does an artillery battery commanded by Captain Braxton Bragg. The American rear guard at Saltillo, moreover, defeats an effort by Mexican cavalry to envelop the American forces. The Mexicans are driven off.

American casualties in the battle total 267 killed, 456 wounded, and 23 missing. The Mexicans lose perhaps 500 dead and 1,000 wounded, along with 300 men and two guns captured. Santa Anna's decision not to continue the battle and withdraw his forces has prompted many historians to deem the engagement a Mexican defeat.

The Battle of Buena Vista marks the end of major fighting in northern Mexico. The fighting now shifts to the central part of the country as Santa Anna begins another forced march, this time to Veracruz.

February 27, 1847

Mexican-American War (continued): Revolt in Mexico City. In the capital of Mexico City, troops loyal to conservative Mexican general Matías de la Peña y Barragán revolt against liberal Mexican vice president Valentín Gómez Farías, who has introduced legislation to tax properties belonging to the Roman Catholic Church. Both sides appeal to Mexican president Antonio López de Santa Anna to resolve the situation. Such political infighting greatly hinders the Mexicans' military effort and is a major factor in their defeat.

February 28, 1847

Mexican-American War (continued): Doniphan's March (continued): Battle of Sacramento. Colonel Alexander W. Doniphan's 1st Regiment of Missouri Mounted Volunteers of 924 men, reinforced by two batteries of artillery, continues its march south, deep into Chihuahua Province. On February 28 at Sacramento, 15 miles north of Chihuahua, Doniphan, outnumbered more than 4 to 1, executes a daring flanking maneuver and defeats 4,200 Mexican infantry and cavalry under Major General José Antonio de Heredia. The Mexicans suffer 169 killed, 300 wounded, and 79 taken prisoner. The Americans also capture 10 Mexican guns and the baggage train. U.S. losses are 4 killed and 8 wounded. Doniphan continues south and captures the provincial capital of Chihuahua City on March 2.

March 9, 1847

Mexican-American War (continued): U.S. forces land at Veracruz. U.S. major general Winfield Scott arrives off the Gulf coast port of Veracruz. Scott's 40 transports are escorted by American warships of the Home Squadron under Commodore David Conner. Using 65 surfboats shipped in the holds of transports, within 24 hours and against only light opposition, the navy puts ashore Scott's entire force of more than 10,000 men, artillery, horses, vehicles, and supplies on Collado Beach three miles southeast of Veracruz in the largest amphibious landing in U.S. military history until World War II.

March 10–29, 1847

Mexican-American War (continued): Siege of Veracruz. Before sunrise on March 10, 1847, U.S. Navy commodore David Conner directs Commander Josiah Tattnall and the schooner *Spitfire* (11 guns) to mount a diversionary attack against the powerful island fortress San Juan de Ulúa, mounting 135 guns and manned by 1,030 men. At the same time, American troops begin to invest Veracruz itself. The city of some 15,000 people is defended by 3,360 soldiers, two-thirds of whom are regulars. They man 86 guns.

By March 13, U.S. forces have entirely isolated Veracruz. American engineers oversee the placement

SIEGE OF VERACRUZ, MARCH 10–27, 1847

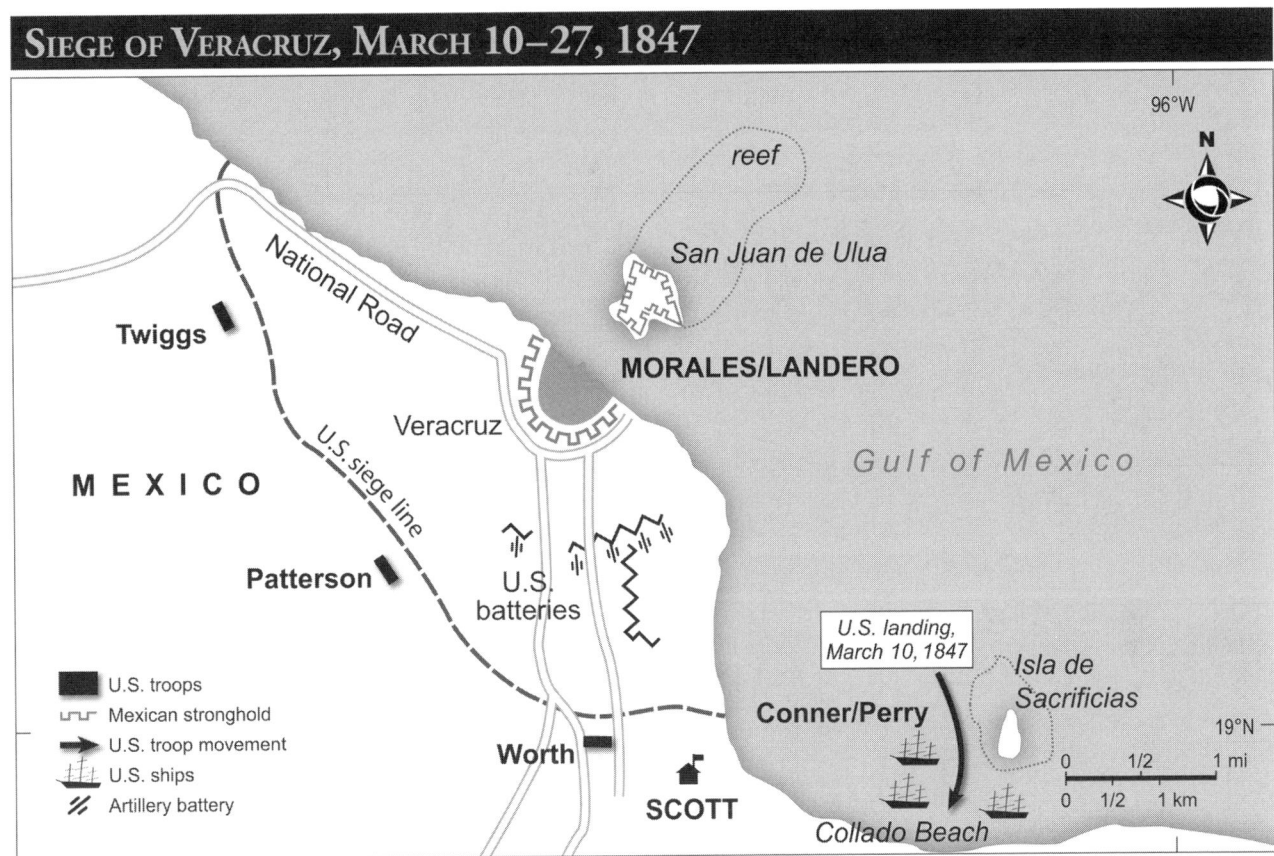

of siege works while U.S. sailors land and man 3 32-pounders and 3 8-inch shell guns from ships of the Home Squadron. By March 21 the batteries are ready to fire. U.S. commander Major General Winfield Scott calls on Mexican commander Major General Juan Morales to surrender. When he refuses, Scott orders the U.S. bombardment to commence on March 22. American warships offshore provide additional gunfire support. They are now commanded by Commodore Matthew C. Perry, just returned from the United States in the steamer *Mississippi* (10 guns). Perry has orders to replace Commodore David Conner as commander of the Home Squadron, which he does on March 11.

The besiegers steadily increase their rate of fire, and after a five-day bombardment the new Mexican commander at Veracruz, General José Juan Landero, who has replaced the ill Morales, asks for terms. Both Veracruz and the San Juan de Ulúa fortress surrender on March 29. The defenders are paroled, and the officers are allowed to retain their sidearms, mounts, and personal effects.

Scott puts American losses at 64 killed or wounded, although some sources claim 82. Mexican losses are more difficult to determine. A neutral British observer claims 80 soldiers and 100 civilians killed. (A recent Mexican study claims that 350 soldiers and 400 civilians died and 250 people were injured.) Scott now has a secure supply line by sea back to the United States, essential for his planned overland march to Mexico City.

March 21, 1847

Mexican-American War (continued). After having returned to San Luis Potosí with the 10,500 men who had fought at Buena Vista, Mexican president and army commander General Antonio López de Santa Anna marches with his two best divisions to the Guadalupe suburb north of Mexico City. There he ends the political dispute between General

Matías de la Peña y Barragán and Vice President Valentín Gómez Farías by sacking the latter and replacing him with general and congressman Pedro María Anaya.

March 30, 1847

Mexican-American War (continued): Capture of San José del Cabo. On March 29, 1847, the U.S. Navy sloop *Portsmouth* (22 guns) under Commander John B. Montgomery arrives off the port of San José del Cabo in Baja California. Montgomery demands its surrender. When the Mexican authorities refuse, on March 30 Montgomery sends ashore 140 sailors and marines under Lieutenant Benjamin F. B. Hunter. There is no resistance.

April 1, 1847

Mexican-American War (continued): U.S. capture of Alvarado. Major General Winfield Scott, commander of U.S. forces at Veracruz, plans to move inland as soon as possible to escape the low-lying coastal region before the arrive of the summer yellow fever season. Scott needs horses and mules to help transport the tons of supplies required to sustain his army in the field. Even if sufficient livestock could have been brought from the United States, the voyage often leaves many unfit for service. The solution is to purchase or seize as many horses and mules as possible locally.

Scott assigns the task of requisitioning livestock to Major General John A. Quitman. Supported by U.S. naval forces, he is to capture the port city of Alvarado, purchase horses and mules, and return to Veracruz. Quitman selects for the assignment the brigade of Georgia, Alabama, and South Carolina volunteer regiments. Supporting them are two companies of dragoons and a section of artillery. Their arrival at Alvarado is to coincide with a landing by U.S. sailors under Commodore Matthew C. Perry.

Quitman's force sets out on March 30, 1847, and reaches Alvarado on April 1. In the meantime, however, U.S. Navy lieutenant Charles G. Hunter in the screw steamer *Scourge* (3 guns) disobeys Perry's orders and upsets the operation's timing. Arriving off Alvarado late on March 30, Hunter opens up with his ship's 32-pounder long gun on the La Vigía Battery guarding the mouth of the river. The *Scourge* again fires on the same battery the next morning, whereupon a white flag appears over the fort. The Mexican captain of the port then informs Hunter that the inhabitants have evacuated the town during the night, that all naval vessels have been burned, and that the Americans are free to enter Alvarado. Hunter then lands a small party to take possession of the port.

Learning that Mexican vessels laden with munitions have withdrawn upriver, Hunter proceeds after them in the *Scourge*. He captures the *Relamago* and three other Mexican schooners, one of which had grounded and has to be burned. Hunter takes the surrender of the village of Tlacotalpán.

Hunter has no authority for these actions, and in fact they lead the Mexicans to drive off horses that the expedition was to secure. Hunter is subsequently found guilty of insubordination and disobeying orders of a superior officer and is sentenced to a reprimand and immediate dismissal from the squadron but not from the navy.

At Alvarado, the Americans secure more than 20 pieces of artillery and a quantity of small arms. According to American accounts, after the initial panic caused by the appearance of the sailors and soldiers subsides, the residents are both friendly and eager to sell livestock. Some 500 horses are acquired from Alvarado and its environs, and Quitman's brigade is back in Veracruz by April 6. U.S. Navy forces garrison Alvarado.

April 3, 1847

Mexican-American War (continued). Mexican president and army commander General Antonio López de Santa Anna departs Mexico City and heads east to take command of three infantry divisions, one cavalry brigade, and some 2,000 militiamen in an effort to block American forces under Major General Winfield Scott from proceeding inland toward the Mexican capital.

April 3, 1847

Mexican-American War (continued). A landing party from the U.S. Navy sloop *Portsmouth* (22 guns) under Commander John B. Montgomery takes possession of the port of San Lucas, Baja California.

April 8, 1847

Mexican-American War (continued): Commencement of Scott's Mexico City Campaign. Mexican general Antonio López de Santa Anna endeavors to pin U.S. forces under Major General Winfield Scott in the coastal yellow fever belt, but as soon as possible after securing Veracruz, Scott moves inland. His subsequent march to Mexico City ranks among the most brilliant in U.S. military history.

With fewer than 10,000 men (less than half the number requested), hampered by numerous problems not of his own making, and often forced to live off the land, Scott marches his men 260 miles without a reverse in six months. His occupation policies include payment for horses and supplies taken from the Mexicans. Although not always followed, his wise occupation policies help secure his line of communication back to Veracruz.

On April 8, Scott's vanguard departs Veracruz on the national highway toward Mexico City. Major General David E. Twiggs commands 2,000 infantrymen, some dragoons, two light field artillery batteries, and a dozen heavier guns. Other forces follow, with Scott himself and the balance of his expeditionary force proceeding on April 11.

April 13, 1847

Mexican-American War (continued). The U.S. Navy sloop *Portsmouth* (22 guns) under Commander John B. Montgomery arrives off the port of La Paz, capital of the state of Baja California. Montgomery sends in a landing party and demands the surrender of La Paz. Collaborationist Mexican governor Colonel Francisco Palacios Miranda complies, and the next day the American flag is raised over La Paz. The articles of capitulation declare the annexation of Baja California to the United States and guarantee the continuation in office of Mexican officials and rights of Baja Californios, a number of whom now openly throw in their lot with the United States.

April 18, 1847

Mexican-American War (continued): Battle of Tuxpan. In early April 1847, Tuxpan is the only important Gulf coast port not in U.S. hands. Lying midway between Tampico and Veracruz, some eight miles up the river of the same name, it is well fortified and garrisoned and is protected by shoal water at the river's mouth.

In preparation for the expedition, Commodore Matthew C. Perry, commander of the U.S. Navy Home Squadron, organizes and drills a naval brigade of more than 2,000 men drawn from the squadron. It is the first such unit in U.S. Navy history. Perry considers the capture of Tuxpan a matter of honor, because the city is defended in part by guns salvaged from the U.S. brig *Truxtun*, which had run aground on Tuxpan bar in a gale on August 14, 1846, and had been captured.

Tuxpan is well situated for defense. Three water batteries protect its approaches, including one known as La Peña atop a 40-foot cliff that juts out into the river and commands a two-mile stretch of the river. It mounts three guns, including two 32-pounder carronades taken from the *Truxtun*. General Don Martín Perfecto de Cos, brother-in-law of Mexican president General Antonio López de Santa Anna, has charge of the 300–400 man garrison.

Perry commits the steamers *Spitfire* (11 guns), *Vixen* (3 guns), and *Scourge* (3 guns); the 1-gun schooners *Bonita*, *Petrel*, and *Reefer;* and the 1-gun bomb brigs *Etna*, *Hecla*, and *Vesuvius*. Other U.S. warships are also present but are off the river's mouth. Perry's landing force, commanded by Captain Samuel L. Breese, numbers 1,489 officers and men and 4 guns from the steamer *Mississippi* (10 guns) and the *Vesuvius* and *Hecla*.

Rendezvousing at Lobos Island on April 13, the expedition arrives off the Tuxpan River on April 17. As there is only eight feet of water at the bar, that night Perry orders that the larger *Spitfire* and *Vixen* be lightened by removing their masts. The frigate *Raritan* (54 guns) lifts these out. With the flagship *Mississippi*

On April 18, 1847, a U.S. naval brigade commanded by Commodore Matthew C. Perry captured the important Mexican Gulf Coast port of Tuxpan, located midway between Tampico and Veracruz and some eight miles up the Tuxpan River. (Naval Historical Center)

anchored well offshore, Perry shifts his flag to the *Spitfire*, commanded by Captain Josiah Tattnall.

The assault begins early on the morning of April 18 when the three steamers cross the bar and steam upriver toward Tuxpan. Each tows a sail gunboat and 10 barges with the landing parties. The *Spitfire* leads.

About 2:30 p.m., the expeditionary force comes under fire from the La Peña battery. A landing party under Commander Franklin Buchanan quickly goes ashore and charges up the cliff, easily taking La Peña. The ships then continue upriver, capturing the other Mexican forts in succession. By 4:00 p.m. the Americans have secured all the Mexican batteries and occupied Tuxpan, at a cost to themselves of 2 dead and 12 wounded.

The next day, the landing parties began disarming Tuxpan. The sailors destroy the forts and spike the guns that they do not carry off. They retrieve the guns taken from the *Truxtun* and take anything of military value. On April 19, Captain French Forrest leads an expedition upriver. Gone only one day, it returns with only a few small prizes.

On April 22 Perry's shore parties withdraw, and the ships return downriver. Perry assigns the sailing sloop *Albany* (22 guns) and the schooner *Reefer* to guard the river mouth. Unfortunately for the navy, the concurrent U.S. land victory at Cerro Gordo (see April 18, 1847) steals the headlines from this successful operation.

April 18, 1847

Mexican-American War (continued): Scott's Mexico City Campaign (continued): Battle of Cerro Gordo. On April 14, 1847, American forces

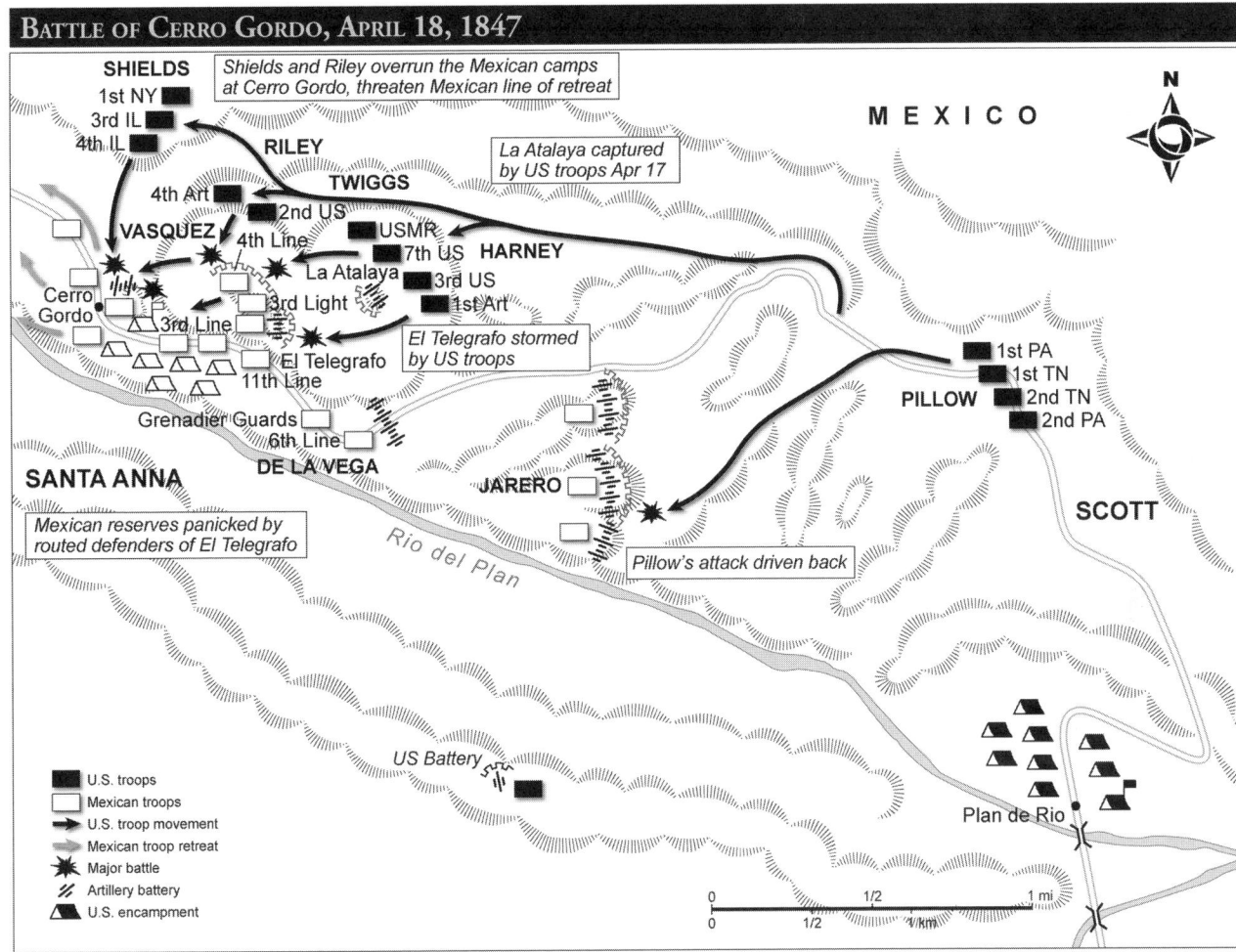

BATTLE OF CERRO GORDO, APRIL 18, 1847

Shields and Riley overrun the Mexican camps at Cerro Gordo, threaten Mexican line of retreat

La Atalaya captured by US troops Apr 17

El Telegrafo stormed by US troops

Mexican reserves panicked by routed defenders of El Telegrafo

Pillow's attack driven back

MEXICO

SHIELDS
1st NY
3rd IL
4th IL
RILEY
TWIGGS
4th Art
2nd US
VASQUEZ 4th Line
USMR
7th US   HARNEY
La Atalaya
3rd US
Cerro   3rd Light   1st Art
Gordo
3rd Line
El Telegrafo
11th Line
Grenadier Guards
6th Line
SANTA ANNA   DE LA VEGA
JARERO

1st PA
1st TN
PILLOW   2nd TN
2nd PA

SCOTT

Rio del Plan

US Battery

Plan de Rio

- U.S. troops
- Mexican troops
- U.S. troop movement
- Mexican troop retreat
- Major battle
- Artillery battery
- U.S. encampment

0   1/2   1 mi
0   1/2   1 km

proceeding west on the National Road reach the fortified pass of Cerro Gordo, held by General Antonio López de Santa Anna and 12,000 men with 43 guns. With the Mexicans occupying strong positions, Scott waits until other units can be brought forward, boosting his strength to some 8,500 men. Meanwhile, U.S. engineers led by Captain Robert E. Lee discover a flanking trail over which infantry and light artillery can be moved.

On the morning of April 17, Major General David E. Twiggs moves his main body along this route, circling north of Santa Anna's position. The American column encounters Mexican resistance at La Atalaya Hill. Twiggs pushes his men forward, enveloping most of the Mexican defenders. The outnumbered Americans withdraw at nightfall back to La Atalaya.

The next morning, April 18, Twiggs resumes his flanking attack while Scott's main force mounts a frontal assault on Santa Anna's position. Fearful of being cut off, the Mexicans flee. In the battle they lose some 1,000 killed or wounded and 3,000 taken prisoner. The Americans also capture 43 guns, 4,000 firearms, and considerable baggage. American losses are 63 killed and 353 wounded. The victory enables Scott to move out of the yellow fever zone and pursue the retreating Mexicans toward Jalapa.

April 20, 1847

Mexican-American War (continued): Scott's Mexico City Campaign (continued). American forces enter Jalapa.

 ## Robert Edward Lee (1807–1870)

U.S. Army and Confederate Army officer. Robert Edward Lee was born on January 19, 1807, in Stratford, Virginia, the third son of American Revolution hero Henry Lee. The younger Lee graduated from the U.S. Military Academy, West Point, in 1829 and was commissioned in the Corps of Engineers. He rose to captain in 1838 and distinguished himself in a variety of engineering assignments along the Mississippi River. Lee saw action during the Mexican-American War (1846–1848), fighting with distinction at Veracruz and Cerro Gordo. After additional fighting at Churubusco and Chapultepec, where he was wounded, he gained a brevet promotion to colonel.

In 1852 Lee became superintendent at West Point, revitalizing its curriculum. In 1855 he left the academy to become lieutenant colonel of the 2nd U.S. Cavalry. In 1859 he was called on to suppress abolitionist John Brown's uprising at Harpers Ferry, which Lee accomplished with a company of marines. He then advanced to colonel of the 1st U.S. Cavalry and was commanding the Department of Texas by 1860.

Lee supported slavery but not secession, and he chose to support his native state of Virginia. When President Abraham Lincoln offered him command of all federal armies at the behest of general-in-chief Lieutenant General Winfield Scott, Lee declined and tendered his resignation in April 1861. By May he was a major general in the Confederate Army, and in August he became a full general. Lee, however, failed in his initial assignment to subdue the western counties of Virginia, due mostly to uncooperative subordinates. Consequently, he became known in some circles as "Granny Lee." President Jefferson Davis, however, assigned him to improve the defenses of the Atlantic coast in the South. Lee was soon back in Richmond as Davis's military adviser, without command responsibilities. In this capacity, Lee suggested to Davis that Union pressure on Richmond might be relieved by reinforcing Major General Thomas J. Jackson in the Shenandoah Valley, which resulted in a brilliant success in the spring of 1862.

Lee's fortunes and those of the Confederacy changed dramatically when he assumed command of the Army of Northern Virginia after General Joseph E. Johnston was severely wounded in the Battle of Seven Pines in May 1862. Lee immediately launched what became his tactical trademark—a relentless series of hard-hitting and punishing attacks. This offensive, known as the Seven Days' Campaign, pushed Union forces away from Richmond. Union forces were never seriously defeated and Confederate losses were heavy, but Lee had correctly gauged Union major general George B. McClellan as overly cautious. In August 1862 following the Peninsula Campaign, Lee caught another Union army under Major General John Pope in the Second Battle of Bull Run (Manassas) and severely defeated it.

Having gained the strategic initiative, Lee then carried the war north into Maryland, and on September 17, 1862, he fought McClellan again in the Battle of Antietam. Lee fought the battle with great skill but was saved largely by McClellan's blunders and the last-minute appearance of Major General Ambrose P. Hill's division. The battle was a strategic defeat for the South. Nevertheless, when McClellan failed to pursue, Lincoln replaced him with Major General Ambrose Burnside.

Burnside attacked Lee in another poorly orchestrated Union effort against the Confederates occupying strong defensive positions at Fredericksburg on December 17, 1862. The battle was Lee's most lopsided victory. The year ended with the Army of Northern Virginia enjoying high morale and an aura of invincibility.

In the spring of 1863, a new commander of the Army of the Potomac, Major General Joseph Hooker, again attacked Lee, at Chancellorsville during May 1–4. Hooker planned a double envelopment of Lee but then halted at the point of success. Lee did not hesitate and, in his most daring gamble, carried out a double envelopment of a double envelopment with a force half the size of his opponent. The ensuing Battle of Chancellorsville was Lee's most brilliant victory, but it was a costly one for the South, with Confederate losses higher than those of the Union in percentage of forces engaged. Jackson was also mortally wounded, and for the remainder of the war Lee was forced to depend on less reliable subordinates.

In June 1863 Lee again led his army north, into Pennsylvania. Major General George Gordon Meade took command of the Army of the Potomac on the eve of battle, with the contending armies colliding at Gettysburg during July 1–3, 1863. Lee committed a major mistake on the final day of the battle, committing 10 brigades in an assault across open ground against the center of the Union line. Suffering heavy losses, Lee retreated back to Virginia beginning on the night of July 4.

In the spring of 1864 Lee was confronted by a new adversary, Lieutenant General Ulysses S. Grant, the Union general-in-chief, who accompanied the Army of the Potomac in the field. When Grant advanced on Richmond in his Overland Campaign, Lee fought a series of battles with him, including the Wilderness, Spotsylvania, and Cold Harbor. Although Grant sustained high casualties, he continued to pursue and hit Lee hard. Grant tried to get in behind Lee at Petersburg, but this effort failed and ended in a long siege.

For nearly a year, Lee maintained his dwindling army in the trenches before Richmond and Petersburg. In February 1865 Lee was appointed general-in-chief of all Confederate forces, but by then the Southern cause was lost. The impasse ended on March 31, 1865, when Major General Philip H. Sheridan broke through Confederate lines at Five Forks. His position untenable, Lee abandoned Richmond and headed west, hoping to link up with General Joseph Johnston in North Carolina. Grant, however, pursued vigorously, and the Army of Northern Virginia was cut off by Union cavalry at Appomattox Court House. Lee surrendered there with great dignity on April 9, 1865.

Following the war, Lee, rejecting more prestigious offers, served as president of Washington College (now Washington and Lee University) in Lexington, Virginia. He transformed the curriculum and created the nation's first departments of journalism and commerce. Lee also urged Southerners to put the war behind them and become loyal citizens of the United States. Lionized by both the North and the South, Lee came to be regarded as the "Marble Man," without blemish. Others came to be blamed for his failures, for example, Lieutenant General James Longstreet for Gettysburg. Lee died in Lexington on October 12, 1870.

SPENCER C. TUCKER

Further Reading

Blount, Roy, Jr. *Robert E. Lee.* New York: Viking, 2003.
Davis, Burke. *Gray Fox: Robert E. Lee and the Civil War.* New York: Gramercy Publishing, 1992.
Gallagher, Gary W., ed. *Lee the Soldier.* Lincoln: University of Nebraska Press, 1996.

April 28, 1847

Mexican-American War (continued): Doniphan's March (continued). Colonel Alexander W. Doniphan's 1st Regiment of Missouri Mounted Volunteers departs Chihuahua and proceeds southeast to join U.S. forces under Brigadier General John E. Wool at Saltillo.

May 6, 1847

Mexican-American War (continued): Scott's Mexico City Campaign (continued): Expiration of volunteer enlistments. As a regiment in U.S. major general Winfield Scott's expeditionary force occupies the abandoned Mexican stronghold of El Penote, seven of Scott's volunteer regiments totaling some 3,000 men depart Jalapa and march east to return to Veracruz, their terms of enlistment having expired. Scott now has only 7,000 men—3,000 of them at Jalapa—to continue his campaign against Mexico City.

May 15, 1847

Mexican-American War (continued): Scott's Mexico City Campaign (continued): Occupation of Puebla. On this date Major General Winfield Scott's army occupies the city of Puebla, some 75 miles from Mexico City. There it remains for three months. This halt is necessary because Scott now has only 5,820 men. Much of his manpower has been lost through the expiration of enlistments and the return home of volunteer units. Scott joins the army at Puebla on May 28.

May 21, 1847

Mexican-American War (continued): Doniphan's March (continued): Arrival at Saltillo. Colonel Alexander W. Doniphan's 1st Regiment of Missouri Mounted Volunteers, having departed Chihuahua City, marches another 750 miles in difficult conditions to Saltillo, arriving there on May 21. With their enlistments now up, the men continue on to Matamoros and board ships to travel to New Orleans. They return to St. Louis in early June 1847, having traveled some 5,500 miles by land and water in slightly more than one year.

May 31, 1847

Mexican-American War (continued). On this date, U.S. Army brigadier general Stephen W. Kearny arrests Brevet Lieutenant Colonel John C. Frémont on charges of insubordination after the latter defies Kearny's direct order to relinquish his post as governor of California. Kearny then transfers his command and administration of California to Colonel Robert B. Mason. On June 16 Kearny and Frémont depart Sutter's Fort for St. Louis, Missouri.

June 14–July 22, 1847

Mexican-American War (continued): Tabasco River Expedition. In June 1847 Commodore Matthew C. Perry, commanding the Home Squadron, mounts another assault on Tabasco. The justification is the movement of supplies for the Mexican Army through the town. In the time since the first U.S. assault a year previously, the Mexicans have considerably strengthened the town's defenses. Perry's assaulting force is consequently much more powerful. The deep-draft ships that are unable to cross the bar all contribute men and boats. Perry flies his flag in the steamer *Scorpion* (4 guns).

On June 14 the ships cross the bar at the mouth of the river and occupy Frontera without resistance. That same day after coaling, they proceed upriver. The *Scorpion* leads, towing the bomb brig *Vesuvius* (1 gun), the Revenue Service cutter *Washington*, and boats from the steamer *Mississippi* (10 guns) and the sloop *John Adams* (22 guns). The steamer *Spitfire* (11 guns) tows the bomb brig *Stromboli* (1 gun), the schooner *Bonita* (1 gun), and boats of the sloop *Albany* (22 guns). Next comes the steamer *Scourge* (3 guns) towing the merchant schooner *Spitfire*, which is carrying explosives to blow up reported river obstacles. The steamer *Vixen* (3 guns) brings up the rear, towing the bomb brig *Etna* (1 gun) and boats of the frigate *Raritan* (54 guns) and the sloops *Decatur* (16 guns) and *Germantown* (22 guns). The 40 ships' boats involved carry 1,173 men. Also included in the tows are 7 surfboats, each transporting a 6-pounder fieldpiece.

The Americans cover 40 miles the first day. On June 16 Perry orders the Naval Brigade ashore below Seven Palms, just above Devil's Bend, to provide flank security and force the Mexicans to abandon the defensive positions built to protect the river obstacles. The entire brigade and its fieldpieces are landed in only 10 minutes. After his land artillery has fired on Fort Acachapan, Perry, sword in hand, personally leads a charge on the fortification. The Naval Brigade routs the defenders, estimated to number some 900 men. The Mexicans sustain 30 casualties; the Americans suffer only 5 men wounded. As the land operation proceeds, the ship crews remove the water obstacles, aided by explosives. Both the land and river forces then proceed to Tabasco, the ships arriving first. With the capture of Tabasco, every Gulf coast Mexican port of consequence is in American hands.

During the course of a week at Tabasco, the Americans destroy contraband, fortifications, and a magazine. They also transfer the guns from the fort to the flotilla. Perry decides to garrison Tabasco with marines, supported by the *Spitfire, Scourge,* and *Etna.* He himself departs on June 22 with the rest of his ships and men.

On June 24, the Mexicans mount a night assault. The Americans defeat this but lack the strength to pursue. When Commander Abraham Bigelow arrives in the *Scorpion* and assumes command at Tabasco on June 26, he requests reinforcements. Perry provides the *Vixen,* 44 marines, 50 sailors, and one gun.

Mexican guerrillas continue to harass the Americans, however. This and yellow fever cause Perry to order a withdrawal. The Americans evacuate Tabasco on July 21–22. They continue to hold Frontera, however, thus cutting off trade to and from the interior.

July 8, 1847

Mexican-American War (continued): Scott's Mexico City Campaign (continued). Major General Winfield Scott's U.S. expeditionary force at Puebla is reinforced by the arrival of some 4,500 American troops under Brigadier Generals George Cadwalader and Gideon J. Pillow.

July 19, 1847

Mexican-American War (continued). Commodore James Biddle transfers command of the Pacific Squadron to Commodore W. Bradford Shubrick.

July 21, 1847

Mexican-American War (continued). The U.S. Navy storeship *Lexington,* commanded by Lieutenant Theodorus Bailey, arrives at La Paz in Baja California and lands 112 men of the 1st New York Volunteer Regiment, commanded by Lieutenant Colonel Henry S. Burton, as a permanent garrison.

July 27, 1847

Mexican-American War (continued). Acting on the orders of Mexican president and army commander General Antonio López de Santa Anna, General Gabriel Valencia arrives with 4,000 troops from San Luis Potosí at Guadalupe, north of Mexico City.

August 6, 1847

Mexican-American War (continued). Brigadier General Franklin Pierce arrives with 2,400 reinforcements at Major General Winfield Scott's encampment at Puebla. That same day, Major F. T. Lilly departs Veracruz with additional reinforcements for Scott in the 1,000-man 9th Infantry Regiment. The men will, however, take nearly two weeks to reach Jalapa because of attacks by Mexican forces led by General Juan Soto.

August 7, 1847

Mexican-American War (continued): Scott's Mexico City Campaign (continued): Resumption of the advance on Mexico City. U.S. major general Winfield Scott, commanding the expeditionary force in the Mexican interior, has received replacements for the volunteer troops whose terms of enlistment had expired. Scott now has some 14,000 men, although 2,500 are sick and 600 others are convalescent. With his supply lines back to Veracruz now under constant Mexican Army harassment, on August 7, 1847, Scott resumes his march on Mexico City. In a daring step, he leaves behind at Puebla his sick and only a small garrison of 400 men under Colonel Thomas Childs, cutting himself off from his base to advance on Mexico City by living off the land. Major General David E. Twiggs's division leads the advance.

August 10, 1847

Mexican-American War (continued): Scott's Mexico City Campaign (continued). Informed that American forces at Puebla have resumed their advance, Mexican general Pedro María Anaya, acting in accordance with instructions of Mexican president and army commander General Antonio López de Santa Anna, departs Mexico City with 7,000 men and begins fortifying El Peñón Hill, 10 miles east of the capital.

August 11–17, 1847

Mexican-American War (continued): Scott's Mexico City Campaign (continued): Scott's arrival at Ayutla. Mexican president and army commander General Antonio López de Santa Anna has gathered some 36,000 men and 100 guns to defend the Mexican capital. Scott has some 10,000 effectives. On August 15 at Ayutla, 15 miles west of Mexico City, Scott discovers that Santa Anna has taken advantage of terrain, especially lakes and marshland, and heavily fortified El Peñón Hill. Rather than meet the strength of the Mexican defenses head-on, Scott opts to approach Mexico City from the south.

August 19–20, 1847

Mexican-American War (continued): Scott's Mexico City Campaign (continued): Battles of Contreras and Churubusco. To avoid encountering the strong Mexican defenses east of the capital, Scott decides to send the bulk of his forces around the Mexican lines in a flanking maneuver to the south. Leaving Major General David E. Twiggs's division at Ayola, 20 miles

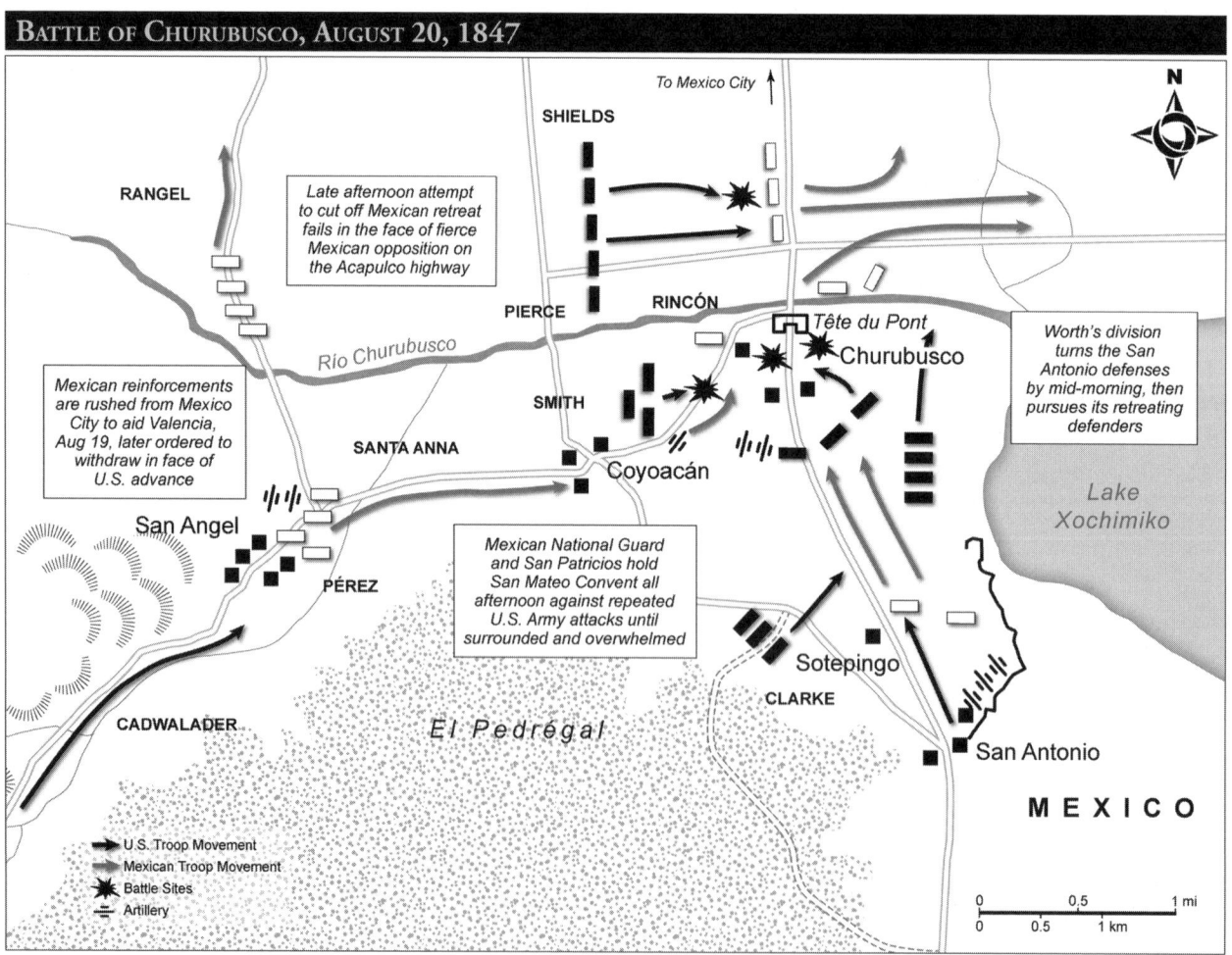

BATTLE OF CHURUBUSCO, AUGUST 20, 1847

SHIELDS

To Mexico City

N

RANGEL

Late afternoon attempt to cut off Mexican retreat fails in the face of fierce Mexican opposition on the Acapulco highway

PIERCE

RINCÓN

Tête du Pont

Churubusco

Worth's division turns the San Antonio defenses by mid-morning, then pursues its retreating defenders

Río Churubusco

Mexican reinforcements are rushed from Mexico City to aid Valencia, Aug 19, later ordered to withdraw in face of U.S. advance

SMITH

SANTA ANNA

Coyoacán

Lake Xochimiko

San Angel

Mexican National Guard and San Patricios hold San Mateo Convent all afternoon against repeated U.S. Army attacks until surrounded and overwhelmed

PÉREZ

Sotepingo

CLARKE

CADWALADER

El Pedrégal

San Antonio

MEXICO

U.S. Troop Movement
Mexican Troop Movement
Battle Sites
Artillery

0   0.5   1 mi
0   0.5   1 km

Battles of Contreras and Churubusco		
Date	August 19–20, 1847	
Location	Contreras and Churubusco, west of Mexico City, Mexico	
Opponents (*winner)	*United States	Mexico
Commander	Major General Winfield Scott	General Antonio López de Santa Anna
#	8,500 men	32,000 men
Casualties	133 killed and 865 wounded	4,197 killed or wounded, 2,637 prisoners, and 3,000 missing; 37 guns captured

east-southeast of Mexico City, Scott sends divisions under Generals William J. Worth, John A. Quitman, and Gideon J. Pillow. The Americans encounter strong Mexican troop concentrations near Contreras and Churubusco, however.

U.S. forces wage two significant battles against Mexican troops under General Antonio López de Santa Anna on August 19–20, 1847. The first occurs near the villages of Contreras and Padierna some 10 miles southwest of the capital. The second is 7 miles to the northeast around the town of Churubusco. The two should properly be considered two parts of the same battle.

In the battles the Americans have to contend with the excellent artillerists of the San Patricio Battalion, made up in large part of U.S. deserters, mostly Irish (hence the name for the battalion of St. Patrick, patron saint of Ireland). During the fighting some 80 San Patricios are taken prisoner, and 51 are subsequently court-martialed and hanged.

The Americans win both the Battle of Contreras and the Battle of Churubusco, and Mexican forces flee north to Mexico City. In the battles, Santa Anna suffers an estimated 4,197 killed or wounded, 2,637 taken prisoner, and 3,000 missing, nearly a third of his force of perhaps 32,000 men. The Americans also take 37 Mexican artillery pieces. Scott's losses are 133 killed and 865 wounded, or about 12 percent of his 8,500 men engaged.

August 22–September 6, 1847

Mexican-American War (continued): Scott's Mexico City Campaign (continued): Armistice. Having suffered major losses in the defeats at Contreras and Churubusco (see August 19–20, 1847), Mexican president and army commander General Antonio López de Santa Anna sends emissaries on August 21, 1847, to U.S. commander Major General Winfield Scott at Tucubaya regarding an armistice to consider peace proposals. Scott agrees the next day. But Santa Anna has entered into the armistice largely to gain time to reconstitute his forces and defenses.

Chief clerk of the U.S. State Department and peace commissioner Nicholas Trist is instructed by President James K. Polk to obtain the Rio Grande boundary for Texas, together with New Mexico and California. Mexican leaders reject these terms, and after two weeks of fruitless talks and upon learning that Santa Anna has violated the armistice terms by the construction of new fortifications, on September 6 Scott informs the Mexicans that the Americans will resume offensive operations the next day.

September 8, 1847

Mexican-American War (continued): Scott's Mexico City Campaign (continued): Battle of Molino del Rey. Major General Winfield Scott sends his forces against the Mexican defenders of a presumed gun foundry and fort near the Chapultepec palace and military academy some two miles southwest of Mexico City. Brigadier General Antonio León

Battle of Molino del Rey		
Date	September 8, 1847	
Location	2 miles southwest of Mexico City	
Opponents (*winner)	*United States	Mexico
Commander	Major General Winfield Scott; Major General William J. Worth	Brigadier General Antonio León
#	3,400 men	4,000 men
Casualties	116 killed, 665 wounded, and 18 missing	269 killed, some 500 wounded, and 852 captured; 4 guns also lost

September 12–13, 1847

BATTLE OF MOLINO DEL REY, SEPTEMBER 8, 1847

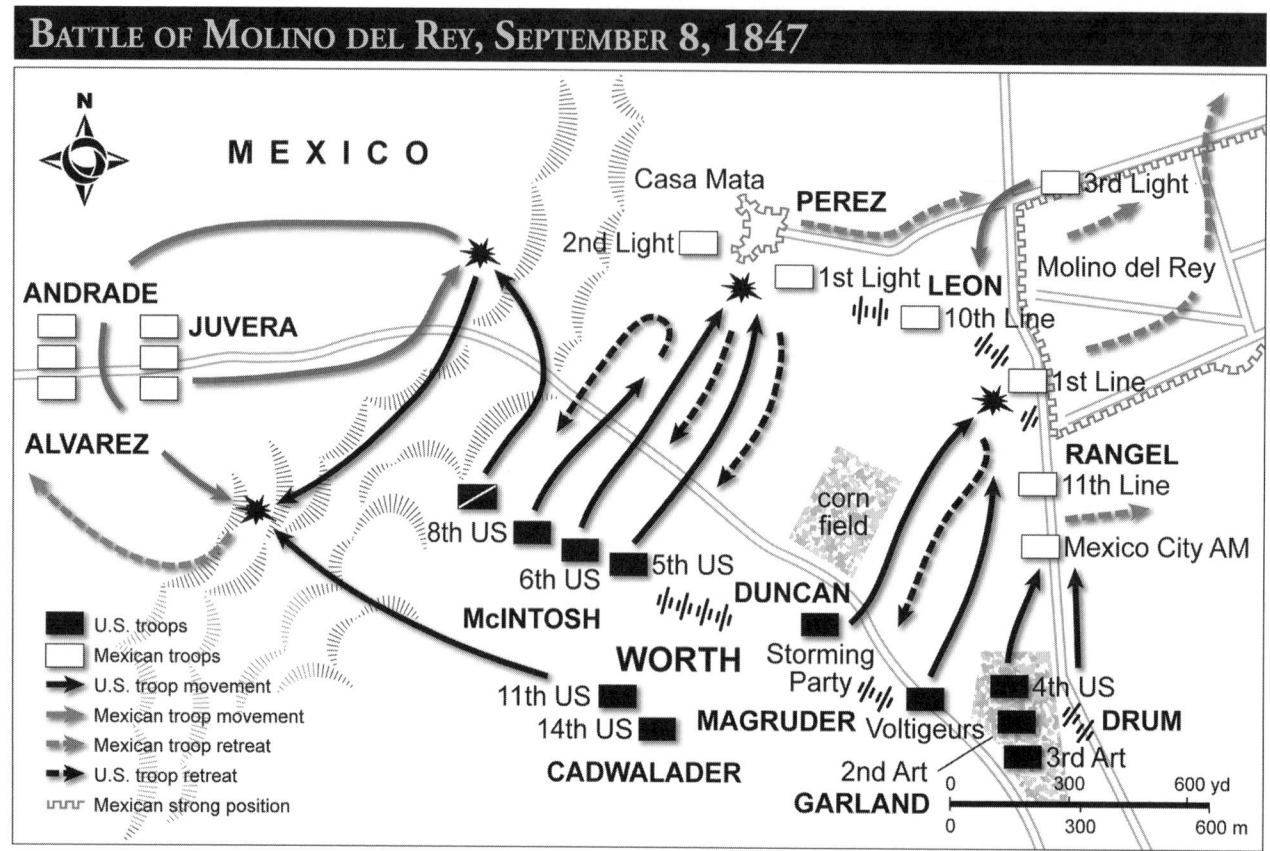

commands some 4,000 Mexican defenders, although there are 8,000–10,000 Mexican troops in the vicinity. The buildings offer excellent defensive positions, but León chooses to deploy his regiments and artillery in front of the buildings rather than sheltering them within the structures.

Major General William J. Worth's 3,400-man division is the U.S. attack force. Expecting the Mexicans to withdraw, Worth orders a frontal assault, and the Americans suffer heavy casualties from the well-entrenched Mexican defenders. Although the Americans ultimately prevail, it is with the highest casualties in percentage of force engaged (some 23 percent) of any battle of the war. U.S. losses are 116 killed, 665 wounded, and 18 missing. Mexican losses are 269 killed, some 500 wounded, and 852 captured. The Americans also secure four Mexican artillery pieces.

The battle brings recriminations on the U.S. side and especially criticism of Worth for inadequate

reconnaissance to detect the location of Mexican artillery positions and strength of the defenders and his ill-conceived headlong assault.

September 12–13, 1847

Mexican-American War (continued): Scott's Mexico City Campaign (continued): Battle of Chapultepec and capture of Mexico City. The last barrier to Mexico City is the fortified hill of Chapultepec, with its summer palace and the Mexican military academy. U.S. major general Winfield Scott now commands some 7,180 effectives. To defend the Mexican capital, president and army commander General Antonio López de Santa Anna has some 15,000 men. About 1,000 of these, including 51 military academy cadets, defend Chapultepec under the command of General Nicolás Bravo.

Scott opens an artillery bombardment on September 12 and launches an assault, complete with scaling

The storming of Chapultepec by U.S. forces on September 13, 1847. Mexico City surrendered the next day. (Library of Congress)

ladders, early the next morning. General Bravo surrenders after about two hours at about 9:30 a.m. Fighting also occurs at the fortified gates of Belén and San Cosme.

U.S. casualties are 116 killed and 669 wounded. The Mexicans lose about 3,000 killed or wounded and 800 taken prisoner. Among the dead are 6 cadets, remembered in Mexican history as the Niños Héros ("Boy Heroes"). The fall of Chapultepec opens the way for the American capture of Mexico City.

Mexico City officials persuade General Santa Anna to evacuate the city to spare it from destruction and civilian casualties. On September 14 General Scott accepts the unconditional surrender of the city, which is then occupied by U.S. troops. Scott appoints Major General John A. Quitman military governor. With the fall of the Mexican capital, peace talks begin anew.

September 14–October 12, 1847

Mexican-American War (continued): Siege of Puebla. Although U.S. major general Winfield Scott has secured Mexico City on September 14, 1847, the war is not yet over. Control of the National Road connecting the port of Veracruz with the Mexican capital is critical to Scott's forces in Mexico City. A series of U.S. garrisons are stationed along the road, with the most important of these at Puebla, roughly the halfway point. There U.S. Army colonel Thomas Childs commands a garrison of slightly more than 400 men. In case of attack, he plans to augment his numbers by pressing into service convalescing U.S. soldiers in the hospitals there.

Mexican Army commander General Antonio López de Santa Anna plans to move against Puebla. While part of his command under General José Joaquín de Herrera withdraws to Querétaro to

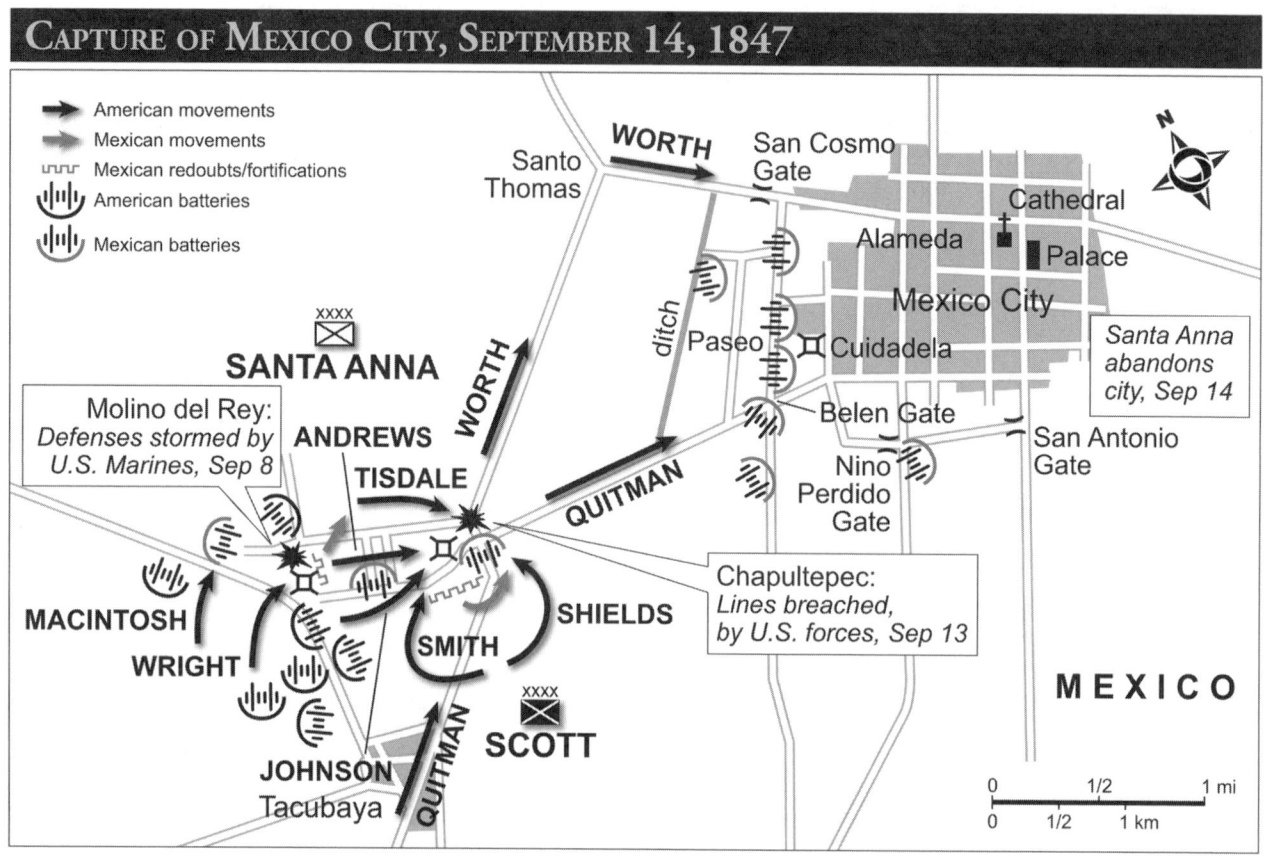

CAPTURE OF MEXICO CITY, SEPTEMBER 14, 1847

- → American movements
- → Mexican movements
- ⌐⌐⌐ Mexican redoubts/fortifications
- ⫿⫿⫿ American batteries
- ⫿⫿⫿ Mexican batteries

WORTH — San Cosmo Gate
Santo Thomas
Cathedral
Alameda
Palace
XXXX SANTA ANNA
Mexico City
ditch
Paseo — Cuidadela
Santa Anna abandons city, Sep 14
Molino del Rey: *Defenses stormed by U.S. Marines, Sep 8*
ANDREWS
WORTH
TISDALE
Belen Gate
San Antonio Gate
QUITMAN
Nino Perdido Gate
MACINTOSH
Chapultepec: *Lines breached, by U.S. forces, Sep 13*
SHIELDS
WRIGHT
SMITH
MEXICO
XXXX SCOTT
JOHNSON
QUITMAN
Tacubaya

0   1/2   1 mi
0   1/2   1 km

regroup, Santa Anna will employ the remainder, led by Brigadier General Joaquín Rea, in a surprise attack on Puebla.

The Americans hold three strategic positions within the city: the citadel of San José, Fort Loretto, and a walled convent. Rea's forces had begun harassing the Americans at Puebla shortly after the bulk of Scott's forces had departed the city on August 7. The Mexicans attacked supply trains and destroyed the aqueduct bringing water into the city. On August 25, Mexican forces had captured most of the garrison's livestock, threatening its food supply.

On September 16, Rea demands that the Americans surrender unconditionally; Childs refuses, and Rea launches two separate attacks by his dragoons in an effort to take the San José citadel, both of which the Americans repulse thanks to devastating artillery fire. Santa Anna arrives at Puebla on September 22 and launches yet another assault, which the Americans also defeat. In spite of the failed attack, Santa Anna

again calls for Childs to surrender. Childs refuses, and Santa Anna renews his attacks on September 27 and continues these for the next five days with little to show for the effort. Rea keeps the Americans inside their fortifications during the next several days but does not provoke further conflict.

Aware that Scott is unable to send reinforcements from the west at Mexico City to Childs because of rain-soaked roads, Santa Anna now shifts his efforts to east of Puebla on the road to Veracruz, where fresh American reinforcements are assembling and from which place they will soon be moving west. On September 30, Santa Anna moves the majority of his men from Puebla to intercept the American relief column. Aware that fewer numbers of men are now manning the Mexican siege lines, Childs mounts several small raids on Mexican strong points, inflicting some casualties.

On September 20, major general of volunteers Joseph Lane and some 1,700 American reinforcements depart from Veracruz for Jalapa. Lane adds

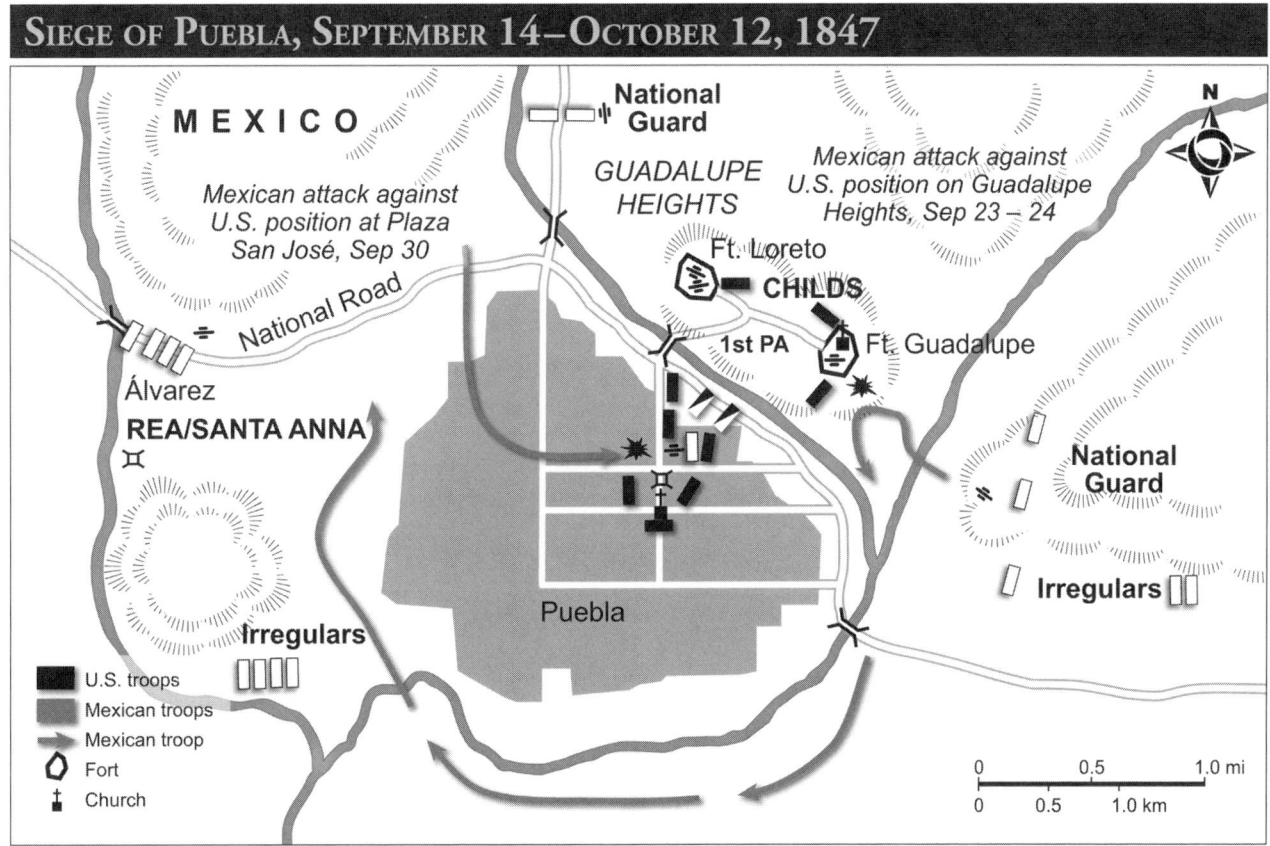

SIEGE OF PUEBLA, SEPTEMBER 14–OCTOBER 12, 1847

men from various garrisons along the way, notably at Perote, bringing his force up to nearly 3,000 men.

Santa Anna engages Lane's column on October 9, just outside the town of Huamantla and northeast of Puebla along the northern branch of the National Road. In the ensuing hard fighting, the Mexicans are driven from the field in disorder following a series of U.S. cavalry charges led by Major Samuel H. Walker and his Texas Rangers and an assault by Lane's infantry, who capture the two Mexican guns. Walker is mortally wounded in the fighting, however. When Lane learns of the death of the popular Walker, he lets loose his poorly disciplined volunteers on the town, which they pillage and destroy—the only instance in the war in which a sizable U.S. force sacks a Mexican town or city.

The next morning, October 10, Lane's troops press on to Puebla, arriving there on October 12. They engage the remainder of the Mexican besiegers and in a brief but hard-fought engagement drive them from the field, lifting the 28-day siege.

American forces under both Childs and Lane have suffered 22 killed, 52 wounded, and 1 missing during the siege. Mexican casualties are unknown. The disorganized remnants of the Mexican Army continue to resist in the Puebla area with guerrilla raids during the next weeks, leading Lane to launch several punitive reprisals. However, the American victory at Puebla marks the end of conventional organized Mexican military opposition in the war.

September 15, 1847

Mexican-American War (continued). At Guadalupe north of Mexico City, General Antonio López de Santa Anna resigns the presidency and is succeeded by Chief Justice Manuel de la Peña y Peña.

September 16, 1847

Mexican-American War (continued). U.S. Army major general Winfield Scott issues General Order No. 20, establishing U.S. military rule throughout occupied Mexico. He imposes on Mexico a $3 million assessment to pay for the occupation.

September 1847–February 1848

Mexican-American War (continued): Prolonged peace negotiations. Following the U.S. capture of Mexico City, peace negotiations open at Guadalupe Hidalgo, north of the capital. Given the U.S. terms, months pass before any Mexican government is willing to negotiate seriously. U.S. president James K. Polk blames his negotiator, Nicholas Trist, and expeditionary force commander, Major General Winfield Scott, for the lack of progress. Polk actually orders Trist home and orders Scott to resume the war. Trist and Scott, now in serious negotiations with the Mexican side, ignore the presidential orders.

October 1, 1847

Mexican-American War (continued): Landing at Mulegé. Departing La Paz, U.S. Navy commander Thomas O. Selfridge arrives off Mulegé in Baja California in the sloop *Dale* (16 guns) on September 30, 1847. Lieutenant Tunis A. M. Craven suggests that they cut out the Mexican schooner *Magdalen,* abandoned in a creek. Selfridge agrees, and Craven leads 50 men in four boats to seize the *Magdalen* and tow it out to the *Dale.* The schooner is found to be unseaworthy, and the Americans burn it.

The next day, October 1, Selfridge calls on Mulegé to surrender all arms and public property. Mexican commander Captain Manuel Pineda refuses. Selfridge bombards the port for 90 minutes and then sends ashore another landing party commanded by Lieutenant Craven. It scatters the 150 Mexican defenders but accomplishes little else, and the men return to the *Dale.* The next day Selfridge sails away, prompting the now-heartened defenders of Mulegé to move against La Paz.

October 5, 1847

Mexican-American War (continued): Landing at Loreto. Departing Mulegé on October 2, 1847, U.S. Navy commander Thomas O. Selfridge arrives off Loreto, Baja California, in the sloop *Dale* (16 guns).

He sends in a landing party under Lieutenant Tunis A. M. Craven to seize two 4-pounder guns and other weapons.

October 17–21, 1847

Mexican-American War (continued): U.S. operations against Guaymas. Commodore William B. Shubrick, commander of the U.S. Pacific Squadron, launches a major amphibious operation against the port of Guaymas in the state of Sonora in northwestern Mexico. This operation on the eastern shore of the Gulf of California is commanded by Captain Elie A. F. Lavallette of the frigate *Congress* (50 guns), accompanied by Commander John B. Montgomery in the sloop *Portsmouth* (22 guns) and the former Chilean brigantine blockade-runner *Argo,* seized by the *Portsmouth* earlier. The three ships arrive off Guaymas on October 17, 1847.

On October 18 Colonel Antonio Campuzano, commanding the 400-man Mexican garrison, rejects a surrender demand, and Lavalette then lands a 32-pounder cannon from the *Congress* on Isle Almagre, placing it in position to control the harbor. At noon on October 19, all preparations to shell Guaymas having been completed, Lavallette sends ashore another surrender demand. When it too is rejected, Lavallette informs Campuzano that he will commence bombarding the city after a delay of two hours to allow women and children to be evacuated. When Campuzano requests a five-hour delay, Lavallette agrees. As it is almost dark on the expiration of the time limit, Lavallette delays his fire until the following morning. During the night of October 19–20, Campuzano withdraws his garrison to Bocachicacampo, four miles up the coast.

On the morning of October 20, the American ships shell Guaymas for an hour, doing considerable property damage and killing one person, an Englishman. The town then surrenders, and Lavallette sends in marines to occupy it. The following day, the landing party destroys Mexican fortifications and collects arms and ammunition from the city's inhabitants.

Lacking the manpower to garrison the town securely, Lavallette charges Commander Thomas O.

Selfridge, captain of the sloop *Dale* (16 guns), which arrives at Guaymas on November 8, to anchor in the roadstead there and maintain order.

November 4, 1847

Mexican-American War (continued). U.S. Navy commodore William B. Shubrick, commander of the Pacific Squadron, issues a proclamation announcing that the United States is about to commence active military operations in Baja California and that it intends to retain possession of this Mexican province at the end of the war.

November 11, 1847

Mexican-American War (continued): U.S. seizure of the port of Mazatlán. Commodore William B. Shubrick, commander of the U.S. Navy Pacific Squadron, arrives off Mazatlán on November 10, 1847. Mazatlán is the busiest port on Mexico's west (Pacific) coast and is second only to Veracruz on the east (Gulf of Mexico) coast. Shubrick flies his flag in the ship of the line *Independence* (56 guns) and is accompanied by Captain Elie A. F. Lavallette in the frigate *Congress* (50 guns) and Commander Samuel F. Du Pont in the sloop *Cyane* (20 guns). The following morning the ships take up positions from which their guns can dominate the city. Mexican lieutenant colonel Rafael Telles, commanding the Mazatlán garrison, has about 560 soldiers but, having made no preparations to repel the Americans, hastily withdraws inland to Palos Prietos. From there he rejects Shubrick's demand to surrender.

On the afternoon of November 11, Lavallette goes ashore with a landing party of 730 men and quickly secures Mazatlán. Shubrick orders the citizens disarmed but otherwise does not interfere with the lives of the townspeople. He installs Lavallette as military governor with a garrison of 400 sailors and marines.

During the next few months, Telles lingers near Mazatlán, occasionally sending out patrols to harass the Americans there. On November 13, a Mexican raiding party enters the town and burns three small boats in the harbor. Americans on patrol are occasionally killed or wounded, but Mexican insurgent forces never make any serious attempt to dislodge the American garrison. In February 1848, the Americans take possession of fortifications laid out by Lieutenant Henry W. Halleck of the U.S. Army engineers. The Americans will return Mazatlán to Mexican control on June 17, 1848.

November 11, 1847

Mexican-American War (continued): Elections occur in the areas of Mexico unoccupied by U.S. troops. On November 14, 1847, Mexican legislators meeting at Querétaro, the temporary seat of the government following the fall of Mexico City, select General Pedro María Anaya to succeed Manuel de la Peña y Peña as president. Anaya holds that post until January 8, 1848.

November 11 and 17, 1847

Mexican-American War (continued): Mexican attacks on La Paz. On November 11, 1847, Mexican captain Manuel Pineda and some 120 men launch an attack against the U.S. 1st New York Volunteer Regiment, commanded by Lieutenant Colonel Henry S. Burton, occupying La Paz on the western shore of the Gulf of California in Baja California. The attackers are driven off by artillery fire. On November 17 Pineda mounts another attack on La Paz and is again driven off, this time with 5 killed and 5 wounded; American losses are 1 killed and 2 wounded.

November 17, 1847

Mexican-American War (continued): Renewed fighting at Guaymas. On November 8, 1847, Commander Thomas O. Selfridge had arrived at the port of Guaymas in southwestern Sonora state in the sloop *Dale* (16 guns) and was charged by Captain Elie A. F. Lavallette of the frigate *Congress* (50 guns) to anchor in the roadstead there and maintain order. Mexican Colonel Antonio Campuzano's men harass the Americans during the next few weeks, and on the night of November 16–17, 350 of them move back into Guaymas.

On November 17 Selfridge leads ashore a landing party of 50 sailors and 17 marines, along with a

Henry Wager Halleck (1815–1872)

U.S. Army general. Born in Westernville, New York, on January 15, 1815, Henry Wager Halleck graduated from the U.S. Military Academy at West Point in 1839 and was assigned to the Corps of Engineers. A report he wrote on the seacoast defenses of the United States won him the favorable attention of commanding general of the army Major General Winfield Scott, who assigned Halleck to travel to Europe in 1844 to study foreign military practices. On his return, Halleck gave a series of lectures at the Lowell Institute, later published as *Elements of Military Art and Science,* that helped win him a reputation as a military intellectual.

During the Mexican-American War (1846–1848) Halleck was sent to California, where he saw limited combat. After the war he continued in California. As military secretary for the territory, he attended the state constitutional convention and played an active role in drafting that document. While retaining his military commission, he became an active partner in a California law firm, resigning from the army only in 1854 when the firm's success was well established. In the years that followed, Halleck expanded his efforts into the real estate and mining businesses and grew wealthy.

When the American Civil War began, Halleck returned to the East and offered his services to the government. On Scott's recommendation, Lincoln nominated Halleck as a major general, one of the highest-ranking officers in the army. Halleck's first assignment was to command the Department of Missouri, where he used his considerable administrative skill to clean up the mess left by his predecessor, Major General John C. Frémont. Halleck was not, however, disposed to advance against the Confederates as Lincoln wanted or to cooperate with Brigadier General Don Carlos Buell, commanding the Department of the Ohio.

In February 1862, Halleck finally gave reluctant permission to his subordinates Brigadier General Ulysses S. Grant and Flag Officer Andrew H. Foote to advance against Confederate Fort Henry on the Tennessee River. Grant and Foote proceeded aggressively and captured not only Fort Henry but also nearby Fort Donelson, controlling the Cumberland River, opening the way for Union advance into the interior of the Confederacy and winning perhaps the most significant victories of the war.

Halleck demanded and received from Lincoln, as a reward for the victories Grant had won, command over all the Union's western armies, including that of his rival Buell. Halleck had planned an advance via the Tennessee and Cumberland Rivers but had wanted to wait until every possible preparation was in place. Now, although he had used Grant's victories for his personal advancement, Halleck was both jealous of Grant's success and unnerved by Grant's aggressiveness. Halleck needlessly reprimanded Grant for failing to communicate frequently with headquarters and reported to the army's new commanding general in Washington, George B. McClellan, that Grant was frequently intoxicated, a report that Halleck knew to be false. Halleck had proceeded to remove Grant from command before Grant's congressman, Elihu B. Washburne, prompted Lincoln to support Grant and force Halleck to restore him. When newspapers criticized Grant after the narrow victory at Shiloh, Halleck seized the opportunity to sideline his subordinate again.

Taking the field for the only time in his career, Halleck pulled together all three field armies within his department, placed Grant in a meaningless second-in-command slot, and with his massed forces advanced with glacial slowness against the Confederate rail hub at Corinth, Mississippi, covering 20 miles in a month. He took the town but let the Confederate army guarding it escape.

Despite such a lackluster result, Lincoln, who was desperately seeking a general to coordinate the movements of all the Union armies, selected Halleck for the post of general-in-chief in July 1862. Halleck's efforts to direct inadequate generals such as Major John Pope and McClellan during the campaign in Virginia that summer proved a dismal failure, and Halleck, who had never been comfortable actually directing operations in the field, all but refused to give further orders to his subordinate generals. A frustrated Lincoln complained that Halleck amounted to little more than "a first-rate clerk." Nonetheless, Halleck performed useful service not only as an adviser to the field commanders but also as a mediator between them and the administration.

In March 1864 when Grant was appointed to supersede Halleck as general-in-chief, he retained Halleck in the de facto role he had already been filling, that of chief of staff. In that capacity Halleck continued to advise generals in the field, including Grant; transmit Grant's wishes into orders to the various armies; and convey the impressions of the president and secretary of war to Grant and other field commanders. In the final analysis, despite his early shortcomings, Halleck made an important contribution to Union victory.

After General Robert E. Lee's April 1865 surrender, Halleck commanded the Military District of the James. That August, he took command of the Division of the Pacific; in 1869, he took control of the Division of the South. Halleck died in Louisville, Kentucky, on January 9, 1872.

STEVEN E. WOODWORTH

Further Reading

Ambrose, Stephen. *Halleck: Lincoln's Chief of Staff.* Baton Rouge: Louisiana State University Press, 1962.

Marszalek, John F. *Commander of All Lincoln's Armies: A Life of General Henry W. Halleck.* Cambridge, MA: Belknap Press of Harvard University Press, 2004.

Woodworth, Steven E., ed. *Grant's Lieutenants: From Chattanooga to Appomattox.* Lawrence: University Press of Kansas, 2008.

6-pounder boat gun. The American landing party at Guaymas is soon pinned down until the *Dale* provides fire support and its guns drive the Mexican forces from the town. Between November 1847 and April 1848, landing parties from the *Dale* harass Campuzano's men near Guaymas until the latter are thoroughly weakened and demoralized. Reportedly, by the end of the war every building in Guaymas has been damaged in the fighting.

November 19, 1847

Mexican-American War (continued). A force of some 150 Mexicans under Captains Vicente Mejía and José Marías Moreno and Mexican Navy lieutenant José Antonio Mijares arrives at San José in Baja California and demands the surrender of Lieutenant Charles Haywood and his 24-man marine garrison. Haywood refuses, and the marines and 20 Baja Californio collaborators take up position in the old mission, where they withstand two nights of Mexican attacks. On the morning of November 21 the Mexican attackers sight two approaching ships and decamp. The ships anchor at San José later in the day and turn out to be two American whalers, the *Magnolia* and *Edward*. On learning of the situation at San José, their captains land crewmen to strengthen the American garrison.

November 25, 1847

November 25, 1847

Mexican-American War (continued). Major General Zachary Taylor departs northern Mexico to return to the United States. Taylor arrives in New Orleans on December 3 to a boisterous reception. Regarded by Americans as a war hero, "Old Rough and Ready" is touted as a possible Whig candidate for president. On Taylor's departure, Major General John E. Wool assumes command of U.S. forces in northern Mexico.

November 26, 1847

Mexican-American War (continued). A launch reaches Mazatlán from San José in Baja California with news of the perilous situation for the small marine force there under Lieutenant Charles Haywood. Commodore William B. Shubrick, commanding the U.S. Navy Pacific Squadron, immediately orders the storeship *Southampton* to depart with additional men, supplies, and equipment. Commanded by Lieutenant Robert D. Thornton, it sails that same day for San José and arrives there on November 26, when Thornton lands 26 men, two guns, and additional supplies and provisions. The whalers *Magnolia* and *Edward* then depart.

November 27, 1847

Mexican-American War (continued): Fighting at La Paz. On this day Mexican Army captain Manuel Pineda leads 350 men in attacking Lieutenant Colonel Henry S. Burton's 1st New York Volunteer Regiment of 112 men. The Americans repulse the attack, Pineda's last attempt during the war to recapture La Paz.

November 29, 1847

Beginning of the Cayuse War: The Whitman Massacre. Dr. Marcus Whitman moved to Oregon Territory in 1836 and later established a Christian mission to convert the Cayuse Indians at Waiilaptu near Fort Walla Walla (present-day Walla Walla, Washington). The Cayuses are not especially drawn to Christianity, and many see the increasing numbers of settlers as a threat. They are also angered by a measles epidemic in November 1847 that kills as many as half of the tribe but affects only a handful of the whites at the

mission. Some blame Dr. Whitman for the deaths of his patients.

On November 29, 1847, a number of Cayuses, led by Chief Tomahas, kill Whitman, his wife Narcissa, and 11 other Christian missionaries at Waiilaptu. The Indians take 60 other people hostage, whom they ransom a month later. This begins the Cayuse War (1847–1855).

The Whitman Massacre ends what had been a period of relatively peaceful relations between immigrants and Native Americans in the Pacific Northwest. A series of wars and uprisings follow. In 1850 the Cayuses finally surrender five men, including Chief Tomahas, accused of perpetrating the massacre. They are tried, convicted, and executed. Fighting continues into 1855, however. Most of the Cayuse lands are confiscated, and most Cayuses are resettled on the Confederated Tribes of the Umatilla Indian Reservation along with the Umatilla and Walla Walla peoples.

January 12, 1848

Mexican-American War (continued). At San Blas in the state of Nayarit on the Mexican Pacific coast, a landing party of 47 men under Lieutenant Frederick Chatard goes ashore from the storeship *Lexington* and its tender, the bark *Wharton*. The men seize cannon at the nearby Castillo de la Entrada and remove them to the shore but find that all but two of them are worthless. They then cut out two schooners. Following this raid, the only Mexican guns along the entire Pacific coast are those in the old fort at Acapulco.

January 22–February 14, 1848

Mexican-American War (continued): Second siege of San José. Taking advantage of the departure of the sloop *Portsmouth* (22 guns), Mexican Army captain Manuel Pineda directs his entire force of up to 350 men against San José in Baja California. The American garrison there counts 27 marines, 15 sailors, and 20 Baja Californio volunteers. With the arrival of Pineda's force, 50 women and children also take refuge with the garrison, which is soon on half rations. The capture of an American foraging party outside San José on January 22, 1848, signals the start of the second siege of that place. Before the garrison is cut off, however, Lieutenant Charles Haywood is able to get word of events to Commodore William B. Shubrick, commander of the U.S. Navy Pacific Squadron, at Mazatlán.

Pinada's forces occupy the town from January 22. Although Haywood's men make several sorties for supplies, they lack the numbers to evict the Mexicans from the town. Finally on February 14 the sloop *Cyane* (20 guns) arrives, and Commander Samuel F. Du Pont lands with 102 officers and men about three miles distant, then marches on San José and raises the siege. The Americans lose 2 men killed in the siege.

January 24, 1848

Gold is discovered at Sutter's Mill in Coloma, California. News of this gets out and begins the California Gold Rush.

January 31, 1848

Mexican-American War (continued). At Fort Leavenworth, Kansas, U.S. Army brevet lieutenant colonel John C. Frémont is court-martialed for disobedience and is cashiered from the service. President James K. Polk voids the sentence and restores Frémont to duty in the Regiment of Mounted Riflemen. Frémont chooses to resign his commission, however. He then undertakes a private western exploring expedition.

February 2, 1848

Mexican-American War (continued): Treaty of Guadalupe Hidalgo. U.S. State Department chief clerk Nicholas Trist proves to be an able negotiator. Aided by bribes, he finalizes the Treaty of Guadalupe Hidalgo on February 2, 1848. In it, Mexico cedes to the United States all Texas to the Rio Grande boundary, New Mexico (including the future states of New Mexico, Arizona, Colorado, Utah, and Nevada), and upper California (including San Diego). Mexicans living in the ceded territories are to be treated as American citizens. The United States also agrees to assume unpaid claims ($3.25 million) by U.S. citizens against the Mexican government and in addition pays $15 million. The U.S.-Mexican border is fixed along the Rio Grande to the southern line of

The Treaty of Guadalupe Hidalgo was signed on February 2, 1848, and ended the Mexican-American War. (Library of Congress)

New Mexico, then westward and northward along the Gila and Colorado Rivers, and then along the line between Upper and Lower California to the Pacific Ocean.

March 10, 1848

Mexican American War (continued): Ratification of the Treaty of Guadalupe Hidalgo by the U.S. Senate. The treaty is submitted on February 23, 1848, and the Senate ratifies it on March 10 in a vote of 38 to 14 (for: 26 Democrats and 12 Whigs; against: 7 Democrats and 7 Whigs). The major issue with the new U.S.

territorial acquisitions becomes whether they will be slave or free, and in this regard the Mexican-American War helps bring on the American Civil War. A motion to add the Wilmot Proviso to the treaty, which would have banned slavery in the territories acquired from Mexico, is defeated in a vote of 38 to 15. Most opposition to the treaty stems from a demand by Secretary of State James Buchanan and some senators, supported by a rising tide of American expansionism, who want to annex all of Mexico.

With ratification of the treaty, U.S. president James K. Polk now does his best to try to humiliate Major General Winfield Scott, who had won the war, and Trist, who had won the peace. Trist is fired. Congress, however, votes Scott a gold medal, which Polk is then forced to present.

March 25, 1848

Mexican-American War (continued): American attack on San Antonio. Lieutenant Colonel Henry S. Burton of the 1st New York Volunteer Regiment is preparing to take the offensive against Mexican forces in the La Paz area of Baja California but is unable to do so because of a lack of manpower until the arrival on March 22 of 115 men in an additional company of the regiment. Three days later, Captain Seymour G. Steele leads a 33-man raiding party from La Paz against Mexican Army captain Manuel Pineda's encampment at San Antonio. The attackers wound Pineda and take prisoner 3 of his men, while releasing 5 Americans.

March 31, 1848

Mexican-American War (continued): American attack on Todos Santos. Departing La Paz, Baja California, on March 23, 1848, eight days later U.S. Army lieutenant colonel Henry S. Burton and 217 men of his 1st New York Volunteer Regiment attack a Mexican troop concentration under Governor Mauricio Castro at Todos Santos, killing 10 and dispersing the remainder. Castro and many of the troops are subsequently captured farther east, at Santiago, by another American force from San José. The action at Todos Santos is the last fighting of the Mexican-American War.

May 25, 1848

The Mexican Congress formally ratifies the Treaty of Guadalupe Hidalgo.

June 11, 1848

U.S. forces return Veracruz to Mexican control.

June 12, 1848

U.S. forces evacuate Mexico City.

June 17, 1848

U.S. forces return Mazatlán to Mexican control.

June 19, 1848

Congress reduces the size of the U.S. Army to its pre–Mexican-American War level. Officers are permitted to keep their wartime ranks, however. Congress also agrees to death benefits for families of deceased enlisted men, with each to receive the equivalent of three months' pay.

June 24, 1848

U.S. forces return Guaymas to Mexican control.

July 4, 1848

U.S. president James K. Polk proclaims the Treaty of Guadalupe Hidalgo in effect.

July 1848

Scott relocates his headquarters to New York City. Commanding general of the army Major General Winfield Scott manages to stay away from President James K. Polk for the remainder of the latter's term, relocating his headquarters to New York City. Sensitive to the fact that Brevet Major General Zachary Taylor, while still on active duty as commander of the Western Department, is also the de facto Whig candidate for president, Scott temporarily gives up command of the entire army and administers only the Eastern Command, leaving Taylor to command the West without having to report to him.

August 2, 1848

Remaining U.S. forces evacuate Veracruz.

August 31, 1848

U.S. forces return La Paz to Mexican control.

November 7, 1848

Taylor elected president. U.S. Army brevet major General Zachary Taylor, commander of the army's Western Division and Whig Party candidate for president, is elected president of the United States. Taylor is the first and only standing military officer to occupy the White House. Although U.S. Army commanding general Major General Winfield Scott does not attend the presidential inaugural, he visits Washington a few days later to call on his army subordinate of 30 years. Scott suggests that he continue to maintain his headquarters in New York City, and Taylor agrees.

March 3, 1849

The U.S. Congress creates the Department of the Interior and transfers to it from the War Department responsibility for Indian affairs. The U.S. military is, however, still responsible for enforcing treaties signed with the Indian tribes.

August 19, 1849

The discovery of gold in California is reported in the *New York Herald,* resulting in the California Gold Rush. Thousands set off across the continent hoping to strike it rich and bringing increasing tensions with Native Americans.

1849–1865

American Indian Wars. Dozens of small wars, battles, and skirmishes occur between the U.S. Army and Native American tribes in the West. The acquisition of California in 1848 and the discovery of gold there lure many American citizens to cross the Great Plains and the Rocky Mountains by land from the east. Construction of the transcontinental railroad in the 1860s and establishment of settler farms on traditional Native American lands exacerbate the situation. Native Americans roam the Plains freely to hunt buffalo, the staple of their subsistence. They do not believe in private landownership, let alone fenced lands. Conflict is inevitable.

During the 1850s, the vast majority of the U.S. Army's 16,000–17,000 men are located in the vast American West. There are numerous small posts of company strength or such patrolling and seeking to keep the peace. The army is involved in numerous small wars against the Yuma, Apache, Arapaho, Cheyenne, Comanche, Kiowa, Mojave, Navaho, Seminole, Sioux, and other Native American tribes. Both sides are guilty of atrocities, although most of those committed by whites are perpetrated by militiamen rather than regular soldiers.

September 2, 1849

Congress abolishes flogging as a punishment in the U.S. Navy.

September 6, 1849

The U.S. Navy sloop *Yorktown* (16 guns), assigned to the Africa Squadron under Commander John Marston, wrecks on Isla de Mayo in the Cape Verde Islands. All crew members are saved.

October 1849–February 1852

Yuma War. This conflict occurs over control of a strategic crossing over the Colorado River near present-day Yuma, Arizona. The importance of the crossing had long been recognized, and Spanish officials had authorized establishment of two missions here. These had been destroyed and the inhabitants massacred (see July 17, 1781). No further effort had been made to control the area before it had passed to U.S. control in early 1848 as a consequence of the Mexican-American War.

In 1849 the U.S. government dispatches to the area a military detail commanded by First Lieutenant Cave J. Couts to survey it and to provide support for the thousands of settlers now crossing the country to reach the goldfields in California. On October 2 Couts establishes Camp Calhoun on the site of the abandoned Spanish La Purisima Concepción mission near Yuma. Almost immediately Yuma Indians commence attacks on Camp Calhoun. A year later, the camp is moved to the banks of the Colorado River, a mile below the mouth of the Gila River, to secure a

Minié Ball

The minié system revolutionized military small arms in the 1850s. Others had experimented with similar ideas, but in 1849 French Army captain Claude Étienne Minié designed the bullet named for him. The French were particularly interested in developing a more rapidly fired rifle to deal with Arab insurgents in Algeria, who sniped at them from long range. The system proved effective, and in 1851 the British Army also adopted it, ordering 23,000 Minié rifled "muskets," many of which saw service in the Crimean War of 1854–1856. Ultimately any rifle with a similar bullet system became known as the "minnie."

The so-called minnie ball, as the bullet was known during the American Civil War, was not a cylindrical ball at all but rather a cylindo-conoidal lead bullet that contained an iron plug set in a hollow in the base of the bullet, which was also cast in a diameter slightly smaller than the gun bore. When inserted into the gun muzzle, the bullet slid easily down the bore, but on the explosion of the gunpowder at the base of the bore, the base plug pushed forward a fraction of a second ahead of the rest of the bullet, expanding its soft lead to grip the rifling and cause the bullet to be fired on an accurate trajectory. A simpler form of the minié bullet simply had a hollowed-out cone base. This had the same effect of expanding the bullet with the discharge of the powder and sealing the bore.

The Minié system combined the ease of loading of the smoothbore musket with the accuracy of the rifle. The new minnie ball rifle could be loaded and fired as fast as the old smoothbore musket (perhaps three times a minute), but it had far greater effective range: at least 400 yards as opposed to 100–200 yards for the smoothbore musket. The two developments of the new bullet and a reliable percussion primer ignition produced a tremendous increase in long-range defensive infantry firepower.

As is usually the case, tactics lagged behind technology. A great many lives would be lost in the wars of the mid-19th century, especially the American Civil War, to the failure to appreciate the effects of long-range rifle fire from defensive positions against charging troops.

Spencer C. Tucker

Further Reading

Blackmore, H. L. "The Percussion System." In *Pollard's History of Firearms*, edited by Claude Blair, 161–187. New York: Macmillan, 1986.

Tunis, Edwin. *Weapons: A Pictorial History.* New York: World Publishing, 1954.

ferry that serves both transiting settlers and the survey team. Established on November 27, 1850, by Captain Samuel P. Heintzelman of the 2nd Infantry Regiment, the installation is named Camp Independence.

Yuma raids increase with the establishment of Fort Independence, resulting in a bona fide war. The Yumas correctly see the ferry as a threat to their control of the region and also oppose the increasing number of settlers transiting their territory. Yuma attacks eventually force the army to relocate Camp Independence to the original site of Camp Calhoun, an easier area to defend. Completed in March 1851, it is named Camp Yuma.

Attacks on Camp Yuma and patrols from it continue during the spring of 1851. That June the government reduces its garrison in an economy measure, but a small force remains there to protect area settlers. With provisions nearly exhausted, that autumn a foraging party leaves the fort to secure provisions, leaving behind only nine men. Hundreds of Yuma warriors lay siege to Camp Yuma. Its small garrison, weakened from near starvation and scurvy, holds out for more than a month before deciding to flee after learning that a relief column has been ambushed and turned back. On December 6, 1851, after hiding or burying what they cannot take with them, they abandon the fort.

Local whites settling in the region also participate in the war, competing with the Yumas to control the river ferry. In one incident, a scalp hunter named John Joel Glanton leads settlers in an attack on Yumas then operating the ferry. An unknown number of natives are killed, and the ferry is destroyed. The Yumas retaliate, killing Glanton and many of his followers.

In February 1852, Captain Heintzelman returns to the area with 150 troops and wins a decisive battle against the Yumas, repelling 300 warriors and retaking Camp Yuma on February 29. The army then undertakes improvements to the camp, which is renamed Fort Yuma. Heintzelman also mounts a successful effort to retake the ferry and to clear the region of hostile Yumas in an approximate 50-mile radius.

Fort Yuma provides security for the region and leads to the creation of the Colorado Ferry Company. The successful pacification effort here and the Gadsden Purchase (1853) make possible completion of a second transcontinental railroad by the Southern Pacific Railroad Company in 1883. Although the Yumas continue sporadic attacks on white settlers and the garrison at Fort Yuma throughout the 1850s, the war for all intents and purposes ends in February 1852.

May 22, 1850–September 30, 1851

First Grinnell Expedition. Wealthy businessman and philanthropist Henry Grinnell finances an expedition to the Arctic to search for a British exploring expedition under Royal Navy captain Sir John Franklin, of which nothing has been heard since 1847. Grinnell furnishes the brigs *Advance* and *Rescue*, which are outfitted for Arctic operations. They are crewed by U.S. Navy volunteers led by Lieutenant Edward J. De Haven. The rescue mission departs New York City on May 22, 1850, and on August 27 they locate the site of Franklin's first winter encampment and the graves of three of his men. Little progress is made thereafter and in mid-September the two ships are frozen in. The members of the expedition experience considerable hardship during the winter. They renew the search in the spring without success and return to New York on September 30, 1851.

MOVING WEST

Conflict with Native Americans, the Mexican-American War, and Manifest Destiny, 1831–1849

DOCUMENTS

Indian Removal Act (1830) [Excerpt]

Introduction

Enacted on May 28, 1830, after one of the most contentious and bitter debates in Congress, the Indian Removal Act proceeded to shift most of the nations of Indian tribes in the eastern United States to what was called Indian Country in present-day Oklahoma. In the most notorious of the Indian removal efforts, President Andrew Jackson ordered the Cherokees off their land in Georgia in 1833. Although the tribe fought against the order in U.S. courts, it was eventually forced to comply. As the Cherokees made their arduous journey to Oklahoma, starvation, illness, and cold resulted in thousands of deaths, and the journey is now remembered as the Trail of Tears.

Primary Source

Be it enacted by the Senate and House of Representatives of the United States of America, in Congress assembled, That it shall and may be lawful for the President of the United States to cause so much of any territory belonging to the United States, west of the river Mississippi, not included in any state or organized territory, and to which the Indian title has been extinguished, as he may judge necessary, to be divided into a suitable number of districts, for the reception of such tribes or nations of Indians as may choose to exchange the lands where they now reside, and remove there. . . .

And be it further enacted, That it shall and may be lawful for the President to exchange any or all of such districts, so to be laid off and described, with any tribe or nation of Indians now residing within the limits of any of the states or territories, and with which the United States have existing treaties, for the whole or any part or portion of the territory claimed and occupied by such tribe or nation, within the bounds of any one or more of the states or territories, where the land claimed and occupied by the Indians, is owned by the United States, or the United States are bound to the state within which it lies to extinguish the Indian claim thereto.

And be it further enacted, That in the making of any such exchange or exchanges, it shall and may be lawful for the President solemnly to assure the tribe or nation with which the exchange is made, that the United States will forever secure and guaranty to them, and their heirs or successors, the country so exchanged with them; and if they prefer it, that the United States will cause a patent or grant to be made and executed to them for the same.

And be it further enacted, That if, upon any of the lands now occupied by the Indians, and to be exchanged for, there should be such improvements as add value to the land claimed by any individual or individuals of such tribes or nations, it shall and may be lawful for the President to cause such value to be ascertained by appraisement or otherwise, and to cause such ascertained value to be paid to the person or persons rightfully claiming such improvements. And upon the payment of such valuation, the improvements so valued and paid for, shall pass to the United States, and possession shall not afterwards be permitted to any of the same tribe.

And be it further enacted, That upon the making of any such exchange as is contemplated by this act, it shall and may be lawful for the President to cause such aid and assistance to be furnished to the emigrants as may be necessary and proper to enable them to remove to, and settle in, the country for which they may have exchanged; and also, to give them such aid and assistance as may be necessary for their support and subsistence for the first year after their removal.

And be it further enacted, That it shall and may be lawful for the President to cause such tribe or nation to be protected, at their new residence, against all interruption or disturbance from any other tribe or nation of Indians, or from any other person or persons whatever.

[. . .]

And be it further enacted, That for the purpose of giving effect to the Provisions of this act, the sum of five hundred thousand dollars is hereby appropriated, to be paid out of any money in the treasury, not otherwise appropriated.

Source: "Indian Removal Act," *U.S. Statutes at Large* 4 (1830): 411.

James K. Polk's War Message (1846) [Excerpt]

Introduction

On May 11, 1846, President James K. Polk delivered a message, excerpted here, to the U.S. Congress asking for a declaration of war against Mexico. Relations between the United States and Mexico had been tense for years, primarily because of Texas's rebellion from Mexican control in 1835 and its subsequent annexation by the United States in 1845. After Mexican troops attacked U.S. Army troops under the command of Brigadier General Zachary Taylor in a border dispute in southern Texas in early May, the two countries moved quickly toward war. Congress complied with Polk's request on May 13, thus beginning the Mexican-American War.

Primary Source

TO THE SENATE AND HOUSE OF REPRESENTATIVES:

[. . .]

The strong desire to establish peace with Mexico on liberal and honorable terms, and the readiness of this government to regulate and adjust our boundary, and other causes of difference with that power, on such fair and equitable principles as would lead to permanent relations of the most friendly nature, induced me in September last to seek the reopening of diplomatic relations between the two countries. Every measure adopted on our part had for its object the furtherance of these desired results. In communicating to Congress a succinct statement of the injuries which we had suffered from Mexico, and which have been accumulating during a period of more than twenty years, every expression that could tend to inflame the people of Mexico, or defeat or delay a pacific result, was carefully avoided. An envoy of the United States repaired to Mexico, with full powers to adjust every existing difference. But though present on the Mexican soil, by agreement between the two governments, invested with full powers, and bearing evidence of the most friendly dispositions, his mission has been unavailing. The Mexican government not only refused to receive him . . . but, after a long-continued series of menaces, have at last invaded our territory, and shed the blood of our fellow-citizens on our own soil.

It now becomes my duty to state more in detail the origin, progress, and failure of that mission. In pursuance of the instructions given in September last, an inquiry was made, on the 13th of October, 1845, in the most friendly terms, through our consul in Mexico, of the minister for foreign affairs, whether the Mexican government "would receive an envoy from the United States intrusted with full powers to adjust all the questions in dispute between the two governments;" with the assurance that "should the answer be in the affirmative, such an envoy would be immediately despatched to Mexico." The Mexican minister, on the 15th of October, gave an affirmative answer to this inquiry, requesting, at the same time, that our naval force at Vera Cruz might be withdrawn, lest its continued presence might assume the appearance of menace and coercion pending the negotiations. This force was immediately withdrawn. On the 10th of November, 1845, Mr. John Slidell, of Louisiana, was commissioned by me as envoy extraordinary and minister plenipotentiary of the United States to Mexico, and was intrusted with full powers to adjust both the questions of the Texas boundary and of indemnification to our citizens. The redress of the wrongs of our citizens naturally and inseparably blended itself with the question of boundary. The settlement of the one question, in any correct view of the subject, involves that of the other. I could not, for a moment, entertain the idea that the claims of our much injured and long suffering citizens, many of which had existed for more than twenty years, should be postponed, or separated from the settlement of the boundary question.

Mr. Slidell arrived at Vera Cruz on the 30th of November, and was courteously received by the authorities of that city. But the government of General Herrera was then tottering to its fall. The revolutionary party had seized upon the Texas question to effect or hasten its overthrow. Its determination to restore friendly relations with the United States, and to receive our minister, to negotiate for the settlement of this question, was violently assailed, and was made the great theme of denunciation against it. The government of General Herrera ... yielded to the storm raised by its enemies, and on the 21st of December refused to accredit Mr. Slidell upon the most frivolous pretexts....

Five days after the date of Mr. Slidell's note, General Herrera yielded the government to General Paredes, without a struggle, and on the 30th of December resigned the presidency. This revolution was accomplished solely by the army ... and thus the supreme power of Mexico passed into the hands of a military leader.

[...]

Under these circumstances, Mr. Slidell, in obedience to my direction, addressed a note to the Mexican minister of foreign relations, under date of the 1st of March last, asking to be received by that government in the diplomatic character to which he had been appointed. This minister, in his reply under date of the 12th of March, reiterated the arguments of his predecessor, and, in terms that may be considered as giving just grounds of offence to the government and people of the United States, denied the application of Mr. Slidell....

Thus the government of Mexico, though solemnly pledged by official acts in October last to receive and accredit an American envoy, violated their plighted faith, and refused the offer of a peaceful adjustment of our difficulties. Not only was the offer rejected, but the indignity of its rejection was enhanced by the manifest breach of faith in refusing to admit the envoy, who came because they had bound themselves to receive him....

In my message at the commencement of the present session, I informed you that, upon the earnest appeal both of the congress and convention of Texas, I had ordered an efficient military force to take a position "between the Nueces and the Del Norte." This had become necessary, to meet a threatened invasion of Texas by the Mexican forces, for which extensive military preparations had been made. The invasion was threatened solely because Texas had determined, in accordance with a solemn resolution of the Congress of the United States, to annex herself to our Union; and, under these circumstances, it was plainly our duty to extend our protection over her citizens and soil.

> Texas had determined, in accordance with a solemn resolution of the Congress of the United States, to annex herself to our Union; and, under these circumstances, it was plainly our duty to extend our protection over her citizens and soil.

Documents

This force was concentrated at Corpus Christi, and remained there until after I had received such information from Mexico as rendered it probable, if not certain, that the Mexican government would refuse to receive our envoy.

Meantime Texas, by the final action of our Congress, had become an integral part of our Union. The Congress of Texas, by its act of December 19, 1836, had declared the Rio del Norte to be the boundary of that republic. Its jurisdiction had been extended and exercised beyond the Nueces. The country between that river and the Del Norte had been represented in the congress and in the convention of Texas; had thus taken part in the act of annexation itself; and is now included within one of our congressional districts. Our own Congress had, moreover, with great unanimity, by the act approved December 31, 1845, recognised the country beyond the Nueces as a part of our territory, by including it within our own revenue system; and a revenue officer, to reside within that district, has been appointed, by and with the advice and consent of the senate. It became, therefore, of urgent necessity to provide for the defence of that portion of our country. Accordingly, on the 13th of January last, instructions were issued to the general in command of these troops to occupy the left bank of the Del Norte. This river, which is the southwestern boundary of the state of Texas, is an exposed frontier; from this quarter invasion was threatened; upon it, and in its immediate vicinity, in the judgment of high military experience, are the proper stations for the protecting forces of the government. In addition to this important consideration, several others occurred to induce this movement. Among these are the facilities afforded by the ports at Brazos Santiago and the mouth of the Del Norte, for the reception of supplies by sea; the stronger and more healthful military positions; the convenience for obtaining a ready and a more abundant supply of provisions, water, fuel, and forage; and the advantages which are afforded by the Del Norte in forwarding supplies to such posts as may be established in the interior and upon the Indian frontier.

The movement of the troops to the Del Norte was made by the commanding general, under positive instructions to abstain from all aggressive acts toward Mexico or Mexican citizens, and to regard the relations between that republic and the United States as peaceful, unless she should declare war, or commit acts of hostility indicative of a state of war. He was specially directed to protect private property, and respect personal rights.

The army moved from Corpus Christi on the 11th of March, and on the 28th of that month arrived on the left bank of the Del Norte, opposite to Matamoras, where it encamped on a commanding position. . . .

The Mexican forces at Matamoras assumed a belligerent attitude, and, on the 12th of April, General Ampudia, then in command, notified General Taylor to break up his camp within twenty-four hours, and to retire beyond the Nueces river, and, in the event of his failure to comply with these demands, announced that arms, and arms alone, must decide the question. But no open act of hostility was committed until the 24th of April. On that day, General Arista, who had succeeded to the command of the Mexican forces, communicated to General Taylor that "he considered hostilities commenced, and should prosecute them." A party of dragoons, of sixty-three men and officers, were on the same day despatched from the American camp up the Rio del Norte, on its left bank, to ascertain whether the Mexican troops had crossed, or were preparing to cross, the river, "became engaged with a large body of these troops, and, after a short affair, in which some sixteen were killed and wounded, appear to have been surrounded and compelled to surrender."

The grievous wrongs perpetrated by Mexico upon our citizens throughout a long period of years remain unredressed; and solemn treaties, pledging her public faith for this redress, have been disregarded. A government either unable or unwilling to enforce the execution of such treaties, fails to perform one of its plainest duties. Our commerce with Mexico has been almost annihilated. It was formerly highly beneficial to both nations; but our merchants have been deterred from prosecuting it by the system of outrage and extortion which the Mexican authorities have pursued against them, whilst their appeals through their own government for indemnity have been made in vain.... Had we acted with vigor in repelling the insults and redressing the injuries inflicted by Mexico at the commencement, we should doubtless have escaped all the difficulties in which we are now involved.

Instead of this, however, we have been exerting our best efforts to propitiate her good-will. Upon the pretext that Texas, a nation as independent as herself, thought proper to unite its destinies with our own, she has affected to believe that we have severed her rightful territory, and in official proclamations and manifestoes has repeatedly threatened to make war upon us, for the purpose of reconquering Texas. In the meantime, we have tried every effort at reconciliation. The cup of forbearance had been exhausted, even before the recent information from the frontier of the Del Norte. But now, after reiterated menaces, Mexico has passed the boundary of the United States, has invaded our territory, and shed American blood upon the American soil. She has proclaimed that hostilities have commenced, and that the two nations are now at war.

As war exists, and, notwithstanding all our efforts to avoid it, exists by the act of Mexico herself, we are called upon by every consideration of duty and patriotism to vindicate with decision the honor, the rights, and the interests of our country.

[...]

In further vindication of our rights, and defence of our territory, I invoke the prompt action of Congress to recognise the existence of the war, and to place at the disposition of the Executive the means of prosecuting the war with vigor, and thus hastening the restoration of peace. To this end I recommend that authority should be given to call into the public service a large body of volunteers, to serve for not less than six or twelve months, unless sooner discharged.

A volunteer force is beyond question more efficient than any other description of citizen soldiers; and it is not to be doubted that a number far beyond that required would readily rush to the field upon the call of their country. I further recommend that a liberal provision be made for sustaining our entire military force and furnishing it with supplies and munitions of war....

Source: James K. Polk, "War Message," May 11, 1846, in *A Compilation of the Messages and Papers of the Presidents*, Vol. 3, edited by James Daniel Richards, 2288–2289 (Washington, DC: Bureau of National Literature and Art, 1897).

Abraham Lincoln's Speech in the U.S. House of Representatives (1848) [Excerpt]

Introduction

As a young congressman from Illinois, Abraham Lincoln rose to national prominence with this speech, which he delivered on the floor of the U.S. House of Representatives on January 12, 1848. In this address, Lincoln repeatedly inquired of President James K. Polk to name the exact spot of U.S. soil that the Mexican Army had supposedly trespassed on to justify the outbreak of the Mexican-American War in 1846.

Primary Source

Mr. Chairman:—Some if not all the gentlemen on the other side of the House who have addressed the committee within the last two days have spoken rather complainingly, if I have rightly understood them, of the vote given a week or ten days ago declaring that the war with Mexico was unnecessarily and unconstitutionally commenced by the President. I admit that such a vote should not be given in mere party wantonness, and that the one given is justly censurable if it have no other or better foundation. I am one of those who joined in that vote; and I did so under my best impression of the truth of the case. How I got this impression, and how it may possibly be remedied, I will now try to show. When the war began, it was my opinion that all those who because of

Abraham Lincoln's Speech in the U.S. House of Representatives (1848) [Excerpt] 739

knowing too little, or because of knowing too much, could not conscientiously approve the conduct of the President in the beginning of it should nevertheless, as good citizens and patriots, remain silent on that point, at least till the war should be ended. Some leading Democrats, including ex-President Van Buren, have taken this same view, as I understand them; and I adhered to it and acted upon it, until since I took my seat here; and I think I should still adhere to it were it not that the President and his friends will not allow it to be so. Besides the continual effort of the President to argue every silent vote given for supplies into an indorsement of the justice and wisdom of his conduct; besides that singularly candid paragraph in his late message in which he tells us that Congress with great unanimity had declared that "by the act of the Republic of Mexico, a state of war exists between that government and the United States," when the same journals that informed him of this also informed him that when that declaration stood disconnected from the question of supplies sixty-seven in the House, and not fourteen merely, voted against it; besides this open attempt to prove by telling the truth what he could not prove by telling the whole truth—demanding of all who will not submit to be misrepresented, in justice to themselves, to speak out, besides all this, one of my colleagues [Mr. Richardson] at a very early day in the session brought in a set of resolutions expressly indorsing the original justice of the war on the part of the President. Upon these resolutions when they shall be put on their passage I shall be compelled to vote; so that I cannot be silent if I would. Seeing this, I went about preparing myself to give the vote understandingly when it should come. I carefully examined the President's message, to ascertain what he himself had said and

> The President, in his first war message of May, 1846, declares that the soil was ours on which hostilities were commenced by Mexico, and he repeats that declaration almost in the same language in each successive annual message, thus showing that he deems that point a highly essential one.

proved upon the point. The result of this examination was to make the impression that, taking for true all the President states as facts, he falls far short of proving his justification; and that the President would have gone further with his proof if it had not been for the small matter that the truth would not permit him. Under the impression thus made I gave the vote before mentioned. I propose now to give concisely the process of the examination I made, and how I reached the conclusion I did. The President, in his first war message of May, 1846, declares that the soil was ours on which hostilities were commenced by Mexico, and he repeats that declaration almost in the same language in each successive annual message, thus showing that he deems that point a highly essential one. In the importance of that point I entirely agree with the President. To my judgment it is the very point upon which he should be justified, or condemned. In his message of December, 1846, it seems to have occurred to him, as is certainly true, that title—ownership—to soil or anything else is not a simple fact, but is a conclusion following on one or more simple facts; and that it was incumbent upon him to present the facts from which he concluded the soil was ours on which the first blood of the war was shed.

Accordingly, a little below the middle of page twelve in the message last referred to he enters upon that task; forming an issue and introducing testimony, extending the whole to a little below the middle of page fourteen. Now, I propose to try to show that the whole of this—issue and evidence—is from beginning to end the sheerest deception. . . .

I now proceed to examine the President's evidence as applicable to such an issue. When that evidence is analyzed, it is all included in the following propositions

(1) That the Rio Grande was the western boundary of Louisiana as we purchased it of France in 1803.

(2) That the Republic of Texas always claimed the Rio Grande as her eastern boundary.

(3) That by various acts she had claimed it on paper.

(4) That Santa Anna in his treaty with Texas recognized the Rio Grande as her boundary.

(5) That Texas before, and the United States after, annexation had exercised jurisdiction beyond the Nueces—between the two rivers.

(6) That our Congress understood the boundary of Texas to extend beyond the Nueces.

Now for each of these in its turn. His first item is that the Rio Grande was the western boundary of Louisiana, as we purchased it of France in 1803; and seeming to expect this to be disputed, he argues over the amount of nearly a page to prove it true, at the end of which he lets us know that by the treaty of 1803 we sold to Spain the whole country from the Rio Grande eastward to the Sabine. Now, admitting for the present that the Rio Grande was the boundary of Louisiana, what under heaven had that to do with the present boundary between us and Mexico? How, Mr. Chairman, the line that once divided your land from mine can still be the boundary between us after I have sold my land to you is to me beyond all comprehension. And how any man, with an honest purpose only of proving the truth, could ever have thought of introducing such a fact to prove such an issue is equally incomprehensible. His next piece of evidence is that "the Republic of Texas always claimed this river [Rio Grande] as her western boundary." That is not true, in fact. Texas has claimed it, but she has not always claimed it. There is at least one distinguished exception. Her State constitution, the republic's most solemn and well-considered act, that which may, without impropriety, be called her last will and testament, revoking all others—makes no such claim. But suppose she had always claimed it. Has not Mexico always claimed the contrary? So that there is but claim against claim, leaving nothing proved until we get back of the claims and find which has the better foundation. Though not in the order in which the President presents his evidence, I now consider that class of his statements which are in substance nothing more than that Texas has, by various acts of her Convention and Congress, claimed the Rio Grande

as her boundary, on paper. I mean here what he says about the fixing of the Rio Grande as her boundary in her old constitution (not her State constitution), about forming Congressional districts, counties, etc. Now all of this is but naked claim; and what I have already said about claims is strictly applicable to this. If I should claim your land by word of mouth, that certainly would not make it mine; and if I were to claim it by a deed which I had made myself, and with which you had had nothing to do, the claim would be quite the same in substance—or rather, in utter nothingness. I next consider the President's statement that Santa Anna in his treaty with Texas recognized the Rio Grande as the western boundary of Texas. Besides the position so often taken, that Santa Anna while a prisoner of war, a captive, could not bind Mexico by a treaty, which I deem conclusive—besides this, I wish to say something in relation to this treaty, so called by the President, with Santa Anna. If any man would like to be amused by a sight of that little thing which the President calls by that big name, he can have it by turning to Niles's Register, vol. 1, p. 336. And if any one should suppose that Niles's Register is a curious repository of so mighty a document as a solemn treaty between nations, I can only say that I learned to a tolerable degree of certainty, by inquiry at the State Department, that the President himself never saw it anywhere else. By the way, I believe I should not err if I were to declare that during the first ten years of the existence of that document it was never by anybody called a treaty—that it was never so called till the President, in his extremity, attempted by so calling it to wring something from it in justification of himself in connection with the Mexican War. It has none of the distinguishing features of a treaty. It does not call itself a treaty. Santa Anna does not therein assume to bind Mexico; he assumes only to act as the President—Commander-in-Chief of the Mexican army and navy; stipulates that the then present hostilities should cease, and that he would not himself take up arms, nor influence the Mexican people to take up arms, against Texas during the existence of the war of independence. He did not recognize the independence of Texas; he did not assume to put an end to the war, but clearly indicated his expectation of its continuance; he did not say one word about boundary, and, most probably, never thought of it. It is stipulated therein that the Mexican forces should evacuate the territory of Texas, passing to the other side of the Rio Grande; and in another article it is stipulated that, to prevent collisions between the armies, the Texas army should not approach nearer than within five leagues—of what is not said, but clearly, from the object stated, it is of the Rio Grande. Now, if this is a treaty recognizing the Rio Grande as the boundary of Texas, it contains the singular feature of stipulating that Texas shall not go within five leagues of her own boundary.

Next comes the evidence of Texas before annexation, and the United States afterwards, exercising jurisdiction beyond the Nueces and between the two rivers. This actual exercise of jurisdiction is the very class or quality of evidence we want. It is excellent so far as it goes; but does it go far enough? He tells us it went beyond the Nueces, but he does not tell us it went to the Rio Grande. He tells us jurisdiction was exercised between the two rivers, but he does not tell us it was exercised over all the territory between them. . . .

But next the President tells us the Congress of the United States understood the State of Texas they admitted into the Union to extend beyond the Nueces. Well, I suppose they did. I certainly so understood it. But how far beyond? That Congress did not understand it to extend clear to the Rio Grande is quite certain, by the fact of their joint resolutions for admission expressly leaving all questions of boundary to future adjustment. And it may be added that Texas herself is proven to have had the same understanding of it that our Congress had, by the fact of the exact conformity of her new constitution to those resolutions.

I am now through the whole of the President's evidence; and it is a singular fact that if any one should declare the President sent the army into the midst of a settlement of Mexican people who had never submitted, by consent or by force, to the authority of Texas or of the United States, and that there and thereby the first blood of the war was shed, there is not one word

in all the which would either admit or deny the declaration. This strange omission it does seem to me could not have occurred but by design. My way of living leads me to be about the courts of justice; and there I have sometimes seen a good lawyer, struggling for his client's neck in a desperate case, employing every artifice to work round, befog, and cover up with many words some point arising in the case which he dared not admit and yet could not deny. Party bias may help to make it appear so, but with all the allowance I can make for such bias, it still does appear to me that just such, and from just such necessity, is the President's struggle in this case.

Sometime after my colleague [Mr. Richardson] introduced the resolutions I have mentioned, I introduced a preamble, resolution, and interrogations, intended to draw the President out, if possible, on this hitherto untrodden ground. To show their relevancy, I propose to state my understanding of the true rule for ascertaining the boundary between Texas and Mexico. It is that wherever Texas was exercising jurisdiction was hers; and wherever Mexico was exercising jurisdiction was hers; and that whatever separated the actual exercise of jurisdiction of the one from that of the other was the true boundary between them. If, as is probably true, Texas was exercising jurisdiction along the western bank of the Nueces, and Mexico was exercising it along the eastern bank of the Rio Grande, then neither river was the boundary: but the uninhabited country between the two was. The extent of our territory in that region depended not on any treaty-fixed boundary (for no treaty had attempted it), but on revolution. Any people anywhere being inclined and having the power have the right to rise up and shake off the existing government, and form a new one that suits them better. This is a most valuable, a most sacred right—a right which we hope and believe is to liberate the world. Nor is this right confined to cases in which the whole people of an existing government may choose to exercise it. Any portion of such people that can may revolutionize and make their own of so much of the territory as they inhabit. More than this, a majority of any portion of such people may revolutionize, putting down a minority, intermingled with or near about them, who may oppose this movement. Such minority was precisely the case of the Tories of our own revolution. It is a quality of revolutions not to go by old lines or old laws, but to break up both, and make new ones.

As to the country now in question, we bought it of France in 1803, and sold it to Spain in 1819, according to the President's statements. After this, all Mexico, including Texas, revolutionized against Spain; and still later Texas revolutionized against Mexico. In my view, just so far as she carried her resolution by obtaining the actual, willing or unwilling, submission of the people, so far the country was hers, and no farther. Now, sir, for the purpose of obtaining the very best evidence as to whether Texas had actually carried her revolution to the place where the hostilities of the present war commenced, let the President answer the interrogatories I proposed, as before mentioned, or some other similar ones. Let him answer fully, fairly, and candidly. Let him answer with facts and not with arguments. Let him remember he sits where Washington sat, and so remembering, let him answer as Washington would answer. As a nation should not, and the Almighty will not, be evaded, so let him attempt no evasion—no equivocation. And if, so answering, he can show that the soil was ours where the first blood of the war was shed,—that it was not within an inhabited country, or, if within such, that the inhabitants had submitted themselves to the civil authority of Texas or of the United States, and that the same is true of the site of Fort Brown, then I am with him for his justification. In that case I shall be most happy to reverse the vote I gave the other day. I have a selfish motive for desiring that the President may do this—I expect to gain some votes, in connection with the war, which, without his so doing, will be of doubtful propriety in my own judgment, but which will be free from the doubt if he does so. But if he can not or will not do this,—if on any pretence or no pretence he shall refuse or omit it then I shall be fully convinced of what I more than suspect already, that he is deeply conscious of being in the wrong; that he feels the blood of this war, like the blood of Abel, is crying to heaven against him; that originally having

some strong motive—what, I will not stop now to give my opinion concerning to involve the two countries in a war, and trusting to escape scrutiny by fixing the public gaze upon the exceeding brightness of military glory,—that attractive rainbow that rises in showers of blood, that serpent's eye that charms to destroy,—he plunged into it, and was swept on and on till, disappointed in his calculation of the ease with which Mexico might be subdued, he now finds himself he knows not where. How like the half insane mumbling of a fever dream is the whole war part of his late message! At one time telling us that Mexico has nothing whatever that we can get—but territory; at another showing us how we can support the war by levying contributions on Mexico. At one time urging the national honor, the security of the future, the prevention of foreign interference, and even the good of Mexico herself as among the objects of the war; at another telling us that "to reject indemnity, by refusing to accept a cession of territory, would be to abandon all our just demands, and to wage the war, bearing all its expenses, without a purpose or definite object." So then this national honor, security of the future, and everything but territorial indemnity may be considered the no-purposes and indefinite objects of the war! But, having it now settled that territorial indemnity is the only object, we are urged to seize, by legislation here, all that he was content to take a few months ago, and the whole province of Lower California to boot, and to still carry on the war to take all we are fighting for, and still fight on. Again, the President is resolved under all circumstances to have full territorial indemnity for the expenses of the war; but he forgets to tell us how we are to get the excess after those expenses shall have surpassed the value of the whole of the Mexican territory. So again, he insists that the separate national existence of Mexico shall be maintained; but he does not tell us how this can be done, after we shall have taken all her territory. Lest the questions I have suggested be considered speculative merely, let me be indulged a moment in trying to show they are not. The war has gone on some twenty months; for the expenses of which, together with an inconsiderable old score, the President now claims about one half of the Mexican territory, and

Abraham Lincoln's Speech in the U.S. House of Representatives (1848) [Excerpt]

that by far the better half, so far as concerns our ability to make anything out of it. It is comparatively uninhabited; so that we could establish land-offices in it, and raise some money in that way. But the other half is already inhabited, as I understand it, tolerably densely for the nature of the country, and all its lands, or all that are valuable, already appropriated as private property. How then are we to make anything out of these lands with this encumbrance on them? or how remove the encumbrance? I suppose no one would say we should kill the people, or drive them out, or make slaves of them, or confiscate their property. How, then, can we make much out of this part of the territory? If the prosecution of the war has in expenses already equalled the better half of the country, how long its future prosecution will be in equalling the less valuable half is not a speculative, but a practical, question, pressing closely upon us. And yet it is a question which the President seems never to have thought of. As to the mode of terminating the war and securing peace, the President is equally wandering and indefinite. First, it is to be done by a more vigorous prosecution of the war in the vital parts of the enemy's country; and after apparently talking himself tired on this point, the President drops down into a half-despairing tone, and tells us that "with a people distracted and divided by contending factions, and a government subject to constant changes by successive revolutions, the continued success of our arms may fail to secure a satisfactory peace." Then he suggests the propriety of wheedling the Mexican people to desert the counsels of their own leaders, and, trusting in our protestations, to set up a government from which we can secure a satisfactory peace; telling us that "this may become the only mode of obtaining such a peace." But soon he falls into doubt of this too; and then drops back on to the already half-abandoned ground of "more vigorous prosecution." All this shows that the President is in nowise satisfied with his own positions. First he takes up one, and in attempting to argue us into it he argues himself out of it, then seizes another and goes through the same process, and then, confused at being able to think of nothing new, he snatches up the old one again, which he has some time before cast off. His mind, taxed beyond its

power, is running hither and thither, like some tortured creature on a burning surface, finding no position on which it can settle down and be at ease.

Again, it is a singular omission in this message that it nowhere intimates when the President expects the war to terminate. At its beginning, General Scott was by this same President driven into disfavor if not disgrace, for intimating that peace could not be conquered in less than three or four months. But now, at the end of about twenty months, during which time our arms have given us the most splendid successes, every department and every part, land and water, officers and privates, regulars and volunteers, doing all that men could do, and hundreds of things which it had ever before been thought men could not do—after all this, this same President gives a long message, without showing us that as to the end he himself has even an imaginary conception. As I have before said, he knows not where he is. He is a bewildered, confounded, and miserably perplexed man. God grant he may be able to show there is not something about his conscience more painful than his mental perplexity. . . .

Source: Abraham Lincoln, "Speech in the United States House of Representatives," in *Abraham Lincoln: Complete Works, Comprising His Speeches, Letters, State Papers, and Miscellaneous Writings,* Vol. 1, edited by John G. Nicolay and John Hay, 100–107 (New York: Century Co., 1907).

Diary Account of Siege at Veracruz (March 1847)

Introduction

On March 9, 1847, Major General Winfield Scott's 15,000-man army, with the help of U.S. naval assets, landed at Collado Beach, some 2.5 miles south of Veracruz, Mexico. Scott's goal was to lay siege to Veracruz, occupy it, and use it as a base for his Mexico City Campaign. Eschewing a frontal infantry assault, Scott decided to direct naval gunfire on Veracruz and also deployed land artillery to shell the city into submission. The bombardment began on March 22. The Mexican commander at Veracruz requested surrender terms on March 25, and the siege ended officially with an unconditional Mexican surrender on March 29. This success allowed Scott an entrée into Mexico's interior before the yellow fever season set in along the coastal lowlands. What follows is a U.S. army officer's account of the final days of the siege.

Primary Source

[March] 23rd. Firing continued from our mortars steadily—fire of enemy by no means so warm as when we opened on the day before. Our mortar platforms were much injured by the firing already. The 24 pounder battery had to be re-revetted entirely—terreplein levelled. During this day and night the magazine was excavated, and the frame put up. Two traverses made—the positions of platforms and embrasures determined. Two platforms laid and the guns run in—the embrasures for them being partly *cut*. One other gun was run to the rear of the battery.

[March] 24th. On duty with Captain Saunders again—could get no directions so I had the two partly cut embrasures marked with sand bags and dirt, and set a party at work to cover the magazine with earth as soon as it was finished. During this day the traverses were finished, the platforms laid, the magazine entirely finished, and a large number of sand bags filled for the revetments of the embrasures. The "Naval Battery" opened today, their fire was fine music for us, but they did not keep it up very long. The crash of the eight inch shells as they broke their way through the houses and burst in them was very pretty. The "Greasers" had had it all in their own way—but we were gradually opening on them now. Remained out all night to take charge of two embrasures. The Alabama Volunteers, who formed the working party, did not come until it was rather late—we set them at work to cut down and

level the top of the parapet—thickening it opposite the third and fourth guns. Then laid out the embrasures and put seven men in each. Foster had charge of two, Coppee of two, and I of two. Mine were the only ones finished at daylight—the Volunteers gave out and could hardly be induced to work at all.

[March] 25th. Mason and Stevens relieved Beauregard and Foster—but I remained. I had the raw hides put on—and with a large party of Volunteers opened the other embrasures. This was done in broad daylight, in full view of the town—yet they had not fired more than three or four shots when I finished and took in the men. The battery then opened. We then gave it to Mexicans about as hotly as they wished. We had ten mortars—three 68s, three 32s, four 24s, and two eight-inch howitzers playing upon them as fast as they could load and fire. Captain Anderson, 3rd Artillery, fired on this morning thirty shells in thirty minutes from his battery of three mortars (No. 1).

As I went to our camp I stopped at Colonel Totten's tent to inform him of the state of affairs—he directed me to step in and report to General Scott. I found him writing a despatch. He seemed to be very much delighted and showed me the last words he had written which were "indefatigable Engineers." Then we were needed and remembered—the instant the pressing necessity passed away we were forgotten. The echo of the last hostile gun at Vera Cruz had not died away before it was forgotten by the Commander in Chief that such a thing existed as an Engineer Company.

Source: George Brinton McClellan, *The Mexican War Diary of George B. McClellan*, edited by William Starr Myers, 68–71 (Princeton, NJ: Princeton University Press, 1917).

MOVING WEST

Conflict with Native Americans, the Mexican-American War, and Manifest Destiny, 1831–1849

STATISTICS

Casualties, Mexican-American War (1846–1848)					
Branch of Service	Number Serving	Total Deaths	Battle Deaths	Other Deaths	Wounded, Not Mortally
Total	78,718	13,283	1,733	11,550	4,152
Army	—	13,271	1,721	11,550	4,102
Navy	—	1	1	—	3
Marines	—	11	11	—	47

Source: Congressional Research Service, CRS Report for Congress, February 6, 2010.

MOVING WEST

Conflict with Native Americans, the Mexican-American War, and Manifest Destiny, 1831–1849

BIBLIOGRAPHY

Altshuler, Constance Wynn. *Cavalry Yellow and Infantry Blue: Army Officers in Arizona between 1851 and 1886.* Tucson: Arizona Historical Society, 1991.

Ballard, Michael B. *Pemberton: A Biography.* Jackson: University Press of Mississippi, 1991.

Bannon, John Francis. *The Spanish Borderlands Frontier, 1513–1821.* New York: Holt, Rinehart, and Winston, 1970.

Bannon, John Francis, ed. *Bolton and the Spanish Borderlands.* Norman: University of Oklahoma Press, 1964.

Barr, Alwyn. *Texans in Revolt: The Battle for San Antonio, 1835.* Austin: University of Texas Press, 1990.

Bauer, K. Jack. *The Mexican War, 1846–1848.* Lincoln: University of Nebraska Press, 1992.

Bauer, K. Jack. *Surfboats and Horse Marines: U.S. Naval Operations in the Mexican War, 1846–48.* Annapolis, MD: United States Naval Institute, 1969.

Baugh, Virgil E. *Rendezvous at the Alamo: Highlights in the Lives of Bowie, Crockett, and Travis.* New York: Pageant, 1960.

Beers, Henry Putney. *The Western Military Frontier, 1815–1846.* Philadelphia: University of Pennsylvania, 1935.

Bemis, Samuel Flagg. *The Latin-American Policy of the United States.* New York: Harcourt, Brace, 1943.

Bill, Alfred Hoyt. *Rehearsal for Conflict: The War with Mexico, 1846–1848.* New York: Knopf, 1947.

Binkley, William C. *The Texas Revolution.* Baton Rouge: Louisiana State University Press, 1952.

Bolton, Herbert E. *The Spanish Borderlands: A Chronicle of Old Florida and the Southwest.* Chronicles of America 23. New Haven, CT: Yale University Press, 1921.

Brack, Gene M. *Mexico Views Manifest Destiny, 1821–1846: An Essay on the Origins of the Mexican War.* Albuquerque: University of New Mexico Press, 1975.

Braider, Donald. *Solitary Star: A Biography of Sam Houston.* New York: Putnam, 1974.

Briggs, Carl, and Clyde Francis Trudell. *Quarterback and Saddlehorn: The Story of Edward F. Beale, 1822–1893.* Glendale, CA: Arthur H. Clark, 1983.

Brooks, Philip Coolidge. *Diplomacy and the Borderlands: The Adams-Onís Treaty of 1819.* University of California Publications in History 24. Berkeley: University of California Press, 1939.

Brown, Gary. *Hesitant Martyr of the Texas Revolution: James Walker Fannin.* Plano: Republic of Texas Press, 2000.

Campbell, Randolph B. *Sam Houston and the American Southwest.* Library of American Biography. New York: HarperCollins College, 1993.

Cantrell, Gregg. *Stephen F. Austin: Empresario of Texas.* New Haven, CT: Yale University Press, 1999.

Caruso, A. Brooke. *The Mexican Spy Company: United States Covert Operations in Mexico, 1845–48.* Jefferson, NC: McFarland, 1991.

Casdorph, Paul D. *Prince John Magruder: His Life and Campaigns.* New York: Wiley, 1996.

Cashion, Ty. *A Texas Frontier: The Clear Fork Country and Fort Griffin, 1849–1887.* Norman: University of Oklahoma Press, 1996.

Bibliography

Chalfant, William Y. *Dangerous Passage: The Santa Fe Trail and the Mexican War.* Illustrated by Mont David Williams. Norman: University of Oklahoma Press, 1994.

Chance, Joseph E. *Jefferson Davis's Mexican War Regiment.* Jackson: University Press of Mississippi, 1991.

Clarke, Dwight L. *Stephen Watts Kearny: Soldier of the West.* Norman: University of Oklahoma Press, 1961.

Clary, David A. *Eagles and Empire: The United States, Mexico, and the Struggle for a Continent.* New York: Bantam Books, 2009.

Clendenen, Clarence C. *Blood on the Border: The United States Army and the Mexican Irregulars.* The Macmillan Wars of the United States. Louis Morton, general editor. New York: Macmillan, 1969.

Connor, Seymour V., and Odie B. Faulk. *North America Divided: The Mexican War, 1846–1848.* New York: Oxford University Press, 1971.

Cotner, Thomas Ewing. *The Military and Political Career of José Joaquín de Herrera, 1792–1854.* The University of Texas Institute of Latin-American Studies, Latin-American Studies 7. Austin: University of Texas Press, 1949.

Crawford, Mark. *Encyclopedia of the Mexican-American War.* Santa Barbara, CA: ABC-CLIO, 1999.

Cutrer, Thomas W. *Ben McCulloch and the Frontier Military Tradition.* Chapel Hill: University of North Carolina Press, 1993.

Davis, William C. *Three Roads to the Alamo: The Lives and Fortunes of David Crockett, James Bowie, and William Barret Travis.* New York: HarperCollins, 1998.

Dawson, Joseph G., III. *Doniphan's Epic March: The 1st Missouri Volunteers in the Mexican War.* Lawrence: University Press of Kansas, 1999.

Dawson, Joseph Martin. *José Antonio Navarro: Co-creator of Texas.* Waco: Baylor University Press, 1969.

del Castillo, Richard Griswold. *The Treaty of Guadalupe Hidalgo: A Legacy of Conflict.* Norman: University of Oklahoma Press, 1990.

DeLay, Brian. *War of a Thousand Deserts: Indian Raids and the U.S.-Mexican War.* New Haven, CT: Yale University Press, 2008.

DePalo, William A., Jr. *The Mexican National Army, 1822–1852.* Texas A&M University Military History Series 52. College Station: Texas A&M University Press, 1997.

Dillon, Lester R., Jr. *American Artillery in the Mexican War, 1846–1847.* Austin, TX: Presidial, 1975.

Dillon, Richard H. *Fool's Gold: The Decline and Fall of Captain John Sutter of California.* New York: Coward-McCann, 1967.

Dimmick, Gregg J. *Sea of Mud: The Retreat of the Mexican Army after San Jacinto; An Archeological Investigation.* Austin: Texas State Historical Association, 2004.

Doña Ana Historical Society, ed. *The Treaty of Guadalupe Hidalgo, 1848.* Las Cruces, NM: Doña Ana County Historical Society and Yucca Tree Press, 1999.

Douglas, C. L. *James Bowie: The Life of a Bravo.* Dallas, TX: Banks, Upshaw, 1944.

Eisenhower, John S. D. *Agent of Destiny: The Life and Times of General Winfield Scott.* New York: Free Press, 1997.

Elliott, Charles Winslow. *Winfield Scott: The Soldier and the Man.* New York: Macmillan, 1937.

Essin, Emmett M. *Shavetails and Bell Sharps: The History of the U.S. Army Mule.* Lincoln: University of Nebraska Press, 1997.

Faulk, Odie B. *Too Far North . . . Too Far South.* Los Angeles: Westernlore, 1967.

Flores, Richard R. *Remembering the Alamo: Memory, Modernity, and the Master Symbol.* Austin: University of Texas Press, 2002.

Foos, Paul. *A Short, Offhand, Killing Affair: Soldiers and Social Conflict during the Mexican-American War.* Chapel Hill: University of North Carolina Press, 2002.

Francaviglia, Richard V., and Douglas W. Richmond, eds. *Dueling Eagles: Reinterpreting the U.S.-Mexican War, 1846–1848.* Fort Worth: Texas Christian University Press, 2000.

Frazer, Robert W. *Forts of the West, Military Forts and Presidios and Posts Commonly Called Forts West of the Mississippi River to 1898.* Norman: University of Oklahoma Press, 1965.

Frazier, Donald D., ed. *The United States and Mexico at War: Nineteenth-Century Expansionism and Conflict.* New York: Macmillan, 1998.

Frémont, John Charles. *The Expeditions of John Charles Frémont.* 3 vols. Edited by Donald Jackson and Mary Lee Spence. Urbana: University of Illinois Press, 1970–1980.

Friend, Llerena. *Sam Houston: The Great Designer.* Austin: University of Texas Press, 1954.

Gambrell, Herbert. *Anson Jones: The Last President of Texas.* Garden City, NY: Doubleday, 1948.

Greer, James Kimmins. *Colonel Jack Hays: Texas Frontier Leader and California Builder.* College Station: Texas A&M University Press, 1987.

Griffen, William B. *Apaches at War and Peace: The Janos Presidio, 1750–1858.* Albuquerque: University of New Mexico Press, 1988.

Griffen, William B. *Utmost Good Faith: Patterns of Apache-Mexican Hostilities in Northern Chihuahua Border Warfare, 1821–1848.* Albuquerque: University of New Mexico Press, 1989.

Grivas, Theodore. *Military Governments in California, 1846–1850.* Glendale, CA: Arthur H. Clark, 1963.

Hackenburg, Randy W. *Pennsylvania in the War with Mexico: The Volunteer Regiments.* Shippensburg, PA: White Mane, 1992.

Haley, James W. *Sam Houston.* Norman: University of Oklahoma Press, 2002.

Hansen, Todd, ed. *The Alamo Reader: A Study in History.* Mechanicsburg, PA: Stackpole, 2003.

Harden, Stephen L. *Texian Iliad: A Military History of the Texas Revolution, 1835–1836.* Illustrated by Gary S. Zaboly. Austin: University of Texas Press, 1994.

Harlow, Neal. *California Conquered: War and Peace on the Pacific, 1846–1850.* Berkeley: University of California Press, 1982.

Hatley, Allen G. *The Indian Wars in Stephen F. Austin's Texas Colony, 1822–1835.* Austin, TX: Eakin, 2001.

Haynes, Sam W. *Soldiers of Misfortune: The Somervell and Mier Expeditions.* Austin: University of Texas Press, 1990.

Henson, Margaret Swett. *Juan Davis Bradburn: A Reappraisal of the Mexican Commander of the Anahuac.* College Station: Texas A&M University Press, 1982.

Hietala, Thomas R. *Manifest Design: Anxious Aggrandizement in Late Jacksonian America.* Ithaca, NY: Cornell University Press, 1985.

Hine, Robert V. *Bartlett's West: Drawing the Mexican Boundary.* New Haven, CT: Yale University Press for the Amon Carter Museum, 1968.

Hogan, Michael. *The Irish Soldiers of Mexico.* Guadalajara: Fondo Editorial Universitario, 1997.

Hughes, Nathaniel Cheairs, Jr., and Roy P. Stonesifer, Jr. *The Life and Wars of Gideon J. Pillow.* Chapel Hill: University of North Carolina Press, 1993.

Hughes, W. J. *Rebellious Ranger: Rip Ford and the Old Southwest.* Norman: University of Oklahoma Press, 1964.

Hughes, William W. *Archibald Yell.* Fayetteville: University of Arkansas Press, 1988.

Hyslop, Stephen G. *Bound for Santa Fe: The Road to New Mexico and the American Conquest, 1806–1848.* Norman: University of Oklahoma Press, 2002.

Jenkins, John H., and Kenneth Kesselus. *Edward Burleson: Texas Frontier Leader.* Austin, TX: Jenkins, 1990.

Johannsen, Robert W. *To the Halls of the Montezumas: The Mexican War in the American Imagination.* New York: Oxford University Press, 1985.

Johannsen, Robert W., John M. Belohlavek, Thomas R. Hietala, Sam W. Haynes, and Robert E. May. *Manifest Destiny and Empire: American Antebellum Expansion.* Edited by Sam W. Haynes and Christopher Morris. The Walter Prescott Webb Memorial Lectures 31. College Station: Texas A&M University Press, 1997.

Johnston, Abraham R., Marcellus B. Edwards, and Philip G. Ferguson. *Marching with the Army of the West, 1846–1848.* The Southwest Historical Series 4. Edited by Ralph P. Bieber. Glendale, CA: Arthur H. Clarke, 1936.

Jones, Howard, and Donald A. Rakestraw. *Prologue to Manifest Destiny: Anglo-American Relations in the 1840s.* Wilmington, DE: Scholarly Resources, 1997.

Kieffer, Chester L. *Maligned General: The Biography of Thomas Sidney Jesup.* San Rafael, CA: Presidio, 1979.

Lander, Ernest McPherson, Jr. *Reluctant Imperialists: Calhoun, the South Carolinians, and the Mexican War.* Baton Rouge: Louisiana State University Press, 1980.

Launius, Roger D. *Alexander William Doniphan: Portrait of a Missouri Moderate.* Columbia: University of Missouri Press, 1997.

Lavender, David. *Bent's Fort.* Garden City, NY: Doubleday, 1954.

Lavender, David. *Climax at Buena Vista: The American Campaigns in Northeastern Mexico, 1846–47.* New York: Lippincott, 1966.

Leckie, William H., and Shirley A. Leckie. *The Buffalo Soldiers: A Narrative of the Black Cavalry in the West.*

Bibliography

Rev. ed. Norman: University of Oklahoma Press, 2003.

Levinson, Irving W. *Wars within Wars: Mexican Guerillas, Domestic Elites, and the United States of America, 1846–1848.* Fort Worth: Texas Christian University Press, 2005.

Lindley, Thomas Ricks. *Alamo Traces: New Evidence and New Conclusions.* Lanham, MD: Republic of Texas Press, 2003.

Lofaro, Michael A., ed. *Davy Crockett: The Man, the Legend, the Legacy, 1786–1986.* Knoxville: University of Tennessee Press, 1985.

Lofaro, Michael A., and Joe Cummings, eds. *Crockett at Two Hundred: New Perspectives on the Man and the Myth.* Knoxville: University of Tennessee Press, 1989.

Long, David F. *Sailor-Diplomat: A Biography of Commodore James Biddle, 1783–1848.* Boston: Northeastern University Press, 1983.

Long, Jeff. *Duel of Eagles: The Mexican and U.S. Fight for the Alamo.* New York: William Morrow, 1990.

Lord, Walter. *A Time to Stand: The Epic of the Alamo.* Lincoln: University of Nebraska Press, 1978.

Marshall, Bruce. *Uniforms of the Alamo and the Texas Revolution and the Men Who Wore Them, 1835–1836.* Atglen, PA: Schiffer, 2003.

Marti, Werner H. *Messenger of Destiny: The California Adventures, 1846–1847, of Archibald H. Gillespie, U.S. Marine Corps.* San Francisco: John Howell, 1960.

Martínez, Oscar J., ed. *U.S.-Mexico Borderlands: Historical and Contemporary Perspectives.* Wilmington, DE: Scholarly Resources, 1996.

McCaffrey, James M. *Army of Manifest Destiny: The American Soldier in the Mexican War, 1846–1848.* New York: New York University Press, 1992.

McFarland, Philip. *Sea Dangers: The Affair of the Somers.* New York: Schocken, 1985.

Meyer, Jack Allen. *South Carolina in the Mexican War: A History of the Palmetto Regiment of Volunteers, 1846–1917.* Columbia: South Carolina Department of Archives and History, 1996.

Miller, Robert Ryal. *Shamrock and Sword: The Saint Patrick's Battalion in the U.S.-Mexican War.* Norman: University of Oklahoma Press, 1989.

Minge, Ward Alan. *Acoma: Pueblo in the Sky.* Albuquerque: University of New Mexico Press, 1976.

Moore, Stephen L. *Eighteen Minutes: The Battle of San Jacinto and the Texas Independence Campaign.* Lanham, MD: Republic of Texas Press, 2004.

Moorhead, Max L. *The Presidio: Bastion of the Spanish Borderlands.* Norman: University of Oklahoma Press, 1975.

Morison, Samuel Eliot. *"Old Bruin": Commodore Matthew C. Perry, 1794–1858.* Boston: Little, Brown, 1967.

Morton, Ohland. *Terán and Texas: A Study in Texas-Mexico Relations.* Austin: Texas State Historical Association, 1948.

Nance, Joseph Milton. *After San Jacinto: The Texas-Mexican Frontier, 1836–1841.* Austin: University of Texas Press, 1963.

Nance, Joseph Milton. *Attack and Counter-Attack: The Texas-Mexican Frontier, 1842.* Austin: University of Texas Press, 1964.

Norris, L. David, James C. Milligan, and Odie B. Faulk. *William H. Emory: Soldier-Scientist.* Tucson: University of Arizona Press, 1998.

Nye, Russell B. *George Bancroft: Brahmin Rebel.* New York: Knopf, 1944.

Ohrt, Wallace. *Defiant Peacemaker: Nicholas Trist in the Mexican War.* College Station: Texas A&M University Press, 1998.

Oliva, Leo E. *Soldiers on the Santa Fe Trail.* Norman: University of Oklahoma Press, 1967.

Owsley, Frank Lawrence, Jr., and Gene A. Smith. *Filibusters and Expansionists: Jeffersonian Manifest Destiny, 1800–1821.* Tuscaloosa: University of Alabama Press, 1997.

Perkins, Dexter. *The Monroe Doctrine, 1826–1867.* Baltimore: Johns Hopkins University Press, 1933.

Peskin, Allan. *Winfield Scott and the Profession of Arms.* Kent, OH: Kent State University Press, 2003.

Peterson, Norma Lois. *The Presidencies of William Henry Harrison and John Tyler.* Lawrence: University Press of Kansas, 1989.

Pinheiro, John C. *Manifest Ambition: James K. Polk and Civil-Military Relations during the Mexican War.* Westport, CT: Praeger Security International, 2007.

Pletcher, David M. *The Diplomacy of Annexation: Texas, Oregon, and the Mexican War.* Columbia: University of Missouri Press, 1973.

Price, Glenn W. *Origins of the War with Mexico: The Polk-Stockton Intrigue.* Austin: University of Texas Press, 1967.

Ramírez, José Fernando. *Mexico during the War with the United States.* Edited by Walter V. Scholes. Columbia: University of Missouri Press, 1950.

Rebert, Paula. *La Gran Línea: Mapping the United States–Mexico Boundary, 1849–1857.* Austin: University of Texas Press, 2001.

Regnery, Dorothy F. *The Battle of Santa Clara, January 2, 1847.* San Jose: Smith and McKay Printing, 1978.

Ricketts, Norma Baldwin. *The Mormon Battalion: U.S. Army of the West, 1846–1848.* Logan: Utah State University Press, 1996.

Roberts, Randy, and James S. Olson. *A Line in the Sand: The Alamo in Blood and Memory.* New York: Free Press, 2001.

Rodriguez, Jaime E., and Kathryn Vincent. *Myths, Misdeeds, and Misunderstandings: The Roots of Conflict in U.S.-Mexican Relations.* Wilmington, DE: Scholarly Resources, 1997.

Rolle, Andrew. *John Charles Frémont: Character as Destiny.* Norman: University of Oklahoma Press, 1991.

Rosebush, Waldo E. *Frontier Steel: The Men and Their Weapons.* Appleton, WI: C. C. Nelson, 1958.

Rosenus, Alan. *General M. G. Vallejo and the Advent of the Americans: A Biography.* Albuquerque: University of New Mexico Press, 1995.

Salas, Elizabeth. *Soldaderas in the Mexican Military: Myth and History.* Austin: University of Texas Press, 1990.

Samora, Julian, Joe Bernal, and Albert Peña. *Gunpowder Justice: A Reassessment of the Texas Rangers.* Notre Dame, IN: University of Notre Dame Press, 1979.

Santoni, Pedro. *Mexicans at Arms:* Puro *Federalists and the Politics of War, 1845–1848.* Fort Worth: Texas Christian University Press, 1996.

Schlicke, Carl P. *General George Wright: Guardian of the Pacific Coast.* Norman: University of Oklahoma Press, 1988.

Schmitz, Joseph William. *Texan Statecraft, 1836–1845.* San Antonio: Naylor, 1941.

Schroeder, John H. *Matthew Calbraith Perry: Antebellum Sailor and Diplomat.* Annapolis, MD: Naval Institute Press, 2001.

Schroeder, John H. *Mr. Polk's War: American Opposition and Dissent, 1846–1848.* 2 vols. Madison: University of Wisconsin Press, 1973.

Shackford, James Atkins. *David Crockett: The Man and the Legend.* Edited by John B. Shackford. Chapel Hill: University of North Carolina Press, 1956.

Silver, James W. *Edmund Pendleton Gaines, Frontier General.* Baton Rouge: Louisiana State University Press, 1949.

Singletary, Otis A. *The Mexican War.* The Chicago History of American Civilization. Edited by Daniel J. Boorstin. Chicago: University of Chicago Press, 1960.

Smith, Gene A. *Thomas Ap Catesby Jones: Commodore of Manifest Destiny.* Annapolis, MD: Naval Institute Press, 2000.

Smith, George Winston, and Charles Judah, eds. *Chronicles of the Gringos: The United States Army in the Mexican War, 1846–1848.* Albuquerque: University of New Mexico Press, 1968.

Smith, Justin H. *The War with Mexico.* 2 vols. New York: Macmillan, 1919.

Spellman, Paul N. *Forgotten Texas Leader: Hugh McLeod and the Texan Santa Fe Expedition.* College Station: Texas A&M University Press, 1999.

Spurlin, Charles D. *Texas Volunteers in the Mexican War.* Austin, TX: Eakin, 1998.

Stegmaier, Mark J. *Texas, New Mexico, and the Compromise of 1850: Boundary Dispute and Sectional Crisis.* Kent, OH: Kent State University Press, 1996.

Thompson, Frank. *The Alamo.* Denton: University of North Texas Press, 2005.

Tinkle, Lon. *13 Days to Glory: The Siege of the Alamo.* College Station: Texas A&M University Press, 1985.

Tutorow, Norman E. *Texas Annexation and the Mexican War: A Political Study of the Old Northwest.* Palo Alto, CA: Chadwick House, 1978.

Wallace, Edward S. *General William Jenkins Worth: Monterrey's Forgotten Hero.* Dallas, TX: Southern Methodist University Press, 1953.

Weber, David J. *The Mexican Frontier, 1821–1846: The American Southwest under Mexico.* Albuquerque: University of New Mexico Press, 1982.

Weems, John Edward. *Dream of Empire: A Human History of the Republic of Texas, 1836–1846.* New York: Simon and Schuster, 1971.

Weems, John Edward. *To Conquer a Peace: The War between the United States and Mexico.* Garden City, NY: Doubleday, 1974.

Bibliography

Welles, Tom Henderson. *Commodore Moore and the Texas Navy.* Austin: University of Texas Press, 1960.

Wessels, William L. *Born to Be a Soldier: The Military Career of William Wing Loring.* Fort Worth: Texas Christian University Press, 1971.

Winders, Richard Bruce. *Mr. Polk's Army: The American Military Experience in the Mexican War.* College Station: Texas A&M University Press, 1997.

Winders, Richard Bruce. *Sacrificed at the Alamo: Tragedy and Triumph in the Texas Revolution.* Abilene, TX: State House Press, 2004.

MATTHEW J. WAYMAN

BROTHER FIGHTING BROTHER

The American Civil War and the Era of Reconstruction, 1850–1877

OVERVIEW

The American Civil War was a struggle to determine whether the United States would survive as a nation and if so what sort of nation it would be. In 1860, Republican candidate Abraham Lincoln won election to the presidency on a platform calling for a ban on the further spread of slavery into western territories where it did not already exist. Realizing that containment would mean the eventual end of the institution of slavery, a majority of political leaders in seven Deep South states—South Carolina, Georgia, Florida, Alabama, Mississippi, Louisiana, and Texas—did not wait for Lincoln's inauguration but hurried to declare their states no longer part of the United States. Lame duck U.S. president James Buchanan did nothing to stop them, and in February 1861 representatives of the seceding states organized themselves into a new government that they called the Confederate States of America. They selected Jefferson Davis of Mississippi as their president and inaugurated him before Lincoln took the oath of office as president of the United States on March 4, 1861.

Lincoln recognized and had often stated publicly that under normal circumstances he had no constitutional authority to end slavery in the states in which it already existed, but he believed that slavery would eventually die out if contained. He also rejected the validity of secession—the idea that any state could leave the Union any time it wanted for any reason or no reason at all. Lincoln believed that such a concept would amount to anarchy and would spell the doom of self-government by demonstrating that a self-governing republic such as the United States was bound to disintegrate. Lincoln therefore used his inaugural address to assure Southerners that he would not take the initiative in seeking to end slavery where it already existed but that he would do his best to maintain federal authority in the rebellious states by holding on to U.S. installations there.

Only three such facilities remained that had not been seized by secessionists: Fort Pickens outside Pensacola Florida, Fort Jefferson in Florida's Dry Tortugas, and Fort Sumter in the harbor of Charleston, South Carolina. Sumter soon became the flash point. South Carolina was dominated by proslavery extremists who demanded that the Confederate government eject the small U.S. garrison from the fort. When Lincoln declined to remove the few dozen men and announced his intention of replenishing their nearly exhausted supply of food, Jefferson Davis telegraphed from the first Confederate capital in Montgomery to his general commanding at Charleston, Brigadier General Pierre G. T. Beauregard, an order to take the fort. At Beauregard's order, Confederate guns around the harbor opened fire at 4:00 a.m. on the morning of April 12, 1861. After 36 hours of bombardment, the fort surrendered.

With war now a reality, both sides called for volunteers to form large armies. Four more states of the upper South—Virginia, North Carolina, Tennessee, and Arkansas—faced with the necessity of fighting either for the Union or for the Confederacy, chose the latter. Three border slave states—Missouri, Kentucky, and Maryland—each experienced sharp internal divisions and provided recruits for both sides' armies. The newly expanded

Confederacy now moved its capital to Richmond, Virginia. Richmond was at that time the most important industrial center in the South, and Virginia had a large population and also carried the prestige of having been the home of such of the nation's founders as George Washington, James Madison, and Thomas Jefferson. Also, its proximity to the U.S. capital in Washington, D.C., made it a natural choice for the Confederate capital.

An initial Union attempt to take Richmond resulted in an embarrassing failure at the July 21, 1861, First Battle of Bull Run (Manassas). Armies of ill-trained volunteers, numbering between 30,000 and 35,000 on each side, clashed along a stream named Bull Run 25 miles southwest of Washington that was not far from an important railroad junction known as Manassas. Taking the offensive, the Union army commanded by Brigadier General Irvin McDowell enjoyed early success but then lost momentum. Stalled by a stout defensive stand led in part by Confederate brigadier general Thomas J. Jackson, who that day won his nickname "Stonewall," the Union army made a disorderly retreat. Many Southerners thought they had won the war, but Northerners buckled down to what they now realized would be a long and hard process of restoring the Union—although none then guessed how long and how hard it would be.

Union offensives west of the Appalachians scored major successes early in 1862. Cooperating with naval forces on the Mississippi, Cumberland, and Tennessee Rivers and led by superior generals such as Brigadier General Ulysses S. Grant, Union armies advanced steadily into the heartland of the Confederacy. On February 6, 1862, Grant, in cooperation with a gunboat flotilla under U.S. Navy flag officer Andrew H. Foote, captured Fort Henry on the Tennessee River, opening that stream to Union vessels. Ten days later, Grant and Foote again teamed up to capture Fort Donelson on the Cumberland, not only opening that river as they had previously done the Tennessee but also helping to bring the fall of Nashville and capturing some 15,000 troops that the Confederacy badly needed.

In an all-out attempt to reverse the Confederacy's waning fortunes in its heartland, General Albert Sidney Johnston led a major counterattack against Grant's army as it lay encamped on the banks of the Tennessee at Pittsburg Landing, 20 miles northeast of Corinth, Mississippi. The armies numbered about 40,000 on each side and were nearly as green as those at Bull Run. The resulting battle, fought April 6–7, 1862, and also known as the Battle of Shiloh for a church building that stood in the midst of the carnage, introduced the nation to bloodshed on a scale it had never previously imagined in any of its wars. Johnston died early in the battle, and Grant held on to his foothold on the west bank of the Tennessee. The Confederacy never really recovered from the losses in territory and personnel that it suffered as a result of its losses at Forts Henry and Donelson and at Shiloh.

Only in Virginia did Union forces seem incapable of making progress. Much was hoped from the dashing young Major General George B. McClellan, who trained and organized the largest of the Union's armies, naming it the Army of the Potomac. Yet McClellan did not seem eager to advance. When he did lead his beloved army—very slowly—to the outskirts of Richmond in the Peninsula Campaign in the spring of 1862, he proved hesitant and irresolute, retreating in the face of attacks from Confederate general Robert E. Lee, whom Davis had recently appointed to command in Virginia in place of Joseph E. Johnston, who had fallen badly wounded in one of the first battles of the campaign. From June 25 to July 1, 1862, Lee pushed McClellan back from the outskirts of Richmond to a position 25 miles farther away.

Lincoln's immense patience was finally wearing thin with McClellan's uninspired generalship, overcaution, and propensity to give uninvited political advice. In the wake of his failed campaign against Richmond, McClellan, a staunch proponent of slavery, wrote Lincoln a letter arguing that it would be morally wrong to take any step toward freeing the slaves. Lincoln's thoughts were very much in a different direction, although for the moment he did not make them public.

At the outset of the war, Lincoln had hoped that the majority of white Southerners had merely been led astray by their strident proslavery political leaders and would return to their allegiance to the United States if they met firm but restrained Union pressure.

By mid-1862, it was becoming increasingly clear that this was not the case. In the face of Southern intransigence, Lincoln determined to raise the stakes and prepared to invoke his war powers as commander in chief to issue the Preliminary Emancipation Proclamation. Persuaded by his cabinet not to issue the document in the wake of McClellan's defeats outside of Richmond, Lincoln placed the document in his desk drawer and awaited a Union victory.

Hoping to find a general whose heart was in the cause, Lincoln shifted command of the Union's troops in Virginia to Major General John Pope. The new general, however, met with defeat at the August 29–30, 1862, Second Battle of Bull Run (Manassas) partially because of his own mistakes, partially because of the prowess of Lee and Jackson, and partially because McClellan and Army of the Potomac generals, loyal to him and eager to see the new commander fail, undermined Pope.

Lee took advantage of the momentum he had gained in the Second Battle of Bull Run and led his army across the Potomac into Maryland, threatening Pennsylvania as well as Union control of Baltimore, with its strongly pro-Confederate population, and even the national capital. Lee believed that the Army of the Potomac was demoralized and would not fight. Lincoln feared as much and believed that only the still-popular McClellan could restore the troops' fighting spirit. Back in command, McClellan received a windfall when a copy of Lee's plans for the campaign fell into his hands, revealing that Lee had his army spread out and vulnerable. Characteristically McClellan moved too slowly, and Lee was able to reunite his army to meet the Federals along Antietam Creek. There on September 17, 1862, the two armies fought to a tactical draw that, with a total of 3,654 killed, 17,292 wounded, and 1,771 missing or captured on both sides, still stands as the bloodiest day of combat in American history.

Despite its inconclusive results on the ground, the Battle of Antietam forced Lee to withdraw his army from Maryland and thus could reasonably be counted as a Union victory. This gave Lincoln the opportunity for which he had been waiting. Five days after the battle, he issued the Preliminary Emancipation Proclamation, declaring that all slaves in areas still in rebellion against the United States as of January 1, 1863, would be forever free. On that date, Lincoln followed through with the actual Emancipation Proclamation, changing the war for Union and eventual emancipation into a war for Union and immediate emancipation.

Union frustration continued in the small and indecisive yet prestigious eastern theater of the war. When McClellan again proved too slow to accomplish anything, Lincoln sacked him in favor of Major General Ambrose Burnside. Although an intelligent and dedicated man, Burnside blundered into a lopsided defeat at the Battle of Fredericksburg (December 13, 1862). When Burnside continued to be ineffective as a commander and unrest began to grow within the army, Lincoln replaced him with Major General Joseph Hooker.

Hooker had a reputation as a fighting general, but he was brash and had recently made a statement to the effect that what the country needed was a dictator. Lincoln alluded to this in a now-famous letter to Hooker shortly after giving him command of the Army of the Potomac. "Of course it was not for this," Lincoln wrote, "but in spite of it, that I have given you the command. Only those generals who gain success can set up dictators. What I now ask of you is military success, and I will risk the dictatorship." But Hooker could not deliver military success. With a good plan and the Army of the Potomac stronger than ever, Hooker in late April 1863 advanced against Lee with the quip "May God have mercy on General Lee, for I will have none." Almost as soon as his troops made contact with Lee's, however, Hooker seemed to slip into a sort of mental paralysis and gave up the initiative. Lee and Jackson then combined to win their greatest victory over him in the Battle of Chancellorsville (May 1–4, 1863). In a somber note for the Confederacy, however, Jackson died several days later of injuries received when he was accidently shot by his own men while returning from a reconnaissance.

Lee had for some time been planning another foray across the Potomac, and as soon as he could get his army ready and gain the somewhat hesitant approval of Jefferson Davis and the Confederate cabinet, Lee

Union soldiers in the trenches during the June 1864–April 1865 siege of the transportation hub of Petersburg, Virginia. Eventual Confederate abandonment of Petersburg and Richmond led to the surrender of the Army of Northern Virginia at Appomattox Court House and the end of the war. (National Archives)

in June 1863 marched through Maryland and into Pennsylvania, plundering the rich farmland and destroying bridges and railroads along his way. When Hooker seemed reluctant to come to grips with Lee, Lincoln replaced him with Major General George G. Meade. The two armies met on July 1 at Gettysburg in southern Pennsylvania and fought a three-day battle.

Miscalculations by Lee, lack of cooperation by his subordinates, and a respectable performance by Meade combined to give the Union its first clear-cut—if largely hollow—victory in the East. Lee's army escaped back into Virginia with enough booty to feed it for several months as well as a number of African American civilians, captured in Pennsylvania and destined to be sold into slavery in the South.

While Union efforts in Virginia had remained mired in futility for the first two years of the war,

west of the Appalachians, Union forces continued to strike punishing body blows to the Confederacy. Simultaneous with the Union victory at Gettysburg, Grant won a far more significant triumph during the Second Vicksburg Campaign (April–July 4, 1863), sundering the Confederacy, reopening the Mississippi River to Union commerce, and capturing 30,000 soldiers that the Confederacy could ill afford to lose. The Union army of Major General William S. Rosecrans maneuvered the Confederates out of the rest of Tennessee and weathered a concerted counterattack in the August–September 1863 Chickamauga Campaign. Union forces in the western theater then combined, under Grant's command, to finish the year's fighting with a dramatic victory in Tennessee in the Battles for Chattanooga (November 23–25).

For the 1864 offensive, Lincoln gave Grant overall command of all Union armies. Grant personally accompanied Meade's army in Virginia, virtually commanding it himself, while Major General William T. Sherman, acting under Grant's orders, led the western Union armies in a drive against Atlanta, Georgia. Grant and Sherman were relentless in their advances, and the Confederate defenders fought desperately. Both armies reached the outskirts of their target cities—Richmond and Atlanta—by midsummer, but casualty lists were long, and Northern civilians began to despair of ever winning the war. Lincoln feared that he might lose that autumn's presidential election to the Democratic candidate, none other than failed Union general George McClellan running on a platform that called the war a failure.

Then on September 2, 1864, Sherman took Atlanta. That success, along with minor Union victories on other fronts, contradicted the Democratic platform's claim that the war could not be won. Lincoln swept into a second term with a resounding win in the November election.

In the months that followed, Lee's army continued its dogged defense of Richmond, but each day Grant pressed it further toward its breaking point. Elsewhere, Confederate power was already near collapse. The Confederacy's main army in the western theater suffered a crippling defeat in a desperate last-gasp offensive into Tennessee, losing the November 29–December 27, 1864, Franklin and Nashville Campaign. Meanwhile Sherman, with most of his forces, marched through Georgia and then the Carolinas, appropriating food and livestock and destroying railroads, depots, and sometimes more. When spring came, Sherman's western armies were moving northward through North Carolina on their way to join Grant in finishing off Lee. Before they could arrive, on April 2, 1865, Lee's lines broke, and Richmond fell. Lee's army fled westward toward the mountains but never reached them. Lee surrendered on April 9, 1865, at Appomattox Court House, Virginia. By that time, his army had become the only truly effective fighting force left to the Confederacy. With it gone, few Confederates seemed to believe that there was any point in fighting on. The remaining remnants of Confederate forces surrendered over the next few weeks.

STEVEN E. WOODWORTH

BROTHER FIGHTING BROTHER

The American Civil War and the Era of Reconstruction, 1850–1877

TIMELINE

April 19, 1850

Clayton-Bulwer Treaty. President James K. Polk is interested in construction of a transisthmian canal across Central America. Polk dispatches special emissary Elijah Hise to Nicaragua to ascertain British intentions in this regard. Responding to an appeal by settlers in British Honduras (present-day Belize), the British government had established a protectorate over the Mosquito Coast claimed by Nicaragua and had driven Nicaraguans from it and forced the Nicaraguan government in January 1848 to renounce all claim to the area of the San Juan River, the intended eastern terminus of a transisthmian canal proposed by the United States.

Hise concludes a treaty with the Nicaraguan government that gives the U.S. government exclusive rights to build and to fortify a canal across the isthmus in return for a U.S. guarantee of the neutrality of the isthmus and protection of Nicaraguan sovereignty. Polk never submits this treaty to the Senate, so it does not enter into force. A similar treaty is negotiated in 1848 by E. G. Squier (an emissary sent by President Zachary Taylor), who also secured for the United States Tiger Island in the Gulf of Fonseca, at the western terminus of the proposed transisthmian canal route. In response, in October 1849 the British seize Tiger Island, rejecting Squier's contention that it now belongs to the United States.

Although he informs the British government that the United States refuses to recognize British control of the Mosquito Coast or the San Juan River, U.S. secretary of state John M. Clayton initiates discussions with British minister to the United States Sir Henry Lytton Bulwer. Their talks result in the Clayton-Bulwer Treaty. The British make the most concessions. Both nations agree to never obtain, exercise exclusive control over, or fortify a transisthmian ship canal; they guarantee the neutrality and security of such a canal; they agree that such a canal will be open to the nationals of both countries on terms of equality; and they pledge not to colonize, occupy, or exercise dominion over any part of Central America.

The Clayton-Bulwer Treaty of April 19, 1850, is ratified by the U.S. Senate in a vote of 42 to 10, with the ratifications formally exchanged on July 5, 1850. It remains in effect until superseded by the Hay-Pauncefote Treaty of 1901.

May 1850–June 1851

Mariposa War. Drawn by the discovery of gold in California, by the spring of 1850 a large number of whites have settled along the Merced, Fresno, and San Joaquin Rivers in the Yosemite Valley region of central California. Local tribes, particularly the Yosemites, Chowchillas, and Nootchus, resent this encroachment on their lands and decide to act.

In May, Yosemites attack a trading post operated by James Savage along the Merced. During the next six months a coalition of tribes led by Yosemite chief Tenieya mounts attacks and ambushes against the settlers. Savage organizes an opposing alliance of tribes under the leadership of José Juarez, chief of the Tularenos, but when Savage slights Juarez, the latter joins the effort to expel the whites. In December 1850, California governor Peter Burnett authorizes U.S. Indian agent Adam Johnston to try to negotiate an end to hostilities. While recognizing the justice of the native position, Johnston reluctantly concludes that force will be necessary.

James Burney, the sheriff of Mariposa, organizes a militia group known as the Mariposa Battalion and in early January 1851 attacks a native encampment near present-day Oakhurst. The Indians suffer about 40 casualties; the Mariposa Battalion loses 6 men. Burney requests additional manpower from new governor John McDougal, and by the end of January the battalion numbers more than 200 men.

In February 1851, Washington dispatches three commissioners to convince the warring tribes to sign treaties and settle on reservations. At the same time, Savage replaces Burney as commander of the Mariposa Battalion. During February to June, it mounts operations along the Sierra Nevada, including three separate expeditions up Mariposa Creek, the Fresno River, and the San Joaquin River. One by one the tribes are subdued, and their leaders agree to treaties negotiated with the commissioners. The last to come to terms are the Yosemites. The war ends in June 1851, and the Mariposa Battalion is disbanded in July.

The treaties bring the removal of the tribes from the central Sierra Nevada area and open it for settlement. Although they were to receive reservations totaling more than 8 million acres of good land, opposition in the state legislature and the U.S. House of Representatives brings major changes in those agreements, and the Native Americans receive few of the promised benefits.

September 9–10, 1850

Congress passes five laws constituting the so-called Compromise of 1850. These provide for the admission of California into the Union as a free state, the redrawing of the Texas boundary to exclude New Mexico as a territory without restriction regarding slavery, establishment of the Utah Territory under identical provisions to that of New Mexico, the Fugitive Slave Act that places fugitive slaves cases under federal jurisdiction and provides for special commissioners to return runaway slaves to their masters (citizens aiding such fugitives are to be subject to arrest, fines, and imprisonment), and abolition of the slave trade in the District of Columbia.

Many hail this legislation as permanently settling the issue of slavery in the United States, but its principal effect seems to have been the breakup of the Whig Party.

August 6, 1851

The U.S. Navy sloop *Dale* (16 guns), under Commander William C. Pearson, arrives off Johanna Island in the Indian Ocean, and Pearson demands an indemnity from King Selim for the earlier temporary detention of a merchant ship captain. When Selim refuses, Pearson orders the *Dale* to shell the town. The king pays the indemnity the next day.

June 1–October 29, 1852

Raousset's Filibustering Expedition into northern Mexico. Mexico is in a chaotic state, and this leads to a number of incursions into that country by private individuals from the United States known as filibusters. In December 1850 French investors, headed by French ambassador to Mexico André Levasseur, persuade Governor José de Agular and the assembly of the northwestern Mexican state of Sonora to grant their Franco-Mexican Restauradora del Mineral de Arizona Mining Company a mining concession from the 31st Parallel to the border of California and Arizona. Although the Mexican national congress disavows the concession, it provides an excuse for armed intervention that the weak Mexican government cannot prevent.

Count Gaston de Raousset-Boulbon, having arrived in California from France and having failed in a series of gold-mining enterprises, recruits a filibustering expedition into northern Sonora to stake out a claim for the aforementioned Franco-Mexican company in Indian country to the Sonoran interior. Securing 600 mercenaries (260 of them Frenchmen) in San Francisco, California, on June 1, 1853, Raousset arrives at the Mexican port of Guaymas in southwestern Sonora.

Raousset organizes his men into six infantry companies, one cavalry company, and an artillery company with four small guns. On June 13, he marches north toward Hermosillo, capital of Sonora. While Raousset and his men are camped at Magdalena, acting

 **Bormann Fuse**

Artillery shell fuse. A major challenge for artillerists to the mid-19th century was the timely ignition of explosive shells above a target. From the 17th century to the mid-19th century, artillerymen simply packed a fuse channel with fine gunpowder. The action of firing the gun ignited this powder train, which then burned to and set off the explosive charge in the shell. Precise timing was impossible because the powder in the fuse was more tightly packed toward the bottom and thus burned more slowly than at the top. This problem was compounded by the compression of the powder train in the action of the shell being fired.

Imprecision in the timing of the shell explosion had not been a major problem until the development in 1784 of spherical case shot (case or shrapnel). Such projectiles, specifically designed for use against troop concentrations, required precise timing of the explosion to be effective, for with a shell moving at 1,200 feet per second, an error of a quarter of a second would mean 300 feet off the target.

Belgian Army captain (later major general) Charles G. Bormann provided the solution. After extensive tests in 1851, the Belgian Army adopted the fuse of his design, which then found its way into worldwide general use. In the United States it was widely employed during the American Civil War by both the Union and the Confederacy, especially in the 12-pounder Napoleon and Dahlgren boat howitzers.

The Bormann fuse consisted of a threaded zinc disc about 0.5-inch thick and 1.5 inches in diameter. Because the fuse train of mealed powder was placed in a channel laterally around the periphery of the fuse, it enabled uniformity in packing the powder and eliminated any effect of the discharge of the gun on the distribution of fuse powder and, hence, timing. Guided by raised indicators on the fuse's face, the gunner set the fuse by perforating its face with a special punch to expose the powder trail at the appropriate mark. The Bormann fuse allowed a maximum timing of 5.25 seconds for a range of 1,200 yards for the 12-pounder gun.

As with much Southern ordnance, Confederate-manufactured Bormann fuses often proved defective on the battlefield. The main trouble lay in the sealing of the underside of the horseshoe channel containing the powder train. The shock of the discharge of the gun tended to dislodge the plug closing the channel and allowed the flame from the composition to reach the main charge without burning around through the fuse. Attempts to correct the problem were unsuccessful. Following numerous casualties from prematurely exploding shells during the Battle of Fredericksburg, the Confederate Army withdrew the Bormann fuse from service on December 24, 1862.

Union forces did not report comparable problems, and the Bormann fuse saw extensive use until it was eventually phased out of service following the war.

SPENCER C. TUCKER

Further Reading
Dickey, Thomas S., and Peter C. George. *Field Artillery Projectiles of the American Civil War*. Atlanta, GA: Arsenal Press, 1980.

governor of Sonora Fernando Cubillas demands that they either accept Mexican citizenship or leave Mexico. Raousset is aware that Cubillas and local Mexican Army commander Gerneral Miguel Blanco are shareholders in a rival Sonora mining company and rejects Cubillas's demand and proclaims Sonora an independent country.

Raousset continues his march and on September 30 defeats Mexican forces under General Blanco and occupies Hermosillo. After four weeks at Hermosillo, Raousset's small and now isolated force withdraws back toward Guaymas, harried en route by Mexican guerrillas under Blanco. Raousset, suffering from dysentery, abandons his men on October 29, arrives at Guaymas, and sails for Mazatlán before returning to San Francisco. The survivors of his expeditionary force surrender to Mexican authorities in return for being able to depart the country and sell their artillery to the Mexican government.

May 30, 1853–July 24, 1855

Second Grinnell Expedition. Wealthy American businessman and philanthropist Henry Grinnell finances a second expedition to the Arctic to search for Captain Sir John Franklin's British exploring expedition, of which nothing has been heard since 1847. Grinnell provides the specially equipped brig *Advance*, crewed by U.S. Navy volunteers and commanded by Dr. Elisha Kent Kane, a navy surgeon, who had been a member of the first expedition (see May 22, 1850–September 30, 1851). Trapped in pack ice later in 1853, the *Advance* is still caught in the ice at the height of the Arctic summer in April 1855, and Kane orders it abandoned and leads his men on an 83-day trek across the ice by sledge to Upernavik, Greenland, where they arrive on July 24, 1855.

June 11, 1853–October 19, 1855

North Pacific Surveying and Exploring Expedition. On July 11, 1853, a U.S. Navy expedition sails from Hampton Roads. Led by Commander Cadwallader Ringgold, it includes the sloops *Vincennes* (20 guns) and *Porpoise* (8 guns), the support steamer *John Hancock* (1 gun), and two other ships. They round the Cape of Good Hope and chart and explore a number of Pacific islands and shoals before arriving in China in March 1854. There Cadwallader becomes insane. In July, Lieutenant John Rodgers (promoted to commander in September 1855) assumes command. After visiting the Bonins, the Ladrones, and the Marianas, the squadron is between Formosa and China when on September 21 the *Porpoise*, with at least 63 men, parts company with the other ships and is never heard from again. It is presumed lost in a typhoon occurring several days later.

In the Bering Sea, the expedition turns south and proceeds along the western coast of North America. The expedition arrives in Puget Sound in March 1856,

John Rodgers Jr. (1812–1882)

U.S. Navy admiral. Born in Havre de Grace, Maryland, on August 12, 1812, John Rodgers Jr. was the son of Commodore John Rodgers Sr., who won renown during the Barbary Wars and the War of 1812. The younger Rodgers joined the navy as a midshipman on April 18, 1828, and served in the Mediterranean in the frigate *Constellation* and the sloop *Concord*. He was promoted to passed midshipman on June 14, 1834. Rodgers attended the University of Virginia for a year before returning to sea. He then served in the Brazil Squadron and participated in the Second Seminole War (1835–1842) before completing additional tours at sea, including in the Mediterranean and off Africa. He was promoted to lieutenant on January 28, 1840.

In 1852 Lieutenant Rodgers assumed command of the North Pacific Exploring Expedition that surveyed the northern Bering Sea. He was promoted to commander on September 14, 1855. Rodgers was in Washington, D.C., compiling and editing the reports of these endeavors when the American Civil War began in April 1861.

Rodgers participated in the botched destruction of the Norfolk Navy Yard, Virginia, in April 1861, and was taken prisoner with others by the Virginia forces. As Virginia had not yet joined the Confederacy, the legislature in Richmond decided to free Rodgers and his fellows. On May 15, Secretary of the Navy Gideon Welles ordered Rodgers to Cincinnati, Ohio, to supervise the conversion into gunboats of civilian vessels purchased by the army. These were the timberclads, the first units of the Mississippi Flotilla. In the course of these endeavors Rodgers clashed with Major General James C. Frémont, commander of the Western Department, who caused his recall.

Assigned to the South Atlantic Blockading Squadron, Rodgers commanded the screw combatant *Flag* in Commodore Samuel F. Du Pont's expedition against Port Royal, South Carolina, of November 1862, and took an active role in the surrender of Confederate Forts Walker and Beauregard. On May 15, 1862, Rodgers led a squadron up the James River and, in the ironclad *Galena,* engaged Confederate shore batteries in the four-hour-long Battle of Drewry's Bluff, in which the *Galena* was badly damaged and the attempt to reach Richmond was rebuffed. Rodgers was promoted to captain on July 16, 1862.

Rodgers rejoined Du Pont's squadron and, in command of the monitor *Weehawken,* led the failed attack on Charleston on April 7, 1863, in which the monitor absorbed a number of hits and was badly damaged. On June 17 in Wassaw Sound, however, Rodgers's repaired *Weehawken* defeated the Confederate ironclad *Atlanta.* Rodgers received promotion to commodore on June 17, 1863, and took command of the monitors *Canonicus* and *Dictator,* both of which were troubled with developmental problems. Rodgers saw no further fighting in the war.

After the war, Rodgers commanded the squadron off Chile and then had charge of the Boston Navy Yard. He was promoted to rear admiral on December 31, 1869. Rodgers commanded the Asiatic Squadron on a diplomatic mission to investigate the imprisonment and murder of American seamen aboard the merchantman *General Sherman.* The U.S. government also wanted a treaty to guarantee proper treatment for shipwrecked sailors but also diplomatic ties and trade relations with Korea. A diplomatic impasse, however, quickly turned into armed conflict. On June 10, 1871, as Rodgers ascended the Taedong River with his ships, a Korean fort opened fire. Rodgers demanded an apology and, with none forthcoming, sent sailors and marines ashore. They stormed three Korean forts and killed several hundred Koreans. This action failed to sway the Koreans to open diplomatic relations. The Americans soon withdrew, and Rodgers returned to the United States in 1872. He subsequently served on various naval boards and also commanded the Naval Observatory before dying in Washington, D.C., on May 5, 1882.

Spencer C. Tucker

Further Reading

Johnson, Robert E. "John Rodgers: The Quintessential Nineteenth Century Naval Officer." In *Captains of the Old Steam Navy,* edited by James C. Bradford, 253–274. Annapolis, MD: Naval Institute Press, 1986.

Johnson, Robert E. *Rear Admiral John Rodgers, 1812–1882.* Annapolis, MD: Naval Institute Press, 1967.

where it assists in the suppression of Indian uprisings threatening to destroy the white settlements and army outposts. The ships return to the Brooklyn Navy Yard on October 19, 1855. The expedition advances knowledge of the western and northern Pacific and helps pave the way for relations between the United States and a number of East Asian nations.

June 21, 1853

Koszta Incident. Martin Koszta, a Hungarian who had taken part in the unsuccessful Hungarian Revolution, immigrated to the United States and in June 1852 declared his intention to become an American citizen. He then travels to Smyrna in the Ottoman Empire, where the American counsel grants him a *tezkereh,* or safe conduct pass. Koszta, however, is seized by men suspected to be in the pay of the Austrian consul and taken aboard the Austrian warship *Hussar.* The U.S. Navy sloop *St. Louis* (18 guns), captained by Commander Duncan N. Ingraham, is also at Smyrna. Informed of events, Ingraham clears his ship for action and sets a deadline for Koszta's release. The *Hussar* and a second Austrian warship in the harbor also clear for action, but in the end Koszta is released. Congress subsequently awards Ingraham a gold medal for upholding the rights of an American citizen.

July 8, 1853

Perry opens Japan. The mistreatment of American shipwrecked sailors and the U.S. desire for trade and a coaling station prompt the government to order a squadron under Commodore Matthew Calbraith Perry to Japan. Sailing from Norfolk, Virginia, on July 8, 1853, Perry arrives at Uraga Harbor near Edo (present-day Tokyo), with the modern side-wheel steam warships *Mississippi* (10 guns) and *Susquehanna* (9 guns) towing the 20-gun sloops *Plymouth* and *Saratoga.* The Americans are met by representatives of the Tokugawa Shogunate, who order Perry to proceed to Nagasaki, the only Japanese port open to foreigners. Perry refuses and demands permission to present a letter to personal representatives of the emperor from U.S. president Millard Fillmore.

With Perry threatening a naval bombardment, the Japanese, who fear the modern weaponry of his so-called Black Ships, agree to let him land. Perry comes ashore on July 14 with an impressive retinue of 300 well-armed men and presents letters to two imperial princes requesting establishment of diplomatic relations between Japan and the United States, better treatment for American shipwrecked sailors, and the opening of one or two treaty ports. Perry then departs, promising to return the next spring with a more powerful squadron for a reply.

October 15, 1853–May 8, 1854

First Walker filibustering expedition. U.S. soldier of fortune and self-proclaimed colonel William Walker dreams of leading a private campaign to conquer parts of Mexico and Central America. On October 16, 1853, he departs California with 45 men in the schooner *Caroline* to conquer the Mexican territories of Baja California and Sonora. On November 3 Walker and his men disembark at La Paz, capital of sparsely populated Baja California, and declare it to be the capital of the Republic of Lower California. Walker proclaims himself president. The constitution of the new state is modeled on that of the U.S. state of Louisiana, which permits slavery.

Street fighting in La Paz in mid-November leads Walker and his followers to withdraw north into Ensenada, just south of Tijuana; he makes Ensenada his new capital. Walker receives reinforcements but is opposed by Mexicans under ranchero Antonio María Meléndez, who on December 2 attack 17 of Walker's men, killing 1 and capturing 2. Meléndez then joins forces with Lieutenant Colonel Luis Castillo Negrete, Mexican commander of the military district of Lower California, against Walker. Together they have 70–75 men.

In March 1854 Walker sets out with only some 100 filibusters to try to conquer the state of Sonora to the northeast. Walker and his men cross the Colorado River into Sonora on April 4, but they are soon forced to withdraw.

With his forces now hounded by the Mexicans under Meléndez and Negrete, Walker is defeated in a skirmish at La Grulla southeast of Ensenada. He and 33 of his men flee north and cross the border into California on May 8, when he is promptly arrested by U.S. authorities and placed on trial in San Francisco on charges of having conducted an illegal war. Given the attitude of the time and the prevalence of Manifest Destiny, in October a jury takes just eight minutes to acquit him.

January 19, 1854

Cyane Expedition. Lieutenant Isaac G. Strain leads 12 officers and 13 seamen from the sloop *Cyane* (20 guns) on an expedition across the Isthmus of Panama to determine the feasibility of a canal connecting the Atlantic and Pacific Oceans. The men set out from Caledonia on the Atlantic coast with the intention of traveling to Darién on the Pacific. They encounter great hardship, in which 9 men die. Lieutenant Strain pushes on alone to reach the coast, then leads a party to rescue the remaining expedition members.

February 13, 1854

Perry's second voyage to Japan. Commodore Matthew Calbraith Perry returns to Edo (present-day Tokyo) Bay, Japan, as promised, this time with seven warships (nearly twice the number of his first visit). Perry has the side-wheel steamers *Mississippi* (10 guns, flagship), *Susquehanna* (9 guns), and *Powhatan* (9 guns); the frigate *Macedonian* (38 guns); the sloops *Saratoga* (22 guns), *Vandalia* (22 guns), and *Lexington* (24 guns); and the storeship *Southampton* (2 guns).

Pressed by Perry and, following three weeks of negotiations, the Tokugawa Shogunate reluctantly signs the Convention of Kanagawa on March 31, 1854. It establishes an American consulate and includes a Japanese pledge to protect shipwrecked American sailors. It also opens two Japanese ports to restricted trade with the United States. Other nations, including Britain and Russia, then negotiate similar treaties with Japan.

March 5, 1854

Army clash with the Apaches. Near Fort Union, New Mexico Territory, Lieutenant David Bell leads a detachment of Lieutenant Colonel Philip Sheridan's 2nd Dragoons Regiment in a clash with Jicarilla Apaches led by Lobo Blanco. The chief and several of his warriors are killed.

March 30, 1854

Army clash with the Apaches. At Cieneguila in northern New Mexico Territory, Jicarilla Apaches led by Chief Chacon ambush a stagecoach escorted by 60 men of the 1st Dragoons Regiment commanded by Lieutenant John W. Davidson. Outnumbered perhaps 4 to 1, Davidson manages to hold out for three hours before withdrawing, with 22 dead. Soldiers under Lieutenant Colonel Philip St. George Cooke of the 2nd Dragoons, assisted by scout Christopher "Kit" Carson, subsequently track the Apaches to a canyon, defeating them and killing 4–5.

April 4–5, 1854

Fighting at Shanghai, China. Fighting between Chinese government troops and Taiping rebels threatens the Western concessions in the city of Shanghai. Commander John Kelly of the sloop *Plymouth* (20 guns) leads a party ashore and joins a British detachment to drive both Chinese warring factions from the city. The fighting claims one American killed and three wounded.

April 8, 1854

Army clash with the Apaches. At Rio Caliente, New Mexico Territory, Lieutenant Colonel Philip St. George of the 2nd Dragoons Regiment detects a Jicarilla Apache ambush and immediately attacks and routs the Indians. The army suffers one dead and one wounded; the Apaches lose five killed and six wounded.

April 25, 1854

The U.S. Senate ratifies the Gadsden Purchase by which the United States acquires the Mesilla Valley from Mexico. The United States had sought this land, not a part of the Mexican Cession of 1848, as the route for a railroad to connect southern California with the rest of the country.

Philip Henry Sheridan (1831–1888)

U.S. Army general. Born in Albany, New York, on March 6, 1831, Philip Henry Sheridan grew up in Somerset, Ohio. He graduated from the U.S. Military Academy, West Point, in 1853 and was commissioned a second lieutenant in the infantry. Sheridan then served with the 1st Infantry Regiment in Texas and with the 4th Infantry Regiment in Oregon, being promoted to first lieutenant in March 1861 on the eve of the American Civil War.

Assigned to the Western theater, Sheridan was promoted to captain in May 1861 and served in the 13th Infantry Regiment in southwestern Missouri, then as quartermaster for Department of the Missouri commander Major General Henry W. Halleck during the latter's Corinth Campaign in May–June 1862. Disliking staff duty, Sheridan secured a transfer to the volunteer establishment as colonel of the 2nd Michigan Cavalry in May. His subsequent victory at Booneville, Mississippi, on July 1, 1862, earned him promotion to brigadier general of volunteers that September.

Sheridan commanded an infantry division and distinguished himself in the Battle of Perryville in Kentucky on October 8, 1862, and especially at Stones River on December 31, 1862–January 2, 1863, where he perhaps saved from defeat Major General William S. Rosecrans's Army of the Cumberland. For this action Sheridan was promoted to major general of volunteers in March 1863. In the Battle of Chickamauga on September 20, 1863, Sheridan garnered laurels for his division's tenacious fighting. His men played a key role in the Union victory at the Battle of Chattanooga on November 23–25, 1863.

When Ulysses S. Grant was promoted to lieutenant general and became the army's general-in-chief, he selected Sheridan to command the Army of the Potomac's cavalry corps of three divisions and 10,000 men. During the spring and summer of 1864, Sheridan's men won a number of victories against the Confederate cavalry. Sheridan's cavalry took part in Grant's Overland Campaign, disrupting Confederate lines of communication, including tearing up sections of railroad track and destroying telegraph lines. Sheridan was victorious in the Battle of Yellow Tavern in Virginia on May 11, 1864, where Confederate cavalry commander Major General James E. B. Stuart was mortally wounded, but Sheridan suffered a rebuff at Trevilian Station on June 11–12, 1864.

In August 1864, Grant gave Sheridan command of the Army of the Shenandoah and instructed him to drive south and destroy any supplies that might be of use to the Confederate Army. Sheridan soon tangled with Confederate forces under Lieutenant General Jubal Early in the Shenandoah Valley. Sheridan defeated Early in the Third Battle of Winchester on September 19, 1864, and at Fisher's Hill on September 22, 1864. For this accomplishment, Sheridan was advanced to brigadier general in the regular army. Sheridan was caught off guard when Early attacked at Cedar Creek on October 18, 1864. Away when the battle began, Sheridan galloped south from Winchester and rallied his men to victory. Sheridan then proceeded to lay waste to the Shenandoah Valley, depriving the Confederates of much-needed supplies. The extent of this destruction is seen in his boast "A crow couldn't fly from Winchester to Staunton without taking its rations along."

Promoted to major general in the regular army in November 1864, Sheridan raided from Winchester to Petersburg during February 27–March 24, 1865, where he rejoined Grant. Sheridan played a major role in the final defeat of General Robert E. Lee's Army of Northern Virginia, defeating the Confederates at Five Forks on April 1 and Sayler's Creek near Farmville, Virginia, on April 6 before trapping Lee's army near Appomattox Court House, leading to the Confederate surrender on April 9, 1865.

Sheridan was then ordered to Texas with a large force to encourage the French to quit Mexico. He remained in Texas as commander of the Military Division of the Gulf from May 1865 to March 1867, then was named commander of the Fifth Military District of Louisiana and Texas in March 1867. Southern complaints about his firm policies soon brought his removal by the Southern-sympathizing president Andrew Johnson in September.

Sheridan then took over the Department of the Missouri in September 1867 and as such was responsible for the federal effort against hostile western Native Americans. In his new position, he aggressively prosecuted a campaign against Native Americans of the Washita Valley in Indian Territory (Oklahoma) and on the southern Plains in 1868–1869. In March 1869 when Grant became president and William T. Sherman moved up to command the army as a full general, Sheridan was promoted to lieutenant general and assumed command of the Military Division of the Missouri.

Sheridan then traveled to Europe, where he was an official observer attached to the Prussian Army during the Franco-Prussian War (1870–1871). Returning to the United States, he directed the campaign against the Sioux that resulted in the Battle of the Little Bighorn on June 25, 1876, and the punitive effort that followed. He also directed the final operations that prevented Chief Joseph and most of his Nez Perces from reaching Canada in 1877. Sheridan then commanded the Military Divisions of the West and Southwest in 1878. He succeeded Sherman as commanding general of the army in 1884 and was promoted to full general in June 1888. He was also a prime mover behind the creation of Yellowstone National Park. Sheridan died at Nonquitt, Massachusetts, on August 5, 1888. Known as "Little Phil," Sheridan was blunt and outspoken. He was also industrious, offensive-minded, aggressive, and a superb tactical commander.

SPENCER C. TUCKER

Further Reading

Hutton, Paul Andrew. *Phil Sheridan and His Army.* Lincoln: University of Nebraska Press, 1985.
Morris, Roy. *Sheridan: The Life and Wars of General Phil Sheridan.* New York: Crown, 1992.

June–August 1854

Return of Raousset to Mexico. Having vainly appealed his expulsion from the state of Sonora before Mexican president Antonio López de Santa Anna in Mexico City, French adventurer Count Gaston de Raousset-Boulbon returns to San Francisco, California, where he recruits another filibustering force, this time only about 300 men and most of them Frenchmen. He again sails for Mexico, arriving at the port of Guaymas in southwestern Sonora state on June 18, 1854. After failing to persuade local Mexican commander General José María Yáñez to join the Ayutla Revolution against Santa Anna, Raousset engages Yáñez in battle on July 31. Raousset's force is defeated, suffering some 100 casualties, and he is among those taken prisoner. Tried and convicted by a military tribunal, Raousset is executed by firing squad at Guaymas on August 12, 1854.

July 11, 1854

Treaty of Naha. U.S. Navy commodore Matthew C. Perry concludes a treaty of peace and amity with the regency of the Loo Choo (Ryukyu) Islands.

August 19, 1854

Grattan Massacre. In Nebraska Territory, responding to complaints by a Mormon traveling the Oregon Trail that a Brulé Lakota (Sioux) named High Forehead has stolen his cow when the farmer had actually abandoned it and High Forehead had killed it for

NORTH AMERICA AND THE EXPANSION OF THE UNITED STATES, 1824–1854

CANADA
(British)

U.S.-Canadian boundary settled 1846

U.S.-Canadian border, 1821

OREGON TERRITORY

UNITED STATES

MEXICAN CESSION (1848)

ALTA CALIFORNIA

U.S.-Mexican border, 1821

SONORA

NUEVO MEXICO

GADSDEN PURCHASE (1853)

REPUBLIC OF TEXAS (annexed 1845)

Final U.S.-Mexican border, 1854

Gulf of Mexico

MEXICO

ME
VT
NH
NY
MA
PA
CT RI
MD NJ
DE
IL IN OH
MO WV VA
KY
TN NC
SC
MS AL GA
LA

ATLANTIC OCEAN

THE BAHAMAS (British)

CUBA (Spanish)

HAITI

JAMAICA (British)

BRITISH HONDURAS

HONDURAS

GUATEMALA
EL SALVADOR

NICARAGUA

PACIFIC OCEAN

50°N
40°N
20°N
10°N

110°W   100°W   90°W

0   900   1800 mi
0   900   1800 km

Native American encampment outside Fort Laramie in Wyoming, the scene of the Grattan Massacre on August 19, 1854. The army demanded that the Sioux turn over a warrior who had stolen and butchered a stray cow, despite a Sioux offer of compensation. Lieutenant John L. Grattan's men opened fire, killing Chief Conquering Bear, but the Sioux then killed Grattan and most of his men. (Hulton Archive/Getty Images)

food, Lieutenant Hugh Fleming, commander at Fort Laramie, calls on Chief Conquering Bear on August 18, 1854, to adjudicate the matter. Both men are aware that according to the Treaty of Laramie of 1851, such issues are to be settled by the Indian agent, who is due to arrive within days, but Fleming presses the matter. Conquering Bear offers the farmer any of his 60 horses. The settler rejects this offer and demands $25. An impasse ensues, whereupon Fleming then demands that High Forehead be surrendered, which Conquering Bear refuses.

The next day, August 19, Fleming sends Second Lieutenant John Grattan to arrest High Forehead. The inexperienced Grattan is spoiling for a confrontation. Departing with 29 men of the 6th Infantry Regiment, an interpreter, and two small artillery pieces, in present-day Goshen County, Wyoming, Grattan's troops encounter the Sioux, who express outrage over the show of force. The interpreter taunts the Indians, and following an angry exchange, the troopers open

fire, shooting Chief Conquering Bear in the back and killing him. In the ensuing general engagement, the Sioux kill Grattan and 29 of his men; the remaining member of his party subsequently dies of his wounds at Fort Laramie.

On August 20 the Sioux mount a token attack on Fort Laramie before abandoning their camp and returning to their hunting grounds. Although Grattan was largely to blame for the clash, U.S. president Franklin Pierce demands that the military punish the Lakotas.

August 20, 1854

American Indian Wars: Ward Wagon Train Massacre. In Canyon County, Idaho, Shoshone Indians attack a wagon train led by Alexander Ward. A number of women are raped; they and others are tortured, with the children most probably burned alive. Eighteen of the 20 members of the wagon train die. The Shoshones also take some 60 head of cattle and $2,000 in gold.

Nathan Olney leads 39 volunteers, assisted by Nez Perce and Umatilla Native Americans, to track the war party and kill a number of them. Four are caught and later hanged. The Shoshone attack leads to the closing of the Hudson's Bay Company's Fort Boise and Fort Hall.

September 21, 1854

Loss of the *Porpoise*. The sloop *Porpoise* (8 guns), one of the ships in the U.S. Navy North Pacific Surveying and Exploring Expedition, parts company with the other ships. It and its crew of 63 men are never heard from again, presumed lost in a typhoon several days later.

September 29, 1854

The U.S. Navy sloop *Albany* (22 guns) with 193 men under Commander James T. Gerry sails from Aspinwall, Panama, for New York and is never seen again.

November 17, 1854

The U.S. Navy sloop *Vincennes* lands sailors and marines in Okinawa in the Loo Choo (Ryukyu) Islands to enforce provisions of the Treaty of Naha.

December 24, 1854

Fort Pueblo Massacre. In the summer of 1854 an outbreak of smallpox decimates the Mouache Utes. Surviving members of the tribe blame it on contaminated goods provided by the government. Seeking retribution, on December 24, 1854, some Utes and Apaches led by Ute chief Tierra Blanca (Blanco) attack Fort Pueblo (present-day Pueblo, Colorado), killing at least a dozen settlers.

February 15, 1855

Commanding general of the U.S. Army major general Winfield Scott is breveted lieutenant general in a special act of Congress, making him the highest-ranking general officer since George Washington.

March 3, 1855

Increase in the size of the U.S. Army. Recognizing the heightened security requirements in the West, Congress increases the size of the army by adding four new regiments (the 9th and 10th Infantry and the 1st and 2nd Cavalry). The latter two regiments are the first in the U.S. Army to bear the "cavalry" designation. They are stationed at Fort Leavenworth, Kansas, and Jefferson Barracks, Missouri, respectively.

March 3, 1855

Congress appropriates funds for the purchase of camels to be used in the U.S. Southwest against hostile Native Americans. With its rough terrain and arid climate, the Southwest seemed an ideal location for what becomes known as the camel experiment. Secretary of War Jefferson Davis approves, and on March 3, 1855, the U.S. Congress appropriates $30,000 for the project.

Major Henry C. Wayne secures the camels, arriving from Smyrna with several dozen camels and their five handlers at Indianola, Texas, on May 14, 1856. A second shipment of 41 camels arrives on February 10, 1857. The camels are driven to Camp Verde via Victoria and San Antonio. The ability of the camels to traverse the rough terrain and go without water for extended periods proves exceedingly useful in a series of surveying missions during 1857–1860. Handlers have difficulty with the camels, however, and they spook horses and mules. With the beginning of the Civil War the Camel Corps comes to an end, with many of the camels being sold to private owners or escaping into western deserts and British Columbia. Feral camels continue to be sighted in the Southwest; the last reported sighting is in 1941.

April 28, 1855

Battle of Poncha Pass. Following their massacre of settlers at Fort Pueblo, Colorado (see December 24, 1854), Ute warriors move into the San Luis Valley, killing settlers at Costilla and carrying off livestock. In February 1855 Colonel Thomas Fauntleroy arrives at Fort Massachusetts from Fort Union, New Mexico, with his 1st Dragoons Regiment. Assisted by some volunteers, Fauntleroy chases some 150 Utes and Jicarilla Apaches across the valley, catching them north of Poncha Pass on March 23, 1855. After several other skirmishes, a decisive battle occurs on April 28 at Poncha Pass when the soldiers surprise the natives at night around a bonfire, killing 40. The Utes sue for peace shortly thereafter.

April 1855

The Delafield Commission sails for Europe. Appointed by Secretary of War Jefferson Davis, the Delafield Commission consists of army officers Major Richard Delafield, Major Alfred Mordecai, and Captain George B. McClellan. They are charged with gathering information on European military developments, including acting as official observers of the Crimean War (1854–1856), with a view toward instituting improvements in the U.S. military.

May 5, 1855–May 7, 1857

Walker's filibustering expedition to Nicaragua. On May 5, 1855, American filibusterer William Walker sails from San Francisco, California, with 60 followers, who style themselves the Immortals, bound for Nicaragua. Walker is still determined to seize a Latin American country and rule it. There is civil war in Nicaragua, and Walker has been invited in by the (liberal) Democratic Party to assist it in ousting the (conservative) Legitimist Party. Walker is promised a grant of 52,000 acres of land in return for his aid.

By June, Walker has landed and been reinforced by another 100 Americans and added some 170 Nicaraguans. Walker's force, the so-called *Falange Americana,* forms the core of the opposition force that defeats the Nicaraguan army at La Virgen on September 1. Seizing a steamer on Lake Nicaragua, Walker takes the capital city of Granada on October 13. He is aided by American tycoon Cornelius Vanderbilt, who wants to secure for his Accessory Transit Company a stable overland communication route across Central America to construct a railroad facilitating the transit of goods from the Atlantic to the Pacific.

Under a compromise agreement following the victory, Patricio Rivas becomes president of Nicaragua, but Walker controls affairs as commander of the Nicaraguan Army. Walker's chief rival, former army commander Ponciano Corral, is tried and executed on a charge of treason after letters are discovered in which he requests intervention by other Latin American governments to oust Walker.

From November 1855 to June 1856, Walker rules Nicaragua through Rivas, supported by some 1,000 Americans brought in by Vanderbilt's company. In May 1856 President Franklin Pierce extends U.S. recognition to the new government.

On June 29, 1856, in a rigged election, Walker is elected president. Taking office on July 12, his goal is to unite all of Central America under his rule, build railroads and ultimately a canal across the isthmus, introduce slavery, and secure admission of Nicaragua to the United States as a slave-holding state. Walker opens Nicaragua to slavery, which had been abolished there in 1824. Covertly backed by the British, leaders of the other Central American states work together to oust Walker.

Offered money and supplies by Vanderbilt rivals Cornelius K. Garrison and Charles Morgan, Walker revokes the charter of the Accessory Transit Company and seizes its ships and property. A furious Vanderbilt now works tirelessly to unseat Walker. Vanderbilt pressures Washington to withdraw its recognition and extends assistance to the other Central American states opposing Walker's rule. Meanwhile, Walker's own aid dries up. Walker appeals to U.S. Southerners for support, but few rally to him.

Coalition forces invade Nicaragua, and Walker is forced to flee. Cornered with a few of his followers, on May 1, 1857, he surrenders to U.S. Navy commander Charles H. Davis of the sloop *St. Mary's* (22 guns) and is delivered to New Orleans, where he is welcomed by proslavery Louisianans.

May 19, 1855

At Shanghai, China, Captain William J. McCluney of the U.S. Navy side-wheel steamer *Powhatan* (9 guns) sends ashore its marine detachment to protect American commercial interests.

August 4, 1855

Battle of Ty-Ho Bay (Hahlam Bay). The U.S. Navy side-wheel steamer *Powhatan* (9 guns), commanded by Captain William J. McCluney, cooperates with the Royal Navy steam sloop *Rattler* and steamer *Eaglet* to rescue 7 captured merchant vessels, most of which are Chinese junks, held by pirates in Ty-Ho Bay near

Richard Delafield (1798–1873)

U.S. Army general. Richard Delafield was born in New York City on September 1, 1798, and graduated from the U.S. Military Academy, West Point, in 1818. Commissioned a second lieutenant in the Corps of Engineers, Delafield was a member of the American commission that helped establish the U.S. boundary with Canada under provisions called for by the Treaty of Ghent of 1814 and fixed by treaty in October 1820.

Promoted to first lieutenant in August 1820, Delafield assisted in the construction of the Hampton Roads defenses in Virginia during 1819–1824 and then had charge of fortifications and surveys in the Mississippi River delta area during 1824–1832 as well as improvements to the Mississippi and Ohio Rivers. He was advanced to captain in May 1828. Delafield next had charge of repair work on the Cumberland Road east of the Ohio River as well as repairs to Fort Mifflin and improvements along the Delaware River during 1832–1838.

Promoted to major in July 1838, Delafield was superintendent of West Point from September 1838 to August 1845. He supervised its reconstruction following the fire of 1838, made substantial physical improvements to the academy, and designed the new cadet uniform. He also introduced horses for the artillery and cavalry instruction of the cadets. During 1846–1855 Delafield superintended the construction of coastal defenses for New York Harbor.

In 1855 Delafield headed a commission, which was named for him and established by Secretary of War Jefferson Davis, to travel to Europe and report on the European military establishments as well as on the Crimean War then in progress. The members of the Delafield Commission, which also included officers George B. McClellan and Alfred Mordecai, observed the siege of Sevastopol during that war. The commission's report detailed the important midcentury changes occurring in military equipment and practices and was subsequently published by Congress. On his return to the United States, Delafield was again superintendent of West Point during 1856–1861, when he revised and considerably improved its curriculum.

During the Civil War, Delafield initially assisted in the raising and equipping of troops in New York state. Promoted to lieutenant colonel in August 1861 and to colonel in June 1863, he had charge of the harbor defenses of New York (1861–1864).

Following the death of Major General Joseph G. Totten, Delafield was promoted to brigadier general in August 1864 and appointed chief engineer of the U.S. Army. He held this post until his retirement on August 6, 1866. He was breveted major general in March 1865 for his meritorious service during the war.

In retirement, Delafield served as a member of the Lighthouse Board during 1864–1870 and was a regent of the Smithsonian Institution. He died in Washington, D.C., on November 5, 1873.

SPENCER C. TUCKER

Further Reading
Crackel, Theodore J. *West Point: A Bicentennial History.* Lawrence: University Press of Kansas, 2003.
Moten, Matthew. *The Delafield Commission and the American Military Profession.* College Station: Texas A&M University Press, 2000.

Hong Kong, China. British and American sailors and marines in 6 armed boats towed by the *Eaglet* battle the pirates and rescue the captured ships, although the latter are so badly damaged that they are subsequently burned. The Americans and British also sink 20 of 36 Chinese armed junks, kill or wound perhaps 500 pirates, and capture 1,000 at a cost to themselves of 9 killed and 6 wounded (the Americans lose 5 killed). This is one of the last major battles between Chinese pirate fleets and Western navies and one of the first joint operations undertaken by the British and Americans.

September 2–3, 1855

Battle of Ash Hollow (Battle of Blue Water Creek). This engagement occurs along the Platte River in present-day Garden County, Nebraska, between U.S. forces commanded by Brevet Brigadier General William S. Harney and Brulé Lakota (Sioux) led by Little Thunder. It is triggered by the so-called Grattan Massacre (see August 19, 1854). President Franklin Pierce demands military action against the Lakotas and enforcement of provisions of the Fort Laramie Treaty of 1851.

Harney sets out in August 1855 with some 600 men formed of elements of the 2nd Dragoons, the 6th and 10th Infantry Regiments, and the 4th Artillery Regiment. On September 1, they come upon a Brulé village along the Platte River in a place called Blue Waters. During the night of September 2, Harney orders Lieutenant Colonel Philip St. George Cooke and Captain Henry Heth to carry out a flanking maneuver and establish a blocking position against which he plans to drive the Sioux. The next morning, Harney advances with the infantry against the native village. Convinced that the Sioux are trapped, Harney commences negotiations with Chief Little Thunder and demands surrender of those responsible for the Grattan Massacre and other outrages.

With the talks in progress and Little Thunder rejecting Harney's demand, the Sioux discover Cooke's men. Aware of this, Harney orders his infantry to attack the Sioux camp. Firing wildly into the village, the soldiers kill many women and children. Some warriors escape on horseback and are pursued

by Heth's men. More than 80 Sioux are killed, and a large number are wounded; 70 are taken prisoner. The army suffers 4 killed, 7 wounded, and 1 missing.

In October 1855, Harney negotiates a treaty with the Sioux, allowing the army to protect settlers traveling the Oregon Trail. This preserves peace for a decade.

September 12–22, 1855

The sloop *John Adams* at Fiji. On September 12, 1855, Commander Edward B. Boutwell, captain of the U.S. Navy sloop *John Adams* (18 guns), sends a party ashore at Nukylau in the Fiji Islands to secure compensation for damages inflicted on American citizens. When nothing is accomplished, on September 22 the Americans seize the king of Viti Levu and take him back to the *John Adams*, where he is forced to sign a treaty promising compensation to the Americans whose property has been damaged or confiscated.

September 1855–September 23, 1858

Yakima-Rogue War. One of the largest conflicts fought between whites and Native Americans in the Pacific Northwest, it actually encompassed two conflicts: that with the Yakima (Yakama) tribe, along the Columbia and Yakima Rivers to the lee of the Cascade Mountains in Washington Territory, and that with the Rogue River tribe to the south in Oregon Territory.

Although they had refused to participate in the 1847–1855 Cayuse War (see November 29, 1847), the Yakimas are soon confronted with growing numbers of settlers and prospectors on their ancestral lands. Shortly after Oregon's reorganization into the Oregon and Washington Territories in 1853, Isaac Stevens, the first governor of the Washington Territory, who is also superintendent of Indian affairs and chief officer of the Northern Pacific Railway Survey, seeks land for a proposed railroad route from the Mississippi River to Puget Sound. Stevens works with Oregon leaders and negotiates several treaties at the 1855 Walla Walla Council with the Walla Walla, Cayuse, Umatilla, Nez Perce, and Yakima tribes. Stevens intimidates 14 tribes into agreeing to move onto a new Yakima Indian Reservation. In return for the cession of some 10.8 million acres, the government promises a full range of services, generous annuities, and the assurance that removal will occur upon ratification of the treaties in about four years. Although most Yakimas sign the agreement on June 9, 1855, Chief Kamiakin and others reject it. Within two weeks of concluding a third treaty, Stevens declares the area east of the Cascades open to white settlement. Tensions escalate when settlers and prospectors flood into the region, exacerbated by the discovery of gold along the border of Yakima land and on the recently established reservation.

In September 1855, 5 Yakima warriors led by Qualchin (son of Kamiakin's uncle Chief Owhi), kill 6 prospectors in retaliation for attacks on the Yakimas. The war begins shortly after Andrew Bolon, the Indian agent sent to investigate the incident, is killed by warriors on September 23. Several tribes unite under Kamiakin's leadership and some 1,500 warriors defeat 102 troops under Major Granville Haller at Toppenish Creek on October 6, where 5 soldiers and 2 Indians are killed.

This success encourages other tribes to ally with Kamiakin, who becomes the target of an expedition led by Brigadier General Gabriel Rains, who disregards Kamiakin's request for peace and in November razes a Catholic mission for supposedly assisting the Native Americans.

The war quickly extends to two fronts when the Rogue River tribe begins raiding from the Table Rock Reservation in response to dismal living conditions there. Following several attacks on settlements along Bear Creek and the Rogue River, on October 8 settler volunteers attack Indians camped on Little Bear Creek who had refused to return to the reservation. The attack occurs while the natives are sleeping, and 23 die, including a number of women and children. This action officially begins the Rogue River War (1855–1856), as other natives who had not previously left the reservation now join the fight.

Raids continue, with some 20 settlers slain, until December, when Lieutenant Colonel James Kelly marches 350 Oregon settler volunteers through the Walla Walla Valley. He discusses peace with Walla Walla chief Piupiumaksmaks. Rumors of deception result in a battle on December 10 in which the settlers lose 8 killed and 18 wounded; the Walla Wallas and Cayutes suffer more than 100 casualties, with Chief Piupiumaksmaks among those slain. News that the chief and 19 other natives have been scalped prompts other tribes to launch attacks throughout the region.

On February 23, 1856, warriors attack settlements along the lower Rogue River, killing 31 whites and destroying more than 60 homes. Brigadier General John E. Wool of the Pacific Division sends 270 regulars in a three-pronged attack, while Oregon Terrritory governor George L. Curry raises 865 Oregon mounted volunteers to pursue the Indians downriver. By late May, with little food or supplies available after a harsh winter, most Native Americans agree to stop fighting and move onto reservations.

Chief Old John remains a formidable opponent. His band of 150 warriors attacks Captain Andrew J. Smith's 80 regulars at Big Meadows (Bend) on May 27, 1856, killing 11 and wounding 20. This could have ended in disaster for the Americans but for a warning by Chief George (Cholcultah) to Smith and the arrival of Captain C. C. Augur's relief force the next day.

In the following weeks, coastal Native Americans and upper and lower Rogue River tribes surrender in greater numbers under relentless pressure from settler volunteers and army regulars. The war essentially ends on June 20, 1856, with the surrender of Old John, who is incarcerated at Fort Alcatraz in San Francisco Bay. Another Indian leader, Enos Thomas, also eventually surrenders; he is hanged in 1857. Other warriors are sent to an area near Fort Hoskins. The remaining members of the Rogue River tribe are relocated to the Grande Ronde and Siletz Reservations. Having lost a third of its male population because of the conflict, the Rogue River tribe ceases to be a military threat, and southern Oregon remains open to white settlement.

On the northern front, renegade Yakimas attack a blockhouse in the Cascades, convincing Wool to send Colonel George Wright and members of the 9th U.S. Infantry Regiment to occupy the Walla Walla and Yakima Valleys. A truce is reached in July following the defeat of Walla Walla and Cayuse Native Americans in the Grande Ronde Valley by militia under

Lieutenant Colonel Benjamin Shaw. To strengthen control over the Yakima Valley, Major Robert Garnett supervises construction of Fort Simcoe.

A steady flow of settlers to the area leads to a renewal of hostilities, and in September 1856 Stevens calls a second Walla Walla council, demanding the unconditional surrender of hostile tribes. Most tribes sign the resultant treaty, but Kamiakin, Owhi, and Qualchin flee. Despite efforts by Wool and Wright to restrain encroachment through 1857, trespassing prospectors trigger several Native American attacks, culminating in major fighting in 1858. This next phase of the Yakima War is also known as the Coeur d'Alene War and the Spokane–Coeur d'Alene–Paloos War: a series of encounters between the Coeur d'Alene, Spokane, Palouse, and Northern Paiute tribes and the U.S. Army and settlers in the Washington Territory (to include present-day Idaho) during 1858.

On May 17, 1858, a combined force of more than 1,000 Coeur d'Alenes, Yakimas, Cayuses, Spokanes, and possibly Walla Wallas defeats 159 soldiers under Lieutenant Colonel Edward Steptoe in the Battle of Pine Creek, near present-day Rosalia, Washington. The soldiers suffer 7 dead and at least 6 wounded. Indian losses are some 9–50 dead and 40–50 wounded. Wright and 570 troops, supported by six howitzers, are now dispatched to deal with the renewed fighting.

Wright decisively defeats the Native Americans in the Battle of Four Lakes near Spokane on September 1, 1858. Howitzers and long-range fire with the new Springfield Model 1855 rifled musket blunt a Native American mounted charge, while U.S. dragoons pursue the dispersed warriors. The soldiers kill 60 Indians and suffer no losses themselves. In a running fight that lasts four additional days, Wright further weakens Indian resistance by killing 800 horses and destroying cattle and food stocks. Kamiakin flees to Montana, while more than a dozen other chiefs are executed or killed trying to escape, including Qualchan and Owhi, after they had surrendered.

On September 23, Wright imposes a treaty relocating most tribes to a reservation south of present-day Yakima, Washington, restoring peace to the Columbia plateau.

October 28–31, 1855

John Adams at Fiji. The U.S. Navy sloop *John Adams* (18 guns) under Commander Edward B. Boutwell returns to Viti Levu in the Fiji Islands. Boutwell learns that the king has not honored the treaty he had been forced to sign in September (see September 12–22, 1855) to compensate Americans for lost and damaged property. Boutwell sends ashore sailors and marines under Lieutenant Louis C. Sartori, and they burn three native villages. The Americans lose one man killed and three wounded.

November 27, 1855

At Montevideo, Uruguay, the U.S. Navy sloop *Germantown* (22 guns) lands 100 sailors and marines to join detachments from the ships of other countries to protect the customhouse and foreign embassies during an insurrection there.

December 20, 1855–March 1858

Third Seminole War. The third and final war waged by U.S. forces to remove the Seminole Indians from Florida to Indian Territory (Oklahoma) begins in 1855. As with the previous two Seminole wars, the Third Seminole War (1855–1858) is sparked by white encroachment on Seminole lands in their informal reservation in southwestern Florida. Florida authorities had been pressing the federal government for the removal of all Seminoles. Although the Indians have tried to limit their contact with the whites, there are serious incidents.

The war begins on December 20, 1855, when Seminoles under Chief Holata Micco (Billy Bowlegs) attack in Big Cyprus Swamp an 11-man reconnaissance patrol commanded by Lieutenant George Hartsuff from Fort Myers; 4 soldiers are killed. The Seminoles then raid isolated farms and plantations.

Clashes continue through 1856, but the 700 soldiers in southern Florida and local militiamen are unable to defeat the elusive Seminoles, who take advantage of their knowledge of the swamps. In September 1856 Brigadier General William S. Harney, a veteran of the Second Seminole War, assumes command in Florida. He employs an attrition strategy, ordering constant army patrols and the use of metal

Alfred Mordecai (1804–1887)

U.S. Army officer. Alfred Mordecai was born in Warrenton, North Carolina, on January 3, 1804. Raised by his parents as an Orthodox Jew, Mordecai entered the U.S. Military Academy, West Point, at age 15 and graduated first in his class in 1823. He became an assistant professor at West Point for two years and was then involved in the construction of Fort Monroe, Virginia. Promoted to captain in May 1832, Mordecai transferred to the newly organized Ordnance Department. In 1836 he assumed command of the Frankfort Arsenal in Philadelphia.

Mordecai pioneered the use of scientific methods to develop and test ordnance and ammunition in the U.S. Army. He also compiled the army's first ordnance manual, *Ordnance Manual for the Use of Officers of the United States Army* (1841, revised in 1850). He also helped reorganize the army's artillery along more rational lines. In 1839 he was appointed to the Ordnance Board, charged with standardizing the army's weaponry, and he subsequently published the important work *Artillery for the Land Service of the United States* (1849), the first uniform artillery system for the U.S. Army.

By 1842 Mordecai was assistant inspector general of arsenals and assistant to the chief of ordnance. He was appointed a member of the West Point Board of Visitors in 1843. During the Mexican-American War (1846–1848), Mordecai commanded the Washington Arsenal. He was promoted to major in 1854.

In 1855 Mordecai was a member of a three-man commission that also included Major Richard Delafield and Captain George B. McClellan dispatched to Europe to study European military developments and also observe the Crimean War (1854–1856). Among Mordecai's important recommendations was that the army adopt the 12-pounder French Napoleon cannon. It became the standard artillery piece of the American Civil War (1861–1865).

With the outbreak of the Civil War, Mordecai faced a difficult choice. Offered several military posts in the Confederacy, he declined. After much soul-searching, in 1861 he resigned his commission so he would not have to break his oath or fight against his native state. This decision undoubtedly cost him a higher place in the pantheon of American history.

Early in the war, Mordecai taught math at a private school in Philadelphia. He was then assistant engineer of the Mexico and Pacific Railroad (1863–1866) and treasurer and secretary of canal and coal companies controlled by the Pennsylvania Railroad Company (1867–1887). Mordecai died in Philadelphia on October 23, 1887. His son Alfred graduated from West Point in 1861 and fought for the Union.

SPENCER C. TUCKER

Further Reading

Abrahams, Robert D. *The Uncommon Soldier: Major Alfred Mordecai.* New York: Farrar, Straus and Cudahy, 1959.

Falk, Stanley L. "Alfred Mordecai, American Jew." *American Jewish Archives* 10(2) (October 1958): 125–132.

Falk, Stanley L. "Divided Loyalties in 1861: The Decision of Major Alfred Mordecai." *Publications of the American Jewish Historical Society* 48 (1959): 1–4.

Falk, Stanley L. "Soldier-Technologist: Major Alfred Mordecai and the Beginnings of Science in the U.S. Army." Unpublished PhD dissertation, Georgetown University, 1959.

Padgett, Juames A., ed. "The Life of Alfred Mordecai as Related by Himself." *North Carolina Historical Review* 22 (1945): 94–122.

shallow-draft 30-foot double-ended alligator boats to penetrate deep into the Everglades. In April 1857 Harney is ordered to Kansas with the 5th Infantry Regiment to combat rising violence there over the issue of slavery.

Harney is replaced by Colonel Gustavus Loomis, who has available only 10 companies of the 4th Infantry Regiment. Ten companies of the Florida Militia are taken into federal service, and by September Loomis has some 800 men under arms. In November they capture 18 members of Billy Bowlegs's band. They also locate and destroy several Seminole towns and burn crops.

On January 1, 1958, the troops move into the Big Cypress Swamp, destroying all Seminole settlements and crops they can locate. A delegation from Indian Territory (Oklahoma) arrives in Florida in January and is able to contact Billy Bowlegs. The Seminoles now have their own reservation in Indian Territory separate from the Creeks, and the U.S. government promises cash payments of $500 to each warrior (more to the chiefs) and $100 to each woman.

On March 15, Seminole bands under Billy Bowlegs and Assinwar accept this offer, and on May 4, 163 Seminoles (including some captured earlier) are sent to New Orleans, from there to proceed to Indian Territory. On May 8, 1858, Colonel Loomis declares the Third Seminole War at an end. The Sam Jones band of fewer than 150 Seminoles is, however, allowed to remain in the Everglades.

January 26, 1856

Native American attack on Seattle. Some 1,000 Nisqually Indians led by Chief Leshi attack Seattle, Washington Territory. The U.S. Navy sloop *Dale* (14 guns) under Commander Guert Gansvoort, having arrived a week before for repairs after striking an uncharted reef, provides both fire support and a small landing party of marines with 2 9-pounder guns to help the settlers repel the attack. Two settlers are killed; Indian losses are unknown.

May 21–September 15, 1856

Bleeding Kansas. Violence erupts within Kansas over the issue of whether this territory will enter the Union as a free or slave state. A proslavery mob sacks the Free-State stronghold city of Lawrence on May 21, 1856, destroying much property. Abolitionist fanatic John Brown then leads a raid on a proslavery settlement on Pottawatomie Creek during May 24–25, hacking 4 men to death with swords. Free-Staters seize the town of Franklin on August 13, while proslavery men drive Brown and his followers from Osawatomie on August 30. In the disorders, 20 people die and much property is destroyed. In mid-September, federal troops restore order.

September 20, 1856

American forces land at Panama City. The U.S. Navy frigate *Independence* (56 guns) and sloop *St. Mary's* (22 guns) land 160 sailors and marines under U.S. Marine Corps captain Addison Garland to protect American citizens in Panama City in the province of Panama, Colombia.

October 23, 1856

U.S. forces land at Guangzhou (Canton), China. In October 1856, fighting begins anew between Britain and China in what is later known as the Second Opium War (sometimes called the *Arrow* War, for a ship of that name) during 1856–1860. Commodore James Armstrong, commander of the U.S. East India Squadron based at Hong Kong, orders ashore at Guangzhou a 120-man landing party drawn from the 18-gun sloops *Portsmouth*, commanded by Commander Andrew H. Foote, and *Levant*, under Commander William Smith.

November 15, 1856

Chinese Barrier forts commanding the Pearl River (Guangdong) below the city of Guangzhou (Canton) fire on the American flag. In October, Chinese gunners fire on the *Cum Fa*, a small chartered steamer flying the U.S. flag and proceeding to Guangzhou from Macao. Although the Chinese may have mistaken the American flag for that of the British, with whom they are at war, U.S. commander Andrew H. Foote of the sloop *Portsmouth* (18 guns) reports to Commodore James Armstrong, commanding the East India Squadron, that the Chinese have failed to provide

 **Andrew Hull Foote (1806–1863)**

U.S. Navy admiral. Born in New Haven, Connecticut, on June 20, 1806, Andrew Hull Foote was the son of a future U.S. representative and later senator. Foote briefly attended the U.S. Military Academy, West Point, during June–December 1822 but resigned to accept an appointment as an acting midshipman in the U.S. Navy on December 4.

Foote served first in the West Indies, then spent three years in the Pacific. He was advanced to passed midshipman on May 24, 1828. His religious conversion in 1827, during another Caribbean cruise, led to a lifelong interest in furthering Christianity and in reform. He was promoted to lieutenant on May 27, 1830. Following cruises in the Mediterranean and around the world during 1837–1841, he spent three years ashore as the executive officer at the Philadelphia Naval Asylum. In 1843 he became the first lieutenant of the frigate *Cumberland* and succeeded in making it the first temperance ship in the U.S. Navy. Foote was undoubtedly the key advocate in the navy for the abolition of the spirit ration, which became reality in 1862.

During 1849–1851 Foote commanded the brig *Perry* off the southwest coast of Africa, protecting U.S. trade and cruising against the slave trade, taking two slavers. After his return to the United States, Foote published a book about his experiences, *Africa and the American Flag* (1854), that was both a plea for enhanced American action against the slave trade and for support of the African colonization movement in Liberia. He was promoted to commander on December 19, 1852.

After five years ashore, where Foote remained active in naval reform, including service on the 1855 Efficiency Board that cut deadwood from the U.S. Navy, Foote returned to sea as commander of the sloop *Portsmouth* in the Asia Squadron. To avenge Chinese firing on U.S. vessels, in November 1856 Foote personally led a force ashore that destroyed four Chinese forts guarding the river approach to Guangzhou (Canton).

On the outbreak of the American Civil War, Foote was commanding the Brooklyn Navy Yard. He was promoted to captain on June 29, 1861. In August 1861 Secretary of the Navy Gideon Welles sent him to command the Union flotilla in the West, replacing Captain John Rodgers. Foote made minor changes only in the gunboats already contracted for and undergoing conversion. His chief accomplishments were to bring the warships to completion; oversee their manning, equipment, and training; and lead them in battle.

Foote got along well with his army counterpart, Brigadier General Ulysses S. Grant. Both men pushed for an attack on Fort Henry, Tennessee, and Foote's flotilla took the leading role in the February 6 Union attack on that Confederate fort and actually secured its surrender before Grant's land force arrived. Foote then sent Lieutenant Seth L. Phelps on a raid up the Tennessee River. In the subsequent Union naval attack on Fort Donelson on the Cumberland River on February 14, Foote's ironclads were rebuffed by the better-sited Confederate shore batteries, and he himself was slightly wounded, although Donelson did fall later to Grant's land troops.

In many ways, Donelson changed Foote. He became much more cautious, and working to strengthen his gunboats, he delayed their participation in attacks against New Madrid and Island No. 10. Foote preferred to use new 13-inch mortars to reduce the Confederate forts. To those who called for his ships to assault the Confederate positions, Foote pointed out the problems involved, including the substantial Confederate land batteries and the risk of losing ships in the flotilla, for unlike Donelson and Henry, any disabled gunboats would drift downriver under the Confederate guns.

Finally, following repeated appeals from Union major general John Pope, Foote did send two ironclads past the Confederate forts to cut off Island No. 10 and operate in conjunction with Pope's Army of the Mississippi. Foote then took the surrender of Island No. 10. Foote and Union troops moved down the Mississippi to Fort Pillow. By now Foote was exhausted and virtually immobile, his leg wound from Fort Donelson having failed to heal. On May 9 Foote went on a leave of absence.

In July 1862 Foote returned to active duty to head the Bureau of Equipment and Recruiting in Washington. One of the first Union naval officers promoted to the new rank of rear admiral, he was unhappy ashore. He did not seek the position, but when Welles relieved Rear Admiral Samuel Du Pont as commander of the South Atlantic Blockading Squadron, Foote agreed to take that post. He was preparing to go to Charleston when he was suddenly struck down by Bright's disease. After a short illness Foote died in New York City on June 26, 1863. Much respected, even beloved, by his men, Foote was a capable administrator and a brave and tenacious commander.

SPENCER C. TUCKER

Further Reading

Hoppin, James M. *The Life of Andrew Hull Foote, Rear Admiral, United States Navy.* New York: Harper and Brothers, 1874.

Milligan, John D. "Andrew Foote: Zealous Reformer, Administrator, Warrior." In *Captains of the Old Steam Navy: Makers of the American Naval Tradition, 1840–1880,* edited by James C. Bradford, 115–141. Annapolis, MD: Naval Institute Press, 1986.

Tucker, Spencer C. *Admiral Andrew H. Foote.* Annapolis, MD: Naval Institute Press, 1999.

an explanation and that if they do not he is prepared to "take such action as circumstances may require, in vindication of the insult offered to our flag."

On November 15, Foote himself is traveling to Guangzhou by boat with a large American flag at its stern when Chinese gunners in two forts fire five shots at the boat, all of which miss. Foote returns fire with the only weapon available, a pistol, and orders the boat to return to his ship, the sloop *Portsmouth* (18 guns). Foote reports the incident to Commodore James Armstrong, commander of the U.S. East India Squadron.

November 16–22, 1856

U.S. attack on the Barrier Forts below Guangzhou (Canton), China. Based on Commander Andrew H. Foote's report of the November 15 incident, the previously cautious Commodore James Armstrong, commanding the U.S. East India Squadron, authorizes Foote to shell the Chinese barrier forts on the Pearl River.

The four forts appear formidable. Their massive stone walls contain a total of 176 guns—many of which are of 8-inch or larger caliber—manned by some 5,000 men. But these are the same forts that the British had occupied and partially neutralized earlier.

On the morning of November 16, Armstrong sends a steamer to Guangzhou to remove most American personnel guarding factories there and bring the ships up to their full complements. He also sends an armed cutter with a pilot to sound the channel near the forts. It closes to within a mile and a half of the forts when it too comes under Chinese fire. This time the gunnery is more accurate, and a sailor is decapitated by a cannonball while heaving the sounding lead.

U.S. Attack on the Barrier Forts, below Guangzhou (Canton), China		
Date	November 16–22, 1856	
Location	On the Pearl River below Guangzhou, China	
Opponents (*winner)	*United States	China
Commander	Commander Andrew H. Foote	Unknown
#	U.S. Navy sloops *Portsmouth* and *Levant* (18 guns each); landing party of 287 men	4 forts mounting a total of 176 guns, manned by perhaps 5,000 men
Casualties	7 dead, 22 wounded	Perhaps 250 dead and wounded, 4 forts and their ordnance captured

The screw steamer *San Jacinto* (6 guns) draws too much water and cannot participate in the operation, so Armstrong distributes most of its men among the 18-gun sloops *Portsmouth* and *Levant*. He orders two hired steamers to tow the two American warships to the forts. The *Levant* grounds and thus is unable to participate in the initial attack. Battle is joined in late afternoon between the Chinese forts and the *Portsmouth*, now at anchor. During a two-hour period the *Portsmouth* fires 230 shells and some grapeshot and is in return hulled six times, with one man seriously wounded.

That night a rising tide refloats the *Levant*, and it takes up position near the *Portsmouth*, which itself grounds in vulnerable position on the morning of November 17. The Chinese fail to take advantage, and the *Portsmouth* is refloated that afternoon. With the Chinese having ceased fire, Armstrong departs for Huangpu (Whampoa) to demand an explanation and apology from Chinese imperial governor Ye Mingchen, warning that if none is forthcoming within 24 hours he will take whatever steps he believes necessary. Ye does not respond to Armstrong within the time limit and then merely requests that in the interest of safety, the Americans withdraw their ships from the river. Armstrong takes a bellicose stance in his reply, accusing Ye of waging war against the United States.

Before he had departed, Armstrong ordered Foote to remain in position near the forts but not to open fire unless first fired upon, in which case he is to take the forts and raze them. When Foote informs Armstrong that the Chinese are now clearly strengthening the forts, the commodore authorizes an attack.

At 6:45 a.m. on November 20 Foote orders his two ships to open fire on the two nearest forts. The Chinese return fire. About an hour later, Foote personally leads 287 officers, sailors, and marines, covered by 4 howitzers in boats, against the first fort. The Chinese soon abandon this position. When a second fort opens fire on the Americans in the first fort, Foote orders his men there to reposition some of its 53 cannon to take the second fort under fire and silence it. At the same time, other men in the landing party set to work spiking other guns and burning buildings. Marine rifle fire drives back a Chinese force from Guangzhou that Foote estimates to number nearly 3,000 men.

During November 21–22, American landing parties take the remaining three Chinese forts, repeating the process of the day before by using the guns of a captured fort against the next. On the afternoon of November 21 a detachment of marines seizes a battery of six guns on the riverbank, then employs boat howitzer fire to repel hundreds of Chinese soldiers advancing toward them from two directions. Foote reports that the three-day operation has claimed American casualties of 7 dead and 22 wounded. The *Portsmouth* is hit 18 times and the *Levant* 22 times, but neither is seriously damaged. Foote estimates Chinese casualties at about 250.

June 1857–April 1858

Utah War. U.S. president James Buchanan is concerned about the practice of polygamy and an apparent theocracy in the Utah Territory under the Church of Jesus Christ of Latter-day Saints (the Mormons), led by Brigham Young. In June 1857 Buchanan declares Utah to be in a state of rebellion and calls up troops. The next month Buchanan appoints Alfred Cumming as the new territorial governor but fails to notify Young of this. Command of the 2,500 troops sent to Utah falls to U.S. Army colonel Albert Sidney Johnston.

John Fulton Reynolds (1820–1863)

U.S. Army officer. Born on September 20, 1820, in Lancaster, Pennsylvania, the son of a newspaper editor, John Fulton Reynolds was a career military officer who fought in both the Mexican-American War and the American Civil War. He graduated from the U.S. Military Academy, West Point, in 1841. Reynolds first served with the U.S. artillery and spent more than five years in garrison assignments prior to the Mexican-American War.

Reynolds joined Major General Zachary Taylor's Army of Occupation at Corpus Christi, Texas, before the start of the Mexican-American War. With the beginning of hostilities, Reynolds's first major action came in the Battle of Monterrey, where his guns shelled Mexican positions as a part of Taylor's successful operation to take the city. Reynolds's unit received high praise for its effort, and Reynolds was breveted captain. During the Battle of Buena Vista in February 1847, Reynolds's guns helped repulse a Mexican effort to flank the American position, causing Mexican general Antonio López de Santa Anna to withdraw. Reynolds was breveted major for his role in the battle.

Following the Mexican-American War, Reynolds was stationed in the American West, where he fought hostile Native Americans in Oregon's Rogue River region in 1856 and served in the Mormon War from 1857 to 1858. Prior to the outbreak of the Civil War, Reynolds returned to West Point in September 1860 as commandant of cadets, a post he held when the Civil War began in 1861.

Reynolds received a commission as a brigadier general of volunteers in August 1861, and his first brigade command came with the Pennsylvania Reserves. While fighting in the Seven Days' Battles in 1862, Reynolds was taken prisoner during the Battle of Gaines' Mill on June 27. He was released in a prisoner exchange on August 13. Reynolds next fought at the Second Battle of Bull Run (Manassas) in August. On November 29, 1862, he received promotion to major general of volunteers and went on to command the Army of the Potomac's I Corps in the Battle of Fredericksburg on December 13, 1862, and at Chancellorsville during May 2–4, 1863. Reynolds was to become one of the mythic heroes of the Battle of Gettysburg (July 1–3, 1863). He was killed just west of the town on July 1 while leading his forces in support of Brigadier General John Buford's cavalry during the opening stages of the battle. Reynolds had helped make it possible for Union forces to establish the strong defensive positions that came to be known as the Fishhook, which proved critical in the battle's outcome.

NICHOLAS A. KREHBIEL

Further Reading

Clary, David A. *Eagles and Empire: The United States, Mexico, and the Struggle for a Continent*. New York: Bantam Books, 2009.

Lavender, David. *Climax at Buena Vista: The American Campaigns in Northeastern Mexico, 1846–1847*. New York: Lippincott, 1966.

Nichols, Edward J. *Toward Gettysburg: A Biography of General John F. Reynolds*. University Park: Pennsylvania State University Press, 1958.

Each side misunderstands the other's intentions, leading to the Utah War (also known as the Utah Expedition and the Mormon Expedition). Informed of the troop movement, Young mobilizes the Utah Militia. Mormon militia units attack and burn several army supply trains. With the arrival of winter, Johnston decides to delay his advance into Utah Territory and establishes camps in Wyoming. In the spring of 1858, 3,000 reinforcements arrive.

Meanwhile, with the permission of Buchanan, in February 1858 Thomas L. Kane arrives in Utah as a mediator. He persuades Young to accept Cumming as governor if there is a peaceful transition. Kane then gets Cumming to proceed to Salt Lake City without military escort. Cumming is received peacefully, and in April Young surrenders the title of governor to him. The troops arrive shortly thereafter and establish themselves in Camp Floyd, more than 30 miles from Salt Lake City. There is no violence, and the troops depart in 1860.

July 29, 1857

American Indian Wars (continued): Battle of Solomon Fork. At the Solomon River in northwestern Kansas near present-day Morland, Colonel Edwin V. Sumner leads 300 men of the 1st and 2nd Dragoon Regiments in an attack on some 300 Cheyenne warriors led by Ice and Dark. The soldiers charge with drawn sabers and scatter the Indians, pursuing them for seven miles. Nine Cheyennes are killed; the soldiers suffer 2 killed and several wounded.

November–December 1857

New Walker filibustering expedition. After having written a book about his adventures, American filibuster William Walker embarks on another filibustering operation. Eluding U.S. authorities, he sails from Mobile, Alabama, in November 1857 with some 150 supporters to try to reclaim the presidency of Nicaragua. Walker comes ashore at Greytown, but Commodore Hiram Paulding, commander of the U.S. Home Squadron, arrives at Punta Arenas in the screw frigate *Wabash* (38 guns) and immediately sends 350 men ashore, arresting Walker without bloodshed on December 8. Walker is again

returned to the United States, his actions applauded by proslavery Southerners and condemned by antislavery Northerners. The next spring Walker is again tried, in New Orleans, for the third time on having violated U.S. neutrality laws. He is again found not guilty.

January 2, 1858

Marines from the U.S. Navy frigate *St. Lawrence* (52 guns) land at Montevideo, Uruguay, to protect U.S. interests following riots there.

June 25, 1858

Treaty of Tianjin in the Second Opium War (1856–1860). Beginning on May 29, 1858, the Chinese government negotiates with representatives of the British, French, Russian, and U.S. governments, and on June 25 the two sides reach agreement. The resulting Treaty of Tianjin (Tientsin) involves the opening of treaty ports, the establishment of Western embassies in Beijing (then closed to foreigners), and other concessions. The Qing government refuses to ratify the treaty, however, and the war continues. The Qing government, however, is forced in the Treaty of Aigun of May 1858 to cede the left bank of the Amur River to Russia.

August 5, 1858

First Atlantic cable. Following an unsuccessful attempt in 1857, the U.S. Navy steam frigate *Niagara* (4 guns), commanded by Captain William L. Hudson and the largest ship built in the United States to that time, works with the Royal Navy second-rate screw steamer *Agamemnon* (91 guns) to lay the first successful Atlantic telegraph cable. The first official transatlantic telegram is a message of congratulations from Queen Victoria to President James Buchanan on August 16. Unfortunately, the cable is destroyed the following month when excessive voltage is applied in an effort to achieve faster operation. The shortness of the period of service undermines public and investor confidence, but a new cable with improved materials is laid in 1865 by the giant British steamer *Great Eastern* and, after some delays, is placed in service on July 28, 1866.

Hiram Paulding (1797–1878)

U.S. Navy officer. Born in New York City on December 11, 1799, Hiram Paulding received a midshipman's warrant on September 1, 1811. He was promoted to lieutenant on April 27, 1816; to master commandant on February 9, 1837; and to captain on February 29, 1844. During 1855–1858 he commanded the Home Squadron as commodore and then flag officer.

From March to September 1861 Paulding was assigned as chief of the Office of Detail in the Navy Department in Washington, D.C., charged with selecting officers for assignments. On April 18, Secretary of the Navy Gideon Welles, furious at the refusal of the commandant of the Norfolk Navy Yard, Captain Charles S. McCauley, to permit the steam frigate *Merrimack* to depart that place, dispatched Paulding to replace him. The yard was then threatened with takeover by the State of Virginia. Paulding arrived back at Norfolk late on April 20 following a quick trip to Washington, only to find that McCauley, believing that the yard was about to be attacked, had ordered the scuttling of all its ships. Paulding then had no choice but to continue the work already begun. He was able to get off only two ships, the screw sloop *Pawnee* towing the sailing sloop *Cumberland,* early on April 21. Once they had departed, Paulding gave the signal to torch the yard and destroy its facilities. The work of destruction on April 21 was at best only haphazard, and the result was a considerable loss not only in ships, including the *Merrimack* (which would be rebuilt by the Confederates into the ironclad *Virginia*), but also in ordnance and supplies. The Confederates' haul included 1,198 guns, including 52 IX-inch Dahlgrens. Both Paulding and McCauley came under considerable criticism in the Northern press for their handling of the situation.

In October, Paulding assumed command of the New York (Brooklyn) Navy Yard. Although he was placed on the retired list on December 21, he continued in this command. Promoted to rear admiral on the retired list on July 16, 1862, Paulding remained in command of the yard until May 1865. During 1866–1869 he was governor of the Philadelphia Naval Asylum and then port admiral of Boston, Massachusetts, until October 1870. Paulding died in Huntington, New York, on October 20, 1878.

SPENCER C. TUCKER

Further Reading

Thompson, Kenneth E. *Civil War Commodores and Admirals: A Biographical Directory of All Eighty-Eight Union and Confederate Navy Officers Who Attained Commissioned Flag Rank during the War.* Portland, ME: Thompson Group, 2001.

Tucker, Spencer C. *Blue and Gray Navies: The Civil War Afloat.* Annapolis, MD: Naval Institute Press, 2006.

October 1, 1858

Engagement at Rush Springs. In Indian Territory (present-day Oklahoma), Captain Earl Van Dorn leads men of the 2nd Cavalry Regiment accompanied by 135 allied Waco, Caddo, and Tonkawa Indians to attack a camp of 500 Comanche Indians under Chief Buffalo Hump at Rush Springs. The troopers kill 56 Indians and burn their lodges, at a cost to themselves of 5 dead. The escaping Comanches join with Kiowas at the Arkansas River.

October 6, 1858

Punitive operation in Fiji. On Waja in the Fiji Islands, Lieutenant C. H. B. Caldwell of the sloop *Vandalia* (20 guns) leads 44 men ashore to destroy a village in retaliation for the murder of 2 American traders.

Telegraph

Telegraph-like systems for the transmission of messages linked parts of the Roman Empire. Signaling stations set up at regular intervals on high ground or on towers could relay messages by flags, mirrors, fires, smoke, or other means. The English operated a system of warning beacons at the time of the Spanish Armada in 1588, while France and then Britain operated semaphore mechanical telegraph systems in the early 19th century. The French system could transmit simple messages across much of Europe in a matter of hours. Such systems were, however, subject to the vagaries of weather or actions by enemy troops and had only limited application at night. They were also costly to operate and maintain.

By about 1830, scientists determined that messages could be transmitted by means of an electrical impulse through wires. While a number of electric telegraphy systems were developed, the American Samuel Morse created a system and a code for it that employed short and long breaks in the electrical current (dots and dashes). Morse received a patent for his invention in 1840, and in 1843 the U.S. Congress appropriated funds to build a pilot 40-mile telegraph line from Baltimore to Washington. In 1844, Morse transmitted his first message over this line—"What hath God wrought!"

The telegraph allowed messages to be transmitted over considerable distances within minutes. Applied initially to the control of railroad traffic, the combination of telegraph and railroad brought about great changes in military operations. The telegraph proved of immense military value in the rapid communication of messages and control of troops during the Crimean War in the 1850s, the American Civil War (1861–1865), and the Austro-Prussian War of 1866. Telegraph lines laid under the ocean by 1866 connected Europe with North America and within decades the rest of the world.

Telegraphy was widely applied in the Boer War (1899–1902) and was used by both sides in World War I. Indeed, the telegraph remained a means of military communication through World War II. Only after 1950 did telegraph usage decline in the face of competition from the telephone. Today few except radio hams use the Morse code. The best-known telegraph signal is S-O-S, a call for assistance, consisting of three dots, three dashes, and three dots again.

SPENCER C. TUCKER

Further Reading
Beauchamp, Ken. *History of Telegraphy.* London: IEE, 2001.
Wilson, Geoffrey. *The Old Telegraphs.* London: Phillimore, 1976.

January 25, 1859
A U.S. squadron arrives in the Rio de la Plata. Flag Officer William B. Shubrick, commanding officer of the U.S. Navy Brazil Squadron, leads to Paraguay a large U.S. squadron to seek redress from the Paraguayan government for the firing on a U.S. survey vessel, the side-wheel steamer *Water Witch* (1 gun), in the Paraguay River in February 1855. The Paraguayan government quickly agrees to pay an indemnity and also concludes a new commercial treaty with the United States.

January–April 1859
Mojave War. The Mojave Native Americans live in the Mojave Valley of the Colorado River, near the convergence of the present-day states of California, Arizona, and Nevada and not far from Las Vegas. Isolated acts of violence had occurred between the

 ## Breech-Loading Field Artillery and Indirect Fire

Dramatic improvements in artillery occurred in the second half of the 19th century. The most important of these occurred in the change from muzzle-loading to breech-loading guns. This was made possible by greatly improved manufacturing techniques and tremendous advances in metallurgy, especially steel alloys. Steel guns appeared, machined to close tolerances.

Two efficient means of sealing the breech developed. The first of these employed a brass cartridge case, in effect itself the seal. This became the established process for smaller fieldpieces employing what was known as fixed ammunition, with projectile, charge, and primer all contained in one case. The second method of sealing the breech was the De Bange system. In it, the projectile, the bag or bags of powder, and the primer (vent tube) were all loaded separately. This system was used in the larger guns and had the advantage of being able to vary the range depending on powder charge utilized. In the De Bange system, a mushroom-shaped piece was driven back by the force of the exploding gunpowder against a soft obturator ring in front of the breechblock. The obturator ring expanded, sealing the breech.

Sliding breechblocks were developed for quick-firing guns. These moved to one side or downward and allowed the breech to be quickly opened and then closed again. Another system employed an interrupted screw breech. In it, the breechblock had a screw thread but with a section cut away. Turning it through a few degrees would either lock or unlock the breech, permitting rapid reloading. Usually the interrupted screw breech was used with the De Bange system.

One of the first modern breech-loading guns was the British 12-pounder (that is, firing a shell weighing 12 pounds) Armstrong field gun of 1859. In this 3-inch–caliber gun, shell and propellent were loaded separately. Some 12-pounder Armstrongs saw service on the Confederate side in the American Civil War. In 1891 both France and Germany developed recoil systems in which the gun recoiled in a slide against springs or hydro-pneumatic buffers that returned it to its original position. This meant that the artillery piece did not have to be reaimed after each round, which produced far more rapid rates of fire as well as improved accuracy. There were also new mechanical fuses, steel-jacketed projectiles, and new high-explosive fillers. Such guns were quick-firing and highly accurate. The howitzer also increased in importance. This midtrajectory weapon could fire at longer ranges than mortars. It came to be the preferred artillery piece in World War I because its high arc of fire allowed highly accurate plunging fire against enemy entrenchments.

Notable light field artillery pieces going into World War I included the French 75-millimeter (mm), dubbed the "Father, Son, and Holy Ghost of Warfare"; the Russian 76.2-mm; the British 13-pounder (3-inch) and 18-pounder (3.3-inch); and the German 77-mm. One trend during the war, however, was the increasing use of heavier guns, which were found necessary to smash through concrete bunkers. Such pieces included the British 4.5-inch and 9.2-inch howitzers and 60-pounder (5-inch) gun; the French howitzer and gun, both of 155-mm caliber; the Russian 122-mm gun; and the German 105-mm howitzer, 150-mm long gun, and 210-mm howitzer. In World War II the standard German and American field howitzers were of 105-mm. Heavier guns included the 155-mm M2 Long Tom employed by the Americans and a number of their allies.

(continued)

(Continued)

In modern artillery, caliber means two different things. It is first the diameter of the bore and second the length of the barrel. Thus, a 16-inch/50-caliber naval gun would have a bore 16 inches in diameter and a gun tube length of 16 inches by 50 or 66.67 feet.

Through the 1860s, artillery was essentially a direct-fire antipersonnel weapon. This was its primary employment in the American Civil War. During that conflict, artillerymen usually fired only at what they could actually see. If infantry were out of sight, they were generally safe from enemy artillery fire.

An important change occurred with the advent of aimed indirect fire. In 1882 the Russian Carl Guk published a system for firing on an unseen target using a compass, an aiming point, and a forward observer. The Japanese refined Guk's method and employed indirect fire with great success against the Russians in the Russo-Japanese War of 1904–1905.

By the 1890s, most European armies had standardized the techniques of artillery fire, allowing for the massing of fire on remote targets. During the 1899–1902 Boer War, the Boers concealed their artillery pieces rather than deploy them in the open, as in British practice. The advent of new smokeless powders meant that a gun's position was more difficult to locate when it was fired. At the same time, new slower-burning powder also produced more thrust against the shell and less pressure on the gun itself, allowing greater ranges.

All of these changes greatly increased the lethality of artillery. It, not the rifle or machine gun, was the great killer of World War I; estimates claim that artillery fire caused up to 70 percent of battlefield deaths in World War I.

SPENCER C. TUCKER

Further Reading

Hogg, Ian V. *The Guns, 1914–1918.* New York: Ballantine, 1971.
Hogg, Ian V. *The Illustrated Encyclopedia of Artillery.* London: Quarto Publishing, 1987.
Jobé, Joseph, ed. *Guns: An Illustrated History of Artillery.* New York: Crescent Books, 1971.

Mojaves and white trappers in the early 19th century, but tensions increase with an influx of settlers following the cession of this territory to the United States with the Mexican-American War. The ordeal of young Mormon Olive Oatman also influences American sentiment toward the Mojaves. Her family is killed, and she is taken prisoner and enslaved at age 13 in 1850 by Native Americans, perhaps the Yavapai people, and traded to the Mojaves. She is released in 1855 after officers at Fort Yuma learn of her presence. The case attracts wide attention from the American press, in part owing to the prominent blue tattooing of Oatman's face by her captors, and hardens the attitude of settlers toward Native Americans.

Increased white settlement on Mojave lands brings clashes. In 1858 after Mojaves attack a wagon train bound for California and force it to turn back, the U.S. government decides to build a fort to secure the Colorado Crossing and protect settlers. In early January 1859, Lieutenant Colonel William Hoffman of the U.S. 6th Infantry Regiment leads a reconnaissance from Fort Tejon, California, during which his men clash with the Mojaves and kill about a dozen of them in a fight at the Colorado River. Hoffman

THE MASSACRE.

Massacre of the Oatman family. In Arizona in 1850, Native Americans attacked and killed six of the nine members of the family. One of the boys survived his wounds and two daughters were kidnapped. One died in captivity, but the story of the other, Olive Oatman, who was rescued five years later, resonated with the American public. (Corbis)

then requests and receives permission for a campaign against the tribe.

In April 1859 in the Colorado River Expedition, Hoffman leads six companies of infantry and an artillery detachment from Fort Yuma into the heart of Mojave territory. The Mojave warriors withdraw on the approach of the soldiers and opt not to challenge them. On April 23, 1859, leaders of the 22 Mojave clans appear at Hoffman's encampment as ordered and agree to peace. Major Lewis Armistead assumes command from Hoffman and oversees construction of a stockade on the eastern bank of the Colorado River that becomes Fort Mojave.

April 21, 1859

At the mouth of the Congo River in West Africa, the U.S. Navy Africa Squadron sloop *Marion* (14 guns)

under Commander Thomas W. Brent captures an African slaver, the first of five taken by the U.S. Navy antislavery patrol in 1859.

June 15–October 1859

Pig War. This boundary dispute between the United States and British North America occurs over the San Juan Islands between Vancouver Island and the U.S. mainland. Because it begins with the shooting of a pig, it is known as the Pig War, but it is also called the Pig and Potato War, the San Juan Boundary Dispute, and the Northwestern Boundary Dispute. The pig is the sole casualty of this otherwise bloodless conflict.

The Oregon Treaty (see June 15, 1846) had settled an earlier boundary dispute that threatened war between the United States and Britain. The treaty also established the border along the 49th Parallel of

George Edward Pickett (1825–1875)

Confederate Army officer. George Edward Pickett was born on January 25, 1825, in Richmond, Virginia. His father was a successful planter and businessman who greatly indulged his son. Pickett entered the U.S. Military Academy, West Point, in 1842. He often challenged the authorities at West Point and graduated last in the class of 1846.

Despite his problems at West Point, Pickett served with distinction during the Mexican-American War (1846–1848). Assigned to the 8th Infantry Regiment, he participated in Major General Winfield Scott's assault against Veracruz. In the march to Mexico City, Pickett distinguished himself at the Battle of Churubusco in August 1847 and was promoted to first lieutenant. At the Battle of Chapultepec, he replaced the Mexican flag with that of the 8th Infantry, earning the respect of his men and a brevet promotion to captain. In 1848 Pickett's regiment was withdrawn from Mexico and assigned to Camp Worth near San Antonio, Texas, campaigning against the Comanches along the Texas frontier. Pickett also served in the Washington Territory during the 1850s.

As the nation drifted toward civil war, Pickett cast his lot with his home state of Virginia, resigning his U.S. Army commission on June 25, 1861, and taking a commission as a colonel in the Confederate Army. In January 14, 1862, Pickett was appointed a brigadier general and assigned to command a brigade under Major General James Longstreet. Pickett earned high praise from Longstreet for his bravery at the Battle of Williamsburg on May 5, 1862. On June 1, 1862, Pickett's brigade suffered heavy casualties in the Battle of Seven Pines (May 31–June 1, 1862). Later that same month, Pickett was wounded at the Battle of Gaines' Mill (June 27, 1862) and was out of action for three months.

On October 10, 1862, Pickett was advanced to major general and given command of a division. He saw only minimal action at the First Battle of Fredericksburg (December 13, 1862) but was destined to play a major role at the Battle of Gettysburg in 1863. Pickett and his division arrived at Gettysburg, Pennsylvania, on the evening of July 2. The next morning Army of Northern Virginia commander General Robert E. Lee, over the objections of Longstreet, ordered Pickett to attack the center of the Union line holding the high ground along Cemetery Ridge. The assault would require approximately 13,000 men to advance three-quarters of a mile across open ground to assault well-fortified Union troops, a seemingly impossible feat. The Confederates concentrated 150 guns for an artillery bombardment of the Union position, but the shelling inflicted little damage on the Union artillery or troops. Pickett's men bravely charged the Union line, but the advance quickly withered under punishing fire. Within 30 minutes, more than half of the some 12,500 men who made the charge were casualties.

While some criticized Pickett for not exercising better leadership, Pickett blamed Lee for the defeat at Gettysburg. Pickett, who was considered somewhat of a dandy with his goatee and ringlets, was never the same after that fateful day at Gettysburg, and his military reputation underwent a steady decline. He saw some additional action in North Carolina and Virginia before being relieved of his command by Lee just days before the end of the war.

Following the war, Pickett engaged in several business ventures, including insurance, that were only marginally successful. In 1870 he met with Lee for the last time, and the two men quarreled over Gettysburg. Pickett died of a liver ailment in Norfolk, Virginia, on July 30, 1875.

RON BRILEY

Further Reading

Gordon. Lesley J. *General George E. Pickett in Life & Legend.* Chapel Hill: University of North Carolina Press, 1998.
Hollingsworth, Alan M. *The Third Day at Gettysburg: Pickett's Charge.* New York: Holt, 1959.
McPherson, James M. *Battle Cry of Freedom: The Civil War Era.* New York: Oxford University Press, 1988.

latitude to the middle of the channel separating the continent from Vancouver Island. Ambiguity over the agreement remains because of poor maps and the precise channel.

In 1856 the United States and Britain establish a boundary commission, but there is no agreement. The Americans want the line drawn through Haro Strait to the west of San Juan Island, the largest of the islands; the British want it to be through Rosario Strait. Both sides thus claim all the San Juan Islands.

The British Hudson's Bay Company sets up operations on San Juan Island, and several dozen American settlers also establish residence there. On June 15, 1859, Lyman Cutlar, an American farmer on the island, kills a large pig that had repeatedly rooted potatoes in his garden. The pig turns out to have belonged to Charles Griffin, an Irish employee of the Hudson's Bay Company. The two men are unable to agree on compensation for the pig, and British authorities threaten to arrest Cutlar. The American settlers appeal to the U.S. government for protection.

Brigadier General William S. Harney, commanding the Department of Oregon, orders Captain George E. Pickett's company of the 9th Infantry Regiment to San Juan Island. The regiment arrives there on July 27. Governor of the Colony of Vancouver Island James Douglas orders British rear admiral Robert L. Boynes to land marines and evict the Americans, by force if necessary. Boynes rejects this course, but both sides steadily build up their forces on the island. By August the Americans have 461 troops and 14 guns there, commanded by Colonel Silas Casey. The British have five warships with 2,140 men. Both commanders issue identical instructions to their men: defend yourself if attacked but absolutely do not fire the first shot. Although each side tries to goad the other into attacking first, no shots are fired.

Both Washington and London express alarm at the escalating situation. Facing a sectional crisis that will soon erupt in civil war, President James Buchanan sends Lieutenant General Winfield Scott to meet with Douglas and bring events to a speedy termination. Scott, who has twice before peacefully resolved boundary disputes with the British, arrives at San Juan Island on October 10. During the next month Scott and Douglas reach agreement on defusing the crisis. Both sides are allowed to maintain troops on the island until the boundary is set: the British in the north and the Americans in the south, but these are to be limited to 100 men each.

The American Civil War puts off resolution of the matter, although in the meantime considerable fraternization occurs between the two camps on the island. Finally on May 8, 1871, British and U.S. representatives sign the Treaty of Washington, resolving a number of boundary disputes between the United States and the Dominion of Canada (established in 1867). The chief boundary issue of sovereignty over San Juan Island is decided by arbitration headed by Kaiser Wilhelm II of Germany, which rules in October 1872 in favor of the U.S. position that the center of Haro Strait is the international boundary line. San Juan Island passes to U.S. control, and both sides withdraw their small garrisons there, the British in 1872 and the Americans in 1874.

June 25, 1859

U.S. naval forces assist the British in China. The Second Opium War (1856–1860) resumes in 1859 after the Qing government refuses to permit the establishment of a British embassy in Beijing, as promised in the Treaty of Tianjin (June 1858). On June 25, 1859, British and French naval forces, now under British rear admiral Sir James Hope, again attack the Dagu (Taku or Peiho) Forts located on the Hai (Beihe) River about 36 miles from Tianjin (Tientsin). These works, destroyed in 1858, had been rebuilt by the Chinese. Hope leads nine gunboats—eight British and one French—against the forts, but the Chinese concentrate their fire on the exact spot through which the gunboats must pass, inflicting heavy casualties.

Commodore Josiah Tattnall, commanding the U.S. East India Squadron, has joined the 21-ship British and French armada for the operation. Because his flagship, the side-wheel steamer *Powhatan* (11 guns), draws too much water, Tattnall charters the steamer *Toeywan*. With the allied landing force in great difficulty, Tattnall violates his orders and American neutrality by assisting the British. Tattnall employs the *Toeywan* to tow British boats with reinforcements into the battle. He then visits the British flagship, the wooden screw gunboat *Cormorant* (4 guns), in his launch, there ordering his men to man one of the guns and shell a Chinese fort. Several eyewitnesses report Tattnall as declaring that "blood is thicker than water," and one witness has him also saying that "he'd be damned if he'd stand by and see white men butchered before his eyes." In the fighting the British lose 3 gunboats as well as 89 men killed and 345 wounded. French losses are 4 killed and 10 wounded. The Americans lose 1 man killed. Chinese casualties are unknown.

Tattnall might have been court-martialed for his actions in exceeding his instructions except for very favorable press coverage in the United States and in the usually anti-American British newspapers lauding his gallantry and humanitarianism but also because of strong British government praise conveyed to Washington. Significantly, Tattnall's action is not mentioned in the annual report of the U.S. secretary of the navy.

July 31, 1859

At the request of the U.S. consul at Shanghai, Captain William C. Nicholson of the side-wheel steamer *Mississippi* (11 guns) lands men to protect American lives and property.

October 16–18, 1859

John Brown's Raid. Abolitionist John Brown and 18 followers seize the Federal Arsenal at Harpers Ferry, Virginia (now in West Virginia). They hope to spark a slave insurrection in the South and then arm the slaves with the seized weapons. The assault is poorly executed, word soon gets to Washington of events, and the slave insurrection fails to occur. Maryland and Virginia militia are called out, with the raiders defeated by 88 marines under U.S. Army colonel Robert E. Lee. The troops lose 1 killed and 1 wounded; civilian losses are 6 killed and 9 wounded, while the raiders sustain 10 killed and 7 captured; 4 others escape. Brown is among the prisoners. They are charged with murder, conspiracy, and treason against Virginia.

Brown rejects his counsel's suggestion of an insanity plea. He is convicted and hanged on December 2. Four other raiders are executed on December 15, and the remaining two are executed on March 16. The raid greatly alarms whites in the South and leads to the establishment of numerous militia companies and thus militarization of the South before the Civil War.

February 6, 1860

On this date, the U.S. Navy sloop *Portsmouth* (16 guns), captained by Commander John Colhoun, captures the first of 13 slave ships taken by the U.S. antislavery patrol this year.

March 1–2, 1860

At Kissembo in present-day Angola, Commander Thomas W. Brent lands 50 seamen and marines from the sloop *Marion* (14 guns) to protect American property.

March 6, 1860

On this date in Washington, D.C., Christopher M. Spencer receives a patent for his breech-loading repeating rifle. This important weapon signals the decline of single-shot muzzle-loading rifles as the primary infantry firearm.

May 12, 1860

Beginning of the Paiute War: Battle of Big Bend. Tensions between whites and the Paiutes in Utah Territory have steadily increased from the onset of the California Gold Rush in 1849 as settlers traverse Paiute territory along the California Trail. By 1860, reports of silver and gold deposits of the Comstock Lode lead to increasing numbers of miners and settlers, bringing their numbers approximately equal to that of the Paiutes. Conflict is virtually unavoidable. The winter of 1859–1860 is a cold one with considerable snow, bringing great hardship to the Paiutes. It also sees the death of old Chief Winnemucca, who was respected by both sides and who had helped keep the peace.

In the spring of 1860 with food in short supply, Paiutes from across the Great Basin gather at Pyramid Lake, some 35 miles northeast of present-day Reno, Nevada, for the spring fish run but also for a war council. A majority of those at the council favor war, but only Chief Numaga understands and voices the futility

Breech-Loading Rifles

The first guns were actually breech-loaders, but the difficulty of effectively sealing the gases at the breech led to their abandonment and the embrace of the muzzle-loader for both cannon and small arms. Improvements in metallurgical techniques and closer tolerances were one factor in changing this. The other was the change from a loose propellent charge in connection with the flint-and-steel method of firing to a metal cartridge case that contained both powder and projectile. Handmade cartridge cases, tailored to the gun so that their fire port matched one drilled through the gun breech, while possible for the very rich, were not practical for the equipment of mass armies.

The discovery of fulminate of mercury and the development of Alexander Forsyth's percussion cap did away with the necessity of striking fire outside the gun. The next step was to incorporate the percussion cap into a cartridge holding both gunpowder and the bullet, while a hinged-block or bolt opening made in the breech allowed the cartridge to be inserted there. Pulling the trigger released a steel pin that jabbed into the percussion cap and ignited it and thus the main charge. The first was the pin-fire cartridge in the 1840s followed by the rimfire cartridge and then by 1860 the central-fire cartridge. Prussia took the lead. In the 1840s it adopted the Dreyse breech-loading rifle, better known as the needle-gun, a bolt-operated weapon that, however, utilized a paper cartridge.

The Spencer carbine of the American Civil War (1861–1865) was another important step forward. First produced in 1860 and issued to units of the Union Army, it featured a magazine, loaded through the butt of the rifle stock, that could hold seven metallic rimfire cartridges. These were fed to the breech by means of a compressed spring. When the trigger guard was lowered, the breechblock dropped down, ejecting the spent cartridge case. As the trigger guard was returned to its normal position, the breechblock moved up, catching a new cartridge and inserting it into the breech. Some 200,000 Spencers were produced.

(continued)

(Continued)

Among the most important weapons utilizing this principle were the .44-caliber rimfire lever-action breech-loading rifle, designed by American Benjamin Taylor Henry in the late 1850s, and the "improved Henry," the Model 1866 lever-action Winchester, its most notable improvement over the Henry being the addition of a patented cartridge-loading gate system that allowed for a closed magazine tube and a wood forearm. The Model 1866 fired the same .44-caliber rimfire round as the Henry rifle; however, cartridge improvements allowed a shorter carbine barrel length. Its follow-on was the Winchester Model 1873, the weapon that is said to have "won the West." Replica Henry and Winchester rifles remain in production.

In 1865 Erskine S. Allin, master armorer at Springfield Armory, came up with a trapdoor breechblock design that allowed conversion of the muzzle-loading U.S. Army rifled muskets, of which there were a vast number, into breech-loaders. These .58-caliber weapons were improved in the 1866 model that utilized an improved .50-caliber center-fire cartridge in place of the .58-caliber rimfire cartridge 1865 model. Some 25,000 of these were converted at the Springfield arsenal, with their barrels relined and then rifled to .50-caliber and the trapdoor system installed. First issued to U.S. troops in 1867, they proved a major factor in the Wagon Box Fight and the Hayfield Fight on the Bozeman Trail of that year when the attacking Indians did not anticipate the greatly increased firing rate.

The breech-loader could be loaded and fired three times as fast as the old muzzle-loader, but its chief advantage was that this could be easily accomplished in the prone position. By the 1870s, breech-loaders had magazines attached from which rounds could be fed to the breech as fast as the rifleman could aim, fire, and work the reloading mechanism that would eject the spent case, feed a new round into the breech, and cock the firing mechanism by either bolt or lever action.

By the first decade of the 20th century, fine bolt-action repeating rifles such as the German Mauser, the British Lee-Enfield, and the American Springfield provided riflemen with greatly enhanced firepower at ranges of up to 1,000 yards or more.

SPENCER C. TUCKER

Further Reading

Blair, Claude, ed. *Pollard's History of Firearms*. New York: Macmillan, 1983.
Smith, W. H. B. *Small Arms of the World*. London: Arms and Armour, 1984.
Westwood, David. *Rifles: An Illustrated History of Their Impact*. Santa Barbara, CA: ABC-CLIO, 2005.

of such a course. In the course of the meeting, word is received that two brothers at the Williams Station trading post on the Carson River had kidnapped and raped two young Paiute girls and that their families then retaliated on May 7 by burning down the station and killing five whites there. This settles the issue of war and peace as news circulates quickly and sends panic throughout whites in the region.

In short order, 105 mounted but poorly armed settler volunteers assemble at Virginia City determined to teach the Paiutes a lesson. They are in four detachments, but Major William M. Ormsby of the Carson City Rangers has overall command. Few have any military experience. Departing Virginia City on the morning of May 9, they arrive at Williams Station the next day, bury the dead from the Paiute attack, and then move to the Big Bend of the Truckee River. On the morning of May 12 they continue north up the Truckee River, only to encounter Paiute warriors led by Numaga.

In the ensuing Battle of Big Bend (First Battle of Pyramid Lake), which begins the Paiute War (Pyramid Lake War), half of the volunteers pursue what they believe to be a small number of Paiutes, only to be surrounded on three sides. Ormsby is among those killed as his men attempt to flee. All the volunteers then take flight. Darkness saves some, but reports put the number of dead whites at 42, with another 30 missing and only 33 reaching their communities. This is the largest number of Euro-Americans killed in a confrontation with Indians in 69 years. The Paiutes claim to have lost only 3 warriors wounded and two horses killed.

June 2, 1860

Paiute War (continued): Second Battle of Big Bend. The Paiute victory in the First Battle of Big Bend (First Battle of Pyramid Lake) in present-day Nevada (see May 12, 1860) brings panic among miners and settlers. Mining operations shut down completely, and many settlers flee the area. The Indian triumph is short-lived, however.

A telegraph appeal to California brings 544 volunteers from that state and Washoe Country under the leadership of Colonel John Coffee Hays. Joining them are 207 army regulars led by Captain Joseph Stewart. These men and Paiute warriors meet in the Second Battle of Big Bend (Second Battle of Pyramid Lake), fought near where the first had occurred. For their protection the Paiute women and children are temporarily relocated in the Black Rock Desert.

The Second Battle of Big Bend lasts three hours and ends in a draw. The volunteers and soldiers lose only three killed; Paiute losses are unknown but are probably light. That night the Paiute warriors slip away, allowing their opponents to claim victory.

Small-scale raids and skirmishes continue into August. With the Paiutes suffering from food shortages, especially through the disruption of fishing at Pyramid Lake (starvation probably claims more Paiute lives than the fighting), Chief Numaga and whites in the area north of Pyramid Lake enter into an informal cease-fire, bringing the Paiute War to a close. However, a number of Paiutes will subsequently take part in the 1878 Bannock War (Bannock-Paiute War).

August–September 12, 1860

Walker's final filibustering operation. After his third trial and acquittal for having violated U.S. neutrality laws, Walker again attempts to return to Nicaragua. The schooner transporting him and his men strikes a reef off Belize. A British warship rescues the filibusters and returns them to Mobile, Alabama. The wreck of his ship fails to deter Walker from yet another attempt. Evading U.S. and British warships, Walker lands his force of 91 men on the Honduran coast and on August 6, 1859, captures Trujillo and begins a march toward Nicaragua. En route, however, they meet opposition from Honduran infantry and sustain major losses. British warships off the coast prevent reinforcements from joining Walker, and his "army" is soon down to 31 men, nearly all of whom, including Walker, are wounded. On September 3 Royal Navy commander Norvell Salmon takes Walker and his men aboard his warship, the screw sloop *Icarus*, personally assuring them of safe conduct.

For reasons that remain unclear, Salmon changes his mind and sails to Trujillo, where he turns Walker and his deputy, Colonel A. F. Rudler, over to Honduran authorities. Rudler is sentenced to four years in the mines, but Walker is condemned to death. Walker is executed by firing squad on September 12. The rest of his men are deposited on the Honduran island of Roatán. Of the original 91 men who accompanied Walker, only 12 return to the United States.

September 18, 1860

The sloop *Levant* (18 guns) under Commander William E. Hunt departs Hilo, Hawaii, for Aspinwall, Colombia, and is lost at sea, probably to a hurricane.

September 27, 1860

At Panama City, Colombia, the sloop *St. Mary's* (22 guns) lands a party of marines to help quell an insurrection.

November 1860

Background to the Civil War: Causes of the war. By 1860, North and South are completely estranged. The essentially agricultural South is the world's largest producer of raw cotton, the vast majority of which is

North and South on the Eve of the Civil War, March 1861		
Area	United States	Confederacy
Number of states	23	11
Population	22.3 million	9.1 million (nearly 4 million slaves)
Industrial capacity	92 percent	8 percent
Banking capital	82 percent	18 percent
Economy overall	Self-sufficient	Export driven, requiring imports of manufactured goods
Railroad track	21,827 miles	8,947 miles
Men under arms	17,000	35,000
Warships (purpose-built)	90	1

exported, chiefly to the United Kingdom. Southerners want a low tariff to be able to purchase cheaper British-manufactured goods. Some 85 percent of the nation's industry is in the North. Northerners want a high tariff to protect their goods against British manufactures. Banking, insurance companies, and railroads are all concentrated in the North. The West is increasingly tied to the North by the expanding railroad net.

There is also a large growing population imbalance between the two regions. New immigrants, unable to compete with slave labor in the South, settle primarily in the North.

Increasingly, Southerners believe that their way of life is threatened as abolitionist movements gain strength worldwide. Most Southerners support the right of a state to secede from the Union, whereas Northerners reject this. Institutions, including churches and political parties, all split along regional lines.

November 1860–April 1861

Canby's Campaign. After the United States establishes its authority in New Mexico following the Mexican-American War, tensions with Navajo Native Americans there steadily escalate. The cause is the seizure of Navajo grazing lands by white settlers, supported by the U.S. Army. Indeed, territorial governor Abraham Rencher (1857–1861) places primary blame on Colonel Benjamin L. Bonneville, who in 1858 forces a treaty on the Navajos that takes away most of their land in New Mexico proper, and on local militiamen who attack the Navajos without authorization. Rencher warns Washington that given this state of affairs, the Navajos will have little recourse but to turn to banditry, making full-scale war inevitable.

As Rencher predicts, hard-pressed Navajo warriors began attacking supply trains in western New Mexico, leading to a vicious cycle of reprisals by the army and white settlers and counterreprisals by the Navajos. Angered that whites have burned his home and killed some 50 of his sheep, on April 20, 1860, Navajo chief Manuelito leads some 1,000 warriors in an attack that nearly overruns Fort Defiance, the chief army post in New Mexico Territory, near present-day Window Rock, Arizona. Rencher has no choice but to seek army assistance, and federal officials order Brevet Lieutenant Colonel Edward R. S. Canby to lead elements of the 10th Infantry Regiment stationed at Fort Garland, New Mexico, to Fort Defiance, where they are to join men of the 5th and 7th Infantry Regiments and the 2nd Dragoon Regiment.

Canby's Campaign begins in November 1860 with his departure from Fort Defiance with 600 soldiers, accompanied by Ute scouts and a small contingent of New Mexico volunteers under Captain Blas Lucero. Canby divides his force into three detachments, leading one himself and placing the others under Major Henry Hopkins Sibley and Captain Lafayette McLaws. During the next month, Canby's men

Edward Richard Sprigg Canby (1817–1873)

U.S. Army officer. Edward Richard Sprigg Canby was born on November 9, 1817, at Platt's Landing, Kentucky. As a boy, he moved with his family to neighboring Indiana. Canby graduated from the U.S. Military Academy, West Point, in 1835. Commissioned a second lieutenant, he saw action in the Second Seminole War (1835–1842) in Florida and then fought in the Mexican-American War (1846–1848), earning promotion to first lieutenant in 1846. He was twice breveted (major and lieutenant colonel) for gallantry in the latter conflict.

In 1855 after numerous staff assignments, Canby was promoted directly to major in the 10th Infantry Regiment. In November 1860 he launched an offensive against the Navajos in New Mexico, known as Canby's Campaign. Commanding under his brevet rank of lieutenant colonel, he led elements of the 10th Infantry Regiment from Fort Garland, New Mexico, to Fort Defiance, where he was to link up with the 5th and 7th Infantry Regiments and the 2nd Dragoon Regiment. The fighting endured through December but was inconclusive. In January 1861 Canby launched another offensive. This time he was more successful, and by April he had negotiated treaties with 54 Navajo leaders, guaranteeing food, clothing, and protection in return for a sustained peace.

In April 1861 when the American Civil War began, Canby was still at Fort Defiance. Within weeks of the start of the conflict, he was named commander of the Department of New Mexico, having been appointed colonel of the new 19th Infantry Regiment. The beginning of the war made it impossible for the U.S. government to fulfill its obligations, and the Navajos renewed their attacks. Now concerned chiefly with the Confederate threat, Canby could do little to respond to the renewed Navajo raids.

When Confederate troops invaded the territory in early 1862, Canby oversaw the Union counteroffensive, but his Union troops were defeated on February 21, 1862, at Val Verde, New Mexico. A month later at the Battle of Glorieta Pass (March 26–28, 1862), sometimes referred to as the "Gettysburg of the West," Canby's force, now reinforced by a contingent of Colorado volunteers, suffered a tactical battlefield defeat.

The battle turned into a strategic victory, however, when Colorado volunteers under Major John M. Chivington captured the Confederate supply train at Johnson's Ranch. This forced a Confederate withdrawal to Santa Fe. Supply shortages, above all of food, then caused the Confederates to quit New Mexico.

Appointed brigadier general of volunteers, Canby went east, serving for almost two years as adjutant general in Washington, D.C. In July 1863 he commanded the Union troops who put down the New York City draft riots. On May 7, 1864, Canby was advanced to major general of volunteers and took command of the Military Division of West Mississippi. In that post he commanded Union troops who helped capture Confederate forts in highly effective cooperation with Union naval forces under Rear Admiral David G. Farragut during the Battle of Mobile Bay on August 5, 1864.

Canby then commanded the land forces attempting to take Mobile, which finally fell on April 12, 1865. On May 26, 1865, more than a month after General Robert E. Lee's surrender at Appomattox Court House, Canby had the distinction of accepting the surrender of the last major Confederate commands, those of Lieutenant General Richard Taylor and General Edmund Kirby Smith.

(continued)

(Continued)

During the army reorganization in 1866, Canby was confirmed in the regular rank of brigadier general. He then held a variety of posts in Washington and in the South before taking command of the Department of the Columbia in 1870. There he oversaw numerous campaigns against and peace initiatives with the Native Americans. In Siskiyou, California, on April 11, 1873, Canby and a civilian negotiator were treacherously murdered and another civilian was badly wounded during peace talks with hostile Modocs. Canby thus became the only full-rank general officer to be killed during the post–Civil War Indian Wars.

PAUL G. PIERPAOLI JR.

Further Reading

Colton, Ray C. *The Civil War in the Western Territories: Arizona, Colorado, New Mexico, and Utah.* Norman: University of Oklahoma Press, 1959.

Cottrell, Steve. *Civil War in Texas and New Mexico Territory.* Greta, LA: Pelican, 1998.

Larson, Carole. *Forgotten Frontier: The Story of Southeastern New Mexico.* Albuquerque: University of New Mexico Press, 1993.

---

kill 35–40 Navajos. They also seize more than 1,000 Navajo horses and kill several thousand Navajo sheep.

Lack of water and forage caused by the severe drought of 1860 forces Canby to return to Fort Defiance in December without securing a peace treaty. In January 1861 he launches a second campaign from Fort Defiance that focuses primarily on destruction of Navajo crops and livestock. By April, Canby has negotiated a series of treaties with 54 Navajo chiefs, guaranteeing food, clothing, and the army's protection in return for peace.

Unfortunately for the Navajos, the outbreak of the American Civil War in April 1861 prevents the federal government from fulfilling its promises. Canby, appointed colonel of the new 19th Infantry Regiment, commands the Department of New Mexico, but his chief concern is to defend it from Confederate attack. The Navajos take advantage of the situation by renewing attacks on white settlements, for which they will be forced to pay a heavy price in the Long Walk (removal) to Bosque Redondo in 1864.

November 1, 1860

The Navy Department announces plans to convert seven of its sailing ships to steamers at a total cost of more than $3 million.

November 6, 1860

Background to the Civil War (continued): Causes (continued): Lincoln elected president. The Republicans win the congressional elections of 1858, and party leaders hope they can take the presidency in 1860. Leaders of the Deep South make it clear, however, that they will not submit to the rule of a "Black Republican" president. At the Republican convention in May, the platform calls for no more slavery in the territories but no interference with slavery in the states, thus rejecting the abolitionists. Abraham Lincoln of Illinois receives the party nomination.

Meanwhile, the Democratic Party splits on the issue of slavery. Southern Democrats insist on a platform supporting positive protection of slavery in the territories and the acquisition of Cuba. With the party not going far enough in support of slavery to suit Southerners, Jefferson Davis of Mississippi leads a secessionist movement. This proves a disaster for the South, because the only possible way it can protect slavery is to elect a Democrat to the presidency. The sectional split renders this impossible.

Davis hopes that he can deny a majority in the Electoral College and throw the presidential election into the Congress. The Democrats nominate Stephen A. Douglas, while the secessionists nominate John C.

Breckinridge. The House is so evenly divided that it would have been deadlocked, but in the Senate the Democrats have a majority and thus can hope to elect a proslavery candidate.

Lincoln wins the election. He is a minority president, receiving a plurality of the popular vote but a majority in the Electoral College. The results are Lincoln, 1,866,452 popular votes and 180 electoral votes; Douglas, 1,376,957 popular votes and 12 electoral votes; Breckinridge, 849,781 popular votes and 72 electoral votes; and John Bell of the National Constitutional Union, 588,879 popular votes and 39 electoral votes. President James Buchanan still has four more months in office, however, and Lincoln is not inaugurated until March 4, 1861.

November 15–December 12, 1860

Background to the Civil War (continued): Events at Charleston. On November 15, 1860, Major Robert Anderson, a Southerner who owns slaves and is thus thought to be able to communicate with the secessionists, is appointed to command the small U.S. Army garrison at Fort Moultrie at Charleston, South Carolina. On November 23 Anderson advises Washington that Moultrie is vulnerable to land attack and requests permission to withdraw his troops to Fort Sumter in Charleston Harbor. On December 11, Anderson receives word from Major Don Carlos Buell that Secretary of War John B. Floyd, a Virginian and secessionist sympathizer, has denied his request for reinforcements. The next day in Washington, President James Buchanan also declines to send reinforcements to avoid provoking a confrontation with South Carolina authorities. This decision leads Secretary of State Lewis Cass to resign.

December 20, 1860

Background to the Civil War (continued): Causes (continued): Secession of South Carolina from the Union. The election of Republican Party candidate Abraham Lincoln as president of the United States on November 6, 1860, prompts the secession from the Union of the Deep South. A South Carolina convention meeting at Charleston on December 20, 1860, passes without dissenting vote a resolution declaring that the union between South Carolina and the United States of America is "dissolved." On December 24 the convention issues a declaration reiterating arguments for state sovereignty and justifying secession on what it claims as the North's long-running attack on slavery, the accession to power of a sectional party (the Republicans), and the election of a president (Lincoln) "whose opinions and purposes are hostile to slavery."

The other states of the Deep South follow suit: Mississippi (January 9, 1861), Florida (January 10), Alabama (January 11), Georgia (January 19), Louisiana (January 26), and Texas (February 1). Waverers on secession are convinced by the argument that the South will be able to conclude better terms out of the Union than in it, renegotiating a new political framework for the United States.

December 26, 1860

Background to the Civil War (continued): Anderson relocates U.S. forces to Fort Sumter. With Fort Moultrie vulnerable to land attack, on the night of December 26 U.S. Army major Robert Anderson relocates his men to the more easily defensible Fort Sumter in Charleston Harbor. This as yet incomplete Third System masonry fort occupies an artificial island of 70,000 tons of granite deposited on a sandbar at the mouth of Charleston Harbor and controlling access to it.

Anderson's action enrages South Carolina authorities, and during the next several days South Carolina forces occupy both Fort Moultrie and Castle Pinckney ringing Charleston Harbor. This constitutes the first act of military aggression by South Carolina against the United States. South Carolina authorities then seize all remaining federal properties in Charleston, with the exception of Fort Sumter.

December 27, 1860

Background to the Civil War (continued). South Carolina militiamen seize the U.S. Revenue Service cutter *William Aiken* in Charleston Harbor.

1860–1862

Frederick T. Ward commands imperial forces in China. With the end of the Second Opium War

Don Carlos Buell (1818–1898)

U.S. Army officer. Don Carlos Buell was born in Marietta, Ohio, on March 23, 1818. He graduated from the U.S. Military Academy, West Point, in 1841 and was commissioned a second lieutenant and posted to the 3rd Infantry Regiment. He first saw fighting in the Seminole War of 1838–1842. During the Mexican-American War (1846–1848), he distinguished himself in service under Major Generals Zachary Taylor and Winfield Scott. Following the war, Buell was assigned to the adjutant general's office as a lieutenant colonel and was posted to California as adjutant general of the Department of the Pacific.

Following the beginning of the American Civil War, Buell was commissioned a brigadier general of volunteers in May 1861 and assigned to help organize the defenses of Washington, D.C. That August he was assigned to the Army of the Potomac to command a division under Major General George McClellan. In November, Buell succeeded Brigadier General William T. Sherman as commander of the Department of the Ohio. Buell was promoted to major general in March 1862. Ordered to Tennessee, his forces moved slowly but captured Nashville on February 25, the first Confederate capital to fall to Union forces. Dispatched to assist forces under Major General Ulysses S. Grant in a drive on Corinth, Mississippi, Buell arrived with his men at Pittsburg Landing on the evening of April 6, 1862, too late to take part in that day's fighting. His reinforcements helped win the Union victory the next day in the bloody Battle of Shiloh (April 6–7). Buell subsequently, and unjustifiably, claimed that he, rather than Grant, was responsible for the victory.

From this point forward things did not go well for Buell. Always a cautious commander, his campaigning in both Tennessee and Kentucky was marked by delays and missed opportunities. In advancing his four divisions toward Chattanooga along the Memphis and Charleston Railway, in three weeks he progressed only 90 miles from Corinth. His movements were further stalled by activities of Confederate cavalry under Brigadier General Nathan Bedford Forrest, who maneuvered behind Buell and attacked Murfreesboro on July 13. Confederate cavalry also attacked a number of bridges south of Nashville. In August 1862, Buell's supply lines were once more struck, this time by Confederate colonel John Hunt Morgan, who blocked a railway tunnel north of Nashville to sever Buell's communications. Buell's evacuation of central Tennessee in September when Confederate forces under General Braxton Bragg and Major General Kirby Smith invaded Kentucky, despite the fact that Buell's force was superior to his enemy in numbers, brought heavy criticism in the Northern press. At the end of September, Buell was informed that Major General George Thomas had been selected to replace him, but Thomas pointed out that Buell was ready to take the offensive, and the order was rescinded.

At Perryville, Kentucky, on October 8, 1862, Buell blundered into General Braxton Bragg's army. Both sides committed troops piecemeal into what became a bloody battle. Ultimately Bragg withdrew back into Tennessee. Buell's failure to pursue Bragg, on a claim of supply shortages, enraged both Washington and the Northern public, and he was relieved of his command on October 24, replaced by Major General William S. Rosecrans. Buell's conduct during this period was investigated by the army, and although a report was produced, it was never officially published.

Buell moved to Indianapolis to await a further command. Although he was offered several postings, he turned them down because he would be serving under officers whom he believed he outranked. Accordingly, on May 23, 1864, he resigned from the volunteers and left the regular army on June 1.

Buell subsequently supported George McClellan in his campaign against Abraham Lincoln in the presidential election of November 1864.

Following the war, Buell lived in Indiana and Kentucky. From 1865 to 1870, he was president of the Green River Iron Company, and during 1885–1889 he served as a government pension agent in Louisville, Kentucky. Buell died in Rockport, Kentucky, on November 19, 1898.

RALPH BAKER AND SPENCER C. TUCKER

Further Reading

Broadwater, Robert P. *Battle of Perryville, 1862: Culmination of the Failed Kentucky Campaign.* Jefferson, NC: McFarland, 2005.

Engle, Steven D. *Don Carlos Buell: The Most Promising of All.* Chapel Hill: University of North Carolina Press 1999.

Prokopowicz, Gerald J. *All for the Regiment: The Army of Ohio 1861–1865.* Chapel Hill: University of North Carolina Press, 2001.

(*Arrow* War) in 1860, Viceroy Zeng Guofan (Tseng Kuo-fan) and Li Hongzhang (Li Hung-chang) work to reform and revitalize the imperial government. They also attempt to subdue the Taiping regime in southern China. Despite their promises of reform that have drawn so many peasants to their banner, the Taipings have become increasingly repressive.

With the Taipings threatening Shanghai, in 1860 wealthy merchants there finance a mercenary army. Initially composed of foreigners, it is commanded by Frederick Townsend Ward, who arrives in the city with his brother that same year. Ward is an American merchant marine officer and soldier of fortune from Salem, Massachusetts, who had been a filibuster in Mexico and had fought in the Crimean War as an officer in the French Army. His Foreign Arms Corps begins with about 100 men and a military reverse but steadily grows in size and comes to be known as the Ever Victorious Army for a series of successful operations.

In 1861 Ward is made a brigadier general in the Imperial Army. During a four-month span he and his army, assisted by British and French forces returning from operations at Beijing, win 11 victories and clear a swath of territory about 30 miles wide around Shanghai. On August 20, 1862, however, Ward is mortally wounded while leading an assault on the walled city of Cixi (Tzeki) in Zhejiang (Chekiang).

January 5, 1861

Background to the Civil War (continued). Alabama militiamen seize control of federal Forts Morgan and Gaines controlling access to Mobile Bay.

January 9, 1861

Background to the Civil War (continued): South Carolina forces fire on the *Star of the West*. In a stiffening of resolve regarding secession, U.S. president James Buchanan finally agrees that something must be done to resupply and reinforce Major Robert Anderson's small federal garrison at Fort Sumter but rejects plans to send the powerful screw sloop *Brooklyn* (10 guns) as too provocative. The War Department contracts for the private side-wheel steamer *Star of the West*, which sails from New York City on January 5, 1861, with supplies and 200 reinforcements. Efforts to keep this operation secret fail when the Northern press publishes news of the ship's sailing and its intended mission. This is telegraphed to Charleston.

When the *Star of the West* arrives off Charleston Harbor and attempts to reach Fort Sumter early on the morning of January 9, cadets of the Military College of South Carolina (the Citadel), manning batteries at Fort Moultrie and Morris Island, open fire. After a shot across its bow, the unarmed *Star of the West* runs up a large American flag. This does not deter the gunners, who hull the ship twice in the first hostile fire of the Civil War. His ship moderately damaged, the captain of the *Star of the West* returns to New York.

January 10, 1861

Background to the Civil War (continued): Federal evacuation of Pensacola, Florida. Lieutenant Adam J. Slemmer, acting commander of the 50-man federal garrison at Fort Barrancas, aware that this installation, designed to protect the Pensacola Navy Yard from naval assault, is vulnerable to land attack, spikes his guns and transfers the garrison and ammunition and supplies by barge to Fort Pickens on Santa Rosa Island. The navy also abandons the Pensacola Navy Yard. On January 12 Florida militiamen occupy the yard and Forts Barrancas and McCree. U.S. troops refuse to surrender Fort Pickens; it remains in federal hands throughout the war.

January 11, 1861

Background to the Civil War (continued). U.S. Army major Robert Anderson, commanding the federal garrison at Fort Sumter, rejects demands from South Carolina governor Francis W. Pickens to surrender Fort Sumter to state authorities. Anderson refuses similar demands on January 15 and 18.

January 11, 1861

Background to the Civil War (continued). At Baton Rouge, Louisiana, U.S. Army major Joseph A. Haskins, commanding two companies of artillerymen, surrenders the U.S. arsenal here after being surrounded by 600 Louisiana militiamen.

January 14, 1861

Background to the Civil War (continued). U.S. Army captain John M. Brannan preemptively occupies Fort Taylor at Key West, Florida. It becomes a primary coaling station for the subsequent U.S. naval blockade of the Confederacy.

January 24, 1861

Background to the Civil War (continued). The U.S. Navy screw sloop *Brooklyn* (10 guns), frigate *Sabine* (48 guns), and sailing sloops *Macedonian* (22 guns) and *St. Louis* (18 guns) depart Fortress Monroe, Virginia, with a troop contingent to reinforce Fort Pickens on Santa Rosa Island off the coast of Pensacola, Florida. To avoid escalating the crisis, on January 29 orders are issued that the reinforcements are not to disembark unless Fort Pickens is attacked.

January 27–February 18, 1861

The Bascom Affair and the start of the Apache Wars. On January 27, 1861, Coyotero Apaches raid John Ward's ranch along Sonoita Creek in present-day Arizona. The Coyoteros steal 20 cattle and abduct Felix, the 12-year-old son of Ward's Mexican mistress, Jesusa Martínez. Learning of the raid, Ward travels to Fort Buchanan and reports events to its commander, Lieutenant Colonel Pitcairn Morrison. The next morning Morrison dispatches inexperienced Second Lieutenant George N. Bascom and a contingent of troops to investigate. Bascom mistakenly concludes that the raid had been carried out by the Chokonen band of Chiricahua Apaches led by Cochise.

On January 29, Morrison orders Bascom and 54 men mounted on mules to proceed to Apache Pass about 150 miles to the northeast and there rescue the boy and secure the stolen cattle. Ward and an interpreter accompany the expedition. On February 3 Bascom's command arrives at Siphon Canyon, a short distance from Cochise's camp at Goodwin Canyon. Learning of Bascom's presence, Cochise, who is friendly toward Americans, and 6 members of his family go to greet Bascom's party. Bascom demands the return of the boy and the cattle. Cochise denies any knowledge of the raid, but Bascom informs Cochise that he is taking him hostage. Following a scuffle, Cochise escapes, but his family members are taken prisoner.

Following a series of skirmishes between Americans and Cochise's followers in the area surrounding Apache Pass and in retaliation for soldiers who have been slain, Bascom's troops execute Cochise's family on February 18. Bascom returns to Fort Buchanan the next day to be commended by Morrison, despite the fact that the kidnapped boy, who is adopted by the White Mountain Apaches and later becomes a U.S. Army scout known as Mickey Free, is not recovered.

As soon as he learns of the murder of his brother and nephews, Cochise, joined by Mangas Coloradas and his Mimbres Apaches, launches the Apache Wars. These continue, with only brief respites, to 1886.

February 8, 1861

Background to the Civil War (continued): Establishment of the Confederate States of America. In Montgomery, Alabama, representatives of the seven seceded states of the Deep South meet and proclaim the Confederate States of America. On February 9 they elect as president Jefferson Davis of Mississippi. He is officially inaugurated on February 18. U.S. president James Buchanan, whose administration still has a month to run, is fearful of offending Virginia and other border states and does nothing. His successor, Abraham Lincoln, also makes no move against the South during his first six weeks in office.

February 18, 1861

Background to the Civil War (continued). Brevet Major General David E. Twiggs, commanding the Department of Texas, surrenders all U.S. Army installations, personnel, supplies, and equipment in the state. Twiggs subsequently secures a commission as a major general in the Confederate Army. Twiggs is the oldest and most senior U.S. Army officer to declare for the Confederacy.

February 20, 1861

Background to the Civil War (continued). The Confederate Congress establishes a Navy Department and declares the Mississippi River a free-trade zone. The next day President Jefferson Davis appoints Stephen R. Mallory, former U.S. senator from Florida and chair of the Naval Affairs Committee, as secretary of the navy. He will hold this post throughout the war.

February 1861

Background to the Civil War (continued): Union forces secure St. Louis. U.S. Army captain Nathaniel Lyon marches his Company D of the 2nd Infantry Regiment from Jefferson Barracks, Missouri, securing the U.S. Arsenal at St. Louis and its 60,000 muskets, 90,000 pounds of powder, 1.5 million ball cartridges, 40 fieldpieces, and machinery for the manufacture of arms.

Jefferson Davis had served as a U.S. representative, senator, and U.S. secretary of war before he accepted the presidency of the Confederate States of America in 1861. (National Archives)

March 3, 1861

Background to the Civil War (continued). Confederate president Jefferson Davis appoints Brigadier General Pierre G. T. Beauregard to command Confederate forces at Charleston, South Carolina, and orders him to begin planning for the reduction of Fort Sumter in Charleston Harbor by force.

March 4, 1861

Background to the Civil War (continued): Lincoln takes the oath of office as president of the United

Pierre Gustav Toutant Beauregard (1818–1893)

Confederate general. Born into a powerful Louisiana family of Creole background in Saint-Pierre Parish on May 28, 1818, Pierre Gustav Toutant Beauregard spoke French before he spoke English. Beauregard graduated from the U.S. Military Academy, West Point, second in his class, in 1838. Commissioned a second lieutenant of engineers, his first assignment was to Fort Adams near Newport, Rhode Island, making first lieutenant in June 1839. Helping to supervise the construction of coastal defenses, he was then stationed at Pensacola, Florida, and in Louisiana.

During the Mexican-American War (1846–1848), Beauregard served on the staff of Major General Winfield Scott and took part in his Mexico City Campaign. Beauregard particularly distinguished himself. He was wounded twice and was also rewarded with a brevet to captain for his role in the Battles of Contreras and Churubusco and to major for the Battle of Chapultepec.

Following the war, Beauregard returned to New Orleans as chief engineer, supervising the draining of the area. He also dabbled in Democratic Party politics. In 1860 Beauregard, a widower, married Catherine Deslonde, sister-in-law of John Slidell, the powerful Democratic senator from Louisiana and later Confederate diplomat.

Beauregard became superintendent of West Point in January 1861. On January 28 only five days after assuming the position, he resigned when Louisiana seceded from the Union. He subsequently resigned his U.S. Army commission, and on March 1, 1861, he secured a commission as brigadier general in the Confederate Army. Assigned to Charleston, South Carolina, he commanded its defenses confronting the Union enclave at Fort Sumter. On April 12, 1861, Beauregard directed the artillery bombardment of Sumter that forced the Union surrender and evacuation and made him a hero in the South but also sparked the Civil War. Beauregard became known as the "Napoleon in Gray."

Arriving in Richmond at the end of May 1861, Beauregard immediately clashed with President Jefferson Davis, who did not want his advice on military matters. Beauregard received orders to Manassas Junction west of Washington, where he created the Confederate Army of the Potomac (subsequently the Army of Northern Virginia). During the First Battle of Bull Run (Manassas) on July 21, 1861, Beauregard commanded its I Corps under General Joseph E. Johnston. Beauregard felt slighted when others captured the public's attention, but he was advanced to full general on August 31, 1861 (with date of rank from July 21). He then commanded the Potomac District of the Department of Northern Virginia (October 1861–January 1862). Continually disagreeing with Davis over military strategy, Beauregard was exiled to the western theater.

Beauregard commanded the Army of the Mississippi during March–May 1862. Together with western theater commander General Albert Johnston, Beauregard planned to attack Union forces under Major General Ulysses S. Grant at Pittsburg Landing, Tennessee. The resulting Battle of Shiloh (April 6–7, 1862) initially went well, but Johnston was mortally wounded on April 6, and at dusk Beauregard, who anticipated the final destruction of the Union army the next day, called off the attack and sent off a triumphant telegram to Jefferson Davis and the Confederate War Department announcing victory. Historians still debate whether the battle might have been won had it been continued that day. The next day, however, Grant, reinforced, launched a counterattack that drove Beauregard's army from the field.

Davis unfairly criticized Beauregard for the Confederate defeat at Shiloh and for his subsequent evacuation of Corinth. When Beauregard became ill in June 1862, he relinquished command to General Braxton Bragg. Beauregard assumed that this was only temporary, but Davis made it permanent, and Beauregard was relegated to command of the Department of South Carolina, Georgia, and Florida, with his headquarters at Charleston, which he ably defended against Union sea and land attacks. In April 1864 Beauregard was assigned command of the Department of North Carolina and Southern Virginia. In this position, he assisted General Robert E. Lee in the defense of Richmond, protecting the southern approaches to the Confederate capital. Beauregard not only contained Union forces under Major General Benjamin F. Butler at Bermuda Hundred in early May 1864 but defeated Butler in the Second Battle of Drewry's Bluff (Fort Darling) on May 16, 1864, and was able to defend the vital railhead of Petersburg sufficiently long enough for forces under General Robert E. Lee to arrive. Beauregard then proposed to Davis that he invade the North, taking a large part of Lee's army, to end the war. Beauregard continued to serve under Lee in an awkward command relationship until September, when Davis ordered Beauregard to assume overall command in the western theater.

The last months of the war found Beauregard in a series of unredeemable situations as his subordinate General John Bell Hood carried out his disastrous campaign into Tennessee in late 1864. Beauregard then tried unsuccessfully, with no immediate forces under his direct command, to arrest Union major general William T. Sherman's March to the Sea. The end of the war found Beauregard second-in-command to General Joseph E. Johnson, powerless to stop Sherman's drive north through North Carolina. Leaving the army when Johnston surrendered in April 1865, Beauregard returned to New Orleans.

In the postwar years, Beauregard declined offers to command the armies of Romania and Egypt. He prospered in a variety of business ventures, wrote his memoirs, and served in several public offices before his death in New Orleans on February 20, 1893.

STEVEN RAMOLD AND SPENCER C. TUCKER

Further Reading

Basso, Hamilton. *Beauregard: The Great Creole.* New York: Scribner, 1933.
Eicher, John H., and Eicher, David J. *Civil War High Commands.* Stanford, CA: Stanford University Press, 2001.
Williams, T. Harry. *P. G. T. Beauregard: Napoleon in Gray.* Baton Rouge: Louisiana State University Press, 1954.
Woodworth, Steven E. *Jefferson Davis and His Generals: The Failure of Confederate Command in the West.* Lawrence: University Press of Kansas, 1990.

States. One of the greatest war presidents in American history, Abraham Lincoln's only military experience was being a company-grade officer in the Black Hawk War, when he saw no action. In his inaugural address Lincoln tells Southerners that he will not interfere with slavery where it exists but that he will not countenance secession.

March 5, 1861

Background to the Civil War (continued). President Abraham Lincoln appoints Gideon Welles of Connecticut secretary of the navy. Welles, who had earlier served as chief of its Bureau of Provisions and Clothing, is well acquainted with naval administration and proves to be both an able strategist and a highly effective administrator. He serves until 1869.

March 6, 1861

Background to the Civil War (continued). Confederate president Jefferson Davis calls for 100,000 volunteers to serve in the new Confederate Army for a one-year period.

March 16, 1861

Background to the Civil War (continued): The Confederate Congress votes to establish a marine corps. The authorized strength of the Confederate Marine Corps is 46 officers and 944 enlisted men. Colonel Lloyd James Bell from Maryland, a U.S. Army major and paymaster who resigns his commission in April 1861, becomes first commandant. Most of the other officers, however, have served with the U.S. Marine Corps. Twenty-two of 67 serving U.S. Marine Corps officers in 1861 resign their U.S. commissions and join the Confederate Marine Corps. The maximum number of Confederate marines at any one time is 571, on October 31, 1864.

March 31, 1861

Background to the Civil War (continued). U.S. secretary of the navy Gideon Welles orders 250 naval personnel transferred from the Brooklyn Navy Yard to Norfolk, Virginia, in anticipation of a Confederate attack on the facility should Virginia secede from the Union.

April 6, 1861

Background to the Civil War (continued). President Abraham Lincoln directs State Department clerk Robert S. Chew to proceed to Charleston, South Carolina, and there inform Governor Francis W. Pickens that Lincoln has ordered supplies sent to Major Robert Anderson's federal garrison holding Fort Sumter in Charleston Harbor. Chew is instructed to inform Pickens that this is "supplies only" and that if no armed attempt is made to thwart this effort, no additional men, arms, or ammunition will be introduced without prior notification or a Confederate attack.

April 7, 1861

Background to the Civil War (continued). Confederate brigadier general Pierre G. T. Beauregard orders all intercourse ended between federal troops holding Fort Sumter and Charleston.

April 12, 1861

Beginning of the Civil War: Confederate bombardment of Fort Sumter. Of the major federal military installations in the Deep South, only Fort Sumter in Charleston Harbor, South Carolina, and Fort Pickens on Santa Rosa Island off Pensacola, Florida, remain in Union hands. Confederate state authorities have also seized cutters belonging to the U.S. Revenue Service in their ports. After a month of seeking a way to resupply Sumter and hoping for a cooling of Southern passions, U.S. president Abraham Lincoln concludes that he must send relief expeditions to these forts or surrender them to the South. The risk is that this may cause Virginia and other border states to secede.

Against the advice of a majority of his cabinet, Lincoln on March 30 orders Secretary of the Navy Gideon Welles to prepare a relief expedition for Fort Sumter based on a plan drawn up by Gustavus V. Fox. The expedition is to be ready to sail by April 6, with Lincoln to make the final decision at that point. Secretary of State William Seward argues against this course of action, which he believes will probably lead to war and cause Virginia to secede; Seward proposes evacuating Sumter and holding on to Pickens.

The Sumter expedition with Fox in charge sails on April 10. It consists of two warships only: the screw sloop *Pawnee* (8 guns) and the U.S. Revenue Service side-wheeler *Harriet Lane* (4 guns). These escort the unarmed troop and supply ship *Baltic*, with 200 men and supplies. The side-wheel steam frigate *Powhatan* (16 guns) was to have been included, but Lincoln secretly diverts this to relieve Fort Pickens without informing Welles. Its absence probably does not affect the outcome at Sumter, but the diversion of the frigate says much about Lincoln administration decision making at the beginning of the war.

Although Lincoln informs the Confederate government that the resupply of Sumter is "of provisions only," Confederate president Jefferson Davis orders Brigadier General Pierre G. T. Beauregard at Charleston to demand the surrender of Fort Sumter. If refused, he is to reduce it. Beauregard makes this demand on April 11. Following an unsatisfactory reply from Sumter's commander, U.S. Army major Robert Anderson, Beauregard orders fire opened before the Union relief expedition can arrive.

On April 12, 1861, at 4:30 a.m., firing commences against Sumter. Beauregard and some 500 men shell the fort with 30 heavy guns and 18 mortars. Anderson has 85 men and 43 civilian engineers. Fort Sumter has 43 guns, but to conserve ammunition, Anderson orders return fire restricted to 6 guns. Although the Union relief expedition arrives off Charleston Harbor, rough weather precludes any attempt to launch boats to resupply Sumter. Without the *Powhatan,* Fox is also reluctant to expose his ships to enemy fire.

With the Confederate batteries holding the federal ships at bay, with Sumter nearly out of food, and with fires having broken out in the fort, following 34 hours of bombardment Anderson arranges a truce on April 13 and formally surrenders on April 14. As part of the capitulation terms, Sumter's garrison begins a last act of firing a 100-gun salute to the U.S. flag. On the 50th shot, however, powder sparks ignite stacked shells, which explode and kill one Union soldier outright (Private Daniel Hough) and wound two others, one (Private Edward Galloway) mortally. These are the only casualties in the battle that begins the bloodiest war in U.S. history. Anderson and his garrison are evacuated by the Union ships off Charleston and return to the North.

The shelling of Sumter galvanizes opinion on both sides. It ends any sympathy in the North for the Confederate cause. With the South having fired on the U.S. flag, a patriotic fervor sweeps the North. Whether Lincoln had intended to maneuver the South into this is unclear, but America is now at war with itself.

April 12, 1861

Civil War (continued): Balance of forces. The North, superior to the South by virtually every economic measure, enjoys tremendous advantages. At the time of American independence, North and South were relatively equal in population, but slavery in the South, with which free men cannot compete economically, leads the large influx of immigrants arriving primarily from Europe to settle in the North. In 1861, the 23 states of the North have 22.3 million people, whereas the 11 seceded states of the South contain only 9.1 million (and nearly 4 million of them are slaves). In white males age 15–40, the Union advantage is perhaps 4.0 million to 1.5 million. The North also has a much higher number of educated

people, an important factor in waging modern war, as Northern resources are far better managed than those of the South.

The North has some 85 percent of the prewar industrial capacity but produces 92 percent of its industrial goods and has a like percentage of the industrial workers. The entire South has less manufacturing capacity than New York City. The South also has no facilities for forging steel and is unable to construct machine tools, major liabilities in the new age of machine war. In 1860, Northern states produced 93 percent of the nation's pig iron and manufactured 97 percent of its firearms. While it will take the North time to mobilize its great industrial assets for military production, the resources are there.

The South possesses abundant natural resources, including substantial iron and coal deposits and vast amounts of timber, but facilities to transport the raw materials to manufacturing sites are inadequate. In 1861 the North has 21,827 miles of railroad; the South only 8,947 miles. And with the South unable during the war to manufacture or secure rails or steam locomotives in any number, its railroads will deteriorate.

The North also has 82 percent of the prewar U.S. banking capital. Overall, the Northern economy is self-sufficient, whereas that of the South is export-driven. The South exports agricultural goods, chiefly cotton but also rice and tobacco, in return for industrial goods, mostly from Great Britain. While the South accomplishes much in the industrial sphere in the course of the war, it proves insufficient. Given all these disparities, the outcome of the war is hardly surprising.

In terms of actual military strength, at the war's onset the regular U.S. Army numbers fewer than 17,000 men; the men are widely scattered, with the bulk of its 19 regiments scattered in small posts across the American West. The Confederacy has 35,000 men under arms, but the vast majority are untrained. In March 1861 the U.S. Navy possesses 90 ships, but only 42 are in commission. The Confederacy has fewer than a dozen ships, only 1 of which is a purpose-built warship, and it is obsolete. The North can also readily purchase and convert merchant shipping, most of which is based there, and it can far more easily build new warships. The South has only limited ability in these areas.

April 12, 1861

Civil War (continued): Strategy and war plans. Confederate leaders plan to remain on the defensive, trusting that Britain and France will come to their assistance because of their need for cotton. Indeed, Confederate president Jefferson Davis makes a major blunder in withholding the Southern cotton crop to force European recognition of the South. This does not work, and the Confederacy misses an opportunity to rush in war supplies before the Union blockade becomes effective. Southerners trust that the North will ultimately tire of the war and let the South go.

Northern strategy is predicated on preserving the Union; it will thus have to invade and defeat the South. On May 2, U.S. Army general-in-chief Lieutenant General Winfield Scott presents a plan for victory: a naval blockade of the Confederate coasts with the concurrent training of a large Union Army, then joint army-navy operations to bisect the South along its great rivers, especially the Mississippi. This is known as the Anaconda Plan for the large South American snake that squeezes its victims to death. It is the basic strategy that will be followed and that brings victory.

Scott is virtually alone in predicting a long, hard struggle. Most Northern leaders, including President Abraham Lincoln, believe that one short campaign will bring victory. Lincoln's chief problem will be finding a general who will execute the Union war plan aggressively and effectively.

The North has to invade and conquer the South, but the distances involved are vast. The Appalachian Mountains and the Mississippi River divide the Confederacy into three parts: the Eastern, Western, and Trans-Mississippi West theaters. The East (Virginia and the Carolinas and Georgia east of the Blue Ridge) will see half of the war's battles. The north-south corridors of the Shenandoah and Cumberland River Valleys form a natural invasion route for both sides. The West, with its abundant natural resources, agriculture, and key railroads, ranks next in importance to the East. Military operations in the trans-Mississippi West are of little importance.

April 13, 1861

Civil War (continued): Reinforcement of Fort Pickens. Union troops and supplies arrive in Pensacola Bay in the screw sloop *Brooklyn* (10 guns), and, their orders changed, the men go ashore at Fort Pickens on Santa Rosa Island on April 13, 1861. Five days later the steam ferry *Atlantic* arrives, followed a few hours later by the side-wheel steam frigate *Powhatan* (16 guns), which had been plagued by defective boilers. Fort Pickens is secure for the Union.

April 15, 1861

Civil War (continued): Lincoln calls for volunteers. Following the Confederate shelling of Fort Sumter, U.S. president Abraham Lincoln declares the existence of an "insurrection" and calls for 75,000 volunteers to serve for three months. Many more than that number volunteer and are turned away. Lincoln is still trying to conciliate Southerners and is in any case limited constitutionally to the 90-day term for militia in federal service to put down the rebellion.

April 17, 1961

Civil War (continued). Using the excuse of Lincoln's call for 75,000 volunteers, Confederate president Jefferson Davis invites applications for letters of marque and reprisal to initiate privateering operations against U.S. merchant commerce.

April 17–May 20, 1861

Civil War (continued): Secession of the border states. As many Northern leaders have feared, President Abraham Lincoln's call for volunteers to suppress the rebellion and decision to reinforce Forts Sumter and Pickens brings the defection of much of the Upper South: Virginia (April 17, 1861), Arkansas (May 6), Tennessee (May 7), and North Carolina (May 20). The loss of Virginia and Tennessee is especially grievous to the North. Virginia has the South's most important manufacturing center in Richmond, with its major iron foundry (the Tredegar Works) and the largest prewar navy yard (the Norfolk or Gosport Yard); it also gives the South some of its finest officers, including Robert E. Lee and Thomas J. "Stonewall" Jackson. Tennessee has considerable natural resources. In a

 ## Thomas Jonathan Jackson (1824–1863)

Confederate States of America general. Born in Clarksburg, Virginia (now West Virginia), on January 21, 1824, Thomas Jonathan "Stonewall" Jackson was orphaned while young and was reared by an uncle. Securing an appointment to the U.S. Military Academy, West Point, he graduated in 1846. Commissioned a second lieutenant in the artillery, he served under Major General Winfield Scott in the Mexican-American War (1846–1848). In 1847 Jackson distinguished himself in fighting at Veracruz on March 27, Cerro Gordo on April 18, and Chapultepec on September 13. Awarded three brevet promotions, he ended the war a major. Following the war he served at military installations in New York and Florida.

Disagreements with his commander at Camp Meade, Florida, and an appointment to teach natural philosophy (physics) and artillery tactics at the Virginia Military Institute in 1851 led Jackson to leave the army shortly thereafter. He commanded the artillery section of the institute's cadets sent as guards to John Brown's execution in December 1859.

When Virginia seceded from the Union in April 1861, Jackson, a major in the Virginia Militia, was ordered to Richmond with a detachment of Virginia Military Institute cadets to serve as drillmasters for the army. Promoted to colonel of infantry in April, Jackson was ordered to Harpers Ferry, Virginia, which he fortified. Jackson was then promoted to brigadier general in the Confederate Army and awarded command of the 1st Virginia Brigade in June.

Jackson and his troops played a key role in the defense of the Confederate railhead at Manassas Junction. In the First Battle of Bull Run (Manassas) on July 21, 1861, the first big battle of the Civil War (1861–1865), Jackson received the sobriquet "Stonewall" for his defense of Henry Hill. Promoted to major general in October, he took command of Confederate forces in the Shenandoah Valley in November.

Ordered to occupy Union troops in the valley and prevent them from reinforcing U.S. Army major general George B. McClellan's advance on the Confederate capital of Richmond in March 1862 from the east, Jackson proceeded, in the Shenandoah Valley Campaign, to wage one of the most brilliant operations in American military history. Over a span of 48 days he marched his men some 350 miles and fought two actions, four skirmishes, and five major battles. Repulsed at Kernstown near Winchester on March 23, he was victorious at Front Royal on May 23, Winchester on May 24–25, Cross Keys on June 8, and Port Republic on June 9. In the process, Jackson tied down three different Union commands, each of which was at least the size of his own force. This campaign made Jackson a Southern military hero.

Jackson then slipped out of the valley with his men to join General Robert E. Lee in the defense of Richmond in June 1862, fighting in the Seven Days' Battles (June 26–July 2, 1862). Fatigue and unfamiliarity with the terrain prevented Jackson from carrying out Lee's plan to corner McClellan. Jackson's command was then moved northwest and played a key role in the subsequent Confederate victory over Union forces under Major General John Pope in the Second Battle of Bull Run (Manassas) (August 29–30, 1862). Jackson accompanied Lee in his subsequent invasion of Maryland. Jackson's troops forced the surrender of the Union garrison at Harpers Ferry on September 15, then rejoined Lee in time to participate in the bloody Battle of Antietam (Sharpsburg) on September 17.

(continued)

(Continued)

Promoted to lieutenant general and given command of II Corps in Lee's Army of Northern Virginia in October 1862, Jackson commanded the Confederate right flank in the Battle of Fredericksburg (December 13, 1862) in Virginia, helping to prevent a Union breakthrough. In the Battle of Chancellorsville (May 1–4, 1863), Lee, outnumbered two to one by Union forces under Major General Joseph Hooker, ordered Jackson to carry out a flanking attack against the Union right. Jackson's brilliant execution of the plan on May 2 caught Union forces off guard and rolled up the Union right. Only darkness prevented Jackson from inflicting greater damage. That night Jackson and his staff, riding out in advance of Confederate lines on a reconnaissance, were mistaken for Union troops on their return and fired upon. Jackson was badly wounded, necessitating amputation of his left arm. He subsequently contracted pneumonia and died at Guiney Station, Virginia, on May 10, 1863. He was buried in Lexington, Virginia. Jackson's death was perhaps the greatest single military personnel loss to befall the Confederacy. Personally brave and extremely self-confident and resolute, Jackson was also extremely religious, hard, and absolutely uncompromising. It has been said of him that he lived in the New Testament but fought in the Old Testament.

SPENCER C. TUCKER

Further Reading

Chambers, Lenoir. *Stonewall Jackson.* 2 vols. New York: William Morrow, 1959.

Freeman, Douglas Southall. *Lee's Lieutenants: A Study in Command.* 3 vols. New York: Scribner, 1942–1944.

Robertson, James I. *Stonewall Jackson: The Man, the Soldier, the Legend.* New York: Macmillan, 1997.

Vandiver, Frank E. *Mighty Stonewall.* College Station: Texas A&M University Press, 1988.

blow to the Confederacy, however, Kentucky declares its neutrality on May 24.

April 18, 1861

Civil War (continued): Eastern theater: Union forces evacuate Harpers Ferry. At Harpers Ferry, Virginia (now West Virginia), Lieutenant Roger Jones of the U.S. Army, defending the important federal arsenal and armory here with just 50 regulars and 15 volunteers, is unable to secure reinforcements and is forced to withdraw this evening on the advance of some 360 Virginia militia from nearby Charles Town. Jones sets fire to the armory and arsenal buildings before retreating across the Potomac River, but the locals manage to save many weapons and the important machine tools and dies for small-arms manufacture. These are subsequently removed to Richmond.

April 19, 1861

Civil War (continued): Eastern theater: Baltimore Riot. In Baltimore, Maryland, sharply divided in sympathies between North and South, pro-Confederacy rioters attack troops of the 6th Massachusetts Regiment in the streets. In what is also known as the Pratt Street Riot and the Pratt Street Massacre, shots are exchanged, during which 4 soldiers and 12 civilians are killed; 36 soldiers and an unknown number of civilians are wounded. Secessionists then cut telegraph lines and rail connections with Washington, D.C., isolating the federal capital for several days.

The Baltimore Riot marks the first real bloodshed in the Civil War and leads President Abraham Lincoln to send troops to Maryland and essentially take possession of the state to prevent it from seceding.

April 19, 1861

Civil War (continued). President Abraham Lincoln proclaims a naval blockade of the Confederate coasts. On April 27 he extends the blockade to include the coasts of Virginia and North Carolina.

At first, ships are few in number. The distances involved are also vast. From Alexandria, Virginia, to the Rio Grande in Texas, the Confederate coastline stretches more than 3,500 miles, and for much of this the Outer Banks present a double coastline. There are 189 harbors, river mouths, or indentations to be guarded. The Mississippi and its tributary rivers count 3,615 miles, and sounds, bayous, rivers, and inlets along the Atlantic and Gulf coasts constitute an additional 2,000 miles. The blockade is never totally effective, but it remains the major focus of the Union effort at sea.

There is general agreement that the blockade has major impact on the war's outcome. The growing number of Union ships capture many blockade-runners and prevent the South from significant export of cotton to pay for needed imports of war supplies and key manufactured goods such as steam engines and railroad rails. The blockade also has an increasingly negative impact on the Southern economy. By far the bulk of Union naval assets are concentrated in blockade operations during the war, and the key to their success is steamships able to intercept the sleek, fast blockade-runners, a number of which are constructed in Britain especially for this purpose.

April 19–May 1861

Civil War (continued): Confederate privateers. In reaction to President Abraham Lincoln's call for 75,000 volunteers, Confederate president Jefferson Davis on April 19, 1861, issues a declaration inviting applications for privateers. He claims that this is legal because the U.S. government had previously refused to adhere to the 1856 international convention banning privateering.

The Confederate Congress approves this step on May 6, and the first commission is issued on May 10. The few Confederate privateers have little impact. Forced to bring their prizes back into Southern ports, most are soon chased down by Union warships.

April 20, 1861

Civil War (continued): Virginia forces seize the Norfolk Navy Yard. This largest of the prewar navy yards

Print showing the U.S. Navy screw frigate *Merrimack* under sail near the entrance to New York Harbor. On their completion in the mid-1850s, the ships of this class were considered among the world's most powerful warships. (Library of Congress)

 ## CSS *Virginia*

With few ships at the beginning of the U.S. Civil War in April 1861, the Confederacy hoped to overcome this in part through new weapons. Confederate secretary of the navy Stephen R. Mallory embraced both the ironclad and the naval mine.

The *Virginia* was the first Confederate ironclad. It was the reincarnation of the U.S. Navy screw frigate *Merrimack,* which had been undergoing repair at the Norfolk Navy Yard in April 1861 when that facility was taken by the State of Virginia. Set on fire by withdrawing Union forces, the *Merrimac* sank in shallow water. Although its upper decks were destroyed, the ship's machinery and hull could be salvaged. The Confederates raised what remained, moved it to the yard's large dry dock, and began converting it into an ironclad.

Lieutenant John M. Brooke drew the basic plans and had charge of the ordnance and armor, Naval Constructor John L. Porter oversaw the reconstruction, and Chief Engineer William P. Williamson dealt with the overhaul of the engines, which remained woefully inadequate, especially for a heavier ironclad.

By mid-July work was well under way, ultimately involving some 1,500 men. Carpenters shortened the ship from 279' to 262'9", then built onto the cut-down hull a main deck 2' above the waterline. On top of this they constructed a central casemate sloping upward and inward 36 degrees on each side so as to deflect shot.

The 170-foot-long casemate extended over the hull and into the water. It was formed of 4 inches of oak laid horizontally, 8 inches of yellow pine laid vertically, and 12 inches of white pine laid horizontally, the whole bolted together. This was then sheathed in iron plate. Unique in Confederate ironclads, both ends were rounded. The casemate was pierced by 14 elliptical gunports, 4 unevenly spaced on port and starboard (to provide greater room for the gun crews to work) and 3 each at bow and stern. The flat top of the casemate, also known as the shield or spar deck, was pierced by the funnel and three iron gratings to provide ventilation to the gun deck below.

The *Virginia* was the first modern warship to completely do away with rigging. Unique to Confederate ironclads was its submerged bow and stern. A 1,500-pound iron ram or beak about three feet long was placed at the bow underwater; it was, however, poorly secured to the ship.

Plans called for the *Virginia* to be ready in November. Had the work proceeded on schedule, the Confederacy would have stolen an important march on the Union. Armoring the ship brought delay, however. Originally the *Virginia* was to have one-inch plate, but in early October Brooke conducted firing tests and discovered that the *Virginia* would require two thicknesses of two-inch plate rather than three thicknesses of one-inch plate. The Tredegar Works in Richmond produced the plate from rolled railroad iron, but the 723 tons required took nearly the entire activity of its rolling mills for five months. Transporting the plate to the yard also proved difficult because of a shortage of freight cars. The last plating did not arrive at the yard until February 12. The *Virginia* was launched five days later, a full week after the launching of the Northern ironclad, the *Monitor.*

Problems were immediately apparent. The *Virginia*'s steering was so sluggish that it took 30–40 minutes and four miles to bring the ship about 180 degrees. Its engines were unreliable and inadequate, with a top speed of only about five knots. Most serious, Porter had miscalculated the ship's displacement, with the result that the *Virginia* rode too high in the water. This was the ship's greatest vulnerability. Adding 150 tons of coal, additional ballast, shot, and supplies lowered the ship in the water somewhat, but the problem was never completely resolved.

The *Virginia* was at least well armed. It mounted 10 guns: 6 IX-inch Dahlgren smoothbores and 2 6.4-inch single-banded Brooke rifles in broadsides and 2 7-inch single-banded Brooke rifles in pivot at bow and stern. When it went into battle, the *Virginia* had shell for all its guns but had shot only for its smoothbores. The Virginia had a crew of 320 men, including 55 marines.

Optimists such as Mallory hoped that the ship might attack New York. Others thought that it might be employed to drive the Union blockaders from the South Atlantic seaboard. Such plans were beyond the ship's capabilities. Its draft was too deep to get up the Potomac, and it is doubtful that even with the best pilot it could have crossed the bar to New York City. Disrupting the North's planned Peninsula Campaign by destroying the Union warships off Fort Monroe was ambitious enough.

On March 8, 1862, the *Virginia* destroyed two powerful Union warships off Fort Monroe. The next day it fought the *Monitor* to a draw. The latter engagement was nonetheless a strategic Union victory, and when the Union forces captured its port of Norfolk, the Confederates scuttled the *Virginia* on May 11, 1862.

SPENCER C. TUCKER

Further Reading

Baxter, James P. *The Introduction of the Ironclad Warship*. Cambridge, MA: Harvard University Press, 1933.

Brooke, George M., Jr. *John M. Brooke: Naval Scientist and Educator*. Charlottesville: University Press of Virginia, 1980.

Quarstein, John V. *C.S.S. Virginia: Mistress of Hampton Roads*. Appomattox, VA: H. E. Howard, 2000.

Still, William N. Still, Jr. *Iron Afloat: The Story of the Confederate Armorclads*. Columbia: University of South Carolina Press, 1985.

boasts a dry dock and extensive shops and stores. Eleven ships are undergoing repair or are in ordinary (laid up), including the modern steam frigate *Merrimack*, having its engines rebuilt.

Yard commander Commodore Charles F. McCauley waits too long to take action, and only two of the ships are gotten off. The dry dock is not destroyed, and although the other ships are burned to the water's edge and sunk, they can be raised. The Confederates secure intact valuable stores, machinery, ammunition, and 2,000 barrels of powder. Most importantly, they obtain 1,195 heavy guns, including 52 modern IX-inchers. Many of these guns are soon on their way to coastal defenses throughout the Confederacy. The Confederates raise the *Merrimack*, take apart and reassemble its machinery, and rebuild it as the ironclad *Virginia*.

Northern forces, however, retain control of Fort Monroe across Hampton Roads, an important staging area during the war.

April 22, 1861

Civil War (continued). North Carolina forces seize the federal arsenal at Fayetteville.

April 23, 1861

Civil War (continued): Trans-Mississippi West theater. Confederate troops seize control of Fort Smith in Arkansas.

April 23, 1861

Civil War (continued): Eastern theater: Lee assumes command of Virginia state forces. On April 20, 1861,

Lieutenant Colonel Robert E. Lee resigns his U.S. Army commission, having previously declined an offer from U.S. Army general-in-chief Lieutenant General Winfield Scott to command all federal forces in the field. Lee opts to go with his native state of Virginia, and on April 23 he assumes command of its state forces as a major general.

April 25, 1861

Civil War (continued): Trans-Mississippi West theater. With the beginning of the war, many federal troops in Texas make their way to the coast, hoping to find transport to the North. On this date some 500 are at Saluria, when 420 of them under Major C. C. Sibley are forced to surrender to Confederate Army colonel Earl Van Dorn. They are paroled and allowed to sail for New York City.

April 26, 1861

Civil War (continued): Western theater: Union forces secure arms from the St. Louis Arsenal. On April 20, 1861, a pro-Confederate mob at Liberty, Missouri, seizes the Liberty Arsenal, securing some 1,000 muskets and rifles. This leads to fears that with Missouri secessionists largely in charge at St. Louis, the Confederacy might secure the much larger stocks of weapons there. U.S. Army captain James H. Stokes secretly arranges to remove arms from the St. Louis Arsenal in the steamer *City of Alton.* At 2:00 a.m. on April 26, the loaded steamer sails for loyalist Alton, Illinois, arriving there three hours later with 10,000 muskets, 100 new rifle carbines, 500 revolvers, 110,000 musket cartridges, and a quantity of cannon, leaving only 7,000 muskets in the arsenal with which to arm the St. Louis volunteers. With the assistance of men, women, and children of

Revolvers

Revolvers are repeating firearms that have revolving cylinders with multiple chambers and at least one barrel. The development of handguns paralleled that of muskets. Alexander Forsyth's patent of mercury fulminates as priming for firearms in 1807 was a great boon in their development.

Handguns proliferated in the 19th century. There were many types, but among notable designs were those of the American Henry Deringer Jr. Deringer opened a business in Philadelphia in 1806 and routinely made flintlock muskets for the federal government. He was one of the first gunmakers to embrace the new percussion cap system, although he did not receive his first government contract for percussion firearms until 1845. Deringer's muzzle-loading rifled percussion cap handguns were of varying bore size and had barrel lengths of 1 inches to six inches. The smaller types could easily be carried concealed and became de rigueur for many men and women, especially in the more lawless American West and South.

So-called pepper-box revolvers also were popular for defensive purposes. They had four to six barrels that were loaded separately from the muzzle end. Most often, the barrels were bored into a single piece of metal that then rotated on a long steel pin. In some of these handguns the barrels had to be turned by hand, but soon the barrels were turned by double action, that is, the action of pulling the trigger turned the barrel and raised and dropped the hammer to fire the weapon.

Samuel Colt of Hartford, Connecticut, invented the modern revolver. In 1836 he formed the Patent Army Manufacturing Company in Paterson, New Jersey. Its first product was a small five-shot .28-caliber revolver, but its most famous early design was the 1838 Colt Holster Model Paterson Revolver No. 5. Better known as the Texas Paterson, it was .36-caliber, had five cylinders, and came in 4-inch to 12-inch barrel lengths. This was the first revolving cylinder handgun in general use. Each chamber was separately loaded from the muzzle end and had its own nipple for the copper percussion cap. The drum chamber moved each time the hammer was cocked. Colt revolvers were adopted by both the army and navy and saw wide service in both the Mexican-American War and the American Civil War as well as in fighting with the American Indians in the West.

At the same time, breech-loading revolvers appeared. Screw-off barrels had appeared early in the development of firearms, but in 1812 Swiss national Samuel J. Pauly, working in Paris, developed a revolver in which the barrel swiveled downward to allow it to be loaded. It utilized a self-contained cartridge of Pauly's invention, one of the most important developments in the history of small arms. Several types of methods were used to fire it.

The development of metal cartridges led to a change from muzzle-loading to breech-loading firearms. Not only were muzzle-loading rifles turned into breech-loaders, but Colt revolvers were similarly transformed. Thus, in the 1870s the Colt Model 1861 navy revolver was converted to a breech-loader. The cylinder was removed for reloading.

There are three principal means of ejecting spent cartridge cases from the cylinder. In the side-gate cylinder, the cartridge cases are pushed rearward out of the cylinder one at a time by means of a hand-operated rod alongside the barrel. In the break-open cylinder, all cartridge cases are ejected at the same time by means of a star-shaped extractor when the revolver is opened. Finally there is the swing-out cylinder, in which all cases are ejected simultaneously by hand with a star-shaped extractor after the cylinder is opened.

The first breech-loading revolver designed specifically for metal cartridges was the Smith and Wesson Model No. 1. Manufactured during 1857 to 1860, it had a rifled barrel and seven chambers and was hinged at the top. It utilized .22-caliber rimfire ammunition. In 1869 Smith and Wesson produced a .44-caliber revolver for the army. Probably the most famous early revolver in U.S. history was the Colt .45 Peacemaker. Still in production, it was widely used in the American West in fighting against the American Indians. The cavalry version had a 7.5-inch barrel and was officially known as the Single Action Army Revolver, Model 1873 Six-shot .45-caliber Colt. Colt also produced another famous sidearm during 1898–1944, the Colt New Service Double Action Revolver, in .45-caliber.

For the most part, at the end of the 19th century .38 was the standard army caliber. It remained thus until after the Philippine-American War of 1898–1902, when the army sought a caliber with greater stopping power. Competition led to adoption of the Colt semiautomatic .45-caliber pistol, which became the standard sidearm of the U.S. military for the next 70 years.

Among other notable revolvers were those in the United Kingdom manufactured by both Webley and Enfield, produced chiefly in .38- and .44-calibers. During World War II Britain purchased some 1 million Smith and Wesson .38-caliber revolvers. In 1953 Colt introduced its more powerful Colt Python in .357-caliber, and a number of other manufacturers followed suit.

Spencer C. Tucker

Further Reading

Blair, Claude, ed. *Pollard's History of Firearms*. New York: Macmillan, 1985.
Kinard, Jeff. *Pistols: An Illustrated History of Their Impact*. Santa Barbara, CA: ABC-CLIO, 2003.
Myatt, F. *Illustrated Encyclopedia of Pistols and Revolvers*. London: Salamander Books, 1980.
Taylorson, A. *The Revolver*. 3 vols. London: Arms and Armour, 1966–1970.

Alton, who are informed of the situation, the arms are soon loaded into freight cars of the Chicago and Alton Railroad, and that night they arrive safely in Springfield, much to the consternation of Missouri secessionists.

April 26, 1861

Civil War (continued): Eastern theater. Confederate brigadier general Joseph E. Johnston arrives at Richmond, Virginia, to assume command of the defenses of the city.

Early May 1861

Civil War (continued): Eastern theater. Virginia forces control Alexandria, just south of Washington, D.C., and their batteries along the Potomac River menace Union shipping. Small clashes occur along the river.

May 3, 1861

Civil War (continued). President Abraham Lincoln issues a call for an additional 42,000 volunteers for the army to serve three-year enlistments as well as an additional 18,000 men for the navy. These will bring totals up to 156,000 soldiers and 25,000 sailors.

May 9, 1861

Civil War (continued): Naval operations. Confederate Secretary of the Navy Stephen R. Mallory orders James D. Bulloch to Great Britain, there to purchase

Joseph Eggleston Johnston (1807–1891)

Confederate Army officer. Born in Farmville, Virginia, on February 3, 1807, Joseph Eggleston Johnston graduated from the U.S. Military Academy, West Point, in 1829 and served in the Second Seminole War and the Mexican-American War. An engineer by training, he served in varying roles with the Topographical Engineers. In 1860, making use of family connections to the secretary of war, Johnston won appointment as quartermaster general of the U.S. Army with the rank of brigadier general.

When Virginia seceded, Johnston resigned his commission and went first into state and then into Confederate service, commanding the defenses of the Shenandoah Valley. When Union forces threatened Brigadier General Pierre G. T. Beauregard's Confederate army at Manassas Junction, Virginia, Confederate president Jefferson Davis ordered Johnston to take his troops to join Beauregard. The presence of Johnston's command was the key factor in the Confederate victory at the Battle of First Bull Run (Manassas) on July 21, 1861.

In September, Davis released his five nominations for the rank of full general. Johnston was furious to find himself fourth on the list. Confederate law stipulated that officers leaving the U.S. Army to join the Confederate Army have the same relative rank in the new service, and Johnston believed that his rank as brigadier general made him the highest-ranking U.S. general to enter Confederate service. What Johnston overlooked in the law was a stipulation that previous staff rank would count for staff appointments in the Confederate service but not for appointments to the line. Since Johnston's Confederate appointment was to the line, his rank was based on his previous highest line rank in the U.S. service, and his standing among Confederate generals was correct. Nevertheless, Johnston sent Davis a 15-page abusive letter. Perhaps unwisely, Davis retained Johnston in his command.

In the spring of 1862, Johnston made an unforced precipitate withdrawal from the outskirts of Washington, D.C., where the Confederate army had wintered, to a position behind the Rappahannock River, causing unnecessary loss of supplies and equipment and further annoying Davis, particularly since Johnston had failed to keep the government apprised of his plans.

When Major General George McClellan's Union army landed on the Virginia peninsula east of Richmond, Johnston dissented strongly from Davis's decision to defend the peninsula, preferring instead to retreat immediately to the outskirts of Richmond. Johnston retreated without fighting or informing the president of his intentions. Under strong pressure from Davis not to give up Richmond without a fight, Johnston attacked McClellan in the May 31 Battle of Fair Oaks (Seven Pines). Late in the badly bungled attack, Johnston was wounded and had to yield command of the army.

By November when Johnston was marginally able to return to duty, General Robert E. Lee was firmly ensconced as the commander of the Army of Northern Virginia, and Davis assigned Johnston to command of the region between the Appalachians and the Mississippi, where he was to supervise the armies of General Braxton Bragg in Tennessee and Lieutenant John C. Pemberton in Mississippi. Johnston immediately complained that the assignment was poorly conceived. As before, he did not communicate sufficiently with Davis or fulfill his responsibilities in the way the president desired. When Davis intervened with direct orders for the movement of troops, Johnston's resentment grew.

In May 1863 Davis sent Johnston to Mississippi to direct Pemberton in the defense of the state against Grant. Johnston went but immediately announced that he was too late and could do nothing. Throughout the siege of Vicksburg, Johnston made no effort to relieve the stronghold even though he had heavy reinforcements and there was constant urging from Richmond.

Despite his displeasure with Johnston's performance in 1863, Davis assigned him to command the Army of Tennessee at Dalton, Georgia, after Bragg's defeat at Chattanooga. In the months that followed, Johnston resisted Davis's urging to take the offensive. Major General William T. Sherman's Union armies advanced in May, and Johnston fell back again and again in the face of Sherman's skillful turning maneuvers. By July, with Sherman on the outskirts of Atlanta and Johnston offering no assurance that he would give battle before giving up the city, Davis relieved him of command.

During the closing months of the war, Davis, at Lee's behest, placed Johnston in command of the Department of North Carolina and Southern Virginia, charged with impeding Sherman's advance northward through the Carolinas. By this time little could be done, but Johnston on March 19 launched an attack—only his second of the war—against one wing of Sherman's forces at Bentonville, North Carolina. After limited initial success Union troops beat off the attack, and Johnston narrowly escaped the entrapment and destruction of his army. After Lee's surrender at Appomattox, Johnston surrendered to Sherman at Durham Station, North Carolina, on April 18, 1865.

Johnston subsequently worked in the insurance business and lived in several cities throughout the South. His 1874 memoirs were an attempt to vindicate his Civil War record. He later served two terms in the U.S. House of Representatives, and he served as railroad commissioner in the first Grover Cleveland administration. Johnston died in Washington, D.C., on March 21, 1891.

STEVEN E. WOODWORTH

Further Reading

Symonds, Craig. *Joseph E. Johnston: A Civil War Biography.* New York: Norton, 1992.

Woodworth, Steven E. *Davis and Lee at War.* Lawrence: University Press of Kansas, 1995.

Woodworth, Steven E. *Jefferson Davis and His Generals: The Failure of Confederate Command in the West.* Lawrence: University Press of Kansas, 1990.

ironclads and ships to be turned into commerce raiders.

May 10, 1861

Civil War (continued). The U.S. Navy screw frigate *Niagara* (12 guns), commanded by Captain William M. McKean, arrives off Charleston Harbor to begin the blockade there.

May 10, 1861

Civil War (continued): Western theater: Camp Jackson Affair. At the beginning of May, Missouri governor Claiborne Jackson, who had favored the South but is now "neutral," calls out the Missouri Militia for "maneuvers." Fearful that this is a secessionist plot and that the militia may have secured artillery, U.S. Army captain Nathaniel Lyon marches out from St. Louis with Union troops to the militia encampment at "Camp Jackson" just north of the city. Although it is unclear how many of the militiamen are secessionists, Lyon is determined they be disarmed. Threatening force, he secures the surrender of 669 militiamen and their commander, Brigadier General David M. Frost.

When the militiamen refuse to take an oath of allegiance to the United States, Lyon brings them back under guard into St. Louis prior to issuing them a parole and releasing them. As the soldiers proceed with their prisoners through St. Louis, they are attacked by angry crowds, many of whom taunt the largely ethnic German troops. In the ensuing melee, 2 soldiers and two dozen civilians are killed, and perhaps 50 others are injured. Missouri remains firmly in Union hands, and Lyon is promoted to brigadier general.

May 13, 1861

Civil War (continued): Western theater. George B. McClellan, a former U.S. Army officer who has established a reputation in the railroad business, is appointed major general and given command of the U.S. Army Department of the Ohio.

George Brinton McClellan (1826–1885)

Union Army officer. Born in Philadelphia on December 3, 1826, George Brinton McClellan graduated from the U.S. Military Academy, West Point, in 1846. He served in the Mexican-American War and received two brevets. After the war McClellan served mainly on the western frontier, performing various surveys and explorations. He was also one of the U.S. observers of the Crimean War (1853–1856) and wrote a much-studied report of his observations. In 1857 McClellan resigned his commission to become a railroad executive.

When the American Civil War began, McClellan became commander of Union troops in Ohio at the rank of major general of volunteers. His first assignment was to secure the western counties of Virginia. Thanks to able subordinates, Confederate miscues, and the support of the local populace, the area was largely secured for the Union by the midsummer of 1861, with McClellan hailed in Northern newspapers as "the Napoleon of the present war."

The fame came at an opportune moment, for in the wake of the July 21 Union debacle at the First Battle of Bull Run (Manassas), Lincoln was looking for a suitable general to replace the discredited Brigadier General Irvin McDowell. Given the job, McClellan showed skill in organizing and training the army and restoring morale. Yet throughout the autumn months, much to the dismay of the president, McClellan did not advance. In November, General-in-Chief Winfield Scott, with whom McClellan had frequently quarreled, went into retirement. McClellan received Scott's duties in addition to his previous ones, but the added authority did not make him any more inclined to move forward. McClellan was also an open Democrat who approved of slavery and made no secret of his contempt for abolitionists and Republicans.

In January 1862, Lincoln ordered McClellan to advance toward Richmond. In response, McClellan finally revealed that he had a scheme for taking the army down Chesapeake Bay by water, landing on the Virginia peninsula between the York and James Rivers, and advancing toward Richmond from the east. Lincoln had misgivings about the plan, and some in Lincoln's cabinet thought that it looked suspiciously like leaving Washington open to a Confederate counterstroke. Nevertheless, the president reluctantly gave his approval, although he relieved McClellan of his duties as general-in-chief, leaving him to command only the Army of the Potomac.

McClellan's Peninsula Campaign (March–August 1862) grew out of his desire to restore the Union with a minimum of damage to Southern society and especially to the institution of slavery. Ironically, his timid implementation of the plan helped prolong the war and accomplish exactly the results that he wished to avoid. After advancing slowly to the outskirts of Richmond, McClellan lost his nerve and retreated after heavy attacks by Confederate forces under General Robert E. Lee.

The president now decided to withdraw McClellan's troops from the peninsula and from McClellan's command, transferring them to the army of Major General John Pope in northern Virginia. McClellan moved so slowly in transferring them that Lee was able to defeat Pope at the Second Battle of Bull Run (Manassas) (August 29–30, 1862) before most of them arrived. Many leading Republicans suspected that McClellan and several of his loyal subordinates had hoped for just such an outcome. Still, with Pope's army demoralized and the victorious Lee advancing into Maryland, Lincoln believed that he had little choice but to restore McClellan to command of the Union forces opposing Lee, hoping that McClellan's popularity with the soldiers would help restore morale.

McClellan's reinstatement did restore morale. Then a stroke of luck gave McClellan a complete copy of Lee's orders for the operation, showing that the Confederate army was spread out and vulnerable. Yet McClellan moved so slowly that Lee was able to regroup his forces and face him behind Antietam Creek in western Maryland. Although McClellan outnumbered Lee by about two to one at Antietam, he overestimated Lee's numbers by a factor of four, as he had done in all his previous operations. Holding almost half his force in reserve, on September 17, 1862, McClellan launched a series of piecemeal attacks that nearly succeeded in driving Lee into the Potomac River. In the end, McClellan allowed Lee to escape. Several weeks later, fed up with McClellan's slowness and lack of drive, Lincoln relieved him of command.

McClellan now plunged into Democratic Party politics and challenged Lincoln unsuccessfully in the 1864 presidential election. McClellan then traveled widely, worked as a civil engineer, wrote a patently self-adulatory memoir, and was governor of New Jersey during 1878–1881. He died in Orange, New Jersey, on October 29, 1885.

STEVEN E. WOODWORTH

Further Reading

Rafuse, Ethan S. *McClellan's War: The Failure of Moderation in the Struggle for the Union*. Bloomington: Indiana University Press, 2005.
Sears, Stephen W. *George B. McClellan: The Young Napoleon*. New York: Ticknor and Fields, 1988.

May 13, 1861

Civil War (continued): Eastern theater: Union troops establish firm control of Baltimore. U.S. Army brigadier general Benjamin Butler arrives by ship at Annapolis with reinforcements and marches the men into Baltimore. Guns are situated on Federal Hill, and troops are stationed at key locations in the city and the surrounding area to maintain order. During the next several months, President Abraham Lincoln orders the military to arrest a number of suspected Southern-sympathizing members of the state legislature, who are held without trial.

May 16, 1861

Civil War (continued): Western theater. U.S. Navy commander John Rodgers Jr. is ordered to assist the U.S. Army in establishing a naval force that will operate on Western waters. The ships of this force, to be purchased by the army, will be commanded by naval officers but will fall under authority of Western Department commander Major General John C. Frémont. This leads to the establishment of the Western Gunboat Flotilla (later known as the Mississippi Squadron).

May 18–19, 1861

Civil War (continued): Eastern theater: Battle of Sewell's Point. In the first fighting of the war in Virginia, the U.S. gunboat conversions *Monticello* (3 guns), commanded by Captain Henry Eagle, and *Thomas Freeborn* (2 guns), commanded by Commander James H. Ward, engage Confederate batteries at Sewell's Point, Virginia. There are few casualties on either side.

 ## Benjamin Franklin Butler (1818–1893)

U.S. Army officer and politician. Benjamin Franklin Butler was born in Deerfield, New Hampshire, on November 5, 1818. His father died five months after his birth, and his mother moved the family to Lowell, Massachusetts, in 1828. The income she earned from operating a boardinghouse there enabled Butler to attend Waterville College (now Colby College) in Maine. Graduating in 1838, he studied law and went into practice in 1840.

Butler soon became active in the Democratic Party, and in 1853 he won election to the Massachusetts House of Representatives. He ran successfully for the state senate in 1859. Butler attended the 1860 National Democratic Convention in Charleston, South Carolina, where his conviction that the U.S. Constitution upheld slavery led him to support Jefferson Davis for the presidential nomination. When the party fractured along regional lines, Butler supported John C. Breckinridge for president. Butler's own 1860 candidacy for governor of Massachusetts ended in defeat.

Despite his acceptance of slavery, Butler opposed secession. He supported the Union when the American Civil War began, cooperating with his former opponent, Governor John Andrew, to organize Massachusetts's troops. Appointed brigadier general of the state militia in April 1861, Butler led the 8th Massachusetts Regiment to Maryland, where he threatened to arrest that state's legislators if they approved an ordinance of secession. On April 25, Butler was named commander of the Military Department of Annapolis. He led troops into Baltimore on May 13, 1861, to forestall violence between Union and Confederate sympathizers.

President Abraham Lincoln appointed Butler major general of volunteers and assigned him to command Fortress Monroe in Hampton Roads, Virginia. To secure his position, Butler ordered an attack on nearby Confederate positions, but his troops were repulsed on June 10 at Big Bethel. Butler also took the Union's first official step against slavery when he declared fugitive slaves who had come into his lines "contraband of war" and refused to return them to their owners. Instead, he put them to work on his fortifications. Lincoln approved the measure. Butler briefly took command of an expedition that captured two forts guarding Hatteras Inlet in North Carolina and then returned to New England to raise more troops.

In February 1862, Butler took command of the army contingent assigned to attack New Orleans. His troops occupied the city at the end of April. Butler aroused considerable controversy by hanging a man who tore down the U.S. flag and declaring in his infamous "General Order No. 28" that any woman who insulted his troops would be treated "as a woman of the town plying her avocation." He also quarreled with foreign diplomats and seized $800,000 from the Dutch consulate because he believed that the money was earmarked for Confederate use. These many controversies resulted in his recall in December 1862.

Lacking a command, Butler spent most of 1863 shoring up his political position with the Radical Republicans. In November 1863 he was placed in command of the Department of Virginia and North Carolina. Butler was named to command the Army of the James in the spring of 1864. Union Army general-in-chief Lieutenant General Ulysses S. Grant assigned him to land on the south bank of the James River and advance toward Petersburg, Virginia, in conjunction with his Overland Campaign against Richmond. Butler landed on the Bermuda Hundred Peninsula on May 5, and the next day he had all of his 33,000 troops ashore. Instead of pushing rapidly toward Petersburg, which was defended by only 2,000 Confederates, Butler paused to entrench. He then spent several days probing the Confederate positions.

On May 16, Butler finally launched a determined attack against General Pierre G. T. Beauregard's Confederates at Drewry's Bluff. Butler's delays, however, had given Beauregard time to increase his force tenfold so that the Union troops were repulsed with a loss of more than 4,000 men, compared to 2,500 Confederate casualties. Butler then withdrew within his Bermuda Hundred fortifications and remained inactive.

Given command of the land contingent in a joint army-navy assault on Fort Fisher, which guarded the only remaining major Confederate port of Wilmington, North Carolina, Butler withdrew his forces on December 27 after only three days ashore and without coordinating with his naval counterpart, Rear Admiral David Dixon Porter. Porter was furious and so was Grant, who dismissed Butler from command in January 1865.

After the war, Butler represented Massachusetts in the U.S. Congress for five terms. He was elected governor of the state in 1882 and was the Greenback Party's presidential candidate in 1884. He won less than 2 percent of the vote, and that along with his failure to win reelection as governor led to his withdrawal from politics. Butler died on January 11, 1893, in Washington, D.C.

JIM PIECUCH

Further Reading

Butler, Benjamin F. *Autobiography and Personal Reminiscences of Major-General Benj. F. Butler: A Review of His Legal, Political, and Military Career.* Boston: A. M. Thayer, 1892.

Hearn, Chester G. *When the Devil Came Down to Dixie: Ben Butler in New Orleans.* Baton Rouge: Louisiana State University Press.

May 20, 1861

Civil War (continued). The city of Richmond, Virginia, becomes the capital of the Confederacy.

May 23, 1861

Civil War (continued): Eastern theater. At Fortress Monroe, Virginia, Brigadier General Benjamin Butler refuses to return three runaway slaves to their masters. He declares them "contraband of war." Although at first not always followed by other U.S. Army and U.S. Navy commanders, this precedent allows thousands of slaves in the South to escape to Union forces and freedom.

May 24, 1861

Civil War (continued): Eastern theater: Union troops occupy Alexandria, Virginia. Commander Stephen C. Rowan of the U.S. Navy screw sloop *Pawnee* (8 guns) demands the surrender of the town, and in the first amphibious expedition of the war, some 13,000 U.S. troops under Brigadier General Samuel P. Heintzelman cross the Potomac River into Virginia, occupying Alexandria and Arlington Heights as part of the Union effort to secure the approaches to Washington, D.C.

Colonel Elmer E. Ellsworth of the 11th New York Regiment is shot dead while removing a Confederate flag from a rooftop, the first U.S. Army officer fatality of the war. The next day, the Union troops tear up railroad tracks between Alexandria and Leesburg.

May 26, 1861

Civil War (continued). The U.S. Navy blockade of the major rivers and bays of the Gulf coast begins when the screw sloop *Brooklyn* (10 guns) under Commander Charles H. Poor takes up position off the mouth of the Mississippi River, and the side-wheel frigate *Powhatan* (16 guns), under Lieutenant David D. Porter, assumes duty off Mobile Bay, Alabama.

David Dixon Porter (1813–1891)

U.S. Navy admiral. Born in Chester, Pennsylvania, on June 8, 1813, David Dixon Porter was the 3rd of 10 children of Commodore David Porter, who had distinguished himself in the War of 1812. The younger Porter's adopted brother was David G. Farragut. Porter first went to sea with his father at age 10. After brief service as a midshipman in the Mexican Navy serving under his father during 1826–1828, in which he was wounded and was briefly a prisoner of the Spanish, Porter joined the U.S. Navy as a midshipman on February 2, 1829. He became a passed midshipman on July 3, 1835, and was promoted to lieutenant on February 27, 1841. Routine assignments followed, including service in the Mediterranean. Porter distinguished himself during the Mexican-American War (1846–1848), especially in operations against Tabasco on June 14–22, 1847, but frustrated by the slow rate of advancement in the U.S. Navy, he took a leave of absence to captain merchant vessels.

Returning to duty with the navy in 1855, Porter received command of the steamer *Supply* and then served ashore at the Portsmouth Navy Yard during 1857–1860. He was on the verge of a second leave of absence from the navy when the secessionist crisis occurred. Porter then secured command of the powerful side-wheel frigate *Powhatan* on April 1, 1861. He circumvented both Secretary of the Navy Gideon Welles and commander of the Brooklyn Navy Yard Captain Andrew H. Foote in carrying out Secretary of War William H. Seward's plan to relieve Fort Pickens in Florida. This removed the *Powhatan* from participation in the effort to relieve Fort Sumter but probably did not in itself ensure the failure of that operation. Despite his having disobeyed orders, Porter received promotion to commander on April 22.

Porter then conducted operations with the *Powhatan* in the Gulf of Mexico. He returned to Washington in early 1862 and convinced Welles and Assistant Secretary of the Navy Gustavus V. Fox that bombardment of Confederate Forts Jackson and St. Philip on the lower Mississippi by a flotilla of mortar boats would be essential to the success of a plan to capture New Orleans. Porter pledged that both forts would be rendered ineffective by shelling from 13-inch mortars within 48 hours. Receiving command of the mortar flotilla under the overall command of his adoptive brother and commander of the West Gulf Coast Blockading Squadron Flag Officer David Farragut, Porter carried out a six-day bombardment of Forts Jackson and St. Philip, which failed to reduce the forts. Farragut then ran past the forts with the ships of his squadron on April 27, while Porter supplied gunfire support. With the two forts then cut off by the Union ships and troops, Porter took their surrender on April 28.

As an acting rear admiral, Porter assumed command of the Mississippi Flotilla, now designated the Mississippi Squadron, on October 15, 1862. Naval activity then sharply increased with the initiation of joint operations against Vicksburg. Porter helped secure Arkansas Post on January 1863, then worked closely and effectively with Major General Ulysses S. Grant and Brigadier General William T. Sherman. Porter was rewarded for his role in the surrender of Vicksburg on July 4 with advancement to permanent rear admiral over many other more senior officers, with the promotion backdated to July 4.

Porter commanded the naval phase of the Red River Expedition during March 12–May 13, 1864, supporting army troops ashore under Major General Nathaniel P. Banks in an effort to capture Shreveport. Banks and Porter did not get along, and low water levels in the Red, in part caused by the Confederates, plagued Porter's operations. Despite myriad problems, Porter succeeded in extraditing his ships and was not blamed for the fiasco, one of the great military blunders of the war.

Porter then assumed command of the North Atlantic Blockading Squadron in September 1864 and assembled in December the most powerful naval force to that point in U.S. history: 61 warships, including 5 ironclads, mounting a total of 635 guns for an attack on Fort Fisher in an effort to close off the port of Wilmington to Confederate blockade-runners. The initial assault on December 24–25 went poorly, thanks to ineffective cooperation on the part of the commander of the Union Army contingent, Major General Benjamin Butler. Union general-in-chief Ulysses S. Grant then sacked Butler and appointed Brigadier General Alfred H. Terry, who established an excellent working relationship with Porter. In a textbook amphibious operation, Fort Fisher fell to Union army and navy forces on January 13–15, 1865. Porter then operated on the James River in April, forcing the Confederate commander to scuttle his squadron there and conducting President Abraham Lincoln on a tour of Richmond.

Following the war, Porter assumed the superintendency of the Naval Academy during 1865–1869, where he introduced extensive reforms. Promoted to vice admiral on July 25, 1866, he was advanced to admiral on August 15, 1870. He then served as head of the Board of Inspection until his death in Washington, D.C., on February 13, 1891.

SPENCER C. TUCKER

Further Reading

Hearn, Chester. *David Dixon Porter: The Civil War Years*. Annapolis, MD: Naval Institute Press, 1996.

Melia, Tamara M. "David Dixon Porter: Fighting Sailor." In *Captains of the Old Steam Navy*, edited by James C. Bradford, 227–249. Annapolis, MD: Naval Institute Press, 1986.

Robinson, Charles M. *Hurricane of Fire: The Union Assault on Fort Fisher*. Annapolis, MD: Naval Institute Press, 1998.

May 26–29, 1861

Civil War (continued): Eastern theater. U.S. Army major general George B. McClellan, commanding the Department of the Ohio, advances three columns to Grafton in western Virginia, securing control of the vital Baltimore and Ohio Railroad, which links Washington, D.C., with the West.

May 28, 1861

Civil War (continued): Eastern theater. U.S. Army colonel Irvin McDowell is promoted to brigadier general and given command of the Department of Northwestern Virginia.

May 29, 1861

Civil War (continued). In Washington, D.C., Dorothea Dix approaches Secretary of War Simon Cameron, offering to organize hospital services for federal forces in the war.

May 29, 1861

Civil War (continued). The U.S. Navy screw steamer *Union* (1 gun), under Commander John R. Goldsborough, initiates the blockade off Savannah, Georgia.

May 29–31, 1861

Civil War (continued). The U.S. Navy Potomac Flotilla under Commander James H. Ward and consisting of the steamers *Thomas Freeborn* (flagship, 2 guns), *Anacostia* (2 guns), and *Resolute* (2 guns) bombards Confederate batteries at Aquia Creek, Virginia.

May 30, 1861

Civil War (continued). U.S. secretary of war Simon Cameron instructs Brigadier General Benjamin Butler at Fortress Monroe, Virginia, not to return fugitive slaves to their owners but instead to employ them as laborers on federal installations.

May 30, 1861

Civil War (continued): Eastern theater. The Confederates begin work to salvage the screw frigate *Merrimack*, scuttled by federal forces abandoning the Norfolk Navy Yard.

June 2, 1861

Civil War (continued): Eastern theater. Confederate major general Pierre G. T. Beauregard assumes command of Confederate forces at Manassas Junction in northern Virginia.

Irvin McDowell (1818–1885)

U.S. Army officer. Irvin McDowell was born in Columbus, Ohio, on October 15, 1818. He received his early education in France; graduated from the U.S. Military Academy, West Point, in 1838; and was commissioned a second lieutenant in the artillery. McDowell performed garrison duty along the Canadian border until 1841, when he returned to West Point as an instructor of tactics.

Promoted to first lieutenant in 1842, in 1845 McDowell joined the staff of Brigadier General John E. Wool in Texas as aide-de-camp, retaining this post throughout the Mexican-American War. McDowell was breveted captain for his performance in the February 1847 Battle of Buena Vista and was promoted to permanent captain in May.

McDowell was then assigned to the Adjutant General's Department in Washington, D.C. Between 1848 and 1861, he was aide-de-camp to general-in-chief Lieutenant General Winfield Scott, earning promotion to major. Following the onset of the American Civil War in April 1861, Scott arranged for McDowell to be promoted to brigadier general of volunteers.

In the anxious early days of the war, it fell to McDowell to organize, train, and lead an army against the Confederate forces in Virginia. Despite his lack of experience commanding large formations, McDowell had by July assembled a force of some 50,000 regulars and raw volunteers around Washington, D.C. Had he possessed sufficient time, he would no doubt have welded this polyglot collection into an effective fighting force. Domestic politics intervened, however.

Goaded by President Abraham Lincoln and others, McDowell was forced to commence offensive operations before his army could competently enact them. He nonetheless concocted a viable scheme for advancing into Virginia. He planned to outflank Confederate forces under Brigadier General Pierre T. Beauregard at Manassas Junction and sever its supply line to Richmond. Politicians in Washington hoped that a crushing Union victory here would end the war.

On July 16, 1861, McDowell led some 37,000 men out of Washington. He proceeded slowly, and as it turned out, his men were unable to execute his plan effectively. In the First Battle of Bull Run (Manassas) on July 21, Beauregard was able to redeploy his 22,000 men to meet the Union envelopment in time, greatly aided by the arrival by rail from the Shenandoah Valley of 11,000 men under Brigadier General Joseph E. Johnston, who tipped the battle in favor of the Confederates. McDowell's forces then broke and ran in a humiliating stampede back to Washington, D.C. Fortunately for the Union, the Confederates were totally disorganized and in no condition to pursue. Nonetheless, the defeat was a national disgrace, and McDowell was relieved of command.

Lincoln, perhaps cognizant of his mistake in rushing McDowell into combat, allowed him to command I Corps in Major General George B. McClellan's newly organized Army of the Potomac. McDowell was promoted to major general of volunteers in March 1862. Throughout McClellan's ineffectual Peninsula Campaign (March–August 1862) during the spring of 1862, I Corps remained fixed in place guarding Washington, D.C.

In July 1862, McDowell's force was redesignated II Corps as part of General John Pope's Army of Virginia. Both commanders subsequently turned in poor performances in the Union defeat at the Second Battle of Bull Run (Manassas) on August 29–30, 1862, and were relieved of command. McDowell, angered at being hung out to dry for a second time, demanded a court of inquiry that cleared him, but his career was effectively finished. He spent the rest of the war in exile commanding the Department of the Pacific beginning in July 1864 before taking command of the Department of California in July 1865.

McDowell took command of the Department of the East in July 1868 and rose to major general in November 1872. After four years commanding the Division of the South, he resumed command of the Department of the Pacific in June 1876. McDowell retired six years later and died on May 4, 1885, in San Francisco. Though the last stage of his career was efficient and commendable, he never lived down the stigma gained at Bull Run 25 years earlier.

JOHN C. FREDRIKSEN

Further Reading

Davis, William C. *Battle at Bull Run: A History of the First Major Campaign of the Civil War.* Baton Rouge: Louisiana State University Press, 1977.

Hankinson, Alan. *First Bull Run, 1861: The South's First Victory.* London: Osprey, 1991.

Hassler, Warren W. *Commanders of the Army of the Potomac.* Westport, CT: Greenwood, 1962.

Dorothea Lynde Dix (1802–1887)

Renowned medical and hospital reformer, nurse, and superintendent of U.S. Army nurses (1861–1865). Dorothea Lynde Dix was born in Hampden, Maine (then part of Massachusetts), on April 4, 1802. At age 12 she moved to Boston to live with her grandmother. Dix worked for a time as a teacher, then operated a finishing school for women in Boston and authored several undistinguished books. In 1834, she traveled to Europe and visited numerous asylums for the mentally ill, hoping to bring reform to such facilities in the United States. Thus began a decades-long crusade to reform institutions for the mentally disabled and poor. Dix spent years lobbying Congress and local politicians to support her reforms, and by the mid-1850s she had secured from Congress legislation that allotted thousands of acres of federal land for the construction of modern—and humane—mental institutions. In the late 1850s Dix returned to Europe to study the management and physical layout of various hospitals, including military facilities.

In April 1861 when the Civil War began, Dix volunteered her services to the War Department. Appointed superintendent of all army nurses on June 10, 1861, she immediately began to recruit and appoint nurses and established efficient systems of management and medical delivery. During the war, she personally appointed more than 3,000 nurses. Dix also had charge of vast quantities of hospital supplies, which were distributed through her office in Washington, D.C. She maintained very stringent standards for nurse recruiting and training, which alienated some would-be nurses and greatly annoyed some army doctors, who did not like to be beholden to a female nurse such as Dix. Some nurses referred to their boss as "Dragon Dix," but most soon came to appreciate her exacting guidelines.

In October 1863, the surgeon general trimmed some of Dix's authority as a result of physicians' complaints. Order No. 351 empowered surgeons to appoint their own employees, including nurses. Dix was, however, undeterred and redoubled her efforts to provide the best nursing care possible among the employees she still controlled. She also tried to prevent her nurses from becoming victims of unwanted advances by male doctors, which infuriated some physicians all the more.

When supplies were short, Dix often raised private funds and purchased them herself. She toured many hospitals during the war and even operated a home where nurses could rest during leaves and furloughs. Dix accomplished all of this without receiving any pay from the government.

After the war, Dix continued her advocacy work on behalf of the mentally ill and indigent and founded a hospital in Trenton, New Jersey, where she died on July 17, 1887.

PAUL G. PIERPAOLI JR.

Further Reading

Brown, Thomas J. *Dorothea Dix: New England Reformer.* Cambridge, MA: Harvard University Press, 1998.
Muckenhoupt, Margaret. *Dorothea Dix: Advocate for Mental Health Care.* New York: Oxford University Press, 2004.

June 3–July 13, 1861

Civil War (continued): Eastern theater. U.S. Army major general George B. McClellan clears western Virginia (later the state of West Virginia) of Confederate forces in the battles of Philippi (June 3, 1861) and Rich Mountain (July 11) and Carrick's Ford (July 13).

June 8, 1861

Civil War (continued). The U.S. Navy side-wheel frigate *Mississippi* (12 guns) initiates the blockade off Key West, Florida.

June 10, 1861

Civil War (continued): Eastern theater: Battle of Big Bethel. In the first battle in present-day Virginia and the first real land battle of the war, Union major general Benjamin F. Butler at Fort Monroe orders converging columns from Hampton and Newport News to attack Confederate outposts at nearby Little Bethel Church and Big Bethel Church in Hampton and York Counties (near present-day

unincorporated Tabb) that have been harassing his troops. Union brigadier general Ebenezer W. Pierce has command of the operation, with about 3,500 troops.

The Confederates abandon Little Bethel and fall back on prepared entrenchments behind Brick Kiln Creek, near Big Bethel Church. Colonel John B. Magruder commands some 1,200 Confederates. In the ensuing battle, Pierce squanders his considerable numerical advantage by expending his inexperienced men piecemeal in frontal assaults against the entrenched Confederates. The 5th New York Zouave regiment crosses Brick Kiln Creek downstream and tries to turn the Confederate left but is repulsed. Pierce then withdraws. Union losses are 18 killed, 60 wounded, and 1 missing. Confederate losses are only 1 killed and 7 wounded.

June 10, 1861

Civil War (continued). Confederate secretary of the navy Stephen R. Mallory orders Lieutenant John M.

U.S. Army first lieutenant John T. Greble and his artillerymen during the Battle of Big Bethel, Virginia, June 10, 1861. Greble was killed in the fighting, the first West Point graduate to die in the Civil War. (William O. Blake, *Pictorial History of the Great Rebellion*, 1866)

John Mercer Brooke (1826–1906)

U.S. and Confederate Navy officer and ordnance designer. The son of U.S. Army colonel George Mercer Brooke, John Mercer Brooke was born at Fort Brooke on the site of present-day Tampa, Florida, on December 18, 1826. He secured a warrant as a midshipman in the U.S. Navy on March 3, 1841, and graduated as a passed midshipman from the Naval Academy, Annapolis, on August 10, 1847. He was promoted to master on September 14, 1855, and to lieutenant on September 15, 1855.

Brooke's intellectual curiosity and scientific bent led to useful inventions, including deep-sea-sounding leads that eventually made possible the laying of an Atlantic cable. Later he led major explorations of the North Pacific and the coast of Japan. He also escorted the first Japanese diplomatic mission to the United States.

On April 20, 1861, three days after the secession of Virginia, Brooke resigned his commission in the U.S. Navy. His wife and close friends seem to have been the key factors in the decision. Future admiral David Dixon Porter stated that he only regretted the loss of two men from the U.S. Navy: Catesby ap Roger Jones and Brooke.

Commissioned a lieutenant in the Virginia Navy on April 23, Brooke became naval aide to commander of Virginia forces General Robert E. Lee. When it was clear that Virginia would be linked to the Confederacy, Brooke applied for a commission in the Confederate Navy, which was granted on May 2.

In a June 1861 meeting with Confederate secretary of the navy Stephen R. Mallory, Brooke assured the secretary that the South could build its own ironclads. Mallory then transferred Brooke to the naval ordnance office, where he supervised work on the armor and guns for CSS *Virginia*. Brooke was

Brooke to draw up plans for an ironclad. Within two weeks, Brooke presents a plan for a casemated vessel with inclined sides.

June 10, 1861

Civil War (continued). U.S. secretary of war James Cameron appoints Dorothea Dix superintendent of nurses for the U.S. Army.

June 17, 1861

Civil War (continued): Eastern theater: Secession of West Virginia from Virginia. The western section of Virginia, tied economically to the Ohio Valley and estranged from the state's Tidewater and Piedmont regions, refuses to recognize the secession of the rest of the state. During June 11–25 a convention meets in Wheeling and organizes a government. On June 17 it unanimously declares West Virginia independent from the rest of Virginia under the temporary name of Kanwaha. On June 20, 1863, the 50 western counties of Virginia are admitted to the Union as the state of West Virginia.

June 17, 1861

Civil War (continued): Western theater: Battle of Boonville. U.S. Army brigadier general Nathaniel Lyon advances on Jefferson City, Missouri, and secures it. At nearby Boonville, Lyon defeats pro-Confederate governor Claiborne Jackson's militiamen and drives them southwest. The clash is more a skirmish than a battle. It lasts only 20 minutes, and each side suffers only about a dozen killed or wounded, responsible for the *Virginia's* slanted armor casemate, subsequently copied in other Confederate ironclads, as well as the idea of bow and stern extensions under water. However, friction between Brooke and constructor John D. Porter, who claimed credit for the *Virginia's* design, contributed to Brooke's subsequent lack of interest in the ironclad program.

Brooke's ordnance achievements are especially remarkable, particularly given his lack of experience in that area. Promoted to commander in September 1862, in March 1863 he was named chief of the Confederate Bureau of Ordnance and Hydrography, a post he held until the end of the war. In this capacity, Brooke designed a variety of guns for the Confederacy. His rifled pieces were perhaps the finest of that type on either side in the war. Brooke also oversaw the establishment of the Confederate Naval Academy at Drewry's Bluff, Virginia.

Following the war, Brooke joined the Virginia Military Institute faculty as a professor of astronomy, meteorology, and geography. He served in that position from 1865 until 1899. Brooke died in Lexington, Virginia, on December 14, 1906.

SPENCER C. TUCKER

Further Reading

Brooke, George M., Jr. *John M. Brooke: Naval Scientist and Educator.* Charlottesville: University Press of Virginia, 1980.

Brooke, John Mercer. "The *Virginia* or *Merrimac:* Her Real Projector." *Southern Historical Society Papers* 19 (January 1891): 3–34.

Conrad, James Lee. *Rebel Reefers: The Organization and Midshipmen of the Confederate States Naval Academy.* Cambridge, MA: Da Capo, 2003.

Olmstead, Edwin, Wayne Stark, and Spencer Tucker. *The Big Guns: Civil War Siege, Seacoast and Naval Cannon.* Alexandria Bay, NY, and Bloomfield, Ontario, Canada: Museum Restoration Service, 1997.

although 80 Confederates are captured. The battle is, however, of major strategic importance, securing Missouri for the Union.

June 18, 1861

Civil War (continued). Balloonist Thaddeus S. C. Lowe, who has claim to being the nation's first aeronaut and had been preparing to attempt a crossing of the Atlantic Ocean by balloon, in a demonstration flight at Washington, D.C., ascends in his balloon *Enterprise* some 500 feet and sends a message via telegraph key to President Abraham Lincoln at the White House. In July, Lincoln appoints Lowe chief aeronaut of the U.S. Army Balloon Corps to provide information on Confederate Army dispositions.

June 18, 1861

Civil War (continued). President Abraham Lincoln signs legislation authorizing establishment of a civilian sanitary commission to assist the Army Medical Corps. Many of the deaths in the army are the result of disease—from dysentery, diarrhea, typhoid, and malaria—due to overcrowded and unsanitary conditions in the field. Preaching the necessity for clean water, good food, and fresh air, the Sanitary Commission presses the Army Medical Department to improve sanitation, build large well-ventilated hospitals, and encourage the recruitment of women in the newly created nursing corps. Despite its work, twice as many soldiers will die from disease as from battle. The commission helps lead to the subsequent establishment of the American Red Cross.

 **Balloons**

French brothers Joseph-Michael and Étienne Montgolfier became fascinated by the rise of paper in updrafts in the family chimney and were convinced that they could send aloft bags of paper by means of building a fire under them (they mistakenly attributed the rise, or levity, to properties in the smoke). Their first known successful trial occurred on April 25, 1783. French physicist Jacques-Alexandre-César Charles, believing that the Montgolfiers had employed hydrogen, caused to be built a balloon of silk, which he filled with that gas and launched from the Champ de Mars in Paris on August 27. The balloon came down some 15 miles distant. Alarmed peasants promptly ripped the balloon to shreds with their pitchforks.

The first aeronauts were Jean-François de Pilâtre de Rozier and François Laurent, Marquis d'Arlandes. Their untethered flight took place on November 21, 1783, in a Montgolfier balloon from the grounds of the Chateau of Versailles in a flight lasting 23 minutes that covered about 10 miles. The first hydrogen-filled balloon ascent was on December 1, 1783, from the Tuileries Garden in Paris. It lasted two hours and covered 27 miles. In 1785, two daring individuals crossed the English Channel in a hydrogen balloon. The French soon used their invention for military purposes. In 1794 during the Wars of the French Revolution, balloon observers provided valuable intelligence to French ground forces. Balloons also provided communication during the German siege of Paris in the Franco-Prussian War of 1870–1871.

During the American Civil War (1861–1865), both the Union and Confederacy employed observation balloons, although most were on the Union side. On June 17, 1861, aeronaut Thaddeus S. C. Lowe ascended in his balloon, the *Enterprise,* over Washington, D.C. President Abraham Lincoln was sufficiently impressed to establish a Balloon Corps headed by Lowe. It served with the Army of the Potomac during 1861–1863, gathering information on Confederate troop movements and deployments and directing artillery fire. In March 1862 a balloon also took part in Union operations against Island No. 10 in the Mississippi River.

Civil War balloons held between 15,000 and 32,000 cubic feet of hydrogen and were up to 45 feet in height, not counting the gondola under the balloons, which could carry as many as five men. Lowe also experimented with the telegraph wire to transmit messages, although written messages tied to rocks usually proved more efficient.

Balloons were regularly employed for communication and observation thereafter and proved of immense importance in artillery spotting and general observation during the fixed fighting that characterized warfare on the Western Front in World War I, and shooting them down became an important task for opposing aircraft and antiaircraft artillery. Wires strung between the balloons foiled low-flying enemy aircraft. Aircraft employed in balloon busting used special incendiary bullets to ignite the hydrogen.

Observation balloon duty was understandably hazardous for its participants. Although equipped with parachutes as early as 1915, the observers were authorized to put these on only when a balloon actually caught fire, when chances of escape were slim.

Barrage balloons were also widely employed during World War II as a defense against low-lying aircraft. Tethered in large numbers over strategic locations, they trailed long steel cables, through which aircraft could not fly. The presence of barrage balloons forced attacking aircraft to fly at higher altitudes, thus reducing bombing accuracy. During the war in Operation FU-GO, the Japanese sent some 9,000

30-foot-diameter hydrogen-filled paper balloons with incendiaries against North America in an effort to start forest fires. Of 258 reported incidents, there were only six fatalities—a woman and five children on a picnic.

Ironically, today's recreation balloons have returned to the Montgolfier hot-air design, employing rip-stop nylon for the envelope with hot air provided by propane gas burners.

SPENCER C. TUCKER

Further Reading

Ege, Lennart A. T. *Balloons and Airships, 1783–1973*. Edited by Kenneth Munson. New York: Macmillan, 1981.
Manceron, Claude. *The French Revolution*, Vol. 3, *Their Gracious Pleasure, 1782–1785*. Translated by Nancy Amphoux. New York: Knopf, 1980.
Rolt, L. T. C. *The Aeronauts: A History of Ballooning, 1783–1903*. New York: Messner, 1958.

June 27, 1861

Civil War (continued). The U.S. Commission of Conference, usually referred to as the Blockade Board or the Strategy Board, begins meetings in Washington, D.C. It recommends dividing the naval blockade into four separate commands and calls for the seizure of points along the Confederate coasts for bases and coaling stations to support the naval blockade.

June 27, 1861

Civil War (continued). The crew of the U.S. Navy screw tug *Resolute* (2 guns) disembarks and burns a Confederate supply depot along the Potomac River. On this date also, landing parties from the U.S. Navy side-wheel steamer *Thomas Freeborn* (2 guns), the Revenue Service screw steamer *Reliance* (6 guns), and the screw sloop *Pawnee* (8 guns) engage Confederate forces at Mathias Point, Virginia. Commander James H. Ward, commanding the Potomac River Flotilla, is mortally wounded while sighting a gun, becoming the first U.S. naval officer killed in action during the Civil War. Four others on the Union side are wounded.

June 28–29, 1861

Civil War (continued). Confederate Navy captain George N. Hollins leads a force disguised as passengers aboard the U.S. steamer *St. Nicholas* and, during its run between Baltimore, Maryland, and Georgetown in Washington, D.C., captures it. The Confederates take three additional U.S. ships the following day: the schooners *Margaret* and *Mary Pierce* and the brig *Monticello*.

June 30, 1861

Civil War (continued): Escape of CSS *Sumter*. In one of the memorable chases of the entire war, Confederate Navy lieutenant Commander Raphael Semmes in the screw steamer *Sumter* (ex-*Habanna*, 6 guns) outruns the U.S. Navy screw sloop *Brooklyn* (10 guns) off the mouth of the Mississippi, escaping into the Gulf of Mexico. The Confederate government had purchased the *Habanna* at New Orleans and converted it into the first Southern commerce raider.

June 30, 1861

Qui Nhon Inident. On June 26, the U.S. Navy side-wheel steamer *Saginaw* under Commander James F. Schneck departs Hong Kong to search for the American bark *Myrtle* and its crew, lost along the Indochina coast the year before. On June 30 the American gunboat arrives at Qui Nhon, Cochin China. Although Schneck hoists the American flag and a white flag and intends to parley with Vietnamese officials, the fort opens fire. After three shots hit close to his ship, Schneck orders fire returned, silencing the fort in an hour's exchange. Lacking sufficient manpower for a landing party, he returns to Hong Kong.

July 2, 1861

Civil War (continued): Eastern theater: Battle of Hoke's Run. On May 24, 1861, U.S. Army general-in-chief Lieutenant General Winfield Scott had ordered commander of the Department of Pennsylvania Major General Robert Patterson to recapture Harpers Ferry and prevent Confederate forces under Brigadier General Joseph E. Johnston in western Virginia from joining the large force gathering west of Washington, D.C. However, Patterson does not cross the Potomac with his 18,000 men until July 2. That same day he engages a Confederate brigade under Colonel Thomas J. Jackson in the Battle of Hoke's Run in Berkeley County (now West Virginia) but here and elsewhere fails to press his great numerical advantage.

During the next several weeks Johnston will outmaneuver Patterson, who occupies Martinsburg, but Johnston makes no other aggressive move until July 15, when he marches to Bunker Hill. Instead of continuing on to Winchester, he moves east to Charles Town and then withdraws to Harpers Ferry.

July 2, 1861

Civil War (continued). The U.S. Navy screw steamer *South Carolina* (5 guns), under Commander James Alden, initiates the blockade off Galveston, Texas.

July 6, 1861

Civil War (continued). Having captured seven U.S. merchantmen, the Confederate commerce raider *Sumter* puts into Havana, Cuba, with its prizes. On July 19, however, Cuban authorities order the prizes released, signaling the difficulty that the Confederates will have with captured ships. With the Union blockade of the Confederate coasts, it is difficult to sail the captured ships to Southern ports. As a consequence, most prizes are burned.

July 7, 1861

Civil War (continued). In Aquia Creek, Virginia, the U.S. Navy screw steamer *Pocahontas* (6 guns) engages

and damages the Confederate Navy side-wheeler *George Page* (2 guns).

July 7, 1861

Civil War (continued): First use of naval mines in the war. The crew of the U.S. Navy screw steamer *Resolute* (2 guns), commanded by Acting Master William Budd, retrieves two torpedoes (naval mines) from the Potomac River. Ultimately the Confederates will employ a wide variety of torpedoes and destroy some 40 Union ships.

July 11 and 13, 1861

Civil War (continued): Battles of Rich Mountain and Corrick's Ford. In western Virginia (now West Virginia) U.S. Army major general George B. McClellan sends Brigadier General William S. Rosecrans south from Clarksburg with a reinforced brigade against some 1,300 Confederates under Lieutenant Colonel John Pegram in the area of Rich Mountain (present-day Randolph County, West Virginia). McClellan also orders Brigadier General T. A. Morris to advance his brigade from Philippi against Confederate forces under Brigadier General Robert S. Garnett at nearby Laurel Hill.

On July 11, 1861, at Rich Mountain, Rosecrans and 2,000 Union troops proceed by a mountain path and seize the Staunton-Parkersburg Turnpike in Pegram's rear. A sharp two-hour battle ensues, with each side suffering about 70 casualties, but the Confederate forces are split. On July 13 Pegram and 555 of his men surrender, including the so-called Sydney Boys (a regiment formed of students from Hampden-Sydney College). His line of communications now threatened, Garnett abandons Laurel Hill. The Federals pursue, and during fighting at Corricks Ford on July 13 Garnett is killed, the first general officer on either side to die in the war. The Confederates sustain 70 casualties; U.S. losses are only 10.

July 14, 1861

Civil War (continued). The U.S. Navy screw steamer *Daylight* (4 guns), under Commander Samuel Lockwood, initiates the federal naval blockade off Wilmington, North Carolina.

William Starke Rosecrans (1819–1898)

Union Army officer. Born in Delaware County, Ohio, on September 6, 1819, William Starke Rosecrans graduated from the U.S. Military Academy, West Point, in 1842. He entered the Corps of Engineers, but in 1854 he left the army to pursue a career in business and engineering.

With the beginning of the American Civil War in 1861, Rosecrans returned to uniform, joining the staff of Major General George B. McClellan. Rosecrans rose to brigadier general in May 1861 and as McClellan's chief subordinate was the real author of most of the success in the autumn 1861 campaign in western Virginia, although McClellan appropriated the credit. An embittered Rosecrans transferred to the Western theater rather than continue service under McClellan.

Assigned to the Army of the Mississippi, Rosecrans took part in the Corinth Campaign (April 29–May 30, 1862), after which he commanded the Army of the Mississippi, under the overall command of Major General Ulysses S. Grant. Rosecrans suggested a two-pronged attack to trap Confederate forces under Major General Sterling Price. In the ensuing Battle of Iuka (September 19–20), however, Rosecrans left an escape route open for the Confederates, who attacked and held him at bay while their force made a getaway. Grant's force, prevented by the wind direction from hearing the sounds of Rosecrans's battle, did not get into the fight.

On October 7–8, Price's army combined with one under Major General Earl Van Dorn in an attempt to recapture Corinth, defended by Rosecrans. Rosecrans handled his troops poorly and showed signs of panic, although the stubbornness of his troops secured victory. Despite positive orders and reinforcements from Grant, Rosecrans made no attempt to pursue the defeated Confederates until it was too late to trap them at the Hatchie River, as Grant had planned.

Nonetheless, because Corinth had been a Union victory, President Abraham Lincoln tapped Rosecrans to take command of the army that Major General Don Carlos Buell had mismanaged during the just-concluded Kentucky campaign. Rosecrans christened it the Army of the Cumberland. Aware that Lincoln wanted aggressive action, when he learned that a Confederate army under General Braxton Bragg had been weakened by the transfer of one-fourth of its infantry to Mississippi, Rosecrans determined to attack. He met Bragg's army just outside Murfreesboro, Tennessee, along the banks of Stones River and in an inspired performance defeated it in battle during December 31, 1862–January 2, 1863.

The victory, coming in the midst of a season of Union defeats, was a political godsend for Lincoln, but the president's gratitude wore thin as Rosecrans kept his army idle for the next six months. At last in late June he advanced again and in a nine-day campaign of maneuver forced Bragg to fall back another 80 miles to Chattanooga.

After another six-week pause, Rosecrans again advanced and again succeeded in turning Bragg and forcing him to retreat another 27 miles to Lafayette, Georgia. Rosecrans, however, thought that Bragg was falling back all the way to Atlanta and pursued aggressively, with his corps widely spread in separate columns. In fact, Rosecrans's previous long delays had allowed Richmond to reinforce Bragg to greater numbers than the Army of the Cumberland. The Confederate counterstroke fell at the September 18–20, 1863, Battle of Chickamauga. On the final day of the battle, Rosecrans gave an ill-conceived

(continued)

(Continued)

order that created a gap in his line just as the Confederates were launching a major assault. His army was routed except for a large contingent under Major General George Thomas, which held its ground until, close to nightfall, Rosecrans ordered it to retreat.

After Chickamauga, Rosecrans was a broken man. He pulled his troops back into Chattanooga and allowed Bragg to place him under virtual siege there. Lincoln observed that Rosecrans was acting "confused and stunned, like a duck hit on the head." The president assigned Major General Ulysses S. Grant to command of all Union armies west of the Appalachians with authority to retain Rosecrans in command of the Army of the Cumberland or to dismiss him. Grant made the obvious choice. Later in the war Rosecrans held a minor command in Missouri. He resigned from the army in 1867.

During 1868–1869, Rosecrans was minister to Mexico. He returned to his California ranch before serving in the U.S. House of Representative during 1881–1885. He then held a position in the Treasury Department until 1893. Rosecrans died in Redondo, California, on March 11, 1898.

STEVEN E. WOODWORTH

Further Reading

Lamers, William M. *The Edge of Glory: A Biography of General William S. Rosecrans, U.S.A.* New York: Harcourt, Brace, 1961.

Woodworth, Steven E. *Nothing but Victory: The Army of the Tennessee, 1861–1865.* New York: Knopf, 2005.

Woodworth, Steven E. *Six Armies in Tennessee: The Chickamauga and Chattanooga Campaigns.* Lincoln: University of Nebraska Press, 1998.

July 16, 1861

Civil War (continued). The U.S. Navy Blockade Board recommends that hulks filled with stone (the so-called stone fleets) be sunk in channels of strategic waterways to impede Confederate shipping and augment the porous Union naval blockade.

July 21, 1861

Civil War (continued): Eastern theater: First Battle of Bull Run (Manassas). Demands in the North for a drive on Richmond and a quick end to the Confederacy lead U.S. president Abraham Lincoln to disregard the advice of general-in-chief Lieutenant General Winfield Scott, who wants more time to train the green Union troops. Brigadier General Irvin McDowell, with 38,000 men, is ordered to advance southwest of Washington to Manassas Junction, Virginia, 22 miles distant, against some 20,000 Confederates under Brigadier General Pierre G. T. Beauregard. McDowell sets out on July 16.

Timorous U.S. major general Robert Patterson with 18,000 men, having been ordered to prevent Confederate brigadier general Joseph E. Johnston from joining his 10,000 men in western Virginia with Beauregard's force, fails to carry out his mission, and McDowell's dilatory advance from Washington allows the Confederates time to concentrate. On July 17 Confederate president Jefferson Davis orders Johnston to join Beauregard, and in the first large troop movement by rail in U.S. history, Johnston evades Patterson and joins Beauregard just in time on July 20.

Believing the Confederate positions too strong for a frontal assault, McDowell decides on a complicated flanking maneuver that proves too difficult for his poorly trained troops to execute effectively. The

The First Battle of Bull Run, July 21, 1861. Inexperienced Union troops were unable to carry out Brigadier General Irvin McDowell's attack plan, and defending Confederate forces under Pierre G. T. Beauregard won a clear-cut victory in this first large battle of the Civil War. (Library of Congress)

resulting First Battle of Bull Run, also known as the First Battle of Manassas (the Union names its battles for the nearest body of water, while the Confederates prefer towns), begins with a Union attack before dawn on July 21. McDowell seems to have carried the day by 3:00 p.m., but the arrival of Confederate reinforcements and a magnificent stand in the vicinity of Henry House Hill by troops under Brigadier General Thomas J. Jackson (which leads to his nickname of "Stonewall") turns an apparent rout into a Confederate victory.

McDowell's men begin an orderly retreat, but this quickly becomes a confused, panicky stampede toward Washington. In the battle the Union side suffers 2,896 casualties (460 killed, 1,124 wounded, and 1,312 captured or missing); the Confederates sustain

First Battle of Bull Run (Manassas)		
Date	July 21, 1861	
Location	Manassas Junction, Virginia, 22 miles west of Washington, D.C.	
Opponents (*winner)	*Confederacy	United States
Commander	Brigadier General Pierre G. T. Beauregard	Brigadier General Irvin McDowell
#	Some 20,000 men engaged	Some 38,000 men engaged
Casualties	1,982 (387 killed, 1,582 wounded, and 13 missing)	2,896 casualties (1,300 of them prisoners); substantial quantities of weapons and supplies captured

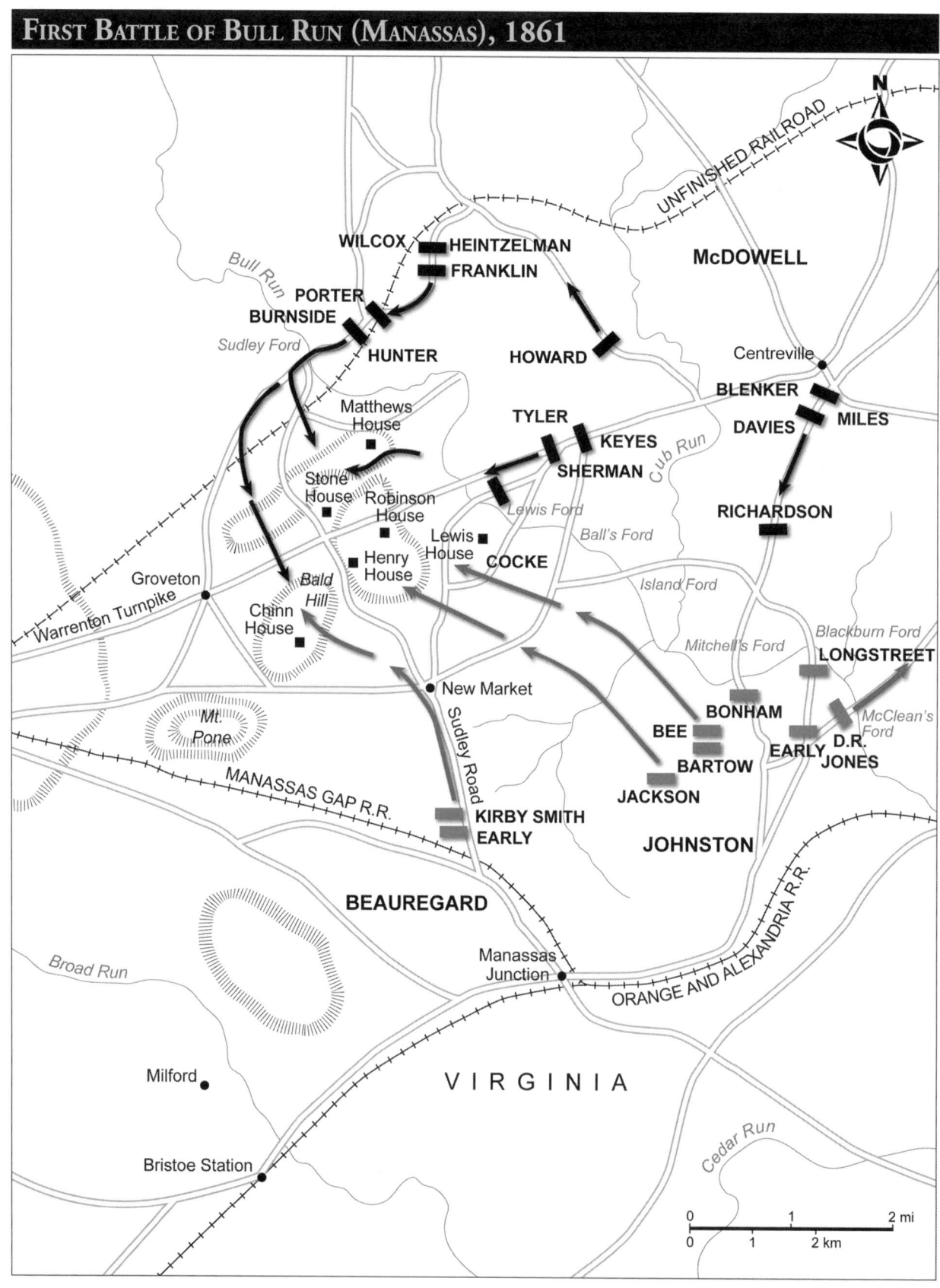

FIRST BATTLE OF BULL RUN (MANASSAS), 1861

1,982 casualties (387 killed, 1,582 wounded, and 13 missing). The Southerners also seize substantial amounts of weapons and supplies. Confederate commanders are later much criticized for their failure to follow up the victory with a march on Washington, but their forces are hardly better organized than those on the Union side.

July 22, 1861

Civil War (continued). With the three-months enlistments of many Union Army volunteers expiring, President Abraham Lincoln signs legislation authorizing 1 million volunteers to serve three-year enlistments.

July 22, 1861

Civil War (continued): Eastern theater: McClellan takes command of the main Union field army. Major General George B. McClellan, having enjoyed success in western Virginia, replaces Major General Irvin McDowell as commander of what becomes the Army of the Potomac. McClellan spends the next six months training it. In November on the retirement of Lieutenant General Winfield Scott, McClellan also becomes general-in-chief. McClellan, however, makes no move to take the offensive, much to President Abraham Lincoln's intense frustration. McClellan's chief contribution to the Union war effort will be in training the army, not in leading it.

July 25–27, 1861

Civil War (continued): Trans-Mississippi West theater: Battle of Mesilla and surrender of Union forces. On the night of July 24, 1861, Confederate Army lieutenant colonel John R. Baylor arrives near Fort Fillmore (present-day New Mexico, then part of Arizona Territory), with 300 men, having come up the Rio Grande from Fort Bliss 40 miles distant. Learning that 1 of his men has warned the Union garrison, Baylor cancels his planned attack but occupies nearby Mesilla, which is strongly pro-Confederate.

On July 25, Union major Isaac Lynde approaches Mesilla from the south with the 7th Infantry Regiment and mounted riflemen: 380 men with four mountain howitzers. Baylor rejects Lynde's demand

for surrender, and Lynde orders his artillery to open fire. A bungled Union charge results in the deaths of 3 Union soldiers; 2 officers and 4 soldiers are also wounded. Lynde then orders a return to Fort Fillmore. There are no Confederate casualties.

The Confederates remain in Mesilla, although Baylor sends to El Paso for artillery and additional manpower. Learning that Baylor has requested artillery, during the night of July 26–27 Lynde orders his men to destroy such public property as they cannot carry off and abandons Fort Fillmore. Because Baylor has blocked the shortest retreat route north up the Rio Grande toward Fort Craig, New Mexico, the Union troops proceed northeast toward San Augustin Pass in the Organ Mountains, making for Fort Stanton. Learning at dawn of Lynde's departure, Baylor pursues and overtakes him later on July 27 at San Augustine Springs, capturing the Union howitzers in a wagon. Despite objections from his officers, Lynde surrenders his 492 men. One Union soldier is killed, allegedly for threatening a Confederate. Lynde's action leaves a large part of New Mexico Territory vulnerable to Confederate invasion. In Mesilla on August 1, Baylor proclaims this as Arizona Territory of the Confederate States of America and names himself governor.

July 25, 1861

Civil War (continued): Western theater. John C. Frémont is appointed to command the U.S. Army's Western Department as a major general.

July 28, 1861

Civil War (continued). In light of the deteriorating Confederate military position in western Virginia, President Jefferson Davis orders General Robert E. Lee to take charge of forces there.

August 3, 1861

Civil War (continued). The first aerial reconnaissance from a warship occurs when John La Mountain makes a balloon ascent from the U.S. steamer *Fanny* in Hampton Roads, Virginia, to observe Confederate artillery batteries at Sewell's Point. The *Fanny* is, in effect, the nation's first aircraft carrier.

August 3, 1861

Civil War (continued). Aware that the Confederates have raised the scuttled screw frigate *Merrimack* and are rebuilding it as an ironclad, the U.S. Congress appropriates $1.5 million for armor-plated warships and authorizes creation of the Ironclad Board to oversee and approve proposals for their design and construction. The board will approve construction of three experimental ironclads: the *Galena*, *Monitor*, and *New Ironsides.*

August 3, 1861

Civil War (continued). The U.S. Congress authorizes the surgeon general to employ women as nurses in army hospitals.

August 5, 1861

Civil War (continued). The U.S. Congress votes to abolish flogging as punishment in the army.

 ## USS *Monitor*

The U.S. Navy *Monitor* was a revolutionary American Civil War warship. The Union side was well aware that the Confederates were rebuilding the former steam sloop *Merrimack* as an ironclad, subsequently christened the *Virginia*. In consequence, in August 1861 the U.S. Congress appropriated $1.5 million for ironclad construction. Swedish American engineer John Ericsson's design was by far the most revolutionary of the three that secured approval. It was approved only because of the perceived threat from the *Virginia* and because Ericsson promised to complete the work quickly. The contract was highly unusual and reflected the serious doubts about the ship, which some dubbed "Ericsson's Folly." Ericsson and his partners had to assume all the risk. If the ship failed in any way—with the navy to determine what constituted failure—then all money advanced for construction was to be returned to the government.

In contrast to the lengthy delays that marked construction of the *Virginia,* the *Monitor* was completed in record time. Laid down in Brooklyn, New York, on October 25, 1861, the ship was ready for its trials on February 19, 1862. It was commissioned six days later.

The *Monitor* revolutionized naval warfare. Entirely of iron, it incorporated such innovations as forced draft ventilation. Of only 987 tons displacement, the ship was 179′ long, with a beam of 41′6″ and a draft of only 10′6″ (half that of the *Virginia*). Its two engines delivered 320 horsepower to a single screw propeller. Design speed was 9 knots, although actual speed was somewhat less.

For all practical purposes, the *Monitor* had two hulls: an upper or armored raft supported by a lower iron hull. The raft portion had 2″ of iron on the deck and 4.5″ on the sides. To shield the hull, the armor extended 3′6″ below the waterline. The *Monitor*'s most visible part was its 120-ton 9′-tall spindle-mounted turret amidships, with an interior diameter of less than 20′. The turret had two side-by-side gun ports and mounted a pair of 9-inch Dahlgren smoothbores. Because it rotated, the ship's gun ports could be protected from enemy fire while the guns themselves were being reloaded. The turret and a small pilothouse (the command center of the ship) located forward and extending only 3′10″ above the deck were both heavily protected. The turret had eight layers and the pilothouse had nine layers of 1″ plating. Most of the ship's machinery was below the waterline.

The turret was a great advantage in that it provided protection for the gun crews and could fire on an opponent with the ship in almost any direction, but because of the turret's great weight, Ericsson designed the *Monitor* with very low freeboard, only 18 inches. The *Monitor* thus came to be called "a hat on the water" or "a cheesebox on a raft." Ericsson simply ignored the contract requirement that the ship sport a sail rig. The *Monitor* and its offspring were coastal vessels rather than seagoing ships. They were also unsuited for blockade duties, as in rough seas the crews had no alternative but to batten down the hatches and remain below.

Following the success of the *Monitor* in its March 9, 1862, battle with the *Virginia* in Hampton Roads, the North was swept up in a so-called monitor mania. Of 56 ironclads laid down by the North during the war, 52 were of the *Monitor* or turreted type. The *Monitor* itself succumbed to a storm while under tow off the Atlantic coast on December 31, 1862. The wreck was located in 1975 and is now protected as the first U.S. National Marine Sanctuary Site. Parts of the ship, including its turret, can be seen at the Mariner's Museum in Virginia.

SPENCER C. TUCKER

Further Reading

Baxter, James P. *The Introduction of the Ironclad Warship*. Cambridge, MA: Harvard University Press, 1933.
Bennett, Frank M. *The Monitor and the Navy under Steam*. Boston: Scribner, 1900.
Miller Edward N. *U.S.S. Monitor: The Ship That Launched a Modern Navy*. Annapolis, MD: Leeward Publications, 1978.

August 7, 1861

Civil War (continued). The U.S. War Department enters into a contract with James B. Eads of St. Louis for construction of seven ironclad river gunboats for use in the Mississippi River Valley. These are the *Cairo, Carondelet, Cincinnati, Louisville, Mound City, Pittsburg,* and *St. Louis* (later *Baron de Kalb*). They and three timberclad gunboats (the *Conestoga, Lexington,* and *Tyler*), so-called because they are reinforced by five-inch-thick oak planking to protect against small-arms fire and are modified by Commander John Rodgers Jr., form the nucleus of the Western Gunboat Flotilla (later the Mississippi Squadron).

August 8, 1861

Civil War (continued): Western theater. Brigadier General Ulysses S. Grant assumes command of the District of Ironton, Western Department.

August 10, 1861

Civil War (continued): Western theater: Battle of Wilson's Creek. Following the Confederate defeat at Boonville, Missouri, Missouri militia Major General Sterling Price, reinforced by Arkansas militia under Brigadier General Ben McCullough, attempts to retake Missouri. At 5:00 a.m. on this date, Union brigadier general Nathaniel Lyon, with 5,500 men, launches a surprise attack on Price and McCullough with some 10,000 men camped at Wilson's Creek, about 15 miles from Springfield.

Lyon's plan to take the Confederate front and rear fails when Colonel Frank Siegel is routed in the rearward attack. Lyon is killed, and the Union troops flee. The Confederates, who suffer 1,230 casualties to 1,317 for the Union, are disorganized and low on ammunition and are thus unable to follow up their victory.

August 12, 1861

Civil War (continued). The Union timberclads *Conestoga* (4 guns), *Lexington* (6 guns), and *Tyler* (7 guns) arrive at Cairo, Illinois, to begin patrolling the strategic confluence of the Mississippi and Ohio Rivers.

 **USS *Cairo***

Lead ship in the seven-vessel Cairo class or City class of Union river gunboats named for towns on the Western rivers. The center-wheel Cairo-class ships were often referred to as "Pook Turtles" for their rectangular casemates and sloped sides that gave them a turtle-like appearance. The ship was designed by Samuel R. Pook and built by James Buchanan Eads. Although underpowered, the *Cairo* and its sister river ironclads were 175′ in length, 51′2″ in breadth, and 6′ in draft. They were capable of 5.5 knots. Heavily armed, they mounted 13 guns: three 8-inch smoothbores, four 42-pounder coast defense rifled guns (7-inch bore), and six 32-pounder rifled guns. Three of the guns fired forward. Each gunboat was protected with 2.5 inches of armor on its casemate and 1.25 inches on the conical pilothouse forward.

Commissioned on June 25, 1862, the *Cairo* participated in the occupation of Clarksville, Tennessee, in February 1862; the bombardment of Fort Pillow; engagements with Confederate gunboats in April and May; and the Battle of Memphis on June 6. Beginning on December 11, the *Cairo* took part in an expedition up the Yazoo River that was part of Major General Ulysses S. Grant's overland campaign to take Vicksburg. On December 12 about a dozen miles up the river as the smaller ships and their boats were sweeping the river for Confederate torpedoes (mines) and believing that they had come under attack, the *Cairo*'s captain, Lieutenant Commander Thomas Selfridge, ordered the ironclad ahead. It struck two Confederate torpedoes and sank.

The navy abandoned efforts to salvage the *Cairo* in 1863, and it remained hidden in the thick Yazoo mud for nearly 100 years. Efforts to locate the wreck paid off in 1956, and in the early 1960s the remains, still largely intact, were raised and moved to the National Battlefield Park at Vicksburg, where they are now displayed. The adjacent *Cairo* Museum houses artifacts recovered from the wreck.

SPENCER C. TUCKER

Further Reading

Bearss, Edwin C. *Hardluck Ironclad: The Sinking and Salvage of the Cairo*. Baton Rouge: Louisiana State University Press, 1966.

Official Records of the Union and Confederate Navies in the War of the Rebellion, Series I, Vol. 23. Washington, DC: U.S. Government Printing Office, 1910.

Tucker, Spencer C. *Blue and Gray Navies: The Civil War Afloat*. Annapolis, MD: Naval Institute Press, 2006.

August 15, 1861

Civil War (continued). Confederate president Jefferson Davis orders all Northern men to leave the South within 40 days.

August 16, 1861

Civil War (continued). U.S. president Abraham Lincoln declares the seceding states to be in a state of rebellion and orders an end to all economic intercourse with them.

August 26, 1861

Civil War (continued): Battle of Kessler's Cross Lanes. In western Virginia, Brigadier General John B. Floyd, commanding Confederate forces in the Kanawha Valley, crosses the Gauley River and surprises and routs Colonel Erastus Tyler's 7th Ohio Regiment encamped at Kessler's Cross Lanes in Nicholas County (now in West Virginia). The Union side sustains 245 casualties, the Confederates only 40. Floyd subsequently withdraws to the river and

Ulysses Simpson Grant (1822–1885)

U.S. general and president of the United States. Born in Point Pleasant, Ohio, on April 27, 1822, Hiram Ulysses Grant grew up on his father's farm. Securing appointment to the U.S. Military Academy, West Point, Grant discovered that his name had been changed to Ulysses Simpson (his mother's maiden name) Grant, which he kept. At West Point, Grant excelled only in horsemanship, graduating in 1843 21st of 39 cadets.

Grant served with distinction in the Mexican-American War (1846–1848). Serving as regimental quartermaster, he saw action under Major General Zachary Taylor in northern Mexico in the Battles of Palo Alto (May 8, 1846), Resaca de la Palma (May 9, 1846), and Monterrey (September 20–24, 1846). Transferred to Major General Winfield Scott's command in March 1847, Grant fought in the Battles of Cerro Gordo (April 17–18, 1847), Churubusco (August 20, 1847), and Molino del Rey (September 1, 1847). After the latter battle, he was breveted a first lieutenant for gallantry. Following the Battle of Chapultepec (September 13, 1847), Grant received a second brevet promotion, to captain.

Following the war, Grant was on duty in California, where he was promoted to captain in August 1853. Bored and upset at being separated from his wife, Grant drank heavily and was forced to resign from the army in July 1854 to avoid a court-martial. He returned to his family in Missouri but was unsuccessful as a farmer and at selling real estate during 1854–1860. His father gave him a position as a clerk in the family leather store in Galena, Illinois.

When the American Civil War began in April 1861, Grant secured a colonelcy of volunteers and command of the 21st Illinois Regiment in June. Promoted to brigadier general of volunteers, he received command of the Southwest Missouri Military District in August. He distinguished himself in the early fighting in Kentucky, where he took Paducah without waiting for authorization in September, and in Missouri, where he fought an indecisive battle against the Confederates at Belmont on November 7 but virtually secured that state for the Union.

In the subsequent Union river campaigns, Grant worked well with his naval counterpart, Flag Officer Andrew Hull Foote. Grant and Foote finally persuaded their superior, Major General Henry Halleck, to allow them to attack Fort Henry on the Tennessee River, which fell to Foote's gunboats on February 6, 1862. Grant then invested nearby Fort Donelson on the Cumberland, forcing it to surrender "unconditionally" on February 16. Now known as "Unconditional Surrender Grant" for the victory, he received promotion to major general of volunteers.

Grant was preparing to attack Corinth, Mississippi, when he was surprised by Confederates under General Albert Sidney Johnston at Shiloh. In the ensuing battle Grant rallied his men and managed to hold on. Reinforced by troops under Major General Don Carlos Buell, Grant then was victorious on April 6–7.

Pressed to relieve Grant over Shiloh, President Abraham Lincoln replied, "I cannot spare this man; he fights." Demoted a second time by a jealous Halleck, Grant served as second-in-command in Halleck's snail-pace advance on Corinth. Given command of the Army of the Tennessee in October, Grant set his sights on capturing the Confederate stronghold of Vicksburg on the Mississippi River. The Confederates rebuffed his efforts to take the city from the north, but Grant then decided to strike from the south. In a daring maneuver and accompanied by Rear Admiral David Dixon Porter's gunboats, Grant passed by Vicksburg on the Louisiana shore, then was ferried across the river to the Mississippi side. Disregarding

(continued)

(Continued)

Halleck's instructions to await reinforcements, Grant cut loose from his base at Grand Gulf and moved north, taking Jackson on May 14, 1863, and then destroying it as a communications center. He then engaged Confederate forces under Lieutenant General John C. Pemberton, which sallied from Vicksburg, winning the Battle of Champion's Hill on May 16 and forcing Pemberton back into Vicksburg. After initial assaults failed, Grant laid siege to Vicksburg, taking the city on July 4, 1863, in one of the biggest Union victories of the war.

Promoted to major general in the regular army and given command of the Military District of the Mississippi on October 4, 1863, Grant directed the relief of the city of Chattanooga, Tennessee, and then, reinforced, broke the Confederate siege of Chattanooga on October 25–28 and drove the Confederates under General Braxton Bragg from both Lookout Mountain and Missionary Ridge on November 24–25.

Named commanding general of the armies of the United States, with the revived rank of lieutenant general in April 1864, Grant opened a multipronged offensive against the Confederacy, with the main effort coming in Virginia against Confederate general Robert E. Lee's Army of Northern Virginia, in the so-called Overland Campaign, beginning in May. Grant campaigned there with Major General George Gordon Meade's Army of the Potomac. A series of bloody rebuffs followed, but Grant kept pressing the attack. Following bloody engagements in the Wilderness on May 4–7, at Spotsylvania Court House on May 8–17, and Cold Harbor on June 3, Grant attempted to get in behind Lee at Petersburg but failed. Grant then laid siege to Petersburg in the longest such operation of the war during August 1864–March 1865. His victory at Five Forks on March 29–31 sealed the fate of Richmond and Petersburg. With his forces being starved into submission, Lee broke free and headed west, but Grant forced him to surrender at Appomattox Court House on April 9, 1865. Grant's generous terms helped the healing process and set the tone for the other surrenders to follow.

Following the war, Grant continued as commanding general of the army and was advanced to full general by act of Congress in January 1866. Grant has been regarded as a controversial figure for his supposed failure as president. Elected in November 1868 as a Republican to the first of his two terms in office (1869–1877), he was personally honest, but his administration was wracked by scandal, and he failed to squelch it. Grant remained popular, however. He was firm in his support for civil rights for blacks in the South, and he took a strong stance against racial violence by such groups as the Ku Klux Klan. He also developed a humane policy toward Native Americans.

Becoming bankrupt after leaving the presidency when a brokerage firm failed, Grant developed throat cancer but struggled to complete his memoirs in order to provide for his family financially. He completed the task only two days before his death at Mount McGregor, New York, on July 23, 1885. The *Memoirs* (1885) proved a great literary success and reveal the depth of his intelligence and character. A bold, aggressive commander who never hunted because he hated killing things, Grant eschewed military ceremonial and dress. A highly effective strategist, he could see the overall situation clearly and determine the correct course of action. His relentless hammering of Confederate forces ended the Civil War.

SPENCER C. TUCKER

Further Reading

Grant, Ulysses S. *The Personal Memoirs of Ulysses S. Grant.* Reprint. Introduction by Brooks D. Simpson. Lincoln: University of Nebraska Press, 1996.

McFeely, William S. *Grant: A Biography.* New York: Norton, 1981.

Perret, Geoffrey. *Ulysses S. Grant: Soldier and President.* New York: Random House, 1997.

assumes a defensive position at Carnifex Ferry, leading to a battle there (see September 10, 1861). Meanwhile, General Robert E. Lee arrives to coordinate the forces of Floyd and Brigadier Generals Henry A. Wise and William W. Loring for an offensive to retake western Virginia.

 **August 29, 1861**

Civil War (continued): Eastern theater: Union capture of Hatteras Inlet. On August 26, the U.S. Navy commences its first significant operation of the war, against Hatteras Inlet, North Carolina, one of several access points to Pamlico Sound and a major staging area for blockade-runners and Confederate privateers. Flag Officer Silas H. Stringham sails from Hampton Roads, Virginia, with the screw frigates *Minnesota* (flagship, 47 guns) and *Wabash* (46 guns), the side-wheel frigate *Susquehanna* (25 guns), the screw sloop *Pawnee* (8 guns), the converted merchant steamer *Monticello* (3 guns), and the ex–Revenue Service cutter *Harriet Lane* (4 guns). The squadron also includes the tug *Fanny* and the chartered steamer transports *Adelaide* and *George Peabody*, carrying some 900 army troops under Major General Benjamin F. Butler. The transports tow schooners carrying surfboats, while the *Monticello* and *Pawnee* tow surfboats only.

Two poorly manned log and earthen forts on Hatteras Island control Hatteras Inlet: Fort Clark, a small earthen works on the ocean side, mounts 5 guns, while Fort Hatteras, a half mile distant on the other side, has 25 guns. Colonel William F. Martin commands the two forts. Unfortunately for the Confederates, the forts are separated from the land by the very sound they protect. Stringham plans to shell the forts from their water face with his ships while Butler's troops assault them from the rear on the land face. The operation is conceived as a raid.

The squadron anchors off Hatteras Inlet on the afternoon of August 27. At 6:45 a.m. the next day, Stringham orders marines and troops ashore in surfboats about two miles east of Fort Clark, beyond range of its guns. Ships' launches with Dahlgren boat howitzers stand ready to provide covering fire, while the *Pawnee, Monticello,* and *Harriet Lane* can provide heavier gunfire support.

At 8:45 a.m., the larger Union ships begin the bombardment of Fort Clark. The *Wabash* leads, towing the newly arrived razee sloop *Cumberland* (24 guns), with the *Minnesota* following. Stringham orders the bombardment ships to steam in a large oval. Fort Clark returns fire for a time. Heavy surf limits the number of men put ashore; by 11:30 a.m., only 320 have been

---

⚔ Dahlgren Guns

Name given to a system of guns developed by U.S. Navy commander John A. Dahlgren and used extensively throughout the American Civil War by both sides. In many ways they marked the apogee of the heavy muzzle-loading gun at sea. Dahlgren first arrived at the Washington Navy Yard in 1844 as a lieutenant, assigned there to conduct ordnance-ranging experiments. Soon he was designing new firing locks for guns and had developed a new system of naval ordnance.

In 1849 Dahlgren produced a new boat howitzer for the navy. Cast of bronze, the howitzer appeared as a 12-pounder (light, 660 pounds, and heavy, 750 pounds) and 24-pounder smoothbore (1,300 pounds). There were also 3.4-inch (12-pounder, 870 pounds) and 4-inch (20-pounder, 1,350 pounds) rifles. Dahlgren boat howitzers were the finest guns of their time in the world and remained in service with the U.S. Navy until the 1880s. They were also copied by other navies.

(continued)

(Continued)

Dahlgren is chiefly remembered, however, for the system of heavy smoothbore muzzle-loading ordnance that bears his name. In January 1850 Dahlgren submitted a draft for a 9-inch gun to the chief of ordnance. The first prototype Dahlgren gun was cast at the Fort Pitt Foundry and was delivered to the Washington Navy Yard in May 1850. The original 9-incher had a more angular form and only one vent. Later the design was modified in favor of a curved shape and a double vent, and in 1856 the side vents were restored. The purpose of the second vent was to extend the life of the gun. Repeated firings enlarged the vent opening, and when this occurred the second vent, which had been filled with zinc, was opened and the original vent itself sealed with zinc.

Dahlgren guns, with their smooth exterior, curved lines, and preponderant weight of metal at the breech, resembled in appearance soda water bottles and were sometimes called "soda bottles." Dahlgren designed them so as to place the greatest weight of metal at the point of greatest strain at the breech. The 9-inch Dahlgren smoothbore remained the most common broadside carriage-mounted gun in the U.S. Navy in the Civil War; the 11-inch, the prototype of which was cast in 1851, was the most widely used pivot-mounted gun. Its 11-inch shell could pierce 4.5 inches of plate iron backed by 20 inches of solid oak.

Dahlgren guns appeared in a variety of sizes: 32-pounder (3,300 and 4,500 pounds), 8-inch (6,500 pounds), 9-inch (12,280 pounds), 10-inch (12,500 pounds for shell and 16,500 pounds for shot), 11-inch (16,000 pounds), 13-inch (34,000 pounds), and 15-inch (42,000 pounds). There was even a 20-inch bore (97,300 pounds) Dahlgren, which did not see service aboard ship during the war. The 15-inch Dahlgren was employed aboard Union monitors.

Dahlgrens also appeared as rifled guns, somewhat similar in shape to the smoothbores. Some of these had separate bronze trunnion and breech straps. Dahlgren rifles appeared in these sizes: 4.4-inch/30 pounder (3,200 pounds), 5.1-inch/50-pounder (5,100 pounds), 6-inch/80-pounder (8,000 pounds), 7.5-inch/150-pounder (16,700 pounds), and 12-inch (45,520 pounds, only three of which were cast). Dahlgren's rifled guns were not as successful as his smoothbores, and in February 1862 most were withdrawn from service.

Apart from the rifles, Dahlgren guns were extraordinarily reliable. They remained the standard muzzle-loading guns in the navy until the introduction of breech-loading heavy guns in 1885.

SPENCER C. TUCKER

Further Reading

Dahlgren, John A. *Shells and Shell Guns.* Philadelphia: King and Baird, 1856.

Olmstead, Edwin, Wayne Stark, and Spencer Tucker. *The Big Guns: Civil War Siege, Seacoast and Naval Cannon.* Alexandria Bay, NY, and Bloomfield, Ontario, Canada: Museum Restoration Service, 1997.

Tucker, Spencer C. *Arming the Fleet: U.S. Navy Ordnance in the Muzzle-Loading Era.* Annapolis, MD: Naval Institute Press, 1989.

landed. Despite this, as a consequence of the naval bombardment, at about noon the Confederates abandon Fort Clark. By 2:00 p.m. the Union troops take possession.

At 4:00 p.m., believing that both Confederate forts have surrendered, Stringham orders the *Monticello* into Hatteras Inlet. Proceeding up the channel, it soon comes under fire from Fort Hatteras but is able to withdraw without major damage. Stringham promptly orders the remainder of his ships in to shell Fort Hatteras.

Deteriorating weather prevents the landing of additional Union troops, and the Union squadron anchors for the night. Meanwhile, Flag Officer Samuel Barron, commanding the naval defenses of Virginia and North Carolina, reaches Fort Hatteras in a steam tug towing a schooner with 230 reinforcements, bringing Confederate strength there to some 650 men. Barron then assumes command from Martin. Additional reinforcements fail to arrive, however, and Barron must drop his plan to retake Fort Clark.

At 8:00 a.m. on August 29, the *Susquehanna, Wabash,* and *Minnesota,* joined an hour later by the *Cumberland,* recommence shelling Fort Hatteras at long range. The *Harriet Lane* also joins. The Confederate guns reply, but their shot falls short.

Barron meets with his officers to consider the situation. A Union shell penetrates the fort's ventilator shaft next to the magazine during the meeting and probably hastens the decision, for not long afterward at 11:00 a.m. the Confederates surrender. The Union secures between 600 and 700 Confederate prisoners. There are no Union casualties. Too late, commandant of the Norfolk Navy Yard Flag Officer French Forrest orders Commander Thomas T. Hunter to prepare an expedition to Hatteras.

The capture of Hatteras Inlet is the first real Union naval triumph of the war, indeed the first noteworthy Union victory on land or at sea. It does much to restore morale in the North, shaken by the earlier defeat on land at the First Battle of Bull Run (Manassas), and also proves the great value of steamships in engaging land forts. Securing the inlet allows the Union to seal off Pamlico Sound to Confederate privateers and

blockade-running. Under Stringham's urging, Union forces retain Hatteras, which becomes a Union blockader base and depot for coal and supplies.

August 30, 1861

Civil War (continued). At St. Louis, Missouri, U.S. Army major general John C. Frémont, commanding the important Western Department and having already declared martial law on August 14, on August 30 announces a conditional emancipation proclamation by which all slaves belonging to Confederate sympathizers in Missouri are declared free. Twelve days later, fearful of its effect on pro-Unionist slave owners, President Abraham Lincoln disavows Frémont's precipitous action. Lincoln sees the general's action as an attempt to transform the war to save the Union into one to free the slaves. Three months later Frémont is relieved of his post.

September 1, 1861

Civil War (continued): Western theater. Brigadier General Ulysses S. Grant assumes command of the District of Southeast Missouri in the Western Department (later the Department of the Missouri).

September 2, 1861

Civil War (continued): Eastern theater. At Pensacola, Florida, Union forces holding Fort Pickens destroy by fire the floating dry dock from the navy yard there that had grounded near the Lincoln and Cameron batteries in May 1861 when its towline broke as Confederate forces were attempting to scuttle it across the harbor mouth.

September 4, 1861

Civil War (continued): Western theater: Confederate forces invade Kentucky. Kentucky has been serving as a shield for the defense of Confederate Tennessee, which the Confederates themselves now undo. In one of the war's major blunders, Confederate major general and Episcopal bishop Leonidas Polk orders Brigadier General Gideon J. Pillow to fortify Columbus, Kentucky, on the Mississippi River 20 miles below Cairo. This violation of Kentucky's neutrality gives the Union side a justifiable excuse to intervene in that state.

September 5, 1861

Civil War (continued): Western theater. Captain Andrew Hull Foote relieves Commander John Rodgers Jr. as the naval officer in charge of riverine operations in the Western theater. Rodgers had clashed with imperious Western Department commander Major General John C. Frémont.

September 6, 1861

Civil War (continued): Western theater: Operations in Kentucky. U.S. brigadier general Ulysses S. Grant, commander of the District of Southwest Missouri, believes that Confederate forces that have occupied Columbus, Kentucky, will soon move against Paducah at the confluence of the Tennessee and Ohio Rivers. He quickly dispatches troops there in transports from Cairo, Illinois. Grant's men occupy first Paducah and then Smithland, at the mouth of the Cumberland River. The timberclads *Lexington* (6 guns) and *Tyler* (7 guns) provide naval support. Union forces now have access to the Ohio, Tennessee, and Cumberland Rivers.

September 10, 1861

Civil War (continued): Eastern theater: Battle of Carnifix Ferry. Following his victory over Lieutenant Colonel Erastus Tyler's 7th Ohio Regiment in the Battle of Kessler's Cross Lanes (see August 26, 1861), Confederate brigadier general John B. Floyd entrenches near Carnifex Ferry in present-day Nicholas County, West Virginia, ignoring General Robert E. Lee's warning that he is in an exposed position and should withdraw across the Gauley River.

At the beginning of September, commander of Union forces in western Virginia Brigadier General William S. Rosecrans leads three brigades of infantry south from Clarksburg to support Tyler's reconstituted regiment. Commanding some 5,000 men, Rosecrans attacks Floyd's position on the afternoon of September 10. Darkness brings the fighting to a close. Union losses are 17 killed and 141 wounded; the Confederates have only several men killed and perhaps 30 wounded. That night Floyd withdraws his 2,000 men by ferry to the south side of the Gauley River and, after destroying the ferry to thwart pursuit, moves east to near Lewisburg.

September 10, 1861

Civil War (continued): Western theater. In an attempt to check Southern advances up the Mississippi River, the timberclad gunboats *Conestoga* (4 guns) and *Lexington* (6 guns) attack a Confederate garrison at Lucas Bend, Missouri, silencing its guns and driving off the Confederate gunboat *Yankee* (2 guns).

September 11–13, 1861

Civil War (continued): Eastern theater: Battle of Cheat Mountain. In his first military operation of the war, Confederate general Robert E. Lee masses some 15,000 troops in an attempt to regain control of western Virginia. After dividing his forces into five separate commands, he is rebuffed by 2,000 Union troops under Brigadier General Joseph J. Reynolds in the Battle of Cheat Mountain in west-central Virginia. The Confederates are thwarted by the rough terrain and the fact that Union prisoners mislead Lee into thinking that he is outnumbered and that Union reinforcements are en route. Union forces suffer about 80 casualties; Confederate losses are perhaps 90.

Lee orders Confederate forces to abandon the westernmost Virginia counties. Lee's failure here brings much criticism in the Southern press. "Granny Lee," as some dub him, is then dispatched to supervise coastal defenses in South Carolina.

September 14, 1861

Civil War (continued). U.S. Navy lieutenant John H. Russell leads 100 marines and sailors in four boats from the screw frigate *Colorado* (44 guns) into Pensacola Harbor. The landing party burns the Confederate schooner *Judah* and spikes several batteries before retiring.

September 14, 1861

Civil War (continued). A landing party from the U.S. Navy screw sloop *Pawnee* (8 guns) captures Beacon Island, North Carolina, sealing off the Oracoke Inlet.

The *New Ironsides* in action off Charleston, South Carolina. The *New Ironsides* was the most successful of the three experimental ironclads ordered in response to the September 16, 1861, report of the U.S. Navy Ironclad Board. Its services off Charleston were unmatched by any other Union warship. (Library of Congress)

September 16, 1861

Civil War (continued). The U.S. Navy Ironclad Board issues its "Report on Iron Clad Vessels." It concludes that what is required are light draft vessels "invulnerable to shot." The report recommends construction of such ships before proceeding to "a more perfect system of large ironclad sea-going vessels of war."

Although it receives proposals for ironclads from some British yards, the board decides to rely on U.S. firms alone. Narrowing 17 proposals submitted to 5, it rejects 2 as too costly. It recommends 3 contracts: to C. S. Bushnell and Co. of New Haven, to Merrick & Sons of Philadelphia, and to John Ericsson of New York. Their completed ships are, respectively, the *Galena*, *New Ironsides*, and *Monitor*.

September 17, 1861

Civil War (continued): Union capture of Ship Island. Union forces arriving in the screw steamer *Massachusetts* (5 guns) secure Ship Island in Mississippi Sound, just abandoned by the Confederates as untenable. Situated about 12 miles south of Biloxi, Mississippi, 60 miles from New Orleans and 40 miles from Mobile, it becomes an important U.S. base on the Gulf coast and the staging area for Flag Officer David G. Farragut's squadron and mortar flotilla in operations against New Orleans.

John Ericsson (1803–1889)

Engineer, inventor, and naval architect. Born in Långbanshyttten, Sweden, on July 31, 1803, John Ericsson joined the Swedish Army in 1817 as a lieutenant of topographical engineers, but he also displayed a great capacity for mechanical engineering. In 1827 Ericsson immigrated to England to study steam propulsion and there designed many novel devices. Foremost among these was a screw propeller. It brought him to the attention of U.S. Navy captain Robert F. Stockton, then in England, who convinced Ericsson to relocate to the United States.

Stockton used his political influence to arrange for Ericsson to design the machinery for the *Princeton*, the world's first steam-driven screw warship. The new ship incorporated such novel ideas as placement of engines below the waterline to shield them from enemy gunfire. It also mounted two large 12-inch wrought-iron guns, one designed by Ericsson dubbed "the Oregon" and manufactured in England and the other designed by Stockton and known as "the Peacemaker." The *Princeton* performed as expected, but during a public demonstration on the Potomac River on February 28, 1844, the Peacemaker exploded, killing eight people, including Secretary of the Navy Thomas W. Gilmer and Secretary of State Abel P. Upshur. Ericsson was exonerated of any blame, but recriminations with Stockton led him to vow never to do work for the navy again. Ericsson spent the next 15 years designing commercial steamships.

It took the American Civil War before Ericsson would again deal with the Navy Department. When word was received that the Confederates had raised the scuttled U.S. Navy steam frigate *Merrimack* at Norfolk and were rebuilding it as an ironclad, the U.S. Navy called for ironclads of its own. David Bushnell, designer of the ironclad *Galena,* convinced Ericsson to submit a design that he made for a revolutionary ship. His experimental new ironclad, christened the *Monitor,* featured many new ideas and ushered in a new age of warfare. It sported a low long hull, was completely armored, and had a single turret that rotated on its axis. Constructed in only 100 days, the *Monitor* was rushed into combat on March 9, 1862, when it fought the *Virginia* to a draw. This engagement ensured protection for the Union blockaders and the eventual fall of Norfolk. Ericsson spent the balance of the war designing and building new classes of monitors. As a patriotic gesture, he made his unpatented plans available to other engineers to facilitate immediate construction.

Ericsson spent the next two decades refining his ideas on steam propulsion and developing torpedo boats. The most significant naval engineer of the 19th century, Ericsson died in New York City on March 8, 1889.

JOHN C. FREDRIKSEN

Further Reading

Canney, Donald L. *The Old Steam Navy.* 2 vols. Annapolis, MD: Naval Institute Press, 1990.

DeKay, James T. *Monitor: The Story of the Legendary Civil War Ironclad and the Man Whose Invention Changed the Course of History.* London: Pimlico, 1999.

Eliasson, Erik. *Captain John Ericsson in New York.* New York: John Ericsson Society, 1988.

Mindell, David A. *War, Technology, and Experience aboard the USS Monitor.* Baltimore: Johns Hopkins University Press, 2000.

September 18, 1861

Civil War (continued): Western theater. Confederate forces under Brigadier General Simon B. Buckner occupy the important transportation center of Bowling Green, Kentucky. Soon a Confederate stronghold, in November it is named the capital of the Confederate state of Kentucky.

September 18, 1861

Civil War (continued). U.S. Navy captain Samuel F. Du Pont is appointed commander of the South Atlantic Blockading Squadron.

September 20, 1861

Civil War (continued): Western theater: Confederate capture of Lexington, Missouri. Confederate major general Sterling Price continues his campaign to secure Missouri for the Confederacy by advancing on Lexington, Missouri, just east of Kansas City, with some 10,000 men of the pro-Confederate Missouri State Guard. Lexington is held by Colonel James Mulligan and some 2,500 Union troops. Skirmishing begins on September 12, but Price delays taking further action until all his men are in place. By September 17 the Confederates have encircled Lexington. They then cut the town's water supply. On September 20 the Southerners advance on the Union fortifications, rolling before them movable breastworks of large bales of hemp, soaked in water so they will not catch fire. As the Confederates slowly advance their lines, Union soldiers begin surrendering. Price secures Lexington at a cost of only 25 men killed and 72 wounded; Union losses are 39 dead and 120 wounded.

Price's victory bolsters pro-Confederacy sentiment in the Missouri Valley region. U.S. Army major general John C. Frémont at St. Louis comes under much criticism for not having dispatched Union reinforcements to Lexington in time.

September 23, 1861

Civil War (continued). U.S. Navy commodore Louis M. Goldsborough assumes command of the North Atlantic Blockading Squadron.

September 25, 1861

Civil War (continued). Secretary of the Navy Gideon Welles authorizes enlistment of African American sailors aboard U.S. Navy ships.

October 1, 1861

Civil War (continued). The Confederate paddle-wheel steamer *Curlew* (1 gun), steam sloop *Raleigh* (2 guns), and screw tug *Junaluska* (2 guns), all under Flag Officer William F. Lynch, capture the U.S. Navy steamer *Fanny* (2 guns) transporting Union troops and stores in Pamlico Sound.

October 1, 1861

Civil War (continued): The Confederate War Department approves a battle flag. It has a blue cross of St. Andrew, with 13 white stars—1 for each Confederate state plus 1 each for Missouri and Kentucky—edged in white and set against a red field. Although never officially approved by the Confederate Congress, it is widely embraced by white Southerners.

October 8, 1861

Civil War (continued): Western theater. U.S. Army brigadier general William T. Sherman succeeds Brigadier General Robert Anderson in command of the Department of the Cumberland.

October 12, 1861

Civil War (continued): Confederate forces attack Union ships at the Head of Passes in the Mississippi River. The Confederate ironclad ram *Manassas* (2 guns), under Commodore George N. Hollins, assisted by the armed steamers *Ivy* (2 guns) and *James L. Day* (armament unknown), attacks the U.S. Navy squadron at the Head of Passes below New Orleans. Commanded by Captain John Pope, the U.S. ships are the screw sloop *Richmond* (19 guns), the sloops *Vincennes* (18 guns) and *Preble* (10 guns), the side-wheel sloop *Water Witch* (5 guns), and the supply ship *Nightingale* (4 guns).

The attack catches the U.S. squadron by surprise. In the effort to escape, both the *Richmond* and *Vincennes* run aground. Mistaking Pope's signal to "get under

John Pope (1822–1892)

U.S. Army officer. John Pope was born in Louisville, Kentucky, on March 16, 1822, but he grew up in Kaskaskia, Illinois. He graduated from the U.S. Military Academy, West Point, in 1842 and then served as a topographical engineer. During the Mexican-American War (1846–1848), he distinguished himself at the Battles of Monterrey and Buena Vista.

After the war, Pope carried out surveys in Minnesota and the American Southwest. In 1856, he was promoted to captain. By the late 1850s, Pope was known as an expert horseman and an intrepid soldier. He was also known for his impetuosity and caustic personality.

When the American Civil War began, Pope was commissioned a brigadier general of volunteers in June 1861. He held various district and field commands until February 1862, when he was assigned to command the Union Army of the Mississippi as a major general of volunteers. Pope's army captured the key Confederate position on the Mississippi River of New Madrid, Missouri, in mid-March 1862 and participated, with the navy, in the capture of Island No. 10 and its 5,000 defenders in early April. These successes earned him promotion to brigadier general in the regular army and a summons to Washington, D.C., to command the new Army of Virginia.

In the Second Battle of Bull Run (Manassas) during August 29–30, 1862, Confederate forces led by Major General Thomas J. "Stonewall" Jackson and Major General James Longstreet convincingly defeated Pope and his army. Pope blamed the loss on his "unsoldierly" officers, most notably Major General Fitz John Porter, who he claimed were more loyal to Major General George B. McClellan than to him. Nevertheless, Pope conducted an orderly retreat to Washington, D.C. President Abraham Lincoln apparently agreed with his commander's assessment. Despite this, Pope was removed from command the following month and assigned to head the Department of the Northwest, where the army had just defeated an uprising by the Santee Sioux in Minnesota. A military tribunal had sentenced 303 Santees to death for their participation in the fighting. Responsibility for reviewing the sentences and carrying out the executions now fell to Pope. Although he favored executing the condemned Santees, he referred the matter to Lincoln, who reduced the number of death sentences to 39.

In 1863 and 1864, Pope supervised operations against other Sioux groups in the Dakotas. Impressed by Pope's leadership, Lieutenant General Ulysses Grant created the Division of Missouri in 1864 that extended Pope's command westward to the Rocky Mountains. Pope considered all of the Plains tribes hostile, rejected the advice of civilian Indian agents to negotiate, and prepared to impose peace by force. Cheyenne, Arapaho, and Sioux attacks in retaliation for the November 20, 1864, Sand Creek Massacre convinced him that his view was correct.

Pope thus organized the army's largest campaign to that date against the Plains tribes. In the spring of 1865, Brigadier General Patrick Connor marched into the Powder River area with three columns of soldiers, Brigadier General Alfred Sully headed an expedition on the upper Missouri River, and Brigadier General James H. Ford moved against the Kiowas and Comanches south of the Arkansas River. All three offensives failed, however, because of supply problems and slow movement.

Pope's inability to defeat the Plains tribes and public horror at the Sand Creek Massacre gave rise to demands that the government make peace. Pope continued to favor military action and argued that civilian interference with the army was a major obstacle to defeating the hostile tribes. He therefore urged that the Bureau of Indian Affairs be placed under the control of the War Department, a view favored by many Westerners but spurned by Congress, which wanted a peace policy. Having alienated many influential officials, Pope was transferred to the South to supervise Reconstruction efforts.

In 1870, Pope returned to the Department of Missouri. From his headquarters at Fort Leavenworth, Kansas, he closely supervised operations during the successful 1874–1875 Red River War. He also developed a more humanitarian attitude toward the Native Americans, advocating a policy of religious conversion and cultural assimilation, although he continued to favor giving the army full authority over Indian affairs.

Pope dispatched troops in the summer of 1879 to quell unrest on the Ute Reservation in Colorado, where fighting broke out in late September. However, Pope rushed more army units to the scene, and their appearance quickly ended the conflict. Because his department included New Mexico, Pope was later involved in directing operations against the Apaches from 1881 to 1883, when he took command of the Division of the Pacific.

In 1886, Pope retired from the army. He died in Sandusky, Ohio, on September 23, 1892.

JIM PIECUCH

Further Reading

Cozzens, Peter. *General John Pope: A Life for the Nation.* Urbana: University of Illinois Press, 2000.

Utley, Robert M. *Frontier Regulars: The United States Army and the Indian, 1866–1890.* New York: Macmillan, 1973.

Warner, Ezra J. *Generals in Blue: Lives of the Union Commanders.* Baton Rouge: Louisiana State University Press, 2006.

way" for "abandon ship," Commander Robert Handy of the *Vincennes* takes off his crew and orders a slow match lit to the ship's magazine. Fortunately for the Union the match fails, and after an appropriate wait, Handy and his crew return to their ship.

Although the Confederate gunboats shell the grounded Union ships, they fail to take advantage of the temporarily abandoned *Vincennes*, and the larger and longer-range guns of the Union squadron soon drive the gunboats back upriver. Finally both Union ships are gotten free, although not before the crew of the *Richmond* has thrown overboard 14 of its 18 guns and much shot. Meanwhile, the Confederates take the collier *Joseph H. Toone*, with 15 tons of coal.

Known as Pope's Run, this embarrassing engagement forces the U.S. Navy to reconsider its blockade policy for the Mississippi and spurs planning for an operation to take the city of New Orleans.

October 15–21, 1861

Civil War (continued): Western theater: Thompson's cavalry raid and the Battle of Fredericktown. Confederate brigadier general Merriwether J. Thompson, soon known as the "Swamp Fox of the Confederacy," commands the First Military District of Missouri, which covers the swampy southeastern quarter of the state from St. Louis to the Mississippi River. On October 15, 1861, Thompson leads a cavalry raid by some 1,500 men to burn the Iron Mountain Railroad bridge over the Big River near Blackwell in Jefferson County. Thompson then withdraws to join his infantry at Fredericktown. Two large Union columns under Colonels J. B. Plummer and William P. Carlin converge on Fredericktown soon afterward, and in the Battle of Fredericktown on October 21 they defeat Thompson's men. Union casualties are unknown; the Confederates suffer 35 killed, 40 wounded, and 80 captured. The battle establishes Union control over southeastern Missouri.

October 21, 1861

Civil War (continued): Eastern theater: Battle of Ball's Bluff. Colonel Edward D. Baker, a U.S. senator turned army officer, leads a Union reconnaissance-in-force across the Potomac River near Leesburg, Virginia. Each side commits about 1,700 men to the ensuing battle, but Baker foolishly sends his men piecemeal against the Confederates under Colonel Nathan G. Evans. Baker's troops, pinned on the south side of the river, suffer heavy casualties, and Baker himself is killed. Union casualties are 49 killed, 158 wounded, and 553 taken prisoner. The Confederates suffer 33 killed, 115 wounded, and 1 missing. The Confederates also secure about 1,500 small arms and 3 cannon.

The defeat at Ball's Bluff stuns the North. Although professional officers correctly blame Baker, some in Congress see a wider plot. They use the defeat to establish the Joint Committee on the Conduct of the War to push for an uncompromising prosecution of the war and a strong stand against slavery.

October 24, 1861

Civil War (continued): Eastern theater: Secession of West Virginia from Virginia. On October 24, 1861, residents of 39 counties in western Virginia approve the formation of a new Unionist state. The accuracy of the election results has been questioned, because Union troops are stationed at many of the polls in order to prevent Confederate sympathizers from voting. The new state is not officially admitted to the Union until June 20, 1863.

November 1, 1861

Civil War (continued). On the retirement of Lieutenant General Winfield Scott as general-in-chief of Union forces on October 31, 1861, President Abraham Lincoln names Major General George B. McClellan as his successor.

November 7, 1861

Civil War (continued): Western theater: Battle of Belmont. U.S. brigadier general Ulysses S. Grant proceeds down the Mississippi River with 2,500 men in transports escorted by gunboats. With Columbus, Kentucky, too strong to attack, early this day Grant lands his men across the river at Belmont, Missouri, to attack a camp of 2,700 Confederates under Brigadier General Gideon J. Pillow. The timberclads *Lexington* (6 guns) and *Tyler* (7 guns) engage the Confederate batteries.

Grant's force defeats the Confederates ashore, but the Union troops then stop to loot the camp, allowing their adversaries an opportunity to regroup. Confederate major general Leonidas Polk dispatches reinforcements across the river, protected by the lower batteries at Columbus, in an effort to cut off the Union soldiers from their transports. With the *Lexington* and *Tyler* providing covering fire, Grant's outnumbered men manage to cut their way through the Confederates and embark. The battle claims 610 Union and 642 Confederate casualties. Although it may be questioned as a Union victory, it reveals Grant's aggressive nature and willingness to take risks in order to achieve results.

November 7, 1861

Civil War (continued): Union capture of Port Royal Sound. Apart from Charleston, the best natural harbor on the southern Atlantic coast is Port Royal, South Carolina, located halfway between Savannah and Charleston. The Confederates are aware of this, and Port Royal is one of the first coastal areas they fortify. Flying his flag in the screw frigate *Wabash* (46 guns), Flag Officer Samuel Du Pont departs Hampton Roads with 50 ships, the largest task force under a single command to this point in U.S. Navy history. His ships carry 16,000 troops commanded by Brigadier General Thomas W. Sherman.

Most of the ships survive a severe storm on November 1, and beginning on November 6 Du Pont directs the shelling first of Confederate Fort Walker and then Fort Beauregard. The two guard the harbor entrance and mount in all 43 guns. Fort Walker surrenders on November 7, and Fort Beauregard surrenders on November 8. Union casualties are 8 killed and 23 wounded. Confederate losses total 11 killed and 48 wounded.

Port Royal's deep harbor provides an ideal base for subsequent South Atlantic Blockading Squadron operations; it is soon a major Union naval station and supply depot. Many Northern leaders now have the mistaken notion that steam warships can defeat all forts.

November 8, 1861

Civil War (continued): The *Trent* Affair. Overzealous U.S. Navy captain Charles Wilkes of the screw frigate *San Jacinto* (12 guns) stops the British mail steamer *Trent* in the Old Bahama Channel and removes Confederate commissioners James M. Mason and John Slidell, who were on their way to England. On November 24 the *San Jacinto* arrives at Boston, and the Confederate diplomats are imprisoned at Fort Warren. Wilkes's precipitous action produces an international crisis, and there are calls in both Britain and the United States for war. President Abraham Lincoln ultimately ends the crisis by agreeing to release the two men. "One war at a time," Lincoln says.

November 9, 1861

Civil War (continued): Western theater. In major Union command changes, Major General Henry W. Halleck is appointed commander of the newly designated Department of the Missouri, and Major General Don Carlos Buell assumes command of the Department of the Ohio.

November 12, 1861

Civil War (continued). The British-built steamer *Fingal* runs the Union blockade to reach Savannah, Georgia. Its cargo is the most important to reach that Southern city by sea during the war and includes 14,000 Enfield rifles; 1 million cartridges; 2 million percussion caps; thousands of sabers, bayonets, rifles, and revolvers; 10 rifled cannon and ammunition; 400 barrels of powder; and assorted medical supplies.

With Savannah tightly blockaded, the *Fingal* cannot again get to sea to return to England. In early 1862 it is cut down at the waterline and rebuilt as the casemated ironclad ram *Atlanta*.

November 24–December 25, 1861

Civil War (continued): Western theater. Confederate colonel Nathan B. Forrest initiates his spectacular Civil War career as a cavalry commander in a prolonged raid that results in the defeat of Union troops at Caseyville and Eddyville, Kentucky.

December 17, 1861

Civil War (continued). The U.S. Navy sinks seven stone-filled hulks in an effort to block the entrance to Savannah Harbor. It is the first attempt to employ stone fleets in the Union naval blockade.

December 17, 1861

French intervention in Mexico and occupation of Veracruz. Seeking to secure payment of debts owed their citizens, the governments of Britain, France, and Spain send naval units and some troops to Mexico. These land at Veracruz and then move to Orizaba. French emperor Napoleon III has more in mind than mere debt recovery, however. Taking advantage of the American Civil War and influenced by Spanish exiles and French religious conservatives but also motivated by the desire to secure Mexican silver resources, Napoleon decides to intervene in force and establish a monarchial regime in Mexico under French influence. The French intervention in Mexico lasts from 1861 to 1867.

December 18, 1861

Civil War (continued): Western theater: Battle of Milford. On this date, a large Union force commanded by Brigadier General John Pope surprises a poorly led force of Confederate regulars and militia near Milford, Missouri, at the Shawnee Mound. The Union force takes some 1,300 Confederates prisoner, along with 1,000 firearms and a number of supply wagons.

December 20, 1861

Civil War (continued). In another use of the stone fleets, U.S. captain Charles H. Davis supervises the sinking of 16 whaling ship hulks at Charleston, South Carolina, in a largely unsuccessful effort to block the shipping channels to that port.

 **Percussion Cap**

The chief military invention of the first half of the 19th century was the percussion cap, made possible by the discovery of fulminate of mercury in 1800. In 1807 Scottish Presbyterian minister Alexander Forsyth patented a gun lock utilizing mercuric fulminates as a priming for firearms. The process brought reliability to the discharge of lethal projectiles.

Before this invention, all guns—individual firearms through the largest cannon—were discharged by lighting a priming charge of finely ground gunpowder. This was first accomplished by a burning rope and later by flint and steel, both outside the touchhole at the end of the bore. Mercury fulminate detonated when struck a sharp blow, and Forsyth's system employed what looked like a perfume bottle, known as the scent bottle, that was mounted on the side of the gun at the breech. It contained sufficient fulminates for perhaps 20 shots and was connected by a fire hole that led to the base of the bore. To prime the scent bottle, it was turned upside down, causing some of the fulminates to drop down onto a flash pan. When the trigger was pulled, a hammer dropped down on top of a firing pin at the end of the scent bottle. The pin came down on the pan, exploding the small amount of fulminates there. The flash from this then passed into the bore of the gun, igniting the main charge.

Joshua Shaw, an English artist living in Philadelphia, simplified the process considerably by 1816. Shaw painted the fulminates on the inside of a small copper cap, which fitted over a nipple containing the fire hole over the base of the bore. When the hammer struck the percussion cap, the exploding fuminates ignited, and the fire raced down the touchhole to explode the main powder charge.

Percussion-cap sidearms could be reloaded and fired more rapidly than a flintlock and were reliable in all weather conditions. In 1834 the British Army tested a musket armed with the new percussion cap against the old Brown Bess flintlock. Each weapon fired 6,000 rounds. The percussion cap weapon failed 6 times, while the flintlock failed to fire nearly 1,000 times. As can be readily imagined, the new system produced a tremendous increase in firepower.

Muzzle-loading rifled muskets fired this way were in general service in the world's armies by 1850. The U.S. Army adopted the percussion cap system in 1842, paying Shaw $18,000 for the use of it. The percussion cap muzzle-loading rifled musket was the standard infantry firearm of the American Civil War.

SPENCER C. TUCKER

Further Reading

Blackmore, H. L. "The Percussion System." In *Pollard's History of Firearms,* edited by Claude Blair, 161–187. New York: Macmillan, 1986.
Tunis, Edwin. *Weapons: A Pictorial History.* New York: World Publishing, 1954.

Nathan Bedford Forrest (1821–1877)

Confederate general and cavalry commander during the American Civil War. Born in modest circumstances on July 13, 1821, near Chapel Hill, Bedford County, Tennessee, Nathan Bedford Forrest was largely self-educated. By dint of his ability he worked himself up from farm laborer to planter and slave trader by 1861. In June 1861 he joined the Confederate Army as a private in the 7th Tennessee Cavalry and rose quickly in responsibility and rank. Commissioned a lieutenant colonel in August, Forrest was promoted to colonel in April 1862, brigadier general in July 1862, major general in December 1863, and lieutenant general in February 1865.

Forrest fought in the defense of Fort Donelson, Tennessee, but refused to surrender and indeed cut his way out with his men on February 16, 1862, before its capitulation. Forrest distinguished himself in the Battle of Shiloh on April 6–7, where he was wounded. On his recovery, he took command of a cavalry brigade under General Braxton Bragg and was given the chance to develop the raiding tactics that he applied with such success from that point forward. Despite his lack of any formal military education, Forrest proved himself a master tactician, employing his cavalry as mounted infantry and often making artillery the lead element.

Beginning in July 1862, Forrest led independent cavalry operations in Tennessee as well as in northern Alabama, Georgia, and Mississippi, striking and destroying Union supply depots and lines of communication. He conducted a daring raid against Murfreesboro, Tennessee, during December 31, 1862–January 2, 1863, and then captured an entire Union cavalry brigade near Rome, Georgia, in April 1863.

Bold and resourceful, Forrest did not shrink from the threat of bloodshed in order to secure the surrender of entire Union commands. In the process he became the most feared Southern cavalry commander. Forrest commanded the right flank of Bragg's forces in the Battle of Chickamauga (September 19–20, 1863), but when Bragg failed to pursue Union forces, Forrest secured a transfer from Confederate president Jefferson Davis and was allowed to raise a new command.

In his repeated raids behind Union lines, Forrest invariably accomplished more than thought possible with the forces available to him. His actions were often controversial. He was widely blamed by the Northern press for the murder of Union African American soldiers following his capture of Fort Pillow, Tennessee, on April 12, 1864.

Two months later in the Battle of Brice's Crossroads (June 10, 1864) in Mississippi, Forrest demonstrated a clear understanding of conventional warfare when he inflicted a major defeat on Union forces under Brigadier General Samuel D. Sturgis. In late 1864 Forrest commanded the cavalry in Confederate general John B. Hood's invasion of Tennessee and successfully commanded the rear guard in the retreat of the remnants of that army after the Battle of Nashville (December 15–16, 1864).

Following the war, Forrest returned to farming and business, as president of the Selma, Marion & Memphis Railroad. He was one of the founders of the Ku Klux Klan that terrorized African Americans in the South and served as its grand wizard. Forrest died in Memphis, Tennessee, on October 29, 1877. Bold, fearless, and resourceful but also brutal toward his enemies, Forrest was a brilliant

(continued)

(Continued)

tactician and strategist who helped revolutionize cavalry tactics. His favorite maxim was "Get there first with the most."

SPENCER C. TUCKER

Further Reading

Hurst, Jack. *Nathan Bedford Forrest.* New York: Knopf, 1993.
Lytle, Andrew Nelson. *Bedford Forrest and His Critter Company.* Nashville: J. S. Saunders, 1993.
Wyeth, John Allen. *That Devil Forrest.* New York: Harper and Row, 1959.

December 21, 1861

Civil War (continued): Institution of the Medal of Honor. On this date the U.S. Congress authorizes the Medal of Honor for petty officers, seamen, and marines who distinguish themselves by "their gallantry and other seamanlike qualities during the present war." Commissioned officers are not eligible for the award until 1915. The army award is not instituted until July 12, 1862. Congress makes it a permanent decoration in 1863.

January 7, 1862

Civil War (continued). The timberclad *Conestoga* (4 guns), commanded by Lieutenant Seth L. Phelps, conducts a reconnaissance of the lower Cumberland and Tennessee Rivers. Phelps reports that the Confederates are fortifying Forts Henry and Donelson. During the following weeks, the *Conestoga, Tyler* (7 guns), and *Lexington* (6 guns) make repeated patrols up both rivers to determine the nature of the Confederate defenses. The intelligence gained is of vital importance to Brigadier General Ulysses S. Grant and Flag Officer Andrew H. Foote in planning their upcoming campaign against the two Confederate forts.

January 9, 1862

Civil War (continued). Captain David G. Farragut is appointed commander of the U.S. Navy West Gulf Blockading Squadron and charged with the capture of New Orleans.

January 10, 1862

Civil War (continued): Eastern theater: Capture of Romney. In western Virginia, Confederate major general Thomas J. Jackson orders Brigadier General William J. Loring to quit his winter encampment at Winchester in the Shenandoah Valley and march northwest with 8,500 men to capture strategically important Romney (now in West Virginia). The troops depart on January 9, with temperatures below zero. Although Loring secures Romney on January 10 when its small Union garrison withdraws, his men suffer greatly from the weather, prompting a bitter quarrel with Jackson.

Jackson orders Loring to hold at Romney, but Loring violates the chain of command and appeals directly to Secretary of War Judah P. Benjamin, who instructs Jackson to withdraw Loring's men from their exposed position. Jackson is furious and submits his resignation from the army but is talked back into service by President Jefferson Davis.

January 11, 1862

Civil War (continued). On the resignation of U.S. secretary of war James Cameron, charged with corruption and mismanagement, President Abraham Lincoln replaces him with the energetic and effective Edwin M. Stanton, then attorney general.

January 11, 1862

Civil War (continued). The U.S. 14-gun river ironclads *Essex*, under commander William D. Porter, and

St. Louis, commanded by Lieutenant Leonard Paulding, engage and drive back to their base at Columbus, Kentucky, Confederate gunboats in the upper Mississippi River.

January 19–20, 1862

Civil War (continued): Western theater: Battle of Mill Springs. In late November 1861, Confederate brigadier general Felix K. Zollicoffer had advanced 70 miles from Cumberland Gap into Kentucky to Mill Springs. His superior, Major General George B. Crittenden, realizing that Zollicoffer is in a dangerous position, crosses the Cumberland River to join him.

Union brigadier general George H. Thomas is ordered to move against the Confederates from Lebanon, Kentucky, and drive them back across the Cumberland. Thomas arrives at Logan's Cross Roads on January 17, where he awaits the arrival of troops under Brigadier General Albin F. Schoepf from Somerset.

Unable to withdraw across the rain-swollen Cumberland, Crittenden decides to attack Thomas, some 10 miles distant, before Schoepf can reinforce him. Crittenden has some 5,900 men, Thomas perhaps 4,400. The resulting battle near present-day Nancy is known as the Battle of Mill Springs or the Battle of Logan's Crossroads in Union terminology and the Battle of Fishing Creek to the Confederates. It is the second-largest engagement fought in Kentucky during the war.

The Confederates march six hours during the night in rain and mud to arrive at the Union position and attack at about 6:30 a.m. on January 19, 1862. Many of their old flintlock muskets prove useless in the weather, but the men give a good account of themselves nonetheless. Zollicoffer, conspicuous in a white rubber

The Battle of Mill Springs, Kentucky (also known as the Battle of Logan's Crossroads). This battle during January 19–20, 1862, ended in a victory for Union troops under Brigadier General George H. Thomas over Confederate forces commanded by Major General George B. Crittenden and gave the Union control of eastern Kentucky. (Library of Congress)

raincoat, mistakenly approaches a Union regiment that he believes to be Confederates firing on their own men and is shot and killed, reportedly by its commander with a pistol. Crittenden is able to restore the line, but the battle is decided in favor of the Union when the 9th Ohio Regiment turns the Confederate left flank.

The retreat that follows becomes a rout, and Crittenden is forced to abandon at his Beach Grove encampment 12 guns, 150 wagons, considerable equipment, and his dead and wounded. The battle claims 533 Confederate casualties, including 120 dead; Union losses are 246 (39 killed). Although the remaining Confederates manage to cross the Cumberland that night by steamboat, they do not halt until they reach Chestnut Mound near Murfreesboro, leaving Union troops in control of Kentucky.

January 22, 1862

Civil War (continued). During a reconnaissance mission up the Tennessee River, the U.S. gunboat *Lexington* (6 guns) exchanges fire with the Confederate garrison at Fort Henry.

January 26, 1862

Civil War (continued). Unable to get along with the Confederate War Department and President Jefferson Davis (a common complaint by his generals), General Pierre G. T. Beauregard is transferred to the Western theater as second-in-command to General Albert S. Johnston. General Joseph E. Johnston is the new commander of Confederate forces in Virginia.

January 27, 1862

Civil War (continued): Lincoln orders offensive action. After months of waiting with no action, President Abraham Lincoln issues General Order No. 1, mandating a general offensive on all fronts by Union land and naval forces to commence on February 22, 1862. Union Army general-in-chief Major General George B. McClellan and other Union commanders ignore the directive.

January 28, 1862

Civil War (continued): Western theater. U.S. Navy flag officer Andrew H. Foote requests approval from commander of the Department of the Missouri Major General Henry W. Halleck to move against Forts Henry and Donelson before the rivers recede. Both Foote and Brigadier General Ulysses S. Grant have been pleading with Halleck for permission to commence operations, but the cautious Halleck repeatedly refuses.

January–March 1862

Civil War (continued): Eastern theater: McClellan's plan to take Richmond. Despite U.S. president Abraham Lincoln's persistent appeals, Union general-in-chief Major General George B. McClellan refuses to act against Richmond. He has available about 180,000 men in or near Washington, D.C. Opposing them west of Washington in the Manassas area are some 50,000 Confederates under General Joseph E. Johnston. Believing that Johnston has 100,000 men (still half his own force), McClellan comes up with a new plan to take Richmond. Rather than a drive south overland that would come up against well-prepared Confederate defenses, McClellan seeks to use Union command of the sea to outflank the Confederates by moving his men by water down the Chesapeake Bay and then up the Rappahannock River to Urbanna, only 45 miles east of Richmond, where they could strike overland. If executed rapidly, this could force the Confederates to quit their positions at Manassas and also isolate Confederate defenders in the eastern peninsulas formed by the Rappahannock, York, and James Rivers.

Lincoln favors the overland approach, but his only real option is to replace McClellan. With no prospective commander in sight, Lincoln yields but insists on holding back a corps to guard the Union capital. McClellan then modifies the plan, making the Union land base not Urbanna on the Rappahannock but rather the more distant (75 miles from Richmond) Fort Monroe on the Chesapeake. The latter has the advantage of already being in Union hands. Operating from that point, where it would be supplied by water, McClellan's army can supposedly move by detachments up the York and James, outflanking the Confederates, who will be forced to withdraw west on Richmond. When McClellan closes on Richmond from the east with 130,000 men, the Union corps of 75,000 men under Major General Irvin McDowell, held back to guard Washington, will push south overland and link up with McClellan to take Richmond and end the war. Toward this end, in late February 1862 the War Department begins securing ships to move the Army of the Potomac to Fort Monroe and Hampton for what becomes known as the Peninsula Campaign, the largest land campaign of the war. McClellan's plan is deeply flawed in both planning and execution, for he is never known for speed.

Well aware that a major Union drive against Richmond is imminent, the Confederates construct significant defenses at Yorktown at the mouth of the York, and in the James River they count on their new ironclad ram, the *Virginia*.

February 1, 1862

Civil War (continued): Trans-Mississippi West theater: Sibley's New Mexico Campaign. Brigadier General Henry H. Sibley, commanding Confederate forces along the upper Rio Grande in Texas, obtains approval from President Jefferson Davis for an offensive. Sibley intends to secure New Mexico and Arizona, only lightly held by Union forces, then subdue California. Confederate success here will deny the North gold and silver needed to fight the war and also divert Union troops required elsewhere. On February 1, 1862, Sibley departs Fort Bliss at El Paso, Texas, with his 3,200-man Army of New Mexico.

February 3, 1862

Civil War (continued). In order to avoid threatened Southern retaliation against captured Union personnel, the U.S. government declares that captured Confederate privateersmen will be designated as prisoners of war rather than pirates.

February 4, 1862

Civil War (continued). The U.S. Congress authorizes President Abraham Lincoln to seize the railroads. Within a week, railroad executive Daniel C. McCallum is commissioned an army brigadier general and empowered to take control of any railroads that might be used in transporting troops, equipment, and

supplies. Throughout the war, the extensive Northern railroad network provides invaluable service to the Union military effort and is far better managed than the Southern lines.

February 6, 1862

Civil War (continued): Western theater: Union capture of Fort Henry. Union brigadier general Ulysses S. Grant and Flag Officer Andrew H. Foote have been pressing for an attack on Confederate Fort Henry on the Tennessee River and Fort Donelson on the Cumberland. They form the linchpin of Confederate general Albert Sidney Johnston's western defenses. After having rejected their earlier requests, Major General Henry W. Halleck, commander of the U.S. Department of the Missouri, finally agrees on learning that the Confederates plan to send reinforcements west. Grant and Foote immediately set out. Grant's troops move by transports, protected by Foote's gunboats, from Cairo, Illinois, to a point on the Tennessee River above Fort Henry.

On February 6 with Grant's troops delayed by the poor state of the roads, Foote begins the attack on Fort Henry alone. His squadron consists of the 14-gun river ironclads *Essex, Carondelet, Cincinnati* (flagship), and *St. Louis,* with a separate division of the timberclads *Conestoga* (4 guns), *Lexington* (6 guns), and *Tyler* (7 guns) under Lieutenant Commander Seth L. Phelps. The outgunned area Confederate commander, Brigadier General Lloyd Tilghman, commanding both Fort Henry and Fort Donelson, surrenders Fort Henry to Foote and the navy before Grant and the Union troops arrive, but Tilghman has fought a successful delaying action, after having sent the fort's entire garrison of 3,400 men, except for its artillerymen, overland to Fort Donelson, 10 miles distant. Union casualties in the battle are 11 killed, 31 wounded, and 5 missing. The Confederates lose 5 killed, 11 wounded, and 94 captured (most of the captured are sick). The battle provides a false impression of the ability of ironclads to reduce land forts, for the defenses at Fort Henry were poorly sited.

Immediately following the surrender of Fort Henry, Foote orders Phelps to take his timberclads in a raid up the Tennessee River. This four-day foray reaches as far as Muscle Shoals in northwestern Alabama and results in the destruction of six Confederate steamers and the capture of three others, including the *Eastport,* which will be converted into a Union ironclad. Phelps also secures substantial quantities of lumber and supplies. The expedition is intended in part to demonstrate the dominance of the U.S. river navy in the Western theater.

February 7–8, 1862

Civil War (continued): Eastern theater: Union capture of Roanoke Island. Union possession of Hatteras Island provides a base for further amphibious operations against eastern North Carolina. West of the Outer Banks are six sounds, the two largest being Pamlico and Albemarle. Shallow-draft Union warships on these sounds could operate against major cities in the region.

Roanoke Island lies at the northern end of Pamlico Sound and controls passage between it and Albemarle Sound to the north and west. Roanoke Island also dominates access to the southern termini of the Dismal Swamp Canal and the Albemarle and Chesapeake Canal, both of which reach to Norfolk, Virginia. Union forces already control Pamlico Sound, and securing Roanoke Island will provide access to Albemarle Sound, with its rivers leading into interior North Carolina and over which railroads run north on bridges to Norfolk, Virginia. From Roanoke Island, Union troops could thus threaten Norfolk.

Flag Officer Louis M. Goldsborough, commanding the North Atlantic Blockading Squadron, and U.S. Army brigadier general Ambrose Burnside command the Roanoke Island operation. Also known as the Burnside Expedition, it departs Hampton Roads in mid-January. Because of the shallow water in which they have to operate, Goldsborough's 20 warships are all converted tugs, river steamers, and ferry boats. Most are lightly armed. Typical is his flagship, the *Philadelphia,* a side-wheeler former passenger steamer armed with two 12-pounder rifled boat howitzers. Command problems are compounded by the fact that Burnside has charge of the army's vessels, including some gunboats. Goldsborough's ships provide protection for some 70 army transports carrying 12,000 troops and their supplies.

A severe storm scatters many of the Union ships. The army loses three: the *City of New York,* with ordnance and supplies; the *Pocahontas,* with 100 horses; and one of Burnside's gunboats, the *Zouave* (4 guns). Once at Hatteras Inlet, a number of the deeper-draft army vessels have to be substantially lightened, and some ships must be kedged over the bar.

The warships and transports get under way early on February 5, but fog and rain delay the advance, with the ships passing west of the southern tip of Roanoke Island into Croatan Sound on the morning of February 7.

Although well aware of Union preparations, Confederate authorities have few warships, guns, or troops available. Brigadier General Henry A. Wise commands Roanoke Island with two North Carolina regiments totaling 1,435 men. Another 800 are in reserve at Nags Head. Roanoke Island has five forts with a total of 30 guns. Wise has also ordered a double line of pilings placed to block the Union advance; on the Union approach, the Confederates also sink a number of small vessels to strengthen this water barrier. Behind it, Flag Officer William F. Lynch commands seven small steamers with a total of only 8 guns.

The Union ships move up Croatan Sound. As the transports prepare to disembark their troops on Roanoke Island, Goldsborough orders his gunboats forward to shell the Confederate forts and ships. The 19 Union gunboats mount a total of 57 guns. Although only six Confederates are wounded in the exchange, damage to Lynch's ships is extensive. The largest, the side-wheeler *Curlew* (1 gun), is holed; its crew runs it ashore. The screw steamer *Forrest* (1 gun) is disabled by a displaced propeller. The Union warships escape serious injury, thanks to constant maneuvering.

Running short of ammunition, Lynch in late afternoon orders his remaining ships to take the *Forrest* in tow and proceed to Elizabeth City, 35 miles up Albemarle Sound. Securing fuel and ammunition sufficient for only two of his ships, Lynch is en route back to Roanoke Island when he learns of its surrender.

Meanwhile, the earthen works of Fort Bartow on Pork Point are hard hit by the Union naval

 ## Ambrose Everett Burnside (1824–1881)

U.S. Army officer. Born in Liberty, Indiana, on May 23, 1824, Ambrose Everett Burnside graduated from the U.S. Military Academy, West Point, in 1847 and was commissioned a second lieutenant. Too late to see action in the Mexican-American War, he served on the southwestern frontier and was wounded in fighting the Apaches. In 1853 he resigned from the army; settled in Providence, Rhode Island; and went into business manufacturing the Burnside Carbine, which he had invented. The carbine was an excellent weapon, and the War Department contracted to make extensive purchases. However, Secretary of War John B. Floyd, apparently bribed by a rival gun maker, broke the contract with Burnside. Burnside lost an 1858 election for Congress, and shortly thereafter his factory burned. His creditors took control of the patents for the carbine, some 55,000 of which were produced during the American Civil War.

When the Civil War began, Burnside raised the 1st Rhode Island Volunteer Regiment and became its colonel. He led a brigade at the First Battle of Bull Run (Manassas) and was promoted to brigadier general in August 1861. Later in the summer, he took command of Union troops operating against the North Carolina coast. On February 7 Burnside and 7,500 men landed on Roanoke Island and the next day forced its 2,500-man Confederate garrison to surrender. Burnside than captured New Bern on March 14. Thereafter Burnside's coastal command was expanded to full corps strength, designated IX Corps.

In recognition of his victories, Burnside was advanced to major general in March 1862. After Major General George B. McClellan's defeat in the Peninsula Campaign, Lincoln offered Burnside command of the Army of the Potomac, but Burnside turned it down both because he was loyal to his friend McClellan and because he believed that he was not competent to command such a large force. Transferred to northern Virginia to support Major General John Pope, Burnside played only a minor role in the Second Battle of Bull Run (Manassas). After Pope's defeat there, Lincoln again offered command of the army to Burnside, but again he refused, saying that he doubted has own capabilities.

At the Battle of Antietam on September 17, 1862, Burnside took most of the day to get around to crossing Antietam Creek, fixating on capturing an arched stone bridge even though the creek was readily fordable at many points. The delay allowed Confederate general Robert E. Lee to shift forces and blunt the Union attacks, although by the narrowest of margins. McClellan never forgave Burnside for what he believed to be his slowness in the battle.

On November 7, 1862, Lincoln, fed up with McClellan's endless delays, removed him from command and ordered Burnside to take over the Army of the Potomac. Well aware that Lincoln expected aggressive operations in the near future, Burnside submitted, and Lincoln approved, a plan to turn Lee's Army of Northern Virginia by passing around its right, crossing the Rappahannock at Fredericksburg, and getting between Lee and Richmond. All went well until the army actually reached Fredericksburg and it was discovered that a low priority had been assigned to the pontoon bridging equipment, which was unready. Rather than attempt an immediate crossing, Burnside chose to wait for the specialized equipment. The delay allowed Lee to arrive on the south bank of the river and take up a strong defensive position on Marye's Heights, blocking southward egress from the town. Burnside finally crossed the river and occupied the town, but in the Battle of Fredericksburg of December 13, 1862, his repeated

(continued)

(Continued)

frontal assaults of Marye's Heights proved futile and produced heavy Union casualties and Lee's most lopsided victory of the war. Burnside withdrew back across the Rappahannock amid bitter and open grumbling from his high-ranking subordinates. Before he could act against them, Lincoln removed Burnside from command.

Burnside's next assignment was as commander of the Army of the Ohio. He captured Knoxville, Tennessee, on September 2 but later was besieged there by Confederate forces under Lieutenant General James Longstreet, who mounted a bloody and futile assault on Burnside's fortified position but then withdrew when a Union relieving army approached from Chattanooga.

In the spring of 1864 general-in-chief Lieutenant General Ulysses S. Grant brought Burnside and his IX Corps east to take part in the campaign in Virginia, where Burnside performed in an uninspired but passable manner. During the deadlock in the Petersburg trenches, some of Burnside's men tunneled under Confederate lines and placed a large explosive charge there. Burnside grossly mishandled the resultant Battle of the Crater on July 30 and was relieved of command on August 14. He never returned to duty.

Burnside resigned his commission in April 1865. He went on to serve as governor of Rhode Island, being elected three times—in 1866, 1867, and 1868. He returned to his previous business activities and in 1874 was elected to the U.S. Senate, serving until his death in Bristol, Rhode Island, on September 13, 1881.

STEVEN E. WOODWORTH

Further Reading

Marvel, William. *Burnside.* Chapel Hill: University of North Carolina Press, 1991.
Rable, George C. *Fredericksburg! Fredericksburg!* Chapel Hill: University of North Carolina Press, 2002.

bombardment. At about 5:00 p.m. with darkness coming on, Goldsborough orders his ships to cease fire. Meanwhile, beginning at 3:00 p.m., Union troops have begun going ashore on Roanoke Island, and by midnight 1,000 are ashore. Launches land six howitzers on field carriages to provide security.

On February 8 the Union soldiers get under way at first light, and by 9:00 a.m. the fighting is general. The Union ships support the land advance by again taking the Confederate forts under fire, but the Union soldiers have little difficulty with the outnumbered Confederates. Pork Point is taken by 4:00 p.m., and the Confederates set fire to the *Curlew* and blow it up. Meanwhile, Union gunboat crews clear a path through the obstructions across the sound, and by 4:00 p.m. the ships have passed into Albemarle Sound. Lynch now withdraws his gunboats up the Pasquotank River.

In the Battle of Roanoke Island, Union navy losses, including those in the boat howitzer battery, are only 6 killed, 17 wounded, and 2 missing. The army sustains just over 250 casualties, 47 of them killed. The Confederates lose 23 killed and nearly 2,000 captured (58 of them wounded), including some 500 reinforcements arriving just in time to surrender. This major Union victory effectively closes Albemarle Sound to the Confederates and brings the eventual abandonment of Norfolk.

February 10, 1862

Civil War (continued): Eastern theater: Battle of Elizabeth City. Early this morning, Commander Stephen

C. Rowan leads 13 Union gunboats with marines from Roanoke Island, North Carolina, up the Pasquotank River to pursue Confederate flag officer William F. Lynch's remaining gunboats. The Confederates are caught by surprise and are unprepared. The *Forrest* (1 gun) is on the ways at Elizabeth City undergoing repairs, and Lynch had sent the *Raleigh* (2 guns) up the Dismal Swamp Canal toward Norfolk to secure ammunition. Union marines land near Cobb's Point to attack the battery guarding access to the gunboats. Lynch directs its defense, but the half dozen militiamen there run away. Lynch orders most of the crew of the *Beaufort* (1 gun) ashore, but the few Confederates can only man two of the fort's 32-pounders.

After a spirited hour-long engagement, Rowan's ships pass the shore battery and close in on the gunboats, sinking the *Sea Bird* (2 guns) and taking its crew prisoner and capturing the *Ellis*. The crew of the steamer *Fanny* (2 guns) run their vessel ashore and set it on fire, and the crew of the schooner *Black Warrior* (2 guns) set their ship on fire as well. Union seamen are unable to save either gunboat.

With the Union gunboats now outflanking the fort, the guns of which cannot be brought to bear, Lynch orders its guns spiked and his men to withdraw. He also orders the *Forrest* at Elizabeth City burned to prevent its capture. The *Beaufort*, *Raleigh*, and *Appomattox* (1 gun) escape. The battle costs Lynch four killed and six wounded.

Driven up the Dismal Swamp Canal, the *Beaufort* and *Raleigh* join the ironclad *Virginia* at Norfolk. The *Appomattox* is too broad for the canal lock above Elizabeth City, however, and Lynch decides to destroy both it and the lock with explosives for fear that the Union forces will pursue.

Rowan, meanwhile, sends men ashore to occupy both Elizabeth City and Edenton and to obstruct the Albemarle and Chesapeake Canal. Others of his men destroy Confederate property and secure ammunition, ordnance, and other useful stores.

February 11, 1862

Civil War (continued). U.S. secretary of war Edwin M. Stanton establishes the U.S. Military Rail Road, run by former rail executive Daniel McCallum. As Southern rail lines steadily deteriorate thanks in part to a shortage of track and steam locomotives, the Northern rail system becomes the world's largest and most unified. It is a key factor in the ultimate U.S. military triumph.

February 13, 1862

Civil War (continued): Western theater. Union forces under Brigadier General Samuel R. Curtis take possession of Springfield, Missouri.

February 13–16, 1862

Civil War (continued): Western theater: Battle of Fort Donelson. Following the capture of Fort Henry on the Tennessee, Union brigadier general Ulysses S. Grant and Flag Officer Andrew H. Foote move against Fort Donelson on the Cumberland River, only some 10 miles by land from Fort Henry. Confederate Western theater commander General Albert Sidney Johnston decides to reinforce Fort Donelson in order to purchase time for his flanking forces to withdraw. Johnson probably intends to make the garrison at Donelson strong enough so that it can cut its way out after the Union gunboats have made the riverfront untenable and sufficient time has been won. Brigadier General John B. Floyd assumes command of Fort Donelson.

Grant marches overland to Donelson from Fort Henry and gradually builds up his forces there. Foote's gunboats attack Fort Donelson's water batteries on February 14. These are situated on high ground, and their shot strikes the slanted armor of the gunboats at right angles. The ironclads are rebuffed; three of the four are put out of action and drift downstream. In the flotilla, 11 men are killed and 43 wounded (including Foote). Grant, however, continues to add to his besieging forces, as Floyd waits too long to do battle with him.

On February 15, Confederate brigadier general Gideon J. Pillow bungles a Confederate escape attempt. He opens the escape route but then expands it into an effort to defeat Grant. The Union lines bend but do not break, and Grant takes advantage of the consequent weakening of the remainder of the Confederate line for Pillow's effort to order an attack

Battle of Fort Donelson		
Date	February 13–16, 1862	
Location	Fort Donelson on the Cumberland River, Tennessee	
Opponents (*winner)	*United States	Confederacy
Commander	Brigadier General Ulysses S. Grant; Flag Officer Andrew H. Foote	Brigadier General John B. Floyd
#	27,000 men	Some 21,500 men
Casualties	500 killed, 2,108 wounded, and 221 captured or missing	1,500–3,500 killed and wounded; up to 15,000 prisoners; 57 guns and considerable numbers of small arms and supplies captured

on the Confederate right, and Union troops under Brigadier General Charles F. Smith penetrate the fort's defensive perimeter. That night the Confederates decide to surrender, although Colonel Nathan Bedford Forrest refuses to do so and escapes with his cavalry through shallow water next to the river, where the Union lines do not yet extend. Floyd and Pillow abandon their men, crossing the Cumberland and leaving Brigadier General Simon B. Buckner to surrender. He asks for terms, but Grant insists on unconditional surrender.

In all some 2,500 Confederates escape, but as many as 15,000 surrender. Union forces also secure a considerable quantity of small arms, 57 light and heavy guns, and equipment and rations. Estimates of Confederate killed or wounded range from 1,500 to 3,500; Union losses are 500 killed, 2,108 wounded, and 221 captured or missing. Grant is lionized in the Northern press as "Unconditional Surrender Grant."

Union theater commander Major General Henry W. Halleck refuses to permit Grant and Foote to move immediately on Nashville, though. This allows the Confederates time to remove stocks of supplies. Nashville falls only on February 25. The fight at Donelson indirectly impacts the subsequent Battle of Shiloh (see April 6–7, 1862), for had the men lost at

Donelson been available there, victory would probably have gone to the Confederates.

February 16–21, 1862
Civil War (continued): Trans-Mississippi West theater: Sibley's New Mexico Campaign (continued). Brigadier General Henry H. Sibley's first objective is U.S. Fort Craig in New Mexico Territory, commanded by his brother-in-law Colonel Edward R. S. Canby with 2,000 men. Fort Craig is too strong for the 3,200 Confederates to capture, and several days of inconclusive fighting there and at nearby Valverde reduce Sibley's force and his supplies. Desperate for food, Sibley bypasses Fort Craig and proceeds north toward Albuquerque, where the Union troops have substantial supplies.

February 25, 1862
Civil War (continued): Western theater. Union troops under the overall command of Department of the Ohio major general Don Carlos Buell occupy Nashville, Tennessee. Brigadier General William "Bull" Nelson arrives on the north bank of the Cumberland River at Nashville on February 24 and, assisted by the Union ironclad *Cairo* (13 guns), occupies the city the next day. The second-largest city in Tennessee, Nashville is the first Confederate state capital captured by Union forces. Buell's slow advance following the capture of Bowling Green, Kentucky, on February 14 and the refusal of Department of the Missouri major general Henry Halleck to permit Brigadier General Ulysses S. Grant and Flag Officer Andrew H. Foote to advance on Nashville immediately after the capture of Fort Donelson nonetheless have given the Confederates time to withdraw stocks of arms and manufacturing facilities from the city.

March 2, 1862
Civil War (continued): Western theater: The Confederates abandon Columbus. With the Union victories at Forts Henry and Donelson, Major General Leonidas K. Polk orders Confederate forces to abandon Columbus, Kentucky. Its garrison and 140 guns are relocated to defend New Madrid, Missouri, and Island No. 10 in the Mississippi River.

March 3, 1862

Civil War (continued). A U.S. Navy expedition under Flag Officer Samuel F. Du Pont captures Fernandina Beach and Amelia Island, Florida. A landing party from the screw gunboat *Ottawa* (4 guns) captures Fort Clinch, the first Union installation retaken in the war.

March 7–8, 1862

Civil War (continued): Trans-Mississippi West theater: Battle of Pea Ridge (Elkhorn Tavern). On February 10, 1862, U.S. major general Samuel R. Curtis had begun a campaign designed to clear Missouri of Confederate forces. The campaign is successful, and Curtis drives some 8,000 Confederates into Arkansas. The Confederates reorganize under aggressive Major General Earl Van Dorn, who now takes the initiative.

On March 6, the van of the advancing Confederate forces engages the Union rear guard, which then falls back on the main Union line. On March 7 Van Dorn and some 17,000 Confederates attack Curtis's 11,000 men entrenched along Pea Ridge, some 10 miles northeast of Bentonville in northern Arkansas. Van Dorn attempts to turn Curtis's left flank near Elkhorn Tavern, but this attack is slow to develop, and although the Union troops eventually give ground, they are able to stabilize their line by nightfall.

Fighting resumes the next day. Believing correctly that the Confederates are running out of ammunition, Curtis attacks and is successful on both flanks, and Van Dorn is forced to withdraw. Curtis has won a decisive victory against superior numbers.

Union losses are 1,384 men against as many as 4,600 Confederates, including 300 prisoners. The Battle of Pea Ridge is the first major Union victory in the Trans-Mississippi West theater and ensures Union control of Missouri for more than two years.

March 8–9, 1862

Civil War (continued): Battle of Hampton Roads. U.S. major general George B. McClellan's massive Peninsula Campaign, directed against Richmond, Virginia, is in jeopardy when Union transports at Hampton Roads are threatened with destruction by the new Confederate ironclad *Virginia*, commanded

Battle of Hampton Roads		
Date	March 8–9, 1862	
Location	Hampton Roads, Virginia	
Opponents (*winner)	*United States (battle is a draw, but this enables the Union Peninsula Campaign to proceed)	Confederacy
Commander	Lieutenant John Worden	Flag Officer Franklin Buchanan; Lieutenant Catesby ap Roger Jones
#	Union squadron of 5 wooden warships and the ironclad *Monitor* (total 204 guns)	Confederate ironclad *Virginia* and 3 small wooden gunboats and 2 wooden tenders of the James River Squadron (total 35 guns)
Casualties	261 killed, 108 wounded; frigate *Congress* and sloop *Cumberland* sunk	7 killed, 17 wounded; *Virginia* damaged

by Flag Officer Franklin Buchanan. The *Virginia*, an ironclad conversion from the former wooden U.S. Navy steam frigate *Merrimack*, which had been scuttled by Union forces at the Norfolk Navy Yard, mounts 10 guns.

On March 8, 1862, the *Virginia* steams from Norfolk on its maiden voyage. Most in the crew believe this to be a shakedown run, but Buchanan is determined to attack the Union warships protecting the vulnerable transports in Hampton Roads, the large basin into which the James, Nansemond, and Elizabeth Rivers empty before Chesapeake Bay. In addition to the *Virginia*, Buchanan is accompanied by two small tenders and three gunboats of the Confederate James River Squadron. These six Confederate ships, mounting a total of 35 guns, face a Union naval force mounting 204 guns. The larger Union ships are the screw frigates *Minnesota* (flagship, 40 guns) and *Roanoke* (40 guns), the sailing frigates *Congress* (50 guns) and *St. Lawrence* (50 guns), and the razee (cut-down) sailing sloop *Cumberland* (24 guns).

 **Naval Gun Turret**

Following the decision to arm ships with a few large-bore pivot-mounted guns as their principal armament, the next step was an armored turret to protect the guns and their crews, especially during the lengthy reloading process. During the Crimean War, Royal Navy captain Cowper Coles designed two floating batteries to engage Russian shore batteries at close range. The second of these mounted a 68-pounder protected by a hemispheric iron shield, which during action proved largely impervious to hostile fire.

In March 1859 Coles patented the idea of turrets aboard ship. He advocated guns mounted on the centerline of the vessel so as to have wide arcs of fire on either side of the ship and halving the number of guns previously required for broadsides fire. Coles's persistence coupled with the powerful support of Prince Albert led the Admiralty in March 1861 to install an experimental armored turret on the floating battery *Trusty*. The test was a success, for 33 hits from 68-pounder and 100-pounder guns failed to disable it.

The Coles turret turned on a circumferential roller path set in the lower deck, operated by two men with a hand crank. Its upper 4.5 feet of armor came up through the main or upper deck and formed an armored glacis to protect the lower part. The crew and ammunition entered the turret from below, through a hollow central cylinder.

The first British seagoing turreted ship was the Coles-inspired *Prince Albert* of 1864. It mounted four 9-inch muzzle-loading rifles, one each in four center-line circular turrets, turned by hand; 18 men could complete a revolution in one minute. The problem of center-line turrets in a ship of high superstructure and sail rig and very low freeboard (the latter the result of a design error) contributed to the disastrous loss at sea of the Coles-designed HMS *Captain* in 1870. Most of its crew drowned, Coles among them.

In the United States, John Ericsson's single revolving turret the *Monitor* entered service in March 1862. The *Monitor* and many follow-on types all had very low freeboard. This lessened the amount of armor required to protect the ship and allowed it to be concentrated in the turret. Unlike the *Captain,* however, the *Monitor* had no high superstructure or sail rig.

Ericsson's turret was all above the upper deck, on which it rested. Before the turret could be turned, it had to be lifted by rack and pinion from contact with the deck. A steam engine operating through gearing turned the turret around a central spindle. The *Monitor*'s engagement with CSS *Virginia* on March 9, 1862, was the first time that a revolving turret had actually been employed in battle.

Sharp disagreement continued between those who favored the revolving turret and those who supported broadside armament. Renewed interest in the ram—in consequence of the 1866 Battle of Lissa—and larger, more powerful guns helped decide this in favor of the turret. The ram meant that ships had to fire ahead as they prepared to attack an opposing vessel; heavier guns meant that ships needed fewer of them and that these should have the widest possible arc of fire. The elimination of sail rigs and improved shop designs heightened the stability of turreted warships.

Turrets continued to undergo design refinement and received new breech-loading guns as well as heavier armor, indeed the thickest aboard ship. Relatively thin top-of-turret armor on British battle cruisers, however, led to the loss of three of them to German armor-piercing shells in the Battle of

Jutland (May 31–June 1, 1916). The battle cruiser turrets also lacked flash protection doors and the means of preventing a shell burst inside the turret from reaching the magazines. The largest battleship ever built, the Japanese *Yamato,* had 25.6-inch steel armor protection on its turrets.

SPENCER C. TUCKER

Further Reading

Hawkey, Arthur. *Black Night off Finisterre: The Tragic Tale of an Early British Ironclad.* Annapolis, MD: Naval Institute Press, 1999.

Hogg, Ian, and John Batchelor. *Naval Gun.* Poole, Dorset, UK: Blandford, 1978.

Hough, Richard. *Fighting Ships.* New York: Putnam, 1969.

Padfield, Peter. *Guns at Sea.* New York: St. Martin's, 1974.

Tucker, Spencer C. *Handbook of 19th Century Naval Warfare.* Annapolis, MD: Naval Institute Press, 2000.

Undeterred, Buchanan heads for the Union warships protecting the transports and uses his ship's ram to sink the nearest, the *Cumberland.* The ram catches in the Union ship, nearly taking the *Virginia* down, but the ram breaks off and frees the ironclad. Buchanan then attacks and burns the *Congress.* Maneuvering to escape, the Union flagship *Minnesota* runs aground.

With darkness coming on, its pilots uncertain of the shoal water that poses a threat to the deep-draft *Virginia* and Buchanan wounded in the exchange with the *Congress,* the *Virginia* retires. Its crew members are confident that they will complete their work of destruction the next day.

As the Confederates depart, the Union ironclad *Monitor* puts into the roads. Commanded by Lieutenant John Worden, it is far more maneuverable than its Confederate opponent, but it is only a fraction of the *Virginia'*s size and mounts but two 11-inch guns in a revolving turret. Hastily completed, the *Monitor* had nearly sunk the day before while under tow south. The crew is exhausted from their labors, and there are serious doubts that it will prove a worthy opponent for the fearsome *Virginia.*

The next morning, March 9, with crowds of civilians and soldiers, North and South, lining the shoreline of Hampton Roads to watch, the *Virginia,* now commanded by Lieutenant Catesby ap Roger Jones, steams out to attack the *Minnesota.* The *Monitor* places itself in front of the grounded flagship.

The battle between the two warships begins about 8:00 a.m. and lasts until noon. It is fought at close range, with both warships constantly in motion. The *Virginia* rams the more nimble *Monitor,* but as the *Virginia* has lost its ram, the blow does little damage. The *Monitor'*s gunners meanwhile try to cripple their antagonist's vulnerable propeller and rudder.

The *Monitor'*s guns can fire only once every seven or eight minutes, but its rotating turret means that they are a target only when they are about to fire. Almost all of the Union ship's shots register, and the *Virginia* sustains damage. Although the *Virginia* fires more shots, most go high and do little damage. Worden, however, is temporarily blinded by a direct hit on the pilothouse. In the resultant confusion the *Monitor* drifts away from the battle; by the time its new commander, Lieutenant Samuel Greene, brings the *Monitor* back into position, the *Virginia* is withdrawing. Jones chooses to interpret the *Monitor'*s actions as retreat, and he returns to Norfolk for repairs.

Tactically the battle is a draw. It might have ended differently had the *Virginia'*s fire been concentrated on the *Monitor'*s pilothouse or if it had fired solid shot instead of shell, the type of projectile suitable against the wooden warships that it had been expected to engage. On the other hand, the *Monitor'*s fire should have been directed at its opponent's waterline, and its 11-inch guns should have used 30-pound powder

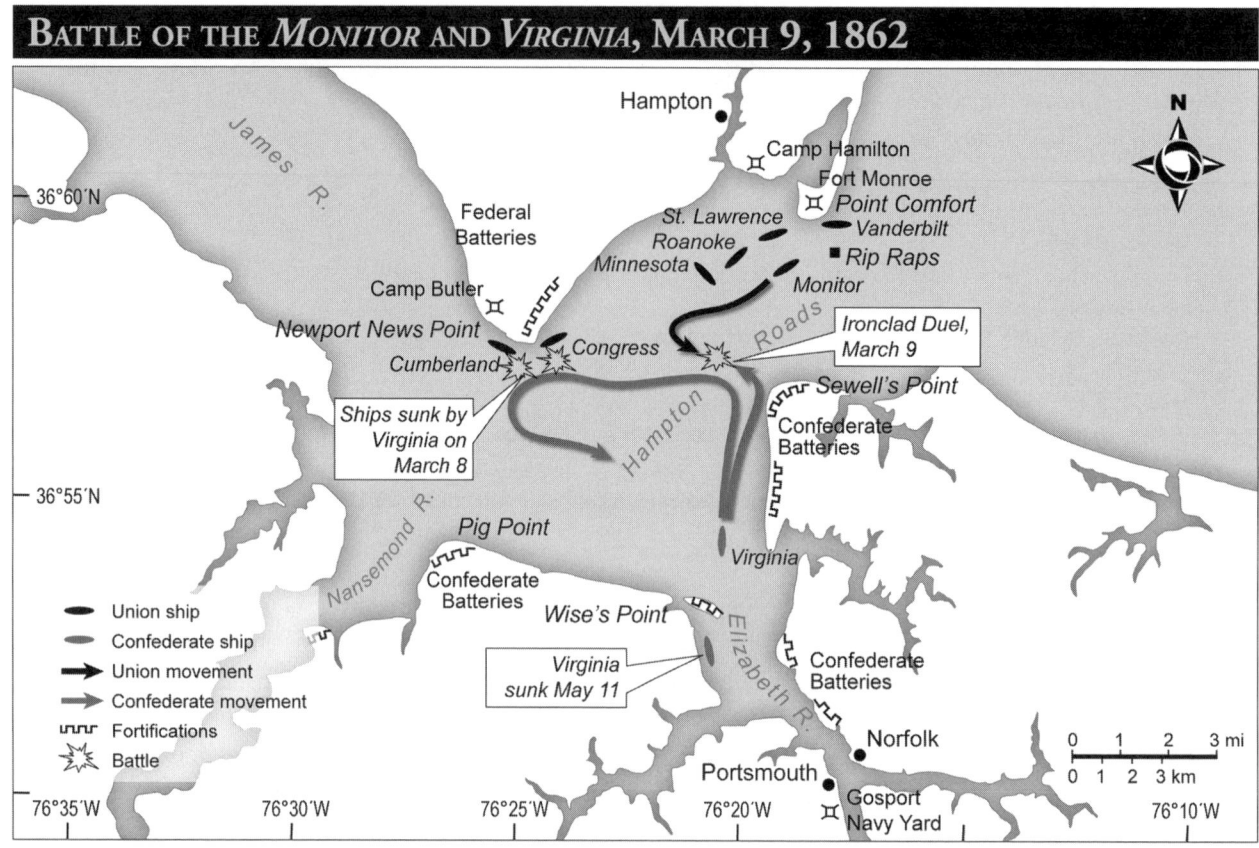

BATTLE OF THE *MONITOR* AND *VIRGINIA*, MARCH 9, 1862

charges, which designer/builder John Ericsson called for, instead of the 15-pound charges decreed as a consequence of the 1844 Peacemaker explosion. But the *Virginia* has been hit 50 times and is leaking. The *Monitor* has sustained only 21 hits and is virtually undamaged. In the two-day engagement the Union suffers 261 killed and 108 wounded; the Confederates lose only 7 killed and 17 wounded.

The battle between the two ironclads is not renewed, but in merely surviving, the *Monitor* ensures the safety of the Union transports and supply ships and hence McClellan's entire operation. The existence of the *Virginia,* however, blocks any Union naval flanking movement up the James River.

The Battle of Hampton Roads, the first-ever engagement between ironclad ships and the first use of a revolving turret in warfare at sea, leads to so-called monitor mania in the North, a clamor for construction of more of this type of ship. In effect, the battle marks a new era in naval warfare. It also sparks

an effort to manufacture larger-caliber guns capable of penetrating the new iron armor.

Union forces soon seize Norfolk. Because the *Virginia*'s deep draft makes passing up the James River impossible, the ship is scuttled on May 11. The *Monitor* also will be lost before the year is out.

March 11, 1862
Civil War (continued). Discouraged by his general-in-chief's lack of aggressiveness, President Abraham Lincoln removes Major General George B. McClellan from command of the Union Army but leaves him in charge of its principal striking force, the Army of the Potomac. No new general-in-chief is named.

At the same time, Lincoln appoints Major General Henry Halleck—who has claimed for himself the laurels won by Brigadier General Ulysses S. Grant and Flag Officer Andrew H. Foote at Forts Henry and Donelson—to command of all Union forces in the Western theater. The new command includes Union forces in 11 states and 3 territories, now renamed the Department of the Mississippi.

March 11, 1862

Civil War (continued). A landing force from the U.S. Navy screw frigate *Wabash* (44 guns) seizes control of St. Augustine, Florida.

March 12, 1862

Civil War (continued): Eastern theater: Union occupation of Winchester, Virginia. With numerically superior Union troops led by Major General Nathaniel P. Banks moving against it, Confederate forces under Major General Thomas J. "Stonewall" Jackson evacuate strategically placed Winchester in the northern Shenandoah Valley.

March 12, 1862

Civil War (continued). A landing force from the U.S. Navy screw gunboat *Ottawa* (3 guns) takes possession of Jacksonville, Florida.

March 13–14, 1862

Civil War (continued): Eastern theater: Union capture of New Bern. Union forces under Commander Stephen C. Rowan and Brigadier General Ambrose E. Burnside mount a joint amphibious assault against New Bern, North Carolina. On March 13, 1862, Burnside lands 12,000 men at Slocum's Creek along the Neuse River, supported by Rowan's 13 gunboats. Burnside then marches inland against New Bern, North Carolina's second-largest city and a key railhead.

Nathaniel Prentice Banks (1816–1894)

Massachusetts governor, U.S. congressman, and U.S. Army general. Nathaniel Prentice Banks was born in Waltham, Massachusetts, on January 30, 1816. Raised in poverty, he was apprenticed in a textile mill but studied law and was admitted to the bar at age 23. His skill as a public speaker assisted his entry into politics. Elected to the state House of Representatives as a Democrat, he served there during 1843–1853; elected to the U.S. House of Representatives, he served during 1853–1857 and was Speaker during 1856–1857. His opposition to the spread of slavery led him to join the new Republican Party, and he was reelected with the help of that party in 1856. He resigned his seat in December 1857 and was governor of Massachusetts during 1858–1861. By now he was probably the most popular political figure in New England.

With the start of the American Civil War, President Abraham Lincoln appointed Banks a major general of volunteers. Although he was a political heavyweight, Banks quickly proved to be a military flyweight. He had no military training and experience, and he followed his own counsel and rejected sound advice offered by his professional officer subordinates. His demonstrated early incompetence included losses to Major General Thomas J. "Stonewall" Jackson in the First Battle of Winchester (May 25, 1862) and at Cedar Mountain (August 9).

Given command of the forces defending Washington, Banks was asked in November 1862 to organize a force of 30,000 New England recruits, and in part because of his excellent political connections, the effort was successful. A month later he sailed for New Orleans with this force to replace Major General Benjamin Butler as commander of the Department of the Gulf.

Laying siege to Port Hudson on the Mississippi, Banks made two unsuccessful assaults on that place, in which he employed African American soldiers for the first time in a major battle during the war.

(continued)

(Continued)

The Confederates surrendered only on July 9, when they were low on food and ammunition and had learned that Union forces had captured Vicksburg upriver.

Although Banks agreed with Major General Ulysses S. Grant that the next Union objective should be Vicksburg, he dutifully followed the plan developed by Major General Henry W. Halleck and Lincoln to move instead against Shreveport. With indications that Banks was considering a run for the presidency in 1864 on the Republican ticket, no doubt Lincoln reasoned that keeping Banks occupied in the Southwest would mean that he was less likely to stir up trouble for his own effort to secure his party's nomination.

The ensuing Red River Campaign (March 10–May 22, 1864) was a disaster. Supremely confident, Banks failed to undertake the detailed staff work necessary for success, was late to move, made poor dispositions, and proceeded toward Shreveport on a route that took him from the protection of Rear Admiral David D. Porter's gunboats on the Red. Caught by the Confederates with his forces in march formation, he was defeated by Confederate forces under Major General Richard Taylor in the Battle of Mansfield (April 8) but was able to withdraw 20 miles and make a stand the next day at the Battle of Pleasant Hill. Despite rebuffing the Confederates in this battle, Banks decided to withdraw. Ultimately Congress investigated the Red River fiasco; its report largely blamed Banks.

Recalled from field command and replaced by Major General Edward R. S. Canby, Banks went on leave in the autumn of 1864. He was mustered out of the army in August 1865. Again elected to Congress, Banks served there during 1865–1873, 1875–1879, and 1889–1891. During 1879–1888 he was a U.S. marshal from Massachusetts. Banks died at Waltham on September 1, 1894.

SPENCER C. TUCKER

Further Reading

Banks, Raymond H. *The King of Louisiana, 1862–1865, and Other Government Work: A Biography of Major General Nathaniel Prentice Banks.* Las Vegas: R. H. Banks, 2005.

Hollandsworth, James G. *Pretense of Glory: The Life of General Nathaniel P. Banks.* Baton Rouge: Louisiana State University Press, 1998.

Joiner, Gary D. *One Damn Blunder from Beginning to End: The Red River Campaign of 1864.* Wilmington, DE: Scholarly Resources, 2003.

On March 14, Brigadier General Lawrence O'Bryan with 4,000 largely untrained and poorly armed men mounts a strong defense for four hours, but when his militia bolts, this forces a general Confederate withdrawal. Burnside's men then occupy New Bern.

The battle costs the Confederates 68 killed, 116 wounded, and some 400 captured or missing; Union losses are 90 killed, 385 wounded, and 1 man captured. The Confederates also lose a number of cannon and considerable equipment and ammunition stores at New Bern. The Union now has a base for operations to the North Carolina interior.

March 16, 1862

Civil War (continued): Western theater: Battle of Pound Gap. U.S. brigadier general James A. Garfield arrives with 500 infantry and 100 cavalry from Pikeville, Kentucky, and attacks 500 men of the 21st Virginia Infantry under Brigadier General Humphrey Marshall entrenched at Pound Gap in the Cumberland Mountains along the Kentucky-Virginia border.

The Confederates flee. Garfield's men destroy the Southern camp and withdraw.

March 16–April 8, 1862

Civil War (continued): Western theater: Siege of Island No. 10. Major General Henry W. Halleck, commanding the Union armies in the West, takes part of Major General Ulysses S. Grant's resources and forms the 18,000-man Army of the Mississippi under Brigadier General John Pope. Halleck orders it to operate with the Union river flotilla under Flag Officer Andrew Hull Foote.

Halleck's goal is to expel the Confederates from the upper Mississippi by securing both New Madrid, Missouri, and nearby Island No. 10. The flotilla will then proceed downriver to meet Union forces advancing from the river's mouth. Union control of the river will cut off the Trans-Mississippi West from the remainder of the Confederacy and allow the transit of goods to the Gulf of Mexico, binding the upper Midwest to the Union cause.

Island No. 10 (which with a shift in the Mississippi River's course is now part of the shore) is in a long bend in the river about 40 miles below Columbus. The Confederates heavily fortify both it and the eastern (Tennessee) shore. In order to take Island No. 10, Union forces must first capture New Madrid, 6 miles downriver and defended by 7,500 men under Brigadier General John P. McCown.

Pope marches his army 50 miles overland and brings New Madrid under siege on March 3. With the arrival of siege guns, on March 13 Pope bombards New Madrid, which McCown abandons that night. This 15-day land campaign claims about 50 killed or wounded on each side, but Island No. 10 is now cut off from most river communication and means of supply.

On March 15 Foote arrives above Island No. 10 with 7 gunboats (his flagship is the powerful new ironclad conversion, the side-wheel steamer *Benton* [16 guns]) and 10 mortar boats accompanied by 1,500 troops and an assortment of steamers and tugs. He opens a bombardment the next day, but the round-the-clock shelling inflicts little damage. Foote rejects repeated requests from Pope to send gunboats past Island No.

10, knowing that if disabled they will drift downriver and be captured. On March 23 work begins on one of the more innovative engineering achievements of the war: a canal to bypass the island entirely. Meanwhile, Brigadier General William W. Mackall assumes command on March 31, replacing McCown.

Foote finally responds to Pope's repeated appeals by sending the gunboat *Carondelet* (14 guns) past Island No. 10 during a thunderstorm on the night of April 4. Another gunboat, the *Pittsburg* (14 guns), follows on the night of April 7. That same day Pope and his men, covered by the two gunboats, cross the river and secure the Tiptonville Road, cutting off Island No. 10.

Mackall now orders a withdrawal. On the evening of April 7 Captain W. Y. C. Hume, commanding Island No. 10, requests surrender terms. Foote demands unconditional surrender, which Hume accepts early on April 8.

The loss of Island No. 10 is a major Confederate defeat. Only about 1,000 of the defenders escape. Union forces take 4,500 prisoners, 5,000 small arms, and 109 cannon and mortars. They also secure four steamers and a floating battery as well as ammunition and supplies. It is a cheap victory in terms of Union casualties: 7 men killed, 14 wounded, and 4 missing, more than half to accidents. Fort Pillow, 60 miles downriver, is the next Union objective.

March 17, 1862

Civil War (continued): Eastern theater. The men of Major General George B. McClellan's 105,000-man Army of the Potomac begin embarking aboard transports at Alexandria, Virginia, for transport to Fortress Monroe in Virginia on Hampton Roads. This marks the opening of what becomes known as the Peninsula Campaign, McClellan's effort to capture the Confederate capital of Richmond by moving up the peninsula formed by the York and James Rivers.

March 22, 1862

Civil War (continued). The first ship built in England for the Confederacy, the steamer *Oreto* sails from Liverpool bound for Nassau, Bahamas, where it will be armed and commissioned as the Confederate Navy commerce raider *Florida*.

March 23, 1862

Civil War (continued): Eastern theater: Jackson's Valley Campaign: First Battle of Kernstown. In one of the most brilliant campaigns in military history, Confederate major general Thomas J. "Stonewall" Jackson, with never more than 18,000 men, ties down more than 64,000 Union troops in the Shenandoah Valley during the period March 23–June 9, 1862.

Union major general Nathaniel P. Banks commands 23,000 Union troops. They are positioned to halt any thrust from the Shenandoah Valley against Washington. In late March, Jackson commands some 4,500 Confederates. Banks is supposed to clear the valley as part of the Peninsula Campaign against Richmond. After defeating Jackson, Banks is to cover Washington, freeing Major General Irvin McDowell's corps of 30,000 men to advance on Richmond from the north. Convinced that Jackson poses no threat, Banks leaves

9,000 men under Brigadier General James Shields to push south against Jackson and himself moves east to Manassas.

Having received a false report on Union strength, in the First Battle of Kernstown, Jackson attacks Shields, who has twice his own strength. Shields repulses the Confederate attack, inflicting 718 casualties against 590 of his own.

Shields reports that Jackson must have been reinforced, and this leads President Abraham Lincoln to order Banks to return to the valley as well as to keep McDowell's corps near Fredericksburg, in effect subtracting some 50,000 soldiers from the Union forces moving against Richmond.

March 26–May 4, 1862

Civil War (continued): Trans-Mississippi West theater: Sibley's New Mexico Campaign (continued):

The First Battle of Kernstown, Virginia, March 23, 1862. Based on a false report of Union strength, Confederate major general Thomas J. "Stonewall" Jackson attacked Union forces here under Brigadier General James Shields and lost the battle, considered to be the opening engagement of Jackson's famed, and thereafter victorious, Shenandoah Valley Campaign. (Library of Congress)

Battle of Glorieta Pass and aftermath. Confederate brigadier general Henry H. Sibley, at the head of 3,200 Texas troops and desperate for supplies, breaks off his effort to capture Fort Craig in order to secure the substantial Union supplies at Albuquerque. When he reaches there, he finds the Union troops gone and the supplies destroyed. Sibley then occupies Santa Fe on March 10, only to discover a similar situation. Meanwhile, the Union retention of Fort Craig cuts Sibley's line of communications back to Texas.

After establishing his headquarters in Albuquerque, Sibley dispatches 200–300 men under Major Charles Lynn Pyron to secure La Glorieta Pass on the Santa Fe Trail. If the Confederates can take the pass they will be able to move onto the High Plains and attack Fort Union, the Union stronghold along the invasion route northward through Raton Pass.

The ensuing Battle of Glorieta Pass on March 26–28, 1862, is the principal engagement of the campaign. Union commander Colonel John P. Slough has some 900 men, while the Confederates have 1,100 men under Lieutenant Colonel William R. Scurry. The Confederates win the running three-day battle. The Union suffers 52 killed, 78 wounded, and 15 taken prisoner; the Confederates sustain 50 killed, 80 wounded, and 92 prisoners.

Colorado volunteers under Major John M. Chivington, however, capture the lightly guarded Confederate supply train at Johnson's Ranch, forcing Scurry to withdraw to Santa Fe. On April 15 Edward R. S. Canby, now a brigadier general and having been reinforced, attacks and defeats one of Sibley's regiments under Colonel Thomas Green at Peralta, 20 miles south of Albuquerque. Supply shortages, above all of food, force Sibley to quit New Mexico. Other small engagements occur until some 1,700 Confederates regain Fort Bliss on May 1, ending the campaign.

April 2, 1862

Civil War (continued): Western theater. As General Albert S. Johnston assembles at Corinth the Army of Mississippi, the largest concentration of Confederate forces to date in the Western theater, skirmishing occurs between the Confederates and Union troops under Major General Ulysses S. Grant who have crossed the Tennessee River and established a bridgehead at Pittsburg Landing, Tennessee.

April 5–May 3, 1862

Civil War (continued): Eastern theater: Peninsula Campaign: Siege of Yorktown. Having assembled some 90,000 men of his Army of the Potomac at Fort Monroe, Major General George B. McClellan prepares to move west against the Confederate capital of Richmond. McClellan's glacial advance leads to him being called "the Virginia Creeper," after the vine of the same name.

Before he can move against Richmond, though, McClellan must first secure Yorktown, held by 15,000 Confederates under Major General John B. Magruder, who buys a valuable month's delay for the Confederates to build up their strength by deceiving McClellan into believing that his force is much larger than is the case, using dummy ordnance (Quaker guns) and false movements. McClellan claims that the Confederates probably have 100,000 men at Yorktown. He slowly builds up his forces and begins positioning heavy siege artillery. Several days before McClellan's planned assault, on the evening of May 3 under cover of an artillery bombardment Magruder slips away. The next morning a Union balloonist confirms that the Confederate trenches are empty. The siege claims some 182 Union and 300 Confederate casualties.

April 6–7, 1862

Civil War (continued): Western theater: Battle of Shiloh. Commander of the Confederate Western theater General Albert Sidney Johnston, stung by a series of reversals, is determined to attack Union forces now preparing to move against the important Southern railhead of Corinth, Mississippi. At Corinth, Johnston assembles some 44,000 men of the Army of Mississippi and at dawn on April 6 launches a surprise attack on Major General Ulysses S. Grant's 39,000-man Army of the Tennessee, encamped just south of the Tennessee River at Pittsburg Landing, where Grant has been ordered to await reinforcement by Major General Don Carlos Buell's 36,000-man Army of the Ohio. Knowing that he will shortly be taking the offensive and assuming

Battle of Shiloh		
Date	April 6–7, 1862	
Location	Hardin County, Tennessee, on the Tennessee River	
Opponents (*winner)	*United States	Confederacy
Commander	Major General Ulysses S. Grant; Major General Don Carlos Buell	General Albert Sidney Johnston; General Pierre G. T. Beauregard
#	Army of the Tennessee (39,000 men); Army of the Ohio (36,000 men)	Army of Mississippi (44,000 men)
Casualties	13,047 (1,754 killed, 8,408 wounded, 2,885 captured/missing)	10,699 (1,728 killed, 8,012 wounded, 959 captured/missing)

that he would be the one initiating any action, Grant had failed to throw up defensive works.

The ensuing Battle of Shiloh (Pittsburg Landing) takes its name from a small local Baptist church named Shiloh, Hebrew for "place of peace." The fighting is fierce, and Union troops are driven back almost into the river, where the timberclads *Tyler* (7 guns) and *Lexington* (6 guns) bombard Confederate positions through the two days and intervening night of intense fighting, securing the Union flank at Dill Branch and denying the Confederate attacks along the riverbanks.

Johnston is mortally wounded early in the afternoon and is succeeded in command by General Pierre G. T. Beauregard, who calls off the attack late in the day, throwing away whatever chance the Confederates have for victory, because that night Buell's men arrive.

When the fighting resumes on April 7, it is Grant who attacks first to regain land lost the day before, much to Beauregard's surprise. Now facing superior Union strength, Beauregard withdraws back on Corinth, abandoning much equipment on the way. In the battle the Confederates sustain 10,699 casualties (1,728 killed, 8,012 wounded, 959 captured or missing); Union losses are 13,047 (1,754 killed, 8,408 wounded, 2,885 captured or missing). Although Grant is roundly criticized in the Northern press,

President Abraham Lincoln defends him, countering that "I cannot spare this man. He fights."

April 8, 1862

French intervention in Mexico (continued). Well aware of French designs to control Mexico and not wishing to be a party to them, the British and Spanish governments withdraw their far smaller troop contingents from Mexico; the French reinforce.

April 9, 1862

Civil War (continued): Eastern theater: Union evacuation of Jacksonville. Having occupied the city in March but finding it impossible to defend, Union forces evacuate Jacksonville, Florida. Many Union sympathizers are forced to leave behind there all that they own.

April 11, 1862

After a heavy bombardment by Union forces, the Confederates surrender Fort Pulaski south of Savannah, Georgia.

April 12, 1862

Civil War (continued): Western theater: Great Locomotive Chase (Andrews' Raid). U.S. major general Ormsby M. Mitchel, commanding Union forces in middle Tennessee, seeks to capture the key Southern railhead of Chattanooga. To accomplish this with the forces at hand, Mitchel must cut off the city from reinforcement by rail from Atlanta. James J. Andrews, a civilian scout and Union spy, proposes a daring plan aimed at destroying the Western and Atlantic Railroad link to Chattanooga. With Mitchel's approval, he recruits another civilian, William H. Campbell, and 22 Union soldiers in Mitchel's command. All are to rendezvous at Marietta, Georgia, by midnight on April 10. To avoid suspicion, the men travel in pairs in civilian clothes.

Bad weather imposes delays, but all reach Marietta by midnight on April 10 except for one who is delayed and two others who are forced to enlist in the Confederate Army (their instructions if questioned are to say they are Kentuckians traveling to join a Confederate artillery unit). Two others oversleep and do not join the raid. On the morning of April 12 at Big

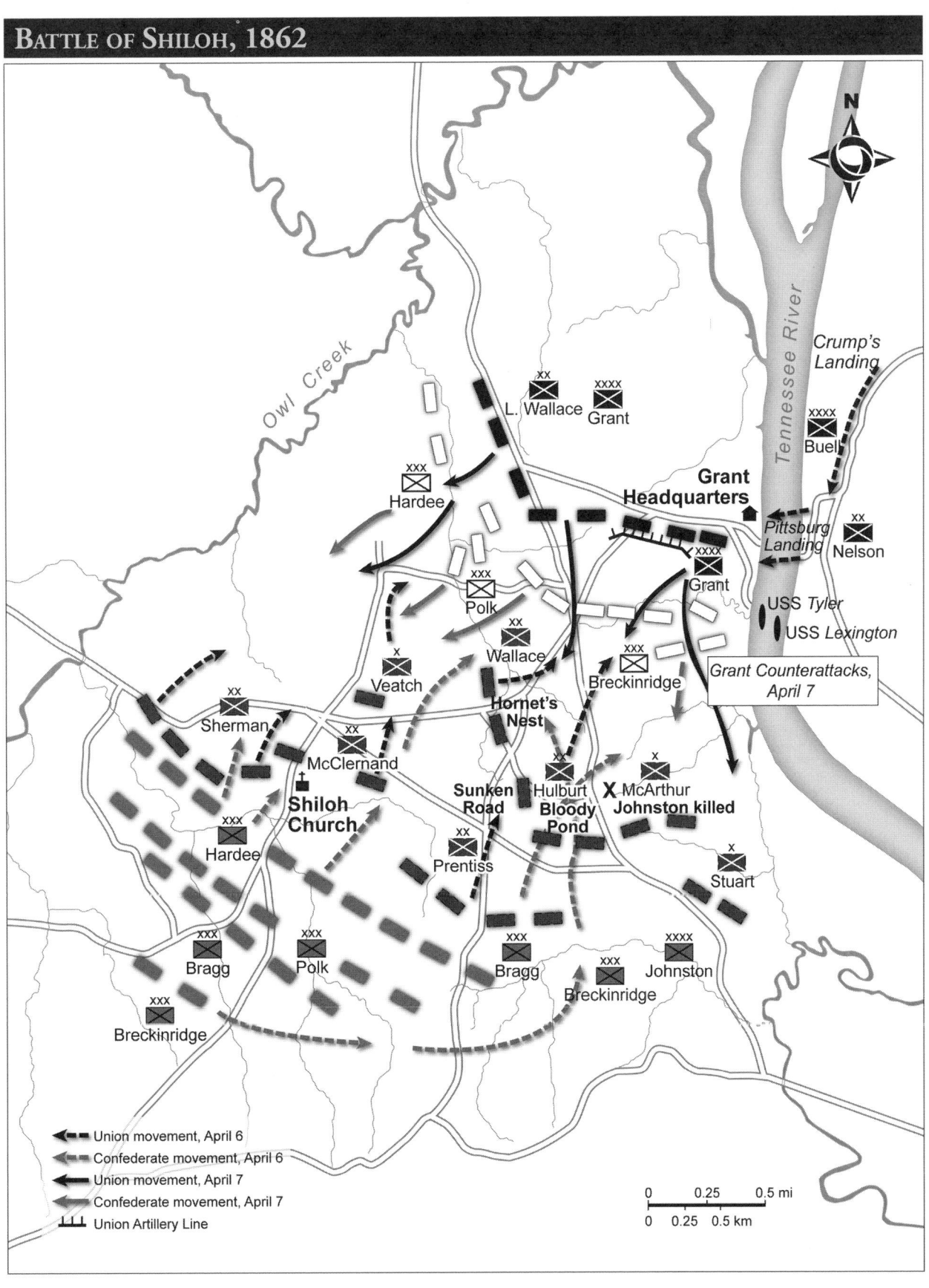

BATTLE OF SHILOH, 1862

Crump's Landing

Tennessee River

xxxx
Buel

xx
L. Wallace

xxxx
Grant

xxx
Hardee

Grant Headquarters

xx
Nelson

Pittsburg Landing

xxxx
Grant

xxx
Polk

xx
Wallace

x
Veatch

xxx
Breckinridge

USS *Tyler*

USS *Lexington*

Grant Counterattacks, April 7

xx
Sherman

Hornet's Nest

xx
McClernand

Shiloh Church

Sunken Road

xx
Hulburt

x
McArthur

X Johnston killed

xxx
Hardee

xx
Prentiss

Bloody Pond

x
Stuart

xxx
Bragg

xxx
Polk

xxx
Bragg

xxxx
Johnston

xxx
Breckinridge

xxx
Breckinridge

Owl Creek

◄━ ━ Union movement, April 6
◄━ ━ Confederate movement, April 6
◄━━ Union movement, April 7
◄━━ Confederate movement, April 7
⊥⊥⊥ Union Artillery Line

0   0.25   0.5 mi
0   0.25   0.5 km

Dynamite

Dynamite is a powerful explosive invented by Swiss chemist and engineer Alfred Nobel in 1866 and patented a year later. Nobel's involvement in heavy construction work in Stockholm led him to try to develop safer methods of blasting rock. In 1846 Italian chemist Ascanio Sobrero had invented nitroglycerine. It consists of a mix of sulfuric acid, nitric acid, and glycerine. A powerful explosive, nitroglycerine soon found application in commercial mining and blasting operations, but it suffered from the drawback of being highly volatile in its liquid state. Even a slight shock can cause nitroglycerin to explode, and it was thus very dangerous to transport and utilize.

Nobel discovered that nitroglycerin could be stabilized when absorbed in diatomaceous earth (kieselguhr). He named his invention dynamite, after the Greek *dynamos* ("powerful"). It was the first safe and predictable explosive with a greater force than gunpowder and was certainly one of the great inventions of the 19th century.

Dynamite consists of three parts nitroglycerin and one part diatomaceous earth as well as a small amount of sodium carbonate. Dynamite most usually is formed into sticks about an inch in diameter and eight inches long and wrapped in paper. These sticks were in this fashion so they could be easily inserted in holes drilled into rock.

Dynamite is classified as a high explosive, meaning that it detonates instead of deflagrating. Nobel sold his explosive as "Nobel's Safety Blasting Powder." In order to detonate the dynamite, Nobel also developed a blasting cap, which he also patented. It was ignited by lighting a fuse.

Dynamite found wide application in such areas as construction, mining all sorts of materials, and digging canals and tunnels. Its military implications were also immense. Dynamite found its way into high-explosive fillers for artillery shells, bombs, and land mines. It was also used in satchel charges.

Nobel made a great fortune from his invention. The Republic of South Africa soon became the largest producer of dynamite, which was widely used in mining for gold. Nobel later used some of his money gained from the invention to establish prizes in the sciences, although the most recognized of these prizes is the Nobel Prize for Peace. Nobel's invention ended centuries of experiment with gunpowder and inaugurated a new era of vastly more powerful high explosives.

SPENCER C. TUCKER

Further Reading

Brown, Stephen R. *A Most Damnable Invention: Dynamite, Nitrates, and the Making of the Modern World.* New York: St. Martin's, 2005.
Fordham, Stanley. *High Explosives and Propellents.* Oxford, UK: Pergamon, 1980.

Shanty (now Kennesaw), Georgia, the remaining men seize the Confederate locomotive *General* and several cars halted there for a breakfast stop. They intend to run the train northward to Chattanooga, destroying railroad bridges en route, then join Mitchel's forces advancing on the city.

William A. Fuller, the train's conductor, and other Confederates pursue the *General*, first on foot, then in a handcar, and finally in a succession of other locomotives. Because the raiders periodically stop to cut telegraph lines, W & A train stations do not know that the *General* has been hijacked and is on a sabotage mission. Meanwhile, the raiders fail in their attempts to burn bridges and dynamite Tunnel Hill.

Finally, a few miles short of Chattanooga, the *General* runs out of steam, and the men take to the woods. Mitchel halts his troops 30 miles short of Chattanooga.

All the men who reached Marietta are subsequently captured, including the two who missed the rendezvous. The raiders are tried as spies and found guilty. Andrews is hanged at Atlanta on June 7, and seven others are hanged at Atlanta on June 18. Eight others then make a remarkable escape and travel hundreds of miles, but all reach safety. The remaining six are exchanged in March 1863. Nineteen soldier participants are subsequently awarded the Medal of Honor, established on July 12.

April 14–June 4, 1862

Civil War (continued): Western theater: Siege of Fort Pillow. The next Union objective on the northern Mississippi after the capture of Island No. 10 is Fort Pillow. Located 60 miles to the south and just north of Fulton on the Tennessee shore, it guards the northern approach to the important railhead of Memphis, 40 miles downriver. The fort's 6,000 defenders turned Fort Pillow into a strong defensive position.

Union flag officer Andrew Hull Foote's naval flotilla and transports carrying Brigadier General John Pope's 20,000-man Army of the Mississippi arrive at Hale's Point above Fort Pillow on the morning of April 14. The Union ironclads drive off five gunboats of the Confederate River Defense Fleet commanded by Captains James E. Montgomery and J. H. Townsend. The latter counts more than a dozen lightly armed and poorly armored gunboats. These mount only one or two guns each, but they are somewhat faster and more agile than their Union counterparts. A number have been fitted with reinforced bows, enabling them to act as rams.

That same afternoon, Union mortar boats open fire on Fort Pillow, and the bombardment continues for the next seven weeks. Unable to get at Fort Pillow by land, Pope and Foote decide to replicate the plan of Island No. 10 by digging a six-mile-long canal on the Arkansas side of the river to pass the

Union gunboats below Fort Pillow. Any possibility of a quick strike at Fort Pillow is dashed, however, when Major General Henry W. Halleck withdraws almost all of Pope's troops on April 17 for his own campaign against Corinth. Pope leaves behind only 1,200 infantry to garrison Fort Pillow should the Confederates evacuate it.

April 16, 1862

Civil War (continued): Confederate conscription. With the Army of the Potomac advancing on the Confederate capital of Richmond and Southern forces hard-pressed for manpower, President Jefferson Davis authorizes mandatory conscription. In the first military draft in American history, all Southern white males ages 18 to 35 are now eligible for 3 years of military service. There is, however, widespread resentment to an exemption for any Southerner owning 20 or more slaves. The Union will not introduce conscription until 1863.

April 18, 1862

Civil War (continued): Western theater: Start of Union operations against New Orleans. With Union forces on the northern Mississippi pushing south, Flag Officer David Glasgow Farragut, commanding the West Gulf Blockading Squadron, has charge of an operation to secure the river's mouth. On April 16, 1862, Farragut moves his 17 ships (mounting 154 guns) and a squadron of 20 mortar boats under Commander David D. Porter up the river to a point below Confederate Forts Jackson and St. Philip, which guard the southern water approach to New Orleans and mount a combined 126 guns.

The Confederates have stretched a chain across the river on hulks. They also have 14 warships, but most are small, and they mount a total of only 40 guns. These include the *Louisiana,* an unfinished ironclad moored along the riverbank with 16 guns, and an ironclad ram, the *Manassas* (1 gun). Major command divisions impede the Confederate defensive efforts, however.

On April 18 Porter's mortar boats open a bombardment of Fort Jackson with their 13-inch shells. The fort is little damaged in five days and nights of bombardment with 16,800 shells; its garrison heroically remains in place.

April 19, 1862

Civil War (continued): Western theater: Union operations against New Orleans (continued): Crewmen of the U.S. Navy 4-gun screw gunboats *Itasca* and *Pinola,* under heavy Confederate fire, breach the Confederate obstructions in the Mississippi River below Forts Jackson and St. Philip, paving the way for Flag Officer David G. Farragut to move his West Gulf Blockading Squadron up the river and take New Orleans.

April 24, 1862

Civil War (continued): Western theater: Union operations against New Orleans (continued): Farragut's squadron passes Forts Jackson and St. Philip. Following careful preparation and a breach in the water barrier, the ships of Flag Officer David G. Farragut's West Gulf Blockading Squadron proceed upriver and engage the Confederate forts, which return a heavy fire, and Confederate ships in the river, including the unfinished ironclad *Louisiana,* moored as a stationary battery along the riverbank. Once the Union ships are past the forts, the fate of New Orleans is sealed.

The toll is 1 Union ship rammed and sunk, while the Confederates lose the *Manassas* and 12 smaller vessels, 2 of them captured. Union casualties are surprisingly light: the total during April 18–26 is 39 killed and 171 wounded.

April 25–26, 1862

Civil War (continued): Eastern theater: Bombardment and capture of Fort Macon. Beginning in late March 1862, Union troops under Brigadier General John G. Park isolate Fort Macon, located on the Outer Banks near Atlantic Beach, North Carolina, and commanded by Colonel Moses J. White. On April 25, U.S. Navy commodore Samuel Lockwood with the coastal combatant *Daylight* (4 guns), the side-wheel combatant *State of Georgia* (9 guns), the screw gunboat *Chippewa* (4 guns), and the bark *Gemsbok* (6 guns) shells Fort Macon. With the fort's

masonry walls collapsing, White surrenders the next day. Park's troops then go ashore and take possession of the fort.

Union losses are 1 killed and 3 wounded. Confederate losses are 7 killed, 18 wounded (2 mortally), and some 400 captured. Two Confederate blockade-runners, the *Alliance* and *Gandar,* are also taken.

April 25–29, 1862

Civil War (continued): Western theater: Union operations against New Orleans (continued): Farragut secures New Orleans. The ships of his squadron having passed Forts Jackson and St. Philip and defeated Confederate naval forces in the lower Mississippi, Flag Officer David G. Farragut arrives with his West Gulf Blockading Squadron at New Orleans just after noon this day. High water places the guns of his ships above the tops of the levees and able to dominate the city. Farragut sends Captain Theodorus Bailey to demand the surrender of New Orleans. The city fathers and Confederate major general Mansfield Lovell, who commands the New Orleans defenses, refuse. Lovell then announces that he and his remaining troops will evacuate the city. That same day the Confederates burn their unfinished ironclad *Mississippi* and scuttle the cottonclad ram *Defiance* (1 gun) and the screw gunboat *McRae* (8 guns).

On the morning of April 26, Bailey again meets with the city leaders. Again they reject his surrender demand. But with the city poorly provisioned and indefensible, they state that they will not resist a Union takeover. At noon on April 29, 200 U.S. marines and several naval officers go ashore and assume official possession, raising the U.S. flag.

April 28, 1862

Civil War (continued): Western theater: Surrender of Forts Jackson and St. Philip. With Fort Jackson now cut off, on April 25 Commander David D. Porter demands that Confederate brigadier general Johnson K. Duncan surrender both that fort and naval vessels in the vicinity, including the ironclad *Louisiana* (16 guns). Duncan refuses, whereupon Porter commences a mortar bombardment. Although neither

Confederate fort had been seriously damaged in the lengthy earlier bombardment, the defenders have now had enough, and early on April 28 many desert. Later that same day Duncan comes aboard Porter's flagship, the *Harriet Lane* (4 guns), to surrender both forts. As this is occurring, Flag Officer John K. Mitchell, the senior Confederate naval commander on the river, sets fire to the *Louisiana* and cuts it free from its moorings to drift downriver. It blows up before it reaches the Union ships. Duncan assures Porter that the ironclad was not under his command and hence not bound by his surrender order.

April 29–May 30, 1862

Civil War (continued): Western theater: Halleck's Corinth Campaign. Major General Henry Halleck, commander of the Department of the Mississippi, takes charge of Union forces at Pittsburg Landing, Tennessee, on April 29, 1862, and proceeds to organize what will become the largest military force in the war to that date. Halleck combines the Army of the Tennessee, the Army of the Ohio, and the Army of the Mississippi into a single unit of more than 100,000 men. Major General Ulysses S. Grant is second-in-command. Halleck's objective is the key Confederate railhead of Corinth, Mississippi, 22 miles distant. Through it run the Memphis and Charleston and the Mobile and Ohio railroads.

General Pierre G. T. Beauregard commands the Confederate Army of Mississippi at Corinth. Following the Battle of Shiloh, on April 7 the army had fallen back to Corinth, abandoning much of its equipment. Beauregard, having only 30,000 men, calls for reinforcements. With the addition of Major General Earl Van Dorn's 14,000-man Army of the West in mid-April and other reinforcements, Beauregard has 70,000 men, but some 20,000 are ill or recovering from wounds.

Rolling terrain separates the two armies. Woody and in places swampy, it is traversed by numerous streams that can pose major obstacles. Indeed, the Union advance is slowed by heavy rains, which wash out roads and bridges and inhibit resupply. Still, Halleck's caution is the primary reason for the glacial Union advance. Halleck inches forward, entrenches, and then inches forward again. Grant is so frustrated that he threatens to leave the army altogether but is talked out of this by his friend Major General William T. Sherman.

By the middle of May, Halleck's army is only several miles from Corinth. Beauregard wants to attack the Union forces, but the attempt never occurs because Van Dorn, who is supposed to lead it off on May 22, fails to move on time. Beauregard sees no way to breach Halleck's lines without incurring heavy casualties. On May 25, he announces that supply shortages and other circumstances leave him no option but to abandon Corinth and save the army. Deceptions, including the use of bands playing music and soldiers cheering when trains arrive empty to evacuate the sick and wounded, Quaker guns to replace real ones in the line, and "deserters" spreading stories about the arrival of reinforcements, all succeed. During May 29–30, most of the Confederates depart, undetected by the Union side. Halleck takes only some 2,000 prisoners.

Halleck had written that Corinth and Richmond were the two strategic centers of the war, and he expresses great satisfaction with his success, despite Beauregard having escaped. Within two months, President Abraham Lincoln will call Halleck to Washington to assume command of the Union armies.

May 1, 1862

Civil War (continued): Western theater. Union troops under Major General Benjamin Butler occupy New Orleans. Butler's subsequent order to hang William B. Mumford, who has taken down a U.S. flag, and his Order No. 28 (the so-called Woman Order in which he orders that any woman who fails to show proper respect to U.S. soldiers is to be treated as a common prostitute) lead to his being known by the locals as "Beast Butler."

May 3, 1862

Civil War (continued): Eastern theater: Peninsula Campaign (continued): First use of land mines in the war. Confederate forces withdrawing from Yorktown, Virginia, leave behind "infernal machines," land mines in the form of shells buried beneath the

 **Land Mines**

Mining, in the sense of digging a tunnel under an enemy fortification in order to collapse it, is as old as siege warfare itself, and the use of gunpowder placed in the mine chambers dates from the second half of the 15th century. The notion of using explosive devises as smaller antipersonnel and later anti-vehicular weapons dates from the 19th century. Mines may be used offensively, as in attacks on vehicle convoys or infantry patrols, or defensively to protect one's own position against enemy attack.

The world's navies had employed so-called torpedoes at sea since the American Revolutionary War, but land torpedoes first appeared during the American Civil War. During his defense of Yorktown in the 1862 Peninsular Campaign, Confederate brigadier general Gabriel James Rains ordered 24-pounder artillery shells equipped with percussion fuses and then buried several inches below ground so that they would explode when stepped on. At the time, many on both sides of the war condemned the practice, the use of such devices being considered barbarous and outside civilized warfare, but as the war increased in severity, such moral prohibitions were largely ignored. Mines are both random and controlled. Random mines detonate when they are tripped. The four basic types of triggering devices are pressure, pressure-release, pull, and pull-release. Controlled mines are command-detonated by electronic means.

Mines were employed in World War I, but they became a defensive mainstay in World War II, especially in North Africa and in some of the great Eastern Front battles. The Germans also laid large numbers of mines as part of their defensive scheme known as the Atlantic Wall to protect against an Allied invasion of France. Mines are laid both in large groups, known as minefields, and individually.

One of the best known of World War II mines was the German Shrapnellmine 35, known to U.S. soldiers as the "Bouncing Betty." Set off either by pull wire or by direct pressure, a propellent charge ejected the mine from the ground. An anchor wire triggered the mine at waist height, and a single pound of explosive hurled 350 ball bearings in every direction. This mine was widely copied, the U.S. counterpart being the M-16.

The Germans had some 40 different types of antitank mines. The Tellermine 35 was typical. Made of steel, it was round in shape, 12.5 inches across, and 3.2 inches thick. It had a handle mounted on the side for ease in carrying. Weighing 20 pounds, it contained an explosive charge of 12 pounds of TNT. Its pressure plate would detonate the mine only with 250 pounds of pressure. It could also be fitted with an antilifting device so that once it was set in place, it would detonate if lifted.

In the post–World War II period new types of mines appeared, such as those of plastic that could not be located by metal detectors. The plastic U.S. M14 antipersonnel mine of the 1950s was designed to explode if stepped on. Antitank mines also became more sophisticated and employed shaped charges. Particularly effective was the new command-detonated direction-type antipersonnel M-18A1 Claymore mine employed by U.S. forces in Vietnam.

Mines continue to be employed in a wide variety of guises. They include the improvised explosive devices that often consist of the primitive rigged artillery shells employed by the insurgents in the Iraq War. It is not essential that antipersonnel mines kill their victims. Indeed, serious wounding is often more desirable; it imposes logistical problems on the enemy force and immobilizes soldiers who go to the aid of the victim.

Mines may be laid by hand, laid by plow behind a vehicle, projected by launch tubes from vehicles, dropped by aircraft, or deployed from special artillery projectiles. Mine detection and clearance is a very difficult and dangerous enterprise. It may be accomplished by hand (the mine probe or stick) and special metal detectors. A path through a minefield might be cleared and the mines set off by means of a flail of heavy chains, rollers, a plow in front of a tank, or an explosive line charge. Soviet marshal Georgi Zhukov told a shocked U.S. general Dwight Eisenhower that the quickest means to clear a minefield was to march penalty troops across it.

The millions of land mines that have been laid in wars and civil wars in several dozen countries around the world continue to claim thousands of innocent victims every year, and there is a world-wide effort to ban their use entirely. Following an effort led by Diana, Princess of Wales, and various human rights groups, representatives of 118 nations met in Ottawa, Canada, in December 1997 and there signed a treaty to ban land mines. As of March 2006, 115 nations had ratified the treaty. The major military powers of Great Britain, the People's Republic of China, Russia, and the United States were not among them.

SPENCER C. TUCKER

Further Reading

Croll, Mike. *The History of Land Mines*. Barnsley, UK: Leo Cooper, 1998.

Monin, L., and A. Gallimore. *The Devil's Gardens: A History of Land Mines*. London: Pimlico, 2002.

Sloan, C. E. E. *Mine Warfare on Land*. London: Brassey's, 1986.

surface. Brigadier General Gabriel J. Rains is criticized by his superiors for employing these, but such criticism is soon forgotten as the war winds on. Rains later develops a contact mine, set off by a pressure of several pounds.

May 5, 1862

Civil War (continued): Eastern theater: Peninsula Campaign (continued): Battle of Williamsburg. Near Williamsburg, Virginia, in the first major fighting of the campaign, a stubborn Confederate rearguard action prevents Union major general George B. McClellan's Army of the Potomac from encountering the main body of Confederate general Joseph Johnston's forces as they are withdrawing toward Richmond. Union brigadier general Winfield S. Hancock in a long flanking attack disrupts Confederate reinforcements, but Major General James Longstreet is able to extricate the Confederates by nightfall. The battle results in 2,239 Union and 1,703 Confederate casualties. Both sides claim victory.

May 8, 1862

Civil War (continued): Eastern theater: Jackson's Valley Campaign (continued): Battle of McDowell. In order to destroy Confederate forces in the northern part of the Shenandoah Valley under Major General Thomas J. "Stonewall" Jackson, U.S. president Abraham Lincoln orders the creation of three separate commands to converge on the Confederates: one under Major General Irvin McDowell, one under Major General Nathaniel Banks, and one under Major General John C. Frémont. No one officer has overall command, and this proves fatal for the Union effort.

General Robert E. Lee, military adviser to Confederate president Jefferson Davis, knowing that General Joseph E. Johnston has only 60,000 men to defend Richmond against Union major general George B. McClellan's 130,000 men, recommends that Jackson, now reinforced to some 17,000 men, demonstrate in the Shenandoah Valley to tie down as many Union troops as possible there. Davis approves.

James Longstreet (1821–1904)

Confederate general. Born in Edgefield District, South Carolina, on January 8, 1821, the son of a farmer, James Longstreet spent his early years in Augusta, Georgia, but on the death of his father moved with his mother to Somerville, Alabama. Longstreet secured an appointment to the U.S. Military Academy, West Point. There he became friends with Ulysses S. Grant. Graduating in 1842, Longstreet was commissioned a second lieutenant in the 4th Infantry Regiment and served in Louisiana and Missouri. He then served with the 8th Infantry Regiment in Florida.

During the Mexican-American War (1846–1848), Longstreet first served under Major General Zachary Taylor in northern Mexico and took part in the Battle of Monterrey on September 20–25, 1846. Longstreet then joined forces under Major General Winfield Scott in the Veracruz to Mexico City Campaign. Longstreet was breveted captain following the Battle of Churubusco (August 20, 1847) and major after the Battle of Molino del Rey (September 8, 1847). He was badly wounded in the Battle of Chapultepec (September 12–13, 1847).

With the beginning of the Civil War, Major Longstreet resigned from the U.S. Army on June 1, 1861, and accepted a commission as a brigadier general in the newly formed Confederate Army on June 17. He commanded troops in fighting at Centreville, Virginia, on July 18, then fought well in the First Battle of Bull Run (Manassas) on July 21. Promoted to major general on October 7, Longstreet commanded a division in the Yorktown Campaign and fought a skillful delaying action at Williamsburg on May 5, 1862. During the Battle of Seven Pines/Fair Oaks on May 31, however, his failure to move swiftly threw off Confederate commander General Joseph E. Johnston's plans, but Longstreet performed well under General Robert E. Lee during the Seven Days' Battles of June 25–July 1, 1862.

In command of five divisions, more than half of Lee's infantry, Longstreet was dispatched to join with forces under Major General Thomas J. Jackson, defeating Major General John Pope's Army of Virginia in the Second Battle of Bull Run (Manassas) (August 29–30, 1862). Although he opposed Lee's invasion of Maryland, Longstreet performed well at South Mountain on September 14 and in the Battle of Antietam (Sharpsburg) on September 17. He was promoted to lieutenant general in October, and in the Battle of Fredericksburg on December 13 his I Corps held Marye's Heights, defending it against numerous costly Union assaults.

In early 1863 Lee sent Longstreet on foraging operations (the Suffolk Campaign), and he thus missed the Battle of Chancellorsville. Following the death of Jackson from wounds sustained in that battle, Longstreet became Lee's chief subordinate, known as Lee's "Old War Horse." Longstreet opposed Lee's decision to fight at Gettysburg on July 1–3 and especially Lee's failed frontal assault (Pickett's Charge) on July 3.

Sent west with his men to reinforce General Braxton Bragg, Longstreet arrived there in time to fight in the Battle of Chickamauga (September 19–20, 1863), where he was able to take advantage of Major General William Rosecrans's critical error that shifted a Union division out of the line. Then while Bragg besieged Chattanooga, Longstreet moved against Union major general Ambrose E. Burnside at Knoxville but failed to dislodge him and had to begin a siege, which denied Bragg support at Chattanooga.

In April 1864 Longstreet rejoined Lee in Virginia, and Longstreet and his men fought effectively against the Union forces in Grant's Overland Campaign of 1864. Wounded in the Battle of the Wilderness on

May 5–6, Longstreet relinquished command to recuperate. Returning to duty in November, he fought in the remaining actions of the war near Petersburg and Richmond, serving with Lee's Army of Northern Virginia to the final surrender at Appomattox Court House on April 9, 1865.

After the war Longstreet alienated Southerners when he became a Republican, renewed his friendship with Grant, and served in a variety of U.S. government posts, including minister to Turkey in 1880. Many proponents of the Lost Cause found it easy to make Longstreet a scapegoat, blaming him, for example, for his delay in attacking on the second day of the Battle of Gettysburg as well as for mistakes made by Lee there. Longstreet wrote extensively to defend his role in that battle, publishing his memoirs in 1896. He initially settled in New Orleans, Louisiana, but he later moved to Gainesville, Georgia, where he died on January 2, 1904. Greatly respected by his men, who called him "Old Pete," Longstreet, while careful and judicious in his planning, was an able commander and tactician with a talent for defensive warfare. A fine corps commander, he lacked the aptitude for independent command.

SPENCER C. TUCKER

Further Reading

Eckenrode, H. J., and Bryan Conrad. *James Longstreet: Lee's War Horse.* Chapel Hill: University of North Carolina, 1986.

Freeman, Douglas Southall. *Lee's Lieutenants: A Study in Command.* 3 vols. New York: Scribner, 1970.

Longstreet, James. *From Manassas to Appomattox: Memoirs of the Civil War in America.* New York: Da Capo, 1992.

Wert, Jeffery D. *General James Longstreet.* New York: Simon and Schuster, 1993.

Jackson is at Swift Run Gap, Virginia. His intelligence is excellent, and his men are capable of such rapid movement that they become known as "Jackson's foot cavalry." Banks is moving slowly south up the valley with some 15,000 men, while Frémont with another 20,000 men is moving on Staunton from the west. Had Frémont and Banks combined forces, Jackson would have been overwhelmed.

Leaving 8,000 men under Major General Richard S. Ewell to contain Banks, on April 30 Jackson departs Swift Run Gap and moves rapidly westward with some 10,000 men to engage Frémont. On May 6, having endured driving rain, he arrives in Staunton with his men, having covered 92 miles on foot and another 25 miles by train. Pushing west, late on the afternoon of May 7 Jackson's leading elements, led by Brigadier General Edward "Allegheny" Johnson, encounter Brigadier General Robert H. Milroy's brigade, the leading element of Frémont's army. Milroy's men withdraw as Brigadier General Robert C. Schneck rushes to his support. Because he is senior to Milroy, Schneck assumes command, deploying his 6,000 Union troops around McDowell as the Confederates occupy the nearby key terrain feature of Stilington's Hill. On May 8 as Jackson is trying to figure out a way to the flank the Union position, Schneck attacks.

In the four-hour Battle of McDowell (also known as the Battle of Stilington's Hill), 2,800 Confederates turn back all assaults by 2,300 Union troops, personally led by Milroy and aimed at driving them from the hill. That night as Jackson personally leads the Stonewall Brigade onto the field, Schneck uses the cover of darkness to withdraw into the Alleghenies.

Jackson pursues the Union troops as far as Franklin (in present-day West Virginia) but gives up the pursuit on May 12 to return to the valley and move against Banks. In the Battle of McDowell, the Confederates lose 45 killed and 423 wounded; Union losses are only 26 killed, 227 wounded, and 3 missing.

May 8, 1862

Civil War (continued): Western theater: Union capture of Baton Rouge. On May 7, 1862, U.S. Navy flag officer David G. Farragut orders Commander James S. Palmer of the screw sloop *Iroquois* (6 guns) to secure both Baton Rouge, Louisiana, and Natchez, Mississippi. That same evening Palmer arrives off the Louisiana state capital. The next day he sends ashore a landing party to seize the arsenal and take possession of Baton Rouge without a shot being fired. Farragut arrives on May 10, landing 1,500 infantry to secure the city.

May 8, 1862

Civil War (continued). On the urging of U.S. president Abraham Lincoln, the U.S. Navy ironclad *Monitor* (2 guns), the 5-gun screw sloops *Dacotah* and *Seminole*, the side-wheel frigate *Susquehanna* (14 guns), and the small screw steamer *Naugatuck* (3 guns) attack Confederate batteries at Sewell's Point, Virginia. Lincoln, who is on the scene, prods Flag Officer Louis M. Goldsborough to make this attack with the hope of landing troops to threaten the Norfolk Navy Yard.

May 8, 1862

Civil War (continued): Siege of Fort Pillow (continued): On May 8 the Confederates send three rams against the Union mortar boats shelling Fort Pillow. These, however, are protected by three Union gunboats and are driven off. With U.S. flag officer Andrew Foote ailing (he has yet to recover from wounds sustained during the attack on Fort Donelson), on May 9 Flag Officer Charles H. Davis replaces him as commander of the Western Gunboat Flotilla.

May 10, 1862

Civil War (continued): Western theater: Siege of Fort Pillow (continued): Battle of Plum Point Bend. The Confederate naval sortie on May 8, 1862, should have been sufficient warning, but on May 10 at 7:00 a.m. with no Union lookouts posted and only one Union ironclad, the *Cincinnati*, protecting a mortar boat firing at Fort Pillow, eight Confederate gunboats suddenly round Craigshead Point. These are the *Little Rebel* (flagship, 3 guns), *General Bragg* (armament unknown), *General Sterling Price* (armament unknown), *General Earl Van Dorn* (1 gun), *General Sumter* (armament unknown), *General Thompson* (armament unknown), *General Beauregard* (5 guns), and *Colonel Lovell* (1 gun). Their commander, Captain James E. Montgomery, hopes to cut out or destroy the mortar boat and/or its covering gunboat. The other Union gunboats upstream endeavor to get under way; an hour later they are able to chase the Confederates downriver, but not before the Confederates have rammed and sunk the 14-gun ironclads *Cincinnati* and *Mound City*.

In the hour-long battle the Union side suffers only 4 wounded, 1 of whom later dies. While the Confederates have two of their gunboats disabled and up to 108 dead (largely as a consequence of burst steam boilers), they have won a tactical victory by temporarily disabling two much more powerful Union gunboats. Refloated, they are returned to Mound City for repairs.

During the course of the next three weeks, Flag Officer Charles H. Davis continues the steady, slow bombardment of Confederate positions.

May 10, 1862

Civil War (continued): Eastern theater: Confederate evacuation of the Gosport (Norfolk) Navy Yard. Confederate forces carry off such valuable equipment as they can, set the buildings afire, and destroy what remains. Union forces quickly retake Norfolk and occupy the nearby Gosport (Norfolk) Navy Yard at Portsmouth, what had been the largest prewar U.S. Navy yard.

May 10, 1862

Civil War (continued): Eastern theater: Confederate evacuation of the Pensacola Navy Yard. Their resources stretched thin and needing the troops and ordnance to defend against Union advances in the Western theater, Confederate authorities decide to evacuate Pensacola. The Confederates remove everything of value they can, then proceed to destroy the navy yard, Forts Barrancas and McRae, the steamer *Fulton*, and an ironclad under construction in the Pensacola River. Union brigadier general Lewis G. Arnold then leads

1,000 men across the bay from Fort Pickens to occupy Pensacola itself on May 12.

May 11, 1862

Civil War (continued). With the destruction of its base of the Gosport (Norfolk) Navy Yard and unable because of their ship's deep draft to make it up the James River, the Confederates blow up the ironclad ram *Virginia* near Craney Island, Virginia, to prevent its capture by advancing Union forces.

May 13, 1862

Civil War (continued). The screw sloop *Iroquois* (6 guns) under Commander James S. Palmer, having steamed from Baton Rouge, takes the surrender of Natchez, Mississippi.

May 13, 1862

Civil War (continued). Robert Smalls, a free African American working as a wheelman on the Confederate side-wheel steamer dispatch boat and transport *Planter* (2 guns), sails it out of Charleston Harbor with his family and a number of slaves, 16 people in all. Raising a white flag, he surrenders the ship to the Union blockader *Onward* (8 guns).

May 15, 1862

Civil War (continued): Eastern theater: First Battle of Drewry's Bluff. With destruction of the Confederate ironclad *Virginia*, President Abraham Lincoln presses Flag Officer Louis M. Goldsborough, commander of the North Atlantic Blockading Squadron, to take action. Goldsborough orders Commander John Rodgers Jr. to proceed up the James River to Richmond with the ironclads *Galena* (flagship, 6 guns), *Monitor* (2 guns), and *Naugatuck* (5 guns); the wooden screw gunboat *Aroostook* (4 guns); and the side-wheel steamer *Port Royal* (8 guns). Rodgers is instructed to shell the Confederate capital into submission.

At 6:30 a.m. on May 15, 1862, Rodgers's squadron arrives at the Confederate defenses at Drewry's Bluff, officially designated Fort Darling. It is an excellent defensive position, as the river takes a sharp bend here and narrows. The Confederates have 3 heavy guns on high cliffs on the south bank. They have

also sunk hulks in the river and used pile drivers to form a barrier of stone cribs and other debris. Commander John R. Tucker of the Confederate James River Squadron scuttles one of his two most powerful ships, the side-wheel steamer *Jamestown*, as an added obstruction, adding its 5 guns to the shore defenses. Tucker also positions the side-wheel steamer gunboat *Patrick Henry* (10 guns) behind the obstructions. Former crewmen of the *Virginia* assist in manning the guns ashore, while an infantry brigade occupies rifle pits along the riverbank. Before the Union crews can work at removing the obstructions, they must neutralize both the shore batteries and the Confederate infantrymen.

The battle opens at 7:45 a.m. and ends at about 11:00. The *Galena* bears the brunt of the fight, as the *Monitor's* guns cannot be sufficiently elevated to engage the guns on the bluff. Also, a Parrott rifle on the *Naugatuck* bursts halfway through the engagement, putting that ship out of action, while the *Port Royal* is kept busy engaging the Confederate infantry along the riverbank. Confederate fire reveals the serious shortcomings in the *Galena's* armor arrangement. Thirteen Confederate shots penetrate the ship, killing 13 crewmen and wounding 11. Corporal John B. Mackie of the *Galena* subsequently receives the Medal of Honor, the first marine so awarded. Southern losses in the battle are 7 killed and 8 wounded.

The Confederate stand here saves the capital. Rodgers claims that had troops been available and been landed, Drewry's Bluff would have been taken, and the campaign against Richmond might have worked out differently. The Confederates subsequently improve their defenses on the upper James, and by 1864 they have three ironclads here as well as an elaborate system of electrically detonated mines developed by Commander Matthew F. Maury.

May 18, 1862

Civil War (continued): Vicksburg refuses to surrender. Despite reservations about taking his big ships there because of the low water and lack of river pilots, commander of the West Gulf Blockading Squadron Flag Officer David G. Farragut orders the ships of his squadron to continue on to Vicksburg. The screw

 **Parrott Gun**

The most widely used rifled gun of the American Civil War (1861–1865), designed by Robert P. Parrott, superintendent of the West Point Foundry. Parrott guns were easy to operate, reliable, accurate, and relatively inexpensive to manufacture. Both sides produced them during the war. The Parrott was essentially a cast-iron rifled gun with a wrought-iron band shrunk over the breech, the point of greatest strain. The band was equal in thickness to half the diameter of the bore.

Parrott's first rifled gun was a 2.9-inch (land diameter) 10-pounder. Prior to the Civil War, Parrott also produced a 3.67-inch (20-pounder) and a 4.2-inch (30-pounder). Neither the U.S. Army nor the U.S. Navy, however, adopted the Parrott guns until after the start of the Civil War. During the war Parrotts were produced in bore diameters of 2.9-inch, 3-inch, 3.3-inch, 3.67-inch, 4.2-inch, 5.3-inch (60 pounder), 6.4-inch (100-pounder, army; 80-pounder, navy), 8-inch (200-pounder, army; 150-pounder, navy), and 10-inch (300-pounder, army; 250-pounder, navy). The guns had spiraled rifling, with from 3 grooves and lands on the 1.9-inch to 15 grooves and lands on the 10-inch.

The smallest U.S. Navy Parrott was the 3.67-inch. The larger guns were better suited to naval service, where weight was also not as much a factor as in field artillery on land. The 6.4-inch Parrott, for example, weighed some 9,800 pounds. With a powder charge of 10 pounds and at 35 degrees of elevation, it could fire its projectile more than five miles. The U.S. Navy employed the 8-inch Parrott in the turrets of some of its monitors, alongside a smoothbore Dahlgren.

The Parrott gun fired an elongated projectile some 3 calibers in length. Cylindro-conical in shape, it had a bronze ring at a contraction in the base. On ignition of the powder charge, the gas expanded the bronze ring into the grooves of the bore, thus imparting a spin to the projectile. Parrott projectiles were fitted with both time and percussion fuses, and there were also variations with hardened noses to pierce armor.

Both the army and the navy experienced problems during the war with Parrott guns bursting, most notably in operations against Charleston and Fort Fisher. Parrott blamed these on premature shell explosions rather than defects in the bore, but clearly these early rifled guns experienced greater problems than did the smoothbores, especially from grit and sand in the bores. Fewer navy guns burst, which was probably attributable to an order that all rifled projectiles be thoroughly greased before they were loaded. The navy did subsequently remove its heaviest Parrotts from service, however.

From the beginning of the war through April 1864, nearly 2,000 Parrotts were manufactured for the U.S. Army and the U.S. Navy, representing about one-fifth of Union guns on land and sea. The Confederates produced their own Parrotts at the Tredegar Iron Works in Richmond in 2.9-inch, 3-inch, 3.67-inch, and 4.2-inch sizes.

SPENCER C. TUCKER

Further Reading

Hazlett, James C., Edwin Olmstead, and M. Hume Parks. *Field Artillery Weapons of the Civil War*. Newark: Delaware University Press, 1983.

Olmstead, Edwin, Wayne Stark, and Spencer C. Tucker. *The Big Guns: Civil War Siege, Seacoast, and Naval Cannon*. Alexandria Bay, NY: Museum Restoration Service, 1997.

Tucker, Spencer C. *Arming the Fleet: U.S. Naval Ordnance in the Muzzle-Loading Era*. Annapolis, MD: Naval Institute Press, 1989.

sloop *Hartford* (flagship, 24 guns) runs aground but is gotten off two days later. The ships of the squadron straggle in and finally collect near Vicksburg.

With their defenses strengthened by the arrival of heavy guns and troops evacuated from New Orleans and other points in Mississippi, on May 18 Confederate authorities at Vicksburg confidently reject a Union surrender demand delivered by the screw sloop *Oneida* (10 guns). Farragut correctly determines that his resources are totally inadequate to take that city. The heavy Confederate guns are on the 200-foot-high bluffs that the Union guns cannot reach, and Vicksburg's several thousand defenders can be quickly augmented by railroad from Jackson. Even if the Union vessels could have shelled Vicksburg into submission, Farragut has only about 1,400–1,500 men under Brigadier General Thomas Williams, a totally insufficient force to hold the city.

On May 30 Farragut returns to New Orleans with most of his ships, leaving behind the troops and only half a dozen gunboats.

May 23, 1862

Civil War (continued): Eastern theater: Jackson's Valley Campaign (continued): Battle of Front Royal. Confederate major general Thomas J. "Stonewall" Jackson moves north, utilizing as a screen the 50-mile-long Massanutten Mountain that bisects the Shenandoah and Luray Valleys. He moves east through its one pass, at New Market, on May 21 and then turns north again. On May 23, his movements effectively screened by Colonel Turner Ashby's cavalry, Jackson attacks Union forces at Front Royal, Virginia, under Colonel John R. Kenly. The Confederates have about 3,000 men engaged; the Union side has 1,063. Forced back through the town, the Federals make a stand on Camp Hill and again on Guard Hill. Outnumbered and outflanked, Kenly withdraws to Cedarville. There two Confederate charges break through the Union lines and force a surrender. The Confederates suffer some 50 casualties; Union losses are 904: 32 killed, 122 wounded, and 750 taken prisoner.

This Southern victory threatens the rear of the Union army under Major General Nathaniel P. Banks and forces him into a rapid retreat northward toward Winchester early on May 24. Jackson follows.

May 24, 1862

Civil War (continued): Eastern theater. President Abraham Lincoln, alarmed by Confederate military successes in the Shenandoah Valley that might presage a descent on Washington, again orders Major General Irvin McDowell's corps to halt at Fredericksburg, thus preventing some 30,000 Union troops from joining Major General George B. McClellan's drive on Richmond.

May 25, 1862

Civil War (continued): Eastern theater: Jackson's Valley Campaign (continued): First Battle of Winchester. Union troops under Major General Nathaniel P. Banks race north to Winchester, closely followed by Confederate forces under Major General Thomas J. "Stonewall" Jackson. Following several skirmishes, Banks attempts to reorganize part of his force in defensive positions to hold the town. Meanwhile, Confederate brigadier general Richard S. Ewell's division drives on Winchester from the southeast, along the Front Royal Pike.

The fighting pits some 16,000 Confederates against 6,500 Union troops. The Confederates flank the Union position. The Union troops panic and flee north through Winchester and across the Potomac River, abandoning thousands of weapons as well as stocks of supplies. Jackson's men are too exhausted to pursue beyond several miles north of Winchester. In addition to the much-needed supplies, Jackson's men capture a large number of Union prisoners. Union casualties in the battle total 2,019; the Confederates lose perhaps 400.

This First Battle of Winchester spreads panic in Washington and fans fears of a descent on the federal capital by Jackson. President Abraham Lincoln recalls Major General Irvin McDowell's corps from its planned juncture with Union forces under Major General George B. McClellan advancing on Richmond from the east. This allows the Confederate defenders of Richmond to concentrate exclusively against McClellan.

Jackson, however, is in danger of being trapped on the Potomac. U.S. brigadier general James Shields, with 10,000 men of McDowell's command, captures Front Royal and moves west, trailed by another 10,000 Union troops. U.S. major general John C. Frémont is again advancing east with 15,000 men, 25 miles southeast of Winchester. Meanwhile, Banks is north of the Potomac reorganizing his command and preparing to move south again.

May 29–30, 1862

Civil War (continued): Western theater. Confederate general Pierre G. T. Beauregard abandons Corinth, Mississippi, for Tupelo. This action leaves Fort Pillow outflanked and untenable, and on June 4 the Confederates evacuate it as well.

May 31–June 1, 1862

Civil War (continued): Eastern theater: Peninsula Campaign (continued): Battle of Seven Pines. By May 14, U.S. major general George B. McClellan's 103,000-man Army of the Potomac reaches its advanced base on the Pamunkey River only 20 miles from Richmond. Opposing it is Confederate general Joseph E. Johnston's 60,000-man Army of the Potomac. Despite his overwhelming strength, McClellan halts to await the arrival from the north of Major General Irvin McDowell's 30,000-man corps, which has been recalled by President Abraham Lincoln.

McClellan's army is extended in a great "V"; the upper leg stretches out to meet McDowell, while the lower reaches just beyond Fair Oaks Station, within five miles of Richmond. Union troops are on both sides of the Chickahominy River: three corps on the north shore to protect his supply line and facilitate a linkup with McDowell and two corps south of it.

On May 31 General Johnston, having been informed that the Union threat from the north posed by McDowell's corps has evaporated with its recall, attacks the two Union corps on the south bank of the Chickahominy isolated from the main part of the Union army by the flooded river. Only the timely arrival of another Union corps that manages to cross the river prevents a disastrous defeat.

In the Battle of Seven Pines (Fair Oaks), each side commits about 42,000 men. McClellan gains a tactical victory. Casualties are heavy. The Union sustains 5,031 casualties (780 killed, 3,594 wounded, and 647 taken prisoner or missing); the Confederates suffer 6,134 (980 killed, 4,749 wounded, and 405 missing or captured). The battle marks a significant turning point in the war, as it ends McClellan's offensive. Also, Johnston is among the severely wounded. He is temporarily succeeded by Major General Gustavus W. Smith, but on June 1 Confederate president Jefferson Davis names General Robert E. Lee commander of the Confederate Army of the Potomac, which now becomes known as the Army of Northern Virginia. The battle also unnerves the overly cautious McClellan, already reluctant to commit his men.

June 4, 1862

Civil War (continued): Western theater. Confederate forces abandon Fort Pillow, Tennessee, allowing Union naval forces to move downriver on the Mississippi against Memphis.

June 6, 1862

Civil War (continued): Western theater: Battle of Memphis. With the Confederates having abandoned Fort Pillow on June 4, the next day Flag Officer Charles H. Davis's Union flotilla, reinforced by the seven converted river steamers of the War Department's new Mississippi Ram Fleet flotilla under Colonel Charles Ellet Jr., steams south past Fort Pillow, arriving just above Memphis that evening.

The battle for Memphis begins early on June 6; it ends with the destruction of seven of eight Confederate gunboats. Only one, the *General Earl Van Dorn* (1 gun), manages to escape southward to Vicksburg. The Confederates surrender Memphis. The Union side suffers only four casualties and one badly damaged ram. Colonel Ellet, one of the wounded, dies two weeks later. The Union has ended Confederate naval power on the Mississippi and added additional shipping to its flotilla. The battle also gives the Union the fifth-largest city in the Confederacy, along with control of four key rail lines and important manufacturing resources, including a naval yard that soon becomes a principal Union base. The Mississippi is now open all the way south to Vicksburg.

June 8, 1862

Civil War (continued): Eastern theater: Jackson's Valley Campaign (continued): Battle of Cross Keys. U.S. president Abraham Lincoln orders Major General Irvin McDowell to send 20,000 men (10,000 each under Brigadier General James Shields and Major General Edward Ord) to Front Royal and Major General John C. Frémont to move east to Harrisonburg. If these two forces can meet at Strasburg, they can cut Confederate major general Thomas J. "Stonewall" Jackson's escape route south up the valley.

Moving swiftly, Jackson avoids the Union trap, withdrawing his 15,000 men along with 2,000 Union prisoners and captured Union supplies. Clearing Winchester on May 31, he passes through Strasburg and gains Harrisonburg on June 5. Jackson leaves Brigadier General Richard S. Ewell to hold Union troops under Frémont at Cross Keys, while he and the rest of his command move to Port Republic to meet the Union forces under Shields.

In the Battle of Cross Keys on June 8, Ewell's three brigades of some 5,000 men repulse Frémont's attack, then occupy the former Union positions. That night most of the Confederates march to aid Jackson at Port Republic. Those who remain fall back the next day.

June 9, 1862

Civil War (continued): Eastern theater: Jackson's Valley Campaign (continued): Battle of Port Republic. Major General Thomas J. "Stonewall" Jackson concentrates his forces at Port Republic, east of the South Fork of the Shenandoah River. Union brigadier general James Shields's division is at Conrad's Store. He sends forward two brigades to probe the Confederate position and appeals to Major General John C. Frémont to hurry to join him. Jackson orders an attack, which is repulsed with heavy casualties. He then sends Brigadier General Richard Taylor's brigade through the woods, turning the Union left and forcing a withdrawal. Jackson, with about 6,000 men, has defeated 3,500 Union troops. The Union suffers

1,008 losses (558 prisoners), but Confederate losses have been heavy, with 816 casualties.

Brigadier General Richard S. Ewell has sent most of his men from Cross Keys to join Jackson at Port Republic. They burn the North River Bridge behind them. Frémont arrives too late to be of assistance at Port Republic and can only watch helplessly from across the rain-swollen river.

The Battle of Port Republic is the final victory in Jackson's remarkable Shenandoah Valley Campaign. During a span of 48 days with never more than 18,000 men, Jackson's men have marched 646 miles and defeated three Union armies totaling four times his own strength in four pitched battles, six large skirmishes, and numerous minor actions. Jackson has inflicted some 8,000 Union casualties for fewer than 2,500 losses of his own.

Jackson now moves swiftly east to take part in the critical battles for Richmond.

June 10, 1862

Civil War (continued): Western theater. U.S. major general Henry W. Halleck, commander of the Armies of the West, authorizes his subordinate commanders to resume independent operations. He restricts Major General Ulysses S. Grant to the Mississippi River Valley and sends Major General Don Carlos Buell into Tennessee.

June 12–16, 1862

Civil War (continued): Eastern theater: Peninsula Campaign (continued): Stuart's Raid. Some 1,200 cavalrymen of the Confederate Army of Northern Virginia, ably commanded by Brigadier General James Ewell Brown ("Jeb") Stuart, set out on a reconnaissance in force. They end up riding around the entire Union Army of the Potomac, further unnerving its commander, Major General George B. McClellan; destroying valuable Union stores; and securing significant intelligence on troop dispositions.

June 17, 1862

Civil War (continued): Western theater. General Braxton Bragg replaces General Pierre G. T. Beauregard in command of the Confederacy's Western theater. To

James Ewell Brown Stuart (1833–1864)

U.S. Army and Confederate Army officer, probably the best-known cavalry commander of the American Civil War on either side. James Ewell Brown ("Jeb") Stuart was born at the family farm of Laurel Hill in Patrick County, Virginia, on February 6, 1833. During 1848–1850 he attended Emory and Henry College but left to enter the U.S. Military Academy, West Point, from which he graduated in 1854.

Commissioned in the Mounted Rifles, Stuart was assigned to Fort Davis, Texas. In 1853 he transferred to the 1st Cavalry Regiment. He spent much of the next six years on frontier duty in so-called Bleeding Kansas. Stuart was promoted to first lieutenant on December 20, 1855.

In November 1859, Stuart traveled to Washington, D.C., to discuss a government contract for a hook he had invented with which to attach a saber to a cavalryman's belt. While there, Colonel Robert E. Lee, who had been superintendent at West Point when Stuart was a cadet, requested and secured him as his aide to go with Lee and a company of marines to Harpers Ferry to subdue the insurrection led by John Brown.

Stuart returned to Kansas and was promoted to captain on April 22, 1861, but with the secession of Virginia he resigned his U.S. Army commission on May 10 and accepted a commission as a lieutenant colonel in the Virginia Infantry. He then organized the 1st Virginia Cavalry Regiment at Harpers Ferry and was commissioned a colonel in the Confederate Army on July 16. Stuart distinguished himself in the First Battle of Bull Run (Manassas) (July 21, 1861), where he led a charge that helped ensure the Confederate victory. Receiving command of a brigade, he was promoted to brigadier general on September 24.

During the March–August 1862 Peninsula Campaign, Stuart was charged with determining whether the Union right flank was vulnerable to attack. Having accomplished this mission rather than simply return to camp, with his 1,200 men he rode entirely around the Union army, covering 150 miles and taking a number of prisoners, horses, and supplies and helping to unnerve already cautious Union commander Major General George B. McClellan. The ride made Stuart famous throughout the South.

Stuart commanded more men during the Seven Days' Campaign (June 25–July 1, 1862) and took part in the pursuit of the withdrawing Union forces. He then took part in the Battle of Malvern Hill (July 1) but prematurely opened fire with an artillery piece that revealed his presence and may have cost the Confederates victory. This did not prevent his promotion to major general on July 25, and he took command of all cavalry in the Army of Northern Virginia.

Stuart raided Union commander Major General John Pope's headquarters at Catlett's Station on August 22–23, covered Major General Thomas J. "Stonewall" Jackson's advance to Bristoe Station and Manassas, and aided him at the Battle of Groveton (August 28). Stuart then took part in the Confederate invasion of Maryland, culminating in the Battle of Antietam (September 17). During October 10–11, he led 1,800 men in a raid on Chambersburg, Pennsylvania, in an unsuccessful effort to destroy the iron bridge over Conococheague Creek but circumnavigated the Army of the Potomac for a second time. During the Battle of Fredericksburg (December 13, 1862), Stuart had command of the artillery on the Confederate right.

That winter Stuart's men held the Confederate line south of the Rappahannock River and provided timely intelligence to Lee on the Union crossing that culminated in the Battle of Chancellorsville (May

1–4, 1863). During that battle Stuart's men helped protect Jackson's flanking movement against Union cavalry. When Jackson was wounded, Stuart took temporary command of his corps. On June 9, 1863, Stuart and his men were surprised by a Union attack led by Major General Alfred Pleasanton that ended in the largest cavalry battle ever fought in North America, at Brandy Station.

Stuart, who until this point had enjoyed Lee's full confidence and praise, played a controversial role in the June–July Gettysburg Campaign. Lee assigned Stuart the task of protecting the right flank of the Army of Northern Virginia in its movement north but gave the always reliable Stuart discretionary powers. But a large Union concentration prevented Stuart from crossing the Potomac until June 27–28 and then farther east than he intended. This cut him off from Confederate forces under Lieutenant General Richard S. Ewell, but rather than trying to close with Ewell, Stuart proceeded north on his own. Stuart's reputation for reliability led Lee to mistakenly assume that the federal Army of the Potomac was still in its camps north of the Rappahannock and led to Lee being forced to fight at Gettysburg (July 1–3, 1863). Stuart arrived only on the afternoon of July 2, incurring a rebuke from Lee.

After Gettysburg, the flamboyant Stuart always remained in close contact with Lee. Stuart's cavalry provided invaluable information on Union movements at the Overland Campaign (May 4–June 12, 1864).

Stuart was mortally wounded in the Battle of Yellow Tavern, Virginia, on May 11, 1864, when his 4,500 cavalrymen attempted to halt 10,000 Union cavalry under Major General Philip H. Sheridan. Stuart died the next day. While the flamboyant Stuart was known as the "Confederate cavalier," he was an uncommonly able cavalry commander who excelled in reconnaissance and the employment of cavalry in support of offensive infantry operations.

SPENCER C. TUCKER

Further Reading

Longacre, Edward G. *The Cavalry at Gettysburg.* Lincoln: University of Nebraska Press, 1986.

Longacre, Edward G. *Lee's Cavalrymen: A History of the Mounted Forces of the Army of Northern Virginia.* Mechanicsburg, PA: Stackpole, 2002.

Wert, Jeffry D. *Cavalryman of the Lost Cause: A Biography of J. E. B. Stuart.* New York: Simon and Schuster, 2008.

Wittenberg, Eric J., and J. David Petruzzi. *Plenty of Blame to Go Around: Jeb Stuart's Controversial Ride to Gettysburg.* New York: Savas Beatie, 2006.

prevent Union major general Don Carlos Buell from securing the important Chattanooga railhead, Bragg shifts most of his forces to southeastern Tennessee.

June 17, 1862
Civil War (continued): Trans-Mississippi West theater. The U.S. Navy ironclad *Mound City* (14 guns) under Commander Augustus H. Kilty is hit and suffers serious damage in an artillery duel with Confederate shore batteries on the White River near Charles City, Arkansas. Other Union ships tow the stricken ship to safety. The shore batteries are neutralized by accompanying troops, and the White River is opened to Union patrols.

June 18, 1862
Civil War (continued): Western theater: Union forces occupy Cumberland Gap. With manpower required elsewhere, the Confederates abandon Cumberland Gap, Tennessee. Union troops under Brigadier General George W. Morgan take possession of the Gap and begin to fortify it.

June 25–July 1, 1862

Civil War (continued): Eastern theater: Peninsula Campaign (continued): Seven Days' Battles. In a move to drive Union major general George B. McClellan's Army of the Potomac of some 103,000 men from the Virginia Peninsula, Confederate commander General Robert E. Lee, having gathered 97,000 men (the largest force he ever commands), plans to send forces under Major General Thomas J. "Stonewall" Jackson, just arrived from the Shenandoah Valley, to attack Major General Fitz John Porter's corps on the north side of the Chickahominy River. With most of his army concentrated just west of Mechanicsville, Lee will move against McClellan's center.

The offensive is poorly handled, though. Jackson, physically spent by the just-concluded Shenandoah Valley Campaign, fails to command effectively and displays uncharacteristic lethargy. His men never get into the fight in the Battle of Mechanicsville on June 26. Porter rebuffs the uncoordinated Confederate assaults and, learning of Jackson's approach, retires to Gaines' Mill.

Lee again attacks Porter on June 27 in the Battle of Gaines' Mill. Jackson is again late arriving and fails to get in behind Porter's right flank as Lee desires. Lee manages to penetrate Porter's left, however. In danger of a double envelopment with the approach of Jackson, Porter withdraws in good order, thanks to the timely arrival of Union reinforcements.

That night on McClellan's order, Porter withdraws to the south bank of the Chickahominy. Ignoring appeals from Brigadier General Philip Kearny and Major General Joseph E. Hooker that Richmond is his for the taking if he will only order offensive action, McClellan withdraws to the James River and protection by Union gunboats. During June 29–30 Lee pursues and suffers sharp rebuffs at the hands of Union forces in battles at Peach Orchard, Savage's Station, White Oak Swamp, and Glendale-Frayser's Farm. Jackson again fails to envelop the Union right flank.

In the Battle of Malvern Hill on July 1, in the absence of McClellan, Porter exercises command, and the Army of the Potomac, supported by the heavy guns in the Union river squadron, withstands Lee's desperate attacks. The Army of Northern Virginia suffers more than 5,000 casualties in the span of a few hours. Although it is a clear Union victory, McClellan orders an immediate retreat to Harrison's Landing. The next day, the Confederates withdraw toward Richmond. The Peninsula Campaign is over.

Casualties in the Seven Days' Battles are Union, 15,855 (1,734 killed, 8,066 wounded, 6,055 missing/captured) and Confederates, 20,204 (3,494 killed, 15,758 wounded, and 952 missing/captured). McClellan has fumbled away victory. With a little more energy, the war might have been ended or drastically shortened. McClellan, however, is so fearful of losing that he will not risk winning.

June 28, 1862

Civil War (continued): Western theater: Farragut's West Gulf Blockading Squadron passes Vicksburg. Under orders from U.S. secretary of the navy Gideon Welles that the Mississippi River be cleared, in late June 1862 West Gulf Blockading Squadron commander Flag Officer David G. Farragut makes yet another attempt against Vicksburg, this time in conjunction with Flag Officer Charles H. Davis's Mississippi River flotilla, which proceeds from the north to just above Vicksburg. This time, Farragut brings with him Captain David D. Porter's flotilla of 12 mortar boats, recalled from Ship Island.

Meanwhile, U.S. Army brigadier general Thomas Williams with 3,000 men is digging a canal across the

Seven Days' Battles		
Date	June 25–July 1, 1862	
Location	West of Mechanicsville near Richmond, Virginia	
Opponents (*winner)	*Confederacy	United States
Commander	General Robert E. Lee	Major General George B. McClellan
#	97,000 men	103,000 men
Casualties	20,204 (3,494 killed, 15,758 wounded, and 952 missing/captured)	15,855 (1,734 killed, 8,066 wounded, 6,055 missing/captured)

Joseph Hooker (1814–1879)

Union Army general. Born in Hadley, Massachusetts, on November 13, 1814, Joseph Hooker graduated from the U.S. Military Academy, West Point, in 1837 and served in the Second Seminole War and the Mexican-American War, winning three brevets for gallantry in action. In 1853 he resigned his commission and spent the next eight years as a farmer in Sonoma, California. As had been his tendency while in uniform, he did a good deal of drinking, wenching, and gambling.

Returning to the army with the outbreak of war in 1861, Hooker received a brigadier general's commission in August, backdated to May, and was soon commanding a division in the Army of the Potomac. During the Peninsula Campaign Hooker established a reputation for skillful and aggressive generalship, winning a promotion to major general for his role in the Battle of Williamsburg on May 5, 1862. Through a newspaper typesetting error he also won the nickname "Fighting Joe" (the headline was supposed to have read "Fighting—Joe Hooker"). The name stuck, much to Hooker's annoyance. He was even more annoyed with and openly critical of his commander, Major General George McClellan, for the timid, halting way in which McClellan conducted the campaign.

Hooker rose to command I Corps during the Antietam Campaign (September 1862) and acted with his usual skill and aggressiveness in the Battles of South Mountain and Antietam, at the latter of which he was forced to leave the field early in the day by a wound in the foot. In October, President Abraham Lincoln removed McClellan from command and replaced him with Major General Ambrose Burnside. Burnside organized the army's seven corps into three grand divisions, with Hooker commanding one of them. In December 1862 Burnside led the Army of the Potomac to defeat at the First Battle of Fredericksburg, sending many of Hooker's troops to their deaths in repeated futile uphill assaults against a strong Confederate line. Hooker's denunciations of Burnside after the battle rose almost to the level of insubordination. Burnside was determined to purge Hooker and other malcontents from the army.

Before Burnside could act, Lincoln removed him from command, elevating Hooker in his place. Hooker set out to improve the army's administration and morale. The troops were soon enjoying better rations and equipment and such morale-building steps as the addition of unit patches to their uniforms. On the other hand, Hooker continued to exercise his long-standing vices, and one officer noted that headquarters was a combination of "a barroom and a brothel." As he prepared for the spring campaign against the Confederate army of General Robert E. Lee, Hooker's dispatches to Washington exuded confidence—even cocksureness—to a degree that worried Lincoln.

When Hooker actually led his army to face Lee in what became known as the Chancellorsville Campaign, Hooker's demeanor changed dramatically. No sooner had his leading elements made contact with the Confederates than he seemed to lose all confidence and pulled his army back into an area known as the Wilderness, where dense foliage negated most of his advantage in numbers and artillery. There he remained inert, almost cowering, leaving the initiative in Confederate hands, while Lee and Major General Thomas J. "Stonewall" Jackson combined to strike his army in flank and attack some of its isolated elements in detail, winning one of the most dramatic long-odds victories in the history of warfare. During the battle, a shell struck Hooker's headquarters, stunning him for hours but making no significant change in his direction of the army. After retreating back to the army's prebattle camps, Hooker loudly blamed several subordinates for the failure.

(continued)

(Continued)

When Lee moved north in what became the Gettysburg Campaign, Hooker followed with the Army of the Potomac, but his messages to Washington betrayed a reluctance to bring the Confederates to battle again. When general-in-chief Major General Henry W. Halleck refused Hooker's demand for authority to withdraw the garrison of Harpers Ferry, Hooker requested to be relieved of command. Lincoln lost no time in granting his request, replacing him with Major General George Gordon Meade.

That autumn Hooker was assigned to command a two-corps detachment of the Army of the Potomac sent to reinforce the Army of the Cumberland at Chattanooga. Hooker performed well in the operation, successfully capturing Lookout Mountain and flanking the Rebel line on Missionary Ridge, though he suffered a severe setback at Ringgold Gap while attempting pursuit of the retreating enemy. The following spring, Hooker commanded a corps in Major General William T. Sherman's army group advancing toward Atlanta. Again Hooker performed well. In July the command of the Army of the Tennessee came open, and Hooker was furious when Sherman chose Major General Oliver O. Howard for the position. Angry at being passed over, Hooker asked to be relieved.

Hooker served out the rest of the war in insignificant commands in the North. When a stroke left him paralyzed on one side of his body, he retired from the army in October 1868. Hooker died in Garden City, New Jersey, on October 31, 1879.

STEVEN E. WOODWORTH

Further Reading

Hebert, Walter H. *Fighting Joe Hooker*. Indianapolis: Bobbs-Merrill, 1944.
Longacre, Edward G. *The Commanders of Chancellorsville*. Nashville, TN: Rutledge Hill, 2005.
Sears, Stephen W. *Chancellorsville*. Boston: Houghton Mifflin, 1996.

mile-wide peninsula formed by the U-shaped bend in the river on which Vicksburg is located in the hopes of bypassing Vicksburg's land batteries.

With the mortar flotilla positioned on both sides of the river and providing covering fire, Farragut's ships begin their passage at 4:00 a.m. on June 28. The squadron includes the steam sloops *Richmond* (22 guns), *Hartford* (24 guns), and *Brooklyn* (26 guns) and 14 gunboats. A three-mile-long exchange between the ships and the Confederate batteries on the bluffs and along the riverbank ensues. By 6:00 a.m., the first of Farragut's ships has passed through the gauntlet of Confederate fire to join Lieutenant Colonel Alfred W. Ellet's Ram Fleet, the leading element of Davis's flotilla that has come downriver from Memphis. The *Brooklyn* and two accompanying gunboats fail to make it through, however. Although Farragut has not lost a ship, his squadron has sustained some damage and 10 killed and 30 wounded; Porter's mortar flotilla suffers 8 killed and 10–12 wounded. At Vicksburg, Brigadier General Martin L. Smith reports that not a single Confederate gun has been lost in the exchange.

While this dash past Vicksburg proves that the Union ships can pass back and forth at relatively slight cost, Farragut is now more convinced than ever that taking Vicksburg is a matter for ground troops. He informs Major General Henry W. Halleck at Corinth, Mississippi, via courier that the Confederates have some 8,000–10,000 ground troops in place, a force sufficient to prevent the relatively small number of Union troops from landing. Farragut requests reinforcements "to carry out the order of the President." This request does not seem unreasonable, given that Halleck commands some 120,000 men, but the latter replies that he can spare no men. Taking Vicksburg must await a more aggressive Union area commander.

July 2, 1862
Civil War (continued). In Washington, D.C., the U.S. Congress passes and President Abraham Lincoln signs into law the Morrill Act for land-grant colleges. The act provides millions of acres of land and other incentives to the individual states for educational purposes—chiefly to establish agricultural colleges and universities. The act is expanded in 1863 to specify that the student curricula must include military science, the forerunner of today's Reserve Officer Training Corps (ROTC).

July 5, 1862
Civil War (continued). The U.S. Navy Department is reorganized with the addition of three new bureaus to the five existing. The new bureaus are Equipment and Recruiting, Navigation, and Steam Engineering.

July 11, 1862
Civil War (continued). President Abraham Lincoln orders Major General Henry Halleck from the Western theater to Washington as general-in-chief, and Major General George B. McClellan is ordered to bring the Army of the Potomac back to Washington (August 3).

July 12, 1862
Civil War (continued). The U.S. Congress makes available for soldiers the Medal of Honor, established in December 1861 for the U.S. Navy and the U.S. Marine Corps.

July 13, 1862
Civil War (continued): Western theater: Forrest's raid on Murfreesboro. Early this morning, Colonel Nathan Bedford Forrest and some 1,500 Confederate cavalrymen descend on strategically important Murfreesboro, Tennessee, garrisoned by 1,040 Union soldiers in two infantry regiments camped one and a half miles apart. Almost immediately the Confederates capture Union commander Brigadier General Thomas T. Crittenden. Forrest then succeeds in convincing the

commander of the 9th Michigan Regiment, Lieutenant Colonel John G. Parkhurst, that the rest of the garrison has been taken and that no quarter will be given should he not surrender immediately. The issue is put to a vote, and the officers decide unanimously to surrender.

Forrest then turns his attention to the 3rd Minnesota Regiment, commanded by Colonel Henry Lester, with four artillery pieces, sending in the same demand. Given proof that the other regiment has surrendered, Lester follows suit. In addition to some 1,100–1,200 prisoners, Forrest secures considerable supplies and the artillery. After burning the railroad depot and the supplies he cannot carry off, Forrest withdraws with his prisoners. His own casualties total some 25 killed and 100 wounded. Union losses are 19–20 killed and 1,100–1,200 prisoners, including 120 wounded.

July 14, 1862
The U.S. Congress passes legislation abolishing the daily spirit (rum) ration for naval personnel. President Abraham Lincoln signs the bill, and it goes into effect on this date. The legislation substitutes a pay increase of five cents per day.

July 15, 1862
Apache Wars (continued): Battle of Apache Pass (Fort Bowie). In early 1862, Colonel James H. Carleton sets out from California with 2,300 men in his California Column to attack Confederate forces in New Mexico Territory. On May 20, Carleton's men roust a small number of Confederates who have taken possession of Tucson. Carleton then prepares to move east via Apache Pass in southeastern Arizona. He sends an advance force under Captain Thomas L. Roberts of 22 cavalrymen and 116 infantry with two 12-pounder howitzers. They also have 21 wagons and 242 mules and horses.

After the troops enter Apache Pass, they come under attack by as many as 500 Apache warriors under Mangas Coloradas and Cochise (and possibly Geronimo). The two howitzers are the difference, inflicting most of the Apache casualties and driving off the attackers. Two soldiers are killed, and 3 are wounded;

the Apaches suffer 66 killed and an unknown number wounded.

July 15, 1862

Civil War (continued): Western theater: CSS *Arkansas* runs past the Union squadrons above Vicksburg. Flag Officers David G. Farragut and Charles H. Davis and Brigadier General Thomas Williams send a reconnaissance force of ships up the Yazoo. The Confederate ironclad ram *Arkansas* (8 guns) had been moved from Memphis up the White to Yazoo City and there completed. The Union ships are the ironclad *Carondelet* (14 guns), the timberclad *Tyler* (7 guns), and the ram *Queen of the West* (4 guns).

On July 15, 1862, rounding a bend in the river, the Union ships suddenly encounter the more powerful *Arkansas,* which immediately attacks. As the Union ships flee back downriver, the *Arkansas* fires on them with its bow guns, scoring 13 hits on the unprotected stern of the *Carondelet* and forcing it into shallow water, where it grounds. The Confederate fire also damages the *Tyler.*

At 8:00 a.m. the *Arkansas* exits the Yazoo into the Mississippi. Steaming south under full power, it passes some 20 unprepared Union ships in the two squadrons without their steam up, trading broadsides with many of them. Perhaps to the surprise of its own crew, the *Arkansas* gets through and docks at Vicksburg.

An embarrassed and angry Farragut attempts to destroy the *Arkansas* as he runs his ships south past Vicksburg later that same day. It is dark when the Union ships reach the city, and the attempt fails, as does an effort by the ironclad *Essex* (6 guns) and the ram *Queen of the West* (4 guns) early on July 22. Farragut returns to the Gulf of Mexico with the bulk of his ships to resume operations there.

July 16, 1862

Civil War (continued). The U.S. Congress authorizes the rank of rear admiral, the first in U.S. history. Four men are promoted: David G. Farragut is first in order of preexisting seniority. He is followed by Louis M. Goldsborough, Samuel F. Du Pont, and Andrew H. Foote. The legislation also establishes the ranks of commodore, heretofore an honorific title, and lieutenant commander.

July 17, 1862

Civil War (continued). Major General Henry W. Halleck arrives in Washington and assumes the position of general-in-chief. His departure from the Western theater enables Major General Ulysses S. Grant to exercise greater freedom of command in western Tennessee.

July 17, 1862

Civil War (continued): Second Confiscation and Militia Acts. The U.S. Congress approves the Second Confiscation Act that frees slaves owned by disloyal citizens, regardless if they are employed in the Confederate war effort or on farms and plantations. This is essentially the same as Major John C. Frémont's emancipation proclamation of the year before (see August 30, 1861). Although limited in scope, it is regarded as the first legal emancipation proclamation. It also authorizes the president to "employ as many persons of African descent as he may deem necessary and proper for the suppression of this rebellion, and for this purpose he may organize and use them in such manner as he may judge best for the public welfare."

At the same time Congress passes the Militia Act, allowing the drafting of some 300,000 militiamen into the U.S. Army. The act also provides that persons of African descent may be enlisted in the U.S. Army "for the purpose of constructing intrenchments, or performing camp service or any other labor, or any military or naval service for which they may be found competent." Eventually some 186,000 blacks comprising 163 units will serve in the Union Army (constituting some 10 percent of the force) and take part in some 449 military engagements during the war. Another 19,000 will serve in the U.S. Navy, constituting 15–16 percent of its personnel.

July 17, 1862

Civil War (continued): Creation of national cemeteries. In Washington, D.C., mounting military deaths lead the U.S. Congress to pass legislation empowering President Abraham Lincoln to purchase grounds as "a national cemetery for the soldiers who shall die in the service of the country." Fourteen national cemeteries are created in 1862. Since that time, more than 3 million burials have taken place in national cemeteries now under jurisdiction of the National Cemetery Administration. In 2011 there were 128 existing national cemeteries with more than 16,000 acres of land.

July 18, 1862

Civil War (continued): Western theater: Confederate Newburgh raid. Captain Adam R. Johnson leads 35 men, mostly partisans and the majority recruited at Henderson, Kentucky, across the Green and Ohio Rivers on a raid against Newburgh, Indiana. The chief prize is an arsenal storing arms for 200 future recruits.

Johnson secures these, and he then bluffs into surrender a U.S. Army medical service colonel named Bethel, commanding a makeshift Union hospital in the nearby Exchange Hotel where 80 wounded Union soldiers are convalescing. Johnson bluffs Bethel into surrendering by telling him that he is both outnumbered and surrounded and that if he refuses to surrender Johnson will shell the town with his cannon. He hands Bethel a spyglass, with which the colonel can see what appear to be two distant guns, actually Quaker guns consisting of a stove pipe and a charred log mounted on two pairs of wheels from an abandoned wagon. The town secured, Johnson paroles the captured Union personnel and escapes back to Kentucky with the weapons and medical supplies. Subsequently, 2 Newburgh residents who had assisted the Confederates are killed by a mob, and 6 others are imprisoned. Johnson, now known as "Stovepipe," receives promotion to colonel. As a consequence of the raid, however, Indiana governor Oliver H. P. T. Morton is able to secure additional arms with which to defend the state.

July 23, 1862

Civil War (continued): Western theater. At Tupelo, Mississippi, General Braxton Bragg oversees the transfer of 31,000 Confederate troops to Chattanooga, 776 miles distant, in the largest movement of Confederate troops by rail during the war.

August 5–6, 1862

Civil War (continued): Western theater: Battle of Baton Rouge and destruction of CSS *Arkansas.* Some 4,000 Confederates of the Vicksburg garrison led by Major General John C. Breckinridge attack Baton Rouge, Louisiana, defended by about 3,200 entrenched Union troops, commanded by Brigadier General Thomas Williams, who were landed there by Rear Admiral David G. Farragut's ships in late July. Many of the Union troops are incapacitated by fever. Although a number leave their sickbeds to join the fight, Williams has a maximum of only about 2,700 men in line. The defenders are supported by four warships, including the ironclad *Essex* (6 guns), protecting the city from the riverside and able to provide artillery support.

The Confederate ironclad ram *Arkansas* (8 guns) is dispatched from Vicksburg to clear the river, even though repairs from the July 22 Union attack are not yet complete, and its engines are in poor shape. The *Arkansas* sets out on August 3 under Lieutenant Henry K. Stevens, but its engines break down several times, and it is unable to reach Baton Rouge in time to support the initial Confederate assault. Nevertheless, the Confederates breach the Union lines and drive the Union troops back against the river. With the *Arkansas* again disabled by another engine breakdown some eight miles above Baton Rouge, the Union gunboats downriver keep up a steady stream of fire against the advancing Confederate troops and drive them back, although General Williams is among the Union dead, killed while urging his men to counterattack. Had the *Arkansas* been on the scene and occupying the Union ships, the battle would probably have gone the other way.

During the night of August 5, Commander William D. Porter of the *Essex* learns of the presence of the *Arkansas* upriver, and at 8:00 a.m. on August 6 he leads his four ships upriver against it. Repairs just completed, the *Arkansas* moves to engage the *Essex,* but its engines break down yet again, and the ironclad drifts back to the shore. Stevens then orders his men to abandon ship and fire it. The burning *Arkansas* drifts back out into the river and downstream for more than an hour until it blows up. In retrospect, the

Arkansas should have been kept at Vicksburg. With its engines properly repaired, it might have disrupted the subsequent passage by Rear Admiral David D. Porter's Mississippi Squadron that made possible Major General Ulysses S. Grant's final operations against Vicksburg.

The destruction of the *Arkansas* influences Breckinridge's decision not to renew the attack. Meanwhile, Colonel Thomas W. Cahill has assumed temporary command of the Union forces at Baton Rouge, and he confines his demoralized men to the city's defensive perimeter for several days. Breckinridge, meanwhile, moves heavy cannon to Port Hudson. Union casualties in the Battle of Baton Rouge are 84 dead and 299 wounded or missing. Confederate losses are 84 dead and 372 wounded or missing. On August 21, the Union troops evacuate Baton Rouge and return to New Orleans.

August 9, 1862

Civil War (continued): Eastern theater: Battle of Cedar Mountain. As part of his general reorganization of the army, U.S. president Abraham Lincoln, disillusioned by the recent Union defeats in the Shenandoah Valley caused in large part by a fragmented command structure, creates from the disparate Union elements there a single force, the Army of Virginia. It is commanded by the overconfident and inept Major General John Pope, reassigned from the Western theater, where he enjoyed success. Confederate general Robert E. Lee, commanding the Army of Northern Virginia, concerned by the threat posed by Pope's army, dispatches Major General Thomas J. "Stonewall" Jackson with 12,000 men to protect the railroad junction at Gordonsville and observe Union movements. Lee follows, leaving only 20,000 men to protect Richmond.

Pope plans an advance toward the Rapidan River. Learning of the Confederate presence there, he deploys on a wide front near Culpeper. On August 9 U.S. major general Nathaniel P. Banks, commanding the leading Union corps, errs in impetuously attacking Jackson with virtually his entire corps of 9,000 men without requesting reinforcements from Pope. Jackson rebuffs Banks and drives him back to Culpeper.

In the Battle of Cedar Mountain, the Union suffers 2,353 casualties; the Confederates lose 1,354.

August 10, 1862

Civil War (continued): Trans-Mississippi West theater. U.S. Navy rear admiral David G. Farragut orders the shelling of Donaldsonville, Louisiana. This is in response to sniper attacks on his ships patrolling the Mississippi. He warns Confederate authorities that if the attacks do not cease, he will order the town destroyed.

August 17, 1862

Civil War (continued). The *Oreto*, the first ship built in Britain for the Confederacy as a commerce raider, is commissioned by Lieutenant John N. Maffitt at Green Cay in the Bahamas as CSS *Florida*.

August 17–December 26, 1862

American Indian Wars (continued): Sioux Uprising (also known as the War of 1862, the Dakota War, and Little Crow's War). Throughout the late 1850s, treaty violations by the United States, including encroachments on Sioux land, and late or unfair annuity payments by Indian agents add to increasing hunger and hardship among the eastern Sioux, or Dakotas. Traders with the Dakotas had insisted that the government give the annuity payments directly to them (introducing the possibility of unfair dealing between the agents and the traders to the exclusion of the Dakotas). In mid-1862 the Dakotas demand the annuities directly from their agent, Thomas J. Galbraith. The traders refuse. In one meeting at the Lower Sioux (Redwood) Agency, Dakota representatives approach trader representative Andrew Jackson Myrick and ask him to sell them food on credit. He refuses, his response reported as "Let them eat grass."

On August 17, 1862, four half-starved Dakota warriors on a hunting expedition steal food and kill five American settlers. Recognizing that this will bring war, that night a council of Dakotas headed by Chief Little Crow (Taoyateduta) decides to attack settlements throughout the Minnesota River Valley in southwestern Minnesota in an effort to drive out the whites.

On August 18 Little Crow leads an attack on the Lower Sioux Agency. Myrick is among the first to be slain. His body is later discovered with grass stuffed into his mouth. In the Battle of Redwood Ferry, Minnesota militia forces sent to quell the uprising are defeated, and 24 are killed. Widespread Sioux attacks occur throughout the region, and the Indians burn settlements at Milford, Leavenworth, and Sacred Heart. The community of New Ulm comes under attack on August 19 and again on August 23, and the Dakotas also attack Fort Ridgely on August 20 and 22, although they are unable to take it.

In the three-hour Battle of Birch Coulee on September 2, Dakotas attack a detachment of 150 soldiers, killing 13 and wounding 47, while only 2 Dakotas are slain. A relief force of 240 soldiers from Fort Ridgely rescues the remainder of the soldiers that afternoon.

Washington finally dispatches troops under Major General John Pope to restore order. The last major battle of the Sioux Uprising occurs on September 23 at Wood Lake (Lone Tree Lake), when Little Crow leads an attack by some 800 warriors on 1,600 troops and volunteers under Colonel Henry H. Sibley. The Dakotas are dispersed by artillery and defeated. Most of the Dakota bands then surrender. The uprising claims 77 U.S. Army and 70–100 Dakotas dead. There is no firm count on the number of settlers killed, but estimates range from 400 to 800.

By late December 1862, more than 1,000 Sioux are being held in Minnesota jails. Following trials and sentencing, 38 of them are publicly hanged in Mankato on December 26, 1862, in the largest public execution in U.S. history. In April 1863 the remaining Dakotas are expelled from Minnesota to Nebraska and South Dakota. Congress abolishes their reservations. Little Crow is shot and killed by a settler on July 3, 1863, while he and his son are gathering berries on the settler's land near Hutchinson, Minnesota.

August 23, 1862

Civil War (continued): Eastern theater: Stuart's Raid. Confederate major general J. E. B. Stuart leads a daring raid by 1,500 cavalrymen to cut the Union supply lines by destroying the Orange & Alexandria Railroad bridge over Cedar Run and simultaneously striking Major General John Pope's headquarters at nearby Catlett's Station, Virginia. Stuart takes 300 Union prisoners, supplies, and $350,000 in cash. He also seizes Pope's personal baggage, uniform, and papers, from which the Confederates learn the important information that Pope's Army of Virginia of 55,000 men will be joined by Major General George B. McClellan's 100,000-man Army of the Potomac.

August 24, 1862

Civil War (continued): Commissioning of CSS *Alabama*. Off the island of Terceira in the Azores, Captain Raphael Semmes commissions the *Enrica*, built by a British firm for the Confederacy, as CSS *Alabama*. During a span of 22 months it will become the most successful Confederate commerce raider.

August 26, 1862

Civil War (continued). Captain Franklin Buchanan is promoted to the rank of rear admiral, making him the first Confederate Navy admiral and its senior-ranking officer.

August 29–30, 1862

Civil War (continued): Eastern theater: Second Battle of Bull Run (Manassas). Learning that Major General George B. McClellan's Army of the Potomac has been ordered to return from the Virginia Peninsula to reinforce Major General John Pope's new Union Army of Virginia, commander of the Confederate Army of Northern Virginia General Robert E. Lee decides on a daring plan. He will march north and attack Pope before the two Union armies (total strength of some 155,000 men) can

Second Battle of Bull Run (Manassas)		
Date	August 29–30, 1862	
Location	Prince William County, Virginia	
Opponents (*winner)	*Confederacy	United States
Commander	General Robert E. Lee	Major General John Pope
#	55,000 men	62,000 men
Casualties	9,197	16,054

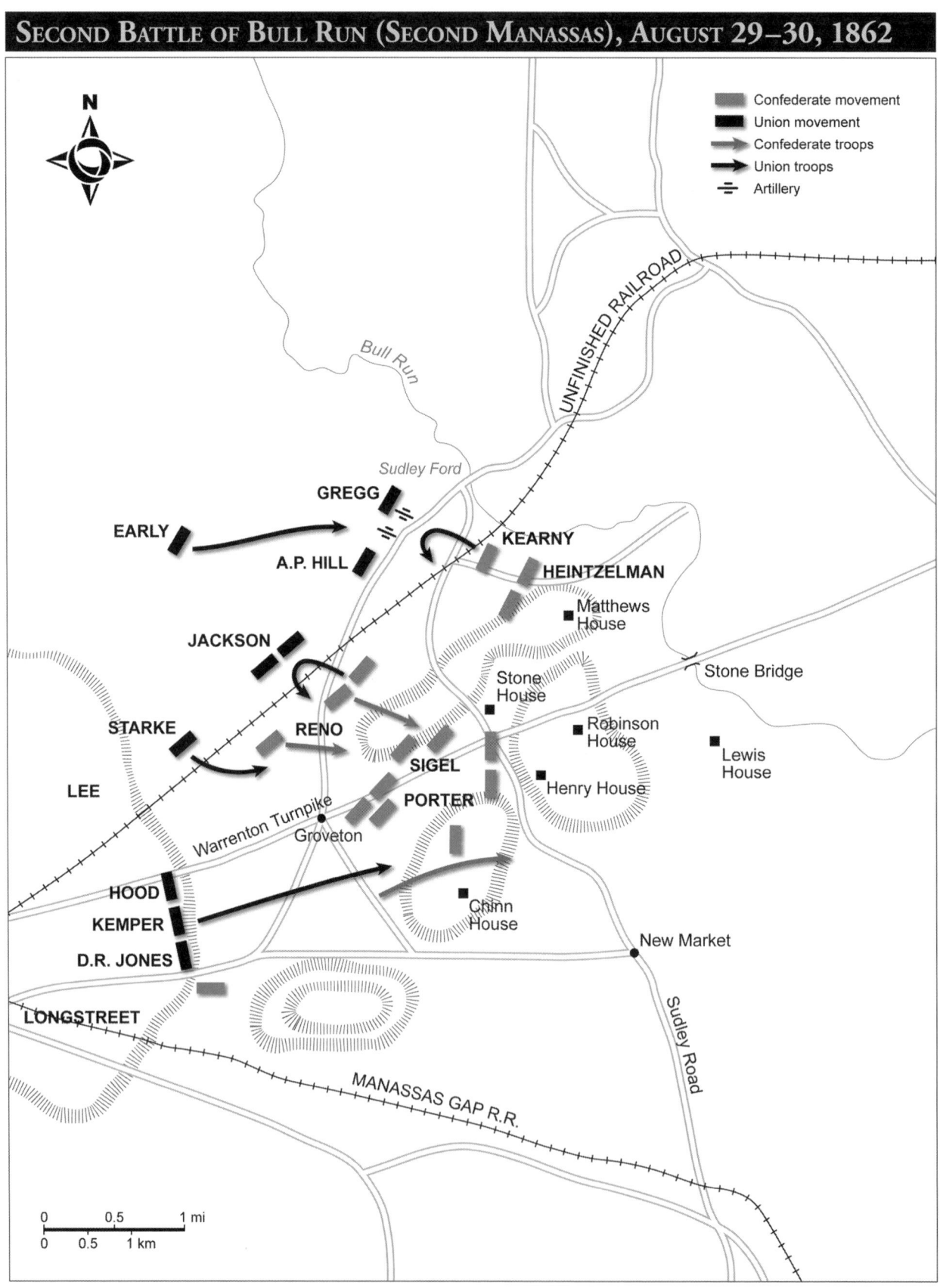

SECOND BATTLE OF BULL RUN (SECOND MANASSAS), AUGUST 29–30, 1862

N

Confederate movement
Union movement
Confederate troops
Union troops
Artillery

UNFINISHED RAILROAD

Bull Run

Sudley Ford

GREGG

EARLY

A.P. HILL

KEARNY

HEINTZELMAN

Matthews House

JACKSON

Stone House

Stone Bridge

STARKE

RENO

SIGEL

Robinson House

Lewis House

LEE

PORTER

Henry House

Warrenton Turnpike

Groveton

HOOD

Chinn House

New Market

KEMPER

D.R. JONES

LONGSTREET

Sudley Road

MANASSAS GAP R.R.

0   0.5   1 mi
0   0.5   1 km

combine against his own army of 55,000. McClellan, who dislikes Pope, delays in transferring men to him as ordered by Washington, withholding his two best corps, giving Pope some 62,000 men. Furious, President Abraham Lincoln subsequently relieves McClellan of command.

In the Second Battle of Bull Run (Manassas), Lee sends Major General Thomas J. "Stonewall" Jackson around Pope's right flank. Covering some 54 miles in only two days, on August 27 Jackson's men fall on Pope's supply base at Manassas Junction and torch it. Pope, embarrassed, sends his entire army against Jackson. Pope locates the Southerners on August 28, when Jackson deliberately attacks a Union division near Groveton to divert Pope's attention from the advancing Confederate corps under Major General James Longstreet. Pope orders a concentration on the former Bull Run battlefield, aiming to destroy Jackson.

On August 29 Jackson holds in a strong defensive position against Pope's badly coordinated attacks. Lee comes up with Longstreet's 30,000-man corps in late afternoon, but Pope refuses to believe reports that Jackson has been reinforced. Pope resumes attacks on August 30. At the climax of the Union assault, Longstreet's men rise from concealment and fall on Pope's flank from the south, sending Union forces reeling back in confusion. Only a stubborn Union defense on Henry House Hill prevents disaster.

The outcome of the battle deservedly discredits Pope as a military commander. His forces have suffered 16,054 casualties while inflicting only 9,197 on Lee's army. The Confederate victory here clears the way for Lee's invasion of the North.

August 29–30, 1862

Civil War (continued): Western theater: Battle of Richmond. On July 31, 1862, Major General Edmund Kirby Smith, commander of the Confederate Department of East Tennessee, meets at Chattanooga with General Braxton Bragg, commander of the Army of Tennessee, and proposes an invasion of Kentucky. Smith hopes to secure control of this key state, divert Union troops from Tennessee, and secure supplies and recruits. Smith commands some 20,000 men, while Bragg commands 30,000 men. On August 13,

Smith advances north from Knoxville into Kentucky. Bragg leave Chattanooga on August 28, moving on a parallel track to the west.

On August 29, Brigadier General Patrick T. Cleburne, leading a small advance division of Smith's force, attacks two Union brigades under Brigadier General Mahlon D. Manson at Richmond. On the continuation of fighting on August 30, both Smith and Union major general William "Bull" Nelson arrive on the battlefield to take charge of their respective armies. The three separate engagements that constitute the Battle of Richmond end in arguably the South's most complete victory of the entire war. Union losses are 206 killed, 844 wounded, and 4,300 missing (most taken prisoner). Southern losses are 78 killed, 372 wounded, and a small number missing. The way is now open for a Confederate advance on Lexington and Frankfort.

September 1, 1862

Civil War (continued): Eastern theater: Battle of Chantilly. Confederate commander of the Army of Northern Virginia General Robert E. Lee sends forces under Major General Thomas J. "Stonewall" Jackson around the right flank of Union major general John Pope's Army of Virginia in order to cut it off from Washington, D.C. Pope discovers this on the night of August 31, countermanding his own attack plan to order his army to withdraw into the Washington defenses. The next day, Jackson encounters forces sent by Pope to block his advance.

The battle occurs in a violent rainstorm. In the Battle of Chantilly (known to the Confederates as Ox Hill), two Union divisions under Brigadier General Isaac Stevens and Major General Philip Kearny check Jackson, although both Union generals are killed. Jackson suffers perhaps 500 casualties, the Union side as many as 1,000. Lee makes no further effort toward Washington.

Pope compounds his unpopularity by blaming his overall defeat in the Second Battle of Bull Run on his capable subordinate Major General Fitz John Porter. In a highly controversial court-martial, Porter is found guilty of insubordination and is dismissed from the service. Pope himself is relieved of command on September 12. His Army of Virginia is by this date absorbed into the Army of the Potomac, and Major General George B. McClellan is recalled to command it. President Abraham Lincoln declares that "We must use the tools we have."

September 1, 1862

Civil War (continued). U.S. Navy rear admiral Samuel P. Lee assumes command of the North Atlantic Blockading Squadron, relieving Rear Admiral Louis M. Goldsborough.

September 4, 1862

Civil War (continued): Eastern theater: Lee's first invasion of the North. Union major general George B. McClellan reorganizes his forces, absorbing the Army of Virginia as three corps of his Army of the Potomac and moving from Washington with 97,000 men to meet Confederate general Robert E. Lee, with 55,000 men. Lee has permission from Confederate president Jefferson Davis for a general invasion of the North. Lee hopes to cut rail lines and isolate Washington, D.C., with Harrisburg, Pennsylvania, as his probable ultimate objective.

Overestimating Confederate strength as usual, McClellan proceeds with his customary caution. On September 7 Lee is concentrated near Frederick, Maryland. On September 9 he orders Major General James Longstreet to advance on Hagerstown, Maryland, while Major General Thomas J. "Stonewall" Jackson returns across the Potomac to capture the Union arsenal at Harpers Ferry, Virginia, and open a new line of communication south.

September 4, 1862

Civil War (continued): CSS *Florida* runs into Mobile Bay. With most of his crew sick with yellow fever, Lieutenant John N. Maffitt, commander of the Confederate commerce raider *Florida* (9 guns), decides on a desperate plan to run his ship past the Union blockaders off Mobile Bay, Alabama. With only a skeleton crew able to work the ship, Maffitt arrives off Mobile Bay, then blockaded by U.S. Navy commander George Preble's squadron of the screw sloop *Oneida* (10 guns), the screw gunboat *Winona* (4 guns), and the schooner *Rachel Seaman* (2 guns). Without hesitation Maffitt

runs for the bay, flying an English ensign. The captains of the *Winona* and *Rachel Seaman*, expecting Preble to handle the situation, hold back. Preble hesitates, wary of a repeat of the *Trent* Affair that might bring war with Britain. Maffitt closes to within 80 yards of the *Oneida* before Preble fires the first of two warning shots.

When Maffitt does not stop, Preble releases a full broadside at point-blank range, but the shot goes too high to inflict major damage. All three Union ships now fire on the *Florida*, but although it is considerably damaged by the Union cannonade and with one man killed and nine wounded, the *Florida* gains the bay and soon anchors under the protecting guns of Fort Morgan. Repaired and with new crew members, the *Florida* escapes to sea again on January 16, 1863.

September 8, 1862

Civil War (continued). U.S. Navy commodore John Wilkes assumes command of the West India Squadron with his flag in the large side-wheel steamer *Vanderbilt* (15 guns). The squadron's primary mission is to seek out and capture Confederate commerce raiders.

September 12–15, 1862

Civil War (continued): Eastern theater: Lee's first invasion of the North (continued): Battle of Harpers Ferry. As part of Confederate commander of the Army of Northern Virginia General Robert E. Lee's invasion of the North, he detaches a substantial portion of his force in three divisions to take Harpers Ferry, Virginia (now part of West Virginia). Major General Thomas J. "Stonewall" Jackson and 11,500 men are to cross the Potomac River and attack Harpers Ferry from the west, a column under Major General Lafayette McLaws of 8,000 men is to take the Maryland Heights, and Brigadier General John G. Walker and 3,400 men are to secure Loudoun Heights. Lee wants to capture the substantial stocks of arms and ammunition at the federal arsenal there but also wants to secure his flank and supply lines as he moves north and during his subsequent withdrawal. Although Lee is being pursued by Union forces under Major General George B. McClellan that outnumber his own army by more than 2 to 1,

Lee takes the risky strategy of dividing his forces because he believes, correctly as it turns out, that McClellan will be slow to move and that he will have time to concentrate his own forces before the major confrontation with McClellan can occur.

McClellan had requested that the Harpers Ferry garrison of 14,000 men under Colonel Dixon S. Miles be added to his own forces, but Union general-in-chief Major General Henry W. Halleck refused, expecting Miles to hold. Miles should have been able to do so, but apparently taking his orders "to hold the town" literally, he insists on keeping most of his men near the town rather than positioning them to hold the critical high ground that commands it. Also, many men in the garrison are new to the army and poorly trained.

The first Confederates arrive on September 12, and inconclusive skirmishing occurs for the weakly defended Maryland Heights. Major Confederate attacks the next day give them that commanding position. The last Confederate troops arrive that afternoon and occupy undefended positions west and south of the town. Jackson carefully positions his artillery around Harpers Ferry and orders Major General A. P. Hill to prepare to attack the Union left.

Meanwhile, Miles rejects suggestions advanced by Colonel Benjamin F. Davis and other subordinate commanders that they attempt a breakout on the night of September 14. Davis is determined to try, with or without permission, and succeeds in escaping that night with 1,400 cavalrymen.

By the morning of September 15, Jackson has some 50 guns in position on the Maryland Heights and at the base of Loudoun Heights. After the artillery barrage begins and just before the infantry attack is to occur, Miles decides that the situation is hopeless and orders a surrender. Before he can personally do so, he is mortally wounded by a shell. In the fighting, the Union suffers 44 killed and 173 wounded. The Confederates sustain 39 killed and 247 wounded. But Jackson takes 12,419 prisoners, 13,000 small arms, 73 cannon, 200 wagons, and considerable stocks of military equipment in what is the largest Union surrender of the war.

Leaving a division to guard the prisoners and equipment, Jackson now proceeds by forced marches with the rest of his men to join Lee at Sharpsburg,

Maryland, arriving there in time to participate in the battle of September 17.

September 14, 1862

Civil War (continued): Eastern theater: Lee's first invasion of the North (continued): Battle of South Mountain. A member of the advance guard of the Union Army of the Potomac discovers, wrapped around some cigars, the entire operational orders of Confederate general Robert E. Lee's Army of Northern Virginia. A Union officer confirms the handwriting as that of Lee's adjutant. Union commander Major General George B. McClellan now knows the entire disposition of Lee's forces. Despite this, McClellan dallies.

Lee's army is spread out over 25 miles and is vulnerable to attack, but McClellan delays a full 18 hours before putting his army in motion to push through the Blue Ridge Mountain passes. It takes him two days to cover the 10 miles from Frederick, Maryland, to the South Mountain passes.

On September 14 in the battles at South Mountain and Crampton's Gap, Confederate forces fight small but intense engagements that hold off the Union advance. Lee orders his scattered legions to concentrate at Sharpsburg, Maryland.

September 17, 1862

Civil War (continued): Eastern theater: Lee's first invasion of the North (continued): Battle of Antietam (Sharpsburg). Confederate general Robert E. Lee divided his Army of Northern Virginia into

Battle of Antietam (Sharpsburg)		
Date	September 17, 1862	
Location	Near Sharpsburg, Maryland	
Opponents (*winner)	*United States	Confederacy
Commander	Major General George B. McClellan	General Robert E. Lee
#	87,000 men	41,000 men
Casualties	2,108 dead, 9,540 wounded, and 753 captured/missing	1,546 dead, 7,752 wounded, and 1,018 captured/missing

Confederate dead along Hagerstown Road, Maryland. The men were killed in the Battle of Antietam on September 17, 1862. (Library of Congress)

three main bodies for the movement north. With Union major general George B. McClellan closing with his much larger Army of the Potomac, Lee considers withdrawal but decides to stand and fight. He orders his army to concentrate at Sharpsburg, Maryland, trusting that McClellan's well-known slowness will allow his own scattered forces to come together in time.

On the afternoon of September 15, the major part of the Army of the Potomac is within easy striking distance of Sharpsburg. Lee has available only 18,000 men, and McClellan possesses 55,000. Lee positions his three available divisions along a low ridge extending about four miles north to south, just east of Sharpsburg and west of Antietam Creek. The hilly terrain allows Lee to mask his inferior resources while he awaits the arrival of his remaining six divisions. The resultant battle is very much a fragmented fight, in large part because of the terrain.

Had McClellan attacked on the afternoon of September 15, he would have driven Lee into the Potomac. But McClellan wants to rest his troops that night, and he spends the next day placing his artillery and infantry and personally inspecting the entire line. While McClellan dallies, Major General Thomas J. "Stonewall" Jackson arrives with his corps on September 16 at midday. This leaves only four of Lee's nine divisions still absent. Even with Jackson's

John Bell Hood (1831–1879)

Confederate general. Born at Owingsville, Kentucky, on June 1, 1831, John Bell Hood graduated from the U.S. Military Academy, West Point, in the stellar class of 1853 that also included Philip Sheridan, James B. McPherson, and John M. Schofield. Commissioned a second lieutenant and assigned to the U.S. 4th Infantry in California, Hood transferred to the new U.S. 2nd Cavalry, an elite unit that included Albert Sidney Johnston, Robert E. Lee, William J. Hardee, and George Thomas among more than a dozen future American Civil War generals. Hood was wounded while commanding a detachment during an engagement with Comanches on the Devil's River in Texas in 1857 and was promoted to first lieutenant the following year.

During the secession crisis, Hood resigned his commission and entered Confederate service as a lieutenant, identifying with Texas since Kentucky remained in the Union. After a brief stint commanding cavalry at Yorktown, Virginia, Hood became colonel of the 4th Texas Infantry in October 1861, and in March 1862 he was commissioned a brigadier general, commanding what came to be known throughout the war as Hood's Texas Brigade. The brigade fought with conspicuous ferocity during the spring 1862 Peninsula Campaign and the Seven Days' Battles, delivering a crushing attack at Gaines' Mill. Hood commanded a division during the Second Battle of Bull Run (Manassas), during which his men again provided a major blow, and again at Antietam (Sharpsburg) in September 1862, where much of his command was sacrificed to buy valuable time for Lee's Army of Northern Virginia. Promoted to major general in October 1862, Hood commanded his division at Fredericksburg and at Gettysburg, where on July 2, 1863, during the momentous second day of that battle, he received a severe wound that left his left arm withered and useless.

After an amazingly brief period of recovery, Hood rejoined his division and most of Lieutenant General James Longstreet's corps when they moved to Georgia in an effort to bolster General Braxton Bragg's forces there. On September 20 on the final day of the Battle of Chickamauga, with Hood in temporary command, Longstreet's corps pierced the Union line, precipitating the near collapse of the Army of the Cumberland. But in that attack Hood sustained a life-threatening wound in his upper right thigh that necessitated the amputation of that limb at the hip, a dangerous operation from which Hood recovered in time to take the field the following spring.

Promoted to lieutenant general in February 1864 and assigned to command a corps in General Joseph Johnston's Army of Tennessee, Hood grew increasingly discouraged with Johnston's unwillingness to confront Major General William T. Sherman's armies as they pushed the Confederates to the outskirts of Atlanta. In July, Confederate president Jefferson Davis removed Johnston and named Hood commander with the rank of full general. Hood fought a series of fierce battles in late July in an effort to hold Atlanta. By the end of August, his situation hopeless, Hood abandoned the vital railroad hub and marched his army northward in a forlorn attempt to draw Sherman's massive force out of Georgia. Undeterred, Sherman soon launched his March to the Sea. That autumn Hood's army foundered in northern Alabama before marching into Tennessee in hope of securing a tide-turning victory. After a lost opportunity to destroy Major General John Schofield's force at Spring Hill on November 30, Hood flung his exhausted army against Schofield's lines at Franklin in one of the most desperate battles of the war. He then pushed on to Nashville, where on the frozen hills south of the city Major General George Thomas attacked on

(continued)

(Continued)

December 15 and 16. Hood's force disintegrated, with the remnants retreating back into Mississippi, where Hood was relieved at his own request. Without another field command for the rest of the conflict, Hood surrendered to federal authorities at Natchez, Mississippi, in May 1865.

After the war Hood engaged in a variety of business ventures in New Orleans, where he married and fathered 11 children. He died there six days after the deaths of his wife and eldest daughter during a yellow fever epidemic on August 30, 1879.

DAVID COFFEY

Further Reading

Coffey, David. *John Bell Hood and the Struggle for Atlanta.* Abilene, TX: McWhiney Foundation Press, 1998.

McMurry, Richard M. *John Bell Hood and the War for Southern Independence.* Lexington: University Press of Kentucky, 1982.

Woodworth, Steven E. *Jefferson Davis and His Generals: The Failure of Confederate Command in the West.* Lawrence: University Press of Kansas, 1991.

corps, though, Lee is outnumbered 41,000 to 87,000. McClellan claims after the battle that he thought Lee had 120,000 men. This is hard to believe, as McClellan plans a double envelopment to hit Lee's flank and then smash the Confederate center.

During the battle, Lee is in position to observe and command throughout. He also gives great latitude to his subordinate commanders. McClellan is more than a mile to the rear, unable to observe the battle in progress and with little idea of what is transpiring. More fatefully, McClellan fails to take advantage of his superior numbers. He withholds an entire corps (20,000 men fail to see battle) and employs a piecemeal rather than simultaneous form of attack. Each Union corps is committed by successive oral orders from headquarters without informing the other corps commanders and without instructions for mutual support. This problem is compounded, as corps commanders likewise send their own divisions to the attack in piecemeal fashion. McClellan also fails to employ his cavalry to cut Confederate lines of communication and prevent Confederate reinforcements from reaching the battlefield from the south. Even a delay of an hour or two would have changed the battle, as Lee's remaining three divisions arrive on the battlefield at about 10:30 a.m. on September 17, with the Union attack already in progress.

The Battle of Antietam opens early on the morning of September 17 with an attack by Major General Joseph Hooker's 12,000-man I Corps against the Confederate left held by Jackson's corps. Hooker's men drive the Confederates back into the West Woods. Lee calls up Brigadier General John Bell Hood's Texas Brigade, which repulses the Union attack. Amid smoke and ground fog, the battle lines are only 30–50 yards apart, and units are destroyed as soon as they begin to fight. In the intense fighting for the cornfield, the 1st Texas Regiment of Hood's Brigade suffers more than 82 percent of its men killed or wounded in 20 minutes, the highest percentage of losses North or South in any regiment of the war. Successive Union attacks on the Confederate left by Major General Joseph Mansfield's XII Corps and Brigadier General Edwin Sumner's II Corps also meet rebuff.

In the Confederate center, though, a crisis develops as some 3,000 Confederates under Major General Daniel H. Hill fight to hold the Sunken Road, which comes to be known as Bloody Lane. Here Union major general William B. Franklin's VI Corps mounts

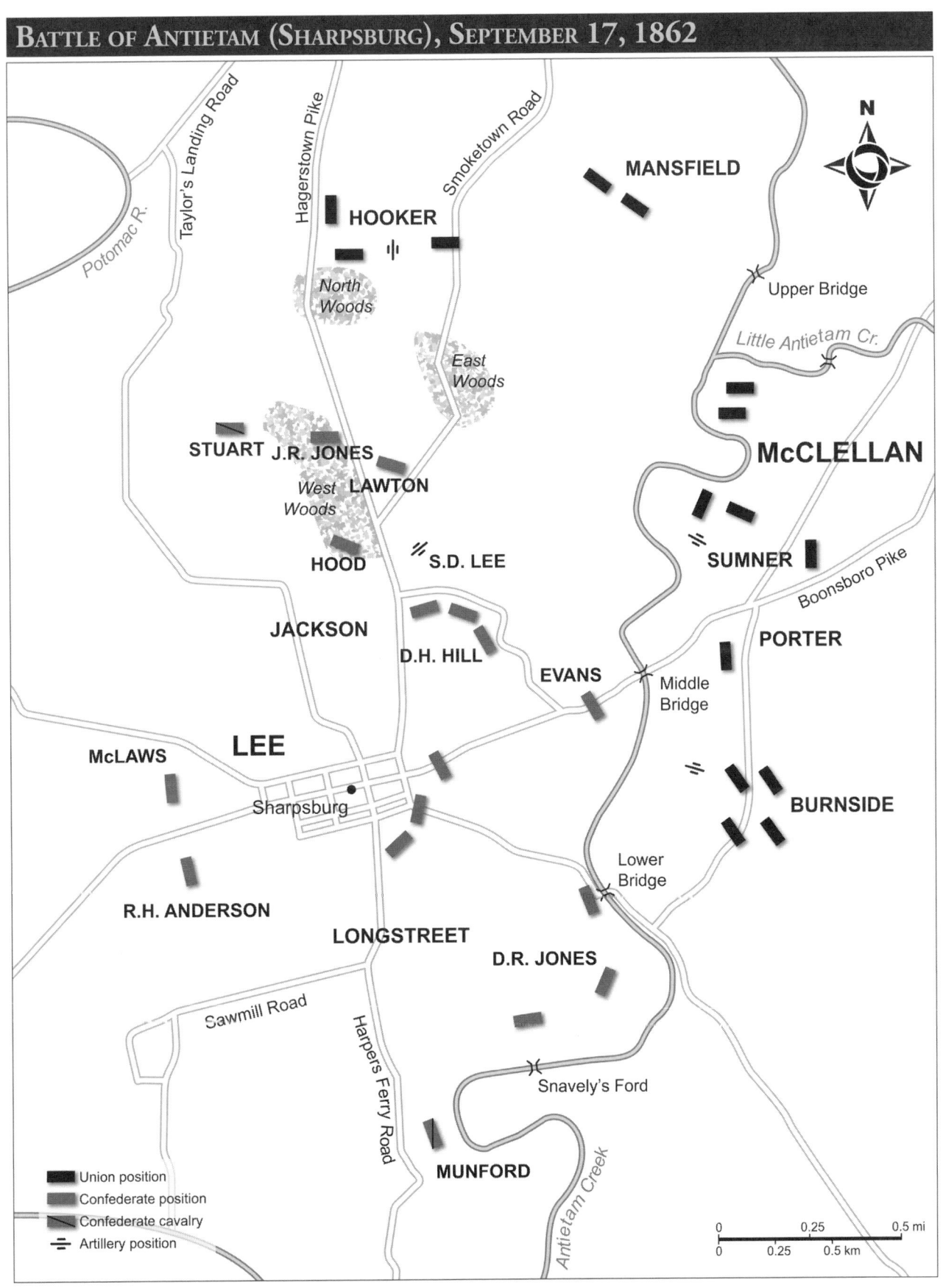

BATTLE OF ANTIETAM (SHARPSBURG), SEPTEMBER 17, 1862

N

Taylor's Landing Road

Hagerstown Pike

Smoketown Road

Potomac R.

MANSFIELD

HOOKER

Upper Bridge

North Woods

Little Antietam Cr.

East Woods

McCLELLAN

STUART J.R. JONES

West Woods LAWTON

SUMNER

Boonsboro Pike

HOOD S.D. LEE

JACKSON

PORTER

D.H. HILL

EVANS Middle Bridge

LEE

McLAWS

BURNSIDE

Sharpsburg

R.H. ANDERSON

Lower Bridge

LONGSTREET

D.R. JONES

Sawmill Road

Harpers Ferry Road

Snavely's Ford

MUNFORD

Antietam Creek

Union position
Confederate position
Confederate cavalry
Artillery position

0   0.25   0.5 mi
0   0.25   0.5 km

three separate assaults; all fail. Then two Union regiments are able to enfilade the Confederate position on the Sunken Road, forcing the Confederates to fall back and opening a gap between the Confederate center and left. Hill's troops manage to plug the hole in time. Lee then orders Jackson to counterattack the Union right, a move that is not successful. McClellan, however, fails to take advantage of the situation and commit his reserves.

On the Union left, Major General Ambrose Burnside's IX Corps spends the morning trying to carry a bridge over Antietam Creek. Union forces finally cross the creek via fords, but the Confederates withdraw to higher ground. By the time Burnside is ready to renew the attack, the last division of Lee's army, that under Major General Ambrose P. Hill, arrives. Although exhausted from their forced march, the men defeat the Union assault. The Battle of Antietam is over.

The loss of life is appalling. Union casualties are 2,108 dead, 9,540 wounded, and 753 captured or missing (15 percent of effectives). Confederate losses are 1,546 dead, 7,752 wounded, and 1,018 captured or missing (26 percent of the force). It is the bloodiest single day of fighting of the entire war.

Lee waits one day and then pulls back into Virginia. McClellan fails to pursue. President Abraham Lincoln is furious at his general's inaction and soon removes McClellan from command again.

The battle, while inconclusive in a military sense, nonetheless has important results. Lee's defeat weakens Confederate hopes of securing recognition from Britain and France. Never again is the Confederacy as close to winning diplomatic recognition abroad. The battle also helps ensure that Democrats do not win control of the House of Representatives in the November elections. A single percentage's shift in the vote would have brought Democratic control and trouble for Lincoln. The Union victory also allows Lincoln the opportunity to issue the Preliminary Emancipation Proclamation.

September 19–20, 1862

Civil War (continued): Western theater: Battle of Iuka. U.S. major general Ulysses S. Grant, commanding the 45,000-man Army of the Tennessee, has his assets stretched over a considerable territory. His chief forces are with him at Corinth, Mississippi, where his lines of communication are threatened by the armies of Confederate major generals Sterling Price (the Army of the West of 15,000 men) and Earl Van Dorn (the Army of West Tennessee with 7,000 men), who hope to unite against him.

Grant does not wait to be attacked but instead moves against Price, who has occupied the Union supply depot of Iuka, Mississippi, on September 14 and is now waiting for Van Dorn to join him. Grant plans a double envelopment. Brigadier General William S. Rosecrans and his Army of the Mississippi are to approach Iuka from the southwest, while three divisions of Grant's own army under Major General Edward O. C. Ord attack out of the northwest against the Confederate front. This goes awry when Rosecrans takes the wrong route and fails to cut the Confederate line of retreat. Grant had ordered Ord to wait until he heard the sounds of Rosecrans in battle south of Iuka before driving from the north.

An acoustic anomaly prevents Ord and Grant from hearing the battle noise, though, and Rosecrans is forced to fight Price alone, which he does successfully. Price then withdraws from Iuka. Grant, however, is critical of Rosecrans for failing to mount an aggressive pursuit of Price, who joins Van Dorn. The Union suffers 790 casualties; Confederates losses are 1,516.

September 23, 1862

Civil War (continued): Preliminary Emancipation Proclamation. President Abraham Lincoln had been seeking a victory so that he could do this from a position of strength, and six days after the Battle of Antietam he issues the Preliminary Emancipation Proclamation. It declares that as of January 1, 1863, slaves in areas of the South still in rebellion will be free. Although the proclamation actually frees no slaves, it resonates in the North and in Europe, where it helps allay the considerable sympathy there for the Confederate cause. It also represents a change in Union war aims, in effect transforming a war to preserve the Union into a struggle for human freedom.

September 25, 1862

Civil War (continued): Trans-Mississippi West theater. The U.S. Navy screw steamer *Kensington* (3 guns), schooner *Rachel Seaman* (2 guns), and mortar schooner *Henry James* (1 mortar) shell Confederate shore positions at Sabine Pass, Texas. Confederate troops stationed at Sabine City near the mouth of the Sabine River withdraw temporarily.

September 1862–October 1863

American Indian Wars (continued): Shoshone War. This struggle for control of the Great Basin of the West is centered on the present-day state of Utah and involves the Shoshone tribe and volunteer troops. Its primary cause is the steady encroachment of white settlers onto the traditional homelands of the Shoshone peoples as a result of an influx of Mormons and the discovery of gold in California and later in Oregon and Montana. Soon bands of Shoshones are raiding the settlers' farms for horses and food.

Fighting actually begins in September 1862. Colonel Patrick Edward Connor and his 3rd California Volunteer Infantry Regiment arrive in the Great Basin to protect the overland route between Carson City and Fort Bridger. Worried about California's vulnerability to Confederate forces, Washington orders Connor to secure the lines of communication and sources of gold and silver vital to the Union war effort. Following the killing by the Shoshones of 12 whites at Gravelly Ford in September 1862, Connor dispatches Major Edward McGarry and two companies of men to the Humboldt River with orders to kill all Shoshones they encounter, resulting in 25 Native American deaths.

Chief Bear Hunter of the Northern Shoshones leads attacks on the mail and stage lines, and he and his followers become the primary target of Connor's efforts. In November 1862 Connor sends McGarry to rescue a boy taken by the Shoshones two years previously. McGarry attacks Bear Hunter's camp, chasing him and others into a canyon, where three Indians die. Bear Hunter surrenders and is held hostage until the boy is returned. In retaliation, the Shoshones kill several miners.

With the Shoshones continuing their attacks on white settlements, Connor orders McGarry to retrieve the stolen stock. At Bear River Crossing on December 6, McGarry takes and executes four Shoshones. A flurry of Shoshone attacks ensues through January 1863, prompting Utah Territory Supreme Court chief justice John F. Kinney to issue arrest warrants for Chiefs Bear Hunter, Sagwitch, and Sanpitch.

Connor decides on a massive assault on the Shoshone's winter camp, sending Captain Samuel Hoyt, 69 infantrymen, 13 wagons, and two howitzers toward Cache Valley on January 22, 1863. Connor waits two days before he and McGarry lead 220 cavalrymen to a rendezvous point in hopes of misleading Shoshone scouts as to his intentions. In the Battle of the Bear River on January 29, 1863 (what some dub the Bear River Massacre), Connor attacks and kills at least 224 Shoshones but more likely 300, wounding 70 others. He also captures 170 horses and destroys winter provisions and supplies. Bear Hunter is among the dead. Sanpitch and Sagwitch escape. The California Volunteers lose 17 men. The engagement precipitates major unrest among the Shoshones.

Eluding U.S. troops for months, the hostile Shoshones carry out numerous small raids. The volunteer troops counterattack, and in early May Captain Samuel Smith kills 53 Goshute Native Americans. During June–October the government negotiates five treaties with the Shoshones. All promise 20 years of annuity payments in exchange for guarantees of safe passage and settlement, bringing the Shoshone War to a close.

October 1, 1862

Civil War (continued). The Western Gunboat Flotilla is formally transferred from War Department control to that of the U.S. Navy. On October 15, 1862, Commander David D. Porter, promoted to acting rear admiral, is placed in command of the newly sanctioned Mississippi Squadron, bringing the brown water navy to equal footing with the oceangoing squadrons.

October 3–4, 1862

Civil War (continued): Western theater: Second Battle of Corinth. At Ripley, Tennessee, on September 28, 1862, the armies of major generals Earl Van Dorn and Sterling Price unite. With a combined strength of some 22,000 men and under Van Dorn's command, they move south from Chewalla in southwestern Tennessee to attack 23,000 Union troops under Major General William Rosecrans, entrenched at Corinth, Mississippi. The Confederates hope to seize this key railroad junction, then undertake an invasion of Tennessee.

In the ensuing bloody Second Battle of Corinth, the Confederates make initial gains but cannot overcome stiffened Union resistance. Union losses are nearly 2,500 killed or wounded; the Confederates suffer 2,470 killed or wounded and another 1,763 missing or deserted during the subsequent retreat to Ripley.

Rosecrans again fails to mount an effective pursuit, despite Grant's order that he move immediately. Nonetheless, Rosecrans is lauded in the Northern press, and President Abraham Lincoln will subsequently reward him with command of XIV Corps, soon renamed the Army of the Cumberland, replacing Major General Don Carlos Buell.

October 8, 1862

Civil War (continued): Western theater: Battle of Perryville. Confederate forces under Major General Edmund Kirby Smith and General Braxton Bragg have invaded Kentucky. Departing Chattanooga with 30,000 men on August 28, 1862, Bragg besieges and takes Mumfordville, Kentucky, during September 14–17, then secures most of Kentucky and organizes a new Confederate government in Frankfort. The Confederates now have some 50,000 troops in Kentucky.

Union major general Don Carlos Buell's Army of the Ohio is of approximately equal size. Buell moves about distractedly and enters Louisville only on September 25. Bragg's preoccupation with establishing a new Kentucky government, however, allows Buell time to reorganize. Substantially reinforced and threatened with removal of command if he fails to act, on October 1 Buell departs Louisville, in the midst of one of the worst droughts in years, to seek battle with Bragg.

The two armies come together in the confused Battle of Perryville (Chaplin Hills) on October 8, both seeking to locate a source of water. Union casualties total 4,276 (894 killed, 2,911 wounded, and 471 captured

or missing); the Confederates lose 3,401 (532 killed, 2,641 wounded, and 228 captured or missing). Tactically a draw, strategically the battle is a Union victory. Bragg is now badly outnumbered, and it is clear that Kentuckians will not now rise en masse in support of the Confederacy. Given this situation, he withdraws back into Tennessee. Buell fails to pursue.

October 9, 1962

Civil War (continued): Trans-Mississippi West theater: Union capture of Galveston. Galveston, Texas, is important to both sides. The largest prewar Texas seaport, with some 7,000 people, it is the state's second-largest city. Much of the state's cotton and sugar is shipped through its port, and Galveston boasts some war industries. In Union hands, it would be an excellent westernmost blockading base and could serve as a staging area for an invasion into the interior.

In October 1862, Union forces attempt to take Galveston. On October 4, Commander William B. Renshaw arrives with the side-wheel steamers *Westfield* (flagship, 6 guns), *Harriet Lane* (4 guns), and *Clifton* (6 guns); the screw gunboat *Owasco* (4 guns); and the mortar schooner *Henry James* (1 mortar). Renshaw demands that the Confederates surrender, and when they delay he orders in his ships. A brief exchange of fire follows, but inadequate defenses lead Confederate commander Colonel Joseph J. Cook to accede to Renshaw's demands on condition of a four-day truce. Renshaw reluctantly agrees to prevent civilian casualties, but much to his chagrin, the Confederates use the truce to remove military personnel, artillery, and equipment. Galveston formally surrenders on October 9.

Renshaw's Galveston forces are strengthened by the arrival of the screw steamer *Sachem* (4 guns) and the sailing schooner *Corypheus* (2 guns) from New Orleans, along with three companies of the 42nd Massachusetts Infantry Regiment. The Union troops take up position in large warehouses at the end of Kuhn's Wharf, which extends north into Galveston Bay from the waterfront. Barricades deny access to it from the waterfront. The troops also remove portions of the wharf in front of the barricades so that only a single plank connects to the waterfront.

October 16, 1862
Civil War (continued): Western theater. Major General Ulysses S. Grant assumes command of the Department of the Tennessee and immediately begins gathering men and supplies for a campaign to capture "the Confederate Gibraltar" of Vicksburg.

October 21, 1862
Civil War (continued): Trans-Mississippi West theater. Crewmen from the U.S. Navy City-class ironclad *Louisville* (14 guns), escorting the army transport *Meteor*, take and burn the towns of Bledsoe's Landing and Hamblin's Landing, Arkansas. This is in response to an attack by Confederate guerrillas on the Union mail steamer *Gladiator*.

October 26, 1862
Civil War (continued): Eastern theater: McClellan crosses the Potomac. Despite the repeated pleas and orders of President Abraham Lincoln and Union Army general-in-chief Major General Henry W. Halleck, Union commander of the Army of the Potomac Major General George B. McClellan has refused to pursue Confederate general Robert E. Lee and his Army of Northern Virginia. Not until five weeks after the Battle of Antietam does McClellan at last cross the Potomac, but he is so cautious that Lee easily transposes his own forces between McClellan and the Union goal of Richmond.

October 27, 1862
Civil War (continued): Western theater. U.S. Army major general William S. Rosecrans replaces Major General Don Carlos Buell as commander of the Army of the Cumberland (formerly the Army of the Ohio).

October 31, 1862
Civil War (continued). The Confederate Congress authorizes the formation of a Torpedo Bureau under the command of General Gabriel J. Rains and a Naval Submarine Battery Service under Lieutenant Hunter Davidson in order to substantially increase the use of naval mines (known at the time as torpedoes) against U.S. warships.

November 4, 1862
Civil War (continued). Dr. Richard J. Gatling of Indianapolis, Indiana, is issued a patent for his new gun, but the U.S. Army fails to adopt the weapon during the Civil War.

November 5, 1862
Civil War (continued): Eastern theater: Relief of McClellan. U.S. president Abraham Lincoln is unhappy with the failure of commander of the Army of the Potomac Major General George B. McClellan to pursue Confederate forces following the Battle of Antietam (see September 17, 1862). When McClellan reluctantly moves to Warrenton, Virginia, but refuses to proceed farther, on November 5 Lincoln removes him from command and replaces him with Major General Ambrose E. Burnside, who only reluctantly agrees to assume command.

November 8, 1862
Civil War (continued): Western theater. At New Orleans, Major General Nathaniel P. Banks replaces Major General Benjamin F. Butler as commander of the U.S. Army Department of the Gulf.

November 13–December 29, 1862
Civil War (continued): Western theater: First Union land campaign against Vicksburg. Commander of the Army of the Tennessee Major General Ulysses S. Grant attempts an overland campaign south from his advanced base at Holly Springs along the Mississippi Central Railroad, hoping thereby to draw out the bulk of Confederate lieutenant general John C. Pemberton's 40,000-man Army of Mississippi, which is defending Vicksburg. At the same time, Grant sends his trusted subordinate, Major General William T. Sherman, and 32,000 men down the Mississippi River in transports covered by Rear Admiral David Dixon Porter's Mississippi Squadron in a surprise attack on the few defenders expected to remain at Vicksburg.

On November 13, 1862, Grant puts his own force in motion, driving back Confederate forces under Pemberton. The farther Grant moves south, however, the more vulnerable are his supply and communication lines. Confederate cavalry under Brigadier

 **Gatling Gun**

The American Civil War (1861–1865) gave rise to a number of new weapons. Among these were several precursors to the modern machine gun, including Wilson Ager's Coffee Mill. It took its name from the means of feeding the ammunition from the top of the weapon by a funnel and crank mechanism, which resembled a coffee mill.

Ager's gun had a single barrel. The ammunition was formed of a steel tube that contained powder and a .58-caliber bullet and a nipple at the end for a percussion cap. Steady turning of the crank dropped a round into the chamber, locked the breechblock in place, dropped a hammer that fired the round, and ejected the spent case. Ager claimed a firing rate of 100 rounds per minute, although the gun barrel could not have long withstood the heat thus generated.

Ager demonstrated his weapon before President Abraham Lincoln, and the U.S. Army eventually purchased 50 of them. The Coffee Mills proved unreliable, however, in combat use and were never employed en masse. Ultimately they were used in the defensives of Washington.

Confederate Army captain D. R. Williams also invented a mechanical gun. Mounted on a mountain-howitzer carriage, it was a four-foot long 1-pounder of 1.57-inch bore. Operated by a hand crank, it utilized paper cartridges and could fire 65 shots per minute. It tended to overheat, and it was also not a true machine weapon in that ammunition was fed into it by hand.

Other such weapons also appeared, but the most famous of mechanical guns was that invented by Dr. Richard Jordan Gatling in 1862. Well aware of problems from the buildup of heat, Gatling designed his gun with six rotating barrels around a central axis. Each barrel fired in turn and each with its own bolt and firing pin. Thus, in a firing rate of 300 rounds per minute, each barrel would have been utilized only 50 times.

The Gatling gun employed a hopper for the ammunition similar to that of the Coffee Mill. The first Gatling gun also employed steel cylinders with a percussion cap at the end, a round, and paper cartridges with the charge. The production model did away with the percussion cap in favor of a rimfire cartridge. Turning the crank rotated the barrels, dropped in the rounds, and fired each barrel in turn. The chief difference from the Coffee Mill was in the rotating multiple-barrel design.

Gatling received a patent for his gun on November 4, 1862, but the U.S. Army's chief of ordnance Colonel John W. Ripley, who was well known for his opposition to innovative weaponry, blocked adoption of the new weapon. Gatling's North Carolina birth also seems to have worked against him. Despite Gatling's appeals to Lincoln, the army never adopted the gun. Its only use in the Civil War came when Major General Benjamin Butler purchased six of them at his own expense and employed them effectively in the Siege of Petersburg at the end of the war.

In 1864 Gatling redesigned the gun so that each barrel had its own chamber, which helped prevent the leakage of gas. Gatling also adopted center-fire cartridges. These and other refinements produced a rate of fire of about 300 rounds per minute. Finally, in 1866 the U.S. Army purchased 100 Gatling guns, equally divided between 6-barrel models of 1-inch caliber and 10-barrel models of .50-inch caliber. Gatling worked out a licensing agreement with Colt Arms to produce the gun.

The Gatling gun provided effective service in the Indian Wars in the American West and in the Spanish American War. The V Corps' Gatling Gun Detachment played an important role in the Santiago Campaign in Cuba, especially in the U.S. victory in the Battle of San Juan Hill of July 1, 1898. Gatling guns were also utilized in the Puerto Rico Campaign.

Gatling guns also served with the U.S. Navy. Tested by the British government in 1870, the Gatling gun outshot its competition by a wide margin and was adopted by both the British Army and the Royal Navy, in .42-caliber and .65-caliber, respectively. The Gatling gun remained the standard mechanical rapid-fire weapon until the introduction of the Maxim gun, the first true machine gun.

During the Vietnam War era Gatling-type weapons returned, this time electrically driven. The 20-millimeter (mm) M-61 Vulcan automatic cannon was first designed as an aircraft weapon but was also used as a ground-based antiaircraft weapon. The smaller 7.62-mm M-134 minigun was primarily a helicopter-mounted weapon.

SPENCER C. TUCKER

Further Reading

Berk, Joseph. *The Gatling Gun: 19th Century Machine Gun to 21st Century Vulcan.* Boulder, CO: Paladin, 1991.
Wahl, Paul, and Don Toppel. *The Gatling Gun.* New York: Arco Publishing, 1965.
Willbanks, James A. *Machine Guns: An Illustrated History of Their Impact.* Santa Barbara, CA: ABC-CLIO, 2004.

General Nathan Bedford Forrest soon threaten these all the way back to Columbus, Kentucky. Forrest's 2,100 men tear up nearly 50 miles of railroad track, seize considerable quantities of military supplies, and inflict some 2,000 Union casualties.

On December 20 an even worse calamity befalls Grant. As Porter prepares to depart Memphis with Sherman's troops and with Grant having drawn off some 20,000 Vicksburg defenders and engaging them outside the town of Granada, Confederate major general Earl Van Dorn captures Grant's supply base of Holly Springs (see December 20, 1862), destroying vast stocks of food and supplies bound for Grant's soldiers. Grant has no choice but to call off his advance and retrace his steps to Grand Junction. He tries to get word to Sherman, but the telegraph lines are disabled, and the message does not get through.

November 15, 1862

Civil War (continued): Eastern theater: Burnside begins offensive operations toward Richmond. Urged on by President Abraham Lincoln, new commander of the Army of the Potomac Major General Ambrose E. Burnside plans an overland movement south against the Confederate capital of Richmond, Virginia. Burnside, with more than 121,000 men and 312 guns, plans to outflank General Robert E. Lee's Army of Northern Virginia of nearly 80,000 men by moving to the east and crossing the Rappahannock River at Fredericksburg, midway between Washington, D.C., and Richmond.

Burnside feints toward Warrenton. Covering 40 miles in two days, he arrives at Falmouth, opposite the heights of Fredericksburg.

November 29, 1862

Civil War (continued): Trans-Mississippi West theater. Major General John B. Magruder assumes command of the Confederate District of Texas and begins assembling men and equipment to retake Galveston.

December 7, 1862

Civil War (continued). Off the coast of Cuba, the Confederate commerce raider *Alabama* (8 guns) seizes

 ## John Clifford Pemberton (1814–1881)

Confederate Army officer. Born in Philadelphia on August 10, 1814, John Clifford Pemberton graduated from the U.S. Military Academy, West Point, in 1837. He served in the Mexican-American War and was breveted twice for gallantry. Afterward, he continued in the regular U.S. Army.

At the beginning of the American Civil War, Pemberton, at the urging of his Virginia-born wife, opted to support the Confederacy, resigning his commission in the U.S. Army and accepting one in the Confederate Army as a brigadier general. His first major assignment was to command the coastal defenses of Charleston, South Carolina. He was advanced to major general in January 1862.

In October 1862, President Jefferson Davis appointed Pemberton lieutenant general and assigned him to command in Mississippi. The main Union target within the state was the town of Vicksburg on the Mississippi River. Perched on high rugged bluffs overlooking a bend in the river, Vicksburg stood as the chief barrier to Union control of the Mississippi. Although it was supported by several subsidiary outposts farther south, the most significant of which was Port Hudson, Louisiana, Vicksburg was the key to the Confederacy's hold on the Mississippi, protecting the flow of supplies from the trans-Mississippi states of Arkansas, Louisiana, and Texas to the Southern states east of the river.

Pemberton's first test came very soon after he assumed command. A Union army commanded by Major Ulysses S. Grant advanced into Mississippi from the north, following the tracks of the Mississippi Central Railroad. Pemberton's army retreated steadily in front of Grant, who advanced through Holly Springs and Abbeville to Oxford, 50 miles into the state. Believing his force inadequate to meet that of Grant, Pemberton called on Davis for reinforcements and meanwhile dispatched Major General Earl Van Dorn to lead a cavalry raid aimed at Grant's supply lines. Both efforts were successful. Van Dorn destroyed Grant's supply depot at Holly Springs on December 20, 1862, forcing a Union withdrawal from the state. Davis, overriding the objections of Western theater commander General Joseph E. Johnston, detached 10,000 men from Bragg's army and sent them to Pemberton.

Before the reinforcements could arrive, Pemberton had successfully dealt with yet another threat. On Grant's orders, Major General William T. Sherman had led a second Union column down the Mississippi to attack Vicksburg directly from the north, hoping that Pemberton would be distracted dealing with Grant's force in the interior. With Grant in retreat, Pemberton was free to turn his full attention to Sherman. However, the most significant factor in Confederate success was the terrain north of Vicksburg, which funneled the Union attack into a few easily defended corridors. The result was a lopsided Confederate victory at the Battle of Chickasaw Bluffs on December 29, 1862.

Thereafter, Grant encamped on the Louisiana bank of the Mississippi, just above Vicksburg, and spent the first three months of 1863 seeking a way of getting at Vicksburg via terrain that allowed some chance of success. That would mean approaching the town from the west or northwest. Pemberton, who had more troops than Grant and made use of the almost impenetrable swamps of the Mississippi Delta region above Vicksburg, foiled all of Grant's attempts during those months.

Then in April 1863 Grant launched a new campaign, sending his gunboats and transports past Vicksburg, then crossing his army into Mississippi below the town and marching for Jackson, squarely in Vicksburg's rear. Despite his advantage in overall numbers within the state of Mississippi, Pemberton was distracted by diversions that Grant planned and was unprepared for the speed and boldness of

Grant's campaign. Pemberton's response was confused and hesitant. Ordered by Johnston to pull all his troops out of fortresses and combine them for an open-field battle against Grant in the interior of the state, Pemberton started to do so. Then he received a cryptic telegram from Davis that Pemberton interpreted to mean he was not to leave Vicksburg or Port Hudson ungarrisoned at any time. Returning the garrisons, he set out to meet Grant with a reduced field force. Grant met and defeated him at the Battle of Champion Hill on May 16, 1863, and defeated him again the next day at the Big Black River Bridge. What was left of Pemberton's field army fled back into the Vicksburg fortifications. Grant followed and laid siege. On July 4, 1863, with food running low and Grant's approach trenches only a few feet outside his breastworks, Pemberton surrendered.

With no suitable command available at his rank, Pemberton resigned his lieutenant general's commission and became a colonel in the artillery. After the war, he retired near Warrenton, Virginia, and then returned to Pennsylvania, where he died in the village of Penllyn on July 31, 1881.

STEVEN E. WOODWORTH

Further Reading

Ballard, Michael B. *Pemberton: A Biography*. Jackson: University Press of Mississippi, 1991.
Bearss, Edwin Cole. *The Campaign for Vicksburg*. 3 vols. Dayton, Ohio: Morningside, 1985–1986.
Shea, William L., and Terrence J. Winschel. *Vicksburg Is the Key: The Struggle for the Mississippi River*. Lincoln: University of Nebraska Press, 2003.

the U.S. steamer *Ariel* with 700 passengers, including 150 U.S. marines.

December 7, 1862

Civil War (continued): Trans-Mississippi West theater: Battle of Prairie Grove. Both sides seek to control northwestern Arkansas, and on December 3, 1862, Confederate major general Thomas C. Hindman leads 11,000 men from Van Buren, Arkansas, to attack Union brigadier general James G. Blunt with 7,000 men near Fayetteville. Blunt appeals for assistance, and Brigadier General Francis J. Herron arrives from Springfield, Missouri, 110 miles distant, with 6,000 reinforcements following a hard three-day march. Hindman sees the chance to get between the two Union forces and defeat each in turn.

Leaving a small force to occupy Blunt, Hindman moves first against Herron, whom he engages near Prairie Grove. Following a series of attacks and counterattacks and with Hindman about to order a third assault, Blunt, who has marched his men to the sound of the guns, arrives and catches Hindman by surprise. Fighting continues until dark, when the Confederates, short on food and ammunition and with most of their artillery having been neutralized, withdraw. Each side suffers about 1,300 casualties.

Blunt pursues Hindman and captures Van Buren at the end of December, securing both northwestern Arkansas and western Missouri for the Union.

December 12, 1862

Civil War (continued): Western theater. The U.S. ironclad *Cairo* (14 guns), commanded by Lieutenant Commander Thomas O. Selfridge, sinks after striking two Confederate torpedoes (naval mines) in the Yazoo River during operations to circumvent the Confederate fortifications at Vicksburg, Mississippi. The *Cairo* is the first U.S. Navy warship sunk by Confederate torpedoes.

 ## CSS *Alabama*

During the American Civil War, the Confederacy resorted to attacking Union merchant shipping in order to drive up insurance costs and build antiwar sentiment in the North. The *Alabama* was the most successful of all the Southern commerce raiders. Built by John Laird & Sons at Liverpool, England, and launched in May 1862 as the *Enrica,* it was sailed to the Azores to skirt British neutrality laws and there outfitted. In August, Captain Raphael Semmes placed it in commission as CSS *Alabama.*

A sleek three-masted bark-rigged sloop of oak with a coppered hull, the *Alabama* was probably the finest cruiser of its day. With a weight of 1,050 tons and a length of 220 feet, the ship could make 13 knots under steam and sail and 10 knots under sail. It had a crew of 148. The *Alabama* mounted six broadside 32-pounders and two pivot-guns: a 7-inch 110-pounder rifled Blakeley and a smoothbore 8-inch 68-pounder amidships.

During the period August 1862 to June 1864 the *Alabama* cruised the Atlantic, the Caribbean, and the Pacific all the way to India. The ship sailed 75,000 miles, took 66 prizes, and sank the Union warship *Hatteras.* Twenty-five Union warships were engaged in searching for the *Alabama.* The ship's exploits were a considerable boost to Confederate morale.

With his ship badly in need of an overhaul, Semmes sailed it to Cherbourg, France. Blockaded there by the Union steam sloop *Kearsarge* with the certainty of additional U.S. warships soon arriving, on June 19, 1864, Semmes took his ship out to do battle. In one of the most spectacular of two-ship Civil War naval engagements, the *Kearsarge* sank the *Alabama.*

In 1984 the French Navy located the *Alabama* within French territorial waters. British preservationist groups want the wreck, if raised, to be displayed at Birkenhead where it was built. The U.S. government had asserted ownership, however, and in 1989 Congress passed a preservation act to protect the wreck.

SPENCER C. TUCKER

Further Reading

Semmes, Raphael. *Memoirs of Service Afloat, during the War between the States.* 1869; reprint, Secaucus, NJ: Blue and Grey, 1987.

Summersell, Charles Grayson. *CSS Alabama: Builder, Captain, and Plans.* University: University of Alabama Press, 1985.

Tucker, Spencer C. *Raphael Semmes and the Alabama.* Abilene, TX: McWhiney Foundation Press, 1996.

December 13, 1862

Civil War (continued): Eastern theater: Battle of Fredericksburg. On November 18, 1862, Major General Ambrose E. Burnside had arrived with his Army of the Potomac of more than 121,000 men and 312 guns at Falmouth across the Rappahannock River from Fredericksburg, then defended by only a token Confederate force.

Instead of crossing immediately, Burnside decides to await the arrival of pontoon bridges. These do not begin reaching the army until November 25, by which time Confederate general Robert E. Lee's Army of Northern Virginia is arriving in force at Fredericksburg. The Confederates have ample time to entrench on the high ground overlooking Fredericksburg.

 ## George Gordon Meade (1815–1872)

U.S. Army general. George Gordon Meade was born in Cádiz, Spain, on December 31, 1815. His father was a U.S. naval agent whose early death and attendant financial problems forced Meade to withdraw from school in Philadelphia and attend one in Washington, D.C., then enter the U.S. Military Academy, West Point. Meade graduated 19th in his class of 56 in 1835 and was commissioned in the artillery. During a brief leave, Meade assisted in a survey for the Long Island Railroad. Assigned to Florida during the Seminole War of 1835–1842, he caught a fever, returned to the North, and resigned from the army in October 1836.

Meade worked as a civil engineer but rejoined the army as a second lieutenant of topographical engineers in May 1842. Assigned to the northwest border survey, he assisted with lighthouse construction in the Delaware Bay area before serving under Major General Zachary Taylor in the Mexican-American War (1846–1848). Meade saw action in the Battle of Palo Alto (May 8, 1846) and the Battle of Resaca de la Palma (May 9, 1846). He was breveted first lieutenant for his role in the siege of Monterrey (September 20–24, 1846). He was then assigned to Major General Winfield Scott at Tampico, but because Scott already had sufficient numbers of topographical engineers, Meade was ordered to Washington. He was then involved in lighthouse work and in surveying the Great Lakes region. Meade was promoted to first lieutenant in August 1851 and to captain in May 1856.

Following the outbreak of the American Civil War (1861–1865), Meade was commissioned a brigadier general of volunteers in August 1861 and given command of one of three Pennsylvania brigades. At first assigned to the defense of Washington, D.C., he fought in Major General George McClellan's Peninsula Campaign during April–July 1862 and was promoted to major in the topographical engineers in the regular army. He was badly wounded in the hip and arm on June 30 during the Seven Days' Battles of June 26–July 2 before Richmond but recovered in time to participate in the Second Battle of Bull Run (Manassas) on August 29–30.

Given command of a division, Meade saw action during the Antietam Campaign in the Battle of South Mountain on September 14, 1862. In the Battle of Antietam (Sharpsburg) on September 17 he won praise for pressing home the attack and took temporary command of I Corps when Major General Joseph Hooker was wounded. Promoted to major general of volunteers in November, Meade commanded the 3rd Division in I Corps in the Battle of Fredericksburg on December 13, where he commanded on the Union left and won a temporary success. Meade briefly commanded the Center Corps that included the former III and VI Corps, then commanded V Corps in the Battle of Chancellorsville on May 1–6, 1863, where his forces were not heavily engaged.

Because Hooker had performed poorly as commander of the Army of the Potomac at Chancellorsville and Meade had a reputation of being unflappable, President Abraham Lincoln replaced Hooker with Meade as commander of the Army of the Potomac, the Union's major field army, on June 28 during Confederate general Robert E. Lee's Army of Northern Virginia's second invasion of the North. The two armies stumbled into a confrontation at Gettysburg, Pennsylvania. Meade fought a masterly defensive battle there on July 1–3, beating back several of Lee's attacks. Following Lee's last effort in Major

(continued)

(Continued)

General George Pickett's charge, Meade refused to stage a counterattack of the Confederate lines. He believed, rightly in the opinion of most historians, that a frontal attack across open ground would be a costly failure. Meade was criticized for his slow pursuit of Lee, who then retreated back to Virginia, bringing off his prisoners and much booty. Nonetheless, Meade had won the battle, handling the Army of the Potomac with cool competence. For the first time the Army of the Potomac was commanded by a general who refused to get rattled when confronting Lee. For his performance, Meade was promoted to brigadier general in the regular army.

Meade continued to command the Army of the Potomac for the remainder of the war, although new Union general-in-chief Lieutenant General Ulysses S. Grant accompanied the army in the field and had direction of its operations during the Overland Campaign against Richmond and the following siege of Petersburg. Despite this awkward situation, the two men worked well together. Meade and Grant engaged Lee in the Battles of the Wilderness (May 5–6, 1864), Spottsylvania Court House (May 8–18), and Cold Harbor (May 31–June 12). The Army of the Potomac then carried out the longest siege operation of the war at Petersburg, south of Richmond, during July 1864–April 1865 and fought in the Appomattox Campaign (March 30–April 9), when Lee endeavored to escape west. Meade, who was promoted to major general in the regular army in August 1864, was present with Grant at the surrender of the Army of Northern Virginia at Appomattox on April 9, 1865.

Meade was disappointed in the years after the Civil War, as his contributions in the war appeared slighted. First serving as commander of the Division of the Atlantic, with headquarters in Philadelphia, he then commanded the Third Military District in the South, consisting of Alabama, Georgia, and Florida, during 1867–1869. It was an assignment he did not wish, but he won the respect of the occupied for his fairness. After Grant became president, Meade was again assigned command of the Division of the Atlantic in 1869 but was slighted when Grant named William T. Sherman commander of the army with the rank of general and gave Sherman's former post not to Meade but instead to Philip Sheridan as a lieutenant general. Still affected by his old war wounds, Meade caught pneumonia and died at Philadelphia on November 6, 1872. Not a brilliant or bold commander, Meade was nonetheless solid and steady. He may have found it difficult to make decisions, but he was also not a man who scared easily and was thus the ideal man to command the Union field forces in the most important battle of the Civil War.

SPENCER C. TUCKER

Further Reading

Cleaves, Freeman. *Meade of Gettysburg.* Norman: University of Oklahoma Press, 1960.

Lyman, Theodore. *With Grant and Meade from the Wilderness to Appomattox.* Lincoln: University of Nebraska Press, 1994.

Meade, George Gordon. *The Life and Letters of George Gordon Meade, Major-General United States Army.* New York: Scribner, 1913.

Rafuse, Ethan Sepp. *George Gordon Meade and the War in the East.* Abilene, TX: McWhiney Foundation Press, 2003.

The First Battle of Fredericksburg, December 13, 1862. Major General Ambrose E. Burnside's Union troops attacked General Robert E. Lee's strong Confederate positions. The attackers were beaten back with 12,653 casualties, three times the losses sustained by Lee's force. (Library of Congress)

Attempts by Union engineers to place the pontoon bridges across the river are slowed by Confederate sharpshooters. The Union troops finally complete their crossing on the evening of December 11. The next day, Burnside organizes his forces for the assault.

The Union attack occurs on December 13. Major General George Gordon Meade's division briefly penetrates the Confederate line under Lieutenant General Thomas J. "Stonewall" Jackson to the southeast of Fredericksburg, but Lee rushes reinforcements there. Burnside's main effort at Fredericksburg, a frontal assault against the strength of Lee's line, is a dismal failure. Fourteen massed assaults against the high ground of Marye's Heights, just beyond the town, result in horrific Union

Battle of Fredericksburg		
Date	December 13, 1862	
Location	Fredericksburg, Virginia	
Opponents (*winner)	*Confederacy	United States
Commander	General Robert E. Lee	Major General Ambrose E. Burnside
#	72,500 men	121,000 men
Casualties	5,377 casualties (608 killed, 4,116 wounded, 653 captured/missing)	12,653 casualties (1,284 killed, 9,600 wounded, 1,769 captured/missing); 11,000 firearms lost

December 13, 1862

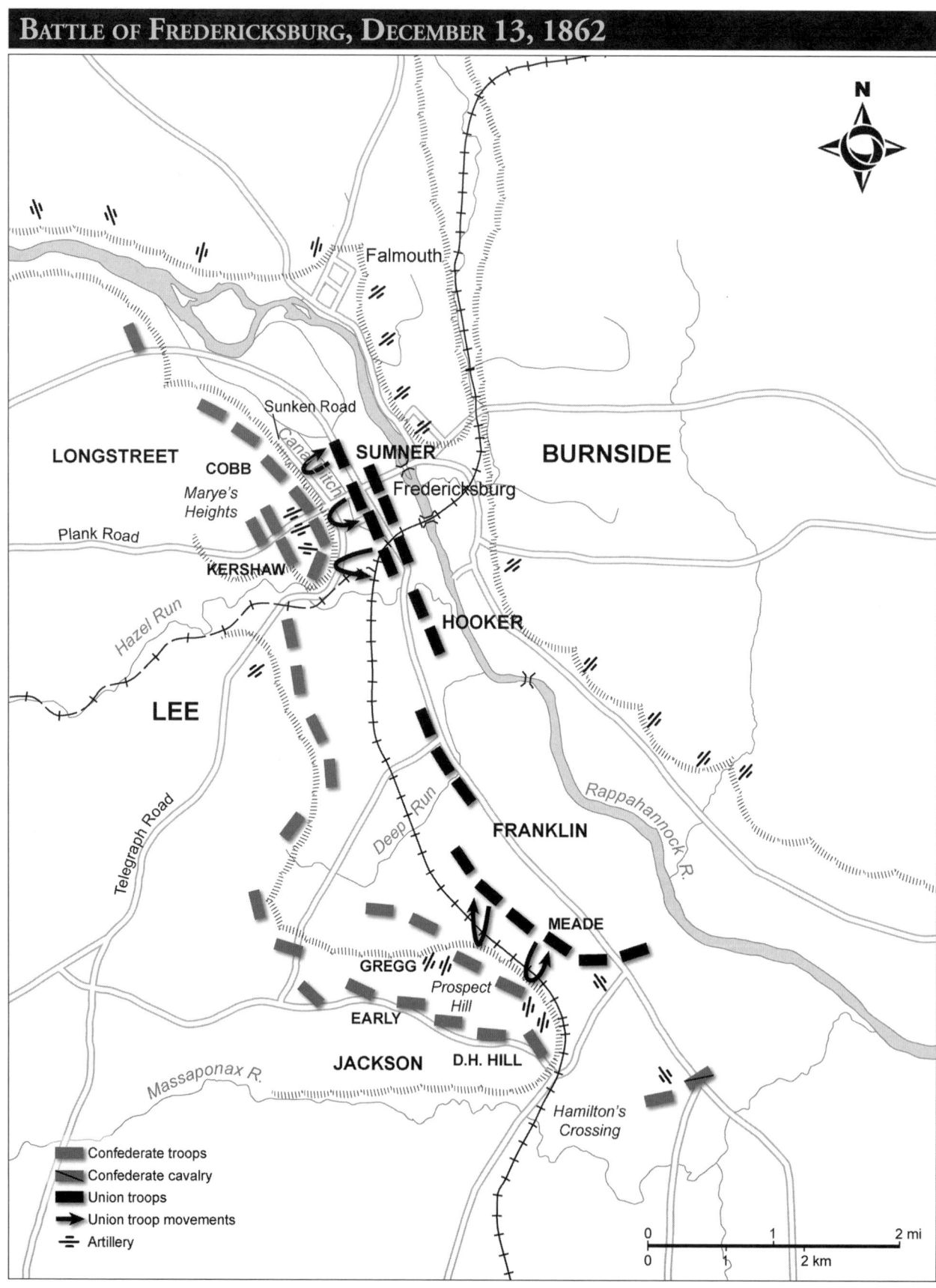

BATTLE OF FREDERICKSBURG, DECEMBER 13, 1862

N

Falmouth

Sunken Road

LONGSTREET

COBB

Marye's Heights

Plank Road

KERSHAW

SUMNER

Fredericksburg

BURNSIDE

Canal Ditch

Hazel Run

LEE

HOOKER

Deep Run

Rappahannock R.

FRANKLIN

Telegraph Road

MEADE

GREGG

Prospect Hill

EARLY

JACKSON   D.H. HILL

Massaponax R.

Hamilton's Crossing

Confederate troops
Confederate cavalry
Union troops
Union troop movements
Artillery

0   1   2 mi
0   1   2 km

casualties. On December 14 Burnside, following objections from his subordinates, agrees to suspend additional attacks. Under cover of a thunderstorm on the night of December 15, he withdraws his army across the Rappahannock, ending the battle and the campaign. A temporary truce that day allows the recovery of those Union wounded surviving two days of cold and rain on the battlefield.

Fredericksburg is Lee's most one-sided victory. The Union side suffers 12,653 casualties (1,284 killed, 9,600 wounded, 1,769 captured or missing). The Confederates also recover 11,000 Union firearms. The Confederates sustain 5,377 casualties (608 killed, 4,116 wounded, 653 captured or missing).

On January 25, 1863, President Abraham Lincoln replaces Burnside as commander of the Army of the Potomac with Major General Joseph E. Hooker.

December 14, 1862

Civil War (continued): Eastern theater: First Battle of Kinston. U.S. Army brigadier general John G. Foster departs New Bern, North Carolina, with 10,000 men, 640 cavalry, and 40 guns to attack the Wilmington and Weldon Railroad at Goldsborough. Some 2,000 Confederates under Brigadier General Nathan Evans contest the Union advance near Kinston Bridge, but heavily outnumbered, they withdraw north of the Neuse River. Union forces suffer 160 casualties, the Confederates 525.

December 18, 1862

Civil War (continued): Western theater: Battle of Lexington. Confederate general Braxton Bragg orders Brigadier General Nathan Bedford Forrest to cut the Union supply lines in western Tennessee. Forrest departs Columbia, Tennessee, with some 2,500 men on December 11 and crosses the Tennessee River two days later. On December 16, Union brigadier general Jeremiah Sullivan dispatches Colonel Robert Ingersoll and 200 men from Jackson to Lexington, Tennessee, where Ingersoll secures 470 reinforcements. Most of the men, however, have no combat experience.

Ingersoll's scouts detect Forrest's approach from the south on December 17. There are two principal roads on which to approach Lexington. Ingersoll orders the destruction of a bridge on one and concentrates the bulk of his forces to defend the other. Forrest attacks on December 18. Ingersoll's scouts had failed to destroy the bridge the day before as ordered, leaving the Confederates easy access to the smaller part of Ingersoll's command. In the ensuing Battle of Lexington, Forrest captures 147 men, including Ingersoll. The rest of the Union force is scattered. Forrest also secures two artillery pieces, 70 horses, numerous small arms, and supplies.

Forrest continues on to Jackson, Tennessee, but finds it too well defended. He then proceeds into Kentucky, destroying bridges and cutting supply lines to Union forces in Mississippi.

December 20, 1862

Civil War (continued): Western theater: Battle of Holly Springs. As part of his campaign against Vicksburg, on November 28, 1862, Union major general Ulysses S. Grant occupies Holly Springs, located on the Mississippi Central Railroad, a key transportation artery running north and south to Jackson. Grant establishes it as his major supply depot.

Grant draws off most Union troops for his drive south, leaving only 1,500 men to hold Holly Springs. Confederate major general Earl Van Dorn and 3,500 cavalry easily capture Holly Springs, take the garrison prisoner, and destroy vast stocks of food and supplies bound for Grant's soldiers and worth an estimated $1.5 million. The Confederates also tear up track and destroy telegraph lines in what is one of the most devastatingly effective cavalry raids of the entire war. Van Dorn then departs just ahead of reacting Union cavalry.

The Holly Springs raid forces Grant to call off his advance the next day. Evacuating Oxford, he retraces his steps to Grand Junction.

December 22, 1862–January 5, 1863

Civil War (continued): Morgan's Christmas Raid. The Louisville and Nashville Railroad is critical to supplying Union major general William S. Rosecrans's Army of the Cumberland. Confederate colonel John Hunt Morgan is determined to disrupt that supply route, with his principal objective being destruction of two railroad trestles at Muldraugh's Hill just north of Elizabethtown in Kentucky. Securing permission from Army of Tennessee commander Braxton Bragg, on December 22 Morgan departs Alexandria, Tennessee, with some 4,000 cavalrymen and seven guns.

Proceeding north, Morgan crosses the state line near Tompkinsville on December 24 and routs the advance guard of a Union cavalry battalion, then continues north through Glasgow. On Christmas Day he defeats a small Union force at Bear Wallow near Cave City, taking most of the men prisoner.

Morgan sends part of his men to burn the Bacon Creek Bridge, taking the stockade defending it and capturing nearly 100 Union soldiers. Farther north, on December 27 Morgan uses his considerable numerical advantage to defeat the 91st Illinois Volunteer Infantry Regiment defending Elizabethtown, securing that place and 650 prisoners. The next day Morgan's men ride to Muldraugh, where they assault and capture the two stockades protecting the two railroad trestles about two miles apart, each some 90 feet high and 500 feet in length, which the raiders then burn. Here Morgan takes another 700 prisoners.

Union troops are now out in force seeking to catch Morgan. On December 29, Colonel John Harlan and 2,300 infantry with a battery of artillery catch up with Morgan at the Rolling Fork River near Boston, but Morgan fights his way across. He then continues due south through Bardstown, New Haven, Springfield, and Campbellsville. At Tebbs Bend, the Confederates burn a stockade and a bridge over the Green River. Morgan arrives at Smithville, Tennessee, on January 5, 1863.

The so-called Christmas Raid is arguably Morgan's most successful of the war. His men kill and wound some 150 Union soldiers and capture and parole more than 1,800. The raiders also destroy several million dollars worth of Union property, tear up 35 miles of track, and burn bridges, railroad depots, and stores. The raid severely cripples the Army of the Cumberland's supply lines; it will be March 1863 before work begins to restore the lost infrastructure. Morgan has accomplished all this at a cost to his own force of only

2 dead and 14 wounded. The raid brings him promotion to brigadier general.

December 23–29, 1862

Civil War (continued): Western theater: Chickasaw Bayou Operation. Aware of the Union defeat at Holly Springs, Mississippi, on December 20 but not of the decision of Major General Ulysses S. Grant to terminate his overland drive on Vicksburg from the north, Rear Admiral David D. Porter and Major General William T. Sherman proceed with their part of the operation. On December 23 Porter and Sherman, with about 30,000 troops in transports, enter the Yazoo River and proceed upstream. On December 26 about 10 miles from the river mouth, three of the four Union divisions disembark.

Sherman's men are only about six miles north of Vicksburg, but before they can assault the city's northern defenses on the bluffs overlooking Chickasaw Bayou, the Union soldiers will have to cross the bayou and a morass of marshy low ground, subsidiary bayous, swamps, thick forest, and felled trees that are well covered by artillery. Heavy rain makes an already difficult situation far worse.

During December 27–28 as Sherman's troops slowly work their way toward the bluffs under covering fire from the Union ships in the river, the Confederate defenders increase their numbers from 6,000 to 12,000 men. Some Union gunboats proceed upriver to feign an attack on Haynes' Bluff, but this fails to draw off the defenders.

The major fighting ashore occurs on December 29, with Porter's gunboats providing diversionary fire. Sherman strikes the center of the Confederate line, advancing his men across open ground against the entrenchments. The Union troops are driven back by heavy fire from the bluffs. Faced with deteriorating weather and resolute Confederate resistance and learning at last of Grant's action, Sherman orders a withdrawal. By the morning of January 2, 1863, his men are again on board ship and on their way to the Mississippi and their base at Milliken's Bend, Louisiana.

Union losses are 175 killed, 930 wounded, and 743 taken prisoner. Confederate casualties number only 63 killed, 134 wounded, and 10 prisoners.

December 31, 1862

Civil War (continued). The U.S. Navy ironclad *Monitor* (2 guns) founders in a storm while under tow and is lost at sea off Cape Hatteras, North Carolina.

December 31, 1862

Civil War (continued): Eastern theater: Battle of Parker's Cross Roads. As Confederate brigadier general Nathan Bedford Forrest's cavalry raid into western Tennessee nears its end, Union brigadier general Jeremiah Sullivan, with two brigades under Colonels Cyrus L. Dunham and John W. Fuller totaling some 3,000 men, attempts to cut off Forrest's 1,800 men before the Confederates can withdraw across the Tennessee River. On December 31, the two meet at Parker's Cross Roads in Henderson County. Confederate artillery secures an early advantage, and Dunham withdraws about a half mile and redeploys, repelling frontal feints until attacked on both flanks and the rear.

Dunham rejects Forrest's demand for unconditional surrender, and Forrest is preparing a renewed assault when Fuller's brigade arrives and surprises the Confederates with an attack on their rear. The Confederates briefly reverse their front, repel Fuller, and then rush past Dunham's men south to Lexington and across the Tennessee River at Clifton. Both sides claim victory. Union casualties total 27 killed, 149 wounded, and 300 prisoners; the Confederates suffer perhaps 60 killed or wounded and 300 prisoners.

December 31, 1862–January 2, 1863

Civil War (continued): Western theater: Battle of Stones River (Murfreesboro). New Union commander of the Army of the Cumberland Major General William S. Rosecrans and Confederate commander of the Army of Tennessee General Braxton Bragg confront one another in Tennessee. Both Washington and Richmond goad their respective commanders into action, but it is Rosecrans who forces action on Bragg along Stones River outside Murfreesboro.

Rosecrans has some 44,000 men to 38,000 for Bragg. Both sides attempt the same maneuver: an envelopment of the other's right flank. Bragg moves first, but while he enjoys initial success, he fails to employ his reserves effectively, and Rosecrans is able to establish a new defensive line. Both sides hold their respective positions the next day with no fighting but redressing their lines. Bragg again attacks on January 2 and is repulsed.

Union casualties are 13,209 among 41,000 engaged; the Confederates lose 10,206 of nearly 35,000 engaged. Although a tactical draw, Stones River is a Union strategic victory, as Bragg, believing that Rosecrans has been reinforced, withdraws to Shelbyville. Rosecrans declines to pursue, contenting himself with occupying Murfreesboro. Based on complaints to Richmond by his subordinate commanders, Bragg is recalled to answer for the campaign.

January 1, 1863

Civil War (continued): Trans-Mississippi West theater: Battle of Galveston. New Confederate commander in Texas Major General John B. Magruder makes recapture of Galveston a priority. His joint army-navy operation commences at 1:00 a.m. on this date.

The Confederate land force is at Virginia Point at the northern end of the railroad bridge to Galveston Island. To assault the 42nd Massachusetts Regiment holding the wharf, Magruder plans to send some 500 men through the shallow water with scaling ladders. Artillery support will come from 6 siege guns, including an 8-inch gun on a railroad flat car, and 14 fieldpieces, moved into position on the night of December 31.

At the same time, Major Leon Smith will lead a flotilla of improvised warships against the Union gunboats. Assembled at Harrisburg on Buffalo Bayou, they are to proceed east to the upper part of the bay, then south to Galveston. Cotton bales to provide limited protection against small-arms fire cause the ships to be dubbed "cottonclads." They are the steamers *Bayou City* (1 gun), *Neptune* (2 guns), *John F. Carr* (2 guns), and *Lucy Gwin* (1 gun?). The steamers carry some 200 "horse marines" of the 5th and 7th Texas Cavalry.

U.S. Navy commander William B. Renshaw has the side-wheel steamer *Westfield* (flagship, 6 guns), *Harriet Lane* (4 guns), *Owasco* (4 guns), and *Clifton* (6 guns); the screw steamer *Sachem* (5 guns); and the schooner *Corypheus* (2 guns). Five supply vessels are anchored offshore. In all, the Union warships mount 30 guns, and these are generally larger than the half dozen in the Confederate warships. Magruder orders Smith to bring his ships in as close as possible without being detected and wait for the land attack to begin. Without the distraction of the land battle, the Confederate ships will have no chance against the far more powerful Union squadron.

The battle does not unfold as Magruder has planned. At about 1:00 a.m. on January 1, Union lookouts spot the Confederate ships west of Pelican Island in the bay and send up signal rockets. Obeying Magruder's orders, Smith orders his ships to withdraw some distance. Renshaw in the *Westfield* tries to cut off the Confederate cottonclads, but the Union flagship grounds near Pelican Island. Renshaw signals to the *Clifton* to come up and assist, but despite the efforts of sailors on both ships, the *Westfield* remains hard aground. This is an immense assist to the Confederates, rendering hors de combat the two most powerful Union warships.

The land battle begins at about 4:00 a.m. as Magruder sends his men against Galveston Island, but with the support of the remaining Union ships, the Confederate attack is rebuffed. The Confederate squadron now steams down the bay and joins the fighting at the wharf, concentrating on the *Harriet Lane*. Although the *Neptune* is sunk, the Confederate ships crash into the *Harriet Lane,* and their more numerous riflemen capture it. Efforts by the other Union ships to retake the *Harriet Lane* are unsuccessful.

Under a flag of truce the captain of the *Bayou City,* Henry Lubbock, brazenly demands that the Union ships surrender, allowing three hours for the decision. If Renshaw agrees, he will be allowed to depart with his men in one of his ships. Convinced that the battle is now lost, the men of the 42nd Massachusetts surrender.

Renshaw orders the remaining Union ships to withdraw from the harbor and escape while he scuttles the *Westfield*. Renshaw sets the ship alight, but its magazine explodes prematurely, killing him and a boat crew. The four remaining Union ships meanwhile escape to sea.

At a cost of one ship lost, 26 men dead and 117 wounded, the Confederates have retaken Galveston and reopened it to blockade-runners. They have destroyed two Union warships, captured two barks loaded with coal and a small schooner, and taken substantial stores and at least 25,000 rounds of small-arms ammunition. Several dozen Union sailors are dead, and 350 sailors and soldiers are prisoners. Although Union naval forces promptly reestablish the blockade off Galveston, the Confederates retain control of that port for the remainder of the war.

January 9–11, 1863

Civil War (continued): Western theater: Battle of Fort Hindman (Arkansas Post). At the beginning of January 1863, U.S. major general John McClernand, a political appointee lacking in military background but senior in rank and thirsting after glory, takes command of river operations against Vicksburg from Major General William T. Sherman. McClernand sends a sizable force up the Arkansas, the largest river emptying into the Mississippi, to destroy Confederate Fort Hindman at Arkansas Post. Located some 50 miles from the river's mouth and mounting 14 guns, it guards the river approach to Little Rock, 117 miles north. Arkansas Post is also an important staging area for Confederate raids threatening Union control of the Mississippi and is held by 5,000 men under Confederate brigadier general Thomas J. Churchill. A Union success here will help restore Union morale following the rebuff of the Battle of Chickasaw Bluffs.

The Union expedition sets out on January 4, 1863, with Rear Admiral David D. Porter heading the naval contingent of eight warships (including three ironclads) escorting a large number of transports carrying some 32,000 men. The troops go ashore near Arkansas Post on the evening of January 9. On January 10 and 11 Porter's warships shell its outer works and then Fort Hindman. With all his guns out of

 ## James Birdseye McPherson (1828–1864)

U.S. Army officer. Born near Clyde, Ohio, on November 14, 1828, to a poor farming family, James Birdseye McPherson earned an appointment to the U.S. Military Academy, West Point, after a local wealthy merchant aided his candidacy. He graduated first in his class in 1853 and was commissioned a second lieutenant in the Corps of Engineers on July 1, 1853. On active duty throughout the 1850s, McPherson was a captain at the outbreak of the American Civil War.

After serving as an aide to Major General Henry Halleck, McPherson became chief engineer for Major General Ulysses Grant. McPherson fought at the Battle of Shiloh (April 6–7, 1862). Promoted to brigadier general on August 19, 1862, he was advanced to major general on October 8, 1862. McPherson commanded XVII Corps of the Army of the Tennessee during December 22, 1862–March 12, 1864.

McPherson distinguished himself in the Second Vicksburg Campaign (April 1–July 4, 1863) in engagements at Jackson (May 14), Champion's Hill (May 16), and Big Black River (May 17). At Champion's Hill, his troops played a critical role in the Union victory, pitching into the Confederate left flank and breaking it after several hours of fierce fighting.

That spring, Major General William T. Sherman, commanding the Union Military Division of the Mississippi at Chattanooga, planned to strike into the interior of the Confederacy, with the aim of defeating the Confederate Army of Tennessee and subsequently assaulting Atlanta. Both Sherman and Grant considered McPherson to be the most promising young general in the Union Army, and on March 26, 1864, McPherson assumed command of the Army of the Tennessee.

On May 9, 1864, McPherson's infantry poured through Snake Creek Gap, moving on Resaca, 15 miles to the Confederate rear. Three days later, his army crossed the Oostanaula River on the way to Atlanta. As Union forces approached the city, McPherson's commands were positioned to the east. On July 22, 1864, a Confederate force struck the Army of the Tennessee as it moved south from Decatur. Sensing that the left flank of his army was in danger, McPherson galloped to the sound of the guns. En route he ordered up a brigade into what he perceived to be a dangerous gap between two Union corps. Ambushed by Confederate cavalry, he was shot dead. Noticing the dead two-star general, a Confederate officer asked who he was. McPherson's orderly is reported to have replied: "It is General McPherson, sir. You have killed the best man in our army." McPherson was the only Union Army commander to be killed in battle during the Civil War.

DAVID M. KEITHLY

Further Reading

Leckie, Robert. *None Died in Vain*. New York: HarperCollins, 1990.

McPherson, James M. *Battle Cry of Freedom*. New York: Oxford University Press, 1988.

Woodworth, Steven E. *Nothing but Victory: The Army of the Tennessee, 1861–1865*. New York: Knopf, 2005.

commission except one, on the afternoon of January 11 Colonel John W. Dunnington surrenders the fort to Porter, while Churchill surrenders the land forces to Sherman.

Confederate losses are about 150 dead and 4,791 prisoners. The Union tally ashore is 79 killed and 440 wounded, while the ships sustain another 30 casualties. The Union troops destroy what remains of the fort and its guns, then return to Milliken's Bend about seven miles above Vicksburg. McClernand takes full credit for the victory.

Concerned about McClernand, Sherman and Porter urge Major General Ulysses S. Grant to come and take personal command of Union operations against Vicksburg. Grant arrives on January 29 and divides his 60,000 men into three corps, commanded by Sherman, McClernand, and Major General James B. McPherson.

January 11, 1863

Civil War (continued). Captain Raphael Semmes of the Confederate commerce raider *Alabama* (8 guns) lures away from the remainder of the U.S. Navy squadron off Galveston, Texas, the side-wheeler *Hatteras* (5 guns), commanded by Lieutenant Commander H. C. Blake. In a quick engagement, the *Alabama* sinks the *Hatteras* and escapes into the Gulf of Mexico.

January 14, 1863

Civil War (continued): Trans-Mississippi West theater: Union attack at Bayou Teche, Louisiana. A joint Union army-navy force under Lieutenant Commander Thomas M. Buchanan and consisting of the coastal combatants *Kinsman* (armament unknown), *Calhoun* (3 guns), and *Diana* (armament unknown) sweeps up Bayou Teche, Louisiana, in an effort to eliminate Confederate resistance above Brashear City (Morgan City). Confederate land forces are forced to withdraw from Franklin, Louisiana, and U.S. ships block the bayou, forcing the destruction of the Confederate gunboat *Cotton* (armament unknown).

January 16–August 23, 1863

Civil War (continued): First cruise of CSS *Florida*. The Confederate commerce raider *Florida* (11 guns),

commanded by Lieutenant John N. Maffitt, repaired and with new crew members, after two failed attempts to escape departs Mobile Bay on the night of January 16–17. At 2:00 a.m. on January 17 in a thick mist, the *Florida* passes two Union blockaders without being detected. Lookouts on a third ship sight the raider as a consequence of sparks from its funnel, and Maffitt orders full steam and all sails set. At 14.5 knots, the *Florida* easily outruns its pursuers. The *R. R. Culyer* (10 guns), the sole blockader capable of overtaking the *Florida*, is sighted at about 5:00 a.m. only 3 miles distant. Maffitt orders sails stricken and engines stopped. The sea is rough, and the waves hide the low-lying raider, enabling it to escape. Both passages of the *Florida* through the blockade are major embarrassments for the U.S. Navy.

In this, its first cruise as a commerce raider, the *Florida* will take 22 Union merchantmen before arriving at Brest, France, on August 23 to refit.

January 20–22, 1863

Civil War (continued): Eastern theater: Mud March. The Union Army of the Potomac commanded by Major General Ambrose Burnside marches west up the northern side of the Rappahannock River in Virginia in an effort to outflank Confederate general Robert E. Lee's Army of Northern Virginia on the southern side of the stream and then drive south on Richmond. Terrible road conditions as a consequence of heavy rain as the troops set out cause it to be known as the Mud March and force Burnside to halt the operation three days later and return the men to their camps at Falmouth.

January 21, 1863

Civil War (continued): Trans-Mississippi West theater. At Sabine Pass, Texas, the Confederate cotton-clad steamers *Josiah H. Bell* (2 guns) and *Uncle Ben* (3 guns) capture the Union blockader sailing ship *Morning Light* (8 guns) and the small schooner *Velocity*, temporarily raising the U.S. Navy blockade there.

January 25, 1863

Civil War (continued): Eastern theater. President Abraham Lincoln relieves Major General Ambrose

Burnside of command of the Army of the Potomac and replaces him with Major General Joseph Hooker, one of Burnside's most outspoken critics.

January 29, 1863

American Indian Wars (continued): Battle of the Bear River. See September 1862–October 1863.

January 31, 1863

Civil War (continued): The first African American regiment is mustered into the U.S. Army. This unit, the 1st South Carolina Volunteer Regiment, is composed of escaped slaves from South Carolina and Florida. Previous efforts to form black units in New Orleans and Kansas have not been officially recognized. Although the regiment sees some combat in coastal operations in Georgia and Florida, it is not involved in any major battles. Its first commander is Colonel Thomas Wentworth Higginson; he and all the other officers are white. Confederate president Jefferson Davis proclaims that if captured, members of the regiment will not be treated as prisoners of war but will be auctioned off as slaves and white officers will be hanged, but this policy is never carried out in practice. The regiment is redesignated the 33rd Infantry Regiment, U.S. Colored Troops, on February 8, 1864.

January 31, 1863

Civil War (continued). The Confederate ironclad rams *Palmetto State* (10 guns) and *Chicora* (6–8 guns) sortie from Charleston, South Carolina, to attack the Union wooden blockaders offshore. The U.S. Navy screw steamer *Mercedita* (9 guns) surrenders, while the side-wheeler *Keystone State* (11 guns) is damaged. The arrival of Union reinforcements, especially the screw sloop *Housatonic* (10 guns), forces the retirement of the Confederate ironclads, and both Union warships are recovered.

Beginning of February–March 1863

Civil War (continued): Western theater: Gunboat operations on the Mississippi. Major General Ulysses S. Grant, now personally commanding Union operations against Vicksburg, rejects another frontal assault on that Confederate fortress, and heavy rain postpones any attempt down the Mississippi until spring. While waiting for the water level in the river to fall, Grant and Rear Admiral David D. Porter, commander of the Mississippi Squadron, mount a series of smaller operations in hopes of positioning Union troops below Vicksburg without having to run the river batteries. These operations are known as the Water Experiments.

Porter also sends the powerful ironclad *Indianola* (4 guns) and the ram *Queen of the West* (4 guns) in daring runs past Vicksburg to operate against Confederate forces between it and Port Hudson to the south. They exact some damage and disrupt Confederate river traffic before their capture: the *Queen of the West* on February 14 and the *Indianola* on February 24.

February 3–April 4, 1863

Civil War (continued): Western theater: Yazoo Pass Expedition. Rear Admiral David D. Porter, commander of the U.S. Navy Mississippi Squadron, believes that he can work around east of Vicksburg from Yazoo Pass and Moon Lake in Mississippi via the connected Coldwater, Tallahatchie, and Yazoo Rivers. Union engineers determine that cutting the Yazoo Pass levee will increase water levels to the point that shallow-draft vessels can navigate the delta waterways.

On February 3 Union engineers blow up the Yazoo Pass levee. Lieutenant Commander Watson Smith has charge of the naval force of the ironclads *Chillicothe* (2 guns) and *Baron de Kalb* (13 guns); the gunboats *Rattler* (flagship, 6 guns), *Marmora* (4 guns), *Signal* (7 guns), *Romeo* (6 guns), and *Forest Rose* (6 guns); the towboat *S. Bayard* with 3 barges of coal; and 13 transports with 6,000 troops under Brigadier General Leonard F. Ross. The expedition gets through the pass without much difficulty, but the Coldwater River is obstructed by trees—many deliberately felled by the Confederates—and widespread underwater growth, all of which have to be dragged clear. The going is easier when the expeditionary force reaches the larger Tallahatchie River, where it is joined by 3 other warships.

Aware of Union intentions, the Confederates erect Fort Pemberton on a narrow neck of land at the confluence of the Tallahatchie and Yalobusha Rivers at Greenwood. Mounting half a dozen guns and manned by 1,500 men under Major General William W. Loring, it commands the water approaches in either direction.

The Union expedition arrives at Fort Pemberton on March 11, and Smith sends his two ironclads against it on March 11, 13, and 16. Each time the ironclads receive the worst of the exchange. With Union troops unable to land, Ross decides to withdraw.

The expeditionary force then meets up with Union reinforcements under Brigadier General Isaac F. Quinby. Senior in rank to Ross, Quinby orders a return to Fort Pemberton. Following other futile attacks, Quinby breaks off the effort for good on April 4, with Union forces retracing their steps north to the Mississippi.

February 14, 1863

Civil War (continued). The Union ram *Queen of the West* (4 guns), commanded by Brigadier General Alfred W. Ellet, is run aground by a Confederate pilot in an expedition up the Red River in Louisiana and abandoned under heavy fire from Confederate shore batteries. Its prize the *De Soto,* which had accompanied the *Queen of the West,* is also lost, with Union seamen finding safety in the *Era No. 5.* The Confederates take possession of the *Queen of the West,* repair it, and employ it to disrupt Union operations below Vicksburg.

February 24, 1863

Civil War (continued): Trans-Mississippi West theater. The Confederate gunboat *William H. Webb* (3 guns) and the recently captured ram *Queen of the West* (4 guns?) attack and capture the powerful Union ironclad *Indianola* (4 guns) in the Mississippi River near the mouth of the Red River. The next day the Confederates, believing a false report that a powerful Union ironclad has come down the Mississippi past Vicksburg (a barge with dummy superstructure to make it appear as if it is an ironclad), destroy the damaged *Indianola* to prevent its recovery by the Union. The Confederates later return and salvage its ordnance.

February 25, 1863

Civil War (continued). The U.S. side-wheeler *Vanderbilt* (15 guns), commanded by Acting Lieutenant Charles H. Baldwin, seizes the British blockade-runner *Peterhoff* off St. Thomas, the Virgin Islands. An international dispute erupts with Great Britain over mail confiscated from the ship.

February 28, 1863

Civil War (continued). The U.S. Navy ironclad monitor *Montauk* (2 guns), under Commander John L. Worden and operating with the 4-gun screw gunboats *Wissahickon* and *Seneca* and the screw combatant *Dawn* (2 guns), destroys the blockade-runner *Rattlesnake* (formerly CSS *Nashville*) at Fort McAllister on the Savannah River in Georgia. Commander of the South Atlantic Blockading Squadron Rear Admiral Samuel F. Du Pont had sent the *Montauk* several times against McAllister in order to test the capability of the monitors against shore installations prior to his assault on Charleston, but the results are disappointing.

March 3, 1863

Civil War (continued): U.S. Draft Act. President Abraham Lincoln signs into law the Enrollment or Federal Draft Act, requiring all able-bodied male citizens and those immigrants who have filed to become citizens who are age 20–45 to register for possible military service. Those eligible may pay substitutes to serve in their place or a fine of $300 to avoid service. This first conscription legislation in U.S. history goes into effect on April 1 and prompts riots in some cities, especially New York in July (see July 13–16, 1863). Only 6 percent of the Union Army is secured through conscription, however, while some 20 percent of Confederate forces are conscripted.

March 5, 1863

Civil War (continued): Western theater: Battle of Thompson's Station. At Thompson's Station in Williamson County, Tennessee, Major General Earl Van Dorn leads 6,000 Confederates against a reinforced Union brigade of 2,857 men under Colonel John Coburn, which had departed Franklin, Tennessee, in a reconnaissance in force toward Columbia. Van

Dorn sends Brigadier General William H. Jackson's dismounted 2nd Division in a frontal attack, while Brigadier General Nathan Bedford Forrest's division sweeps around the Union left and into its rear. After three attempts and hard fighting, Jackson carries the Union hilltop position as Forrest captures Coburn's wagon train and blocks the road to Columbia. Out of ammunition and surrounded, Coburn surrenders. Union casualties total 1,906, while Confederate losses are only 300.

March 8, 1863

Civil War (continued): Eastern theater. In one of the most daring raids of the war, near Fairfax Court House, Virginia, Confederate partisans commanded by Colonel John S. Mosby capture in his bed Brigadier General Edwin H. Stoughton, commanding a brigade of Vermont regiments within the defenses of Washington, D.C. The Confederates also capture 2 captains, 30 soldiers, and 58 horses.

March 10, 1863

Civil War (continued). President Abraham Lincoln signs a general amnesty proclamation that, however, requires soldiers presently absent without leave (AWOL) to return to their units by April 1, 1863.

March 14, 1863

Civil War (continued): Western theater: Union operation against Port Hudson. In early March, West Gulf Blockading Squadron commander Rear Admiral David G. Farragut and commander of the

John Singleton Mosby (1833–1916)

Confederate Army officer and successful guerrilla leader. John Singleton Mosby was born on December 6, 1833, at McLaurrine Place, Cumberland County, Virginia. In 1840 his family moved to Charlottesville. Mosby entered the University of Virginia in 1849, but on March 29, 1850, he shot a fellow student and was sentenced to 12 months in jail. This ended his formal schooling. While in prison, Mosby studied law and joined a law firm upon his release. He was practicing law in Bristol, Virginia, when the American Civil War began, and he immediately joined the Confederate cavalry as a private.

Mosby fought in the First Battle of Bull Run (Manassas) (July 21, 1861). Brigadier General J. E. B. Stuart noted Mosby's performance and secured his promotion to first lieutenant and requested that he join Stuart's cavalry scouts. Mosby played a prominent role in the Confederate cavalry's movement around Major General George B. McClellan's Union forces (the so-called Ride around McClellan) in the Seven Days' Battles near Richmond during June 25–July 1, 1862. However, Mosby was captured by Union cavalry soon thereafter and imprisoned in Washington, D.C.

Exchanged 10 days later, during his return to Confederate lines Mosby gathered much valuable information about the Union reinforcements from North Carolina, led by Major General Ambrose Burnside and destined for Major General John Pope's Union command, and personally relayed this information to General Robert E. Lee.

In January 1863, General Stuart authorized Mosby to form the 43rd Battalion, Partisan Rangers, of the 1st Virginia Cavalry. In what was certainly Mosby's most daring and famous exploit, he and 29 of his men raided the Fairfax County, Virginia, courthouse on March 9, 1863, and captured three high-ranking Union officers, including Brigadier General Edwin H. Stoughton. On August 13, 1864, Mosby and his

(continued)

(Continued)

men ambushed a large Union wagon train at Berryville, Virginia. And on October 24, 1864, Mosby carried out the Greenback Raid at Harpers Ferry, West Virginia, in which a Union train was purposefully derailed. Mosby and his rangers took off with $173,000 sent via rail for soldiers' pay.

Mosby was promoted to colonel on December 7, 1864. Now known as the "Gray Ghost," he caused widespread disruption to Union lines of communication. In all, he staged more than 100 separate attacks on Union troops, supply lines, and depots. The destructive results of these activities led to Lieutenant General Ulysses S. Grant's order to summarily execute any captured partisans attached to Mosby's unit. By Mosby's own account, his outfit may have kept as many as 30,000 Union soldiers from reaching the front lines.

When some of Mosby's men were executed in Front Royal, Virginia, under the orders of Brigadier General George Custer, Mosby wrote to Grant protesting this, and Grant stayed further executions. Never having more than 800 or so men under his command, Mosby was wounded seven times in the course of the war.

Upon the surrender of Confederate forces at Appomattox on April 9, 1865, Mosby disbanded his command. He then returned to the practice of law in Warrenton, Virginia, and embarked on a political career in the Republican Party, eventually working as a campaign manager for General Grant. Mosby served as the U.S. consul in Hong Kong from 1878 to 1885, and in 1904 he was appointed assistant attorney general of the United States, a post he held until 1910. Mosby died in Washington, D.C., on May 30, 1916.

RALPH BAKER AND PAUL G. PIERPAOLI JR.

Further Reading

Jones, Virgil C. *Gray Ghosts and Rebel Raiders*. Charlottesville, VA: Howell, 1998.
Siepel, Kevin H. *Rebel: The Life and Times of John Singleton Mosby*. Cambridge, MA: Da Capo, 1997.

Department of the Gulf Major General Nathaniel P. Banks agree to mount a joint attack on Port Hudson, with Banks providing 25,000 troops from Baton Rouge. Port Hudson is 115 miles downriver from Vicksburg at a sharp bend in the river.

Farragut assembles a powerful force of seven warships accompanied by mortar boats. The Union ships make their run on the night of March 14 but discover an unwelcome surprise in the form of a series of locomotive headlights placed by the Confederates along the eastern bank. These silhouette the Union ships and allow the shore gunners to deliver accurate fire. Only the first two of Farragut's ships, the flagship steam sloop *Hartford* and the gunboat *Albatross*, make

it past. The rest are damaged, and the side-wheeler *Mississippi* is destroyed, with 89 casualties.

A good deal of the responsibility for the failure of the operation rests with Banks. Although his forces probe the Confederate defenses, he fails to mount an attack in sufficient force timed to occupy the Confederate gunners. Learning of Farragut's failure, Banks then calls off his own assault. Farragut's two warships, however, sweep Confederate shipping from the central section of the Mississippi.

March 14–27, 1863

Civil War (continued): Western theater: Steele's Bayou Expedition. Mississippi Squadron

A Union artillery battery at Port Hudson, Louisiana, during the siege of March–July 1863. Confederate major general Franklin Gardner surrendered Port Hudson on July 9, following the Union victory at Vicksburg, Mississippi. (National Archives)

commander Rear Admiral David D. Porter hopes to secure entrance to the Yazoo and land troops above Haynes' Bluff in order to turn the Confederate flank at Vicksburg. Porter sets out with five warships, four mortar schooners, and four tugs. U.S. major general William T. Sherman and 10,000 troops follow in transports.

Progress in Black Bayou is blocked by trees that have to be dragged aside, although in 24 hours the expedition advances four miles. The ships reach the Yazoo on March 16. Progress there is easy, but at Rolling Fork trees and undergrowth as well as Confederate sharpshooters impede progress. As the flotilla approaches the Sunflower River, a Confederate transport brings both troops and light artillery.

With some 4,000 men, the Confederates fell trees in an attempt to cut off Porter from Sherman. Porter contemplates scuttling his ships, but Sherman's troops arrive and drive the Confederates from both banks, allowing the Union ships to retrace their steps to safety. Although it advanced 70 miles, the March 14–27 expedition ends in failure.

March 21, 1863

Civil War (continued): Eastern theater. U.S. major general Joseph Hooker, commanding the Army of the Potomac, orders his chief of staff Major General Daniel Butterfield to create distinctive shoulder patches and insignias for the various corps of the army. This becomes standard army practice. (Some also credit Butterfield as having originated the bugle call "Taps.")

March 25, 1863

Civil War (continued): Western theater: Battle of Brentwood. Confederate brigadier general Nathan B. Forrest with two brigades attacks and takes the surrender of the Union garrison at Brentwood, Tennessee, commanded by Lieutenant Colonel Edward Bloodgood. The Union soldiers had been guarding a key supply depot on the Nashville and Decatur Railroad (also known as the Tennessee and Alabama Railroad). The Confederates destroy a bridge over the Little Harpeth River and take 785 prisoners, then engage and drive off Union cavalry under Brigadier General Green C. Smith. The Confederates suffer 59 casualties; the Union loss is nearly 800, most of them prisoners.

March 25, 1863

Civil War (continued): Western theater: Loss of the U.S. ram *Lancaster*. The *Lancaster* and *Switzerland* (armaments unknown) of the U.S. Army's ram fleet, commanded by Colonel Charles R. Ellet, attempt to run south past Vicksburg on the Mississippi to join Rear Admiral David D. Porter's ships below that Confederate fortress. Proceeding under full steam, the two Union ships encounter heavy fire from Confederate shore batteries. Although the *Switzerland* is disabled by a shot through its steam boiler, the ship floats to safety. The *Lancaster* is not as fortunate. A plunging shot tears a huge hole in the hull of the ship, and it sinks almost immediately.

March 29, 1863

Civil War (continued): Western theater: Beginning of Grant's Second Vicksburg Campaign. Commander of the Union Army of the Tennessee Major General Ulysses S. Grant, his subordinate Major General William T. Sherman, and Mississippi Squadron commander Rear Admiral David D. Porter meet at Milliken's Bend above Vicksburg and develop a new plan to take Vicksburg. With winter over, Grant resurrects an earlier plan now feasible because of receding water. Union troops will march south down the Louisiana

side of the river past Vicksburg to New Carthage. Porter's ships will then run past Vicksburg and ferry Grant's men across the river to Grand Gulf in Mississippi, allowing Grant to approach Vicksburg from the south. The plan is risky, but Grant is determined to try.

On March 29 Grant sets out down the Louisiana shore. Many areas are still flooded, necessitating the laying of log roads for the wagon trains.

April 3, 1863

Civil War (continued): Western theater. U.S. Navy forces under Lieutenant Commander LeRoy Fitch including the timberclad *Lexington* (8 guns) and tinclads *Alfred Robb* (4 guns), *Brilliant* (4 guns), *Silver Lake* (6 guns), and *Springfield* (6 guns) attack and destroy the town of Palmyra, Tennessee, in retaliation for recent attacks by Confederate guerrillas against Union shipping.

April 7, 1863

Civil War (continued): Du Pont's attack on Charleston. Leaders in Washington are especially anxious to take Charleston, South Carolina, font of the rebellion and the most important Southern seaport. Commander of the South Atlantic Blockading Squadron Rear Admiral Samuel Du Pont wants a combined land-sea assault, but Secretary of the Navy Gideon Welles and Assistant Secretary Gustavus V. Fox are convinced that this can be accomplished by ironclads alone, and they pressure Du Pont accordingly. Never confident of the outcome especially after a trial against Confederate Fort McAllister near Charleston, Du Pont plans to enter the harbor with nine ironclads and shell Fort Sumter into submission. Well aware of Union designs, the Confederates work to strengthen Charleston's seaward defenses by a combination of forts mounting heavy guns, mines (known as torpedoes), and obstructions.

The Union assault on April 7, 1863, is a complete failure, with the monitors absorbing heavy punishment. Because the monitors mount relatively few guns, they fire only 139 rounds, while the Confederates fire 2,229. The Union ironclad *Keokuk* (2 guns), hit more than 90 times in the engagement, sinks off Morris Island the next day. Du Pont informs

Washington that Charleston cannot be taken by naval attack alone. He also fears the capture of one of his ironclads, which the Confederates might then use to break the blockade. Welles rather unfairly removes Du Pont from command.

April 9–October 28, 1863

Civil War (continued): Cruise of CSS *Georgia*. Confederate Navy commander William L. Maury commissions the commerce raider *Georgia*. It is the former fast merchant ship *Japan* that his father, Commander Matthew F. Maury, purchased for the Confederacy in Scotland and that then rendezvoused with a merchant ship bearing its armament off Ushant, France. The *Georgia* (5 guns) takes nine U.S. prizes during a cruise to the Cape of Good Hope but, proving unsatisfactory for commerce raiding, is decommissioned and sold after its return to Europe.

April 12–13, 1863

Civil War (continued): Trans-Mississippi West theater: Battle of Fort Bisland. On April 9, 1863, U.S. major general Nathaniel P. Banks, commander of the Department of the Gulf, launches an operation by the three divisions of his XIX Corps up Bayou Teche in western Louisiana in order to capture Confederate Fort Bisland at Irish Bend. Major General Richard Taylor, commander of the Confederate District of Western Louisiana, commands forces opposing him. Two Union divisions cross Berwick Bay from Brashear City to the west side at Berwick. On April 12, the third division proceeds up the Atchafalaya River to land in the rear of Franklin and intercept any forces withdrawing from Fort Bisland or turn the Confederate position. Taylor dispatches a regiment under Colonel Tom Green to ascertain Union strength and delay the advance. Late on April 12, Union troops arrive at the fort, and the two sides engage in an artillery duel, forcing the attackers back to camp for the night.

On the morning of April 13, Union forces resume the attack, with fighting continuing until dusk. The Confederate gunboat *Diana* (armament unknown) assists the defenders. The U.S. gunboats *Estrella* (5 guns), *Arizona* (6 guns), and *Calhoun* (3 guns) join

the fray in late afternoon. They engage and destroy the Confederate ram *Queen of the West* (4 guns?). That same night, Taylor learns that Brigadier General Cuvier Grover's division of Banks's corps sent up the Atchafalaya has landed in his rear and is poised to cut off a Confederate retreat. Taylor immediately begins evacuating men, weapons, and supplies, leaving only a small force to retard Union movements. On the morning of April 14, Union troops discover Fort Bisland abandoned. In the fighting, U.S. forces suffer 234 casualties, the Confederates 450.

April 14, 1863

Civil War (continued): Trans-Mississippi West theater: Battle of Irish Bend. In Louisiana, U.S. major general Nathaniel P. Banks moves the three divisions of his XIX Corps up Bayou Teche to capture Confederate Fort Bisland at Irish Bend. While the other two Union divisions move across Berwick Bay toward the fort, Brigadier General Cuvier Grover's division proceeds up the Atchafalaya River into Grand Lake in order to prevent a Confederate retreat. On the morning of April 13, the division lands in the vicinity of Franklin and scatters Confederate forces there. That night Grover orders his men to cross Bayou Teche and prepare for an attack toward Franklin at dawn. Confederate major general Richard Taylor sends forces to meet Grover. On the morning of April 14, Taylor and his men are at Nerson's Woods just above Franklin. Grover's lead brigade encounters the Confederates, and heavy fighting ensues. Aided by the gunboat *Diana* anchoring their right flank, the Confederates force the brigade to withdraw. The Confederates are outnumbered, however, and as Grover prepares to attack, they decamp. This Union victory, along with that at Fort Bisland two days earlier, ensures the success of the expedition into western Louisiana. U.S. forces suffer 353 casualties; Confederate losses are unknown. On April 18 the Confederates burn the gunboats *Diana* and *Hart* to prevent their capture.

April 16, 1863

Civil War (continued): Western theater: Grant's Second Vicksburg Campaign (continued): Porter's ships run past Vicksburg. Late on this date, Mississippi

Squadron commander Rear Admiral David Porter's squadron of eight warships, a tug, and three army transports pass the Vicksburg batteries under heavy Confederate fire. Although all Union ships are struck, only the transport *Henry Clay* is lost, and all of its men are saved. The Union casualty toll is 12 men wounded. Porter's ships then arrive at New Carthage, Louisiana. Other ships subsequently make the passage.

A few days later, six transports with barges carrying supplies float past Vicksburg; only one, the *Tygress*, is lost. At the same time, Union major general James B. McPherson's corps marches south along the west bank of the Mississippi to New Carthage, while forces under Major General William T. Sherman demonstrate against the Chickasaw Bluffs north of Vicksburg in order to hold Confederate defenders there.

April 17–May 2, 1863

Civil War (continued): Western theater: Grierson's Raid. To divert the attention of Confederate lieutenant general John C. Pemberton at Vicksburg from his move south from Milliken's Bend, Louisiana, Union major general Ulysses S. Grant arranges for two cavalry raids. The raid under Colonel Abel D. Streight from Tuscumbia during April 26–May 3, 1863, is defeated by Confederate brigadier general Nathan B. Forrest. In occupying Forrest, however, Streight helps ensure the success of the second raid under Colonel Benjamin H. Grierson, who leads 1,700 cavalry from La Grange in southern Tennessee more than 600 miles through the heart of Mississippi. The raiders tear up railroad track, destroy rolling stock, and burn stores.

Pemberton disperses his men, casting a wide net for the raiders, but they slip through it and enter Union lines at Baton Rouge, Louisiana, on May 2, 1863. Union casualties total just 27 men; Confederate losses are some 600, including 500 captured and paroled. Two thousand weapons are also taken, and some 50 miles of railroad track and telegraph lines are destroyed. Grierson's men have disrupted Confederate communications, but more important, they have diverted Pemberton's attention from Grant's move south. An entire Confederate division is deployed to defend the Vicksburg–Jackson railroad and is thus

unavailable to stop Grant's landing on the east bank of the Mississippi below Vicksburg.

April 18, 1863

Civil War (continued): Trans-Mississippi West theater: Battle of Fayetteville. Confederate brigadier general William L. Cabell leads 900 mounted men and two guns against Fayetteville, Arkansas, held by 1,100 Union troops under Colonel M. LaRue Harrison. The defenders repulse the Confederate attack. Low on ammunition and convinced that he cannot break through the Union lines, Cabell withdraws. Union losses are 4 killed, 26 wounded, and 39 missing (at least 26 of these are captured and paroled by the Confederates). Confederate losses are some 20 killed, 30 wounded, and 20 missing.

April 24, 1863

Civil War (continued): Western theater: Grant's Second Vicksburg Campaign (continued). Major General Ulysses S. Grant's Army of the Tennessee arrives at Hard Times Plantation, Louisiana, on the Mississippi River.

April 26–May 3, 1863

Civil War (continued): Western theater: Streight's Raid. To divert the attention of Confederate forces at Vicksburg from his own move south, Union major general Ulysses S. Grant arranges for two cavalry raids: those by Colonels Benjamin H. Grierson (see April 17–May 2, 1863) and Abel D. Streight. Streight has 1,700 men, but because of a shortage of horses, many of his men are mounted on mules, a major reason for the raid's failure. Departing Nashville in transports on April 19, the men and their mounts proceed down the Mississippi to Eastport, where a stampede scatters some 400 mules, imposing further delay.

At Tuscumbia, Streight joins Brigadier General Grenville Dodge and his 8,000 cavalry, who are to screen Streight's movement. Streight departs Tuscumbia on April 26. At Mount Hope in Lawrence County, Streight learns from Dodge that the two commands will not meet at Moulton as previously planned, but Dodge assures Streight that he has driven Confederate brigadier general Nathan

Bedford Forrest to the north, clearing a path for Streight to continue unmolested. However, Dodge has not deterred the Confederate cavalry commander, who closely pursues the "Jackass Brigade."

On April 30 the raiders clash with the Confederates at Day's Gap. Other engagements follow. Streight comes close to reaching his objective of Rome, Georgia, but with many of his men now dismounted, he is surrounded by Forrest's men at nearby Cedar Bluff. Although he has only some 500 men, Forrest convinces Streight that he is outnumbered, and with much of his ammunition useless, the Union commander surrenders on May 3. Although the raid is a failure, it helps ensure the success of the second Union raid under Grierson.

April 27, 1863

Civil War (continued): Eastern theater: Beginning of the Chancellorsville Campaign. At Falmouth, Virginia, Major General Joseph Hooker sets the Union Army of the Potomac in motion, westward along the northern shore of the Rappahannock River. Hooker plans to cross the river into a wooded area known as the Wilderness, outflank Confederate general Robert E. Lee's Army of Northern Virginia, and drive south on Richmond. With 134,000 men, Hooker enjoys a numerical advantage of more than 2 to 1.

On April 29, Hooker dispatches his 10,000-man Cavalry Corps under Major General George Stoneman on a major raid against Confederate supply and communication lines. A major mistake, it deprives Hooker of valuable intelligence regarding Lee's subsequent movements.

April 29, 1863

Civil War (continued): Western theater: Battle of Grand Gulf. With Union major general Ulysses S. Grant hoping to cross his forces from Louisiana to the east bank of the Mississippi River at Grand Gulf, Mississippi, 25 miles south of Vicksburg, Mississippi, Squadron commander Rear Admiral David D. Porter attacks the Confederate river defenses with the ironclads *Benton* (17 guns), *Louisville* (14 guns), *Carondelet* (14 guns), *Mound City* (14 guns), *Pittsburg* (14 guns), *Tuscumbia* (10 guns), and *Lafayette* (12 guns).

The engagement lasts more than six hours, and the Union ships fire more than 1,000 rounds. Although the Union shelling soon silences the Confederate lower battery and causes upper battery fire to slacken, most of the ships are damaged, and 18 Union sailors are killed and 56 are wounded.

Informed by an escaped slave of another landing site at Bruinsburg, Mississippi, six miles downstream, Grant decides to cross the river there. That evening Porter's warships safely escort all the transports to the crossing point.

April 29–May 2, 1863

Civil War (continued): Western theater: Grant's Second Vicksburg Campaign (continued): Sherman's diversion. To confuse Confederate commander at Vicksburg Lieutenant General John C. Pemberton and prevent him from sending forces south, U.S. major general William T. Sherman carries out a simultaneous diversion with his corps above Vicksburg in ships left behind for this purpose. Sherman employs 8 warships, 3 tugs towing mortar boats, and 10 large transports up the Yazoo River, disembarking troops at Haynes' Bluff. This causes Pemberton to recall men sent south to reinforce against Major General Ulysses S. Grant and dispatch them by forced marches to Haynes' Bluff. The raid by Colonel Benjamin H. Grierson causes Pemberton to divert other resources as well.

April 30, 1863

Civil War (continued): Eastern theater: Chancellorsville Campaign (continued). In Virginia, U.S. major general Joseph Hooker's Army of the Potomac, having moved 30 miles up the northern shore of the Rappahannock River, crosses the river and by this date is 10 miles beyond Confederate general Robert E. Lee's position at Fredericksburg. The operation has gone well to this point, and Lee is caught off guard.

April 30–May 1, 1863

Civil War (continued): Western theater: Grant's Second Vicksburg Campaign (continued): Union forces cross the Mississippi. In the largest amphibious operation to this point in American history, the ships of

Rear Admiral David D. Porter's Mississippi Squadron commence ferrying the two corps under Major Generals John A. McClernand and James B. McPherson across the river from Louisiana to Bruinsburg, Mississippi, enabling Major General Ulysses S. Grant to operate against the Confederate defenders of Vicksburg from the south and east.

May 1, 1863

Civil War (continued): Western theater: Second Vicksburg Campaign (continued): Battle of Port Gibson. With 24,000 Union troops having crossed the Mississippi River, Major General Ulysses S. Grant's first objective is Port Gibson, a crossroads village 10.5 miles east of the Mississippi River and 22 miles south of Vicksburg. Only 5,200 Confederates defend Port Gibson. In the Battle of Port Gibson, Grant forces the defenders to retreat toward Grand Gulf, at a cost of 875 Union casualties to 834 for the Confederates.

May 1–4, 1863

Civil War (continued): Eastern theater: Battle of Chancellorsville. U.S. major general Joseph E. Hooker has the bulk of his Army of the Potomac across the Rappahannock and west of Fredericksburg, planning to attack Confederate general Robert E. Lee's Army of Northern Virginia at Chancellorsville, Virginia. Hooker has 134,000 men, while Lee has fewer than 61,000. Hooker intends to carry out a double envelopment. He will strike with the larger part of the army to Lee's west, while an eastern pincer

Battle of Chancellorsville		
Date	May 1–4, 1863	
Location	Spotsylvania County, Virginia	
Opponents (*winner)	*Confederacy	United States
Commander	General Robert E. Lee	Major General Joseph E. Hooker
#	61,000 men	134,000 men
Casualties	13,303 (1,665 killed, 9,081 wounded, 2,018 missing)	17,197 (1,606 killed, 9,672 wounded, 5,919 missing)

under Major General John Sedgwick simultaneously attacks Lee at Fredericksburg.

By the evening of April 30, some 75,000 Union troops occupy the Wilderness, an area of thick woods and underbrush 10 miles west of Fredericksburg to Lee's east and rear, while Sedgwick and 40,000 men threaten Lee's right at Fredericksburg. Hooker has erred, however, in sending his 10,000-man Cavalry Corps under Major General George Stoneman in a wide sweep south below Fredericksburg to destroy the Confederate supply depots. This action uncovers the Union right wing and denies Hooker vital intelligence regarding Lee's intentions.

On May 1 Lieutenant General Thomas J. "Stonewall" Jackson's corps arrives near Chancellorsville and engages Union pickets. This action unnerves Hooker, who hesitates and withdraws his men into the Wilderness. The aggressive Lee responds with a daring maneuver. Learning from his own cavalry commander, Major General J. E. B. Stuart, that Hooker's right flank is "in the air," Lee plans a double envelopment of a double envelopment. It is, in fact, a military masterpiece, with a smaller force attempting to surround a much larger one. With 17,000 men, Lee plans to demonstrate in front of the Union line to hold Hooker in place while Jackson, with 28,000 men, marches around the Union right flank. Success depends on Hooker failing to exploit the Confederate separation or determine Jackson's intentions.

Jackson sets off on May 2, the march taking most of the day. His force is detected disengaging, but this is interpreted to mean that Lee is about to withdraw. Hooker therefore orders Union major general Daniel Sickles, commander of III Corps, to attack. Sickles's halfhearted advance further weakens the Union line, however. Meanwhile, Major General Oliver O. Howard, whose XI Corps occupies the far Union right flank, fails to make defensive preparations, despite Hooker's instructions that he do so.

When Jackson's attack comes at about 5:30 p.m., it is a complete surprise and enfilades the Union line. Union troops are sent reeling back in confusion. Darkness, increasing Union resistance, and the loss of Confederate unit cohesion in the woods all help

Union artillerymen before the Battle of Chancellorsville, May 1–4, 1863. The battle was Confederate general Robert E. Lee's military masterpiece, but it also brought the death of Lieutenant General Thomas J. "Stonewall" Jackson. (Library of Congress)

prevent a Union catastrophe. That evening, Jackson is wounded by his own men in front of his lines in the woods while returning from a reconnaissance. On May 3 Stuart, replacing Jackson, resumes the Confederate attack, further constricting Hooker's lines.

The second part of the battle, sometimes known as the Second Battle of Fredericksburg, unfolds at the same time. On the night of May 2, Hooker orders Sedgwick to attack. Although he has four times the strength of Major General Jubal A. Early's 10,000 defending Confederates, Sedgwick believes that he is outnumbered and has failed to move from the Fredericksburg heights. On May 3, however, he advances with 25,000 men from Fredericksburg. Breaking through the Confederate positions, he moves against Early at Salem Church.

Lee now feints again. Leaving just a small force against Hooker, Lee turns east to deal with the new threat. Hooker vastly outnumbers Lee but fails to move. Sedgwick, surrounded on three sides and unaided, is forced to retire back across the Rappahannock during the night of May 4. On May 5 Hooker

withdraws his army back across the Rappahannock as well. The battle is over.

Although Chancellorsville is Lee's military masterpiece, it also might have been the South's costliest victory. Union losses are 17,197 (1,606 killed, 9,672 wounded, and 5,919 missing); the Confederates sustain only 13,303 (1,665 killed, 9,081 wounded, and 2,018 missing). But Union losses are 13 percent of effectives, while Confederate casualties are 22 percent of theirs. It will be much more difficult for the Confederates to replace their losses than it will be for the Union. The loss of Jackson is particularly grievous. He dies on May 10 of pneumonia following amputation of an arm. The Army of Northern Virginia is never quite the same.

May 3, 1863

Civil War (continued): Western theater: Second Vicksburg Campaign (continued). The ships of Rear Admiral David D. Porter's Mississippi Squadron assist Major General Ulysses S. Grant's ground troops in forcing the Confederate evacuation of Grand Gulf,

Oliver Otis Howard (1830–1909)

U.S. Army officer. Oliver Otis Howard was born in Leeds, Maine, on November 8, 1830. Graduating from Bowdoin College in 1850 and the U.S. Military Academy, West Point, in 1854, Howard was a first lieutenant teaching mathematics at West Point when the American Civil War began. He resigned his regular commission to become colonel of the 3rd Maine Regiment. Howard led a brigade during the First Battle of Bull Run (Manassas) on July 21, 1861, and helped cover the Union retreat. His performance won him promotion to brigadier general of volunteers. In the spring of 1862, Howard was conspicuous for his bravery at Seven Pines on May 31 during the Peninsula Campaign, being wounded twice. His right arm was amputated close to the shoulder. (For his actions at Seven Pines, Howard received the Medal of Honor in 1893.)

During his convalescence, Howard became convinced that God had spared his life for the purpose of liberating the slaves. Back in command, Howard fought with distinction in the Second Battle of Bull Run (Manassas) (August 28–30, 1862) and the Battle of Antietam (September 17, 1862). Promoted to major general of volunteers, he led his division in the desperate frontal assault in the First Battle of Fredericksburg on December 13, 1862.

In April 1863 Howard took command of XI Corps, composed largely of German immigrants. Hit on May 2 by Confederate lieutenant general Thomas "Stonewall" Jackson's flank attack in the Battle of Chancellorsville, Howard's corps virtually disintegrated. Notwithstanding this defeat and the considerable controversy about his role in it, Howard retained his command. During Confederate general Robert E. Lee's second invasion of the North, on July 1, 1863, Howard selected Cemetery Ridge as the key defensive position at Gettysburg. Although the performance of his troops during the next two days of battle could best be called mediocre, Howard enjoyed the satisfaction of receiving the thanks of Congress for his actions in the battle (July 1–3, 1863).

Howard then shifted to the Western theater, commanding a corps at Chattanooga. During the Atlanta Campaign, Major General William T. Sherman chose him to command the Army of the Tennessee following the death of Major General James McPherson. At both Ezra Church and Jonesboro, Howard's army won easy victories.

When Sherman marched from Atlanta for Savannah in November 1864, he assigned Howard the honor of commanding the right wing of the army. In the Carolinas, Howard's army impressed all with the rapidity of its movement over flooded swamp country. Although Howard publicly justified the harsh treatment meted out to Southerners during the march, he attempted to check gratuitous violence. In North Carolina, his army fought at Bentonville and Goldsboro. At the close of the war he was appointed brigadier general in the regular army.

Throughout the war, Howard won the admiration of his men for his great personal bravery. He also attracted attention for his churchgoing and for his puritanical ways—he opposed profanity, drinking, and gambling. Certainly Howard saw more than his share of battle and was, in Sherman's eyes, the consummate soldier.

Howard's straight-laced demeanor led President Andrew Johnson to appoint him head of the Bureau of Refugees, Freedmen, and Abandoned Lands in May 1865. While in this post, Howard championed African Americans in various ways. In 1867 he became the key figure in the establishment of one of the earliest black institutions of higher education, which was named Howard University in his honor; he served as its first president until 1874.

Howard also played an active role in the settlement of the West. In 1872 he had traveled with an aide and three civilian guides (two of whom were Apaches) to the remote camp of the Chiricahua Apaches who had taken up arms against the whites. He entered the camp unarmed and, following 11 days of talks, negotiated a lasting peace settlement with Chiricahua leader Cochise.

In 1874 Howard assumed command of the Department of the Columbia, going west to Fort Vancouver. Here he was forced to deal with white settler demands that the Nez Perces under Chief Joseph be removed from the Wallowa Valley. Howard ordered his adjutant, Major Henry Clay Wood, a trained lawyer, to study the treaties involved. Wood concluded that the Nez Perces had legal claim to the land. Howard supported this position, but it was not to be.

First Wood in 1876 and Howard himself in 1877 met with the Nez Perces. In the course of the second meeting Howard reportedly lost his temper and, in the words of Yellow Wolf, "showed the rifle." (In Chief Joseph's famous speech in Washington, D.C., in 1879, he said that if Howard had given him sufficient time to gather his stock, there would have been no war.)

When war broke out later in 1877, Howard sought a quick end to the hostilities, and in the Battle of the Clearwater River his men outnumbered the Nez Perces some six to one. However, the Nez Perces escaped through Lolo Pass and began their epic 1,500-mile flight in an attempt to find refuge in Canada. Howard's forces pursued Joseph's small band, but they never directly engaged the Nez Perces in battle again, and Howard was soon the target of public criticism. Four months later, Joseph surrendered to Colonel Nelson A. Miles at Bear Paw, Montana.

Howard's last Indian war took place in 1878, when his forces quickly and easily defeated the Bannock Indians, some of whom had served as scouts for the army in the Nez Perce War. Howard was superintendent of the U.S. Military Academy during 1881–1882 and was promoted to major general in 1886. After various other peacetime assignments, he retired from active duty in 1894. Howard died in Burlington, Vermont, on October 26, 1909.

MALCOLM MUIR JR.

Further Reading

Greene, Jerome A. *Nez Perce Summer, 1877: The U.S. Army and the Nee-Me-Poo Crisis.* Helena: Montana Historical Society Press, 2000.
Howard, Oliver O. *Autobiography of Oliver Otis Howard.* New York: Baker and Taylor, 1908.
Howard, Oliver O. *My Life and Experiences among Our Hostile Indians: A Record of Personal Observations, Adventures, and Campaigns among the Indians of the Great West.* 1907; reprint, New York: Da Capo, 1972.
McCoy, Robert. *Chief Joseph, Yellow Wolf, and the Creation of Nez Perce History in the Northwest.* New York: Routledge, 2004.

Mississippi, securing Grant's position on the east bank of the Mississippi River.

May 5, 1863
Civil War (continued): Trans-Mississippi West theater: Capture of Fort De Russy. U.S. Navy Mississippi Squadron commander Rear Admiral David D. Porter proceeds up the Red River with the ironclads *Benton* (17 guns), *Lafayette* (12 guns), and *Pittsburg* (14 guns); the gunboat *General Price* (4 guns, the former Confederate warship *General Sterling Price*, sunk in the Battle of Memphis but raised, repaired, and commissioned as a U.S. warship); the ram *Switzerland* (armament unknown); and the tug *Ivy*. These are

joined en route by the gunboats *Estrella* (5 guns) and *Arizona* (6 guns).

On the evening of May 5 the expeditionary force arrives at Fort De Russy, four miles north of Marksville, Louisiana, the principal Confederate military works defending the lower Red River Valley. Faced with this powerful Union force, the Confederate defenders abandon the works. After removing a river obstruction, the U.S. Navy takes possession.

May 6–June 27, 1863

Civil War (continued): Read's commerce raiding cruise. Off the coast of Brazil on May 6, 1863, the Confederate commerce raider *Florida* (11 guns), commanded by Lieutenant John N. Maffitt, takes as a prize the U.S. merchant brig *Clarence*, whereupon 23-year-old Lieutenant Charles W. Read secures permission to undertake a daring mission in it to Hampton Roads, Virginia, and there cut out a Union gunboat or a steamer.

Read sets out the same day with 20 men, his ship armed with a single 12-pounder howitzer, planning to sail the 3,400 miles from Brazil to Norfolk. A month later, he takes and burns his first prize. Others followed, but from the crewmen taken he learns that Union security precautions preclude entrance to Hampton Roads.

Having taken six prizes in the *Clarence*, on June 12 Read shifts operations to one of them, the *Tacony*. It is faster than the *Clarence*, which he burns. Taking other prizes in the *Tacony*, Read is soon forced to release his growing number of prisoners, who reveal his presence.

Continuing north, Read reaches the New England fishing grounds in late June, there taking and burning a half dozen schooners and capturing a large clipper ship. By now Read has exhausted his ammunition, and there are some 40 U.S. warships searching for him. Read, however, takes 15 prizes in the *Tacony* before he burns that ship on June 25, after transferring to yet another prize, the small fishing schooner *Archer*.

On June 26 Read boldly sails the *Archer* into Portland, Maine, where he captures the U.S. revenue cutter *Caleb Cushing* and manages to sail it out of the harbor. Union officials arm two steamers and set out in pursuit. Read is unaware of the location of the cutter's ample ammunition supply and, following a brief gunfight, scuttles the ship and surrenders. Read and his men have taken 21 prizes, burning 15 of them and causing widespread panic along the North Atlantic seaboard.

May 7–15, 1863

Civil War (continued): Trans-Mississippi West theater. Ships of Rear Admiral David D. Porter's Mississippi Squadron, having taken Fort De Russy, proceed up the Red River and take the surrender of Alexandria, Louisiana. Unable to proceed farther because of low water, Porter returns to Fort De Russy, which he partially destroys on May 9, 1863, by cannon fire from the powerful ironclad *Benton* (17 guns). Leaving most of his ships in the Red, Porter returns to Grand Gulf, Mississippi, on May 15.

May 7–19, 1863

Civil War (continued): Western theater: Second Vicksburg Campaign (continued): Big Black River Campaign. Reinforced east of the Mississippi by Major General William H. Sherman's corps on May 8, U.S. major general Ulysses S. Grant defies instructions from Union general-in-chief Major General Henry W. Halleck to await reinforcements from Natchez under Major General Nathaniel P. Banks. Grant knows that this will give his opponents time to both reinforce and fortify. Instead, he marches inland with 20,000 men, carrying as much ammunition as possible along with five days' worth of food and supplies in confiscated conveyances, initiating one of the most brilliant campaigns in American military history.

Grant's movement east and the capture of Port Gibson force the Confederates to abandon Grand Gulf to the north. Confederate lieutenant general John C. Pemberton, at Vicksburg, is largely ignorant of Grant's movements, as General Joseph E. Johnston has stripped away much of his cavalry. (Johnston, recovered from his wounds sustained in the Peninsula Campaign, had assumed command of the Western theater the previous November.) Urged by Johnston to join him in an effort to defeat Grant in open battle but at the same time ordered by Confederate president Jefferson Davis to defend Vicksburg "at all cost," Pemberton chooses to obey Davis.

May 12, 1863

Civil War (continued): Western theater: Second Vicksburg Campaign (continued): Battle of Raymond. Union major general Ulysses S. Grant moves his army northeast, planning to secure the Southern Railroad and isolate Vicksburg from resupply from Jackson, Mississippi, to the east, and then close on Vicksburg from that direction. At Vicksburg, Confederate commander of the Department of Mississippi and East Louisiana Lieutenant General John C. Pemberton orders a brigade of 4,100 men under Brigadier General John C. Gregg to hit Grant in the flank. Gregg hopes to catch Grant unawares but is himself surprised when on May 12 he runs into the head of one of Grant's three corps columns: Major General James P. McPherson's 12,000-man XVII Corps. In the Battle of Raymond in Mississippi, McPherson defeats Gregg. The Union sustains 446 casualties; the Confederates lose 820. Gregg withdraws back on Jackson.

May 14, 1863

Civil War (continued): Western theater: Second Vicksburg Campaign (continued): Grant captures Jackson. Following the Battle of Raymond, Major General Ulysses S. Grant quickly moves against Jackson, Mississippi, the key railhead and logistics center for Vicksburg held by Brigadier General John Gregg and 6,000 Confederates. Early this day Confederate Western theater commander General Joseph E. Johnston, who had arrived the day before and realizes that two Union corps are advancing against him, orders Jackson abandoned. (The decision is a controversial one, for by dawn on May 15 Johnston could have assembled as many as 15,000 men against Grant's 20,000.) Leaving Major General William T. Sherman and one corps to complete the destruction of Jackson's railroad facilities and industry, Grant heads west for Vicksburg with his remaining two corps. Union casualties at Jackson are some 500 men; the Confederates lose 800.

May 16, 1863

Civil War (continued): Western theater: Second Vicksburg Campaign (continued): Battle of Champion Hill. U.S. major general Ulysses S. Grant learns in an intercepted message that Confederate general Joseph E. Johnston has ordered Lieutenant General John C. Pemberton to march east in order to crush Grant's force between their two forces. Grant moves rapidly west to engage Pemberton before he can close on Jackson, Mississippi.

At Champion Hill on May 16, 1863, Grant, with some 29,000 men, overcomes early mistakes by corps commander Major General James P. McPherson and defeats Pemberton with 22,000 men. Pemberton holds the high ground, and the fighting is heavy. Champion Hill plantation changes hands three times before the Confederates retire back toward Vicksburg. Union casualties total 2,457; the Confederates lose 3,840. Grant's troops pursue.

Pemberton fights a delaying action at Big Black River Bridge on May 17, then crosses the Big Black, destroying bridges behind him. U.S. major general Ulysses S. Grant's engineers span the river, and by May 19 Grant's three corps have invested Vicksburg.

Grant's Big Black River Campaign of May 1–19 must be counted as one of the most brilliant military campaigns ever fought on American soil. In just 19 days, Grant has marched 200 miles and has been victorious in half a dozen battles over a numerically larger theater force. He inflicts some 8,000 casualties for 4,400 of his own and traps 30,000 of the enemy at Vicksburg.

May 21–July 9, 1863

Civil War (continued): Western theater: Siege of Port Hudson. Beginning on May 21, Union forces commanded by Major General Nathaniel P. Banks lay siege to Port Hudson, Louisiana, on the Mississippi River below Vicksburg. Banks ultimately commands 30,000 men; Confederate major general Franklin Gardner has about 7,500 defenders.

Two Union assaults on May 27 and June 14 are poorly handled and costly for the attackers. When news of the fall of Vicksburg (July 4) arrives on July

8, however, Gardner agrees to surrender the next day. Union losses in the siege total some 5,000 men. The Confederates lose only some 400 men dead (equally divided between combat and disease), but the entire garrison is taken prisoner. Of these, 5,593 are paroled, and some 500 others are retained in hospitals.

With the fall of Port Hudson, Union forces control the entire Mississippi, cutting off the Trans-Mississippi West from the remainder of the Confederacy.

May 23–July 4, 1863

Civil War (continued): Western theater: Second Vicksburg Campaign (continued): Siege of Vicksburg. Following unsuccessful Union frontal assaults against the "Confederate Gibraltar" on May 19 and 22, U.S. major general Ulysses S. Grant goes over to siege warfare. At Vicksburg, Lieutenant General John C. Pemberton has some 33,000 men; Grant ultimately has 77,000. Grant releases some of his steadily increasing manpower to Major General William T. Sherman to tear up roads and destroy bridges and forage, stymieing efforts by Confederate Western theater commander General Joseph E. Johnston to relieve Vicksburg. Johnston has some 31,000 men raised specifically to lift the siege only two days' march to the east, at Jackson. Grant, however, counters with a heavily manned line facing eastward, and despite the urging of Confederate authorities, Johnston never tests it.

Rear Admiral David D. Porter's Mississippi Squadron plays a key role in the siege. The squadron provides important logistics support, lands heavy guns and crews to work them, and furnishes naval gunfire support from the river, and its mortar boats lob thousands of shells into the city. Porter's warships prevent Confederate resupply from the west, and they move up the Yazoo River and torch the Yazoo City navy yard and its shops and sawmills and destroy Confederate warships and shipping.

Grant's forces increase daily in strength, and his siege lines gradually constrict. Food in Vicksburg is in short supply. Confederate soldiers and civilians seek refuge in caves to escape relentless Union shelling. The besiegers explode two large mines under the Confederate lines, but neither has the desired effect, and the Confederate lines hold.

With food stocks near exhaustion and even drinking water in short supply, on July 3 Pemberton meets with Grant to request terms. Grant extends generous terms, including parole of the garrison. Pemberton surrenders Vicksburg the next day. Union casualties in the siege are 4,835 killed or wounded. Confederate losses are 3,202 killed or wounded. The Union takes 29,495 prisoners, along with 172 cannon. Grant also gains 60,000 small arms. However, many of the Confederates violate their paroles and rejoin the fight against the Union at Chattanooga.

Union casualties in the entire Vicksburg Campaign of October 1862–July 1863 amount to around 9,000 men. The Confederates lose some 10,000, not counting prisoners. The capture of Vicksburg leads to the fall of Port Hudson, and the Trans-Mississippi West is for all intents and purposes cut off from the remainder of the Confederacy. Midwestern farmers can now use the Mississippi to ship their goods, and this brings that region solidly behind the Northern war effort. As President Abraham Lincoln puts it, "The Father of waters again goes unvexed to the sea."

May 27, 1863

Civil War (continued). The U.S. Mississippi Squadron ironclad *Cincinnati* (14 guns) is sunk by Confederate land batteries at Fort Hill near Vicksburg, Mississippi, suffering 25 killed or wounded and 15 possible drownings.

Siege of Vicksburg		
Date	May 23–July 4, 1863	
Location	Vicksburg, Mississippi	
Opponents (*winner)	*United States	Confederacy
Commander	Major General Ulysses S. Grant	Lieutenant General John C. Pemberton
#	77,000 men	33,000 men
Casualties	4,835 killed or wounded	3,202 killed or wounded; 29,495 prisoners; 172 cannon and 60,000 small arms taken

SIEGE OF VICKSBURG, MAY 23–JULY 4, 1863

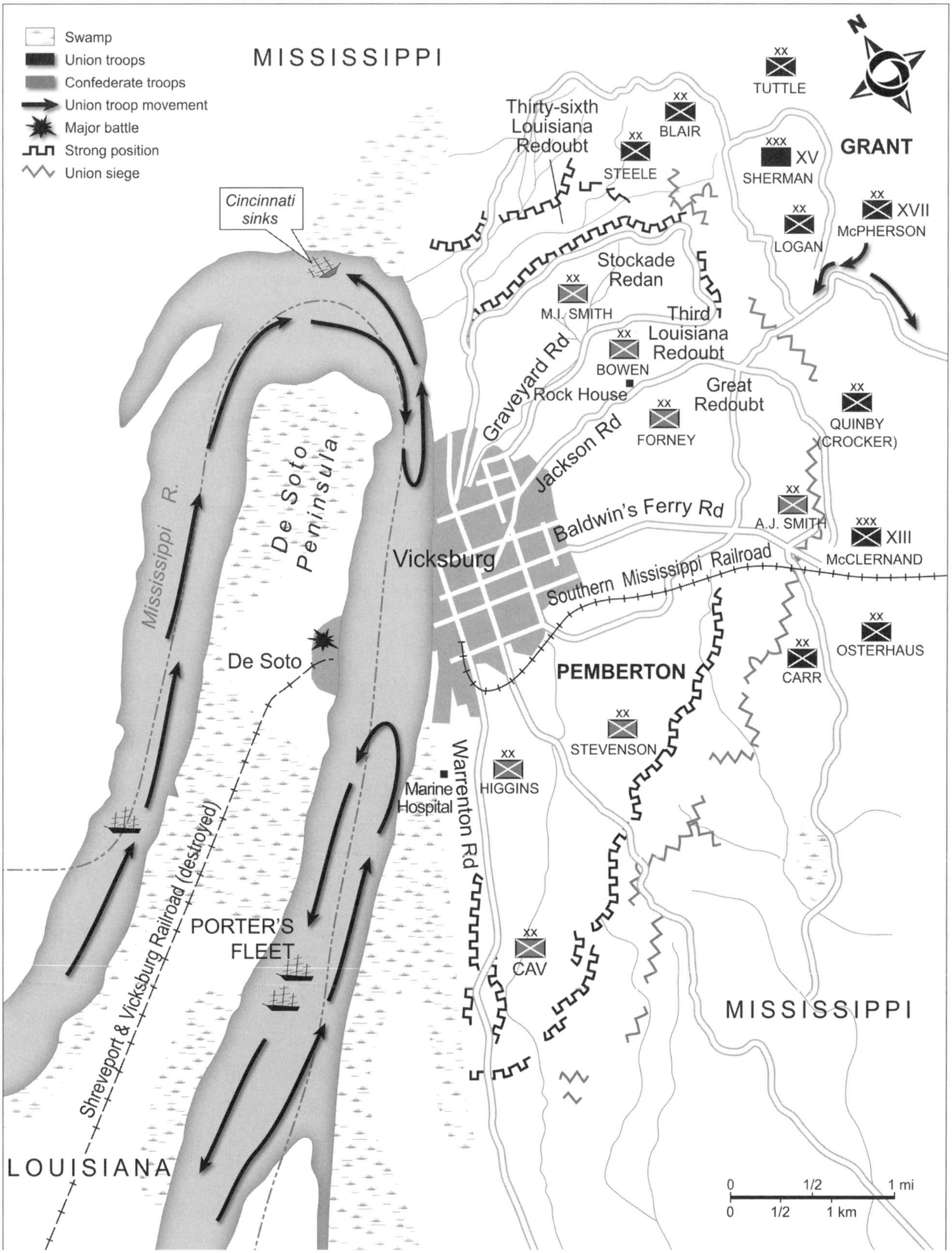

Legend

- Swamp
- Union troops
- Confederate troops
- Union troop movement
- Major battle
- Strong position
- Union siege

MISSISSIPPI

N

Cincinnati sinks

Thirty-sixth Louisiana Redoubt

XX TUTTLE

XX BLAIR

XX STEELE

XXX XV SHERMAN

GRANT

XX XVII McPHERSON

XX LOGAN

Stockade Redan

XX M.L. SMITH

Graveyard Rd

Third Louisiana Redoubt

XX BOWEN

Rock House

Great Redoubt

XX FORNEY

XX QUINBY (CROCKER)

Jackson Rd

De Soto Peninsula

Mississippi R.

Baldwin's Ferry Rd

XX A.J. SMITH

XXX XIII McCLERNAND

Vicksburg

De Soto

Southern Mississippi Railroad

PEMBERTON

XX CARR

XX OSTERHAUS

XX STEVENSON

Marine Hospital

Warrenton Rd

XX HIGGINS

Shreveport & Vicksburg Railroad (destroyed)

PORTER'S FLEET

XX CAV

MISSISSIPPI

LOUISIANA

| 0 | 1/2 | 1 mi |
| 0 | 1/2 | 1 km |

May 30, 1863

Civil War (continued): Eastern theater. Following the death of Lieutenant General T. J. "Stonewall" Jackson, Confederate general Robert E. Lee reorganizes the Army of Northern Virginia. The army is formed into four corps: I Corps under Lieutenant General James Longstreet, II Corps under Lieutenant General Richard S. Ewell, III Corps under Lieutenant General Ambrose P. Hill, and the Cavalry Corps under Major General J. E. B. Stuart.

June 3, 1863

Civil War (continued): Eastern theater: Lee begins his second invasion of the North. Confederate general Robert E. Lee rebuffs suggestions that part of his Army of Northern Virginia be sent west to reinforce Vicksburg, which he believes to be lost, and presents President Jefferson Davis with his own plan: an invasion of Pennsylvania. Not an effort to take pressure off Vicksburg or to support a Southern peace offensive, it is instead a spoiling attack to give Virginia a temporary respite by delaying a new offensive by the Union Army of the Potomac. Lee also hopes to secure needed supplies from resource-rich Pennsylvania.

At the end of May, Lee's army is south of the Rappahannock River in and near Fredericksburg, with U.S. major general Joseph E. Hooker's Army of the Potomac just north of the river keeping watch. Contrary to Lee's expectation, Hooker is not being reinforced; in fact, he is losing strength as enlistments of some volunteer regiments expire and their men head home. Hooker still has the advantage in terms of men and logistical support, but the numbers are much closer than they have been or will be again. Hooker commands some 85,000–90,000 men, Lee perhaps 70,000.

On June 3 Lee sets his army in motion west toward Culpeper, Virginia. Lee's plan is to cross into the Shenandoah Valley, then move north with Major General J. E. B. Stuart's cavalry screening his eastern (right) flank. Lee will then cross the Potomac River and be in position to threaten Philadelphia and Baltimore. This will pressure Hooker to attack him, and Lee can fight a defensive battle in circumstances of his choosing.

June 9, 1863

Civil War (continued): Eastern theater: Battle of Brandy Station. Commander of the Union Army of the Potomac Major General Joseph E. Hooker learns of commander of the Army of Northern Virginia General Robert E. Lee's movements when he sends his Cavalry Corps under Brigadier General Alfred Pleasanton and two infantry brigades across the Rappahannock River in a surprise attack on Confederate major general J. E. B. Stuart's cavalry cantonment. The ensuing Battle of Brandy Station is a widely dispersed and confused action extending over a 70-square-mile area. Each side disposes about 8,000 cavalry, although Pleasanton has the advantage of 3,000 infantry, while Stuart has none.

In what is not only the largest cavalry battle of the war but also the largest cavalry engagement ever for the U.S. Army and in the history of North America, the Confederates finally drive the Union troops back across the Potomac. The Union side suffers 865 casualties, the Confederates only 582. To this point, the Confederates have enjoyed superiority in cavalry, but here the Union cavalry establishes its equality.

June 13–15, 1863

Civil War (continued): Eastern theater: Lee's second invasion of the North (continued): Second Battle of Winchester. Confederate general Robert E. Lee, commander of the Army of Northern Virginia, orders II Corps commander Lieutenant General Richard S. Ewell to clear the lower (northern) Shenandoah Valley of Union forces to open the way for Lee's invasion of the North. Winchester is a major road hub and depot of the Baltimore & Ohio Railroad. Ewell commands almost 20,000 troops, while Union major general Robert H. Milroy defends Winchester with 6,900 men. Milroy does not believe initial reports of approaching Confederates and that they can have evaded the Army of the Potomac.

Rebuffing the initial Confederate attack on June 13 and believing that his forces can hold, Milroy ignores suggestions from Washington to pull his troops back to Harpers Ferry. Too late, early on June 15 Milroy attempts to break out. He encounters Ewell's forces, which have carried out a night flank march. Although

Milroy himself escapes, most of his men are taken prisoner.

The Confederates suffer fewer than 300 casualties; Union losses are 443 men killed or wounded and 3,358 missing or captured. Ewell also captures many weapons, 23 cannon, and some 300 wagons of supplies. The Confederate victory opens the way for Lee to move into Maryland and also returns the entire Shenandoah Valley to Confederate control, providing much-needed food and supplies for Lee's army.

June 15–28, 1863

Civil War (continued): Eastern theater: Lee's second invasion of the North (continued): Lee's forces cross the Potomac. Finally convinced that Confederate general Robert E. Lee plans an invasion of the North, on June 13, 1863, Union major general Joseph E. Hooker puts his Army of the Potomac into motion. He takes a path parallel to Lee's Army of Northern Virginia, keeping his forces between Lee and Washington. Hooker never has a good chance to attack Lee on the march north.

Lee's army pushes across the Potomac during June 15–24 and by June 28 reaches Carlisle and York, Pennsylvania. Lee is unaware of Hooker's movements because of the absence of Major General J. E. B. Stuart's right-flank cavalry screen. Stuart's reputation for reliability leads Lee to assume that the Army of the Potomac is still in its camps in Virginia. Stuart, however, has been forced to move farther east and, taking advantage of discretionary orders, swings wide around the rear of the Union army during June 26–July 2. Determined to circuit Hooker's army, Stuart is slowed by captured wagons.

Lee's army is now dangerously spread out over some 45 miles. On the evening of June 28, Lee learns that Hooker's entire army is massed in the vicinity of Frederick, Maryland, closer to the separate parts of his own army than these are to each other. Lee must concentrate at once or be destroyed. He orders the Army of Northern Virginia to assemble immediately at Gettysburg, a major crossroads.

June 17, 1863

Civil War (continued): Eastern theater: Battle of Wassaw Sound. In Wassaw Sound, Georgia, the Confederate ironclad ram *Atlanta* (4 guns), captained by Commander William A. Webb and escorted by the wooden steamers *Isomdiga* and *Resolute*, engages the U.S. Navy monitors *Weehawken* (2 guns) and *Nahant* (2 guns) under Captain John Rogers. During the battle the *Atlanta* grounds on a bar and is subsequently forced to surrender with its crew of 145 men.

June 23–July 3, 1863

Civil War (continued): Western theater: Tullahoma Campaign. Following the Battle of Stones River, Union major general William S. Rosecrans reorganizes his 60,000-man Army of the Cumberland around Murfreesboro, Tennessee. Opposing Rosecrans along the Duck River, with his headquarters at Tullahoma, is Confederate general Braxton Bragg and his Army of Tennessee of 43,000 men. Fearful that troops will be sent from Bragg's command west to Vicksburg, Union officials in Washington press Rosecrans to take the offensive. He finally agrees on June 23.

In a series of well-executed flanking marches, Rosecrans maneuvers Bragg out of Tennessee at a cost of only 560 men while taking 1,634 Confederates prisoner. He also captures 11 cannon and quantities of supplies.

June 24, 1863

Civil War (continued). U.S. Navy rear admiral John A. Dahlgren is detached from duty at the Washington Navy Yard and ordered to take command of the South Atlantic Blockading Squadron, relieving Rear Admiral Samuel F. Du Pont.

June 25–July 20, 1863

Japan: Shimonoseki Incidents. Although the Tokugawa Shogunate has opened relations with the Western powers, many Japanese feudal lords are strongly opposed. The opposition intensifies when Emperor Kōmei breaks with tradition and takes an active role in matters of state, ordering the expulsion of foreigners from Japan.

The Shimonoseki-based Chōshū clan sides with the emperor against the shogunate and opens fire on foreign ships transiting the narrow Shimonoseki

John Adolph Bernard Dahlgren (1809–1870)

U.S. Navy admiral and developer of a system of ordnance that bears his name. Born in Philadelphia on November 13, 1809, John Adolph Bernard Dahlgren was the son of the Swedish consul in that city. The elder Dahlgren died suddenly in 1824, placing his family in dire financial straits. That winter, John Dahlgren applied to become a midshipman, but the U.S. Navy rejected his application. Dahlgren then shipped as a merchant seaman to gain experience. This and letters from influential connections helped him secure appointment as an acting midshipman in February 1826. Following cruises in the frigate *Macedonian* and the sloop *Ontario,* on April 28, 1832, Dahlgren was advanced to passed midshipman.

Assigned in 1834 to the Coast Survey, Dahlgren showed a great interest in math and science. He spent three years there, making lieutenant on March 8, 1837. But this duty caused serious eye problems and led to two years ashore detached from duty.

Returned to active duty, during 1843–1844 Dahlgren was assigned to the frigate *Cumberland* in the Mediterranean. On his return to the United States, he was given direction of ordnance activities at the Washington Navy Yard. Here he found his true calling. Dahlgren designed a new lock for firing guns, an improved primer, and sights graduated in yards. In 1848 he tested 32-pounders and 8-inch guns and recorded the results, the first time that ranging data was available on these guns.

In 1849 Dahlgren produced a new howitzer for the navy. These appeared as 12- and 24-pounder smoothbores and as a 4-inch (20-pounder) rifle. These were the finest boat guns of their time in the world and remained in service with the U.S. Navy until the 1880s. Dahlgren is, however, chiefly remembered for the system of heavy smoothbore muzzle-loading ordnance that bears his name. These new guns appeared in a variety of sizes, from 32-pounders to 15-inch bore and even—after the American Civil War—20-inch bore. Dahlgren also designed rifled guns, although these were not as successful as his smoothbores, and most were withdrawn from service in 1862.

Dahlgren was promoted to commander on September 14, 1855. When the commandant of the Washington Navy Yard, Captain Franklin Buchanan, joined the Confederacy early in 1861, Dahlgren replaced him. Promoted to captain on July 10, Dahlgren was named a rear admiral on February 7, 1863.

Dahlgren became close friends with President Abraham Lincoln, who often visited the yard. Dahlgren very much wanted the glory of command at sea. Never popular with his brother officers because of his relentless pursuit of recognition and his self-promotion, he used his influence with Lincoln to his advantage. When Secretary of the Navy Gideon Welles replaced Rear Admiral Samuel Du Pont as commander of the South Atlantic Blockading Squadron, Dahlgren sought that command, but Welles, who disliked Dahlgren, gave it to Rear Admiral Andrew H. Foote instead. A tentative arrangement was worked out whereby Dahlgren would be assigned to the squadron with Foote, although Dahlgren insisted that he have separate command of vessels for the attack on Charleston. All this was moot, because on his way to take up his command in June 1863 Foote suddenly became ill and died in New York City, whereupon Lincoln prevailed on Welles to appoint Dahlgren in his stead.

Most of Dahlgren's time with the South Atlantic Blockading Squadron was spent at sea off Charleston trying to seal off that harbor and protect his squadron from Confederate attack. Dahlgren personally led monitor attacks on the Confederate forts, but as with Du Pont before him, he was unable to take Charleston. Like Du Pont, Dahlgren was unwilling to run risks and rejected an attempt to force the inner harbor. A boat attack on Fort Sumter on the night of September 8, 1863, was a dismal failure. Dahlgren's lack of success partly resulted from the lack of coordination between army and navy. Dahlgren did assist Union land forces in taking Savannah and ultimately Charleston. He also directed an expedition up the St. Johns River in Florida. Dahlgren suffered a personal loss when his son Ulrich, an army colonel, was killed in a raid on Richmond in 1864.

After the war Dahlgren commanded the South Pacific Squadron for two years. He then returned to command the Bureau of Ordnance. During his naval career he was a prolific author on ordnance subjects. At the time of his death on July 12, 1870, in Washington, D.C., Dahlgren commanded the Washington Navy Yard.

SPENCER C. TUCKER

Further Reading

Dahlgren, John A. *Shells and Shell Guns*. Philadelphia: King and Baird, 1856.

Dahlgren, Madeleine Vinton. *Memoir of John A. Dahlgren, Rear-Admiral United States Navy*. Boston: James R. Osgood, 1882.

Schneller, Robert J., Jr. *A Quest for Glory: A Biography of Rear Admiral John A. Dahlgren*. Annapolis, MD: Naval Institute Press, 1996.

Tucker, Spencer C. *Arming the Fleet: U.S. Navy Ordnance in the Muzzle-Loading Era*. Annapolis, MD: Naval Institute Press, 1989.

Straits between the islands of Honshū and Kyūshū that connect the Inland Sea with the Sea of Japan. The first such incident occurs on June 25, 1863, when the Chōshūs fire on the U.S. merchant steamer *Pembroke*, inflicting only slight damage. Soon the Chōshūs fire on ships of most foreign nations trading with Japan.

The United States is the first to take retaliatory action. Learning of the attack on the *Pembroke*, on July 16 Commander David McDougal of the U.S. screw sloop *Wyoming* (8 guns) sails to the straits and engages three Chōshū warships: a steamer, a sailing brig, and a bark. The *Wyoming* sinks the brig and renders the steamer dead in the water by exploding its boilers but suffers damage itself as well as four dead and seven wounded (one mortally), largely as a consequence of land fire. Without charts and because of the swift current and narrow straits, McDougal withdraws without engaging the shore batteries. On July 20 two French warships, the *Tancrède* and *Dupleix*, shell a Chōshū town and land a party to spike the guns of a shore battery.

June 28, 1863

Civil War (continued): Eastern theater. U.S. president Abraham Lincoln replaces Major General Joseph E. Hooker with Major General George Gordon Meade as commander of the Army of the Potomac. Hooker has been quarreling with Washington and appears baffled in army command, especially when dealing with Confederate general Robert E. Lee. Meade has proven himself as a steady corps commander who does not rattle easily.

June 28, 1863

Civil War (continued): Eastern theater: Lee's second invasion of the North (continued): Engagement at Rockville, Maryland. Confederate major general J. E. B. Stuart captures 125 Union supply wagons near Rockville, Maryland, but in his most costly blunder of the war, he chooses to bring them into General Robert E. Lee's lines rather than burn them and move quickly back to the army.

Having sacrificed mobility for a relatively insignificant prize, Stuart is thus caught behind Union lines when the Army of the Potomac marches out of Washington, D.C., and is unable to carry out Lee's prime directive of screening the right flank of the Army of Northern Virginia in its march into Pennsylvania. The lack of intelligence from his chief of cavalry forces Lee to concentrate his forces prematurely and to fight the subsequent Battle of Gettysburg without the quality of reconnaissance to which he is accustomed.

June 1863–1864

American Indian Wars (continued): Carleton's Campaign. Although Brevet Lieutenant Colonel Edward R. S. Canby established peace with the Navajos in early 1861, the Civil War prevents the U.S. government from fulfilling its promises to the Navajos to provide food, clothing, and protection. Canby, appointed brigadier general of volunteers and given command of the Department of New Mexico, is also preoccupied with defending New Mexico against a Confederate invasion mounted by Brigadier General Henry Hopkins Sibley in 1862. The Navajos take advantage of the situation by raiding white settlements and disrupting mail service to California. Unfortunately for the Navajos, once the Confederate invasion is defeated, the full force of regional U.S. military strength can be directed against them.

Brigadier General James H. Carleton, who succeeds Canby in September 1862, is determined to crush Native American resistance in New Mexico. Having under his command the 1st New Mexico Cavalry, led by Colonel Christopher "Kit" Carson, the 1st California Cavalry, the 5th U.S. Infantry, the 1st New Mexico Infantry, and the 1st and 5th California Infantry, Carleton moves against the Mescalero Apaches in the spring of 1863, then turns his attention to the Navajos, ordering Navajo chiefs Barboncito and Delgadito to relocate to the new reservation established for the Mescalero Apaches at Bosque Redondo near Fort Sumner along the Pecos River in eastern New Mexico.

When the Navajos refuse to submit to this order, Carleton orders Carson to lead the 1st New Mexico Cavalry to Fort Wingate (near present-day Grants, New Mexico) and Fort Defiance (near present-day Window Rock, Arizona), renamed Fort Canby,

in preparation for a campaign against the Navajos. Beginning in June 1863, Carson's men, greatly assisted by friendly Ute and Zuni warriors, attack Navajo farms and seize livestock. During the next six months, Carson maintains steady pressure on the Navajos, killing a reported 78 warriors and destroying crops, orchards, and dwellings. By January 1864, the majority of the Navajos, now starving, have been forced into their traditional stronghold of Canyon de Chelly, which Carson and his men enter on January 12, 1864.

By mid-March, with the Navajos on the verge of starvation, some 6,000 assemble at Fort Wingate and Fort Canby to surrender. Approximately 2,400 Navajos are then marched to Bosque Redondo, with at least 200 dying en route. By the end of 1864, almost 8,000 Navajos have surrendered and relocated to Bosque Redondo.

Although Carleton's Campaign has effectively crushed the Navajos, his attempt to "civilize" them at Bosque Redondo is a failure. There is insufficient land available to support them and their livestock, and the attempt to force the Navajos to live alongside the Mescalero Apaches, their traditional enemy, results in continued turmoil. Indeed, the Mescalero Apaches flee the reservation in late 1865, and Carleton is relieved of his command in the autumn of 1866. Even hard-nosed Lieutenant General William Tecumseh Sherman, who meets with Navajo leaders at Fort Sumner in 1868, recognizes the futility of the Bosque Redondo experiment and agrees to a new treaty with the Navajos on June 1, 1868, allowing them to return to their traditional homeland.

July 1–3, 1863

Civil War (continued): Eastern theater: Lee's second invasion of the North (continued): Battle of Gettysburg. On June 30, 1863, U.S. major general George Gordon Meade's Army of the Potomac probes toward Emmitsburg and Hanover in Pennsylvania. Advance units of the Union and Confederate armies come together northwest of the crossroads of Gettysburg. Part of Confederate lieutenant general Ambrose Powell Hill's III Corps comes in from the west-northwest to confront Union brigadier general

A wood engraving of a drawing by A. R. Waud in 1863 depicting Pickett's Charge against Union positions on Cemetery Ridge at Gettysburg on July 3, 1863. The Battle of Gettysburg was a turning point in the American Civil War. (Library of Congress)

John Buford's dismounted cavalry division arriving from the southeast. Both sides then build up their forces toward what will become the greatest clash of arms ever on American soil.

On July 1 Hill's corps and Lieutenant General Richard S. Ewell's II Corps drive Union forces back on Gettysburg. Union major general John F. Reynolds reaches that town in midmorning with his I Corps infantry and moves forward to replace Buford's dismounted cavalry division, which is trying to hold off the Confederates.

Reynolds's men purchase just enough time to enable Union reinforcements to come up, although Reynolds himself is killed while placing his units. In the early afternoon, Union major general Oliver Howard's XI Corps reaches the field. In the fierce fighting that follows, however, the Confederates drive the Union troops back through Gettysburg into strong positions on Cemetery Hill and Culp's Hill.

This stand by Reynolds and Buford allows Union forces time to occupy an excellent defensive line, which comes to be known as the Fishhook for its shape. It is the greatest single advantage for the Union side in the battle. The Fishhook is anchored on the right by Culp's Hill. The line runs west to Cemetery Hill, then south along Cemetery Ridge to the two Round Tops. Union cavalry screen the flanks.

The Confederates, meanwhile, occupy Seminary Ridge, a long partially wooded rise to the west that parallels Cemetery Ridge. The first day's battle goes to the Confederates; two-thirds of the 18,000 Union troops engaged are casualties.

 **Napoleon Gun**

The U.S. 12-pounder smoothbore Napoleon gun was the standard fieldpiece of the Union and Confederate Armies in the American Civil War. It was, in effect, the epitome of five centuries of field artillery development. Officially known in the U.S. Army as the "light 12-pounder gun," this fieldpiece was most often referred to on both sides in the war as the "Napoleon." The gun was named not for French emperor Napoleon I but for his nephew, Emperor Napoleon III (1852–1870). A perceptive student of artillery, Napoleon III conceived a lightweight weapon of uniform caliber that would replace guns and howitzers of differing calibers for field service. Such a weapon would have the great advantage of standardization in ammunition. The new weapon was basically a gun without the powder chamber of the howitzer but able to fire shells at howitzer trajectories if need be. By 1856, gun howitzers had been adopted by France, Prussia, Russia, and other European countries.

The first American Napoleon gun was produced in 1857 by the Ames Manufacturing Co. of Chicopee, Massachusetts. During the war, five northern foundries cast the gun. By the time production ceased in 1864, they had produced 1,157 guns, of which almost 500 survive. Seven Confederate arsenals cast some 535 Napoleons during the Civil War, of which 133 survive.

Dozens of varieties of Napoleons existed. Although some were rifled, the vast majority were smoothbores of bronze (at the end of the war with bronze in short supply, the Tredegar foundry in Richmond cast some Napoleons in iron). Napoleons had a bore diameter of 4.62 inches and a bore length of approximately 64 inches, or 14 calibers (the bore being 14 times as long as its bore diameter).

Napoleons were characterized by a smooth exterior appearance without the rings of older guns and with only a slight muzzle swell (the best-known Confederate version had no muzzle swell). They weighed about 1,200 pounds, or 100 times the weight of their round shot. Several dozen of the earliest Union Napoleons had handles over their trunnions for lifting the guns, but these were eliminated in late 1861. Of the surviving Union Napoleons, only 5 are rifled.

Napoleons fired a variety of ammunition, including solid shot, shell, spherical case, grapeshot, and canister. A powder charge of 2.5 pounds gave its solid shot projectile a range of 1,600 yards, more than sufficient for the line-of-sight firing in mixed country that characterized most Civil War battles. Grapeshot fired at intermediate ranges was especially effective against cavalry charges, while canister from the Napoleon fired at close ranges proved deadly against attacking infantry.

The Napoleon gun was extraordinarily safe for its crews, with few if any recorded instances of the gun bursting. By the end of the Civil War, Napoleons comprised four-fifths of Union artillery. The remaining guns were Parrott rifles.

Spencer C. Tucker

Further Reading

Hazlett, James C., Edwin Olmstead, and M. Hume Parks. *Field Artillery Weapons of the Civil War*. Cranbury, NJ: Associated University Presses, 1983.

Ripley, Warren. *Artillery and Ammunition of the Civil War*. New York: Van Nostrand Reinhold, 1970.

The second day of battle, July 2, reveals the advantage of the Fishhook. Meade can operate from interior lines and more easily shift troops and supplies than can Lee on the exterior. Confederate lieutenant general James Longstreet, commanding I Corps, urges Lee to secure the Round Tops south of the Union defensive line and then swing around behind the Union forces, threatening Baltimore and Washington. Longstreet believes that this will draw Meade from his defensive positions. Lee, however, decides on a two-pronged attack on the Union flanks.

The Confederate attacks are not simultaneous, however, enabling Meade to contain both. Longstreet's march to avoid Union observation posts takes much of the afternoon. Nonetheless, his two-division attack against Major General Daniel Sickles's III Corps on the Union left is initially successful. Sickles had foolishly abandoned Cemetery Ridge and moved in advance of the rest of the Union line, forming a salient where he was completely unsupported. Meade shifts forces south to compensate, and although Sickles's men are driven back to Cemetery Ridge, they hold there.

The Confederates also fail to take Little Round Top. Colonel Joshua Chamberlain's badly outnumbered 20th Maine Regiment arrives there just in time and, in desperate fighting, manages to preserve it for the Union. Had the Confederates been successful at Little Round Top, Longstreet could have enfiladed the entire Union line.

The fighting then shifts to the Union center. Although Hill attacks with insufficient numbers, one Confederate brigade briefly secures a lodgment on Cemetery Ridge. To the north at twilight, Union defenders push back two Confederate brigades from Cemetery Hill. Ewell's attack on Culp's Hill is also rebuffed. The second day's fighting ends in a draw.

Although Longstreet expresses his opposition, Lee now plans a massive attack from Seminary Ridge against the center of the Union line, held by Major General Winfield Scott Hancock's II Corps. At the same time, Confederate cavalry under Stuart, which had arrived only the day before, will sweep around the Union line from the north.

At about 1:00 p.m. on July 3 the Confederates begin a massive artillery barrage by some 160 guns

Battle of Gettysburg		
Date	July 1–3, 1863	
Location	Gettysburg, Pennsylvania	
Opponents (*winner)	*United States	Confederacy
Commander	Major General George Gordon Meade	General Robert E. Lee
#	94,000 men	74,000 men
Casualties	23,055 (3,155 killed, 14,531 wounded, and 5,369 captured/missing)	23,231 (4,708 killed, 12,693 wounded, and 5,830 captured/missing); may be as high as 28,000

from Seminary Ridge. More than 100 Union guns on Cemetery Ridge reply in a two-hour cannonade. The guns then fall silent, and the Confederates begin their attack over a mile of open ground in ranks a mile wide, battle flags flying as if on parade. Three divisions take part in the charge, with Major General George E. Pickett's in the center. The other two divisions melt away and stream back toward the Confederate lines, leaving Pickett's men alone and exposed to enfilading Union fire.

Only a few hundred Confederates reach the Union line and there are halted. Confederate losses total 8,000–10,000 men of 12,000–13,500 attackers. The Confederate cavalry meanwhile is defeated five miles east of the battlefield by Union cavalry.

Lee then shortens his line but remains in place along Seminary Ridge the next day hoping that Meade will attack him, but the Union commander refuses to take the bait. On the night of July 4 Lee decamps, taking advantage of darkness and heavy rain to mask his withdrawal. Lee proceeds down the Cumberland Valley with captured booty and 6,000 prisoners.

In the Battle of Gettysburg, Meade suffers 23,055 casualties (3,155 killed, 14,531 wounded, and 5,369 captured or missing) of 94,000 men. Lee's losses are at least 23,231 (4,708 killed, 12,693 wounded, and 5,830 captured or missing) but may actually have been as high as 28,000 men, or more than one-third of his

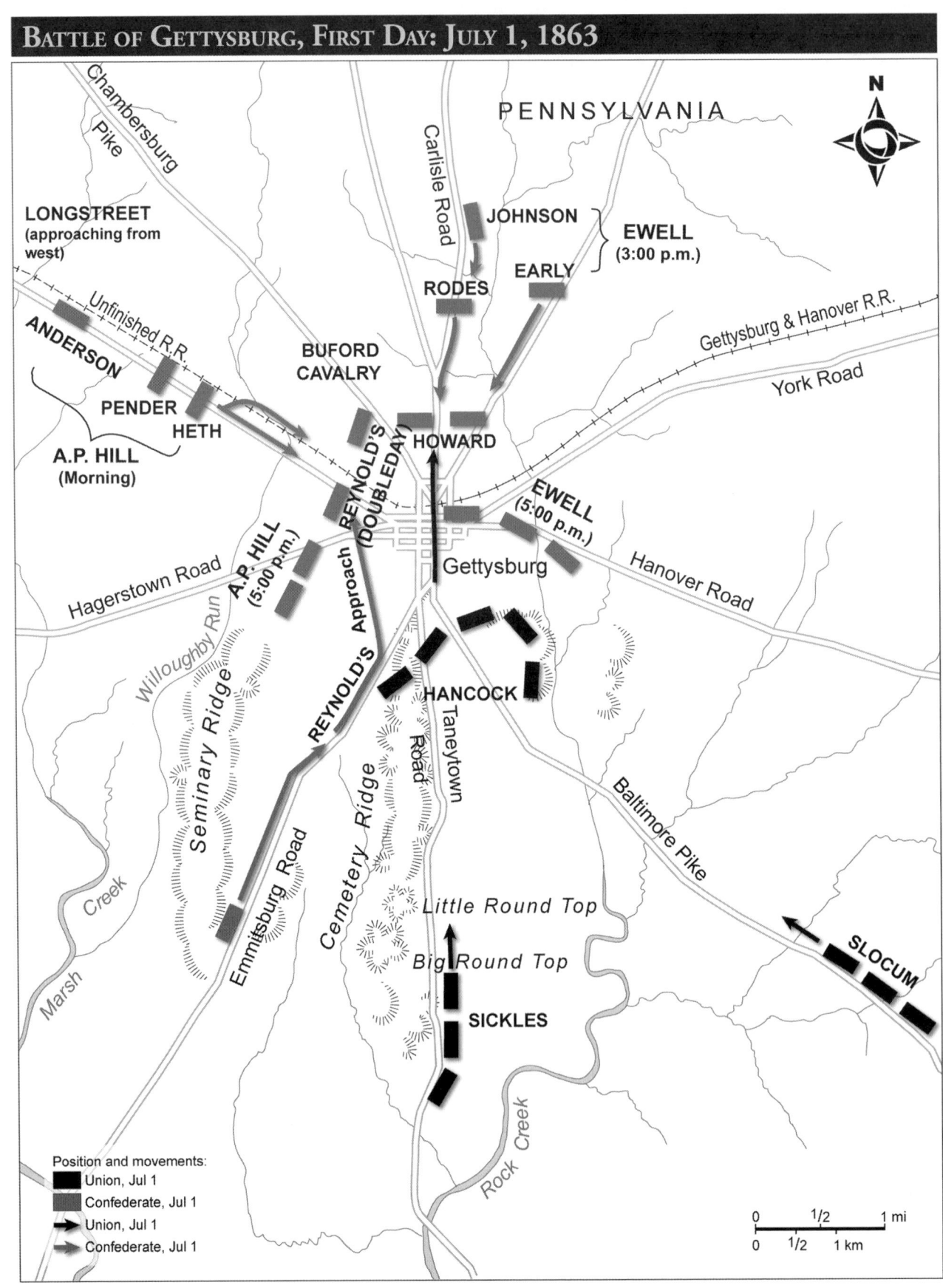

BATTLE OF GETTYSBURG, FIRST DAY: JULY 1, 1863

PENNSYLVANIA

Chambersburg Pike

Carlisle Road

JOHNSON

EWELL
(3:00 p.m.)

EARLY

LONGSTREET
(approaching from
west)

RODES

Unfinished R.R.

ANDERSON

BUFORD
CAVALRY

Gettysburg & Hanover R.R.

PENDER

York Road

HETH

REYNOLD'S
(DOUBLEDAY)

HOWARD

A.P. HILL
(Morning)

EWELL
(5:00 p.m.)

Hagerstown Road

A.P. HILL
(5:00 p.m.)

Hanover Road

Willoughby Run

Gettysburg

REYNOLD'S Approach

HANCOCK

Seminary Ridge

Taneytown Road

Baltimore Pike

Creek

Emmitsburg Road

Cemetery Ridge

Little Round Top

SLOCUM

Big Round Top

Marsh

SICKLES

Rock Creek

Position and movements:
▮ Union, Jul 1
▮ Confederate, Jul 1
→ Union, Jul 1
→ Confederate, Jul 1

0   1/2   1 mi
0   1/2 1 km

army of some 74,000. Although the South trumpets a victory, cooler heads can see that it is a Confederate defeat. The twin Union victories of Gettysburg and Vicksburg decisively tip the military-diplomatic balance in favor of the North.

July 2–26, 1863

Civil War (continued): Western theater: Morgan's Ohio Raid. Defying orders from Confederate general Braxton Bragg that he operate only south of the Ohio River, Brigadier General John Hunt Morgan believes that the war can be won only by carrying it into the North and decides to invade Ohio. Morgan crosses the Cumberland River near Burkesville with some 2,500 mounted men and four guns. Moving through Lebanon on July 5, he takes 400 Union soldiers prisoner. He then crosses the Ohio River on July 8 at Brandenburg. He reaches the suburbs of Cincinnati, covering 90 miles in only 35 hours, the longest continuous march of the war, and is at Pomeroy on July 18.

Although experiencing near constant combat, Morgan has thus far had almost everything go his way, but on July 19 a strong Union column under Brigadier General Edward H. Hobson defeats Morgan's men at Buffington Island, Ohio. Some 700 Confederates are captured while trying to cross the Ohio River into West Virginia. Hobson continues the pursuit of the remainder of Morgan's men, capturing them and Morgan at New Lisbon on July 26.

Morgan covered more than 700 miles in only 25 days. The raiders left in their wake a swath of destruction abetted by Confederate stragglers, who terrorize the local population. They had taken and then paroled 6,000 Union troops, diverted 14,000 regulars from other duties, and forced the calling up of 120,000 militia in two states. In addition to the destruction of public buildings, ransoms exacted, and outright looting, Morgan's raid brings the destruction of 34 bridges and some 60 railroad cuts.

Morgan's raid and the ensuing destruction and financial exactions serve to turn the support of possible Copperheads (Peace Democrats) against the South. The raid also revives spirits in the South, creates panic in the North, and delays the establishment of Union control over eastern Tennessee.

July 4, 1863

Civil War (continued): Trans-Mississippi West theater: Battle of Helena. U.S. major general Benjamin M. Prentiss, commander of the District of Eastern Arkansas, had established his headquarters at the federal enclave of Helena on the Mississippi River. Union troops had occupied Helena in July 1862, and it soon became a major logistical base. To protect it against attack, the city boasts extensive defensive works to include a semicircle of breastworks and rifle pits supported by four artillery batteries and the timberclad *Tyler* (7 guns) in the river. Prentiss, however, has been obliged to send most of his 20,000 troops south to assist in Union operations against Vicksburg so that in early July, Helena is held by only 4,129 men.

Confederate lieutenant general Theophilus H. Holmes, commander of the District of Arkansas, aware of the depletion of Union strength, is determined to retake Helena and prevent it being used as a base for further Union movement into Arkansas. Receiving permission from Lieutenant General Edmund Kirby Smith, commander of the Confederate Trans-Mississippi Department, Holmes assembles some 7,600 men. He plans a converging attack by three columns. Brigadier General John S. Marmaduke will move with his 1,700 dismounted cavalry from the north, Major General Sterling Price will strike with 3,100 infantry from the west, and Brigadier General James Fleming Fagan will attack with 1,300 men from the southwest. Holmes's plan of attack is made without adequate intelligence regarding the strongly fortified Union defensive line and with Prentiss aware of an impending Confederate attack.

Although Holmes had ordered the attack to commence at dawn on July 4, 1863, firing begins between pickets at 3:00 a.m. Despite faulty coordination and poor communications, the Confederates penetrate the Union defenses in several places. But Holmes fumbles away a chance for victory when he is unable to decide which of the attacks to strengthen with his reserves, and the temporary Confederate advantage is soon lost. Union land artillery and the guns of the *Tyler* (which fires 413 rounds in support of the defenders) help turn the tide. By late morning the Confederates have been driven back. The Battle of Helena claims 239 Union and 1,614 Confederate casualties. Although overshadowed by the far larger battles at Vicksburg and Gettysburg, the Battle of Helena is an important Union victory, securing eastern Arkansas for the Union.

July 4, 1863

Civil War (continued): Western theater: Surrender of Vicksburg, Mississippi. See May 23–July 4, 1863.

July 4–14, 1863

Civil War (continued): Eastern theater: Lee's retreat from Gettysburg. Following the repulse of his attack of July 3, 1863, Confederate general Robert E. Lee, commander of the Army of Northern Virginia, waits in vain for the Union troops to attack him. Major General George Gordon Meade, commander of the Army of the Potomac, refuses to take the bait, saying that he will not "play their old game of shooting us behind breastworks."

On the dark and stormy night of July 4–5 Lee decamps, and the Army of Northern Virginia begins the long retreat down the Cumberland Valley toward Hagerstown and Williamsport, Maryland, to return to Virginia with captured booty and some 6,000 Union prisoners.

The Potomac River is up, and for a time it looks as if Meade might catch Lee and pin him against the river. But Meade is slow to move. The Union infantry follows cautiously the next day, converging on Middletown, Maryland. On July 7, Confederate forces under General John D. Imboden stop Brigadier General John Buford's Union cavalry from occupying Williamsport and destroying Confederate baggage trains. Meanwhile, Union cavalry under Brigadier General Hugh J. Kilpatrick drive two Confederate cavalry brigades through Hagerstown before being forced to retire by the arrival of the remainder of Confederate major general J. E. B. Stuart's command.

Lee's infantry, meanwhile, reaches the rain-swollen Potomac River but cannot cross because the pontoon bridge has been destroyed in a Union cavalry raid. On July 11, Lee entrenches at Williamsport. Meade reaches there the next day and probes the Confederate defenses. Heavy skirmishing occurs the next day, with Meade positioning his forces for an assault.

Fortunately for Lee, the river has now receded sufficiently for Confederate engineers to be able to construct a bridge. Lee begins crossing the Potomac on it after dark on July 13. On the morning of July 14, Kilpatrick's and Buford's cavalry divisions attack the rearguard Confederate division of Brigadier General Henry Heth still on the north bank, taking more than 500 prisoners. The Gettysburg Campaign is over.

July 9, 1863

Civil War (continued): Western theater. Port Hudson, Louisiana, the last remaining Confederate Mississippi River bastion, surrenders following an extended siege (see May 21–July 9, 1863).

July 10–September 7, 1863

Civil War (continued): Eastern theater: Continued Union efforts against Charleston. New commander of the South Atlantic Blockading Squadron Rear Admiral John Dahlgren maintains a bombardment of Charleston's defenses. Then on July 10 his ships land 3,000 troops under Brigadier General Quincy A. Gillmore on Morris Island below Fort Sumter. The men work their way toward Fort Wagner (also known as Battery Wagner), carrying out the first assault on July 11. It fails with losses of 49 killed, 123 wounded, and 167 missing; Confederate losses are only 6 dead and 6 wounded. Gillmore now settles in for a siege that ultimately involves some 6,000 men against about 1,300 Confederate defenders. The U.S. Navy supports the land effort with shore bombardments.

When Union troops finally work their way close enough for an assault, the Confederates evacuate Fort Wagner on September 7. Gillmore also commences a long-range shelling of the waterfront area of the city of Charleston, which he holds to be a valid target because of its war industries.

July 13, 1863

Civil War (continued): Western theater: Capture of Yazoo City, Mississippi. The last Confederate naval base operating near Vicksburg, Mississippi, Yazoo City succumbs to a joint army-navy expedition led by Lieutenant Commander J. G. Walker that includes the ironclad *Baron de Kalb* (13 guns), the gunboat

Kenwood (6 guns), the tinclads *Black Hawk* (5 guns) and *Signal* (7 guns), and the river service craft *New National* (4 guns) convoying some 5,000 Union troops under Major General Francis J. Herron. Union forces arrive at Yazoo City on the afternoon of July 13. The leading Union ship, the *Baron de Kalb,* strikes a torpedo (mine) and sinks within 15 minutes.

Confederate Navy officer in charge at Yazoo City Commander I. M. Brown meanwhile orders the scuttling of Confederate ships rather than see them fall into Union hands, leading to the sinking of 15 ships in the Yazoo and another 4 in the Sunflower River. U.S. forces do capture 1 ship, the *St. Mary.* Of the many ships that had sought refuge in the Yazoo, the Confederates now have only 4, in the Tallahatchie and Yalobusha Rivers.

July 13–16, 1863

Civil War (continued): New York City Draft Riots. These riots against the draft laws are the largest civil insurrection in U.S. history, apart from the Civil War itself. The rioters, numbering as many as 50,000 people, are overwhelmingly poor and Irish. They resent the exemption in the legislation that allows the wealthy to escape service by paying a $300 fee, and they fear that blacks will take their jobs while they are being forced to serve in the army.

After attacking government offices and homes of the rich, the rioters turn on blacks, murdering men, women, and children. President Abraham Lincoln orders several regiments of militia and volunteer troops, some of them fresh from the Battle of Gettysburg, to the city. Order is finally restored on July 16.

In the violence some 50 buildings are burned, including 2 Protestant churches and an orphanage. Damage estimates are between $1 million and $5 million. At least 120 people are killed, and more than 1,000 are injured.

July 18, 1863

Civil War (continued): Eastern theater: New Union assault on Battery Wagner. Six ironclads in Rear Admiral John A. Dahlgren's South Atlantic Blockading Squadron shell Confederate Battery Wagner on Morris Island, South Carolina, and Union troops

then assault the fort. Despite the naval cannonade, the defenders repulse the Union infantry assault that is spearheaded by Colonel Robert G. Shaw's 54th Massachusetts Regiment of African American soldiers with white officers. The attackers acquit themselves with honor but suffer an appalling 1,515 casualties. Shaw is among the dead. (Sergeant William H. Carney of the 54th Massachusetts Regiment will be the first African American soldier awarded the Medal of Honor.) The Confederates sustain only 36 dead, 133 wounded, and 5 missing.

July 1863

Civil War (continued): Establishment of the Confederate Naval Academy. On February 20, 1861, the Confederate Congress had authorized creation of a naval academy. Unlike the U.S. Naval Academy, with a formal grounds and a dedicated training ship, the Confederacy opts for a training ship to serve as the academy's entire school: the former passenger liner and freight ship *Yorktown* is converted into a warship renamed the *Patrick Henry* and is the home of the naval academy.

The ship is placed under the James River Squadron and based below Drewry's Bluff on the James River about seven miles below Richmond. Establishing the school takes two years, and it is not until July 1863 that 56 of the Confederacy's 106 midshipmen receive orders to report to the *Patrick Henry.*

Commander John Mercer Brooke, chief of the Office of Ordnance and Hydrography, organizes the academy and has overall supervision. Its first superintendent is Lieutenant William H. Parker.

August 17–21, 1863

Civil War (continued). South Atlantic Blockading Squadron commander Rear Admiral John Dahlgren's squadron of seven ironclads and eight gunboats carries out a five-day bombardment of Charleston Harbor.

August 21, 1863

Civil War (continued): Western theater: Lawrence Massacre. William C. Quantrill leads 300–400 Confederate irregulars against the town of Lawrence in Douglas County, Kansas. He targets Lawrence because

Robert Gould Shaw (1837–1863)

Union Army officer. Robert Gould Shaw was born into a prominent Boston, Massachusetts, family on October 10, 1837. He enrolled at Harvard University in 1856 but dropped out in his junior year to work in his uncle's mercantile firm in New York City. When war seemed imminent in the spring of 1861, Shaw joined an elite military company as a private. Shortly after hostilities commenced, he returned home and was commissioned a second lieutenant in the 2nd Massachusetts Infantry Regiment. Promoted to captain in August 1862, he participated in the First Battle of Winchester (May 25, 1862), the Battle of Cedar Mountain (August 9), and the Battle of Antietam (September 17). Shaw was promoted to major on March 31, 1863.

Massachusetts governor John A. Andrew, a leading abolitionist, prevailed on U.S. president Abraham Lincoln to allow him to recruit an African American regiment for federal service. The 54th Massachusetts Volunteer Infantry was the first such organization raised in a free state. Andrew appointed Shaw colonel of the 54th Massachusetts Volunteer Infantry on April 17, 1863. Shaw was one of the few white officers who believed that minorities might make effective soldiers. He supported a boycott by his men, who received less pay then white soldiers, in which the enlisted men of the 54th Massachusetts Volunteer Infantry (and the sister 55th Massachusetts Volunteer Infantry) refused pay until Congress granted them pay at the white pay rate (which occurred in August 1864).

Following training, the 54th Massachusetts Volunteer Infantry paraded through Boston, Massachusetts, in May 1863 and embarked for Charleston, South Carolina. Following a baptism of fire on July 16, 1863, in which the 54th Massachusetts Volunteer Infantry performed effectively, Major General Quincy A. Gillmore, commanding Union Army operations against Charleston, offered Shaw the opportunity to spearhead another assault on Fort Wagner, the heavily armed Confederate fortification on Morris Island. Eager to prove his men in combat and resentful over how the army had discriminated against his soldiers, Shaw readily assented.

A Union naval bombardment lasting several hours failed to reduce the Confederate defenses at Battery Wagner, and when the Union troops attacked, they were slaughtered by the Confederate defenders. Undaunted, the 54th Massachusetts Volunteer Infantry surged forward, with Shaw at their head, and gained a foothold on the parapet. Shaw stood there urging his men on until struck in the heart by a bullet and killed. When Union reinforcements failed to arrive, the surviving members of the 54th Massachusetts Volunteer Infantry were forced to withdraw. Of 5,300 Union troops engaged that day, 1,515 were casualties. The 54th Massachusetts Volunteer Infantry alone lost 9 killed, 147 wounded, and 100 missing and presumed dead, almost 40 percent of its strength. The defenders suffered only 175 casualties.

When a flag of truce was sent out to recover Shaw's body, Confederate garrison commander Brigadier General Johnson Hagood allowed the bodies of the other officers to be taken away but not that of Shaw. Hagood declared that he would have returned the body had Shaw been in command of white troops, but he would be "buried with his niggers." This callous act, which nonetheless pleased Shaw's parents, who believed it was what he would have wanted, helped elevate Shaw and his men to the status of martyrs in the eyes of abolitionists throughout the North. Moreover, the heroic performance of the 54th Massachusetts Volunteer Infantry proved that African Americans could fight beside their white comrades in arms, and additional black units were raised. In 1882 Shaw was honored by an elaborate stone mural in Boston carved by Augustus Saint-Gaudens.

JOHN C. FREDRIKSEN

Further Reading

Burchard, Peter, *"We'll Stand by the Union": Robert Gould Shaw and the Black 54th Massachusetts.* New York: St. Martin's, 1993.

Duncan, Russell, ed. *Blue-Eyed Child of Fortune: The Civil War Letters of Colonel Robert Gould Shaw.* Athens: University of Georgia Press, 1992.

Duncan, Russell, ed. *Where Death and Glory Meet: Colonel Robert Gould Shaw and the 54th Massachusetts Infantry.* Athens: University of Georgia Press, 1999.

Wise, Stephen R. *Gate of Hell: Campaign for Charleston Harbor, 1863.* Columbia: University of South Carolina Press, 1994.

of its strong support for the abolition of slavery and its reputation as a center of Jayhawkers and Redlegs, the free-state militia and vigilante groups that have been raiding Missouri's proslavery western counties.

The attack is well planned and carefully timed. In the span of only four hours the attackers pillage and set fire to Lawrence, burning 185 buildings. They also systematically execute most of its male population of men and boys, murdering between 185 and 200 in the largest atrocity against civilians of the war.

In retaliation, in the weeks and months to follow Jayhawkers largely destroy five counties in western Missouri.

August 23–25, 1863

Civil War (continued): Eastern theater: Capture of USS *Reliance* and *Satellite.* On August 23, 1863, off Windmill Point in the Rappahannock River, Virginia, some 80 Confederates in four boats commanded by Lieutenant John T. Wood attack and capture the U.S. Navy screw tug *Reliance* (2 guns), commanded by Acting Ensign Henry Walter, and the side-wheel combatant *Satellite* (2 guns), commanded by Acting Master John F. D. Robinson. On August 25 Wood employs the captured ships to take the merchant schooners *Golden Rod, Coquette,* and *Two Brothers,* then moves all five ships up the river, strips them of useful materials, and burns them.

September 2, 1863

Civil War (continued): Western theater. Some 15,000 Union troops under Major General Ambrose E. Burnside, commander of the Department of the Ohio, occupy Knoxville, Tennessee.

September 3, 1863

American Indian Wars (continued): Battle of Whitestone Hill. Following Chief Little Crow's Sioux Uprising in Minnesota in 1862, some Santee Sioux manage to escape Colonel Henry H. Sibley's volunteers and join with Teton Sioux in the Dakota Territory. Brigadier General Alfred Sully organizes 1,200 soldiers at Fort Ridgely to join Sibley in what becomes the 1863–1864 Sioux Campaign.

After nearly two weeks of searching, Sully learns that the hostile Sioux are along the James River searching for food. Sully dispatches Major A. E. House and 300 men of the 6th Iowa Cavalry Regiment ahead of his main body to locate the Sioux camp. On September 3, 1863, they discover a large camp of nearly 500 lodges near Whitestone Hill in present-day Merricourt, North Dakota.

House immediately sends couriers to report this information to Sully but also decides to move most of his command forward in an effort to contain the village and prevent the Sioux from escaping. Only subsequent to this decision does House realize that the

Ambrose Powell Hill (1825–1865)

Confederate Army officer. Ambrose Powell Hill, widely known as A. P. Hill, was born in Culpepper County, Virginia, on November 9, 1825. He graduated from the U.S. Military Academy, West Point, in 1847 and was commissioned a second lieutenant in the 1st Artillery. He saw service in the Mexican-American War (1846–1848).

Hill was promoted to first lieutenant in September 1851. During 1855–1860, he was assigned to the Coast Survey and participated in the Third Seminole War (1855–1858). In October 1860 Hill was granted a leave of absence from the army, and in March 1861 he resigned his commission in response to the deepening crisis over secession. When Virginia left the Union, he was commissioned a colonel and given command of the 13th Virginia Regiment. He distinguished himself in the First Battle of Bull Run (Manassas) on July 21, 1861.

Advanced to brigadier general in February 1862, Hill took command of a brigade in the Army of Northern Virginia. In the 1862 Peninsula Campaign, he saw action at the Battle of Williamsburg on May 5. Promoted to major general that May, he received command of a division, again distinguishing himself in the Seven Days' Battles (June 25–July 1). Hill's Light Division was actually one of the largest divisions in General Robert E. Lee's Army of Northern Virginia. At Mechanicsville on June 26, Hill led the main attack that was repulsed. His division also spearheaded attacks at Gaines' Mill (June 27) and Frayser's Farm (June 30).

Hill's division fought effectively in the Battle of Cedar Run on August 9, 1862, and in the Second Battle of Bull Run (Manassas) on August 29–30. His troops participated in the capture of Harpers Ferry in September, where 11,000 Union troops were taken prisoner and vast amounts of valuable supplies were secured. Hill's division also fought well in the Battle of Antietam on September 17 and at Fredericksburg on December 13, 1962, as part of Lieutenant General Thomas Jackson's II Corps.

During the Battle of Chancellorsville (May 1–4, 1863), Hill's division formed part of Jackson's flanking attack, and Hill assumed command of the corps after Jackson was mortally wounded. Hill was himself subsequently wounded in the battle. In the reorganization of Lee's army following Jackson's death, Hill was promoted to lieutenant general in late May and given command of the new III Corps.

Hill and his corps participated in Lee's second invasion of the North, which terminated in the Battle of Gettysburg (July 1–3, 1863). While he had performed magnificently as a brigade and divisional commander, Hill's performance at the corps level was utterly undistinguished. The actions of his corps led to the premature start of the battle against the explicit orders of Lee, whose forces were then still dispersed. Hill was ill and largely passive for most of the next two days of fighting. On October 14, 1863, he was soundly beaten at Bristoe Station, where he took heavy casualties in frontal assaults against a well-dug-in Union corps, believing that he was attacking a Union rear guard. Hill's troops fought in the Battle of the Wilderness (May 5–7, 1864), but he was again ill and relinquished command, missing the Battles of Spotsylvania Court and Cold Harbor. He returned to service to participate in the Siege of Petersburg but was again ill in the winter of 1864–1865.

During the Siege of Petersburg on April 2, 1865, only a week before Lee's surrender, as Hill rode to the front line accompanied by a staff officer, he was shot and killed by a Union soldier. Following the war,

Hill's frequent illnesses were the subject of considerable debate. Some have attributed this to mental problems, while others contend the illnesses were brought on by complications from venereal disease contracted while he was a West Point cadet.

RALPH BAKER AND SPENCER C. TUCKER

Further Reading

Hassler, William W. *A. P. Hill: Lee's Forgotten General*. Chapel Hill: University of North Carolina Press, 1957.
Martin, David G. *Gettysburg July 1*. Conshohocken PA: Combined Books, 1996.
Robertson, James I. *General A. P. Hill: The Story of a Confederate Warrior*. New York: Vintage Books, 1992.

Sioux camp holds an estimated 1,200 Santee, Yanktonai, Blackfoot, and Hunkpapa warriors. Seeking to delay until Sully can arrive, he enters into negotiations with the warriors. The Sioux, believing they are facing only House's command, then attack.

Just as the Sioux launch their attack, Sully's main column arrives. The Sioux promptly turn their attention to Sully's larger force, enabling House to escape, rejoin the rest of the 6th Iowa Cavalry Regiment, and then launch a counterattack. Pressed from both sides, the Sioux are forced to divide their forces. A charge by the 6th Iowa Cavalry Regiment fails to break the more numerous Sioux, while the Sioux fail in their effort to flank the soldiers' positions.

In the fighting the Sioux suffer more than 100 dead, many more wounded, and 156 captured. After nightfall, the remaining Sioux make good their escape. Sully has sustained 20 dead and 38 wounded. That night, Sully's soldiers torch some 300 lodges and an estimated 400,000 pounds of buffalo meat. Sully also orders the destruction of any Native American lodges and food stocks in the area; as a consequence, some additional fighting occurs during the next several days.

September 6, 1863

Civil War (continued): Eastern theater. Confederate forces abandon Battery Wagner and evacuate Morris Island off Charleston Harbor, South Carolina, following almost two months of Union land and naval bombardments.

September 8, 1863

Civil War (continued): Battle of Sabine Pass. A Union expeditionary force of 4,000 troops under Major General William B. Franklin attempts to take Sabine Pass, Texas. The Union transports are accompanied by four shallow-draft gunboats: the side-wheel steamers *Clifton* (8 guns), *Granite City* (7 guns), and *Arizona* (6 guns) and the coastal screw combatant *Sachem* (5 guns). The Confederate gunboat *Uncle Ben* (3 guns) and shore batteries at Fort Griffin turn back the Union assault. Both the *Clifton* and the *Sachem* are disabled and forced to surrender, with the loss of 315 men. The remaining Union ships recross the bar and return to New Orleans.

September 9, 1863

Civil War (continued): Western theater: Union capture of Chattanooga. After another long delay, at Tullahoma, Tennessee, Major General William S. Rosecrans advances with his Army of the Cumberland against Confederate general Braxton Bragg's Army of Tennessee. At the same time, Union major general Ambrose E. Burnside moves from Lexington, Kentucky, against Knoxville with his Army of the Ohio.

Bragg digs in at Chattanooga to guard the Tennessee River crossings, but again Rosecrans outmaneuvers him. Crossing the river well to the southwest near Bridgeport, he threatens Bragg's line of communications to Atlanta and on September 8 forces the Confederate general to withdraw from the key rail center of Chattanooga, gateway to the heart of the Confederacy. Troops of the Union XXI Corps enter Chattanooga the next day. Bragg moves 28 miles south to Lafayette, Georgia, there to await reinforcements.

September 16, 1863

Civil War (continued). Willie Johnson, a 13-year-old drummer boy in Company D of the 3rd Vermont Infantry Regiment, is awarded the Medal of Honor for bravery during the Seven Days' Battles of 1862. Johnson remains the youngest person ever to receive the nation's highest decoration for bravery.

Union major general William S. Rosecrans commanded the Army of the Cumberland in the Western Theater, but his orders, based on faulty imformation, brought defeat in the Battle of Chickamauga during September 19–20, 1863, leading to his removal from command. (National Archives)

September 19–20, 1863

Civil War (continued): Western theater: Battle of Chickamauga. Following the Union capture of the key railhead of Chattanooga, Confederate general Braxton Bragg withdraws with his Army of Tennessee to Lafayette, Georgia, about 28 miles to the south. Confederate president Jefferson Davis rushes Lieutenant General James Longstreet and a corps to reinforce Bragg, bringing his strength up to about 66,000 men.

U.S. major general William S. Rosecrans now advances with his 57,000-man Army of the Cumberland against Bragg. Confederate soldiers, posing as deserters, inform Rosecrans that Bragg is in full retreat. Without bothering to ascertain the truth of these reports, Rosecrans pushes his forces ahead, splitting them into three detachments sufficiently separated that they cannot support each other. Meanwhile, Bragg is lying in wait along Chickamauga Creek in excellent defensive positions.

The Battle of Chickamauga opens on September 19 with the Confederates attacking. There is heavy fighting all day on a four-mile front. Generally, the Union lines hold.

On September 20 Bragg again attacks, trying to drive between the Union forces and their base at Chattanooga. The Union lines again hold until misinformation causes Rosecrans to order an entire division to shift its position; this creates a great gap in the Union line into which the Confederates under Longstreet

Battle of Chickamauga		
Date	September 19–20, 1863	
Location	Catoosa County and Walker County, Georgia	
Opponents (*winner)	*Confederacy	United States
Commander	General Braxton Bragg	Major General William S. Rosecrans
#	66,000 men	57,000 men
Casualties	18,454 (2,312 killed, 14,674 wounded, 1,468 captured/missing)	16,170 (1,657 killed, 9,756 wounded, 4,757 captured/missing)

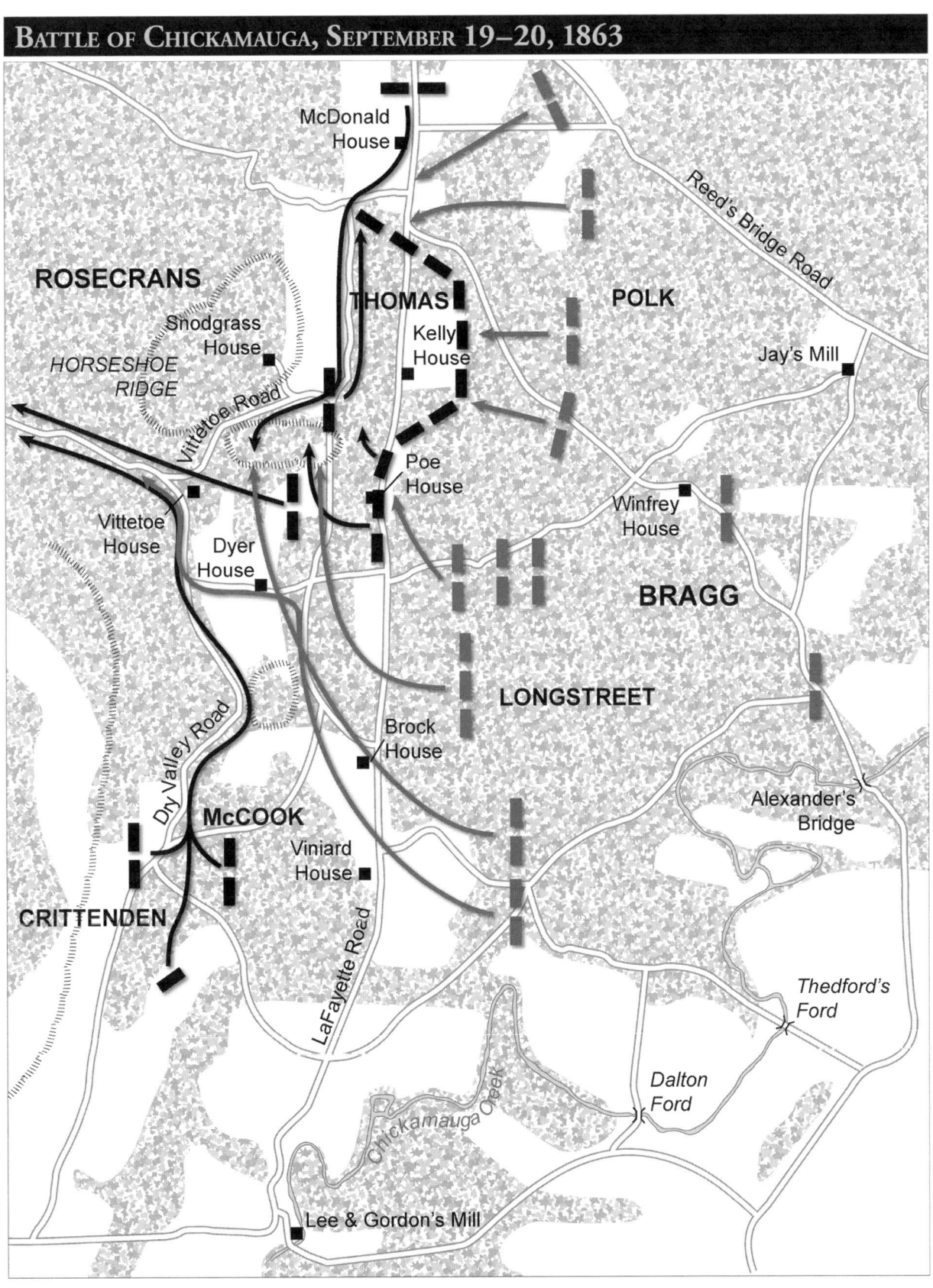

BATTLE OF CHICKAMAUGA, SEPTEMBER 19–20, 1863

ROSECRANS

Snodgrass House

HORSESHOE RIDGE

Vittetoe Road

THOMAS

Kelly House

POLK

Jay's Mill

Poe House

Winfrey House

Vittetoe House

Dyer House

BRAGG

LONGSTREET

Brock House

McDonald House

Dry Valley Road

McCOOK

Viniard House

Reed's Bridge Road

Alexander's Bridge

CRITTENDEN

LaFayette Road

Thedford's Ford

Dalton Ford

Chickamauga Creek

Lee & Gordon's Mill

smash, routing Rosecrans and half his army. Union major general George Thomas takes charge of the remaining Union troops and holds, however, earning him the sobriquet "Rock of Chickamauga." Rosecrans withdraws into Chattanooga.

Chickamauga is one of the most costly battles of the war. Union casualties total 16,170 (1,657 killed, 9,756 wounded, and 4,757 captured or missing); the Confederates lose 18,454 (2,312 killed, 14,674 wounded, and 1,468 captured or missing).

September 23–November 25, 1863

Civil War (continued): Western theater: Siege of Chattanooga. Following his defeat in the Battle of Chickamauga (see September 19–20, 1863), Army of the Cumberland commander Major General William S. Rosecrans digs in at Chattanooga, Tennessee. Confederate general Braxton Bragg, commanding the Army of Tennessee, does not order an immediate assault, which would have been foolhardy; on September 23, however, his men seize the surrounding heights of Missionary Ridge to the east, Lookout Mountain to the southwest, and Raccoon Mountain to the west. They then connect these three positions.

Bragg expects Rosecrans to evacuate Chattanooga. When he does not, Bragg commences siege operations. From the high ground, the Confederates can easily direct artillery fire against Union entrenchments and sever the major rail and water routes into the city. A Confederate cavalry raid under Major General Joseph Wheeler during October 1–9 destroys Union wagon trains trying to reach Chattanooga, and resupply remains tenuous. The troops and inhabitants of the city are soon in dire straits.

Washington orders Major General Ambrose E. Burnside from Knoxville to reinforce Chattanooga and also sends there two corps of the Army of the Potomac under Major General Joseph Hooker. Burnside is stalled by lack of supplies, while Hooker arrives at Bridgeport, 30 miles distant, in mid-October.

On October 17 Union major general Ulysses S. Grant is named commander of the Western theater. He immediately proceeds to Chattanooga. En route, on October 19 he removes Rosecrans as commander of the Army of the Cumberland, replacing him with Major General George Thomas, who declares that the city will be held.

Grant arrives at Chattanooga on October 23. Three days later he puts into action a plan to slip men across the Tennessee River on pontoon bridges to open a gap in the Confederate line. Utilizing this so-called Cracker Line, Hooker's men are able to move to Chattanooga with supplies. Grant also orders Major General William T. Sherman and 17,000 men of the Army of the Tennessee to Chattanooga from Memphis. They arrive on November 14, making it possible for Grant to take the offensive in the Battle of Chattanooga during November 23–25.

October 5, 1863

Civil War (continued): Eastern theater. The semi-submersible Confederate torpedo boat *David*, commanded by Lieutenant William T. Glassell with three other individuals, slips out of Charleston, South Carolina, and detonates a spar torpedo (an explosive charge at the end of a long spar mounted at the vessel's bow) against the powerful U.S. Navy ironclad *New Ironsides* (20 guns). The ironclad sustains only modest damage in the attack but is forced to quit the Charleston station for repairs.

October 9, 1863

Civil War (continued): The British government seizes the two Laird Rams. In June 1862, Commander James D. Bulloch, the Confederate agent in Britain, had contracted with the firm of John Laird and Sons for two armored ships. Identified as hulls 294 and 295, they are best known as the Laird Rams. Their intended names in Confederate service were the *North Carolina* and *Mississippi*. Launched in July and August, respectively, they are designed to mount four 9-inch rifled guns in two rotating iron turrets, and each has a 7-foot iron ram at the bow.

Bullock puts out the cover story that the ships have been ordered by the Egyptian government, but U.S. agents are not fooled, and heavy pressure from Washington, assisted by changing Southern military fortunes in the summer of 1863, leads the British government to seize both ships in the Mersey River. In February 1864 the government purchases them for the Royal Navy.

 **Torpedo Boats**

Development of the automotive torpedo meant that for the first time in naval history, small vessels could threaten large ships. Torpedo boats launched their "fish" (torpedo) from the bow, presenting the smallest silhouette to enemy fire. All navies developed such small, fast boats specifically to launch torpedoes, leading to some discussion in the 1880s as to whether the battleship had been rendered obsolete.

The first purpose-built torpedo boat was the Royal Navy *Lightning,* built by the firm of John I. Thornycroft in 1877. Displacing just 27 tons, it was 84.5 feet long and 11 feet in beam. Powered by a 478-horsepower engine, it could make 19 knots and was fitted with a bow-launching tube for a single 14-inch torpedo. The French were almost first. Their *Torpilleur No. 1* was actually ordered in 1875 but not completed until 1878. Heavily influenced by the thinking of the so-called *jeune école* ("young school") concept that emphasized smaller ships, France built the largest number of torpedo boats. By 1890 France had 220, Britain had 186, Russia had 152, Germany had 143, and Italy had 129. But torpedoes became standard armament on all classes of warships. All Royal Navy ships launched after 1872 carried them.

The first U.S. Navy torpedo boat was the *Cushing* (TB-1). Built at Bristol, Rhode Island, and commissioned in 1890, it displaced 116 tons. Propelled by two screws, it was capable of 23 knots. It was 138'9" in length and only 14'3" in beam. It mounted three 18-inch torpedo tubes and carried three 1-pounder guns. It had a crew complement of 23 men. Effective only in calm waters, it saw service in the Spanish-American War of 1898.

Early torpedo boats were too small to be effective. Their poor performance during maneuvers led to the construction of larger vessels. Torpedo boats were made about 50 percent longer while at the same time preserving their slim, narrow lines. These craft were technically capable of ocean work, although their crews often did not think so. In 1889 France ordered larger boats of about 125 tons each to accompany squadrons at sea. In 1895 the 136-ton 144.4-foot *Forban* reached 31 knots, a world record.

The threat posed by torpedo boats was partially countered by the development of quick-firing Nordenfelt and Gatling machine guns, which became part of the standard armament of even the largest warships. At night these were paired with the newly developed searchlight. The torpedo boat destroyer (later simply known as the destroyer) also appeared; its task was to search out and destroy the torpedo boats before they could close within range. During World War I, the Italian Navy operated nearly 300 torpedo-armed motorboats in the Adriatic Sea against the Austro-Hungarian Navy. The Royal Navy also employed coastal motorboats in home waters and in raids against Ostend and Zeebrugge, Belgium, in April 1918.

The major powers continued to employ torpedo boats during World War II. For the most part these small, fast, highly maneuverable wooden-hulled shallow-draft vessels operated in coastal waters. The Germans had E boats, while the British employed motor torpedo boats. Perhaps the best known of all these craft, however, were the U.S. Navy patrol torpedo boats, popularly known as PT boats. They were 77 feet long with an average speed of 27.5 knots in rough waters and mounted two 21-inch torpedo tubes. They also carried two .50-caliber machine guns in twin turrets. During the war the U.S. Navy deployed 350 PT boats in the Pacific theater, 42 in the Mediterranean, and 33 in the English Channel. They were not very effective against Japanese ships, because early U.S. torpedoes proved defective and

(continued)

(Continued)

were difficult to fire accurately while maneuvering at high speed. PT boats were much more effective in coastal work, where they attacked and destroyed large numbers of Japanese landing craft, landed small forces, and—armed with rockets, mortars, or a 40-millimeter gun—provided support to troops ashore. The successors of such craft were effectively employed in riverine operations during the Vietnam War, while North Vietnamese torpedo boats triggered the Gulf of Tonkin Incident of August 1964.

SPENCER C. TUCKER

Further Reading

Bulkley, Robert J., Jr. *At Close Quarters: PT Boats in the United States Navy*. Washington, DC: Naval Historical Division, 1962.

Nelson, Curtis L. *Hunters in the Shallows: A History of the PT Boat*. Washington, DC: Brassey's, 1998.

Preston, Anthony. *Destroyers*. Englewood Cliffs, NJ: Prentice Hall, 1977.

Ropp, Theodore. *The Development of a Modern Navy: French Naval Policy, 1871–1904*. Edited by Stephen S. Roberts. Annapolis, MD: Naval Institute Press, 1987.

Tucker, Spencer C. *Handbook of 19th Century Naval Warfare*. Annapolis, MD: Naval Institute Press, 2000.

October 14, 1863

Civil War (continued): Eastern theater: Battle of Bristoe Station. Attempting to outflank U.S. major general George G. Meade's Army of the Potomac, Lieutenant General Ambrose P. Hill hastily commits his men to battle against Union major general Gouverneur K. Warren's II Corps at Bristoe Station, Virginia. Because of Hill's stubborn failure to reconnoiter, Union forces, which have been concealed behind a railroad track, exact a heavy toll. The battle costs the Confederates 1,300 casualties and the Union side only 548.

October 18, 1863

Civil War (continued): Western theater. Union major general Ulysses S. Grant meets with Secretary of War Edwin M. Stanton at Louisville, Kentucky, and is informed that he has been appointed commander of the Military Division of the Mississippi. Grant's new command includes the Army of the Tennessee, the Army of the Cumberland, and the Army of the Ohio.

October 19, 1863

Civil War (continued): Eastern theater: Battle of Buckland Mills. Near Buckland Mills in Broad Run, Virginia, Army of Northern Virginia cavalry commander Major General J. E. B. Stuart and Major General Wade Hampton's cavalry division are covering the withdrawal of General Robert E. Lee's infantry following the Confederate defeat in the Battle of Bristoe (see October 14, 1863), when Union cavalry under Brigadier General Judson Kilpatrick attack the Confederates. Major General Fitzhugh Lee's cavalry division then falls on the Union flank. The Union troopers are routed and flee five miles to Haymarket and Gainesville. The battle is also known as the Battle of Chestnut Hill, although the Confederates call it "The Buckland Races."

October 26, 1863

Civil War (continued). Rear Admiral John Dahlgren's Union ironclads commence an intensive two-week bombardment of Fort Sumter in Charleston Harbor. They are joined by Union batteries on Morris Island, but the embattled Confederate defenders hold out.

November 2–4, 1863

Civil War (continued): Trans-Mississippi West theater. A U.S. expeditionary force of the screw sloop *Monongahela* (9 guns) and screw gunboats *Owasco*

(4 guns) and *Virginia* (7 guns) escorts units of the army's XIX Corps in a successful amphibious landing at Brazos Santiago, Texas. The Confederates evacuate Brownsville. This U.S. action is designed in part to send a message to France, which has intervened militarily in Mexico.

November 6, 1863

Civil War (continued): Western theater: Battle of Droop Mountain. Union forces plan a two-pronged raid to destroy the Confederate East Tennessee and Virginia Railroad. On November 1, 1863, Brigadier General William W. Averell leads 5,000 cavalry and infantry southward from Beverly, West Virginia, into the Allegheny Mountains, and on November 3 Brigadier General Alfred N. Duffié departs Charleston, West Virginia, with 1,700 men. They are to join at Lewisburg, West Virginia.

Harassed by Confederate forces en route, Averell's men reach Huntersville at noon on November 4 and there learn that some 600 Confederates of Colonel William L. Jackson's command are at Marling's Bottom. Averell sends two cavalry regiments to cut them off. Jackson's men elude the Union troopers and relocate at Mill Point, as Jackson requests reinforcements. The next day when Averell again tries to cut him off, Jackson withdraws to Droop Mountain, just north of Lewisburg in Pocahontas County.

At 9:00 a.m. on November 6, Brigadier General John Echols arrives from Lewisburg at the summit of Droop Mountain with the 1st Brigade of the Army of Southwestern Virginia. In all the Confederates have some 1,700 men. Averell comes up later that same morning. Following an artillery duel, Averell deploys his infantry to turn the Confederate left, and at about 1:30 p.m. when they attack, he also mounts a frontal assault with four regiments of dismounted troops. Echols's men hold their positions until about 3:00, when they break and retreat down the south slope of the mountain.

Confederate casualties are not as great as initially thought, as many of the men later straggle back in. In all the Confederates lose some 175 killed, wounded, or captured. Averell sustains 6 killed, 112 wounded, and 1 missing, for a total of 119 casualties.

The defeated Confederates withdraw through Lewisburg toward Monroe. Averell arrives at Lewisburg on November 7, Duffié having reached there only hours before after an uneventful march. The combined Union force initially proceed toward Dublin where Echols is re-forming but then decides to abandon the raid. Duffié returns to Beverly on November 12, Averell on November 17. Averell has won a minor battle and captured some equipment and supplies, but the two Union commanders have failed to carry out their mission to destroy the railroad.

November 7, 1863

Civil War (continued): Eastern theater: Battles of Kelly's Ford and Rappahannock Station. Confederate general Robert E. Lee, commander of the Army of Northern Virginia, has withdrawn his forces south of the Rappahannock River expecting to hold that line over the winter but maintains two bridgeheads north of the river about five miles apart at Kelly's Ford and Rappahannock Station to allow him to resume offensive operations.

Pushed by Washington to undertake offensive action, Union major general G. Gordon Meade sends units of his Army of the Potomac against the two Confederate bridgeheads. At Kelly's Ford, Union major general William H. French sends men of his III Corps against Major General Robert Rodes's division. The Confederates are caught by surprise and suffer 349 casualties, many of them captured. At Rappahannock Station, the Confederates suffer a greater reverse. There Brigadier General David A. Russell's division of Major General John Sedgwick's VI Corps also catches by surprise Major General Robert Hoke's division. In hard fighting, the Union troops wipe out the bridgehead and take 1,600 prisoners. Total Confederate losses in the two locations are 2,023, while the Union suffers 370. His defensive line breached, Lee withdraws toward Culpeper Court House.

November 17–December 4, 1863

Civil War (continued): Western theater: Siege of Knoxville. At Chattanooga, Tennessee, Confederate general Braxton Bragg and Lieutenant General James Longstreet are at odds as to how to proceed against

Union troops occupying the city. In part to reduce tensions between the two men and in part to draw off attention from the siege, Confederate president Jefferson Davis orders Longstreet to advance on and capture Knoxville, then held by some 20,000 Union troops under Major General Ambrose E. Burnside. Bragg will continue the siege of Chattanooga with 40,000 men while Longstreet proceeds to Knoxville with 17,000 men, including 5,000 cavalry.

Longstreet sets out on November 4 and arrives at the Little Tennessee River near Loudon on November 14. Burnside then hurriedly withdraws his force of the IX and XXIII Corps in the Loudon area. Longstreet hopes to engage the withdrawing Union troops near Lenoir but fails. Both sides then race to Campbell's Station, strategically situated on the Kinston Road to Knoxville, but the Union forces arrive there just ahead of the Confederates and fight a skillful delaying action there on the afternoon of November 16. Union casualties are 318; the Confederates lose 174. Union troops withdraw into the fortified Knoxville lines that night.

The Confederate siege of Nashville commences on November 17, with Longstreet probing the Union defenses. The Confederates target Fort Sanders on the northwest, but several planned attacks are postponed pending arrival of reinforcements. After some indecision as to the objective, Longstreet launches a major attack on Fort Sanders at dawn on November 29 in what is the principal battle of the siege. A deep ditch around the fort, made slick by rain and ice, helps thwart the assault. Longstreet, observing the attack that claims 813 Confederate casualties to only 13 for the Union, wisely calls off a second attempt.

Although Longstreet receives a telegram from Bragg on November 29 announcing his own withdrawal from Chattanooga into Georgia and ordering Longstreet to reinforce him, intelligence reports indicate that Union troops are on the march. Uncertain whether these are proceeding against Bragg or his own forces, Longstreet decides to remain where he is for the time being. The Confederate siege of Knoxville continues until the night of December 4, when on the approach of Union forces under Major General William T. Sherman, Longstreet withdraws. Union brigadier general James N. Shackelford with about 4,000 cavalry then begins an effort to locate Longstreet, resulting in the Battle of Bean's Station (see December 14, 1863). Casualties in the entire Knoxville Campaign total 681 for the Union and 1,296 for the Confederates. The decision to try to capture Knoxville is a major blunder, for it has weakened the Confederate forces at Chattanooga. All it has accomplished is to deny the Confederates the possibility of a victory at either location.

November 23–25, 1863

Civil War (continued): Western theater: Battle of Chattanooga. Union Western theater commander Major General Ulysses S. Grant initiates the Battle of Chattanooga (which includes Orchard Knob, Lookout Mountain, and Missionary Ridge). On November 23, two Union divisions of IV Corps of Major General George H. Thomas's Army of the Cumberland, dressed as if for parade, suddenly rush Confederate positions on Orchard Knob below Missionary Ridge, seizing it from the astonished Confederates. Union troops then occupy the position.

The next day, November 24, the two sides fight an all-day battle for control of 1,100-foot Lookout Mountain that ends with Union troops under Major General Joseph Hooker in control. On November 25, Union troops also take Missionary Ridge, forcing Confederate general Braxton Bragg to retreat toward Dalton, Georgia.

Battle of Chattanooga		
Date	November 23–25, 1863	
Location	Chattanooga, Tennessee	
Opponents (*winner)	*United States	Confederacy
Commander	Major General Ulysses S. Grant	General Braxton Bragg
#	56,000 men	44,000 men
Casualties	5,824 Union casualties (753 killed, 4,722 wounded, and 349 missing)	6,667 (361 killed, 2,160 wounded, and 4,146 missing, mostly prisoners); may be higher; Grant claims to have taken 6,142 prisoners

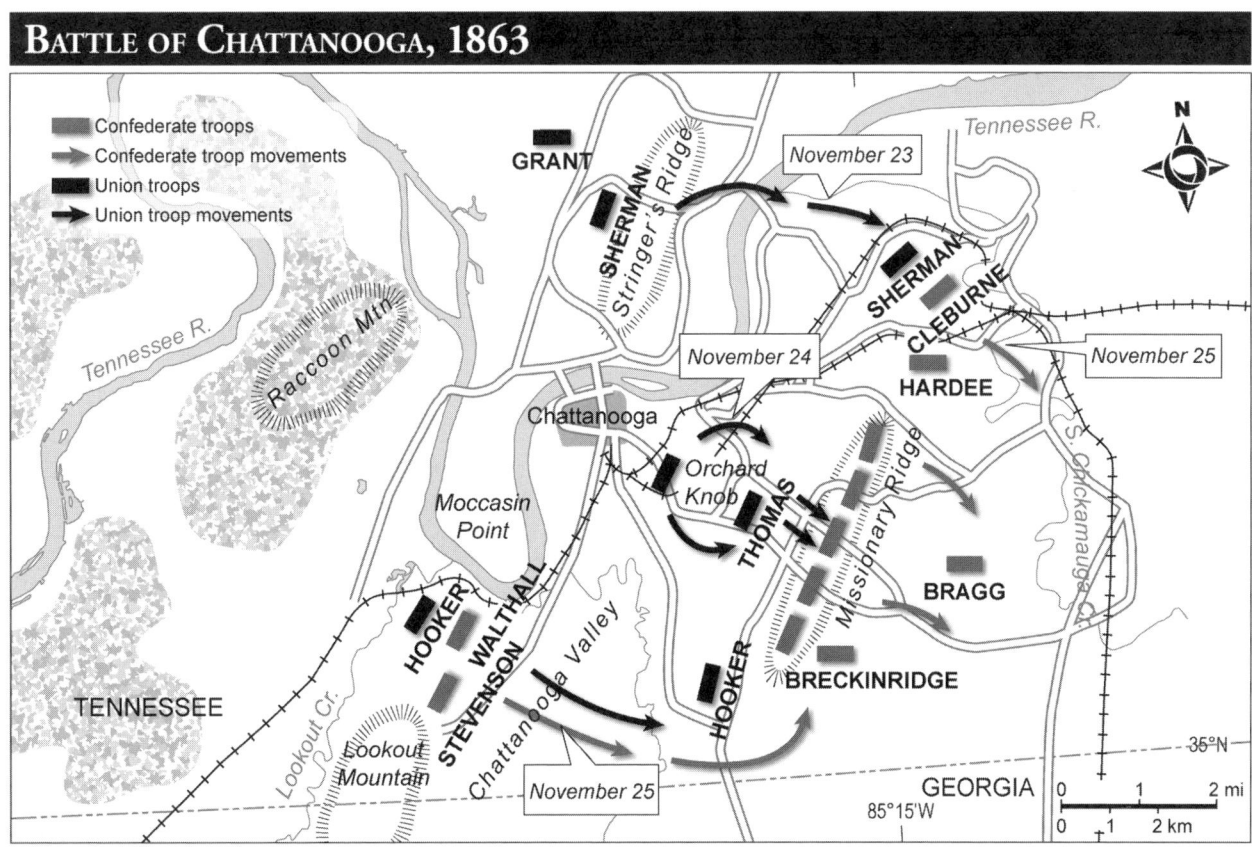

BATTLE OF CHATTANOOGA, 1863

The battle includes some 56,000 Union troops and 44,000 Confederates and results in 5,824 Union casualties (753 killed, 4,722 wounded, and 349 missing) and Confederate losses of 6,667 (361 killed, 2,160 wounded, and 4,146 missing, mostly prisoners); Confederate losses may have been higher, as Grant claims 6,142 Confederates taken prisoner. As a result of the battle, the Union armies of the West are poised to bisect the upper and lower South by marching across Georgia to the sea.

November 26–December 2, 1863

Civil War (continued): Eastern theater: Mine Run Campaign. Union Army of the Potomac commander Major General George Gordon Meade endeavors to turn the right flank of Confederate general Robert E. Lee's Army of Northern Virginia south of the Rappahannock River. Meade hopes to use his 85,000 men to strike and defeat Lee's widely dispersed army before it can concentrate. On November 26, 1863, Union troops take advantage of fog to cross the Rapidan

River. Largely owing to the slow advance of Meade's lead corps under Major General William H. French, Lee is able during the next few days to prepare strong positions along the west bank of Mine Run. Learning of this, Meade sensibly calls off the attack, which would have produced heavy Union casualties. Union losses are 1,653 men; the Confederates suffer 745.

November 27, 1863

Civil War (continued): Taylor's Ridge engagement. After his defeat at Missionary Ridge, Confederate general Braxton Bragg withdraws from the vicinity of Chattanooga, Tennessee, and heads for safety in Georgia. When Union forces under Major General Ulysses S. Grant pursue, Bragg detaches Major General Patrick Cleburne's division to provide rearguard cover. Cleburne posts his 4,157 men in Ringgold Gap and on the surrounding high ground locally known as Taylor's Ridge, southeast of Ringgold, Georgia.

Major General Joseph Hooker commands Union forces making contact with Cleburne's Confederates.

Hooker lacks artillery support but launches poorly coordinated infantry assaults and attempts flanking movements. All are repulsed. Cleburne then slips away, and Hooker decides not to pursue. The Union sustains 507 casualties, the Confederates 221. Bragg's army escapes.

December 6, 1863

Civil War (continued): Eastern theater: Loss of the *Weehawken*. The U.S. Navy Pessaic-class monitor *Weehawken*, commanded by Commander James M. Duncan, is moored to a buoy inside the bar of Charleston Harbor. It has just taken on a load of ammunition, which greatly reduces the ship's freeboard forward. In a strong ebb tide, water washes down an open hawse pipe and hatch. The pumps are unable to handle the flow, and the ship founders. Some two dozen members of the crew drown.

December 7–17, 1863

Civil War (continued): Confederate capture of the *Chesapeake*. Off Cape Cod, Massachusetts, 17 Confederates led by John C. Braine posing as passengers seize control of the U.S. steamer *Chesapeake,* which had sailed from New York City bound for Portland, Maine. In the brief exchange of gunfire taking over the ship, they kill the second engineer. The conspirators had hoped to run the ship through the Union blockade at Wilmington, North Carolina, but on December 17 the *Chesapeake* is recovered by the Union gunboat *Ella and Annie* (later named the *Malvern* [12 guns]) while it is coaling off Nova Scotia. Most of the Confederates escape ashore. The ship is taken to Halifax, where a vice admiralty court restores it to its owners.

December 14, 1863

Civil War (continued): Western theater: Battle of Bean's Station. Following the withdrawal of Confederate forces besieging Knoxville on the night of December 4, 1863, Union major general John G. Parke pursues. Parke detaches Brigadier General James M. Shackelford and some 4,000 cavalry to discover Confederate Lieutenant General James Longstreet's whereabouts. Longstreet has moved off to the northwest to Rogersville, where he resupplies and rests his men. He then backtracks southeast for a dawn attack on December 14 by three columns on Shackelford near Bean's Station, Tennessee, on the Holston River. By 2:00 a.m., however, one of the Confederate columns encounters Union pickets, and the ensuing skirmishing warns Shackelford, who then deploys his men to meet the Confederate assault. Fighting continues for most of the day, but the Union cavalry holds out until nightfall and the arrival of Southern reinforcements, at which point the Union troops retire through Bean's Gap. Despite the intensity of the fighting, casualties are no more than 200 for each side. Longstreet pursues, but the next day, finding the Union troops well entrenched at Blain's Cross Roads and with Union reinforcements coming up, he withdraws.

December 16, 1863

Civil War (continued). Confederate president Jefferson Davis appoints General Joseph E. Johnston to succeed General Braxton Bragg as commander of the Army of Tennessee. Bragg, loser of the Battle of Chattanooga, is ordered to Richmond, where he serves out the remainder of the war as military adviser to Davis. Johnston assumes his new command at Dalton, Georgia, on December 27.

February 2, 1864

Civil War (continued): Eastern theater. A Confederate small boat expedition led by Commander John T. Wood surprises and captures the U.S. Navy sidewheel steamer *Underwriter* (4 guns), commanded by Acting Master Jacob Westerveldt and anchored in the Neuse River near New Bern, North Carolina. Westerveldt is killed in the fighting. Unable to move the ship because it does not have steam up and with it under fire from Union shore batteries, the Confederates destroy the *Underwriter* and escape.

February 9–10, 1864

Civil War (continued): Eastern theater: Escape from Libby Prison. This night, 109 Union officers held in the Libby Prison in Richmond, Virginia, having dug a 50-foot tunnel under the street, make their escape in the largest and most famous such enterprise of the war. Forty-eight are recaptured, 2 drown in the nearby James River, and 59 reach Union lines.

February 12–October 7, 1864

Civil War (continued): Second cruise of the *Florida*. The Confederate commerce raider *Florida* (11 guns), commanded by Lieutenant Charles M. Morris, slips out of Brest, France, where it has undergone repairs, escaping past the blockading Union screw sloop *Kearsarge* (8 guns), commanded by John A. Winslow. The *Florida* will take 15 additional prizes before its capture on October 7.

February 14, 1864

Civil War (continued): Western theater: Union forces capture Meridian. Because of Major General William T. Sherman's feints, Confederate lieutenant general Leonidas Polk, commander of the Army of Mississippi, believes that the Union troops are headed for Mobile, Alabama, and falls back to Demopolis, Alabama. Sherman is thus able to enter Meridian, the temporary Confederate capital of Mississippi, unopposed. He remains there a week. Sherman's men destroy the railroad lines at Meridian and burn its arsenal, storehouses, and many other buildings. They then return to Vicksburg.

February 17, 1864

Civil War (continued): Eastern theater: Sinking of the *Housatonic*. Off Charleston, South Carolina, the Confederate submarine *H. L. Hunley*, commanded by Confederate Army lieutenant G. F. Dixon, attacks and sinks with a spar torpedo the Union screw sloop *Housatonic* (13 guns). Five men are killed. It is the first time in the history of warfare that a submarine has sunk a warship. The *H. L. Hunley* is itself lost in the attack. Its entire crew of eight men perish.

February 20, 1864

Civil War (continued): Eastern theater: Battle of Olustee. In the one large land campaign of the Civil War in Florida, on February 7, 1864, Brigadier General Truman Seymour debarks with some 5,500 men from transports at Jacksonville, Florida, and moves west toward the Suwannee River. Near the railroad depot of Olustee, some 50 miles southwest of Jacksonville, commander of the District of East Florida Brigadier General Joseph Finegan awaits with 5,000 Confederates.

The ensuing Battle of Olustee (or Ocean Pond, for a large nearby lake) ends in an overwhelming Confederate victory that claims 1,860 Union casualties and only 946 Confederates. The pursuit of Seymour's force is handled poorly, and the surviving Union troops reach Jacksonville on February 23.

February 22, 1864

Civil War (continued): Western theater: Battle of Okolona. To divert attention from his Meridian Campaign, on February 1 Union major general William T. Sherman orders Brigadier General William Sooy Smith to depart Collierville, near Memphis, Tennessee, with 7,000 cavalry and raid from Pontotoc, Mississippi, to the Memphis & Ohio Railroad. Smith is then to strike south and join Sherman at Meridian on February 10. Waiting for reinforcements, Smith departs far behind schedule on February 11 with 11,000 men and 20 guns.

Smith's men inflict considerable damage and free many slaves before heading south. North of Meridian on February 20 they encounter some of Confederate major general Nathan Bedford Forrest's 2,500 cavalry. Daunted by Forrest's reputation and uncertain how many men he is facing, Smith withdraws, planning to return to Tennessee.

On February 22 Confederate forces attack Smith about four miles south of Okolona. On the brink of victory and with the Confederates out of ammunition, Smith withdraws. In the fighting during February 20–22, the Confederates suffer 144 casualties (27 killed, 97 wounded, and 20 missing); Union losses are 388 (54 killed, 179 wounded, and 155 missing). Smith arrives back at Collierville on February 26.

February 28–March 3, 1864

Civil War (continued): Eastern theater: Kilpatrick-Dahlgren Raid. Brigadier General Judson Kilpatrick and Colonel Ulrich Dahlgren lead 4,000 cavalry in a raid to free some 15,000 Union prisoners being held

 ## CSS *H. L. Hunley*

The Confederate submarine *H. L. Hunley* was the first submersible to sink a warship. During the American Civil War, Southerner Horace L. Hunley was involved in the building of the *Pioneer,* an experimental submarine at New Orleans. Following the Union capture of that city, Hunley continued experiments at Mobile, Alabama. In mid-February 1863 he and his associates tested another submarine. It went down in rough water in Mobile Bay, but no lives were lost.

Undaunted, Hunley and his associates built a third submarine. On August 15, 1863, it arrived by rail at Charleston, South Carolina, then under Union naval blockade. Built from an iron steam boiler with tapered bow and stern sections added, the *H. L. Hunley* resembled a long, thin cigar. It was 39'6" in length, with a beam of 3'10" and height of a 4'. It was designed for a crew of nine men: one to steer and eight positioned along the length of the center section to power the submarine by hand-turning a crankshaft that moved the propeller, propelling it at about four knots. The submarine was to run awash until close to its target, when it would submerge with the aid of rudders. The submarine was difficult to control, and fresh air was available only when it was awash.

On August 29 after several practice dives in Charleston Harbor, as a result of human error the submarine sank at the dock, and five men drowned. It was promptly raised and refitted. Another crew volunteered, this time with Hunley in charge, but on October 15 the submarine again went down; evidently Hunley had left the valve to the front ballast tank open. This time Hunley and seven others perished. The submarine was again recovered, and a third crew, commanded by infantry Lieutenant George F. Dixon, volunteered.

After training, on the night of February 17, 1864, the *H. L. Hunley* attacked the 1,934-ton screw sloop *Housatonic.* The submarine's destructive force came from a spar torpedo, possibly designed by Confederate Army commander at Charleston General Pierre G. T. Beauregard. Mounted to the bow, a spar held a 130-pound mine (known as a torpedo), which terminated in a barbed lance-head. The barb was to be driven into the target warship below the waterline, and the submarine then would back off, exploding the torpedo by means of a long lanyard.

The Union sloop was prepared. The ship was in shallow water, Captain Charles Pickering had lookouts posted, steam in the engine room was up, and crewmen were ready to slip the ship's cable at a moment's notice. At about 9:00 p.m., lookouts on the *Housatonic* spotted the *H. L. Hunley*'s two hatches above water and its slight wake, but the alarm was too late for anything except small-arms fire. As the sloop was getting under way, the spar torpedo exploded. Only five Union sailors were lost; most of the sloop's crew simply climbed into the rigging to await rescue.

The *Housatonic* was the first ship sunk by a submarine in the history of warfare. The crew of the *H. L. Hunley* signaled by lantern that they were returning to land, but probably damaged in the blast, it sank shortly thereafter with all hands. It was located in 1995. Raised in August 2000, it is currently undergoing conservation.

SPENCER C. TUCKER

Further Reading

Bak, Richard. *The CSS Hunley: The Greatest Undersea Adventure of the Civil War.* Dallas, TX: Taylor, 1999.
Campbell, R. Thomas. *The CSS Hunley: Confederate Submarine.* Shippensburg, PA: Bond Street, 2000.
Ragan, Mark K. *Union and Confederate Submarine Warfare in the Civil War.* Mason City, IA: Savas, 1999.
Roland, Alex. *Underwater Warfare in the Age of Sail.* Bloomington: Indiana University Press, 1978.

in Richmond, Virginia. Kilpatrick runs into opposition and turns back, while high water prevents Dahlgren's 500 men from crossing the James River and entering Richmond from the south as planned.

On March 2 Dahlgren and some 100 of his men who become separated are ambushed. Dahlgren is killed, and most of those with him are taken prisoner. Papers allegedly found on Dahlgren's body that indicate plans to assassinate Jefferson Davis and burn Richmond become a propaganda coup for the South.

March 9, 1864

Civil War (continued): Grant named general-in-chief. President Abraham Lincoln elevates Major General Ulysses S. Grant to the position of Union general-in-chief, giving him full charge over army operations. Grant is appointed to the revived rank of lieutenant general, authorized by Congress for him on March 2. This rank had been awarded previously only on two other times: a full rank to George Washington and a brevet to Winfield Scott. Grant transfers his headquarters to the East and installs his trusted friend Major General William T. Sherman as commander of the Military Division of the Mississippi. Grant's former commander, Major General Henry W. Halleck, who had previously tried to ruin Grant but is an able administrator, becomes Grant's chief of staff and assumes the task of day-to-day army operations. Grant immediately begins planning major coordinated offensives to hammer the Southern armies and end the war.

March 12, 1864

Civil War (continued): Trans-Mississippi West theater: Start of the Red River Campaign. The last major Union riverine operation of the war, the Red River Campaign of March–May 1864 is also the largest combined operation to that point in U.S. military history and one of the war's major military fiascos. U.S. president Abraham Lincoln had approved the plan by Major General Henry W. Halleck for an expedition up the Red River against Shreveport, Louisiana, before Lieutenant General Ulysses S. Grant can assume his post as Union general-in-chief. Although Grant opposes siphoning off critical resources for an objective so far from the

decisive theaters of war, Halleck sets the campaign in motion before Grant can interfere.

The plan calls for the capture of Shreveport, the capital of Confederate Louisiana and a thriving Southern manufacturing center, located on the west bank of the Red River. This will open a route for Union forces to operate against Texas. Lincoln is anxious to secure the abundant cotton of the region for idled New England textile mills, shoring up his political support in the Northeast for the November 1864 presidential election. Emperor Napoleon III has sent a sizable French expeditionary force to Mexico, and U.S. policy makers favor operations against Texas to forestall possible French designs there.

Washington commits sizable resources to the operation, including the most powerful assembly of naval power on inland waters of the entire war (13 ironclads, 12 gunboats, and 1 ram) and 42,900 ground troops. Three-quarters of the Union troops, under the inept and grandstanding Major General Nathaniel P. Banks, are to move north toward Shreveport along the Red River, supported by the gunboats of Rear Admiral David D. Porter's Mississippi Squadron. Another 10,000 men from Major General Frederick Steele's Department of Arkansas (VII Corps) are to move concurrently against Shreveport from the north.

Unfortunately for the Union side, exceptionally dry weather and Confederate defensive diversion schemes reduce water levels considerably. On March 12 the Union naval squadron enters the Red River and begins its progress upriver.

March 14, 1864

Civil War (continued): Trans-Mississippi West theater: Red River Campaign (continued): Capture of Fort De Russy. During the preceding months, Confederate brigadier general William R. Boggs has supervised construction of an extensive defensive system of works and obstacles to protect against a Union attack up the Red River against Shreveport, Louisiana. These are centered on Fort De Russy, situated at the only real defensible position on the river south of Alexandria on the western bank of a U-turn in the river midway between the river's mouth and Alexandria.

De Russy has earthen walls that are 40 feet thick and 12 feet high and are reinforced by railroad iron, all surrounded by a deep, wide ditch. The fort mounts eight heavy guns and two fieldpieces, but it is designed to defend the water approaches. Eight miles below De Russy at another hairpin turn in the Red, the Confederates erect in the river two rows of heavy pilings. Felled trees are then allowed to build up against it.

U.S. Navy rear admiral David D. Porter, commander of the Mississippi Squadron, and U.S. Army brigadier general Andrew J. Smith, commanding 10,000 troops operating with Porter, decide that the troops will assault Fort DeRussy from the land side, while Porter's men remove the river obstructions and use ironclads to attack De Russy from the water. Confederate major general John Walker's division of Texas troops—3,300 men and 12 artillery pieces—defends the lower Red River area. As the Union troops move through Simmesport, Walker sends word to Major General Richard Taylor, commander of the District of West Louisiana, who orders the troops evacuated. This decision dooms Fort De Russy but saves the bulk of the Texans for the more important battles to come.

General Smith's troops arrive at Fort De Russy on the afternoon of March 14. In midmorning, meanwhile, Lieutenant Commander Seth Ledyard Phelps reaches the water barrier with the ironclad *Eastport* (8 guns), the ironclad river monitor *Osage* (3 guns), and the tinclads *Fort Hindman* (7 guns) and *Cricket* (7 guns) and immediately begins dismantling it. By late afternoon a path has been opened, and at dusk the Union ships arrive at Fort DeRussy, just as the Union troops commence their land assault.

The Union ships immediately open fire on the fort, and at 6:00 p.m. De Russy surrenders. Of its 300 defenders, 185 are taken prisoner; the remainder escape. Union casualties total 38 dead or wounded. The Union troops then rejoin the transports to proceed upriver to Alexandria.

Porter, who now abandons his own effort up the Atchafalaya River, employs the *Benton* (17 guns) and *Eastport* in a second effort to destroy Fort De Russy, but even fire from point-blank range fails to destroy its well-constructed casemates.

March 15, 1864

Civil War (continued): Trans-Mississippi West theater: Red River Campaign (continued): The U.S. Navy river monitor *Osage* (3 guns) forces the surrender of Alexandria, Louisiana, the largest municipality in central Louisiana. The town is occupied by Union troops shortly thereafter.

Mississippi Squadron commander Rear Admiral David D. Porter now reaches Alexandria and there waits for the ground troops under Major General Nathaniel P. Banks, who is behind schedule. The Union delay is of immense benefit to the Confederates, for it gives them ample time to prepare, including schemes to lower the water level of the Red River. When Union forces finally unite on March 29, Porter manages to get a dozen of his ships above the rapids at Alexandria and heads up the Red toward Shreveport. Coordination is poor between Banks and Porter.

March 25, 1864

Civil War (continued): Western theater: Battle of Paducah. Confederate major general Nathan Bedford Forrest leads some 2,800 men from Columbus, Mississippi, against the Union base of Paducah, Kentucky. Forrest quickly occupies Paducah as U.S. colonel Stephen G. Hicks and his garrison of 650 men immediately retire to Fort Anderson, west of the town, where they are supported by two gunboats in the Ohio River. Forrest and his men seize horses and mules and what supplies they can carry off, destroying the remainder. Part of his command attacks Fort Anderson but is rebuffed. Forrest then withdraws. Union casualties total 90; the Confederates suffer 50.

April 8, 1864

Civil War (continued): Trans-Mississippi West theater: Red River Campaign (continued): Battle of Mansfield. At Grand Ecore, Union ground force commander Major General Nathaniel P. Banks foolishly decides on a march route inland that removes gunboat support in the Red River. Rear Admiral David D. Porter's gunboats are to proceed alone, with the two forces meeting at Shreveport.

On April 8, 1864, in the Battle of Mansfield (Pleasant Grove, Sabine Crossroads), Confederate major general Richard Taylor with 8,800 men attacks Banks's far larger Union force, but Banks's men are strung out in march formation over 20 miles. Threatened by a double envelopment, the Union troops panic and decamp. Only a stand by Brigadier General William Emory's division 3 miles back prevents complete disaster. Of 12,000 Union troops actually engaged, 2,235 are casualties, including hundreds taken prisoner. Taylor also takes 250 wagons, nearly 1,000 draft animals, and thousands of small arms. Taylor's own losses of 1,500 men are actually heavier in terms of numbers of men engaged, but he has ended the Union drive on Shreveport. The Union troops continue their withdrawal during the night, finally taking up position 14 miles to the south at Pleasant Hill.

April 9, 1864

Civil War (continued): Trans-Mississippi West theater: Red River Campaign (continued): Battle of Pleasant Hill. Retreating to Pleasant Hill, Louisiana, 14 miles south of Mansfield, Union major general Nathaniel P. Banks's men establish strong defensive positions. They come under attack early on April 9 by the reinforced but still much smaller forces of Major General Richard Taylor. Union counterattacks nullify the initial Southern success, and the fighting ends at nightfall. Union losses are 1,506, Southern casualties some 700. Despite having won a tactical victory in the Battle of Pleasant Hill, Banks believes that his army is threatened with destruction. After meeting with his subordinate commanders, he decides to withdraw completely. All Union troops retire at night to Grand Ecore and from there to Alexandria. Taylor has saved Shreveport and driven Union forces from eastern Louisiana.

Learning of events, Union naval commander Rear Admiral David D. Porter has no choice but to withdraw as well. His ships must fight their way south in falling river levels against hastily placed Confederate shore batteries.

April 9, 1864

Civil War (continued): Grant's strategic plan. In Washington, D.C., Union army general-in-chief Lieutenant General Ulysses S. Grant finalizes his plans for a multifaceted simultaneous offensive to defeat the Confederacy. In the Western theater, Major General William T. Sherman with three field armies will drive against General Joseph Johnston's Army of Tennessee then move across Georgia to Savannah, while Major General Nathaniel P. Banks will take Mobile. Major General George Gordon Meade's Army of the Potomac, the major Union field force of some 115,000 men, will drive south from Culpepper, Virginia, on Richmond in what is known as the Overland Campaign. Grant plans to accompany Meade. At the same time, Major General Benjamin F. Butler's 39,000-man Army of the James is to move up the south bank of the James River and cut off Confederate general Robert E. Lee's Army of Northern Virginia from the lower South. Finally, Brigadier Generals George Crook and William W. Averell are to move against the Shenandoah Valley from the west, while Major General Franz Sigel moves south to clear the Shenandoah Valley and seize the railheads of Staunton and Lynchburg.

To meet Grant, Lee has 60,000 men and is supported by General Pierre G. T. Beauregard with 30,000 men in the Richmond-Petersburg area.

April 12, 1864

Civil War (continued): Trans-Mississippi West theater: Red River Campaign (continued): Action at Blair's Landing. Following the land battles of Mansfield and Pleasant Hill and the decision of Union major general Nathaniel P. Banks to withdraw, Rear Admiral David D. Porter begins moving his ships on the Red River back toward Alexandria. On this date, the river monitor *Osage* (3 guns), lashed to the large tinclad steamer *Black Hawk* (13 guns), grounds. As Union seamen work to free the ship, Confederate troops with some artillery gather nearby. Lieutenant Commander Thomas O. Selfridge orders the timber-clad *Lexington* (6 guns) to move downriver and open an enfilading fire.

The Confederate infantry advances to the river and commences small-arms fire. The *Osage* responds with grape and canister and finally with shrapnel and fuses cut to only one second. The fight lasts about an hour and a half until the Confederates withdraw, reportedly suffering some 300 casualties, while the Union

George Crook (1828–1890)

U.S. Army officer. George Crook was born near Dayton, Ohio, on September 8, 1828. He graduated from the U.S. Military Academy, West Point, in 1852 and was commissioned a second lieutenant and assigned to the Pacific Northwest. Promoted to first lieutenant in 1856 and to captain in 1861, following the outbreak of the American Civil War, in September 1861 Crook entered the volunteer establishment as colonel of the 36th Ohio Infantry Regiment and participated in actions in western Virginia. On May 23, 1862, he was wounded at Lewisburg, Virginia; he was promoted to brigadier general of volunteers on September 7, 1862. Crook commanded a brigade in the Kanawha Division in the Battle of South Mountain (September 14, 1862) and in the ensuing Battle of Antietam (September 17). In the early months of 1863, he played a prominent role in operations in eastern Tennessee before assuming command of the 2nd Cavalry Division in the Army of the Cumberland in July 1863.

Given command of the Kanawha District in February 1864, Crook led a series of operations to disrupt Confederate communications between eastern Tennessee and Lynchburg, Virginia. During Major General Philip Sheridan's Shenandoah Valley Campaign (August 7, 1864–March 2, 1865), Crook commanded the Department of Western Virginia and the Army of Western Virginia (VIII Corps) and played a conspicuous role in the succession of Union victories during that campaign. In October 1864 he was promoted to major general and continued to command the Department of Western Virginia from his headquarters in Cumberland, Maryland. On February 21, 1865, Crook and Brigadier General Benjamin Kelley were taken prisoner by Confederate partisans in a daring raid. Exchanged on March 20, Crook subsequently led a cavalry division in the Army of the Potomac as it drove toward Appomattox. He was breveted major general in the regular army on March 27, 1865.

After the Civil War, Crook reverted to lieutenant colonel in the regular army and assumed command of the 23rd Infantry Regiment. He spent the next few years fighting the Paiutes in the Idaho Territory. In 1871 in a controversial move, Crook was assigned to command the Department of Arizona, while still a lieutenant colonel. There he met Captain John G. Bourke, an outstanding officer who would later immortalize Crook in such books as *On the Border with Crook* and *With General Crook in the Indian Wars*.

In Arizona, Crook developed three key methods that helped him to become, in the view of many, the nation's premier Indian fighter. First, he employed Native Americans not only as scouts but also to provide insight into the possible courses of action of his foes. Second, he discarded his wagons and used only mule trains, giving him greater flexibility and speed. Third, he followed his adversaries wherever they went, even into northern Mexico, until he could bring them to battle. After the notable success of his 1872–1873 campaign, in another controversial move he was promoted directly to brigadier general. Crook's approach paid off, and by early 1875 the hostile Apaches had been temporarily subdued. Crook then worked to improve the lot of the Apache people and show them that the benefits of peace outweighed those of war.

In March 1875 Crook was named commander of the Department of the Platte, headquartered in Omaha, Nebraska. He participated in the Sioux War of 1876–1877 and commanded one of three converging columns during the army's spring offensive. In the Battle of the Rosebud (June 17, 1876), Crook's men engaged Native Americans under Chief Crazy Horse in a spirited stand-up fight, unusual for Native Americans, and were forced to fall back and regroup, rendering Crook unable to support the other columns or to communicate news of his setback. Following the devastating defeat of Lieutenant

Colonel George A. Custer's 7th Cavalry at the Little Bighorn, Crook largely directed the army's response, including Colonel Ranald S. Mackenzie's destruction of Cheyenne chief Dull Knife's village.

In 1882 Crook returned to Arizona, where he again employed his innovative approaches, including a heavy reliance on Indian scouts and small expeditions, but his efforts to deal with the Apaches encountered strong opposition from civilian agents and his old roommate, now rival, Lieutenant General Philip Sheridan. Crook's opponents were strengthened when Geronimo led a group of Chiricahuas off the San Carlos Agency on May 17, 1885. Crook's forces wore Geronimo down, however, and the Apache leader finally agreed to surrender. Sheridan rejected Crook's terms and demanded Geronimo's unconditional surrender. Geronimo and some of his men again fled U.S. control, and Sheridan blamed Crook and his Apache scouts. Crook was replaced by Brigadier General Nelson A. Miles.

Crook spent the last years of his life attempting to win the return of Apaches from prison in Florida to Arizona and battling with Miles and Sheridan in print. President Grover Cleveland promoted Crook to major general in April 1888 and assigned him to command the Division of the Missouri. Crook died in Chicago on March 21, 1890, still on active duty.

ALAN K. LAMM

Further Reading

Aleshire, Peter. *The Fox and the Whirlwind: General George Crook and Geronimo, A Paired Biography.* New York: Wiley, 2000.

Crook, George. *General George Crook: His Autobiography.* Edited by Martin F. Schmidt. Norman: University of Oklahoma Press, 1960.

Hutton, Paul A. *Phil Sheridan and His Army.* Lincoln: University of Nebraska Press, 1985.

Hutton, Paul A., ed. *Soldiers West: Biographies from the Military Frontier.* Lincoln: University of Nebraska Press, 1987.

side has but 7 wounded. Among the Confederate dead is able cavalry commander Brigadier General Thomas Green, who nonetheless had led the impetuous advance.

Porter now requests and receives troops from Banks to keep Confederate soldiers away from the river, where the crews on his gunboats frequently have to free Union transports that ground on sandbars. The large transports pose a constant problem and limit the progress of Porter's ships to about 20 miles a day. Although the Union flotilla is never in any immediate danger from the Confederates, a far more serious threat looms in the falling water level of the Red River.

April 12, 1864

Civil War (continued): Western theater: Confederate capture of Fort Pillow. In late March 1864 Confederate major general Nathan Bedford Forrest with about 1,500 men raids into Kentucky as far as Paducah. On his return he captures Fort Pillow, Tennessee, held by about 550 Union troops, half of them African Americans. The Confederates lose 14 killed and 86 wounded; Union losses are 231 killed, 100 wounded, and 226 captured. Union soldiers later assert that Forrest's men killed a number of the African American troops after they surrendered. The Northern public calls it the Fort Pillow Massacre.

April 15, 1864

Civil War (continued): Trans-Mississippi West theater: Red River Campaign (continued). In the Red River, the ironclad *Eastport* (8 guns), the largest U.S. Navy combatant in the expeditionary force, strikes a Confederate torpedo a short distance downstream from Grand Ecore, Louisiana. Damage is extensive, but the *Eastport* is taken under tow.

April 17, 1864

Civil War (continued). U.S. Army general-in-chief Lieutenant General Ulysses S. Grant orders all prisoner exchanges suspended until questions are answered regarding the Vicksburg and Port Hudson paroles (although they have given their word not to, a number of the surrendered Confederates simply rejoin the army) and the matter of exchange of African American troops has been arranged. This imposes severe hardships on the growing number of Union prisoners because of limited Southern resources and a transportation system in collapse, but Grant is determined to put maximum pressure on the South and its dwindling supply of manpower and opposes any step that will increase Confederate Army manpower. Southern military resources are dwindling, and giving Confederate general Robert E. Lee 40,000 additional men might prolong the war indefinitely, for nearly every Confederate prisoner released returns to the ranks, while a large proportion of the Union prisoners held by the South are men whose enlistment terms have expired. Few would have returned to the ranks even if their physical condition permitted it.

On October 1, 1864, Lee again proposes a prisoner exchange. Grant inquires whether Union African American soldiers who had been slaves will be exchanged. Lee, acting under instructions, says that blacks belonging to citizens are not considered subjects of exchange, whereupon Grant declines any further discussion.

April 17–20, 1864

Civil War (continued): Battle of Plymouth. Major General Robert F. Hoke leads 7,000 Confederate troops in an attack on the Union-held supply base of Plymouth, North Carolina, held by Brigadier General Henry W. Wessells with 3,000 men. On April 19 the Confederate ironclad *Albemarle,* under Commander James W. Cooke, issues from the Roanoke River and attacks the U.S. warships there that have been helping hold the Confederates at bay. The *Albemarle* sinks the U.S. Navy side-wheeler *Southfield* and forces the withdrawal of three other Union warships. With Union land forces bereft of naval support, Hoke's troops recapture Plymouth the following day.

April 21, 1864

Civil War (continued): Trans-Mississippi West theater: Red River Campaign (continued). Unable to bring the unwieldy damaged ironclad *Eastport* (8 guns) farther without also jeopardizing the ships accompanying it, U.S. Mississippi Squadron commander Rear Admiral David D. Porter orders the ship destroyed near Montgomery, Louisiana.

April 25, 1864

Civil War (continued): Battle of Marks' Mills. This battle, sometimes known as the Slaughter of Marks' Mills, occurs in Cleveland County, Arkansas. Confederate major general Sterling Price is conducting a modified siege of Camden, held by Union troops under Major General Frederick Steele.

With Union supplies dwindling and the road from Camden to Pine Bluff open, Steele orders Lieutenant Colonel Francis M. Drake to proceed with a brigade and 240 wagons to Pine Bluff and secure supplies there. Drake commands perhaps 1,800 men, including some cavalry and artillery. Some white civilians and perhaps 300 African Americans accompany the Union column.

Confederate major general James Fagan learns of Drake's movement and prepares an ambush with some 4,000 cavalrymen at the intersection of the Camden–Pine Bluff and Warren Roads. The Battle of Marks' Mills begins when Confederate brigadier general William L. Cabell's division blocks Drake's advance. Brigadier General Joseph O. Shelby's division then smashes into the Union left. Overwhelming Confederate numbers force Drake, who is wounded in the fighting, to surrender.

Fagan gives Confederate casualties as 293 (41 killed, 108 wounded, and 144 missing). Estimates of Union casualties vary widely from 1,133 and 1,600, most of them prisoners. The Confederates also take prisoner some 150 African Americans and are accused of killing some 100 others, and they capture some 200 wagons.

The Battle of Marks' Mills effectively cuts the Union supply line to Camden. It and the arrival of Confederate reinforcements compel Steele to abort the campaign. He abandons Camden on April 26, 1864, and marches his command north to Little Rock.

April 26–27, 1864

Civil War (continued): Trans-Mississippi West theater: Red River Campaign (continued). Mississippi Squadron commander Rear Admiral David D. Porter, bringing his ships back to Alexandria, Louisiana, fights a running battle with Confederate artillery batteries along the banks of the Red River. The tinclads *Cricket* (7 guns) and *Juliet* (6 guns) are badly damaged in the exchange. The stern-wheeler pump boats *Champion No. 3* and *Champion No. 5* are both lost. Clouds of steam from a pierced steam boiler in *Champion No. 3* kill 3 crewmen and wound another. Of 150–200 escaped slaves taken on board, only 15 survive. The ships of the Mississippi Squadron above the falls at Alexandria are now effectively trapped by the low waters of the Red.

April 30, 1864

Civil War (continued): Trans-Mississippi West theater: Red River Campaign (continued): Battle of Jenkins' Ferry. As part of the Red River Campaign to capture Shreveport, Louisiana, Major General Frederick Steele, commander of the Department of Arkansas (VII Corps), was to move against that city from the north with 10,000 men. Steele aids the campaign only in that he keeps occupied Confederate cavalry units in the region that otherwise could have been dispatched southward against the main Union drive from the south.

Some three weeks behind schedule, Steele reaches Camden, Arkansas, on April 26, 1864, only to learn that the Confederates have taken and destroyed the Union wagon train on its way from Camden to Pine Bluff. Steele also discovers that Confederate general Edmund Kirby Smith and Major General Sterling Price have joined forces against him. Steele orders a withdrawal to Little Rock, and the Union troops set out the next morning. The Confederates quickly retake Camden, but delay is imposed on them by the need to cross the rain-swollen Ouachita River. The Union head start is partially nullified when the Confederates then cover 52 miles in only 46 hours, despite steady rain.

Before dawn on April 30, Confederate brigadier general John S. Marmaduke's advance force makes contact with Steele's pickets some two miles from Jenkins' Ferry. Steele had reached the Saline River early the day before but cannot cross his men over that rain-swollen river until a pontoon bridge can be built. In the meantime he has some 4,000 men in prepared defensive positions to protect the crossing site.

Fighting continues for most of the day on April 30 as the Union troops slowly cross the river and Price commits his men piecemeal to the battle. By 3:00 p.m. Steele is able to cross all his men, artillery, and supply wagons that are not mired in the mud and escape his pursuers.

Union casualties total some 700, including captured stragglers, while the Confederates lose as many as 1,000 of 6,000 men committed. Although the battle is considered a Union tactical victory, it opens the way for the Confederates to invade Missouri.

April 1864–October 1867

American Indian Wars (continued): Cheyenne-Arapaho War (also known as the Colorado War). The Colorado gold rush brings a large number of miners, traders, and settlers to the central Great Plains. They take over the fertile river valleys and grasslands essential for the survival of the buffalo, in the process impoverishing the Cheyennes and Arapahos of the region. Seeking statehood for Colorado and prompted by personal ambition, Colorado officials—foremost among them Governor John Evans and local military commander and Methodist minister John M. Chivington—provoke a war. They want the Native Americans either removed to reservations or destroyed. One goal is to move the Indians to the Upper Arkansas Reservation, created by the Fort Wise Treaty of 1861. Few Cheyennes and Arapahos, however, recognize this agreement, which had forced the two tribes to relinquish most of their territory. In preparation for anticipated warfare, the settlers raise the volunteer 3rd Colorado Cavalry Regiment.

Fighting begins in April 1864 when troops exchange fire with Cheyennes suspected of stealing horses. In mid-May, soldiers attack a group of Cheyennes on their way to hunt buffalo and kill 28. In response to scattered Indian raids during the summer, many Coloradans demand more aggressive action, while at the same time many of the Native Americans want negotiations. Indeed, some Cheyennes under Black Kettle and Arapahos under Little Raven and Left Hand agree to settle near Fort Lyon, where they believe they are under government protection. Here they come under attack by the Colorado volunteers in the so-called Sand Creek Massacre (see November 29, 1864).

The Sand Creek attack outrages the Cheyennes, Arapahos, and some Sioux. During the winter of 1865 they intensify attacks on white settlements and travelers, twice sacking the town of Julesburg and striking ranches, wagon trains, and stage stations. They also destroy telegraph lines, cutting off Denver from communication with the East. At least 30 soldiers, freighters, travelers, and settlers die in the assaults. In consequence, even official Washington accepts the plan of military subjugation.

In the summer of 1865, the U.S. Army launches its largest offensive to date against the Plains tribes, but many Cheyennes and Arapahos have moved north. The army columns also face massive logistical difficulties, and peace again becomes an option. Black Kettle, whose Cheyennes have moved south of the Arkansas River to avoid the fighting, on October 14, 1865, signs the Little Arkansas Treaty. The Cheyennes give up the Sand Creek Reservation and rights to the hunting grounds of western Kansas and are confined south of the Arkansas River. Still, a majority of Native Americans see the vast central Plains as their birthright, and the summer of 1867 brings another futile army campaign. Finally, the Medicine Lodge Treaty, signed by Kiowas, Comanches, Apaches, Southern Cheyennes, and Arapahos on October 21 and 28, 1867, calls for permanent relocation and creates a combined Cheyenne-Arapaho reservation on Creek and Seminole lands in Indian Territory (Oklahoma). The treaty theoretically brings an end to the Cheyenne-Arapaho War. Sporadic fighting involving some Southern Cheyennes and Arapahos and settlers continues, although army campaigns in 1868–1869 drive most of them to the reservations.

May 1, 1864

Civil War (continued): Trans-Mississippi West theater: Red River Campaign (continued). Confederate land artillery sinks the U.S. Army Quartermaster Corps transports *Emma* and *City Belle* and the dispatch boat *John Warner* at Egg Bend on the Red River, below Alexandria, Louisiana.

May 4, 1864

Civil War (continued): Trans-Mississippi West theater: Red River Campaign (continued). Confederate land artillery sinks the Union tinclads *Covington* (8 guns) and *Signal* (8 guns) below Egg Bend on the Red River.

May 5, 1864

Civil War (continued): Western theater: Atlanta Campaign. Union Western theater commander Major General William T. Sherman departs Chattanooga, Tennessee, for Atlanta, Georgia, with an army group numbering nearly 100,000 men in the Atlanta Campaign (May–August 1864). His forces consist of Major General George H. Thomas's Army of the Cumberland (61,000 men), Major General James B. McPherson's

Atlanta Campaign		
Date	May 5–September 2, 1864	
Location	Northwestern Georgia and the area around Atlanta	
Opponents (*winner)	*United States	Confederacy
Commander	Major General William T. Sherman	General Joseph E. Johnston, then General John B. Hood
#	98,500–112,000 men	50,000–65,000 men
Casualties	31,687 (4,423 dead, 22,822 wounded, and 4,442 missing or captured)	34,979 (3,044 killed, 18,952 wounded, and 12,983 missing or captured)

John McAllister Schofield (1831–1906)

U.S. Army general. John McAllister Schofield was born in Gerry, New York, on September 29, 1831. Raised in Illinois, Schofield graduated from the U.S. Military Academy, West Point, in 1853. Commissioned a second lieutenant, he served for two years in the 1st U.S. Artillery, then returned to West Point as an instructor of experimental philosophy (physics). He was promoted to first lieutenant in 1855, but disillusioned by the lack of promotion, he secured a leave of absence in 1860 and took a position teaching physics at Washington University in St. Louis.

On the beginning of the American Civil War in April 1861, Schofield was commissioned a major in the 1st Missouri Volunteers. He favorably impressed Major General Nathaniel Lyon, the local Union commander, who appointed Schofield his chief of staff. In this capacity Schofield accompanied Lyon in a series of small Union victories over Southern forces but advised against engaging numerically superior Confederate forces at Wilson's Creek on August 10, 1861. Lyon attacked anyway and was killed. Schofield particularly distinguished himself in the battle and in 1892 was formally awarded the Medal of Honor for his role in it.

On November 21, 1861, Schofield was advanced to brigadier general of volunteers. In October 1862 he took command of the Army of the Frontier and the District of Southwest Missouri and enjoyed some success driving Southern guerrillas from Missouri and Kansas. On May 12, 1863, Schofield was named major general of volunteers and given command of the Department and Army of the Ohio. He then participated in Major General William T. Sherman's Atlanta Campaign, during which Schofield did battle with Confederate forces under General John B. Hood's Confederates. Hood invaded Tennessee and attempted to cut off Schofield's smaller force from Nashville. Schofield eluded Hood and entrenched at Franklin. In the Battle of Franklin on November 30, 1864, Schofield's men destroyed the attacking Confederates. For this victory, Schofield was advanced to brigadier general in the regular army to date from the battle.

Moving his forces by sea to Fort Fisher, North Carolina, Schofield occupied Wilmington on February 22, 1865, and then fought at Kinston on March 8–10. Schofield ended the war cooperating closely with Sherman against the remaining Confederate forces under General Joseph E. Johnston.

Following the war, President Andrew Johnson appointed Schofield a confidential agent of the State Department and sent him to France, charged with negotiating with Emperor Napoleon III the withdrawal of French forces from Mexico. This mission accomplished, Schofield commanded the Department of the Potomac from August 1866 to June 1868. President Johnson then appointed him secretary of war. In March 1869 Schofield advanced to major general of regulars and took charge of the Department of the Missouri until May 1870. He then commanded the Division of the Pacific, and in 1873 under secret orders of Secretary of War William Belknap, Schofield traveled to Hawaii to evaluate the strategic usefulness of those islands to the United States. Upon his recommendation, the government purchased Pearl Harbor as a naval facility. In September 1876 Schofield returned to West Point as superintendent, remaining there until January 1881, when he succeeded to command of the Division of the Gulf. In 1878 he also headed a board that reconsidered the court-martial of Major General Fitz John Porter and absolved him of misconduct at the Second Battle of Bull Run (Manassas) in 1862.

(continued)

(Continued)

After successive tours with the Division of the Pacific and the Division of the Missouri, in August 1888 Schofield succeeded Lieutenant General Philip H. Sheridan as commanding general of the army. During his seven-year tenure, Schofield pressed for improvements in the life of common soldiers through better rations, higher pay, and improved standards of living. He also sought to foster professionalism among the officer corps by a system of examinations for promotion, the creation of post libraries, and strong support for service schools.

In sharp contrast with his predecessors Sherman and Sheridan, Schofield disagreed with the prevailing national policy toward Native Americans. Indeed, he urged that they be allowed to join the military as regular soldiers. He believed that in this capacity Native Americans and their dependents could be cared for while at the same time performing useful national service. Owing to the racism prevalent at the time, however, this policy was never adopted.

Schofield proved to be an able administrator. He clarified the military chain of command by ending a long feud with the secretary of war whereby he subordinated the post of commanding general to the secretary's office and agreed to function as his senior military adviser. Schofield's final act was to advocate the adoption of a general staff on the German model to better formulate grand strategic planning. This scheme was not adopted. Schofield retired from the army on February 5, 1895, advanced to lieutenant general.

In 1902 Schofield appeared before a congressional committee to support the creation of a general staff concept, contrary to the opinions of commanding general Major General Nelson A. Miles. Schofield also argued strongly in favor of U.S. intervention in Cuba in order to end the suffering of the Cuban people. During the Spanish-American War, President William McKinley, who distrusted both Miles and Secretary of War Russell Alger, often sought the counsel of the retired Schofield regarding military issues. Schofield also played a major role in McKinley's decision to call for an increase in the size of the regular army. Schofield died in St. Augustine, Florida, on March 4, 1906. He is generally regarded as one of the finest peacetime commanding generals of the army. Schofield Barracks at Pearl Harbor, Hawaii, is named for him.

JOHN C. FREDRIKSEN AND SPENCER C. TUCKER

Further Reading

Connelly, Donald B. *John M. Schofield and the Politics of Generalship.* Chapel Hill: University of North Carolina Press, 2006.

McDonough, James L. *John M. Schofield: Union General in the Civil War and Reconstruction.* Tallahassee: University of Florida Press, 1972.

Schofield, John M. *Forty-Six Years in the Army.* 1897; reprint, Norman: University of Oklahoma Press, 1999.

Army of the Tennessee (24,500 men), and Major General John M. Schofield's Army of the Ohio (13,500 men). Opposing Sherman is Confederate general Joseph E. Johnston's Army of the Tennessee of some 60,000 men. Although Confederate cavalry under capable major generals Nathan B. Forrest and John H. Morgan harass Sherman's rear areas and supply lines, Johnston can do little more than delay Sherman.

May 5, 1864

Civil War (continued): CSS *Albemarle* enters Albemarle Sound. On the afternoon of May 5, 1864, the Confederate ironclad *Albemarle* (2 guns), commanded by Commander James W. Cooke, descends the Roanoke River with the tenders *Bombshell* (4 guns) and *Cotton Plant* (armament unknown) to engage the Union squadron commanded by Lieutenant

Commander F. A. Roe in Albemarle Sound and consisting of the side-wheel gunboats *Sassacus* (12 guns), *Wyalusing* (14 guns), and *Mattabesett* (10 guns). The Union ships soon take the *Bombshell* (which the Confederates had raised and captured from the Union side earlier), and the *Cotton Plant* retires back up the Roanoke. The *Albemarle*, however, disables the *Sassacus* and continues to engage the other Union warships for three hours until the onset of darkness brings an end to the action. The *Albemarle*, little damaged in the fighting, retires up the Roanoke, and the Union ships move into position to try to block its reentry into the sound.

May 5, 1864

Civil War (continued): Trans-Mississippi West theater: Red River Campaign (continued): Engagement at Dunn's Bayou. On this date the small U.S. Navy light-draft gunboats *Signal* (8 guns) and *Covington* (6 guns) are convoying the Quartermaster Corps steamer *Warner* down the Red River when they enter into a fierce firefight with Confederate infantry and artillery positioned at Dunn's Bayou below Alexandria. At point-blank range, all three Union ships suffer heavily. When the *Warner* hoists a white flag and Lieutenant George Lord of the *Covington* sends men to burn that vessel, the army colonel in charge begs him not to do so because of 125 wounded aboard. Lord then permits the *Warner* to surrender.

With the *Signal*'s steam pipe cut and that ship disabled, Lord takes it in tow and heads upriver when the rudder of his own ship becomes disabled. Lord then has the *Signal* anchor and, with the steam pipe soon cut on his own vessel, runs it ashore on the opposite bank. He continues to fire on the Confederates until he has exhausted his ammunition and his boat howitzers are disabled. With many of his crew killed or wounded, Lord spikes the guns, lands his men, and fires his vessel. He and his crew manage to make it by land back to Alexandria. The *Signal* has too many wounded to follow suit and is captured. The Confederates remove its guns and sink the *Signal* as a river obstruction. The engagement lasts some five hours.

May 5–7, 1864

Civil War (continued): Eastern theater: Overland Campaign: Battle of the Wilderness. On May 4, 1864, Union major general George Gordon Meade's 115,000-man Army of the Potomac initiates the Overland Campaign when it crosses the Rapidan River to turn the right flank of General Robert E. Lee's 60,000-man Army of Northern Virginia and drive on Richmond. Union Army general-in-chief Lieutenant General Ulysses S. Grant accompanies the army in the field. The next day, the Union forces are locked in battle with the Confederates in the densely wooded area known as the Wilderness. Lee attacks Grant's left flank, using the terrain to partially nullify the Union numerical advantage. The ensuing fighting is intense, and many wounded burn to death in brush fires.

In the end Lee outmaneuvers his opponent, inflicting 17,500 Union casualties (15 percent of the force engaged) for Confederate casualties estimated to number some 7,500 (12 percent of force). The battle is, however, a strategic victory for the Union. Lee has failed to stop Grant, who continues south.

May 5–16, 1864

Civil War (continued): Eastern theater: Bermuda Hundred Campaign. As part of Lieutenant General Ulysses S. Grant's multipronged offensive in Virginia, while General Robert E. Lee's Army of Northern Virginia is occupied to the north dueling with Grant and Major General George Gordon Meade's Army of the Potomac, Union major general Benjamin Butler is to advance up the James River with his 39,000 man Army of the James, land between Richmond and Petersburg, and threaten either or both cities.

On May 5, one day after Grant has begun his own offensive, Butler's army lands at Bermuda Hundred, a neck of land north of City Point at the confluence of the James and Appomattox Rivers and only 15 miles south of Richmond. The way to the capital appears open. Richmond and Petersburg are virtually undefended, the garrison of the two cities then being only about 5,000 men. Butler fumbles away this golden opportunity.

That same day, General Pierre G. T. Beauregard, commander of the Confederate Department of

Union major general Benjamin Butler's headquarters at Bermuda Hundred, Virginia, in 1864. Butler commanded the Army of the James during the Petersburg Campaign. (Library of Congress)

North Carolina and Southern Virginia, with 18,000 men assumes direction of Confederate defenses at Petersburg. He delegates Major General George E. Pickett to contain Butler. Butler is slow to move, and Pickett rushes men to Bermuda Hundred. The Confederates construct a line across its narrowest point, bottling up Butler.

May 6, 1864

Civil War (continued): Eastern theater. The side-wheel steamer ex–ferry boat *Commodore Jones* (8 guns), commanded by Acting Lieutenant Thomas Wade, is destroyed in the James River in Virginia by an electronically detonated 2,000-pound Confederate torpedo (mine). Some 40 crew members are killed. This is the first ship sunk by an electronically detonated mine in the history of warfare.

May 6, 1864

Civil War (continued): Eastern theater: Sortie by CSS *Raleigh*. This afternoon the Confederate ironclad *Raleigh* (4 guns), commanded by Flag Officer William F. Lynch, sorties from the Cape Fear River in North Carolina and engages the Union side-wheel steamers *Britannia* (5 guns) and *Nansemond* (3 guns), forcing them to withdraw and allowing a Confederate blockade-runner to escape to sea. Early the next morning the *Raleigh* resumes the engagement, this time exchanging fire with four Union warships. At 6:00 a.m. Lynch breaks off the action, but in attempting to cross the bar at the mouth of Cape Fear, the *Raleigh* grounds and is damaged to the extent that Lynch orders it destroyed.

May 7–10, 1864

Civil War (continued): Western theater: Atlanta Campaign (continued): Battle of Rocky Face Ridge. Three armies under U.S. major general William T. Sherman, commanding the Military Division of the Mississippi, are driving on Atlanta, Georgia. Comprising some 112,000 men, they confront the Confederate Army of Tennessee, commanded by General Joseph E. Johnston and numbering some 62,000 men. The first major clash between the two occurs at Rocky Face Ridge in Whitfield County, Georgia.

Johnston's forces are entrenched along Rocky Face Ridge and eastward across Crow Valley. Sherman assigns Major General George H. Thomas's Army of the Cumberland the task of taking Rocky Face. Thomas takes Tunnel Hill on May 7 but the next day is turned back in an effort to capture well-entrenched Confederate forces at Dug Gap, two miles to the south. Sherman also sends Major General James B. McPherson's Army of the Tennessee in a flanking maneuver through Snake Creek Gap to strike the Western & Atlantic Railroad at Resaca.

Meanwhile, Confederate cavalry under Major General Joseph Wheeler harass Major General John Schofield's Army of the Ohio, moving south from Red Clay. On May 9 at Prater's Mill, Wheeler surprises and defeats Union cavalry sent to engage him, taking 150 prisoners and handing the Union side its first defeat of the campaign. At the same time the Confederates rebuff five separate assaults by Thomas to take Rocky Face Ridge.

McPherson's men pass through Snake Creek Gap and on May 9 advance to the outskirts of Resaca, where they find the Confederates entrenched. McPherson then withdraws back to Snake Creek

Gap. On May 10, Sherman decides to concentrate his forces in assisting McPherson and taking Resaca. Thomas demonstrates against the Confederate line that day, but early on May 11 Sherman's army withdraws from in front of Rocky Face Ridge and moves south to support McPherson. Discovering that the entire Union force has decamped, Johnston has no choice but to retire south to Resaca himself on May 12. Sherman will employ similar flanking movements to dislodge the Confederates many times during the next several months.

May 7–21, 1864

Civil War (continued): Eastern theater: Overland Campaign (continued): Battle of Spotsylvania Court House. Following the Battle of the Wilderness, Union Army general-in-chief Lieutenant General Ulysses S. Grant continues southeast toward Richmond with the 100,000-man Army of the Potomac. Grant tries to outflank General Robert E. Lee's 52,000-man Army of Northern Virginia at the crossroads village of Spotsylvania Court House. Lee anticipates Grant's move and gets there first, however. His men quickly throw up entrenchments, and bloody trench warfare ensues.

On May 10, Grant throws three corps against the Confederate lines. That evening on a very narrow front at the so-called Mule Shoe salient in the center of the line, Colonel Emory Upton masses 12 regiments, and following an intense and concentrated artillery bombardment, they manage to break through at this point. The attackers are unable to exploit the situation, however. Upton receives immediate promotion to brigadier general.

Upton's limited success persuades Grant to try the same tactic with an entire corps—Major General Winfield Scott Hancock's II Corps—at the tip of the salient. Grant's inactivity on May 11 in preparation for this leads Lee to believe that Grant is preparing to withdraw, and Lee shifts artillery from the area of the Mule Shoe, where Hancock attacks with his 20,000-man corps in a predawn assault on May 12. His men enjoy initial success, taking 4,000 prisoners and shattering Major General Edward Johnson's division of Lee's II Corps. Johnson and one of his brigadier

Emory Upton (1839–1881)

U.S. Army officer and military theorist. Emory Upton was born on August 27, 1839, to a farming family in Batavia in upstate New York. After a year at Oberlin College (Ohio), he entered the U.S. Military Academy, West Point, in 1856. Graduating near the top of his class in May 1861, Upton was commissioned a first lieutenant of artillery.

Upton fired the opening gun of the battle and was wounded at the First Battle of Bull Run (Manassas) (July 21, 1861). He fought in the Peninsula Campaign (March–August 1862) and at the Battle of Antietam (September 17, 1862). To avoid an assignment teaching at West Point, Upton transferred to the infantry as a colonel of the 121st New York Volunteer Regiment. His unit participated in the Battle of Fredericksburg (December 13, 1862), the Battle of Chancellorsville (May 1–4, 1863), and the Battle of Gettysburg (July 1–3, 1863).

Just before the Battle of Gettysburg, Upton received command of a brigade in VI Corps, which he led with great effectiveness there and at Rappahannock Station (November 7, 1863). Upton especially distinguished himself during Lieutenant General Ulysses S. Grant's Overland Campaign of 1864 that brought the Union Army to the gates of Richmond.

Upton's battlefield experiences led him to advocate an important change in infantry tactics, chiefly advancing the men in columns close to the enemy line, when they would deploy in line and charge. Applying this method, Upton led 12 regiments in breaking through Confederate defenses during the Battle of Spotsylvania Courthouse (May 7–19, 1864). The attack ultimately failed for lack of support, but Upton had demonstrated its potential for breaking through a strongly defended position.

Still only 24 years old, Upton was rewarded with promotion to brigadier general, to date from May 12, 1864. Given command of an infantry division a few months later in Major General Philip H. Sheridan's Shenandoah Valley Campaign, Upton was wounded at Opequon and breveted major general. He was then transferred to Nashville, where he led a cavalry division in the largest cavalry raid of the war, into Alabama and Georgia.

Following the war Upton reverted to his permanent rank of captain, but in July 1866 he was appointed lieutenant colonel of the 25th Infantry Regiment. One of the army's leading intellectuals and reformers, during 1866–1867 Upton was assigned to West Point as an instructor. There he produced *A New System of Infantry Tactics* (1867), which was adopted by the army the same year. To solve the dilemma of greatly enhanced infantry defensive firepower, Upton emphasized reliance upon open formations, the basic unit being a squad of four men. Operating under simplified commands, the squads could easily form a battle line in any direction. Attacking infantry would form a skirmish line about 150 yards from the enemy, building it up by squads to a point where an attacking column could advance to about 200 yards away and then rapidly deploy into line and charge. This system essentially served the army in the Spanish-American War and into the two 20th-century world wars.

From 1870 to 1875, Upton was commandant of cadets and instructor in tactics at West Point. With the United States then involved in fighting the Native Americans in the West, General William T. Sherman, commanding general of the U.S. Army, sent Upton on a yearlong world tour to visit Asia and Europe to study warfare there, especially the British India campaigns. Upton returned as an admirer of the German model of a strong standing army, with a large officer cadre and skeleton formations. In time of need, such an army could be rapidly expanded. This system would do away with volunteer units entirely, for all volunteers would serve in the regular army under its officers. He also applauded the German general staff system and its frequent rotation of officers between staff and line assignments. Upton was also an advocate of conscription but dared approach this only indirectly. He chiefly wanted the United States to abandon its dual system of federal and state control in favor of assigning all military duties to the regular army. He also argued against civilian control of the military.

Upton presented these views in his report, published as *The Armies of Asia and Europe* (1878) and in an influential manuscript work, *The Military Policy of the United States*. The latter, the nation's first professional military history, was published posthumously in 1904. Congress and the country largely ignored his recommendations.

In 1880 Colonel Upton took command of the 4th Artillery Regiment at the Presidio, San Francisco, where on March 15, 1881, plagued by agonizing headaches perhaps caused by depression heightened by the death of his wife, he took his own life.

NEIL HEYMAN AND SPENCER C. TUCKER

Further Reading

Ambrose, Stephen E. *Upton and the Army*. Baton Rouge: Louisiana State University Press, 1964.

Michie, Peter S. *The Life and Letters of Emory Upton, Colonel of the Fourth Regiment of Artillery, and Brevet Major-General, U.S. Army*. New York: D. Appleton, 1885.

Reardon, Carol. *Soldiers and Scholars: The U.S. Army and the Uses of Military History, 1865–1920*. Lawrence: University Press of Kansas, 1990.

Upton, Emory. *The Military Policy of the United States*. Washington, DC: U.S. Government Printing Office, 1904.

Weigley, Russell F. *Towards an American Army: Military Thought from Washington to Marshall*. New York: Columbia University Press, 1962.

Wert, Jeffry. *The Sword of Lincoln: The Army of the Potomac*. New York: Simon and Schuster, 2005.

generals, George H. Steuart, are taken prisoner. The Union attack then loses steam, in part because Grant does not have reserves readily available to exploit the situation. Grant orders VI Corps, now commanded by Brigadier General Horatio Wright on the death on May 9 from a sniper's bullet of Major General John Sedgwick, and IX Corps under Major General Ambrose G. Burnside to support Hancock, but their attacks are not coordinated, and Lee is able to bring up sufficient manpower to plug the gap.

Lee now withdraws to a newly prepared line at the base of the salient. Grant assaults that line six days later on May 18, only to be repulsed. On May 19 Lee demonstrates against the Union right, leading to renewed savage combat. Two days later Grant decamps, again attempting to outflank Lee's right.

Estimates of losses in the Spotsylvania fighting vary widely, but one has Union casualties totaling 14,267 men (14 percent of forces engaged). Lee's losses are actually heavier in terms of percentage of men engaged: more than 10,000 (19 percent).

May 9, 1864

Civil War (continued): Eastern theater: Battle of Cloyd's Mountain. In southwestern Virginia, U.S. brigadier general George Crook advances with his 6,155-man Army of West Virginia. Crook's objective, operating in conjunction with another Union force under Brigadier General William W. Averell, is destruction of the Virginia & Tennessee Railroad. Brigadier General Albert G. Jenkins has charge of Confederate area forces but had only assumed command of the Department of Western Virginia at the beginning of May.

Jenkins gathers some 2,400 men and decides to stand at Cloyd's Mountain. Arriving there, Crook determines that the Confederate position is too strong for a frontal assault and elects to send one of his three brigades in a flanking movement through woods on the Confederate right, with the other two brigades to mount a frontal assault once the flanking attack is under way. Savage hand-to-hand combat ensues in which superior Union numbers gradually tell. Jenkins falls mortally wounded and is captured. Colonel John McCausland assumes command of the defenders and manages to extract most of them. In the battle the Union side suffers more casualties—688 men—but these represent only about 10 percent of the Union strength; Confederate losses of 538 men are fewer but constitute 23 percent of their force engaged. Crook is able to continue his mission, and he destroys several railroad bridges, including that over the New River, severing the only rail connection between Virginia and eastern Tennessee.

May 11, 1864

Civil War (continued): Eastern theater: Overland Campaign (continued): Battle of Yellow Tavern. During the Battle of Spotsylvania Court House, Union major general Philip H. Sheridan's 10,000-man cavalry corps raids south. At Yellow Tavern about six miles above Richmond, Sheridan encounters 4,500 Confederate cavalry led by Major General J. E. B. Stuart. Sheridan drives the Confederates from the field. Stuart is mortally wounded, a major loss for the Confederacy. Union casualties total 625, while the Confederates lose about 1,000, including 300 taken prisoner.

May 13–15, 1864

Civil War (continued): Western theater: Atlanta Campaign (continued): Battle of Resaca. U.S. major general William T. Sherman, commanding the Military Division of the Mississippi, is driving on Atlanta, Georgia. His three armies are confronted by Confederate general Joseph E. Johnston's Army of Tennessee. Sherman had decamped from in front of Rocky Face Ridge and moved his army to the hills around Resaca, Georgia, on the Oostanaula River, a flanking movement that forced Johnston to also withdraw and move to Resaca.

On May 13, 1864, Union forces test the Confederate lines at Resaca. Heavy fighting occurs the next day, with the Union troops generally stymied except on the Confederate right, where Sherman nonetheless fails to press his advantage. Fighting continues into May 15 without result until Sherman deploys newly delivered pontoon bridges and sends men across the Oostanaula River at Lay's Ferry. Faced with another Union flanking movement, Johnston is again forced to withdraw.

Johnston decamps early on May 16, burning both the railroad bridge and a wagon bridge. Sherman's men repair the bridges and, passing men over them, continue their pursuit, triggering the Battle of Adairsville on May 17. In the Battle of Resaca the Union suffers 3,500 casualties, and the Confederates sustain 2,600.

May 14, 1864

Civil War (continued): Trans-Mississippi West theater: Red River Campaign (continued): Escape of Porter's squadron at Alexandria and end of the campaign. Following the loss of several of his ships to Confederate fire and the falling water level in the river, Union rear admiral David D. Porter arrives with his remaining ships above Alexandria only to discover that the water level is too low to pass his ships over the rapids there. Facing the destruction of his squadron, Porter is persuaded by Union Army engineer Lieutenant Colonel Joseph Bailey to pursue a daring scheme that few think will work.

With the assistance of 3,500 Union troops and several hundred wagons, wing dams are constructed to raise the water level nearly seven feet and create a chute for the ships. Although the dams give way prematurely and have to be rebuilt, the scheme works, and Porter is able to pass all his remaining ships to safety by May 13, averting catastrophe. Union forces evacuate Alexandria the next day. Although the bulk of Union forces escape, the Red River Expedition has been a fiasco.

Union gunboats float through a section of a dam on the Red River in Louisiana. Union lieutenant colonel Joseph Bailey suggested building the dam after Rear Admiral David D. Porter's Mississippi Squadron was stranded by low water and in danger of being lost. Bailey's wing dams raised the water level and allowed the Union ships to escape destruction. (John Clark Ridpath, *Ridpath's History of the World*, 1901)

May 15, 1864

Civil War (continued): Eastern theater: Battle of New Market. As part of the overall Union offensive scheme, in early May 1864 Union major general Franz Sigel, commander of the Department of West Virginia, departs Winchester and moves south in the Shenandoah Valley with 6,500 men. His orders are to tie down Confederate forces and clear the valley. Assigned to stop Sigel, Major General John C. Breckinridge assembles a scratch force of some 5,000 men, including 279 members of the Corps of Cadets of the Virginia Military Institute (VMI).

At the crossroads of New Market, Virginia, 50 miles south of Winchester, Sigel meets and engages Breckinridge. The Confederate commander is forced to commit the VMI cadets, who had been held in reserve. The cadet charge turns the tide, and Sigel withdraws. There are 831 Union casualties and 577 Confederates (57 of them cadets, a 20 percent casualty rate).

The threat to the Shenandoah Valley is ended, at least temporarily. Sigel is relieved of command on May 19 and replaced by Major General David Hunter. Breckinridge moves his troops, minus the cadets, east to aid in the defense of Richmond.

May 16, 1864

Civil War (continued): Eastern theater: Second Battle of Drewry's Bluff. On May 5, 1864, Union major general Benjamin Butler's 39,000-man Army of the James had landed at Bermuda Hundred, a neck of land north of City Point at the confluence of the James and Appomattox Rivers and only 15 miles south of Richmond. The way to the capital appeared open, with only 5,000 Confederate defenders, but for a week Butler remains largely inactive near his landing place.

Not until May 12 does Butler begin to move his army toward Richmond. Although Union forces reach near Drewry's Bluff, the last major Confederate defensive position on the James before Richmond, Confederate area commander General Pierre G. T. Beauregard has arrived and has gathered sufficient reinforcements to allow him to meet Butler on more than equal terms, for Butler has with him only 16,000 men, and Beauregard has mustered 18,000.

On May 16, Beauregard launches a surprise attack against a weak point in the Union line near Drewry's Bluff. In the fighting the Confederates suffer 2,506 casualties; Union losses are 4,160. Although he fails in his effort to cut Butler off from his base in Bermuda Hundred, Beauregard has won an important victory. He has saved Richmond and prevented Butler from linking up with the Army of the Potomac driving south. Butler withdraws and constructs a defensive line between the James and Appomattox Rivers.

Beauregard strikes again on May 20 at Ware Bottom Church, but the Confederate attack is repulsed at a cost of 700 Confederate and 800 Union casualties. The Confederates now construct the Howlett Line, effectively bottling up Butler. The Army of the James will remain inactive in Bermuda Hundred until the Army of the Potomac crosses the James River in mid-June.

May 17, 1864
Civil War (continued): Western theater: Atlanta Campaign (continued): Battle of Adairsville. U.S. major general William T. Sherman, commanding the Military Division of the Mississippi with three armies, continues his drive on Atlanta, Georgia, confronted by Confederate general Joseph E. Johnston's Confederate Army of Tennessee. Following the May 13–15 Battle of Resaca, Johnston withdraws south. The two armies meet again at Adairsville, just northeast of Rome, Georgia. Johnston hopes to draw Sherman's far more numerous force into a costly frontal assault, but the terrain there proves unsuitable for a defensive stand, and Johnston is obliged to continue his withdrawal. A series of skirmishes ensue, but there is no pitched battle. Union casualties total some 200; Confederate losses are unknown.

May 23–26, 1864
Civil War (continued): Eastern theater: Overland Campaign (continued): Battle of the North Anna. The Union Army of the Potomac continues its drive on Richmond. Again, Union general-in-chief Lieutenant General Ulysses S. Grant endeavors to move the Army of the Potomac around the right flank of Confederate general Robert E. Lee's Army of Northern Virginia in order to cut it off from Richmond. Again, Lee anticipates Grant's move. Lee establishes strong positions on the North Anna River on May 22, the day before Grant arrives. The ensuing battle is a series of small engagements. Grant suffers 1,973 casualties, Lee perhaps 2,017.

Grant retains the strategic initiative, and on May 27 he again puts the Army of the Potomac in motion, moving eastward. With Lee content to remain inside his entrenchments, Grant assumes that his attrition strategy has worked and that the Army of Northern Virginia is on its last leg. He will learn at Cold Harbor a week later that this is not the case.

May 25–26, 1864
Civil War (continued): Western theater: Atlanta Campaign (continued): Battle of New Hope Church. Major General William T. Sherman, commanding the Union Military Division of the Mississippi, continues his drive on Atlanta, Georgia, against General Joseph E. Johnston's Confederate Army of Tennessee. On May 19–20 Johnston withdraws to Allatoona Pass, but Sherman realizes that any assault here will be costly, and he again seeks to outflank Johnston, proceeding around his left to move on Dallas. Anticipating Sherman's move, Johnston shifts his army into Sherman's path and establishes a new line at New Hope Church. Mistakenly believing that he is confronting only a small part of the Confederate army, Sherman orders Major General Joseph Hooker's XX Corps to attack. Hooker moves with his three divisions along parallel routes, driving the Confederates

back for three miles until he encounters Johnston's principal defensive line.

The terrain prevents Hooker from effectively coordinating his attacking divisions, and on May 25 they sustain severe casualties, especially from Confederate artillery fire. On May 26 both sides entrench, and skirmishing continues throughout the day. Union losses in the battle are 1,665 to only 350 for the Confederates.

May 27, 1864

Civil War (continued): Western theater: Atlanta Campaign (continued): Battle of Pickett's Hill. Union major general William T. Sherman, commander of the Military Division of the Mississippi, attacks the northern end of the defensive line of Confederate general Joseph E. Johnston's Army of Tennessee at Pickett's Mill in Paulding County, Georgia, on May 27, 1864. Sherman orders Major General Oliver O. Howard and his 14,500-man IV Corps to strike Johnston's seemingly exposed right flank. The attack falls chiefly on Major General Patrick Cleburne's division. The Confederates are ready for the Union assault, which does not unfold as planned because supporting troops do not arrive. The Union attackers are repulsed, suffering some 1,600 casualties to only 200 for the Confederates. Nonetheless, Sherman is now only 25 miles northeast of his goal of Atlanta.

May 28, 1864

Civil War (continued): Eastern theater: Overland Campaign (continued): Battle of Haw's Shop, Virginia. Finding Confederate general Robert E. Lee's position too strong, Union Army general-in-chief Ulysses S. Grant tries to outflank him to the east. A delay during Grant's crossing at the Pamunkey River, however, gives Lee time to again place his Army of Northern Virginia between Richmond and the Union Army of the Potomac.

Union and Confederate cavalrymen clash in the Battle of Haw's Shop (also called Hawe's Shop—the historic spelling—or Enon Church) in Hanover County, each side suffering about 300 casualties.

May 28–30, 1864

Civil War (continued): Eastern theater: Overland Campaign (continued): Battle of Totopotomoy Creek (Battle of Bethesda Church or Battle of Hanovertown). Union general-in-chief Lieutenant General Ulysses S. Grant continues his southeastward flanking movement. While the Union army crosses the Pamunkey River without incident, Confederate general Robert E. Lee again moves faster than Grant expects. Indeed, Lee's Army of Northern Virginia is already in a strong defensive position along Totopotomoy Creek.

On May 29, Union forces dig in on the opposite bank of the Totopotomoy. Following cavalry engagements and minor infantry skirmishes during May 28–29, Grant orders a general advance on May 30. Major General Winfield Scott Hancock's II Corps of the Army of the Potomac captures some entrenchments in the center of the Confederate lines but is unable to advance farther. On the Union right, Major General Horatio G. Wright's VI Corps becomes bogged down in a swamp, while on the Union left, Major General Gouverneur K. Warren's V Corps probes Lee's right flank. Lee orders Major General Jubal A. Early on the Confederate right to strike at Warren's corps. Major General Richard Anderson, ordered to assist Early, fails to arrive in time, and Early's attack is repulsed.

Once again Grant orders another flanking maneuver south, toward the town of Cold Harbor. The Battle of Totopotomoy Creek results in 731 Union casualties; the Confederates lose 1,159.

May 31–June 12, 1864

Civil War (continued): Eastern theater: Overland Campaign (continued): Battle of Cold Harbor. Union Army general-in-chief Lieutenant General Ulysses S. Grant slips eastward with the

Battle of Cold Harbor		
Date	May 31–June 12, 1864	
Location	Hanover County, Virginia	
Opponents (*winner)	*Confederacy	United States
Commander	General Robert E. Lee	Lieutenant General Ulysses S. Grant
Approx. #	59,000 men	108,000 men
Casualties	4,600	13,000

Jubal Anderson Early (1816–1894)

Prominent Confederate general. Jubal Anderson Early was born in Franklin County, Virginia, on November 3, 1816. He attended local schools and then graduated from the U.S. Military Academy, West Point, in 1837 and was commissioned in the artillery. Early served in the Second Seminole War in Florida in 1838 but resigned from the army and took up a legal career, which he pursued in both Franklin and Floyd Counties in Virginia during 1840–1846. He also served one term in the state legislature during 1841–1842.

During the Mexican-American War (1846–1848), Early was a major in the 1st Virginia Regiment, although his unit saw little action. Following the war, he returned to his legal career and became a delegate to the Virginia General Assembly; he also served as Commonwealth attorney until 1852.

Early opposed secession and voted against it in the Virginia Convention of 1861. When his state seceded, however, he offered his services. Appointed a colonel in Virginia's forces, Early was sent to Lynchburg to help raise troops. He entered Confederate service as commander of the 24th Virginia Regiment. Early commanded a brigade and fought well at the First Battle of Bull Run (Manassas) (July 21, 1861). He also distinguished himself at Blackburn's Ford (August 18, 1851) and that month was advanced to brigadier general.

In the spring of 1862, Early's brigade was assigned to General Joseph E. Johnston's forces to help stop the advance of Union forces under Major General George B. McClellan toward Richmond in the Peninsula Campaign. In fighting at Williamsburg on May 5, 1862, Early was wounded while leading an attack. On recovery, he commanded a brigade under Major General Thomas J. "Stonewall" Jackson at Malvern Hill on July 1, but Early's men became lost in woods and took little part in the battle.

Early fought well at both Cedar Mountain on August 9, 1862, and the Battle of Second Bull Run (Manassas) on August 28–30. During the Battle of Antietam on September 17, he assumed command of a division. In the First Battle of Fredericksburg on December 13, 1862, Early played an important role in counterattacking Union units that were about to break the Confederate line.

Promoted to major general to rank from January 1863, Early commanded a division at both Chancellorsville (May 1–3, 1863) and Gettysburg (June 1–3). During the winter of 1863–1864, Early was based in the Shenandoah Valley. In 1864, he fought in the Battle of the Wilderness (May 5–7), taking command of III Corps. He also fought at Spotsylvania Court House (May 7–20). On May 31, 1864, Early was promoted to lieutenant general. He then fought in the Battle of Cold Harbor (May 30–June 12).

Early returned to the Shenandoah Valley and, thanks to a ruse, defeated Major General David Hunter in the latter's effort to take Lynchburg (June 17–18, 1864). Early then led the last Confederate invasion of the North during the war. Its intention was to relieve pressure on the Confederacy by threatening Washington, D.C. With some 15,000 men, Early moved quickly up the valley. He defeated Union forces at Monocacy, Maryland, on July 9 but was turned back at Washington by its strong defenses.

Early's forces burned Chamberstown, Pennsylvania, during July 30–31, 1864, and then withdrew into the Shenandoah Valley. Union forces under Major General Philip Sheridan defeated Early at Winchester (September 19) and Fisher's Hill (September 22). At Cedar Hill on October 19, Early launched a surprise attack on Union forces and was almost successful. Most of his II Corps then joined General Robert E. Lee's Army of Northern Virginia at Petersburg.

Early's remaining forces were nearly destroyed at Waynesboro, Virginia, on March 2, 1865, and Early narrowly escaped capture. Lee relieved him of his command at the end of March. Although Early had held large numbers of Union troops at bay for a number of months, he was blamed for the devastation wrought by Sheridan in the Shenandoah Valley. Early possessed a difficult, argumentative personality and was of fiery disposition, but few Confederate generals were as popular with their men as "Jube" or "Old Jubal" Early.

After the war, Early fled first to Texas and then into Mexico. From there he sailed to Cuba and then to Canada. He finally settled in Toronto to write his memoirs, in which he was critical of many Confederate senior officers, chiefly Lieutenant General James Longstreet, whom Early blamed for the Confederate defeat at Gettysburg.

Early returned to Virginia in 1869 and resumed the practice of law. He became president of the Southern Historical Society in 1869, using it as a platform from which to criticize his enemies. In 1877 he became commissioner of the Louisiana Lottery. Returning to Virginia, he died in Lynchburg on March 2, 1894.

RALPH BAKER AND SPENCER C. TUCKER

Further Reading

Early, Jubal A. *War Memoirs*. Edited by Frank E. Vandiver. Bloomington, IN: Bobbs-Merrill, 1960.

Freeman, Douglas Southall. *Lee's Lieutenants: A Study in Command*. 3 vols. New York: Scribner, 1942–1944.

Osborne, Charles C. *Jubal: The Life and Times of General Jubal A. Early, C.S.A., Defender of the Lost Cause*. Chapel Hill, NC: Algonquin Books, 1992.

Wert, Jeffry D. *From Winchester to Cedar Creek: The Shenandoah Campaign of 1864*. Carlisle, PA: South Mountain, 1987.

108,000-man Army of the Potomac, again endeavoring to turn the right flank of General Robert E. Lee's Army of Northern Virginia. Lee has been reinforced by 14,000 men drawn from the Shenandoah Valley and operations along the James River and now commands some 59,000 troops. Lee is able to fortify and entrench, and the result is a stinging rebuff to Grant in one of the bloodiest battles of the war.

On June 3 Grant hurls three corps in a frontal assault against Lee. Within a matter of minutes the Union troops suffer some 7,000 casualties. Grant admits that it is a major mistake. Casualty estimates for the battle vary greatly but are probably on the order of some 13,000 Union troops to 4,600 Confederates.

June 5, 1864

Civil War (continued): Eastern theater: Battle of Piedmont. As part of his multifaceted offensive to keep Confederate forces under General Robert E. Lee off balance and prevent Lee from receiving reinforcements, Union general-in-chief Lieutenant General Ulysses S. Grant had ordered a Union advance south in the Shenandoah Valley. However, Major General Franz Sigel met defeat in the Battle of New Market (see May 15, 1864), and on May 21 Grant replaces him with Major General David Hunter as commander of the Department of West Virginia. On May 26 Hunter again puts Union forces in motion south. His immediate goal is the Confederate railroad and logistics center of Staunton. Hunter is determined to live off the rich Shenandoah Valley farms as much as possible, and his forces destroy much of what they themselves cannot use.

This rapid Union response following New Market catches the Confederates by surprise, with most of their forces in the valley having recently been moved east to join the hard-pressed Army of Northern Virginia before Richmond. Only a small cavalry brigade under Brigadier General John D. Imboden and reserves remain to confront Hunter, and they can do little except impose delay.

Confederate general Robert E. Lee calls on Brigadier General William E. "Grumble" Jones, commanding the Department of Southwest Virginia and East Tennessee. Jones soon arrives at Mount Crawford with reinforcements and takes command from Imboden. In all, Jones has some 5,600 men.

On June 5, Hunter moves south from Port Republic with some 8,500 men toward Mount Meridian. Early that morning his cavalry drives in Imboden's far weaker force, and the Confederates fall back on the village of Piedmont in Augusta County. Imboden, an area native, had urged Jones to set up defenses at Mowry's Hill in more favorable terrain, and is surprised to find him at Piedmont. Jones, the senior officer, wins the argument, and the Confederates make their stand at Piedmont instead.

In the ensuing battle, superior numbers of Union artillery systematically neutralize most of the few Confederate guns. When Jones attempts a concentration of troops for a counterattack, the Union troops exploit a gap in the Confederate line. Jones is killed. Although the Confederates sustain perhaps 1,600 casualties, a successful rearguard action at New Hope allows the remnants of his army to escape. The Union side suffers 863 casualties.

Hunter's army camps for the night. The next day, June 6, it enters its immediate objective of Staunton, the first Union troops to accomplish this during the war.

June 6–18, 1864

Civil War (continued): Eastern theater: Hunter's movement to Lynchburg and the Battle of Lynchburg. Union forces under commander of the Department of West Virginia Major General David Hunter enter the important railroad center of Staunton, Virginia, on June 6. The next day his men destroy its rail facilities, considerable public property, and much private property. On June 8 Hunter is joined at Staunton by Union forces under Brigadier Generals William

W. Averell and George Crook. This brings Hunter's combined strength up to 18,000 men and 30 guns. Resuming their movement south, Hunter's men enter Lexington on June 11. Hunter tarries there for three days, burning the Virginia Military Institute and other property.

Not until June 17 does Hunter arrive at his objective of the key Confederate railroad, supply, and hospital center of Lynchburg. Hunter's delay in Lexington and poor tactical decisions enable the Confederates to reinforce Lynchburg just in time with Lieutenant General Jubal Early's II Corps of some 8,000 men. With perhaps 14,000 defenders, many of whom are poorly armed, Early mounts an elaborate deception that convinces Hunter that he has more men in place than is the case. Had Hunter arrived the day before, Lynchburg would have been his. Now, deep in Confederate territory and far from his own base and with ammunition and supplies low, Hunter launches only a cautious attack on June 18, throwing away an excellent chance for victory.

Hunter abandons the effort to take the city the next day. Early pursues, and Hunter withdraws behind the Allegheny Mountains, leaving the Shenandoah Valley virtually empty of Union troops and leaving Washington, D.C., uncovered.

June 10, 1864

Civil War (continued): Western theater: Battle of Brice's Cross Roads. Union Division of the Mississippi commander Major General William T. Sherman orders Brigadier General Samuel D. Sturgis to find and defeat Confederate cavalry commanded by Major General Nathan Bedford Forrest. Sturgis departs Memphis with 8,100 cavalry and infantry and 22 guns manned by 400 artillerists. At Brice's Cross Roads, Mississippi, Forrest, outnumbered nearly 3 to 1 with only 3,000 men, holds the Union force in place and then carries out a brilliant double envelopment with an attack on the Union rear. Union forces panic. The Union suffers 1,240 casualties (223 killed, 394 wounded, and 623 missing or captured) and loses 16 guns, 1,500 small arms, and 192 wagons, against Confederate casualties of only 39 killed and 396 wounded.

June 11–12, 1864

Civil War (continued): Eastern theater: Overland Campaign (continued): Battle of Trevilian Station. U.S. general-in-chief Lieutenant General Ulysses S. Grant prepares to send the Army of the Potomac across the James River. Grant sends Major General Philip H. Sheridan with two divisions of his Cavalry Corps west into Louisa County to cut the Virginia Central Railroad and join with Union forces in the Shenandoah Valley, now commanded by Major General David Hunter.

Grant plans for the combined forces of Hunter and Sheridan to take the key Confederate rail center of Lynchburg and then join him at Richmond. Lee counters by sending his own cavalry commander, Major General Wade Hampton, and two cavalry divisions after Sheridan. He also dispatches Lieutenant General Jubal A. Early to Lynchburg to check Hunter.

During June 11–12 Sheridan and Hampton clash in a confused battle at Trevilian Station. Sheridan enjoys success on the first day, but the tables are turned on June 12 when the dismounted Confederate cavalrymen turn back several determined dismounted Union attacks. Sheridan withdraws after destroying about six miles of the Virginia Central Railroad. He never does link up with Hunter.

In nearly six weeks of fighting, the Army of the Potomac has suffered perhaps 55,000 casualties against 32,000 casualties for the Army of Northern Virginia. Grant has been attacking, however. Lee's casualties are also greater than those sustained by Grant as a percentage of forces engaged, and Lee's army never quite recovers from the hammering received.

June 15, 1864

Civil War (continued). The U.S. Congress passes legislation providing equal pay for African American soldiers, who previously have been paid less than their white Union Army counterparts.

June 16–18, 1864

Civil War (continued): Eastern theater: Overland Campaign (continued): Battle of Petersburg. Feinting an attack on Richmond, Union general-in-chief Lieutenant General Ulysses S. Grant sends one corps across the James River by naval transport, and in a considerable engineering feat the bulk of the Union troops cross the James from Windmill Point to Fort Powhatan on a 2,100-foot-long pontoon bridge erected by Union engineers in only eight hours on June 14. Confederate Army of Northern Virginia commander General Robert E. Lee still expects a Union thrust on the site of the former Seven Days' battlefield. Grant, however, orders Major General Benjamin F. Butler and his 39,000-man Army of the James at Bermuda Hundred to capture the important railhead of Petersburg, eight miles distant and then only lightly held. Butler fails in two separate attempts, stymied by his own inept generalship and the effective response of Confederate general Pierre G. T. Beauregard, who rushes all available resources forward. Grant comes up and, with the Army of the Potomac arriving, orders the offensive renewed.

Lee, now fully alerted to Grant's push behind him, hurries to meet the Union troops. On June 18 Grant sends 65,000 men against the Petersburg entrenchments, now fully manned by Lee's 40,000 veterans. The Union troops are rebuffed, and Grant begins siege operations. The three-day Battle of Petersburg claims 8,150 Union and 4,752 Confederate casualties.

June 19, 1864

Civil War (continued): Battle between the *Kearsarge* and the *Alabama*. Captain Raphael Semmes has sailed the Confederate raider *Alabama* (8 guns) to Cherbourg, France. The *Alabama*, the most successful Confederate commerce raider of the war, has sailed some 75,000 miles, sent to the bottom a Union warship (the *Hatteras*), and taken 62 Union prizes, most of them burned, but it has been at sea nearly two years and is now in need of repairs.

Informed of the *Alabama*'s arrival, Captain John A. Winslow of the U.S. Navy screw sloop *Kearsarge* (8 guns) takes up station off the French port. Knowing that other Union warships will surely follow, Semmes decides to fight. On paper the two ships are evenly matched, but Winslow enjoys the advantages of a freshly serviced ship, superior speed, and better protection. On June 19, 1864, Semmes sails out to meet

USS *Kearsarge* **versus CSS** *Alabama*		
Date	June 19, 1864	
Location	English Channel off Cherbourg, France	
Opponents (*winner)	*United States	Confederacy
Commander	Captain John A. Winslow	Captain Raphael Semmes
#	some 150 men; 7 guns with a total throw weight of 364 pounds	some 170 men; 8 guns with a total throw weight of 274 pounds
Casualties	3 wounded (1 mortally)	21 killed (12 drowned); 70 prisoners (including 20 wounded); Semmes and the remainder escape, taken aboard a British yacht

Winslow. In an engagement lasting about an hour in international waters off the French coast, the *Kearsarge* sinks the *Alabama*. The *Alabama* sustains 21 killed (12 drowned) and 70 prisoners (20 wounded); the *Kearsarge* has 3 men wounded (1 mortally). Semmes is among those Confederates who escape capture, taken aboard a British yacht observing the battle.

June 19, 1864–April 2, 1865

Civil War (continued): Eastern theater: Siege of Petersburg. Following his failure to take Petersburg, Virginia, by assault, Union general-in-chief Lieutenant General Ulysses S. Grant begins a siege of this important railhead south of Richmond. Grant steadily expands the Union siege lines, with entrenchments of both sides presaging those of the Western Front in World War I.

The 10-month siege is marked by regular shelling and occasional sorties and assaults; the most spectacular event is the Battle of the Crater (see July 30, 1864). Ultimately the Union entrenchments are supported by a 21-mile railroad line that runs their entire length and links Grant's besiegers to their large base at City Point. Confederate troops and the civilians of Petersburg and Richmond increasingly suffer from dwindling stocks of food and supplies.

June 21–23, 1864

Civil War (continued): Eastern theater: Siege of Petersburg (continued): Weldon Railroad Operations. Having begun the siege of Petersburg, Union general-in-chief Lieutenant General Ulysses S. Grant moves to sever the railroad lines connecting Petersburg and Richmond to the south and west. The first operation is against the Weldon Railroad connecting with North Carolina. Grant commits Major General David Birney's II Corps, Major General Horatio G. Wright's VI Corps, and a cavalry division.

Confederate lieutenant general Ambrose P. Hill takes advantage of a gap between the two Union corps to attack the exposed flank of II Corps. In the wide-ranging June 22–23, 1864, Battle of Jerusalem Plank Road (also known as the First Battle of Weldon Railroad), the Union infantry and cavalry fail to secure the rail line and suffer 2,962 casualties, including some 1,600 prisoners; Confederate losses are 572.

June 23–July 6, 1864

Civil War (continued): Eastern theater: Early's Washington Raid. Following his rebuff at Lynchburg, Virginia, Union major general David Hunter had withdrawn on June 19, 1864, and retired behind the Allegheny Mountains. This leaves the Shenandoah Valley virtually empty of Union troops and leaves Washington, D.C., uncovered.

Beginning on June 23, Confederate lieutenant general Jubal A. Early and his II Corps of some 13,000 men move north hoping to force Union general-in-chief Lieutenant General Ulysses S. Grant to detach forces from his siege of Petersburg in order to defend the federal capital. Early crosses the Potomac River into Maryland on July 5. He then occupies Frederick and exacts a ransom of $200,000 from Frederick and $20,000 from Hagerstown.

June 27, 1864

Civil War (continued): Western theater: Atlanta Campaign (continued): Battle of Kennesaw Mountain. Through seven weeks of the Atlanta Campaign, commander of the Union Division of Mississippi Major General William T. Sherman has employed the same tactic of slipping around the left flank of Confederate commander General Joseph E. Johnston's Army of Tennessee. Impatient with flanking maneuvers and discovering his opponent dug in on high ground about two miles northwest of Marietta, Georgia, Sherman decides on a frontal assault of the center of the Confederate line.

Sherman's men pay a heavy price for his change in tactics. In the Battle of Kennesaw Mountain, a hail of Confederate rifle and artillery fire turns back two desperate Union assaults. By noon the battle is over, Sherman having suffered some 3,000 casualties and Johnston only 750. Sherman then carries out another flanking movement around the Confederate left.

June 28, 1864

Civil War (continued): Arlington National Cemetery. The best known of all the national cemeteries, Arlington is established on the 624 acres that was formerly the estate of the family of Confederate general Robert E. Lee's wife Mary Anna (Custis) Lee, a great granddaughter of Martha Washington.

July 9, 1864

Civil War (continued): Eastern theater: Early's Washington Raid (continued): Battle of the Monocacy River. East of Frederick, Maryland, Lieutenant General Jubal A. Early's II Corps encounters a scratch Union force of 5,800 men under Major General Lew Wallace drawn up along the Monocacy River. Although outnumbered more than 2 to 1, Wallace resists Confederate attacks for most of the day, purchasing valuable time for troops to man the defenses of Washington. Union casualties total 1,294; the Confederates lose 700–900 men.

July 11–12, 1864

Civil War (continued): Eastern theater: Early's Washington Raid (continued): Early tests the Washington defenses. Heat, exhaustion, and Union troops exact a toll on the Confederates of Lieutenant General Jubal A. Early's II Corps advancing on Washington, D.C. On July 11 the Confederates reach Fort Stevens, part of the defensive belt protecting Washington. In this first major military threat to the U.S. capital since

1814, federal authorities issue arms to some 20,000 citizens to assist in the defense.

Early is too late, however, for Union general-in-chief Lieutenant General Ulysses S. Grant has rushed north his VI Corps from the Siege of Petersburg. On July 12 Early probes the Union's Washington defenses at a cost of 400 casualties. Judging them too strong, he retires. Although burdened by booty and captured supplies, Early's men rebuff the inept Union pursuit and return to the Shenandoah Valley.

July 14–15, 1864

Civil War (continued): Western theater: Battle of Tupelo. On the orders of Union commander of the Division of the Mississippi Major General William T. Sherman, on July 5, 1864, Major General Andrew J. Smith leads 14,200 Union infantry and cavalry against Major General Nathan B. Forrest's 6,000 Confederate cavalry in northern Mississippi. Smith is to prevent Forrest from attacking the rail lines supplying Union forces moving against Atlanta. Confederate lieutenant general Stephen D. Lee orders Forrest not to attack Smith until Lee can reinforce with 2,000 men, whereupon Lee assumes command.

Having located the Union line on July 13, Lee orders an attack the next day. In the Battle of Tupelo (Harrisburg) the Confederates mount several uncoordinated assaults, all of which fail. Smith then counterattacks and probably would have destroyed the Confederates, but he breaks off the attack because of a shortage of rations and withdraws on July 15. In the battle the Confederates lose 1,300 men (including Forrest, wounded) as opposed to only 674 for the Union. Although Sherman is disappointed with the result and orders a new offensive, Smith has accomplished his mission.

July 17, 1864

Civil War (continued): Atlanta Campaign (continued): Johnston relieved of command. Surprised to find Confederate general Joseph E. Johnston's Army of Tennessee drawn up on the north bank of the Chattahoochee River rather than south of that stream, U.S. major general William T. Sherman again moves quickly with his three armies to outflank Johnston. Sherman sends his

One of a number of installations protecting Washington, D.C., during the Civil War, Fort Stevens was the focus of fighting during July 11–12, 1864, during Confederate lieutenant general Jubal Early's raid on Washington. President Abraham Lincoln witnessed the fighting from the confines of the fort. (National Archives)

men across the Chattahoochee and turns the Confederate left. Johnston falls back on Peachtree Creek, just north of Atlanta, and prepares a counterattack.

On July 17, though, after Johnston has waged a defensive campaign that has restricted Sherman's advance to only about a mile a day with minimum loss to his own forces, he has given no reassurance that he will defend Atlanta. In fact he appears prepared for another retreat, which is unacceptable to Confederate president Jefferson Davis, who replaces him in command of the Army of Tennessee with impulsive, aggressive corps commander General John Bell Hood.

July 20, 1864

Civil War (continued): Atlanta Campaign (continued): Battle of Peachtree Creek. Confederate commander of the Army of Tennessee General Joseph E. Johnston had been planning a counterstroke against Union major general William T. Sherman's army group advancing on Atlanta when he was relieved of command on July 17, 1864. His successor, General John B. Hood, carries out that attack, surprising U.S. major general George H. Thomas's Army of the Cumberland.

In the Battle of Peachtree Creek about three miles north of Atlanta, stubborn Union resistance and the uncoordinated nature of the Confederate attacks give Union forces victory. The Confederates sustain 4,796 casualties of 19,000 engaged; the Union suffers only 1,779 casualties of 20,000 engaged. The Union advance on Atlanta continues, and Hood is forced to withdraw into the Atlanta defenses.

July 22, 1864

Civil War (continued): Atlanta Campaign (continued): Battle of Atlanta. Despite his defeat at Peachtree Creek, Confederate commander of the Army of Tennessee General John B. Hood is determined to try again. He plans a sortie from the Atlanta defenses against investing Union forces under Major General William T. Sherman. Hood's plan is a bold one. While Lieutenant General Alexander P. Stewart occupies Union forces north and northeast of Atlanta, Hood will send two corps under Lieutenant General William J. Hardee and Major General Benjamin F. Cheatham to attack the left flank of Sherman's armies, Major General James B. McPherson's Army of the Tennessee moving westward to Atlanta from Decatur.

The Confederates achieve surprise and enjoy initial success, but the Union troops rally and, despite McPherson's death in the battle (he is the sole Union Army commander to be killed in action in the war), they repel the Confederates. The attack costs the Confederates some 8,000 casualties; Union losses are 3,722.

July 24, 1864

Civil War (continued): Eastern theater: Second Battle of Kernstown. Following his raid on Washington, D.C., Confederate lieutenant general Jubal A. Early had escaped with his II Corps to the Shenandoah Valley virtually unscathed. Union brigadier general George Crook with some 8,500 men (including 1,500 cavalry) now occupies Winchester, Virginia, in the northern part of the valley. Following a cavalry skirmish on July 23, the next day Early advances against Crook. The ensuing Second Battle of Kernstown is at a draw until Confederate major general John C. Breckenridge's division manages to enfilade the Union left flank.

The Union retreat becomes a rout, with the loss of much of the baggage train. The Union sustains 1,185 casualties (including 479 prisoners); Early's losses are only some 200. The Union defeat opens up the lower (northern) Shenandoah Valley to the Confederates and convinces Union authorities that a change is needed. Two weeks later, Major General Philip Sheridan assumes command of the new Army of the Shenandoah (Middle Military Division), formed specifically to defeat Early.

July 26–September 10, 1864

Civil War (continued): Atlanta Campaign (continued): Union and Confederate cavalry raids. Union Western theater commander Major General William T. Sherman's forces are closing in on Atlanta. Finding it too strongly fortified and too extensive to invest, Sherman decides to send cavalry both east and west of the city to destroy lines of communication between Atlanta and the remainder of the Confederacy, forcing the Confederates to abandon the city.

Sherman orders Major General George Stoneman, with three brigades of some 6,500 men, to proceed east of Atlanta, while Brigadier General Edward M. McCook and 3,500 men move west of the city. The two are to join forces at Lovejoy's Station, then cut the Central of Georgia Railroad, the major rail link supplying Army of Tennessee commander General John B. Hood's forces at Atlanta. Sherman also authorizes Stoneman, on the latter's request, to proceed farther south in an effort to release some 30,000 Union prisoners of war being held at Macon and Andersonville, but on condition that the rail connection has been severed first.

Stoneman sets out on July 26 but ignores Sherman's orders and heads for Macon first. On July 27 Stoneman detaches Brigadier General Kenner Garrard's division, sending him to Flat Rock to protect his rear. Stoneman crosses the Ocmulgee River near Covington and proceeds toward Macon. As a consequence of Stoneman's decision, Confederate major general Joseph Wheeler is able to employ his 10,000 cavalry to defeat each of what are now three Union columns. On July 28 Wheeler's men rout Garrard's division.

On July 30, meanwhile, part of Stoneman's command wrecks railway facilities at Griswold Station, destroying 17 locomotives and more than 100 cars as well as a long railroad bridge over the Oconee. At Macon, Stoneman is turned back by strongly entrenched Georgia militia, however. Attempting to withdraw early on July 31, he is brought to bay at Sunshine Church 19 miles northeast of Macon by 1,300 Confederate cavalry under Brigadier General Alfred Iverson Jr. Tricked into believing that he is surrounded by a superior force, Stoneman covers the escape northward of two of his brigades, then surrenders with about 700 men. (Stoneman thus has the distinction of being the highest-ranking Union officer taken by the Confederates in the war; he is exchanged several months later.)

McCook, meanwhile, crosses the Chattahoochee River below Campbelltown by his pontoon bridge, then marches to Lovejoy's Station. With no sign of Stoneman, McCook sets to work tearing up two miles of track, burning two trains of cars, and cutting five miles of telegraph lines. He also comes across a Confederate wagon train, burning 500 wagons and killing 800 mules as well as capturing 422 Confederates. On July 30, however, in the Battle of Brown's Mill near Newnan he is surrounded by Confederate cavalry and infantry and forced to abandon his prisoners and fight his way out. McCook loses about 600 men killed and captured before he and the remainder of his men are able to return to Turner's Ferry.

The Confederates quickly repair the damage inflicted. Sherman's cavalry have failed in their mission and have lost some 2,000 men in what is a significant morale boost to the Atlanta defenders. The raid also reinforces Sherman's already low opinion of cavalry.

Hood then dispatches Wheeler's cavalry on a monthlong (August 10–September 10) raid against Union supply lines. This action fails to deter Sherman, however.

July 27–29, 1864

Civil War (continued): Eastern theater: Siege of Petersburg (continued): First Battle of Deep Bottom. U.S. Army general-in-chief Lieutenant General Ulysses S. Grant sends Major General Winfield Scott Hancock and the II Corps of the Army of the Potomac and two divisions of Major General Philip H. Sheridan's Cavalry Corps across the James River at Deep Bottom by pontoon bridge. Deep Bottom is an area of the James River in Henrico County, some 11 miles southeast of Richmond and a crossing point from the Bermuda Hundred area on the south side of

the river. Brigadier General Robert S. Foster's division of X Corps of the Army of the James had previously crossed the river just upstream on a pontoon bridge and secured a bridgehead on the north side of the river.

Grant's plan calls for Sheridan and Hancock to pass through Foster's bridgehead. Hancock is to pin the Confederates at Chaffin's Bluff in order to prevent reinforcements from opposing Sheridan's cavalry in its drive on Richmond. If possible, Sheridan is to take Richmond, although Grant believes it more likely that Sheridan will at least be able to ride around the capital city and cut the Virginia Central Railroad supplying it from the west. At the very least, Grant anticipates that this thrust will draw off some of the Confederate forces defending Petersburg in advance of a Union attack there, to be preceded by the explosion of a large mine under the Confederate lines. Indeed, rumors of just such a Union move cause Confederate general Robert E. Lee to send forces under Major General Joseph B. Kershaw north on July 23.

Union forces begin crossing the James at 3:00 a.m. on July 27. The ensuing First Battle of Deep Bottom is also known as the Battle of Darbytown, Strawberry Plains, New Market Road, and Gravel Hill. Hancock's men initially break through the Confederate lines on New Market Road, capturing four guns and moving toward Long Bridge Road. The Confederates are ready, however. They counterattack, holding Hancock east of Deep Bottom Run. Confusion in the Confederate command prevents coordinated action. Lieutenant Generals Richard H. Anderson, commanding I Corps, and Richard S. Ewell, commanding the Richmond defenses, cannot agree on who is in charge.

Shielded by Hancock's infantry, Sheridan meanwhile pushes his two cavalry divisions northward. Supported by a cavalry division from the Army of the James, Sheridan probes the Richmond defenses at Darbytown Road but is unable to advance farther, the Confederates there strengthened by the arrival of Major General Henry Heth's division.

Grant arrives on the scene in the afternoon. Surprised by the strength of the Confederate defenders, he orders for the next day an envelopment of the

Winfield Scott Hancock (1824–1886)

Prominent Union Army general. Winfield Scott Hancock was born on February 14, 1824, in Montgomery County near Harristown, Pennsylvania. Hancock graduated from the U.S. Military Academy, West Point, in 1844 and was assigned to the 6th Infantry Regiment as a brevet second lieutenant. He was advanced to full second lieutenant in 1846. Hancock fought in the Mexican-American War and was breveted first lieutenant for his role in the Battles of Contreras and Churubusco (August 19–20, 1847).

Following the war, Hancock served in various posts and was promoted to captain in 1855. He was then assigned to Florida, where he fought in the Third Seminole War (1855–1858). He was next assigned to Kansas and to Utah, where his 6th Infantry arrived after the so-called Mormon War had ended. Posted to California, he was serving there as chief quartermaster at Los Angeles when the American Civil War began.

Called east, Hancock arrived in Washington, D.C., in the late summer of 1861. On September 23 he was promoted to brigadier general of volunteers and given command of a brigade in the Army of the Potomac. Hancock fought with his unit in Major General George B. McClellan's 1862 Peninsula Campaign, notably in the Battle of Williamsburg (May 5) and the Battle of Seven Pines (Fair Oaks) near Richmond (May 31–June 1). Hancock then fought in the Battle of Antietam (September 17, 1862). When Major General Israel Richardson was mortally wounded in the fighting at "Bloody Lane," Hancock replaced him as commander of the 1st Division of II Corps. Hancock performed well in the battle, and in November he was advanced to major general of volunteers.

Hancock's division fought in the Battle of Fredericksburg on December 13, 1862, taking part in the disastrous Union assault on the stone wall at Marye's Heights. At the Battle of Chancellorsville (May 1–4, 1863), Hancock again performed with distinction, showing considerable initiative and directing a rear-guard action that protected the withdrawal of the remainder of the army. Later Hancock testified before the congressional Joint Committee on the Conduct of the War that had the Army of the Potomac pushed forward at Chancellorsville, it would have been successful.

In June 1863, Hancock was appointed commander of II Corps in the Army of the Potomac. He played an important role in the Battle of Gettysburg of July 1–3, 1863. In the first day's fighting he took charge of the field and selected the strong positions (the so-called Fishhook) from which Union forces would fight the battle. On the second day (July 2), Hancock and his II Corps fought on the Union left on Cemetery Ridge. On July 3, Hancock's men met the brunt of General Robert E. Lee's last major effort of the battle, an assault of the Union center led by Major General George E. Pickett. Hancock rode his horse among his men, inspiring them and redirecting units to weak points in the line as necessary. Wounded when a bullet hit his saddle and forced pieces of it and a small nail into his thigh, he refused treatment until victory was ensured. Hancock's role on the third day's fighting was crucial to the Northern victory.

Hancock never completely recovered from his wound, but he returned to active service with the Army of the Potomac in March 1864 to participate in the Overland Campaign. His II Corps participated in the Battle of the Wilderness (May 4–5) and at Spotsylvania (May 8–18). In the Battle of Cold Harbor (June 3–12), Hancock's corps suffered a disastrous rebuff when ordered to attack entrenched Confederate lines. Some 3,000 men of II Corps fell in the assault.

(continued)

(Continued)

Continued problems from the wound he had received at Gettysburg forced Hancock from the field, but he returned later in June to participate in the Siege of Petersburg (June 15, 1864–April 2, 1865). In November 1864 Hancock was promoted to brigadier general in the regular army and breveted major general. Health problems forced him to yield command of II Corps, however. He ended the war in command of the Union defenses of Washington, where he worked to build the Veteran Volunteer Corps.

Promoted to major general in the regular army in July 1866, Hancock assumed command of the Department of Missouri that August. During 1866–1867 he was involved in operations against Indians on the south Great Plains, most notably the Cheyennes. He then commanded the Fifth Military District of Louisiana and Texas (1867–1868), the Division of the Atlantic (1868–1869), and the Department of Dakota (1869–1872). His final commands were those of the Military District of the Atlantic (1872–1876) and the Department of the East (1877–1886).

A popular Democrat, Hancock's frequent clashes with radical Republican politicians led him to accept the Democratic Party nomination for president in the 1880 election, but he lost a close race to Republican James A. Garfield. Hancock remained on active duty with the army and died at his headquarters on Governors Island in New York Harbor on February 9, 1886.

MARY LYNN CLUFF AND SPENCER C. TUCKER

Further Reading

Jordan, David M. *Winfield Scott Hancock: A Soldier's Life.* 3rd ed. Bloomington: Indiana University Press, 1996.
Tucker, Glenn. *Hancock the Superb.* Dayton, OH: Morningside, 1980.

Confederate right flank to spring Sheridan's cavalry. Before this can occur, however, at about 10:00 a.m. on July 28 Kershaw attacks Sheridan's dismounted troopers. The latter repel the assault and then counterattack with their repeating rifles, capturing some 300 Southerners, but the Confederates re-form and block the cavalrymen on New Market Road, causing Sheridan's cavalry raid to be aborted.

On July 29 Union forces recross the river, ending the battle. Lee's swift action has probably saved Richmond. While the Union forces have failed to achieve their principal objectives, they have at least drawn off some Confederates from the Petersburg lines prior to the Battle of the Crater. Union losses in the battle are 486; the Confederates lose 679.

July 28, 1864

American Indian Wars (continued): Battle of Killdeer Mountain. After establishing Fort Rice at the mouth of the Cannonball River in North Dakota, on July 19, 1864, U.S. Army brigadier general Alfred Sully leads some 2,200 men in two brigades from there, accompanying a caravan of 123 wagons destined for the Montana goldfields. Sully is determined to engage hostile Native Americans massing between the Heart and Cannonball Rivers. The ensuing Battle of Killdeer Mountain (also known as the Battle of the Tahkahokuty Mountains), near present-day Killdeer, North Dakota, pits Sully's men against some 1,800 Sioux warriors (Dakotas, Yanktonais, and Lakotas). The battle is the culmination of two years of fighting that began when Sioux warriors attacked Minnesota settlements in response to treaty violations.

When his Native American scouts spot the Sioux on July 28, Sully forms his soldiers into a hollow square extending one and a quarter miles on a side with the artillery battery, wagons, and every fourth man holding four horses each in the middle of the formation. Sioux warrior Long Dog leads the attack. Sully's phalanx holds, and his artillery fire scatters the attackers. Only 2 soldiers die in the battle, while Sully claims 100–150 warriors killed (the Indians claim to have suffered considerably fewer casualties).

The Native American survivors withdraw to the Badlands, a tangle of nearly impassable buttes and canyons. Believing pursuit to be too risky, Sully orders the soldiers to destroy everything in the abandoned Sioux camp of some 1,600 lodges. Hostile activity in the area then convinces Sully to return to Fort Rice. The civilian wagon train proceeds on ahead without a military escort, only to be ambushed by Native Americans a short time later.

While the Battle of Killdeer Mountain scatters hostile Dakota and Lakota bands and eliminates the immediate threat posed by the region's hostile tribes, the Sioux regroup and continue their efforts to drive encroaching settlers from the Dakota Territory.

July 28, 1864

Civil War (continued): Atlanta Campaign (continued): Battle of Ezra Church. Lacking the strength to bring Atlanta under effective siege and blocked by defending Confederate forces north and east of the city, commander of the Division of the Mississippi U.S. major general William T. Sherman decides to move his army group west to destroy railroads into the city. During July 25–27 Sherman transfers Major General Oliver O. Howard's Army of the Tennessee from his left wing to his right wing. Sherman assigns it the task of cutting the rail line to the southwest.

Informed of Howard's move, General John Bell Hood, commanding the Confederate Army of Tennessee, guesses Sherman's intent and sends two corps under Lieutenant Generals Stephen D. Lee and Alexander P. Stewart to intercept. Howard is prepared, though, and the Confederates run into Major John A. Logan's barricaded XV Corps defending against a flank attack from the east. The Southern charge is turned back with frightful cost: some 3,000 Confederates are casualties, against only 562 Union losses.

Although Hood keeps open his only rail line into Atlanta, the Battle of Ezra Church ends the possibility of Southern offensive operations against Sherman.

July 30, 1864

Civil War (continued): Eastern theater: Burning of Chambersburg. On July 27 Confederate lieutenant general Jubal A. Early orders Brigadier General John McCausland to lead 2,800 cavalry in a raid on Chambersburg in the Cumberland Valley of southern Pennsylvania. Early instructs McCausland to demand $100,000 in gold or $500,000 in U.S. currency as compensation for property, including the Virginia Military Institute, destroyed during Union major general David Hunter's May–June Lynchburg Campaign in Virginia. Failing this, Chambersburg is to be burned. Early had employed the same technique in his raid on Washington, D.C., extracting $200,000 from the residents of Frederick, Maryland.

On July 30 when the town leaders refuse to pay, McCausland orders Chambersburg torched. As many as 550 buildings are burned, with damage estimated at more than $1.6 million. McCausland and Early defend the raid as a legitimate act of war, but Northern public opinion sees it quite differently. The raid hardens Union attitudes and brings further Union destruction in the Shenandoah Valley under Major General Philip Sheridan.

July 30, 1864

Civil War (continued): Eastern theater: Siege of Petersburg (continued): Battle of the Crater. With the Union siege of Petersburg, Virginia, apparently stymied, Lieutenant Colonel Henry Pleasants, a mining engineer before the war, secures approval from Army of the Potomac commander Major General George G. Meade and Union army general-in-chief Lieutenant General Ulysses S. Grant to tunnel under the Confederate lines with the intention to explode a large mine under a fort known as Elliott's Salient, after which Union troops will rush the resultant gap in an effort to take Petersburg and end the siege.

For more than a month, Pleasants' regiment, chiefly composed of Pennsylvania coal miners, digs a 511-foot tunnel 50 feet under the Confederate lines in the Union IX Corps sector commanded by Major General Ambrose E. Burnside. Rumors of Union tunneling prompt Confederate sector commander Major General John Pegram to order construction of

Battle of the Crater

Date	July 30, 1864	
Location	Petersburg, Virginia	
Opponents (*winner)	*Confederacy	United States
Commander	Major General John Pegram	Major General Ambrose E. Burnside
#	9,500 men	16,500 men
Casualties	1,491 (361 killed, 727 wounded, 403 missing or captured)	3,798 (504 killed, 1,881 wounded, 1,413 missing or captured)

a supplemental line of trenches and artillery positions to the rear. The depth of the tunnel prevents detection, however.

Meanwhile, a division of the U.S. Colored Troops, commanded by Brigadier General Edward Ferrero, trains for the assault. Its two brigades are to move to either side of the crater and be followed by Burnside's other two divisions in an effort to move on and take Petersburg itself. The day before the attack, however, Meade, who fears adverse publicity in the North were the attack to fail with heavy African American casualties, orders Burnside not to employ Ferrero's division as its lead element.

At 4:45 a.m. on July 30, 1864, the Union troops detonate the mine of four tons of gunpowder. The resulting blast creates a huge crater 170 feet long, 68–80 feet wide, and 30 feet deep in their lines. Some 250–350 Confederates are killed outright.

Brigadier General James H. Ledlie's untrained white division leads the assault, but the attackers reportedly delayed for 10 minutes before leaving their entrenchments. No footbridges or scaling ladders have been prepared, imposing further delay. Rather than moving around the crater, they see it as cover and move into it, promptly bunching up. As masses of Union troops struggle to extricate themselves, Confederate brigadier general William Mahone rallies the defenders, who shoot down the attackers, much like fish in a barrel. With the plan having already failed, Burnside commits Ferraro's division to the battle. Under considerable flanking fire, many of them also

seek cover in the crater. All efforts to push beyond the crater are turned back. For several hours the Confederates, now aided by artillery, slaughter the Union troops before the battle comes to an end.

The Union sustains 3,798 casualties (504 killed, 1,881 wounded, and 1,413 missing or captured) of some 16,500 engaged, the Confederates only 1,491 (361 killed, 727 wounded, and 403 missing or captured, including those in the initial blast) of some 9,500 engaged. As a result of the fiasco, both Ferrero and Burnside are relieved of command, and Ledlie is dismissed from the service. Later Meade, whose order to change the attack plan at the last minute was a major factor in its failure, is censured by the congressional Joint Committee on the Conduct of the War. Pleasants, who had no role in the actual attack, is breveted brigadier general. The Siege of Petersburg continues for another eight months.

August 5, 1864

Civil War (continued): Western theater: Battle of Mobile Bay. Mobile Bay and the port of Mobile, Alabama, are vital to the Confederate war effort. Alabama is an important center for iron manufacturing, including heavy guns and rolled iron plate, and Mobile is one of the few deep-water ports still available to the Confederacy in 1864 and an important transshipment point for goods carried by blockade-runners. After having taken New Orleans in

Battle of Mobile Bay

Date	August 5, 1864	
Location	Mouth of Mobile Bay, Alabama	
Opponents (*winner)	*United States	Confederacy
Commander	Rear Admiral David G. Farragut	Rear Admiral Franklin Buchanan
#	18 ships (4 of them ironclad monitors)	4 ships (1 ironclad and 3 wooden gunboats)
Casualties	1 ironclad and 1 wooden ship sunk; 145 men killed and 170 wounded	1 gunboat sunk; 1 ironclad and 1 gunboat captured; 12 men killed and 123 captured (20 wounded)

The powerful Confederate ironclad *Tennessee*, captained by Commander James D. Johnston, served as Rear Admiral Franklin Buchanan's flagship in the Battle of Mobile Bay, August 5, 1864, when it fought the Union squadron virtually alone. Captured in that battle, the *Tennessee* was taken into the U.S. Navy. (Library of Congress)

early 1862, U.S. Navy rear admiral David G. Farragut wanted to proceed against Mobile with his Gulf Coast Squadron but was forced to operate on the Mississippi, principally against Vicksburg. This delay gives the Confederates time to strengthen Mobile's defenses.

In June 1864 Major General Edward R. S. Canby replaces the inept Major General Nathaniel P. Banks as commander of the U.S. Division of West Mississippi. On June 17, Canby meets with Farragut aboard the screw sloop *Hartford* (24 guns) off Mobile Bay. They develop a plan in which Farragut's ships are to run past the forts guarding the mouth of the bay and destroy the Confederate squadron in the bay itself. After this, a joint army-navy assault will secure Forts Morgan and Gaines. Union land forces would then advance on Mobile from Pascagoula, while the navy secures Fort Powell at Grant's Pass in the Mississippi Sound. Canby commits 20,000 men to the operation. Meanwhile, Farragut is awaiting the arrival of ironclads, which he deems essential to the success of the naval portion.

These plans have to be shelved when Union general-in-chief Lieutenant General Ulysses S. Grant orders Canby to send 20,000 men east to assist in his Overland Campaign against Richmond. On July 9, however, Canby again meets with Farragut and offers to make available perhaps 4,000 men to operate against the Confederate forts. Although clearly insufficient to take Mobile, this force enables Farragut to proceed with operations to secure Mobile Bay.

The revised plan calls for some 3,000 Union troops with artillery to come ashore on the Gulf beach about three miles behind Fort Morgan at the same time that the fleet passes into the bay through the main channel. The soldiers will then work to within a mile of the fort and entrench. As Farragut's ships enter the bay, the troops will open up artillery fire against the fort from that direction. A reserve of 1,500 men will remain in Mississippi Sound. After the fleet has entered the bay, some of the troops will land on Dauphin Island to attack Fort Gaines in conjunction with Farragut's ships.

Early on the morning of August 5, 1864, Farragut leads 18 ships, including 4 ironclad monitors, against Mobile Bay. Shortly after 6:00 a.m., the Union ships cross the bar. Four monitors form a column to the right of another column of wooden ships to mask them from the Confederate Fort Morgan. Farragut orders his 7 smallest wooden ships lashed to the port sides of the larger wooden screw steamers for additional protection.

Situated at the tip of Mobile Point, a long neck of land that juts out into the bay, Fort Morgan controls the entrance into the bay from the east. The fort mounts 40 heavy guns; another 19 guns are in exterior batteries.

Shortly before 7:00 a.m. the lead Union ironclad, the *Tecumseh* (2 guns), opens fire at Fort Morgan, and the engagement becomes general. Rear Admiral Franklin Buchanan, in command of the small Confederate squadron in the bay, moves to attack the advancing Union ships. Buchanan has the powerful ironclad ram *Tennessee* (flagship, 6 guns), also known as the *Tennessee II*, supported by the gunboats *Gaines* (5 guns), *Morgan* (5 guns), and *Selma* (3 guns).

Captain Tunis A. Craven, commander of the *Tecumseh*, makes right for the *Tennessee*. Suddenly there is a great explosion as the Union monitor strikes a submerged torpedo (mine) and sinks in only half a minute with the loss of Craven and 92 of its crew (21 men are saved). This halts the Union squadron in front of the guns of Fort Morgan. Secured to the rigging of the *Hartford*, Farragut sees the sloop *Brooklyn* (26 guns) in front of him slow and then reverse engines. The Union ships also begin to bunch up as Fort Morgan continues to fire on them.

This is the decisive point in the battle, and Farragut chooses to risk additional mines with his own ship, calling out "I shall lead." The *Hartford* gets up speed, and as it passes the *Brooklyn*, Farragut shouts, "What's the trouble?" "Torpedoes" (mines) is the reply. "Damn the torpedoes," Farragut yells. He then orders his ship to get up speed; finally, he calls to the captain of the gunboat lashed to the side of the *Hartford*, "Go ahead, Jouett, full speed!" Farragut's words pass into history as "Damn the torpedoes; full speed ahead."

Although men below decks on the *Hartford* can hear primers going off beneath them, none of the remaining Confederate mines explodes. Some of the Union warships are damaged by Confederate shore fire, but all pass safely into the bay and beyond the range of the fort's guns.

Spotting Farragut's pennant, Buchanan orders the *Tennessee* to attack the *Hartford*. His gunboats also join. The *Tennessee* does not have sufficient speed up to ram, however. It passes by the Union flagship, firing at the remaining pairs of Union ships and inflicting some damage and casualties. Farragut then orders his smaller ships cut free to attack the Confederate gunboats, which haul off and steam up the bay. The *Selma*

surrenders, and the *Gaines* is hit several times below the waterline and sinks; the *Morgan* escapes, first to the protection of Fort Morgan and later to Mobile.

The *Tennessee* gains the protection of Fort Morgan, where Buchanan considers his next move. Rather than wait to be attacked, at 9:00 a.m. he brings his flagship back into action alone against the entire Union squadron. Confederate artillerymen at Fort Morgan cheer on the ram in what seems a suicide mission: the *Tennessee* with 6 guns faces 157 Union guns. Buchanan hopes to inflict what damage he can, return to Fort Morgan, and there ground the *Tennessee* as a stationary battery to assist in repelling attacks on the fort. In any case, he does not want a repeat of what had happened to the ironclad *Virginia* in the James River, when it had been scuttled without a fight.

After ineffectual attempts on both sides to ram, the *Tennessee* is surrounded and pummeled by the Union guns. It is holed only once, but Union shot jam its port shutters and cut its exposed steering chains. With his ship dead in the water and ammunition nearly expended, Buchanan, who is wounded, surrenders.

The Battle of Mobile Bay is the bloodiest naval engagement of the Civil War. It costs the Union side 145 killed and 170 wounded. Many of Farragut's wooden ships are heavily damaged, but only one is lost: a supply vessel hit by fire from Fort Morgan as it attempted to follow the fleet into the bay. The Confederates lose 12 killed and 20 wounded, and the crews of the *Tennessee* and *Selma* are captured.

Union troops under Canby come ashore after the battle. Confederate Fort Gaines, on the eastern tip of Dauphin Island to the west of the channel and mounting 27 guns, surrenders on August 8. Following two weeks of bombardment in which the *Tennessee*, now recommissioned as a U.S. Navy ship of the same name, participates, Fort Morgan finally surrenders on August 23.

For all practical purposes, the Battle of Mobile Bay ends Confederate blockade-running in the Gulf of Mexico. The battle also helps ensure the reelection of President Abraham Lincoln. Mobile, located 30 miles from the Gulf, is not taken until the end of the war, in April 1865, in a joint army-navy operation.

August 6–23, 1864

Civil War (continued). The Confederate steamer *Tallahassee* under Commander John Taylor Wood escapes from Wilmington, North Carolina and in one of the most destructive commerce raiding cruises of the war takes 31 prizes before again passing through the Union blockade and returning to Wilmington.

August 7, 1864

Civil War (continued): Eastern theater: Sheridan takes command in the Shenandoah Valley. Realizing the vulnerability of Washington, D.C., as long as Confederate forces under Lieutenant General Jubal A. Early remain in the Shenandoah Valley, on August 7, 1864, Union general-in-chief Lieutenant General Ulysses S. Grant secretly withdraws the VI and XIX Corps from the defense of Washington and concentrates them near Harpers Ferry. They are organized along with a large Cavalry Corps, and two divisions from the Army of West Virginia as the Army of the Shenandoah under Major General Philip H. Sheridan, commander of the new Middle Military Division. Grant orders Sheridan to move south, defeat Early, and destroy any supplies in the valley that might be of use to the Confederate Army, to the point that "crows flying over it . . . will have to carry their own provender."

August 14–20, 1864

Civil War (continued): Eastern theater: Siege of Petersburg (continued): Second Battle of Deep Bottom. Confederate general Robert E. Lee has dispatched Major General Joseph B. Kershaw's infantry division of Lieutenant General Richard H. Anderson's corps and the cavalry division under Major General Fitzhugh Lee to Culpepper, Virginia, there to act against Major General Philip Sheridan's newly created Army of the Shenandoah yet be able to return to defend Richmond or Petersburg if needed.

Union general-in-chief Lieutenant General Ulysses S. Grant learns of this movement and falsely assumes that Anderson's entire corps has been moved. He decides to again send a force across the pontoon bridge at Deep Bottom, an area of the James River in Henrico County, Virginia, 11 miles southeast of the city of Richmond where Union forces had crossed to the north shore of the river on a pontoon bridge and established a bridgehead. Grant's initial effort here during July 27–29, 1864, had largely failed. Grant's goal is to take Richmond and at least weaken Confederate forces defending Petersburg. The ensuing engagement is known as the Second Battle of Deep Bottom, the Battle of Fussel's Mill, the Battle of New Market Road, the Battle of Bailey's Creek, the Battle of Charles City Road, and the Battle of White's Tavern.

Grant commits some 28,000 men, commanded by Major General Winfield S. Hancock. On the night of August 13–14, 1864, the II and X Corps cross the James at Deep Bottom. On August 14, X Corps advances on New Market Heights, while II Corps extends Union lines along Bailey's Creek. That night Union forces are shifted to the Union right flank near Fussell's Mill. The ensuing Union assault on August 16 here enjoys initial success but is then halted by Confederate counterattacks. Following additional skirmishing, the Union troops withdraw across the James on the night of August 20. The battle claims 2,890 Union casualties and some 1,500 Confederates.

August 18–21, 1864

Civil War (continued): Eastern theater: Siege of Petersburg (continued): Weldon Railroad Operations (continued): Battle of Globe Tavern. During June 22–23, 1864, Union general-in-chief Lieutenant General Ulysses S. Grant had attempted to sever the railroad lines connecting Petersburg and Richmond to the south and west. This effort had failed against stubborn Confederate resistance.

In mid-August in an effort to draw off Confederate resources from the Shenandoah Valley, Grant again orders operations against the Weldon Railroad and other Confederate rail lines north of the James River. Major General Gouverneur K. Warren's V Corps carries out the attack early on August 18 against Confederate forces commanded by Lieutenant General Ambrose P. Hill.

In the ensuing August 18–21 Battle of Globe Tavern, also known as the Second Battle of the Weldon

Railroad, both sides reinforce. Grant sends three divisions of IX Corps and one division from II Corps. The Union suffers 4,455 casualties of 20,289 men engaged; the Confederates sustain only 1,619 casualties of some 14,000 men engaged. The fighting ends with Union troops controlling a portion of the Weldon line, however. Grant has cut this vital Confederate supply link.

August 21, 1864

Civil War (continued): Western theater: Forrest attacks Memphis. At 4:00 a.m. this day, Major General Nathan Bedford Forrest leads three brigades of Confederate cavalry against Memphis, Tennessee. Forrest had set out from Oxford, Mississippi, with 2,000 men but lost perhaps a third of his force from exhausted mounts. His goal is not to take Memphis, which is held by 6,000 Union troops under Major General C. C. Washburn, but to capture the senior Union commanders, free Confederate prisoners held in Irving Block Prison, and force the recall of Union troops from northern Mississippi.

Surprise is essential for the plan to succeed. Taking advantage of heavy fog, the Confederates neutralize Union sentries and enter the city. They withdraw some two hours later with prisoners, captured horses, and significant quantities of supplies. The total Union loss is 15 killed, 65 wounded, and 116 captured or missing. Forrest places his own losses at 20 killed or wounded. The raid does achieve Forrest's strategic goal of inducing the recall of Union forces from northern Mississippi to defend Memphis.

August 25, 1864

Civil War (continued): Eastern theater: Siege of Petersburg (continued): Battle of Ream's Station. With troops of U.S. major general Winfield Scott Hancock's II Corps destroying sections of the Weldon Railroad, the vital supply link for General Robert E. Lee's Army of Northern Virginia at Petersburg, Virginia, Lee orders Lieutenant General Ambrose P. Hill to challenge Hancock. The battle sees some 8,000–10,000 Confederates attacking 9,000 Union troops. The Confederates enjoy considerable success,

including putting Major General John Gibbon's division to flight and driving the Union troops from Ream's Station. Still, a considerable amount of the railroad track has been destroyed, causing further difficulties for Lee's troops in the Richmond-Petersburg area. Union casualties in the battle total 2,747; the Southerners sustain only 814.

August 31–September 1, 1864

Civil War (continued): Western theater: Atlanta Campaign (continued): Battle of Jonesboro. Leaving a corps to protect his lines of communication, Western theater commander Major General William T. Sherman moves with his three armies south of the city of Atlanta to cut the main rail lines supplying Atlanta from that direction. Commander of the Confederate Army of Tennessee General John B. Hood sends half of his army under Lieutenant General William J. Hardee to block Sherman at Jonesboro. Hardee assaults the Union troops on August 31, 1864.

The Confederates attack piecemeal and are thrown back with staggering losses. In the fighting that day, the entrenched Union troops lose just 178 men; the Confederates sustain nearly 2,000 casualties.

The next day, September 1, Sherman attacks Hardee. The Union attacks are poorly coordinated, and the Confederates hold. Union casualties are 1,274 of 20,460 engaged; the Confederates lose 911 of 12,661 engaged. Despite this rebuff, the Union troops have severed the rail line and effectively trapped the Confederates. Hardee has no option but to abandon his position, and Hood has no choice but to withdraw from Atlanta.

September 1–October 1864

Civil War (continued): Trans-Mississippi West theater: Confederate invasion of Missouri. On September 1, 1864, some 13,000 Confederates under Major General Sterling Price invade Missouri from Arkansas. Driving on St. Louis, Price finds it too well defended and turns toward Kansas City. He defeats Union forces under Major General James G. Blunt at Lexington, Missouri, on October 19 and at Independence on October 22.

September 2, 1864

Civil War (continued): Atlanta Campaign (continued): Union troops occupy Atlanta. With rail connections to Atlanta, Georgia, having been severed by Union forces as a consequence of the August 31–September 1, 1864, Battle of Jonesboro in Georgia, on the night of September 1 Confederate general John Bell Hood, commander of the Army of Tennessee, orders all supplies that cannot be removed burnt and evacuates Atlanta. The next morning U.S. Army major general William T. Sherman's forces take possession. Sherman's victory brings rejoicing in the North and buoys Abraham Lincoln's sagging November reelection prospects; many in the South now realize that defeat is inevitable.

In the May 7–September 2, 1864, 100-mile long drive from Chattanooga, Union forces have suffered 31,687 casualties (4,423 dead, 22,822 wounded, and 4,442 missing or captured); Confederate losses are 34,979 (3,044 killed, 18,952 wounded, and 12,983 missing or captured).

September 5–10, 1864

Bombardment of Shimonoseki, Japan. The Western powers assemble a powerful squadron of 10 British, 4 Dutch, 4 French, and 1 American warship. (The Americans have no suitable warship available but are anxious to participate. They therefore charter a steamer and mount a gun in it.) The ships, commanded by British vice admiral Sir Augustus Kuper and carrying some 2,000 troops, depart Yokohama on August 29 and steam to Shimonoseki Strait. Kuper intends to silence once and for all the Chōshū forts that have been shelling Western merchant ships and disrupting trade through the straits.

Beginning on September 5, the allied ships shell the fortifications and land shore parties to take possession of the batteries. By the evening of September 10 all the captured guns are embarked on the allied ships. A Chōshū envoy promises to erect no more batteries and to keep the strait open. Ultimately the Japanese agree to pay an indemnity of $3 million. Allied casualties are 12 killed and 60 wounded. Two British warships are damaged in the exchange of fire.

September 7, 1864

Civil War (continued): Western theater. U.S. major general William T. Sherman establishes his headquarters in Atlanta, Georgia, and issues Special Order No. 67. It requires the evacuation of the city by all civilian inhabitants. When confronted by vehement protests from Confederate officials and civilians, Sherman asserts that a hostile civilian population would not only impede military activities but also unnecessarily burden the Union army.

September 19, 1864

Civil War (continued): Eastern theater: Third Battle of Winchester. Union major general Philip H. Sheridan, commanding the new Army of the Shenandoah, moves into the Shenandoah Valley to engage Lieutenant General Jubal A. Early's II Army of Valley. Sheridan commands some 39,200 men; Early has only about 21,000. Moreover, Confederate forces are widely dispersed in a defensive line extending from Winchester, Virginia, to Martinsburg, West Virginia. Sheridan moves against Winchester, the scene of two previous Union defeats.

On September 19 Union cavalry, followed by Sheridan's infantry, cross Opequon Creek east of Winchester. Early concentrates his own forces, and the Third Battle of Winchester (Opequon Creek) begins before noon with a Union frontal assault on Early's entrenched men. The Confederates halt the attack and then drive into a gap between the Union VI and XIX Corps. The timely arrival of Union reinforcements halts the Confederate counterattack. Union numbers and a late cavalry charge prove the difference.

Early withdraws—the first time his corps has been driven from the battlefield. Sheridan takes Winchester, but the Union side has suffered 5,020 casualties, the Confederates only 3,610. Early continues to resist Sheridan's advance into the valley.

September 22, 1864

Civil War (continued): Eastern theater: Battle of Fisher's Hill. Following the Third Battle of Winchester (Opequon Creek), Union major general Philip H. Sheridan and his Army of the Shenandoah continue their pursuit of Confederate lieutenant general Jubal A. Early's II Corps of the Army of Northern Virginia. On September 22 Sheridan attacks Early at Fisher's Hill, 21 miles south of Winchester. With fewer than 9,000 men, Early is outnumbered at least 3 to 1 and is unable to fully defend the span of the Shenandoah Valley.

Sheridan sends two divisions under Brigadier General George Crook around and behind Early's left. By 4:00 p.m. they are perpendicular to Early's left. The cheering Union troops then attack, immediately rolling up the Confederate left. Sheridan's other forces then assault the center of the Confederate line, forcing Early into a hasty withdrawal along the Valley Turnpike toward Woodstock. Darkness saves the bulk of Early's force. In the battle the Union side suffers 456 casualties, the Confederates some 1,250, along with the loss of 14 guns. The Confederates are forced back to Waynesboro. Sheridan now institutes the Burning, a 13-day campaign that destroys much of Shenandoah Valley's agriculture assets.

September 27, 1864

Civil War (continued): Western theater: Centralia Massacre. William "Bloody Bill" Anderson leads some 80 Confederate guerrillas, some dressed in stolen Union Army uniforms, in an attack on Centralia, Missouri. They plunder the town, robbing civilians of their possessions. They also capture a train and its 125 passengers, 23 of whom are unarmed U.S. Army musicians. The guerrillas order the soldiers to strip off their uniforms and then summarily execute all but 1 of them, a sergeant whom Anderson plans to exchange, and mutilates their bodies. That afternoon U.S. Army major A. V. E. Johnson arrives in Centralia with 155 recruits of the newly formed 39th Missouri Infantry Regiment (mounted). Despite warnings by the townspeople, Johnson pursues the guerrillas, soon encountering them. Johnson insists on fighting the guerrillas on foot, and Anderson then orders a mounted charge. The soldiers, armed with muzzle-loading rifles, are no match for the guerrillas, who are armed with revolvers and kill Johnson and 122 of his men.

September 29–30, 1864

Civil War (continued): Eastern theater: Siege of Petersburg (continued): Battle of Chaffin's Farm and New Market Heights (also known as Laurel Hill). U.S. general-in-chief Lieutenant General Ulysses S. Grant plans semisimultaneous attacks against both flanks of Confederate general Robert E. Lee's Army of Northern Virginia. Major General Benjamin Butler is to attack to the east at Chaffin's Farm with his 35,000-man Army of the James (X and XVIII Corps and a cavalry division). Grant anticipates that this will force Lee to shift resources to defend north of the James, enabling Grant to strike to the west of the Confederate line. At best Butler will take Richmond,

 **Muzzle-Loading Rifles**

The rifle is an individual shoulder-fired firearm. The first muzzle-loading rifles were identical to the smoothbore musket in firing mechanism, means of loading, and general outward appearance. The difference was that the rifle had a spiral twist of lands and grooves on the internal surface of the barrel. Known as rifling, these imparted spin to the round ball and gave it far greater accuracy at much greater distances. Ironically, rifling seems to have been designed not to improve accuracy but rather to collect fouling, which occurred with the black powder, and to ease the loading of the bullet, which had to be pushed down the bore with a ramrod. Rifling proved to be one of the most important inventions in the history of weaponry.

While the range at which an individual with a smoothbore musket would be expected to hit a man-sized target might be only 50–100 yards, the rifle had an effective range of up to 200 or even 300 yards. Such advantage, however, was offset by its much slower rate of fire because of the reduced windage (the difference between the diameters of the ball and of the bore) in order that the soft lead ball would take to the rifling. The difficulty of loading meant that the rifle could fire only about one shot per minute, as opposed to three to four shots per minute for a well-trained soldier with the smoothbore musket. Hence, rifles were not suited for the tactics of the day that stressed massed close-in fire.

Rifling was probably invented in Germany as early as the late 15th century, but it came into widespread use in the first quarter of the 16th century. The earliest extant rifle dates from 1547. Although spiral grooves and lands became the most accepted form of rifling, straight grooves and lands also existed. The first centers of rifle manufacture were Scandinavia and Northern Europe, perhaps because the big game for which these weapons were especially useful in hunting were to be found chiefly in these regions. The Germans first employed rifles for military purposes in 1631. The men armed with rifles were known as Jaegers, from the German word for "hunter." Many riflemen were former gamekeepers and foresters. King Frederick II ("Frederick the Great," r. 1740–1786) raised the first permanent corps of Jaegers in the Prussian Army.

Rifles were especially favored in America, where their long-range accuracy made them ideal for hunting game, especially on the frontier. They probably first arrived in America in the late 17th century and by the 1740s were being manufactured in Pennsylvania and other colonies, chiefly the southern colonies. Most colonists, however, preferred the more robust and less demanding musket, which provided sufficient accuracy for most hunting and effective self-defense.

American rifles of the period usually had octagonal barrels of greater than 40 inches in length. Calibers varied widely but most usually were .52 to .65, making them somewhat smaller than those of smoothbore muskets. Their stocks were often of maple with brass furniture. They also featured wooden ramrods and patchbox cover. The rifle was loaded with loose powder from a powder horn that was poured down the barrel, followed by the ball wrapped in a greased cloth patch, which was then rammed home. The most common firing mechanism was the flintlock, also employed on the musket.

The importance of rifles in America has been exaggerated, but they were employed by some militia and used in the colonial wars, most notably the French and Indian War (1754–1763). Some Native Americans, notably the Shawnees and Delawares, also employed them. Rifles were not equipped either with slings or with lugs for mounting the bayonet.

During the American Revolutionary War, the Continental Army boasted special units armed with the so-called Pennsylvania or Kentucky rifle as skirmishers to fire on British officers from long range. More limited numbers of opposing British and German soldiers were also armed with this weapon, although French troops who fought in America seem not to have been similarly equipped.

SPENCER C. TUCKER

Further Reading

Blair, Claude, ed. *Pollard's History of Firearms*. New York: Macmillan, 1983.

Brown, M. L. *Firearms in Colonial America: The Impact on History and Technology, 1492–1792*. Washington, DC: Smithsonian Institution Press, 1980.

but Grant hopes at least to take advantage of Lee's weakened line to secure the South Side Railroad, a critical supply line into Petersburg.

Butler has made a special effort to recruit African Americans, and his Army of the James has the largest concentration of U.S. Colored Troops (USCT) of any Union army. Blacks constitute a brigade of Major General William Birney's X Corps, while Brigadier General Charles J. Paine's 3rd Division of the XVIII Corps is made up of three all-USCT brigades: the 1st Brigade led by Colonel John Holman, the 2nd Brigade commanded by Colonel Alonzo G. Draper, and the 3rd Brigade of Colonel Samuel Duncan. All USCT units have white officers.

Butler is not content with drawing off Lee's troops from Petersburg and wants instead to take Richmond. Before dawn on September 29, two divisions of Major General Edward O. C. Ord's XVIII Corps on Butler's left are to throw a pontoon bridge across the James for a surprise crossing at Aiken's Landing and then move up the Varina Road to capture Confederate Fort Harrison, the strongest point in the Confederate line. Ord is then to wheel west and destroy the Confederate bridges at and above Chaffin's Bluff and advance on the Osborn Turnpike to Richmond.

Simultaneously, Butler's right wing of Birney's X Corps, plus Paine's USCT regiments detailed from XVIII Corps, are to cross the James River on the original pontoon bridge at Deep Bottom, advance from there and carry New Market Heights, then head for Richmond on the New Market Road. Finally, Brigadier General August V. Kautz's cavalry division will move to the Darbytown Road and, once New Market Heights is cleared, ride hard for the Confederate capital. Butler assigns to Paine's black soldiers the task of spearheading the attack on New Market Heights in order to prove that his efforts to bring African Americans into the army has been a wise policy and that they can fight effectively.

Although Butler hopes to catch the Confederates by surprise, it is impossible to conceal the movements of so many men, and early on September 29 the well-entrenched Confederate defenders are ready and waiting. New Market Heights is held by some 2,000 veteran troops under Brigadier General John Gregg.

Although the initial Union assault by the USCT is repulsed, Birney reinforces, attacks again, and in desperate fighting takes New Market Heights. Meanwhile, Ord's XVIII Corps has been successful to the west, capturing Fort Harrison. Ord is wounded and U.S. Army brigadier general Hiram Barnham is killed in the attack; the Union troops rename the fort in his honor. News of the fall of Fort Harrison, meanwhile, has led Gregg to order his men to redeploy and reinforce the Confederates defending the Varina Road between Forts Harrison and Gilmer.

There can be no doubt as to the bravery of the African American troops and their devastating losses in the fighting for New Market Heights. Duncan's brigade loses 68 killed, almost 300 wounded, and 22 missing. Draper's brigade sustains 63 dead, 366 wounded, and 23 missing. And for some of the men of Draper's brigade, the day's fighting is not yet over, for Paine orders its remnants to support the attack on Fort Gilmer. The regiment suffers another 100 casualties in that unsuccessful effort. Union forces also fail to take Fort Gregg.

Although his attempt to take Richmond is a failure, Butler has the answer as to the performance of black troops. Butler's subsequent effort to secure commissions for some of the African American noncommissioned officers is denied, however. He then pushes for other recognition. Of 1,520 Medals of Honor awarded during the Civil War, 16 go to African American soldiers and 5 to African American sailors. Fourteen of these are presented for the fighting at New Market Heights.

Following the initial Union successes at New Market Heights and Fort Harrison, Lee personally accompanies 10,000 Confederates under Major General Charles Field north from Petersburg. On September 30 he orders a counterattack against Fort Barham (the former Fort Harrison), now commanded by Union major general Godfrey Weitzel, who has replaced the wounded Ord. The Union defenders repel four poorly coordinated Confederate attacks. The Union troops entrench, and the Confederates then erect a new line of works cutting off the captured forts.

In the fighting at Chaffin's Farm and New Market Heights, the Union side suffers 3,372 casualties; Confederate losses are some 2,000.

September 30–October 2, 1864

Civil War (continued): Eastern theater: Siege of Petersburg (continued): Battle of Peebles' Farm (Poplar Springs Church). At the same time that Major General Benjamin Butler's Army of the James attacks the eastern flank of Confederate general Robert E. Lee's Army of Northern Virginia (see September 29–30, 1864), Union general-in-chief Lieutenant General Ulysses S. Grant plans to attack the presumed weakened western end of the Confederate line. He will employ Major General Gouverneur K. Warren's V Corps and Brigadier General David McM. Gregg's cavalry division, supported by units of II and IX Corps. Grant hopes thereby to relieve Confederate pressure on Fort Harrison, which Butler had taken and is holding against Lee's counterattack, and to secure the key South Side Railroad, supplying Lee at Petersburg, Virginia.

Warren's attack is directed against the fortifications guarding the Boydton Plank Road, which carries supplies into Petersburg from the Confederate railhead at Stony Creek to the south and which the Confederates are working to extend to the vicinity of the Union flank at Globe Tavern. While the work is in progress, the Confederates hold a temporary line along Squirrel Level Road.

On September 30, Warren and Gregg begin moving along the Poplar Springs Road toward the Squirrel Level line in the area of Peebles' Farm and Poplar Springs Church. Grant is correct in his assumption that Lee has taken forces from this part of his line, commanded by Lieutenant General Ambrose P. Hill, for a counterattack on Fort Harrison this same day.

The Union attack begins around 1:00 p.m. near the Poplar Springs Church. Union troops quickly capture Fort Archer on the extreme Confederate flank and breach the Squirrel Level line. Warren then halts to fortify the new position and not advance too far in front of the IX Corps under Major General John G. Parke on the left. Junctures between two units in line is difficult in battle, and they fail to make effective contact. Late in the afternoon, Confederate major general Henry Heth mounts a counterattack here, routing IX Corps and forcing the surrender of one of its brigades.

Warren helps rally the remains of IX Corps, checking Heth's advance this day and another counterattack the next day, October 1. The Union troops also repel a cavalry attack led by Major General Wade Hampton. On October 2 Brigadier General Gershom Mott's division from II Corps reinforces the Union line and that same day attacks in an effort to secure the Boydton Plank Road. This results in the capture of Confederate Fort McRae, but the attack is checked before it can reach Boydton Plank Road. Union casualties in the three days of fighting here total 2,889; the Confederates lose 1,239.

September–October 1864

Civil War (continued): Western theater: Maneuvers around Atlanta. Union Western theater commander Major General William T. Sherman, having made Atlanta his chief base, finds it difficult to come to grips with Confederate forces around the city. His 400-mile-long supply line to Nashville is being harassed by Confederate cavalry under Major Generals Joseph Wheeler and Nathan B. Forrest. Sherman must also deal with a major operation by Confederate commander of the Army of Tennessee General John B. Hood.

October 2, 1864

Civil War (continued): Eastern theater: Battle of Saltville (Saltville Massacre). Union brigadier general Stephen Burbridge leads cavalry and infantry to destroy the saltworks at Saltville in far southwestern Virginia. Burbridge's force includes 400 African American troopers of the 5th U.S. Colored Cavalry and part of the 6th U.S. Colored Cavalry. The saltworks is immensely important to the Confederate military, for without salt, beef can not be preserved for army rations. Burbridge is delayed at Clinch Mountain and Laurel Gap by makeshift Confederate forces, enabling Brigadier General Alfred E. Jackson to concentrate forces near Saltville.

In the ensuing Battle of Saltville on the morning of October 2, the Confederates occupy the high ground. Although after five to six hours of fighting Union forces drive the Confederates back on Saltville, they run short of ammunition, and the Confederates, reinforced throughout the day, manage to hold, despite a valiant assault by the 5th U.S. Colored Cavalry on Chestnut Ridge. In late afternoon Burbridge withdraws, his retreat hastened by news that Confederate major general John C. Breckinridge has arrived with additional cavalry. Burbridge abandons some 350 Union dead or wounded on the battlefield. The next day vengeful Confederates, upset by the presence of the black U.S. troops and led by Confederate bushwhacker Samuel "Champ" Ferguson, scour the battlefield and kill in excess of 100 African American wounded and their white officers in one of the worst battlefield atrocities of the war. (Ferguson is arrested after the war, tried on charges of murdering 53 people, convicted, and executed in October 1865.)

The works at Saltville will be destroyed in December in the course of another Union raid (see December 10–29, 1864).

October 5, 1864

Civil War (continued): Western theater: Battle of Allatoona. In early October 1864 commander of the Confederate Army of Tennessee General John B. Hood takes the offensive. Hoping to force Union Western theater commander Major General William T. Sherman to evacuate Atlanta, Hood crosses the Chattahoochee River and marches north against the Western & Atlantic Railroad, Sherman's principal supply route. The Confederates destroy some track, with Allatoona Pass the focus of the fighting.

Sherman orders reinforcements from Rome, Georgia, via signal flag. Some 2,000 Union troops hold against a Confederate division, which then withdraws. The Union suffers 706 casualties in the battle; the Confederates lose about 800.

October 7, 1864

Civil War (continued): Capture of CSS *Florida*. On October 4 the Confederate commerce raider *Florida* (9 guns), commanded by Lieutenant Charles M. Morris, puts into Bahia, Brazil. The U.S. Navy screw sloop *Wachusett* (8 guns), commanded by Lieutenant Napoleon Collins, is in the port, and Collins soon learns the identity of the new arrival. The U.S. consul urges Collins to attack, but he is loath to violate Brazilian

neutrality. With the Confederate raider much faster than his own ship, there is little chance that Collins will be able to catch the *Florida* once it puts to sea. Collins puts it to his officers, and they overwhelmingly urge an attack.

Early on the morning of October 7, 1864, the *Wachusett* rams the *Florida*, but it does not sink. Collins then demands the Confederate ship's surrender, and with many of its crewmen ashore and its guns unloaded, Lieutenant T. K. Porter, commanding in the absence of Morris, has no choice but to comply. The *Wachusett* tows the *Florida* out of the harbor as Brazilian shore batteries open fire on the *Wachusett*, to no effect.

October 19, 1864

Civil War (continued): Trans-Mississippi West theater: Confederate invasion of Missouri (continued): Battle of Lexington. Confederate major general Sterling Price and some 13,000 men are moving slowly along the Missouri River, giving Union forces a chance to trap him, but Major General William S. Rosecrans, commanding the U.S. Department of the Missouri, is unable to communicate with Major General Samuel R. Curtis, commander of the U.S. Department of Kansas, to formalize a plan. Many of Curtis's troops are Kansas militiamen who refuse to enter Missouri, but 2,000 men under Major General James G. Blunt set out for Lexington.

The two sides do battle at Lexington. Price's men eventually drive the Union troops back through the town. Casualties are unknown. Blunt has failed to stop Price but does slow his march.

October 19, 1864

Civil War (continued): Eastern theater: Battle of Cedar Creek. Following the Battle of Fisher's Hill, U.S. major general Philip Sheridan wreaks considerable destruction in the Shenandoah Valley, largely without interference from Confederates under Lieutenant General Jubal A. Early.

On October 19, 1864, however, Early, temporarily reinforced to 18,400 men, launches a surprise predawn attack on Sheridan's 31,000-man Army of the Shenandoah bivouacked at Cedar Creek, 20 miles south of Winchester, Virginia. Sheridan is away, having departed for a strategy meeting in Washington.

During the attack some Union troops panic and withdraw, but Major General Horatio G. Wright rallies the remainder. Sheridan rushes to the battle from Winchester, arriving in midmorning and inspiring his men. In late afternoon he counterattacks and defeats Early, driving the Confederates back to New Market. The Union suffers 5,665 casualties, the Confederates only 2,900. Sheridan now has a firm grip on the valley, however. His men continue destruction of its crops and livestock, preventing vital stores from reaching General Robert E. Lee's Army of Northern Virginia, as most of Early's men return to Lee at Petersburg.

October 19, 1864

Civil War (continued): Commissioning of CSS *Shenandoah*. Off the Portuguese Madeira islands, Lieutenant James I. Waddell commissions the former English steamer *Sea King* as CSS *Shenandoah*. This commerce raider takes 38 prizes and virtually wipes out the New England whaling fleet.

October 22, 1864

Civil War (continued): Trans-Mississippi West theater: Confederate invasion of Missouri (continued): Battle of Independence. Confederate major general Sterling Price's men are moving west toward Kansas City. They pass the night of October 21 at Independence. Resuming their march westward the next morning, they encounter U.S. major general Alfred Pleasonton's cavalry division. The Union troops are driven back. The Confederates sustain 140 casualties; Union losses are unknown.

October 23, 1864

Civil War (continued): Trans-Mississippi West theater: Confederate invasion of Missouri (continued): Battle of Westport. Union troops arrive from St. Louis and Georgia to reinforce Major General James G. Blunt's forces along the Missouri-Kansas line. In the Battle of Westport in Missouri, some 7,000 Union cavalry under Major General Alfred Pleasonton, supplemented by troops from Kansas, attack and defeat the invading Confederates under

Major General Sterling Price. Each side loses about 1,500 men.

October 27, 1864

Civil War (continued): Eastern theater: Destruction of CSS *Albemarle*. The Confederate shallow-draft ironclad ram *Albemarle* (2 guns), a major factor in the April 1864 recapture of Plymouth, North Carolina, dominates the North Carolina sounds.

On the night of October 27, however, U.S. Navy lieutenant William B. Cushing and 14 other volunteers attack the *Albemarle* at its base of Plymouth in a small steam launch with a spar torpedo. His approach detected and under heavy Confederate fire, Cushing runs the steam launch over the protecting wooden boom and detonates the spar torpedo. The explosion sinks the *Albemarle* and ends the threat to Union naval domination of the sounds. Of the 15 men in the launch, only Cushing and 1 other man escape; 2 drown, and 11 are captured.

October 27–28, 1864

Civil War (continued): Eastern theater: Siege of Petersburg (continued): Battle of Boydton Plank Road. In an effort to sever communication between Petersburg and Richmond and the remainder of the Confederacy, Union general-in-chief Lieutenant General Ulysses S. Grant sends three infantry corps and one cavalry division (43,000 men in all) against Boydton Plank Road and the South Side Railroad. In the ensuing battle (also known as the Battle of Burgess Mill or First Hatcher's Run), the Confederates rebuff the attacks and force a Union withdrawal the next day. The Union side suffers 1,758 casualties; Confederate losses are some 1,300. This action concludes Union offensive operations around Petersburg for the time being, as Grant goes into winter quarters.

October 28, 1864

Civil War (continued): Trans-Mississippi West theater: Confederate invasion of Missouri (continued): Battle of Newtonia. Major General Sterling Price's Confederates are withdrawing from Missouri when they stop to rest about two miles south of Newtonia. Shortly thereafter Union major general James G.

William Barker Cushing (1842–1874)

U.S. Navy officer who led the daring attack during the American Civil War on the Confederate ironclad ram *Albemarle*. Born in Delafield, Wisconsin, on November 4, 1842, William Barker Cushing won appointment to the U.S. Naval Academy, Annapolis, on September 23, 1857. However, his failure to apply himself to his studies forced him to resign in March 1861 before graduation. When the Civil War began, Cushing was appointed a master's mate aboard the ship of the line *Minnesota*. In October he again received an appointment as a midshipman and was assigned to the North Atlantic Blockading Squadron. On July 16, 1862, he was promoted to lieutenant.

In October 1862, now commanding the armed tug *Ellis,* Cushing raided Tybee Inlet, North Carolina, to destroy a Confederate saltworks there. He then led a raid on Jacksonville, North Carolina, in which he was forced to destroy the *Ellis* in New River inlet on November 25 to prevent its capture. By now Cushing was regarded as a daring and resourceful commander. He then commanded in succession the ex-ferryboats and side-wheeler fourth-rates *Commodore Barney* and *Shokokon*. In September 1863 he took command of the screw steamer *Monticello,* and in February and June 1864 he led night missions behind Confederate lines.

On July 5, 1864, Rear Admiral Samuel P. Lee, commanding the North Atlantic Blockading Squadron, asked Cushing to lead an effort to destroy the powerful Confederate ironclad ram *Albemarle* based at Plymouth, North Carolina. Lee approved Cushing's plan for an attack by two launches fitted with spar torpedoes. Cushing then traveled to Washington, D.C., to secure final approval from Secretary of the Navy Gideon Welles.

Cushing obtained two steam launches in New York City and supervised their fitting out. One was lost in the trip south and was captured. Cushing arrived in the North Carolina Sounds with *Steam Picket Boat No. 1* on October 24. The new commander of the North Atlantic Blockading Squadron, Rear Admiral David D. Porter, approved Cushing's request that he be allowed to undertake the mission with the one launch only.

The attack on the night of October 27 was successful. While firing its boat howitzer against Confederates on shore, Cushing ran the steam launch up over a log barrier protecting the *Albemarle* and exploded the spar torpedo against the hull of the ironclad, sinking it in place. Only Cushing and another man in the attacking party escaped; 2 others drowned, and 11 were captured. For the deed, Cushing received the thanks of Congress and promotion to lieutenant commander.

Commanding the *Monticello,* Cushing participated in the successful Union assault on Fort Fisher in January 1865. He spent the last months of the war supervising the removal of Confederate mines. Cushing continued on active service with the navy after the war. Promoted to commander in 1872, the next year while in command of the screw sloop *Wyoming* he threatened to open fire on Santiago, Cuba, to prevent the killing of additional American sailors detained there from the *Virginius,* a ship that had been running arms to rebels on the island and had been captured by the Spanish. A congressional committee later vindicated Cushing for "upholding the honor of the American flag."

Assigned as executive officer of the Washington Navy Yard in August 1874, Cushing suffered a mental and physical collapse in late November and died at the Government Hospital for the Insane in

Washington, D.C., on December 17, 1874. Cushing's brother, U.S. Army first lieutenant Alonzo Cushing, was killed in the Battle of Gettysburg in July 1863, but his bravery there earned him hero status in the North and posthumous promotion to lieutenant colonel.

SPENCER C. TUCKER

Further Reading

Elliott, Robert G. *Ironclad of the Roanoke: Gilbert Elliott's Albemarle.* Shippensburg, PA: White Mane, 1999.
Schneller, Robert J., Jr. *Cushing: Civil War SEAL.* Washington, DC: Brassey's, 2004.

Blunt's division surprises the Confederates and drives them back until halted by Brigadier General Joseph O. Shelby's division, which covers the withdrawal of the other Confederates. The arrival of Union reinforcements under Brigadier General John B. Sanborn, however, convinces Shelby to retire. U.S. casualties total some 400; the Confederates sustain perhaps 250. Price retires into Arkansas, but his army is in disarray, and he has only about half of his original force of 13,000 men.

October 28–November 19, 1864

Civil War (continued): Cruise of CSS *Chickamauga.* The former blockade-runner *Edith* is converted into the Confederate Navy screw steamer *Chickamauga* (5 guns). Commanded by Lieutenant John Wilkinson, it slips out of Wilmington, North Carolina. Three weeks later it returns to Wilmington at night, having taken seven Union prizes (burning four and boarding three).

October 29–November 1, 1864

Civil War (continued): Union recapture of Plymouth, North Carolina. Capitalizing on the destruction of the Confederate ironclad *Albemarle,* Commander William H. Macomb leads six Union warships in the recapture of Plymouth, again closing the North Carolina sounds to the Confederacy. Macomb takes 37 prisoners, 22 cannon, 200 stands of arms, supplies, and the sunken *Albemarle.*

October 29–November 7, 1864

Civil War (continued): Cruise of CSS *Olustee.* The former Confederate raider *Tallahassee,* renamed the *Olustee* (5 guns) and commanded by Lieutenant William H. Ward, sails from Wilmington, North Carolina, and passes through the Union blockaders. Although detected and damaged in an exchange of fire, the *Olustee* continues on its cruise and takes six prizes before it slips back past the Union blockaders at night.

November 4, 1864

Civil War (continued): Western theater: Confederate attack on Johnsonville. Major General Nathan Bedford Forrest leads a raid on the major Union supply depot at Johnsonville, Tennessee, on the Tennessee River, destroying much of it and also causing destruction there of the U.S. Navy stern-wheel steamer *Key West* (9 guns) and tinclads *Tawah* (10 guns) and *Elfin* (8 guns).

November 8, 1864

Lincoln reelected. U.S. President Abraham Lincoln is reelected, with running mate Andrew Johnson, a Democrat senator from Tennessee. They defeat a Democrat ticket headed by former Union major General George B. McClellan by a comfortable margin.

November 15–December 21, 1864

Civil War (continued): Western theater: Sherman's March to the Sea. Frustrated by his inability to close with and defeat General John B. Hood's Confederate Army of Tennessee, Union Western theater commander Major General William T. Sherman receives permission from general-in-chief Lieutenant General Ulysses S. Grant to abandon Atlanta. Sherman orders

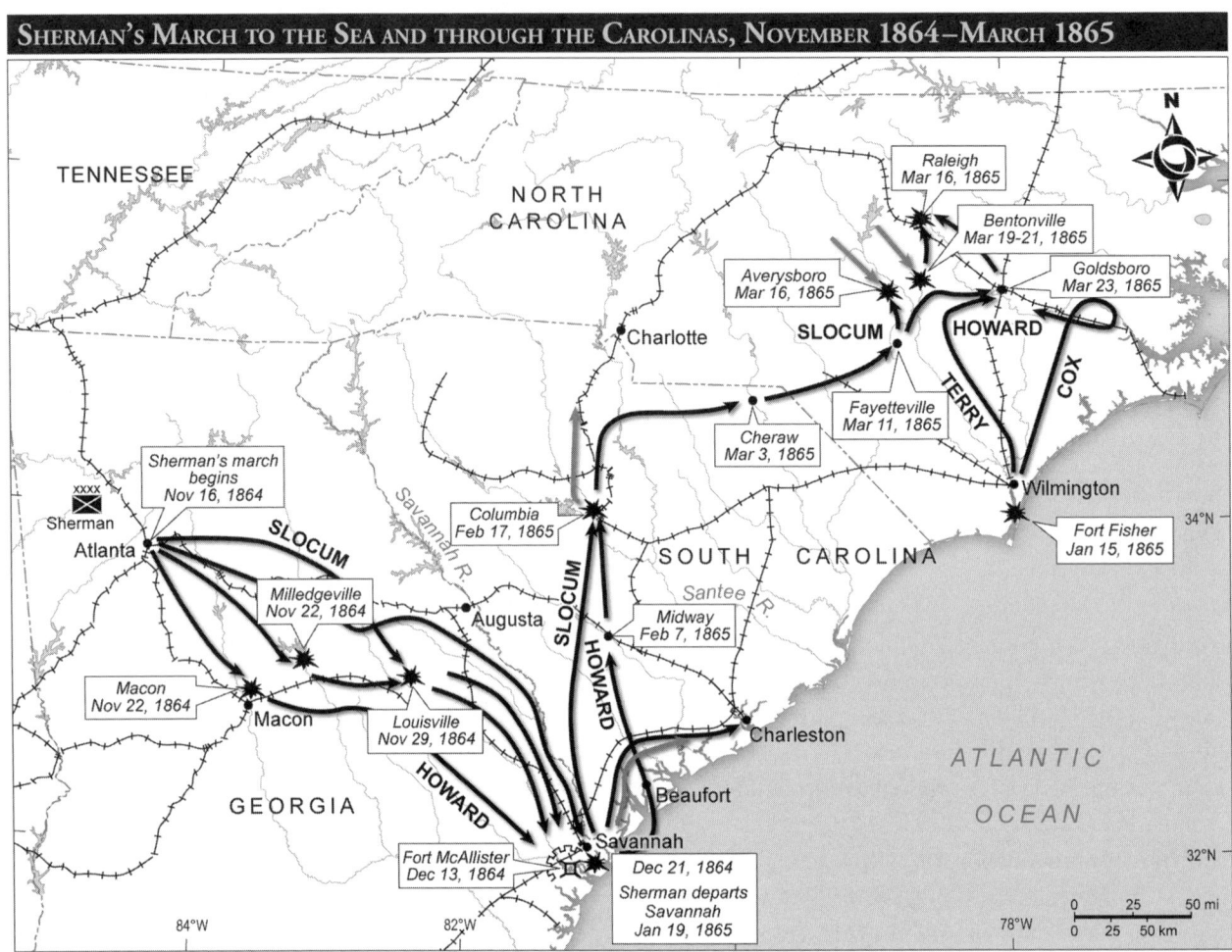

SHERMAN'S MARCH TO THE SEA AND THROUGH THE CAROLINAS, NOVEMBER 1864–MARCH 1865

Major General George H. Thomas's Army of the Cumberland and Major General John M. Schofield's Army of the Ohio to restrain Hood and defend Tennessee. Sherman then destroys any confiscated supplies in Atlanta that might be of use to the Confederates and evacuates the city, striking east on November 15 with 62,000 men in his March to the Sea.

Sherman organizes his army into two wings, the first under Major General Oliver O. Howard with XV and XVII Corps, Army of the Tennessee, and the second under Major General Henry W. Slocum with XIV and XX Corps, formerly of the Army of the Cumberland now re-designated the Army of Georgia. Sherman cuts a wide swath of destruction some 300 miles in length and 60 miles in width. Union troops systematically destroy factories, some public buildings, warehouses, bridges, and rail lines. The troops tear up and twist the

track, making so-called Sherman neckties, that the South cannot replace. The Union troops are encouraged to forage liberally on the countryside, and there is some looting and wanton destruction. Sherman contends that the destruction will bring the war to an end faster and that it is better than loss in lives.

The Confederates have only a maximum of 13,000 men to contest the march, and the Union advance is largely unopposed. Sherman's men reach the outskirts of Savannah on December 10, take Fort McAllister guarding access to the Savannah River on December 13, and occupy the city of Savannah on December 21.

November 25, 1864
American Indian Wars: First Battle of Adobe Walls. The Adobe Walls trading post was established in 1843 near the Canadian River in the Texas Panhandle in

what is today Hutchinson County, Texas. Originally built of logs, it becomes Fort Adobe when it is converted into a rectangular structure 80-feet on a side with 9-foot-high adobe walls. By 1864, however, it is in ruins, with only the walls remaining.

In early November 1864 U.S. Army colonel Christopher "Kit" Carson departs Fort Bascom, New Mexico, to reestablish control of the Santa Fe Trail, which has been subjected to repeated attacks by Comanches, Kiowas, and Kiowa-Apaches, threatening the lines of communication and supply between New Mexico and the East. Carson commands 300 California and New Mexico volunteers, accompanied by some 70 allied Ute and Apache Native Americans.

On the morning of November 25, Carson's advance force of mostly cavalry supported by two 12-pounder mountain howitzers attacks a Kiowa village of some 150 lodges near old Fort Adobe, routing the Native Americans. Carson's men then encounter a large native force of 3,000–7,000 Kiowa, Comanche, and Kiowa-Apache warriors operating from nearby villages, the presence of which had been unknown to Carson. Carson seeks refuge in the ruins of Fort Adobe, repulsing a series of determined attacks led by Kiowa chief Dohasan. The defenders beat these back largely because of fire from their two howitzers.

After turning back the last Native American assault, Carson's men burn the nearby Kiowa village and destroy its stocks of winter foodstuffs and other supplies. Concern for his trailing infantry and lengthy supply train, however, prompts him to withdraw. Carson suffers 2 dead and 10 wounded. Native American casualties are estimated at 50–150 killed or wounded.

Although this First Battle of Adobe Walls ends in a victory, Carson has failed to achieve his overall objective, for the Santa Fe Trail remains subject to Native American attacks.

November 29, 1864

American Indian Wars: Cheyenne-Arapaho War (continued): Sand Creek Massacre. In June 1864 during the Cheyenne-Arapaho War, Colorado Territory governor John Evans issues a proclamation inviting all "friendly Indians" to certain designated forts, where they are to be fed and allowed to camp under military protection. Those who fail to comply will be considered hostile and subject to punitive raids. With most regular troops away fighting the Confederates, Evans calls for civilians to join the new 3rd Colorado Cavalry Regiment for 100 days to carry out his plan, stressing that "any man who kills a hostile Indian is a patriot." Colonel John M. Chivington, a Methodist minister turned soldier and politician who had taken part in the defeat of Confederate forces in the Battle of Glorieta Pass in New Mexico in 1862, commands the 3rd Colorado Cavalry.

Cheyenne leader Black Kettle and six other chiefs decide to accept Evans's invitation and travel with Major Edward Wynkoop, commander of Fort Lyon, to Denver to meet with Evans and Chivington. At Camp Weld on September 28, the Native Americans are told to submit to military authority at Fort Lyon in southeastern Colorado. Black Kettle believes that he has secured peace and security for his own band and others. Unbeknownst to them, however, Chivington receives an order that same day from Major General Samuel R. Curtis, commanding officer of the Department of Kansas, instructing him not to make peace.

On November 4, Major Wynkoop is replaced in command of Fort Lyon by Major Scott Anthony, who orders the Indians away from the fort and instructs them to camp along Sand Creek. Chivington, meanwhile, moves his regiment of nearly 600 men down the Arkansas River toward Fort Lyon, arriving there

Sand Creek Massacre		
Date	November 29, 1864	
Location	Sand Creek, Kiowa County, Colorado	
Opponents (*winner)	*United States	Cheyennes and Arapahos
Commander	Colonel John M. Chivington	Chief Black Kettle
#	725 men, 4 mountain howitzers	450 Cheyennes; 40 Arapahos (men, women, and children)
Casualties	9 killed, 38 wounded	148 killed (60 men and the remainder women and children)

on November 28. The enlistment of his 100-day volunteers is about to expire, and many of them are disappointed at not having experienced battle. Chivington has also been criticized in the press for his inactivity. Accompanied by 125 soldiers under Major Anthony and with four mountain howitzers, the volunteers head for Black Kettle's camp that same evening. They cover the 40 miles to the village that night.

Black Kettle's camp contains some 450 Southern Cheyennes and 40 Arapahos. Most of the Indians are still asleep when the volunteers attack at dawn on November 29. As the soldiers and Colorado volunteers attack from all directions, the mountain howitzers on the south bank of the creek fire grapeshot into the fleeing Native Americans. Black Kettle tries unsuccessfully to halt the slaughter by tying an American flag he had received in Denver and a white flag of truce to a lodge pole but has no choice but to try to escape.

Chivington's men chase the remaining Indians up Sand Creek, killing as many as they can find. Black Kettle is among those who manage to escape. Returning to the village, the Colorado volunteers then kill all the remaining Native Americans wounded and mutilate their bodies. On December 1 the remains of the village and its inhabitants are put to the torch, and the Colorado volunteers depart. Chivington's casualties at Sand Creek are 9 killed and 38 wounded. Cheyenne and Arapaho dead number 148, only 60 of them men.

Although Chivington and his volunteers are initially praised for their actions, soon stories about what really had occurred at Sand Creek convince the U.S. Congress to order a formal investigation. No one is ever formally punished for the massacre, however.

November 30, 1864

Civil War (continued): Western theater: Battle of Franklin, Tennessee. On November 21, 1864, a week after Union General William T. Sherman's departure from Atlanta, Confederate general John B. Hood leads 31,000 infantry and 8,000 cavalry on Nashville. Hood hopes that by threatening Sherman's lines of communication, he can force Sherman to break off his offensive and return to Tennessee. The operation is delayed, however, by the absence of cavalry under Major General Nathan Bedford Forrest, giving Major General George H. Thomas, commanding Union forces in middle Tennessee, time to strengthen the Nashville defenses.

Union major general John M. Schofield, with some 28,000 men of the IV and XIII Corps, marches toward Nashville. He escapes a Confederate trap at Columbia on November 26–27 and a night battle at Spring Hill on November 29, arriving at Franklin early on November 30. There his tired men establish a defensive position.

Hood arrives in early afternoon. Hoping to destroy Schofield before he can unite his forces with Thomas's Army of the Cumberland at Nashville, Hood orders a frontal assault of the Union line across two miles of open ground. He claims that a head-on attack builds character, but the results are devastating for the Confederates. Fighting continues until that night, when Schofield orders a hurried withdrawal. The next morning Schofield's exhausted men reach Nashville. Hood's stupid assault of the entrenched Union positions has virtually destroyed the Army of Tennessee, costing it 6,200 casualties and the Union side only 2,326.

December 9–21, 1864

Civil War (continued): Eastern theater: Union siege of Savannah. Union Western theater commander Major General William T. Sherman's 62,000-man army group reaches its objective of Savannah, Georgia, nearly 300 miles from Atlanta, on December 9. Union troops close around the city, held by 10,000 Confederates commanded by Lieutenant General William J. Hardee. On December 13 Union forces capture Fort McAllister on the Ogeechee River, south of the city, allowing the navy to provide Sherman with supplies and siege guns. With the outcome now certain, Hardee saves his army by constructing a pontoon bridge across the Savannah River and passing his men over it on the night of December 20. The next day Union troops occupy Savannah, and Sherman presents the city as a "Christmas gift" to President Abraham Lincoln.

December 10–29, 1864

Civil War (continued): Eastern theater: Stoneman's Southwestern Virginia Raid. After the October 1864 defeat of a Union force under Brigadier General Stephen G. Burbridge at Saltville in southwestern Virginia, Major General George Stoneman leads a force from eastern Tennessee in a second attempt to destroy this important Confederate saltworks. Stoneman departs Knoxville on December 10 with some 4,200 cavalry and horse artillery under Burbridge and a brigade of 1,500 Tennessee horsemen commanded by Brigadier General Alvan C. Gillem.

At Kingsport, Tennessee, on December 13, the Union raiders defeat an understrength Confederate cavalry brigade commanded by Brigadier General Basil W. Duke. The next day near Bristol, Stoneman defeats another Confederate cavalry unit under Brigadier General John C. Vaughan, preventing it from linking up with the rest of the Confederate forces under Major General John C. Breckinridge at Saltville and securing some 300 prisoners. Stoneman occupies Bristol and then Abington, Virginia, on December 15, where he burns a number of buildings. He then bypasses Saltville to move against lead mines at Wytheville. In an effort to stop him, Breckinridge moves from Saltville to Marion, and on December 17–18 at Marion, the Confederates hold their own against vastly superior Union numbers before withdrawing that evening southward toward North Carolina. Stoneman then destroys the lead works and mines.

On December 20 the Union soldiers enter Saltville, now defended only by local militia and teamsters. The Union cavalrymen destroy the works and a considerable quantity of salt. They depart on December 22 and return to Knoxville on December 29. For only minimal losses of his own, Stoneman captures almost 900 Confederates, 19 guns, 3,000 muskets, and some 3,000 horses and mules. He has also destroyed bridges, factories, and ironworks.

December 15–16, 1864

Civil War (continued): Western theater: Battle of Nashville. U.S. major general John M. Schofield, having delayed Confederate general John B. Hood's Army of Tennessee, joins his forces (the IV and XIII Corps) with Major General George H. Thomas's conglomerate command at Nashville. Hood arrives there on December 2. Thomas rejects calls from Washington to attack Hood with his far larger army and instead busies himself accumulating supplies and cavalry horses. Finally ready, on December 15 Thomas strikes Hood's left flank, which is exposed because Hood has sent Major General Nathan B. Forrest's cavalry to Murfreesboro.

On December 16 Thomas completes the envelopment of both of Hood's flanks. Union losses total 3,061 of nearly 50,000 men engaged, while the Confederates lose 4,350 of 31,000 engaged as well as 150 guns. The battle completes the destruction of the Army of Tennessee as a fighting unit.

Citizens of Savannah, Georgia, evacuate the city on December 21, 1864, as Union troops move in. The Union capture of Savannah marked the end of Major General William T. Sherman's March to the Sea. (Library of Congress)

December 23, 1864

Civil War (continued). U.S. Navy rear admiral David G. Farragut becomes the first American naval officer promoted to the newly established rank of vice admiral, equivalent to army lieutenant general.

December 24–25, 1864

Civil War (continued): Eastern theater: First Union assault on Fort Fisher. The destruction of the Confederate ram *Albemarle* facilitates Union plans to move against Wilmington, North Carolina, the last remaining major Confederate port for blockade-runners and principal overseas supply link for the Army of Northern Virginia. In December 1864 North Atlantic Blockading Squadron commander Rear Admiral David D. Porter assembles the most powerful naval force to this point in U.S. history: 61 warships, including 5 ironclads, mounting 635 guns. The army provides two divisions of 6,500 men under Major General Benjamin Butler.

Before they can proceed against Wilmington, the Union forces must take or destroy Fort Fisher, a powerful earthen works on a narrow spit of land at the entrance to the Cape Fear River. Colonel William Lamb and 1,900 men defend Fisher with 45 heavy guns and numerous smaller pieces.

The Union attempt to blow up a ship under Fisher's walls to damage the fort fails. The *Louisiana,* filled with 150 tons of powder, explodes as planned at about 1:00 a.m. on December 24 but too far from the fort to effect damage. At about noon Porter opens a heavy bombardment, silencing Fisher's guns.

On December 25 Porter resumes the bombardment, while 17 of his smaller warships cover the unopposed landing of 2,000 of Butler's troops. Late that afternoon some of Butler's men, protected by naval gunfire, work their way to within several hundred yards of the fort from the north. They report that it is virtually undamaged. Following a brief demonstration but without attempting an assault or consulting with Porter, on December 27 Butler embarks his men and sails back to Fort Monroe.

1864–1868

American Indian Wars (continued): Snake War. During 1864–1868 a series of small clashes occur between Native Americans and white settlers in California, Nevada, Oregon, Utah, and Idaho. This conflict waged by the Northern Paiutes and Shoshones—called Snakes by early French explorers—is precipitated by the steady influx of white settlers into these regions.

The opening of new gold mines in Idaho leads to even more settlers, and in 1864 open warfare erupts, pitting white settlers, volunteer militias, and the army against various Native American bands in southwestern Idaho, northern California, northern Nevada, Utah, and eastern Oregon. Among tribal leaders waging war against the whites and the U.S. military are Chief Egan of the Paiutes in Owyhee Canyon and Nevada; Howluck, one of the principal chiefs of the Shoshones in Oregon; and Wewawewa, the principal Shoshone leader in southern Idaho.

The war is a series of skirmishes, best characterized as guerrilla warfare. Most of the actions are directly attributable to volunteer militia led by inexperienced and overly enthusiastic junior officers, along with groups of armed citizens. The majority of the troops deployed during the initial stages of the Snake War are volunteer regiments from California and the surrounding states, but the conclusion of the Civil War in 1865 brings a return of regular army units to the West.

In 1866 after a plea by the governor of Idaho to halt the Native American attacks, Lieutenant Colonel George Crook, commanding the 23rd Infantry Regiment, is dispatched to Fort Boise. He arrives on December 11 and initiates a relentless campaign. He gives his foe no time to rest, regroup, or accumulate supplies, carrying out operations in the winter and establishing temporary posts at strategic locations within hostile territory.

In May 1868 the Indian Peace Commission dispatches Brigadier General C. C. Augur to Fort Bridger, Wyoming, to negotiate with the warring tribes. Crook, meanwhile, continues action against them. That same month Chief Egan and his Paiutes are taken prisoner, while in June Howluck and 60 of his people are captured in eastern Oregon. These actions prompt Shoshone leader Wewawewa to sue for peace and surrender to Crook at Fort Harney, Idaho, on July 1, 1868, bringing the Snake War to an end. The war is costly in terms of casualties, with some

1,750 whites and Native Americans killed, wounded, or captured.

January 1, 1865

Civil War (continued). The screw frigate *San Jacinto* (12 guns), commanded by Captain Richard W. Meade, wrecks on a reef at Green Turtle Cay, Abaco, in the Bahamas. All hands are saved, and Meade is able to salvage much of the ship.

January 8, 1865

American Indian Wars (continued): Battle of Dove Creek. A number of Kickapoo Indians are on their way to Mexico to escape being preyed upon by both sides in the Civil War and there join other members of the tribe. On this date some 160 Confederates and 325 Texas militiamen commanded by Captains Henry Fossett, N. M. Gillintine (Gillentine), and S. S. Totten (Totton) attack the Kickapoo encampment, which has an estimated 400 warriors, in a thicket some 20 miles southwest of present-day San Angelo, Texas. The Texans assume the Indians to be either hostile Comanches or Kiowas.

Following a sharp combat, the Texans are routed, suffering at least 22 dead and 19 wounded. Fossett reports 23 Indians killed, but the latter, who cross the Rio Grande near Eagle Pass, claim only 12 killed and 2 wounded, who die after their arrival in Mexico.

January 11, 1865

Civil War (continued): Eastern theater: Battle of Beverly. In bitter cold weather, Confederate major general Thomas L. Rosser leads some 300 men 80 miles from McDowell, Virginia, west across the mountains in a daring attack on some 1,100 men of the 8th and 34th Ohio Regiments under Colonel Robert Youart at Beverly, West Virginia. The fight is brief—barely half an hour—and ends in a complete Confederate victory. Rosser takes 587 prisoners, including Youart, as well as 600 rifles, 100 horses, and a considerable quantity of rations. The remaining Union troops escape to Buckhannon.

January 13–15, 1865

Civil War (continued): Eastern theater: Second Union assault on Fort Fisher. North Atlantic Blockading Squadron commander Rear Admiral David D. Porter is furious at Major General Benjamin Butler's unilateral withdrawal and the end of the first expedition against Fort Fisher, North Carolina, and demands Butler's removal from command. U.S. Army general-in-chief Lieutenant General Ulysses S. Grant complies and on January 3, 1865, appoints Brigadier General Alfred H. Terry to replace Butler.

Porter keeps his ships in the Wilmington-Beaufort area and periodically shells Fisher to stymie any Confederate rebuilding while he awaits the arrival of Terry. The second Union assault on Fort Fisher is a textbook operation. Porter commands 59 warships, while Terry has 8,000 troops.

Terry lands north of the fort on January 13, 1865. He deploys some of his men to build a strong defensive line across the upper neck of the peninsula to keep some 6,000 Confederates under General Braxton Bragg and Major General Robert F. Hoke at bay in the Wilmington area.

On January 14 Porter's ships again bombard the fort's eastern (seaward) side. This time Porter assigns each bombardment ship a specific target. The shelling inflicts some 300 casualties and is far more effective than previous efforts.

At noon on January 15 under cover of Union shelling, Porter puts ashore some 400 marines and 1,600 sailors for a simultaneous assault against the fort's northern sea face. Their assault fails, but it diverts Confederate attention from the main attack, which is delayed. Supported by naval gunfire, three Union brigades push through the palisade and up the parapet on the land face. The fighting is intense and the outcome in doubt until early evening, when Terry commits his reserve brigade. At about 9:00 p.m. on January 15 the Confederates surrender. The attackers suffer some 1,000 casualties, the defenders half that number.

Fort Fisher is the most heavily fortified position taken by amphibious assault during the war. Union forces go on to capture all surrounding works, with 139 guns. They then advance up the Cape Fear River. Wilmington surrenders on February 12. The Army of Northern Virginia is starved of essential supplies.

 ## Alfred Howe Terry (1827–1890)

U.S. Army officer. Alfred Howe Terry was born into a wealthy family in Hartford, Connecticut, on November 10, 1827. After briefly attending Yale University Law School during 1848–1849, he served as a law clerk for the New Haven County Superior Court from 1854 until the outbreak of the American Civil War in 1861.

Terry raised a volunteer regiment in Connecticut and was commissioned its colonel. The regiment saw action in the First Battle of Bull Run (Manassas) in Virginia (July 21, 1861). Terry subsequently recruited and led another Connecticut volunteer regiment, helping to secure Port Royal, South Carolina, for the Union on November 7, 1861. On April 11, 1862, Terry's regiment helped to capture Fort Pulaski, at the mouth of the strategic Savannah River.

On April 26, Terry was promoted to brigadier general of volunteers. He then commanded a division of X Corps and took part in operations against Charleston, including the capture of Fort Wagner in September 1863. In 1864, X Corps was assigned to Major General Benjamin Butler's Army of the James in Virginia, and Terry saw extensive action in the Bermuda Hundred Campaign. On the death of Major General David B. Birney in October, Terry briefly commanded X Corps before it was disbanded.

Terry's greatest recognition during the Civil War came when he received command of a provisional corps, later X Corps, for an attack on Fort Fisher. He and Rear Admiral David D. Porter worked well together, and Fort Fisher fell to Union forces on January 15, 1865. His success won him an official thanks from the U.S. Congress, a brigadier general's commission in the regular army, and a major general's commission in the volunteer army. Terry's promotion to brigadier general in the regular army was a rare accomplishment for someone who had not graduated from the U.S. Military Academy. He ended the war in the Carolinas, where he was part of Major General John M. Schofield's Army of the Ohio, which was operating under Major General William T. Sherman.

After the Civil War, Terry commanded the Department of Dakota from 1866 to 1868 and again from 1873 to 1886. He was a key architect of the 1867 Medicine Lodge Treaty that temporarily ended the fighting with the Southern Plains Kiowa, Apache, and Cheyenne, and Arapaho tribes. Terry also took part in the 1868 Treaty of Fort Laramie negotiations, which helped to end the fighting in the northern Plains known as Red Cloud's War (1866–1868).

In 1873 Terry returned to command the Department of Dakota and participated in the Sioux War (Black Hills War) of 1876–1877. He commanded one of the three converging columns designed to locate and destroy the hostile Native Americans. This led to the disastrous Battle of the Little Bighorn on June 25, 1876, in which the 7th Cavalry Regiment, commanded by Lieutenant Colonel George A. Custer, spearheading Terry's column, attacked without waiting for the supporting columns and suffered a devastating defeat, including the annihilation of Custer and the men with him. Afterward Terry refused to say anything that might tarnish Custer's reputation.

In October 1877, Terry went to Canada to negotiate the surrender of the Sioux leader Sitting Bull. These talks were not successful, but in 1881 Terry was the man to whom Sitting Bull surrendered. Still commander of the Department of Dakota during the Nez Perce War of 1877, Terry sent troops to help intercept Chief Joseph and his people. In 1878 Terry joined Major General John Schofield and Colonel

George W. Getty on the so-called Schofield Commission, a board charged with reexamining the Civil War court-martial of Major General Fitz John Porter.

In 1886 Terry was promoted to major general, one of only three men to hold that rank in the army at the time. He was also the first Civil War volunteer officer to attain that rank in the regular army. Terry received command of the Division of the Missouri, with headquarters in Chicago. He retired from the army in 1888 and died on December 16, 1890, in New Haven, Connecticut.

ALAN K. LAMM

Further Reading

Bailey, John W. *Pacifying the Plains: General Alfred Terry and the Decline of the Sioux, 1866–1890.* Westport, CT: Greenwood, 1979.

Hutton, Paul Andrew. *Phil Sheridan and His Army.* Lincoln: University of Nebraska Press, 1985.

Utley, Robert M. *Custer: Cavalier in Buckskin.* Norman: University of Oklahoma Press, 2001.

Warner, Ezra J. *Generals in Blue: Lives of the Union Commanders.* Baton Rouge: Louisiana State University Press, 1964.

January 15, 1865

Civil War (continued): Eastern theater: Loss of the *Patapsco*. The U.S. monitor *Patapsco* (2 guns), commanded by Lieutenant Commander Stephen P. Quackenbush, strikes a torpedo (mine) near the entrance to the lower harbor at Charleston and sinks immediately with the loss of 64 men, more than half of its crew. It is the fourth monitor lost in the war, two of which have been lost to mines. Thereafter only small boats and tugs are used to search for obstructions.

January 16, 1865

Civil War (continued). With Southern hopes for victory now all but gone and confidence in President Jefferson Davis fast fading, the Confederate Congress passes a resolution calling for General Robert E. Lee to be appointed general-in-chief and General Joseph E. Johnston to be restored to his former position as commander of the Confederate Army of Tennessee.

January 23–24, 1865

Civil War (continued): Eastern theater: Battle of Trent's Reach. The Confederate James River Squadron under Flag Officer John K. Mitchell attempts to move down the James River to attack General Ulysses S. Grant's supply hub of City Point, Virginia. The attack ends when the Confederate ironclads *Virginia II* (4 guns) and *Richmond* (4 guns) ground. The ships are at last floated free and escape back upriver, but the small gunboat *Drewry* (2 guns) blows up when a mortar shell from a Union shore battery explodes its magazine, and the torpedo boat *Scorpion* (1 spar torpedo) is captured.

January 24, 1865

Civil War (continued). U.S. Army general-in-chief Lieutenant General Ulysses S. Grant reverses himself and permits renewal of prisoner exchanges on the assumption that this will create hardship for the Confederate forces suffering from serious food shortages.

February 3, 1865

Civil War (continued): Hampton Roads Peace Conference. U.S. president Abraham Lincoln meets with Confederate commissioners led by Vice President Alexander H. Stephens to discuss peace. It is the first meeting with Southern leaders to which Lincoln has agreed since the start of the war. The talks are held in Hampton Roads, Virginia, on board the Union transport *River Queen*. Northern demands include an end to secession and the emancipation of slaves.

Lincoln offers in return a complete amnesty, but the Southern leaders will only accept independence, and the talks fail.

February 3, 1865

Civil War (continued): Lee named Confederate Army general-in-chief. Although it is far too late to have any significant military impact, Confederate president Jefferson Davis yields command of the army to General Robert E. Lee as general-in-chief. Lee immediately names General Joseph E. Johnston to command Southern forces in the Carolinas against Union forces under Major General William T. Sherman. Johnston takes over previously separated forces under Generals Braxton Bragg and Pierre G. T. Beauregard and Lieutenant General William J. Hardee.

February 5–7, 1865

Civil War (continued): Eastern theater: Siege of Petersburg (continued): Battle of Hatcher's Run. At Petersburg, Virginia, Union general-in-chief Lieutenant General Ulysses S. Grant maintains pressure on Confederate forces under general-in-chief General Robert E. Lee. In the Army of the Potomac and the Army of the James, Grant has some 90,000 well-supplied troops in the Petersburg-Richmond area, while Lee can muster only about 60,000 poorly fed and supplied soldiers defending 37 miles of entrenchments. Lee's Army of Northern Virginia can still fight effectively, however, as demonstrated in the Battle of Hatcher's Run (also known by the names of Dabney's Mill, Rowanty Creek, Armstrong's Mill, and Vaughan Road).

Grant orders that Union lines be extended to the south and west against the Boydton Plank Road, committing 34,500 troops to the operation, but some 14,000 Confederates under Lieutenant General Ambrose P. Hill and Major General John B. Gordon stop the Union effort. Although Union forces gain some ground, they abandon a tentative hold on Boydton Plank Road. Lee, however, has been forced to extend his already thin lines farther to his right. The operation costs Grant 1,512 casualties; Confederate losses number perhaps 1,200.

February 17, 1865

Civil War (continued): Eastern theater: Burning of Columbia. Union forces occupy the South Carolina capital of Columbia. That same night the city is engulfed in flames, and perhaps one-third of it is destroyed. Much of the destruction can be attributed to the chaos surrounding the Confederate evacuation, the availability of large stocks of liquor, and windy conditions. Confederates setting fire to cotton bales stacked in the streets are partly to blame, for sparks from this spawn fires elsewhere. Although the destruction of Columbia remains controversial, it is clear that Union major general William T. Sherman did not set out to destroy the city.

February 17–18, 1865

Civil War (continued): Confederate forces depart Charleston. On February 17, 1865, the same day that Confederate forces under Lieutenant General William J. Hardee abandon Charleston, South Carolina, ships of the U.S. Navy's South Atlantic Blockading Squadron land troops at Bull's Bay, and Major General William T. Sherman's powerful army group approaches from the west. Union forces under Brigadier General Alexander Schimmelfenning enter the city the next day, bringing to a close the long Union naval blockade of the city. Union forces capture some 250 heavy guns.

February 22, 1865

Civil War (continued): Union occupation of Wilmington. Union general-in-chief Lieutenant General Ulysses S. Grant dispatches troops under Major General John M. Schofield against Confederate forces commanded by General Braxton Bragg near Wilmington, North Carolina. Schofield forces Bragg to abandon that city and moves into central North Carolina.

February 25, 1865

Civil War (continued): Eastern theater. General Joseph E. Johnston arrives at Charlotte, North Carolina, and assumes command of the remnants of the Confederate Army of Tennessee and elements from several other commands, reduced to only 25,000 men and short of both supplies and equipment.

March 2, 1865

Civil War (continued): Eastern theater: Battle of Waynesboro. On March 2, 1865, at Waynesboro, Virginia, about 12 miles east of Staunton, Brigadier General George A. Custer's cavalry, part of Major General Philip H. Sheridan's Army of the Shenandoah, attacks and destroys the remnants of Confederate lieutenant general Jubal A. Early's Valley command of some 1,700 men.

Both sides suffer fewer than 100 killed or wounded, although the Union troopers also take 1,500 prisoners, 11–14 guns, and several hundred wagons. Early and some of his staff manage to escape. The battle brings to a close organized Confederate resistance in the valley and marks the end of Sheridan's Shenandoah Valley Campaign, which began on August 7, 1864.

With the Shenandoah Valley secured for the Union, Sheridan continues south to take Lynchburg, then ravages the area north of the James River, closing this vital supply artery to Confederate general-in-chief General Robert E. Lee's forces at Petersburg. Sheridan then rides east to join Union general-in-chief Lieutenant General Ulysses S. Grant at Petersburg for what will be the Appomattox Campaign.

March 7–10, 1865

Civil War (continued): Eastern theater: Battle of Wyse Fork (Second Battle of Kinston). Commander of the Union Army of the Ohio Major General John M. Schofield moves north from Wilmington, North Carolina, with Brigadier General Alfred H. Terry's Expeditionary Corps, while Major General Jacob D. Cox's XXIII Corps proceeds by sea and lands at New Bern, North Carolina. Reinforced at New Bern to three divisions, Cox then moves inland toward Goldsboro, repairing the railroad that will supply Major General William T. Sherman's army group in its movement north.

George Armstrong Custer (1839–1876)

U.S. Army officer. George Armstrong Custer was born on December 5, 1839, in New Rumley, Ohio, although he spent part of his childhood in Monroe, Michigan. At age 16 he was admitted to the U.S. Military Academy, West Point, and performed just well enough to graduate last in his class in 1861.

Despite his mediocre record as a student, Custer excelled during the American Civil War. Shortly after graduation he fought in the First Battle of Bull Run (Manassas) (July 21, 1861). His daring reconnaissance patrols and valor brought him to the attention of Union Army general-in-chief Major General George B. McClellan. As a captain and staff officer for McClellan and Major General Alfred Pleasonton, Custer demonstrated his potential to such an extent that he was promoted to brigadier general on June 29, 1863, and given command of the 2nd Brigade of the 3rd Cavalry Division at age 23.

With a flamboyant uniform that Custer himself designed and with his long flowing reddish hair, he became a national hero. From the Battle of Gettysburg (July 1–3, 1863) through the end of the war, he was renowned for his fearless and often decisive cavalry charges. In October 1864 he took charge of the entire 3rd Cavalry Division and became a close confidant of Major General Philip Sheridan during the Shenandoah Valley Campaign (August 7, 1864–March 2, 1865). Custer also led his men in the Third Battle of Winchester (September 19, 1864) and at Fisher's Hill (September 22, 1864) and Five Forks (April 1, 1865), among other battles. By the end of the war, he had been promoted to major general and was considered one of the most brilliant cavalry officers in the army.

(continued)

(Continued)

Following the war, Custer returned to the regular army with the permanent rank of lieutenant colonel and was assigned to the 7th Cavalry Regiment. Because his commanding officer was frequently absent, Custer was for all intents and purposes in command and quickly made a name for himself on the Great Plains. Dressed in fringed buckskin instead of a traditional uniform, he was the embodiment of the dashing Indian fighter. His best-selling book *My Life on the Plains* (1874) and several popular magazine articles helped to reinforce his reputation as a military genius. Yet the Custer myth did not always square with reality.

Indeed, Custer's first experience fighting Native Americans in 1867 ended in humiliating failure during a campaign against the Cheyennes. Not only did he fail to defeat any Indians, but he was court-martialed and sentenced to a year's suspension from rank and pay for being absent without leave. He rebounded from this setback in 1868 when he surprised Chief Black Kettle's Cheyenne village in a brutal and strategically questionable attack at the Battle of the Washita (November 27, 1868) that burnished Custer's public reputation.

In 1874 Custer and the 7th Cavalry escorted a large exploratory expedition that located gold in the Black Hills of the Dakota Territory. When its subsequent effort to buy the Black Hills from the Sioux failed, the government essentially appropriated the land and attempted to confine the Sioux and Northern Cheyennes to significantly reduced reservations. But in the spring of 1876 thousands of Sioux and Cheyennes departed for hunting grounds in the Powder River and Yellowstone River Valleys, which gave U.S. officials the justification to send in the military in the Sioux War of 1876–1877. The 7th Cavalry spearheaded Brigadier General Alfred Terry's column, part of a large three-pronged campaign to subdue the Indians.

On June 25, 1876, Custer's scouts located a massive Indian village on the Little Bighorn River in southwestern Montana. Perceiving an opportunity, Custer divided his 7th Cavalry into three battalions and, without waiting for the commands of Terry and Colonel John Gibbon to arrive, rashly attacked the village of Sioux leaders Sitting Bull and Crazy Horse. Sending a battalion under Major Marcus Reno to strike the village directly, Custer led his battalion of some 225 men in an effort to outflank the Sioux. Reno's force was quickly repulsed with heavy losses but managed to retreat to a ridge, where survivors were joined by the third battalion, that of Captain Frederick Benteen, and held out until the Indians withdrew.

Custer was outnumbered 10 to 1 and was surrounded. In one of the most famous and controversial engagements in American history, the Sioux slaughtered Custer and all of his men. Among the dead in the battle were Custer's brothers Boston and Thomas. Custer's Last Stand stunned Americans and attached to Custer an immortality that he probably did not deserve but that fit with his reputation and public persona.

ANDY JOHNS

Further Reading

Ambrose, Stephen E. *Crazy Horse and Custer: The Parallel Lives of Two American Warriors*. New York: Doubleday, 1975.

Monaghan, Jay. *Custer: The Life of General George Armstrong Custer*. Lincoln: University of Nebraska Press, 1971.

Wert, Jeffrey D. *Custer: The Controversial Life of George Armstrong Custer*. New York: Simon and Schuster, 1996.

Confederate general Joseph E. Johnston's Army of Tennessee is too distant to attack Schofield's now divided army, but General Braxton Bragg's forces, which had withdrawn from Wilmington, are within striking distance. To be reinforced by veterans of the Army of Tennessee and North Carolina reserves, all under Major General Daniel H. Hill, Bragg marches against Cox near Kinston in Lenoir County. Bragg has some 8,500 men; Cox has 12,000.

On March 7, Union advance units encounter Bragg's entrenched forces along Southwest Creek east of Kinston. Bragg's position not only blocks Cox's path but also threatens a vital crossroads and the New Bern–Goldsboro Railroad. Now reinforced, Bragg takes the offensive the next day. He sends a division under Major General Robert F. Hoke to outflank the Union left, while Hill undertakes a similar move against the Union right. Hoke's attack is successful, and he takes an entire Union regiment prisoner.

Hill also enjoys success and Cox is on the brink of disaster when Bragg halts Hill's advance and sends him in another direction to intercept the supposedly retreating Union troops. By the time Hill returns from this wild goose chase, Cox has moved up his reserve division under Major General Thomas H. Ruger, and the Confederate assault falters. Skirmishing continues until Hoke again tries to turn the Union left flank on March 10. Cox has strongly fortified there, and Union artillery quickly rebuffs the assault. Hill then moves against the Union center, but Union artillery repulses this attack as well. With the remaining elements of the Union XXIII Corps, which has just arrived in New Bern from Tennessee, now moving on Kinston, Bragg withdraws. Total Union losses in the Battle of Wyse Fork are 1,001; Confederate casualties amount to some 1,500.

March 10, 1865

Civil War (continued): Eastern theater: Battle of Monroe's Crossroads. As U.S. major general William T. Sherman's army group advances into North Carolina, Brigadier General Hugh Judson Kilpatrick's 3rd Division of cavalry of some 4,500 men is screening its left flank. Torrential rains have made the advance difficult, and on the evening of March 9, 1865, Kilpatrick

camps in the vicinity of the house of Charles Monroe in Cumberland (now Hoke) County, North Carolina (presently on the grounds of Fort Bragg). Learning of Kilpatrick's precise dispositions through the interrogation of a captured Union officer, Confederate lieutenant general Wade Hampton, who with some 5,800 cavalrymen is screening General Joseph E. Johnston's army, decides to attack.

Early on March 10 Hampton, assisted by Major General Matthew C. Butler and Joseph "Fighting Joe" Wheeler, advances on the Union encampment. Kilpatrick had assigned each of his three brigades the corner of a triangle crossing likely Confederate routes of march but also making it possible for them to be mutually supporting, but Butler discovers in the course of reconnaissance that Kilpatrick has not posted pickets to protect the Union rear.

At daybreak on March 10 Butler, with Wheeler circling around to take the Union troops from the rear, is able to ride right up to the Union camps and catch them by surprise. The attackers drive the Union troops back in confusion and capture both wagons and artillery. Some of the attackers are sent to surround the Monroe house, knowing that Kilpatrick is lodged there with his traveling companion, the comely Mary Boozer. Kilpatrick, clad only in his nightshirt, manages to escape capture through a ruse, however.

The Confederates stop to plunder, giving Kilpatrick and the Union troops time to regroup and counterattack. Thanks to their horse artillery and repeating carbines, the Union troops retake the camps at the end of three hours of fighting, and with Union reinforcements on the way, Hampton withdraws to Fayetteville. Casualty reports of the battle, also known as the Fayetteville Road Fight and popularly as Kilpatrick's Shirttail Skedaddle, are contradictory and incomplete. Kilpatrick gives his losses as 19 dead, some 70 wounded, and 103 taken prisoner. He also states that his men killed more than 80 Confederates and had taken 30 prisoners and 150 horses. Wheeler claims to have taken more than 350 Union prisoners, while General Johnston put the total at 500, along with 173 freed Confederates captured by Kilpatrick earlier.

Hampton has opened the road to Fayetteville and joins Lieutenant General William J. Hardee there

Spencer Repeating Rifle/Carbine

Designed by Christopher M. Spencer and patented by him on March 6, 1860, the Spencer repeating rifle was a manually operated lever-action repeating rifle. It had a tube magazine in the wooden buttstock, which was easily removed for loading and held seven copper cartridges. As with the later Winchester rifle, the trigger guard was the actuating mechanism. Once the cartridge in the chamber had been fired, the operator pulled down on the trigger guard, which both rotated the breechblock and at the same time extracted the spent cartridge case, ejecting the latter when the trigger guard reached the terminus of its travel.

When the trigger guard was at its lowest position, the breechblock engaged with the rear of a cartridge in the magazine. The action of pulling the trigger guard back up to its original position seated the cartridge case in the breech of the rifle. The hammer needed to be cocked manually for every shot, but apart from this, all the user had to do was to aim and fire. The rifle weighed 10 pounds and was 47 inches in length with a barrel length of 22 inches. The cavalry version was shorter, with a weight of 8.25 pounds and an overall length of 39 inches. It had a 20-inch barrel. Both were of .52-caliber and used rimfire cartridges. The bullet was 285 grains, and the powder charge was 48 grains.

Conservatism in the Ordnance Department, headed by Colonel James W. Ripley ("Ripley Van Winkle" as he was known to his detractors), delayed adaptation of the Spencer by the military. However, Spencer was eventually able to gain an audience with President Abraham Lincoln, who subsequently invited him to demonstrate the weapon. Much impressed, Lincoln ordered it be placed in production. The Spencer rifle was first adopted by the U.S. Navy, then ordered by the army. It did not reach the army in significant numbers until 1863, and it never did replace the standard-issue muzzle-loading Springfield rifle. The Spencer did become, however, the favored weapon for cavalry units, who used the shorter, lighter carbine version. The Confederates occasionally captured Spencers, but with the South unable to manufacture the cartridges because of a shortage of copper, the Confederates could only make limited use of them.

The Spencer proved itself in the June 24, 1863, Battle of Hoover's Gap, when Union mounted troops under Colonel John T. Wilder, who had purchased the Spencer with their own funds, easily defeated a force of Confederates. Spencers also played an important role in cavalry engagements in the Battle of Gettysburg on July 1–2, 1863. Whereas a soldier with a rifled muzzle loader could fire only 2–3 shots a minute, one armed with the Spencer could fire as many as 20 shots a minute—more if he was able to take advantage of a cartridge box that contained as many as 14 preloaded magazines. Not only could the soldier with a Spencer put down a greater volume of fire, but these could be aimed rounds. The only disadvantage of the Spencer was the relatively small powder charge in the cartridge, which limited its range. Effective range was 200–500 yards.

The rifle cost the government $37.50 each, and the carbine sold for $25.50. The Spencer proved to be very reliable under combat conditions. In 1869, the Spencer Repeating Rifle Company was sold to the Fogerty Rifle Company and ultimately to Winchester. In all, some 200,000 rifles and carbines were manufactured. The Spencer marked the first adoption of a removable magazine-fed infantry rifle by any country. Many Spencer carbines were later sold as surplus to France and saw service in the Franco-German War of 1870–1871.

SPENCER C. TUCKER

Further Reading

Coates, Earl J., and Dean S. Thomas. *An Introduction to Civil War Small Arms.* Gettysburg, PA: Thomas Publications, 1996.

Marcot, Roy M., and Roy Marcot. *Spencer Repeating Firearms.* 3rd. Rev. ed. Irvine, CA: Northwood Heritage Press, 1995.

Westwood, David. *Rifles: An Illustrated History of their Impact.* Santa Barbara, CA: ABC-CLIO, 2005.

that night. The Battle of Monroe's Crossroads enables Hardee to carry out an organized crossing with his infantry corps across Cape Fear and join General Joseph E. Johnston, setting the stage for the Battle of Bentonville.

March 13, 1865

Civil War (continued): The Confederate Congress authorizes the arming of slaves. On January 11, 1865, Confederate Army general-in-chief General Robert E. Lee had written to the Confederate Congress urging them to arm and enlist black slaves in exchange for their freedom. On March 13 the Confederate Congress enacts legislation to raise African American soldiers. This legislation is promulgated by President Jefferson Davis in General Order No. 14 on March 23, 1865. The emancipation, however, rests on the master's consent, specifying that "No slave will be accepted as a recruit unless with his own consent and with the approbation of his master by a written instrument conferring, as far as he may, the rights of a freedman." In any case, such legislation comes too late.

March 17, 1865

Civil War (continued): Opening of the Union offensive against Mobile. U.S. Army major general Edward R. S. Canby advances on Mobile, Alabama, at the head of 32,000 men of the XIII and XVI Corps. Another Union column under General Edward Steele proceeds there from Pensacola, Florida. Altogether there will be some 45,000 Union troops operating against Mobile. Confederate major general Dabney H. Maury has only some 9,000 men to defend the important Confederate manufacturing center.

March 19–21, 1865

Civil War (continued): Battle of Bentonville. On March 15, 1865, Union major general William T. Sherman, learning that General Joseph E. Johnston has assumed command of Confederate forces in the Carolinas and is concentrating them, departs the seacoast with his army group to move against Johnston. On March 8 Sherman crosses into North Carolina, advancing toward Goldsborough (present-day Goldsboro) with some 60,000 men. His army group is in two major formations: a left wing of the Army of Georgia under Major General Henry W. Slocum and a right wing of the Army of the Tennessee commanded by Major General Oliver O. Howard. Both Union armies are proceeding separately on parallel axes.

On March 19 Johnston surprises Sherman at Bentonville, near the present-day town of Four Oaks, North Carolina, attacking Slocum and the Union left wing. Johnston has only some 21,000 men, but he believes erroneously that the two Union armies are a day's march apart and that his only hope is to achieve

Battle of Bentonville		
Date	March 19–21, 1865	
Location	Bentonville, North Carolina	
Opponents (*winner)	*United States	Confederacy
Commander	Major General William T. Sherman	General Joseph E. Johnston
#	60,000 men	21,000 men
Casualties	1,527 (194 killed, 1,112 wounded, and 221 missing or captured)	2,606 (239 killed, 1,694 wounded, and 673 captured/missing)

The Battle of Bentonville, North Carolina, during March 19–21, 1865, was the last major Confederate attempt to arrest Union major general William T. Sherman's advance northward through the Carolinas. (Library of Congress)

victory over the Army of Georgia before Sherman can concentrate the rest of his force against him. Both Slocum and Sherman initially underestimate the strength of the attackers. Confederates under Major General Daniel H. Hill rout two Union divisions, but their attacks are uncoordinated, and the rest of Slocum's men manage to hold until Union reinforcements come up. Fighting continues until nightfall, when Johnston withdraws to his original position and entrenches.

Little fighting occurs the next day as Sherman reinforces. On March 21 Union major general Joseph A. Mower, commanding a division on the Union right flank, secures permission for a "reconnaissance" but instead launches a full-scale attack on the Confederates defending Mill Creek Bridge and gets to within a mile of that crossing before Sherman recalls him, perhaps missing a chance to entrap and destroy Johnston's entire army and shortening the war by several weeks.

That night Johnston withdraws his men across Mill Creek toward Smithfield, burning the bridge behind him. Sherman does not pursue but instead continues his march toward Goldsborough, where on March 23 he joins forces under Major Generals Alfred H. Terry and John M. Schofield.

The Battle of Bentonville is the last major engagement between the armies of Sherman and Johnston. Although Johnston's initial attack was well planned and effectively executed, he simply lacked the strength to succeed. Confederate losses in the three-day battle are 2,606 (239 killed, 1,694 wounded, and 673 captured or missing); Union casualties are 1,527 (194 killed, 1,112 wounded, and 221 missing or captured).

March 22–April 20, 1865

Civil War (continued): Western theater: Wilson's raid into Alabama. U.S. major general James H. Wilson leads 13,500 cavalrymen—the largest cavalry force in U.S. history—from Gravelly Springs, Alabama, against Confederate cavalry led by Lieutenant General Nathan Bedford Forrest. Moving quickly before Forrest can concentrate his scattered forces, Wilson routs the Confederates. Wilson's goal is the important Southern manufacturing center of Selma. For the first time in the war, a Union force has outmaneuvered Forrest. Selma falls on April 2, 1865 (see April 2–20, 1865).

March 23, 1865

Civil War (continued): Eastern theater. At Goldsborough, North Carolina, U.S. Army major general William T. Sherman joins his army group to Major General John M. Schofield's Army of the Ohio. Sherman's march of some 425 miles in only 50 days constitutes a logistical masterpiece. Realizing the futility of further resistance, Confederate general Joseph E. Johnston soon opens surrender talks with Sherman.

March 24, 1865

Civil War (continued): CSS *Stonewall* sails from Ferrol, Spain. The powerful Confederate ironclad ram *Stonewall* (3 guns) had been constructed at Bordeaux, France, for the Confederate government, but when the tide of war turned, it was sold to Denmark instead, only to be refused by that government and then sold to the Confederates. Commanded by Captain Thomas J. Page and manned by many of the crew of CSS *Florida*, the *Stonewall* undergoes repairs at Ferrol, Spain, then departs for Lisbon for coal.

On March 24 the *Stonewall* clears Ferrol Harbor, with Page attempting to engage the U.S. Navy wooden steam frigate *Niagara* (35 guns), under Captain Thomas T. Craven, and the screw sloop *Sacramento* (10 guns), under Captain Henry Walke. Craven believes his adversary too powerful and refuses battle, for which he will be court-martialed, found remiss in refusing to engage the ironclad, and sentenced to two years' suspension from duty with pay (Secretary of the Navy Gideon Welles regards this as a "paid vacation" and restores Craven to duty).

Page sails again from Lisbon on February 28 and easily outdistances Craven's warships. Page hopes to attack Port Royal, South Carolina, but contrary winds

lead him to steam to Nassau and then to Havana. In the latter port, he learns that the war is over. He turns the ship over to Cuban authorities in return for money to pay off his crew.

March 25, 1865

Civil War (continued): Siege of Petersburg (continued): Battle of Fort Stedman. Learning of Union major general Philip Sheridan's victories over Lieutenant General Jubal A. Early in the Shenandoah Valley, Confederate general-in-chief General Robert E. Lee realizes that Sheridan can now combine his Army of the Shenandoah with the Army of the Potomac against the Army of Northern Virginia at Richmond and Petersburg. Lee therefore decides on a desperate surprise attack against the besiegers under Union general-in-chief Lieutenant General Ulysses S. Grant. The attack is to be mounted east of Petersburg. Lee hopes that success here will force Grant to shift resources, allowing at least some of Lee's men to escape to join Confederate forces under General Joseph E. Johnston in North Carolina.

The attack is led by Major General John B. Gordon with almost half of Lee's 60,000-man army. Its goal is the capture of Fort Stedman, a key redoubt on the Union's far right flank. The Confederate attack enjoys initial success. Stedman is taken, and a hole three-quarters of a mile wide is opened in the Union line. The Confederates then mount a desperate attempt to take the Union supply base at City Point. Although initially slow to respond, Union troops turn back the Confederate advance, recapture Fort Stedman, and restore the Union line at a cost of some 4,000 Confederate casualties (600 killed, 2,400 wounded, and 1,000 missing or captured) to only 1,044 for the Union (72 killed, 450 wounded, and 522 missing or captured). Lee's final offensive of the war is a failure.

Sheridan arrives at Petersburg the next day, March 26, bringing Grant's strength up to 122,000 men, more than double that of Lee.

March 25–April 12, 1865

Civil War (continued): Western theater: Siege of Mobile. In the siege of Mobile, Alabama, U.S. major general Edward R. S. Canby assembles some 45,000 troops, with Rear Admiral Henry K. Thatcher having charge of the naval effort. Army-navy cooperation is excellent. The main land attack moves up the Gulf coast, while a simultaneous diversionary effort proceeds by water to a point on the opposite side of Mobile Bay to prevent Confederate reinforcements from reaching the city. The navy will lose seven ships to Confederate torpedoes (underwater mines) in a five-week span.

Beginning on March 21, Union gunboats support a landing at Donnelly's Mills on the Fish River in Alabama. Thatcher furnishes six tinclads, all the light-draft vessels available. With gunboats bombarding Mobile's forts from the water, the land forces work their way to the main Confederate position at Spanish Fort. A steady Union bombardment forces the Confederates to evacuate that post on April 8. Batteries Tracy and Huger, up the Blakely River from Spanish Fort, fall three days later. On April 12 Major General Dabney Maury's 9,200 Confederate defenders abandon their defenses, and Mobile surrenders.

March 29, 1865

Civil War (continued). During the siege of Mobile, the U.S. Navy river monitor *Osage*, commanded by Commander William M. Gamble, is lost to a Confederate torpedo (mine) in the Blakely River in Alabama. Three men are killed and eight are wounded in the blast.

March 29–31, 1865

Civil War (continued): Eastern theater: Siege of Petersburg (continued): Battles of Dinwiddie Courthouse and White Oak Road. With an overwhelming numerical advantage, Union general-in-chief Lieutenant General Ulysses S. Grant decides to end the siege of Petersburg by mounting a final offensive against Confederate general-in-chief General Robert E. Lee's weak right flank, sending 7,000 men of two corps under Major Generals Gouverneur K. Warren and Andrew A. Humphreys. Grant also dispatches Major General Philip Sheridan's 13,000 cavalry in a wider envelopment of the Confederate right.

Anticipating Grant's move, Lee attempts an encirclement of the encirclement, sending 19,000 infantry and cavalry under Major General George E. Pickett and Major General Fitzhugh Lee toward the vital crossroads of Five Forks. The fighting during March 29–31, 1865, is inconclusive, and casualties are relatively light: Union losses are 354, while the Confederates sustain 760. The engagement nonetheless sets the stage for the decisive action at Five Forks on April 1.

April 1, 1865

Civil War (continued): Eastern theater: Siege of Petersburg (continued): Battle of Five Forks. Union cavalry under Major General Philip H. Sheridan, reinforced by the infantry of Major General Gouverneur K. Warren's V Corps, strike Confederates under Major General George E. Pickett holding Five Forks, which Confederate general-in-chief General Robert E. Lee has ordered held "at all hazards." Sheridan, with a manpower advantage of two to one, personally directs the attack and achieves a significant victory.

The Union side suffers 830 casualties, and the Confederates sustain 2,950. Lee's right flank has been turned, and what remains of Pickett's command is cut off from Lee's main army. The Union capture of Five Forks also threatens Lee's last supply line, the South Side Railroad, as well as Lee's entire right flank. On April 2 Lee informs Confederate president Jefferson Davis that Petersburg and Richmond must be evacuated.

April 2, 1865

Civil War (continued): Eastern theater: Siege of Petersburg (continued): Grant's assault on Petersburg. Following his victory in the Battle of Five Forks, Union major general Philip H. Sheridan moves northwest, over and beyond the vital Confederate supply line of the South Side Railroad. At the same time, three Union corps break through Confederate general-in-chief General Robert E. Lee's thinned right flank west of Petersburg. Confederate lieutenant general Ambrose P. Hill is killed while riding to rally his men. Only Major General John B. Gordon is able to hold against the Union onslaught, and Lee rushes forces under Lieutenant General James Longstreet down from Richmond to strengthen him.

The next day Lee abandons Petersburg and Richmond and breaks out to the west. The long siege of Petersburg is over.

April 2–20, 1865

Civil War (continued): Wilson's raid into Alabama (continued): Battle of Selma and end of the raid. On March 22, 1865, Union major general George H. Thomas, commander of the Department of the Cumberland, had sent his cavalry corps of three divisions (13,500 men), now reorganized under Brigadier General James H. Wilson, against the important Southern arms and munitions manufacturing center of Selma, Alabama. It contains one of two foundries in the South capable of producing heavy cannon. Wilson's troopers constitute the largest cavalry force ever in the history of North America.

Wilson covers the 300 miles to Selma by April 2, getting the better of Confederate lieutenant general Nathan Bedford Forrest's cavalry in several engagements en route. Selma is defended by 5,000 men behind prepared defenses and is anticipating a Union attack. Shortly before evening and fighting dismounted, some 1,500 of Wilson's men under Brigadier General Eli Long breach the Confederate right flank, while Union brigadier general Emory Upton leads his division through a swamp and gaps on the Confederate left.

Although Forrest does his best to hold Selma, the city is in Union hands that evening. Forrest and many other Confederates escape, but Wilson's men take 2,700 prisoners along with 102 cannon and substantial military stores. Confederate casualties are some 4,000, while Union losses are only about 400.

The interior of the Confederacy is now entirely open, and following destruction of the Confederate foundries and military stores, during the next month Wilson moves into middle Georgia, taking other cities and thousands of prisoners. Wilson ends his raid at Macon on April 20, where he learns of the war's end.

April 3, 1865

Civil War (continued): Eastern theater: Beginning of the Appomattox Court House Campaign. Confederate general-in-chief General Robert E. Lee abandons Petersburg and Richmond and strikes west with the Army of Northern Virginia, hoping to join Confederate forces under General Joseph E. Johnston in North Carolina. Pursuing with his own forces, Union Army general-in-chief Lieutenant General Ulysses S. Grant parallels Lee to the south. This same day, Major General Godfrey Weitzel's XXV Corps, composed largely of U.S. Colored Troops, occupies Richmond.

April 3, 1865

Civil War (continued): Destruction of the Confederate James River Squadron. With Confederate troops abandoning Richmond, Secretary of the Navy Stephen R. Mallory orders the destruction of the James River Squadron followed by a directive for its officers and men to join the troops withdrawing westward. Early this morning Confederate rear admiral Raphael Semmes, commander of the squadron, orders the ironclads *Virginia II* (4 guns), *Fredericksburg* (4 guns), and *Richmond* (4 guns) fired and the five wooden gunboats moved upstream to Richmond. The explosions of their magazines and shells shake houses in Richmond. Reaching the city, the men of the squadron find that the school-ship *Patrick Henry* has also been fired. The crews then set fire to the gunboats and set them adrift in the James. The *Beaufort* (1 gun) fails to sink, and Union forces take possession of both it and the unfinished ironclad *Texas*.

April 5, 1865

Civil War (continued): Eastern theater: Appomattox Court House Campaign (continued): Confederate general-in-chief General Robert E. Lee is joined at Amelia Court House, Virginia, by forces under Lieutenant General Richard S. Ewell.

Union major general Philip H. Sheridan, meanwhile, reaches Jetersville on this day in time to prevent Lee from moving southwest. Lee then continues west, now under constant harassment from Sheridan's cavalry.

April 6–7, 1865

Civil War (continued): Eastern theater: Appomattox Court House Campaign (continued): Battle of Sayler's Creek. For four days Confederate general-in-chief

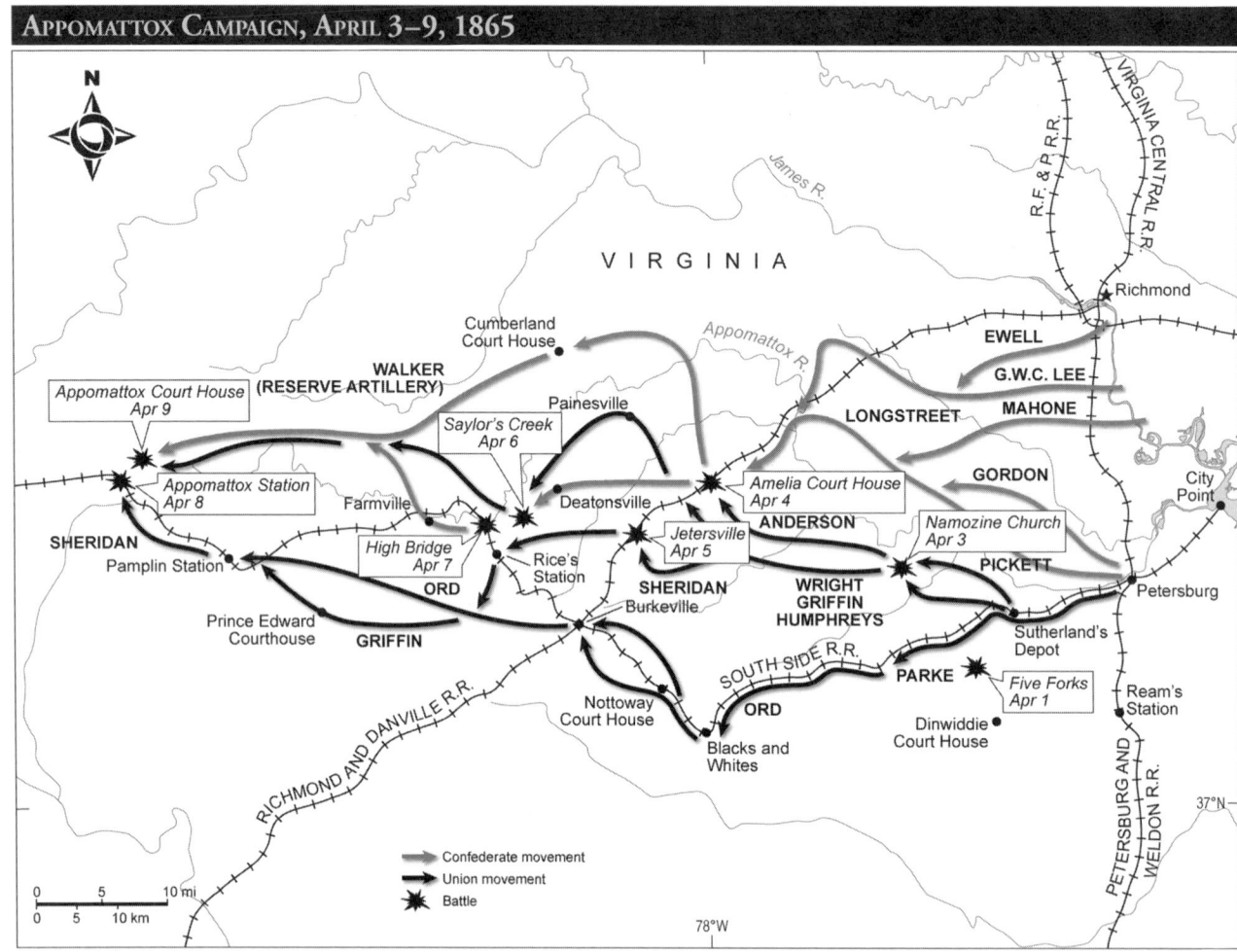

APPOMATTOX CAMPAIGN, APRIL 3–9, 1865

General Robert E. Lee and the Army of Northern Virginia have struggled westward from Petersburg and Richmond, harassed by Union major general Philip H. Sheridan's cavalry. At Sayler's Creek, however, a gap develops midway in the long Confederate line, and Sheridan manages to isolate the rearward Confederate forces under Lieutenant Generals Richard H. Anderson and Richard S. Ewell.

The Confederates are savaged by Sheridan's Cavalry and the Union VI Corps, and some 8,000 are captured, including Ewell; it is the largest number of prisoners ever taken in a battle in North America. Union losses are 166 killed and 982 wounded. Lee's army has lost a quarter of its strength in one afternoon. It now numbers fewer than 30,000 men. The Confederates remember the Battle of Sayler's Creek as "Black Thursday."

Lee now heads with his remaining half-starved troops for the Confederate railhead of Lynchburg by way of Appomattox. Sheridan, anticipating Lee's move, reaches Appomattox ahead of Lee on April 8 as Lee's leading troops approach Appomattox Court House, two miles to the northeast.

April 9, 1865

Civil War (continued): Eastern theater: Appomattox Court House Campaign (continued): Battle of Appomattox. Confederate general-in-chief General Robert E. Lee with the Army of Northern Virginia orders his cavalry commander Major General Fitzhugh Lee and Major General John B. Gordon to attack Union cavalry under Major General Philip H. Sheridan. The attack is halted when, following an all-night march, Union infantry comes up and deploys. Both sides are exhausted, but Union general-in-chief General Ulysses S. Grant enjoys a tremendous advantage in manpower, and Lee's men are near starvation from want of supplies. Realizing that the game is up, Lee requests terms.

That same day, the two men meet in a private residence at Appomattox Court House. Grant's terms are generous. The men are paroled to return home, and officers are permitted to retain their sidearms. All are allowed to keep private horses and mules. All equipment is to be surrendered. In midafternoon Lee surrenders the 28,356 remaining men of the Army of Northern Virginia. The Union soldiers then issue rations to the Confederates.

Although small-scale fighting continues for six weeks in other theaters (the last Confederate unit surrenders on May 26), the war is for all intents and purposes over.

April 12, 1865

Civil War (continued): Eastern theater: Appomattox Court House Campaign (continued). At Appomattox Court House, Virginia, three days after Confederate general-in-chief General Robert E. Lee's surrender, the Army of Northern Virginia formally surrenders. Major General John B. Gordon, commander of II Corps of the Army of Northern Virginia, leads more than 28,000 Confederates in laying down their arms along the Richmond-Lynchburg Stage Road.

April 14, 1865

Civil War (continued): Assassination of Lincoln. In Washington, D.C., U.S. president Abraham Lincoln, attending a play at Ford's Theater with his wife, is shot and mortally wounded by actor and Southern sympathizer John Wilkes Booth. Lincoln dies the next day. This deed, far from creating the chaos that the half dozen conspirators hoped, leads to harsher Reconstruction policies in the South under Lincoln's successor, Andrew Johnson.

April 14, 1865

Civil War (continued): Eastern theater. Major General Robert Anderson, who had commanded the Union Army garrison at Fort Sumter on April 14, 1861, receives the surrender of that Confederate fort in Charleston Harbor.

April 16, 1865

Civil War (continued): Western theater. U.S. Army major general James H. Wilson's cavalrymen brush aside Confederate militiamen, take 1,200 prisoners, and occupy Columbus, Georgia. Unaware of the end of the war, Wilson's men burn several factories, a large quantity of cotton, and 200 railroad cars.

April 16–25, 1865

Civil War (continued): Trans-Mississippi West theater: Passage of CSS *Webb*. The Confederate sidewheel ram *Webb* (3 guns) is on the Red River above

Joshua Lawrence Chamberlain (1828–1914)

College professor, politician, and Union Army officer during the American Civil War. Joshua Lawrence Chamberlain was born on September 8, 1828, in Brewer, Maine. He attended Bowdoin College in Brunswick, Maine, graduating in 1852. An aspiring minister, he later earned a master's degree from Bangor Theological Seminary. He then returned to Bowdoin as a professor of rhetoric and modern languages. When the Civil War began, Chamberlain accepted a commission as a lieutenant colonel of the 20th Maine Volunteers Infantry Regiment. Chamberlain's outfit remained with the Army of the Potomac.

(continued)

(Continued)

Chamberlain and the 20th Maine were present at but did not participate in the September 17, 1862, Battle of Antietam, having formed part of the reserve held back by Major General George McClellan. The unit engaged Confederate forces three days later at Sheperdstown (in western Virginia), where Chamberlain had the first of six horses shot out from under him during the war. Chamberlain then fought in the First Battle of Fredericksburg (December 13, 1862) and the Battle of Chancellorsville (May 1–4, 1863). He was promoted to colonel that same month. Chamberlain then took part in the Battle of Gettysburg (July 1–3, 1863).

At Gettysburg on July 2, Chamberlain was assigned to Little Round Top, one of two small critical elevations on the Union's left flank. If the Confederates could control these, they could enfilade the Union line. Immediately realizing its critical importance, Chamberlain was determined to hold Little Round Top. After turning back several Confederate charges that day and extending his line, and with ammunition running low, Chamberlain ordered a downhill bayonet charge. This action shocked the Confederates and forced their retreat. He was wounded in the action. For his heroism and tenacity, Chamberlain was awarded the Medal of Honor 30 years later, on August 11, 1893.

Chamberlain was promoted to brigadier general in June 1864 and breveted to major general in March 1865. He participated in the Spotsylvania Court House Campaign (May 7–18, 1864), the Second Battle of Cold Harbor (June 1–3, 1864), and the Petersburg Campaign (June 15, 1864–April 3, 1865). During another intrepid assault at Petersburg in June 1864, Chamberlain was wounded for a fourth time, nearly fatally. Defying all odds, he recovered sufficiently enough to return to duty. For his actions, he was breveted brigadier general in June 1864. Chamberlain was breveted major general in March 1865.

Upon the surrender of General Robert E. Lee's Army of Northern Virginia at Appomattox, Virginia, Lieutenant General Ulysses S. Grant selected Chamberlain to preside over the ceremony and receive the Confederate surrender on April 12, 1865. As the Confederate troops passed by and laid down their arms, Chamberlain saluted them. Although criticized by some in the Union for this, he was remembered in the South as one of the most gallant soldiers of the Union Army.

After the war, Chamberlain served as a Republican governor of Maine (1866–1870) and the president of Bowdoin College (1871–1883). He died in Portland, Maine, on February 24, 1914. Chamberlain was a central figure in Michael Shaara's 1975 Pulitzer Prize–winning historical novel *The Killer Angels,* which treats the Battle of Gettysburg.

Claude G. Berube

Further Reading

Desjardin, Thomas A. *Stand Firm, Ye Boys from Maine: The 20th Maine and the Gettysburg Campaign.* New York: Oxford University Press, 1995.

Perry, Mark. *Conceived in Liberty: Joshua Chamberlain, William Oates, and the American Civil War.* New York: Viking, 1997.

Wallace, Willard R. *Soul of the Lion: A Biography of General Joshua L. Chamberlain.* New York: Thomas Nelson and Sons, 1960.

Alexandria, Louisiana. Its commander, Lieutenant Charles W. Read, hits on a daring scheme. Disguising it as a Union warship, he fills the *Webb* with cotton. He plans to proceed down the Red River and then 300 miles down the Mississippi and into the Gulf of Mexico to Cuba, where he will sell the cotton and use the proceeds to purchase arms for the Confederacy.

Read slowly makes his way down the Red. At Alexandria, he learns of General Robert E. Lee's surrender at Appomattox and the assassination of President Abraham Lincoln, but he continues on regardless. On the evening of April 23, Read surprises Union ships guarding the mouth of the Red, then dashes down the Mississippi. The fast-moving *Webb* outdistances three pursuing Union warships and passes by New Orleans as planned in darkness at about midnight on April 24. Read stops to send men ashore to cut telegraph lines, dresses his crew in U.S. Navy uniforms, and flies the U.S. flag at half mast in honor of President Lincoln, but Union forces downriver have been alerted by at least one telegraph message, and federal gunboats at New Orleans open fire on the *Webb*, damaging the spar torpedo at its bow and forcing Read to jettison it. Read then orders the Confederate flag raised, and the *Webb* continues downstream. But about 25 miles below the city it encounters the powerful U.S. Navy steam sloop *Richmond* (25 guns). Trapped between it and the gunboats, Read runs the *Webb* ashore at McCall's Point, where its crew sets it on fire and escapes into the swamps on foot. The majority of the officers and men of the *Webb*, including Read, are soon captured.

April 26, 1865

Civil War (continued): Western theater: General Johnston surrenders in North Carolina. Learning of the surrender of Confederate general-in-chief General Robert E. Lee at Appomattox Court House, Virginia, Confederate general Joseph E. Johnston decides to meet with Major General William T. Sherman, commanding U.S. armies in North Carolina. The two men meet between the lines at a small farm known as Bennett Place, near present-day Durham, North

Carolina, on both April 17 and 18. At the second meeting they agree and sign terms, but Washington then rejects these as being more generous than those accorded Confederate general-in-chief General Robert E. Lee earlier by Union general-in-chief Lieutenant General Ulysses S. Grant. Sherman is ordered to grant terms identical to those of Grant, and Johnston agrees to these in the course of a third meeting, on April 26.

Johnston surrenders not only the 37,000 men of the Army of Tennessee but all remaining Confederate forces still active in North Carolina, South Carolina, Georgia, and Florida. Totaling 89,270 men, it is the largest surrender of the war. Following it, Sherman orders 10 days of rations issued to the hungry Confederate soldiers.

April 27, 1865

Civil War (continued): Western theater: The *Sultana* disaster. Early this morning, the boiler explodes in the side-wheel steamer *Sultana*, which sinks in the Mississippi River a few miles north of Memphis, Tennessee. It is the largest maritime disaster of the Civil War, claiming some 1,700–1,800 Union soldiers, most of whom had been recently released from Confederate prison camps at Andersonville and Cahaba. The ship had a legal capacity of 376 passengers, but the men had crowded aboard in their effort to return to their homes. There is speculation that the blast may have been caused by a Confederate coal torpedo (a grenade disguised as a piece of coal).

May 1, 1865

Civil War (continued). In Washington, D.C., the War Department issues orders demobilizing the 1,052,038 volunteers and regulars comprising the Union Army.

May 4, 1865

Civil War (continued): Western theater. At Citronelle, Alabama, Lieutenant General Richard Taylor surrenders all Confederate forces east of the Mississippi River to Major General Edward R. S. Canby. The terms are identical to those granted the Confederates at Appomattox Court House, Virginia, in April.

In what is considered the worst naval disaster of the Civil War, on April 27, 1865, in the Mississippi River near Memphis a boiler exploded in the Union steamer *Sultana*, which was filled with released Union prisoners of war (POWs). Some 1,700–1,800 died. (Library of Congress)

May 10, 1865

Civil War (continued): Davis taken prisoner. Near Irwinville in southern Georgia, troopers of the 4th Michigan Cavalry surprise the encampment of Confederate president Jefferson Davis and his party who are attempting to reach Texas. Davis and the others are taken prisoner.

May 12–13, 1865

Civil War (continued): Trans-Mississippi West theater: Battle of Palmito (Palmetto) Ranch. Despite the fact that there is a general understanding by each side in Texas that nothing further is to be gained by an attack on the other, Union colonel Theodore H. Barrett, who is without combat experience but the new commander of a brigade at Brazos Santiago Island at the mouth of the Brazos River in the Gulf of Mexico, orders it into combat against the Confederates at Palmito Ranch, near Fort Brown outside of Brownsville.

The reasons for the attack remain unclear, but apparently Barrett seeks to win military glory before the end of the war. The Union attacking force consists of 250 men of the 62nd U.S. Colored Troops and 50 dismounted members of the 2nd Texas Cavalry Battalion, all commanded by Lieutenant Colonel David Branson. These men cross from Brazos Santiago to the mainland during a storm on the night of May 11. Although they fail to achieve surprise, on May 12 the attackers enjoy some success until Confederate cavalrymen under Captain William N. Robinson drive them back to White's Ranch, where the fighting stops for the night. Both sides then appeal for reinforcements. Barrett sends 200 men of the 34th Indiana Infantry Regiment.

The next day, Barrett attacks westward until he encounters Confederate colonel John S. Ford with the remainder of his cavalry and six guns. The Confederates now have some 300 men. Ford attacks, employing his artillery to good effect, and the Union troops withdraw. The Union side suffers 4 killed, 12–14 wounded, and 101 prisoners. The Confederates report only 5–6 wounded. The Battle of Palmito Ranch is the last combat of the war west of the Mississippi River.

May 23–24, 1865

Civil War (continued): The Grand Review of the Armies. In Washington, D.C., more than 80,000 men of the Union Army parade down Constitution Avenue to the accolades of onlookers and reviewing politicians, officials, and prominent citizens, including President Andrew Johnson. Flags fly at full mast for the first time in four years. None of the 106 African American regiments raised during the war are permitted to take part.

May 26, 1865

Civil War (continued): Buckner surrenders at New Orleans. Although commander of Confederate forces in the Trans-Mississippi theater Lieutenant General Kirby Smith has ordered his deputy, Lieutenant General Simon B. Buckner, to consolidate remaining forces at Houston, Texas, Buckner travels to New Orleans, Louisiana, and there surrenders the Trans-Mississippi Department to Union major general Peter J. Osterhaus, deputy to Major General Edward R. S. Canby, commander of the Military District of West Mississippi. This action eliminates all Confederate forces west of the Mississippi River.

May 29, 1865

Civil War (continued): Official end of the war. President Andrew Johnson's proclamation of amnesty and pardon to any former Confederates submitting to a loyalty oath officially brings to an end the Civil War.

June 2, 1865

At Galveston, Texas, Confederate lieutenant general Edmund Kirby Smith formally endorses the surrender of Confederate forces west of the Mississippi River tendered by his deputy, Lieutenant General Simon B. Buckner, at New Orleans on May 26.

June 6, 1865

On the Red River at Alexandria, Louisiana, Confederate Navy lieutenant Jonathan H. Carter surrenders the ironclad Missouri (4 guns) to the U.S. Navy large tinclad Ouachita (39 guns), commanded by Lieutenant William E. Fitzhugh. The Missouri is the last Confederate ironclad to surrender.

June 23, 1865

At Doaksville in Indian Territory (present-day Oklahoma), Confederate brigadier general Stand Watie surrenders the Confederate Cherokees, the last Confederate land force to lay down its arms.

June 28, 1865

The Confederate commerce raider Shenandoah (8 guns), commanded by Lieutenant James Waddell, captures 11 American whalers in the Bering Strait in the North Pacific.

July 6, 1865

In an effort to curb rising violence in the South by whites against former African American slaves, U.S. Army commander General Ulysses S. Grant orders military personnel to arrest civilians suspected of violence against either blacks or U.S. soldiers.

August 2, 1865

The Confederate commerce raider Shenandoah sails for England. In the Aleutian Islands after communicating with a British ship, Confederate Navy lieutenant James Waddell, commander of the commerce raider Shenandoah (8 guns), decides that the Civil War is indeed over. Rather than surrender to a U.S. flag vessel, Waddell decides to undertake a nonstop voyage to Liverpool, England, via Cape Horn. On November 6 after a 123-day voyage, the Shenandoah arrives at Liverpool, and Waddell turns over his ship to British authorities.

August 11–September 24, 1865

American Indian Wars (continued): Connor's Powder River Expedition. At Fort Leavenworth, Kansas, Major General Grenville Dodge, commander of the Departments of Missouri and Kansas, orders Brigadier General Patrick E. Connor to command

Stand Watie (1806–1871)

Cherokee leader and the only Native American to hold the rank of brigadier general in the Confederate Army. Stand Watie (also known as Isaac S. Watie) was born near present-day Rome, Georgia, in 1806 and was named Degataga (meaning "to stay" or "stand firm"). He was educated at a Moravian mission school in Springplace, Georgia, and subsequently served as a clerk for the Cherokee Supreme Court. He was also Speaker of the Cherokee National Council.

In the early and mid-1830s when the Cherokee Nation split over the decision to accede to their forcible removal to Indian Territory (present-day Oklahoma) by the U.S. government, Watie sided with the faction that opted to move west and vacate the Cherokees' ancestral lands in Georgia. Watie was one of the signatories to the 1835 Treaty of New Echota, which provided federal compensation for Cherokee lands in the East and established land for their relocation to Indian Territory. Watie and others who supported the removal believed that it was the only way to keep the Cherokee Nation from being irreparably harmed by white encroachment. Many vehemently rejected Watie's reasoning and asserted that personal greed fueled his decision.

Once he had resettled in Oklahoma, Watie became a successful planter and the de facto leader of the Cherokee faction in Oklahoma. When the American Civil War began in 1861, the Cherokee Nation declared its neutrality, but by late August of 1861, Watie decided to ally his Cherokee faction with the Confederacy. He proceeded to assemble a volunteer regiment, the Cherokee Mounted Rifles, and was named colonel of the unit.

Operating mostly in Indian Territory, Watie proved to be an intrepid cavalry raider who enjoyed great success in numerous hit-and-run guerrilla-style raids against Union troops and their Native American allies. Watie's force played a significant role in the March 7–8, 1862, Battle of Pea Ridge in Arkansas, capturing Union artillery and covering the ultimate Confederate retreat. Indeed, Watie virtually ensured that the war in the region would be waged using unconventional warfare, and in May 1864 he was promoted to brigadier general for his efforts.

In June 1864, Watie led a successful raid on the Union steamer *J. R. Williams* that was plying the Arkansas River. The taking of that vessel resulted in the capture of valuable Union supplies, estimated to be worth some $120,000. On September 19, 1864, Watie's force seized a major Union wagon supply train at the Second Battle of Cabin Creek; the loot from that raid is believed to have been worth more than $1 million.

Watie's daring and successful raids bolstered Confederate morale in the region and won him many accolades from his superiors. He was the last Confederate general to surrender to the Union, laying down his arms on June 23, 1865.

After the war, Watie returned to Oklahoma and again took up his successful planting enterprise. In 1866 he served as a delegate for the Southern Cherokee faction during the negotiations that led to the 1866 Cherokee Reconstruction Treaty. After that, he retired from public life. He died in present-day Delaware County, Oklahoma, on September 9, 1871.

PAUL G. PIERPAOLI JR.

Further Reading

Cunningham, Frank. *General Stand Watie's Confederate Indians*. Norman: University of Oklahoma Press, 1998.

Franks, Kenny A. *Stand Watie and the Agony of the Cherokee Nation*. Memphis, TN: Memphis State University Press, 1979.

a three-pronged punitive expedition to the Powder River against Sioux, Cheyennes, and Arapahos who have been raiding the Bozeman Trail.

Connor has some 2,400 men, most of them volunteers from California, Kansas, and Nebraska. Colonel Nelson Cole's column is to proceed up the Loup Fork of the Platte River to the forks of the Little and Big Powder Rivers and then to the Tongue River, where it will join with Lieutenant Colonel Samuel Walker's column, which is to move north from Fort Laramie, then proceed west of the Black Hills. Connor commands the third column, which will move from the north bend of the North Platte River to the Powder River.

Connor arrives at the Powder River on August 11 and there oversees construction of a stockade, named Fort Connor, before advancing to the Tongue River. Arriving at the Tongue River on the morning of August 29, Connor attacks Chief Black Bear's camp of some 500 Arapahos. Catching the natives by surprise, Connor employs his mountain howitzers with devastating effect, killing approximately 60 Arapahos, including Black Bear's son.

Connor then waits in vain for the arrival of his other two columns, both of which have gotten lost. By the time Connor's scouts locate them on September 19, Cole's and Walker's men are on the verge of starvation, primarily because Connor has most of the supplies.

While Connor is debating how to proceed, a courier arrives on September 24 with orders relieving him of his command. The expedition then straggles back to Fort Laramie. The limited success of the expedition, its high cost, and outrage over Connor's order that all Indian males over age 15 should be summarily shot all contribute to the decision to pursue a peace policy with the Plains tribes. While Connor's campaign ends Arapaho attacks on the overland trails for a time, it accomplishes little against the Sioux. Indeed, the fighting along the Powder River eventually grows into Red Cloud's War.

October 1865

The U.S. Navy Academy returns to Annapolis, Maryland, from Newport, Rhode Island, where it had been located during the Civil War.

November 10, 1865

Former Confederate Army captain Henry Wirz, commander of the notorious Camp Sumter prisoner of war camp (better known for its location of Andersonville, Georgia), is executed by hanging in Washington, D.C. Wirz has been tried and found guilty of the mistreatment of Union prisoners. He is the only person executed after the war for war crimes committed during it.

November 11, 1865

Mary E. Walker becomes the first woman awarded the Medal of Honor, the nation's highest military honor, for her service in the Civil War. It is presented on January 24, 1866.

1865–1890

American Indian Wars (continued). Disputes between Native Americans and white settlers seeking land and trying to fence in their property lead to widespread conflict. Native Americans do not believe in private landownership, and they oppose fences, which prevent the migratory grazing of the great herds of buffalo that they depend on for their livelihood. Various civilian agencies, peace commissions, and the Bureau of Indian Affairs in the Department of the Interior all attempt to persuade the Native Americans to accept great land cessions, change their way of life, and enter white society or live on reservations set aside for them. Many Native Americans resist this by force of arms.

The Civil War had drawn off a number of troops from the West, allowing the Indians to reclaim many of their ancestral lands. This is especially true on the northern Great Plains. The return of peace in 1865 allows Washington to send resources westward, making clashes between settlers and the U.S. Army on the one side and the Indians on the other almost inevitable. About 5,000 U.S. Army troops in scattered posts of a single company or less hold the northern Great Plains; another 4,000 troops, equally scattered, garrison the southern Great Plains.

Perhaps 270,000 Native Americans live in the West in 1865; some 100,000 are in tribes determined to fight. In the Plains Indians, the U.S. Army encounters some of the greatest natural horsemen in

Mary Edwards Walker (1832–1919)

Physician, humanitarian, women's rights advocate, and the only woman to be awarded the Medal of Honor. Mary Edwards Walker was born in Oswego, New York, on November 26, 1832. Encouraged by her parents to pursue her education beyond the primary level, for a brief time she worked as a teacher before deciding on a career as a medical doctor, a profession that at the time was almost completely closed to women. Through sheer perseverance, she gained acceptance at the Syracuse Medical College and graduated with an MD degree in 1855, only the second American women to achieve the degree. Married while in medical school, she refused to adopt her husband's surname and opened a medical practice in Rome, New York, that soon failed because most people refused to accept a female physician. From there she went to Cincinnati, Ohio, to practice medicine but enjoyed little success.

When the American Civil War began in 1861, Walker volunteered her services to the Union Army, which permitted her to work as a nurse but not as a physician. She worked mostly in a hospital in Washington, D.C. In early 1864, the 52nd Ohio Infantry Regiment hired her as a contract surgeon for a period of six months, and in October 1864 the Union Army hired her as an assistant surgeon, a commission she held until she resigned in June 1865. Her position enabled her to move freely between Union and Confederate lines, and she actively sought to treat civilians on both sides. There is conjecture that she performed espionage work for the Union side, but this has never been substantiated. Nevertheless, as she was treating a wounded Confederate soldier in 1864, she was charged with spying. She spent four months as a prisoner before being released. During her war service, Walker adopted the Union officer's uniform but wore her hair in curls to ensure that she was not mistaken for a man.

On November 11, 1865, Walker became the first woman to be awarded the Medal of Honor, thanks to the recommendations of Major Generals William T. Sherman and George Thomas, for her meritorious work during the war. Following the war, Walker continued to work as a physician, published two books, and actively campaigned for women's rights, improved health care, and temperance. She also advocated the direct election of U.S. senators. Walker was known for her adoption of the Bloomer costume, an outfit that incorporated both a skirt and trousers. Arrested many times because of her penchant for wearing male attire, she later wore men's suits exclusively. In 1897 Walker tried unsuccessfully to establish an all-female colony, which she called Adamless Eden. Because she spurned the prescribed gender roles of the era, she was considered highly controversial and militant. Most women did not support her activities, and even her own family ostracized her.

In 1919 the federal government revoked Walker's Medal of Honor, and despite demands by the U.S. Army that she return the medal, she refused, responding, "You can have it, over my dead body." Walker died alone and penniless on February 21, 1919, in Oswego, New York. In 1977, President Jimmy Carter signed a proclamation posthumously restoring the Medal of Honor. In 1982, Walker was depicted on a U.S. postage stamp that listed her as an army surgeon and a Medal of Honor recipient.

Wendy A. Maier

Further Reading

Graf, Mercedes. *A Woman of Honor: Dr. Walker and the Civil War.* Gettysburg, PA: Thomas Publications, 2001.
Walker, Dale. *Mary Edwards Walker: Above and Beyond.* New York: Forge Books, 2005.

the world. The Native Americans are also often better armed, with repeating Winchester rifles.

The principal hostiles are the Sioux, on the northern Great Plains; the Kiowas, Comanches, Cheyennes, and Arapahos, on the southern and central Plains; and the Apaches, in the Southwest. During 1865–1890 the army fights nearly 1,000 engagements in 12 separate campaigns. Most engagements are quite small (and not included here). The American Indians excel at hit-and-run tactics. For a variety of reasons, however, they are usually unable to organize larger sustained campaigns.

The first of the U.S. Army's campaigns against the Native Americans occurs during 1865–1868, with widespread fighting in southern Oregon, northern California, Nevada, and Idaho.

January 1, 1866

The U.S. Navy armed tug *Narcissus* (2 guns), commanded by Acting Ensign Isaac S. Bradbury, wrecks off Egmont Key, Florida. All 32 crew members are lost.

June 20, 1866

At Chwang, China, with local authorities unwilling to intervene, Lieutenant John W. Philip, commanding the steam sloop *Wachusett* (10 guns), lands 100 sailors and marines to arrest a Chinese bandit chieftain who assaulted the American consul.

Mid-July 1866–November 6, 1868
American Indian Wars (continued): Red Cloud's War (Powder River War). This war—the most successful ever fought by Native Americans against the U.S. Army—pits Sioux and Northern Cheyennes against settlers and the U.S. Army. It is fought for control of the Powder River country of the Great Plains in northeastern Wyoming Territory, through which the Bozeman Trail passes to the Montana goldfields.

The discovery of gold in Idaho and Montana in 1862 and 1863 opens a new area of conflict between white settlers and the Plains Indian tribes. Despite the Civil War, the gold discoveries bring thousands of fortune seekers to the area, and pressure mounts to establish more direct access to the Virginia City, Montana, goldfields. Army officials adopt the route pioneered by John Bozeman, which proceeds from Fort Laramie on the North Platte River and the Oregon Trail northwestward along the eastern base and around the northern shoulder of the Bighorn Mountains and on to Virginia City. The Bozeman Trail is nearly 400 miles shorter than other routes to the goldfields, but it cuts through hunting grounds reserved for the Sioux, Northern Cheyennes, and Arapahos by the Harney-Sanborn Treaties of 1865.

In the late spring of 1866, U.S. government representatives, under considerable public pressure but also lured by the region's gold that might relieve the

---

Red Cloud (ca. 1821–1909)

Oglala Sioux war leader. Red Cloud (Makhpyia-luta) was born in 1821 or 1822, possibly near the forks of the Platte River in present-day Nebraska. In conflicts against the Pawnees, Crows, and other rival tribes, he demonstrated great courage and earned the position of war leader for the Teton Lakota Sioux, which included Red Cloud's Oglala band.

The discovery of gold in Montana drew numerous white immigrants to the Bozeman Trail that passed through the Powder River region of Wyoming and Montana, territory claimed by the Sioux, Arapahos, and Northern Cheyennes. The influx began in 1864, and by early 1865 the Sioux, at Red Cloud's urging, had begun to attack these interlopers.

(continued)

(Continued)

American peace commissioner E. B. Taylor invited the Sioux to Fort Laramie in Wyoming Territory for talks. Red Cloud, Man-Afraid-of-His-Horses, and other leaders arrived in June 1866. During the negotiations, Colonel Henry Carrington arrived with troops to build forts along the Bozeman Trail. Red Cloud denounced this as treachery, promised to fight anyone who intruded onto Sioux lands, and promptly left the conference.

Throughout the summer and autumn of 1866, Sioux, Cheyenne, and Arapaho warriors under Red Cloud and other leaders attacked travelers and the soldiers building three forts along the trail. The raids culminated in the Fetterman Massacre of December 21, 1866. Lured from Fort Phil Kearny by a Sioux decoy party, Captain William Fetterman and his 79 men were ambushed and annihilated.

Native raids continued during 1867, including an unsuccessful assault against woodcutters from Fort Phil Kearny that Red Cloud led in person. Meanwhile, after much debate, the U.S. government agreed to a conciliatory approach to the Native Americans of the Powder River region.

Red Cloud, on the advice of Man-Afraid-of-His-Horses, rejected an invitation to a peace conference in November 1867. When Red Cloud received a second invitation the following spring, he agreed to attend on the condition that the soldiers first evacuate the forts on the Bozeman Trail. American officials complied, and the forts were evacuated in July and August 1868. Red Cloud and his followers then burned the abandoned forts.

In November, Red Cloud arrived at Fort Laramie for negotiations. The resulting treaty ended the war and recognized Sioux claims to a vast tract of land in Montana and Wyoming and set aside most of present-day western South Dakota as the Great Sioux Reservation.

Red Cloud apparently chose to ignore the terms of the treaty by remaining near Fort Laramie, regardless of government efforts to have him move to the reservation. In 1870, he visited Washington, D.C., and met with President Ulysses Grant. In 1873 the government created the Red Cloud Agency for Red Cloud and his followers in northwestern Nebraska, but in 1878 the agency was relocated within the confines of the old Great Sioux Reservation in Dakota Territory and redesignated the Pine Ridge Agency. There Red Cloud feuded with the Indian agent, Dr. Valentine T. McGillycuddy, who wanted the Sioux to abandon hunting and take up farming.

Despite his conflict with McGillycuddy, repeated violations of the Fort Laramie Treaty by the U.S. government, and pressure from Sioux militants to join them in armed resistance, Red Cloud played no role in the Great Sioux War (1876–1877) or the Ghost Dance Movement that ended with the tragedy at Wounded Knee. For the remainder of his life Red Cloud honored his commitment to keep the peace. He died on December 10, 1909, at Pine Ridge.

JIM PIECUCH

Further Reading

Brown, Dee. *Bury My Heart at Wounded Knee: An Indian History of the American West*. New York: Holt, Rinehart and Winston, 1970.

Olson, James C. *Red Cloud and the Sioux Problem*. Lincoln: University of Nebraska Press, 1965.

Utley, Robert M. *The Indian Frontier of the American West, 1846–1890*. Albuquerque: University of New Mexico Press, 1984.

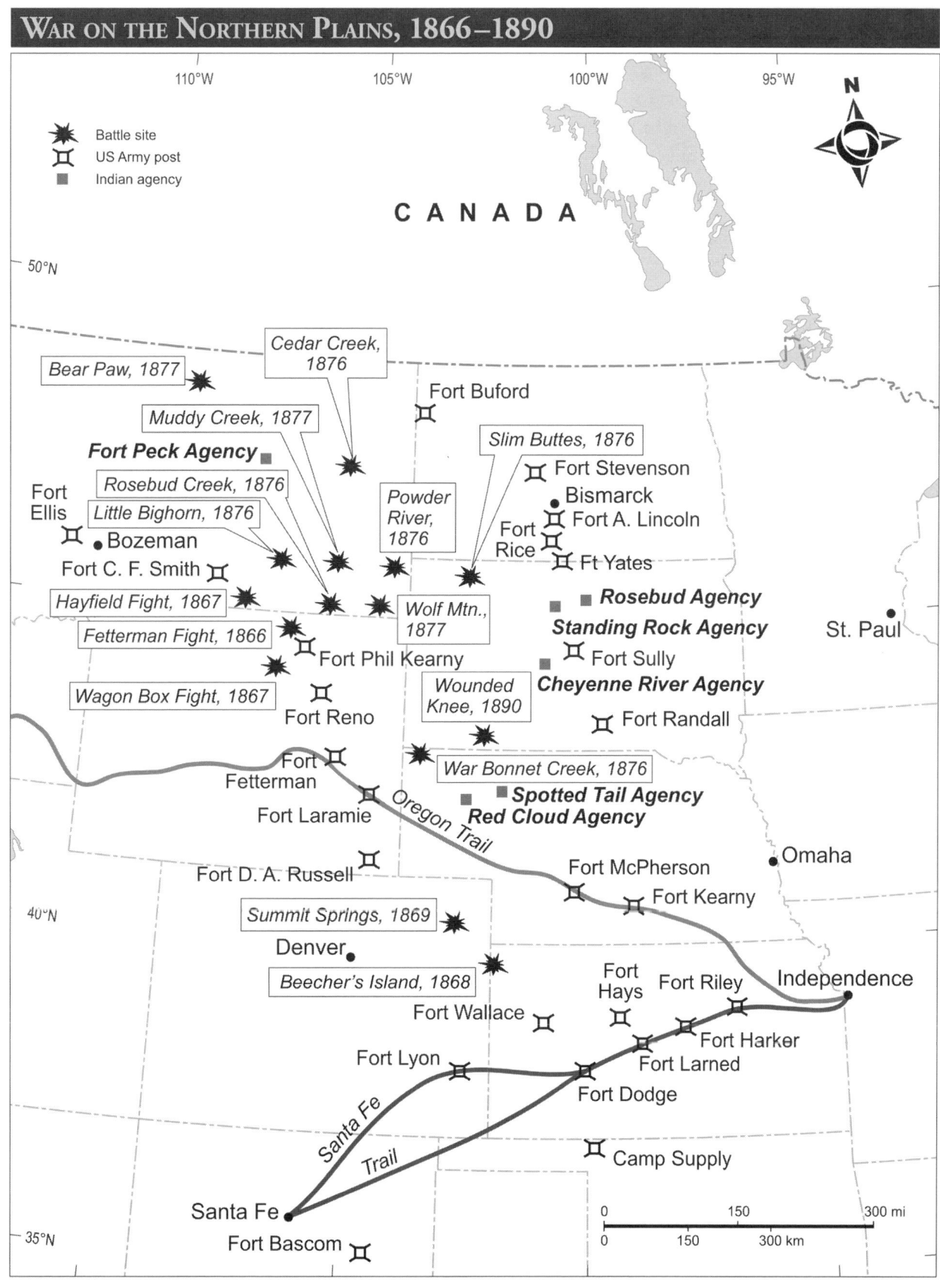

WAR ON THE NORTHERN PLAINS, 1866–1890

Battle site
US Army post
Indian agency

110°W
105°W
100°W
95°W

N

50°N

CANADA

Bear Paw, 1877
Cedar Creek, 1876
Muddy Creek, 1877
Fort Buford
Fort Peck Agency
Slim Buttes, 1876
Fort Stevenson
Fort Ellis
Rosebud Creek, 1876
Bismarck
Little Bighorn, 1876
Powder River, 1876
Fort A. Lincoln
Bozeman
Fort Rice
Fort C. F. Smith
Ft Yates
Hayfield Fight, 1867
Rosebud Agency
Fetterman Fight, 1866
Wolf Mtn., 1877
Standing Rock Agency
St. Paul
Fort Phil Kearny
Fort Sully
Wagon Box Fight, 1867
Wounded Knee, 1890
Cheyenne River Agency
Fort Reno
Fort Randall
Fort Fetterman
War Bonnet Creek, 1876
Spotted Tail Agency
Fort Laramie
Oregon Trail
Red Cloud Agency
Fort D. A. Russell
Fort McPherson
Omaha
Fort Kearny
40°N
Summit Springs, 1869
Denver
Fort Hays
Fort Riley
Independence
Beecher's Island, 1868
Fort Wallace
Fort Harker
Fort Lyon
Fort Larned
Santa Fe
Fort Dodge
Trail
Camp Supply
Santa Fe
0   150   300 mi
0   150   300 km
35°N
Fort Bascom

financial burden caused by the Civil War, call a conference to engage the tribes in negotiations in an effort to gain passage through their lands. The conference occurs in June at Fort Laramie, Wyoming. Although a few chiefs sign new treaties at Fort Laramie, others refuse, angered that the army has already dispatched Colonel Henry B. Carrington and his 18th Infantry Regiment to establish a series of posts along the Bozeman Trail before agreements have been reached with all the tribes. Oglala Lakota chief Red Cloud leads the opposition and begins mobilizing warriors to oppose the army incursion.

On June 17, 1866, Carrington, with about 700 men of the 18th Infantry plus several cavalry units and hundreds of mule teams hauling large amounts of supplies and equipment, departs Fort Laramie for the Bighorn Mountains. At Fort Reno on the Powder River and many miles from the nearest telegraph station, Carrington relieves two companies of the 5th U.S. Volunteers, comprised of former Confederate prisoners who have agreed to frontier service in exchange for their freedom. Farther to the northwest some 225 miles from Fort Laramie on the Piney tributary of the Powder River, Carrington orders construction of a new fortification, which he names Fort Phil Kearny. Carrington bases five companies here; the remaining two march another 90 miles and establish Fort C. F. Smith on a bluff some 500 yards from the Bighorn River.

Almost immediately in mid-July 1866 Fort Phil Kearny comes under Native American attack and remains in an almost continual state of siege. On December 21 Red Cloud's warriors attack soldiers cutting wood six miles from the fort. Captain William Fetterman, who holds the Indians in contempt, disobeys orders and leads 80 men into a carefully executed ambush. His entire force is annihilated (see December 21, 1866).

The army is more successful in two other notable actions on the Bozeman Trail. In August 1867 Cheyenne and Sioux warriors launch separate but seemingly coordinated attacks that become known as the Hayfield and Wagon Box Fights (see August 1, 1867, and August 2, 1867).

Despite these modest army victories, the days of the Bozeman Trail are numbered. Red Cloud's determined resistance leads to the abandonment of the Bozeman Trail and the three army forts there. Following eight months of negotiations, the majority of the tribal leaders agree to the terms of the Treaty of Fort Laramie on April 29, 1868, but it is not until November 6, 1868, when Red Cloud signs the document at Fort Laramie that the war officially comes to an end. The Indians achieve virtually all of their demands. Meanwhile, the army quits Fort Phil Kearny, with the last troops departing there on July 31, 1868. Shortly thereafter the fort is burned to the ground, probably by the Cheyennes.

July 25, 1866

Congress creates the rank of admiral and confers it on Vice Admiral David G. Farragut in recognition of his service to the nation during the Civil War. On this date as well, Ulysses S. Grant is promoted to the newly created rank of general of the army of the United States.

July 28, 1866

Congress fixes the post–Civil War U.S. military establishment at 45 infantry and 6 cavalry regiments, totaling 54,302 men. The act also authorizes creation of 4 regiments of "Colored Troops," with African American enlisted men and white officers. These are the 38th, 39th, 40th, and 41st Infantry Regiments, and they recruit their members mainly from Civil War veterans of the U.S. Colored Troops.

September 21, 1866

Creation of the 9th and 10th Cavalry Regiments. In August 1866 Major General Philip Sheridan, commander of the Military Division of the Gulf, obtains authorization from the War Department to raise an African American cavalry regiment. On September 21, 1866, at Greenville, Louisiana, the 9th United States Cavalry Regiment comes into being, commanded by Colonel Edward Hatch. On the same day at Fort Leavenworth, Kansas, the 10th Cavalry Regiment is also organized, commanded by Colonel Benjamin H. Grierson. Both regimental commanders are celebrated Civil War veterans. The two regiments draw their men entirely from African American recruits; all their officers are white. These two cavalry regiments and two African American infantry regiments—the

24th and 25th Regiments (reorganized from the four African American infantry regiments on November 1, 1869) distinguish themselves in service in the American West, becoming known as the Buffalo Soldiers. (The name is reportedly given to them by the Cheyennes, who assert that the black soldiers fight as fiercely and courageously as a wounded buffalo.)

December 21, 1866

American Indian Wars (continued): Red Cloud's War (continued): Fetterman Massacre. The U.S. Army constructs a series of forts along the Bozeman Trail, with Fort Phil Kearny the major installation. Colonel Henry Carrington, commander of the 18th Infantry Regiment garrisoning the Bozeman Trail forts, has his headquarters here. It is strategically located but is several miles away from the nearest stand of timber, required as fuel in the winter. Each day a small detachment of soldiers is sent about an hour distant to secure wood, and usually they come under Native American attack.

Captain William Fetterman of the 18th Infantry holds the Native Americans in contempt. He also believes that Carrington is too timid and that more aggressive action is needed against the area's hostile tribes. Indeed, Fetterman boasts that with just 80 soldiers he can defeat the entire Sioux Nation.

By early December 1866, Oglala Sioux chief Red Cloud and Northern Cheyenne chief Roman Nose have gathered several thousand warriors (mainly Sioux, Northern Cheyennes, and Arapahos) a mere 50 miles from the fort. When another army wood train ventures out on December 6, a large party of warriors attacks it and then nearly defeats a relief party dispatched by Carrington, who now prohibits any more retaliatory operations.

On December 19 another wood train comes under attack and is rescued by a detachment under Captain James Powell that drives off the attackers, but as ordered, Powell refuses to pursue the warriors and fall into a trap. The next day a heavily armed wood-gathering detachment accomplishes its mission without incident. Carrington plans one final wood train before a break during the winter.

That last wood train heads out on December 21 and, once again, comes under attack. According to the

Fetterman Massacre		
Date	December 21, 1866	
Location	Near Fort Phil Kearny, Wyoming	
Opponents (*winner)	*Oglala Sioux, Northern Cheyennes, and Arapahos	United States
Commander	Chief Red Cloud	Captain William Fetterman
#	2,000 warriors	80 soldiers
Casualties	Unknown	80 killed

most widely accepted account, Captain Fetterman insists that he be permitted to lead the rescue party. Carrington agrees but orders Fetterman not to pursue the warriors beyond Lodge Trail Ridge. Fetterman's relief party of cavalry and infantry has exactly 80 men, ironically the precise number Fetterman has claimed he would need to defeat the entire Sioux Nation.

When Fetterman arrives on the scene, the warriors break off their attack and begin to withdraw. One, an Oglala Lakota Sioux named Crazy Horse, stops to check his horse to entice the pursuing soldiers. Others follow Crazy Horse's lead and taunt the soldiers with insults and obscene gestures. Ignoring orders, Fetterman orders a pursuit beyond Lodge Trail Ridge until he and his men suddenly find themselves confronted by as many as 2,000 warriors. Within 20 minutes, Fetterman's entire force is annihilated in the greatest U.S. Army loss in any battle with Native Americans west of the Mississippi to this date.

When a relief force arrives, they find that the 80 dead soldiers have been stripped and their bodies mutilated. This news causes near panic at Fort Phil Kearny with its women and children, but the Native Americans do not attempt to attack the fort.

April 19, 1867

American Indian Wars (continued): Hancock's destruction of Pawnee Fork. In March 1867, Major General Winfield S. Hancock, commander of the Military Department of the Missouri, leads an expedition of 1,400 men across the southern Plains to intimidate Native Americans of the region. The troops march across Kansas without opposition, but several

Crazy Horse (ca. 1840–1877)

Lakota Sioux war chief. Paradoxically, Crazy Horse remains one of the most mysterious figures in American history. Most sources accept that Crazy Horse was born sometime in 1840. His father, who survived him and became one of the major sources of information about him, had also been called Crazy Horse, but when his son reached maturity and wished to take that name, his father took the name Worm. The tribal affiliation of Crazy Horse's mother is also somewhat ambiguous: most sources identify her as a Brule Sioux, but some contend that she was a Miniconjou Sioux.

As a young warrior, Crazy Horse earned a reputation for skill and fearlessness in battle against the Lakotas's tribal enemies: the Arikaras, Blackfeet, Crows, Pawnees, and Shoshones. After the Lakotas allied themselves with the Cheyennes, Crazy Horse distinguished himself in his first battles against the U.S. military, at Red Buttes and Platte River Bridge Station. He first came fully to the attention of the U.S. military and of the American public during Red Cloud's War (1866–1868). In violation of existing treaties, the U.S. Army had constructed forts along the Bozeman Trail, which provided an eastern route to gold-rich Virginia City, Montana. On December 21, 1866, Crazy Horse led a small number of warriors who lured cavalry and infantry units away from Fort Phil Kearny and into a trap sprung by many more Indians. Outnumbered more than 10 to 1, the 80 soldiers were wiped out in what became known as the Fetterman Massacre, named for the commander of the doomed unit, Captain William Fetterman. It was to this point the worst defeat suffered by the army during the Plains Indian Wars.

On August 2, 1867, Crazy Horse attempted to repeat the Fetterman Massacre when he led an attack on a wood-cutting party sent out from Fort Phil Kearny. But in what became known as the Wagon Box Fight, the soldiers surprised and eventually drove off the Lakotas with the much-enhanced firepower provided by their recently issued breech-loading rifles.

Ten years later during what became known as the Sioux War, or Great Sioux War (1876–1877), Crazy Horse led about 1,500 Lakota and Cheyenne warriors against Brigadier General George Crook's roughly equal force of cavalry, infantry, and Native American allies in the Battle of the Rosebud on June 17, 1876. Although neither side committed fully enough to the battle to sustain sizable losses, Crook's advance into Sioux territory was temporarily checked, delaying his rendezvous with the 7th Cavalry Regiment under Lieutenant Colonel George A. Custer.

All Native American sources agree that Crazy Horse had a decisive role in the annihilation of Custer's men at the Battle of the Little Bighorn (June 25–26, 1876). But nothing is known about Crazy Horse's specific actions during the engagement. Nonetheless, his notoriety following the massacre of Custer and his troopers made him a prime target of the forces sent to subdue the Sioux and Cheyennes.

After his surrender in May 1877, Crazy Horse was held at Camp Robinson, Montana. Rumors of a possible insurrection among the Lakotas led to an order for his arrest. On September 5, 1877, Crazy Horse was bayoneted when resisting arrest. He died that night.

MARTIN KICH

Further Reading

Ambrose, Stephen E. *Crazy Horse and Custer: The Parallel Lives of Two American Warriors.* New York: Anchor Books, 1996.

Blevins, Winfred. *Stone Song: A Novel of the Life of Crazy Horse.* New York: Forge, 1995.

Matthiesen, Peter. *In the Spirit of Crazy Horse.* New York: Viking, 1991.

McMurtry, Larry. *Crazy Horse.* New York: Lipper/Viking, 1999.

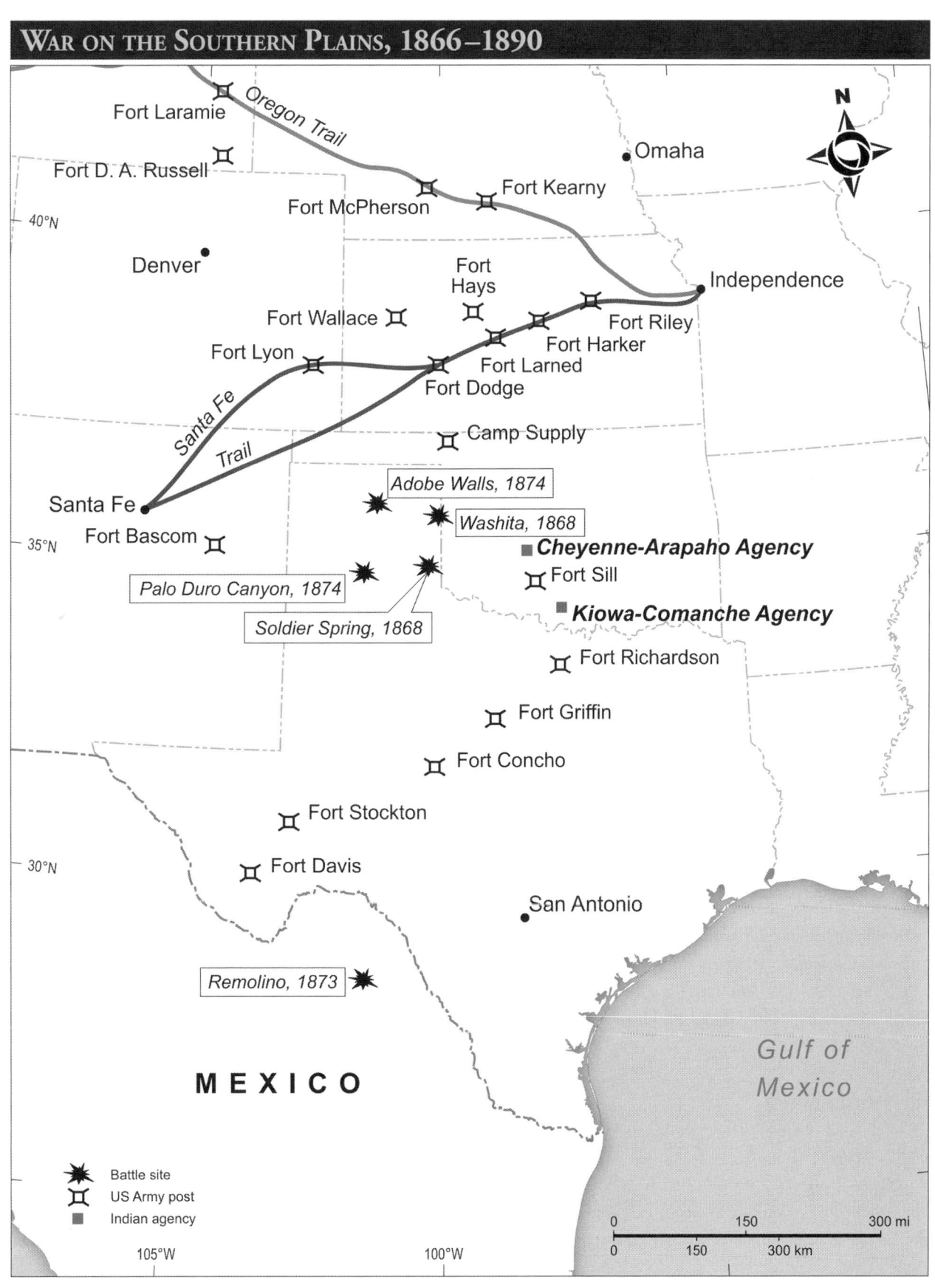

WAR ON THE SOUTHERN PLAINS, 1866–1890

Fort Laramie

Oregon Trail

Fort D. A. Russell

40°N

Fort McPherson

Fort Kearny

Omaha

Denver

Independence

Fort Hays

Fort Wallace

Fort Riley

Fort Lyon

Fort Harker

Santa Fe

Fort Larned

Fort Dodge

Trail

Camp Supply

Adobe Walls, 1874

Santa Fe

35°N

Washita, 1868

Fort Bascom

Cheyenne-Arapaho Agency

Fort Sill

Palo Duro Canyon, 1874

Kiowa-Comanche Agency

Soldier Spring, 1868

Fort Richardson

Fort Griffin

Fort Concho

Fort Stockton

30°N

Fort Davis

San Antonio

Remolino, 1873

MEXICO

Gulf of Mexico

Battle site

US Army post

Indian agency

0   150   300 mi

0   150   300 km

105°W   100°W

meetings with Cheyenne and Sioux leaders Tall Bull and Pawnee Killer in mid-April 1867 frustrate Hancock, as the Native Americans attend reluctantly. Hancock narrowly escapes death at one conference when Cheyenne leader Roman Nose is dissuaded by another chief from killing him.

On April 12 the Indian leaders slip away, and in retaliation Hancock orders their village burned. The Indians take this as a declaration of war and commence widespread raiding. On April 19 Hancock burns an abandoned Cheyenne and Sioux encampment at Pawnee Fork, sparking retaliatory attacks against nearby settlers.

June 13, 1867

Taiwan (Formosa) expedition. The U.S. Navy screw sloops *Hartford* (24 guns) and *Wyoming* (6 guns) land 181 men under Commander George C. Belknap to attack aborigines on Taiwan who had murdered the crew of the merchant bark *Rover*. In the fighting, Lieutenant Commander Alexander S. Mackenzie is mortally wounded.

June 19, 1867

The screw sloop *Sacramento* (9 guns), commanded by Captain Napoleon Collins, grounds at the mouth of the Godavari River in the state of Madras, India, and is a total loss. All hands are saved.

July 1, 1867

The British North America Act (the Constitution Act) establishes the Dominion of Canada. On the heels of the American Civil War and following several constitutional conferences, the British Parliament and the Canadian Parliament agree to the British North America Act (known as the Constitution Act). It officially creates the Canadian Confederation, "one Dominion under the name of Canada," consisting of the four provinces of Ontario, Quebec, Nova Scotia, and New Brunswick.

July 2, 1867

American Indian Wars (continued): Kidder Massacre. On June 1, 1867, U.S. Army lieutenant colonel George A. Custer departs Fort Hays, Kansas, with his 7th Cavalry Regiment of some 1,100 men to clear the area of the Platte and Arkansas Rivers of bands of hostile Sioux and Cheyenne warriors. The Indians easily evade the cavalry, and after patrolling north to Fort McPherson on the Platte River near present-day North Platte, Nebraska, Custer turns south to the forks of the Republican River near Benkleman, Nebraska. Again Custer fails to make contact.

On June 29 Major General Philip H. Sheridan, then commanding at Fort Sedgwick near Julesburg, Colorado, sends dispatches to Custer via a cavalry detachment of 10 troopers commanded by Lieutenant Lyman S. Kidder of the 2nd Cavalry Regiment, accompanied by Sioux guide Red Bead. Kidder expects to meet Custer at the forks of the Republican River, some 90 miles to the southeast. Kidder reaches Custer's campsite on the evening of July 1 but discovers it abandoned. Custer is off scouting to the south and then to the northwest. Kidder mistakes the trail of a wagon train that Custer has sent to Fort Wallace for Custer's own trail and follows it.

Around noon on July 2, a group of Lakotas discover Kidder's party north of Beaver Creek, a tributary of the Republican River. The Lakotas alert nearby Cheyennes, and the far more numerous warriors close on the soldiers. Kidder and his men try to escape to Beaver Creek, 12 miles north of present-day Edson, Kansas. Some cavalrymen are shot down on a ridge above the creek, but the remainder establish a defensive position near Beaver Creek. The soldiers are hopelessly outnumbered, and Kidder, his men, and Red Bead are all slain, some of them tortured before their deaths. The Indians mutilate and burn the bodies. Two of the Lakotas also die in the battle, one of them Chief Yellow Horse.

Having received no word from Sheridan, Custer begins a movement toward Fort Sedgwick. Arriving at Riverside Station some 40 miles to the west, he telegraphs the fort for orders and only then learns of the Kidder patrol and immediately returns south. On July 12 his men come across the decomposed bodies of Kidder and his party.

August 1, 1867

American Indian Wars (continued): Red Cloud's War (continued): Hayfield Fight. In July 1867, Fort C. F.

Smith in Montana Territory, established by Colonel Henry Carrington of the 18th Infantry Regiment to protect travelers along the Bozeman Trail, acquires several mowing machines for cutting hay, allowing the fort's garrison to gather its own hay rather than have to purchase it from local farmers.

On July 29 garrison commander Lieutenant Colonel Luther P. Bradley orders a mowing party of 6 civilians with the new machines to cut hay for the fort's animals. He assigns newly arrived Lieutenant Sigismund Sternberg and 19 soldiers to serve as an escort for the mowers at a meadow some three miles from the fort. Crow Indian scouts have repeatedly warned of an impending attack from hostile Cheyenne and Sioux warriors in the area, but with only two clashes having occurred in the last seven months, Bradley proceeds.

Oglala Sioux chief Red Cloud, meanwhile, has assembled nearly 1,000 warriors to resume attacks

 ## Springfield Model 1861 Rifled Musket

The Springfield Model 1861 .58-caliber was the most widely used infantry weapon of the American Civil War. In 1855, U.S. secretary of war Jefferson Davis, later president of the Confederacy, approved adoption by the army of the .58-caliber muzzle-loading rifled musket. The new weapon combined the percussion cap system of ignition with the minié ball. Such weapons had come into widespread use in the world's armies at midcentury. The percussion cap greatly increased reliability of fire and hence firepower, while rifling increased the effective range from some 80–100 yards to 300 yards. Thanks to the invention of the expanding cylindro-conoidal bullet known as the minié ball, the rifle could now be loaded as rapidly as the smoothbore musket. The 1861 model came to be named for the Springfield Arsenal, its original production facility.

The Model 1861 Springfield was 56 inches in length with a 40-inch barrel and weighed 9.5 pounds. It had a flip-up leaf sight and fired a bullet of 500 grains at a muzzle velocity of 950 feet per second and had a maximum effective range of 300 yards. The Model 1863 was essentially the same weapon but incorporated redesigned barrel bands and a new hammer. The Springfield's heavy, slow-moving lead bullet could exact frightful damage, tumbling in flight and flattening on impact, tearing away chunks of bone, which necessitated amputations.

With its attached 18-inch bayonet, the weapon stood taller than the average soldier of the time. The Springfield Model 1861 could be loaded and fired about three times per minute. The standard issue of ammunition going into combat was 40 paper cartridges per man, which would therefore provide only about a dozen minutes of sustained rapid fire.

The Springfield Arsenal could not produce the requisite number required, and some 20 firms also contracted to build the weapon. During the war approximately 1.5 million Models 1861 and 1863 were produced by a wide variety of manufacturing facilities, but Southern firms accounted for less than 1 percent of the total.

SPENCER C. TUCKER

Further Reading

Bilby, Joseph. *Civil War Firearms: Their Historical Background and Tactical Use.* New York: Da Capo, 2005.
Edwards, William B. *Civil War Guns.* Gettysburg, PA: Thomas Publications, 1997.
Graf, John F. *Standard Catalog of Civil War Firearms.* Iola, WI: Krause, 2009.

along the Bozeman Trail. Learning from his scouts of the hay-cutting party, he immediately convenes a war council to formulate an attack plan for the morning of August 1.

At the mowing site, the soldiers construct a makeshift corral of brush and logs to serve as both a pen for the draft animals and an improvised fortification. At 11:00 a.m. on August 1, warriors attack the civilian laborers working the mowing machines and chase them into the corral. The Native Americans then employ decoys in an attempt to lure the soldiers from their makeshift fort. When this fails, they assault the corral. The Indians expect to encounter slow-firing muzzle-loading muskets with long pauses between volleys of fire. The soldiers, however, have just been issued Model 1866 Springfield-Allin Trapdoor breech-loading .50-caliber rifles, supplied to the military in the West in consequence of the Fetterman Massacre. These have quadruple the rate of fire of the old muzzle-loaders. Nonetheless, the warriors mount four attacks on the corral, the last on foot. Refusing to take cover, Lieutenant Sternberg is mortally wounded early in the fight. With the detail's only noncommissioned officer, Sergeant James Norton, severely wounded shortly thereafter, command passes to civilian Don Colvin, a Civil War veteran.

When a messenger arrives at the fort with news of the battle, Bradley hesitates to send reinforcements, remembering the trap set during the Fetterman Massacre the previous December. At 3:30 p.m., however, he dispatches a mounted reconnaissance party, which confirms the severity of the fighting. Bradley then assembles a relief force of two infantry companies with a light howitzer. Their arrival forces the Indians to withdraw after nearly six hours of assaulting the corral. In the battle the army suffers 3 killed and 3 wounded. Estimates of Indian casualties are 18–23 killed and several dozen wounded.

August 2, 1867

American Indian Wars (continued): Red Cloud's War (continued): Wagon Box Fight. On August 2, 1867, Captain James Powell and 31 men from the 27th Infantry Regiment, guarding a party of 50–60 men cutting wood for Fort Phil Kearny along the Bozeman Trail in Wyoming Territory, come under attack from some 1,500 Sioux warriors led by Oglala Sioux chief Red Cloud. Powell's men seek refuge in a defensive perimeter created by positioning 14 wagons in an oval. During the ensuing five-hour fight, Powell loses 3 men killed and 2 wounded but reports Native American losses of as many as 60 killed and 120 wounded. The survival of so many of the soldiers is primarily due to the recent issuance of the Springfield Model 1866 Trapdoor .50-caliber breech-loading rifle. In his attack plan, Red Cloud had counted on the long reloading time of muzzle-loading weapons. The battle ends with the arrival of a relief force from Fort Phil Kearny.

August 28, 1867

The United States annexes Midway Island. Uninhabited Midway Atoll (Midway Islands or Midway Island) was sighted on July 5, 1859, by Captain N. C. Middlebrooks (commonly known as Brooks) of the merchant sailing ship *Gambia*. The uninhabited atoll is some 2.5 square miles in area. The islands are first known as the "Middlebrook Islands" or the "Brook Islands." Brooks claimed Midway for the United States under the Guano Islands Act of 1856, which authorized Americans to occupy uninhabited islands temporarily to obtain guano or fertilizer. On August 28, 1867, Captain William Reynolds of the screw sloop *Lackawanna* (15 guns) formally takes possession for the United States as a coaling station.

On December 28 the U.S. government formally annexes the islands. The name changes to "Midway" sometime later. This is the first overseas territory annexed by the United States. Formally known as the Unincorporated Territory of Midway Island, it is administered by the U.S. Navy.

October 18, 1867

Formal transfer of Alaska to the United States. In late 1866 the Russian government informs the U.S. government that it is interested in selling Alaska, which it regards as an economic liability. Ardent expansionist Secretary of State William H. Seward submits to the Senate a treaty providing for the transfer for the sum of $7.2 million. Vigorous debate follows over

 ## Breech-Loading Modern Heavy Guns at Sea

Ordnance experiments in the 1870s involving testing pressures in gun bores revealed that performance could be significantly enhanced by utilizing slower-burning gunpowder and longer barrels. Slow-burning large-grain powder, known as prismatic powder, prolonged the length of time that the charge acted on the projectile and thus increased both muzzle velocity and range. The problem with this was that the projectile left the barrel before all the powder was consumed. This could be solved by longer barrels, but that made muzzle-loading next to impossible. The slower-burning powders also required a powder chamber of diameter larger than that of the bore. All these factors and the need to protect gun crews during the loading process prompted a renewed search for an effective breech-loading gun.

Although breech-loaders had been tried at sea in the modern era, beginning in 1858 with the French *Gloire* and later in the Royal Navy *Warrior,* problems led to them being discarded. In 1864 the Royal Navy reverted definitively to muzzle-loading ordnance, but other nations, especially France, moved ahead with breech-loaders.

The old problem of ineffective sealing at the breech was only slowly overcome. In 1872 a French Army captain named de Bange came up with a "plastic gas check" that helped prevent escape of gases at the breech, and in 1875 France adopted the breech-loader. At the same time brass cartridge cases, already used for small arms, came into use for the smaller breech-loading guns.

An accident aboard the British battleship *Thunderer* in the Sea of Marmora in January 1879 helped prompt the Royal Navy's return to breech-loaders. Simultaneous firing was under way, with the main guns fired in salvo; during this, one of the battleship's 12-inch muzzle-loading guns misfired. This was not detected from the force of the discharge of the one gun, and both guns were run back in hydraulically to be reloaded. When they were again fired the double-charged gun blew up, killing 11 men and injuring 35 others. This could not have happened with a breech-loading gun, and in May the Admiralty set up a committee to investigate the merits of breech-loading versus muzzle-loading guns. In August 1879 after a committee of officers examined new breech-loaders, the Royal Navy decided to utilize the breech-loader in three battleships entering service in 1881–1882. The U.S. Navy steel cruisers *Atlanta, Boston,* and *Chicago,* authorized in the naval construction act of 1883 and marking the beginning of the modern U.S. Navy, were also the first equipped with modern breech-loading guns.

Guns also came to be described by a combination of their caliber (such as 12-inch) and length in calibers. Thus, a 12-inch/50 would be a gun with a bore diameter of 12 inches and a length of 50 feet from breech face to muzzle. Another change in the period was to guns of steel, which accompanied enormous increases in gun size. Krupp in Germany began producing cast steel rifled guns in 1860. The change to steel guns was made possible by the production of higher-quality steel. A steel jacket was shrunk over a steel tube, and layers of steel hoops were then shrunk over this. The system of jackets and hoops over an inner steel tube was followed by one in which steel wire was spun on under tension varying with the distance from the bore. This helped eliminate barrel droop. Bore lengths of the guns increased from 35 to 45 calibers and even to 40 to 45 calibers.

(*continued*)

(Continued)

The larger guns of the period required mechanized ammunition hoists and complex breech-loading gear. Their metal carriages recoiled on inclined metal slides that pivoted under the gun port. The slides were trained laterally by means of transverse truck wheels moving on racers, or iron paths set into the ship's deck.

SPENCER C. TUCKER

Further Reading

Hogg, Ian, and John Batchelor. *Naval Gun.* Poole, Dorset, UK: Blandford, 1978.

Lambert, Andrew, ed. *Steam, Steel & Shellfire: The Steam Warship, 1815–1905.* Annapolis, MD: Naval Institute Press, 1992.

Padfield, Peter. *Guns at Sea.* New York: St. Martin's, 1974.

Tucker, Spencer C. *Handbook of 19th Century Naval Warfare.* Annapolis, MD: Naval Institute Press, 2000.

what many call "Seward's Folly," but the Senate ratifies the treaty on April 19, 1867, and formal transfer takes place on October 18, 1867. On July 14, 1868, the House of Representatives approves the necessary monetary bill. Alaska adds 663,268 square miles of territory to the United States.

On October 29, U.S. troops enter Alaska. A battalion of troops commanded by Major Charles O. Wood from the 9th Infantry Regiment establishes a post at Sitka.

October 21 and 27, 1867

American Indian Wars (continued): Medicine Lodge Treaties. In October 1867, U.S. government peace commissioners meet with representatives of the Arapahos, Comanches, Kiowas, Kiowa-Apaches, and Southern Cheyennes along Medicine Lodge Creek, 60 miles south of Fort Larned, Kansas. There on October 21 and 27 the principal leaders of the southern Plains tribes sign three treaties promising to move onto two reservations in western Indian Territory (present-day Oklahoma) and to take no action to impede the construction of nearby railroads, wagon roads, and government facilities. In exchange for their compliance, the government promises to provide the signatory tribes agricultural implements, clothing, education for their children, and annuity payments and to prohibit white settlement on reservation land.

February 4, 1868

At Hiogo, Japan, the U.S. Navy screw sloop *Oneida* (12 guns) lands men to protect American lives and property.

February 7–26, 1868

At Montevideo, Uruguay, Rear Admiral Charles H. Davis lands detachments from five ships of the U.S. South Atlantic Squadron to safeguard foreign lives and property during an insurrection.

February 8, 1868

At Nagasaki, Japan, a party from the U.S. Navy screw sloop *Shenandoah* (9 guns) lands to protect American lives and property.

April 4, 1868

At Yokohama, Japan, 25 marines from the U.S. Navy screw sloop *Iroquois* (7 guns) and the side-wheel steamer *Monocacy* (10 guns) are landed to protect American interests.

April 29, 1868

American Indian Wars (continued): Red Cloud's War (continued): Fort Laramie Treaty. Signed between Major General William T. Sherman for the U.S. government and various bands of Lakota Sioux, Yanktonai Sioux, Santee Sioux, and Arapahos, the Fort

Signing of the Fort Laramie Treaty on April 29, 1868, by Major General William T. Sherman for the United States and various Sioux and Arapaho chiefs. The treaty ended Red Cloud's War of 1866–1868. (National Archives)

Laramie Treaty of April 19, 1868, largely ends Red Cloud's War (1866–1868), although Red Cloud himself does not sign until October. The treaty meets almost all Sioux demands, including the abandonment of Forts Reno, Phil Kearny, and C. F. Smith, and the closing of the Bozeman Trail. The treaty also recognizes Native American dominion over the Powder River country and vast hunting grounds in Wyoming and Montana, and it sets aside most of the Dakota Territory west of the Missouri River as the Great Sioux Reservation. For the first time in its history, the U.S. government has negotiated a peace that concedes everything demanded by the opposing party and secures nothing in return.

The Fort Laramie Treaty is one of the last important treaties signed between the U.S. government and the Plains Indians. The failure of the federal government to live up to its terms and the inability of the

signing tribes to enforce the treaty on all their members lead to the Great Sioux War (Black Hills War) of 1876–1877 and eventual removal of the Black Hills from Lakota ownership.

May 30, 1868

First celebration of Memorial Day. Former U.S. Army major general John A. Logan, now a U.S. representative from Illinois who was instrumental in founding the Grand Army of the Republic, calls on Union soldiers and veterans to decorate with flowers the graves of military dead. First known as Decoration Day, it is later named Memorial Day.

July 9, 1868

Loss of USS *Suwanee*. Off Vancouver Island in Queen Victoria Sound, British Columbia, the U.S. Navy side-wheel steamer *Suwanee* under Commander

Richard S. Law hits an uncharted rock and is lost. All its crew are saved.

September 17–25, 1868

American Indian Wars (continued): Battle of Beecher's Island (Arikaree Fight). In the summer of 1868, Oglala Sioux and Cheyenne war parties move east through northwestern Kansas to battle their traditional enemies, the Pawnees. While passing through the Solomon and Saline River Valleys, the warriors attack a number of farms, murdering scores of settlers, burning farms, and taking a white woman captive. In response, U.S. Army major general Philip Sheridan, commander of the Department of the Missouri, authorizes his longtime aide Major George A. Forsyth, with Lieutenant Henry Ward Beecher as second-in-command, to raise a company of settlers and pursue the hostiles. This unit, known as "Solomon Avengers," is well armed with Spencer repeating carbines.

On September 10 Forsyth's command of 50 men departs Fort Wallace in western Kansas to intercept a party of raiders. Four days later his men come across an Indian trail, which the scouts follow westward along the Arikaree Fork of the Republican River. On the morning of September 17 the scouts come under attack along the Arikaree in northeastern Colorado, near present-day Wray, by as many as 600 Arapaho, Northern Cheyenne, and Oglala Sioux warriors led by Northern Cheyenne warrior Roman Nose. Realizing that they will be ridden down or shot down if they attempt escape, the scouts take shelter on an island in the nearly dry Arikaree streambed.

Despite suffering several casualties, including Beecher (for whom the island and battle are named) mortally wounded, the men dig shallow entrenchments in the sandy soil and hold off several Native American attacks. That night, badly outnumbered, still surrounded, and with all their horses dead, Forsyth sends two men—Jack Stilwell and Pierre Trudeau—to get word to Fort Wallace 85 miles distant. They arrive there on September 22. The remaining scouts on Beecher Island employ their repeating Spencer carbines to good advantage and manage to hold off successive Indian assaults, surviving mainly on horse flesh, until the arrival on September 25 of Captain Louis Carpenter and the Buffalo Soldiers of Troop H of the 10th Cavalry Regiment.

In the battle Forsyth loses 6 killed and 15 wounded. Native American losses are estimated at 9 to more than 30 killed, including Roman Nose, and perhaps 60–70 wounded. The battle helps convince Sheridan that small units of militia are insufficient to maintain peace on the frontier.

November 18, 1868–March 28, 1869

American Indian Wars (continued): Washita Campaign. In October 1867, leaders of five Indian nations had signed the Medicine Lodge Treaties (see October 21 and 27, 1867). Of the five nations represented, the Southern Cheyennes are the least united in support of the treaty. Chief Black Kettle had been reluctant to sign the document until the militant Cheyenne Dog Soldiers agreed to its terms. Unable to convince war chief Roman Nose and his band of the merits of peace, Black Kettle nonetheless affixed his mark to the treaty, and he and his followers settled into reservation life on lands below the Arkansas River.

During the winter of 1867–1868, food stores from the autumn buffalo hunts sustain the reservation Cheyennes. With the approach of spring, however, supplies dwindle, and the promised government support fails to arrive in adequate quantities. Most disconcerting for the Cheyennes is the absence of promised guns and ammunition needed for hunting. Although Indian agent Edward W. Wynkoop tries to reassure the disaffected, some young Cheyennes, angered by what they regard as the duplicity of the white peace commissioners, leave the reservation and travel north to join Roman Nose and the other resistant factions.

In response to the growing defiance of the U.S. government's reservation policy among the Indians on the southern Plains, Major General Philip H. Sheridan, commanding the Department of the Missouri—with the full support of Lieutenant General William Tecumseh Sherman, commander of the Military Division of the Missouri—institutes a strategy to bring about Native American compliance. Sheridan plans a winter operation utilizing converging columns of cavalry and infantry to round up warriors rendered largely immobile by lack of supplies and fodder for their horses.

On November 18, 1868, Major Andrew W. Evans departs Fort Bascom, New Mexico, with 563 men and marches eastward down the South Canadian River. Two weeks later Major Eugene A. Carr departs Fort Lyon, Colorado, with 650 men and, guided by William "Buffalo Bill" Cody, proceeds southward toward Antelope Hills in Indian Territory. On November 23, the third and largest column of 800 men of the 7th Cavalry Regiment, under Lieutenant Colonel George A. Custer, departs Camp Supply, a depot on the North Canadian River 100 miles south of Fort Dodge, Kansas, and heads south toward the Washita River. Sheridan instructs Custer to follow a fresh trail in the snow, suspecting that it has been made by a Cheyenne raiding party returning from Kansas.

Following the Battle of the Washita in which his 7th Cavalry Regiment attacks and destroys Black Kettle's peaceful camp (see November 27, 1868), Custer continues operations. The Washita Campaign officially ends on March 28, 1869, when the 7th Cavalry returns to Camp Supply.

November 27, 1868

American Indian Wars (continued): Sheridan's Washita Campaign (continued): Battle of the Washita (Washita Massacre). In the autumn of 1868, Chief Black Kettle of the Southern Cheyennes and his followers establish an encampment at a bend of the Washita River, 40 miles east of the Antelope Hills and 2 miles from present-day Cheyenne, Wyoming. Its 51 lodges contain women, children, and elders as well as recently returned young warriors who are more willing to accept the peaceful ways of Black Kettle following the death of Roman Nose in the Battle of Beecher's Island (see September 17–25, 1868). There are additional Arapaho, Kiowa, and Cheyenne camps downriver.

Learning that U.S. troops are on the move to force compliance with the Medicine Lodge Treaties (see October 21 and 27, 1867), Black Kettle and other Cheyenne and Arapaho leaders travel 100 miles to Fort Cobb and there meet with its commander, Brigadier General William B. Hazen, to seek protection for their people. To their dismay, Hazen maintains that he does not have the authority to allow the Cheyenne and Arapaho bands to move closer to the fort. He instructs the Indian leaders to return to their camps.

On November 26 one of the army's three converging columns, that of the 800 men of the 7th Cavalry Regiment led by Lieutenant Colonel George A. Custer, approaches Black Kettle's camp undetected. On Sheridan's instructions, the soldiers are following a trail in the snow, which the general suspects has been made by a Cheyenne raiding party and leads directly to Black Kettle's encampment. Without bothering to determine the identify of his presumed foe, Custer orders an attack for the following morning.

Just before daybreak on November 27, troopers from the 7th Cavalry, with the regimental band playing "Garryowen," charge into the sleeping village from four directions. The surprised Cheyennes can do little except attempt to escape. A few warriors vainly fight back. Black Kettle and his wife attempt to escape across a ford in the river, only to be shot down. Within 10 minutes, the men of the 7th Cavalry control the village.

Estimates vary, but it is probable that 103 Cheyenne men, women, and children die in the attack; another 53 women and children are taken captive of the total camp population of some 250 people. Custer loses 21 killed and 13 wounded, most of these commanded by

Battle of the Washita (Washita Massacre)		
Date	November 27, 1868	
Location	2 miles from Cheyenne, Wyoming	
Opponents (*winner)	*United States	Cheyennes
Commander	Lieutenant Colonel George A. Custer	Chief Black Kettle
#	800 7th Cavalry Regiment troopers	250 Native Americans (total camp population)
Casualties	21 killed, 13 wounded	103 Cheyenne men, women, and children killed; 53 women and children taken captive

Soldiers of the 7th Cavalry Regiment under Lieutenant Colonel George Armstrong Custer attack Chief Black Kettle's peaceful Cheyenne encampment along the Washita River on November 27, 1868. A reproduction of an 1878 painting by James E. Taylor. (Library of Congress)

Major Joel H. Elliott. Attempting to corral a group of Indians fleeing downriver, Elliot and his men are themselves surrounded and killed by members of the nearby Arapaho and Cheyenne camps coming to Black Kettle's aid.

As more and more mounted warriors arrive on the scene, Custer's troopers set up a defensive perimeter and then systematically set fire to Black Kettle's lodges, destroying the supply of winter food and clothing. The cavalrymen also slaughter more than 800 Cheyenne ponies and mules. To escape an increasingly foreboding environment, Custer abandons efforts to locate Major Elliott, in late afternoon feigns an attack against Indian encampments downriver, and departs across the river after dark. The 7th Cavalry returns triumphantly to Camp Supply on the North Canadian River on December 2.

The Battle of the Washita, more of a massacre than a battle, deals a debilitating blow to the Southern Cheyennes. With their winter supplies destroyed, along with their herd of mules and ponies, the majority have little choice but to submit to reservation life. The Battle of the Washita also demonstrates to noncompliant Plains tribes that they can no longer count on winter to provide some security from army attack.

January 7, 1869

Establishment of Fort Sill, Indian Territory. Located near present-day Lawton, Oklahoma, Fort Sill serves as a base for operations against nearby hostile Kiowa and Comanche Indians. It is today the only active installation of all the army forts of the southern Plains during the Indian Wars and houses the U.S. Army's Field Artillery School.

March 3, 1869

Congress reduces the U.S. Army's 45 infantry regiments to 25. The 4 regiments of African Americans become 2 regiments: the 38th and 41st Infantry Regiments are consolidated into the 24th Infantry regiment, while the 39th and 40th Regiments become the 25th Infantry Regiment.

March 8, 1869

Four days after he is inaugurated president of the United States, Ulysses S. Grant appoints Lieutenant General William T. Sherman to succeed him as commanding general of the army as a full general.

July 8, 1869

American Indian Wars (continued): Skirmish on the Republican River. Three U.S. Army soldiers, led by Corporal John Kile and assisted by Pawnee Indian scout Sergeant Mad Bear (Co-rux-te-chod-ish), are attacked by eight hostile Indians near the Republican River in Kansas. Mad Bear charges ahead to secure a prisoner. Although wounded by friendly fire, he continues fighting. Later Kile and Mad Bear are both awarded the Medal of Honor. Mad Bear is the first Indian recipient of the nation's highest award for valor.

July 11, 1869

American Indian Wars (continued): Battle of Summit Springs. On July 9, 1869, Major Eugene A. Carr departs Fort McPherson, Nebraska, with some 500 men: 244 members of the 5th Cavalry Regiment and a battalion of Pawnee Indian scouts. Among the participants is scout William F. "Buffalo Bill" Cody. Carr's mission is to stop hostile Cheyenne Indians from raiding into western Kansas and move them to a reservation in Indian Territory (Oklahoma). Unaware that they are being closely pursued, some 200 Cheyennes under Chief Tall Bull make camp at Summit Springs in present-day Logan County in northeastern Colorado while they wait for the South Platte River to subside before crossing. Believing that they are not in danger, the Cheyennes allow their horses to graze at a distance.

In midafternoon on July 11, troopers of the 5th Cavalry and the Pawnee scouts locate the Cheyennes and charge in two parallel columns from about one mile distant. The Pawnees reach the Cheyenne encampment first, while the cavalrymen encircle the camp to prevent the Dog Soldiers from gaining their horses. The Indian women and children flee to a ravine leading to the river. Chief Tall Bull and about 20 warriors fight to cover their escape.

In the battle, the cavalrymen sustain only 1 man wounded. Carr reports 52 Cheyennes, including Tall Bull, killed and 17 women and children taken prisoner. The soldiers also recover 2 captured white women, but they find the bodies of another and her young son, apparently killed during the attack. Carr's men then destroy 84 lodges, along with military supplies, food, clothing, and camp equipment; 274 Cheyenne horses and 144 mules are herded away. The loss of their supplies and horses renders the remaining Cheyennes virtually powerless.

The Battle of Summit Springs ends Cheyenne Dog Soldier occupation of western Kansas and eastern Colorado. Although White Horse and some other survivors join the Northern Cheyennes, most move south under Bull Bear and surrender at Camp Supply.

January 23, 1870

American Indian Wars (continued): Marias Massacre (Baker Massacre). The growing number of whites settling on the northern Plains brings increasing tension with Indians of the region. In 1867, a Blackfoot (Piegan) Sioux named Owl Child purportedly steals several horses from white trader Malcolm Clark. Owl Child claims that Clark had stolen his horses and that he simply replied in kind. Clark and his son hunt down Owl Child and severely beat him. In August 1869 Owl Child and several other Blackfeet murder Clark and seriously wound his son, whereupon area settlers demand retribution.

The army insists that Owl Child be turned over to U.S. authorities, dead or alive, in two weeks' time. Owl Child goes into hiding, protected by Blackfoot chief Mountain Chief. With the expiration of the deadline and Owl Child still in hiding, Major Eugene M. Baker leads a detachment of the 2nd Cavalry Regiment to find Owl Child and punish those who have given him refuge.

On January 23, 1870, Baker learns that Mountain Chief's clan is camped along the Marias River in Montana. Learning of the cavalry presence, Mountain Chief flees with his people. The encampment that Baker attacks this day is not that of Mountain Chief but instead is the encampment of Chief Heavy Runner, who has generally enjoyed friendly relations with whites. Reportedly Baker ignores word from his scouts that the encampment might not be that of Mountain Chief.

On this day most of the men in the village are out hunting, leaving behind chiefly women, children, and the elderly. In the ensuing rapid army attack, at least 173 Blackfeet perish (33 men, including Chief Heavy Runner; 90 women; and 50 children); another 140 are taken prisoner. There is only 1 army casualty, a cavalryman killed in a fall from his horse. Following reports in the Eastern press, Baker comes under scrutiny for what critics call the Marias Massacre (often also called the Baker Massacre), but the army concludes that Baker had only followed orders, and there is no official investigation.

January 24, 1870

Loss of USS *Oneida*. The screw sloop *Oneida* under Commander Edward P. Williams sinks with the loss of 125 lives when it is struck by the British P & O steamer *City of Bombay* on the evening of January 24, 1870, as it is exiting Yokohama Harbor, Japan. Japanese fishermen save 65 crew members, but the *City of Bombay* continues on its way without rendering assistance (its captain is later suspended).

June 17, 1870

On the Pacific coast of Mexico, Lieutenant Willard H. Brownson leads boats from the U.S. Navy screw sloop *Mohican* to attack pirates in the Teacapan River.

The seamen and marines disperse the pirates and burn their ship, the former British screw gunboat *Forward*, sold out of the navy the year before.

July 12, 1870

American Indian Wars (continued): Battle of the Little Wichita River. Frustrated by the confinement of their people to a reservation in southeastern Indian Territory (Oklahoma) and its lack of adequate resources, some Kiowa warriors begin raiding across the Red River into northern Texas. Their success exacerbates already tense relations with white settlers and undercuts the authority of tribal leaders counseling peace.

Chief Kicking Bird is among Kiowa tribal leaders accused of cowardice for attempting to establish close relations with whites. To restore his prestige, in late June or early July he leads about 100 warriors across the Red River into Wichita County, Texas, to do battle with the army. A small group of young warriors breaks off from the main body and, disregarding Kicking Bird's orders forbidding hostile contact with civilians, attacks and robs a mail stage in Jack County. Word of this reaches Fort Richardson on the morning of July 6.

Captain Curwen B. McClellan of the 6th Cavalry Regiment promptly assembles 55 troopers, 2 officers, a surgeon, and a civilian scout to find the hostiles. Moving northwest, McClellan pursues the Indians' trail for five days and about 50 miles, finally locating the main body on the evening of July 11.

At 10:00 a.m. on July 12, McClellan's men attack the Kiowa camp, but the soldiers soon realize that they are outnumbered 2 to 1 and that the Kiowas are armed with Spencer rifles, which are superior to their own weapons. McClellan is fortunate to lose only 3 men killed and 11 wounded in several hours of combat before he is finally able to extricate his men and escape across the West Fork of the Trinity River. He estimates Kiowa casualties at 15 killed and an unknown number of wounded. That night the troops are reinforced by cowboys from Terrell Ranch and 20 cavalrymen stationed at nearby Jean. On July 14, McClellan and his men arrive back at Fort Richardson. Returning home with his reputation restored,

Kicking Bird dedicates himself to restoring peaceful relations between his people and the whites.

October 29, 1870

Loss of USS *Saginaw*. The U.S. Navy side-wheel steamer *Saginaw* under Commander Montgomery Sicard strikes a reef and is lost at Ocean Island (now Green Island, Kure Atoll) in the mid-Pacific. The crew gets ashore, but prospects of rescue appear remote, and on November 18 the ship's executive officer, Lieutenant John G. Talbot, sets out in the gig with five volunteers to sail the 1,500 miles to Hawaii. Thirty-one days later the gig swamps in the surf while approaching Kauai. Talbot and four of the men drown, but Coxswain William Halford survives to secure the rescue of the remaining members of the *Saginaw*'s crew.

March 3, 1871

Indian Appropriation Act. President Ulysses S. Grant signs the Indian Appropriation Act, part of his so-called Quaker Peace Policy. The legislation nullifies previous treaties with the Indians and ends the practice of treating the tribes as sovereign nations. It directs that all Indians be treated as individuals and legally designated as "wards" of the federal government. The act is justified as a means to avoid misunderstandings in treaty negotiations, where whites have too often wrongly assumed that a chief is also that tribe's chief of state, but its practical effect is another step toward dismantling tribal structure. Under Grant's assimilationist policy, the Department of the Interior embarks on a number of education and medical programs, and large quantities of food, clothing, and books are donated by churches and relief organizations to the various tribes. Housing on reservations is sharply increased, as is the number of schools and teachers. Land under cultivation and quantities of livestock are also dramatically increased.

April 30, 1871

American Indian Wars (continued): Camp Grant Massacre. Following a number of raids by hostile Chiricahua Apaches in southern Arizona Territory, Tucson residents plot revenge, and William Oury and Jesus Maria Elías lead 6 Anglo-Americans, 48 Mexican Americans, and 92 Tohono O'odham warriors in an attack on a peaceful village of Apaches, most of whom are women and children, who had surrendered to the U.S. Army at Camp Grant. The village is located up Aravaipa Creek, five miles from Camp Grant and too distant for the soldiers there to be aware of what is transpiring. The attackers murder more than 100 of the villagers; some 30 children are taken captive, and most of them are sold into slavery at Sonora, Mexico.

Although there is jubilation among residents of Tucson concerning the deed, newspapers in the East express outrage, and President Ulysses S. Grant threatens to impose martial law to prosecute those responsible. Under this pressure, on October 23, 1871, a grand jury hands down 111 indictments. Following a weeklong trial in December, the jury quickly returns a not guilty verdict.

Meanwhile, the survivors of the massacre have dispersed. In 1872 they return to Camp Grant and agree to settle on the San Carlos River to the north. Their lands in the San Pedro Valley are taken by Anglo-Americans and Mexican Americans.

May 8, 1871

Treaty of Washington. In Washington, D.C., British and U.S. representatives sign a treaty to resolve outstanding boundary disputes between the United States and the Dominion of Canada. They agree to the establishment of a commission. The chief boundary issue of sovereignty over San Juan Island is to be decided by arbitration headed by Kaiser Wilhelm II of Germany. He then appoints a three-man commission that meets in Geneva, Switzerland, for nearly a year, and he then rules on October 21, 1872, in favor of the U.S. position that the center of Haro Strait is the international boundary line. San Juan Island passes to U.S. control, and both sides withdraw their small garrisons there, the British in 1872 and the Americans in 1874.

May 18, 1871

American Indian Wars (continued): Warren Wagon Train Raid. While on an inspection tour of Texas, commanding general of the army General William T.

Sherman and a small escort pass along the Jacksboro-Belknap road unmolested by a large Kiowa raiding party lying in wait near Salt Creek, eight miles west of Fort Richardson, and led by Chiefs Satanta (White Bear), Satank, and Big Tree. Unaware of Sherman's presence, the hostiles opt not to attack the soldiers but to attack instead, less than an hour later, a large private contractor wagon train carrying supplies to forts in western Texas. The Kiowas torture to death seven teamsters, then mutilate the bodies. Sherman subsequently visits the scene of the attack, prompting him to intensify military activity on the southern Plains. Satanta, who boasts of his role in the raid, is arrested on May 27 at the Fort Sill Agency, along with Satank and Big Tree. The three are sent to Fort Richardson for trial, although Satank is killed en route while attempting escape. The other two chiefs are tried, convicted of murder, and sentenced to be executed. The punishment is subsequently reduced to life in prison, and in October 1873 the two are paroled.

May 30–July 3, 1871

U.S. naval expedition to Korea. Washington dispatches a squadron of five warships under Rear Admiral John Rodgers Jr. in support of an effort to investigate the imprisonment and murder by Koreans of American seamen from the merchantman *General Sherman*. Rodgers flies his flag in the screw frigate

Battle for the Citadel		
Date	June 11, 1871	
Location	Han River estuary, near Chemulpo (present-day Inchon, Republic of Korea)	
Opponents (*winner)	*United States	Kingdom of Korea
Commander	Commander Lewis A. Kimberly	Unknown
#	575 sailors, 109 marines	Unknown
Casualties	3 killed, 11 wounded	243 killed, 20 prisoners, many of them wounded; 481 cannon captured, along with numerous firearms

Colorado and also has the screw gunboat *Alaska*, the screw sloop *Benita*, the side-wheel gunboat *Monocacy*, and the screw tug *Palos*. With him is U.S. minister to China Frederick Low. Their mission is to secure a treaty that will guarantee proper treatment for shipwrecked American sailors but also to establish diplomatic ties and trade relations with Korea.

On May 30, 1871, Rodgers's squadron anchors near Chemulpo (present-day Inchon) at the mouth of the channel leading to the Han River. Low refuses to meet with lower-level officials, informing them that only when those of the first rank present themselves will he reveal the purpose of the visit, although he assures the Koreans that the Americans mean no harm. The effort to treat with the Korean government soon turns into armed conflict, for on May 31 one of five Korean forts on Gan-ghwa (Kanghwa) Island in the Han River estuary opens fire on the *Palos*. The American warships return fire. The only American casualties before the forts cease fire are two seamen, wounded in a launch.

Rodgers demands an apology from the Koreans. With none forthcoming, on June 10, 1871, Rodgers sends ashore at Gan-ghwa a naval brigade under Commander Lewis A. Kimberly, consisting of 575 sailors under Lieutenant Commander Silas Casey Jr. and 109 marines under Captain McLane Tilton, with seven guns. The *Monocacy* and *Palos* provide covering fire for the landing party. The Koreans manning the first two forts withdraw following only token resistance.

On June 11 the brigade advances against the principal fort, known as the Citadel, and its two supporting forts. Fierce fighting follows before the Citadel is taken. The Americans count 243 Koreans killed; 20 are taken prisoner, many of them wounded. The landing party sustains 3 killed and 11 wounded. The Americans also capture 481 cannon of varying types and calibers, along with hundreds of matchlock muskets. The Americans then demolish the forts.

Ignoring this American military success, the Korean government refuses to resume negotiations, claiming that there is no possibility of relations between two such distant nations. Indeed, the Korean government strengthens its policies against treating

Matchlock

The matchlock was the successor to the primitive early individual hand gonne known as the harquebus (arquebus). The first illustration of a matchlock mechanism dates to 1475, and matchlocks were in general use in Europe by the 1500s. The Portuguese then transported the technology to India, China, and Japan. As with most individual firearms through at least the mid-19th century, the matchlock had a long wooden stock. One end of the stock fitted against the individual's shoulder, while the stock itself held the long cast-iron barrel and firing mechanism. Unlike the primitive hand gonne, the matchlock had a trigger mechanism. On the trigger being pulled, its mechanism plunged the glowing tip of the match (really a very slow-burning fuse) into priming powder in a pan, which then ignited the main charge in the barrel. A great many varieties of matchlocks existed, but in most cases the priming pan had to be opened by hand before the trigger was pulled.

Matchlocks did not immediately supplant bows or crossbows. Indeed, matchlocks had many limitations. The match proved susceptible to rain and wind, and it could reveal troop positions at night, compromising ambushes and surprise attacks. Matchlocks initially had great psychological impact against native peoples unfamiliar with firearms. The natives soon overcame their fear of the great smoke, noise, and flame from the matchlocks and before long were trading for or capturing these weapons for themselves. The matchlock was also far slower to load and fire than longbows and crossbows and could not compete with them in terms of accuracy. There was also the concern of an accidental discharge. The matchlock's successors were the wheel-lock and the far more reliable flintlock. The matchlock's simplicity and ready availability kept it in service in European armies until about 1720. It was eventually replaced by the flintlock as the chief infantry armament.

Spencer C. Tucker

Further Reading

Blair, Claude, ed. *Pollard's History of Firearms*. New York: Macmillan, 1983.

Brown, M. L. *Firearms in Colonial America: The Impact on History and Technology, 1492–1792*. Washington, DC: Smithsonian Institution Press, 1980.

Lenk, Torsten. *The Flintlock: Its Origin and Development*. New York: Bramhall House, 1965.

Peterson, Harold L. *Arms and Armor in Colonial America, 1526–1783*. New York: Bramhall House, 1956.

with foreigners. Rodgers's squadron departs Korean waters on July 3, having failed in its mission.

April 20, 1872

American Indian Wars (continued): Gonzales Wagon Train Fight. At Howard's Well in Crockett County, Texas, a large number of Kiowas under Big Bow and Comanches led by White Horse attack a government wagon train led by a man named Gonzales. All 16 teamsters are killed; the wounded are tied to the wagon train wheels, doused with kerosene, and set

on fire. A woman and her small child are captured, but the child is soon killed, its head bashed against a wagon wheel.

Captain N. Clooney and two cavalry companies then arrive on the scene. They drive off the Indians but at a cost to themselves of 1 officer and 1 trooper killed.

September 14, 1872

Settlement of the *Alabama* Claims. The U.S. government has long held that the construction during the

Civil War of Confederate commerce raiders in the United Kingdom, although the ships were not armed there, was illegal. The U.S. government presses the British government for compensation for the destruction that the raiders caused to the U.S. merchant marine. Following the German victory over France in 1871, British leaders conclude that it might be wise to reach some accommodation with the United States against the possibility of a German drive for world hegemony.

An international tribunal meets in Geneva to discuss what became known as the *Alabama* Claims, and on September 14, 1872, the tribunal awards the U.S. government $15.5 million in damages. This comes to be regarded as an important step in the peaceful settlement of international disputes and victory for the world rule of law.

September 29, 1872

American Indian Wars (continued): Battle of the North Fork of the Red River (McClellan Creek). Despite the government's Quaker Peace Policy, commanding general of the army General William T. Sherman is determined to end hostile actions by non-reservation Indians in the Texas Panhandle. On July 28, 1872, Colonel Ranald S. Mackenzie, commanding the 4th Cavalry Regiment, sets out against Indians of the Llano Estacado with 284 men of the 4th Cavalry and 24th Infantry Regiments, 2 surgeons, 20 Tonkawa scouts, and a Comanchero prisoner named Polonia Ortiz.

Mackenzie's men proceed to Fort Sumner, New Mexico, then north to Fort Bascom in mid-August, after which they turn east into the Panhandle, following Tierra Blanca Creek to near present-day Canyon, Texas. They have had no significant contacts with hostile Indians, Comancheros, or cattle thieves.

After a period of rest at a supply base, on September 21 Mackenzie proceeds to the Red River headwaters. Following his return route of nearly a month before, he arrives at the Salt Fork of the Red River about five miles north of present-day Clarendon. Leaving behind his supplies with a detachment to protect them, Mackenzie proceeds north with 222 officers and men and 9 Tonkawa scouts, crossing the south prong of McClellan Creek.

On the afternoon of September 29, Mackenzie's scouts locate a large Indian village in a valley on the south bank of the North Fork of the Red River, six miles southeast of present-day Lefors. The village of 262 lodges is headed by Kotsoteka Comanche chief Mow-way, who is away at the Wichita Agency near Fort Sill. In his absence, the subchief Kai-wotche has charge. The Indians, busy at normal daily tasks, are taken by surprise when the troopers charge. Within a half hour the soldiers overcome all resistance.

Mackenzie reports 23 Comanches killed, including Kai-wotche and his wife. Another 130, mostly women and children, are taken prisoner, some of them wounded. The number of Indian dead is probably higher because the warriors reportedly threw some of their dead into a deep pool to keep the bodies from being scalped by the Tonkawas. Mackenzie loses 2 men killed and 2 seriously wounded. The soldiers round up between 800 and 3,000 horses and mules. They discover substantial evidence of the band's depredations, including proof that a number of the mules had been stolen. The troops burn the lodges, food stocks, equipment, and most of the Indians' possessions.

Soon after dark, Mackenzie moves about two miles distant and camps. That night and the next, however, the Comanches are able to recover many of their horses as well as those of the Tonkawa scouts. Mackenzie has, however, dealt a crippling blow to the renegades and has mastered the terrain over which future battles will be fought. His victory ends the Llano Estacado as an Indian sanctuary. Shortly after the battle, Mow-way and Parra-o-coom (Bull Bear) move their own bands to the vicinity of the Wichita Agency. Nokoni chief Horseback, who has relatives among the Indian prisoners, persuades the Comanches to trade stolen livestock and white captives for their own women and children held by the army. This is completed by June 1873.

November 29, 1872

American Indian Wars (continued): Beginning of the Modoc War: Battle of the Lost River. In July 1872 in the Oregon Territory, Superintendent T. B. Ordenal is ordered by the Bureau of Indian Affairs to relocate the

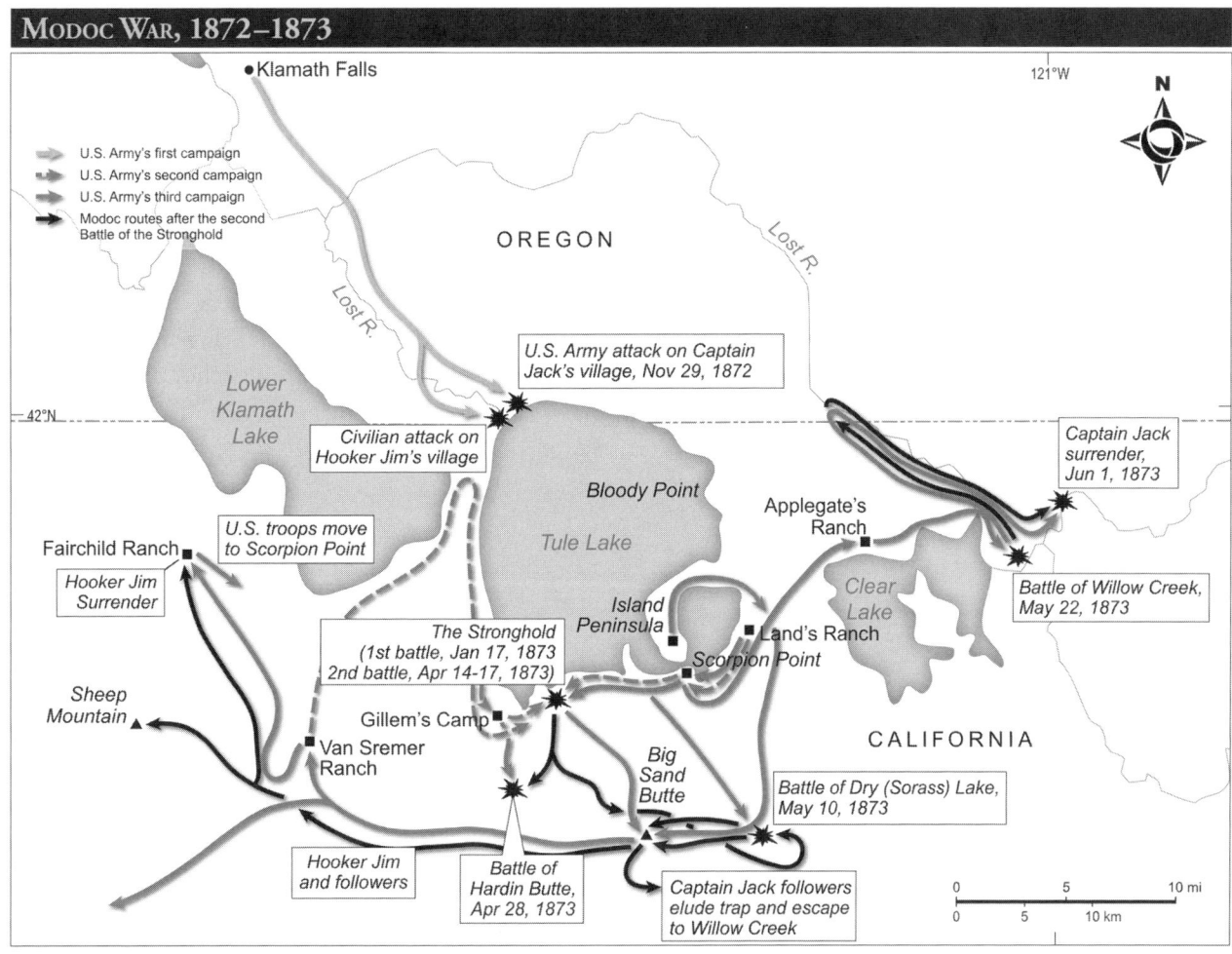

MODOC WAR, 1872–1873

- U.S. Army's first campaign
- U.S. Army's second campaign
- U.S. Army's third campaign
- Modoc routes after the second Battle of the Stronghold

Klamath Falls

121°W

N

OREGON

Lost R.

Lost R.

Lower Klamath Lake

42°N

U.S. Army attack on Captain Jack's village, Nov 29, 1872

Civilian attack on Hooker Jim's village

Bloody Point

Applegate's Ranch

Captain Jack surrender, Jun 1, 1873

Fairchild Ranch

Hooker Jim Surrender

U.S. troops move to Scorpion Point

Tule Lake

Battle of Willow Creek, May 22, 1873

Island Peninsula

Clear Lake

Land's Ranch

Scorpion Point

Sheep Mountain

The Stronghold (1st battle, Jan 17, 1873 2nd battle, Apr 14-17, 1873)

Gillem's Camp

Van Sremer Ranch

CALIFORNIA

Big Sand Butte

Battle of Dry (Sorass) Lake, May 10, 1873

Hooker Jim and followers

Battle of Hardin Butte, Apr 28, 1873

Captain Jack followers elude trap and escape to Willow Creek

0   5   10 mi
0   5   10 km

Modoc Indians to the Klamath Reservation, by force if necessary. The Modocs refuse to live on a reservation next to their traditional enemies, the Klamaths, however. Modocs led by Captain Jack (Kintpuash) leave Fort Klamath for their homeland on Tule Lake in California.

Along the Lost River on November 29, 1872, 40 troopers of the 1st Cavalry Regiment under Captain James Jackson, having left from Fort Klamath the day before, come on Captain Jack's camp. Jackson demands that the Modocs return to the reservation. Captain Jack is loath to fight and agrees to go to the reservation, but the situation becomes tense when Jackson demands that the Indians disarm. Captain Jack finally agrees, but as his followers are laying down their weapons, one warrior and an army sergeant begin arguing, and shots are exchanged. The

Modocs then attempt to recover their weapons, and a short battle occurs before the Modocs flee south toward California. Jackson orders his men to await reinforcements. In the Battle of Lost River, U.S. casualties are one killed and seven wounded; the Modocs suffer two killed and three wounded.

Captain Jack and the remaining Modocs continue on toward Tule Lake, but some of the band, led by Hooker Jim, split off and on November 29 and 30 attack and kill 13–18 settlers in the Tule Lake area.

December 28, 1872

American Indian Wars (continued): Battle of Skull Cave. Troopers of the 5th Cavalry Regiment under Major William M. Brown, assisted by Apache scouts, locate and trap Tonto Apache Indians in Skull Cave along Salt River Canyon in Arizona Territory. The

Apaches appear to be in an impregnable position and refuse to surrender; they also reject demands that they send out their woman and children, saying that they will fight to the death. The Apaches fire arrows high in the air in order to reach the soldiers hidden behind rocks, but this is to little effect. Brown in turn orders his men to fire bullets at the roof of the cave; these ricochet and hit a number of the Indians.

Some 20 warriors charge the soldiers, only to be shot down. Six or 7 are slain, and the remainder are driven back. The soldiers then resume firing at the roof of the cave before they themselves mount a successful charge. Seventy-six of the Tontos are dead. Nearly all the surviving 35 women and children are wounded. The cave is found to be well provisioned with food and ammunition seized on raids.

The battle has virtually wiped out one of the most destructive of the Tonto bands. It also establishes beyond doubt the value of Apache scouts working with the army and the fact that they can locate even the most obscure Apache strongholds. Following this Tonto defeat and a few other battles, most Apaches surrender to U.S. forces under Department of Arizona commander Lieutenant Colonel George Crook at Camp Verde. Crook then employs a number of them as scouts.

January 17, 1873

American Indian Wars (continued): Modoc Wars (continued): First Battle of the Stronghold (First Battle of the Lava Beds). Modocs led by Captain Jack have withdrawn into the area known as the Stronghold, a vast labyrinthine lava bed on the south shores of Tule Lake in northern California. On January 13, 1873, in a thick fog, 300 infantry (soldiers and Oregon militiamen) and 100 cavalry supported by two howitzers, all under Lieutenant Colonel Frank Wharton, attack the Modocs in this virtually impregnable rocky fortress. Although there are no more than 160 Modocs and only 53 of them are warriors, the defenders use the natural formations to advantage, and their determined resistance forces Wharton to withdraw, with 9 killed and 28 wounded. The dead are abandoned on the battlefield, providing the Modocs with additional rifles and ammunition.

There are apparently no Modoc losses. Colonel Alvan C. Gillem replaces Wharton in command, and the army brings up reinforcements. In the meantime, however, the army begins peace negotiations.

April 11, 1873

American Indian Wars (continued): Modoc Wars (continued): Murder of General Canby. On April 11, 1873, Brigadier General Edward R. S. Canby, commander of the Department of the Columbia, meets with renegade Modoc leader Captain Jack and some of his followers at Siskiyou County in northernmost California to discuss peace terms. Canby dismisses reports that Captain Jack might try to murder him during the talks and sits down with the Modoc leader unarmed. After the talks have begun, the usually astute Captain Jack, apparently led to believe that the soldiers will end operations against his people if their leader is killed, suddenly pulls out a pistol and shoots to death both Canby and civilian negotiator Reverend Eleaser Meacham. Another civilian is badly wounded. Canby thus becomes the only general officer killed in fighting during the post–Civil War Indian Wars.

The death of the popular Canby outrages the army. Although Captain Jack gets away, he and four others will subsequently be caught, tried, convicted of the deed, and hanged. On May 2 Brigadier General Jefferson C. Davis succeeds Canby.

April 15–17, 1873

American Indian Wars (continued): Modoc War (continued): Second Battle of the Stronghold (Second Battle of the Lava Beds). Colonel Alvan C. Gillem had replaced Lieutenant Colonel Frank Wharton following the army's defeat by Modoc warriors in the First Battle of the Stronghold. With the assassination during peace negotiations of Brigadier General Edward R. S. Canby by Modoc leader Captain Jack on April 11, 1873, Gillem resumes operations against the Modoc positions, known as the Stronghold, in the lava beds along the south shore of Tule Lake in northern California. Within this natural fortress are 160 Modocs, of whom only 53 are warriors.

Commanding 675 men, Gillem attacks on April 15. On the night of April 16 the soldiers succeed in cutting off the Modoc water supply. Fighting continues the next day, and on April 17, with everything in readiness for a final assault on the Stronghold, the Modocs escape through an unguarded crevice. Army casualties total 7 killed and 13 wounded; the Modocs lose 1 boy, killed when he attempted to open an unexploded shell with an ax.

April 26, 1873

American Indian Wars (continued): Modoc War (continued): Thomas-Wright Massacre (Battle of Hardin Butte). Following the Second Battle of the Stronghold, local army commander Colonel Alvan C. Gillem sends out patrols to try to locate the escaped Modocs. On April 26, 1873, he orders Captains Evan Thomas and Thomas Wright to lead 67 officers and men who are to be joined by 13 Warm Spring Scouts on a reconnaissance of the lava beds on the south shore of Tule Lake in northern California. Stopping for a noon meal, the soldiers are surprised by a Modoc attack led by Scarface Charley. Perhaps half of the soldiers panic and flee. Those who remain are either killed or wounded; Thomas and Wright are among the dead. The army casualty toll in the two-hour engagement is 23 dead and 19 wounded. Of 6 officers, 4 are killed outright and 2 are wounded, 1 mortally. There are no Modoc losses.

May 7–12, 1873

In the Colombian province of Panama, 200 men from the U.S. Navy screw sloop *Tuscarora* go ashore to protect American lives and property during a revolutionary outbreak.

May 10, 1873

American Indian Wars (continued): Modoc War (continued): Battle of Dry Lake. On May 7, 1873, army troops and Captain Jack's band of Modocs skirmish at Scorpion Point in northern California. Brigadier General Jefferson C. Davis, commanding troops operating against the Modocs, orders a reconnaissance to locate the hostiles. Now vastly outnumbered, short of supplies, and lacking horses, Captain Jack's followers begin to desert. Hooker Jim leads one band to Fairchild Ranch, where he knows and trusts the ranch owner and there surrenders.

More aggressive Modocs urge an attack on the soldiers, and on May 10 those remaining attempt an ambush of soldiers at Dry Lake. The ensuing battle is a turning point in the war. The soldiers counterattack and rout the Modocs. Army casualties are 5 killed, 2 of whom are Warm Springs Scouts, and 12 wounded; the Indians suffer 5 killed, including Ellen's Man, one of their leaders. The Modocs also lose 24 pack animals with most of their ammunition.

May 18, 1873

American Indians Wars (continued): Battle of Nacimiento. During the American Civil War, both the Union and the Confederacy had sought the aid of the various Indian tribes. Attempting to avoid involvement with either side, many Kansas and Indian Territory Kickapoos traveled through Texas to join their relatives in northern Mexico. Believing them to be hostile Kiowas or Comanches, Texas forces attacked a large Indian encampment in southern Texas in the Battle of Dove Creek (see January 8, 1865). The Texans had been routed, and the Kickapoos continued on to northern Mexico, but for years the Kickapoos used the Dove Creek attack as justification for raids from Mexico across the Rio Grande into southern Texas.

By the early 1870s these cross-border depredations have become such a serious problem that the army is called in. On May 13, 1873, Colonel Ranald S. Mackenzie, under orders from Lieutenant General Philip H. Sheridan, commander of the Military Division of the Missouri, departs Fort Clark (in Brackettville, Texas) with his 4th Cavalry Regiment of some 400 men. Mackenzie has planned his operation to coincide with a major Kickapoo hunt, when most of the men will be away. The cavalrymen cross the Rio Grande and fall on the hostile Kickapoo camp at Nacimiento, Mexico. The soldiers kill 19 Kickapoos, mostly women and children, at a cost to themselves of 4 wounded (1 mortally). Forty prisoners are marched to San Antonio, then transferred to Fort Gibson in Indian Territory, where they are held hostage to encourage the surrender of fugitive Kickapoos. The 317 who give up are removed to Indian Territory, but most of the tribe refuse to leave and gather anew at Nacimiento.

June 3, 1873

American Indian Wars (continued): Modoc War (continued): Capture of Captain Jack. Renegade Modoc leader Captain Jack and his band, now numbering fewer than three dozen warriors, continue to elude army forces searching for them. At Big Sand Butte, Captain Jack escapes an army trap by more than 300 soldiers. But one by one the Modocs surrender or are captured. Hooker Jim, one of his chief lieutenants, and his small band are taken prisoner, and Hooker Jim agrees to assist in the capture of Captain Jack, who surrenders near the Lost River on June 3, 1873, officially bringing to a close the Modoc War, which has claimed the lives of some 83 whites and 17 Indians. Captain Jack and 3 others are subsequently tried, convicted, and hanged (October 3, 1873) for the murder of the peace commissioners, while 2 other Modocs have their sentences commuted to life imprisonment. The rest of the Modocs are removed to a reservation in Indian Territory (Oklahoma).

August 4, 1873

American Indian Wars (continued): Tongue River Engagement. Along the Tongue River in Montana, Lieutenant Colonel George A. Custer, his brother First Lieutenant Thomas W. Custer, and 20 mounted scouts, come under attack by some 300 Sioux and Cheyenne warriors. Custer's men hide in the grass, rising to fire several volleys at point-blank range, and drive off the attackers. The remainder of the 7th Cavalry then arrives, rescuing Custer and the scouting party.

August 5, 1873

American Indian Wars (continued): Battle of Massacre Canyon (Pawnee Scouts Massacre). Facing starvation largely because of inadequate U.S. government rations, the Pawnees of Nebraska receive approval from their Indian agent to leave their agency in Nebraska for a buffalo hunt. On July 3, 1873, as many as 400 Pawnees (about 250 men, 100 women, and 50 children), led by Sky Chief, a former Pawnee scout, and accompanied by Indian agents John W. Williamson and L. B. Platte, depart on the hunt.

Following a successful hunt along the Republican River, the Pawnees turn north to begin the journey home. At Frenchman's Creek near present-day Trenton, Nebraska, the Pawnees are warned by some white buffalo hunters that a large number of their Sioux enemies are headed in their direction. Sky Chief's men have seen no sign of Sioux being nearby. Distrusting the white hunters, he decides to continue on. Unknown to Sky Chief, however, a large party of Brulé Sioux, augmented by Ogalas, have been trailing the Pawnees for several days and are determined to attack. Their accompanying agents, Nick Janis and Stephen F. Estes, do little to dissuade them.

On July 3, the Sioux surprise the Pawnees in their camp and attack. The Pawnees withdraw into a nearby canyon, where they are able to hold off their attackers until the Brulé Sioux arrive. Now vastly outnumbered (there may be as many as 2,000 Sioux present), the Pawnees panic and try to get their women and children to safety. Some manage to escape on horseback as the Sioux stop to loot, kill the Pawnee wounded, and mutilate the dead. The escaping Pawnees encounter a detachment of the 3rd Cavalry Regiment under Captain Charles Reinhold from Fort McPherson, but when the soldiers reach the canyon, the Sioux have departed. Reinhold counts 20 men, 39 women, and 10 children dead at the scene, but the actual Pawnee death toll is more than 100. The Sioux have lost 5–6 killed.

Massacre Canyon is the last Native American battle in Montana. Although the Sioux finally agree to release the Pawnees they had taken prisoner, the outcome of the battle is a turning point in Pawnee history. It so dispirits the tribe that its members move to a reservation in Indian Territory (Oklahoma).

August 11, 1873

American Indian Wars (continued): Clash between the army and the Sioux near the mouth of the Bighorn River in Montana. In a second engagement between the 7th Cavalry Regiment, led by Lieutenant Colonel George A. Custer, and Lakota Sioux, Custer attacks a Sioux village at present-day Hysham, Montana, near the mouth of the Bighorn River. Some 1,000 Sioux warriors then close in from the rear, but Custer reverses direction and charges, causing them to scatter. Custer, who seems to lead a charmed existence, is not hurt but has his 11th horse shot from under him. His orderly John H. Tuttle is among 3 cavalrymen killed; 4 others are wounded. Sioux casualties are estimated at 40 killed or wounded.

September 23–October 9, 1873

A landing party of 190 men from the U.S. Navy screw *Pensacola* and the screw sloop *Benicia* goes ashore in the Colombian province of Panama to protect American lives and property during a revolutionary outbreak.

October 31, 1873

The *Virginius* Affair. During the Ten Years' War (1868–1878), insurgents in Cuba seek money and weapons from Americans sympathetic to the cause of Cuban independence. In 1870 Cuban insurgent general Rafael Quesada had arrived in the United States and arranged with U.S. citizen John F. Patterson to purchase the small, fast iron side-wheel steamer *Virginius*. The ship had been built in Scotland in 1864 as a blockade-runner during the American Civil War. Captured by the U.S. Navy in 1865, it had been sold. Patterson registered the *Virginius* in New York as an American ship.

During the next three years, the *Virginius* delivers to Cuban insurgents quantities of weapons, munitions, and other supplies, all under the American flag. Spanish authorities are unable to stop the fast ship. In June 1873 at Aspinwall, Colombia (today in Panama), a Spanish gunboat intercepts and almost seizes the *Virginius*, but the U.S. Navy screw steamer *Kansas* intervenes, and the *Virginius* escapes.

In October 1873 the *Virginius*, commanded by former Confederate Navy officer Joseph Fry, secures arms and munitions at Kingston, Jamaica, and in

Illustration from *Frank Leslie's Illustrated Newspaper* depicting the arrival of the Spanish steamer *Tornado* with the captured American steamer *Virginius* at Santiago de Cuba on October 31, 1873. (Corbis)

Haiti and sails for Cuba. It has a crew of 52 and 103 passengers, including prominent Cuban insurgent officers and leaders and several American and British nationals.

Informed as to the *Virginius*'s anticipated route, on October 31, 1873, the Spanish corvette *Tornado* intercepts the ship off Cuba, then chases it down and forces its surrender in Jamaican territorial waters. Spanish authorities take all on board to Santiago de Cuba and charge them with piracy. The governments of both the United States and Great Britain protest, but Spanish officials refuse to allow their consuls to visit the prisoners, and all crew members and passengers of the *Virginius* are tried and sentenced to death. On November 4, 4 Cuban insurrectionist officials are shot by a firing squad, and three days later Captain Fry and other members of the crew meet the same fate. The following day, 12 passengers are also executed. In all, 37 crew members and 16 passengers, including several U.S. and British citizens, are executed.

On November 8 the British steam sloop *Niobe* arrives off Santiago de Cuba. Its captain, Sir Lambton Loraine, threatens to shell the port unless the executions end. There is also a great wellspring of anger in the United States, bringing it to the brink of war with Spain.

Political events in Spain make resolution of the crisis difficult. The monarchy had been overthrown in February 1873, the new republican government is disorganized, and civil war has begun. The U.S. ambassador to Spain, former Union general Daniel Sickles, makes the situation worse by his intemperate stance. Finally, U.S. secretary of state Hamilton Fish works out an agreement with Spain's ambassador to the United States José Polo de Bernabé, signed on November 29, 1873.

Spain agrees to release the *Virginius* and return its surviving crew members and passengers. Spain also consents to salute the American flag on December 25 and to prosecute its officers if the *Virginius* is proven to have been legitimately flying the American flag at the time of its capture, but a U.S. Circuit Court subsequently finds that the *Virginius* was the property of Rafael Quesada and had therefore fraudulently flown the American flag.

On December 16, 1873, the Spanish Navy turns the *Virginius* over to the U.S. Navy screw sloop *Ossipee*. (The *Virginius*, which had been damaged during the fight with the *Tornado*, sinks off Cape Hatteras, North Carolina, while under tow from the *Ossipee* during a storm on December 26.) On December 18 Spain releases the remaining prisoners. On March 5, 1875, the Spanish government agrees to pay $80,000 to the families of the executed Americans and a smaller indemnity to the British government.

The *Virginius* Affair fuels American animosity toward Spain and also has a major impact on the U.S. Navy. During the crisis a Spanish ironclad happened to be anchored in New York Harbor, and the U.S. Navy then had no ship capable of defeating it. The crisis prompts the construction of five new ironclads, all of which will take part in the Spanish-American War of 1898, and fuels public support for the creation of a more modern steel navy.

November 24, 1873

A government patent is issued to Joseph F. Glidden for barbed wire; it will play a key role in the history of the American West and become a fixture of land warfare.

February 12, 1874

At Honolulu, Hawaii, 150 officers and men are landed from the sloop *Portsmouth*, under Commander Joseph K. Skerrett, and the screw sloop *Tuscarora*, under Commander George E. Belknap, to protect American lives and property in rioting following the coronation of King Kalakaua.

June 16, 1874

Congress reduces the size of the U.S. Army to 25,000 men.

June 27–July, 1874

American Indian Wars (continued): Second Battle of Adobe Walls. The Adobe Walls site near the Canadian River in the Texas Panhandle in what is today Hutchinson County, Texas, remained abandoned following the battle there of November 25, 1864, until 1874, when merchants established stores there to

Barbed Wire

From the first domestication of animals, men sought to find effective barriers to contain them. Fences of both wood and stone appeared, but by the second half of the 19th century ranchers in the vast expanse of the North American West employed fences of smooth wire strung between posts. Wire was easily erected, relatively inexpensive, would not rot, and was unaffected by fire. Smooth wire was not terribly effective as a barrier, however, as cattle could push through it. By the 1860s manufacturers experimented with adding sharp points to the wire. In 1868 American Michael Kelly invented a wire with points that was used in quantity until 1874, when Joseph Glidden of DeKalb, Illinois, came up with a process whereby barbs were placed at intervals on smooth wire and fixed in place by a twisted second wire. Subsequently, hundreds of patents were issued on thousands of varieties of barbed wire on this principle.

The British used barbed wire to protect their military encampments during the Boer War (1899–1902), but World War I saw its extensive employment. Once the front lines on the Western Front stabilized at the end of 1914, both sides erected wire barriers to break up enemy attacks and to prevent trench raids to secure prisoners.

Wire became a ubiquitous feature of no-man's-land. Almost every night parties of soldiers ventured forth to lay additional wire and repair breaks in existing wire that had been cut by enemy sappers. At first the wooden stakes holding the wire had to be hammered into the earth. The noise from this, however, alerted opposing troops, with obvious ill effects for the wire layers. Someone then came up with the idea of a metal stake with a corkscrew tip that allowed it to be screwed into the earth noiselessly.

The wire was laid not singly but in belts. The Germans, who were for the most part standing on the defensive on the Western Front, laid particularly thick bands of wire. These were often more than 50 feet deep, and in some places on the Hindenburg Line they were 100 yards in depth.

The belief that artillery could blast holes in the wire proved false. More often than not, even prolonged shelling merely rearranged the entanglements. Barbed wire thus contributed greatly to the heavy casualties of the war. The need to deal with barbed wire obstacles was one of the motives behind British and French development of the tank. Specialized explosive charges such as the bangalore torpedo were also developed and were used extensively in World War II to blast holes in a defender's wire.

During World War II, barbed wire was a feature of concentration camps and prisoner of war facilities. More lethal razor wire was developed and utilized during the Vietnam War and other late-20th-century conflicts.

SPENCER C. TUCKER

Further Reading

Ellis, John. *Eye-deep in Hell: Trench Warfare in World War I.* New York: Pantheon Books, 1977.

McCallum, Henry D., and Frances T. McCallum. *The Wire That Fenced the West.* Norman: University of Oklahoma Press, 1965.

Simpson, Andy, ed. *Hot Blood and Cold Steel: Life and Death in the Trenches of the First World War.* London: Tom Donovan, 1993.

MILITARY POSTS IN THE WEST, 1874

CANADA

N

50°N

Vancouver
Barracks

Department
of the Columbia

Blackfoot

Nez Perce

Department
of Dakota

Klamath

Bannock

Department
of the Platte

Lakota

St. Paul

40°N

Modoc

Paiute

Northern
Cheyenne

San
Francisco

Shoshoni

Omaha

Chicago

Department
of California

Ute

St.
Louis

Department
of the Missouri

Ft.
Leavenworth

Prescott

Navajo

Kiowo

Southern
Cheyenne

Department
of Arizona

Comanche

Arapaho

30°N

Apache

Department
of Texas

PACIFIC
OCEAN

San
Antonio

New
Orleans

MEXICO

Gulf of
Mexico

⭐ Division headquarters
☆ Department headquarters
— Department boundary
▨ Division of the Pacific
▨ Division of the Missouri
▨ Division of the Atlantic
▨ Indian territory transferred to
Department of the Missouri (1875)

0   200   400 mi
0   200   400 km

100°W

90°W

trade in buffalo hides. A number of buffalo hunters begin operating in the area, leading to the Second Battle of Adobe Walls.

Early on the morning of June 27, 1874, Quanah Parker, Lone Wolf, and Stone Calf lead a war party of some 300 Comanche, Cheyenne, and Kiowa Indians against the outpost. They kill several people on their approach, alerting the remaining 28 buffalo hunters, who seek safety in Adobe Walls. The hunters employ accurate rifle fire to hold off their attackers.

The warriors then institute a siege. On July 29, additional Buffalo hunters arrive, bringing the defenders up to some 100 men. The Indians withdraw shortly thereafter. This Second Battle of Adobe Walls claims 4 buffalo hunters dead; 16 Indians perish. Adobe Walls is again abandoned.

June 27, 1874–June 2, 1875

American Indian Wars (continued): Red River War. Attacks on white settlements by hostile elements of the Kiowa, Cheyenne, Arapaho, and Comanche tribes on the southern Great Plain lead the U.S. government to call in the army in 1874. Commanding general of the army General William T. Sherman announces an end to the Grant administration's so-called Quaker Peace Policy toward Native Americans and calls on Lieutenant General Philip H. Sheridan to go after all hostile tribes. In its subsequent military operations, the army is aided by the fact that the Native Americans never present a united front, and there are peace factions within the tribes themselves.

In what becomes known as the Red River War, some 3,000 U.S. troops are gathered in five converging columns from bases in Texas, New Mexico, and Indian Territory (Oklahoma) under the overall command of Colonel Nelson A. Miles. The U.S. troops chase down the Indians and force them to settle on reservations in Indian Territory. One of the most effective army leaders is Colonel Ranald S. Mackenzie, commander of the 4th Cavalry Regiment.

The most notable battle is that of Palo Duro Canyon, Texas (see September 28, 1874), in which Mackenzie's men destroy the Native American camp there and kill 1,000 horses, thereby depriving the Native Americans of mobility. The Red River War breaks the power of the Native Americans in the southern Great Plains and brings the confinement of the southern Plains Indians of the Comanches, Kiowas, Kiowa Apaches, Cheyennes, and Arapahos on reservations in Indian Territory (present-day Oklahoma).

July 2–August 30, 1874

Custer's Black Hills expedition. Lieutenant Colonel George A. Custer departs Fort Abraham Lincoln in Dakota Territory with his 7th Cavalry Regiment on an expedition to verify the presence of valuable mineral deposits, especially gold, in the Black Hills. The troopers are accompanied by a number of geologists and scientists. Custer also employs Crow scouts, headed by Bloody Knife.

Three weeks later Custer's men enter the Black Hills, an area sacred to the Sioux. Custer's Crow scouts, fearing retaliation by the Sioux, depart. On August 2, Custer confirms the presence of gold deposits in the Black Hills, an announcement that will lead to a considerable influx of white miners and bring on the Great Sioux War (Black Hills War) of 1876–1877. Having covered more than 1,200 miles in 60 days, Custer's men return to Fort Abraham Lincoln on August 30.

August 30, 1874

American Indian Wars (continued): Red River War (continued). Colonel Nelson A. Miles's initial operation against renegade Cheyenne, Comanche, and Kiowa bands along the Red River in Indian Territory (present-day Oklahoma) ends on this date in a running skirmish and stand by warriors at Tule Canyon. Short of supplies, Miles is forced to withdraw.

September 9–12, 1874

American Indian Wars (continued): Red River War (continued): Battle of the Upper Washita. Having been forced to break off for want of supplies his pursuit of recalcitrant Cheyenne, Comanche, and Kiowa Indians along the Red River, Colonel Nelson A. Miles sends Captain Wyllys Lyman with 36 empty wagons and a protective detail of 104 men to meet a wagon train from Camp Supply at Commission Creek in present-day Ellis County, Oklahoma. Transferring

Nelson Appleton Miles (1839–1925)

U.S. Army general. Nelson Appleton Miles was born on a farm near Westminster, Massachusetts, on August 8, 1839. After attending public school, he moved to Boston in 1856, where he worked as a store clerk. Interested in the military, Miles received some instruction from a retired French colonel.

At the outbreak of the American Civil War, Miles recruited men for the 22nd Massachusetts Regiment and was commissioned a first lieutenant of volunteers (September 9, 1861). Considered too young for battlefield command, he initially served in a staff position during the March–August 1862 Peninsula Campaign. Miles soon demonstrated a natural capacity for battlefield leadership and began a meteoric advance in rank. Following the Battle of Seven Pines (May 31–June 1), he was promoted to lieutenant colonel in the 61st New York Infantry. He fought in the Seven Days' Campaign (June 25–July 1) and in the Battle of Antietam (September 17) and was promoted to colonel (September 30). Miles was wounded four times in the war, including in the Battle of Fredericksburg (December 13) and the Battle of Chancellorsville (May 1–4, 1863). For his actions at Chancellorsville, he later (1892) received the Medal of Honor. Miles commanded a brigade of II Corps in the May 4–June 12, 1864, Overland Campaign and saw combat in the Battle of the Wilderness (May 5–7) and the Battle of Spotsylvania Court House (May 8–21), for which he was promoted to brigadier general of volunteers to date from May 12.

Miles commanded a division in the Siege of Petersburg (June 15, 1864–April 3, 1865) and briefly (at age 26) a corps. Miles suffered his fourth wound of the war in the First Battle of Ream's Station (June 19, 1864).

Following the war, in October 1865 Miles was advanced to major general of volunteers and assumed command of II Corps. In the reorganization of the army in 1866, he became colonel of the 40th Infantry Regiment, an African American unit. In 1869 he took command of the 5th Infantry Regiment. Miles saw extensive service in the American West and became renowned as one of the army's finest commanders in the ensuing Indian Wars. He was conspicuously active in the Red River War of 1874–1875. In 1876 and 1877 he played prominent roles in the Sioux War and the Nez Perce War, personally accepting the surrenders of Sioux war chief Crazy Horse and Nez Perce chief Joseph.

Miles was promoted to brigadier general in the regular army in December 1880. From 1880 to 1885 he commanded the Department of the Columbia, and from 1885 to 1886 he had charge of the Department of the Missouri. In 1886 he took command of the Department of Arizona. There he discontinued the wise practice of his predecessor, Brigadier General George Crook, of employing Apaches as scouts, choosing instead to rely mostly on U.S. troops. Following several months of failure, he reintroduced Crook's practice and oversaw the final surrender of Geronimo and the Chiricahua Apaches in September 1886. Miles then engaged in a public dispute with Crook over the subsequent exile of the Apaches, including the loyal scouts, to Florida.

In 1888 Miles took command of the Division of the Pacific. Promoted to major general in April 1890, he directed the suppression of the Sioux Ghost Dance Uprising in the Dakota Territory but was angered by the bloodshed at Wounded Knee on December 29, 1890. Miles wanted to court-martial Colonel James W. Forsyth, who commanded during that action. Although Miles relieved Forsyth from command, the War Department soon reinstated him.

In 1894 Miles was called upon to employ troops in suppressing the Pullman Strike and then commanded the Department of the East. On October 5, 1895, he succeeded Lieutenant General John M. Schofield as commanding general of the army. Miles opposed the Spanish-American War, believing that diplomacy could resolve the differences between Spain and the United States. When the war began in 1898, he favored using regulars in Cuba rather than volunteer forces, which he believed should remain in the United States and maintain its defenses against a possible Spanish attack. He also opposed an invasion of Cuba until the Spanish naval squadron had been destroyed but convinced President William McKinley to shift the main American land assault from Havana to Santiago de Cuba. Once Santiago was secured, Miles received approval to proceed with his own invasion of Puerto Rico, an assignment he had sought early on. Miles conducted a highly successful campaign in Puerto Rico that was cut short by the armistice of August 12, which denied him the capture of San Juan.

After the war, Miles was the central figure in the notorious Embalmed Beef Scandal, in which he alleged that the Commissary Department had issued spoiled beef to the troops. He was subsequently reprimanded by the Dodge Commission for making charges that were proven to be substantially unfounded.

In June 1900 Miles was promoted to lieutenant general. President Theodore Roosevelt, who called Miles a "brave peacock" for his love of excessive uniform display, crossed swords with Miles, as did Secretary of War Elihu Root, who found Miles to be in sharp opposition to his plan to create a General Staff and do away with the position of commanding general of the army, substituting for it the new position of chief of staff.

Miles retired from the army on August 8, 1903. Combative, vain, and ambitious, he was, with Ranald Mackenzie, one of the finest field commanders during the Indian Wars, amassing a record second to none. Despite Miles's leadership qualities in battle, he was a commanding general who displayed little political sense and did not fit well in the new 20th-century army. In 1917 when the United States entered World War I he offered his services, but the offer was not accepted. In retirement, he wrote articles and several books, including a two-volume memoir. Miles died at Washington, D.C., on May 15, 1925.

JERRY KENNAN AND SPENCER C. TUCKER

Further Reading

DeMontravel, Peter R. *A Hero to His Fighting Men: Nelson A. Miles, 1839–1925*. Kent, OH: Kent State University Press, 1998.

Johnson, Virginia. *The Unregimented General: A Biography of Nelson A. Miles*. Boston: Houghton Mifflin, 1962.

Miles, Nelson A. *Personal Recollections and Observations of General Nelson A. Miles*. 2 vols. Lincoln: University of Nebraska Press, 1992.

Wooster, Robert. *Nelson A. Miles and the Twilight of the Frontier Army*. Lincoln: University of Nebraska Press, 1993.

the supplies to his own wagons, Lyman begins the return trip.

In the course of the return, the wagon train encounters Lieutenant Frank D. Baldwin and 3 scouts with a white Kiowa captive named Tehan, whom they had taken prisoner while skirting Lone Wolf's camp. They leave Tehan with Lyman so that Miles can question him, then continue on toward Fort Supply. Lyman is well aware of the danger of attack, and he forms his wagons in a double column protected by 40 infantrymen on either side and his 13 cavalrymen at the front.

Discovering that Tehan is missing, the Indians search for him and discover the wagon train and begin firing at it from a distance. Lyman's defensive arrangements allow the wagon train to continue another 12 miles south to about 1 mile from the Washita River in Hemphill County, Texas, when in midafternoon on September 9, 1874, as it emerges from a steep ravine, the wagon train comes under sudden attack by some 70 warriors. The Kiowa and Comanche attackers are led by Lone Wolf, Satanta, and Big Tree. The ensuing fight is one of the longest and most publicized events of the Red River War.

Lyman is able to form the wagons into a circle, and that night the soldiers dig protective rifle pits and secure water from a pool about 400 yards distant. The Indians, numbering some 400, institute a siege.

On the afternoon of September 10, Lyman sends out an appeal by a scout on foot to Camp Supply for reinforcements. Tehan, meanwhile, escapes and returns to the Kiowas. Probably because of his advice, the Indians fortify the water hole, placing Lyman's men in dire straits. By September 12, however, a number of the Kiowas depart to continue their intended trek south toward Palo Duro Canyon, probably influenced by the distant approach of a relief column under Major William R. Price. Lyman's men remain within the protection of the wagons until Price's arrival early on September 14. Later that same day, Lyman continues on to join Miles on the Washita.

Lyman's losses are 2 killed and 3 wounded; Indian casualties are 13 or more. On the recommendation of Colonel Miles, 13 soldiers receive the Medal of Honor for their actions in the fight; Lyman is promoted.

September 28, 1874

American Indian Wars (continued): Red River War (continued): Battle of Palo Duro Canyon. By late September 1874 a large number of recalcitrant Indians are camped in Palo Duro Canyon in the Texas Panhandle near present-day Amarillo, Texas, where Kiowa shaman Maman-ti has promised that they will be safe. Aware of their location, Colonel Ranald S. Mackenzie leads his U.S. 4th Cavalry up from the south, with his men first chasing several small Comanche bands into Tule Canyon and there defeating them. Early on the morning of September 27, 1874, some 300 Arapahos, Cheyennes, Comanches, and Kiowas attack Mackenzie's camp. At daylight Mackenzie orders a charge by two troops of his cavalry, driving off the Indians.

Guided by Tonkawa chief Johnson, the 4th Cavalry reaches the edge of the canyon the next day. Mackenzie orders his scouts to locate a path to the canyon floor, which they quickly do. Mackenzie plans a surprise attack for sunrise on September 28, but Comanche leader Red Warbonnet discovers the soldiers and fires a warning shot before he is killed by the Tonkawas. Leadership of the several Indian bands on the floor of the canyon falls to Cheyenne chief Iron Shirt, Comanche leader Poor Buffalo, and Kiowa chief Lone Wolf. Because their camps are scattered over a wide area, the Indians are unable to mount a united defense, and the ensuing battle is actually a series of skirmishes against a number of war parties, each of which lacks the strength to defeat the attackers.

The soldiers and scouts first attack and destroy Red Warbonnet's encampment, an act that spreads panic among the other camps. The Tonkawa scouts, accompanied by their women, carry out most of the destruction of Comanche property and secure an enormous amount of loot. Many Indians attempt to flee the canyon on foot. Some fight back, sniping at the soldiers, but their resistance is weak, and by nightfall the soldiers and Tonkawa scouts have captured all of the Indian camps.

Casualties are surprisingly light: three warriors and one soldier killed. Mackenzie's troops also capture

Battle of Palo Duro Canyon		
Date	September 28, 1874	
Location	Palo Duro Canyon in the Texas Panhandle	
Opponents (*winner)	*United States	Arapahos, Cheyennes, Comanches, and Kiowas
Commander	Colonel Ranald S. Mackenzie	Iron Shirt, Poor Buffalo, and Lone Wolf
#	450 troopers of the 4th Cavalry and Native American scouts	More than 1,000 people, perhaps a quarter of them warriors
Casualties	1 killed	3 killed; 1,400 ponies captured

more than 1,400 Indian ponies. Of these, 40 are given to Chief Johnson and another 300 to the other scouts. The remaining ponies are shot by the soldiers so that they cannot be recovered. Most of the Indian possessions, including their entire winter food supply, are also destroyed.

The Battle of Palo Duro Canyon is the major military engagement of the Red River War. Although the loss of life has been remarkably small, the Battle of Palo Duro Canyon renders the southern Plains Indians largely immobile and is their last major military resistance against white settlement in the region.

June 12, 1875
American Indians Wars (continued). Chiricahua Apache chief Taza, the son of chief Cochise, relocates his people to the San Carlos Reservation in New Mexico Territory. Some 400 holdouts, including Geronimo, choose to flee to northern Mexico.

June 18, 1875
The side-wheel sloop *Saranac*, commanded by Captain Walter W. Queen, strikes a rock and is lost in the Seymour Narrow off Vancouver Island, British Columbia. All hands are saved.

February 8, 1876
American Indian Wars (continued): Beginning of the Great Sioux War. The Sioux are a confederation, numbering in 1876 about 30,000 people in the Dakotas and Wyoming. Unlike most Native Americans, they can on occasion unite and field large forces in sustained operations. Part of this is attributable to their leaders Red Cloud, Sitting Bull, and Crazy Horse. Following the sustained Sioux investment of Fort Phil Kearny during 1866–1868, the U.S. government had agreed to halt construction of the Bozeman Trail, and the Sioux accepted a reservation in southern Dakota Territory with rights to hunt as far as Wyoming Territory.

Geronimo (1829–1909)

Chiricahua Apache war leader and medicine man. Geronimo, named Goyahkla at birth, was born on June 16, 1829, on the upper Gila River near the present Arizona–New Mexico border. The Mexicans gave him the name Geromino, Spanish for Jerome, with Saint Jerome being the Catholic saint of lost causes. Legend has it that Mexican soldiers invoked Saint Jerome's name when they fought against Geronimo's raiding parties, and the name eventually stuck. Geronimo was born into the Bedonkohe band, which was closely associated with the Chiricahuas. As a youth, he honed his skills as a hunter and marksman and learned survival skills that would serve him well throughout his storied career.

In 1850 when he was 21, Geronimo went with the Mimbres Apache war leader Mangas Coloradas to Janos, Mexico, where they raided several Mexican settlements. During Geronimo's absence, Mexicans attacked his family's encampment; Geronimo's mother, wife, and three young children were all slain. The tragedy instilled in Geronimo a deep hatred of Mexicans.

After the 1850 expedition, Geronimo continued to develop warrior and raiding skills under Mangas Coloradas. Geronimo engaged in a number of raids against both Mexicans and Americans and is thought to have been a participant in the Battle of Apache Pass in July 1862. He began associating with other notable Apache leaders such as Victorio, Juh, and Cochise and lived among the followers of Cochise. In 1871 during a particularly bloody battle in Arizona against U.S. military forces, Geronimo may have been responsible for the death of Lieutenant Howard B. Cushing. In the meantime, Geronimo continued to raid settlements on both sides of the U.S.-Mexican border.

(continued)

(Continued)

Geronimo eventually allied himself with Victorio and in 1877 took up residence with his followers at the Ojo Caliente Reservation in New Mexico. Shortly after Geronimo's arrival, the reservation agent had him arrested and placed in irons. This began a long series of intrepid breakouts and arrests. By 1878, Geronimo was back in Mexico and allied with the Nednhi Apache war chief Juh. Geronimo participated in numerous raids conducted by Juh and his followers, who subsequently took up residence at the San Carlos Reservation in southern Arizona, where Juh and Geronimo were forbidden to leave by U.S. authorities. Nevertheless, in 1881 Geronimo escaped along with Juh and their followers, who settled in Mexico's Sierra Madre for about a year. In 1882 Geronimo and Juh led a daring raid on the San Carlos Reservation, ostensibly to win the release of Chief Loco, but several hundred Native Americans located there decided to follow Geronimo and Juh.

In 1884 after Geronimo had again returned to San Carlos, he voluntarily surrendered to American authorities; however, less than two years later, he eluded officials and was again on the run. He remained at large until March 1886, when he surrendered, this time to Brigadier General George Crook at Cañon de los Embudos, just south of the U.S.-Mexican border. Geronimo and his followers halted temporarily in southeastern Arizona, where an unscrupulous liquor salesman clandestinely entered the encampment and proceeded to provide enough liquor to inebriate Geronimo and his followers. The salesman then convinced Geronimo that if he and his followers did not leave the area at once, they would likely be killed by U.S. forces.

Geronimo and his people fled and were on the run for at least six months; meanwhile, Geronimo continued to conduct raids. U.S. forces pursued Geronimo and the Apaches tenaciously, however, and by the late summer of 1886 the Native Americans were exhausted, sick, and hungry. Thus, in early September 1886, Geronimo sent word that he would surrender. He met personally with Brigadier General Nelson A. Miles in Skeleton Canyon, Arizona, to discuss the terms. On September 4, the Apaches formally surrendered. Geronimo and some of his followers remained at Fort Bowie until September 8, at which time they were placed on a train bound for Florida.

Eventually Geronimo and other Apache leaders were detained at Fort Marion in St. Augustine; their families, however, were sent to Fort Pickens near Pensacola, some 300 miles distant. This violated the terms of the surrender, which guaranteed that families would not be split up. By May 1888, the Apaches were reunited in Mount Vernon, Alabama. Geronimo embraced his new life, cooperating with U.S. officials and missionaries, converting to Christianity, and even becoming a local justice of the peace. In 1892 the Apaches were relocated again, this time to Indian Territory (Oklahoma). Geronimo died at the age of 80 at Fort Sill, Oklahoma, on February 26, 1909.

PAUL G. PIERPAOLI JR.

Further Reading

Debo, Angie. *Geronimo: The Man, His Time, His Place.* Norman: University of Oklahoma Press, 1976.

Skinner, Woodward B. *The Apache Rock Crumbles: The Captivity of Geronimo's People.* Pensacola, FL: Skinner Publications, 1987.

Stockel, H. Henrietta. *Survival of the Spirit: Chiricahua Apaches in Captivity.* Reno: University of Nevada Press, 1993.

Sitting Bull (ca. 1831–1890)

Hunkpapa Lakota chief and holy man. Sitting Bull (Tatanka-Iyotanka) was born around 1831 at a place the Lakota called "Many Caches" on the Grand River in present-day South Dakota. He received the name Tatanka-Iyotanka, which describes a buffalo bull sitting on its hind legs. At age 14 he experienced his first battle in a raid against the Crow Nation. He first encountered American soldiers in June 1863 during a campaign in retaliation for the Minnesota Sioux Uprising in which the Lakotas had not participated. The next year Sitting Bull fought U.S. volunteers at the Battle of Killdeer Mountain, and in 1865 he led a siege of Fort Rice in present-day North Dakota. Widely respected for his bravery and insight, he became head chief of the Lakota Nation around 1868.

In 1874 U.S. Army lieutenant colonel George Armstrong Custer led an expedition that confirmed the presence of gold in the Black Hills of the Dakota Territory, an area sacred to many native tribes and placed off-limits to whites by the 1868 Fort Laramie Treaty. Despite this ban, white prospectors moved into the area and provoked the Lakotas into defending their land. The U.S. government tried to purchase the Black Hills, but the tribes refused to sell. The government then set aside the Fort Laramie Treaty and decreed that all Lakotas must return to their reservation by January 31, 1876, or be considered hostile. Sitting Bull and his people refused to return to the reservation.

In March 1876, Brigadier Generals George Crook and Alfred Terry and Colonel John Gibbon led separate army columns into the Yellowstone Valley. At his camp on Rosebud Creek in Montana Territory, Sitting Bull led the Lakota, Cheyenne, and Arapaho Nations in the sun dance ritual, during which he had a vision of soldiers falling into the Lakota camp from the sky.

Inspired by Sitting Bull's vision, Oglala Lakota war chief Crazy Horse, with 500 warriors, surprised Crook's troops on June 17, forcing them to retreat at the Battle of the Rosebud. The Lakotas now moved their camp to the valley of the Little Bighorn River, where 3,000 more Native Americans who had left the reservations joined them. On June 25 in the Battle of the Little Bighorn, the badly outnumbered 7th Cavalry Regiment, commanded by Custer, attacked the camp, only to be overwhelmed. Custer and a large portion of the regiment were annihilated.

After this disaster, the army sent thousands of troops into the Yellowstone Valley and the Black Hills and, during the next year, relentlessly pursued the Lakotas. Because the Lakotas had split up after the Battle of the Little Bighorn, the army was able to defeat them piecemeal. However, the defiant Sitting Bull led his band into Canada in May 1877. There he refused a pardon offered by General Terry, who had traveled to Canada for that purpose, in exchange for settling on a reservation.

After three years Sitting Bull, unable to feed his people, returned to the United States and surrendered at Fort Buford in Montana on July 19, 1881. The army sent him to the Standing Rock Reservation and soon afterward farther down the Missouri River to Fort Randall, fearful that he might inspire a new uprising. Sitting Bull and his followers remained there as prisoners for almost two years. In May 1883 Sitting Bull rejoined his tribe at Standing Rock, where he was forced to work in the fields.

In 1885 Sitting Bull joined Buffalo Bill Cody's Wild West Show but was unable to tolerate white society and left the show after only four months. Sitting Bull returned to Standing Rock and lived in a cabin on the Grand River, near where he had been born. There he maintained his traditional ways.

(continued)

(Continued)

Soon after his return, Sitting Bull had another vision in which a meadowlark sat beside him on a hill and said to him that a Lakota would kill him. In the autumn of 1890 Sitting Bull learned about the Ghost Dance, a ceremony that promised to rid the land of white people and restore the Native Americans' way of life. Because many Lakotas at the Pine Ridge and Rosebud Reservations had already adopted the ceremony, U.S. Indian agents called for troops to control the growing movement. Some authorities at Standing Rock, fearing that Sitting Bull would join the Ghost Dancers, sent 43 Lakota policemen to apprehend him. Before dawn on December 15, 1890, the policemen forced their way into Sitting Bull's cabin and dragged him outside. During an ensuing gunfight between Sitting Bull's supporters and the Lakota policemen, one of the policemen shot Sitting Bull in the head, killing him.

ROBERT B. KANE

Further Reading

Larson, Robert W. *Gall: Lakota War Chief.* Norman: University of Oklahoma Press, 2007.

Michno, Gregory F. *Lakota Moon: The Indian Narrative of Custer's Defeat.* Missoula, MO: Mountain Press, 1997.

McMurtry, Larry. *Oh What a Slaughter: Massacres of the American West 1846–1890.* New York: Simon and Schuster, 2005.

Utley, Robert M. *The Indian Frontier of the American West, 1846–1990.* Albuquerque: University of New Mexico Press, 1985.

The discovery of gold in the Black Hills in 1874 and the failure of efforts by the army to prevent incursions into Sioux lands by growing numbers of mining parties searching for gold lead to the Great Sioux War (1876–1877), also known as the Black Hills War and the Sioux and Northern Cheyenne War. In May 1875 Sioux leaders Red Cloud, Lone Horn, and Spotted Tail travel to Washington in an effort to prevent what appears to be an inevitable war by convincing the Ulysses S. Grant administration to abide by its treaties and stop the flow of miners into the Black Hills. They meet with Grant, Secretary of the Interior Columbus Delano, and Bureau of Indian Affairs commissioner Edward Smith. The Sioux leaders reject an offer of $25,000 for the Black Hills and relocation to Indian Territory (present-day Oklahoma). In autumn the government sends a commission to each of the Indian agencies in order to convince the Sioux to bring pressure on their leaders to accept a new treaty that will cede the Black Hills, but this is a failure.

The Lakotas are also resentful of wagon trains and U.S. proposals to run the Northern Pacific Railroad across Lakota buffalo hunting grounds. Trouble is also brewing between the U.S. government and the Cheyennes, and there had been a series of army attacks on Cheyenne encampments before 1876. Indeed, some believe that the ensuing war is intended to target the Cheyennes rather than the Sioux.

With its diplomatic efforts having failed, the Grant administration seeks alternative solutions. Division of the Missouri commander Lieutenant General Philip H. Sheridan is called to Washington in November 1875, and plans are drawn up for military action against the bands of Sioux and Northern Cheyennes who have refused to come to the Indian agencies or who have simply left the reservations.

Concerned at the prospect of being seen as launching an unprovoked war, the Grant administration instructs Indian agents to insist that the Indians return to the reservations by January 31, 1876, or face military action. A number of the Sioux not on the reservations, including Hunkpapa Lakota Sioux medicine man Sitting Bull, insist that they must first hunt buffalo and will return to the reservations in the spring, but government leaders refuse any extension in the deadline to placate the Sioux or the Indian agents, who point out that weather conditions will not allow the Lakotas to meet it.

On February 1, 1876, Secretary of the Interior Zachariah Chandler confirms that hundreds of Sioux under Oglala Lakota leader Crazy Horse and Sitting Bull have refused to report to reservations as ordered. Chandler turns matters over to the War Department to round them up. On February 8, Sheridan issues orders for the subjection of the recalcitrant Sioux and their return to the reservations. The resultant Great Sioux War is the toughest Native American challenge for the army since before the War of 1812.

Sheridan's plan involves three converging columns. Brigadier General Alfred H. Terry, in charge of the Department of the Dakota, has overall command. He is to move from the east along the Yellowstone River. At the same time, Brigadier General George Crook will proceed north, while Colonel John Gibbon and a third force march in from the west. Sheridan's plan for a winter campaign is stymied by delays, however.

March 17, 1876

American Indian Wars (continued): Great Sioux War (continued): Battle of the Powder River. The first army column to go into action against the Sioux and Cheyennes is that under Brigadier General George Crook. On March 1, 1876, Crook departs Fort Fetterman, Wyoming, with 883 soldiers and some Indian scouts. A blizzard leaves a foot of snow on the ground, and it and bitter cold weather make going difficult. On the evening of March 16, however, Crook sends Colonel Joseph J. Reynolds with the 3rd Cavalry and some companies of the 2nd Cavalry on a night march against a Northern Cheyenne village led by Little Wolf of more than 100 lodges and an immense herd of at least 800 ponies along the Powder River in eastern Montana.

The next morning, March 17, Reynolds attacks the village, but he fails to commit his entire command, and the warriors are able to hold the attackers at bay until all the women and children escape across the river. They subsequently join the villages of war chiefs Hunkpapa Lakota Sioux Sitting Bull and Oglala

Lakota Crazy Horse farther up the Powder River. Reynolds sets to work destroying the village and its ample weapons, supplies, and food stocks. By midafternoon, Reynolds orders his men to withdraw. In his premature haste, he leaves behind the bodies of three soldiers as well as a badly wounded private, who is subsequently tortured to death. (Reynolds's command decisions in this battle will bring his court-martial and retirement the next year.)

In the fighting the Indians lose 1 killed and 1 wounded and several women and children frozen to death. Army casualties are 10 dead and 16 wounded. Although the troopers carry off the Indians' pony herd, the Indians recover it the next day during a snowstorm. Terrible weather leading to frostbite cases among his men forces Crook to withdraw.

June 17, 1876

American Indian Wars (continued): Great Sioux War (continued): Powder River–Bighorn–Yellowstone Campaign Battle of the Rosebud (Battle of Rosebud Creek). Division of the Missouri commander Lieutenant General Philip H. Sheridan's plan for the campaign against the Sioux and Northern Cheyennes involves three converging columns. Brigadier General Alfred H. Terry, in charge of the Department of the Dakota, has overall command and with 1,000 men will move from the east along the Yellowstone River. Brigadier General George Crook will proceed north from Fort Fetterman, Wyoming, with 1,000 soldiers and some 260 allied Shoshone and Crow Indians, while Colonel John Gibbon with another 450 men marches from Fort Ellis and the west. The three columns are to converge on the Yellowstone River. With nearly 3,000 men committed, army leaders are confident of victory.

Crook's column is the first to make contact with the hostiles. On June 17, 1876, while proceeding up the south bank of the Rosebud River in present-day Bighorn County, Montana, Crook fights an unusual sustained six-hour battle with at least 1,500 and as many as 4,000–6,000 Lakota Sioux and Cheyennes led by Oglala Lakota Sioux war chief Crazy Horse. The battle is inconclusive. The Indians, aware of the forces converging against them, withdraw. Never

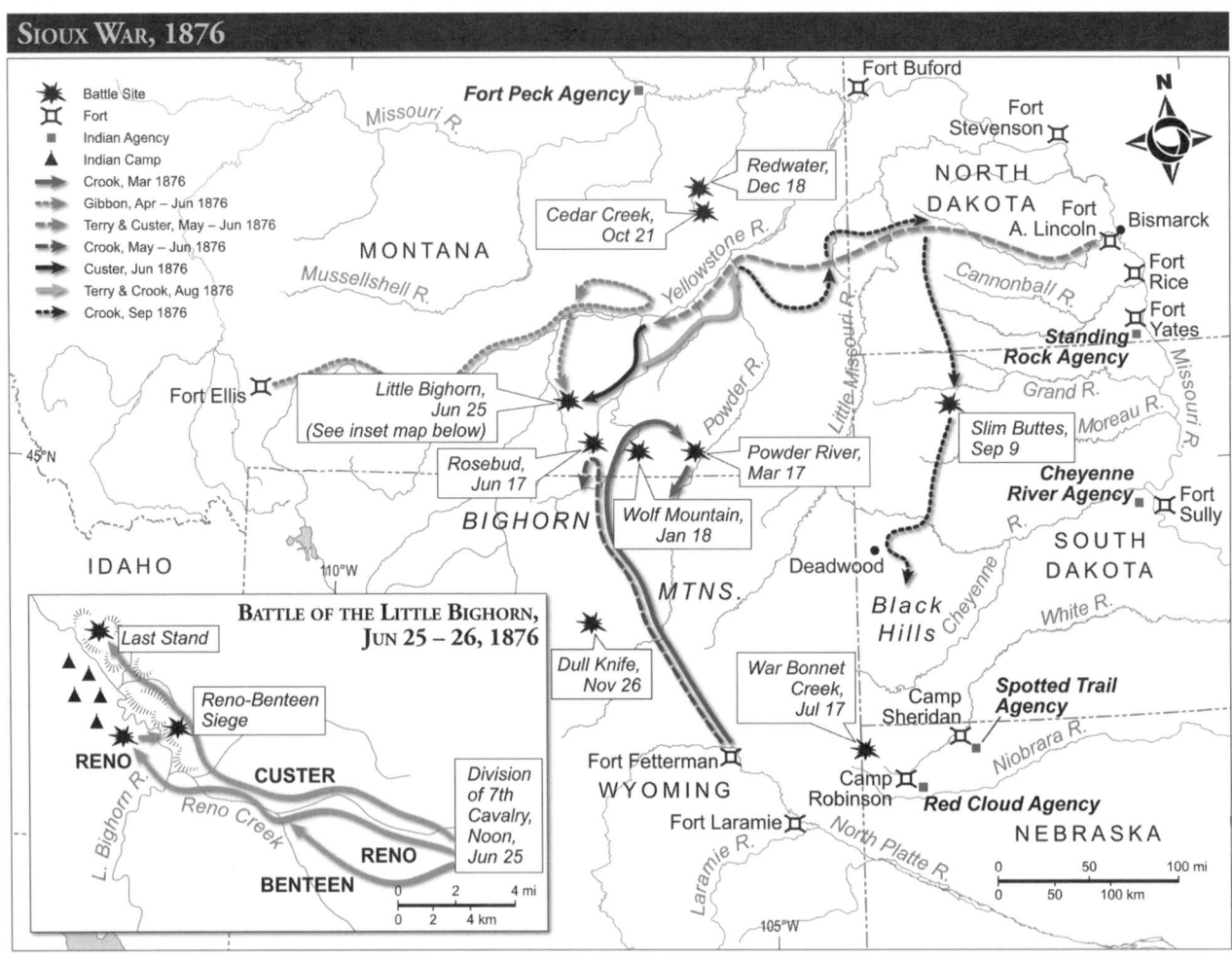

SIOUX WAR, 1876

Battle Site
Fort
Indian Agency
Indian Camp
Crook, Mar 1876
Gibbon, Apr – Jun 1876
Terry & Custer, May – Jun 1876
Crook, May – Jun 1876
Custer, Jun 1876
Terry & Crook, Aug 1876
Crook, Sep 1876

BATTLE OF THE LITTLE BIGHORN, JUN 25 – 26, 1876

before, however, have the Plains Indians fought such a prolonged battle or demonstrated such willingness to accept casualties to achieve their ends.

In the Battle of the Rosebud, the soldiers suffer 32 dead and 21 wounded; Indian casualties are 21 dead and 63 wounded. While Crook claims a victory, it is a hollow one, for he is forced to retire and regroup. He will spent the next seven weeks at his camp on Goose Creek awaiting reinforcements. His adversaries in the battle are, however, able to take part in the subsequent major Battle of the Little Bighorn.

June 25–26, 1876

American Indian Wars (continued): Great Sioux War (continued): Powder River–Bighorn–Yellowstone Campaign (continued): Battle of the Little Bighorn. Commander of U.S. Army forces in the campaign Major General Alfred H. Terry presses on with his 1,000 men, unaware of Brigadier General George Crook's rebuff on the Rosebud River. Terry and Colonel John Gibbon unite their columns and, learning that the Sioux are camped along the Little Bighorn River, proceed in that direction. In the advance is Lieutenant Colonel George A. Custer with his 7th Cavalry Regiment. A general in the American Civil War and a veteran of the Plains fighting, Custer is also an inveterate glory seeker frustrated that he has not yet regained his former rank. He also denigrates Native American fighting abilities.

Custer is unaware that he is approaching probably the largest assemblage of Indian power ever: some 10,000–15,000 people, at least 4,000 of them warriors. Ordered to scout the Rosebud and Bighorn River Valleys, Custer and his 647 men, including 35 scouts,

Battle of the Little Bighorn		
Date	June 25–26, 1876	
Location	Near the Little Bighorn River, Big Horn County, Montana	
Opponents (*winner)	*Oglala Sioux, Cheyennes, and Arapahos	United States
Commander	Chief Crazy Horse	Lieutenant Colonel George A. Custer
#	Some 1,800 warriors	647 troopers of the 7th Cavalry Regiment
Casualties	At least 200 killed or wounded	268 killed, 55 wounded

come upon the camp on June 25, 1876. Ignoring orders that call for him not to attack until the command can be concentrated, Custer proceeds alone. He divides his 12 companies into three columns, with the plan to attack the camp from three different directions. Major Marcus Reno receives command of 3 companies, and Captain Frederick Benteen takes command of 3 others, but the largest body of 6 companies of 212 troops proceeds under Custer's direct command.

In the ensuing Battle of the Little Bighorn, none of Custer's columns gets very far. Reno's smaller column is halted by Native American fire. It is subsequently joined by the other smaller column under Benteen, the arrival of which probably saves Reno's men from annihilation. The cavalrymen construct a defensive position on bluffs (known today as Reno Hill). Digging rifle pits, they are able to hold out here until rescued by Terry two days later.

Custer, meanwhile, is surrounded by more than 1,000 warriors led by Oglala Lakota Sioux war chief Crazy Horse. Many of the warriors have repeating Winchester rifles and are thus better armed than Custer's men, who have the slower-firing Trapdoor Springfield. Within two hours, Custer's force is wiped out; all 212 men are killed. More than 100 are killed or wounded in the other two columns. In all, 268 are killed and 55 wounded. Indian casualties probably total 200 or more.

Terry and Gibbon reach the field two days later, on June 27, and bury the dead. Lacking the logistical capability to sustain a larger force in the field for long, the Native Americans have moved off, separating into smaller bands. Had they stayed together, they might have defeated Terry and Gibbon as well.

The disaster on the Little Bighorn shocks the American people. Washington immediately dispatches reinforcements to the region and directs the army to hunt down the "hostiles." Although it takes time to locate the elusive bands, the Native Americans soon fall victim to their pursuers. Many are starving and come in voluntarily to army posts.

July 17, 1876
American Indian Wars (continued): Battle of Warbonnet Creek. Colonel Wesley Merritt and 200 men of his 5th Cavalry Regiment intercept at Warbonnet Creek in Nebraska Territory a band of some 800 Northern Cheyennes fleeing the Red Cloud Agency. In a brief skirmish, Scout William F. "Buffalo Bill" Cody shoots and kills subchief Yellow Hair, then scalps him. There are no other casualties on either side, as the remainder of the Indians turn and flee back to the agency.

September 9, 1876
American Indian Wars (continued): Great Sioux War (continued): Battle of Slim Buttes. Reinforced at last, Brigadier General George Crook again takes the field from his base at Goose Creek. He briefly joins forces under Brigadier General Alfred H. Terry, but bad weather and muddy conditions lead to the column separating again on August 18. Unable to locate any large Sioux or Northern Cheyenne encampment and desperately short of supplies, Crook's men—now on half rations—head south to mining settlements to find food in what becomes known as the Starvation March.

En route on September 8, Crook's advance force under Captain Anson Mills comes across a village of some 800 Minneconjou Sioux led by American Horse at Slim Buttes near present-day Reva, South Dakota. The next day, September 9, they attack, catching the Indians by surprise and killing those who resist. Those Sioux who escape reach neighboring Sans Arc, Brulé Sioux and Northern Cheyenne villages, informing

Wesley Merritt (1836–1910)

U.S. Army officer. Wesley Merritt was born in New York City on June 16, 1836. He attended the U.S. Military Academy, West Point, graduating in the middle of his class in 1860. Commissioned a second lieutenant, Merritt served in Utah with the 2nd Dragoons. The American Civil War brought Merritt's transfer to the East, where he twice served as aide to Major General George Stoneman, commander of cavalry in the Army of the Potomac. Merritt turned out to be a superb cavalry officer. As a captain, he distinguished himself in the Gettysburg Campaign at the Battle of Brandy Station (June 9, 1863), the largest cavalry engagement in the history of North America, and in other engagements and was breveted brigadier general of volunteers. For the remainder of the Gettysburg Campaign, he commanded the reserve cavalry of the Army of the Potomac.

Assigned temporary command of a division in May 1864, Merritt again fought with distinction in the Battle of Todd's Tavern on May 7, the largest dismounted cavalry engagement of the war. He also distinguished himself in other battles and was rewarded with permanent command of the 1st Cavalry Division of Sheridan's Army of the Shenandoah, leading it with distinction in subsequent battles, including Tom's Brook. During the Appomattox Campaign, Merritt commanded Major General Philip Sheridan's cavalry corps as a brevet major general of volunteers.

Following the Civil War, Merritt remained with the regular army as a lieutenant colonel and commander of the 9th Cavalry Regiment, one of two African American regiments in the army. This began 17 years of service on the frontier and extensive fighting against the Mescalero Apaches, Kickapoos, Sioux, Cheyennes, and Utes, with campaigning from Texas to Montana. His experience earned him a position as cavalry adviser to the Schofield Board in 1869, where he helped develop army tactics and equipment for the Indian Wars.

In 1876 Merritt received promotion to colonel and took command of the 5th Cavalry Regiment. During the Great Sioux War of 1876, he commanded all the cavalry in Brigadier General George Crook's Bighorn and Yellowstone Expedition, fighting in the Battle of War Bonnet Creek and the Battle of Slim Buttes. During 1877–1878 he took part in the pursuit of the Nez Perces and in the Bannock War (1877–1878). In 1879 he participated in the Ute War. Under Merritt's command, the 5th Cavalry Regiment was recognized as one of the top cavalry units in the U.S. Army.

In 1882 Merritt became superintendent of West Point, serving in that position until his promotion to brigadier general in 1887. He then assumed command of the Department of the Missouri at Fort Leavenworth, Kansas. From 1895 to 1897 he commanded the Departments of the Missouri, Dakota, and the East, respectively. In 1893 he wrote a book, *The Armies of Today*. In it and in articles, Merritt advocated a large modern regular U.S. Army. He also supported U.S. imperial expansion.

At the beginning of the Spanish-American War in 1898, Major General Merritt was the second-ranking officer in the army and received command of VIII Corps, dispatched to the Philippines. He arrived there in late July. Following negotiations with the Spanish, Merritt staged a small symbolic battle on August 13 to satisfy Spanish honor. His forces then occupied Manila.

At the end of August, Merritt gave up his command to travel to Paris to brief the U.S. peace commissioners there, where he urged that the United States annex the Philippines. In December 1898 Merritt assumed command of the Department of the East. He retired from the army in 1900 and died in Natural Bridge, Virginia, on December 10, 1910.

DAWN OTTEVAERE NICKESON AND SPENCER C. TUCKER

Further Reading
Alberts, Don E. *General Wesley Merritt: Brandy Station to Manila Bay.* Columbus, OH: General's Books, 2001.
Feuer, A. B. *America at War: The Philippines, 1898–1913.* Westport, CT: Praeger, 2001.
Starr, Stephen Z. *The Union Cavalry in the Civil War.* 3 vols. Baton Rouge: Louisiana State University Press, 1979–1985.

Oglala Laokota Sioux war leader Crazy Horse and other Native American leaders of the attack.

Crazy Horse and some 600–800 warriors immediately ride to the area of the battle, only to discover that Crook's main column has since arrived. The warriors open fire from the bluffs on Crook's men below, but Crook immediately establishes a defensive perimeter around his horses and mules. Crook orders the village set on fire and then has his men advance on the bluffs dismounted. The soldiers soon drive most of the warriors from the high ground. In their destruction of the village, the troopers discover numerous weapons and other artifacts from the Battle of the Little Bighorn. Provisions taken here also provide for Crook's starving men. In the two days of fighting at Slim Buttes the Sioux lose 10 killed, an unknown number of wounded, and 20 captured (among them are 3 mortally wounded, including American Horse); army casualties are 3 killed and 13 wounded.

Crook departs on September 10, leading his men toward the Black Hills and promised food and supplies. The Sioux harass the cavalrymen during the next few days before Crook finally reaches a supply column on September 15.

October 21, 1876
American Indian Wars (continued): Great Sioux War (continued): Battle of Cedar Creek (Big Dry Creek or Big Dry River). In the summer of 1876, Colonel Nelson A. Miles and some 400 men of his 5th Infantry Regiment proceed from Fort Leavenworth, Kansas, by ship up the Missouri River to the Yellowstone River to join the search for Sioux and Northern Cheyenne Indians who had participated in the Battle of the Little Bighorn. That autumn Miles joins with Brigadier General Alfred H. Terry on the Rosebud and moves up that river to join with Brigadier General George Crook. Crook then splits off at the mouth of the Powder River, and Terry and Miles continue on to Glendive in Montana Territory, where Miles has established a temporary base.

In mid-October after the arrival at Glendive of a supply train led by Colonel Elwell S. Otis of more than 100 wagons (which had been forced to fend off two Sioux attacks en route), two Indian emissaries make contact with Otis and suggest peace talks with Hunkpapa Lakota Sioux leader Sitting Bull. Miles agrees, and he and Sitting Bull meet on October 20 and 21 at Cedar Creek. But with Miles presenting the government position that Sitting Bull must surrender and his followers must return to the reservation and with Sitting Bull adamant that the soldiers must depart and there be no more wagon trains through Sioux territory, the talks collapse after the second day. Fighting again soon breaks out. Sitting Bull orders the tall grasslands set on fire and villages abandoned. Miles orders his 5th Infantry Regiment to pursue the fleeing natives. In subsequent fighting, two soldiers are wounded and five Indians are slain. The soldiers pursue the Indians for more than 40 miles, collecting quantities of abandoned equipment and broken-down ponies along the way as Sitting Bull and his followers head for Canada and sanctuary.

November 25, 1876

American Indian Wars (continued): Great Sioux War (continued): Powder River Expedition and Dull Knife Fight (also known as the Battle of Bates Creek). On November 14, 1876, Brigadier General George Crook departs Fort Fetterman, Wyoming, with nearly 1,500 men in the 2nd, 3rd, 4th, and 5th Cavalry Regiments and the 4th, 9th, 14th, and 25th Infantry Regiments. Some 400 Pawnee, Shoshone, and Arapaho scouts and 300 civilian teamsters with 168 wagons accompany the soldiers. On November 22 Crook's Indian scouts locate and reconnoiter a Northern Cheyenne camp led by Dull Knife and Little Wolf along Bates Creek, near the North Fork of the Powder River west of present-day Kaycee, Wyoming. Many of the warriors had taken part in the annihilation of Lieutenant Colonel George A. Custer's command in the Battle of the Little Bighorn, and Crook orders Colonel Ranald S. Mackenzie and some 1,100 men of the 2nd, 3rd, 4th, and 5th Cavalry Regiments to attack the encampment of some 200 lodges, destroy the Indians' food supply, and capture their ponies.

Following a difficult night march on November 24–25, the troopers attack at dawn on November 25. The Northern Cheyennes had been celebrating a victory over a band of Shoshones, and surprise is complete. In frigid weather conditions, Mackenzie's troopers drive some 400 warriors and their families from their lodges. The Indians flee westward down the valley, abandoning their ponies. Some warriors take up a position in a draw near a butte in the middle of the valley, and hand-to-hand combat here produces the bulk of the battle's casualties.

Most of the Cheyennes escape, with a small group of warriors on the bluffs covering the withdrawal. In the battle, the Indians suffer 40 killed and an estimated equal number of wounded. Mackenzie sustains 7 killed and 26 wounded. The Dull Knife Fight is the last major engagement of the Great Sioux War.

The cavalrymen then burn the village along with its food stocks. They also take away nearly 600 ponies. Temperatures that night drop to about 30 degrees below zero. Without shelter and with little more than the clothes on their backs, the Cheyennes face brutal conditions in their effort to reach Oglala Lakota Sioux war chief Crazy Horse's band. Dull Knife and Little Wolf finally surrender their remaining followers at the Red Cloud Agency on May 5, 1877.

Meanwhile, harsh winter conditions force Crook to terminate the Powder River Expedition in December and return to Fort Fetterman. The destruction of Dull Knife's village in effect ends Northern Cheyenne resistance. Crook's campaign coincides with similar efforts by other army elements in the region against the Sioux.

January 8, 1877

American Indian Wars (continued): Great Sioux War (continued): Battle of Wolf Mountain. Colonel Nelson A. Miles, with 500 infantry and two light guns, locates Oglala Sioux war chief Crazy Horse's encampment on a bluff. The surprise shelling of the heights by army howitzers causes the Indians to flee. Casualties on both sides are light, but the loss of their winter encampment is a heavy blow to Crazy Horse and his followers.

April 24, 1877

President Rutherford B. Hayes orders army forces from New Orleans, Louisiana. This removal of the last soldiers from the South in effect brings to a close the period in American history known as Reconstruction following the Civil War.

May 6, 1877

American Indian Wars (continued): Great Sioux War (continued). Oglala Lakota war chief Crazy Horse and some 800 of his followers surrender at Camp Robinson in Nebraska Territory, officially bringing the Great Sioux War to a close. Virtually all hostile Sioux and Northern Cheyennes have surrendered except for several hundred Sioux led by Hunkpapa Lakota leader Sitting Bull who have taken refuge in Canada. The surrendering Indians are sent to reservations, where they must depend on the government for subsistence.

June 14, 1877

Henry Flipper becomes the first African American to graduate from the U.S. Military Academy, West Point. He is commissioned a second lieutenant of infantry.

Henry Ossian Flipper (1856–1940)

First African American graduate from the U.S. Military Academy. Henry Ossian Flipper was born in Thomasville, Georgia, on March 21, 1856, into slavery as the eldest of five sons of two slave parents. Growing up in Georgia, he attended schools operated by the American Missionary Association in Atlanta. In 1873 he accepted an appointment to the U.S. Military Academy, West Point, where he suffered ostracism from his fellow cadets because of his race. Flipper overcame the prejudice to become the first African American to graduate from West Point in June 1877. He was commissioned a second lieutenant and assigned to Company A of the 10th Cavalry.

Flipper served at various posts on the frontier carrying out assorted missions, including scouting, patrolling, and combating local belligerent Native Americans. During his time at Fort Davis in Texas, he led his company in several small skirmishes and expeditions against the Apache war chief Victorio in 1880. While a capable field commander, Flipper excelled particularly in engineering projects at these outposts, working as a surveyor and construction planner. At Fort Sill, Oklahoma, he and his troops drained all of the mosquito-ridden ponds on the installation, which improved the health of the garrison. Flipper's Ditch, which he designed to remove the contaminated water, remains and is now a national historic landmark. He also successfully applied his West Point engineering education in various other projects, such as stringing telegraph lines, constructing roads, and erecting post buildings.

While at Fort Davis, Texas, Flipper also performed auxiliary duties such as serving as acting assistant quartermaster, post quartermaster, and acting commissary of subsistence, which made him responsible for the installation's supplies and facilities. Once he took on these positions, Flipper left himself exposed to plots by racist white officers to force him out of the army. In 1881 he discovered post funds missing from his quarters and attempted to conceal the loss until he could find or replace the money. Post commander Colonel William R. Shafter of the 1st Infantry accused Flipper of embezzling the money and of conduct unbecoming of an officer and a gentleman. Shafter relieved him of his duties. A court-martial exonerated Flipper of embezzlement but convicted him on the latter charge, resulting in his dismissal from the army on June 30, 1882.

Flipper went on to a successful career as an engineer in Mexico, South America, and Arizona working on several lucrative surveying, railroad, and mining projects over the next 30 years. Ironically, the same federal government that stripped him of his army career hired Flipper as an engineering and cultural adviser for the Justice Department, the Department of the Interior, and the Senate Committee on Foreign Relations. However, Flipper continued to battle with the government over his conviction, asserting his innocence. He spent the rest of his life lobbying for vindication from his court-martial, including an unsuccessful attempt to have Congress reinstate his commission so that he might participate in the Spanish-American War in 1898.

To bolster his cause, Flipper published two books, one an account of his military academy experiences and the other about his ordeal with the army, the second published posthumously. He retired from his

(continued)

(Continued)

engineering career in 1931 and died in Atlanta, Georgia, on May 3, 1940. President William Clinton officially pardoned Flipper on February 19, 1999.

BRADFORD A. WINEMAN

Further Reading

Dinges, Bruce J. "The Court-Martial of Lieutenant Henry O. Flipper." *American West* 9 (January 1972): 12–17.
Flipper, Henry Ossian. *The Colored Cadet at West Point.* New York: Arno/New York Times, 1969.
Harris, Theodore D., ed. *Negro Frontiersman: The Western Memoirs of Henry O. Flipper.* El Paso: Texas Western College Press, 1963.

June–October 1877

American Indian Wars (continued): Nez Perce War. One of the most extraordinary episodes in American military history, the Nez Perce War takes place over a span of some 1,500 miles and involves more than 1,000 soldiers, all to subdue Nez Perce bands numbering at most 800 people, only 300 of them warriors. The war is caused by the desire of white settlers to secure the rich lands held by the Nez Perces in the Wallowa Valley in northeastern Oregon.

A treaty of 1855 between the Nez Perces and the U.S. government established a reservation acknowledging the ancestral homelands of the Nez Perce people. The discovery of gold in 1860, however, changes all this, as increasing numbers of miners and settlers move into the area. Despite this, the Nez Perces remain peaceful. Responding to settler pressure, however, in 1863 the U.S. government forces a new treaty on the tribe that reduces Nez Perce lands by some 90 percent. A number of Nez Perce leaders refuse to sign the new treaty, and they and their followers continue to live in peace outside the boundaries set by it. Among these is the Wallowa (Wal-lam-wat-kain) band of Nez Perces led by Chief Joseph.

Negotiations fail between Chief Joseph and Brigadier General Oliver O. Howard, commander of the Department of the Columbia, and Howard gives Joseph and his followers 30 days to surrender their lands and move onto a reservation in Idaho where other Nez Perces had been removed earlier. Joseph reluctantly yields and prepares to move to the reservation. Later he will claim that had Howard been more accommodating, there would have been no war.

On June 13, 1877, however, 3 youths from White Bird's Nez Perce band, seeking revenge for the 1875 murder of the father of one of them, kill 4 white settlers. The war that Joseph hoped to avoid now occurs. Word reaches Howard at Fort Lapwai, and he immediately dispatches troops to protect settlers in the Salmon River area. The killing of the 4 whites ignites the desire for vengeance among other Nez Perces, however, and the soldiers are unable to prevent the deaths of another 15 settlers.

Well aware that Howard will be sending soldiers, by June 16 Joseph relocates his band of some 800 Nez Perces to the more easily defended White Bird Canyon in north-central Idaho Territory. The next day the Nez Perces defeat Captain David Perry and 117 of the 1st Cavalry troopers and Idaho volunteers (see June 17, 1877). Another battle occurs on July 11 at the Clearwater River (see July 11–12, 1877) when the Nez Perce rebuff Howard and some 500 men. The warriors hold Howard at bay until their families can escape. The Nez Perces then cross the Bitterroot Mountains into Montana.

The Nez Perces stop to rest at the Big Hole Basin. There on August 9 they are surprised by another army column unexpectedly arriving from the east under Colonel John Gibbon. The soldiers attack, but again

FLIGHT OF THE NEZ PERCE, JUNE 18–OCTOBER 5, 1877

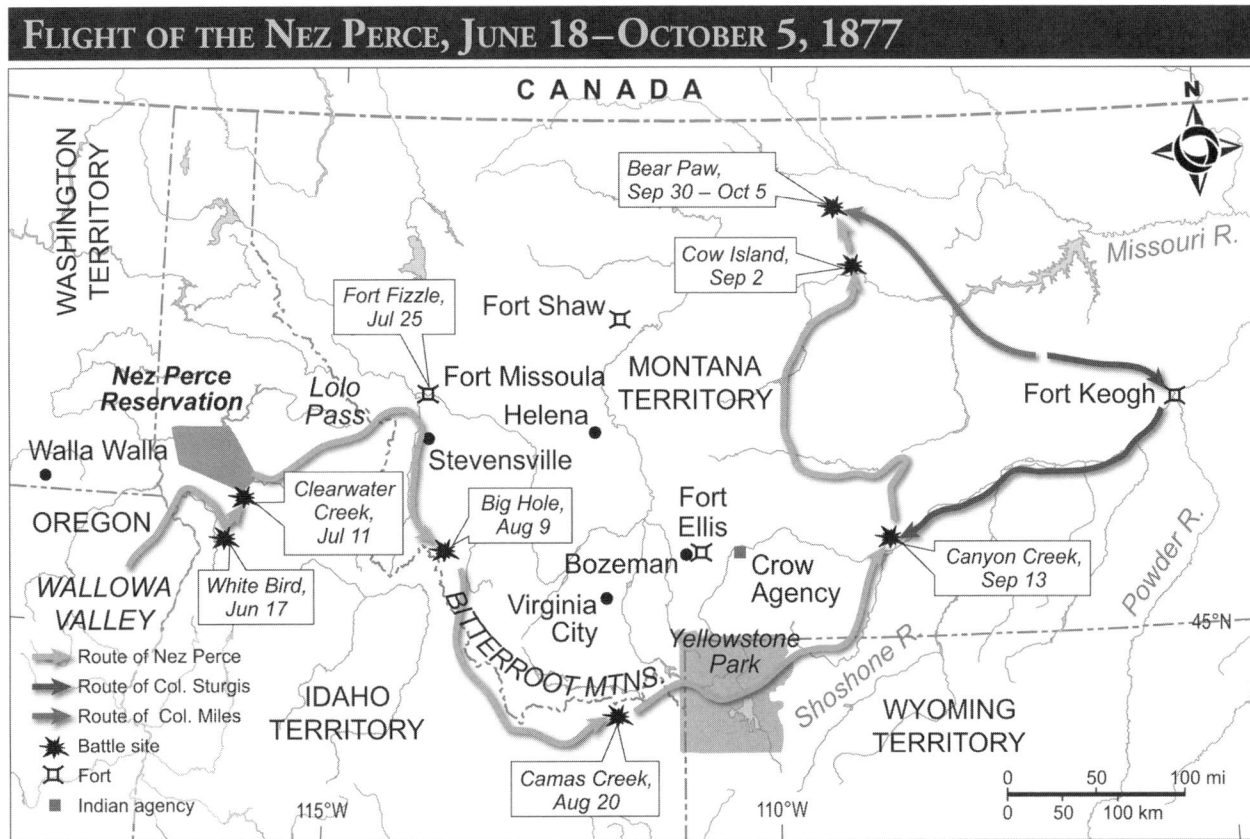

the Native Americans rally and drive the soldiers back (see August 9–10, 1877). The Nez Perces withdraw as Howard and his men arrive.

Following a skirmish at Camas Meadow, the Nez Perces move through present-day Yellowstone National Park, then turn north in an attempt to reach Canada. On September 13 at Canyon Creek north of the Yellowstone River, they beat back an attack by Colonel Samuel Sturgis and six troops of the 7th Cavalry. The Nez Perce then continue their extraordinary trek, still pursued by Howard. On September 30 only about 40 miles short of their goal, the Nez Perces are cut off by yet another army column near Bear Paw Mountain in northern Montana (see September 30–October 5, 1877).

After fighting against 10-to-1 odds during five days and with many of their leaders dead, about 400 Nez Perces surrender to Colonel Nelson A. Miles on October 5. Some of the Nez Perces manage to make it across the border into Canada and safety.

Colonel Miles had promised Joseph that he and his people would return to reservations in their homeland. The Nez Perces are instead sent to Kansas and to Indian Territory (Oklahoma), under protest from both Miles and Howard. In 1885 the Nez Perces are permitted to return to Washington but not to the Wallowa River Valley.

June 17, 1877

American Indian Wars (continued): Nez Perce War (continued): Battle of White Bird Canyon. Chief Joseph and his band of Nez Perces have moved into north-central Idaho Territory. Knowing that Brigadier General Oliver O. Howard, commander of the Department of the Columbia, will be sending soldiers against them, by June 16 Joseph relocates his people to the more easily defended White Bird Canyon near the Salmon River. That night, Nez Perce scouts report the approach from the north of Captain David Perry and 106 men of the 1st Cavalry Regiment with 11

Chief Joseph (1840–1904)

Nez Perce chief, Wallowa headman, and leader during the Nez Perce War of 1877. Chief Joseph, also known as Young Joseph or Hin-mah-too-yah-lat-kekt, was born in Oregon's Wallowa Valley in 1840, the son of the Christianized Nez Perce chief Old Joseph. His son was baptized as a child and renamed Young Joseph. Young Joseph spent a short time at the Spalding Mission School. He developed diplomatic and leadership skills by accompanying his father to councils and other negotiations. Old Joseph, however, refused to sign an 1863 treaty with the United States, renounced Christianity, and influenced his son to reject any white attempts to purchase Nez Perce land. When Old Joseph died in 1871, Young Joseph became chief of the Wallowa Band.

Growing friction between settlers and the Nez Perces prompted U.S. Army brigadier general Oliver Otis Howard to meet with headmen in July 1876. Chief Joseph and his brother Ollokot represented the non-treaty Nez Perces and presented testimony regarding settlers' crimes against their people. Chief Joseph was not satisfied with Howard's response, which virtually ignored the charges brought by Joseph. In January 1877 Howard gave Joseph an ultimatum: Joseph and the Wallowas were to leave for a reservation in Idaho by April 1, 1877, or face forcible removal. Joseph's refusal prompted Howard to send two companies of the 1st Cavalry from Fort Walla Walla (Washington) to the mouth of the Wallowa Valley.

Despite constant infringements on their lands, Joseph counseled his people to be patient and restrain their actions. Joseph and Howard again met, this time negotiating at Fort Lapwai in early May. Under threat of military reprisal, Joseph finally agreed to move his people to the reservation.

On June 14, 1877, three Nez Perce warriors killed four settlers, and the war that Chief Joseph had hoped to avoid erupted. He decided that he would not take his people to the reservation and embarked with them on a trek that ultimately covered more than 1,500 miles in an effort to reach Canada.

On June 17 troopers of the 1st Cavalry caught up with Joseph's small band in White Bird Canyon. Joseph, Ollokot, and about 60 warriors defeated the soldiers and began what turned out to be a three-month trek through Oregon, Idaho, Wyoming, and Montana toward the Canadian border. Leading about 800 people, Joseph evaded or engaged U.S. Army detachments throughout June and July. He earned a reputation as a civilized fighter, allowing noncombatants to escape and refusing to scalp or mutilate dead soldiers.

On August 7, 1877, at Big Hole, Montana, Colonel John Gibbon, with the 7th Infantry and the 2nd Cavalry, fought another battle, attacking the Nez Perces when they were encamped. The tactical draw at Big Hole was followed by fierce fighting with Howard at Canyon Creek. Colonel Nelson Miles's command joined the pursuit, chasing Joseph to the Bear Paw Mountains, Montana, where he was forced to surrender with about 400 of his followers on October 5, just 30 miles south of Canada. Some 300 Nez Perces managed to escape into Canada. Chief Joseph told Miles on his surrender that "From where the sun now stands I will fight no more forever."

The government dispersed the Nez Perces, and Joseph was eventually sent to the Colville Reservation in Washington. He remained a staunch advocate for his people for the rest of his life, always seeking to return to Wallowa, where his father was buried. Chief Joseph died on September 12, 1904, in Colville, Washington.

DAWN OTTEVAERE NICKESON

Further Reading

Gidley, M. *Kopet: A Documentary Narrative of Chief Joseph's Last Years.* Seattle: University of Washington Press, 1981.

Greene, Jerome A. *Nez Perce Summer, 1877: The U.S. Army and the Nee-Me-Poo Crisis.* Helena: Montana Historical Society Press, 2000.

McCoy, Robert. *Chief Joseph, Yellow Wolf, and the Creation of Nez Perce History in the Northwest.* New York: Routledge, 2004.

Moulton, Candy. *Chief Joseph.* New York: Tom Doherty and Associates, 2005.

Idaho settler volunteers. The Nez Perces decide to attempt peace negotiations with the understanding that should these fail, they will fight.

On June 17 Perry's advance party, including the Idaho volunteers, approaches the Nez Perce camp. They encounter 6 warriors under a flag of truce. For some unknown reason, 1 of the volunteers opens fire on the Nez Perce truce party. General fighting then ensues. Some 70 Nez Perce warriors already occupy excellent defensive positions; an equal number are asleep.

Perry then comes up with the main body and tries to organize a charge, but the Nez Perces are excellent marksmen and attack the soldiers from both flanks. Perry also has difficulty communicating his orders. A command to consolidate is misinterpreted as one for general retreat, producing near panic and stranding some soldiers on the battlefield. The soldiers and volunteers then begin a hasty withdrawal along two routes. The Nez Perces trap one of the groups and, when its members run out of ammunition, kill those in it. Perry manages to regroup the remaining troopers at a nearby ranch and withdraw them under fire to nearby Mount Idaho, where they are reinforced by additional volunteers.

The Battle of White Bird Canyon results in 34 U.S. soldiers killed and 2 wounded; 2 Idaho volunteers are also wounded. The Nez Perce losses are only 3 warriors wounded. The Nez Perces also secure a number of weapons and some ammunition.

July 11–12, 1877

American Indian Wars (continued): Nez Perce War (continued): Battle of the Clearwater River. Following the victory of the Nez Perces under Chief Joseph in the Battle of White Bird Canyon (see June 17, 1877), Brigadier General Oliver O. Howard, commander of the Department of the Columbia, assumes personal command and sets out with some 500 men. Chief Looking Glass has combined his own band with that of Chief Joseph, and the Nez Perces now number about 800 people, of whom perhaps 300 are warriors.

On July 11, 1877, Howard's soldiers surprise the Nez Perces camped along the Clearwater River in north-central Idaho. Howard's men charge into an Indian camp at the bottom of a ravine. Soon other Nez Perces counterattack the soldiers and force Howard's men back.

The fighting lasts for several hours until the army can bring up howitzers. The Nez Perces manage to capture several of them, but Lieutenant Charles F. Humphrey of the 4th Artillery leads a charge that retakes the howitzers, for which he is subsequently awarded the Medal of Honor.

The battle continues into the night and the next day, ending only when additional troops approach from Fort Klamath. Joseph and the Nez Perces then escape across the Clearwater.

The army suffers 17 killed and 27 wounded. The Nez Perces lose 4 killed and 6 wounded. Instead of launching an immediate pursuit, Howard waits until the next day, giving the Nez Perces a considerable lead as they move across Idaho and into Montana. Although Howard's command had sustained the greater number of casualties, the army claims victory because the Nez Perces have been forced from Idaho into Montana.

August 9–10, 1877

American Indian Wars (continued): Nez Perce War (continued): Battle of Big Hole. Following the Battle of the Clearwater River (see July 11–12, 1877), the Nez Perces under Chiefs Joseph and Looking Glass move up the Bitterroot Valley in Montana. On August 6 they reach the Big Hole Basin along the north fork of the Big Hole River in present-day Beaverhead County, Montana. Here Looking Glass, believing that they are sufficiently ahead of the army column under Brigadier General Oliver O. Howard, insists that they stop for a time to rest. Although Joseph and others protest, Looking Glass is adamant.

Unknown to the Nez Perces, a second army column, led by commander of the District of Montana Colonel John Gibbon, is also pursuing the Indians. Proceeding from Missoula, Gibbon has 161 army personnel and 45 volunteers. His scouts locate the Nez Perce encampment on August 8. The remainder of his men then come up, and Gibbon attacks at sunrise on August 9. Believing themselves safe, the Nez Perces have not posted guards and are caught by surprise.

The soldiers charge the camp as the warriors attempt to purchase time for the women and children to take refuge in nearby woods. Within 20 minutes Gibbon's command has secured the encampment and is attempting to burn it when the Indians counterattack and force Gibbon to withdraw. The soldiers then dig in. Some warriors hold Gibbon's soldiers at bay throughout the remainder of that day and the next, while the rest of the Nez Perces again take flight. On the night of August 10 the remaining warriors break contact and slip away to join the others. The following day Howard arrives with his column, and the pursuit resumes.

In the two-day Battle of Big Hole, Gibbon sustains 28 dead (22 soldiers, 1 civilian guide, and 5 civilian volunteers). Another 39, including Gibbon, are wounded. Nez Perce losses are 60–90 dead, most in the initial assault and many of them women and children. The number of wounded is unknown. The remaining Nez Perces move east into Yellowstone National Park before turning north toward Canada.

August 15, 1877

American Indian Wars (continued): Nez Perce War (continued): Battle of Birch Creek (Birch Creek Massacre). Following the Battle of Big Hole (see August 9–10, 1877), Nez Perce chief Joseph and his followers cross the Continental Divide at Bannock Pass into the Lemhi Valley, moving south. On August 15 as some 60 Nez Perce warriors traverse the Birch Creek Valley in present-day Clark County, Idaho, they encounter a supply train bound for Salmon City and consisting of eight wagons and 30 mules, with three teamsters and five others.

The warriors lead the wagon train to their camp about two miles upriver, where they arrange to purchase goods, including whiskey, which the natives then consume, becoming more belligerent in the process. One of the freighters escapes, and apparently the Nez Perces permit three Chinese passengers to depart, but conflict ensues with the remaining teamsters and passengers, resulting in the deaths of four whites.

August 20, 1877

American Indian Wars (continued): Nez Perce War (continued): Battle of Camas Meadows. U.S. Army troops under Brigadier General Oliver O. Howard have been in pursuit of the Nez Perces led by Chiefs Joseph and Looking Glass, who are attempting to reach Canada. With Colonel John Gibbon's force still recovering from the Battle of Big Hole just days earlier (see August 9–10, 1877), Howard is on his own in the effort to overtake the Nez Perces before they can gain the border.

On the evening of August 19 Howard and his cavalry, which is in advance of the infantry, camp at a site used by the Nez Perces the previous night near the confluence of East Camas and Spring Creeks at present-day Kilgore in eastern Idaho. Before dawn on August 20, some 200 Nez Perce warriors ride back to their abandoned camp and there secure some 150 mules. When they approach the heavily guarded horses, however, they are discovered and forced into a fighting withdrawal. Some cavalrymen give chase and recapture a few of the mules but are soon forced back by superior numbers.

The army suffers 2 killed and 11 wounded. No Nez Perce losses are reported. Although a small skirmish, the Battle of Camas Meadows is noteworthy because the loss of his pack animals sharply reduces Howard's maneuverability and permits the Nez Perces to continue their flight for Canada.

September 2, 1877

American Indian Wars (continued): Apache escape from San Carlos. Victorio, a leader of the Eastern Chiricahua Apaches, often known as the Warm Springs or Mimbreño Apaches, and more than 300 of his followers escape into the wilderness from the San Carlos Reservation in Arizona Territory. Within a month many give themselves up at Fort Wingate in New Mexico Territory, but Victorio and 80 warriors remain in the mountains. Victorio hopes to settle his people at the Mescalero Reservation at Ojo Caliente in western New Mexico, but negotiations toward that end fail.

September 5, 1877

American Indian Wars (continued): Death of Crazy Horse. A rumor spreads that Oglala Lakota war chief Crazy Horse, who had surrendered the previous May, is planning an uprising among the Indians at Fort Robinson, Nebraska. An army detail is sent to arrest him. Crazy Horse resists and is bayoneted, dying that night.

September 13, 1877

American Indian Wars (continued): Nez Perce War (continued): Battle of Canyon Creek. In Yellowstone National Park, Montana, Nez Perce Indians under Chief Joseph attempting to reach Canada abduct some tourists, killing two and injuring others. Meanwhile, Nez Perce chief Looking Glass sends out envoys to the Crow Indians. They return with the unwelcome news that the Crows have sided with the United States and will not give the Nez Perces refuge. Looking Glass then dispatches the envoys to Canada to seek safety with the Sioux already there under Chief Sitting Bull.

On September 13 along Canyon Creek near the park, some 350 troopers of the 7th Cavalry Regiment,

led by Colonel Samuel D. Sturgis, encounter the Nez Perces. Sturgis orders his men to dismount and begin a slow advance. The two sides exchange long-distance rifle fire. Before combat ends, the soldiers have sustained 3 killed and 11 wounded. Nez Perce losses are 1 killed and 3 wounded. While the Nez Perces escape, Crow Indians assist the cavalry in securing 400 of the slowest Nez Perce animals. Sturgis is subsequently sharply criticized for his handling of the engagement.

September 30–October 5, 1877

American Indian Wars (continued): Nez Perce War (continued): Battle of Bear Paw Mountain (Battle of Bear Paw). Some 40 miles from sanctuary in Canada, Nez Perce chief Looking Glass, believing that they have outmaneuvered pursuing army troops under Brigadier General Oliver O. Howard, again insists that the fleeing Nez Perces rest from their pursuers at Snake Creek just north of the Bear Paw Mountains, some 16 miles south of present-day Chinook, Montana. Once again Looking Glass errs, for the halt enables troops under Colonel Nelson A. Miles to come up.

On September 30, 1877, Miles and 400 men of the 2nd and 7th Cavalry and 5th Infantry (mounted), accompanied by 40 Indian scouts, attack the unsuspecting Nez Perce camp while at the same time capturing all of their ponies. Again the Nez Perces prove

Battle of Bear Paw Mountain		
Date	September 30–October 5, 1877	
Location	Blaine County, Montana	
Opponents (*winner)	*United States	Nez Perces
Commander	Colonel Nelson A. Miles; Brigadier General Oliver O. Howard	Chief Joseph
#	525 soldiers	700 Native Americans (men, women, and children)
Casualties	36 killed, 47 wounded	25 killed, 46 wounded, 418 prisoners

Fighting in the Battle of Bear Paw Mountain—which led to the surrender of Chief Joseph on October 5, 1877, during the Nez Perce War—by U.S. Army soldiers under Colonel Nelson A. Miles. From sketches by G. M. Holland, an illustration from *Frank Leslie's Illustrated Newspaper*, November 3, 1877. (Library of Congress)

their discipline under fire, and both sides take heavy casualties, causing Miles to break off the attack and settle in for a siege.

By day's end, Miles has encircled the Nez Perce camp. A stalemate ensues until Howard arrives on October 4 with reinforcements. Howard, however, leaves Miles in command.

The Nez Perce leaders debate what course of action to follow. Joseph wants negotiations, while White Bird and Looking Glass favor an attempt to break out. On October 5, an army sniper kills Looking Glass. Joseph then decides to meet with Howard and Miles. That same day, he hands his rifle to Miles with the words "I am tired; my heart is sick and sad. From where the sun now stands I will fight no more forever."

During their trek, the Nez Perces have covered some 1,500 miles and fought 18 engagements, most of which they have won. Joseph surrenders 87 men, 184 women, and 147 children. White Bird disagrees with the decision; he and some 300 others manage to elude the soldiers during the battle and siege and reach Canada. In the battle and siege the army suffers 36 dead and 47 wounded; Nez Perce losses are 25 dead (2 of them women) and 46 wounded. Sickness and death will claim additional Nez Perces during a prolonged exile in Kansas and Indian Territory (present-day Oklahoma). Although some Nez Perces return to a diminished reservation at Lapwai in 1885, Joseph and 150 of his followers are settled on the Colville Reservation in central Washington.

November 24, 1877

The sloop-rigged iron screw steamer *Huron,* under Commander George P. Ryan, wrecks in a storm off Nags Head, North Carolina. Ninety-eight members of its crew of 132 are lost.

BROTHER FIGHTING BROTHER

The American Civil War and the Era of Reconstruction, 1850–1877

DOCUMENTS

Abraham Lincoln, Proclamation Calling the Militia and Convening Congress (1861) [Excerpt]

Introduction

Immediately after news reached him regarding the fall of Fort Sumter to Confederate forces on April 12, 1861, President Abraham Lincoln issued this proclamation on April 15 calling out the militia and convening a special session of the U.S. Congress. Such actions indicated that the federal government did not intend to let the seceding Southern states leave the Union without a fight, marking the opening of the Civil War.

Primary Source

BY THE PRESIDENT OF THE UNITED STATES A PROCLAMATION.

Whereas the laws of the United States have been for some time past, and now are opposed, and the execution thereof obstructed, in the States of South Carolina, Georgia, Alabama, Florida, Mississippi, Louisiana and Texas, by combinations too powerful to be suppressed by the ordinary course of judicial proceedings, or by the powers vested in the Marshals by law,

Now therefore, I, Abraham Lincoln, President of the United States, in virtue of the power in me vested by the Constitution, and the laws, have thought fit to call forth, and hereby do call forth, the militia of the several States of the Union, to the aggregate number of seventy-five thousand, in order to suppress said combinations, and to cause the laws to be duly executed. The details, for this object, will be immediately communicated to the State authorities through the War Department.

I appeal to all loyal citizens to favor, facilitate and aid this effort to maintain the honor, the integrity, and the existence of our National Union, and the perpetuity of popular government; and to redress wrongs already long enough endured.

I deem it proper to say that the first service assigned to the forces hereby called forth will probably be to re-possess the forts, places, and property which have been seized from the Union; and in every event, the utmost care will be observed, consistently with the objects aforesaid, to avoid any devastation, any destruction of, or interference with, property, or any disturbance of peaceful citizens in any part of the country.

And I hereby command the persons composing the combinations aforesaid to disperse, and retire peaceably to their respective abodes within twenty days from this date.

Deeming that the present condition of public affairs presents an extraordinary occasion, I do hereby, in virtue of the power in me vested by the Constitution, convene both Houses of Congress. Senators and Representatives are therefore summoned to assemble at their respective chambers, at 12 o'clock, noon, on Thursday, the fourth day of July, next, then and there to consider and determine, such measures, as, in their wisdom, the public safety, and interest may seem to demand. . . .

ABRAHAM LINCOLN

Source: Abraham Lincoln, "Proclamation," in *A Compilation of the Messages and Papers of the Presidents, 1789–1897,* edited by James D. Richardson, 13–14 (Washington, DC: Authority of Congress, 1900).

Abraham Lincoln, Proclamation Declaring a Blockade of Southern Ports (1861)

Introduction

One of the most effective Union measures in defeating the Confederacy during the Civil War, U.S. president Abraham Lincoln's imposition of a massive federal blockade around the South on April 19, 1861, virtually cut the Confederacy off from the rest of the world. Not only could Southerners no longer import the supplies they needed to wage the war, but neither could they export their crops (most notably cotton). However, blockade-runners managed to bring at least some supplies and material into the South.

> I deem it proper to say that the first service assigned to the forces hereby called forth will probably be to re-possess the forts, places, and property which have been seized from the Union.

Primary Source

Whereas an insurrection against the Government of the United States has broken out in the States of South Carolina, Georgia, Alabama, Florida, Mississippi, Louisiana, and Texas, and the laws of the United States for the collection of the revenue cannot be effectually executed therein conformably to that provision of the Constitution which requires duties to be uniform throughout the United States:

And whereas a combination of persons, engaged in such insurrection, have threatened to grant pretended letters of marque to authorize the bearers thereof to commit assaults on the lives, vessels, and property of good citizens of the country lawfully engaged in commerce on the high seas, and in waters of the United States:

And whereas an Executive Proclamation has been already issued, requiring the persons engaged in these disorderly proceedings to desist therefrom, calling out a militia force for the purpose of repressing the same, and convening Congress in extraordinary session to deliberate and determine thereon:

Now, therefore, I, ABRAHAM LINCOLN, President of the United States, with a view to the same purposes before mentioned, and to the protection of the public peace, and the lives and property of quiet and orderly citizens pursuing their lawful occupations, until Congress shall have assembled and deliberated on the said unlawful proceedings, or until the same shall have ceased, have further deemed it advisable to set on foot a blockade of the ports within the States aforesaid, in pursuance of the laws of the United States and the law of nations in such case provided. For this purpose a competent force will be posted so as to prevent entrance and exit of vessels from the ports aforesaid. If therefore, with a view to violate such blockade, a vessel shall approach, or shall attempt to leave either of the said ports, she will be duly warned by the commander of one of the blockading vessels, who will indorse on her register the fact and date of such warning, and if the same vessel shall again attempt to enter or leave the blockaded port, she will be captured and sent to the nearest convenient port, for such proceedings against her and her cargo as prize, as may be deemed advisable.

And I hereby proclaim and declare that if any person, under the pretended authority of the said States, or under any other pretence, shall molest a vessel of the United States, or the persons or cargo on board of her, such person will be held amenable to the laws of the United States for the prevention and punishment of piracy.

Source: Abraham Lincoln, "Proclamation Declaring a Blockade of Southern Ports," April 19, 1861, United States Department of State, in *Papers Relating to the Foreign Relations of the United States,* Vol. 3 (Washington, DC: U.S. Government Printing Office, 1874), 319.

Abraham Lincoln, Correspondence Relieving George B. McClellan of Command (1862)

Introduction

Since the First Battle of Bull Run (Manassas) (July 21, 1861), President Abraham Lincoln had grown increasingly frustrated with Major General George B. McClellan's tentativeness and inaction. The general also routinely harangued Lincoln with his Democratic Party viewpoints and his belief that slavery should continue, even after the war was over. Lincoln had already relieved McClellan of certain command responsibilities once before, reinstating them only under political pressure. When McClellan allowed the Confederate Army of Northern Virginia to escape from the September 17, 1862, Battle of Antietam relatively unscathed, Lincoln decided to sack McClellan for good. What follows is correspondence from Lincoln to McClellan that culminated in the general's dismissal.

Primary Source

WAR DEPARTMENT, Washington City, October 24, 1862.

Major-General McCLELLAN:

I have just read your dispatch about sore-tongued and fatigued horses. Will you pardon me for asking what the horses of your army have done since the battle of Antietam that fatigues anything?

A. LINCOLN.

* * *

EXECUTIVE MANSION, Washington, November 5, 1862.

By direction of the President, it is ordered that Major-General McClellan be relieved from the command of the Army of the Potomac, and that Major-General Burnside take the command of that army.

Also that Major-General Hunter take command of the corps in said army which is now commanded by General Burnside. That Major-General Fitz John Porter be relieved from the command of the corps he now commands in said army, and that Major-General Hooker take command of said corps.

The General-in-Chief is authorized, in discretion, to issue an order substantially as the above, forthwith, or so soon as he may deem proper.

A. LINCOLN.

> **Source:** U.S. War Department, *War of the Rebellion: A Compilation of the Official Records of the Union and Confederate Armies*, Ser. I, Vol. XIX (Washington, DC: U.S. Government Printing Office, 1900), 485–545.

Robert E. Lee: Official Reports on the Battle of Gettysburg (1863) [Excerpt]

Introduction

In this series of official reports to Confederate president Jefferson Davis, Confederate general Robert E. Lee details the events at and immediately after the momentous Battle of Gettysburg (July 1–3, 1863). Although the battle had cost both the Union Army and the Confederate Army greatly, the Confederates suffered more in the long run, as they no longer had the manpower to replace those who had fallen. Many historians consider this battle as the turning point of the Civil War.

Primary Source

Near Gettysburg, Pa., July 4, 1863.

Mr. PRESIDENT:

After the rear of the army had crossed the Potomac, leading corps, under General Ewell, pushed on to Carlisle and York, passing through Chambersburg. The other two corps closed up at the latter place, and soon afterward intelligence was received that the army of General Hooker was advancing. Our whole force was directed to concentrate at Gettysburg, and the corps of

Generals Ewell and A. P. Hill reached that place on the 1st July the former advancing from Carlisle and the latter from Chambersburg. The two leading divisions of these corps, upon reaching the vicinity of Gettysburg, found the enemy, and attacked him, driving him from the town, which was occupied by our troops. . . .

On the 2nd July, Longstreet's corps, with the exception of one division, having arrived, we attempted to dislodge the enemy, and, though we gained some ground, we were unable to get possession of his position. The next day, the third division of General Longstreet having come up, a more extensive attack was made. The works on the enemy's extreme right and left were taken, but his numbers were so great and his position so commanding, that our troops were compelled to relinquish their advantage and retire.

> We captured at Gettysburg about 6,000 prisoners, besides the wounded that remained in our hands after the engagements of the 1st and 2d. Fifteen hundred of these prisoners and the wounded were paroled.

It is believed that the enemy suffered severely in these operations, but our own loss has not been light. . . .

Very respectfully, your obedient servant,

R. E. LEE, General.

* * *

HAGERSTOWN, July 7, 1863.

Mr. PRESIDENT:

My letter of the 4th instant will have informed you of the unsuccessful issue of our final attack on the enemy in the rear of Gettysburg. Finding the position too strong to be carried, and, being much hindered in collecting necessary supplies for the army, by the numerous bodies of local and other troops which watched the passes, I determined to withdraw to the west side of the mountains. This has been safely accomplished with great labor, and the army is now in the vicinity of this place.

One of my reasons for moving in this direction, after crossing the mountains, was to protect our trains with the sick and wounded, which had been sent back to Williamsport, and which were threatened by the enemy's cavalry. Our advance reached here yesterday afternoon in time to support our cavalry in repulsing an attempt of the enemy to reach our trains. . . . We captured at Gettysburg about 6,000 prisoners, besides the wounded that remained in our hands after the engagements of the 1st and 2d. Fifteen hundred of these prisoners and the wounded were paroled. . . . The rest have been sent to Williamsport. . . . We were obliged to leave a large number of our wounded who were unable to travel, and many arms that had been collected on the field at Gettysburg.

[. . .]

Very respectfully, your obedient servant,

R. E. LEE, General.

* * *

Near Hagerstown, Md., July 8, 1863.

MR PRESIDENT:

My letter of yesterday will have informed you of the position of this army. Though reduced in numbers by the hardships and battles through which it has passed since leaving the Rappahannock, its condition is good, and its confidence unimpaired. Upon crossing the Potomac into Maryland, I had calculated upon the river remaining fordable during the summer, so as to enable me to recross at my pleasure, but a series of storms, commencing the day after our entrance into Maryland, has placed the river beyond fording stage, and the present storm will keep it so for at least a week. I shall, therefore, have to accept battle if the enemy offers it, whether I wish to or not. . . . I deem it prudent to make every arrangement in our power to meet any emergency that may arise.

From information gathered from the papers, I believe that the troops from North Carolina and the coast of Virginia, under Generals Foster and Dix, have been ordered to the Potomac, and that recently additional re-enforcement have been sent from the coast of South Carolina Banks. If I am correct in my opinion, this will liberate most of the troops in those regions, and should Your Excellency have not already done so, I earnestly ask that all that can be spared be concentrated on the Upper Rappahannock, under General Beauregard. . . . This command will answer the double purpose of affording protection to the capital at Richmond and relieving the pressure upon this army.

I hope Your Excellency will understand that I am not in the least discouraged, or that my faith in the protection of an all-merciful Providence, or in the fortitude of this army is at all shaken. . . .

I am, most respectfully, your obedient servant,

R. E. LEE, General.

* * *

July 10, 1863.

Mr. PRESIDENT:

Since my letter of the 8th instant, nothing of importance, in a military point of view, has transpired. The Potomac continues to be past fording, and, owing to the rapidity of the stream, and the limited we have for crossing, the prisoners and wounded are not yet over. I hope they will be able to cross to-day. I have not received any definite intelligence of the movements or designs of the enemy. A scout report that a column which followed us across the mountain has reached Waynesborough, Pa., and other bodies are reported as moving by way of Fredericksburg from Emmitsburg, as if approaching in this direction. If these reports be correct, it would appear to be intention of the enemy to deliver battle, and we have no alternative but to accept it if offered. The army is in good condition, and we have a good supply of ammunition. . . .

[. . .]

Very respectfully, your obedient servant,

R. E. LEE, General.

* * *

Bunker Hill, Va., July 16, 1863.

Mr. PRESIDENT:

I have received your letter of the 12th instant, and thank you for the kind terms you speak of the army, and for your consideration of myself. I inclose a copy of my letter of the 7th instant, which failed to reach you. The army is encamped around this place, where we shall rest today. The men are in good health and spirits, but want shoes and clothing badly. I have sent back to endeavor to procure a supply of both, and also horseshoes, for want of which nearly our cavalry is unserviceable. As soon as these articles are obtained, we shall be prepared to resume operations.

I shall not need the pontoon train now, as the boats used at Falling Waters have been brought away, excepting the new ones constructed by us, which were too heavy and too large for transportation. I have accordingly ordered the train of which you speak to come no farther. The attack on the coast may have been caused by the information contained in the captured letter. I think that all these demonstrations of the enemy are designed to retain troops from the field, and while he must be resisted and a force kept at threatened points sufficient to secure them, we should endeavor to avoid being misled as to his numbers and real intentions, and thus enable him to accomplish his purpose. I do not know that I shall need any more troops here, and they had better be kept in front of Richmond, to secure it from attack and protect our railroads.

[. . .]

I am, with great respect, Your Excellency's obedient servant,

R. E. LEE, General

Source: U.S. War Department, *War of the Rebellion: A Compilation of the Official Records of the Union and Confederate Armies,* Ser. I, Vol. XXVII (Washington, DC: U.S. Government Printing Office, 1900), 298–302.

BROTHER FIGHTING BROTHER

The American Civil War and the Era of Reconstruction, 1850–1877

STATISTICS

Branch of Service	Number Serving	Total Deaths	Battle Deaths	Other Deaths	Wounded, Not Mortally
Total	2,213,363	364,511	140,414	224,097	281,881
Union forces					
Army	2,128,948	359,528	138,154	221,374	280,040
Navy	84,415	4,523	2,112	2,411	1,710
Marines	—*	460	148	312	131
Confederate forces					
All services	600,000–1,500,000	259,821–264,821**	74,524	85,297–91,000**	—

* Marines serving included in navy total.
**Includes 26,000–31,000 who died in Union prisoner-of-war camps.
Source: Congressional Research Service, CRS Report for Congress, February 6, 2010.

BROTHER FIGHTING BROTHER

The American Civil War and the Era of Reconstruction, 1850–1877

BIBLIOGRAPHY

Adams, George Worthington. *Doctors in Blue: The Medical History of the Union Army in the Civil War.* New York: Schuman, 1952.

Anderson, Bern. *By Sea and by River: The Naval History of the Civil War.* New York: Knopf, 1962.

Ashdown, Paul, and Edward Caudill. *The Myth of Nathan Bedford Forrest.* American Crisis Series 16. Lanham, MD: Rowman and Littlefield, 2005.

Ayers, Edward L. *What Caused the Civil War? Reflections on the South and Southern History.* New York: Norton, 2005.

Bailey, Anne J. *War and Ruin: William T. Sherman and the Savannah Campaign.* American Crisis Series 10. Wilmington, DE: Scholarly Resources, 2003.

Ballard, Michael B. *Vicksburg: The Campaign That Opened the Mississippi.* Civil War America. Chapel Hill: University of North Carolina Press, 2004.

Bearss, Edwin C. *The Campaign for Vicksburg.* Dayton, OH: Morningside, 1986.

Beatie, Russel Harrison. *The Army of the Potomac.* Cambridge, MA: Da Capo, 2002.

Bennett, Michael J. *Union Jacks: Yankee Sailors in the Civil War.* Civil War America. Chapel Hill: University of North Carolina Press, 2004.

Beringer, Richard E. *The Elements of Confederate Defeat: Nationalism, War Aims, and Religion.* Athens: University of Georgia Press, 1988.

Beringer, Richard E. *Why the South Lost the Civil War.* Athens: University of Georgia Press, 1986.

Bernstein, Iver. *The New York City Draft Riots: Their Significance for American Society and Politics in the Age of the Civil War.* New York: Oxford University Press, 1990.

Bilby, Joseph G. *A Revolution in Arms: A History of the First Repeating Rifles.* Yardley, PA: Westholme, 2006.

Boritt, Gabor S., ed. *Why the Confederacy Lost.* New York: Oxford University Press, 1992.

Brown, Kent Masterson. *Retreat from Gettysburg: Lee, Logistics, and the Pennsylvania Campaign.* Civil War America. Chapel Hill: University of North Carolina Press, 2005.

Brown, Walter Lee. *A Life of Albert Pike.* Fayetteville: University of Arkansas Press, 1997.

Bruce, Robert V. *Lincoln and the Tools of War.* Indianapolis: Bobbs-Merrill, 1956.

Bunting, Josiah. *Ulysses S. Grant.* American Presidents Series. New York: Times Books, 2004.

Burnham, Philip. *So Far from Dixie: Confederates in Yankee Prisons.* Lanham, MD: Taylor Trade, 2003.

Carmichael, Peter S. *Audacity Personified: The Generalship of Robert E. Lee.* Baton Rouge: Louisiana State University Press, 2004.

Carpenter, John A. *Ulysses S. Grant.* Twayne's Rulers and Statesmen of the World Series 14. New York: Twayne, 1970.

Carter, Arthur B. *The Tarnished Cavalier: Major General Earl Van Dorn, C.S.A.* Knoxville: University of Tennessee Press, 1999.

Carter, Samuel. *The Final Fortress: The Campaign for Vicksburg, 1862–1863.* New York: St. Martin's, 1980.

Casdorph, Paul D. *Confederate General R. S. Ewell: Robert E. Lee's Hesitant Commander.* Lexington: University Press of Kentucky, 2004.

Catton, Bruce. *America Goes to War.* Middletown, CT: Wesleyan University Press, 1958.

Bibliography

Catton, Bruce. *The Civil War.* New York: American Heritage, 1971.

Catton, Bruce. *The Coming Fury.* The Centennial History of the Civil War. Garden City, NY: Doubleday, 1961.

Catton, Bruce. *Grant Moves South.* Boston: Little, Brown, 1960.

Catton, Bruce. *Grant Takes Command.* Boston: Little, Brown, 1969.

Catton, Bruce. *Never Call Retreat.* The Centennial History of the Civil War 3. Garden City, NY: Doubleday, 1965.

Catton, Bruce. *A Stillness at Appomattox.* The Army of the Potomac 3. Garden City, NY: Doubleday, 1953.

Catton, Bruce. *Terrible Swift Sword.* The Centennial History of the Civil War 2. Garden City, NY: Doubleday, 1963.

Catton, Bruce. *This Hallowed Ground: The Story of the Union Side of the Civil War.* Mainstream of America Series. Garden City, NY: Doubleday, 1956.

Catton, Bruce. *U.S. Grant and the American Military Tradition.* The Library of American Biography. Boston: Little, Brown, 1954.

Cavanaugh, Michael Arthur, and William Marvel. *The Petersburg Campaign: The Battle of the Crater "The Horrid Pit," June 25–August 6, 1864.* The Virginia Civil War Battles and Leaders Series. Lynchburg, VA: H. E. Howard, 1989.

Cleaves, Freeman. *Meade of Gettysburg.* Norman: University of Oklahoma Press, 1960.

Coddington, Edwin B. *The Gettysburg Campaign: A Study in Command.* New York: Scribner, 1968.

Coffey, David. *Sheridan's Lieutenants: Phil Sheridan, His Generals, and the Final Year of the Civil War.* The American Crisis Series 18. Wilmington, DE: Rowman and Littlefield, 2005.

Cozzens, Peter. *Battles and Leaders of the Civil War,* Vols. 5 and 6. Urbana: University of Illinois Press, 2002.

Cunningham, Horace Herndon. *Doctors in Gray: The Confederate Medical Service.* Baton Rouge: Louisiana State University Press, 1958.

Daniel, Larry J. *Cannoneers in Gray: The Field Artillery of the Army of Tennessee, 1861–1865.* University: University of Alabama Press, 1984.

Daniel, Larry J. *Days of Glory: The Army of the Cumberland, 1861–1865.* Baton Rouge: Louisiana State University Press, 2004.

Davis, Burke. *Sherman's March.* New York: Random House, 1980.

Davis, William C. *Battle at Bull Run: A History of the First Major Campaign of the Civil War.* Garden City, NY: Doubleday, 1977.

Davis, William C. *The Imperiled Union: 1861–1865.* Garden City, NY: Doubleday, 1982.

Davis, William C., and Time-Life Books. *Death in the Trenches: Grant at Petersburg.* The Civil War. Alexandria, VA: Time-Life Books, 1986.

Detzer, David. *Donnybrook: The Battle of Bull Run, 1861.* Orlando, FL: Harcourt, 2004.

DiNardo, R. L., and Albert A. Nofi, eds. *James Longstreet: The Man, the Soldier.* Conshohocken, PA: Combined Publishing, 1998.

Donald, David Herbert, ed. *Why the North Won the Civil War.* Baton Rouge: Louisiana State University Press, 1960.

Dowdey, Clifford. *The Seven Days: The Emergence of Lee.* Boston: Little, Brown, 1964.

Drake William F. *Little Phil: The Story of General Philip Henry Sheridan.* Prospect, CT: Biographical Publishing, 2005.

Eicher, David J. *The Longest Night: A Military History of the Civil War.* New York: Simon and Schuster, 2001.

Faust, Drew Gilpin. *This Republic of Suffering: Death and the American Civil War.* New York: Knopf, 2008.

Fellman, Michael. *The Making of Robert E. Lee.* New York: Random House, 2000.

Fellman, Michael, Lesley J. Gordon, and Daniel E. Sutherland. *This Terrible War: The Civil War and Its Aftermath.* New York: Longman, 2003.

Foote, Shelby. *The Civil War: A Narrative.* New York: Random House, 1974.

Fowler, William M. *Under Two Flags: The American Navy in the Civil War.* New York: Norton, 1990.

Freeman, Douglas Southall. *Lee's Lieutenants: A Study in Command.* New York: Scribner, 1944.

Freeman, Douglas Southall. *Robert E. Lee: A Biography.* New York: Scribner, 1935.

Fuller, John Frederick Charles. *Grant & Lee: A Study in Personality and Generalship.* Civil War Centennial Series. Bloomington: Indiana University Press, 1957.

Furgurson, Ernest B. *Chancellorsville, 1863: The Souls of the Brave.* New York: Knopf, 1992.

Gallagher, Gary W. *Lee and His Army in Confederate History.* Civil War America. Chapel Hill: University of North Carolina Press, 2001.

Gallagher, Gary W. *Lee the Soldier.* Lincoln: University of Nebraska Press, 1996.

Gallagher, Gary W. *The Shenandoah Valley Campaign of 1862.* Military Campaigns of the Civil War. Chapel Hill: University of North Carolina Press, 2003.

Gallagher, Gary W. *The Shenandoah Valley Campaign of 1864.* Military Campaigns of the Civil War. Chapel Hill: University of North Carolina Press, 2006.

Gallagher, Gary W., and Joseph T. Glatthaar, eds. *Leaders of the Lost Cause: New Perspectives on the Confederate High Command.* Mechanicsburg, PA: Stackpole, 2004.

Gilmore, Donald L. *Civil War on the Missouri-Kansas Border.* Gretna, LA: Pelican, 2006.

Glatthaar, Joseph T. *General Lee's Army: From Victory to Collapse.* New York: Free Press, 2008.

Glatthaar, Joseph T. *The March to the Sea and Beyond: Sherman's Troops in the Savannah and Carolinas Campaigns.* The American Social Experience Series 1. New York: New York University Press, 1985.

Glatthaar, Joseph T. *Partners in Command: The Relationships between Leaders in the Civil War.* New York: Free Press, 1994.

Goss, Thomas Joseph. *The War within the Union High Command: Politics and Generalship during the Civil War.* Modern War Studies. Lawrence: University Press of Kansas, 2003.

Gott, Kendall D. *Where the South Lost the War: An Analysis of the Fort Henry–Fort Donelson Campaign, February 1862.* Mechanicsburg, PA: Stackpole, 2003.

Govan, Gilbert E., and James Weston Livingwood. *A Different Valor: The Story of General Joseph E. Johnston, C.S.A.* Indianapolis: Bobbs-Merrill, 1956.

Grant, Susan-Mary, and Brian Holden Reid. *The American Civil War: Explorations and Reconsiderations.* New York: Longman, 2000.

Grant, Ulysses S. *Ulysses S. Grant: Warrior and Statesman.* New York: Morrow, 1969.

Griffith, Paddy. *Battle Tactics of the Civil War.* New Haven, CT: Yale University Press, 1989.

Grimsley, Mark. *And Keep Moving On: The Virginia Campaign, May–June 1864.* Great Campaigns of the Civil War. Lincoln: University of Nebraska Press, 2002.

Hagerman, Edward. *The American Civil War and the Origins of Modern Warfare: Ideas, Organization, and Field Command.* Bloomington: Indiana University Press, 1988.

Harsh, Joseph L. *Taken at the Flood: Robert E. Lee and Confederate Strategy in the Maryland Campaign of 1862.* Kent, OH: Kent State University Press, 1999.

Hattaway, Herman, and Archer Jones. *How the North Won: A Military History of the Civil War.* Urbana: University of Illinois Press, 1983.

Hauptman, Laurence M. *Between Two Fires: American Indians in the Civil War.* New York: Free Press, 1995.

Hazlett, James C., and Edwin Olmstead. *Field Artillery Weapons of the Civil War.* Newark: University of Delaware Press, 1983.

Henderson, George Francis Robert. *Stonewall Jackson and the American Civil War.* New York: Longmans, Green, 1936.

Hennessy, John J. *Return to Bull Run: The Campaign and Battle of Second Manassas.* New York: Simon and Schuster, 1993.

Hess, Earl J. *Field Armies and Fortifications in the Civil War: The Eastern Campaigns, 1861–1864.* Civil War America. Chapel Hill: University of North Carolina Press, 2005.

Hess, Earl J. *The Union Soldier in Battle: Enduring the Ordeal of Combat.* Modern War Studies. Lawrence: University Press of Kansas, 1997.

Hesseltine, William Best. *Civil War Prisons: A Study in War Psychology.* American Classics. New York: F. Ungar, 1930.

Holzer, Harold, and Tim Mulligan, eds. *The Battle of Hampton Roads: New Perspectives on the USS Monitor and CSS Virginia.* New York: Fordham University Press, 2006.

Horigan, Michael. *Elmira: Death Camp of the North.* Mechanicsburg, PA: Stackpole, 2002.

Hughes, Nathaniel Cheairs. *General William J. Hardee: Old Reliable.* Southern Biography Series. Baton Rouge: Louisiana State University Press, 1965.

Huston, James L. *Calculating the Value of the Union: Slavery, Property Rights, and the Economic Origins of the Civil War.* Civil War America. Chapel Hill: University of North Carolina Press, 2003.

Bibliography

Hutton, Paul Andrew. *Phil Sheridan and His Army.* Lincoln: University of Nebraska Press, 1985.

Johnson, Robert Underwood, and Clarence Clough Buel. *Battles and Leaders of the Civil War: Being for the Most Part Contributions by Union and Confederate Officers.* New York: T. Yoseloff, 1956.

Jones, Archer. *Civil War Command and Strategy: The Process of Victory and Defeat.* New York: Free Press, 1992.

Jordan, David M. *Winfield Scott Hancock: A Soldier's Life.* Bloomington: Indiana University Press, 1988.

Josephy, Alvin M. *The Civil War in the American West.* New York: Knopf, 1991.

Knight, Wilfred. *Red Fox: Stand Watie and the Confederate Indian Nations during the Civil War Years in Indian Territory.* Glendale, CA: A. H. Clark, 1988.

Korda, Michael. *Ulysses S. Grant: The Unlikely Hero.* Eminent Lives. New York: Atlas Books/Harper-Collins, 2004.

Linderman, Gerald F. *Embattled Courage: The Experience of Combat in the American Civil War.* New York: Free Press, 1987.

Longacre, Edward G. *Fitz Lee: A Military Biography of Major General Fitzhugh Lee, C.S.A.* Cambridge, MA: Da Capo, 2005.

Longacre, Edward G. *The Man behind the Guns: A Biography of General Henry Jackson Hunt, Chief of Artillery, Army of the Potomac.* South Brunswick, NJ: A. S. Barnes, 1977.

Luvaas, Jay, and Harold W. Nelson, eds. *The U.S. Army War College Guide to the Battle of Antietam: The Maryland Campaign of 1862.* Carlisle, PA: South Mountain, 1987.

Luvaas, Jay, and Harold W. Nelson, eds. *The U.S. Army War College Guide to the Battle of Gettysburg.* New York: Perennial Library, 1986.

Luvaas, Jay, and Harold W. Nelson, eds. *The U.S. Army War College Guide to the Battles of Chancellorsville & Fredericksburg.* Carlisle, PA: South Mountain, 1988.

Maney, R. Wayne. *Marching to Cold Harbor: Victory and Failure, 1864.* Shippensburg, PA: White Mane, 1995.

Marszalek, John F. *Commander of All Lincoln's Armies: A Life of General Henry W. Halleck.* Cambridge, MA: Belknap Press of Harvard University Press, 2004.

Marszalek, John F. *Sherman: A Soldier's Passion for Order.* New York: Free Press, 1993.

Marszalek, John F. *Sherman's March to the Sea.* Civil War Campaigns and Commanders Series. Abilene, TX: McWhiney Foundation Press, 2005.

Martin, Samuel J. *The Road to Glory: Confederate General Richard S. Ewell.* Indianapolis: Guild Press of Indiana, 1991.

Marvel, William. *Andersonville: The Last Depot.* Civil War America. Chapel Hill: University of North Carolina Press, 1994.

Marvel, William. *Lee's Last Retreat: The Flight to Appomattox.* Civil War America. Chapel Hill: University of North Carolina Press, 2002.

Matter, William D. *If It Takes All Summer: The Battle of Spotsylvania.* Chapel Hill: University of North Carolina Press, 1988.

McDonough, James L. *Chattanooga: A Death Grip on the Confederacy.* Knoxville: University of Tennessee Press, 1984.

McDonough, James L. *Nashville: The Western Confederacy's Final Gamble.* Knoxville: University of Tennessee Press, 2004.

McDonough, James L. *Shiloh: In Hell before Night.* Knoxville: University of Tennessee Press, 1977.

McDonough, James L., and James Pickett Jones. *"War So Terrible": Sherman and Atlanta.* New York: Norton, 1987.

McKnight, Brian Dallas. *Contested Borderland: The Civil War in Appalachian Kentucky and Virginia.* Lexington: University Press of Kentucky, 2006.

McMurry, Richard M. *Two Great Rebel Armies: An Essay in Confederate Military History.* Chapel Hill: University of North Carolina Press, 1989.

McPherson, James M. *Abraham Lincoln and the Second American Revolution.* New York: Oxford University Press, 1990.

McPherson, James M. *Battle Cry of Freedom: The Civil War Era.* The Oxford History of the United States 6. New York: Oxford University Press, 1988.

McPherson, James M. *Drawn with the Sword: Reflections on the American Civil War.* New York: Oxford University Press, 1996.

McPherson, James M. *For Cause and Comrades: Why Men Fought in the Civil War.* New York: Oxford University Press, 1997.

McPherson, James M. *Ordeal by Fire: The Civil War and Reconstruction.* New York: Knopf, 1982.

McPherson, James M. *Tried by War: Abraham Lincoln as Commander in Chief.* New York: Penguin, 2008.

McWhiney, Grady. *Battle in the Wilderness: Grant Meets Lee.* Civil War Campaigns and Commanders Series. Fort Worth, TX: Ryan Place Publishers, 1995.

McWhiney, Grady. *Braxton Bragg and Confederate Defeat.* New York: Columbia University Press, 1969.

McWhiney, Grady, and Perry D. Jamieson. *Attack and Die: Civil War Military Tactics and the Southern Heritage.* Tuscaloosa: University of Alabama Press, 1982.

Merrill, James M. *The Rebel Shore: The Story of Union Sea Power in the Civil War.* Boston: Little, Brown, 1957.

Miers, Earl Schenck. *The Web of Victory: Grant at Vicksburg.* New York: Knopf, 1955.

Mitchell, Reid. *Civil War Soldiers.* New York: Viking, 1988.

Murfin, James V. *The Gleam of Bayonets: The Battle of Antietam and the Maryland Campaign, September 1862.* New York: T. Yoseloff, 1965.

Nevins, Allan. *Ordeal of the Union: Emergence of Lincoln.* New York: Scribner, 1971.

Nichols, David A. *Lincoln and the Indians: Civil War Policy and Politics.* Columbia: University of Missouri Press, 1978.

Nichols, Edward J. *Toward Gettysburg: A Biography of General John F. Reynolds.* University Park: Pennsylvania State University Press, 1958.

Nosworthy, Brent. *The Bloody Crucible of Courage: Fighting Methods and Combat Experience of the Civil War.* New York: Carroll and Graf, 2003.

Parish, Peter J. *The American Civil War.* New York: Holmes and Meier, 1975.

Pfanz, Donald. *Richard S. Ewell: A Soldier's Life.* Civil War America. Chapel Hill: University of North Carolina Press, 1998.

Pfanz, Harry W. *Gettysburg: The Second Day.* Chapel Hill: University of North Carolina Press, 1987.

Priest, John M. *Antietam: The Soldiers' Battle.* Shippensburg, PA: White Mane, 1989.

Prushankin, Jeffery S. *A Crisis in Confederate Command: Edmund Kirby Smith, Richard Taylor, and the Army of the Trans-Mississippi.* Baton Rouge: Louisiana State University Press, 2005.

Rafuse, Ethan Sepp. *McClellan's War: The Failure of Moderation in the Struggle for the Union.* Bloomington: Indiana University Press, 2005.

Randall, J. G., and David Herbert Donald. *The Civil War and Reconstruction.* 2nd ed. Lexington, MA: Heath, 1969.

Reid, Brian Holden. *The Origins of the American Civil War.* Origins of Modern Wars. New York: Longman, 1996.

Rhea, Gordon C. *The Battle of the Wilderness, May 5–6, 1864.* Baton Rouge: Louisiana State University Press, 1994.

Rhea, Gordon C. *The Battles for Spotsylvania Court House and the Road to Yellow Tavern, May 7–12, 1864.* Baton Rouge: Louisiana State University Press, 1997.

Rhea, Gordon C. *Cold Harbor: Grant and Lee, May 26–June 3, 1864.* Baton Rouge: Louisiana State University Press, 2002.

Rhea, Gordon C. *To the North Anna River: Grant and Lee, May 13–25, 1864.* Baton Rouge: Louisiana State University Press, 2000.

Rhoades, Jeffrey L. *Scapegoat General: The Story of Major General Benjamin Huger, C.S.A.* Hamden, CT: Archon, 1985.

Rhodes, James Ford. *History of the Civil War, 1861–1865.* American Classics. New York: Ungar, 1961.

Roberts, William H. *Now for the Contest: Coastal and Oceanic Naval Operations in the Civil War.* Great Campaigns of the Civil War. Lincoln: University of Nebraska Press, 2004.

Robertson, James I. *General A. P. Hill: The Story of a Confederate Warrior.* New York: Random House, 1987.

Robertson, James I. *Robert E. Lee: Virginian Soldier, American Citizen.* New York: Atheneum Books for Young Readers, 2005.

Robertson, James I. *Soldiers Blue and Gray.* American Military History. Columbia: University of South Carolina Press, 1988.

Robertson, James I. *Stonewall Jackson: The Man, the Soldier, the Legend.* New York: Macmillan, 1997.

Roland, Charles Pierce. *Albert Sidney Johnston, Soldier of Three Republics.* Austin: University of Texas Press, 1964.

Bibliography

Roland, Charles Pierce. *An American Iliad: The Story of the Civil War.* Lexington: University Press of Kentucky, 1991.

Royster, Charles. *The Destructive War: William Tecumseh Sherman, Stonewall Jackson, and the Americans.* New York: Knopf, 1991.

Rutkow, Ira M. *Bleeding Blue and Gray: Civil War Surgery and the Evolution of American Medicine.* New York: Random House, 2005.

Sanborn, Margaret. *Robert E. Lee.* Philadelphia: Lippincott, 1967.

Sanders, Charles W. *While in the Hands of the Enemy: Military Prisons of the Civil War.* Conflicting Worlds. Baton Rouge: Louisiana State University Press, 2005.

Sears, Stephen W. *George B. McClellan: The Young Napoleon.* New York: Ticknor and Fields, 1988.

Sears, Stephen W. *Landscape Turned Red: The Battle of Antietam.* New Haven, CT: Ticknor and Fields, 1983.

Sears, Stephen W. *To the Gates of Richmond: The Peninsula Campaign.* New York: Ticknor and Fields, 1992.

Shea, William L., and Terrence J. Winschel. *Vicksburg Is the Key: The Struggle for the Mississippi River.* Great Campaigns of the Civil War. Lincoln: University of Nebraska Press, 2003.

Sheehan-Dean, Aaron Charles. *The View from the Ground: Experiences of Civil War Soldiers.* New Directions in Southern History. Lexington: University Press of Kentucky, 2007.

Smith, Jean Edward. *Grant.* New York: Simon and Schuster, 2001.

Speer, Lonnie R. *Portals to Hell: Military Prisons of the Civil War.* Mechanicsburg, PA: Stackpole, 1997.

Stampp, Kenneth M. *And the War Came: The North and the Secession Crisis, 1860–1861.* Baton Rouge: Louisiana State University Press, 1950.

Stampp, Kenneth M. *The Causes of the Civil War.* Englewood Cliffs, NJ: Prentice Hall, 1965.

Starr, Stephen Z. *The Union Cavalry in the Civil War.* Baton Rouge: Louisiana State University Press, 1985.

Steere, Edward. *The Wilderness Campaign.* Civil War Campaigns. Harrisburg, PA: Stackpole, 1960.

Swanberg, William Andrew. *First Blood: The Story of Fort Sumter.* New York: Scribner, 1957.

Sword, Wiley. *Shiloh: Bloody April.* New York: Morrow, 1974.

Symonds, Craig L. *Joseph E. Johnston: A Civil War Biography.* New York: Norton, 1992.

Tanner, Robert G. *Stonewall in the Valley: Thomas J. "Stonewall" Jackson's Shenandoah Valley Campaign, Spring 1862.* Garden City, NY: Doubleday, 1976.

Thomas, Emory M. *Robert E. Lee: A Biography.* New York: Norton, 1995.

Thomas, Emory M. *The Confederacy as a Revolutionary Experience.* New Insights in History. Englewood Cliffs, NJ: Prentice Hall, 1971.

Thompson, Jerry D. *Henry Hopkins Sibley: Confederate General of the West.* Natchitoches, LA: Northwestern State University Press, 1987.

Tucker, Glenn. *High Tide at Gettysburg: The Campaign in Pennsylvania.* Indianapolis: Bobbs-Merrill, 1958.

Tucker, Spencer C. *Andrew Foote: Civil War Admiral on Western Waters.* Annapolis, MD: Naval Institute Press, 2000.

Tucker, Spencer. *Blue and Gray Navies: The Civil War Afloat.* Annapolis, MD: Naval Institute Press, 2006.

Turner, George Edgar. *Victory Rode the Rails: The Strategic Place of the Railroads in the Civil War.* Indianapolis: Bobbs-Merrill, 1953.

Warner, Ezra J. *Generals in Blue: Lives of the Union Commanders.* Baton Rouge: Louisiana State University Press, 1964.

Warner, Ezra J. *Generals in Gray: Lives of the Confederate Commanders.* Baton Rouge: Louisiana State University Press, 1959.

Weddle, Kevin John. *Lincoln's Tragic Admiral: The Life of Samuel Francis Du Pont.* A Nation Divided. Charlottesville: University of Virginia Press, 2005.

Weigley, Russell Frank. *A Great Civil War: A Military and Political History, 1861–1865.* Bloomington: Indiana University Press, 2000.

Weitz, Mark A. *More Damning Than Slaughter: Desertion in the Confederate Army.* Lincoln: University of Nebraska Press, 2005.

Wert, Jeffry D. *General James Longstreet, the Confederacy's Most Controversial Soldier: A Biography.* New York: Simon and Schuster, 1993.

Whan, Vorin E. *Fiasco at Fredericksburg.* University Park: Pennsylvania State University Press, 1961.

Wiley, Bell Irvin. *The Life of Billy Yank: The Common Soldier of the Union.* Indianapolis: Bobbs-Merrill, 1952.

Wiley, Bell Irvin. *The Life of Johnny Reb: The Common Soldier of the Confederacy.* Indianapolis: Bobbs-Merrill, 1943.

Williams, Kenneth Powers. *Lincoln Finds a General: A Military Study of the Civil War.* New York: Macmillan, 1959.

Williams, Thomas Harry. *Lincoln and His Generals.* New York: Knopf, 1952.

Williams, Thomas Harry. *P. G. T. Beauregard: Napoleon in Gray.* Southern Biography Series. Baton Rouge: Louisiana State University Press, 1954.

Woodworth, Steven E. *Beneath a Northern Sky: A Short History of the Gettysburg Campaign.* The American Crisis Series 12. Wilmington, DE: SR Books, 2003.

Woodworth, Steven E. *Grant's Lieutenants: From Cairo to Vicksburg.* Modern War Studies. Lawrence: University Press of Kansas, 2001.

Woodworth, Steven E. *Grant's Lieutenants: From Chattanooga to Appomattox.* Modern War Studies. Lawrence: University Press of Kansas, 2008.

Woodworth, Steven E. *Jefferson Davis and His Generals: The Failure of Confederate Command in the West.* Modern War Studies. Lawrence: University Press of Kansas, 1990.

MATTHEW J. WAYMAN

EXPANSION AT HOME AND ABROAD

The Later Indian Wars, the Spanish-American War, and the Philippine-American War, 1878–1913

OVERVIEW

The Spanish-American War and the Philippine-American War stemmed from international dislocations that began during the 1890s. These global discontents eventually led to a long era of global warfare, including the Cold War, from 1914 to 1991. At this time the international balance of power, which had been largely stable though dynamic after the Napoleonic Wars, began to destabilize, a consequence of imposing changes during the 19th century. Among these unsettling developments were the urban Industrial Revolution, the rise of strong nation-states in the Western world that enjoyed the loyalty of their citizenry, and the expansion of European empires in Africa and Asia.

The Spanish Empire, once the greatest in the world, largely disappeared during the Napoleonic era, leaving only a few colonies in Africa (Morocco), the West Indies (Puerto Rico and Cuba), and the Pacific Ocean (the Philippines and smaller island groups, among them the Carolines and Marianas). During the latter years of the 19th century, anticolonial movements emerged in the most important of Spain's possessions, the Philippines and Cuba. Spain's Restoration monarchy, which had been established in 1875, decided to put down these insurgencies rather than grant either autonomy or independence. The Spanish Army crushed the first outbreaks, the Ten Years' War (1868–1878) in Cuba, and the First Philippine Insurgency (1896–1897). A second insurgency in Cuba, which began in 1895, evolved into extended guerrilla warfare that proved most troublesome for the Spanish Army, although by the end of 1897

The Naval Battle of Santiago de Cuba, July 3, 1898, during the Spanish-American War. Ships of the U.S. Navy Blockading Squadron destroyed a Spanish cruiser squadron attempting to escape from Santiago. (Library of Congress)

General Valeriano Weyler, known as "the Butcher" because of his stern methods, had succeeded in largely containing it.

This success, however, came too late. Spain's Conservative Party, led by Antonio Cánovas de Castillo, had authorized drastic measures in Cuba to counter the insurgents' recourse to partisan tactics. This initiative aroused growing opposition in the United States, especially after Weyler ordered a cruel reconcentration of rural civilians in urban areas to deprive the insurgents of support in the countryside. The United States did not have large investments and commercial interests in Cuba, but anti-Spanish sentiment grew as newspapers published reports of terrible civilian suffering and aroused latent dislike of Spain.

President William McKinley, who took office in April 1897, exerted increasing pressure on Spain to adopt reforms that would at least grant Cuba a significant degree of autonomy. When an anarchist assassinated Cánovas in 1897, Spain's Liberal Party, headed by Práxedes Mateo Sagasta, soon took power, recalled Weyler, and finally granted home rule to both Cuba and Puerto Rico. This gesture, however, came too late. The Cuban leaders rejected autonomy, sensing that this concession signaled Spanish weakness and that perseverance might soon lead to independence.

The Cuban question, although of growing importance, was but one of several great issues that concerned Americans at this time, but a stirring event suddenly transformed the situation. On February 15, 1898, the battleship *Maine,* which had been sent to Havana Harbor to establish a U.S. naval presence, exploded and sank, causing the deaths of 266 crew members and many injuries among the survivors. Thereafter the Cuban question dominated public attention. The nation jumped to the conclusion that the Spanish had placed a mine in the harbor to destroy the *Maine*. A naval inquiry confirmed this view, although years later it became clear that internal combustion in the ship's coal bunkers adjacent to stockpiles of ammunition had probably caused the disaster.

The cautious McKinley opposed armed intervention, seeking instead to emphasize economic reforms, but public pressures eventually forced him to call for Cuban independence. His supporters in the business community, the most important constituency in the Republican Party, were concerned chiefly with the monetary system and the tariff. They feared the unsettling effects that might stem from war, which often leads to unexpected and undesirable outcomes for business.

When Spain did not bow to the American demand for Cuban independence, the U.S. Congress authorized armed intervention but also adopted the Teller Amendment, which proclaimed that the purpose of armed intervention was to help Cuba achieve independence, a resounding repudiation of imperialist intentions. For various reasons many Democrats supported war, which influenced McKinley. He reluctantly went along with Congress, in all probability fearing that his failure to do so would compromise the Republican Party in the autumn elections and eventually return the Democratic Party, the champion of free silver and free trade, to power in Washington.

Spain attempted to gain support from the great powers of Europe but failed to do so. The nation had no international ties of importance, having followed a policy of isolation from other nations during many years of internal political challenges, notably the agitation of Carlists, Basques, Catalonians, and other groups. Widespread domestic unrest raised fears of revolution and the fall of the Restoration monarchy. Given these domestic challenges, Spain did not involve itself in external affairs. The European powers, preoccupied with great issues of their own including difficulties with their own empires, refused to help Spain, having no obligations and no desire to earn the enmity of the United States. Bereft of European support, Spain had to fight alone against a formidable enemy.

Popular emotions influenced the Madrid government to some extent; many Spaniards believed that the empire had been God's gift as a reward for the expulsion of the Moors from Europe and believed that no Spanish government could surrender the remaining colonies without dishonoring the nation. War seemed a lesser evil than looming domestic tumult. In addition, many believed that Spain could give a good account of itself because the Americans seemed unprepared for war. Spain possessed a large army, already in place in the likely combat zones, and also possessed a respectable navy, which it deemed superior to that of the United States. Even if Spain experienced defeat, an honorable military effort rather than craven acceptance of the American demands might preserve the established order.

Spain declared war on April 23, 1898, and the United States followed on April 25, predating its action to April 21 because it had already begun naval operations.

Spain adopted a defensive strategy to back up its policy of retaining its colonies, hoping to repel American attacks on Cuba, Puerto Rico, and the Philippines. The most important decisions made in Madrid during the early days of the war were to dispatch a naval force to help defend Cuba and to organize another to reinforce its garrison in the Philippines.

To achieve its sole war aim—the independence of Cuba—the United States adopted an offensive strategy, a product of prewar planning. There was no thought of acquiring Spanish colonies. Recognizing the limited size of the regular U.S. Army (28,000 men), the United States would first conduct naval operations on the peripheries of Spanish power in the Caribbean Sea and in Philippine waters. The United States sought to intimidate the enemy by launching prompt and vigorous campaigns in the hope of achieving an early cessation of hostilities. Lacking sufficient trained troops under arms, the nation could not immediately dispatch large armies to the theaters of war. Of course it could call upon immense numbers of militia and volunteers, but these men lacked military training. It would take a year to mobilize, train, equip, and deploy a huge volunteer army. For the moment the government could only contemplate rather modest army expeditions to the Caribbean Sea and the western Pacific Ocean in support of naval operations.

As soon as war was declared, Commodore George Dewey's small but competent Asiatic Squadron, which had been ordered from Japan to Hong Kong in anticipation of possible hostilities, departed for the Philippines. The squadron did so in accordance with prescriptions in the navy's prewar plans in the event of war with Spain. On May 1 the U.S. squadron entered Manila Bay. Dewey's warships consisted of the protected cruisers *Olympia, Baltimore, Raleigh,* and *Boston* and the gunboats *Concord* and *Petrel.*

This force, which mounted 54 heavy guns of which 10 were 8-inch breech-loading rifles, engaged Admiral Patricio Montojo y Pasarón's Spanish squadron of two large cruisers, four unprotected cruisers, and one gunboat, which mounted only 37 heavy guns, the largest being 6.3-inch rifles (7 total). This weak aggregation bereft of armor anchored in shallow water off the naval base at Cavite rather than near Manila to avoid an American bombardment of the city and to limit casualties during the impending battle.

When Dewey located the antiquated and unarmored Spanish squadron, he simply steamed past it several times and fired on it at will. The guns of the American vessels outnumbered those of the enemy and outranged them. Dewey's gunfire sank three vessels and severely damaged the other four. The crippled

ships were scuttled and joined the others on the shallow bottom. After the battle, the *Petrel* set fire to them. Three were later raised, repaired, and placed in American service. Montojo's crews suffered heavy casualties, with 161 killed and 210 wounded. The unprotected cruiser *Reina María Cristina,* Montojo's flagship, attempted to sortie against the American squadron but was soon forced to return to its anchorage. It took more than half of the Spanish losses. Dewey's crews sustained only 9 wounded and none killed.

The victorious Dewey lacked troops to conduct operations on land. He stationed his squadron off Manila and soon brought in the former leader of the defeated Philippine insurgency, Emilio Aguinaldo, and encouraged him to resume hostilities. Aguinaldo organized an army and instituted successful operations against the Spanish garrisons located elsewhere on Luzon and on other islands, but the Americans did not allow him to attack Manila. He also established a civil government in anticipation of gaining independence.

Meanwhile, the North Atlantic Squadron, commanded by Rear Admiral William T. Sampson, left its base at Key West and immediately established an effective blockade of Cuba, initially at Havana but soon extended to other ports. Another naval force, the Flying Squadron, then at Hampton Roads, Virginia, received instructions to deal with an enemy naval attack on the East Coast. As in the Philippines, no land force was available to conduct early and extensive operations on land. In any event, an attack on Cuba had to await assurance that Spain's navy could not compromise such an operation.

Spain attempted to counter the early American successes with naval initiatives. Sagasta's government immediately ordered Admiral Pascual Cervera y Topete's small squadron of only seven vessels (four armored cruisers and three destroyers) to proceed to Cuban waters. The best of these ships, the armored cruiser *Cristóbal Colón,* lacked its main battery of 10-inch guns. Minus one of his destroyers, Cervera arrived on May 19 at Santiago de Cuba, a port on the southeastern coast of the island several hundred miles from Havana. The principal Spanish land forces were far distant in western Cuba. A Spanish garrison at Santiago de Cuba of just over 10,000 troops held off a smaller force of Cuban insurgents.

The Spanish government also organized a naval squadron commanded by Admiral Manuel de la Cámara y Libermoore to relieve the Philippines, but necessary preparations delayed its departure for about two months. Meanwhile, the U.S. Navy sent important naval reinforcements to Manila Bay.

The United States took immediate steps to follow up its initial naval operations. McKinley decided to dispatch modest army expeditions to both Cuba and the Philippines, seeking to maintain pressure on the Spanish defenders. Representatives of the United States made contact with Cuban military leaders, and the insurgents received shipments of arms. When the navy's Flying Squadron, with Commodore William T. Schley in command, managed to blockade Cervera in port at Santiago de Cuba on May 29, McKinley authorized a modest expedition to seize the port and destroy the Spanish vessels.

Major General William R. Shafter was made commander of the army's V Corps, which was hurriedly concentrated at Tampa on the west coast of Florida amid considerable confusion. The expedition received orders to go to Santiago de Cuba as soon as possible. V Corps eventually included 12 regular army regiments, 4 of them black units. It also contained 5 volunteer organizations including the 1st Volunteer Cavalry, dubbed the Rough Riders, and militia from New York, Massachusetts, and Michigan, for a grand total of about 17,000 men. After a muddled delay in Tampa, the expedition departed for Cuba on June 15 and arrived off Santiago de Cuba on June 20. Shafter made contact with the local Cuban commander, General Calixto García y Iñiguez, and landed almost immediately at Daiquirí and Siboney, located east of Santiago de Cuba, without opposition. Fearful that tropical disease, especially yellow fever and malaria, would infect his troops and that Spanish reinforcements might soon bolster the enemy garrison, Shafter decided to move quickly against Santiago de Cuba along an inland route. He rejected Admiral Sampson's proposal to seize the Spanish batteries located near the Morro Castle at the harbor entrance, an operation that would bottle up Cervera.

Rivalry between the U.S. Army and the U.S. Navy at Santiago de Cuba arose frequently, with unfortunate consequences.

On June 3 Sampson attempted to block the channel with an old ship, the *Merrimac*. Naval constructor Richmond P. Hobson commanded this bold enterprise. The ship came to rest outside the channel, but this brave failure brought fame to Hobson and his small crew, who were taken prisoner.

On June 24 Shafter advanced eastward from his landing locations to the small village of Las Guásimas on a miserable road known as the Camino Real. His men soon encountered Spanish troops, who inflicted the first casualties on the American troops. After a brief firefight, the Spaniards withdrew toward San Juan Heights just west of the city. Shafter moved his headquarters to a location named El Pozo and prepared to attack the Spanish defenders to their front, who were stationed in two locations: the village of El Caney and San Juan Heights. These strong points lay in advance of a line of fortifications, the main line of resistance that protected the city.

Seeking to prevent Cuban insurgents from entering Santiago de Cuba, the Spanish commander, General Arsenio Linares y Pombo, posted his troops, including a large contingent of sailors from Cervera's squadron, along a semicircular perimeter of about 20 miles. This arrangement resulted in small concentrations of troops in numerous positions. Only 500 troops occupied El Caney. Another 500 held San Juan Heights, which included a small rise called Kettle Hill and a larger elevation named San Juan Hill.

Shafter's plan of operations specified two attacks. One of the infantry divisions, commanded by Brigadier General Henry W. Lawton, received orders to seize El Caney, thereby preventing a highly unlikely flank attack from the enemy left. After quickly accomplishing this presumably simple mission, Lawton would immediately join the rest of the troops on the right of the line in front of San Juan Heights. At this time an infantry division and a dismounted cavalry division would make a second attack, sweeping the enemy from San Juan Heights. Then these two units and Lawton's division would press forward immediately to occupy Santiago de Cuba.

Meanwhile, volunteer troops from Michigan were detailed to advance along the coast toward Aguadores, which was located near the entrance to the bay of Santiago de Cuba, and demonstrate against the Spanish infantry and artillery around the Morro Castle. Shafter hoped to convince the enemy that the main attack would come at the entrance to the mouth of the harbor. Such an operation would also prevent reinforcements from moving northward from that area to engage the Americans who were to attack San Juan Heights.

This unduly elaborate plan, which did not make adequate use of naval support, unraveled immediately. Lawton's division proved unable to overcome the resistance of General Joaquín Vara del Rey y Rubio and his small force until afternoon. The Americans took a large number of casualties. This delay forced Shafter, who had fallen ill, to begin the assault on San Juan Heights at 1:00 p.m. without Lawton, who did not join the other two divisions until the next day.

When V Corps advanced toward San Juan Heights, it attracted artillery fire from Spanish batteries. An observation balloon that approached the front helped the Spanish locate the American troop concentrations. The Spanish fire caused some troops to hesitate, including men of the 71st New York, a volunteer regiment. A regular army regiment passed through them and moved up San Juan Hill along with other advancing units.

Meanwhile, the Rough Riders, with Lieutenant Colonel Theodore Roosevelt in command, and a regular army regiment, the black dismounted 10th Cavalry, assaulted Kettle Hill, which was located northeast of San Juan Hill. These units evicted the defenders of Kettle Hill without serious opposition and then came to the assistance of the troops moving up the adjacent San Juan Hill. The 500 Spanish defenders on the hilltop at first resisted, but when a battery of three Gatling guns sited at El Pozo opened fire for eight minutes, the enemy troops quickly withdrew to the main line of resistance behind them, leaving the Americans in possession of the heights. The Gatling guns decided the outcome, although the attacking units, which vastly outnumbered the resisting enemy, would most probably have taken San Juan Heights without this assistance.

The projected advance into Santiago de Cuba did not materialize. The delays and difficulties that V Corps encountered at El Caney and San Juan Heights precluded further operations that day. Instead, the exhausted troops constructed field fortifications on San Juan Hill and prepared to repulse a possible counterattack.

Shafter and his subordinate commanders did not grasp the extent of their victory. Deeming their position on San Juan Heights quite dangerous, they contemplated withdrawal and called for reinforcements. When McKinley and the War Department learned of the possible retreat, they immediately ordered Shafter to hold his position, recognizing the negative reaction that might follow any such move. The War Department rapidly sent reinforcements to augment the force at Santiago de Cuba.

General Linares was wounded on July 1, and General José Toral y Vázquez succeeded to the Spanish command. He received reinforcements from Manzanillo, 2,700 troops under Colonel Federico Escario García, who succeeded in getting past the Cuban insurgents assigned to stop them, but this augmentation increased the difficulty of supplying the besieged army and probably did more harm than good. Toral devoted himself principally to negotiations with the Americans during his brief tenure, recognizing the weakness of his position.

When Spanish governor-general Ramón Blanco y Erenas in Havana learned of the defeat on San Juan Heights, he directed Admiral Cervera to leave Santiago de Cuba immediately. Cervera opposed this order, recognizing that he had little or no chance of escaping through the strong American blockade. Blanco persisted, however, and Cervera resigned himself to the probable catastrophe that lay ahead. He rejected a nocturnal departure, which might have allowed him to achieve surprise, because of navigational difficulties in the narrow channel. At 9:00 a.m. on Sunday, July 3, in broad daylight, his vessels began to pass in single file through the channel to the open sea.

By unlucky chance, Admiral Sampson absented himself from the blockade that morning, having steamed in his flagship, the *New York*, eastward toward Siboney to confer with General Shafter. This circumstance left Commodore Schley, the commander of the Flying Squadron, in his flagship *Brooklyn* in charge when the Spanish squadron made its appearance. Sampson reversed course and joined the battle in its final phase but made only a minor contribution.

As the Spanish vessels exited the channel, they came under heavy fire from the blockading squadron, which that morning included seven ships (the battleships *Indiana, Oregon, Iowa,* and *Texas;* the armored cruiser *Brooklyn;* and the converted yachts *Gloucester* and *Vixen*). An equal number of vessels were absent, including the flagship *New York* and two accompanying gunboats, the battleship *Massachusetts,* two cruisers, and a tender.

Nevertheless, the remaining vessels reacted effectively. All except the fastest of Cervera's six vessels, the armored cruiser *Cristóbal Colón,* were sunk or forced to beach on the coast shortly after clearing the channel one after another and immediately coming under fire. Only the speedy *Cristóbal Colón* managed to slip past the blockaders. It fled on a westerly course toward Cienfuegos, with Schley in hot pursuit. The *Brooklyn,* which turned away from the Spanish warships at the beginning of the battle, a serious mistake, led the pursuit. The Spanish ship eventually ran out of good coal and lost headway, allowing the *Brooklyn* to approach within range. The commander of the *Cristóbal Colón* then beached his ship about 50 miles west of Santiago de Cuba. The naval battle at Santiago de Cuba ended like the one at Manila; the American ships destroyed the entire Spanish squadron.

The outcome of the naval battle had profound consequences; the Spanish government decided to seek a cessation of hostilities. To this end it recalled Admiral Cámara's squadron, which had finally begun its voyage to the Philippines, and soon inaugurated peace negotiations with the United States through the good offices of the French government.

At Santiago de Cuba, General Shafter and General Toral engaged in exchanges that eventually led to a capitulation on July 17. The Cuban leader, General García, was not allowed to participate in the negotiations. To reach a settlement, the United States agreed to finance the repatriation of Spanish troops in Cuba. This outcome came none too soon. Tropical disease appeared among the Americans and quickly disabled large numbers. A hurried evacuation of V Corps to Montauk, Long Island, soon began, and other troops arrived to occupy Cuba.

During this time Major General Nelson A. Miles, the commanding general of the U.S. Army, stopped briefly at Santiago de Cuba with a large complement of troops on its way to invade Puerto Rico. He was supposed to land at Fajardo near San Juan, but instead he steamed to the south coast of the island to achieve surprise. After landing his troops at Ponce and other ports, he launched several columns on northward routes toward San Juan. These groups encountered little resistance but did not reach the capital city before August 12, the date when the belligerents signed a protocol in Washington that ended the war. Critics later argued that Miles would have encountered little resistance at Fajardo and San Juan and should have followed the original plan.

Meanwhile, the United States sent about 10,000 troops, mostly volunteers, to Manila in three phases during June and July, achieving a much more orderly process than the expedition to Santiago de Cuba. During the voyage of the first contingent the U.S. Navy escort occupied Guam, the southernmost island in the Marianas. Of greater importance was the annexation of the Hawaiian Islands. These acquisitions improved the long line of communications across the Pacific Ocean to the Philippines.

After assembling his troops, Major General Wesley Merritt prepared to attack Manila. Admiral Dewey, however, managed to negotiate the capitulation of the Spanish garrison. A new governor-general, Don Fermín Jáudenes y Alvarez, decided to give up after Dewey agreed to a sham battle to preserve the honor of the Spanish Army and promised to prevent Aguinaldo's insurgents from entering Manila. The army brigade commanders who led the assault were not informed of this charade, which involved some casualties during the largely unopposed advance that led to the occupation of the city.

As it happened, the capitulation came on August 13, a day after the signing of the Protocol of Peace. Spain later argued that this circumstance invalidated an American claim to the islands based on the right of conquest, but the United States rejected this contention despite support for it in international law. Although Aguinaldo's army continued to expand its control of areas outside of Manila, Major General Elwell S. Otis, who led the American occupation, followed orders not to recognize the Philippine government, a policy that led to growing tensions.

Meanwhile, the United States and Spain conducted peace negotiations in Paris. The protocol of August 12 specified most of the principal elements of the settlement, including Cuban independence and the American acquisition of Puerto Rico and Guam, but left the disposition of the Philippines to the peace conference.

McKinley did not immediately respond to growing pressure to acquire the archipelago. After undertaking a speaking tour to test national sentiment, he ultimately decided to authorize annexation, arguing that responsibility to humanity along with national unity, duty, and destiny required this action. As in April 1898 when he reluctantly supported armed intervention in Cuba, he bowed to public opinion, again seeking to safeguard the Republican Party's control of the government and the pursuit of various domestic reforms of interest to his political constituency. In the peace treaty of December 10, 1898, the United States agreed to purchase the Philippines for $20 million. Spain sold its other insular possessions in the Pacific to Germany.

Opponents of overseas expansion publicized cogent arguments against an imperialist policy, among other things claiming the unconstitutionality of overseas territorial acquisitions, the reversal of sound anti-imperialist traditions, the policy's inconsistency with isolationist foreign policy, and disturbance of racial tensions, but these contentions failed to overcome the burst of enthusiasm for expansion after the defeat of Spain. This short-lived but fairly intense reaction to the victory over Spain stemmed from expectation of outlets for trade and investment, the example of European empires, the recent rise to great-power status, and certain irrational feelings such as overblown patriotism and nationalism that stimulated expansionist sentiment.

The turn toward overseas expansion led to difficulties that gradually cooled interest in the modest new empire composed of Puerto Rico, the Philippines, Hawaii, and various small islands in the Pacific, including Midway Island, Wake Island, Guam, and American Samoa. Chief among the developments that inspired disenchantment were the failure of anticipated trade and investment to materialize and the outbreak of an insurgency in the Philippines that exposed the burdens associated with imperialist adventures.

The decision to annex the Philippines greatly exacerbated the festering animosity of Aguinaldo and his supporters. A threatening force of insurgents, denied entrance into the walled city, lay outside the gates in Manila. On February 4, 1899, an American soldier shot a Filipino, an act that precipitated the outbreak of an insurrection against the United States, which today is called the Philippine-American War. This event also influenced the U.S. Senate's consideration of the Treaty of Paris; the Senate was divided in its views. Two days later the Senate gave its advice and consent by a close vote of 57 to 27, barely achieving the required two-thirds margin. The president soon ratified the settlement. The Spanish Cortes (parliament) refused its approval, but the queen regnant of Spain overrode this act and ratified the treaty on March 19, 1899.

After winning the Second Battle of Manila, General Otis began a campaign of pacification. The Filipino commander, General Antônio Narciso Luna de St. Pedro, decided to wage conventional warfare, a decision that played into the hands of the Americans. The cautious Otis conducted methodical attacks that gradually wore down Luna's ill-equipped and poorly trained troops. Luna was assassinated, probably with the connivance of Aguinaldo. By the end of 1899, Aguinaldo decided to abandon conventional warfare in favor of guerrilla operations. Otis incorrectly concluded that the insurgency had been defeated, and he returned to the United States.

Otis's successor, Major General Arthur MacArthur, forced to quell revived opposition, faced a difficult task. Small guerrilla bands operated from secure areas in the countryside where they gained support, either voluntary or coerced, from the local civilian populations. They avoided pitched battles in favor of harassing American garrisons established in many locations throughout the island of Luzon without giving battle. The Americans had to decentralize their forces to cope with widely separated pockets of resistance, which required considerable reinforcements and increased costs.

The development of significant anti-imperialist sentiment in the United States in 1900, spearheaded by the Democratic presidential candidate William Jennings Bryan, led the insurgents to hold out, hoping that the defeat of McKinley would lead to an eventual American withdrawal. This expectation failed to materialize. Filipino resistance suffered after McKinley gained reelection in November 1900, blasting insurgents' hopes for an early grant of independence.

In March 1901 Brigadier General Frederick Funston led a group of pro-American Macabebe tribesmen to Aguinaldo's headquarters in a remote area of Luzon and captured him. Aguinaldo soon swore allegiance to the United States and urged his followers to give up.

This outcome was part of a tactic known as attraction, an application of a policy of benevolent assimilation that included efforts to gain the backing of influential Filipinos and undermine popular support for the insurgency. American efforts to improve education and sanitation gained favorable public notice. A civilian commission headed by William Howard Taft contributed importantly to pacification. Taft later became the first civilian administrator of the Philippines.

Meanwhile, local field commanders developed various means of dealing effectively with the insurgency in differing combat environments. A resort in certain locations to reconcentration of civilians provided a means of depriving the insurgents of essential support. Also in some cases U.S. troops used torture to extort information from captives, a crime that patently violated American law and ethics. Congressional investigations called attention to these acts and aroused considerable public criticism.

After the insurgents attacked a small American garrison in Balangiga on the island of Samar in September 1901, killing 48 Americans and wounding 22, Brigadier General Jacob Smith ordered severe retaliations that caused considerable suffering in the Philippines and extensive public criticism in the United States.

Slowly but surely, isolated bands of insurgents were forced to abandon the field. Among the last leaders to surrender, ending three and a half years of resistance, were General Vicente Lukban on Samar (February 1902) and General Miguel Malvar on Luzon (April 1902).

On July 4, 1902, President Theodore Roosevelt declared an official end to the Philippine-American War, although some pockets of resistance still existed in scattered locations. On the large island of Mindanao, a Muslim population sustained a long resistance that persisted until 1913, but the pacification achieved by 1902 endured in almost all other places.

When the short-lived burst of imperialist enthusiasm came to an end, the idea of granting independence to the Filipinos began to take root and by stages became public policy. In 1934 the Tydings-McDuffie Act authorized commonwealth status for the Philippines and eventual independence. Japan occupied the Philippines during World War II, but the Philippines finally gained its independence in 1946.

The Spanish-American War and the Philippine-American War were minor events at the outset of an international crisis that bred a long century of death and destruction. The costs and dangers of overseas expansion soon became apparent to the American people, and the imperialist experiment at the beginning of the 20th century came to an early end.

The international agenda for the United States at the outset of the 20th century ought to have included extensive and sustained participation in international politics with an eye to the restoration and preservation of a just and lasting balance of power by peaceful methods. To support such a policy, the United States had to maintain credible armed forces. Almost half a century passed before the United States finally recognized that it must accept an extensive and continuing role in world politics. Future statecraft would have to guarantee the future of all peoples and places and preclude the possibility of another resort to general warfare, an event that would surely cause inconceivable destruction and suffering everywhere.

A turn to such a policy did not occur until the exigencies of World War I forced the United States into the struggle. The postwar departure from the prescription for a revolution in American statecraft and the creation of effective international peacekeeping and reform contributed most importantly to a renewal of warfare from 1939 to 1945 and the long and dangerous aftermath that endured until about 1991. Then, after the dissolution of the Soviet Union, the international balance was finally restored on a reasonably firm foundation. During the 20th century the great Eurasian empires all fell by the wayside, along with the hegemonic ambitions that had flowered on all too many occasions during a long era of unprecedented international instability and total war.

DAVID F. TRASK

EXPANSION AT HOME AND ABROAD

The Later Indian Wars, the Spanish-American War, and the Philippine-American War, 1878–1913

TIMELINE

May 30–September 20, 1878

American Indian Wars (continued): Bannock War. Members of the Bannock tribe and the Northern Shoshones, having agreed in 1868 to be removed to the Fort Hall Reservation in Idaho, go to war under Chief Bull Horn because of settlers moving onto their ancestral lands and also because of famine, the result of white poachers killing their cattle and the inadequacy of government rations.

In the spring of 1878, several Bannock bands congregate on the Camas Prairie in southern Idaho to gather camas roots, a major part of their diet, only to discover that white settlers have encroached on the land and decimated the root fields by grazing hogs and cattle. On May 30, 1878, a Bannock shoots and kills 2 white herders and wounds another. This incident, which begins the Bannock War, sharply divides the tribe, however. Most members leave for the reservation at Fort Hall, but some 200 warriors under the leadership of Buffalo Horn are determined to drive out the white settlers by force.

News of what has transpired reaches Boise Barracks, where Captain Reuben F. Bernard of the 1st U.S. Cavalry prepares to track down the renegades. Colonel Orlando Robbins of the territorial militia also calls up men. Brigadier General Oliver O. Howard, commander of the Department of the Columbia, receives orders to round up all the Bannocks and remove them to the Yakima Indian Reservation in eastern Washington. While resources are being mobilized against them, Buffalo Horn and his warriors set out on a path of destruction toward eastern Oregon. They loot and burn white settlements and homes, attack wagon trains, and kill whites indiscriminately.

Near South Mountain on June 8, a civilian volunteer company of 20 men under Captain Harper from Silver City, Idaho, is searching for the Bannocks when it is suddenly attacked by Buffalo Horn and some 50 warriors. In the ensuing brief fight, 4 volunteers are killed before the remainder get away, but in a major blow to the Bannocks, Buffalo Horn is mortally wounded. Some of his followers now return to the reservation, while those remaining withdraw to Stein's Mountain in an effort to recruit support from other tribes. Disaffected Paiute, Umatilla, and Cayuse warriors join them, while new leadership is provided by Malheur Paiute chief Egan (Pony Blanket).

Robbins and Bernard continue their chase of the hostiles, now led by Egan, and catch up with them at Silver Creek, near present-day Riley in south-central Oregon, on June 22, 1878. There are nearly 2,000 Paiutes and Bannocks, of whom 700 are warriors. The soldiers and volunteers are considerably outnumbered, but Bernard leads a surprise attack on the morning of June 23 with his 250 troopers. Five soldiers are killed, as opposed to as many as 100 Indians; among them Egan is desperately wounded.

Survivors of the battle, now under the leadership of Chief Oytes, escape to the John Day River, where they hope to join warriors from other tribes. General Howard, meanwhile, assumes leadership of the forces in the field. On June 25 he dispatches scouts ahead of the main body to locate the remaining hostiles. On July 8 Howard learns from the scouts that the renegade Bannocks and Paiutes have established a defensive position high on the cliffs above Birch Creek near Pilot Butte, an extinct volcano in present-day Deschutes County, Oregon. There the troops outflank the Indians, forcing them to withdraw again.

Howard moves north to Fort Walla Walla in an attempt to cut off the natives' retreat. The Indians change course, however, and move southward to the Umatilla Reservation in an attempt to coerce that tribe's support. Captain Evan Miles, leading soldiers of the 21st Infantry Regiment and learning of their presence, abandons the plan to join Howard and instead proceeds against the hostiles.

On July 12 nearly 500 hostiles launch a surprise attack on Miles's exhausted troops, but the soldiers quickly regroup and counterattack, and their superior firepower causes the Indians to flee southward. The neutral Umatillas, who observed the battle, waiting to side with the victor, now offer their services to the army in exchange for amnesty. On July 15 a band of Umatillas approaches the camp of the retreating Bannocks under the guise of joining them and then open fire, killing Chief Egan and cutting off his head as proof of the deed.

The hostiles now split. The Bannocks move east, while the Paiutes proceed south in small groups. The surrender of Chief Oytes on August 12 marks the end of Paiute hostilities. The Paiutes are held at Camp Harney in Oregon and later sent to the Yakima Reservation.

Bannock resistance continues, with the remaining bands attacking and occasionally murdering local whites and destroying their property. On September 4, troops under Colonel Nelson A. Miles defeat a Bannock band attempting to retreat through the Yellowstone Valley. On September 20 along the John Day River, Lieutenant Colonel James W. Forsyth and men of his 1st Cavalry Regiment subdue the last hostile contingent. The remaining 131 Bannocks surrender shortly thereafter. After a brief detention at Fort Keogh, they are moved permanently to the Fort Hall Reservation in Idaho.

September 9, 1878

American Indian Wars (continued): Dull Knife Outbreak. Northern Cheyenne leaders Morning Star, better known as Dull Knife (the name given him by the Lakotas), and Little Wolf are among Cheyennes who had allied with the Lakota (Sioux) and taken part in the Battle of the Little Bighorn (see June 25–26, 1876). Pursued by the army, they and their followers had surrendered in May 1877 and were relocated to Indian Territory (Oklahoma).

It is soon clear to the Northern Cheyennes that the promises of adequate resources on the reservation are untrue. Game is nearly nonexistent, promised government rations fail to arrive on time and in sufficient quantity, and many Cheyennes either starve to death or perish of fever, probably malaria. In August 1878 with perhaps half of the Cheyennes who had been sent to Indian Territory now dead, Dull Knife and Little Wolf plead with U.S. Indian agent John Miles to let the survivors return to their ancestral homes in the Powder River basin of Wyoming and Montana. On the orders of his superiors, Miles refuses.

Dull Knife and Little Wolf take matters into their own hands. On September 9 they lead some 350 Indians from the reservation and begin a march on foot to their homelands. There are perhaps only 70 warriors among them. Pursuing cavalry and Arapaho scouts catch up with the renegades on the Little Medicine Lodge River, but the Cheyennes refuse to surrender. Three soldiers and 1 Arapaho scout are killed, and the Northern Cheyennes continue their trek, repelling attacks and securing arms and food from settlements they encounter.

The Indians cross the Arkansas and South Platte Rivers, and at White Clay Creek, Nebraska, they split into two groups. Little Wolf leads 115 Cheyennes to the Sand Hills, while Dull Knife plans to lead the remainder to the Red Cloud Agency in Nebraska, where they will surrender. Dull Knife's band arrives at the Red Cloud Agency, only to find it abandoned. They then trek to Fort Robinson, where they surrender on October 23. Dull Knife and his band are there for two months, and they are then informed that they will be returned to Indian Territory. Dull Knife refuses.

Denied food, water, and heat until they relent, on the night of January 9, 1879, the Northern Cheyennes kill 2 guards in an escape attempt. Some 50 Indians are shot down by soldiers as they run from the fort, and others are discovered nearby in the course of the next days and ordered to surrender. Many choose to fight to the death. Fewer than 100 are herded back to Fort Robinson. Dull Knife and his wife and son, traveling at night on foot, manage to make it to the Pine Ridge Agency 18 days later. They and their few remaining followers are eventually allowed to stay there until they receive a reservation of their own, a year after Dull Knife's death in 1883.

Meanwhile, Little Wolf and the remaining Cheyennes had arrived in the Nebraska Sand Hills and there survive the winter of 1878–1879. Along the Little Missouri River in Montana on March 27, 1879, Little Wolf surrenders his band to Lieutenant William P. Clark of the 2nd Cavalry Regiment. The Indians are escorted to Fort Keogh, where Little Wolf and many of his followers sign on to help the army fight the Sioux.

May–October 1879

American Indian Wars (continued): Sheepeater War. At the conclusion of the 1878 Bannock War, a small band of Native Americans, primarily from the Bannocks, Weisers, and Shoshones and known as the Sheepeaters, withdraw into the mountains of central Idaho to continue resistance against white settlers. This takes the form of raiding livestock and stealing horses. Although U.S. government authorities lack proof, they blame renegade Sheepeaters for the murder of five Chinese miners in Oro Grande and two ranchers on the South Fork of the Salmon River. Brigadier General Oliver O. Howard, commander of the Department of the Columbia, orders a detachment of troops to apprehend the guilty parties for prosecution.

This campaign, which begins in late May 1879, opens the so-called Sheepeater War. Three separate army columns converge on the Sheepeaters' stronghold at Payette Lake, near present-day McCall, Idaho. Captain Reuben Bernard leads 56 men of the 1st Cavalry Regiment north from Boise Barracks,

Lieutenant Henry Catley leads 48 mounted soldiers from the 2nd Infantry Regiment south from Camp Howard, and 28 scouts and sharpshooters under Lieutenant Edward S. Farrow march eastward from the Umatilla Reservation in Oregon.

Bad weather with deep snow and the rugged terrain hinder the troops, but there is some fighting in late July. The three columns unite at Elk Creek on August 11 and, with reinforcements under Captain Albert G. Forse from Camp Howard, return to the site of an earlier engagement with the Sheepeaters at Big Creek. In a running fight on August 2, one soldier is killed, the only army casualty of the campaign. Bernard, Farrow, and Forse continue to track the Sheepeaters during the course of the next several weeks without making contact. Having lost a number of horses through exhaustion, being short on rations, and with winter in the offing, Bernard and Forse return to their home posts in early September. Farrow continues the campaign, capturing several dozen Sheepeater women and children.

On September 25, Farrow and his men make contact with Tamanmo (known as War Jack), leader of the renegades, who offers to surrender his people. It takes several weeks to bring the Indians out of the remote mountains, but by October they have been moved to the Columbia River. Farrow then sends them to Vancouver for internment. The following spring, they are transferred to Fort Hall.

The few remaining Sheepeater warriors never admit to the murders of which they are accused, but they are kept in prison under presumed guilt. The Sheepeater War marks the end of Native American resistance in the Pacific Northwest. All the remaining tribes are forced onto reservations.

August 7, 1879–March 23, 1882

Jeannette Expedition to the North Pole. *New York Herald* publisher James Gordon Bennett gives the U.S. Navy the steam bark *Jeannette*, with a specially reinforced hull, for an expedition to reach the North Pole through the Bering Strait. The ship's crew, commanded by Lieutenant George Washington DeLong, numbers 28 navy officers and seamen and 3 civilians; all are volunteers.

The *Jeannette* sails from San Francisco on August 7, 1879. The ship reaches the Arctic in early September but is almost immediately trapped in pack ice and remains thus for 21 months. During this period, the men conduct scientific experiments.

On June 13, 1881, however, shifting ice crushes the ship's hull, and the men are forced to set out over the ice. On September 12 the expedition finally reaches the edge of the ice pack, and the men launch three boats that they have dragged across the ice with them. One broaches and sinks with all hands; the other two, commanded by DeLong and Chief Engineer George W. Melville, are launched successfully but become separated.

Melville's boat reaches the western edge of the Lena Delta, Siberia, where the men are cared for by natives. DeLong's boat makes landfall on the uninhabited eastern bank of the Lena. The men attempt to continue on overland, but their condition gradually deteriorates. DeLong makes camp and sends the 2 strongest men on ahead. They eventually secure help, but when they return on March 23, 1882, to the camp, they find DeLong and 14 others of the party all frozen to death. They recover the expedition's records, which prove useful for subsequent Arctic explorers.

September 3, 1879–October 15, 1880

American Indian Wars (continued): Victorio's War. Victorio is a leader of the Eastern Chiricahua Apaches, often known as the Warm Springs or Mimbres Apaches. In the 1850s he had participated in raids into northern Mexico with Nana and Geronimo. Victorio is believed to have joined Mangas Coloradas in 1862 and, after the latter's death in 1863, emerged as the leader of a band of some 300 Eastern Chiricahua and Mescalero Apaches. In 1869 Victorio and his followers settled near Fort Craig in New Mexico Territory, there to await the completion of a new reservation near Ojo Caliente.

On April 20, 1877, however, the government ordered Victorio and his followers removed to the San Carlos Reservation in Arizona Territory. Victorio protested leaving his crops but had obeyed the order. Conditions at San Carlos prove intolerable, however, and when Poinsenay, another Apache leader who had

been raiding in Mexico, tells Victorio of his successes, Victorio on September 2, 1877, leads several hundred Apaches off the reservation toward Mexico, beginning three years of intermittent raiding in Mexico, Texas, and New Mexico.

Although Victorio eventually surrenders at Fort Stanton, asking to return to Ojo Caliente, the historic home of the Warm Springs Apaches, the government rejects his request, and he is informed that he and his people will be returned to Arizona Territory. Victorio then quits Fort Stanton and the Mescalero Reservation and in September 1879 begins what becomes known as Victorio's War.

Victorio operates principally in the area between Fort Davis and El Paso in Texas. He is pursued principally by the African American (Buffalo Soldiers) troopers of the 9th and 10th Cavalry Regiments, commanded by Colonel Edward Hatch and Lieutenant Colonel Benjamin H. Grierson, respectively. Some Texas Rangers also mount forays against Victorio, as do Mexican Army units.

On September 3, 1879, Victorio attacks a unit of the 9th Cavalry Regiment at Ojo Caliente, capturing 50 cavalry horses and 18 mules and killing five troopers and three civilians guarding the animals. This sparks an all-out effort to bring in Victorio and his followers.

Troopers of the 9th Cavalry Regiment track Victorio and his followers up Las Animas Creek in the Black Range in New Mexico Territory. On September 18, Victorio attacks two companies of the 9th Cavalry under Captain Ambrose Hooker and First Lieutenant Byron Dawson, who are following Navajo guides. In so-called Massacre Canyon, the Apaches ambush the troopers, killing eight and making off with 46 cavalry horses.

In January 1880 Victorio returns to U.S. soil from Mexico. A series of small engagements follows during the spring and summer in the New Mexico and Arizona Territories and in Texas. During most of the summer of 1880 Victorio makes camp in various sites in the Quitman, Carrizo, and Guadalupe Mountains in far western Texas.

That August, Grierson learns that Victorio is proceeding north from the Rio Grande toward the

CAMPAIGNS AGAINST THE APACHES, 1880'S

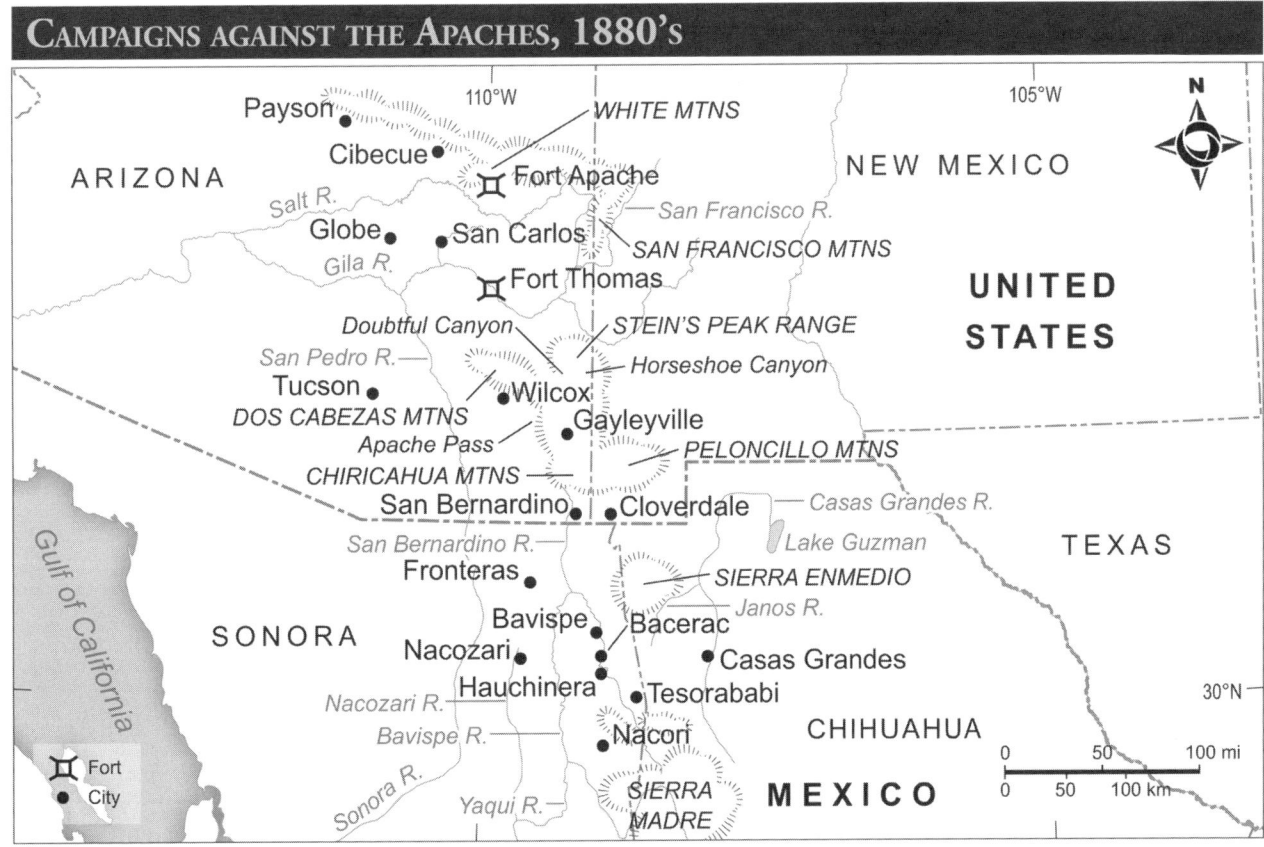

Guadalupe Mountains, and he leads his men from Fort Quitman, Texas, hoping to trap the Apaches near the Rattlesnake Springs watering place. On August 8 in the Battle of Rattlesnake Springs, Grierson's troopers fight a three-hour battle with the Apaches, who then flee westward into the Carrizo Mountains and on into Mexico. As many as 4 soldiers die; the Apaches lose up to 30 killed or wounded.

Grierson spends the remainder of the autumn searching for Victorio but, failing to locate him and his band, returns to Fort Concho. Texas Rangers are also involved in the hunt, even crossing into Mexico until forced to withdraw by Mexican troops led by Colonel Joaquín Terrazas, leader of the Chihuahua state militia, who is also pursuing Victorio.

In October 1880 Terrazas and his volunteers track the Apaches to the Tres Castillas mountain range some 60 miles south of the border in Mexico. On October 15, they surround Victorio and during the course of the next two days kill him and his band

(see October 15–16, 1880), bringing Victorio's War to a close.

September 29–October 5, 1879

American Indian Wars (continued): Ute War (White River War, Siege of Milk Creek/Meeker Massacre). By the 1870s, the remaining Ute bands are living on reservations along the Colorado, San Juan, and White Rivers in western Colorado and eastern Utah. The Utes have a long history of peaceful relations with settlers in the region, but the discovery of silver on their lands in the 1870s brings increased demands for their removal to Indian Territory (Oklahoma). The situation is exacerbated by delays in government shipments to the Utes of clothes and provisions and by the appointment in 1878 of Nathan C. Meeker as Indian agent at the White River Agency.

Meeker has no experience treating with Native Americans and attempts to turn the Utes into farmers. The Utes consider farming degrading; Meeker's insistence that they have too many horses and that they must plow up pastures to grow crops threatens the survival of their pony herds. An altercation leads Meeker to call in the army.

Major Thomas T. Thornburgh leads as many as 200 men (most of them from the 5th Cavalry Regiment but including some soldiers of the 4th Infantry Regiment) south from Fort Fred Steele, Wyoming, to the White River Agency. On his arrival, Thornburgh moves with his cavalry to Milk Creek, where on September 29 he is confronted by 100 Ute warriors. Although it initially appears that conflict might be avoided by talks between the two sides, a single gunshot from an undetermined source sparks the Battle of Milk Creek.

Following the initial exchange of fire, the soldiers fall back to their wagon train. Army casualties are heavy, with 13 killed (including Thornburgh) and another 43 wounded. Captain John Payne takes command. The soldiers take up a defensive position but are pinned down there for six days.

On October 2 Captain Francis Dodge arrives with 40 men of the 9th Cavalry Regiment to reinforce Payne. On October 5 following a forced 170-mile march from Fort D. A. Russell near Cheyenne, Wyoming, Colonel Wesley Merritt appears with 254 men of the 5th Cavalry Regiment, and the Utes abandon the battlefield. They have sustained 23 dead.

During the Battle of Milk Creek, Ute warriors also attack and burn the White River Agency, overrunning it on September 30 and in the so-called Meeker Massacre killing Meeker and 11 others and taking captive 3 women and 2 children. Eventually Charles Adams, a former agent to the Utes, and Ouray, the chief of the Uncompahgre band, negotiate an end to hostilities, with the Utes agreeing to surrender their captives. Although the government had planned to prosecute a number of Utes for the massacre of Meeker and his subordinates, none ever stand trial. In August 1881, however, the Utes lose most of their lush lands in Colorado and are forced to settle on small arid reservations in southwestern Colorado and eastern Utah.

July 20, 1880

American Indian Wars (continued): Sitting Bull surrenders. His people starving in Canada, Hunkpapa Lakota Sioux chief Sitting Bull surrenders himself to federal authorities at Fort Buford in Dakota Territory, along with 45 warriors, 67 women, and 73 children. They are held at Fort Randall for two years until they are relocated onto a reservation at Standing Rock in Dakota Territory.

October 15–16, 1880

American Indian Wars (continued): Battle of Tres Castillos. Victorio, a leader of the Eastern Chiricahua Apaches, often known as the Warm Springs or Mimbres Apaches, has been involved in protracted warfare with the U.S. Army since September 1879 in what is known as Victorio's War (see September 3, 1879–October 15, 1880). For some time he successfully evades both American and Mexican forces. But by early autumn, he has been forced across the border into Mexico to keep ahead of pursuing U.S. troops.

By mid-October, Victorio and as many as 150 warriors are camped in northern Chihuahua, Mexico, some 60 miles from the U.S. border amid three small rocky peaks that the Mexicans call Tres Castillos. Mexican militiamen, led by Colonel Joaquín Terrazas, leader of the Chihuahua state militia, who is pursuing Victorio, come on the Apache camp on October 15, 1889. Catching the Apaches by surprise, Terrazas orders his men to scatter Victorio's horses to prevent the Apaches from escaping and immediately launches a full-scale assault on the encampment.

The Apaches climb one of the three peaks and engage in a firefight with the Mexicans well into the night. Victorio attempts to escape, but finding this impossible, he orders his men to erect makeshift stone fortifications and vows a fight to the death. At dawn on October 16, the Mexicans rush the Apache defenses and engage in close combat, much of it hand to hand. The Mexicans are victorious, and the Apaches suffer 78 dead, Victorio among them. Almost 100 young women and children are taken prisoner as slaves. Only 17 escape. The Battle of Tres Castillos marks the end of the Victorio War.

May 21, 1881

American Red Cross. In Washington, D.C., Clara Barton establishes the American Red Cross. Barton, known as the "angel of the battlefield" for her work with wounded during the American Civil War, is its first president. The Red Cross is a volunteer-led humanitarian organization providing emergency assistance, disaster relief, and education inside the United States and is today the designated U.S. affiliate of the International Federation of Red Cross and Red Crescent Societies.

July 1881–June 22, 1884

Lady Franklin Bay Expedition (Greely Expedition). The first International Polar Year is established for 1882–1883, with 11 nations pledging to create 15 new observation stations in the Arctic and Antarctic. The most remote location is the U.S. station at Lady Franklin Bay, to be commanded by U.S. Army lieutenant Adolphus Washington Greely. Besides

Clara (Clarissa) Harlowe Barton (1821–1912)

Nurse, philanthropist, and founder of the American Red Cross (1881). Clara (Clarissa) Harlowe Barton was born in Oxford, Massachusetts, on December 25, 1821, into a middle-class family. She was educated at home, began teaching at age 15, and founded a free public school in Bordentown, New Jersey. Prior to the American Civil War, her only medical experience came while caring for a sickly brother for two years.

By 1861, Barton was living in Washington, D.C. Employed by the U.S. Patent Office, she decided to organize relief aid for soldiers of the 6th Massachusetts Regiment, who had been involved in the April 19, 1861, Baltimore Riots. Her efforts began a lifelong commitment to humanitarian aid. Upon learning that many soldiers who had fought in the First Battle of Bull Run (Manassas) (July 21, 1861) had died because of a lack of basic medical supplies, she took out an advertisement in the *Spy*, a Worcester, Massachusetts, newspaper, to solicit donations for wounded Union soldiers. The response was nearly instantaneous and gratifying, and she was soon head of a highly successful relief organization.

In 1862, U.S. surgeon general William Hammond gave Barton a travel pass so that she could accompany army ambulances to distribute aid and nurse ailing soldiers. Hammond's move was highly unusual for the time, as most women were barred from being on or near battlefields. For the next three years, Barton traveled extensively in Virginia and South Carolina, caring for wounded and dying soldiers and supervising relief and donation drives.

Barton carried out extensive nursing at hospitals in Fredericksburg, Virginia, as well as field hospitals, where she cared for wounded soldiers in May 1864 both during the Battle of the Wilderness and at Bermuda Hundred, not far from Richmond. Her good work drew national attention and admiration on both sides of the conflict. In late 1864 and early 1865, Barton held her only official post during the Civil War when she served as Major General Benjamin Butler's superintendent of nurses. She also expanded her role and mission when she went to Camp Parole, Maryland, to establish a system for locating men listed as missing in action or captured by the enemy. There she conducted extensive interviews with Union soldiers returning from captivity in Southern prisons and was many times able to determine the status or whereabouts of men missing in action. She then passed the information along to families.

It is believed that Barton helped locate some 30,000 such soldiers. When the war was over, she traveled to Andersonville, Georgia, in an effort to identify and properly mark the graves of Union soldiers who

(continued)

(Continued)

had been buried there. Barton went to considerable lengths to locate missing servicemen, including the publication of lists of names in newspapers and direct communication with missing soldiers' families and friends.

All of this work proved to be the beginning of a lifelong commitment to humanitarian causes. In 1870 during a visit to Western Europe, Barton became active in the International Red Cross (founded in 1864), which led her to found the American Red Cross in 1881. Before long, Barton had broadened the scope of the Red Cross to include not only neutral aid in wartime but also responses to other emergencies and natural disasters. She tried to go to Cuba during the Spanish-American War but was prevented from doing so by U.S. military officials. Instead, she cared for Spanish prisoners of war and refugees in Key West, Florida. Her sometimes brusque demeanor and reluctance to delegate authority eventually led to her resignation in 1904, when she retired to her home outside Washington, D.C.

In addition to her humanitarian efforts, Barton was active in the women's suffrage movement and the African American fight for civil rights. She also authored several books, including a volume on the early history of the American Red Cross. Barton died in Glen Echo, Maryland, on April 12, 1912.

PAUL G. PIERPAOLI JR.

Further Reading

Hutchinson, John F. *Champions of Charity: War and the Rise of the Red Cross.* Boulder, CO: Westview, 1996.
Pryor, Elizabeth Brown. *Clara Barton, Professional Angel.* Philadelphia: University of Pennsylvania Press, 1987.

scientific observations, its less publicized goal is to reach the North Pole or at least establish a new farthest-north record. The expedition of 22 officers and men with 2 civilians sets out in the ship *Proteus* in early July 1881. The *Proteus* reaches Lady Franklin Bay on August 11, deposits the men and their equipment, and departs. The summer of 1881 is unusually warm, leading to an underestimation of the problems of reaching Lady Franklin Bay. The men establish a station that they call Fort Conger. Although some members of the expedition achieve a new farthest-north record, the expedition's tenure is marred by difficult conditions, clashing personalities, and failed supply efforts. The supply ship *Neptune* is forced to turn back in the summer of 1882, and new rescue efforts by the *Proteus*, commanded by Lieutenant Ernest Garlington, and the *Yantic*, commanded by Commander Frank Wilde, both fail. The *Proteus* is crushed by the ice but is able to leave 40 days of supplies at Camp Sabine on Littleton Island, which

Greely and his men reach in October and where they are forced to spend the winter.

In the spring of 1884, Secretary of the Navy William E. Chandler orchestrates a new relief expedition. Led by Commander Winfield S. Schley and consisting of the steamers *Thetis* and *Bear*, assisted by the British ships *Alert* and *Loch Gerry*, it sails during April 22–May 10. On June 22, they rescue Greely and six others, all near death from starvation. The remaining members of the expedition have succumbed to hypothermia, starvation, or drowning; Greely had also ordered one man shot.

August 30, 1881

American Indian Wars (continued): White Mountain Apache Rebellion (Incident at Cibecue Creek/Battle of Cibecue Creek). Colonel Eugene Carr, commanding the 6th Cavalry Regiment, arrives at Cibecue Creek in Arizona Territory with 85 soldiers and 23 Indian scouts and arrests White Mountain Apache medicine man Nochedelklinne on charges that he is inciting revolt. News of this arrest brings as many as 100 warriors from the nearby San Carlos Agency, who then crowd into the army camp. Shooting breaks out, and a scout kills Nochedelklinne to prevent his recapture, reportedly on Carr's orders. This, however, causes the other native scouts to mutiny. As many as 18 Apaches are killed in the fighting; 8 soldiers are killed, and 2 are wounded. The remaining Apaches are rounded up and returned to the San Carlos Agency.

This fighting touches off a general Apache outbreak in which Chiricahua and Warm Springs Apaches such as Naiche, Juh, and Geronimo leave the reservation, plunging the Arizona and New Mexico Territories and part of northern Mexico into two years of turmoil.

April 1882

American Indian Wars (continued). Chiricahua Apache leaders Geronimo and Juh, having left the San Carlos Reservation in Arizona Territory along with several hundred followers, initiate a series of attacks on whites in Texas and the Arizona Territory. Chased by troopers of Lieutenant Colonel George Forsyth's 6th Cavalry Regiment, they manage to reach northern Mexico.

July 6, 1882

American Indian Wars (continued). On this date near the San Carlos Agency in Arizona Territory, a party of about 60 White Mountain Apache warriors, led by Natiotish, waylay and kill chief of Indian scouts J. L. Colvig and a half dozen members of his Indian police.

July 14, 1882

U.S. forces land at Alexandria, Egypt. Opposition to foreign control of Egypt brings a rebellion in February 1881 led by Ahmet Arabi (Urabi). Their position in Egypt threatened, the British and French governments plan a joint military intervention. Both nations dispatch powerful squadrons to Alexandria in May, but a change of government in France leads to the belated decision in Paris not to participate, and London proceeds alone.

On July 11 following antiforeign riots in Alexandria and the deaths of 68 Europeans, British admiral Sir Frederick Beauchamp Paget Seymour subjects Alexandria to shelling by his 14-ship squadron. The British suffer 5 killed, 28 wounded, and slight damage to their ships but inflict considerable damage to the shore defenses and the city and inflict 300–2,000 casualties. British marines and seamen then occupy Alexandria.

On July 14, U.S. Marine Corps captain Henry C. Cochrane leads 133 seamen and marines ashore from the U.S. Navy gunboat *Nispic*, screw sloop *Lancaster*, and screw steamer *Quinnebang* to protect the U.S. consulate and assist the British in maintaining order.

July 17, 1882

American Indian Wars (continued): Battle of Big Dry Fork (Big Dry Wash). In the middle of July 1882, White Mountain Apache renegade leader Natiotish is leading some 60 followers up Cherry Creek in Arizona Territory heading for General Springs. Discovering that they are being trailed by a single troop of cavalry, Natiotish decides to lay an ambush seven miles north of General Springs where a fork of East Clear Creek cuts a gorge into the Mogollon Rim. Captain Adna R. Chaffee Sr., commanding the pursuing cavalry, is warned by scout Al Sieber of an ambush. That night Chaffee is reinforced by four additional cavalry companies from Fort Apache under Major Andrew W. Evans, bringing army strength up to about 350 men. The 2 officers now develop a plan to try to trap the Indians.

Early on July 17 one cavalry troop opens fire from the rim to pin down the Apaches, while Chaffee sends two troops upstream and two others downstream. Between 16 and 27 Apaches are killed, including Natiotish. Lieutenant George H. Morgan and 1 other cavalrymen are killed in what is the last major battle between the army and the Apaches, although armed conflict between Apaches and white settlers in the Arizona Territory continues as late as 1900.

July 26, 1882

The United States ratifies the Geneva Convention. Building on the work of Swiss businessman Henri

Adna Romanza Chaffee Sr. (1842–1914)

U.S. Army officer and army chief of staff. Born on April 14, 1842, in Orwell, Ohio, Adna Romanza Chaffee Sr. served in the U.S. Army from 1861 to 1906, taking part in the American Civil War, the Indian Wars, the Spanish-American War, and the 1900 Boxer Uprising. At the outset of the Civil War, Chaffee enlisted in the Union Army. On July 22, 1861, he was assigned to the 6th Cavalry as a private; he would remain with the same regiment for more than a quarter century. Chaffee won promotion to sergeant for his performance in the 1862 Peninsula Campaign. He fought in the Battle of Antietam (September 17, 1862) and in May 1863 was commissioned a second lieutenant. Wounded at the Battle of Gettysburg (July 1–3, 1863), he narrowly escaped capture. In February 1865 he was promoted to first lieutenant, and because of his valor at the Battle of Dinwiddie Court House on March 31, 1865, he was breveted captain.

Chaffee remained in the army following the war. Promoted to captain in 1867, he was posted to Fort Griffin in 1868. In March 1868 he was breveted major following an engagement against the Comanches at Paint Creek, Texas. For three decades, he fought in a series of Indian wars on the Great Plains and in the Southwest against the Cheyennes, Kiowas, and Apaches.

In 1888 Chaffee was promoted to major and transferred to the 9th Cavalry Regiment, composed of African American enlisted men (the famed Buffalo Soldiers). In 1894 he was assigned to Fort Leavenworth, where he taught military tactics for two years. In 1897 he was transferred to the 3rd Cavalry Regiment and promoted to lieutenant colonel.

Following the beginning of the Spanish-American War in April 1898, Chaffee was promoted to brigadier general of volunteers and assumed command of a brigade of volunteers in May. After his important role in the U.S. victory in the Battle of El Caney on July 1, 1898, he was promoted to major general of volunteers. From the conclusion of the Spanish-American War to May 1900, Chaffee served as chief of staff to Lieutenant General Leonard Wood, the U.S. military governor of Cuba.

In July 1900 Chaffee was assigned to command the U.S. Army's China Relief Expedition, a force of 2,500 men charged with relieving the foreign legations at Beijing during the Boxer Uprising. His troops entered the city on August 14, 1900.

Promoted to major general in the regular army in 1901, from July to October 1902 Chaffee served as military governor of the Philippines during the latter part of the Philippine-American War. Returning to the United States, he commanded the Department of the East from October 1902 to October 1903. Promoted to lieutenant general in January 1904, he served as army chief of staff during 1904–1906. In that position, he implemented significant organizational reforms. Chaffee retired from active duty in February 1906 and died of typhoid on November 1, 1914, in Los Angeles, California.

MICHAEL R. HALL

Further Reading

Barr, Ronald J. *The Progressive Army: US Army Command and Administration, 1870–1914.* New York: St. Martin's, 1998.

Carter, William H. *The Life of Lieutenant General Chaffee.* Chicago: University of Chicago Press, 1917.

Cosmas, Graham A. *An Army for Empire: The United States Army in the Spanish-American War.* College Station: Texas A&M University Press, 1994.

Dunant, who publicized the plight of wounded in battle, the Swiss government had invited nations to send representatives to a conference in Geneva. Sixteen countries participated, and on August 22, 1864, the conferees adopt the first Geneva Convention "for the Amelioration of the Condition of the Wounded in Armies in the Field." Representatives of 12 states sign the convention, by which they agree to guarantee neutrality to medical personnel, expedite medical supplies for their use, and adopt the identifying emblem of a red cross on a white field. The United States finally agrees to the Geneva Convention on July 26, 1882.

September 1882

American Indian Wars (continued). Brigadier General George Crook resumes command of the Department of Arizona, then crosses the Mexican border to pursue Chiricahua Apache leader Geronimo. Crook develops the tactics that will bring the army victory. These include employing friendly Apaches as guides, dispensing with wagon trains in favor of more mobile mule trains, and, once on the trail of a hostile force, continuing the chase no matter where it leads, even into Mexico.

February 18, 1883

The U.S. Navy side-wheel gunboat *Ashuelot*, under Commander Horace H. Mullan, grounds and is lost near Shantou (Swatow), China. Eleven members of its crew perish.

March 3, 1883

Congress authorizes construction of the protected cruisers *Atlanta, Boston,* and *Chicago* and the dispatch gunboat *Dolphin*. The first 3 are known as protected cruisers because they have steel decks up to three inches thick to prevent plunging fire from penetrating their vital engine areas. The ABCDs, as the 4 are known (they are also called the White Squadron), are the first really modern ships to enter the navy since the Civil War. They are constructed of steel and have compound steam engines as well as full sail rigs. They also are the first to mount modern breech-loading guns. Their heaviest armament is two modern breech-loading rifled 8-inch guns. They also mount six 6-inchers and a half dozen smaller guns.

Construction of these 4 ships is generally regarded as the beginning of the modern U.S. Navy. During 1885–1899 Congress authorizes 30 new warships of different classes, totaling nearly 100,000 tons.

This same act changes the navy rank of master to lieutenant (junior grade).

March 21–April 1, 1883

American Indian Wars (continued). Chiricahua Apache leader Geronimo launches lightning raids throughout northern Mexico, southeastern Arizona Territory, and New Mexico Territory, killing some 26 settlers.

May 1, 1883

American Indian Wars (continued). In northern Mexico, Captain Emmet Crawford, part of army forces under Brigadier General George Crook, pursues Chiricahua Apache leader Geronimo into the northern Mexico highlands and, assisted by 150 loyal Apache scouts, locates the Apache base camp and attacks it while the warriors are away raiding. Apaches at the camp and others nearby ultimately surrender, and 325 are escorted back to the San Carlos Reservation in Arizona Territory. Geronimo himself communicates to Crook that he is willing to give up, but he does not voluntarily return to San Carlos until March 1884.

May 17, 1884

American Indian Wars (continued). Chiricahua Apache leader Geronimo again escapes the San Carlos Agency along with some 140 other Apaches, including Chihuahua, Naiché, Nana, and Mangas. Eluding cavalry stationed by Brigadier General George Crook along the Mexican border, they escape into the Sierra Madre. Crook relocates his headquarters to Fort Bowie in New Mexico Territory and ultimately deploys some 2,000 men across the U.S. Southwest and in northern Mexico in the search for his elusive foe.

October 6, 1884

Establishment of the Naval War College. Secretary of the Navy William E. Chandler establishes the U.S. Naval War College at Newport, Rhode Island. Its first

Stephen Bleeker Luce (1827–1917)

U.S. admiral. Born on March 25, 1827, in Albany, New York, Stephen Bleeker Luce entered the navy in 1841. As a midshipman, he joined the frigate *Congress* in the Mediterranean. In 1845, he served in the frigate *Columbus* in Captain James Biddle's mission to China and Japan. Luce attended the Naval Academy during 1848–1849 and served in the sloop *Vandalia* in the Pacific in 1849–1852 and in the side-wheeler steamer *Vixen* during 1853–1854, followed by duty with the Coast Survey 1854–1857 and in the sloop *Jamestown* in the Caribbean in 1857–1860. He became seamanship and gunnery instructor at the Naval Academy in 1860, following it from Annapolis to Newport at the start of the American Civil War.

At Newport, Luce revised W. H. Parker's textbook *Naval Light Artillery* (1862). Ordered temporarily to the screw frigate *Wabash* in the South Atlantic Blockading Squadron during 1861–1862, Luce returned to the academy to write *Seamanship* (1862), the U.S. Navy's first text on the subject. *Seamanship* remained the standard manual to 1901. In 1863 Luce took command of the training ship *Macedonian* and then the monitor *Nantucket* and the side-wheeler gunboats *Sonoma* and *Pontiac* during 1864–1865. In 1865–1868 he returned to the Naval Academy as commandant of midshipmen, then commanded the side-wheeler gunboat *Mohongo* in 1868–1869 and the sloop *Juniata* in 1869–1870.

While serving at the Boston Navy Yard, Luce wrote what became the lead article in the first issue of the newly established Naval Institute *Proceedings*. In 1874 he played a key role in outfitting the sloop *St. Mary's* to become the New York State Maritime School. After commanding the screw sloop *Hartford* during 1875–1877 and the screw frigate *Minnesota* during 1877–1881, he commanded the Naval Training Squadron, establishing its base at Newport in 1883.

In 1884 Luce founded the Naval War College, becoming its first president. Inspired by Emory Upton, John Laughton, and others, Luce focused the college on the study of strategy, tactics, international law, naval history, and war-gaming, gathering James Soley, William McCarty Little, and Alfred Thayer Mahan to carry out this work.

Luce commanded the North Atlantic Station during 1886–1889. Following retirement in March 1889, he was an active writer and lecturer, serving on the War College faculty during 1901–1910, and in January 1909 President Theodore Roosevelt appointed him to the Moody Commission on naval reorganization. Luce died in Newport, Rhode Island, on July 28, 1917.

JOHN B. HATTENDORF

Further Reading

Cherpak, Evelyn. *Register of the Papers of Stephen B. Luce.* Manuscript Register Series, 14. Newport, RI: Naval Historical Collection, Naval War College, 1986.

David Foote Sellers, Stephen B. Luce: A Register of Their Papers in the Library of Congress. Naval Historical Foundation Collection, Part 7. Washington, DC: Library of Congress, 1969.

Hayes, John D., and John B. Hattendorf, eds. *The Writings of Stephen B. Luce.* Newport, RI: Naval War College Press, 1975.

president is Commodore Stephen B. Luce. Among the institution's first faculty members are Tasker H. Bliss, a future U.S. Army chief of staff, and Captain (later Rear Admiral) Alfred Thayer Mahan, who soon becomes renowned for his writings on naval strategy.

November–December 1885

American Indian Wars (continued): Apache raid into Arizona Territory. In early November, Chiricahua Apache leader Chihuahua sends his younger brother Josanie and a dozen warriors into Arizona Territory in what will be one of the most daring raids of the Apache wars. Apparently the objectives are to try to release relatives captured by the army the previous June and to punish those Western Apaches who have agreed to live on reservations and especially the families of Apache scouts working with the army.

The raiders are sighted near Fort Apache, and scouts and cavalry are soon in pursuit. Josanie and his fellows cut telegraph lines and then attack the Fort Apache Reservation, killing Apaches there with the exception of some women whom they carry off. Although the scouts manage to attack Josanie's camp and take their horses and equipment, the next day the raiders attack a ranch, killing 2 men there and securing new horses. Later the renegades ambush the cavalry troop pursuing them. Returning to Mexico four weeks later, Josanie and his men will have ridden some 1,200 miles, killed 38 people, and stolen and worn out some 250 horses, all for the loss of only 1 of their own.

January 11, 1886

American Indian Wars (continued): Apache ambush of U.S. Army forces in northern Mexico. In December 1885, Captain Emmett Crawford of the 6th Cavalry Regiment reenters northern Mexico with a large number of Chiricahua Apache scouts and the now usual pack train in pursuit of elusive Chiricahua Apache leader Geronimo. On January 10, 1886, the scouts locate and attack Geronimo's encampment on the Rio Aros in the Sierra Madre. The Indians escape but lose all of their horses and considerable stocks of equipment and provisions. Demoralized

by the discovery of Chiricahua Apaches working as scouts with the army against them, Geronimo, Chihuahua, and Nachez agree to meet with Crawford the next day.

The next morning, a force of Mexican scalp hunters opens fire on the American camp. In the exchange of fire, Crawford is mortally wounded. Some 14 die on the Mexican side. Geronimo then meets with Crawford's successor, Lieutenant Marion Maus, and agrees to meet with Brigadier General George Crook in "two moons" and surrender to him.

January 18, 1886

The gunboat *Alliance* lands 12 marines at Aspinwall (present-day Colón) on the Atlantic coast of the Colombian province of Panama to protect the terminus of the transisthmian railroad and American interests.

March 16–May 25, 1886

U.S. forces intervene in Panama. With the absence of most Colombian forces in Buenaventura and the state of Bolívar, a revolution occurs in the Colombian province of Panama. The revolutionaries block free transit of the isthmus, to which the United States is entitled by treaty with Colombia. On April 14, the Bogotá government formally requests U.S. military intervention to maintain Colombian control of Panama, but American forces have already intervened. Acting Rear Admiral James E. Jouett's Atlantic Squadron is ordered to Aspinwall (now Colón). Other forces under Commander Bowman McCalla are also dispatched. On March 26 the screw sloop *Galena* sends ashore a landing party at Aspinwall, which is soon joined by detachments from the *Iroquois*, *Shenandoah*, and *Swatara*. On April 12, 232 marines under Lieutenant Colonel Charles Heywood arrive at Aspinwall from the United States and reopen the transisthmian railroad to Panama City and the Pacific. Three days later they are joined by two battalions of marines and seamen under Commander McCalla, who takes command of the expeditionary brigade. It remains ashore until Colombian forces crush the Panamanian revolution.

March 25, 1886

American Indian Wars (continued): Geronimo again agrees to surrender. On March 25, 1886, Brigadier General George Crook meets with Chiricahua Apache leader Geronimo again, this time at Embudo Canyon a dozen miles inside Mexico. Crook accepts Geronimo's surrender as well as those of Nana, Naiche, and others. It is the Apaches, not Crook, who set the terms. They will go east to join their families for two years, return to the reservation as before, or continue the war. Crook accepts the first option. As in

Geronimo was a pivotal figure in the final phase of the Apache Wars of the late 19th century. He was the last major recalcitrant Indian leader to surrender. His final surrender was to Brigadier General Nelson A. Miles on September 4, 1886. (National Archives)

1883, Crook then proceeds north without Geronimo, who has promised he would be along soon. Lieutenant Marion Maus is to escort the Chiricahua Apache leader back to the United States. The fighting seems to be over, but again this is not the case.

Two days after the conference and the surrender, the Chiricahuas secure some mescal and have second thoughts about their surrender. Lieutenant Maus returns to Fort Bowie in New Mexico Territory with old Nana, Chihuahua, and about 60 other Apaches, mainly women and children. Geronimo, Naiche, 18 other men, 13 women, and 6 children return to the Sierra Madre.

Crook has already telegraphed commanding general of the army Lieutenant General Philip H. Sheridan to report Geronimo's capture. Sheridan, however, rejects as unacceptable the surrender agreement and wires Crook to insist on unconditional surrender. This is unacceptable to Crook, who had always kept his word to the Apaches, and on April 1 he wires Sheridan and requests that he be relieved of his command. Sheridan immediately accepts this (Crook returns to his former post as commander of the Department of the Platte) and names Brigadier General Nelson A. Miles to replace Crook.

Miles commands some 5,000 men, roughly one-fourth of the entire U.S. Army at the time. Following Sheridan's suggestion, Miles dismisses most of the Apache scouts and divides the border area into districts, each with a garrison. He also sets up a system of heliograph stations on mountaintops; once operational, it can flash a 25-word message 400 miles and receive a response within only four hours. To pursue Geronimo into Mexico, Miles forms at Camp Bowie a unit of some 100 men under Captain Henry W. Lawton of the 4th Cavalry Regiment and at Fort Huachuca with Lieutenant Stanton and surgeon Leonard Wood. Lawton sets out on May 5. He will spend the next four months searching for the elusive Apache leader.

April 27, 1886

American Indian Wars (continued): Geronimo raids Arizona Territory. On this date Chiricahua Apaches led by Geronimo raid a number of ranches near Casita

Leonard Wood (1860–1927)

Doctor, U.S. Army general, and chief of staff of the U.S. Army. Born on October 9, 1860, in Winchester, New Hampshire, the son of a family doctor who died before his children reached adulthood, Leonard Wood was forced by finances to earn a living. Opting for medicine, he earned a degree from Harvard in 1884. He was accepted as an intern at Boston City Hospital but was fired for insubordinate behavior before completing his internship.

Wood joined the army as a contract surgeon in 1885 and participated in the protracted pursuit of Apache leader Geronimo through the mountains of southern Arizona and northern Mexico, for which Wood ultimately received the Medal of Honor. In 1895 after a time at Fort McPherson in Atlanta during which Wood helped organize and served as first coach of the Georgia Tech football team, he was assigned to Washington, D.C. When William McKinley was elected president, Wood became personal physician to McKinley's wife. Wood also became a close friend of the new assistant secretary of the navy, Theodore Roosevelt.

Wood and Roosevelt encouraged McKinley to support war with Spain in 1898, and when he did, they received permission to recruit their friends from both the western territories and the eastern aristocracy into the 1st Volunteer Cavalry Regiment, which was nicknamed the Rough Riders. Wood was colonel and commander, and Roosevelt was lieutenant colonel and second-in-command.

Wood commanded the Rough Riders in their first skirmish of the war at Las Guásimas, after which he was promoted to brigadier general. He commanded the 2nd Cavalry Brigade in the Battle of San Juan Hill. Shortly after the Spanish surrendered Santiago, he was named military governor of the city and then of the province. He used his medical training to bring disease and starvation under control and proved to be an exceptional and exceptionally stern administrator. His success in Cuba coupled with his Washington ties and a talent for political machinations led to his being named military governor of Cuba in December 1899. As governor, he made notable strides in education, public health, and prison reform and established a fiscally responsible republican government. Perhaps his most notable accomplishment was his sponsorship of and acceptance of responsibility for Walter Reed's yellow fever experiments. Immediately after Reed demonstrated the mosquito's role as a vector for the disease, Wood used his autocratic power to authorize draconian insect control measures carried out by his chief surgeon, Major William Gorgas. The campaign transformed Havana from one of the most dangerous cities in the world to one of the healthiest.

Wood had attained the rank of major general in the volunteer army but was still a captain in the medical corps until 1901 when, in a controversial move, Roosevelt, now the president, secured his promotion to brigadier general in the regular army over 509 more-senior officers.

Wood turned the government of Cuba over to an elected government in 1902 and was named commander of the Department of Mindanao, where he fought to control Islamic insurgents. He was promoted to major general in 1904 and was named commander of the Division of the Philippines in 1906. During his tenure in the Philippines, he was involved in a number of actions against insurgents, several of which were controversial and resulted in the deaths of large numbers of civilians.

(continued)

(Continued)

Wood was named commander of the Division of the East in 1903 and chief of staff of the army in 1910. In the latter position, which he held until 1914, he rescued the General Staff system from department heads determined to prevent its implementation, introduced techniques of scientific management to the military, and worked to professionalize the officer corps.

From 1914 to 1917, Wood returned to the Department of the East as its commander. Convinced as early as 1910 that the United States would participate in a European war, Wood became a vocal advocate of military preparedness and led the Plattsburg Movement, which was designed to train civilians who could be officers in such a war. He advocated universal military training and was a vocal opponent of Woodrow Wilson's pacifism. In 1916 Wood, who repeatedly crossed the traditional line separating military officers from politics, was briefly considered as the Republican candidate for president.

When the United States entered World War I, Wood was passed over for command of the American Expeditionary Force in favor of his former subordinate, General John J. Pershing. Wood was relegated to training the 89th Division at Camp Funston, and when that unit was sent to Europe in May 1918, he was (at Pershing's specific request) relieved and reassigned to train the 10th Division. In January 1918 while on an inspection tour of the Western Front, Wood received a minor injury from a mortar shell. In spite of the fact that he never was formally assigned a combat role, he was the most-senior American officer actually wounded by fire.

When Theodore Roosevelt died unexpectedly in 1919, Wood became his political heir and narrowly missed receiving the Republican nomination for president in 1920, even though he was still a general officer on active duty. From 1919 until 1921, he commanded the Central Division and then served on a special mission to the Philippines. He retired from active service in late 1921 and then returned to the Philippines, serving as governor-general until 1927. Wood died in Boston on August 7, 1927, during surgery to remove a benign brain tumor.

JACK MCCALLUM

Further Reading

Hagedorn, Hermann. *Leonard Wood: A Biography.* 2 vols. New York: Harper and Brothers, 1931.
Lane, Jack. *Armed Progressive: General Leonard Wood.* San Rafael, CA: Presidio, 1978.
McCallum, Jack. *Leonard Wood: Rough Rider, Surgeon, and Architect of American Imperialism.* New York: New York University Press, 2006.

in Arizona Territory, killing more than 30 people and taking hostages. U.S. cavalry units set out in pursuit.

July 20, 1886

American Indian Wars (continued): Pursuit of Geronimo. Renegade Chiricahua Apaches under Geronimo retire to northern Mexico, where they are pursued by Captain Henry W. Lawton of the 4th Cavalry Regiment and his 100 scouts and soldiers. On July 20, 1886, guided by his Apache scouts, Lawton attacks Geronimo's camp, but the renegades escape into the nearby hills.

August 6, 1886

Congress orders construction of the *Maine*, originally designated a heavy cruiser and later a second-class battleship, and the *Texas*, designated from the first as an armored battleship. Although rated at the time

 ## USS *Maine* (ACR-1)

The *Maine* was the U.S. Navy's second commissioned predreadnought battleship. Although classified as a second-class battleship, it was originally designated an armored or heavy cruiser (ACR-1). Authorized on August 3, 1886, it was built at the New York Navy Yard, supposedly on the design of the *Riachuelo,* built by Samuda for Brazil. The *Maine* was laid down in October 1888, launched in November 1889, and commissioned on September 17, 1895.

The *Maine* displaced 6,843 tons. It had an overall length of 324′4.5″, a beam of 57′3″, and a depth of hull of 30′3″. Its two shafts and two vertical triple expansion steam engines with eight boilers drove the ship at a speed of 16.5 knots. It had a 12′7″ steel armor belt and was armed with four 10-inch guns in twin en echelon turrets and six 6-inch guns on broadside. Typical of capital ships of the day, it had a range of armaments to enable it to fight at long, medium, and close ranges. Thus, it also carried seven 6-pounders, four 1-pounders, and four Gatling guns. It had a crew complement of 374 officers and men. Its coal capacity largely limited the ship to a coast-defense role.

The renewal of fighting in Cuba between revolutionaries bent on independence and Spanish troops determined to prevent that created concern for the security of U.S. interests in Cuba and fears that a European power, most probably Germany, might seek to take advantage of the situation. On January 24, 1898, President William McKinley ordered Captain Charles Sigsbee of the *Maine* to steam from Key West, Florida, to Havana supposedly to protect U.S. interests in Cuba but actually to pressure Spain to change its policies there and to enforce the 1823 Monroe Doctrine. This was certainly a provocative act, much resented by Spain, although Madrid had reluctantly agreed to it. The *Maine* arrived in Havana Harbor on January 25.

Although Spanish authorities in Havana extended full courtesies to the *Maine*'s crew, Sigsbee refused to allow the sailors shore leave in order to avoid a possible incident. At 9:30 p.m. on February 15, the *Maine* blew up and sank in Havana Harbor when its forward magazines, containing nearly five tons of powder charges, exploded. The sinking claimed 266 lives.

On March 28 a naval court of inquiry reported that the explosion had resulted from an external mine, a clear implication of Spanish responsibility. This finding was confirmed in a careful examination of the wreck in 1911 by a board of U.S. Navy and U.S. Army officers. Although the precise cause will probably never be established, in the 1970s Admiral Hyman Rickover and his staff cited stress studies of metal in underwater explosions to conclude that spontaneous combustion of bituminous coal in one of the ship's bunkers ignited ammunition in an adjacent magazine. It is also hard to see what the Spanish might have thought they could gain from planting a mine; nonetheless, there are those who claim that the explosion came from a mine set by Spanish extremists.

The loss of the *Maine* provided a rallying point for Americans who wanted war. The cry "Remember the Maine—to hell with Spain!" swept the country, and the day after the board of inquiry's report, President McKinley sent Madrid an ultimatum that ultimately led to the April 25, 1898, U.S. declaration of war against Spain.

SPENCER C. TUCKER

(continued)

(Continued)

Further Reading
Blow, Michael. *A Ship to Remember: The Maine and the Spanish-American War.* New York: William Morrow, 1992.
Friedman, Norman. *U.S. Battleships: An Illustrated Design History.* Annapolis, MD: Naval Institute Press, 1985.
Rickover, Hyman. *How the Battleship Maine Was Destroyed.* Washington, DC: U.S. Government Printing Office, 1976.
Samuels, Peggy, and Harold Samuels. *Remembering the Maine.* Washington, DC: Smithsonian Institution Press, 1995.
Weems, John Edward. *The Fate of the Maine.* New York: Henry Holt, 1985.

as a battleship, the *Maine* belongs to the type later identified as armored cruisers; its largest guns are four 10-inchers, while the *Texas* mounts two 12-inchers.

September 4, 1886

American Indian Wars (continued): Surrender of Geronimo. Brigadier General Nelson A. Miles, commanding the 5,000 troops searching for Chiricahua Apache renegade leader Geronimo and his followers, soon learns what his predecessor, Brigadier General George Crook, has long known, that it is simply impossible for army troops to keep up with and wear down the Apaches. If their horses are captured, the Apaches simply raid nearby towns and ranches and secure others. Only Apache scouts unencumbered by supply trains can keep up with the hostiles in the mountains. Miles now resurrects his predecessor's tactics and also his policy of negotiated surrender.

With the renegades worn down by Captain Henry W. Lawton's constant pursuit and ready to talk peace, First Lieutenant Charles B. Gatewood, who knows the Apaches and their language, meets with Geronimo and carries on the negotiations that lead to his decision to surrender. The Apache leader says that he will surrender only to Miles, who reluctantly travels to Skeleton Canyon in Arizona Territory. Following two days of negotiations, Geronimo formally surrenders with 33 followers, including Nachez, on September 4 under terms that Miles knows the government will not honor. Miles ignores two directives from President Grover Cleveland, first by giving Geronimo

terms and second by sending him and his followers to Fort Marion, Florida, rather than incarcerating them in the nearest fort or prison, there to stand trial.

Miles had not been honest with Geronimo, for the general promised Geronimo and his followers protection from prosecution, reunion with their families and a well-stocked reservation in Arizona. The Cleveland administration is now faced with a dilemma and ultimately decides that the Apache men would be held at Fort Pickens and the women and children at Fort Marion. Even less defensible than separation of families is the incarceration at Fort Marion of 17 Apache scouts who had served effectively with the army.

The surrender of Geronimo marks the end of formal warfare between the Native Americans and the U.S. Army. Only Apache leader Mangus and a dozen or so followers remain at large. In October, Captain Charles L. Cooper and 20 men of the 10th Cavalry Regiment and 2 scouts from Fort Apache locate them in an open area near the Black Mountains and capture the entire party, the only time this has occurred during the entire campaign.

November 5, 1887

American Indian Wars (continued). On the Crow Agency in southern Montana, Sword Bearer, who claims mystical powers that will protect him and his followers against the whites and enable him to kill all those opposing him with one sweep of a sword, attracts several dozen followers. They threaten the agency, firing several shots into its buildings, although no one is hurt. Director Henry E. Williamson calls for support, and Brigadier General T. H. Roger dispatches troops from nearby Fort Custer. When the hostile Crows refuse to surrender and charge the soldiers, an engagement occurs. Medicine Tail, an agency policeman, shoots and wounds Sword Bearer, who rides off in an attempt to escape. Several Native American agency policemen catch up with him and taunt him over his supposed invulnerability to bullets, and one kills him by shooting him in the back of the head with a pistol. Sword Bearer's death ends the affair.

June 19, 1888

At Chemulpo (present-day Inchon), Korea, the U.S. Navy screw steamer *Essex* lands 25 men under First Lieutenant Robert D. Wainwright to proceed to Seoul and there protect American interests.

November 14, 1888

At Apia, Upolu Island, Samoa, the U.S. Navy gunboat *Nipsic* lands marines to protect American traders during a civil war.

March 15–16, 1889

Tensions over Samoa, eased by a hurricane. The strategically placed 14 islands of the Samoan group located on the trade route to Australia had long been of interest to the United States, and in 1878 the U.S. government had secured a treaty allowing it to establish a coaling station at Pago Pago in return for a pledge to use its good offices should Samoa become involved in a dispute with a third power. In 1879 the United States, Germany, and Great Britain all establish consulates in the capital at Apia to guarantee equal economic opportunities. All three powers actively intervene in Samoan politics, however, supplying arms and in some cases troops to warring Samoan factions. Despite New Zealand's concerns, the British support a German protectorate for Samoa, hoping for recognition by Germany of their paramount position in Egypt in return.

When the American consul in Samoa proclaims an American protectorate, U.S. secretary of state Thomas F. Bayard denounces this and invites Germany and Great Britain to resolve the Samoan issue

at a conference in Washington in June 1887. Both countries accept, while at the same time continuing secret negotiations of their own. Indeed, Great Britain agrees to recognize Germany's paramount interests in Samoa, hoping that Germany will support its position in Egypt. The United States refuses to accept German control over Samoa, however, and the Washington conference ends without result.

In August 1887, however, German troops engineer a coup d'état in Samoa and establish martial law, making Samoa a de facto German possession. The United States demands an immediate return to the status quo, but Great Britain, hoping to gain Tonga in Africa, publicly protests yet privately accepts Germany's actions. Tensions mount, and the United States and Germany seem on a collision course that might lead to war. The Grover Cleveland administration takes a hard line, and both nations dispatch warships to the islands, the United States sending three ships under Pacific Squadron commander Rear Admiral Lewis A. Kimberly.

Tensions abate thanks to an act of nature. On March 15–16, 1889, a hurricane strikes Apia Harbor, where one British, three American, and three German warships, along with six merchantmen, are anchored. The British screw corvette *Calliope* is the only ship to make it out of the harbor. The captain of the U.S. Navy gunboat *Nipsic* is able to beach his ship, but Kimberly's flagship steamer *Trenton* and the screw sloop *Vandalia* are both sunk, along with all three German warships—the *Adler, Eber,* and *Olga*—and all six merchantmen. In all 150 seamen are lost, including 49 Americans.

Meanwhile, German chancellor Otto von Bismarck, who has publicly criticized the German consul's actions, invites the British and U.S. governments to send representatives to a conference in Berlin. In June 1889, they agree to establishment of a three-power protectorate. This lasts only until 1899, when the islands are divided between and annexed by the United States and Germany.

June 21, 1889

Maxim guns are test-fired at Annapolis, Maryland. American Hiram Maxim, working for the British

Maxim Gun

If any one weapon symbolized World War I, it was the machine gun. Efficient manually operated rapid-firing small arms were in service in the 1860s and 1870s, including the Agar "Coffee Mill" (ca. 1860) and the Gatling gun (1862) employed at the end of the American Civil War (1861–1865). The French utilized the 25-barrel Mitrailleuse (1869) in the Franco-Prussian War (1870–1871). But the Maxim gun of 1884, named for American Hiram Maxim, was the first truly automatic machine gun. Development of the metallic cartridge made possible rapid loading at the breech.

Maxim's innovation was to use some of the energy of the firing to operate the weapon. Using the recoil energy, which he called blowback, Maxim designed a fully automatic rifle fed by a revolving magazine. He then applied the same principle to a machine gun, which fired as long as the trigger was depressed. In the Maxim gun, the firing of the cartridge drove back the bolt, compressing a spring that in turn drove the bolt forward again, bringing a new round into position for firing. The Maxim gun was both self-loading and self-ejecting.

Maxim first demonstrated his prototype machine gun in 1884. It weighed 60 pounds (the Mitrailleuse had weighed 2,000 pounds because it was mounted on a towed field carriage, like an artillery piece). The Maxim gun was both belt-fed and water-cooled. Maxim addressed the problem of overheating by adding a water jacket around the barrel. He also mounted the weapon on a tripod instead of wheels. It fired a .45-caliber bullet at a rate of up to 600 rounds per minute and could be operated by a crew of only five men. The gun was fired principally by a single gunner. The others assisted in carrying it and in bringing up belts of ammunition for it. Aided by the British firm of Vickers, Maxim had his gun largely perfected before the end of the 1880s.

The British Army adopted the Maxim gun in 1889, originally in .45-caliber and later in .303-caliber. The British employed the Maxim gun with great success against the Zulus in South Africa and the Dervishes in the Sudan. Rudyard Kipling proclaimed the importance of the new weapon when he wrote that "Whatever else, we have got the Maxim Gun, and they have not." Maxim was later knighted by Queen Victoria for "services to humanity," in the false assumption that the machine gun would make wars shorter and thus more humane. The U.S. military also adopted the Maxim gun.

Despite the experiences of the Boer War (1899–1902) and the Russo-Japanese War (1904–1905), almost all armies had failed to come to terms with the new lethality of the increased firepower by the start of World War I in 1914. At 450–600 rounds per minute, one machine gun could equal the fire of 40–80 riflemen. The machine gun also had a greater range than the rifle, enabling indirect fire in support of an attack. In the German Army, machine guns initially were deployed in companies as opposed to dispersing them among infantry formations, but as the war progressed, the Germans altered their tactics and organization to make the light machine the centerpiece of the German infantry squad. Light machine guns, such as the excellent Lewis gun, appeared later and saw widespread service in World War I. The Vickers machine gun was an improved and redesigned Maxim gun. Introduced into the British Army in 1912, the Vickers machine gun remained in service until 1968.

Spencer C. Tucker

Further Reading

Goldsmith, Duff L., and R. Blake Stevens. *The Devil's Paintbrush: Sir Hiram Maxim's Gun.* 2nd ed. Toronto: Collector Grade Publications, 1993.

Willbanks, James H. *Machine Guns: An Illustrated History of Their Impact.* Santa Barbara, CA: ABC-CLIO, 2004.

firm of Vickers, has been perfecting his new weapon in England since 1884. The U.S. military subsequently adopts the Maxim.

July 30, 1889
Following disturbances at Honolulu in the Kingdom of Hawaii, the U.S. Navy screw gunboat *Adams* lands marines to protect American lives and property.

April 23, 1890
At Bristol, Rhode Island, the U.S. Navy commissions its first torpedo boat, the *Cushing* (TB-1).

June 30, 1890
Congress authorizes construction of the first U.S. Navy first-class battleships. They are the *Indiana*, *Massachusetts*, and *Oregon*.

Alfred Thayer Mahan (1840–1914)

U.S. Navy officer, prominent naval historian and strategist, and staunch proponent of U.S. imperialism. Born at West Point, New York, on September 27, 1840, Alfred Thayer Mahan was the son of West Point professor Dennis Hart Mahan, who initiated the study of military theory in the United States and exerted a profound impact on officers in the American Civil War (1861–1865).

Mahan attended Columbia College for two years. Securing a warrant as an acting midshipman on September 30, 1856, he entered the U.S. Naval Academy, Annapolis, graduating second in his class, and was promoted to midshipman on June 9, 1859. He served in the U.S. Brazil Squadron, and during the Civil War he was posted to the South Atlantic Blockading Squadron and was promoted to lieutenant on August 31, 1861; to lieutenant commander on June 7, 1865; and to commander on November 20, 1872. In 1883 he published *The Gulf and Inland Waters,* a book treating U.S. Navy operations during the war. This impressed Captain Stephen Luce, and in 1885, Luce, president of the newly established Naval War College, invited Mahan to lecture there on naval tactics and history. Mahan was promoted to captain on September 23 that same year.

In 1890 Mahan published his lectures under the title *The Influence of Sea Power upon History, 1660–1783*. This important book is a history of British naval development in its most crucial period, a treatise on war at sea, and a ringing defense of a large navy. It had particular influence in Britain, Germany, and Japan, but Mahan's lectures and magazine articles on current strategic problems also won an ever-widening audience in the United States with such individuals as Theodore Roosevelt.

Mahan argued that the United States needed a strong navy to compete for the world's trade. He claimed that there was no instance of a great commercial power retaining its leadership without a large navy. He also criticized traditional U.S. "single ship, commerce raiding" (the *guerre de course*), which could not win control of the seas. Mahan argued for a seagoing fleet, an overbearing force that could beat down an enemy's battle line, its strength in battleships operating in squadrons. Mahan believed in the concentration of forces, urging that the fleet be kept in one ocean only. He also called for U.S. naval bases in the Caribbean and in the Pacific. Mahan overlooked new technology, such as the torpedo and the submarine, and he was not concerned about speed in battleships.

Mahan was president of the Naval War College during 1886–1889 and 1889–1893. He commanded the cruiser *Chicago,* flagship of the European Station during 1893–1896, and was publically feted in

(*continued*)

(Continued)

Europe and recognized with honorary degrees from Oxford University and Cambridge University. An important apostle of the new navalism, Mahan retired from the navy in 1896 to devote himself full-time to writing.

Mahan was called back to active duty with the navy in an advisory role during the 1898 Spanish-American War. He was a delegate to the 1899 Hague Peace Conference, and he was promoted to rear admiral on the retired list in 1906. Mahan wrote a dozen books on naval warfare and more than 50 articles in leading journals, and he was elected president of the American Historical Association in 1902. He died in Washington, D.C., on December 1, 1914.

SPENCER C. TUCKER

Further Reading

Hughes, Wayne P. *Mahan: Tactics and Principles of Strategy.* Newport, RI: Naval War College, 1990.
Livezey, William E. *Mahan and Sea Power.* Norman: University of Oklahoma Press, 1947.
Mahan, Alfred Thayer. *The Influence of Seapower upon History, 1660–1783.* Boston: Little, Brown, 1890.
Quester, George R. *Mahan and American Naval Thought since 1914.* Newport, RI: Naval War College, 1990.
Puleston, William D. *Mahan: The Life and Work of Captain Alfred Thayer Mahan.* New Haven, CT: Yale University Press, 1939.

July 30, 1890

At Buenos Aires, Argentina, the U.S. Navy side-wheel steamer *Tallapoosa* lands marines to guard the U.S. legation during civil unrest.

December 29, 1890

American Indian Wars (continued): Ghost Dance and the Battle of Wounded Knee (Massacre of Wounded Knee). In the 1870s, influential Northern Paiute medicine man Jack Wilson, known as Wovoka, began preaching a belief system that called for highly moral behavior combined with the practice of traditional Native American customs and cooperation among Native American groups. Above all, Wovoka denounces violence. Wovoka predicts a peaceful end to white expansion onto Indian lands and advocates cooperation between Indians and whites. The new religion sweeps across the American West. Its outward manifestation is the traditional Indian circular dance.

Kicking Bear, a subchief among the Minneconjou Sioux, is believed to have introduced the concept of Ghost Shirts into the ritual. These are special shirts, perhaps the result of Mormon influence, that it is claimed will protect the pious wearer from danger. Lakota tradition also holds that all whites will be removed from Native lands, whereas Wovoka had encouraged harmonious relations between Indians and whites living together.

In February 1890, meanwhile, the federal government breaks a treaty with the Lakotas in reworking the territory of the Great Sioux Reservation of South Dakota, which formerly encompassed the majority of their territory. In order to accommodate white settlers, the one large reservation is broken up into five smaller reservations. The land is distributed on the basis of 320-acre plots for individual households, and the Lakotas are encouraged to farm and raise livestock. To promote assimilation, the Lakotas are also encouraged to send their children to boarding schools, where they will be instructed in white American cultural practices to the exclusion of traditional Indian culture.

In addition to anger over these developments, the Bureau of Indian Affairs has sharply cut subsidies to the Sioux, failing to provide adequate food and supplies during the transition period, nor does it provide

 ## Indiana-Class Battleships

The three Indiana-class battleships—the *Indiana, Massachusetts,* and *Oregon*—were the first U.S. Navy modern battleships. Authorized by Congress on June 30, 1890, as "sea-going coast-line battleships," these ships were a third again as large as the *Maine* and *Texas* (subsequently designated second-class battleships). The Indiana-class battleships displaced 10,288 tons and were 350'11" in length overall and 69'3" in beam. Propelled by two screws, they were capable of a speed of 16.8 knots. They had crew complements of 473 officers and men. Typical of capital ships of the day, they had a mixed armament. They mounted 4 13-inch guns in what now became standard center-line turrets. They also had 8 8-inch and 4 6-inch guns as well as 20 6-pounders, 6 1-pounders, 2 3-inch field guns, 2 Colt machine guns, and 5 18-inch torpedo tubes (the *Indiana* had only 4 torpedo tubes). With 8" to 16" side armor and up to 17" turret armor, they were more heavily protected and more powerfully armed than their European counterparts. They had very low freeboard, however, and rolled heavily until fitted with bilge keels in 1897.

The *Indiana* (BB-1) was laid down on May 7, 1891, and commissioned on November 20, 1895. The *Massachusetts* (BB-2) was laid down on June 25, 1891, and commissioned on June 10, 1896. The *Oregon* (BB-3) was laid down on November 19, 1891, and commissioned on June 15, 1896. The *Indiana* and *Massachusetts* were both built by the firm of Wm. Cramp and Sons, Philadelphia, while the *Oregon* was built at Union Iron Works. All three ships took part in the blockade of Cuba during the Spanish-American War, the *Oregon* making a historic 14,500-mile voyage from the Pacific coast to Key West in 46 days, at an average speed of almost 12 knots. All three ships took part in the bombardment of Santiago, and the *Indiana* and *Oregon* both participated in the Battle of Santiago Bay on July 3, 1898. The *Oregon* also took part in the Philippine-American War. The *Indiana* was decommissioned on January 31, 1919; the *Massachusetts* was decommissioned on March 29, 1919; and the *Oregon* was decommissioned on June 12, 1919. The *Indiana* and *Massachusetts* were both sunk as artillery target ships. Originally preserved as a museum ship, the *Oregon* was sold for scrap during World War II. This was subsequently halted, and the stripped hulk was used as an ammunition barge during the Battle for Guam. The hulk was finally sold for scrap in 1956. In 1920 when hull numbers were retroactively assigned to battleships in 1920, the Indiana-class ships were designated BB 1 through BB 3.

SPENCER C. TUCKER

Further Reading

Friedman, Norman. *U.S. Battleships: An Illustrated Design History.* Annapolis, MD: Naval Institute Press, 1985.
Silverstone, Paul H. *The New Navy, 1883–1922.* New York: Routledge, 2006.

sufficient farmer trainers. The Bureau of Indian Affairs also fails to take into account the shorter growing season and semiarid nature of the region. With the great herds of bison all but eliminated, the Sioux are in danger of starvation.

The Sioux embrace the Ghost Dance and distort it into a more militant doctrine against white oppression. Many Lakotas, long fed up with the inept administration at the Pine Ridge Agency, take up the Ghost Dance and move off the reservation. Indian agents and army officers charged with maintaining order on the northern Great Plains express concern that other Sioux bands might join the Pine Ridge contingent. Thousands of additional troops arrive.

The Ghost Dance, performed by the Sioux. The Ghost Dance was a new religious movement believed to reunite the spirits of the living with the dead and bring about a new era of peace and prosperity. (Library of Congress)

Their presence only increases the prospects of armed confrontation.

Brigadier General Nelson A. Miles, commander of the Division of Missouri, orders the arrest of 2 prominent Sioux leaders who it is feared might bring about a wider Indian alliance: spiritual leader Sitting Bull and Chief Big Foot (also known as Spotted Elk). On December 15, 1890, at the Standing Rock Agency in South Dakota Territory, Apache police attempt to arrest Sitting Bull. A scuffle ensues, and Sitting Bull is killed. Enraged tribesmen then open fire, and 13 Indians are killed in the ensuing exchange.

Big Foot, whose Miniconjou band is located at the Cheyenne River Agency, is invited by the chiefs of the Pine Ridge Agency to travel there to try to ease tensions between Oglalas and Brules and not to promote violence. On December 27, Big Foot and his band of some 350 men, women, and children are overtaken by Major Samuel M. Whiteside of the 7th Cavalry and ordered to set up camp at Wounded Knee Creek, near the Pine Ridge Agency, where they might be easily watched. Big Foot, ill with pneumonia, agrees. Whiteside sends his surgeon to attend Big Foot and orders rations distributed to the hungry Indians.

On the evening of December 28, Colonel James W. Forsyth arrives at Wounded Knee with the remainder of the 7th Cavalry. Ordered to disarm Big Foot's village, some 500 troopers surround the encampment on the morning of December 29. The Sioux warriors are then lined up and ordered to hand over all weapons. Despite being outnumbered and with four artillery pieces positioned to fire into the encampment if need be, the Indians refuse to surrender their Winchester repeating rifles. Tension grows as troopers begin to go through the lodges and as a medicine man known as Yellow Bird begins to dance and incite the Sioux to

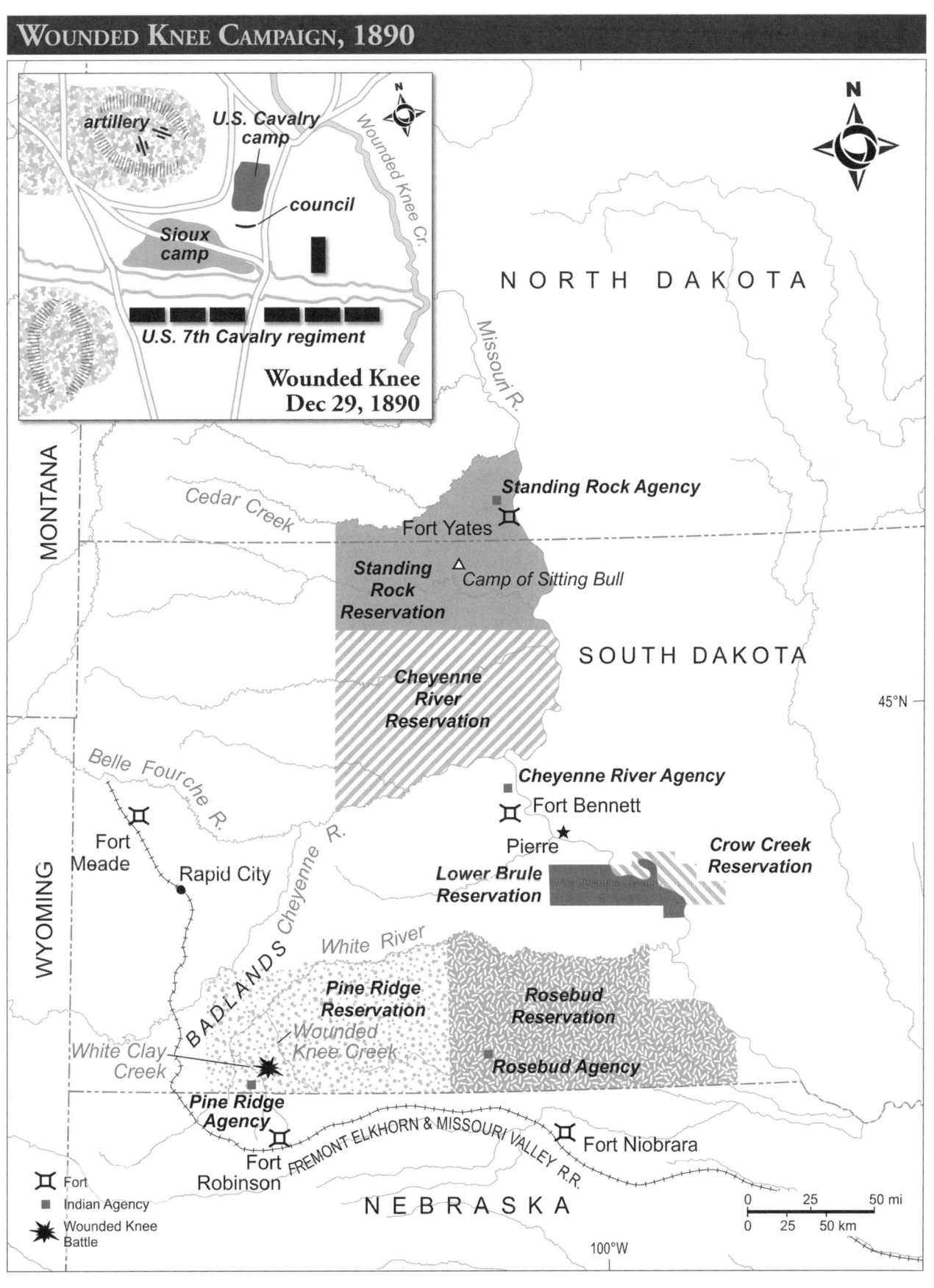

WOUNDED KNEE CAMPAIGN, 1890

Wounded Knee
Dec 29, 1890

artillery

U.S. Cavalry camp

council

Sioux camp

U.S. 7th Cavalry regiment

Wounded Knee Cr.

NORTH DAKOTA

Missouri R.

MONTANA

Cedar Creek

Standing Rock Agency

Fort Yates

Standing Rock Reservation

Camp of Sitting Bull

SOUTH DAKOTA

45°N

Cheyenne River Reservation

Belle Fourche R.

Cheyenne River Agency

Fort Bennett

Pierre

Fort Meade

Rapid City

Cheyenne R.

Lower Brule Reservation

Crow Creek Reservation

WYOMING

BADLANDS

White River

Pine Ridge Reservation

Wounded Knee Creek

Rosebud Reservation

White Clay Creek

Rosebud Agency

Pine Ridge Agency

Fort Robinson

FREMONT ELKHORN & MISSOURI VALLEY R.R.

Fort Niobrara

Fort

Indian Agency

Wounded Knee Battle

0   25   50 mi
0   25   50 km

NEBRASKA

100°W

Battle of Wounded Knee (Wounded Knee Massacre)		
Date	December 29, 1890	
Location	Wounded Knee Creek, South Dakota	
Opponents (*winner)	*United States	Miniconjou Sioux
Commander	Colonel James W. Forsyth	Chief Big Foot (Spotted Elk)
#	500 soldiers, 4 artillery pieces	350 Native Americans (men, women, and children)
Casualties	25 killed, 35 wounded	At least 146 killed

action. Someone fires a shot, and a number of warriors fire into a line of soldiers.

Brief hand-to-hand combat ensues, involving firearms as well as knives and clubs. Once the fight is over, the artillery shells the village. A total of 146 Native Americans are dead, including Big Foot and 83 other men, 44 women, and 18 children (some estimates place the number of killed higher). Another 150 Indians manage to escape, but many of these subsequently freeze to death. Army casualties in the fighting are 25 killed and 39 wounded.

A related skirmish occurs the following day at Drexel Mission Church, four miles north of Wounded Knee, where a group of Sioux who had escaped the slaughter burn some sheds. They also ambush a 7th Cavalry patrol, killing one trooper and wounding six others. Native casualties are not known. The patrol is rescued by members of the 9th Cavalry Regiment, trailing the Sioux from the White River.

General Miles, hoping to coerce the Pine Ridge tribes back to their reservations without further violence, surrounds the disgruntled Native Americans with some 3,500 soldiers at a distance and employs a mix of diplomacy and the threat of force to secure their surrender on January 15, 1891.

Word of what has occurred causes considerable outrage in the East, and Colonel Forsyth is relieved of command. A court of inquiry concludes that he had not anticipated a fight and that the soldiers did indeed try to avoid killing women and children, but their presence made these deaths unavoidable. It remains unclear which side fired first. Forsyth is exonerated, but Miles, who had warned against endangering the troops by placing them too close to the Indians, charges him with dereliction of duty, although Forsyth is later restored to command.

The Battle of Wounded Knee is usually cited by historians as marking the close of the Indian Wars. The nomadic Plains Indian way of life was bound to end, even without the army (although the wars certainly aid the process). Commercial hunters have quite literally wiped out the buffalo on which the Plains Indians have depended for their livelihood. Other factors in the defeat of the Native Americans include their disunity, the arrival of the railroads, the larger number of settlers, and superior white organization and technology.

January 1, 1891
American Indian Wars (continued): Battle of Little Grass Creek. Along the north bank of the White River near the mouth of Little Grass Creek in South Dakota Territory, troopers of the 6th Cavalry Regiment under Captain John B. Kerr engage several hundred Brulé Sioux Indians attempting to flee the Pine River Agency. The soldiers lose one dead and one wounded; the Indians suffer six killed. Five members of the 6th Cavalry are awarded the Medal of Honor for this engagement.

June 2, 1891
At Navassa Island, Hawaii, the U.S. Navy screw sloop *Kearsarge* lands marines to preserve order.

August 28, 1891
At Valparaiso, Chile, the U.S. Navy cruisers *Baltimore* and *San Francisco* land marines to protect the U.S. consulate during the 1891 Chilean Civil War.

October 16, 1891–January 1892
Crisis between the United States and Chile (the *Baltimore* Affair). On October 16, 1891, with the captain of the U.S. Navy protected cruiser *Baltimore*,

Commander Winfield S. Schley, having permitted liberty to some of its crew, fighting breaks out at the True Blue Saloon in Valparaiso between the sailors and a mob of Chileans. Two Americans are killed, and 17 are injured. Offensive remarks by the Chilean foreign minister stoke the fires, and by December, war between Chile and the United States becomes a possibility. In this crisis, Americans are surprised to learn that the Chilean Navy is larger than that of the United States and might threaten the U.S. Pacific coast.

On January 25, 1892, U.S. president Benjamin Harrison threatens a break in diplomatic relations unless there is a Chilean apology for the foreign minister's remarks. The crisis is resolved when the Chilean government promptly agrees to the apology and the payment of $75,000 to the families of the two dead sailors.

July 1892

Coeur d'Alene, Idaho, labor strike of 1892. During the 1880s, silver miners in the Coeur d'Alene, Idaho, area organize local unions, and the mine owners respond by forming a Mine Owners' Association. To reduce rising costs, the mine owners agree both to reduce wages and increase working hours. In 1892 the miners declare a strike, but the mine owners bring in replacement workers. To protect the latter, infiltrate the unions, and help break up the strike activity, the owners hire Pinkerton and Thiel Detective Agency personnel.

On July 10 shooting occurs at the Frisco mine between miners and guards, each claiming that the other had fired first. In the ensuing violence here and at other mines, several company employees are killed and a number of guards are taken prisoner by the union men. At the behest of the miners, on July 14 Idaho governor N. B. Willey declares martial law and orders in six companies of the Idaho National Guard to "suppress insurrection and violence." U.S. Army troops are also brought in, and they hold some 600 miners without formal charges. Some are later sentenced to prison for violating injunctions or obstructing the U.S. mail. Military rule lasts for four months. These events lead to the formation of the Western Federation of Miners at Butte, Montana, on May 15, 1893.

August 1892

The U.S. Army adopts the Norwegian Krag-Jørgensen rifle.

January 17, 1893

U.S. intervention in the Hawaiian Islands. Hawaiian queen Liliuokalani attempts to assert authority over the interests of the powerful plantation owners who have arisen in the islands. Liliuokalani is not successful, for on January 17, 1893, she is overthrown by a cabal of plantation owners and merchants in Honolulu, almost all of whom are Europeans and Americans. The rebellion has the immediate support of U.S. minister to Hawaii John Stevens, who has the protected cruiser *Baltimore,* then at Honolulu, land 150 marines and sailors, ostensibly to protect the U.S. legation but in reality to secure the islands and prepare them for eventual annexation to the United States.

Lame-duck president Benjamin Harrison favors annexation, but his term ends only six and a half weeks after the overthrow of the queen in Hawaii, an insufficient time frame to secure congressional annexation. Harrison's successor, Democrat Grover Cleveland, opposes U.S. overseas expansion. He repudiates the overthrow in a message to Congress on December 18, 1893, but does nothing to restore the status quo ante.

August 1, 1893

The U.S. Navy's first armored cruiser, the *New York* (CA 2; the *Maine* [CA 1] was designated a battleship before its completion) is commissioned at Philadelphia. It displaces 8,200 tons and sets a world speed record of 21.09 knots in its trials. It is armed with 6 8-inch guns, 12 4-inch guns, 8 6-pounders, 2 1-pounders, and 3 18-inch torpedo tubes. It has a complement of 556 men. In 1911 the ship is renamed the *Saratoga,* and in 1917 it becomes the *Rochester.*

November 3, 1893

The U.S. Congress authorizes the War Department to assign 100 army officers to college campuses to teach military science.

Krag-Jørgensen Rifle

With rapid changes in infantry small arms, including the introduction of bolt action repeating rifles, the U.S. Army sought to replace its current infantry rifle, the single-shot Spring Model 1873. A competition was held in 1892 at Governors Island, New York, involving 53 different designs to select the new army rifle. The finalists were three foreign firms: Lee of Great Britain, Krag of Norway, and Mauser of Germany.

In August 1892 the U.S. Army adopted the Norwegian Krag-Jørgensen rifle. A .30-caliber (7.62-millimeter [mm]) weapon, it was much admired for its smooth action. It had a five-round clip and an effective range of 984.251 yards (900 meters). The rifle had a barrel length of 30 inches and a total length of 49 inches. Its loaded weight was 9.2 pounds. Its .30-caliber cartridge was the first smokeless powder round adopted by the U.S. military, but its civilian name (.30-40) retains the caliber-charge designation of earlier black powder cartridges. The .30-40 Krag thus utilized a .30-caliber (7.62-mm) bullet propelled by 40 grains (3 grams) of smokeless powder.

During 1894–1904, the U.S. Springfield Arsenal in Massachusetts produce about 500,000 Krags for the army. The Krag saw service in the Spanish-American War, the Philippine-American War, and the Boxer Uprising. It was replaced by the Model 1903 Springfield. During World War II under German demand, occupied Norway produced Krags for the German Army. A number remain in use as sporting rifles.

SPENCER C. TUCKER

Further Reading

Blair, Claude, ed. *Pollard's History of Firearms.* New York: Macmillan, 1983.
Smith, W. H. B. *Small Arms of the World.* London: Arms and Armour, 1984.

February 2, 1894
The old U.S. Navy screw sloop *Kearsarge*, under Commander Oscar F. Heyerman, wrecks on Roncador Reef between Cuba and the Mexican and Nicaraguan coasts. All crew members are saved.

May 11–July 20, 1894
Pullman Strike. On May 11, 1894, some 3,000 employees of the Pullman Palace Car Company at Pullman, Illinois, begin a wildcat strike to protest a reduction in their wages by management following a drop in sales of Pullman railroad cars, owing to the economic panic of 1893. On June 26 Eugene V. Debs, leader of the American Railway Union (the nation's first industry-wide union), calls for a formal strike against the Pullman Company and for members of the union to refuse to run Pullman cars. By the end of June the strike has tied up all midwestern railroads. The strike ultimately involves some 250,000 workers in 27 states.

The railroads begin hiring replacement workers; many are African Americans, adding a racial element to the conflict. When violence occurs, the railroad owners appeal to U.S. president Grover Cleveland for government intervention. On July 2, a federal court issues an injunction forbidding interference with the movements of the mail or interstate commerce. (Such injunctions will be increasingly employed to halt strikes.)

Despite the protests of Illinois governor John P. Atgeld and with Cleveland's own cabinet divided over whether he has the authority to do so, Cleveland orders in U.S. marshals and 12,000 federal troops under Major General Nelson A. Miles to restore order. Before the violence ends, 31 strikers are killed and more than 50 injured. There is also considerable damage to railroad property. Although the strike is broken and calm is restored, his decision to send in troops costs Cleveland the Democratic Party renomination for the presidency in 1896. Arrested and tried on charges of violating an injunction, Debs is imprisoned for six months.

July 6, 1894

At Bluefields, Nicaragua, the U.S. Navy cruiser *Columbia* lands sailors and marines to safeguard American lives and property.

July 24, 1894

At Chemulpo (present-day Inchon), Korea, the U.S. Navy cruiser *Baltimore* lands 150 marines and sailors under U.S. Marine Corps captain George F. Elliott to travel to Seoul and safeguard the American legation there during the Sino-Japanese War when the Japanese send troops to Korea.

September 17, 1894

Battle of the Yalu River. During the Sino-Japanese War of 1894, Philo McGiffen, an 1882 graduate of the U.S. Naval Academy now serving in the Imperial Chinese Navy, becomes the first American to command a modern battleship in action when, as executive officer, he takes command from the captain of the *Chen Yuen* during the Battle of the Yalu River (Haiyang); the battle is also known as the Battle of the Yellow Sea. Through skillful maneuvering, he is able to force a Japanese withdrawal. McGiffen is severely wounded during the battle and subsequently returns to the United States.

February 25, 1895–April 1898

Background of the Spanish-American War: Insurrection in Cuba against Spanish rule. The failure of the Spanish government to grant promised reforms in Cuba following the Ten Years' War (1868–1878) and the Small War (1879–1880) leads directly to a widespread war known as the Cuban Insurrection (also known as the Cuban War of Independence). Spanish captain general Valeriano Weyler attempts to put down the rebellion by compartmentalization of the island through *trochas* (fortified lines) and establishment of concentration camps to isolate the insurgents from support.

Widespread press coverage in the United States of the war and exaggerations by the so-called yellow press of Spanish policies, especially under Weyler, help bring about war between the United States and Spain in April 1898.

August 15, 1895

The first U.S. Navy battleship, the *Texas*, is commissioned.

November 20, 1895

The U.S. Navy battleship *Indiana* (BB 1) is commissioned.

May 2–4, 1896

At Corinto, Nicaragua, the U.S. Navy gunboat *Alert* lands a party to safeguard American citizens and interests.

February 7, 1898

During revolutionary disturbances at San Juan del Sur, Nicaragua, the U.S. Navy gunboat *Alert* lands marines and sailors to protect American lives and property.

February 9, 1898

Background of the Spanish-American War (continued): Publication of the Dupuy de Lôme Letter. Spanish ambassador to the United States Enrique Dupuy de Lôme writes a personal letter to an acquaintance, José Canalejas, in Cuba covering events there for a Spanish newspaper. Dupuy de Lôme is sharply critical of U.S. president William McKinley, characterizing him as "weak" and a "low" politician pandering to the "rabble." Cuban revolutionaries intercept the dispatch and turn it over to the Hearst publishing empire. The letter is published in the *New York Journal* on February 9, 1898, and increases popular support in the United States for war against Spain. Dupuy de Lôme promptly resigns his post and returns to Spain.

February 15, 1898

Background of the Spanish-American War (continued): Destruction of USS *Maine*. Washington dispatches the second-class battleship *Maine* to Havana, Cuba, ostensibly to protect American interests in the island but actually to intimidate Spain into granting concessions to Cuban guerrillas opposing Spanish rule in Cuba. Commanded by Captain Charles Sigsbee, the *Maine* arrives on January 25, 1898.

At 9:30 p.m. on February 15 the *Maine* is at anchor in Havana Harbor when its forward magazines containing nearly five tons of powder charges explode. The blast sinks the ship and kills 266 crew members. Sigsbee and most of the officers survive because their quarters are located in the aft section.

A subsequent naval court of inquiry concludes that the blast was caused by an external mine. More recent scientific research concludes that it was spontaneous combustion in a coal locker next to a magazine. Although it is hard to imagine any gain for Spain in the sinking of the ship, many Americans at the time hold the Spanish responsible. The incident, fanned by the sensationalist yellow press in the United States, fuels anti-Spanish sentiment and helps bring war between the United States and Spain two months later.

March 8, 1898

Background of the Spanish-American War (continued). Congress passes a $50 million national defense appropriation bill, the money to be spent at the discretion of the president. President William McKinley signs the bill into law the next day.

March 17, 1898

Background of the Spanish-American War (continued): Proctor's speech to Congress. Moderate Republican senator Redfield Proctor, having returned from an inspection trip to Cuba, delivers a major speech before the U.S. Senate and denounces the brutal methods of repression adopted by the Spanish

authorities there. His speech helps convince many that the United States has a humanitarian duty to intervene in Cuba.

March 18, 1898

Background of the Spanish-American War (continued): Creation of the Flying Squadron. In view of the great possibility of war with Spain, the U.S. Navy establishes the Flying Squadron to defend the U.S. East Coast. Acting Commodore Winfield Scott Schley takes command of the Flying Squadron on March 28. It includes the armored cruiser *Brooklyn* (flagship), the battleships *Massachusetts* and *Texas,* and the cruisers *Columbia* and *Minneapolis.*

March 19–May 24, 1898

Background of the Spanish-American War (continued): Voyage of the *Oregon.* On March 19, 1898, the U.S. Navy battleship *Oregon* sails from San Francisco for the East Coast, proceeding around Cape Horn. At the time the newest and most powerful U.S. warship, the *Oregon* arrives at Jupiter Inlet, Florida, on May 24, after a voyage of some 14,500 miles at an average speed of almost 12 knots.

On June 1 the *Oregon* joins the North American Squadron in the naval blockade of Cuba. Its epic voyage, which would have required just 21 days had a canal existed across Central America versus the actual 66 days it took, serves as a powerful argument for construction of an isthmian canal across Central America.

March 24, 1898

Background of the Spanish-American War (continued). U.S. Navy captain William T. Sampson assumes command of the North Atlantic Squadron as a rear admiral.

March 29, 1898

Background of the Spanish-American War (continued). Under considerable pressure from the American public, eager for war with Spain, U.S. president William McKinley sends an ultimatum to Madrid demanding, among other matters, that the Spanish quit Cuba. The Spanish government's reply, received

VOYAGE OF USS *OREGON*, MARCH 19–MAY 24, 1898

NORTH AMERICA

Puget Sound

San Francisco

UNITED STATES

Gulf of Mexico

Jupiter Inlet

Key West

Bahamas

ATLANTIC OCEAN

San José

Panama City

Barbados

Belém

Cape São Roque

SOUTH AMERICA

Callao

Bahia

Rio de Janeiro

PACIFIC OCEAN

Valparaiso

Montevideo

Sandy Point

Port Tamar

Strait of Magellan

40°N

20°N

0°

20°S

40°S

120°W 100°W 80°W 60°W 40°W

USS *Oregon* traveled 67 days and 14,700 miles
— Course of USS *Oregon*
-- Course of USS *Marietta*

0   400   800 mi
0   400   800 km

William Thomas Sampson (1840–1902)

U.S. Navy admiral. Born in Palmyra, New York, on February 9, 1840, William Thomas Sampson became an acting midshipman on September 24, 1857. He graduated first in his class from the United States Naval Academy and was promoted to midshipman on June 1, 1861. Sampson began his naval career as an instructor at the academy and was promoted to lieutenant on July 16, 1862.

Although he saw only limited action during the American Civil War, he nearly lost his life while serving on the monitor *Patapsco* in the South Atlantic Blockading Squadron. On January 15, 1865, the monitor struck a large mine or mines off Charleston, South Carolina, and sank in only about 15 seconds, taking down 62 officers and men. Only 5 officers and 38 men were saved, Sampson among them.

After the Civil War, Sampson served on the steam frigate *Colorado* in the European Squadron and was promoted to lieutenant commander on July 15, 1866. During the three decades between the end of the Civil War and the outbreak of the Spanish-American War, Sampson enhanced his reputation as an outstanding officer and a man of considerable intellect. He was again an instructor at the Naval Academy and served in the Bureau of Navigation and in the screw sloop *Congress*. Promoted to commander on August 9, 1874, he was assigned to the Naval Observatory and then had charge of the Naval Torpedo Station at Newport, Rhode Island. On September 9, 1886, he became superintendent of the Naval Academy. Promoted to captain on April 9, 1889, Sampson fitted out the protected cruiser *San Francisco* at the Mare Island Navy Yard and then assumed command of the ship on its commissioning that November. In June 1892 he was assigned as inspector of ordnance at the Washington Navy Yard, and in January 1893 he became chief of the Bureau of Ordnance.

In June 1897 Sampson assumed command of the new battleship *Iowa*. After the battleship *Maine* blew up in Havana Harbor on February 15, 1898, President William McKinley named Sampson to head the naval board charged with investigating the disaster. On March 26, 1898, Sampson was advanced to temporary rear admiral and took command of the North Atlantic Squadron, replacing Rear Admiral Montgomery Sicard, who had taken ill. Sampson's promotion may have planted the seed of his later troubles with Commodore Winfield Scott Schley, who, along with a number of other officers, was senior to Sampson. Evidence suggests that Sampson was not in the best of health at the time, a fact that he apparently managed to conceal from all but those closest to him. He may have suffered from what we now identify as multiple infarct dementia, caused by a succession of small strokes that can reduce the victim's mental acuity but do not affect the personality. This did not affect his strong leadership of the squadron in the Caribbean theater of war.

On April 29, 1898, a week after the U.S. declaration of war on Spain, Spanish rear admiral Pascual Cervera y Topete sailed with his squadron from the Cape Verde Islands to Cuba. Meanwhile, Sampson had put to sea from Key West for Cuba, his flag in the armored cruiser *New York*.

After establishing the blockade of Cuba, Sampson sailed with a small task force for San Juan, Puerto Rico, hoping to locate Cervera. Arriving off that port on May 12, Sampson failed to find Cervera and, following a brief bombardment of San Juan's defenses, returned to Key West, where he arrived on May 18 just after Commodore Schley and his Flying Squadron. Schley was then ordered to Santiago but was dilatory in carrying out that order, not establishing a blockade of that port until May 28. Cervera, who in the meantime had arrived at Santiago, failed to depart while he had the opportunity, and Sampson arrived on June 1 with his own ships and established a strong presence there. With the Spanish squadron now effectively neutralized, Sampson provided support to the landing of Major General William R. Shafter's U.S. V Corps at Daiquirí and Siboney.

Early on the morning of July 3, 1898, Sampson headed east from Santiago in the *New York* for a conference with Shafter. As luck would have it, Cervera chose that time to attempt a breakout. In Sampson's absence, Schley had command of the blockading ships and led the attack on the Spanish ships as they emerged from the sanctuary of Santiago Harbor.

Learning of the battle by means of smoke and signal flags, Sampson headed back at flank speed. But the *New York* did not make it back in time to contribute to the near total destruction of the Spanish squadron. Officially Sampson was credited with the naval victory, which he announced in a cable to Washington as "The fleet under my command offers the nation as a Fourth of July present the whole of Cervera's fleet." It was Schley who received the plaudits in the press, however. Claims and counterclaims over responsibility for the victory led to subsequent controversy and much ill will in the navy.

After the war, Sampson was appointed Cuban commissioner on August 20, 1898. He assumed command of the Atlantic Fleet that December. In October 1899 he took command of the Boston Navy Yard. All the while his health had continued to deteriorate, and he retired on February 9, 1902. Sampson died in Washington, D.C., on May 6, 1902.

SPENCER C. TUCKER

Further Reading

Dawson, Joseph G., III. "William T. Sampson: Progressive Technologist as Naval Commander." In *Admirals of the New Steel Navy: Makers of the American Naval Tradition, 1880–1930,* edited by James C. Bradford, 149–179. Annapolis, MD: Naval Institute Press, 1990.

Dawson, Joseph G., III. "William T. Sampson and Santiago: Blockade, Victory, and Controversy." In *Crucible of Empire: The Spanish-American War and Its Aftermath,* edited by James C. Bradford, 47–68. Annapolis, MD: Naval Institute Press, 1993.

Trask, David F. "The Battle of Santiago." In *Great American Naval Battles,* edited by Jack Sweetman, 198–218. Annapolis, MD: Naval Institute Press, 1998.

---

two days later, is conciliatory but does not address Cuban independence.

April 11, 1898

Background of the Spanish-American War (continued). U.S. president William McKinley asks Congress for a declaration of war against Spain.

April 19, 1898

Background of the Spanish-American War (continued). The U.S. Congress passes a joint resolution regarding Cuba. It recognizes the independence of Cuba, demands the withdrawal of Spanish armed forces from the island, calls on the president to use the U.S. armed forces to carry out these demands, and disclaims any U.S. intention to exercise sovereignty over the island (the Teller Amendment). President William McKinley signs the resolution on April 20.

April 22, 1898

Background of the Spanish-American War (continued). U.S. president William McKinley orders a naval blockade of Cuba. This same morning, U.S. Navy rear admiral William Sampson orders his North Atlantic Squadron from Key West for Cuba to initiate the blockade. The U.S. Navy gunboat *Nashville* fires several shots across the bow of the Spanish merchant ship *Buenaventura* and seizes the ship off Havana in

The U.S. Navy gunboat *Nashville* captures the Spanish merchantman *Buenaventura* off Key West, Florida, on April 22, 1898. Drawing by Carlton T. Chapman. (*Harper's Pictorial History of the War with Spain*, 1899)

the first ship capture of the war. By April 23, the U.S. Navy has established a blockade off Havana, Mariel, Matanzas, Cárdenas, and Cienfuegos.

April 23, 1898

Spanish-American War: Spanish declaration of war on the United States. The Spanish government regards the U.S. congressional resolution signed by President William McKinley and delivered to the Spanish ambassador to the United States on April 20 as a de facto declaration of war. Spain breaks diplomatic relations with the United States on April 21, and its diplomats quit the United States for Canada. Spain mobilizes 80,000 reserve troops and orders 5,000 troops to the Canary Islands. Then on April 23, Spain formally declares war on the United States.

April 25, 1898

Spanish-American War (continued): Formal U.S. declaration of war against Spain and U.S. preparedness. The United States declares war on Spain. The

resolution makes the declaration retroactive to April 21. The United States goes to war with the stated purpose of freeing Cuba. Indeed, the Teller Amendment, which is attached to the joint resolution authorizing the war with Spain, declares that the United States supports Cuban independence and will maintain a presence on the island until it is entirely pacified. The amendment also specifically declares that the United States has no long-term claims of sovereignty or jurisdiction over Cuba.

Although the U.S. Navy is ready for war, the small U.S. Army is not. The army is minuscule by European standards, numbering just 2,143 officers and 26,040 enlisted men. Its largest unit is the infantry regiment, of which there are 25. Many of its units are also poorly trained and are equipped with obsolete equipment. The regular army is immediately increased in size to 65,000 men, while a volunteer force largely drawn from the National Guard of 125,000 men is created for the duration of the conflict. By May 1898, regular and volunteer strength totals 168,929 men; that number rises to 274,717 by August.

April 27, 1898

Spanish-American War (continued): Dewey sails for the Philippines. Commodore George Dewey's U.S. Asiatic Squadron is at Hong Kong when Dewey is informed on April 23, 1898, by the acting British governor of Hong Kong, Major General Wilsone Black, that war has been declared between the United States and Spain. Black issues a proclamation of British neutrality and orders Dewey's ships to leave Hong Kong territorial waters by noon the next day.

Dewey steams to Mirs Bay, an anchorage near Hong Kong but in Chinese waters. There he receives a cablegram from Secretary of the Navy John D. Long ordering him to the Philippines to destroy or capture the Spanish squadron there.

Dewey's squadron consists of the protected cruisers *Olympia* (flagship), *Baltimore*, *Boston*, and *Raleigh*; the gunboats *Concord* and *Petrel*; and the *McCulloch*, a revenue cutter that had been pressed into service. Two colliers accompany the squadron.

George Dewey (1837–1917)

U.S. admiral. Born in Montpelier, Vermont, on December 26, 1837, the son of a prominent physician, George Dewey wanted to go to the U.S. Military Academy, West Point, but ended up attending the U.S. Naval Academy, Annapolis, instead. He graduated in 1858. Promoted to lieutenant in April 1861, during the American Civil War he served aboard the steam frigate *Mississippi* and soon became its executive officer. He took part in the passage of Flag Officer David Farragut's fleet up the Mississippi River to New Orleans on April 24–25, 1862, and in operations against Port Hudson on March 14, 1863. Dewey then served in the North Atlantic Blockading Squadron, and as the executive officer aboard the steam frigate *Colorado,* he took part in operations against Fort Fisher during December 1864–January 1865. Dewey ended the war as a lieutenant commander aboard the steam sloop *Kearsarge* in European waters.

During the next two decades Dewey held a number of assignments. Promoted to commander in 1872, he moved to Washington, D.C., in 1875 and served for seven years on the Lighthouse Board. Dewey returned to sea as captain of the steam sloop *Juniata* in 1882. While in the Mediterranean, he became ill and spent a year in a British hospital on Malta. He did not fully recover and return to duty with the navy until 1884. Promoted to captain in September 1884, he received command of one of the navy's first steel ships, the gunboat *Dolphin,* which was still under construction. Frustrated at the delays in its commissioning, Dewey secured command of the steam sloop *Pensacola,* flagship of the European Squadron, during 1885–1889.

Dewey returned to Washington as chief of the Bureau of Equipment during 1889–1893 and then as president of the Bureau of Inspection and Survey during 1895–1897. On his promotion to commodore in February 1896, he was entitled to command a squadron. Both Dewey and Commodore John A. Howell sought the post of commander of the U.S. Asiatic Squadron. Relations with Spain were deteriorating over Cuba, and should there be war the Philippines would figure prominently in it. With the support of his friend Assistant Secretary of the Navy Theodore Roosevelt, Dewey received the coveted position. He officially took up his command at Nagasaki, Japan, aboard the cruiser *Olympia* in January 1898.

(continued)

(Continued)

When the battleship *Maine* exploded and sank in Havana Harbor on February 15, 1898, Dewey's squadron was on its way to Hong Kong. Dewey had already begun preparations for a possible attack on the Spanish squadron in the Philippines. The United States declared war on Spain on April 25, and three days later under telegraph orders from the Navy Department, Dewey's squadron steamed for the Philippines.

Dewey boldly led his squadron into Manila Bay on the night of April 30, despite the threat from mines. Although a risk, he took this decision to avoid fire from Spanish batteries guarding the entrance to the bay and to catch the Spanish off guard. Dewey insisted that the flagship *Olympia* be the lead warship.

Early the next morning, May 1, Dewey discovered the Spanish squadron of Rear Admiral Patricio Montojo y Paráson anchored off Cavite and commenced operations against it and the shore batteries. In one of the memorable quotes in U.S. Navy history, Dewey told his flag captain Charles V. Gridley, "You may fire when ready, Gridley." In a matter of six hours, Dewey's squadron of four cruisers, two gunboats, and a revenue cutter had reduced the seven smaller Spanish warships to scrap, at a cost of only seven men wounded for the Americans. News of the victory in the Battle of Manila Bay made Dewey a hero in the United States and led to his promotion to rear admiral that same month.

Unable to capture Manila itself because of the lack of U.S. ground troops, Dewey waited for their arrival. His squadron then supported the army's capture of Manila on August 13 and subsequent operations in the Philippines. In recognition of his services, Congress advanced Dewey to admiral of the navy in March 1899. He remains the only U.S. Navy officer to have held that rank.

Dewey returned to the United States on September 26, 1899, and four days later led a victory parade through New York City. In the spring of 1900 he made a brief bid for the presidency but dropped out to become president of the newly formed Navy General Board. Exempted from retirement due to age, Dewey served in this post for 16 years and played an important role in U.S. Navy expansion. He also supported President Theodore Roosevelt's plan for a circumnavigation of the globe by the Great White Fleet during 1907–1909. Dewey then published his autobiography in 1913.

Secretary of War Elihu Root and Secretary of the Navy William Moody established the Joint Army-Navy Board in 1903, and Dewey became its chair, serving on this board and the Navy General Board until his death in Washington, D.C., on January 16, 1917. Intelligent, thorough in his preparations, and a bold commander, Dewey was a natural leader who was greatly respected by those he commanded.

SPENCER C. TUCKER

Further Reading

Dewey, George. *The Autobiography of George Dewey.* 1913; reprint, Annapolis, MD: Naval Institute Press, 1987.

Spector, Ronald. *Admiral of the New Empire: The Life and Career of George Dewey.* Baton Rouge: Louisiana University Press, 1974.

Williams, Vernon L. "George Dewey: Admiral of the Navy." In *Admirals of the New Steel Navy: Makers of the American Naval Tradition, 1880–1930,* edited by James C. Bradford, 222–249. Annapolis, MD: Naval Institute Press, 1990.

Wukovits, John F. "George Dewey: His Father's Son." In *The Great Admirals: Command at Sea, 1587–1945,* edited by Jack Sweetman, 306–325. Annapolis, MD: Naval Institute Press, 1997.

An hour before the squadron sails, former U.S. consul to the Philippines Oscar Williams briefs Dewey and his commanders on board the *Olympia*. Williams confirms that the American squadron is superior to that of the Spanish. He believes that the Spanish squadron will most likely be found in Subic Bay, 30 miles from Manila.

That same afternoon, April 27, the American ships depart Chinese waters.

April 27, 1898

Spanish-American War (continued): First action of the war. Off Matanzas, Cuba, the armored cruiser *New York* (flagship of Rear Admiral William T. Sampson's North Atlantic Squadron), the cruiser *Cincinnati*, and the monitor *Puritan* engage and silence, at no cost to themselves, two Spanish shore batteries that had previously fired on the U.S. Navy gunboat *Foote*.

April 29, 1898

Spanish-American War (continued): Naval engagement off Cienfuegos. This morning U.S. Navy commander Bowman H. McCalla of the unprotected cruiser *Marblehead*, in company with the gunboats *Nashville* and *Eagle*, arrives off Cienfuegos, Cuba, to enforce the U.S. naval blockade. The *Nashville* runs down and captures the Spanish steamer *Argonauto*, transporting mail, munitions, and some Spanish Army officers and men.

The Spanish torpedo-gunboat *Galicia* then appears at the head of the harbor supported by two small gunboats, covered by light shore batteries. The Spanish ships exchange fire with the *Eagle*. With the arrival of the *Marblehead*, the *Galicia* withdraws deeper into the harbor. The only damage in the exchange of fire is from two shells that strike a small village and a Spanish hit on the *Galicia* that inflicts light damage. This skirmish is nevertheless considered the first naval action of the war.

April 29, 1898

Spanish-American War (continued): Cervera's squadron sails from the Cape Verde Islands for the West Indies. Spanish rear admiral Pascual Cervera y Topete's Cádiz Squadron arrives in the Cape Verde

Islands on April 9, 1898. It consists of the armored cruisers *Infanta María Teresa*, *Vizcaya*, *Almirante Oquendo*, and *Cristóbal Colón* and the torpedo boat destroyers *Furor*, *Plutón*, and *Terror*. Cervera holds a captain's council on April 20, and all present disagree with the decision reached in Madrid to order the ships on to West Indies. Cervera sends to Madrid the captains' report as well as his own recommendation that the order be voided, calling the plan a "useless sacrifice." Nonetheless, a majority of a government council, largely composed of naval officers, disagrees, and Cervera is ordered to proceed. He departs on April 29 for Puerto Rico. On May 12, the *Terror* is left behind at Martinique because of mechanical problems. The squadron then stops at Curaçao before arriving at Santiago, Cuba, on May 19.

May 1, 1898

Spanish-American War (continued): Battle of Manila Bay. At daybreak on April 30, 1898, Commodore George Dewey's U.S. Asiatic Squadron makes landfall at Cape Bolineau, Luzon. It consists of four protected cruisers: the *Olympia* (flagship; main battery of 4 8-inch and 10 5-inch guns), *Baltimore* (4 8-inch and 6 6-inch guns), *Boston* (2 8-inch and 6 6-inch guns), and *Raleigh* (1 6-inch and 10 5-inch guns); the gunboats *Concord* (6 6-inch guns) and *Petrel* (4 6-inch guns); and the *McCulloch*, a revenue cutter. There are also two colliers.

Battle of Manila Bay		
Date	May 1, 1898	
Location	Manila Bay, Philippine Islands	
Opponents (*winner)	*United States	Spain
Commander	Commodore George Dewey	Rear Admiral Patricio Montojo y Pasarón
#	Engaged: 4 protected cruisers, 2 gunboats	Engaged: 2 protected cruisers, 5 light cruisers
Casualties	8 wounded	All ships sunk; 167 killed, 214 wounded

 ## Destroyers

Destroyers are relatively small, lightly armed and armored (even unprotected) warships capable of high speed. They were specifically developed to deal with the threat posed to the battle fleet by torpedo boats. First known as the torpedo boat destroyer, later the new ship was called simply a destroyer. The precursor was the Royal Navy *Polyphemus* of 1881. Known as a torpedo ram, it displaced 2,640 tons, was 240 feet in length with a beam of 40 feet, and capable of a speed of 18 knots. It carried a 2-pounder gun and 18 torpedoes for its five torpedo tubes.

To counter the large number of torpedo boats built by the rival French Navy and Russian Navy, in 1898 the Royal Navy contracted for what became known as a torpedo boat destroyer. Early types, however, lacked the speed to hunt down and destroy torpedo boats. That changed with the *Havock* of 1893, generally regarded as the first modern torpedo boat destroyer. Displacing 275 tons, it was 180 feet by 19 feet and was capable of nearly 27 knots. It was armed with a 12-pounder and three 6-pounder guns as well as three 18-inch torpedo tubes.

Each subsequent design registered improvements. The new ships were capable of sustained operations with the battle fleet.

With their excessive vibration, wet conditions, and excessive rolling, destroyers were difficult ships for their crews. Some of these negatives were mitigated in later designs that altered both superstructure and weight displacement; in addition, the new turbine engine made them at 37 knots the fastest ships in the fleet.

The U.S. Navy destroyer *Bainbridge* (DD-1), completed in 1902, began the U.S. Navy numbering system for destroyers. Commissioned on November 24, 1902, it had a raised forecastle and two widely displaced funnels, displaced 630 tons at full load, was 250′3″ in overall length with a beam of 23′5″, and was capable of a speed of 28.4 knots. It had a crew complement of 75 men and was armed with two 3-inch and five 6-pounder guns and two 18-inch torpedo tubes. The last ship in this U.S. Navy numbering system was DD-997, the Spruance-class *Hayler* in 1983.

In 1914 destroyers were the most numerous warships of the world's navies, with Britain operating 221, Germany operating 90, France operating 81, Russia operating 42, and the United States and Japan operating about 50 each. Destroyers assumed the role of torpedo boats in attacking the capital ships of an enemy fleet, but they also were charged with providing perimeter protection for one's own capital ships against enemy destroyers.

During World War I, Allied destroyers provided protection for the vital convoys. With the advent of the submarine, destroyers became the primary antisubmarine vessel. Equipped with depth charges and hydrophones in 1917 and sonar (asdic) in 1918, they proved to be highly effective sub hunters. They also provided gunfire support for amphibious operations.

Destroyers continued in these same roles in World War II, in addition to a new role as antiaircraft platforms. Probably the best known of World War II destroyers were the 150 U.S. Navy Fletcher-class ships. Launched during 1942–1945 and displacing 2,325 tons, they were 376 by 40 feet in size and were capable of a speed of 38 knots. They carried an armament of five single-mount 5-inch guns along with four 4-millimeter (mm) and four 20-mm guns and 10 21-inch torpedo tubes. They had a crew complement of 273 men. Considered some of the best destroyers ever built, the Fletchers played an important role in the Pacific theater.

Destroyers remained in service after the war and fought in the Korean War. In 1957 the United States launched the *Coontz,* the first purpose-built guided-missile destroyer. The Soviet Union followed the American lead in 1958. In August 1964 two U.S. destroyers were the focus of the Gulf of Tonkin Incidents. During the 1982 Falklands War, British destroyers protected troopships from Argentine submarine and air attack.

In the first decade of the 21st century, destroyers are the heaviest surface combatants in general use, with only four navies—those of the United States, the Russian Federation, France, and Peru—still operating cruisers and none having battleships in active service. Modern destroyers, also known as guided-missile destroyers, are equivalent in tonnage but are substantially superior in firepower to World War I–era cruisers.

SPENCER C. TUCKER

Further Reading

George, James L. *History of Warships: From Ancient Times to the Twenty-First Century.* Annapolis, MD: Naval Institute Press, 1998.

Lambert, Andrew, ed. *Steam, Steel & Shellfire: The Steam Warship, 1815–1905.* Annapolis, MD: Naval Institute Press, 1992.

Preston, Anthony. *Destroyers.* Englewood Cliffs, NJ: Prentice Hall, 1977.

Smith, Peter. *Hard Lying: The Birth of the Destroyer, 1893–1913.* Annapolis, MD: Naval Institute Press, 1971.

Tucker, Spencer C. *Handbook of 19th Century Naval Warfare.* Annapolis, MD: Naval Institute Press, 2000.

After a quick search of Subic Bay reveals no trace of the Spanish squadron, Dewey, confident that the Spanish ships are off Manila, orders the squadron to enter Manila Bay on the night of April 30. He ignores the threat of mines and the fortifications guarding the entrance to the bay, selects Boca Grande Channel, and orders his ships to steam through in single file with as few lights as possible. Not until the squadron has passed the El Fraile rock do the Spanish discover the American presence. The two sides then exchange a few shots but without damage. The American ships are now into the bay. Detaching his two supply ships and the *McCulloch,* Dewey proceeds ahead, intending to engage the Spanish after dawn.

The Spanish have some 40 naval vessels in and around Manila, but most are small gunboats. Rear Admiral Patricio Montojo y Pasarón's squadron consists of 7 ships: the large cruisers *Reina Cristina* and the wooden *Castilla* of about 3,000 tons each and the small cruisers *Don Juan de Austria, Don Antonio de Ulloa, Isla de Cuba, Marqués del Duro,* and *Isla de Luzon.* The main battery of the *Reina Cristina* consists of six 4.7-inch guns, while the *Castilla* mounts four 5.9-inch and two 5.7-inch guns. Each of the small cruisers is less than 1,200 tons, and none has more than four 4.7-inch guns in its main battery. Other ships are undergoing repairs. Not only are the Spanish warships greatly inferior in armament to the American ships, but the American crews are better trained.

Montojo had his ships at Subic Bay during April 26–29, but the promised shore batteries were not yet in place, and the harbor entrance had not been mined. The water there is also 40 feet deep. Pessimistic about his chances and reportedly deciding that if his ships are to be sunk he would prefer it to occur in shallower water, Montojo returned them to Manila Bay, his captains concurring in the decision.

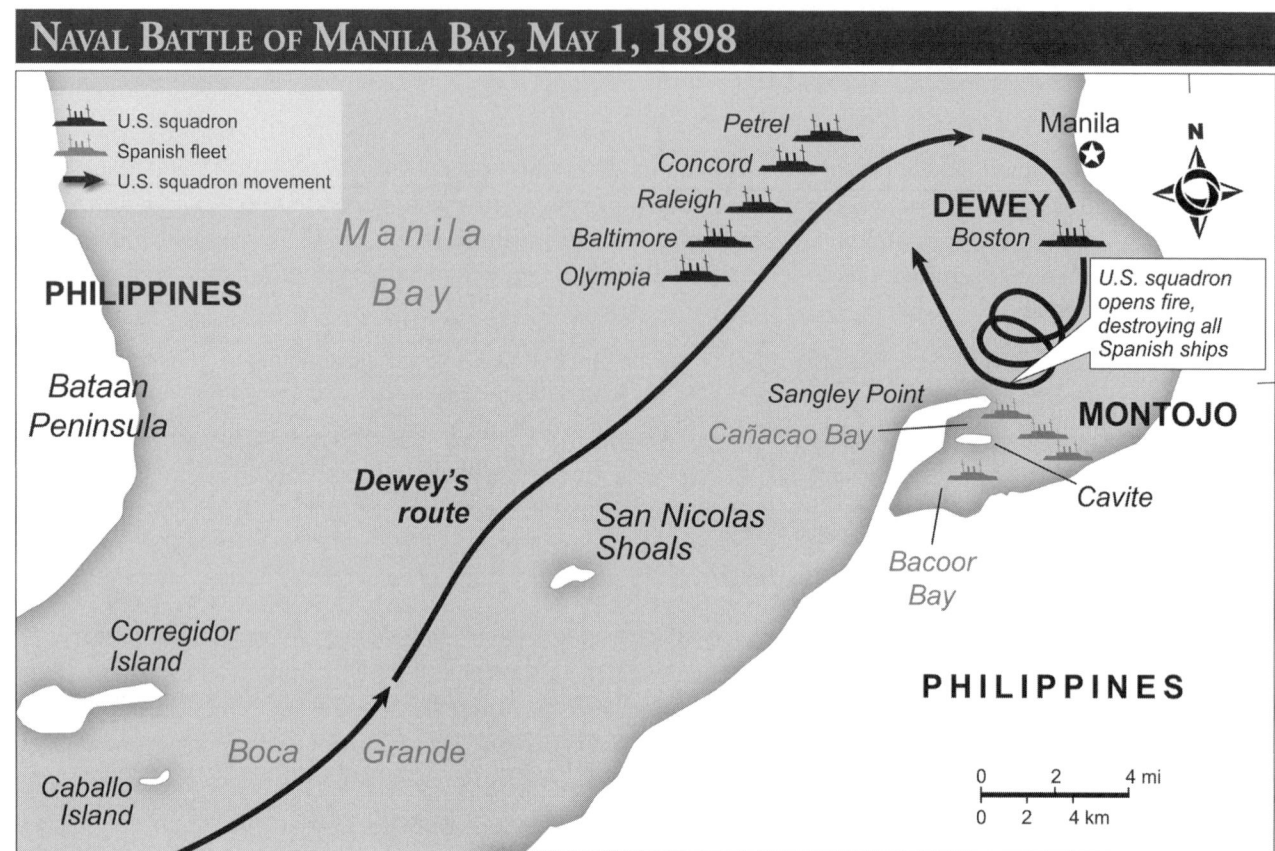

NAVAL BATTLE OF MANILA BAY, MAY 1, 1898

- U.S. squadron
- Spanish fleet
- U.S. squadron movement

Manila Bay

PHILIPPINES

Bataan Peninsula

Petrel
Concord
Raleigh
Baltimore
Olympia

Manila

DEWEY
Boston

U.S. squadron opens fire, destroying all Spanish ships

Sangley Point
Cañacao Bay

MONTOJO

Cavite

Dewey's route

San Nicolas Shoals

Bacoor Bay

PHILIPPINES

Corregidor Island

Boca   Grande

Caballo Island

0   2   4 mi

0   2   4 km

To help offset his weakness in firepower, Montojo anchors his ships in Cañacao Bay, just south of Manila off the fortified naval yard of Cavite in order to be supported by land batteries. The water is only 25 feet deep, and if the ships are sunk or have to be scuttled, their crews will stand a better chance of escape.

Early on May 1, Dewey's ships steam toward Manila. The *Olympia* leads, followed by the *Baltimore*, *Raleigh*, *Petrel*, *Concord*, and *Boston*. With the U.S. ships off Manila a little after 5:00 a.m., the Spanish shore batteries open up with wildly inaccurate fire that inflicts no damage. The *Boston* and *Concord* return fire. Dewey then turns his ships toward the Spanish squadron. As the American ships advance in single line, two Spanish mines explode at some distance from the *Olympia* but without effect. Closing to about 5,000 yards of the Spanish line, at 5:40 Dewey turns to his flag captain Charles Gridley of the *Olympia* and says, "You may fire when you are ready, Gridley."

The ships of the American squadron then close to about 3,000 yards and turn to the west, running parallel back and forth along the Spanish line and pounding it with their fire. The 150-pound shells fired by the 8-inch guns on the U.S. cruisers exact the most damage. The Spanish ships and shore batteries respond but fail to inflict significant damage. Dewey then calls a halt to assess damage and the status of ammunition stocks, also ordering breakfast served to the crews.

At 11:16 a.m. the American ships stand in again to complete their work of destruction. Within little more than an hour, they have sunk the remaining Spanish warships and secured the surrender of the naval station at Cavite. Dewey sends a message to the Spanish commander at Manila that if the shore batteries do not cease fire, he will shell the city and destroy it. Shortly thereafter, Manila's guns fall silent.

The Spanish lose 167 dead and 214 wounded, all but 10 aboard the ships. The Americans later salvage

Illustration of the Battle of Manila Bay, May 1, 1898. The U.S. Navy's destruction of the Spanish squadron off Manila made possible the U.S. conquest of the Philippines. (Library of Congress)

and press into service three of the Spanish ships. The Americans suffer only 8 wounded. Rarely has a victory been more cheaply obtained. Dewey takes Cavite and blockades the city of Manila while awaiting troops to take and occupy it.

May 2, 1898
Spanish-American War (continued). In the Philippines near Manila, the U.S. Navy gunboat *Petrel* lands men to take possession of the Cavite naval base.

May 2, 1898
Spanish-American War (continued). U.S. president William McKinley authorizes the dispatch of ground troops to the Philippine Islands. They will be sent in

several convoys from the West Coast, principally San Francisco, during succeeding weeks.

May 8, 1898
Spanish-American War (continued). Commanding general of the U.S. Army major general Nelson A. Miles begins organizing 70,000 regular and volunteer troops for a U.S. military descent upon Cuba.

May 11, 1898
Spanish-American War (continued): Engagement off Cienfuegos, Cuba. On the morning of April 29, 1898, Commander Bowman H. McCalla of the unprotected cruiser *Marblehead* returns to Cienfuegos with the revenue cutter *Windom* and collier *Saturn* to attempt

a cable-cutting operation near the harbor entrance. With the *Marblehead* and the patrol vessel *Nashville* close to shore providing covering fire, 52 men led by Lieutenant Cameron M. Winslow in two steam and two sailing launches close on the shore.

Winslow's men locate two large cables and one small one. They drag up the two large cables and cut both. Spanish small-arms fire and fire from the shore increase as the operation proceeds, and the Americans thus do not attempt to cut the small cable, which provides telegraphic communication with Jamaica and continues to operate throughout the war. The lighthouse at Cienfuegos, also used by the Spanish for a firing position, is destroyed by gunfire from the two supporting warships, joined by the *Windom*.

In the operation, three Americans are killed and several more are wounded. Spanish losses are unknown but are believed to have been higher. The men in the launches who took part in the actual cable cutting are each awarded the Medal of Honor.

May 11, 1898

Spanish-American War (continued): Naval engagement off Cárdenas. On this date the U.S. Navy gunboats *Wilmington* and *Macias*, the torpedo boat *Winslow*, and the revenue cutter *Hudson* arrive off Cárdenas, Cuba. There they duel with the Spanish shore batteries, the gunboats *Alerta* and *Ligera*, and the armed tug *Antonio López*. The *Winslow* is seriously damaged by fire from a Spanish shore battery and has to be towed to sea by the *Hudson*. U.S. casualties aboard the *Winslow* are five dead and three wounded. Among the dead is Ensign Worth Bagley, the only U.S. naval officer killed in the war. On the Spanish side, two warships are damaged, part of the town of Cárdenas is set on fire, and seven people are killed.

May 12, 1898

Spanish-American War (continued): U.S. Navy bombardment of San Juan. U.S. Navy rear admiral William T. Sampson sails from Havana, Cuba, to San Juan with his North American Squadron in search of Spanish rear admiral Pascual Cervera y Topete's Cádiz Squadron, known to be at sea. Sampson arrives

off San Juan, Puerto Rico, in the early morning of May 12. Cervera's ships are not there, but at 5:20 a.m. Sampson commences a bombardment of Spanish military positions. The American warships involved are the cruiser *Detroit*, followed by the battleships *Iowa, Indiana*, and *New York;* the double-turreted monitors *Amphitrite* and *Terror;* and the unprotected cruiser *Montgomery*.

In three bombardment circuits before breaking off the engagement at 7:45 a.m., the American warships fire a total of 1,360 shells. The Spanish shore batteries fire only 441 shells in reply. American gunnery is abysmal, with only some 20 percent of shells hitting the general target area, and many of these failing to explode. The U.S. ships suffer some minor damage, with 1 man killed and 7 wounded. Spanish casualties are 13 killed and perhaps 100 wounded, most of these civilians.

The shelling is controversial, for international law clearly requires that noncombatants be warned before such an event, but Sampson subsequently claims that his ships were firing not on the city but instead on its military installations, and thus no prior notification was required. The shelling makes little sense, however. Sampson later justifies it as a means to ascertain Spanish military "positions and strength." Spanish governor-general of Puerto Rico Manuel Macías y Casado and the island press trumpet the exchange of fire as the first Spanish victory of the war. Sampson, meanwhile, takes his squadron first to Haiti and then on to Key West, Florida, arriving there on May 18.

May 19, 1898

Spanish-American War (continued): Arrival of Cervera's squadron at Santiago, Cuba. On April 29, Spanish rear admiral Pascual Cervera y Topete had sailed from the Cape Verde Islands with his squadron of four cruisers and three torpedo boat destroyers. Although forced to leave one of the latter behind at Martinique because of mechanical problems, Cervera successfully evades efforts by U.S. rear admiral William T. Sampson's North Atlantic Squadron to locate his ships and engage them at sea. Cervera arrives at Santiago, Cuba, on May 19.

May 24, 1898

Spanish-American War (continued): Aguinaldo establishes a provisional government in the Philippines. Filipino revolutionary General Emilio Aguinaldo y Famy arrives back in the Philippines on May 19, 1898, in the U.S. revenue cutter *McCulloch*. He then meets with U.S. rear admiral George Dewey, who provides both arms and ammunition with which to fight the Spanish. Establishing his headquarters at Malolos 30 miles north of Manila, on May 24 Aguinaldo announces the formation of a provisional government.

May 25, 1898

Spanish-American War (continued). The first U.S. troopships depart San Francisco for Manila in the Philippine Islands. They carry the 2,500 men of Brigadier General Thomas M. Anderson's 2nd Division, the vanguard of Major General Wesley Merritt's VIII Corps.

May 29, 1898

Spanish-American War (continued): U.S. Flying Squadron arrives off Santiago de Cuba. By May 20, U.S. secretary of the navy John Davis Long knows that Spanish rear admiral Pascual Cervera y Topete had sailed from the Cape Verde Islands with his squadron of cruisers and torpedo boat destroyers. Long orders Commodore Winfield Scott Schley and his Flying Squadron, formed to protect the U.S. East Coast from Spanish attack, to proceed to Santiago and there blockade Cervera. Schley receives the orders on May 24.

Not convinced that Cervera is at Santiago, Schley dithers off Cienfuegos, Cuba, before steaming slowly toward Santiago. It is fortunate for the Americans that Cervera does not sortie in the interval, for Schley arrives off Santiago only on May 26. There the Flying Squadron consists of the cruiser *Brooklyn* (flagship); the battleships *Iowa*, *Massachusetts*, and *Texas*; the protected cruiser *Marblehead*; the auxiliary warships *Vixen* and *Hawk*; and the collier *Merrimac*. Other warships soon join.

May 31, 1898

Spanish-American War (continued): Naval skirmish at Santiago, Cuba. On this day, Commodore Winfield Scott Schley approaches the port of Santiago, Cuba, with ships of his Flying Squadron to take under fire the ships of Spanish rear admiral Pascual Cervera y Topete's squadron in the harbor. Schley has the battleships *Massachusetts* (temporary flag) and *Iowa* and the protected cruiser *New Orleans*. Approaching the harbor entrance, he takes under fire the cruiser *Cristóbal Colón*, which has come down from the inner harbor. The American warships, firing from a range of 8,000–9,000 yards while steaming at 9–10 knots, inflict no damage on either the Spanish ship or the Cuban shore fortifications.

June 1, 1898

Spanish-American War (continued). U.S. rear admiral William T. Sampson arrives off the port of Santiago, Cuba, adding the ships of his North Atlantic Squadron to those of Commodore Winfield Scott Schley's Flying Squadron, already there. Together these two units form the North Atlantic Fleet. The U.S. blockading warships include five battleships, two armored cruisers, and a number of smaller cruisers and auxiliaries.

June 3, 1898

Spanish-American War (continued): U.S. effort to block the mouth of the Santiago Bay channel. Rear Admiral William T. Sampson, commander of the North Atlantic Fleet, authorizes an attempt to position and sink a ship in the channel to Santiago Bay to prevent the departure of Rear Admiral Pascual Cervera y Topete's squadron from Santiago. Lieutenant Richmond Hobson leads a volunteer crew of six men (one other man stows away) in the collier *Merrimac* for what is regarded as a virtual suicide mission.

Early on June 3, 1898, the *Merrimac* gets under way, towing a lifeboat in which the crew members are to escape. With his ship hit by Spanish torpedoes and shore fire, Hobson scuttles it with explosive charges inside the harbor entrance but fails to block the channel. All involved are taken prisoner. Later they are awarded the Medal of Honor.

June 9, 1898

Spanish-American War (continued): U.S. marines land at Guantánamo Bay. Some 45 miles east of

June 9, 1898

NAVAL BLOCKADE OF SANTIAGO, 1898

N

Santiago

20°N

Santiago Bay

C U B A

Cayo Ratón

Punta Gorda Battery

Cayo Smith

USS *Merrimac*

Lower Socapa Battery

Estrella Battery

Upper Socapa Battery

Morro Castle

Morro Battery

San Juan R.

Caribbean Sea

Sunken ship
Mine (electrical)
Battery

0   1/2   1 mi
0   1/2   1 km

76°W

Santiago de Cuba, Guantánamo is situated on one of several well-protected bays on the Cuban southeastern coast. This city of some 8,000 people has a Spanish garrison of 5,592 men, commanded by General Félix Pareja Mesa. Pareja has his men build extensive defenses around the town.

On June 9 the auxiliary cruisers *Marblehead* and *Yankee,* under Commander Bowman H. McCalla, enter Guantánamo Bay, and the next day they bombard Spanish strong points guarding the harbor entrance. A few hours later, 21 officers and 615 men of the 1st Marine Battalion, commanded by Lieutenant Colonel Robert W. Huntington, and 4 attached sailors begin the U.S. invasion of Cuba when they come ashore on the east side of the outer harbor.

June 11–17, 1898

Spanish-American War (continued): Battle of Guantánamo. On June 9, 1898, the U.S. Marine Battalion of 636 officers and men commanded by Lieutenant Colonel Robert W. Huntington came ashore at Guantánamo, Cuba, about 45 miles east of Santiago de Cuba. In addition to small arms, the marines have a machine gun and a battery of four 3-inch rifled guns. Supported by warships offshore, including the battleship *Oregon,* the marines advance to a nearby hill and there establish Camp McCalla. When the Spanish fire on their camp on June 11, the first land battle of the war begins. On June 12, 60 Cuban insurgents join the marines. In three days of fighting the marines sustain 3 dead and 3 wounded;

During the first land battle of the Spanish-American War, U.S. marines raise the American flag at Guantánamo, Cuba, on June 12, 1898. (Library of Congress)

Quick-Firing Naval Gun

The development of relatively small caliber (4- to 6-inch) quick-firing guns was of great importance to naval warfare at the end of the 19th century. All navies utilized machine guns, but they were of limited range and effectiveness. The quick-firing gun was a larger-caliber weapon specifically developed to deal with the threat of torpedo boat attacks and to be able to riddle the unprotected portions of ships.

The quick-firing gun operated on the principle of fixed ammunition, cartridge cases utilized in small arms that contained propellent, primer, and projectile. Fixed ammunition had the advantages of ease and rapidity of loading, protection of the powder charge, reducing erosion on the chamber of the gun, and sealing the breech. Quick-firing guns had sliding breechblocks and a recoil mechanism that rapidly returned the gun into firing position with a minimum of displacement. Besides their rapid rate of fire, such guns required smaller crews—only three men each for the lesser calibers.

The quick-firing gun resulted from an 1881 Royal Navy advertisement for a gun to fire 12 aimed shots a minute. The 47-millimeter (mm) revolving Hotchkiss gun, which fired a 2.37-pound high-explosive shell out to a range of 4,000 yards, was subsequently adopted by several major navies. The 53-mm Hotchkiss fired a 3.5-pound shell out to 5,500 yards but failed to achieve the popularity of the smaller model.

In 1886, 57-mm (2.24-inch) 6-pounder single-barrel guns by Hotchkiss and Nordenfelt were introduced in Britain. Later the quick-firing gun was made larger to deal with armored vessels. A 4.7-inch quick-firing gun was tested and proven successful on the cruiser *Piemonte*, constructed in Britain for Italy in 1887. By the end of the decade, Hotchkiss had built a 33-pounder and had a design for a 55-pounder; Armstrong had 4.72-inch, 5.5-inch, and even 6-inch rapid-fire guns. Such larger quick-firing guns soon became standard secondary armament on British battleships.

Because of the short battle ranges that prevailed in prerangefinder days, the quick-firing 6-inch gun could easily riddle the unarmored sections of the old battleships. Henceforth to use wood as material for a ship's superstructure was to invite disaster, as the Chinese learned during their war with Japan in 1894.

SPENCER C. TUCKER

Further Reading

Brodie, Bernard. *Sea Power in the Machine Age.* Princeton, NJ: Princeton University Press, 1941.

Hogg, Ian, and John Batchelor. *Naval Gun.* Poole, Dorset, UK: Blandford, 1975.

Lambert, Andrew, ed. *Steam, Steel & Shellfire: The Steam Warship, 1815–1905.* Annapolis, MD: Naval Institute Press, 1992.

Tucker, Spencer C. *Handbook of 19th Century Naval Warfare.* Annapolis, MD: Naval Institute Press, 2000.

the Spanish suffer some 60 casualties, including 20 prisoners.

Following the Battle of Cuzco Hill and U.S. naval gunfire support, by June 15 the Spanish have been driven from the eastern coast of the lower bay. Huntington then orders an attack on a well supplying the Spanish with water. Supported by gunfire from

the U.S. Navy gunboat *Dolphin*, Huntington's men destroy the well and take 20 Spanish soldiers prisoner.

In the meantime, the Spanish gunboat *Sandoval*, protected by a minefield, ferries men and supplies across the bay. To counter this and to destroy a small Spanish fort, Rear Admiral William T. Sampson dispatches the battleship *Texas* to join the *Marblehead* and the gunboat *Suwanee* to shell the Spanish shore positions on June 15. In an hour of shelling, the ships silence the fort. Fighting essentially ends by June 17, with a total cost to the marines of 6 dead and 16 wounded. Once the mines are removed, Guantánamo Bay becomes an anchorage for coaling and resupply operations and a staging point for the future invasion of Puerto Rico.

June 12, 1898

Spanish-American War (continued). At Malolos 30 miles north of Manila, an assembly of Filipino nationalists proclaims the establishment of an independent Philippine Republic. On June 23, Emilio Aguinaldo y Famy forms a new government with himself as president, holding that post until April 1, 1901.

June 14, 1898

Spanish-American War (continued). Using its 15-inch dynamite guns, the U.S. Navy dynamite cruiser *Vesuvius* shells Morro Castle, Cuba, on the eastern side of the entrance to the harbor of Santiago de Cuba but without significant effect. Because the Spanish coastal defense guns greatly outrange its own pneumatic launch tubes, the *Vesuvius* is employed only at night. On three separate occasions the *Vesuvius* will lob three projectiles in the direction of the entrance to Santiago Harbor and then speed away. Accuracy is understandably poor. There is no evidence for the American claim that these bombardments have "great psychological effect."

June 14, 1898

Spanish-American War (continued). Escorted by U.S. Navy warships army Major General William Shafter sails from Tampa, Florida, for Cuba with his V Corps expeditionary force of 16,888 men, a combination of regulars (15 regiments) and volunteers (3 regiments).

June 16, 1898

Spanish-American War (continued). Spanish rear admiral Manuel de la Cámara y Libermoore departs Cádiz, Spain, with his squadron, bound for the Suez Canal with the ultimate destination of the Philippine Islands. Cámara's squadron consists of the battleship

Pelayo; the armored cruiser *Emperador Carlos V;* the unprotected cruisers *Patriota* and *Rápido;* the torpedo boat destroyers *Audaz, Proserpina,* and *Osado* (which are under orders to return to Spain when the squadron reaches the Suez Canal); the transports *Buenos Aires* and *Isla de Panay* (lifting a total of 4,000 troops); and four colliers carrying 20,000 tons of coal. Informed of the squadron's formation by intelligence operatives in Spain, in an effort to force the squadron's recall the U.S. Navy establishes the Eastern Squadron and also commences a disinformation campaign to the effect that U.S. warships will attack the coasts of Spain.

The Spanish squadron arrives off Port Said, Egypt, on June 26. The British government, however, has instructed authorities in Egypt, which is under British control, to pursue a policy of strict neutrality and not to allow coaling on the grounds that the squadron has sufficient coal to allow it to return to its home port. Unaware of the British decision, Ethelbert Watts, deputy U.S. consul general in Cairo, secures a lien on all coal available at Suez. On June 29, Cámara is informed that he cannot coal in Egyptian territorial waters and will have to depart Port Said in 24 hours.

Cámara's squadron passes through the Suez Canal during July 5–6 and proceeds into the Red Sea. Following the Spanish defeat in the naval battle at Santiago Bay on July 3, however, on July 7 Madrid recalls Cámara and his squadron to Spain with all possible speed so that it might protect the Spanish coasts against a possible U.S. naval attack. The squadron returns to Cartagena on July 23 and then makes its way back to Cádiz.

June 20, 1898

Spanish-American War (continued): U.S. seizure of Guam. Escorting troopships en route to the Philippines and acting under orders opened only when at sea, U.S. Navy captain Henry Glass of the cruiser *Charleston* arrives at Agana, the capital of Guam, on June 20, 1898, along with the troopships *City of Peking, City of Sydney,* and *Australia.* The *Charleston* lobs 13 shells at the fort there. There is no return fire, and many inhabitants assume that the ship is merely firing a salute. Spanish governor Juan Marina has received no mail or other communication from

 **Dynamite Gun**

The dynamite gun utilized compressed air for launching its projectile. In 1882 D. M. Mefford in the United States patented a compressed-air gun "for discharging projectiles filled with dynamite or other detonating powders." Hoping to provide a less jarring initial shock for the projectile to enable it to have a dynamite filler, in 1884 Mefford demonstrated a 2-inch-caliber gun made from brass tubing. It fired a 5-pound solid shot for half a mile, where it penetrated 26 inches into a concrete target. Mefford believed that some redesign of the gun was necessary, but before he could do this, G. H. Reynolds patented a design taken from Mefford's work but sufficiently different to avoid patent infringement. U.S. Army lieutenant E. L. Zalinski, present at the Mefford trial, resigned from the service and teamed up with Reynolds to form the Pneumatic Dynamite Gun Company.

Eventually the company produced a 15-inch-caliber smoothbore gun that fired a variety of dynamite-filled projectiles, from a 12-inch of 966 pounds to an 8-inch of 298 pounds. The projectiles had fins to aid in stability in flight, and the smaller ones had wooden sleeves to bring them up to the gun caliber.

The U.S. government purchased a number of these guns for coast defense purposes, and the navy fitted three 15-inch dynamite guns aboard the so-called dynamite cruiser *Vesuvius,* authorized in 1886 and completed in 1890. Mounted at fixed angle on the fore deck, its dynamite guns were aimed by turning the ship; range was regulated by the amount of air pressure on the shell. All the necessary compressing equipment left little room for anything else.

The dynamite gun's chief failing was its relatively short range. Advances in slower-burning powder that produced longer pressure on the projectile quickly brought its eclipse. The only use of this weapon in battle came during the Spanish-American War of 1898, when the *Vesuvius* shelled Morro Castle, Cuba, without significant effect.

In 1897 a Zalinksi dynamite gun was also mounted on the first American submarine, the *Holland* (SS-1). It was removed in 1900. The government also purchased 16 Sims-Dudley fieldpieces for use by the army, one of which saw service—with mixed results—during the Siege of Santiago in the Spanish-American War. Its chief advantage seems to be that it did not give away the firing location. During 1894–1901, the U.S. Army also purchased several 15-inch dynamite guns to be used as coastal artillery pieces. These had a range of 2,000–5,000 yards, depending on the weight of the projectile (from 50 to 500 pounds). The equipment to operate the guns, including the steam boiler, compressor, and other equipment, weighed more than 200 tons. The batteries were scrapped in 1904.

SPENCER C. TUCKER

Further Reading

Gardiner, Robert, ed. *Conway's All the World's Fighting Ships, 1860–1905.* Annapolis, MD: Naval Institute Press, 1979.

Hogg, Ian, and John Batchelor. *Naval Gun.* Poole, Dorset, UK: Blandford, 1978.

Madrid since April 9 and is thus unaware of the war. Informed of the situation, Marina promptly surrenders, and a small U.S. garrison takes possession of the island. The acquisition of Guam is confirmed in the Treaty of Paris ending the war.

June 22, 1898
Spanish-American War (continued): U.S. landing at Daiquiri. On June 22, 1898, Major General William R. Shafter's V Corps begins coming ashore at Daiquiri on the southeast coast of Cuba, about 16 miles east of Santiago. Supported by U.S. warships, that day in a chaotic operation some 6,000 men come ashore. In all, Shafter commands 16,888 men. Spanish lieutenant general Arsenio Linares y Pomba commands the Santiago area. Despite having some 12,000 men in the immediate vicinity, Linares allows the U.S. landings to occur largely unopposed. Even a small Spanish force might have inflicted significant casualties.

Following the initial landing, on June 23 Shafter sends one of his divisions to secure Siboney, which proves to be as deserted as Daiquiri. Seven miles closer to Santiago, Siboney becomes Shafter's headquarters for the assault on Santiago.

June 22, 1898
Spanish-American War (continued). Arriving off San Juan, Puerto Rico, to establish the blockade there, the U.S. Navy auxiliary cruiser *St. Paul*, commanded by Captain Charles D. Sigsbee, engages and damages the Spanish cruiser *Terror*.

June 24, 1898
Spanish-American War (continued): Battle of Las Guásimas. Following the landing of Major General William R. Shafter's V Corps at Daiquirí beginning on June 22, Brigadier General Henry Ware Lawton's division moves toward Siboney in order to repel any Spanish attack down El Camino Real (the Royal Road). When Lawton reports that Siboney is abandoned, Shafter orders the troops there to advance toward Santiago. This order is not addressed specifically to Lawton but instead goes to the senior officer present, Major General Joseph "Fighting Joe" Wheeler, the ex-Confederate general appointed by President William McKinley who commands the expeditionary force's lone cavalry division.

Wheeler seeks to exploit what appears to be a golden opportunity. Proceeding with a small detachment of U.S. soldiers and Cuban guerrillas, Wheeler discovers that the Spanish troops who had evacuated Siboney are digging in along a high ridge at Las Guásimas, three miles from Siboney along the El Camino Real to Santiago. Wheeler prepares an attack for the next day. Angry at being upstaged, Lawton attempts to inform Shafter and have the attack called off, but the commanding general is still aboard ship and cannot be contacted in time.

Wheeler is apparently aware through Cuban revolutionaries commanded by General Demetrio Castillo that General Arsenio Linares, Spanish commander at Santiago, fearful that the troops at Las Guásimas might be cut off, has ordered them to retire to Santiago. Wheeler has Brigadier General Samuel B. M. Young's brigade of the U.S. 1st and 10th Regular Cavalry Regiments and the U.S. 1st Volunteer Cavalry (better known as the Rough Riders), together with a four-gun battery of mountain fieldpieces. Cuban General Castillo promises some 800 revolutionaries to support the attack, but they never materialize.

Young's troops reach Las Guásimas at 5:40 a.m. on June 24. At 8:00 a.m. Young's fieldpieces open up, but they are soon silenced and forced to withdraw as a result of effective long-range Spanish rifle fire. The attack proceeds without artillery support. Young divides his brigade into two columns. The 1st and 10th Regular Cavalry Regiments are under his personal command on the right flank, while the Rough Riders, under Colonel Leonard Wood and Lieutenant Colonel Theodore Roosevelt, are on the left.

The Spanish line is strong. Brigadier General Antero Rubín Homet commands some 1,500 men and two guns against only 1,000 Americans. The Spanish riflemen exact a considerable toll with their Mauser rifles, which have smokeless powder cartridges that make their positions difficult to locate. Wood directs Roosevelt to take three companies of the Rough Riders and work around behind the Spanish position. Supported by fire from the other two regiments in Young's brigade, the Rough Riders

Smokeless Gunpowder

The standard propellent for firearms, large and small, from its introduction into Europe in the 13th century up to the late 19th century was black powder. Its principal liabilities were the residue it produced on burning (known as fouling), which necessitated considerable windage (the difference between the diameters of the bore and the projectile) and the dense cloud of smoke it gave off on firing. The latter immediately revealed the weapon's location on the battlefield. After a half dozen shots, the smoke also obscured observation of the target. With the development of rapid-firing firearms and artillery, this became a serious liability.

Attempts were made to develop a substitute for black powder, especially after the mid-19th century. In 1846 the French government appointed a commission to report on the feasibility of using nitrated cotton, which was found to burn without smoke and might be suitable for small-arms use. In 1884 French chemist Paul Vielle produced a successful nitrocellulose powder for small arms. His next type, which came to be designated Poudre B, was the first successful smokeless powder adopted by any nation. Weapons utilizing it also had a much higher velocity than those with ordinary gunpowder.

Similar experiments were carried out by Alfred Nobel in Sweden with what came to be known as ballistite, a compound of nitroglycerine and nitrocellulose. Nobel employed camphor to harden the powder grains. The British were aware of Nobel's work and sought to develop a powder using nitroglycerine and acetone as a solvent for guncotton but without using camphor. British scientists used petroleum jelly to help with stabilizing and antifouling. The British powder, formed in pale brown stands, came to be called cordite. The chief problem with cordite was a more rapid erosion of the weapon's bore. These new powders also proved less dangerous in bulk than the old black powder. In the United States, in 1890 a patent for smokeless powder was obtained by Hudson Maxim.

Smokeless powder proved its worth in the Boer War (1899–1902). Using it in new German Krupp artillery and long-range Mauser rifles, the Boers were able to open fire at long range on the British positions without revealing their own. This was also the case during the Spanish-American War when U.S. volunteer troops, many of them armed with the old single-shot Trapdoor Springfield with black powder cartridges, came up against dug-in Spanish troops equipped with the 1893 Mauser bolt-action rifle with smokeless powder cartridges. Smokeless powder greatly influenced tactics and led to renewed interest in camouflage.

SPENCER C. TUCKER

Further Reading

Blair, Claude, ed. *Pollard's History of Firearms*. New York: Macmillan, 1983.
Cocroft, Wayne. *Dangerous Energy: The Archaeology of Gunpowder*. London: English Heritage Publications, 2000.
Kelly, Jack. *Gunpowder: Alchemy, Bombards, and Pyrotechnics; The History of the Explosive That Changed the World*. New York: Basic Books, 2004.
Partington, James Riddick. *A History of Greek Fire and Gunpowder*. Baltimore: Johns Hopkins University Press, 1998.

advance. Roosevelt commands on the left, Wood controls the center, and Wheeler, having arrived on the scene, takes personal charge on the right.

Following two hours of combat, General Rubín, in accordance with his orders, halts the action and effects a clean withdrawal to Santiago. Young's command incurs 16 dead and 52 wounded; Spanish casualties are 10 killed and 25 wounded.

June 28, 1898

Spanish-American War (continued). U.S. president William McKinley extends the blockade to all of Cuba and San Juan, Puerto Rico.

June 28, 1898

Spanish-American War (continued). Off San Juan, Puerto Rico, the U.S. Navy auxiliary cruiser *St. Paul,* under Commander William H. Emory and manned by the Michigan Naval Militia, intercepts the Spanish transport *Antonio Lopez* laden with supplies for the island's garrison. Despite efforts by the Spanish cruisers *Isabel II* and *Alfonso XIII* and a torpedo boat to protect the transport's arrival, the *St. Paul* is able to drive the *Antonio Lopez* onto a reef and destroy it by some 200 rounds from its 5-inch guns, but the Spaniards later salvage much of the cargo, including a dozen or so large guns.

June 30, 1898

Spanish-American War (continued): First U.S. troops disembark in the Philippines. On May 25, 1898, the first 2,500 troops of U.S. major general Wesley Merritt's VIII Corps arrive by ship from San Francisco at Manila Bay in the Philippines and come ashore at Cavite beginning on June 30. By the end of July all of Merritt's 10,800 men are on hand, including the general himself.

July 1, 1898

Spanish-American War (continued): Battles of San Juan Ridge and El Caney. U.S. V Corps commander Major General William R. Shafter and North Atlantic Fleet commander Rear Admiral William T. Sampson cannot agree on a plan to attack the city of Santiago and destroy Rear Admiral Pascual

Cervera y Topete's Spanish squadron there. Although Spain has some 200,000 troops in Cuba, fewer than 35,000 are in the Santiago area, and the garrison defending the city numbers only 13,000. Spanish lieutenant general Arsenio Linares y Pomba, commanding the Santiago area, makes no effort to concentrate his forces to meet the Americans.

After U.S. forces defeat the Spaniards in the Battle of Las Guásimas on June 24, 1898, Shafter moves to take the high ground east of Santiago known as San Juan Heights (Ridge), including the prominent points of San Juan Hill and Kettle Hill. If U.S. forces can control this terrain, they will control access to Santiago.

Shafter's plan calls for Brigadier General Jacob Ford Kent's division to attack San Juan Hill while Brigadier General Samuel Sumner's dismounted cavalry assaults nearby Kettle Hill. At the same time, Brigadier General Henry Lawton's division will take nearby El Caney. Shafter expects the latter operation to take about two hours, which will allow Lawton's division to rejoin the others and take part in the general attack on the San Juan Heights. As it turns out, Lawton is caught up in a daylong fight and thus is unable to participate in the San Juan Ridge attack.

Following a morning artillery duel on July 1, 1898, in which the more modern Spanish guns soon silence those of the Americans, the ground assault opens at 1:00 p.m. American elan, leadership, and superior numbers overcome Spanish firepower. In the attack, Lieutenant Colonel Theodore Roosevelt wins renown for leading the dismounted 1st Volunteer Cavalry Regiment (the Rough Riders) up Kettle Hill. In the battle

Battles of San Juan Ridge and El Caney		
Date	July 1, 1898	
Location	Near Santiago, Cuba	
Opponents (*winner)	*United States	Spain
Commander	Major General William R. Shafter	Lieutenant General Arsenio Linares y Pomba
#	15,000	13,000
Casualties	1,572 killed or wounded	850 killed or wounded

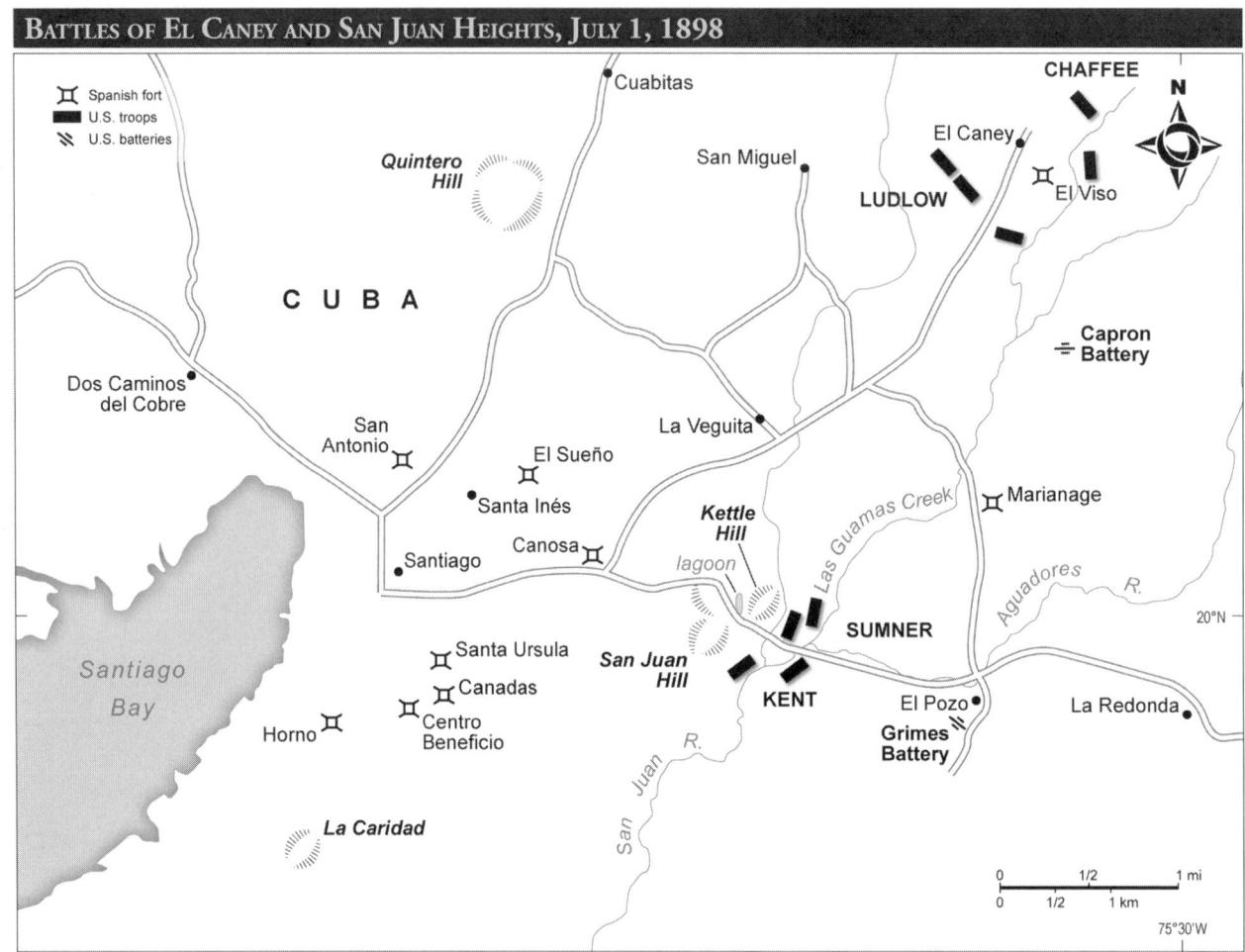

BATTLES OF EL CANEY AND SAN JUAN HEIGHTS, JULY 1, 1898

Naval Battle of Santiago de Cuba		
Date	July 3, 1898	
Location	Santiago de Cuba	
Opponents (*winner)	*United States	Spain
Commander	Rear Admiral William T. Sampson; Captain Winfield Scott Schley	Rear Admiral Pascual Cervera y Topete
#	4 battleships, 1 armored cruiser, 3 auxiliary cruisers	4 armored cruisers, 2 torpedo boat destroyers
Casualties	1 killed, 10 wounded	323 killed, 151 wounded; all ships sunk or scuttled

for San Juan Ridge and El Caney, the Americans lose 1,572 killed or wounded; Spanish losses are 850.

July 3, 1898

Spanish-American War (continued): Battle of Santiago de Cuba. With the American land forces closing on Santiago from the east, Madrid orders Rear Admiral Pascual Cervera y Topete to sortie from Santiago with his squadron of the armored cruisers *Infanta María Teresa, Vizcaya, Almirante Oquendo,* and *Cristóbal Colón* and the torpedo boat destroyers *Furor* and *Plutón.* At 9:35 a.m. on July 3, 1898, the Spanish ships begin exiting the channel. The cruisers lead, followed by the torpedo boat destroyers.

The powerful U.S. Navy blockading squadron off Santiago consists of the battleships *Indiana, Iowa, Oregon,* and *Texas;* the armored cruiser *Brooklyn;* and

LAND BATTLE OF SANTIAGO, JULY 1–17, 1898

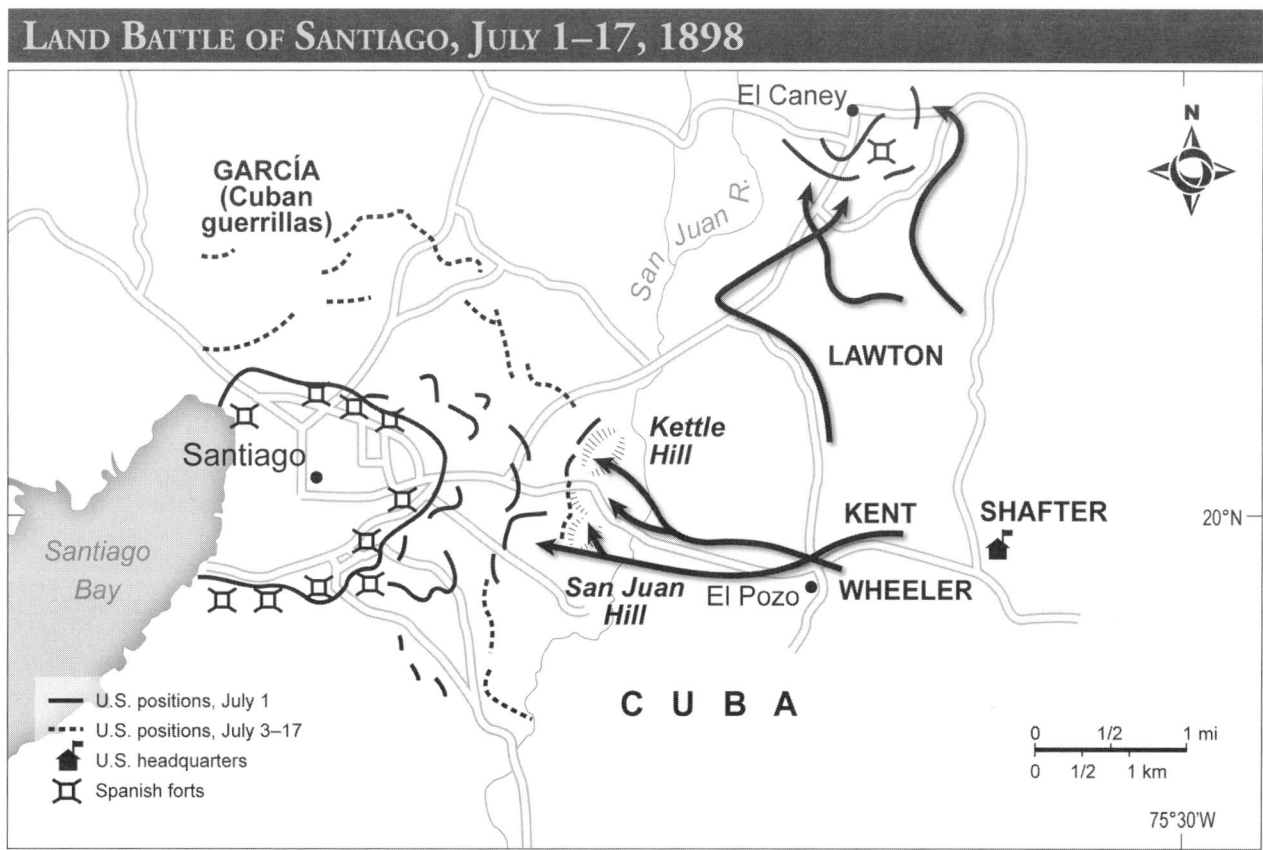

the armed yachts (auxiliary cruisers) *Gloucester, Hist,* and *Vixen.* Its commander, Rear Admiral William T. Sampson, has just departed in another battleship, the *New York,* for a conference with ground force commander Major General William R. Shafter to discuss the latter's request that the navy force the entrance to Santiago Harbor. Commodore William T. Schley exercises command in Sampson's absence. Although Sampson quickly returns with the *New York* and the torpedo boat *Ericsson* once the battle begins, it is already decided on his arrival.

The Spanish ships are plagued by fouled bottoms and faulty guns and ammunition. The battle opens with the *Infanta María Teresa* engaging the *Brooklyn,* but the Spanish ships are quickly overwhelmed by the superior U.S. firepower. The ships try to make the shore, and the Americans soon turn to rescuing their crews. The battle ends by 1:15 p.m. when the last Spanish ship, the *Cristóbol Cólon,* is overtaken by the *Oregon* and the *Brooklyn* and run aground. In the

four-hour Battle of Santiago de Cuba the Spaniards lose all six ships either sunk or scuttled; 323 men are killed, and another 151 are wounded; 1,720 are taken prisoner, including Cervera. American casualties are 1 dead and 10 wounded. Later there is a bitter public controversy as Schley feuds with Sampson over who should receive credit for the victory.

July 4, 1898

Spanish-American War (continued). After nightfall the Spaniards attempt to block water access to Santiago, Cuba, by scuttling in the channel to Santiago Harbor the cruiser *Reina Mercedes,* which had been serving as a guard ship at Santiago since 1895. This effort is detected, and the Spanish ship is hit five times by gunfire from the U.S. battleships *Massachusetts* and *Texas.* The crew of the *Reina Mercedes* manages to set off the scuttling charges, but the ship takes too long to sink and drifts out of the channel before grounding.

July 7, 1898

Spanish-American War (continued): The United States annexes Hawaii. While Grover Cleveland remained president, he checked all efforts to annex the Hawaiian Islands. Cleveland's successor William McKinley is open to annexation, however. Agreeing to a treaty with representatives of the Republic of Hawaii (signed on June 16, 1897), he submits it to the Senate for approval. Democrats and anti-imperialist Republicans block ratification, however.

A political shift occurs following the American victory in the Battle of Manila Bay on May 1, 1898. Although there is considerable question regarding the future disposition of the Philippines, the advantages of permanent U.S. naval access to a mid-Pacific coaling station in the Hawaiian Islands are obvious. During a secret session of the U.S. Senate on May 31, 1898, advocates of annexation tout the advantages of the Hawaiian Islands as a coaling station and base for military operations in the Philippines.

In order to prevent defeat under the two-thirds vote required for ratification of treaties by the Senate, legislators seeking annexation resurrect an earlier alternative of a bill introduced into both houses of Congress and said to be equivalent to a treaty of annexation. This joint resolution, known as the Newlands Resolution, is passed by the House on June 15, 1898, in a vote of 209 to 91 and by the Senate on July 6, 1898, in a vote of 42 to 21. President McKinley signs the legislation on July 7, 1898, officially annexing Hawaii. On April 30, 1900, Congress declares the Hawaiian Islands to be a U.S. territory.

July 10, 1898

Spanish-American War (continued). The U.S. battleships *Massachusetts* and *Texas* and the armored cruiser *Brooklyn* bombard Santiago de Cuba, hitting the city with more than 100 shells.

July 17, 1898

Spanish-American War (continued): Surrender of Santiago. On July 1, 1898, Spanish general of brigade José Toral y Vázquez succeeds Lieutenant General Arsenio Linares y Pomba (wounded in the Battle of San Juan Ridge) in command of the Santiago area.

Toral is unaware that the U.S. forces under Major General William R. Shafter blockading Santiago from the land are rapidly falling prey to disease. On July 3 following the Battle of Santiago Bay, Shafter demands that Toral surrender. After a bombardment of the city during July 10–11 by land and water and with freshwater cut off and supplies running low, Toral finally surrenders on July 17, Shafter having offered to return to Spain at U.S. expense all prisoners taken. The siege of Santiago claims 1,614 U.S. casualties; Spain suffers some 2,000 dead or wounded and 11,500 prisoners. Eight Spanish vessels, including the gunboat *Alvarado*, are captured in the harbor. The surrender of Santiago largely ends the fighting in Cuba.

July 18, 1898

Spanish-American War (continued): Engagement in Manzanilla Harbor. On this date in the Philippines, the U.S. gunboats *Wilmington* and *Helena*, the auxiliary cruisers *Hist* and *Scorpion*, and the armed tugs *Osceola* and *Wompatuck* enter Manzanilla Harbor and there engage and sink the Spanish gunboats *Cuba Española*, *Delgado Perado*, *Estrella de Guantánamo*, *Guardián*, *José Garcia*, *María Pantón*, and *Sentinel Delago*, along with the blockade-runner *El Purísima Conceptión*.

July 21, 1898

Spanish-American War (continued). Off Nipe in northern Cuba, the U.S. gunboats *Annapolis* and *Topeka*, the auxiliary cruiser *Wasp*, and the armed tug *Leydon* shell the Spanish coastal defenses. The Spanish auxiliary cruiser *Jorge Juan* sorties to engage the American warships and is promptly sunk.

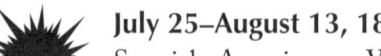 July 25–August 13, 1898

Spanish-American War (continued): Puerto Rico Campaign. U.S. land operations on Puerto Rico occur late in the war. Initially, both commanding general of the army Major General Nelson A. Miles and his predecessor, Major General John Schofield, acting as a military adviser to President William McKinley, had favored a campaign in Puerto Rico over an invasion of Cuba. Miles believed that it made more sense strategically to strike Puerto Rico

OPERATIONS IN PUERTO RICO, 1898

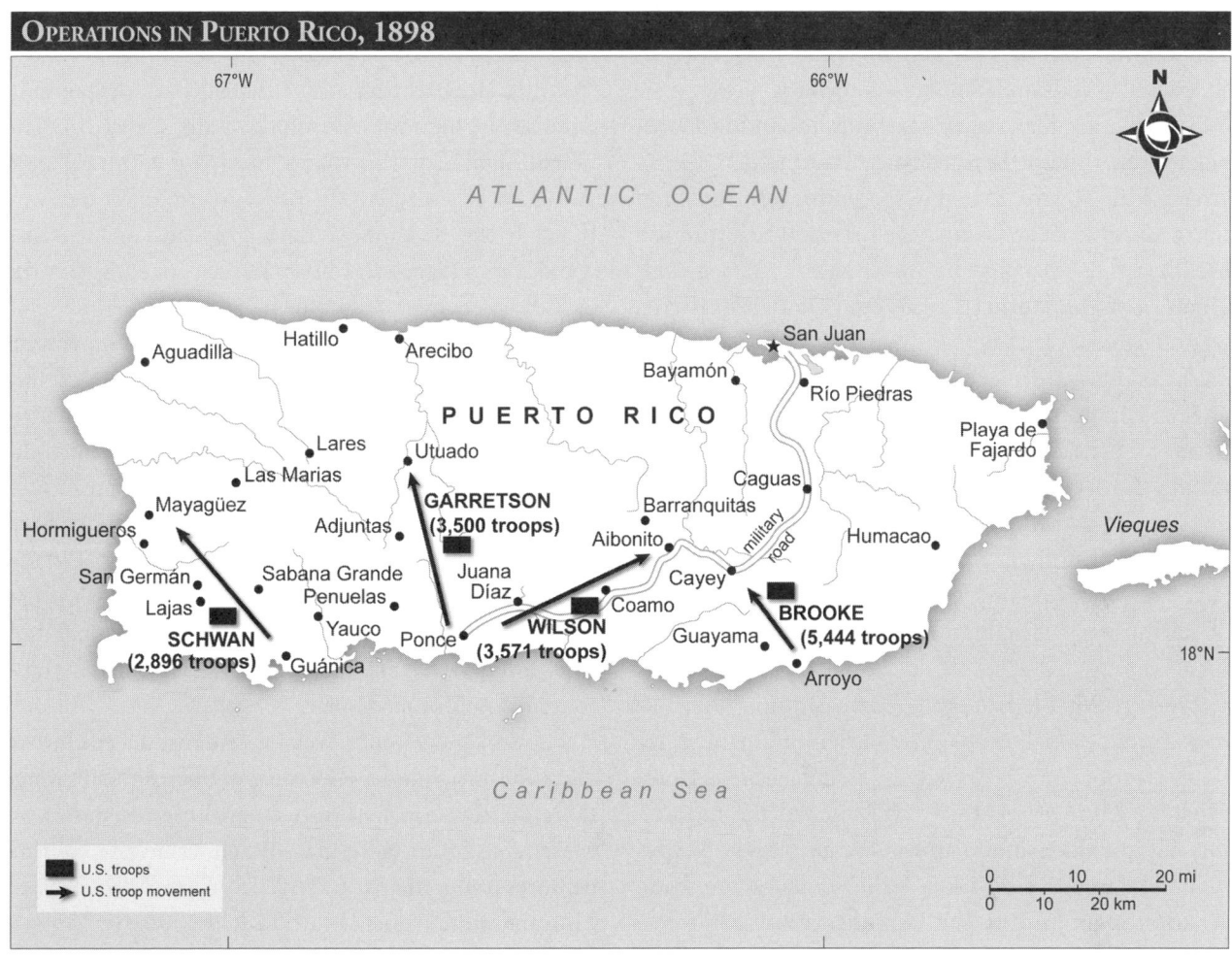

first, wait until the yellow fever season in Cuba had ended, and then send the navy to defeat the Spanish squadron there.

In late May 1898 when Rear Admiral Pascual Cervera y Topete's Spanish squadron arrived at Santiago and was blockaded there, Miles again pressed for a Puerto Rico Campaign, followed by an invasion of Cuba. However, McKinley chose to invade Cuba first as a means of supporting the navy in its effort to destroy the Spanish squadron, which remained the primary U.S. strategic objective. Such a move, it was reasoned, would have an immediate and compelling effect on Spain.

Although the Spanish squadron is destroyed on July 3, the land campaign against Santiago bogs down, and McKinley directs Miles to proceed to Cuba and support the Santiago operation if needed. Miles sails

from Charleston, South Carolina, on July 8 with 3,500 men and proceeds to Santiago. With the capitulation of Santiago on July 17, the next day Miles receives authorization to proceed against Puerto Rico.

Miles's earlier opposition to a Cuban invasion during the fever season was well founded, for by the time Santiago surrenders, a large number of men have fallen prey to yellow fever and malaria. Miles had originally planned to include part of V Corps in his Puerto Rico Campaign, but the men are in no shape for more campaigning. Miles has wisely kept his troops with him on ship so as not to expose them to tropical fevers. He now sails from Guantánamo, Cuba, on July 21 with 3,415 infantry, two companies of engineers, and one signal company in the transports *Columbia, Macon,* and *Yale.* Captain Francis J. Higginson commands the naval escort of the battleship *Massachusetts* (flagship), the cruiser *Dixie,* and the armed yacht *Gloucester.* This initial force will be followed by more than 13,000 additional troops and supporting artillery.

The original plan called for Miles to land at Cape Fajardo on the northern coast of Puerto Rico. Once at sea, Miles learns that the Spaniards are expecting him to land at Fajardo and have prepared accordingly. He therefore changes the objectives to Ponce and Guánica on the southern coast. Ponce is Puerto Rico's second-largest city, only 70 miles from San Juan, and offers a ready source of supplies.

Spanish governor-general of Puerto Rico Manuel Macías y Casado is fully aware of the U.S. intent to invade the island, even though the landing point is unknown. His orders are to offer stout resistance in order to strengthen Spain's bargaining position in peace negotiation, and Macías concentrates the bulk of his military resources around the capital of San Juan.

On July 25, a U.S. landing party captures without resistance the small deep-water harbor of Guánica, 15 miles west of Ponce. On July 27, a detachment from Guánica advances on Ponce. It is joined the following day by some 3,600 troops under Brevet Major General James H. Wilson, which had sailed from Charleston on July 20. The combined American force compels the Spanish to surrender the city. On July 26, a column under Brigadier General George Garretson moves on Yauco, a few miles north of Guánica. Following a brief skirmish with Spanish troops, the column captures the town and nearby railroad line.

Although the population of Puerto Rico has not risen up against Spanish rule as was the case in Cuba, they do not strongly support the Spanish. Militarily, throughout the campaign Miles stresses maneuver in order to flank and isolate Spanish positions rather than mounting direct frontal assaults.

By August 5, additional troops have landed under Major General John R. Brooke and Brigadier General Theodore Schwan with 4,000 and 2,900 men, respectively. Miles now has some 17,000 troops. Spanish troop strength numbers more than 8,200 regulars and some 9,100 volunteers. Unlike General Shafter's V Corps in Cuba, the various elements of Miles's command had left the United States fully equipped for the campaign. Miles has 106 mortars, howitzers, and field and siege guns as well as 10 Gatling guns.

Miles learns that the Spanish are organizing defenses in the low mountainous area separating the northern half of the island from the southern half. Aibonito is a key strong point; it guards a gateway through the mountains leading to San Juan. Miles decides to advance in four columns, sweep across the island, and converge on San Juan.

General Schwan is to move from Ponce northwest along the left flank to Mayagüez and Arecibo. Garretson will proceed due north to Adjuntas and then to Arecibo, where he and Schwan will form one column under Brigadier General Guy Henry and move directly on San Juan. A third column under Wilson will march northeast from Ponce to Aibonito. Finally, Brooke is directed to march to Cayey, at which point he would be behind the Spanish defenders at Aibonito, forcing the defenders to retire and leaving the route from Aibonito open.

Schwan gets under way on August 6, aiming to clear western Puerto Rico of any Spanish forces, but there are few Spanish troops and little resistance. In the course of an eight-day march, Schwan's column captures nine towns and has a sharp fight only at Hormigueros, 7 miles south of Mayagüez, on August 10, suffering 1 killed and 16 wounded. Brooke, meanwhile, moves west from Arroyo toward Guayama, where he encounters significant resistance and sustains several casualties before finally capturing that Spanish position on August 5. On August 9, Brigadier General Oswald H. Ernst's men of Wilson's force have a stiff fight at Coamo, some 17 miles east-north-east of Ponce. This action is brought to an end when the 16th Pennsylvania Regiment moves around the Spanish and flanks the defenders out of position, then inflicts heavy casualties on them. Some 40 Spaniards are killed or wounded, and 170 are captured. American losses are only 6 men wounded.

On August 12, Wilson's forces have a brief skirmish at the Asomante Hills near the town of Aibonito on the main road from Ponce to San Juan. The last combat of the Puerto Rico Campaign is another skirmish, at Las Marías, on August 13, a day after the Protocol of Peace had been signed but before word of it had been received. There are no American casualties, but the Spanish suffer 5 killed, 14 wounded, and 56 taken prisoner.

The entire Puerto Rico Campaign is conducted amid an impending cease-fire. With Wilson preparing to attack Aibonito following rejection of a surrender demand, Miles receives word that the Protocol of Peace has been signed, thereby concluding the campaign on August 13. Brief though it is, the Puerto Rico Campaign has moved along far more effectively than Shafter's effort in Cuba. In Puerto Rico there are no tropical diseases to debilitate the troops, and the various columns have made surprisingly good time in difficult terrain. By the time of the armistice, U.S. forces have fought six engagements, suffering only 3 dead and 40 wounded, and have captured half of the island. Spanish casualties are at least 10 times that number.

The campaign ensures the U.S. acquisition of Puerto Rico as part of the peace negotiations of 1898 and limits Spanish bargaining power at the conference table. Had the campaign taken longer and proven costlier, it might well have worked to Spain's advantage.

July 26, 1898

Spanish-American War (continued). Peace talks, requested by the Spanish government through the good offices of France, begin in Washington, D.C. On August 2, with some reservations concerning the future status of the Philippine Islands, Spain accepts the U.S. demands.

August 12, 1898

Spanish-American War (continued): An armistice goes into effect. On August 11, 1898, U.S. State Department officials and French ambassador to the United States Jules-Martin Cambon successfully negotiate the formal Protocol of Peace. An armistice goes into effect the next day.

August 13, 1898

Spanish-American War (continued): First Battle of Manila. This last battle of the Spanish-American War pits troops of the U.S. Army VIII Corps against Spanish forces. It is waged after the Protocol of Peace goes into effect on August 12, because the cable linking Manila with Hong Kong has been cut and field commanders here are unaware of the truce agreement.

Manila, the capital and most important city of the Philippines, is located on the east side of Manila Bay on the island of Luzon. Following his victory in the Battle of Manila Bay on May 1, 1898, U.S. Navy commodore George Dewey realized that Manila can and should be seized. But with no landing force available to undertake such a mission, Dewey can only establish a coaling station ashore at Cavite and await the arrival of troops.

The Philippine Expeditionary Force (VIII Corps) reaches the Philippines in three contingents from San Francisco. The first—2,500 men under Brigadier General Thomas Anderson—arrives at the end of June, followed in mid-July by 3,500 men under Brigadier General Francis V. Greene. The final contingent of 4,800 troops under Brigadier General Arthur MacArthur reaches the islands at the end of July, along with VIII Corps commander Major General Wesley Merritt.

The Spaniards still control Manila and much of its environs. The city proper is split by the Pasig River, south of which is the old walled city of Fort Santiago. The Spanish defensive line, known as the Zapote Line, is one and a half miles to the south from a large

First Battle of Manila		
Date	August 13, 1898	
Location	Manila, Luzon, Philippine Islands	
Opponents (*winner)	*United States	Spain
Commander	Major General Wesley Merritt	Captain-General Fermín Jáudenes y Alvarez
#	More than 10,000 men	13,000 men
Casualties	5 dead, 43 wounded	150 dead or wounded; 13,000 prisoners; 22,000 small arms also taken

The U.S. flag flies over Fort San Antonio de Abad (also known as Fort Malate) following its capture by American forces during their assault on Manila on August 13, 1898. (Naval Historical Center)

blockhouse, Number 14, on the Pasay Road and extends west to a stone structure, known as Fort San Antonio de Abad, near the shore of Manila Bay. A line of entrenchments connects these two strong points.

Opposing the Spaniards are some 10,000 Filipino nationalist troops under Emilio Aguinaldo y Famy, who had formally proclaimed the Republic of the Philippines on June 12. Nationalist forces have managed to isolate Manila from its source of supplies, in effect placing it under siege. In Manila, food is scarce. Although both sides exchange fire, there are no serious offensive movements.

During the course of the U.S. buildup, General Greene's troops construct a series of entrenchments and move into some of the works of the nationalists, who abandon them only reluctantly. In places, nationalist forces occupy trenches between the Americans and the Spaniards. Artillery and rifle fire between the

Americans and the Spaniards produces growing casualties. Relations between the Americans and Aguinaldo's men also begin to deteriorate as the latter grow increasingly suspicious of U.S. intentions regarding the Philippines.

In late July, Dewey, now a rear admiral, becomes convinced that the Spanish can be made to surrender Manila through negotiations, and he meets with Spanish commander Captain General Basilio Augustín y Dávila and then with his successor, Fermín Jáudenes y Alvarez, to explore possibilities. Nevertheless, Greene urges naval gunfire on Spanish positions to relieve pressure on his command. His troops had dug a line of trenches south of Fort Abad and are taking casualties daily from Spanish fire. Merritt supports Greene in this request, but Dewey is reluctant to open fire from his warships, fearful that this will end any chance of securing Manila by negotiation. Dewey

Arthur MacArthur (1845–1912)

U.S. Army general. Arthur MacArthur was born in Chicopee Falls, Massachusetts, on June 2, 1845. At an early age he moved with his family to Milwaukee, Wisconsin, and was educated in the local schools. With the start of the American Civil War, MacArthur secured a commission as first lieutenant with the 24th Wisconsin Regiment of Volunteers and soon distinguished himself in fighting. He was breveted captain following his performance in the Battle of Perryville (October 8, 1862). He also fought effectively at Stone's River (December 31–January 2, 1863), Chickamauga (September 18–20, 1863), and Kennesaw Mountain (June 17, 1864). He was severely wounded at the Battle of Franklin (November 30, 1984) in Tennessee. MacArthur received brevet promotions for gallantry and was advanced to major (January 1864), lieutenant colonel (March 1865), and colonel (May 1865). By the end of the war, MacArthur, not yet 20 years old, was commanding the 24th Wisconsin. In 1890, he was belatedly awarded the Medal of Honor for his actions in the Union assault on Missionary Ridge.

With the end of the Civil War, MacArthur joined the regular army as a second lieutenant in the 17th Infantry Regiment in February 1866 and was immediately promoted to first lieutenant. He made captain that July. During the next 20 years, he served in various posts throughout the country. At first posted to Louisiana during Reconstruction, he then commanded a unit that protected the builders of the Union Pacific Railroad in Nebraska and Wyoming. He was also a cavalry recruiting officer in New York and commanded an outpost in the Utah and New Mexico Territories. In 1886, Captain MacArthur was posted to the Infantry and Cavalry School at Fort Leavenworth, Kansas. In July 1889, he was promoted to major and assigned to the adjutant general's department. MacArthur won promotion to lieutenant colonel in May 1898.

Shortly after the U.S. declaration of war on Spain, MacArthur was appointed brigadier general of volunteers in May 1898 and assigned to the U.S. expeditionary force sent to the Philippines. He commanded the 1st Brigade of the 2nd Division in Major General Wesley Merritt's VIII Corps. MacArthur led his brigade in the First Battle of Manila (August 13, 1898). Cited for gallantry, he became the provost marshal general and civil governor of Manila.

Promoted to major general of volunteers, MacArthur then commanded the 2nd Division, the chief field force opposing Filipino insurgents led by Emilio Aguinaldo y Famy in the Philippine-American War. MacArthur's forces pacified all of Luzon. Promoted to regular army brigadier general in January 1900, he succeeded Major General Elwell S. Otis as commanding general of the Division of the Philippines and military governor of the Philippine Islands. MacArthur was promoted to major general in the regular army that July. In pacifying the Philippines, he combined vigorous military action with civic action, including advances in education, health care, and legal reform.

MacArthur was, however, slow to yield control to the civilian administrators headed by William H. Taft. MacArthur and Taft clashed repeatedly, and before the year was out, President Theodore Roosevelt had replaced MacArthur with a more pliable military governor. MacArthur's disagreements with Taft and Roosevelt ultimately cost MacArthur the position of commanding general of the U.S. Army.

Returning to the United States, MacArthur commanded in turn the Department of Colorado, the Department of the Lakes, and the Department of the East. In 1905, he went to Manchuria as a military observer

(continued)

(Continued)

for the last stage of the Russo-Japanese War (1904–1905) and then for a few months was the U.S. military attaché in Tokyo. He toured Asia during November 1905–August 1906. On his return to the United States, he commanded the Department of the Pacific, was promoted to lieutenant general, and was the senior officer in the army (September 1906). When Taft, then secretary of war and still bearing a grudge against his old nemesis, named a more junior officer as chief of staff, MacArthur returned to Milwaukee to await orders. When none were forthcoming, he retired in July 1909. MacArthur died in Milwaukee on September 5, 1912, while giving a speech during the reunion of the 24th Wisconsin Regiment. His son, Douglas MacArthur, was later chief of staff of the army and rose to the rank of general of the army. Like his father, Douglas MacArthur would have an equally stormy relationship with his superiors.

WESLEY MOODY, PAUL G. PIERPAOLI JR., AND SPENCER C. TUCKER

Further Reading

Linn, Brian McAllister. *The Philippine War, 1899–1902*. Lawrence: University Press of Kansas, 2000.

Young, Kenneth Ray. *The General's General: The Life and Times of Arthur MacArthur*. Boulder, CO: Westview, 1994.

does agree to support Greene should this prove absolutely necessary.

President William McKinley instructs Merritt not to involve the nationalists in taking Manila, because this would mean accepting them as partners in negotiations with Spain over the future of the islands. Jáudenes, meanwhile, has orders to hold the city, as Spain's bargaining position in the peace talks will be weakened by a surrender.

On August 9, 1898, Merritt and Dewey send an ultimatum to Jáudenes demanding that he surrender Manila and threatening an attack if he refuses. Jáudenes summons a meeting of his subordinate commanders and puts the issue to a vote. Seven favor immediate negotiations for a surrender, but an equal number are opposed. Jáudenes breaks the tie, deciding to continue delaying tactics. He informs the Americans that he has no authority to surrender and asks to be able to communicate with Madrid through Hong Kong. On August 10, Dewey and Merritt reject this.

Dewey continues separate negotiations with Jáudenes through Belgian consul in Manila Edouard André. Jáudenes agrees to consider surrendering Manila to U.S. forces, but he insists that to salvage Spanish honor, it must appear that a genuine effort has been made to defend the city. Most important, Filipino nationalists must not be allowed to enter the city, as Jáudenes fears that they will show no mercy to the defenders, and it must not appear that Spanish troops are surrendering to Filipinos. Thus, both Spain and the United States have their own reasons for keeping Aguinaldo's men from entering Manila.

The two sides finally reach agreement that the Spaniards will offer a token defense of their outer works but not of the walled city itself. Neither of the U.S. commanders who are to lead the attack, Generals Greene and MacArthur, are made aware of the pact, because Merritt fears that had they known of it, their attacks would have lacked authenticity.

The axis of the attack is to be south to north, in two essentially parallel columns. Greene's brigade will advance along the northern flank nearest Manila Bay, while MacArthur's brigade will move along the southern flank. By prearrangement, Dewey's flagship, the cruiser *Olympia*, will fire a few token rounds at the heavy stone walls of Fort San Antonio de Abad before raising the international signal flag calling for surrender.

On the morning of August 13 amid a heavy rain, the naval bombardment of Fort San Antonio de Abad occurs as agreed, the American land artillery opens

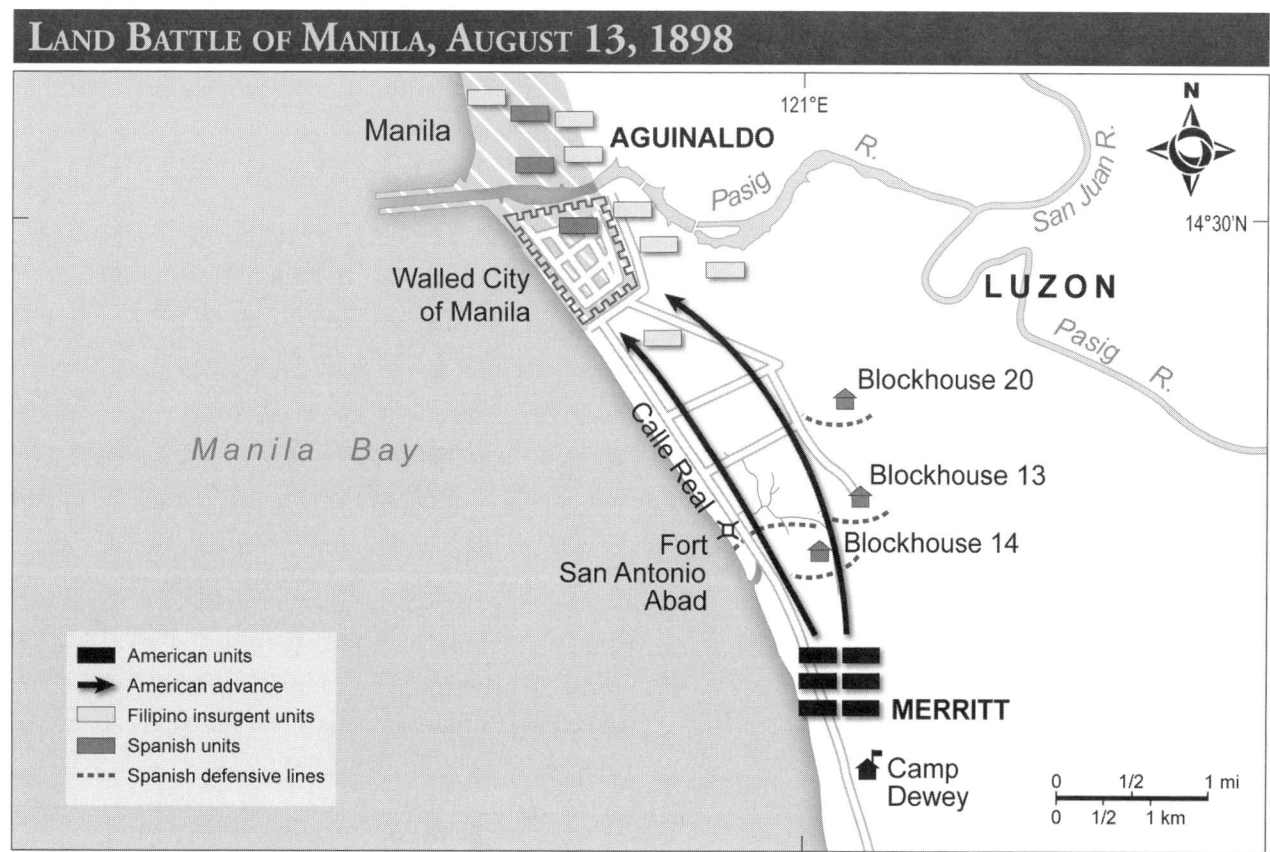

LAND BATTLE OF MANILA, AUGUST 13, 1898

fire, and the assault commences, with the U.S. troops advancing under what becomes a deluge. Spanish resistance is heavier than Merritt had expected although not sufficient to thwart the advance. The defenders gradually fall back, and Greene moves into the city unopposed to accept the surrender.

On the right flank MacArthur finds the going much tougher, complicated by Filipino nationalist forces determined to take part in the capture of the city. As MacArthur's troops move north along the Singalong Road, Spanish infantry in a blockhouse inflict numerous casualties. MacArthur's biggest challenge, however, is in keeping nationalist forces from entering the city. As the U.S. troops move closer to Manila, their ranks become increasingly intermingled with those of the Filipinos, and MacArthur is compelled to have his commanders hold the nationalists back from the city.

By the end of the day, U.S. troops have occupied all of Manila proper, but outside the city

Aguinaldo's troops are in an ugly mood. Fortunately for the Americans, the heavy tropical storm helps defuse hostile crowds. On August 14, a joint group of American and Spanish officers agrees to a formal capitulation agreement supplementing a preliminary agreement signed by Merritt and Jáudenes the day before.

In the battle, U.S. forces suffer 5 dead and 43 wounded. Spanish casualties total some 150 dead or wounded and 13,000 prisoners. In addition, the United States secures 22,000 stands of small arms, 10 million rounds of ammunition, and 70 artillery pieces. Because Manila is seized after the Protocol of Peace, Spanish negotiators at the formal peace talks in Paris will argue that it is invalid.

August 30, 1898

Spanish-American War (continued). Having requested that he be relieved of command, U.S. major general Wesley Merritt is succeeded as commander of

VIII Corps and military governor of the Philippines by Major General Elwell S. Otis.

November 4, 1898
At Beijing (Peking), China, 15 U.S. marines from the cruisers *Baltimore, Boston,* and *Raleigh* establish a guard at the U.S. legation.

December 10, 1898
Spanish-American War (continued): Treaty of Paris. Following the armistice of August 13, 1898, Spanish and U.S. negotiators meet in Paris to bring the war to a formal close. The only sticking point is the future of the Philippines, but on October 26 President William McKinley instructs the U.S. delegation to demand cession of the islands. In the Treaty of Paris, Spain relinquishes sovereignty over Cuba, cedes to the United States the islands of Puerto Rico and Guam, and sells the Philippine Archipelago to the United States for $20 million. The decision to acquire the Philippines makes the United States a Pacific power, but it touches off the Philippine-American War and sets up a future confrontation with Japan.

January 17, 1899
U.S. Navy commander Edward D. Taussig, captain of the gunboat *Bennington*, claims unoccupied Wake Island (Wake Atoll) in the North Pacific for the United States. This coral atoll has a 12-mile coastline and is 2,300 miles west of Honolulu, Hawaii, and 1,510 miles east of Guam.

January 23, 1899
Proclamation of the Malolos Constitution of the First Philippine Republic. Initially, Filipinos considered the Americans to be allies in their revolutionary war against Spain. U.S. policy regarding the Philippines is unclear, however, and both Rear Admiral George Dewey and Major General Wesley Merritt had kept Filipino nationalist troops under Aguinaldo y Famy out of the capital city of Manila and excluded him from the Spanish surrender in August 1898.

In December 1898 the United States formally acquires the Philippines from Spain. Aguinaldo, though, has already initiated in September a constitutional convention in the town of Malolos, north of Manila. It establishes the First Philippine Republic, proclaimed on this date by Aguinaldo.

February 4–March 17, 1899
Beginning of the Philippine-American War: The Second Battle of Manila and beginning of the Luzon Campaign. Following the First Battle of Manila (see August 13, 1898), relations sharply

---

 **Camouflage**

Camouflage is a method of deception whereby men and their equipment are concealed from an enemy both on and off the battlefield. This process had existed since ancient times, with individuals wearing animal skins and employing foliage to conceal their location. With the development of mass armies maneuvering on the battlefield in compact formations, however, camouflage seemed of little worth.

The arrival of the long-range rifle in the second half of the 19th century changed all that. Its bullets were able to reach much farther into the battlefield than ever before, and personal concealment now became a major concern. Also, new smokeless powder meant that firing a rifle did not mean the immediate appearance of a telltale cloud of black smoke. It was thus much more difficult for opposing forces at greater range to detect an enemy position. Both developments heightened interest in cover and concealment. Uniforms, heretofore brightly colored in part to instill confidence in one's own side and intimidate an opponent, gave way to drab khaki and gray that blended in with the landscape. Cheap and fast chemical dye processes aided the process. Aerial observation, which came into its own in World War I, heightened the need to conceal one's own dispositions, even well behind the front lines.

Camouflage, first widely practiced by the Boers against the British in the Boer War (1899–1902), was widely practiced in World War I. Camouflage seeks to reduce the effect of color and blend an object into the background. Properly applied, it also transforms shapes, changing them from rectangular man-made forms to the indiscriminate. Camouflage also involves removing the shine from metal equipment. Faces too might be colored, either by burned cork or by mud. White suits were introduced for alpine troops so that they would blend in against the snow.

Screens of green canvas with different-colored shapes applied to them and the netting were also widely employed beginning in World War I. Dummy tree trunks and other common objects also appeared, overnight replacing real tree trunks on the battlefield. These concealed snipers or observation outposts. At the same time, dummy heads or body shapes were used to attract enemy fire where it could do no harm to real troops.

Ships and aircraft were not immune from this process. Experiments revealed that aircraft were less prone to observation from above if they were painted in a disruptive pattern in matt colors, mainly olive green and very dark green, while the same was true from below if the undersides of fuselages and wings were painted a sky blue or light gray color. Aircraft while on the ground were parked in revetments with their own camouflage netting.

At sea, attempts were made to disrupt the silhouette of a vessel by painting it in alternating dark and light gray blocks of color. This type of dazzle camouflage was intended not to conceal the presence of a vessel, which was impossible, but instead to obscure its size, type, and orientation.

Camouflage, which came into its own in World War I, reached new levels of sophistication in World War II. Painted screens and face blackening, especially among elite raiding troops, came into wide use, as did helmet nets to hold foliage. Uniforms varied in color depending on the battlefield, from jungle to desert. Factories received paint that appeared to alter their shape from the air, while painted forms could give the impression of a bomb crater on an otherwise undamaged runway. Lights at night in open uninhabited positions were used to attract enemy aircraft, while night-fighter aircraft were painted black to render them more invisible. Aircraft also dropped aluminum strips, or chaff, to give false readings on radar. Today there are stealth aircraft and even stealth ships designed so as to be invisible to conventional radar.

As infrared sights and observation equipment came into wider use, new materials were introduced for uniforms and camouflage netting that absorbed, rather than reflected, the infrared rays. Special paint for vehicles and equipment also absorbs infrared. Camouflage continues to be an important element of modern war.

SPENCER C. TUCKER

Further Reading

Hartcup, Guy. *Camouflage: A History of Concealment and Deception in War.* New York: Encore Editions, 1980.
Hodges, P. *Royal Navy Warship Camouflage.* London: Almark, 1973.
Stanley, R. M. *To Fool a Glass Eye: Camouflage versus Photoreconnaissance in World War II.* Shrewsbury, UK: Airlife, 1998.

deteriorate between U.S. troops, now commanded by Major General Elwell S. Otis, and the Filipino Army of Liberation headed by Emilio Aguinaldo y Famy. Following their capture of Manila, the Americans insist that the Filipino Army of Liberation retract its lines from in front of Manila to avoid possible exchanges with U.S. troops. Aguinaldo grudgingly agrees, but there are frequent verbal exchanges between Americans and Filipinos.

The Second Battle of Manila begins on the night of February 4, 1899. How the fighting starts remains a matter of dispute, but certainly the war that ensues is largely inevitable, given the fact that the United States is determined to retain control of the islands, while the nationalist side is no less determined to secure independence.

In the Santa Mesa District northeast of Manila, a patrol of U.S. troops fires on some Filipino troops, supposedly in retaliation for their incursion into what has been agreed to as a neutral zone. The exchange sets off what will be a three-year war (1899–1902) between the United States and Aguinaldo's republican forces. This conflict is known as the Philippine-American War, the War for Philippine Independence, and—at the time in the United States—the Philippine Insurrection. At the onset, U.S. forces number little more than 20,000 men, but by 1902 the United States will have sent 126,000 troops to the Philippines.

The initial U.S. response to the fighting is rapid. The next day, February 5, Brigadier General Arthur MacArthur, commander of the 2nd Division, orders attacks on Army of Liberation positions along his front. Supported by artillery and naval gunfire, elements of the division encounter minimal opposition as they advance through rice paddies to seize Filipino positions. Other units have to contend with more difficult terrain and heavy Filipino fire. By the end of the second day of fighting, MacArthur's troops have secured the high ground north of the city.

On February 6 also, Brigadier General Thomas Anderson's division attacks Filipino positions south of Manila. Anderson's troops—composed largely of volunteers—are supported by artillery. At an old Spanish position on the Pasig River, strong Filipino fire briefly stalls the advance, but Filipino Army of Liberation forces are soon in full retreat. U.S. cohesiveness is soon lost, however, and Anderson fails to trap the Filipino forces between his two brigades. In the Second Battle of Manila, U.S. forces suffer 50–60 dead and 225 wounded; Filipino nationalist forces sustain some 2,000 casualties (killed, wounded, or captured).

Pockets of Filipino resistance remain, and fighting continues in the Luzon Campaign until March 17, 1899. On February 16, Filipino forces attack one of Anderson's brigades but are halted by American defensive firepower. On February 19, U.S. forces, supported by the gunboat *Laguna de Bay*, devastate Filipino positions south of Manila.

U.S. warships play an important role in the Philippines fighting. Most U.S. naval operations involve gunboats shelling insurgent positions, then landing detachments of marines and sailors to occupy coastal villages. The navy also intercepts insurgent vessels transporting men and supplies.

Most Army of Liberation troops fall back to Caloocan, a dozen miles north of Manila. MacArthur's plan to strike there is postponed because of a threatened uprising in Manila itself. Finally, on February 10 MacArthur's division, supported by naval gunfire, attacks Caloocan. By day's end the Americans have secured this important rail center on the line to Malolos, the newly proclaimed capital of the Philippine Republic.

Meanwhile, U.S. authorities learn through captured nationalist documents about the planned uprising in Manila, enabling U.S. forces to arrest known revolutionaries and shut down the revolt before it can really get started. Although some street fighting occurs, it falls far short of full-scale revolt.

U.S. military commander in the Philippines Major General Elwell S. Otis concludes that the key to winning the war lies in securing Luzon, north of Manila. Otis is convinced that the insurrection is centered in the Tagalog population in the provinces of southern Luzon. He believes that these areas will be difficult to subjugate but that ethnic groups north of Manila will welcome the Americans. His assessment is based on a misguided understanding of Filipino opposition to the U.S. presence.

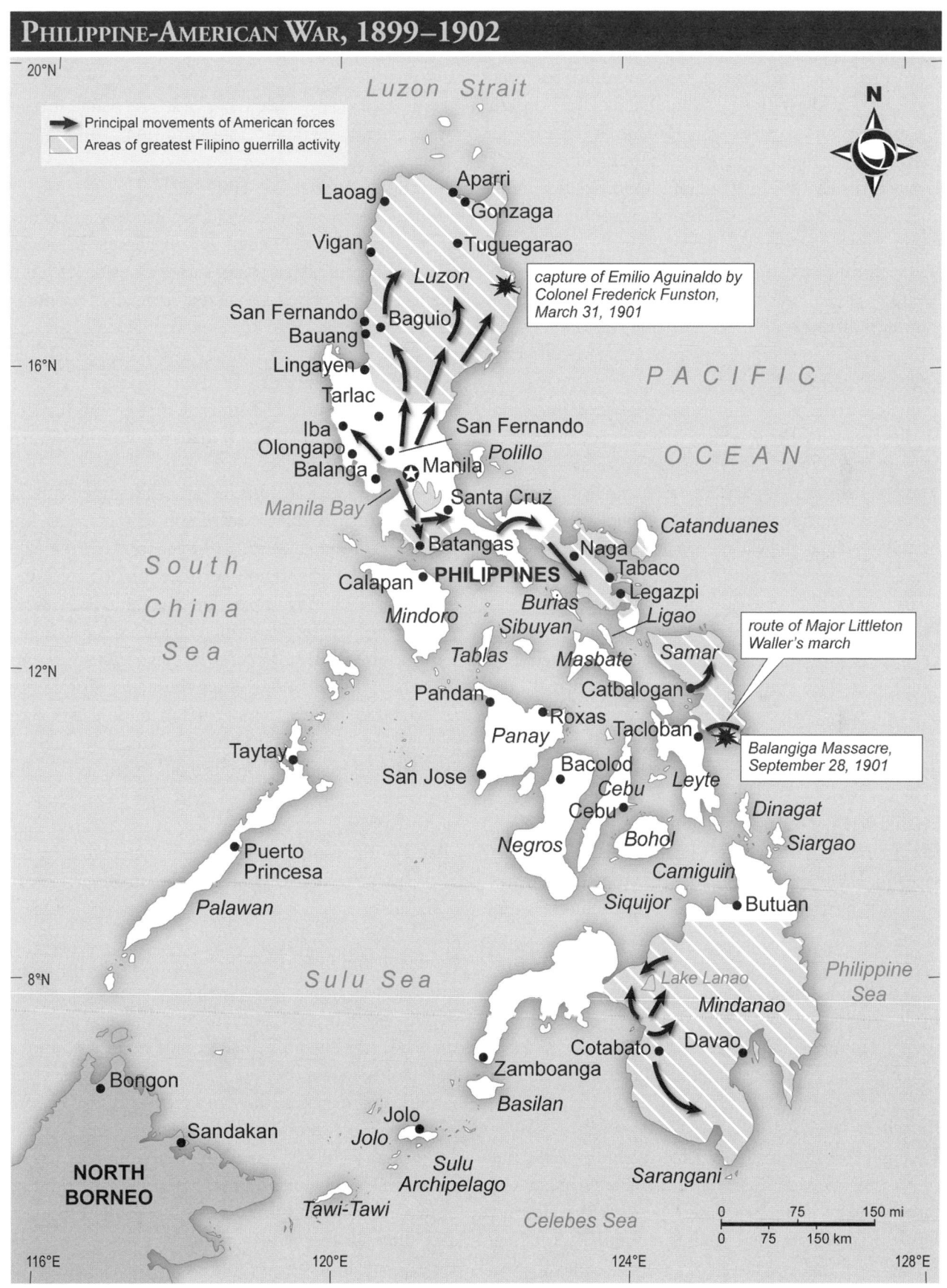

PHILIPPINE-AMERICAN WAR, 1899–1902

Principal movements of American forces

Areas of greatest Filipino guerrilla activity

N

Luzon Strait

Aparri

Laoag

Gonzaga

Vigan

Tuguegarao

Luzon

capture of Emilio Aguinaldo by
Colonel Frederick Funston,
March 31, 1901

San Fernando

Baguio

Bauang

Lingayen

P A C I F I C

Tarlac

San Fernando

Iba

Polillo

O C E A N

Olongapo

Balanga

Manila

Santa Cruz

Manila Bay

Catanduanes

Batangas

Naga

Tabaco

PHILIPPINES

S o u t h

Calapan

Legazpi

C h i n a

Mindoro

Burias

Ligao

route of Major Littleton
Waller's march

S e a

Sibuyan

Masbate

Samar

Tablas

Catbalogan

Pandan

Tacloban

Roxas

Balangiga Massacre,
September 28, 1901

Taytay

Panay

Bacolod

Leyte

San Jose

Cebu

Dinagat

Cebu

Siargao

Negros

Bohol

Puerto
Princesa

Camiguin

Siquijor

Butuan

Palawan

*Philippine
Sea*

S u l u S e a

Lake Lanao

Mindanao

Bongon

Cotabato

Davao

Zamboanga

Jolo

Basilan

Jolo

Sandakan

**NORTH
BORNEO**

*Sulu
Archipelago*

Sarangani

Tawi-Tawi

Celebes Sea

0   75   150 mi

0   75   150 km

Otis's strategy has two parts. The first is severing insurgent supply lines. On March 12, Brigadier General Lloyd Wheaton leads a provisional brigade east and south of the city to Laguna de Bay. His orders are to clean out pockets of nationalist resistance and destroy crops that might supply Aguinaldo's forces. During March 12–17 Wheaton, supported by a gunboat and land artillery, delivers a crippling blow to nationalist forces south of the capital.

The second part of Otis's strategy is the capture of Malolos, the newly proclaimed capital of the Philippine Republic.

February 6, 1899

Spanish-American War (continued): U.S. ratification of the Treaty of Paris. Senate debate over the treaty ending the war reveals the sharp divisions in the country between imperialists and anti-imperialists. Following considerable spirited debate, the Senate narrowly ratifies the Treaty of Paris by a 2-vote margin: 52 to 27.

February 8–12, 1899

Philippine-American War (continued): Iloilo Campaign. Although securing Luzon is the principal U.S. military objective in 1899, steps are also taken to establish control over other important islands. Iloilo on Panay is occupied on February 11.

February 11, 1899

Philippine-American War (continued): Action at Ho-Ho. The U.S. Navy gunboat *Petrel* shells an insurgent fort on the island of Panay, then lands men to occupy it.

February 22, 1899

Philippine-American War (continued). A landing party from the U.S. Navy gunboat *Petrel* takes possession of the Philippine island of Cebu.

March 2, 1899

Philippine-American War (continued): Creation of new volunteer units. With the expiration of the term of service for Spanish-American War troops, Washington creates new volunteer regiments totaling 35,000 men to serve two-year enlistments. These replace the state volunteer units previously in service and include 1 cavalry and 24 infantry regiments. The army also receives authorization to add 3,000 men to bring existing regiments up to full strength.

March 24–August 16, 1899

Philippine-American War (continued): Malolos Campaign. This campaign is carried out by Major General Arthur MacArthur's 2nd Division of 9,000 men in three brigades under Brigadier Generals Lloyd Wheaton, Harrison Otis, and Irving Hale. Otis and Hale proceed north along the rail line from Caloocan, supported by an artillery battery and a section of Colt machine guns. The advance is slow and fighting is fierce as the troops work their way through nearly impenetrable brush.

Meanwhile, Wheaton's brigade, designated a flying column, gets under way on March 25, moving to the west of Otis and Hale. Otis hopes to catch the Filipino Army of Liberation between these two forces. On March 26 Wheaton's troops capture Malinta, though not in time to seal off Emilio Aguinaldo y Famy's withdrawing forces. Five days later on March 31, MacArthur's troops enter the nationalist capital of Malolos, which the departing nationalists have burned and largely destroyed. Although Malolos is now in U.S. hands, the plan has failed in that the Army of Liberation has escaped. The Americans go on to capture Pampagna on May 5 and San Isidro on May 15. The campaign ends with the capture by the 12th Infantry Regiment of Angeles on August 16.

April 1–25, 1899

Samoan uprising. Late in 1898 intertribal warfare begins in the Samoan islands, which are jointly administered by the United States, Britain, and Germany. American and British personnel are sent ashore to guard the consulates at Apia on Upolu island. The Americans are from the protected cruiser *Philadelphia* and are commanded by Lieutenant Philip Van Horn Lansdale. On April 1, 1899, Samoan insurgents ambush a joint American-British patrol near Apia, killing four Americans (including Lansdale) and three Britons and wounding seven others. The uprising is put down by April 25 through naval shelling and punitive land operations.

April 8–17, 1899

Philippine-American War (continued): Laguna de Bay Campaign. U.S. troops under Major General Henry W. Lawton proceed south. Capturing Santa Cruz in the Laguna de Bay region on April 10, they return to Manila on April 17.

April 21–May 30, 1899

Philippine-American War (continued): San Isidro Campaign. U.S. troops under Major General Henry W. Lawton advance from La Lona Church on San Isidro, dispersing insurgent forces there. Lawton's forces return to Manila on May 30.

June 13, 1899

Philippine-American War (continued): Zapote River Campaign. Brigadier General Henry W. Lawton's men overrun Filipino insurgent field fortifications along the Zapote River.

June 30, 1899

The U.S. Army Signal Corps purchases several electric-powered trucks to test them as transport vehicles. The tests prove unsuccessful, as the trucks' batteries prove incapable of holding a charge for a sufficient period of time.

July 1899

Philippine-American War (continued). U.S. forces in the Philippines lose some 8,000 U.S. volunteer troops when their enlistments expire. Military operations by VIII Corps in the Philippines must proceed with only 20,000 men until the arrival of reinforcements in autumn.

September 6, 1899

U.S. proclamation of the Open Door Policy regarding China. U.S. secretary of state John Hay sends the first of a series of notes to the British, German, and Russian governments. Similar notes are also sent to Japan, Italy, and France. Hay calls for equality of access to commercial opportunity in China and asks the governments involved to declare formally that they will uphold Chinese territorial and administrative integrity within their spheres of influence and will not interfere with the free use of the treaty ports. Other than the United Kingdom, which supports the note, the other powers all give noncommital responses.

September 18–23, 1899

Philippine-American War (continued). A U.S. navy squadron of the monitor *Monterey*, the cruisers *Baltimore* and *Charleston*, the gunboat *Concord*, and the transport *Zafro* shells Filipino insurgent positions ashore, and a landing party then takes possession of Olongapo, securing Subic Bay on the west coast of Luzon.

September 25, 1899

Philippine-American War (continued): Loss of the *Urdaneta*. The U.S. Navy patrol boat *Urdaneta*, commanded by Naval Cadet Welborn C. Wood, is ambushed by Filipino insurgents in the Pampanga River near Orani, Luzon. In the ensuing firefight, Wood and four of his eight-man crew are killed; the remaining four are taken prisoner. The *Urdaneta* is the only U.S. Navy warship lost during the Philippine-American War.

October 7–13, 1899

Philippine-American War (continued): Cavite Campaign. With the arrival of the annual summer monsoon rains, active campaigning comes to a temporary end in Luzon. The character of U.S. forces in the Philippines changes with the arrival of new volunteer regiments and the organization of the Philippine Scouts, Filipino units that provide highly effective support on the U.S. side.

The autumn of 1899 brings the beginning of the dry season and with it a resumption of campaigning. In the Cavite Campaign, forces under Brigadier Generals Lloyd Wheaton and Theodore Schwan wipe out nationalist resistance in Cavite and adjacent provinces. A 400-man U.S. Marine Corps battalion also takes part, attacking Filipino entrenchments at the coastal town of Novaleta from the land side on October 8.

October 15–November 19, 1899

Philippine-American War (continued): San Isidro Campaign. U.S. forces begin a three-pronged offensive in northern Luzon involving forces under Brigadier Generals Henry W. Lawton, Arthur MacArthur, and Lloyd Wheaton, with the primary objective of trapping nationalist leader Emilio Aguinaldo y Famy in hopes of ending the nationalist resistance. Aguinaldo's Army of Liberation numbers perhaps as many as 80,000 men. Although his men are certainly not as well equipped as the U.S. forces and lack a cadre of veteran leaders, they are tough, courageous, and determined. They also have the great advantage of being familiar with the territory.

In the San Isidro Campaign of October 15–November 19, 1899, Lawton and Brigadier General Samuel B. M. Young proceed north up the Rio Grande de la Pampanga, closing off the mountain passes of the Sierra Madre in order to prevent Filipino nationalist forces from escaping. They capture San Isidro on October 19.

Lawton decides to dispatch a mixed force of infantry and cavalry from San Isidro under Young to push ahead in advance of the main column. Lawton is also concerned about Wheaton, from whom he had heard nothing, and fears that if their two commands do not unite as planned, Aguinaldo will again escape. Lawton's command pursues the nationalist forces aggressively, covering more than 100 miles of extremely harsh terrain during a six-week period. They skirmish with Aguinaldo's rear guard but are unable to capture the Filipino leader. Lawton's men approach San Fabian on the Lingayen Gulf on November 18.

November 2, 1899

Philippine-American War (continued). The U.S. Navy protected cruiser *Charleston*, commanded by Captain George W. Pigman, is lost on an uncharted reef near Camiguin Island in the Philippines. All hands are saved.

November 5–20, 1899

Philippine-American War (continued): Tarlac Campaign. Brigadier General Arthur MacArthur advances from San Fernando along a rail route that runs through the fertile valleys and plains of central Luzon. His men capture Tarlac on November 12 and reach Dagupan on November 20.

November 6–19, 1899

Philippine-American War (continued): San Fabian Campaign. Finally, a third force under Brigadier General Lloyd Wheaton of 2,500 men sails from Manila on November 6, 1899, coming ashore at San Fabian the next day. It promptly gets bogged down, however. Routing an insurgent force at San Jacinto on November 12, it links up with U.S. forces under Brigadier General Arthur MacArthur at Dagupan only on November 20, despite the fact that it is only a dozen miles from San Fabian. Even though some of Young's scouts alert Wheaton to the urgency of the situation, he fails to act with dispatch. Finally moved to action, he captures nationalist leader Emilio Aguinaldo y Famy's mother and infant son, but Aguinaldo himself escapes with about 1,000 followers.

November 1899

Boxer Uprising. The nationalist uprising in China, known to contemporaries as the Boxer Rebellion and today as the Boxer Uprising or Boxer Movement, is initiated by the secret organization the Righteous and Harmonious Fists. Its members practice martial arts—hence their name in the West as the Boxers. The movement begins in Shandong Province of northern China in March 1898. It takes place in the context of drought, famine, and resentment of aggressive Christian missionaries and at the legal privileges enjoyed by Chinese Christians, whose association with foreign missionaries gives them advantage in the settlement of legal disputes.

The Boxers seek the removal of all foreign influences, including Christianity. They want an end to European control of Chinese territory and trade and termination of such concessions as extraterritoriality, whereby foreigners are not subject to Chinese law. The Boxers also initially oppose the imperial government, but after they are badly defeated in a clash with imperial troops in October 1898, they halt their anti-imperial government campaign and concentrate on expelling the foreigners and ending foreign influence.

The imperial court, controlled by Dowager Empress Cixi (Tz'u Hsi), claims not to be able to control the Boxers; in fact, it incites them to operate against the foreigners.

December 2, 1899
Philippine-American War (continued): Battle of Triad Pass. On December 2, elements of Brigadier General Lloyd Wheaton's command under Major Peyton March attack Filipino nationalist leader Emilio Aguinaldo y Famy's rear guard at Triad Pass, killing General Gregorio del Pilar, Aguinaldo's close friend and adviser. This action ends the U.S. Army's major campaigns in Luzon; only scattered insurgent elements remain active in the island thereafter. Considerable fighting is yet to be done, but Aguinaldo realizes that he cannot now wage a conventional war against the U.S. Army with any real hope of success. As a result, from December 1899 until Aguinaldo's capture on March 23, 1901, the U.S. Army is obliged to fight a protracted guerrilla war that does not come to a formal end until 1902.

January 7, 1900
Philippine-American War (continued): Battle of Imus. Near Imus in Cavite Province on the island of Luzon, members of Colonel William E. Birkhimer's 28th Volunteer Infantry Regiment engage a large force of Filipino insurgents in a two-hour battle. Birkhimer reports Filipino casualties of 65 dead and more than 40 wounded, for 8 American wounded.

January 26, 1900–April 27, 1902
Philippine-American War (continued): U.S. operations in Samar. The island of Samar is the easternmost and largest of the Visayan group in the central Philippines. Some 5,000 square miles in size, it is situated across the San Jacinto Straits north of Leyte. U.S. military operations here prove difficult because of the island's dense jungle interior, lack of roads, and few navigable rivers, all of which greatly aid Filipino insurgent General Vicente Lukban in carrying out guerrilla warfare.

There is little U.S. military activity on Samar early in the war. Rope shortages make pacification of the island, with its significant hemp production, a priority. On January 26, 1900, U.S. military governor of the Philippines Major General Elwell Otis orders Brigadier General William Kobbe to occupy Calbayog and Catbalogan with the 43rd Infantry Regiment. This forces Lukban and his men to withdraw into the interior. Colonel Arthur Murray and Major Henry Tureman Allen attempt to establish civil order on Samar through benevolent assimilation, but Lukban's guerrillas prevent many civilians from collaborating with the Americans through intimidation, the burning of towns, and the killing of sympathizers.

Although Allen mounts offensive operations, Major General Arthur MacArthur, who assumes command of U.S. forces in the Philippines on May 15, 1900, visits the island that same month and returns the American troops to their defensive garrisons. By July 1900, the first major campaign to secure Samar has failed.

Colonel E. E. Hardin replaces Murray in July 1900 and attempts to interdict trade between Leyte and Samar through naval blockade. By early 1901, however, the small U.S. occupation force on Samar barely holds the hemp ports of Calbayog and Catbalogan. This changes in May 1901 when Leyte is turned over to the Philippine Commission. The pacification of Samar now becomes a priority, for the rebels across the narrow straits in Samar threaten the pacification of Leyte.

On May 13, 1901, MacArthur transfers Samar to Brigadier General Robert P. Hughes and orders him to "clean up" the island "as soon as possible." A quick inspection trip to Samar convinces Hughes that the situation there is indeed poor, with American troops largely confined to their occupation posts. In June, Hughes extends the U.S. naval blockade to all the ports of Samar and orders occupation forces to seize all island boats except those used for fishing. Hughes also orders sweeps of the interior and the destruction of rebel towns and crops. The navy assists with amphibious operations. These actions deprive the local population of supplies and lead to widespread starvation but fail to break the back of the guerrilla resistance.

On September 28, 1901, insurgent forces attack and massacre unarmed members of Company C of the 9th Infantry Regiment at Balangiga. In the attack (see September 28, 1901), 59 of the soldiers are either killed outright or die of their wounds. An American relief force discovers the town deserted and burns it to the ground.

The so-called Balangiga Massacre brings immediate demands for revenge, and Major General Adna Chaffee Sr. dispatches 4,000 soldiers to Samar, while Rear Admiral Frederick Rodgers sends a marine battalion under Major Littleton W. T. Waller. In October 1901, Chaffee selects Brigadier General Jacob H. Smith to take command of operations in Samar. Smith, who is well known for his harsh methods, instructs Waller to take no prisoners, to "kill and burn," and to turn Samar into "a howling wilderness."

Waller soon locates Lukban's headquarters in the interior on the Sohotón Cliffs along the Cadacan River. Waller plans a land and amphibious operation against the insurgents. In a successful operation, the marines take the rebel headquarters, killing 30 insurgents for no losses of their own.

Waller then mounts another operation to the interior. He starts out from Lanang on the east coast, planning to cross Samar from east to west. The jungle proves virtually impenetrable, and the marines soon run out of food. Filipino bearers claim not to know what is edible in the jungle and refuse to help. Waller then sends half of his men back to Lanang under Captain David D. Porter and pushes on with the remainder. Porter is forced to leave some of his weakened marines behind on the march. An army rescue team subsequently finds 9 of them dead, and 1 is never located. Learning that the rest of the bearers had allowed a marine lieutenant to be killed by a bearer, Porter has all 10 of the bearers arrested and sent to Basey.

Waller, now ill, also makes it to Basey, where Lieutenant John H. A. Day has discovered a conspiracy to repeat the Balangiga Massacre. Day has the mayor arrested and executed and the local priest imprisoned. Day also secures permission from a delirious Waller to execute all of the bearers arrested earlier. The 10 men are shot in the town square.

On his recovery, Waller reports all of this to Smith, who sends it on to Chaffee, who then forwards it to the War Department. The news shocks the American public and empowers U.S. anti-imperialists. Indeed, at the end of January 1902, the U.S. Senate begins committee hearings (the Committee on the Philippines, otherwise known as the Lodge Committee) regarding military atrocities in the Philippines.

U.S. forces capture Lukban on February 18, 1902, and continue pressuring the guerrillas, who are by now suffering from starvation and lack the ability to sustain combat operations. Brigadier General Joseph Grant accepts their surrender on April 27, 1902.

Meanwhile, reaction to U.S. actions on Samar brings Waller's arrest and court-martial. He remains loyal to Smith and refuses to reveal the latter's orders to him but instead bases his defense on American Civil War General Order 100 that authorizes actions against guerrillas and civilians who aid them. When Smith testifies against Waller, however, and perjures himself by claiming that the latter had acted on his own responsibility, Waller breaks his silence and reveals Smith's written orders. A parade of witnesses confirms Waller's testimony. This results in Waller's acquittal and Smith's arrest, court-martial, and conviction.

March 30, 1900

The General Board of the Navy is established. Under the presidency of Admiral George Dewey, this board of senior naval officers is to provide advice to the secretary of the navy regarding policy and operations.

April 30, 1900

Congress grants territorial status to the Hawaiian Islands, to take effect on June 14, 1900. Hawaii becomes the 50th state of the United States on August 21, 1959.

May 15, 1900

Philippine-American War (continued). Major General Arthur MacArthur assumes command of U.S. forces in the Philippines from Major General Elwell Otis.

May 27, 1900

Boxer Uprising (continued): Foreign reinforcements are dispatched to Beijing. Chinese nationalists, known as the Society of Righteous and Harmonious Fists (the Boxers), intensify their actions against foreign interests and influence. The Chinese imperial court is unwilling to take action against them and indeed issues edicts in defense of the Boxers, drawing protests from foreign diplomats.

Given this situation, beginning in April 1900 the Western powers build up their naval presence on the Chinese coast and land 4,500 men to safeguard their interests in Tianjin (Tientsin). On May 31, 1900, 430 marines and sailors from the Eight-Nation Alliance are dispatched to Beijing to reinforce the legations there. Nations sending troops to China include Japan, Russia, the United Kingdom, France, Germany, Italy, Austria, and the United States.

Most of the foreign embassies in Beijing are located in a compound near the Forbidden City (the Qing Imperial Palace). This compound is now fortified and becomes a refuge for foreign citizens in the Chinese capital.

June 10–26, 1900

Boxer Uprising (continued): First relief expedition to Beijing. On June 9, 1900, members of the Chinese nationalist Society of Righteous and Harmonious Fists (the Boxers) cut the telegraph line to Beijing (Peking). The next day, British vice admiral Sir Edward Seymour sets out with some 2,100 men, mostly marines and sailors, and 19 guns, gathered from the warships at Tianjin (Tientsin), to march to Beijing to aid the few foreign forces already in place defending the foreign legations in the imperial capital.

Encountering heavy resistance from far more numerous imperial forces and having sustained some 300 casualties, Seymour's men are forced to withdraw. They return to their ships at Tianjin.

June 13–August 14, 1900

Boxer Uprising (continued). Chinese nationalists, known as the Society of Righteous and Harmonious Fists (the Boxers), in June 1900 invade the city of Beijing, where they kill some 230 non-Chinese. In the provinces, mostly Shandong (Shantung) and Shanxi (Shensi), they also kill tens of thousands of Chinese Christians. Foreigners and some Chinese Christians seek safety in the legations quarter of Beijing.

June 17, 1900

Boxer Uprising (continued): Capture of the Dagu Forts. Imperial Chinese troops reinforce the Dagu (Taku or Peiho) Forts at the mouth of the Hai River, cutting off the foreign force sent to reinforce the legations compound at Beijing from their ships at Tianjin (Tientsin). On June 16 the foreign troops present the Chinese with an ultimatum, demanding the surrender of the forts. Instead of waiting for the expiration of the ultimatum, the Chinese open fire on the allied ships early on June 17. This initiates a heavy exchange of fire, and allied landing forces assault the forts, taking them. Naval boarding parties headed by Royal Navy lieutenant Roger Keyes also capture four Chinese destroyers.

June 20–August 14, 1900

Boxer Uprising (continued): Siege of the foreign legations in Beijing. On June 19, 1900, Chinese empress Cixi (Tz'u-hsi) demands that the foreign legations relocate to Tianjin. The diplomatic corps responds with a request for additional time and an adequate military escort. The next day, however, the Chinese nationalists, known as the Society of Righteous and Harmonious Fists (the Boxers), kill German minister Baron von Kettler in Beijing. They then lay siege to the foreign legations. That same day the Chinese government declares war on the foreign governments for the Western seizure of the Dagu (Taku or Peiho) Forts on June 17.

All the legations are located in the same area of Beijing, within the so-called Tatar City section. The ministers of Austria-Hungary, Belgium, France, Germany, the United Kingdom, the Netherlands, Spain, and the United States meet and decide to abandon the Belgian and Netherlands legations, which are believed too difficult to defend, and withdraw into a quadrilateral formed by the remainder. All the women and children are collected at the large British legation, which is less exposed to attack. At the same time the defenders occupy portions of the Beijing city wall, which runs nearby, in order to observe Chinese troop movements.

The Beitang (Pei-t'ang), or Northern Cathedral, of the Catholic archbishop of Beijing is another

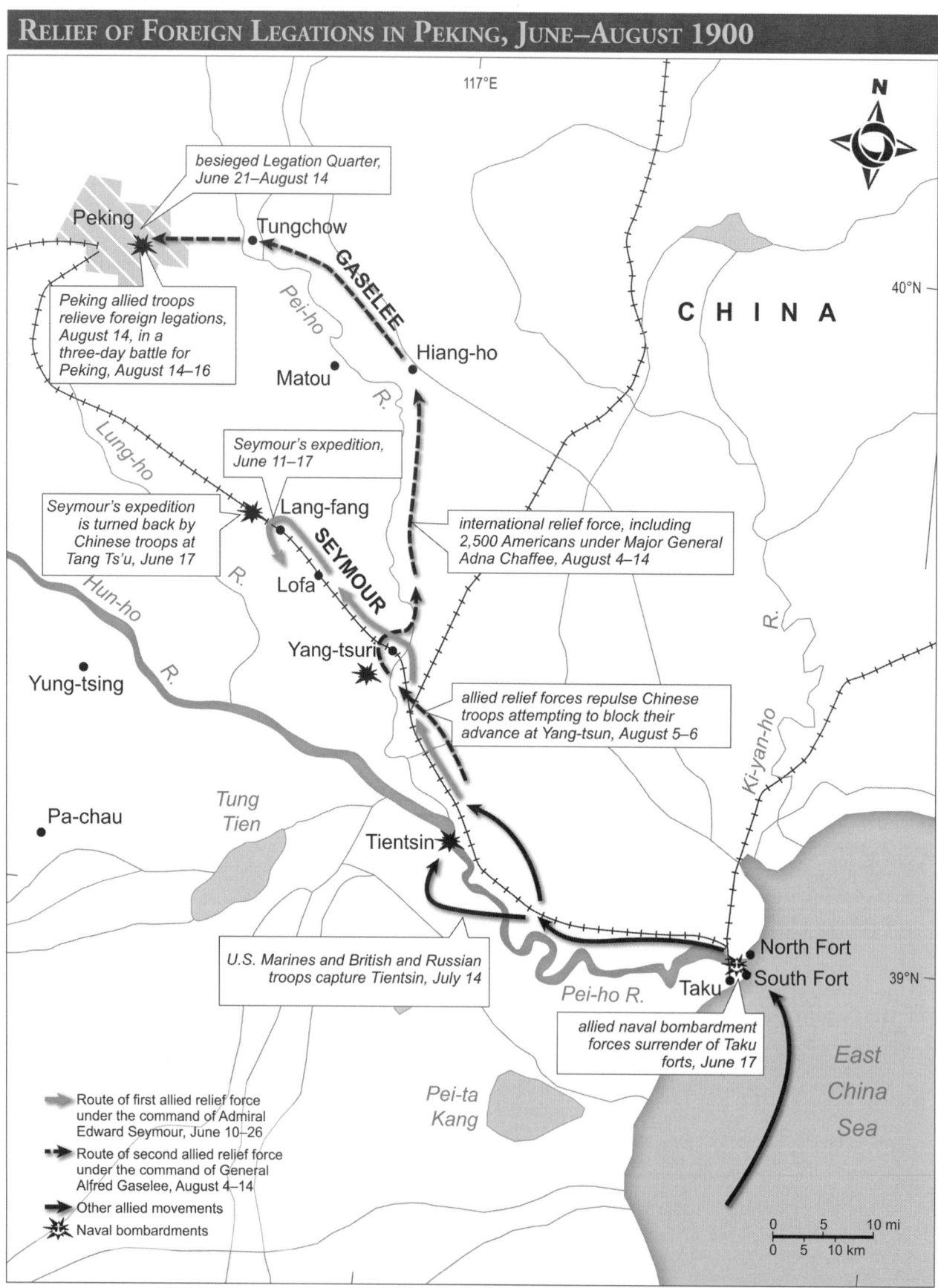

RELIEF OF FOREIGN LEGATIONS IN PEKING, JUNE–AUGUST 1900

117°E

40°N

CHINA

besieged Legation Quarter, June 21–August 14

Peking

Tungchow

GASELEE

Pei-ho R.

Hiang-ho

Peking allied troops relieve foreign legations, August 14, in a three-day battle for Peking, August 14–16

Matou

Lung-ho

Seymour's expedition, June 11–17

Seymour's expedition is turned back by Chinese troops at Tang Ts'u, June 17

Lang-fang

SEYMOUR

Hun-ho R.

Lofa

international relief force, including 2,500 Americans under Major General Adna Chaffee, August 4–14

Yung-tsing

Yang-tsun

allied relief forces repulse Chinese troops attempting to block their advance at Yang-tsun, August 5–6

Ki-yan-ho R.

Pa-chau

Tung Tien

Tientsin

U.S. Marines and British and Russian troops capture Tientsin, July 14

North Fort

South Fort

Taku

39°N

Pei-ho R.

allied naval bombardment forces surrender of Taku forts, June 17

East China Sea

Pei-ta Kang

Route of first allied relief force under the command of Admiral Edward Seymour, June 10–26

Route of second allied relief force under the command of General Alfred Gaselee, August 4–14

Other allied movements

Naval bombardments

0   5   10 mi

0   5   10 km

gathering point for foreigners. Isolated from the legations, it is defended by French sailors and some Italians.

The defenders dig trenches and construct barricades. There are only 364 foreign troops: 72 Russians, 61 British marines, 51 Italians, 50 U.S. sailors, 45 French, 31 Italians, 30 Austrians, and 24 Japanese. They have only small arms, one machine gun, and several small artillery pieces. A number of European civilian men living in Beijing as well as some Chinese assist in the defense of both Beitang and the legations.

On the afternoon of June 20, the imperial ultimatum to depart having expired, a force that ultimately reaches some 18,000 regular Chinese troops surrounds the legation quadrilateral. These regular forces, led by Dong Fuxiang (Tung Fu-hsiang), open fire on the legations, in effect making common cause with the Boxers. The Chinese attacks, most of which are mounted by the Boxers, are only halfhearted, however. Evidence suggests that some of the Qing commanders, who did not support the Boxers, purposely refrain from using their most advanced weapons. In mid-July a truce is arranged, and the empress sends in several wagons of food to the besieged, who are fast running out of provisions.

On August 9 the regular Chinese forces depart, leaving the siege to Manchu troops, a sign that an allied relief column from Tianjin is on the way. The 55-day siege ends early on August 14.

June 25, 1900

Major Walter Reed of the Army Medical Corps arrives in Cuba. Alarmed by the number of U.S. deaths caused by yellow fever during the Spanish-American War, in May 1900 the army appoints Reed to head the Yellow Fever Commission in Cuba. Reed and his team, which includes James Carroll in charge of bacteriology, Jesse Lazear in charge of experimental mosquitoes, and Aristides Agramonte in charge of pathology, arrive in Havana on June 25. Volunteers are infected with yellow fever, which allows Reed to prove the hypothesis that mosquitoes cause the disease. Reed renders his conclusions in October, and on December 21, 1900, Brigadier General Leonard Wood issues General Order No. 6, setting measures to be used for mosquito control on all U.S. Army posts in Cuba. William Gorgas ultimately applies these to the civilian populated areas of the island.

Reed's work was based on a theory first postulated by Cuban physician Carlos Juan Finlay in 1881 that identified mosquitoes as the carriers of yellow fever, but until Reed verifies Finlay's hypothesis, it was commonly held that yellow fever was contracted by contact with clothing and bedding soiled by the excrement and body fluids of yellow fever victims. Reed also conducts controversial experiments to determine if survivors are immune to the disease from subsequent mosquito bites.

Reed's experiments, Wood's policies, and Gorgas's action sharply reduce deaths from yellow fever and facilitate the construction of the Panama Canal from 1904 to 1914. A vaccine to protect against yellow fever is eventually developed in 1937.

July 14, 1900

Boxer Uprising (continued): Capture of Tianjin. Their capture of the Dagu (Taku or Peiho) Forts on June 17, 1900, provides the forces of the Eight-Nation Alliance a staging area from which to relieve their troops at Tianjin (Tientsin) and advance to Beijing. By early July, 51 warships (18 of them Japanese) from the eight nations are deployed in the mouth of the Hai River.

The members of the alliance now have 4,750 marines and naval landing forces plus almost 50,000 other troops, the great majority from Japan (20,840), Russia (13,150), and Britain (12,020). Smaller contingents come from France (3,520), the United States (3,420), Germany (900), Italy (80), and Austria-Hungary (75).

This force assaults the city of Tianjin on July 13, capturing it the next day. U.S. forces involved consist of two battalions of the 9th Infantry Regiment and the 1st Marine Regiment. Colonel Emerson H. Liscum, commanding the 9th Infantry Regiment, is mortally wounded in the battle. Total American losses are 18 dead and 22 wounded. This is the first time since the American Revolutionary War that American troops have participated in an allied operation in the field.

Walter Reed (1851–1902)

U.S. Army doctor. Walter Reed was born on September 13, 1851, in Belroi, Virginia. He earned an MD degree from the University of Virginia in 1869. At the time, he was the youngest person to earn such a degree at the university. Reed earned a second medical degree from the Bellevue Hospital Medical College in 1870. On June 26, 1875, he was appointed as an assistant surgeon in the U.S. Army Medical Corps with the rank of first lieutenant. His first assignment was Fort Lowell, Arizona.

In 1880 after serving at various posts in the West, Reed was promoted to captain and transferred to Fort McHenry, Maryland. During the early 1880s, he attended lectures at Johns Hopkins University in Baltimore. He also studied bacteriology and pathology under the guidance of William Henry Welch, the foremost bacteriologist in the United States. In 1893 after being promoted to major, Reed was appointed professor of bacteriology at the U.S. Army Medical School. He also taught at George Washington University.

Alarmed by the number of U.S. deaths caused by yellow fever during the Spanish-American War, in May 1900 the U.S. Army appointed Reed to head the Yellow Fever Board in Cuba. Reed and his team, which included James Carroll in charge of bacteriology, Jesse Lazear in charge of experimental mosquitoes, and Aristides Agramonte in charge of pathology, arrived in Havana on June 25, 1900. Volunteers were infected with yellow fever, which allowed Reed to prove the hypothesis that mosquitoes caused the disease. He made his conclusions by October of that year. His tests were based on a theory first postulated by Cuban physician Carlos Juan Finlay in 1881 that identified mosquitoes as the carriers of yellow fever. Until Reed had verified Finlay's hypothesis, it had been commonly held that yellow fever was contracted by contact with clothing and bedding soiled by the excrement and body fluids of yellow fever victims. Reed also conducted experiments to determine if survivors were immune to the disease from subsequent mosquito bites. These generated considerable controversy when nurse Clara Maass died of yellow fever on August 24, 1901.

As a result of Reed's efforts, Colonel William Crawford Gorgas, the U.S. Army's chief sanitary officer in Cuba, was able to virtually eliminate yellow fever from Cuba by destroying the mosquitoes' breeding grounds. In 1901 Reed returned to Washington, D.C., to resume his duties at the U.S. Army Medical School and George Washington University. Reed died on November 23, 1902, of peritonitis following an appendectomy.

Reed's pioneering research stymied the mortality rates caused by yellow fever and facilitated the construction of the Panama Canal during 1904–1914. Although there is still no cure for the disease, a vaccine to protect against yellow fever was eventually developed in 1937. Opened in 1909, the Walter Reed General Hospital (Walter Reed Army Medical Center) in Washington, D.C., is named in his honor.

MICHAEL R. HALL

Further Reading

Bean, William. *Walter Reed: A Biography.* Charlottesville: University of Virginia Press, 1982.

Pierce, John R., and James V. Writer. *Yellow Jack: How Yellow Fever Ravaged America and Walter Reed Discovered Its Deadly Secrets.* New York: Wiley, 2005.

August 4–14, 1900

Boxer Uprising (continued): Allied advance on and relief of Beijing. On August 4, 1900, some 17,000 troops of the Eight-Nation Alliance (Austria-Hungary, France, Germany, Italy, Japan, Russia, the United Kingdom, and the United States) begin the 72-mile movement from Tianjin (Tientsin) to Beijing. There is no overall allied commander, although the various national forces do cooperate. The troops move in two columns: 7,000 Japanese troops in the first and 10,000 British, French, German, Italian, Russian, and U.S. troops in the second. Brigadier General Adna R. Chaffee Sr. commands the U.S. expeditionary force of two infantry regiments, two cavalry troops, and one artillery battery. Total U.S. force involved includes the battleship *Oregon*, the cruiser *Newark*, 295 marines, and 3,125 army personnel.

Opposing the allies are some 70,000 imperial troops and 50,000–100,000 members of the Society of Righteous and Harmonious Fists (Boxers). During August 5–6, 1900, the allies defeat some 10,000 imperial troops at Yangcun (Yang-ts'un) about 20 miles from Beijing, with British troops and the U.S. 14th Infantry Regiment taking the lead. U.S. losses in the fighting are 7 dead and 65 wounded.

The allied force reaches Beijing on August 13. The Chinese repel an immediate attack by Russian forces, who are in the lead. On August 14 they also turn back a Japanese attack, but that same day soldiers of the 9th and 14th U.S. Infantry Regiments reach the

American, British, and Japanese troops storm Beijing, China, on August 14, 1900, during the Boxer Rebellion. The effort by the nationalist Boxers to drive Westerners from China was derailed by an international expeditionary force that advanced on Beijing. (Library of Congress)

30-foot-high Tartar Wall of the Outer City. Corporal Calvin P. Titus, a bugler, volunteers to scale the wall. He discovers that it is undefended, and the rest of the men follow, planting the American flag. With the Japanese and Americans having drawn Chinese forces away from the walled city, Sikh soldiers in the British force penetrate the Water Gate and are the first to enter Beijing.

That afternoon the siege of the foreign legations comes to an end, with the next phase the taking of the Imperial City and the Forbidden City. During the 55-day siege of the foreign legations, compound defenders sustain 65 killed (12 civilians) and 168 wounded (23 of them civilians).

The allies also liberate the defenders at the Catholic cathedral, where 40 French and Italian marines have protected a half dozen priests and nuns and some 3,000 Chinese Christians against determined Boxer attacks. Seven of the marines, 4 priests, and perhaps 400 of the Christians die in the defense.

The capture of Beijing marks the end of significant U.S. involvement in crushing the Boxer Uprising. In the operation, U.S. forces have suffered fewer than 200 casualties.

August 15, 1900

Boxer Uprising (continued). The imperial court flees to Xi'an (Sian) in Shaanxi (Shensi) Province. This same day, American artillery blasts open the gate to the Forbidden City (the Qing Imperial Palace), but the allied troops do not enter it until August 28. They subsequently embark on wholesale looting.

September 1900–May 1901

Boxer Uprising (continued): Allied expeditionary forces operate elsewhere in China. In September the Russians rush 10,000 troops to Manchuria to solidify their hold over that Chinese province. Other Allied troops spread out over northern China, breaking up small concentrations of the Society of Righteous and Harmonious Fists (the Boxers) where they can be found.

On December 26 Dowager Empress Cixi (Tz'u Hsi) announces her acceptance of all allied demands. On February 1, 1901, the imperial government officially abolishes the Boxers. Meanwhile, the allies mount a series of destructive punitive attacks in the Beijing area. The troops of the Eight-Nation Alliance are guilty of considerable wanton destruction and looting of Chinese property as well as rapes.

September 13, 1900

Philippine-American War: Battle of Massiquisie. The town of Massiquisie is on the island of Marinduque. Only about 400 square miles in size with some 50,000 people, Marinduque lies just off the southern coast of Luzon. In April 1900, Major General John C. Bates, commanding U.S. forces in southern Luzon, dispatches a battalion of the 29th U.S. Volunteer Infantry Regiment to Marinduque. Despite regular army patrols to the interior, the guerrillas refuse to engage the troops in pitched battle.

Captain Devereux Shields, commander of Company F of the 29th Regiment, establishes a base at Santa Cruz in northeastern Marinduque and mounts 13 operations during July and August. None of these extend more than 10 miles from Santa Cruz, however. Aided by the local populace and the island's rugged terrain, the guerrillas simply avoid contact.

In early September, the presence of the U.S. Navy (ex-Spanish) gunboat *Villalobos* provides Shields with the opportunity to deploy forces to Torrijos on Marinduque's southeastern coast. Ordering First Lieutenant M. H. Wilson and 41 soldiers to defend Santa Cruz, Shields and 51 others proceed via the gunboat to near Torrijos and land on September 11. The Americans scatter some 20 guerrillas and destroy their base. On September 13, Shields and his troops proceed into the interior, intending to return to Santa Cruz. Insurgent leader Lieutenant Colonel Máximo Abad masses virtually the entire insurgent force on the island—some 250 men with rifles and another 2,000 men with bolos—and ambushes the Americans. Following several hours of fighting, Shields orders a withdrawal to prevent an envelopment. Retreating more than three miles, the Americans take up position behind dikes in a rice paddy close to the town of Massiquisie.

Vastly outnumbered, Shields is forced to surrender. Four Americans have been killed in the fighting, and all others are taken prisoner, 6 of them (including

USS *Holland*

Irish immigrant to the United States John P. Holland invented the first really practical submarine. Holland arrived in America in 1873 with a hatred of the English. He hoped that his submarine might end British dominance at sea and perhaps its hold on Ireland. Holland planned to use water ballast to submerge the submarine and horizontal rudders to make it dive. Navy Department officials were unimpressed, and so Holland approached the Fenian Brotherhood, an organization dedicated to independence for Ireland. In 1876 Holland demonstrated a 30-inch model of his submarine to Fenian supporters at Coney Island, New York, and they agreed to advance money for the project.

The one-man *Holland I* was lozenge-shaped with a length of 24′6″ and a beam of 12′6″. It had a square conning tower. The submarine promptly sank when launched, unoccupied, on May 22, 1878. It was easily recovered, and a week later Holland took it out on a successful trial.

Holland's next submarine, the *Holland II,* was also funded by the Fenians. Weighing 19 tons, it was powered by a 15-horsepower (hp) combustion engine. Utilizing horizontal rudders while under way, it actually dived beneath the surface, unlike its predecessor, which simply sank in place. The *Holland II* was also equipped with a pneumatic cannon to fire a torpedo. Twice Holland entered and won U.S. Navy submarine design competitions, but his steam-powered *Plunger* of 1897 proved unsuccessful. Believing the navy specifications to be unrealistic, Holland decided to build a submarine to his own specifications.

Holland built his sixth submarine, at Elizabeth, New Jersey, during 1896–1897. The *Holland VI,* which made its first surface run in February 1898, is usually known simply as the *Holland.* Forerunner of all modern submarines, it was powered by an internal combustion 45-hp gasoline engine for running on the surface with hatches open and an electric motor for submerged operation. While it was running, the gasoline engine powered a generator that recharged the batteries. The *Holland* was the first submarine to be so equipped, with this system becoming common on submarines for the next half century.

The *Holland* had a length of 53′10″ and a breadth of 10′3″. It displaced only 63.3 tons on the surface and 74 tons submerged. It was armed with a single 18-inch torpedo tube and could carry two reload torpedoes. It was also equipped with an 8-inch pneumatic dynamite gun mounted forward. The *Holland* could travel at eight knots on the surface and five to six knots submerged. It was designed for a crew of five.

Its stability while submerged and greater range put the *Holland* in a class by itself. Recognizing the importance of the design, in April 1900 the navy purchased the submarine, commissioning it that October. Later it was assigned hull number SS-1 as the U.S. Navy's first submarine. In September 1900 during North Atlantic Squadron war games off Newport, Rhode Island, the *Holland* carried out mock torpedo attacks against the battleship *Kearsarge,* during which the latter was ruled to have been sunk. A month earlier, Washington had signed a contract with the Holland Torpedo Boat Company for six additional submarines, the first of which was launched in July 1901. Given names, they were known as the Adder class. The *Holland* itself became a training vessel and was finally scrapped in 1913.

SPENCER C. TUCKER

Further Reading

Morris, Richard Knowles. *John P. Holland, 1841–1914: Inventor of the Modern Submarine.* Annapolis, MD: Naval Institute Press, 1965.

U.S. Navy. *Dictionary of American Naval Fighting Ships.* 8 vols. Washington, DC: Naval History Division, Department of the Navy, 1960–1981.

Shields) wounded. Shields estimates insurgent deaths at 30, but this figure is never confirmed. The Battle of Massiquisie brings additional U.S. troops to the island and a number of punitive raids that, however, do little to cripple guerrilla activities.

October 3, 1900

Boxer Uprising (continued). Much of U.S. Army brigadier general Adna R. Chaffee Sr.'s American Expeditionary Force embarks aboard ship to return from China to the Philippines, although some men remain behind to protect lines of communication.

October 12, 1900

The U.S. Navy commissions its first submarine, the *Holland* (SS-1), commanded by Lieutenant Harry H. Caldwell.

October 21–23, 1900

Philippine-American War (continued): Battle of Loac. At Loac on Luzon, some 300 Filipino insurgents ambush Captain George W. Biegler's 19-man patrol of the 28th Volunteer Regiment. Biegler's men defeat the insurgents, killing 75 of them at a cost to themselves of 4 wounded. Biegler is subsequently awarded the Medal of Honor.

February 2, 1901

Congress passes the Army Reorganization Act. On this date, with the deadline for the temporary forces in the Philippines rapidly running out, Congress fixes the regular army at 30 regiments of infantry and 15 of cavalry, 3 battalions of engineers, and a "corps" of artillery that includes both 50 field batteries and 126 companies of coastal artillery. Total army strength would vary between 60,000 and 100,000 men at the discretion of the president.

Section 19 of the Army Reorganization Act establishes the Army Nurse Corps as a permanent part of the Medical Department. Dr. Anita Newcomb McGee, director of the Daughters of the American Revolution Hospital Corps, who was instrumental in providing highly qualified nursing graduates for appointment as army contract nurses during the Spanish-American War, authors the bill that becomes

Section 19 and is thus known as the "Founder of the Army Nurse Corps." McGee is subsequently appointed acting assistant surgeon general in charge of the Nurse Corps Division.

March 2, 1901

Platt Amendment. An amendment drafted by U.S. secretary of war Elihu Root and presented to the Senate by Connecticut Republican Orville H. Platt is attached to the Army Appropriations Act passed by the U.S. Congress on March 2, 1901. The Platt Amendment in effect supersedes the 1898 Teller Amendment, which had prohibited American annexation of Cuba. U.S. troops have been stationed in Cuba since the Spanish-American War of 1898. The Platt Amendment outlines both provisions for their withdrawal and defines future Cuban-U.S. relations.

The Platt Amendment stipulates that Cuba may never enter into any treaty with a foreign power that will impair its independence, that it must not acquire foreign debt beyond its ability to pay from its own revenues, that the United States has the right to intervene to preserve Cuban independence and to preserve law and order, that Cuba must agree to cede or lease land to the United States for the purposes of naval or coaling stations (the Guantánamo Bay Naval Base), and that Cuba include the provisions of the Platt Amendment verbatim in its new constitution. In effect the Platt Amendment gives the United States a virtual protectorate over Cuba.

Under considerable U.S. pressure, the Cuban Constitutional Convention includes the Platt Amendment provisions in its constitution on June 12, 1901. Following the withdrawal of U.S. troops in May 1902, the United States and Cuba incorporate the Platt Amendment into a formal treaty between the two nations on May 22, 1903. Acting under the Platt Amendment, the United States intervenes in Cuba in 1906, 1909, 1912, and 1917–1923 to protect American interests. Congress repeals the Platt Amendment in 1934 as part of President Franklin D. Roosevelt's Good Neighbor Policy to improve relations with Latin American and Caribbean nations. All its provisions, except for the U.S. rights to Guantánamo Bay, are nullified. The American Guantánamo Bay base

Elihu Root (1845–1937)

U.S. secretary of war and secretary of state. Elihu Root was born in Clinton, New York, on February 15, 1845. He graduated from Hamilton College in Clinton in 1864 and obtained his law degree from New York University Law School in 1867. He then became a successful corporate attorney. Root served as U.S. district attorney for the southern district of New York from 1883 to 1885.

President William McKinley appointed Root as secretary of war in 1899, and he served in this post until 1904. Root's immediate problem was to secure adequate manpower to crush the Filipino insurgency, and he pushed for a larger U.S. military establishment to meet the expanded U.S. overseas commitments. In February 1901, Congress fixed the regular army at between 60,000 and 100,000 men at the discretion of the president. That same year Root secured creation of the Army War College by Executive Order.

Theodore Roosevelt became president in September 1901 on the death of McKinley. Although chiefly interested in the navy, he supported Root's reforms, and in 1903 Congress passed Root's recommended bills that established a General Staff and reformed the National Guard. The new legislation replaced the hollow office of commanding general with the position of chief of staff, with control of the staff bureaus and appointment for a limited term only. The Dick Act of 1903 repealed the Militia Act of 1792 and recognized the wholly volunteer National Guard as the "organized militia" and the nation's first-line military reserve. The National Guard was to be organized, trained, and equipped as the regular army. The federal government would provide its weapons and equipment and furnish regular army officers as instructors. The act also imposed minimum standards of weekly drill and an annual encampment. Root also oversaw the introduction of new weapons, including the Model 1903 .30-caliber Springfield rifle and new artillery.

During 1905–1909, Root served as secretary of state. He improved relations with Latin America and Japan. In 1908, he secured the Root-Takahira Agrement with Japan to confirm the U.S. Open Door Policy in China.

During 1909–1915, Root was a U.S. senator but also served as chief U.S. consul of the International Court of Justice at The Hague in the North Atlantic fisheries arbitration case, which settled the dispute between the United States and Great Britain over Canadian and U.S. territorial fishing rights in the North Atlantic. In recognition of his work as secretary of state and at The Hague, Root received the 1912 Nobel Peace Prize.

A strong proponent of the defeat of Germany in World War I, Root was critical of President Woodrow Wilson's policy of neutrality. After the war, Root advocated U.S. membership in the League of Nations. In 1920, he helped to create the League of Nation's Permanent Court of International Justice. As president of the Carnegie Endowment for International Peace from 1910 to 1925, Root worked for the free international exchange of scientific knowledge. In 1921 he was a delegate to the International Conference on the Limitation of Armaments in Washington, D.C. (commonly known as the Washington Naval Conference). Root died in Clinton, New York, on February 7, 1937.

Spencer C. Tucker

Further Reading

Cosmas, Graham. *An Army for Empire: The United States Army in the Spanish-American War.* College Station: Texas A&M University Press, 1998.

Jessup, Philip C. *Elihu Root.* 2 vols. New York: Dodd, Mead, 1938.

Leopold, Richard W. *Elihu Root and the Conservative Tradition.* Boston: Little, Brown, 1954.

continues to rankle, but the lease can be revoked only with the joint consent of Cuba and the United States.

March 23, 1901

Philippine-American War (continued): Capture of Aguinaldo. U.S. Army brigadier general Frederick Funston learns through captured dispatches that Filipino nationalist leader Emilio Aguinaldo y Famy has requested that 400 insurgent reinforcements proceed to his jungle headquarters. Funston quickly devises a raid in which Macabebe Scouts under his command pose as the reinforcements, escorting 5 American officers, including Funston, as their supposed prisoners. Totaling 89 men, the raiding force consists of 79 Macabebe Scouts in captured insurgent uniforms, 4 rebel defectors, the 5 U.S. officers, and a Spanish intelligence officer working with the Americans. Proceeding through 100 miles of jungle, the force is so convincing that Aguinaldo's honor guard welcomes them. The Macabebe Scouts then quickly take Aguinaldo prisoner.

Aquinaldo is taken to Manila. Perhaps believing that further resistance against the United States is futile or simply realizing that his own influence has deteriorated too much to warrant continuation of the struggle, on April 1 Aguinaldo signs an oath of allegiance to the United States and encourages his followers to do the same.

July 4, 1901

Philippine-American War (continued). The U.S. military government in the Philippines is replaced by a civilian administration headed by William Howard Taft. Although Governor-General Taft supports strong military action where required, he believes strongly in civilian control and that a reforming civilian administration winning the support of the Filipino people is more likely to bring about law and order than an autocratic military administration. Taft soon clashes with Major General Arthur MacArthur, commander of the Division of the Philippines and, until Taft's arrival, military governor of the islands. Following disagreements, MacArthur departs. Taft proves highly popular with the Filipinos.

September 7, 1901

Boxer Uprising (continued): Boxer Protocol. On September 7, 1901, the Chinese imperial government signs the Boxer Protocol (also known as the Peace Agreement between the Eight-Nation Alliance and China). The Qing government agrees to the execution of 10 named officials accused by the allied governments as linked to the uprising and guilty of the killing of Westerners. China is forced to pay reparations of 450 million taels of silver ($333 million, £67.5 million), to be paid largely by raising the tariff rate. Russia will receive the largest sum (30 percent). Britain and the United States subsequently allocate much of their portions for the education of Chinese students.

The humiliating defeat of the Qing government by the Western powers greatly aids the growth of Chinese nationalism, anti-Manchu sentiment, and movements dedicated to the nation's modernization and overthrow of the Qing dynasty.

September 28, 1901

Philippine-American War (continued): Balangiga Massacre. Elements of the 9th U.S. Infantry Regiment arrive at Balangiga on Samar in the Eastern Visayas in the late summer of 1901 at the request of Mayor Pedro Abayan, who is actually working for Filipino insurgent General Vicente Lukban.

Captain Thomas W. Connell's Company C of the 9th Regiment duly occupies Balangiga, and Connell sets about trying to clean up the town. He establishes local work details that, unknown to him, soon involve some 100 of Lukban's men. To promote a more peaceful atmosphere, Connell prohibits the carrying of firearms except by sentries. On September 27 the insurrectionists smuggle in weapons in coffins containing the bodies of children who have died in a cholera epidemic, and a number of guerrillas also gain access to Balangiga disguised as women carrying the coffins.

On the morning of September 28, the rebels attack. They seize an American sentry's weapon and shoot him, then rush the mess hall where most of Connell's men, who are unarmed, are eating breakfast. Some soldiers escape to the arsenal and then by boat to Basey, held by Company G. But 59 of the soldiers, including Connell, are either killed in the attack or die of their wounds on the way to Basey. When an American relief force arrives at Balangiga, it finds the town deserted and, after attending to the American dead, burns it to the ground.

Some newspapers in the United States compare Balangiga to Custer's Last Stand, and there are immediate demands for revenge. This occurs under new U.S. commander in Samar Brigadier General Jacob H. Smith (see January 26, 1900–April 27, 1902).

November 16, 1901

Lieutenant William S. Sims writes President Theodore Roosevelt regarding naval gunnery reform. U.S. Navy gunnery in the Spanish-American War had been abysmal (it is subsequently determined that only about 3 percent of shells had hit their marks).

A number of naval reformers, most notably Lieutenant Commander Bradley A. Fiske, urge adoption of new firing techniques developed by Royal Navy gunnery expert Captain Percy Scott. Lieutenant William S. Sims, to whom Scott has personally explained his gunnery system, takes the daring step of bypassing the chain of command and writing directly to President Roosevelt, a former assistant secretary of the navy who has a keen interest in naval affairs. Roosevelt is won over and secures Sims's appointment as inspector of target practice. Over the next half decade Sims, Fiske, and Lieutenant Commander Albert P. Niblack revolutionize American naval gunnery.

November 18, 1901

Hay-Pauncefote Treaty. U.S. pressure to modify the terms of the Clayton-Bulwer Treaty of 1850

William Sowden Sims (1858–1936)

U.S. Navy admiral. Born in Port Hope, Ontario, Canada, on October 15, 1858, William Snowden Sims was the son of an American father and a Canadian mother. His family moved to Pennsylvania when Sims was 10 years old, and he graduated from the U.S. Naval Academy, Annapolis, in 1880. The transformation of the U.S. Navy in this period to new steel ships and breech-loading guns marked the beginning of his lifelong interest in enhancing naval equipment, technology, and doctrine. He then served largely in assignments at sea during 1880–1897.

Intelligence reports that Sims sent the Office of Naval Intelligence during the Sino-Japanese War of 1894–1895 carefully analyzed the performance of the various vessels involved and drew lessons as to how the effectiveness of the American fleet might be enhanced. Sims was U.S. naval attaché to France and Russia during 1897–1900. The information on European naval innovations that he provided and extensive espionage operations against Spain that he mounted during the Spanish-American War (1898) favorably impressed Assistant Secretary of the Navy Theodore Roosevelt, who became president in 1901. Sims served on the staff of the commander of the U.S. Asiatic Fleet in 1901 and there became friends with British captain Percy Scott, learning from him of new gunnery techniques introduced into the Royal Navy. Sims's efforts to interest the U.S. Navy in these were not successful, leading him to write to President Roosevelt, technically an act of insubordination.

Recalled to Washington in 1902 and appointed inspector of target practice as a lieutenant commander in November 1902, Sims achieved tremendous success in U.S. naval ordnance reform, reducing the firing time for large-caliber guns from five minutes to 30 seconds while at the same time improving

(continued)

(Continued)

accuracy. As an observer during the Russo-Japanese War (1904–1905), Sims reported on the effectiveness of new armor and the ability of battleships to engage smaller ships.

Promoted to commander in July 1907, Sims became naval aide to President Roosevelt in November. Sims then commanded the battleship *Minnesota* during 1909–1911. Promoted to captain in March 1911, he was an instructor at the Naval War College during 1911–1912, then commanded the Atlantic Torpedo Flotilla during 1913–1915 and the battleship *Nevada* during 1915–1917. He briefly served as president of the Naval War College and commander of the Second Naval District during January–March 1917.

Promoted to rear admiral (to date from August 1916) and with war between the United States and Germany looming, Sims was ordered to Britain to discuss naval cooperation with the Allied powers in March 1917. The United States declared war on Germany on April 6 before his arrival. Promoted to temporary vice admiral in May and made commander of U.S. naval forces in European waters, Sims bombarded Washington with recommendations on convoying, antisubmarine warfare, intelligence gathering, and strategic planning. He urged the immediate implementation of convoys, which gained the support of British prime minister David Lloyd George, and also urged that American battleships be assigned primarily to escort duties convoying supplies and men for the Allies, ventures that brought drastic reductions in Allied shipping losses but generally involved resigning overall control of American naval operations in Europe to British admirals.

Sims's attitude and his excellent relations with his British counterparts led Washington officials, including Secretary of the Navy Josephus Daniels and Chief of Naval Operations William Shepherd Benson, to consider him an Anglophile. For his part, Sims ascribed the navy's initially somewhat disappointing wartime performance to his superiors' failure to implement some of his suggestions and what he viewed as their earlier reluctance to prepare the navy for a major conflict, charges that he aired to Congress in 1920 during an investigation that he largely precipitated, which provoked bitter feuding within the navy.

Within eight months of U.S. entry into the war, Sims and his staff were supervising the operations of 350 ships and 75,000 men. Promoted to temporary admiral in December 1918, Sims returned to the United States and reverted to his permanent rank of rear admiral. He then headed the Naval War College during April 1919–October 1922 until his retirement. He continued to speak out on naval and defense issues, publishing his wartime memoirs, *The Victory at Sea* (1920), which won the Pulitzer Prize for History. Sims also forcefully urged the development of naval aviation. A dynamic and energetic reformer and proponent of naval expansion, in later life Sims's unfortunate tendency to demonize those who opposed him vitiated his numerous concrete achievements. Sims died in Boston on September 25, 1936.

PRISCILLA ROBERTS

Further Reading

Hagan, Kenneth J. "William S. Sims: Naval Insurgent and Coalition Warrior." In *The Human Tradition in the Gilded Age and Progressive Era,* edited by Ballard C. Campbell, 187–203. Wilmington, DE: Scholarly Resources, 2000.
Morison, Elting E. *Admiral Sims and the Modern American Navy.* Boston: Houghton Mifflin, 1942.
Sims, William S. *The Victory at Sea.* 1920; reprint, Annapolis, MD: Naval Institute Press, 1984.
Simpson, Michael, ed. *Anglo-American Naval Relations, 1917–1919.* Brookfield, VT: Gower, 1991.

regarding construction of a transisthmian canal in order to secure exclusive U.S. rights results in discussions between U.S. secretary of state John Hay and British minister plenipotentiary to the United States Sir Julian Pauncefote. The British government, alarmed by the growing strength of the German Navy, is anxious to reach agreement with the United States, and the talks bring the signing on February 5, 1900, of the first Hay-Pauncefote Treaty. Britain renounces all rights to such a canal, which the United States is to construct, maintain, and control. The United States pledges in turn to maintain the neutrality of the canal and never to fortify it. On December 20, 1900, the U.S. Senate ratifies the treaty but with modifications that permit the United States to fortify the canal and with other provisions unacceptable to the British.

Negotiations with Britain resume in April 1901, and on November 18 the Second Hay-Pauncefote Treaty is concluded. The Senate ratifies it on December 16. The treaty abrogates the Clayton-Bulwer Treaty of 1850 and permits the United States to construct, control, and maintain the canal, which will be open to the ships of all nations under equal auspices. In a separate memorandum of August 3, the British concede the right of the United States to fortify the canal. The way is now clear diplomatically for the United States to construct a canal.

November 24–December 4, 1901

U.S. intervention in Colombia. The U.S. battleship *Iowa* and the gunboats *Concord, Machias,* and *Marietta* land marines to protect American interests, particularly the transisthmian railway, during one of the frequent revolts in the province of Panama against Colombian rule. The marines are withdrawn after Captain Thomas Perry of the *Iowa* negotiates a pledge from the opposing forces to respect American lives and property.

November 27, 1901

Establishment of the Army War College. In the wake of criticism leveled at the army, much of this from within the ranks, during the Spanish-American War, in General Order No. 155 Secretary of War Elihu Root establishes the Army War College to train staff officers. An adjunct to the army staff, the college is to advise the president, devise war plans, acquire information, and direct intellectual exercises for the army. The first class of six captains and three majors of the U.S. Army and the U.S. Marine Corps convenes on November 1, 1904. Initially located at Washington Barracks (now Fort Lesley J. McNair), in Washington, D.C., the college is today located at Carlisle, Pennsylvania.

May 1902–November 1903

Philippine-American War: Lake Lanao Campaigns. The area around Lake Lanao in western Mindanao is the scene of hard fighting between U.S. troops and Muslim insurgents during 1902–1903. The Spaniards call the 100,000 Muslims of Mindanao and the nearby Sulu Archipelago Moros, believing that they resemble the Moors of North Africa. Perpetually troublesome to the Spaniards, the recalcitrant Moros pose a threat to U.S. pacification efforts.

In August 1899 U.S. Army brigadier general John C. Bates had concluded a treaty with the sultan of Sulu providing for recognition of U.S. sovereignty in return for noninterference in the religion and customs of the Moro people and subsidy payments to the sultan and his principal chieftains. The treaty secured Moro neutrality in the Philippine-American War and enabled the United States to establish some military outposts in Moro territory.

By 1901, the army has established camps in Mindanao and has begun moving into the Lake Lanao region with the goals of civilizing the natives and securing harmonious relations. The Moros, meanwhile, have grown increasingly resentful. Although some Moro datus (chieftains) are on more or less friendly terms with U.S. authorities, many are overtly hostile, and attacks on small parties of U.S. soldiers grow more frequent.

In September 1901, impressed with Captain John J. Pershing's views and work, Brigadier General George W. Davis, commander of the Department of Mindanao-Jolo, appoints Pershing commander of the remote post of Iligan on the north-central coast of Mindanao, not far from the northern shore of Lake

American troops rest in a field while on a march to Marahui, near Lake Lanao, in the Philippines. (Library of Congress)

Lanao. Pershing had sought the assignment, regarded as a particularly difficult undertaking.

In May 1902 Colonel Frank D. Baldwin, commanding Camp Vicars on the southern shore of Lake Lanao and favoring force to subdue the Moros, responds to Moro harassment of his work parties building a road inland from the coast to Lake Lanao by launching a punitive strike from Malabang with the 27th Infantry Regiment and 25th Mountain Artillery Battery. Baldwin's policy of shooting first and talking later brings fierce fighting and the eventual destruction of the Moro forts, or cottas, at Bayan and Binadayan. Some 400–500 Moros are reportedly slain, including the sultans of Bayan and Pandapatan; American casualties are 10 dead and 44 wounded.

Despite this military success, Baldwin's superiors, Brigadier General George W. Davis and Major General Adna R. Chaffee Sr. (military governor of the Philippines), believe that he had acted too aggressively and failed to work hard enough to achieve harmonious relations with the Moros. Thus, in June 1902 they replace Baldwin with Pershing, who has through patience and hard work established good rapport with the Moros on the north side of Lake Lanao.

Pershing, only a captain, commands a regimental-size force at Camp Vicars, but in spite of his best efforts a number of Moros continue to ambush patrols and attack army camps at night to secure weapons. Pershing decides that punitive action is necessary.

John Joseph Pershing (1860–1948)

General of the Armies of the United States and commander of U.S. forces in France during World War I. Born in Laclede, Missouri, on September 13, 1860, John Joseph Pershing worked odd jobs and taught school to support his family until receiving an appointment to the U.S. Military Academy, West Point, in 1882. Commissioned a second lieutenant on graduation in 1886, he joined the 6th Cavalry Regiment in New Mexico and saw limited action in the final subjugation of the Apache Indians. Pershing also participated in the campaign to quiet the Sioux in 1891 following the tragic confrontation at Wounded Knee.

Pershing became professor of military science at the University of Nebraska in 1891, where he also studied law. He completed a law degree in 1893 and, frustrated by the lack of military advancement, considered a legal career. He returned to the field in 1895 with the 10th Cavalry, an African American unit. Pershing joined the staff of Commanding General Nelson A. Miles in Washington in 1896 and then was an instructor of tactics at West Point in 1897. Here, cadets unhappy with his dark demeanor and rigid style labeled him "Black Jack," a derogatory reference to Pershing's 10th Cavalry posting.

During the Spanish-American War in 1898, Pershing rejoined the 10th Cavalry for the Cuba campaign. His men performed well during the fight for the San Juan Heights on July 1–3, and he drew praise for his own coolness and bravery under fire. Returning to the United States, Pershing oversaw the War Department's new Bureau of Insular Affairs. He was then assigned to the Philippines in September 1899. As a captain, he successfully campaigned against the Moros in 1901, attracting further recognition.

Pershing returned to the United States for General Staff service and to attend the Army War College in 1903. As military attaché to Japan during 1905–1906, he became an official military observer of the Russo-Japanese War of 1904–1905. Impressed with Pershing, President Theodore Roosevelt nominated him for direct promotion from captain to brigadier general in September 1906, vaulting him ahead of 862 more-senior officers. Pershing spent most of the next eight years in the Philippines, where he continued to display effective leadership as the military commander of Moro Province. Returning to the United States, he commanded briefly at the Presidio, San Francisco, before moving to Fort Bliss near El Paso, Texas, in 1914 to confront problems associated with the Mexican Revolution. His wife Frances Warren and their three daughters, who remained at the Presidio, died in a house fire in 1915.

Following the raid by Mexican revolutionary leader Francisco "Pancho" Villa on the small border town of Columbus, New Mexico, on March 9, 1916, Pershing took charge of the Punitive Expedition of 10,000 men into Mexico, with orders to capture or kill Villa and his followers while avoiding conflict with Mexico. It lasted 10 months, cut deep into northern Mexico, and threatened all-out war. Although Villa escaped, Pershing tested new technologies, including machine guns, aircraft, motorized transport, and radio.

Following the U.S. declaration of war on Germany on April 6, 1917, President Woodrow Wilson named Pershing, promoted to major general only in September 1916, to command the American Expeditionary Forces in France on May 12, 1917. Pershing, promoted to full general in October 1917, stubbornly refused to have his forces broken up in smaller units as fillers for British and French forces, but during the crisis occasioned by Germany's 1918 Spring (Ludendorff) Offensives, Pershing offered individual U.S. divisions to the Allied command, and the Americans quickly proved their worth.

(continued)

(Continued)

Pershing directed American forces in the Aisne-Marne Offensive of July 25–August 2, 1918, and the Saint-Mihiel Salient Offensive of September 12–17. He hoped to follow up this latter victory with a drive on Metz and beyond, but Allied commander General Ferdinand Foch favored a broad-front strategy and refused. Pershing then redirected American efforts into the massive Allied Meuse-Argonne Offensive of September 26–November 11. Pershing opposed the armistice of November 11, preferring to fight until Germany surrendered, but was overruled.

After overseeing the demobilization of American forces, Pershing returned to the United States a hero in 1919. Congress confirmed him as general of the armies in September. After service as army chief of staff during 1921–1924, Pershing retired. Active in public life thereafter, he received the Pulitzer Prize for his memoir, *My Experiences in the World War* (1931). Pershing died at Washington, D.C., on July 15, 1948. A stern disciplinarian with high standards and a superb administrator with an ability to pick able subordinates, Pershing was also a military diplomat of high order and among the most significant leaders in American military history.

DAVID COFFEY

Further Reading

Cooke, James J. *Pershing and His Generals: Command and Staff in the AEF.* Westport, CT: Praeger, 1997.

Smith, Gene. *Until the Last Trumpet Sounds: The Life of General of the Armies John J. Pershing.* New York: Wiley, 1999.

Smythe, Donald. *Guerrilla Warrior: The Early Life of John J. Pershing.* New York: Scribner, 1973.

Smythe, Donald. *Pershing: General of the Armies.* Bloomington: Indiana University Press, 1986.

Vandiver, Frank E. *Black Jack: The Life and Times of John J. Pershing.* 2 vols. College Station: Texas A&M University Press, 1977.

In late September 1902, Pershing mounts a campaign that utilizes American artillery to good advantage and destroys Moro cottas at Guaun and Bayabao. Pressing on toward Maciu, Pershing dispatches emissaries, but efforts to negotiate are rebuffed. He is, however, forced to pull back when he is unable to cross an inlet of Lake Lanao separating Maciu, Sauir, and Talub.

Returning with engineers, Pershing orders a road constructed around the inlet, and by October 1 he confronts the hostile cottas. American artillery makes short work of the Moro forts, and on October 3 Pershing returns to Camp Vicars, having destroyed 10 cottas and inflicted heavy casualties for few losses of his own. In November, he renews efforts to persuade Moro leaders, notably the sultan of Bacolod, to accept U.S. terms. Although these are rejected, offensive operations do not resume until the following spring.

Authorized to move against the intractable sultan of Bacolod, Pershing departs Camp Vicars on April 3, 1903. Three days later after maneuvering over rugged terrain, Pershing surrounds the powerful Moro cotta at Bacolod on a ridge above Lake Lanao. On April 7 he attacks in a heavy rainstorm. By dark, the cotta is ablaze from artillery fire. Moro casualties are again heavy, but Pershing allows many Moros to escape, hoping that having experienced American military might, they will persuade other Moros that further resistance is futile.

In May, Pershing continues to sweep the area around Lake Lanao, defeating the Moros at Taraca and destroying more cottas. American gunboats on the lake support the mission and attack the Moro vintas (a type of canoe). By May 10 Pershing is back at Camp Vicars, the first American to lead an expedition completely around Lake Lanao.

Pershing's honesty and compassion but readiness to inflict punishment when necessary bring resolution of the problem. In November 1903, Moro Province governor Leonard Wood leads a final punitive military campaign in the Lake Lanao area. These campaigns break organized Moro resistance, although some harassment by individuals continues.

July 4, 1902

President Theodore Roosevelt declares the Philippine-American War at an end. Sporadic opposition to American rule continues throughout the archipelago, however. The Moros in Mindanao and Jolo prove particularly intractable, and there is warfare into 1913. During the official period of the war (1899–1902), perhaps 80,000–100,000 Filipinos had fought U.S. forces in some 2,811 recorded actions and had suffered an estimated 16,000 military deaths. Some 250,000–1 million Filipinos die as a consequence of the war. Another 100,000 Filipino civilians die in the Moro Rebellion. U.S. forces suffer 4,325 dead between 1898 and 1902, 1,500 of them in actual combat. Another 2,818 are wounded.

September 18–November 18, 1902

U.S. forces landed in Colombia. At Colón, Colombia, on September 18, 1902, the U.S. cruiser *Cincinnati* sends a landing party to protect American lives and property. The next day the U.S. Navy survey ship *Ranger* does the same at Panama City in the Colombian province of Panama.

On September 23, a battalion of U.S. marines under Lieutenant Colonel B. R. Russell lands at Colón, Panama. Rear Admiral Silas Casey, commanding U.S. naval forces, refuses to permit Colombian troops to cross the isthmus to attack the Panamanian rebels and is able to arrange a tentative peace.

November 24, 1902

The U.S. Navy commissions its first destroyer, the *Bainbridge* (DD 1). It sees extensive service in the European theater in World War I. Decommissioned in July 1919, it is sold and broken up for scrap.

December 1902–January 1903

Venezuelan Crisis. When Venezuelan dictator Cipriano Castro defaults on debt payment to European creditors, Germany and Great Britain, later joined by Italy, dispatch warships to the coast of that country. They blockade several Venezuelan ports and seize several Venezuelan gunboats, while the Germans shell several coastal forts and sink two Venezuelan gunboats. Determined to prevent European military intervention in the Western Hemisphere, President Theodore Roosevelt sends U.S. naval forces to the Caribbean and takes a leading role in negotiations that cause the creditor nations to submit their claims to the International Court of Justice at The Hague (Hague Tribunal), which rules in February 1904 that Venezuela must pay.

January 21, 1903

Congress passes the Militia Act of 1903. The Spanish-American War and the Philippine-American War reveal major weaknesses in the U.S. military establishment. As a part of reform and reorganization undertaken by Secretary of War Elihu Root, U.S. senator Charles W. F. Dick (a major general in the Ohio National Guard and chair of the Committee on the Militia) introduces legislation that when passed replaces the Militia Act of 1792.

The Militia Act of 1903, also known as the Dick Act, states that the militia of the United States includes all able-bodied male citizens between the ages of 18 and 45. They are divided into two classes: the "Organized militia," to be known as the National Guard, and the "Reserve militia."

The National Guard is to be organized, trained, and equipped the same as the regular army. Members must attend 24 weekly drills and a five-day annual encampment. The federal government provides its pay, weapons, and equipment, and regular army officers serve as instructors.

Still, Washington can call the National Guard into service only for the constitutional purposes of keeping internal order or repelling invasion. In case of overseas service, Washington can only ask that its members volunteer. The presumption is that in the event of need, the National Guard will volunteer en masse.

January 22, 1903

Hay-Herrán Treaty. The need for a canal across Central America, which would dramatically cut shipping time between the Atlantic and Pacific coasts of the United States and therefore costs, had been amply demonstrated in the 66-day cruise of the U.S. Navy battleship *Oregon* during the Spanish-American War (see March 19–May 24, 1898). Had there been a canal, the trip would have taken a third the time. U.S. president Theodore Roosevelt is determined to build such a canal.

On this date, U.S. secretary of state John Hay and Columbian chargé d'affaires Tomás Herrán conclude a treaty, under the terms of which for payment of $10 million and an annual subsidy of $250,000, Colombia agrees to grant the United States a 100-year lease on land for the construction and operation of a canal across the Isthmus of Panama. Although the U.S. Senate approves the treaty in March 1903, in August the Columbian Senate rejects it.

February 14, 1903

The U.S. Congress authorizes creation of a general staff. Part of the extensive military reforms undertaken by Secretary of War Elihu Root, this eliminates the position of commanding general, who in times of war had little authority over field generals and in time of peace had nothing to command, as administration resided in the heads of the staff bureaus of engineers, ordnance, quartermaster, commissary, and adjutant general—all of which are under the civilian secretary of war. The chiefs of these bureaus had permanent tenure, and their bureaus were staffed by officers who spent their entire careers within their respective corps. Their chief goals in peacetime were economy and bureaucratic efficiency, not preparation for war.

Root secures the replacement of the office of commanding general with the position of chief of staff as the highest-ranking army officer. He is the head of the military hierarchy and serves as senior military adviser to the president and his civilian deputy, the secretary of war. The chief of staff has authority over the staff bureaus, which will carry out planning, training, the development of new weapons systems, and logistical support necessary for a war, the tactics and strategy of which will be set by the field commanders. This far more efficient system also provides that the chief of staff will serve a fixed term only. Typically the commanding general had been the most senior officer in the army and, once appointed, held that post for the remainder of his military career. The new arrangement makes it possible to select the most capable individuals for this post. Also, the officers in the new General Staff Corps serving the chief of staff will also serve fixed terms, so that planning, weapons design, and administrative policy will be in close contact with the "using arms." Lieutenant General Samuel B. M. Young is the U.S. Army's first chief of staff. He assumes the position in August 1903 and holds it until his retirement in January 1904.

February 23, 1903

Under terms of the Platt Amendment (see March 2, 1901), the United States leases 45 square miles of land and water at Guantánamo Bay at the southeastern end of Cuba, where it establishes the Guantánamo Bay Naval Base.

March 21–April 16, 1903

Following a revolution in Honduras, the United States dispatches the gunboat *Marietta*, the transport *Panther*, and the cruisers *Olympia*, *Raleigh*, and *San Francisco* to operate off the Honduran coast; marines are landed to protect the U.S. embassy.

April 1–19, 1903

The U.S. Navy cruiser *Atlanta* lands a detachment of marines to guard the U.S. consulate at Santo Domingo following an insurrection in the Dominican Republic.

June 23, 1903

The U.S. Army formally adopts the Springfield .30-caliber M1903 rifle as its first semiautomatic infantry firearm.

M1903 Springfield .30-Caliber Rifle

In 1900 the U.S. government Springfield Arsenal produced a prototype new infantry rifle. On June 23, 1903, the U.S. Army formally adopted the Springfield .30-caliber M1903 rile as its first semiautomatic infantry firearm. It replaced the Norwegian Krag-Jørgensen rifle that had been adopted in 1892. After the Springfield went into production, President Theodore Roosevelt objected to its rod-type bayonet. Other modifications were also effected, and the new model was accepted on June 21, 1905. During the Spanish-American War, the U.S. Army had secured a number of Spanish Model 93 Mauser rifles, and the Springfield utilized a Mauser-type action. (Mauser Werke brought suit because of this, and the U.S. government was subsequently forced to pay royalties to Mauser for patent infringement.) In addition to becoming the standard army rifle, the Springfield replaced rifles in service with the U.S. Navy and the U.S. Marine Corps.

The bolt-action Springfield weighed some 8.67 pounds and had a barrel length of 24 inches and an overall length of 43.9 inches. Comparable in performance to the British Lee-Enfield, the Springfield had a 5-shot clip. A trained rifleman could fire 15 rounds a minute.

The Springfield utilized a cartridge with a 150-grain (9.7 grams) bullet fired at 2,800 feet per second designated "Cartridge, Ball, Caliber .30, Model of 1906." The M1906 cartridge is based on the German *spitzer* ("boat-tail") bullet design of a relatively light bullet with pointed nose and better long-range ballistics. This .30-06 ammunition is used in many rifles and machine guns and is still among the world's most popular sporting rifle cartridges.

Officially replaced by the eight-round semiautomatic M1 Garand in 1937, the Springfield nonetheless continued in service with the army in the early period of U.S. involvement in World War II because there were initially insufficient numbers of Garands to equip U.S. troops. The Springfield saw service as a sniper rifle throughout World War I, World War II, and the Korean War and early in the Vietnam War. It remains a popular civilian firearm today.

SPENCER C. TUCKER

Further Reading

Bishop, Chris. *The Encyclopedia of Weapons of World War II*. New York: Orbis Publishing, 1998.
Blair, Claude, ed. *Pollard's History of Firearms*. New York: Macmillan, 1983.
Brophy, William. *The Springfield 1903 Rifles*. Mechanicsburg, PA: Stackpole, 1985.
Westwood, David. *Rifles: An Illustrated History of Their Impact*. Santa Barbara, CA: ABC-CLIO, 2005.

September 7–13 and October 10–17, 1903
U.S. intervention in Beirut. Following unrest in Beirut in the Turkish province of Syria, the cruiser *Brooklyn* lands marines and sailors to protect American students at the American University. During October 10–17 following additional disorders in Beirut, other seamen and marines are also landed from the cruiser *San Francisco.*

November 3–6, 1903
Revolution in Panama. With the failure of the Colombian Senate to approve the Hay-Herrán Treaty (see January 22, 1903), whereby the United States would have secured a 100-year lease on land for construction of a canal across the Isthmus of Panama, stockholders of the failed New Panama Canal Company stand to lose everything. Philippe Bunau-Varilla, head of the

John Archer Lejeune (1867–1942)

U.S. Marine Corps general. Born on January 10, 1867, in Pointe Coupée Parish, Louisiana, John Archer Lejeune entered Louisiana State University in 1881 but transferred to the U.S. Naval Academy, Annapolis, in 1884. Graduating as a midshipman in 1888, he was assigned to the cruiser *Vandalia,* which sank in a typhoon off Samoa in March 1889. When he learned that he was to become a naval engineer because of his high grades at the academy, Lejeune appealed to the secretary of the navy and won his case, being commissioned in the U.S. Marine Corps in July 1890.

Lejeune then held a series of ship assignments and had command of the marine detachment on board the cruiser *Cincinnati* during the Spanish-American War. He was promoted to captain in 1899 and to major in 1903, when he took command of the Floating Battalion of the Atlantic Fleet. Lejeune served in Panama and from 1907 to 1909 commanded the Marine Brigade in the Philippines.

Promoted to lieutenant colonel in 1908, Lejeune became the first U.S. Marine Corps officer to graduate from the Army War College (in 1910). He commanded the Advanced Base Brigade during 1913–1914 and was promoted to colonel in 1914. Lejeune then took part in the 1914 occupation of Veracruz, Mexico, where he organized its first motorized unit and also conducted the first U.S. Marine Corps air operations.

Appointed assistant to the commandant of the U.S. Marine Corps in 1915, on August 29, 1916, Lejeune won promotion to brigadier general. He lobbied both for increases in marine personnel and for deployment of marines to France following U.S. entry into the war in April 1917. That September, Lejeune assumed command of the Marine Barracks at Quantico, Virginia.

Lejeune deployed to France in June 1918. The senior marine in France, he asked American Expeditionary Forces commander John Pershing to create a marine division. Pershing refused. Lejeune went on to prove himself as an effective commander of a National Guard Brigade and then the 4th Marine Brigade in the 2nd Division in July. Only three days after Lejeune assumed the latter command, Pershing named the 2nd Division commander, Major General James C. Harbord, to be director of supply, and on July 29 Lejeune, promoted to major general, took over from Harbord to become the first marine to command a U.S. Army division in combat.

Lejeune's 2nd Division was considered one of the army's best. It distinguished itself in the Saint-Mihiel Offensive in September; in the Battle for Mont Blanc Ridge in October, where the division breached the Hindenburg Line and took more than 3,300 prisoners and 121 guns; and in the Meuse-Argonne Offensive. Lejeune emerged from World War I as one of the most decorated U.S. officers. After the armistice, the 2nd Division moved into southern Belgium and then crossed into Germany, taking up occupation duties at Koblenz until its return to the United States in July 1919.

Lejeune then resumed command of Quantico. In June 1920 he was appointed major general commandant of the U.S. Marine Corps. During three terms as commandant until March 1929, Lejeune emphasized education and modernization, established professional military schools for all ranks, adopted modern amphibious tactics, and strengthened the aviation sector of the U.S. Marine Corps. Many regard him as the architect of the modern U.S. Marine Corps.

Lejeune retired from the U.S. Marine Corps in November 1929 and became superintendent of the Virginia Military Institute in Lexington, Virginia. He held this post until 1937. In February 1942 he was promoted to lieutenant general on the retired list. Lejeune died at Baltimore, Maryland, on November 20, 1942. Camp Lejeune, North Carolina, is named in his honor.

DEREK W. FRISBY AND SPENCER C. TUCKER

Further Reading

Bartlett, Merrill L. *Lejeune: A Marine's Life, 1867–1942*. Columbia: University of South Carolina Press, 1991.

Lejeune, John A. *The Reminiscences of a Marine*. Quantico, VA: Dorrance, 1930.

Lewis, Charles Lee. *Famous American Marines*. Boston: L. C. Page, 1950.

Millett, Allan R. *Semper Fidelis: The History of the United States Marine Corps*. Rev. and expanded ed. New York: Free Press, 1991.

company, which had assumed control of the assets of the failed earlier French Panama Canal Company, had arranged to sell these to the United States for $40 million. But the Spooner Act of 1902 appropriating the money was contingent on approval of the Hay-Herrán Treaty.

To safeguard his investment and that of other stockholders, Bunau-Varilla arranges for a revolution in Panama, confident of the full support of U.S. president Theodore Roosevelt's administration. While Washington does not actively plot with the revolutionaries in Panama who desire independence from Colombia, the timing of the revolutionaries' operation and its success clearly rest on U.S. actions. Bunau-Varilla meets with U.S. officials in Washington, who infer that support will be forthcoming. Only then does Bunau-Varilla, operating from New York City, alert the revolutionaries of U.S. support.

The revolt begins in Panama City on November 3, 1903. Already Roosevelt has directed the Navy Department to send ships toward Panama. That same day but hours before the official beginning of the revolution, Commander John Hubbard of the U.S. Navy gunboat *Nashville*, who is ordered to prevent the landing of Colombian troops, anchors at the Atlantic coast port of Colón, still officially Colombian territory. Hubbard lands a small detachment and, supported by the American

superintendent of the Panama Railroad, prevents some 450–500 Colombian soldiers from being able to take the railroad to Panama City to crush the revolution.

On November 5, a battalion of U.S. marines under Major John A. Lejeune arrives at Colón in the transport *Dixie*. Lejeune sends two of his companies ashore, and Colombian troops there yield to superior force and embark in a ship to return home. The next day, November 6, the United States officially recognizes Panamanian independence.

On November 16 Bunau-Varilla is received in Washington, D.C., as the new ambassador of Panama. On November 18 he signs a treaty with U.S. secretary of state John Hay. It is ratified by the U.S. Senate on February 22, 1904, in a vote of 66 to 14. Under the terms of the Hay–Bunau-Varilla Treaty, the United States promises to maintain the independence of Panama and receives a grant in perpetuity of a zone 10 miles wide across Panama in which the canal will be constructed. For this, the U.S. government agrees to pay Panama $10 million and an annuity of $250,000. In public remarks in March 1911, former president Roosevelt will proudly boast, "I took Panama." Recognizing U.S. culpability in the independence of Panama, in the Treaty of Bogotá of February 1921 the United States agrees to pay Colombia $25 million.

December 17, 1903

Wright brothers' first manned heavier-than-air flight. During a span of several hours at Kitty Hawk, North Carolina, Orville and Wilbur Wright of Dayton, Ohio, carry out the world's first manned flights in the *Flyer*, a powered heavier-than-air craft built by them. Orville's initial flight covers 120 feet in 12 seconds and the last 856 feet in 59 seconds. These flights inaugurate a new era.

January 3, 1904

The U.S. Navy cruiser *Detroit* lands its marine detachment to protect American interests during an insurrection at Puerto Plata in the Dominican Republic.

January 5–April 23, 1904

At Chemulpo (present-day Inchon), Korea, on January 5, 1904, the U.S. Navy transport *Zafiro* lands 103 marines and seamen to guard the U.S. legation in

---

 **Wright Military Flyer**

Although men had flown in gliders, balloons, and airships, the first powered and manned heavier-than-air flight was achieved by Wilbur and Orville Wright, two bicycle builders in Dayton, Ohio. In their accomplishment they owed substantial debt to others, most notably Samuel Langley, who made significant advances in aerodynamics. On December 17, 1903, at Kitty Hawk, North Carolina, Orville Wright accomplished the first manned powered flight. During a 12-second span, he flew the biplane *Flyer* a distance of 120 feet. (Since 1949, *Flyer I* has been displayed by the Smithsonian Institution as the world's first piloted powered airplane in which man made controlled and sustained flight.)

The Wright brothers continued to improve their design. In 1908 they built the *Military Flyer*. Purchased by the U.S. Army Signal Corps in August 1909 for $30,000 ($25,000 and a $5,000 bonus, as it flew faster than the 40 miles per hour [mph] required), it was designated Signal Corps Airplane No. 1 and was the world's first military heavier-than-air flying machine. Employed in pilot instruction, it was retired in March 1911 and is now in the Smithsonian Institution.

The *Military Flyer* had a length of 28'11", a wingspan of 36'6", and a height of 7'10.5". It weighed 740 pounds. A biplane, it had a double horizontal front rudder. Powered by a four-cylinder 30.6-horsepower engine, the *Military Flyer* was capable of a speed of 42 mph and had a maximum endurance of approximately one hour.

Signal Corps airplanes played a role in Brigadier General John J. Pershing's expedition into Mexico in 1916, scouting ahead and then dropping messages to troops on the ground. The U.S. Navy was also the first to take a plane off from a ship and the first to land an aircraft on a ship. The military implications of this were enormous, but although the United States was the first to experiment with military aviation, it soon fell behind other powers in this regard. Actually, the first use of airplanes in war was by the Italians during the Tripolitan War of 1911–1912 with the Ottoman Empire. The Italians used their aircraft for scouting purposes and also dropped a few primitive bombs, which caused some panic but did little damage. Military aviation came into its own during World War I.

SPENCER C. TUCKER

Further Reading

Chandler, Charles deForest, and Frank P. Lahm. *How Our Army Grew Wings.* New York: Ronald, 1943.
McFarland, Marvin W., ed. *The Papers of Wilbur and Orville Wright.* New York: McGraw-Hill, 1953.

---

nearby Seoul. Although most are withdrawn in April, 25 remain there until November 11, 1905.

January 7–February 27, 1904

U.S. forces land in the Dominican Republic during a revolution there. On January 7, 1904, the cruiser *Detroit* lands men to protect American lives and property at Sosúa. On January 17 the *Detroit* and the old screw sloop *Hartford* send ashore seamen and marines at Puerto Plata. On February 11 when insurgent forces in Santo Domingo fire on the U.S. Navy cruiser *New York*, the cruisers *Columbia* and *Newark* send ashore 300 sailors and marines under Lieutenant Commander James P. Parker. Supported by covering fire from the *Newark*, they drive the insurgents from Santo Domingo, returning to their ships that evening. During February 25–27, marines from the training ship *Yankee* go ashore to protect the U.S. consulate at Santo Domingo.

January 7–February 16, 1904

U.S. marines sent to Panama. As a show of force, Washington dispatches three additional marine battalions to Panama to reinforce the one commanded by Major John A. Lejeune already there. The marines land on January 7, 1904, and form a provisional brigade under U.S. Marine Corps commandant Brigadier General George F. Elliott. This is the first time a U.S. Marine Corps commandant has commanded units in the field. When it becomes evident that Colombia is not prepared to go to war over the independence of Panama, the brigade is disbanded on February 16.

May 4, 1904

Work commences on the Panama Canal, which will take 10 years to complete.

May 30, 1904

U.S. marines land at Tangier. When naturalized American citizen Ion Perdicaris is kidnapped by bandit chieftain Raisouli, U.S. president Theodore Roosevelt informs the Moroccan government that he wants "Perdicaris alive or Raisouli dead." The marine detachment of the cruiser *Brooklyn* lands at Tangier, and Raisouli releases Perdicaris.

December 6, 1904

Roosevelt Corollary. The Venezuelan Debt Crisis (see December 1902–January 1903) is a major influence behind President Theodore Roosevelt's decision to announce in the course of his address to Congress what becomes known as the Roosevelt Corollary to the Monroe Doctrine. Roosevelt declares that the United States may be forced, "however reluctantly, in flagrant cases of such wrongdoing or impotence, to the exercise of an international police power."

The Roosevelt Corollary is first invoked in December 1905 following the debt crisis in the Dominican Republic. The application of the Roosevelt Corollary generates considerable ill will with Latin American nations, especially when combined with the Platt Amendment's authorization of the right of American intervention in Cuba and the U.S. role in orchestrating a revolution in Panama to secure the Panama Canal Zone. President Franklin D. Roosevelt's Good Neighbor Policy of 1933 marks abandonment of the Roosevelt Corollary.

January 20, 1905

Dominican customs agreement. When the Dominican Republic faces a default on its debts in 1905, President Theodore Roosevelt invokes the Roosevelt Corollary, declaring that the United States will not permit a European nation to forcibly collect debts in the Western Hemisphere and that the United States will assume the responsibility of ensuring that states fulfil their debt obligations. On January 20, 1905, U.S. Navy and U.S. Marine Corps officers assume control of the customs service of the Dominican Republic. American officers arrange for 55 percent of receipts to be applied to debt payment, and by 1907 the Dominican Republic's foreign debts have been paid.

July 29, 1905

Taft-Katsura Memorandum. Based on conversations on July 27 in Tokyo between U.S. secretary of war William Howard Taft and Japanese prime minister Katsura Taro, the United States recognizes Japan's sphere of influence in Korea, while Japan recognizes the U.S. sphere of influence in the Philippine Islands. Intended as a memorandum to maintain

 ## William Crawford Gorgas (1854–1920)

U.S. Army surgeon and surgeon general of the United States. Born on October 3, 1854, in Mobile, Alabama, William Crawford Gorgas was the son of the former Confederate chief of ordnance and grandson of a former governor of Alabama. Gorgas was raised on the family plantation near Mobile, and unable to obtain an appointment to the U.S. Military Academy, West Point, he decided to join the Army Medical Corps after obtaining a medical degree from Bellevue Medical College in New York. In the 1880s while stationed at Fort Brown, Texas, he met Marie Doughty, his future wife, while they were both recovering from yellow fever. Because he was subsequently immune to the disease, Gorgas spent much of the next two decades in posts where yellow fever was common. In 1898 during the Spanish-American War, he was sent to Cuba to be the director of sanitation.

Working under Brigadier General Leonard Wood, who was both a physician and Cuba's military governor, Gorgas applied the research carried out by Walter Reed's Yellow Fever Commission into a coordinated effort to rid Cuba of mosquitoes. The resultant mosquito-control program, which included draconian punishments for leaving standing water, virtually eradicated yellow fever and dramatically reduced the incidence of malaria within less than three years. Since the legs of hospital beds were placed in flat dishes filled with water to keep crawling bugs from getting onto patients, Gorgas treated the water and placed screens around patients to keep the disease from spreading.

In 1904 the United States acquired the rights to the Panamanian isthmus and bought the equipment left by the French after their failed effort to dig a canal. Realizing that the death rate among workers from yellow fever and malaria had been a major factor in the French failure, the army sent Gorgas to take charge of sanitation in the Panama Canal Zone. Unfortunately, the Canal Commission and Colonel George Goethals were unwilling to spend any money on improving sanitary conditions and controlling mosquito breeding. An outbreak of yellow fever in late 1904, however, convinced the Canal Commission to fund Gorgas's attempts at mosquito control. Because of insufficient funding, it was not until late 1905 that yellow fever and malaria were eradicated in the Panama Canal Zone. Following President Theodore Roosevelt's visit to the zone, Gorgas was made a member of the Canal Commission. Determined to see the completion of the Panama Canal, he refused an offer in 1911 to become president of the University of Alabama. Gorgas was the only U.S. official who remained on the canal project from beginning to end.

In 1914, Gorgas was promoted to brigadier general and named surgeon general of the United States, an office he held through World War I. He is credited with having made the medical corps more efficient and with standardizing medical evaluation of new recruits.

Retiring from the army in 1918, Gorgas accepted an offer from the Rockefeller Foundation to travel to South America to advise on the eradication of yellow fever and malaria. He also served as president of the American Medical Association and the American Society of Tropical Disease. Gorgas died in London on July 4, 1920, shortly after suffering a stroke. Following a large funeral in St. Paul's Cathedral, his body was returned to the United States and buried in Arlington National Cemetery.

MICHAEL R. HALL AND JACK MCCALLUM

Further Reading

Gibson, John M. *Physician to the World: The Life of General William C. Gorgas.* Durham, NC: Duke University Press, 1989.

Gorgas, Marie Cook. *William Crawford Gorgas: His Life and Work.* Garden City, NY: Doubleday, 1935.

Gorgas, William Crawford. *Conquest of Malaria: The Views of Surgeon-General Gorgas.* N.p.: Argus, 1914.

cordial Japanese-U.S. relations and not a binding treaty, the Taft-Katsura Memorandum (also known as the Taft-Katsura Agreement) is nonetheless kept secret until 1924.

September 5, 1905

Treaty of Portsmouth (New Hampshire), ending the Russo-Japanese War of 1904–1905. Both Russia and Japan accept the invitation of U.S. president Theodore Roosevelt to a peace conference held at the Portsmouth Navy Yard. By terms of the Treaty of Portsmouth of September 5, 1905, Japan fails to secure an indemnity to pay for the war but takes over Russia's lease of the Liaodong (Liaotung) Peninsula, its railway from Lüshunkou (formerly Port Arthur) north to Changchun, and its mining rights in southern Manchuria. This in effect converts southern Manchuria into a Japanese sphere of influence. Russia also recognizes Japan's preponderant interest in Korea and its right to control and protect the Korean government. Russia also surrenders to Japan the southern half of Sakhalin Island, which Japan occupied during the war. The terms halt Russia's expansion in the Far East and mark the arrival of a new Great Power in Asia. The Japanese victory also rocks all Asia in that it shatters the myth of European military supremacy.

March 5–8, 1906

Moro Rebellion: First Battle of Bud Dajo. Following the revocation by the United States in March 1904 of the Bates Treaty (see May 1902–November 1903), the Moros renew resistance to U.S. authority. This takes the form of sporadic violence and refusal to pay taxes. The governor of Moro Province, Major General Leonard Wood, has been unsuccessful in pacifying Jolo Island, and insurgent Moro attacks there become more frequent.

Hundreds of Moros, including women and children, now establish themselves at Bud Dajo, the crater of an extinct volcano about six miles from the city of Jolo. Legend holds that spirits here will assist warriors in times of need. Rising some 2,100 feet with steep, jungle slopes, the crater is accessible only by three narrow paths and is thus easily defended. It is also well stocked with provisions.

When negotiations by several friendly datus (chiefs) fail to bring about an insurgent surrender, Wood commences military operations on March 5, 1906, sending Colonel Joseph W. Duncan with some 790 U.S. and Philippine Constabulary troops to put down 800–1,000 Moros at Bud Dajo.

The battle begins on March 6. Supported by artillery fire, the attackers work their way through dense jungle and up the slope, attacking the cottas (forts) and other Moro positions. They take Bud Dajo on March 8. Once the outer rim has been secured, artillery—worked to the top with block and tackle—and machine guns are employed against the remaining Moros. Wood reports that "All the defenders were killed as near as could be counted."

In the battle, 18 Americans are killed and another 52 are wounded. Wood estimates Moro dead at 600, including women and children, although some estimates run to 900. U.S. authorities consider this a significant victory and commend Wood. Wood's friend, President Theodore Roosevelt, who had served under him in Cuba in 1898, sends him a congratulatory telegram, and Secretary of War William Howard Taft also approves of Wood's actions. Some in the press, however, believe that it is little more than a massacre, particularly given the number of noncombatants killed. Moro practice is for warriors to take their wives and children with them, but some in the press write that Wood should have simply laid siege to the mountain. The controversy soon dies down as local datus

Battle of Bud Dajo		
Date	March 5–8, 1906	
Location	Bud Dajo, Jolo Island, Philippine Islands	
Opponents (*winner)	*United States	Moro insurgents
Commander	Major General Leonard Wood; Colonel Joseph W. Duncan	Unknown
#	790 U.S. and Philippine Constabulary troops	800–1,000 men, women, and children
Casualties	18 killed, 52 wounded	600 or more killed

and the sultan of Sulu, religious leader of the region, seek stability. Moro resistance continues, however, leading to Brigadier General John J. Pershing's Bud Dajo Campaign of December 1911 and the Battle of Bud Bagsak in June 1913 (see June 11–15, 1913).

April 18, 1906

Following the catastrophic San Francisco, California, earthquake of this date, military units organized by Brigadier General Frederick Funston, to include his 22nd Infantry and 6th Cavalry Regiments and the California National Guard as well as sailors and marines from Mare Island Navy Yard, assist in fighting fires and carrying out rescue and relief operations.

August 13–14, 1906

Brownsville Raid of 1906. Three companies of the African American 25th Infantry Regiment stationed at Fort Brown, Brownsville, Texas, beginning in late July 1906 are immediately subjected to racial discrimination as well as some physical abuse. A reported attack on a white woman during the night of August 12 leads Major Charles W. Penrose, after consultation with town authorities, to declare an early curfew the following day. Around midnight, shootings occur that take the life of bartender Frank Natus and wound police lieutenant M. Y. Dominguez. Some residents claim, despite it being dark and they being distant, to have seen soldiers in the streets shooting.

Several military and civilian investigations occur, presuming the guilt of the soldiers without identifying any culpable individual. A citizens' committee secures the removal of the troops. Meanwhile, Major Augustus P. Blocksom, who is charged with investigating the incident, declares the soldiers to be uncooperative and urges their dismissal if they refuse to give evidence, but the men deny any knowledge of the shootings. Texas Rangers captain William Jesse McDonald arrests 12 enlisted men for conspiracy, but a Cameron County grand jury refuses to return indictments. Inspector General Ernest A. Garlington charges that there is a "conspiracy of silence" by the soldiers and urges that Blocksom's recommendation be carried out. Accordingly, on November 5 President Theodore Roosevelt summarily discharges "without honor" all 167 enlisted men previously garrisoning Fort Brown.

Roosevelt's decision shocks African Americans across the country and focuses national attention on the affair. The Constitution League, a civil rights organization, condemns what it calls the lack of due process and the timing of the action, which closely follows congressional elections. Republican senator Joseph B. Foraker of Ohio, an enemy of Roosevelt, calls for a Senate investigation. The Senate Military Affairs Committee, of which Foraker is a member, conducts hearings, while courts-martial clear Major Penrose and another officer of alleged negligence. The majority report of the Senate committee, issued in March 1908, supports the White House decision, but one minority report of four Republicans finds the evidence inconclusive, and yet another minority report, by Foraker and another Republican, asserts the soldiers' innocence.

Submitting to public pressure, the administration appoints a board of retired army officers, headed by former army chief of staff Lieutenant General Samuel B. M. Young, to review African American applications for reenlistment. After interviewing somewhat more than half the applicants, the Court of Military Inquiry in 1910 inexplicably approves only 14. This decision, along with William H. Taft's presidential victory, Roosevelt's retirement, and Foraker's failure to win renomination, ends the matter for more than 60 years.

In 1972, convinced by recent research critical of government handling of the affair, Representative Augustus Hawkins, a Democrat from California, urges reinstatement of the dismissed soldiers. The Richard Nixon administration concurs and awards the men honorable discharges without back pay. This incident remains the largest single summary dismissal in U.S. Army history.

September 13, 1906–January 28, 1909

U.S. military intervention in Cuba. Widespread political unrest occurs in Cuba following the fraud-ridden reelection of General Tomás Estrada Palma as president of Cuba in September 1905. This and endemic corruption lead to revolutionary outbreaks in August 1906. Palma formally requests U.S. intervention on September 8. Faced with the prospect of chaos in Cuba and with some 60 percent of rural holdings there controlled by U.S. interests, President Theodore Roosevelt concludes that the United States must intervene. This action comes only four years after the end of the occupation of Cuba during 1899–1902.

Roosevelt dispatches the light cruiser *Denver* and the gunboat *Marietta* to Cuba and names Secretary of War William H. Taft and Assistant Secretary of State Robert Bacon to investigate the situation. During September 13–14, 120 sailors and marines land from the *Denver* at Havana to restore order. Other U.S. warships also soon arrive. On September 18 a battalion of marines arrives in the transport *Dixie* to protect U.S. interests at Cienfuegos, and five additional marine battalions are subsequently dispatched to the island.

Palma resigns on September 28, and the next day Taft issues a proclamation on behalf of Roosevelt informing the Cuban people that the United States is seizing political control of the island under terms of the Platt Amendment "to restore order and protect life and property."

On October 1, Colonel Littleton W. T. Waller organizes the two marine regiments presently at Havana into a provisional brigade of 2,900 men. The marines occupy some two dozen strategic points across the island and proceed to disarm insurgent forces. On October 6 the first U.S. Army units arrive in Cuba. Ultimately rising to 6,000 men, these units are formed into the Army of Cuban Pacification. It consists of seven regiments under Brigadier General Frederick Funston. The marine brigade is soon disbanded, although the 1st Regiment remains in Cuba.

On October 13, civilian Charles E. Magoon replaces Taft as provisional governor of Cuba. The insurgents cooperate with the U.S. forces, and Magoon begins the work of revising the Cuban political system and reconstructing the economy. The United States also reorganizes the Cuban military establishment. The Liberal opposition party wins the general elections of May and November 1908, and on January 28, 1909, Magoon transfers authority to the new Cuban government and departs that same day in the battleship *Maine* (BB-10). Forces of the U.S. Army of Cuban Pacification remain on the island to ensure an orderly transition but are withdrawn in April. Unfortunately for Cuba, the modest reforms enacted during the U.S. occupation of 1906–1909 do little to reverse the practice of Cuban leaders using political office for personal gain, and the strengthened Cuban military establishment created by the United States repeatedly interferes in political affairs, leading to the subsequent military dictatorships of Gerardo Machado y Marales and Fulgencio Batista y Zaldívar.

December 30, 1906

The U.S. War Department orders that all soldiers be issued metal identification tags with their names and serial numbers, the origin of the so-called dog tags.

January 8, 1907

Designation of "USS" for United States ship. From the beginnings of the U.S. Navy, there has been no standard designation for a navy ship. President Theodore Roosevelt ends this in Executive Order 549, which states that all U.S. Navy ships are to be referred to as "The name of such vessel, preceded by the words, United States Ship, or the letters U.S.S., and by no other words or letters." Henceforth "USS" is the ship prefix used to identify a commissioned ship of the U.S. Navy. "USS" only applies to a ship while it is in commission. Before commissioning or after decommissioning, it is referred to by name only, with no prefix.

February–December 1907

War between Honduras and Nicaragua. The Nicaraguans win the war and occupy the Honduran capital of Tegucigalpa. Both the U.S. and Mexican governments intervene, and the Washington Conference of December 1907 leads to the establishment of the Central American Court of Arbitration for the peaceful adjudication of disputes.

April 28–June 8, 1907

The U.S. Navy gunboat *Paducah* lands its 12-man marine detachment to protect American interests, first at Laguna and then inland at Choloma, Honduras.

May 20–21, 1907
Anti-Japanese riots in San Francisco reignite a crisis with Japan. A war scare lasts to September.

December 16, 1907–February 22, 1909
Voyage of the Great White Fleet. On June 27, 1907, President Theodore Roosevelt announces his intention to transfer all 16 battleships of the Atlantic Fleet to the Pacific sometime in October, supposedly so they can engage in maneuvers. In August he reconfirms the decision to send the ships via the Strait of Magellan, with the return route to be decided later. Roosevelt's primary goal is to demonstrate to the world the strength of the U.S. Navy. He especially intends to impress Japan, with which relations have deteriorated since anti-Japanese riots on the Pacific coast in May.

The battleships, painted a brilliant white with top hamper an orangish yellow and known as the Great White Fleet, depart from Hampton Roads, Virginia, on December 16. They are the *Connecticut, Georgia, Illinois, Kansas, Kearsarge, Kentucky, Louisiana, Minnesota, Missouri, Nebraska, New Jersey, Ohio, Rhode Island, Vermont, Virginia,* and *Wisconsin.* Rear Admiral Robley D. Evans has command. Four auxiliaries accompany them, along with six torpedo boats. Once the fleet reaches the Caribbean, Evans notifies the sailors that this is a voyage not just to San Francisco but around the world. No cruise of this duration has previously been attempted by steam-powered steel battleships, and many claim that it is technologically impractical.

The ships travel through the Strait of Magellan around Cape Horn, arriving at Magdalena Bay on the west coast of Mexico, where they conduct gunnery practice before proceeding on to California. At San Francisco, Evans, suffering from severe gout, is relieved. Shortly afterward, his replacement, Rear Admiral Charles M. Thomas, dies of heart failure, and Rear Admiral Charles S. Sperry assumes command for the remainder of the voyage.

The ships cross the Pacific and pay port calls at Australia and New Zealand. Some sailors are so impressed by their reception here that hundreds desert. The Great White Fleet then sails for the Philippines, but planned shore leave here is not possible because of a cholera epidemic. On the way to Japan, the Fourth Division becomes separated in a typhoon but rejoins the fleet in Tokyo Bay. Later a sailor on the *Georgia* comes down with smallpox, and that ship is quarantined at Ceylon (present-day Sri Lanka).

After passage through the Indian Ocean, the ships enter the Red Sea, then pass through the Suez Canal into the Mediterranean. Here the fleet's four divisions separate to carry out diplomatic assignments. They reunite at Gibraltar and return to Hampton Roads, Virginia, on February 22 (George Washington's birthday) in 1909, where a jubilant Roosevelt greets them aboard his presidential yacht.

While the 14-month 45,000-mile cruise is virtually incident-free without a single breakdown and is a diplomatic success, it also reveals potential problems. The ships have been forced to rely heavily on foreign ports and supplies, particularly coal. Subsequent Senate hearings also expose problems with ammunition magazines located directly below gun turrets, increasing the danger of explosion.

April 23, 1908
Establishment of the Army Reserve. Formed to provide a reserve of medical officers for the army in time of need, the U.S. Army Reserve is today the federal reserve force of the U.S. Army. Together, the U.S. Army Reserve and the Army National Guard constitute the Reserve Components of the U.S. Army.

May 13, 1908
The U.S. Navy Nurse Corps is established. Twenty women are subsequently selected as its first members. The so-called Sacred Twenty are the first women to serve formally as members of the U.S. Navy.

September 9, 1908
U.S. Army lieutenant Frank P. Lahm becomes the first military passenger in a powered aircraft, during a flight in a Wright Flyer that lasts six and a half minutes and is piloted by Orville Wright outside the nation's capital at Fort Myer, Virginia.

September 17, 1908

At Fort Myer, Virginia, U.S. Army first lieutenant Thomas Selfridge becomes the first military airplane fatality when one of the propellers on the Wright Flyer piloted by Orville Wright breaks apart and the plane loses control and crashes from a height of 75 feet. Selfridge fractures his skull in the crash and dies that evening. Wright also suffers severe injuries and is hospitalized.

April 6, 1909

Peary claims to have reached the geographic North Pole. On July 6, 1908, Commander Robert E. Peary of the U.S. Navy Civil Engineer Corps sails from New York City on his seventh Arctic expedition with 23 other men in the steamer *Roosevelt* under Captain Robert Bartlett. They pass the winter on Ellesmere Island and set out on their trek for the pole on February 28–March 1, 1909. On the final stage of the journey toward the North Pole only 5 of Peary's men—his faithful companion Matthew Henson and 4 Eskimos—accompany him. On April 6 he establishes Camp Jesup allegedly within five miles of the pole, which he claims in his diary entry of April 7 to have reached. This is immediately disputed by Dr. Frederick A. Cook, who had been a surgeon on an 1891–1892 Peary expedition, and claims to have reached the pole several months before. Peary's claim is widely credited for most of the 20th century, although today it is doubted.

August 2, 1909

The U.S. Army accepts delivery of its first airplane, purchased from Orville and Wilbur Wright for $25,000 plus a $5,000 bonus for the Wright *Flyer* having reached 42.5 miles per hour (mph), thus exceeding the contract speed requirement of 40 mph. The plane weighs 800 pounds and is powered by a 30-horsepower engine. Included in the contract is the requirement that the Wright Brothers train and certify two military officers as pilots.

October 26, 1909

First military pilot. At College Park, Maryland, after three hours of training, U.S. Army Signal Corps lieutenant Frederick E. Humphreys becomes the first military pilot to solo in an aircraft when he takes aloft the army's Wright *Flyer*. Lieutenant Frank Lahm also solos the same day.

December 1909–March 1910

U.S. military intervention in Nicaragua. In October 1909 a revolt breaks out in Nicaragua against President José Santos Zelaya, who orders the execution of two U.S. citizens who aided the rebels. Washington breaks diplomatic relations with Nicaragua over what

Smedley Darlington Butler (1881–1940)

U.S. Marine Corps officer. Smedley Darlington Butler was born into a prominent Quaker family in West Chester, Pennsylvania, on July 30, 1881. His father, Thomas Stalker Butler, was a lawyer and for 31 years a U.S. congressman. The younger Butler attended the Haverford School, but he dropped out on the occasion of the war with Spain and joined the U.S. Marine Corps on April 8, 1898, while still 16 years old. His first assignment was to the Philippines, and in 1900 he participated in the expedition to Peking (Beijing) to crush the Boxer Uprising, during which he was wounded twice. For a singular act of heroism helping wounded comrades during the campaign, Butler received the U.S. Marine Corps Brevet Medal, which until 1914 was the highest decoration for U.S. Marine Corps officers. In 1908,

(continued)

(Continued)

Butler was diagnosed with a nervous condition and went on leave for nine months; he then returned to the U.S. Marine Corps.

Butler earned two Medals of Honor as a major: the first during the U.S. occupation of Veracruz, Mexico, in 1914 and the second for the capture of Fort Rivière, Haiti, in 1915. He was the only U.S. Marine Corps officer ever to earn the U.S. Marine Corps Brevet Medal and two Medals of Honor. From 1909 to 1912, Butler was stationed in Nicaragua. Appointed to command the Gendarmerie d'Haiti in December 1915, he was given the rank of Haitian major general. Butler enthusiastically took up the project, creating by the time of his departure in 1918 a force of 120 American officers and 2,600 Haitian enlisted men.

Much to his disappointment, Butler did not see combat during World War I. Advanced to temporary brigadier general in 1918, he commanded the debarkation depot of Camp Pontanezen, Brest, France, from October 1918 to July 1919. He was appointed permanent brigadier general on March 5, 1921. As commander of the U.S. Marine Corps Barracks, Quantico, Virginia, from 1919 to 1924, Butler was an enthusiastic advocate of enlisted education.

During January 1924–December 1925, Butler was on temporary leave of absence from the U.S. Marine Corps to serve as director of the Department of Safety in Philadelphia, Pennsylvania, where he achieved considerable success in a full-scale assault on crime in the city. From 1927 to 1929, Butler commanded the Marine Expeditionary Force in China. He returned from China to be promoted to major general on July 5, 1929, and resumed command of Quantico, which he made the showplace of the U.S. Marine Corps.

Many expected Butler, as the senior marine general, to be named commandant of the U.S. Marine Corps in 1930, but he failed to receive the appointment and retired from the U.S. Marine Corps at his own request on October 1, 1931. In his later years he became an outspoken opponent of U.S. interventions abroad. Butler was one of the first to write about the military-industrial complex (*War Is a Racket,* published in 1935). A frequent speaker at meetings organized by pacifists and church groups, Butler spoke out against war profiteering and what he regarded as the growth of fascism in the United States. For a time in the mid-1930s he acted as a spokesman of the American League Against War and Fascism. Butler ran unsuccessfully as a candidate for the Republican nomination for the U.S. Senate from Pennsylvania in 1932. In 1934, he claimed that a group of wealthy industrialists planned to overthrow the U.S. government and the administration of President Franklin D. Roosevelt. Butler died in the Naval Hospital, Philadelphia, Pennsylvania, on June 21, 1940.

SPENCER C. TUCKER

Further Reading

Heinl, Robert Debs, Jr. *Soldiers of the Sea: The United States Marine Corps, 1775–1962.* Baltimore: Nautical and Aviation Publishing, 1991.

Millett, Allan R. *Semper Fidelis: The History of the United States Marine Corps.* New York: Free Press, 1982.

Schmidt, Hans. *Maverick Marine: General Smedley D. Butler and the Contradictions of American Military History.* Lexington: University Press of Kentucky, 1987.

Venzon, Anne Ciprion. *General Smedley Darling Butler: The Letters of a Leatherneck, 1898–1931.* New York: Praeger, 1992.

it regards as the "murder" of U.S. citizens. Strong U.S. criticism of Zelaya aids the rebels.

On December 18, a U.S. Marine Corps provisional battalion commanded by Colonel E. J. Mahoney embarks on the transport *Buffalo* for Corinto on the Nicaraguan Atlantic coast and is there joined by the Panama Battalion under Major Smedley D. Butler. On December 20 with the marines still aboard ship off Corinto, Zalaya agrees to step aside in favor of fellow Liberal Party member José Madriz, but the U.S. State Department continues nonrecognition of the Nicaraguan regime. The situation gradually returns to normal, and in March 1910 the marines are withdrawn.

January 4, 1910

Commissioning of the battleship *Michigan*, the first U.S. Navy dreadnought.

May 19, 1910

U.S. armed intervention in Nicaragua. New Nicaraguan president José Madriz continues the fight against Nicaraguan rebels and is on the point of victory at the Atlantic coast town of Bluefields when the U.S. government again dispatches marines, ostensibly to protect U.S. property there. On this date the gunboats *Dubuque* and *Paducah* land men to prevent government forces from attacking the town, while the gunboats also prevent the Nicaraguan government gunboat *Venus* from bombarding Bluefields from the sea. On May 30 the Panama Battalion, commanded by Major Smedley D. Butler, comes ashore from the gunboat *Dubuque* and establishes a neutral zone around the town from the land side.

This U.S. action weakens the government forces and strengthens the revolutionaries. Madriz resigns the presidency on August 20, 1910, and the insurgents take power. The marines depart on September 4.

June 30, 1910

Demonstration of aerial bombing. On this date, aviation pioneer Glenn Curtiss, employing his Curtiss pusher airplane at Keuka Lake, New York, drops dummy bombs (actually sections of lead pipe) into a ring formed of buoyed flags in the shape of a battleship. Navy observers record hits by 15 of the 17 dummy bombs dropped.

November 14, 1910

The U.S. Navy flies the first plane off a ship. The United States leads the world in development of naval aviation. Although the navy has no airplanes in 1910, Captain Washington Irving Chambers, in charge of aviation matters for the navy, arranges a series of tests, noting the value of aircraft in locating an enemy battle fleet and adjusting over-the-horizon naval gunfire. Flying a Curtiss pusher aircraft, civilian Eugene B. Ely becomes the first pilot ever to fly a plane off a ship. He takes to the air from a wooden platform mounted over the bow of the light cruiser *Birmingham* at Hampton Roads, Virginia.

January 7, 1911

First bomb dropped from a powered aircraft. During the San Francisco Air Meet, held at the Tanforan Race Track, U.S. Army lieutenant Myron Sydney Crissy, flying in a Wright biplane piloted by Philip O. Parmalee, drops a live bomb weighing 36 pounds from an altitude of 1,500 feet. The bomb hits within the 20-foot target area in a distant part of the field. The first bomb dropped from a powered aircraft during combat operations occurs on November 1 by an Italian aircraft in the Tripolitan War.

January 18, 1911

First shipboard landing by an aircraft. Civilian pilot Eugene B. Ely, the first man to fly an aircraft off a ship, becomes the first to land on a ship when he lands his Curtiss pusher aircraft on a jury-rigged wooden platform aboard the armored cruiser *Pennsylvania* in San Francisco Bay.

January 21, 1911

The first radio-telegraphic transmission from an airplane occurs on this date when U.S. Army lieutenant Paul W. Beck sends a message from a transmitter of his own design at an altitude of 100 feet over Selfridge Field, Michigan, to a receiver one and a half miles distant.

USS *Michigan* (BB-27)

The *Michigan* was the U.S. Navy's first dreadnought battleship. The dreadnought made all other battleships obsolete. Named for the prototype Royal Navy battleship *Dreadnought,* these capital ships were driven at high speed with steam turbine engines and had central gunnery control. Dreadnoughts mounted an all big-gun armament, making them the equivalent in firepower of as many as four or five older battleships.

Plans for the two South Carolina–class battleships *South Carolina* (BB-26) and *Michigan* (BB-27) had actually been developed in 1904, and this had helped spur construction of the *Dreadnought,* which had been built in the record time of one year and entered service in 1906. The *Michigan* was not laid down until December 17, 1906. It was launched on May 26, 1908, and commissioned on January 4, 1910. (Respective dates for the *South Carolina* are December 18, 1906; July 11, 1908; and March 1, 1910.) Displacing 167,000 tons (17,617 tons full load) and with an overall length of 452'9", a beam of 80'2", and a draft of 24'6", the two ships were capable of 18.5 knots and had a crew complement of 521 officers and 818 men. The first battleships to be equipped with superimposed turrets, they also had all their main guns on the centerline. They mounted a main armament of 8 12-inch guns. They were also equipped with 22 3-inch guns and 2 21-inch torpedo tubes.

Assigned to the Atlantic Fleet, the *Michigan* embarked on a shakedown cruise first to Europe and then to the Caribbean. During 1913 and again in 1914, the *Michigan* took part in operations off the Gulf of Mexico coast and landed a battalion of marines at Veracruz in April 1914. Following U.S. entry into World War I, the *Michigan* was stationed along the Atlantic seaboard. The *Michigan* was decommissioned at the Philadelphia Navy Yard on February 11, 1922, and stricken from the naval register on November 10, 1923. In accordance with provisions of the Washington Naval Treaty, the *Michigan* and four other battleships were scrapped in 1924.

SPENCER C. TUCKER

Further Reading

Friedman, Norman. *U.S. Battleships: An Illustrated Design History.* Annapolis, MD: Naval Institute Press, 1985.
Silverstone, Paul H. *The New Navy, 1883–1922.* New York: Routledge, 2006.

January 26, 1911
In the first U.S. seaplane flight, U.S. aviation pioneer Glenn Curtiss attaches floats to a biplane, then takes off and lands on the water.

February 1, 1911
The U.S. Navy cruiser *Tacoma* lands men to protect American interests at Puerto Cortez, Honduras.

February 14, 1911
The U.S. Army officially adopts the Colt .45 semiautomatic pistol.

February 17, 1911
Aviation pioneer Glenn Curtiss demonstrates his seaplane for the U.S. Navy. Curtiss taxies his seaplane alongside the cruiser *Pennsylvania,* which then lifts the seaplane aboard with its crane, then returns it to the water, whereupon Curtiss takes off.

March 7, 1911
U.S. president William H. Taft, concerned about increasing instability along the Mexican border following revolution in that country, orders 20,000 troops deployed there.

 **Radio**

Both the telegraph and then the telephone had major impacts on the conduct of war. The follow-on communications method of wireless telegraphy, or radio, produced a communications revolution. In the 1870s the Briton James Clerk Maxwell first theorized that electrical waves traveled over distances, and the German Heinrich Hertz then demonstrated that these waves traveled in straight lines and could be reflected. The Italian Guglielmo Marconi, however, is generally credited with the invention of radio around 1895. By 1896 Marconi had developed or adapted the equipment to enable a Morse code radio message to be beamed across the English Channel, and in 1901 he managed to send the Morse code signal, three dots for the letter "S," across the Atlantic.

The implications of radio in war were not immediately apparent to many military leaders, but in 1899 the Royal Navy used radio between ships and shore during fleet maneuvers. Despite its limited initial range, however, the world's navies eventually adopted radio for communication. For the first time in naval history, communications could be effected between vessels over the horizon from one another. The first operational application of wireless in war came during the 1904–1905 Russo-Japanese War.

Progress in adapting wireless to land warfare was slower because the first radios were very bulky and prone to malfunction. In the course of World War I, however, radios were adopted to use in tanks as well as in aircraft communicating with the ground. Improved modes of transmission allowed the use of voice signals and not merely code. By World War II, all major armies had developed man-portable radios that accompanied troops in the field. During the first two postwar decades, the transistor and then integrated circuits miniaturized radios and made them far more durable. So-called burst transmissions also make it more difficult for enemy forces to detect the location of the sending source.

In addition to helping commanders control events on the battlefield, radios have also greatly aided search-and-rescue operations. Radio also became an important propaganda tool in the hands of governments, a means to communicate policy objectives at home and abroad. The great importance of radio in war led to the development of so-called jamming to interrupt communication by this means.

SPENCER C. TUCKER

Further Reading

Burns, Russell W. *Communications: An International History of the Formative Years*. London: Institute of Electrical Engineers, 2004.

Hezlet, Sir Arthur. *Electronics and Sea Power*. New York: Stein and Day, 1975.

Snyder, Thomas S., ed. *Air Force Communications Command, 1938–1991: An Illustrated History*. Scott Air Force Base, IL: Office of History, 1991.

Wedlake, G. E. C. *SOS: The Story of Radio Communication*. North Pomfret, VT: David and Charles, 1973.

 ## Browning (Colt) .45 Semiautomatic Pistol

Identified in 1940 for the original model as Automatic Pistol, Caliber .45, M1911, and one of the most famous firearms and probably the most enduring pistol in history, this pistol was designed by American John M. Browning for the Colt Patent Firearms Manufacturing Company and was actually a semiautomatic, firing one shot each time the trigger was pulled. Born in 1855, Browning, the son of a gunsmith, was perhaps the most innovative firearms designer in history. Among his other weapons are the M2 .50-caliber machine gun and the Browning automatic rifle.

By the 1890s Browning had developed a self-loading pistol, initially in .38-caliber, that he demonstrated for officials at Colt. In 1896 the two parties agreed that Colt would develop, manufacture, and distribute Browning's designs in the United States, while Browning struck a similar deal with the Belgian firm of Fabrique Nationale in Europe.

Browning's first Model 1900 semiautomatic pistol was the basis of the later M1911 .45-caliber pistol. It fired a .38-caliber rimless cartridge and had a seven-round detachable box magazine. The barrel was attached to the receiver with corresponding grooves and lugs. When the weapon was fired, the barrel moved to the rear just slightly and simultaneously pivoted downward slightly, which caused the locking grooves to disengage. The slide continued moving back to the rear. As it did so, it ejected the spent cartridge and cocked the exposed hammer. It continued rearward until it hit the positive stop on the receiver, when the operating spring then returned the slide into battery, stripping a new round from the magazine as it did so.

The Model 1902 and a shorter-barrel Model 1903 followed. The Model 1903 .32-caliber pistol, with a 4-inch (later 3.75-inch) barrel, was highly successful. With its slide lock and concealed hammer and weighing only 23 ounces, it remained in production until 1946. Browning also designed a Model 1908 .38-caliber and a .25-caliber that was produced until 1941.

But Colt and other firearms manufacturers were most interested in winning the competition for a new U.S. government sidearm. The army's experience during the Philippine War (Insurrection) of 1899–1902, in which its .38-caliber pistols had not been able to halt hard-charging Moro insurgents, led to the decision by the Ordnance Bureau that the new weapon could be no less than .45-caliber. Following extensive tests, including those in the field and against cadavers and animals, it won out over a half dozen other designs to enter service in May 1911. It replaced a wide range of revolvers and semiautomatic pistols to equip all the U.S. armed forces.

Although heavy at 39 ounces with an empty magazine and having a hefty recoil, the .45-caliber pistol was absolutely reliable and accurate. It also had great knock-down power, thanks to the large 230-grain relatively slow-moving bullet (muzzle velocity of 830 feet per second). Magazine capacity was eight rimless .45 rounds. The M1911 also featured both a thumb-operated and grip safety.

With World War I, demand for the pistol increased tremendously, and 380,000 were manufactured between April 1917 and November 1918 alone. In 1927 the M-1911 was improved slightly and redesignated the M-1911A1. During World War II, the government ordered 1.9 million produced. The M-1911 and M-1911A1 remained in service with the U.S. military (and many foreign militaries) from

1911 until 1985 and the changeover to the standard 9-millimeter North Atlantic Treaty Organization (NATO) model Beretta.

SPENCER C. TUCKER

Further Reading

Kinard, Jeff. *Pistols: An Illustrated History of Their Impact.* Santa Barbara, CA: ABC-CLIO, 2004.

Smith, W. H. B. *Small Arms of the World.* 9th ed. Harrisburg, PA: Stackpole, 1969.

March 13, 1911

At Guantánamo Bay, Cuba, a provisional marine battalion under Major George C. Thorpe is landed to protect American interests.

April 11, 1911

The U.S. Army establishes its first permanent aviation school, at College Park, Maryland. Operations commence there in June, but after several difficult winters there the school is relocated to San Diego, California.

April 12, 1911

Lieutenant T. Gordon Ellyson becomes the first U.S. Navy aviator following completion of training at the Glenn Curtiss Aviation Center in San Diego, California. Ellyson goes on to register a number of other firsts in a distinguished naval career.

May 8, 1911

Beginning of U.S. naval aviation. U.S. Navy captain Washington Irvin Chambers, who has charge of aviation matters for the navy, completes contract specifications for the first two U.S. Navy aircraft. Although bidding invitations do not go out to potential contractors for several weeks (the contracts are awarded to Glenn Curtiss), this is officially considered the birth date of U.S. naval aviation.

July 1, 1911

Glenn Curtiss successfully demonstrates the 80-horsepower A-1 Triad hydroplane, the first aircraft purchased by the navy. He takes off and lands on Lake Keuka at Hammondsport, New York. Curtiss makes four flights in the A-1 that day. Fitted with retractable wheels as well as floats, it is the first amphibian aircraft.

September 1911

Establishment of the first naval air station. The U.S. Navy aviation encampment is established at the Naval Engineering Experiment Station in Annapolis, Maryland, across the Severn River from the U.S. Naval Academy.

October 10, 1911–January 19, 1914

A battalion of marines commanded by Major Philip M. Bannon arrives at Beijing (Peking), China. Dispatched from the Philippines, the battalion reinforces the guard at the American legation in Beijing during the Chinese Revolution beginning on October 10, 1911 (the Xinhai Revolution), which overthrows the Manchu dynasty and establishes the Chinese Republic. A number of marines and then army troops are dispatched to China, along with other foreign troops.

November 4–14, 1911

At Shanghai, China, the U.S. Navy cruiser *Albany* and the transport *Rainbow* land 24 marines to protect the cable station there.

November 24, 1911

The U.S. Navy armored cruiser *New York* sails from Shanghai, China, with a company of marines to protect American missionaries at Taku.

December 3–26, 1911

Moro Rebellion (continued): Bud Dajo Campaign. Moro Province in the southern

Moro War, 1898–1913

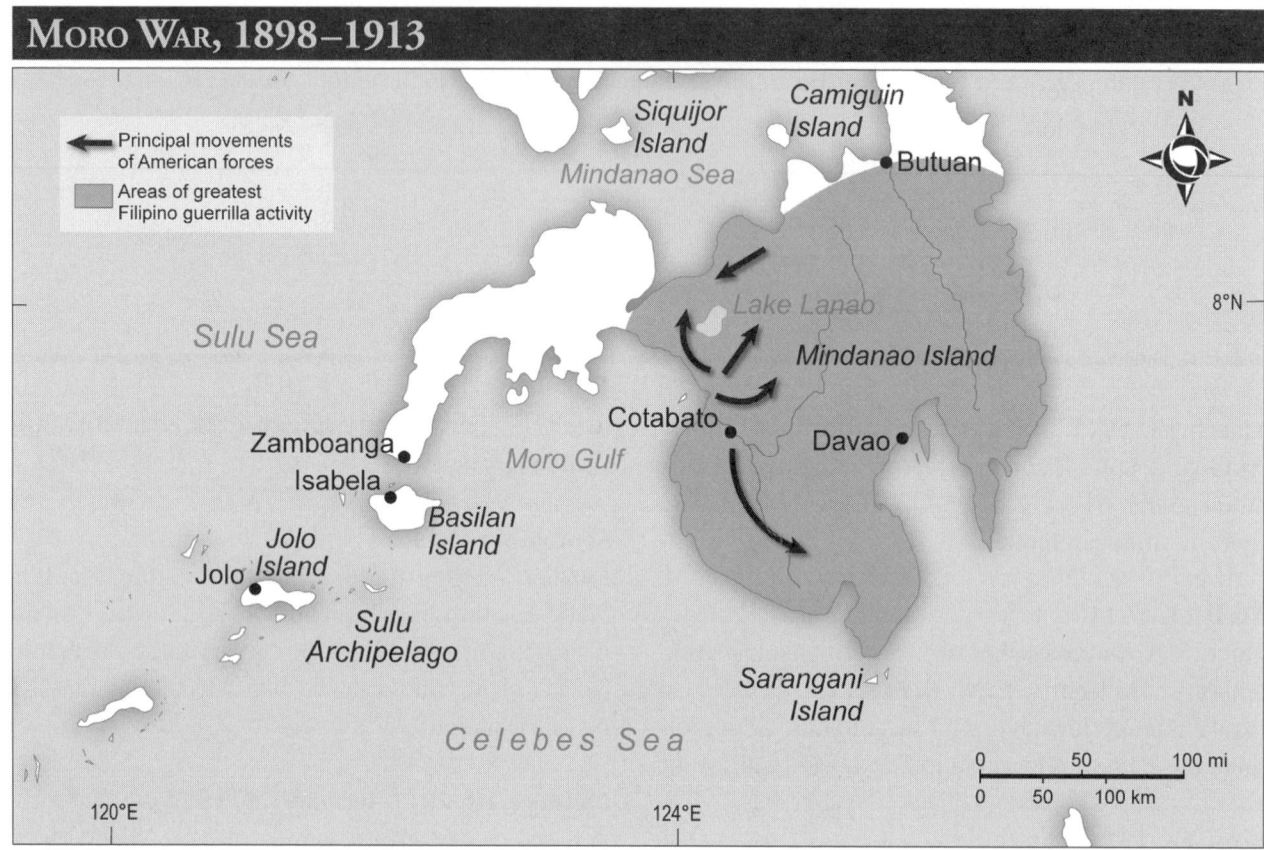

Philippines has become notorious for attacks by the largely Muslim population on Christians as well as for murders, robbery, slavery, and general lawlessness. For these reasons, the governor of the province, U.S. Army brigadier general John J. Pershing, decides to disarm the Moros. Pershing is determined to spare noncombatants as much as possible, but it is practice for Moro warriors to take their wives and children with them on campaign.

Pershing understands the risks, for some Moros are bound to resist disarmament, and this can bring war. He orders the construction of new roads and the improvement of other roads to ensure that his men will be able to reach all areas of the province and protect cooperative Moros. He also meets with moderate Moro leaders to convince them of the wisdom of complete disarmament.

Pershing issues his disarmament order, Executive Order No. 24, on September 8, 1911. This makes it unlawful for a Moro to possess either a gun or a cutting weapon. December 1 is the deadline for turning in guns and receiving cash payments. Even Moros friendly to the government expect a general uprising if the order is enforced, but Pershing is determined to proceed.

Trouble indeed occurs on Jolo, where militant Moros mount a night attack on the U.S. camp at Seit Lake, killing one American and wounding three others. Pershing immediately departs for Jolo to take personal charge. He divides his command into two field forces, sending one east to Seit Lake and the other west to Taglibi, eight miles west of Jolo City. Because the latter area has been rife with anti-American sentiment, Pershing suspects a Moro attack here. As a precaution the troops entrench, string barbed wire, and clear fields of fire. On the night of November 18, the Moros do indeed strike. Although no Americans are killed, Pershing is determined to teach the Moros a lesson while at the same time sparing noncombatants as much as possible.

On December 3, Pershing orders three columns out in the Taglibi area. The Moros attack but are driven back. Two days later, Pershing sends out five columns in different directions to comb the area. The Moros appear to be impressed by this show of force, and on the afternoon of December 5 an influential Moro reports that the militants are ready to disarm. Pershing suspects a trick but orders a suspension of operations pending negotiations, which drag on without result.

On December 14 Pershing learns that many Moros are occupying Bud Dajo, their sacred mountain. An extinct volcano, it has steep sides and will be difficult to assail. Some 800 Moros, armed with between 150 and 250 rifles in addition to cutting weapons, take up position in the crater and fortify it.

Pershing assumes personal command of operations. Determined to avoid unnecessary loss of life, especially of noncombatants, he orders up reinforcements in the form of three American infantry companies, three companies of Philippine Scouts, and one machine-gun platoon, giving him about 1,000 men. After a personal reconnaissance of the three Bud Dajo approaches, Pershing orders camps established at each in order to cut off supplies to the Moros. By December 22, Bud Dajo is completely isolated.

The Moro decision to occupy Bud Dajo had been a precipitate one, and the Moros soon run short of food and supplies. Meanwhile, Pershing orders his men to avoid contact if possible and not to return fire. He employs friendly Moros to send messages to those on the mountain, and during the next few days hundreds of Moros surrender. On December 23, Pershing informs the remaining Moros that the next day there will be no chance for them to surrender except unconditionally. He then prepares for an assault.

On the morning of December 24, Pershing again sends friendly Moros up the mountain. They return with word that the holdouts, perhaps 60–100 in all, have left the crater. Rushing the crater with two companies of Philippine Scouts, Pershing traps the insurgent Moros in woods and then fortifies, expecting the Moros, without food or water, to try to escape that night. They do so, but few make it. The operation concludes on December 26. Pershing reports 300 Moros taken prisoner. Casualties for the entire campaign on the American side are 3 wounded. On the Moro side, 12 are killed and a few others wounded. Pershing sends the prisoners to Mindanao to be tried for insurrection. Later he decides to drop charges against a prisoner if his friends can collect sufficient arms for his release.

Although this has been a very successful operation, Moro resistance ends only with the Battle of Bud Bagsak (see June 11–13, 1913).

December 1911–March 1938

The U.S. 15th Infantry Regiment begins arriving in Tianjin (Tientsin) in December 1911 and is fully in place, minus one of its battalions, the next month. The troops are there to show the flag, provide additional security for the foreign interests in China, and support other regional international forces. Although never firing a shot in anger, the 15th Regiment will remain in Tianjin for 26 years, until March 1938. George C. Marshall, then a colonel, commands the regiment during 1924–1927.

1911

U.S. Army lieutenant colonel Isaac Newton Lewis invents the Lewis machine gun.

February 14, 1912

Commissioning of the submarine *Skipjack* (SS-24), later renamed *E-1*. Built by the Fore River Shipyard in Quincy, Massachusetts, the submarine's commander is Lieutenant (later Fleet Admiral) Chester W. Nimitz. Displacing 292 tons surfaced and 347 tons submerged and 135'3" in length and 14'7" in beam, the *E-1* is the first U.S. submarine with diesel engines and the first to cross the Atlantic Ocean under its own power. It carries out experiments with submerged radio transmission and is the first to use the Sperry gyrocompass.

March 1, 1912

U.S. Army captain Albert Berry becomes the first person to parachute from a powered airplane when he jumps from a Benoist pusher biplane flown by Anthony Jannus at an altitude of 1,500 feet over Jefferson Barracks, Missouri. Berry's 36-foot-diameter

George Catlett Marshall (1880–1959)

U.S. Army general, chief of staff of the army, secretary of state, and secretary of defense. Born in Uniontown, Pennsylvania, on December 31, 1880, George Catlett Marshall graduated from the Virginia Military Institute in 1901. Commissioned in the infantry in 1902, he then served in a variety of assignments, including in the Philippines. He attended the Infantry and Cavalry School, Fort Leavenworth, in 1906 and was an instructor in the Army Service Schools during 1907–1908.

After the United States entered World War I, Marshall went to France with the American Expeditionary Forces as operations and training officer of the 1st Division in June 1917. Promoted to lieutenant colonel in 1918, he became deputy chief of staff for operations of the U.S. First Army in August and was the principal planner of the Saint-Mihiel Offensive of September 12–16. He earned admiration for his logistical skills in directing the repositioning of hundreds of thousands of men quickly across the battlefront after that success for the Meuse-Argonne Offensive of September 26–November 11. After working on occupation plans for Germany, Marshall reverted to his permanent rank of captain and during 1919–1924 became aide to General John J. Pershing, who served as chief of staff of the army during 1921–1924. Marshall was promoted to major in 1920 and lieutenant colonel in 1923.

Marshall served in Tianjin (Tientsin), China, with the 15th Infantry Regiment during 1924–1927. He was assistant commandant in charge of instruction at the Infantry School, Fort Benning, Georgia, during 1927–1932, where he helped to train many officers who would serve as generals during World War II. Promoted to colonel in 1932, he served in various assignments in the continental United States, including instructor with the Illinois National Guard from 1933 to 1936. He advanced to brigadier general in 1936 and assumed command of the 5th Infantry Brigade.

Marshall became head of the War Plans Division in Washington, D.C., with promotion to major general in July 1938, then deputy chief of staff in October. President Franklin D. Roosevelt advanced him over many more senior officers to appoint him chief of staff of the army on September 1, 1939, the day that German armies invaded Poland. Marshall was promoted to major general and simultaneously to temporary general the same day he became chief of staff.

As war began in Europe, Marshall worked to revitalize the American defense establishment. Supported by pro-Allied civilian senior leaders, such as Secretary of War Henry L. Stimson, Marshall instituted and lobbied for programs to recruit and train new troops; expedite munitions production; assist Great Britain, China, and the Soviet Union in resisting the Axis powers; and coordinate British and American strategy. After the United States entered the war on December 7, 1941, Marshall presided over an increase in U.S. armed forces from a mere 200,000 troops to a wartime maximum of 8.1 million men and women. Marshall stressed the tactical basics of firepower and maneuver, and he supported mechanization and the most modern military technology. For all this he became known as the "Organizer of Victory."

Marshall was a strong supporter of opening a second front in Europe as early as possible, a campaign that was deferred by strategic necessity until June 1944. Between 1941 and 1945 he attended all the major Allied wartime strategic conferences, including those at Placentia Bay, Washington, Quebec, Cairo, Tehran, Malta, Yalta, and Potsdam. Marshall was the first to be promoted to the newly authorized five-star rank of general of the army in December 1944. Perhaps Marshall's greatest personal disappointment was that he did not hold field command, especially that of the European invasion forces.

Roosevelt and the other wartime chiefs wanted him to remain in Washington, and Marshall bowed to their wishes. Marshall was a major supporter of the U.S. Army Air Forces, and he advocated employment of the atomic bomb against Japan in August 1945.

On the urging of President Harry S. Truman, Marshall agreed to serve as special envoy to China during 1945–1947. He was secretary of state during 1947–1949, when he advanced the Marshall Plan to rebuild Europe, and was president of the American Red Cross during 1949–1950. Truman persuaded Marshall yet again to return to government service as secretary of defense in September 1950. Marshall worked to repair relations with the other agencies of government that had become frayed under his predecessor and to build up the U.S. military to meet the needs of the Korean War (1950–1953) and commitments in Europe, while at the same time maintaining an adequate reserve. Marshall opposed General Douglas MacArthur's efforts for a widened war with China and supported Truman in his decisions to fight a limited war and to remove MacArthur as commander of United Nations forces.

Marshall resigned in September 1951, ending 50 years of dedicated government service. Awarded the Nobel Prize for Peace in 1953 for the Marshall Plan, he was the first soldier so honored. Marshall died in Washington, D.C., on October 16, 1959. If not America's greatest soldier, Marshall was one of the nation's most capable military leaders and statesmen and certainly one of the most influential figures of the 20th century.

SPENCER C. TUCKER

Further Reading
Cray, Ed. *General of the Army: George C. Marshall, Soldier and Statesman.* New York: Norton, 1990.
Pogue, Forrest C. *George C. Marshall.* 4 vols. New York: Viking, 1963–1987.
Stoler, Mark A. *George C. Marshall: Soldier-Statesman of the American Century.* Boston: Twayne, 1989.

parachute is in a metal canister attached to the underside of the aircraft. Berry leaves his seat and lowers himself to a trapeze bar attached to the underside of the aircraft. When Berry drops from the aircraft, his weight pulls the parachute from the canister. Berry falls 500 feet before the parachute opens.

May 22, 1912
Beginning of U.S. Marine Corps aviation. U.S. Marine Corps second lieutenant Alfred A. Cunningham reports to the aviation encampment at the Naval Engineering Experiment Station in Annapolis, Maryland, for flight training and soon qualifies as the first U.S. Marine Corps pilot.

May 28–August 1912
U.S. military intervention in Cuba. Blacks in Cuba rebel, protesting injustice, racism, and exclusion from politics. U.S. president William H. Taft, fearful that the Cuban government headed by President José Miguel Gómez will not be able to protect the extensive U.S. economic interests in the island, orders a "preventive" military intervention to protect that property. On May 23, the Taft administration dispatches the transport *Prairie* with 500 marines to join two other U.S. warships already at Guantánamo. Other U.S. ships soon also arrive at Havana and Nipe Bay. The 1st Provisional Marine Regiment is hastily organized and landed at Guantánamo on May 28 from the transport *Prairie*. Another marine regiment lands on June 5, and a provisional brigade is organized under Colonel Lincoln Karmany. The marines garrison some two dozen towns in the vicinity of Guantánamo and Santiago.

Gómez protests the U.S. action, which Washington claims does not constitute "intervention" and

Chester William Nimitz (1885–1966)

U.S. Navy admiral. Born far from the sea in Fredericksburg, Texas, on February 24, 1885, Chester William Nimitz graduated from the U.S. Naval Academy, Annapolis, in 1905. He then served with the U.S. Asiatic Fleet, steadily advancing in rank and position. Promoted to lieutenant in 1910, he assumed command of the submarine *Skipjack* in 1912. He studied diesel engine construction in Europe, then supervised construction of the U.S. Navy's first diesel ship engine. Upon U.S. entry into World War I in April 1917, Lieutenant Commander Nimitz served as chief of staff to the commander of submarines in the Atlantic Fleet during 1917–1919.

Following the war, Nimitz was appointed to the Navy Department staff in Washington and then transferred to Pearl Harbor in 1920 to oversee the construction of a new submarine base there. Over the next 20 years he served in a wide variety of submarine billets as well as aboard battleships and destroyers. He also served several tours in Washington and helped establish the first Naval Reserve Officer Training Corps programs in American universities. He was promoted to rear admiral in 1938.

At the time of the Japanese attack on Pearl Harbor on December 7, 1941, Nimitz was chief of the Bureau of Navigation. On the recommendation of Secretary of the Navy Frank Knox, President Franklin Roosevelt promoted Nimitz to full admiral on December 31 and appointed him commander of the U.S. Pacific Fleet, replacing Admiral Husband E. Kimmel at Pearl Harbor. Although a single U.S. command in the Pacific would have been far more advantageous, General Douglas MacArthur would not agree to serve under a naval officer. As a result, two commands emerged. As commander in chief, Pacific Ocean Area, Nimitz directed all U.S. military forces in the Central Pacific and provided support to MacArthur and his Southwest Pacific forces. Nimitz left actual tactical command in the hands of able subordinates.

Although the Allies made the war against Japan secondary to their Europe-first strategy, Nimitz did not delay his plans to halt Japanese expansion, retake their gains, and push the war to the Japanese homeland. Using information provided by American code breakers about Japanese plans, Nimitz orchestrated the halting of the Japanese invasion of Port Moresby in the Battle of the Coral Sea on May 7–8, 1942, and the Japanese effort to take Midway on June 2–6. The latter battle transferred the initiative to the Americans. Nimitz and MacArthur then cooperated in a series of island-hopping campaigns that progressed toward the Japanese home islands. Nimitz's forces took the Gilbert Islands in November 1943, the Marshall Islands in February 1944, and the Mariana Islands in August 1944. Nimitz's accomplishments were recognized by his promotion to the newly established five-star rank of admiral of the fleet in December 1944. In early 1945 Nimitz directed the offensives against Guam, Iwo Jima, and Okinawa. His forces were preparing to invade Japan when the Japanese surrendered. Nimitz signed the formal Japanese surrender aboard the battleship *Missouri* in Tokyo Bay on September 2.

Nimitz returned to Washington in October 1945 and assumed the post of chief of naval operations. For the next two years he supervised the postwar demobilization of men and ships while also providing input into the development of nuclear-powered submarines. Following his retirement in December 1947, Nimitz briefly served as adviser to the secretary of the navy and for two years was the United Nations commissioner for Kashmir. Nimitz died near San Francisco on February 20, 1966. An officer of considerable experience and an exceptional theater commander, Nimitz directed overall strategy while giving wide latitude to his subordinates.

JAMES H. WILLBANKS

Further Reading

Brink, Randall. *Nimitz: The Man and His Wars*. New York: Penguin, 2000.

Driskell, Frank A., and Dede W. Casad. *Chester W. Nimitz, Admiral of the Hills*. Austin, TX: Eakin, 1983.

Potter, Elmer B. *Nimitz*. Annapolis, MD: Naval Institute Press, 1976.

is only to protect U.S. property. As many as 3,000 Cubans may have died in the uprising, but with the Gómez government able to restore order, on July 25 the marines receive orders to withdraw, ending the "preventive" intervention.

June 7, 1912

First firing of a machine gun from an airplane. U.S. Army captain Charles DeF. Chandler and Lieutenant T. D. Milling carry out the first firing of a machine gun from an aircraft in flight. The plane is a Wright B model, and the weapon is a Lewis gun. Chandler scores five hits and several misses on the target, a six-by-seven-foot piece of cheesecloth.

July 27, 1912

In the first radio communication between an aircraft and a ship, U.S. Navy lieutenant John Rodgers flying the Wright B-1 hydroplane over Chesapeake Bay near Annapolis, Maryland, transmits the letter "D" in Morse code to the torpedo boat *Bailey* more than a mile distant.

August 4, 1912–January 17, 1913

U.S. military intervention in Nicaragua. A revolution begins against President Adolfo Díaz of Nicaragua, who enjoys U.S. government support. On August 4, 1912, 100 sailors and marines from the U.S. Navy gunboat *Annapolis* come ashore at Corinto on the Nicaraguan Pacific coast, then march inland to guard the U.S. legation in Managua. For the third time since 1909, U.S. Marine Corps major Smedley D. Butler's

battalion is ordered to Nicaragua. The battalion arrives from Panama at Corinto on August 14. Other landing parties come ashore at Nicaraguan Atlantic and Pacific ports during the next few weeks from the cruisers *Tacoma*, *California*, *Denver*, and *Colorado*. On September 4, the 1st Provisional Marine Regiment of 700 men under Colonel Joseph H. Pendleton arrives at Corinto from Philadelphia in the transport *Philadelphia*. Pendleton assumes command of all U.S. forces in Nicaragua, now some 2,000 men. They take control of the chief transportation artery in the country, the railroad from Corinto through Managua to Granada.

On September 22, Butler with two marine battalions and an artillery battery raises the rebel siege of Granada. Returning from Granada, during October 22–24 Butler's force tangles with rebels under General Zeledón along the rail line near Masaya. Pendleton arrives during the fight with another battalion, and early on October 4 the marines storm the rebel position on Coyotepe Hill. The battle claims more than 60 rebel dead, including General Zeledón, apparently shot by his own men; the marines sustain 18 casualties.

On October 6, 1,200 seamen and marines under Lieutenant Colonel C. G. Long capture the rebel-held city of León, at a cost of 6 casualties. This marks the effective end of the revolution, although mopping-up operations continue into early November. On November 21, Pendleton's provisional regiment embarks at Bluefield on the transport *Buffalo*. Long remains at León with a marine battalion until January

 **Lewis Gun**

By 1910, machine guns shared the basic characteristics of being belt-fed, water-cooled, and tripod-mounted. The Maxim and Vickers machine guns had a minimum three-man crew, however, and there was a persistent need for a light machine gun capable of being carried in the attack by one man. The first true light machine gun, the Madsen, which was employed by the Russians in the Russo-Japanese War of 1904–1905, demonstrated the important role that such a weapon could play in offensive operations.

Hotchkiss in Paris developed a light machine gun, subsequently adopted by both the French and British cavalry. The U.S. Army also purchased some. A lighter version of the regular Hotchkiss design, it remained in service in some reserve units until 1949. But the most significant new light machine-gun design was advanced by Americans Samuel McClean and U.S. Army lieutenant colonel O. M. Lissak. The two developed several gas-operated designs, which they described as automatic rifles. Unable to interest the army in their work, they sold the patents to the Automatic Arms Company of Buffalo, which in turn approached U.S. Army lieutenant colonel Issac Lewis about turning the designs into a workable product. Lewis took the McClean design and transformed it from a water-cooled tripod-mounted medium gun into an air-cooled shoulder-fired light model. By 1911, Lewis had developed a number of working models and demonstrated them before U.S. Army officials, who then turned them over to the Board of Ordnance for testing.

Here Lewis ran up against the obstacle of chief of ordnance Major General William Crozier, who took umbrage at the fact that Lewis had worked on the gun while in the army. Although Lewis resigned his commission in 1913, he could not overcome Crozier's opposition. Lewis then set up his own company in Belgium, Armes Automatiques Lewis, to produce the gun.

The gas-operated air-cooled Lewis gun was an excellent weapon. Weighing 27 pounds and firing a .303-caliber round, the Lewis gun was easily carried into battle by one man, although all machine guns have at least an assistant gunner. It had a 47-round circular, horizontally mounted drum magazine. Cooling was effected by a tubular jacket over the barrel covering aluminum fins. When the gun was fired, muzzle draft drew air forward over the fins, cooling the barrel. Lewis licensed the Birmingham Small Arms Company (BSA) in Britain to make the weapon. The Lewis gun was easy to manufacture, with six produced in the time it took to make one Vickers. At the beginning of World War I in 1914, the BSA could not keep up with demand, and the Savage Arms Company in the U.S. also produced the Lewis gun.

The Lewis gun was the best light machine gun of its time and became standard issue with the British Army and the Belgian Army. In April 1916 the U.S. Navy ordered 3,500 Lewis guns, which became standard issue for the U.S. Marine Corps. Shortly thereafter the U.S. Army ordered 18,500 Lewis guns. Employed during the Punitive Expedition into Mexico in 1916–1917, the Lewis gun was also widely used by U.S. forces when they entered World War I and was modified to use .30-06-caliber ammunition. In 1915 British infantry battalions on the Western Front each had four Lewis guns; by 1917 each battalion was equipped with 46. The Germans referred to the gun as the "Belgian Rattlesnake."

The Lewis gun also saw extensive use in aircraft, both in fixed and flexible mountings, with a 97-round drum. In the air the cooling system was discarded, reducing the gun's weight to only 20 pounds. The Lewis gun was also used in armored cars, in tanks, and even on motorcycles.

During World War II the British returned 50,000 Lewis guns in reserve stocks to service, and the weapon also saw widespread use in the armies of other nations. In the U.S. Army, the Lewis gun was replaced by the Browning automatic rifle.

Spencer C. Tucker

Further Reading

Skennerton, Ian. *.303 Lewis Machine Gun*. Eastbourne, East Sussex, UK: Arms and Armour, 2001.
Truby, J. David. *The Lewis Gun*. 2nd ed. Boulder, CO: Palladin, 1978.
Willbanks, James H. *Machine Guns: An Illustrated History of Their Impact*. Santa Barbara, CA: ABC-CLIO, 2004.

17, 1913. A legation guard of 100 men is maintained at Managua until August 1925.

August 12, 1912

Army aircraft participate in military maneuvers for the first time. Three U.S. Army Signal Corps aircraft take part in army maneuvers at Bridgeport, Connecticut, employed in a reconnaissance role.

August 24 and 26, 1912

Near Shanghai, China, a company of marines is landed from the U.S. Navy transport *Rainbow* to protect American lives and property.

November 12, 1912

First U.S. Navy catapult launching of an aircraft. The first attempt by the navy to launch an aircraft using a compressed-air catapult failed on July 31, 1912, when a Curtiss A-1 hydroplane with Lieutenant T. Gordon Ellyson at the Santee Wharf at the U.S. Naval Academy in Annapolis, Maryland, is not secured properly and is cartwheeled into the Severn River. Ellyson escapes unscathed.

Undeterred, Ellyson tries again on November 12, this time from a stationary barge in the Anacostia River off the Washington Navy Yard. The attempt, in a new Curtiss A-1, is successful.

November 30, 1912

First flight by a U.S. Navy flying boat. On this date, U.S. Navy lieutenant T. Gordon Ellyson successfully flies the navy's first flying boat, the Curtiss C-1, on Lake Keuka at Hammondsport, New York. The navy had taken delivery of it three days before.

January 6, 1913

For the first time, U.S. Navy aircraft take part in fleet maneuvers, off Guantánamo Bay, Cuba.

March 26, 1913

U.S. Corps of Engineers assigned flood control duties. Widespread floods in Ohio and Indiana during March 23–27 lead to the members of the U.S. Army Corps of Engineers being assigned permanently to flood control. The National Guard is called out, and western Indianapolis is placed under martial law to protect lives and property.

June 11–15, 1913

Moro Rebellion: Battle of Bud Bagsak. The Lati Moros on Jolo Island in the southern Philippines continue their attacks, despite earlier attempts, mostly successful, at disarmament in 1912 by American authorities. Insurgent Moro successes prompt a new military operation in January 1913 designed to defeat the Moros that is spearheaded by Brigadier General John J. Pershing, who is also the governor of Moro Province.

In several early engagements, the Americans—working in concert with Philippine Scouts and the Philippine Constabulary—attempt to pacify the region. Two Moro cottas (forts) are seized, but the

 ## Director Fire Control and New Range-Finding at Sea

The Battle of Tsushima Straits in May 1905 during the Russo-Japanese War (1904–1905) demonstrated that the big gun was the key at sea; only the largest shells could inflict crippling damage on an armored ship's superstructure. Navies therefore paid increasing attention to gunnery practice and methods, and over the next decade naval gunnery was transformed. Longer-base-length range finders appeared, capable of accurate range measurement out to 10,000 yards, and early analogue computer systems helped solve the considerable problem of calculating the precise location of the target ship when the shells arrived. Such systems took into account range, drift, and speed of the ship and of its target, deflection (lead angle), gun elevation, and forces exerted on the projectile.

The most important figure in the dramatic change in naval gunnery practice was Royal Navy captain Percy Scott, "the pocket Hercules." In 1898 while commanding the cruiser *Scylla* in the Mediterranean, Scott invented a technique of continuous aiming. In the Mediterranean Fleet annual firing competition, the average for the ships participating was only 30 percent hits, but the *Scylla* scored 80 percent. Scott also introduced salvo firing.

Then in 1905 Scott perfected a system of director firing. Taking advantage of new electrical circuitry, he came up with a system that concentrated control of all the big guns in the hands of one man: the director, or first gunnery officer. The director and his assistants were located in a director tower high in the foremast to remain clear of funnel and gun smoke, blast, and sea spray. From this observation platform with its master sight, cables ran to a central transmitting station, which produced firing data for the director, and to the individual turrets. The director controlled the laying and firing of all the main guns. In emergency circumstances or if the director tower was out of action, individual turrets could still fire on their own.

The Admiralty long resisted this change, but in November 1912 the superdreadnought *Thunderer,* fitted for director firing, achieved a hit ratio six times that of its sister ship, *Orion,* which employed the older independent method. Nonetheless, the Admiralty moved so slowly that at the beginning of World War I, only a third of Royal Navy dreadnoughts were fitted with director towers. The Royal Navy also turned down a privately developed fire-control computer system, an early analogue computer, designed by a civilian, Arthur Pollen, in favor of an inferior and less-sophisticated system developed by Admiral Sir Frederic Dreyer.

By World War I nonetheless, capital ships could engage their opponents at ranges out to five miles or more, double that of Tsushima. Elevation in ship guns reflected this change. In the Royal Navy, maximum gun elevation was 13.5 degrees until 1909, when in new ships it became 15 degrees. In 1911 it became 20 degrees and in 1915 was increased to 30 degrees. By 1912 with assistance from instruments to plot range changes (the dumaresq or trigometric slide rule developed in 1902 by Royal Navy lieutenant John S. Dumaresq), Vickers range clocks to determine changes of range rate, and new Barr & Stroud range finders, British capital ships could conduct firing practice out to 14,000 yards.

The U.S. Navy followed the British lead, thanks to the energetic efforts of Lieutenant William S. Sims and Lieutenant Commanders Bradley A. Fiske and Albert P. Niblack and the enthusiastic support of President Theodore Roosevelt. If ships during World War I scored about the same number of hits as the

U.S. Navy had registered at Manila Bay and Santiago during the Spanish-American War of 1898, it was in considerably more difficult circumstances and at up to 10 times the range.

SPENCER C. TUCKER

Further Reading
Brown, David K. *The Eclipse of the Big Gun: The Warship, 1906–45.* Annapolis, MD: Naval Institute Press, 1992.
Hogg, Ian, and John Batchelor. *Naval Gun.* Poole, Dorset, UK: Blandford, 1978.
Padfield, Peter. *Guns at Sea.* New York: St. Martin's, 1974.
Tucker, Spencer C. *Handbook of 19th Century Naval Warfare.* Annapolis, MD: Naval Institute Press, 2000.
Wrigley, Walter, and John Hovorka. *Fire Control Principles.* New York: McGraw-Hill, 1959.

leaders of the insurgency, Naquib Amil, Sahipa, and Jami, elude capture. During the next several months, as many as 10,000 Lati Moros, mostly women and children, gather at Bud Bagsak, a fortified extinct volcano mountaintop and site of earlier battles. Many are herded here against their will.

With an attack on the mountaintop likely to result in the slaughter of many noncombatants, Pershing is able to secure an agreement whereby Moro civilians are allowed to return to their homes if they wish. Approximately 400 Moros refuse to disarm, however, causing Pershing to act decisively to force their surrender.

On June 11, Pershing's force of U.S. Army infantry and Philippine Scouts arrives undetected on the scene and cuts off the belligerents from most of the noncombatants. For almost five days, intense fighting, some of it hand to hand, occurs. Equipped with two mountain guns and the new Colt .45 pistol, Pershing's troops withstand several Moro charges with krises (Malayan-style daggers) and go on to destroy the Moro cottas beneath the main stone fortress. On June 15 the mountain guns shell the main Moro fort, then soldiers assault it. Following hand-to-hand combat, the soldiers are successful. Government forces suffer 14 killed and 13 wounded, while nearly all Moro defenders are killed.

Although several American newspapers describe the Battle of Bud Bagsak as a massacre, claiming that more than 2,000 have perished, little comes of these allegations, which are clearly exaggerated. The U.S. Army supports Pershing, asserting that he has acted properly in accordance with the rules of engagement. The battle largely ends Moro resistance on Jolo and brings the Moro Rebellion to a close.

July 7, 1913
At Shanghai, China, the U.S. Navy protected cruiser *Albany* lands its marine detachment to protect American interests.

EXPANSION AT HOME AND ABROAD

The Later Indian Wars, the Spanish-American War, and the Philippine-American War, 1878–1913

DOCUMENTS

Charles Sigsbee, Testimony to the Naval Court of Inquiry on the Destruction of the *Maine*, 1898 [Excerpt]

Introduction

Although President William McKinley hoped to avoid going to war with Spain over the fate of Cuba, mounting tensions between the two nations led him to send the U.S. battleship *Maine* to Havana, supposedly as a gesture of friendship. Spain, however, saw the gesture for what it was—a show of strength. The *Maine* arrived in Havana Harbor on January 25, 1898, under the command of Captain Charles Sigsbee. Over the ensuing days, American and Spanish officers exchanged salutes and friendly visits. On the night of February 15, however, the *Maine* exploded, killing 266 American sailors. Captain Sigsbee sent a carefully worded telegram urging Americans not to jump to conclusions. The U.S. Navy held a court of inquiry into the cause of the explosion; Sigsbee's excerpted testimony and the court's conclusions are shown here. The court concluded that the explosion could only have been caused by an external mine. Historians now believe that the explosion was due to an internal cause, but the cause cannot be known with certainty.

Primary Source

Q. Regarding strangers being in the ship, at what time were they compelled to leave the ship?

A. I think Lieutenant-Commander Wainwright was rather severe on desultory visitors. Very few visited the ship, except people of the highest social standing in the city. They came commonly from 2 to say 5 o'clock. They were always accompanied about the ship by officers, and of course under the supervisory orders of the master at arms and sergeant of marines. People were allowed to visit the ship from about 10 to 12, and about 1 to 4. I think there were but two visits of Spanish military officers. Once, about two weeks ago, a party of five or six Spanish officers came on board during my absence. They were reported to me as having been constrained, and not desirous to accept much courtesy....

Q. Among the precautions which you took was the fact of having extra lookouts on the deck. Was there ever any report of any unauthorized boats attempting to approach the ship and being ordered off?

A. Never, to my knowledge.

Q. On the night of the disaster, were all your extra precautions in force? I mean, in regard to quarter watches?

A. I assume that they were; they were never rescinded, and up to the night of the explosion, as far as my observation could go, my knowledge is that they were carried out....

[...]

Q. What kind of a night was it at the time of the explosion?

A. It was a very quiet and warm night, and I remember distinctly that the echoes of the bugle at tattoo were singularly distinct and pleasant: A little rain fell after the explosion, which may have been precipitated by the concussion of the explosion.

Q. Was it a dry night?

A. There were stars, but I think it was somewhat overcast. I think I saw several stars after the accident, but it was somewhat overcast according to my recollection.

Q. How was the *Maine* heading at the time of the explosion?

A. Approximately northwest. She pointed toward the shears—somewhat to the right of the shears, near the admiral's residence.

Q. Where were you at the time?

A. I was writing at my port-cabin table, after side. I was dressed.

Q. Please give your experience in full.

A. I was just closing a letter to my family when I felt the crash of the explosion. It was a bursting, rending, and crashing sound or roar of immense volume, largely metallic in its character. It was succeeded by a metallic sound—probably of falling debris—a trembling and lurching motion of the vessel, then an impression of subsidence, attended by an eclipse of the electric lights and intense darkness within the cabin. I knew immediately that the *Maine* had been blown up and that she was sinking. I hurried to the starboard cabin ports, thinking it might be necessary for me to make my exit in that way. Upon looking out I decided that I could go by the passage leading to the superstructure. I therefore took the latter route, feeling my way along and steadying myself by the bulkheads. The superstructure was filled with smoke, and it was dark; nearing the outer entrance I met Private Anthony, the orderly at the cabin door at the time. He ran into me and, as I remember, apologized in some fashion, and reported to me that the ship had been blown up and was sinking.

I reached the quarter-deck, asked a few questions of those standing about me—Lieutenant Commander Wainwright, I think, for one—then I asked the orderly for the time. He said that the exact time

> I was just closing a letter to my family when I felt the crash of the explosion. It was a bursting, rending, and crashing sound or roar of immense volume, largely metallic in its character.

of the explosion was 9.40 p.m. I proceeded to the poop deck, stood on the side rail, and held on to the main rigging in order to see over the poop awning, which was baggy and covered with debris; also in order that I might observe details in the black mass ahead. I directed the executive officer to post sentries all around the ship, but soon saw that there were no marines available, and no place forward to post them. Not being quite clear as to the condition of things forward, I next directed the forward magazine to be flooded if practicable, and about the same time shouted out myself for perfect silence everywhere. This was, I think, repeated by the executive officer. The surviving officers were about me at the time on the poop. I was informed that the forward magazine was already under water, and after inquiring about the after magazine was told that it was also under water, as shown by the condition below reported by those coming from the wardroom and steerage.

About this time fire broke out in the mass forward, over the central superstructure, and I inquired as to the spare ammunition in the captain's pantry. That region was found to be subsiding very fast. At this time I observed, among the shouts or noises apparently on shore, that faint cries were coming from the water, and I could see dimly white, floating bodies, which gave me a better knowledge of the real situation than anything else. I at once ordered all boats to be lowered, when it was reported that there were only two boats available, namely, the gig and whaleboat, both were lowered and manned by officers and men, and by my direction they left the ship and assisted in saving the wounded jointly with other boats that had arrived on the scene from the Spanish man-of-war, from the steamer *City of Washington*, and from other sources. Later—I can not state precisely how long—these two boats of the *Maine* returned to the starboard quarter alongside, and reported that they had gathered in from the wreck all the wounded that could be found and had transferred them to the other boats—to the *Alfonso XII* or to the *City of Washington*. The poop deck of the *Maine*, the highest point, was by that time level with the gig's gunwale while she was afloat in the water alongside. The fire amidships was burning more fiercely and the spare ammunition in the pilot house was exploding in detail. We had done everything that could be done so far as I could see. Lieutenant Commander Wainwright whispered to me that he thought the 10 inch magazine forward had been thrown up into the burning mass, and might explode in time. I directed him then to get everybody into the boats over the stern, and this was done, although there was some little delay in curbing the extreme politeness of the officers, who wanted to help me into the boat. I directed them to go first, as a matter of course, and I followed and got into the gig. We proceeded to the steamer *City of Washington,* and on the way I shouted to the boats to leave the vicinity of the wreck, and that there might be an explosion. I got Mr. Sylvester Scovell to translate my desire to one or two boats which were at that time somewhat nearer the fire than we ourselves were.

Having succeeded in this, I went on board the *City of Washington,* where I found our wounded all below in the dining saloon on mattresses, covered up, and being carefully attended by the officers and crew of that vessel. Every attention that the resources of the vessel admitted was being rapidly brought into use. I then went on deck and observed the wreck for a few minutes, and gave directions to have a muster taken on board the *City of Washington* and other vessels, and sat down in the captain's cabin and dictated a telegram to the Navy Department. At this time various Spanish officers—civil, military, and naval—appeared on board, in their own behalf and in representative capacity, expressing sympathy and sorrow for the accident. The representatives of General Blanco and of the admiral of the station came on board, and the civil governor of the province was on board in person. I asked them to excuse me for a few minutes, until I completed my telegram to the Navy Department. After finishing the telegram and putting it in the hands of a messenger to be taken on shore, I conversed for a few minutes with the various Spanish gentlemen around me, thanking them for the visit and their sympathy. I was asked by many of them the cause of the explosion, and I invariably answered that I must await further investigation.

For a long time the rapid-fire ammunition continued to explode in detail. The number of the wounded was reported to me later. I have some difficulty in remembering figures, I think we found about 84 or 85 men that night who survived. It was also reported to me that the wounded on board Spanish vessels had been taken to the hospitals on shore, as were also the survivors who had reached the machina, in the neighborhood of the shears on shore. To keep a clear head for the emergency I turned in about 2 o'clock, getting little sleep that night, owing to the distressing groans of the wounded.

Q. By the time you reached the quarter-deck, were all the large explosions over?

A. So far as my experience is concerned there was simply one impression of an overwhelming explosion. I do not recollect details. I have already stated the explosions of minor character.

[...]

Q. You state in your story that the *City of Washington* attended to the wounded. Did not the Spanish man-of-war also do the same?

A. I am not very sure personally, but the reports were that they were doing all that was possible. . . .

[...]

Q. From your examination of the wreck, as far as you have been able to make, what magazines or shell rooms, if any, should you say were blown up?

A. From the appearance of things about the wreck it is extremely difficult to come to any conclusion. The center of the explosion appears to have been beneath and a little forward of the conning tower, and on the port side. The forward part of the superstructure has been thrown upward backward over the after part and toward the starboard side, indicating an explosion on the port side of the ship. In the region of the center or axis of explosion was the 6 inch reserve magazine, which contained very little powder—probably, I am informed, about 300 pounds. The 10 inch magazine is in the general region, but it is on the starboard side, under the forward turret, which is well out on the starboard side. Over the 10-inch magazine in the loading room of the turret, and in the adjoining passage, and well on the starboard side, were a number of 10-inch shell, permanently placed. There were also several additional shell in the loading room. It is difficult, therefore, to conceive that the explosion involved the 10-inch magazine, because of the location of the explosion, and because I have had no reports that any 10 inch shell were hurled into the air by the explosion. The violence of the explosion, although not its immediate locality, indicates that the 10-inch magazine may have been involved.

Q. Where was the 10-inch shell room?

A. The 10-inch shell room was abreast the 10-inch magazine on the port side. It opened on the port side of the vessel.

Q. Was it not between the reserve 6-inch and 10-inch magazines?

A. It was.

Q. Do you know the thickness of the bulkhead between those three divisions?

A. I can not recollect. I should say that it was of ordinary metal, the thickness of a bulkhead of similar construction in other parts of the ship.

Q. Do you know what was between the coal bunker and the magazine?

A. I think nothing but the ordinary steel plate. It is so aft.

[...]

TWENTY-THIRD DAY. U.S.S. IOWA (1st rate), Key West, Fla., Monday, March 21, 1898—10 a.m.

The court met pursuant to the adjournment of yesterday.

Present: All the members and the judge-advocate.

The record of last day's proceedings was read over and approved.

The court was then cleared for deliberation.

After full and mature consideration of all the testimony before it, the court finds as follows:

1. That the United States battle ship *Maine* arrived in the harbor of Habana, Cuba, on the 25th day of January, 1898, and was taken to buoy No. 4, from 5½ to 6 fathoms of water by the regular Government pilot.

The United States consul-general at Havana had notified the authorities at that place the previous evening of the intended arrival of the *Maine.*

2. The state of discipline on board the *Maine* was excellent, and all orders and regulations in regard to the care and safety of the ship were strictly carried out.

All ammunition was stowed in accordance with prescribed instructions, and proper care was taken whenever ammunition was handled.

Nothing was stowed in any one of the magazines or shell rooms which was not permitted to be stowed there.

The magazines and shell rooms were always locked after having been opened, and after the destruction of the *Maine* the keys were found in their proper place in the captain's cabin, everything having been reported secure that evening at 8 p.m.

The temperatures of the magazines and shell rooms were taken daily and reported. The only magazine which had an undue amount of heat was the after 10-inch magazine, and that did not explode at the time the *Maine* was destroyed.

The torpedo war heads were all stowed in the after part of the ship, under the ward room, and neither caused nor participated in the destruction of the *Maine.*

The dry gun-cotton primers and detonators were stowed in the cabin aft, and remote from the scene of the explosion.

Waste was carefully looked after on board the *Maine* to obviate danger. Special orders in regard to this had been given by the commanding officer.

Varnishes, driers, alcohol, and other combustibles of this nature were stowed on or above the main deck and could not have had anything to do with the destruction of the *Maine*.

The medical stores were stowed aft, under the ward room, and remote from the scene of the explosion.

No dangerous stores of any kind were stowed below in any of the other storerooms.

The coal bunkers were inspected daily. Of those bunkers adjacent to the forward magazines and shell rooms four were empty, namely: B3, B4, B5, B6. A15 had been in use that day, and A16 was full of New River coal. This coal had been carefully inspected before receiving it on board. The bunker in which it was stowed was accessible on three sides at all times, and the fourth side at this time on account of bunkers B4 and B6 being empty. This bunker, A16, had been inspected that day by the engineer officer on duty.

The fire alarms in the bunkers were in working order, and there had never been a case of spontaneous combustion of coal on board the *Maine*.

The two after boilers of the ship were in use at the time of the disaster, but for auxiliary purposes only, with a comparatively low pressure of steam, and being tended by a reliable watch.

These boilers could not have caused the explosion of the ship. The four forward boilers have since been found by the divers, and are in a fair condition.

On the night of the destruction of the *Maine* everything had been reported secure for the night at 8 p.m. by reliable persons, through the proper authorities, to the commanding officer. At the time the *Maine* was destroyed the ship was quiet, and, therefore, least liable to accident caused by movements from those on board.

EXPLOSIONS.

3. The destruction of the *Maine* occurred at 9.40 p.m. on the 15th day of February, 1898, in the harbor of Havana, Cuba, she being at the time moored to the same buoy to which she had been taken upon her arrival. There were two explosions of a distinctly different character, with a very short but distinct interval between them, and the forward part of the ship was lifted to a marked degree at the time of the first explosion. The first explosion was more in the nature of a report like that of a gun, while the second explosion was more open, prolonged, and of greater volume. This second explosion was, in the opinion of the court, caused by the partial explosion of two or more of the forward magazines of the *Maine*.

CONDITION OF THE WRECK.

4. The evidence bearing upon this, being principally obtained from divers, did not enable the court to form a definite conclusion as to the condition of the wreck, although it was established that the after part of the ship was practically intact, and sank in that condition a very few minutes after the destruction of the forward part.

The following facts in regard to the forward part of the ship are, however, established by the testimony:

A portion of the port side of the protective deck, which extends from about frame 30 to about frame 41, was blown up, aft, and over to port. The main deck, from about frame 30 to about frame 41, was blown up, aft, and slightly over to starboard, folding the forward part of the middle superstructure over and on top of the after part.

This was, in the opinion of the court, caused by the partial explosion of two or more of the forward magazines of the *Maine*.

5. At frame 17 the outer shell of the ship, from a point 11½ feet from the middle line of the ship, and 6 feet above the keel when in its normal position, has been forced up so as to be now about 4 feet above

the surface of the water, therefore about 34 feet above where it would be had the ship sunk uninjured.

The outside bottom plating is bent into a reversed V shape (^), the after wing of which, about 15 feet broad and 32 feet in length (from frame 17 to frame 25), is doubled back upon itself against the continuation of the same plating, extending forward.

At frame 18 the vertical keel is broken in two, and the flat keel bent into an angle similar to the angle formed by the outside bottom plating. This break is now about 6 feet below the surface of the water, and about 30 feet above its normal position.

In the opinion of the court this effect could have been produced only by the explosion of a mine situated under the bottom of the ship at about frame 18 and somewhat on the port side of the ship.

6. The court finds that the loss of the *Maine* on the occasion named was not in any respect due to fault or negligence on the part of any of the officers or members of the crew of said vessel.

7. In the opinion of the court the *Maine* was destroyed by the explosion of a submarine mine, which caused the partial explosion of two or more of the forward magazines.

8. The court has been unable to obtain evidence fixing the responsibility for the destruction of the *Maine* upon any person or persons.

W. T. SAMPSON,
Captain, U.S.N., President.
A. MARIX,
Lieut. Com., U.S.N., Judge-Advocate.

The court having finished the inquiry it was ordered to make, adjourned at 11 a.m., to await the action of the convening authority.

W. T. SAMPSON,
Captain, U.S.N., President.

A. MARIX,
Lieut.-Com., U.S.N., Judge-Advocate.
U.S. FLAGSHIP NEW YORK,
Off Key West, Fla., March 22, 1898.

The proceedings and findings of the court of inquiry in the above case are approved.

M. SICARD,
Rear Admiral, Commander in Chief of the United States Naval force on the North Atlantic Station.

Source: U.S. Congress, *Papers Relating to the Foreign Relations of the United States with the Annual Message of the President Transmitted to Congress December 5, 1898* (Washington, DC: U.S. Government Printing Office, 1901), 1026–1029.

Spanish and American Declarations of War (April 23 and 25, 1898) [Excerpt]

Introduction

President William McKinley hoped to resolve the Cuban conflict without resorting to war, but the events of early 1898—including the February explosion of the battleship *Maine*—made war virtually inevitable. In March the U.S. ambassador to Spain issued an ultimatum demanding an armistice in Cuba, an end to the concentration camps, and eventual Cuban independence. Spain also wished to avoid war and in early April declared a cease-fire in Cuba and ended the reconcentration system but did not commit to Cuban independence. Two days later on April 11, 1898, McKinley delivered an address to the U.S. Congress asking for the authority to use whatever means necessary, including military intervention, to bring about peace and stability in Cuba. On April 19, 1898, Congress passed a resolution recognizing Cuba's independence, calling for Spain to withdraw, and authorizing American military intervention. Spain responded with a declaration of war on April 23. Spain's declaration was issued as a royal decree by Queen Regent María Cristina and detailed Spain's intentions regarding shipping, privateering, and maritime law. The United States responded with its own declaration of war two days later and made it retroactive to April 21.

Primary Source
FOREIGN OFFICE, May 8, 1898.

The secretary of state for foreign affairs has received, through Her Majesty's embassy at Madrid, the following translation of a decree issued by the Spanish Government on the 23d of April, 1898:

ROYAL DECREE.

In accordance with the advice of my council of ministers, in the name of my son, King Alfonso XIII, and as Queen Regent of the Kingdom, I decree as follows:

ARTICLE I. The state of war existing between Spain and the United States terminates the treaty of peace and friendship of the 27th October, 1795, the protocol of the 12th January, 1877, and all other agreements, compacts, and conventions that have been in force up to the present between the two countries.

ART. II. A term of five days from the date of the publication of the present royal decree in the Madrid Gazette is allowed to all United States ships anchored in Spanish ports, during which they are at liberty to depart.

ART. III. Notwithstanding that Spain is not bound by the declaration signed in Paris on the 16th April, 1856, as she expressly stated her wish not to adhere to it, my Government, guided by the principles of international law, intends to observe and hereby orders that the following regulations for maritime law be observed:

(a) A neutral flag covers the enemy's goods, except contraband of war.

(b) Neutral goods, except contraband of war, are not liable to confiscation under the enemy's flag.

(c) A blockade to be binding must be effective; that is to say, maintained with a sufficient force to actually prevent access to the enemy's coast.

ART. IV. The Spanish Government, while maintaining their right to issue letters of marque, which they expressly reserved in their note of the 16th May, 1857, in reply to the request of France for the adhesion of Spain to the declaration of Paris relative to maritime law, will organize for the present a service of "auxiliary cruisers of the navy," composed of ships of the Spanish mercantile navy, which will cooperate with the latter for the purposes of cruising, and which will be subject to the statutes and jurisdiction of the navy.

ART. V. In order to capture the enemy's ships, to confiscate the enemy's merchandise under their own flag, and contraband of war under any flag, the royal navy, auxiliary cruisers, and privateers, if and when the latter are authorized, will exercise the right of visit on the high seas and in the territorial waters of the enemy, in accordance with international law and any regulations which may be published for the purpose.

ART. VI. Under the denomination contraband of war the following articles are included:

Cannons, machine guns, mortars, guns, all kinds of arms and firearms, bullets, bombs, grenades, fuses, cartridges, matches, powder, sulphur, saltpeter, dynamite and every kind of explosive, articles of equipment like uniforms, straps, saddles, and artillery and cavalry harness, engines for ships and their accessories, shafts, screws, boilers, and other articles used in the construction, repair, and arming of war ships, and in general all warlike instruments, utensils, tools, and other articles, and whatever may hereafter be determined to be contraband.

ART. VII. Captains, commanders, and officers of non-American vessels or of vessels manned as to one-third by other than American citizens, captured while committing acts of war against Spain, will be treated as pirates, with all the rigor of the law, although provided with a license issued by the Republic of the United States.

ART. VIII. The minister of state and the minister of marine are charged to see the fulfillment of the present royal decree and to give the orders necessary for its execution.

MARIA CRISTINA.
MADRID, April 23, 1898.

EXECUTIVE MANSION, WASHINGTON
April 25, 1898.

To the Senate and House of Representatives of the United States of America:

I transmit to the Congress for its consideration and appropriate action, copies of correspondence recently had with the representative of Spain in the United States, with the United States minister at Madrid, and through the latter with the Government of Spain, showing the action taken under the joint resolution approved April 20, 1898, "for the recognition of the independence of the people of Cuba, demanding that the Government of Spain relinquish its authority and Government in the island of Cuba, and to withdraw its land and naval forces from Cuba and Cuban waters, and directing the President of the United States to use the land and naval forces of the United States to carry these resolutions into effect."

[…]

I commend to your especial attention the note addressed to the United States minister at Madrid by the Spanish minister of foreign affairs on the 21st instant, whereby the foregoing notification was conveyed. It will be perceived therefrom that the Government of Spain, having cognizance of the joint resolution of the United States Congress, and in view of the things which the President is thereby required and authorized to do, responds by treating the reasonable demands of this Government as measures of hostility, following with that instant and complete severance of relations by its action which by the usage of nations accompanies an existent state of war between sovereign powers.

The position of Spain being thus made known, and the demands of the United States being denied, with a complete rupture of intercourse, by the act of Spain, I have been constrained, in the exercise of the power conferred upon me by the joint resolution aforesaid, to proclaim, under date of April 22, 1898, a blockade of certain ports of the north coast of Cuba, between Cardenas and Bahia Honda, and the port of Cienfugos, on the south coast of Cuba, and to issue my proclamation dated April 23, 1898, calling forth volunteers.

I now recommend the adoption of a joint resolution declaring that a state of war exists between the United States of America and the Kingdom of Spain, that the definition of the international status of the United States as a belligerent power may be made known and the assertion of all its rights in the conduct of a public war may be assured.

DECLARATION OF WAR WITH SPAIN

Be it enacted by the Senate and House of Representatives of the United States of America in Congress assembled, First. That war be, and the same is hereby, declared to exist, and that war has existed since the 21st day of April, A. D. 1898, including said day, between the United States of America and the Kingdom of Spain. Second. That the President of the United States be, and he hereby is, directed and empowered to use the entire land and naval forces of the United States and to call into the actual service of the United States the militia of the several States to such extent as may be necessary to carry this act into effect.

Approved, April 25, 1898.

Source: "Spanish and American Declarations of War, Transmitted by Ambassador Hay," *London Gazette*, May 3, 1898.

George Dewey, Official Report of the Battle of Manila (May 4, 1898) [Excerpt]

Introduction

On April 25, 1898, the day that the United States declared war on Spain, Commodore George Dewey, commander of the U.S. Navy's Asiatic Squadron, received President William McKinley's order to move against the Spanish fleet at Manila, capital of the Philippines. On April 30 Dewey's six ships entered Manila Bay, and the next morning the Americans destroyed the entire Spanish Pacific fleet without losing a single man. In the space of a few hours, the Spanish lost all their vessels and suffered nearly 400 casualties. However, with only 1,700 sailors, Dewey could not hope to capture the city of Manila. It would be two months before land forces arrived from the United States. In the meantime Dewey blockaded Manila, while the Filipino rebel leader Emilio Aguinaldo harassed the Spanish troops. Dewey's official report, excerpted here, briefly recounts the action and commends a number of individuals for their conduct. News of the complete and dramatic victory inspired the American public and elevated Dewey to the status of hero.

Primary Source

Flagship Olympia, May 4, 1898.

... The squadron left Mirs Bay on April 27.... Arrived off Bolinao on the morning of April 30, and finding no vessels there, proceeded down the coast and arrived off the entrance to Manila Bay on the same afternoon. The *Boston* and *Concord* were sent to reconnoitre Port Subic.... A thorough search of the port was made by the *Boston* and the *Concord*, but the Spanish fleet was not found....

Entered the south channel at 11:30 P.M., steaming in column at eight knots. After half the squadron had passed, a battery on the south side of the channel opened fire, none of the shots taking effect. The *Boston* and *McCulloch* returned the fire.

The squadron proceeded across the bay at slow speed and arrived off Manila at daybreak and was fired upon at 5:15 A.M., by three batteries at Manila and two near Cavite, and by the Spanish fleet anchored in an approximately east and west line across the mouth of Baker Bay, with their left in shoal water in Canacao Bay.

The squadron then proceeded to the attack, the flagship *Olympia*, under my personal direction, leading, followed at distance by the *Baltimore, Raleigh, Petrel, Concord,* and *Boston,* in the order named, which formation was maintained throughout the action.

The squadron opened fire at 5:41 A.M. While advancing to the attack, two mines were exploded ahead of the flagship, too far to be effective. The squadron maintained a continuous and precise fire, at ranges varying from 5,000 to 2,000 yards. ... The enemy's fire was vigorous but generally ineffective.

[...]

At 7 A.M. the Spanish flagship *Reina Christina* made a desperate attempt to leave the line and come out to engage at short range, but was received with such galling fire, the entire battery of the *Olympia* being concentrated upon her, that she was barely able to return to the shelter of the point.

The fires started in her by our shells at this time were not extinguished until she sank.... The three batteries at Manila had kept up a continuous report from the beginning of the engagement, which fire was not returned by this squadron....

At this point I sent a message to the Governor-General to the effect that if the batteries did not cease firing the city would be shelled. This had the effect of silencing them.

> The squadron opened fire at 5:41 A.M. While advancing to the attack, two mines were exploded ahead of the flagship, too far to be effective. The squadron maintained a continuous and precise fire, at ranges varying from 5,000 to 2,000 yards.

At 7:35 A.M. I ceased firing and withdrew the squadron for breakfast. At 11:16 A.M. returned to the attack. By this time the Spanish flagship and almost the entire Spanish fleet were in flames. At 12:30 P.M. the squadron ceased firing, the batteries being silenced and the ships sunk, burnt, and deserted. At 12:40 P.M. the squadron returned and anchored off Manila, the *Petrel* being left behind to complete the destruction of the smaller gunboats, which were behind the point of Cavite.

[. . .]

I am unable to obtain complete accounts of the enemy's killed and wounded, but believe their losses to be very heavy. The *Reina Christina* alone had one hundred and fifty killed, including the captain, and ninety wounded. I am happy to report that the damage done to the squadron under my command was inconsiderable. There were none killed and only seven men in the squadron slightly wounded. . . .

Several of the vessels were struck and even penetrated, but the damage was of the lightest, and the squadron is in as good condition now as before the battle.

I beg to state to the department that I doubt if any commander-in-chief was ever served by more loyal, efficient, and gallant captains than those of the squadron now under my command.

[. . .]

The conduct of my personal staff was excellent. Commander B. P. Lamberton, chief-of-staff, was a volunteer for that position and gave me most efficient aid. Lieutenant Brumby, flag lieutenant, and Ensign W. P. Scott, aide, performed their duties as signal officers in a highly creditable manner.

[. . .]

I desire specially to mention the coolness of Lieutenant C. G. Calkins, the navigator of the *Olympia,* who came under my personal observation, being on the bridge with me throughout the entire action, and giving the ranges to the guns with an accuracy that was proven by the excellency of the firing.

[. . .]

Source: United States Adjutant-General's Office, *Correspondence Relating to the War with Spain . . .* (Washington, DC: Center of Military History, 1993), 330, 379.

Congressional Hearings on the War in the Philippines, Testimony Regarding the Use of Torture (1902) [Excerpt]

Introduction

After occupying the Philippines as a result of the Spanish-American War, U.S. soldiers resumed fighting on February 4, 1899, to put down Philippine resistance. As the war intensified, President William McKinley sent additional troops. The Filipino rebels used mostly guerrilla tactics. The U.S. Army scored notable successes in the first year of fighting, and the commanding general believed that the rebellion had been suppressed. However, determined resistance in outlying provinces continued to inflict significant casualties. Reports filtered back to the United States about American cruelty, including scorched-earth tactics and the use of torture. Prowar senator Henry Cabot Lodge, chairman of the Senate Committee on the Philippines, was forced to conduct hearings on the allegations of war crimes. Excerpted here are the eyewitness testimony of Private William L. Smith and Lieutenant Grover Flint. They describe in detail U.S. soldiers and Philippine Scouts under their command applying the infamous water cure, the force-feeding of large volumes of water. Although the testimony was published, no further action was taken.

Primary Source
TESTIMONY OF WILLIAM LEWIS SMITH.
(Sworn by the chairman.)

By Senator RAWLINS:

Q. Were you at Igbaras, Iloilo Province, island of Panay, on or about the 27th of November, 1900?—A. Yes, sir. Q. What regiment were you connected with?—A. Twenty-sixth Volunteer Infantry.

Q. How long had you been in the service at that time?—A. Since July 17, 1899.

Q. Where is your home?—A. Athol, Mass. Q. You may state whether or not you witnessed what is known as the water cure.—A. I did, sir.

Q. And where did you see it?—A. At the town of Igbaras.

Q. On what day?—A. November 27, 1900.

Q. Upon whom was it inflicted?—A. Upon the presidente of the town and two native police.

Q. Did you observe it inflicted more than once?—A. I saw part of it at one time and the whole of it the second time.

Q. Describe what you saw on the first occasion.—A. We arrived at the town about daylight in the morning. It was just breaking day. There was an outpost put all over the town, so that no people could leave town by the gates, and we proceeded to quarters. A detachment of our company was stationed there.... We proceeded to quarters, and I was one of a detail that was sent out to ask the presidente to come over to the quarters. On the way we met him and proceeded to the house of the padre, the priest of the town, to get him. He was not at home.

The presidente went along over to the quarters. When I got back to the quarters, the boys were sitting around, and I went upstairs, and the first that I saw of the presidente was that he was stripped. He had nothing on but his pants. His shirt and coat were off, and his hands were tied behind him, and Lieutenant Conger stood over him, and also a contract doctor by the name of Dr. Lyons, and as we stopped there they proceeded to give him what is known as the water cure. It was given from a large tank.... He was thrown on his back, and these four or five men, known as the water detail of these Gordon Scouts, held him down. Water was administered by the opening of the faucet. We could not get close enough to see exactly how it was done, because if we would congregate there at all the officers would tell us to pass on....

The second time I saw it after he had confessed what they wanted—I do not know whether he confessed or not, I only saw a part of that—but downstairs they asked him through an interpreter, they all stood over him at the time, and they asked him if he sent any word out to the insurgents when the troops arrived in town. One of the native police in the meantime disclosed that he had, that he had sent him personally, so in order to get that from him Lieutenant Conger called for the water detail. This time it was given by means of a syringe. Two men went out to their saddlebags and obtained two syringes, large bulbs, a common syringe, about 2 feet of common hose pipe, I should think, on either end. One was inserted in his mouth and the other up his nose. We could all stand by there and see that. When this doctor said to get a pail of water, and they started into the building with him, Captain Glenn was there, and he said, "No, this is good enough right here on the outside." So we all had a chance to witness it that time....

[...]

The CHAIRMAN. Did the men subjected to this torture die?

The WITNESS. I never saw a man die. But I saw a man who I thought was going to die once, and I had indirect evidence that a man had died in another case; but nothing that I could testify to.

Senator VARMACK. That men have died in other cases, you say?

The WITNESS. Yes, sir.

By Senator CULBERSON:

Q. Apparently you were about to detail what you actually saw the next morning?—A. Yes.

Q. You stated the night before you only casually saw it, and then you were going on to state what you saw in the morning?—A. In the morning I actually witnessed it. I saw men thrown down and heard their groans and that sort of thing.

Documents

Q. Please tell the committee what you actually saw?—A. That is, you want me to describe one individual case of a man being put through the water cure?

Q. Yes; I would like you to do that, sir.—A. Very good, sir. A man is thrown down on his back and three or four men sit or stand on his arms and legs and hold him down, and either a gun barrel or a rifle barrel or a carbine barrel or a stick as big as a belaying pin—that is, with an inch circumference—

Senator BEVERIDGE. As big in its diameter?

A. (Continued.) Yes; is simply thrust into his jaws and his jaws are thrust back, and, if possible, a wooden log or stone is put under his head.

Senator PATTERSON. Under his head or neck?

A. (Continued.) Under his neck, so he can be held firmly.

Senator BURROWS. His jaws are forced open, you say? How do you mean, crosswise?

The WITNESS. Yes, sir; as a gag. In the case of very old men I have seen their teeth fall out—I mean when it was done a little roughly. He is simply held down, and then water is poured onto his face, down his throat and nose from a jar, and that is kept up until the man gives some sign of giving in or becomes unconscious, and when he becomes unconscious he is simply rolled aside and he is allowed to come to. That is as near a description as I think I can give. All the cases were alike I saw on that occasion.

By Senator CULBERSON:

Q. Is the water allowed to remain in the man or is it any way expelled from him, by any method?—A. Well, I know that in a great many cases, in almost every case, the men have been a little roughly handled; they were rolled aside rudely, so that water was expelled. A man suffers tremendously; there is no doubt about it. His suffering must be that of a man who is drowning, but who cannot drown.

Source: U.S. Congress, Committee on the Philippines, *Affairs in the Philippine Islands: Hearings before the Committee on the Philippines, 57th Cong., Part II* (Washington, DC: U.S. Government Printing Office, 1902), 1538–1539, 1766–1767.

Black Elk's Account of the Wounded Knee Massacre (December 29, 1890) [Excerpt]

Introduction

Confined to their South Dakota reservation and suffering from inadequate rations, in 1890 the Sioux embraced the rapidly spreading Ghost Dance religion with particular fervor. The U.S. agent at Pine Ridge Reservation demanded military protection, fearing that a violent uprising was imminent. The army ordered the arrest of Sitting Bull, and he was killed on December 15, 1890. His people then fled the reservation but returned to surrender two weeks later. Black Elk, a Sioux medicine man and a cousin of Crazy Horse, was a leading participant in the Ghost Dance movement. In this excerpt he describes the December 29, 1890, massacre of his people at Wounded Knee. Most of the surrendering Indians had stacked their arms, but the soldiers were confiscating the weapons that a few men had concealed. A concealed rifle went off, a scuffle ensued, and a soldier was shot. U.S. troops turned their guns on the Indians at close range and mowed them down, then pursued and killed those who tried to flee. They killed more than 150 Sioux, many of them women and children.

Primary Source
Black Elk's Account

Then I rode over the ridge and the others after me, and we were crying: "Take courage! It is time to fight!" The soldiers who were guarding our relatives shot at us and then ran away fast, and some more cavalrymen on the other side of the gulch did too. We got our relatives and sent them across the ridge to the northwest where they would be safe. I had no gun, and when we were charging, I just held the sacred bow out in front of me with my right hand. The bullets did not hit us at all. We found a little baby lying all alone near the head of the gulch. I could not pick her up just then, but I got her later and some of my people adopted her. I just wrapped her up tighter in a shawl that was around her and left her there. . . .

Expansion at Home and Abroad

The soldiers had run eastward over the hills where there were some more soldiers, and they were off their horses and lying down. I told the others to stay back, and I charged upon them holding the sacred bow out toward them with my right hand. They all shot at me and I could hear bullets all around me, but I ran my horse right close to them, and then swung around. Some soldiers across the gulch began shooting at me too, but I got back to the others and was not hurt at all. By now many other Lakotas, who had heard the shooting, were coming up from Pine Ridge, and we all charged on the soldiers. They ran eastward toward where the trouble began. We followed down along the dry gulch, and what we saw was terrible. Dead and wounded women and children and little babies were scattered all along there where they had been trying to run away. The soldiers had followed along the gulch, as they ran, and murdered them in there. Sometimes they were in heaps because they had huddled together, and some were scattered all along. Sometimes bunches of them had been killed and torn to pieces where the wagon guns hit them. I saw a little baby trying to suck its mother, but she was bloody and dead. There were two little boys at one place in this gulch. They had guns and they had been killing soldiers all by themselves. We could see the soldiers they had killed. . . .

When we drove the soldiers back, they dug themselves in, and we were not enough people to drive them out from there. In the evening they marched off up Wounded Knee Creek, and then we saw all that they had done there. Men and women and children were heaped and scattered all over the flat at the bottom of the little hill where the soldiers had their wagon-guns, and westward up the dry gulch all the way to the high ridge, the dead women and children and babies were scattered. When I saw this I wished that I had died too, but I was not sorry for the women and children. It was better for them to be happy in the other world, and I wanted to be there too. But before I went there I wanted to have revenge. I thought there might be a day, and we should have revenge.

After the soldiers marched away, I heard from my friend, Dog Chief, how the trouble started, and he was right there by Yellow Bird when it happened. This is the way it was: In the morning the soldiers began to take all the guns away from the Big Foots, who were camped in the flat below the little hill where the mound and burying ground are now. The people had stacked most of their guns, and even their knives, by the tepee where Big Foot was lying sick. Soldiers were on the little hill and all around, and there were soldiers across the dry gulch to the south and over east along Wounded Knee Creek too. The people were nearly surrounded, and the wagon guns were pointing at them. Some had not yet given up their guns, and so the soldiers were searching all the tepees, throwing things around

> Dead and wounded women and children and little babies were scattered all along there where they had been trying to run away. The soldiers had followed along the gulch, as they ran, and murdered them in there.

and poking into everything. There was a man called Yellow Bird, and he and another man were standing in front of the tepee where Big Foot was lying sick. They had white sheets around and over them, with eyeholes to look through, and they had guns under these. An officer came to search them. He took the other man's gun, and then started to take Yellow Bird's. But Yellow Bird would not let go. He wrestled with the officer, and while they were wrestling, the gun went off and killed the officer. Wasichus and some others have said he meant to do this, but Dog Chief was standing right there, and he told me it was not so.

As soon as the gun went off, Dog Chief told me, an officer shot and killed Big Foot who was lying sick inside the tepee. Then suddenly nobody knew what was happening, except that the soldiers were all shooting and the wagon-guns began going off right in among the people. . . .

Source: Reprinted by permission from *Black Elk Speaks: Being the Life Story of a Holy Man of the Oglala Sioux; The Premier Edition*, edited by John G. Neihardt, 88–211, the State University of New York Press © 2008, State University of New York. All rights reserved.

F. F. Girard, Account of Battle of Little Bighorn (ca. 1920) [Excerpt]

Introduction

On June 25, 1876, Lieutenant Colonel George Armstrong Custer and his 7th Cavalry discovered the major Sioux encampment on Little Bighorn Creek. Custer apparently did not realize how large a force he confronted and, without waiting for reinforcements, ordered Major Marcus Reno and his detachment to charge. As the outnumbered Reno was fought to a standstill, Custer's force charged from another direction. Custer and all of his more than 200 men died in the ensuing combat. The nation was shocked by the defeat. Custer's judgment and Reno's actions came under scrutiny, but most importantly, the army turned its full might against the Indians of the northern Plains.

Primary Source

F. F. GIRARD'S STORY OF THE CUSTER FIGHT (From *The Arikara Narrative*)

ON JUNE 22d, Custer's command left the mouth of the Rosebud looking for Indians. On June 24th, we broke camp and marched all day and in evening went into camp. The men had supper and grazed their horses and then marched all night till 4 A.M., when a halt was called. The horses remained saddled but the soldiers slept on the ground as best they could. Two Arikara scouts arrived from Lieutenant Varnum, who had been sent out to reconnoitre and locate Indian camps. They brought word of a very large camp down in Little Big Horn Valley, but the Indians had discovered us and were on the run. Custer ordered me to go with him and the two Arikara scouts who had come in from Varnum and two of our scouts, to where Lieutenant Varnum was. About daybreak we reached Varnum and could see the large black mass moving in front and down the Little Big Horn and a dense cloud of dust. The camp we had found was the smaller camp (the larger camp was downstream farther), and was on the way to the larger camp and this led us all to believe that the Indians were stampeded. Custer

and his party with Varnum and his scouts started back to rejoin the command at a sharp gait. Before reaching his troops, about half way back, Tom Custer met us at the head of the troops and Custer addressed him saying: "Tom, who in the devil moved these troops forward? My orders and intentions were to remain in camp all day and make a night attack on the Indians but they have discovered us and are on the run." After joining the troops, Custer with his officers held a consultation and decided it would be better to follow the Indians so he divided his command into three battalions, one under his own command, Benteen in command of the second, and Reno of the third. Benteen he sent to the left of the command to overlook the ridges as we marched down the valley. He then ordered Reno to take his command and try to overtake the Indians and bring them to battle while he himself would support him. Custer said: "Take the scouts with you." Reno started on the double quick down the valley until he came to the Little Big Horn. Up to that time we were all still under the impression that the Indians were running away. Upon reaching the ford of the Little Big Horn, I discovered that the Indians were coming back to give us battle and called Reno's attention to this change in their movements. Reno halted for a few seconds and ordered the men forward. Thinking that Custer should know of this change of front on the part of the Indians, I rode back at once to tell Custer the news. At an abrupt turn I met Cook [*sic*], Custer's adjutant, ahead of his command, who said: "Girard, what's up?" On hearing the news he ordered me back to Reno's command and rode to inform Custer of the change in the front on the part of the Indians. I rejoined Reno's command just as he was drawing up his men on the skirmish line. The men were almost six feet apart along the brow of a hill. As the Indians came charging back the men used the timber for cover and the Indians rode by on the left and around to the higher ground at the rear and left. Not more than four rounds had been fired before they saw Custer's command dashing along the hills one mile to their rear. Reno then gave the order: "The Indians are taking us in the rear, mount and charge." This was then about 1:30 P.M. I was surprised [at] this change of position as we had excellent cover and could hold off the Indians indefinitely, but the orders were to mount and charge. Charley Reynolds was killed as he rode up the slope at the left and Isaiah a little farther out. Reno led his men in Indian file back to the ford above which he had seen Custer's command pass. The Indians picked off the troops at will; it was a rout, not a charge. All the men were shot in the back, some men fell before high ground was reached. As soon as the hill was gained, Benteen and his command came up and the demoralization of Reno's men affected his own men and no attempt was made to go to Custer's aid. They remained where they were though it was about 2 P.M. and no Indians attacked them for more than an hour.

After Reno's command left, I found in the timber Lieutenant de Rudio, Sergeant O'Neill and Wm. Jackson, the half-breed Blackfoot scout, who were also cut off from the command. All the afternoon we could hear the troop volleys, but the scattering fire of the Indians gradually predominated till we were sure that the Indians had won. . . .

Source: O. G. Libby, ed. *The Arikara Narrative of the Campaign against the Hostile Dakotas* (Cedar Rapids, IA: Torch, 1920), 171–175.

EXPANSION AT HOME AND ABROAD

The Later Indian Wars, the Spanish-American War, and the Philippine-American War, 1878–1913

STATISTICS

American Indian Demographic Change by Region						
	Notable Tribes	Date of Initial Estimate	Number of Tribes at Initial Estimate	Number of Tribes in 1907	Population at Initial Estimate	Population in 1907
Northern Atlantic Region	Abenakis, Iroquois, Delawares	1600	24	10	55,600	21,900
Southern Atlantic Region	Cherokees, Powhatans, Tuscaroras	1600	35	15	52,200	2,170
Gulf Coast Region	Creeks, Miamis, Seminoles	1650	39	12	114,400	62,700
Central Region	Illinois, Shawnees, Yuchis	1650	12	10	75,300	46,130
Southwest Region	Kiowas, Navajos, Pueblos	1680	25	19	72,000	53,830
Southern Plains Region	Apaches, Comanches, Kickapoos	1690	12	7	41,000	2,860
California Region	Chumash, Miwoks, Shastas	1770	45	36	260,000	18,800
Northern Plains Region	Dakota Sioux, Missouris, Sauks	1780	20	19	100,800	50,480
Northwest Region	Chinooks, Modocs, Suquamish	1780	95	83	88,800	15,430
Central Mountains Region	Arapahos, Cheyennes, Sashonis	1845	6	6	19,300	11,540

Sources: Paul Stuart, *Nations within a Nation: Historical Statistics of American Indians* (Westport, CT: Greenwood, 1987); Russell Thornton, *We Shall Live Again: The 1870 and 1890 Ghost Dance Movements as Demographic Revitalization* (New York: Cambridge University Press, 1986).

Statistics

Casualties, Spanish-American War (1898–1901)					
Branch of Service	Number Serving	Total Deaths	Battle Deaths	Other Deaths	Wounded, Not Mortally
Total	306,760	2,446	385	2,061	1,662
Army	280,564	2,430	369	2,061	1,594
Navy	22,875	10	10	—	47
Marines	3,321	6	6	—	21

Source: Congressional Research Service, CRS Report for Congress, February 6, 2010.

EXPANSION AT HOME AND ABROAD

The Later Indian Wars, the Spanish-American War, and the Philippine-American War, 1878–1913

BIBLIOGRAPHY

Adams, Alexander B. *Geronimo: A Biography.* New York: Putnam, 1971.

Adams, George Rollie. *General William S. Harney: Prince of Dragoons.* Lincoln: University of Nebraska Press, 2001.

Alberts, Don E. *Brandy Station to Manila Bay: A Biography of General Wesley Merritt.* Austin, TX: Presidial, 1981.

Alip, Eufronio Melo. *In the Days of General Emilio Aguinaldo: A Study of the Life and Times of a Great Military Leader, Statesman, and Patriot Who Founded the First Republic in Asia.* Manila: Alip, 1969.

Allen, Douglas. *Frederic Remington and the Spanish-American War.* New York: Crown, 1971.

Allen, Helena G. *The Betrayal of Liliuokalani: Last Queen of Hawaii, 1838–1917.* Glendale, CA: Arthur H. Clark, 1982.

Altshuler, Constance Wynn. *Cavalry Yellow and Infantry Blue: Army Officers in Arizona between 1851 and 1886.* Tucson: Arizona Historical Society, 1991.

Altshuler, Constance Wynn. *Chains of Command: Arizona and the Army, 1856–1875.* Tucson: Arizona Historical Society, 1981.

Ambrose, Stephen E. *Crazy Horse and Custer: The Parallel Lives of Two American Warriors.* Garden City, NY: Doubleday, 1975.

Anderson, William L., ed. *Cherokee Removal: Before and After.* Athens: University of Georgia Press, 1991.

Balfour, Sebastian. *The End of the Spanish Empire, 1898–1923.* Oxford: Clarendon, 1997.

Beale, Howard K. *Theodore Roosevelt and the Rise of America to World Power.* Baltimore: Johns Hopkins University Press, 1956.

Beede, Benjamin R. *The War of 1898 and U.S. Interventions, 1898–1934: An Encyclopedia.* New York: Garland, 1994.

Beisner, Robert L. *Twelve against Empire: The Anti-Imperialists, 1898–1900.* New York: McGraw-Hill, 1968.

Beisner, Robert L. *The United States and Cuba: Hegemony and Dependent Development, 1880–1934.* Pittsburgh: University of Pittsburgh Press, 1977.

Benjamin, Jules R. *The United States and the Origins of the Cuban Revolution: An Empire of Liberty in an Age of National Liberation.* Princeton, NJ: Princeton University Press, 1990.

Berner, Brad K. *The Spanish-American War: A Historical Dictionary.* Lanham, MD: Scarecrow, 1998.

Blackhawk, Ned. *Violence over the Land: Indians and Empires in the Early American West.* Cambridge, MA: Harvard University Press, 2006.

Blow, Michael. *A Ship to Remember: The Maine and the Spanish-American War.* New York: Morrow, 1992.

Bouvier, Virginia M., ed. *Whose America? The War of 1898 and the Battles to Define the Nation.* Westport, CT: Praeger, 2001.

Bradford, James C., ed. *Crucible of Empire: The Spanish-American War and Its Aftermath.* Annapolis, MD: Naval Institute Press, 1993.

Braisted, William Reynolds. *The United States Navy in the Pacific, 1897–1909.* Austin: University of Texas Press, 1958.

Bibliography

Burton, David H. *Theodore Roosevelt: Confident Imperialist.* Philadelphia: University of Pennsylvania Press, 1968.

Callicott, Wilfred H. *The Caribbean Policy of the United States, 1890–1920.* Baltimore: Johns Hopkins University Press, 1942.

Campbell, Charles S. *The Transformation of American Foreign Relations, 1865–1900.* New York: Harper and Row, 1976.

Cannon, Joseph Gurney, and L. White Busbey. *Uncle Joe Cannon: The Story of a Pioneer American.* St. Clair Shores, MI: Scholarly Press, 1970.

Carlson, Paul H. *"Pecos Bill": A Military Biography of William R. Shafter.* College Station: Texas A&M University Press, 1989.

Carter, Samuel, III. *Cherokee Sunset: A Nation Betrayed: A Narrative of Travail and Triumph, Persecution and Exile.* Garden City, NY: Doubleday, 1976.

Challener, Richard D. *Admirals, Generals, and American Foreign Policy, 1898–1914.* Princeton, NJ: Princeton University Press, 1973.

Chidsey, Donald Barr. *The Spanish-American War: A Behind-the-Scenes Account of the War in Cuba.* New York: Crown, 1971.

Cirillo, Vincent J. *Bullets and Bacilli: The Spanish-American War and Military Medicine.* New Brunswick, NJ: Rutgers University Press, 2004.

Coates, Austin. *Rizal: Philippine Nationalist and Martyr.* New York: Oxford University Press, 1968.

Coletta, Paolo Enrico. *Admiral Bradley A. Fiske and the American Navy.* Lawrence: Regents Press of Kansas, 1979.

Coletta, Paolo Enrico. *Bowman Hendry McCalla: A Fighting Sailor.* Washington, DC: University Press of America, 1979.

Coletta, Paolo Enrico. *French Ensor Chadwick: Scholarly Warrior.* Lanham, MD: University Press of America, 1980.

Collin, Richard H. *Theodore Roosevelt's Caribbean: The Panama Canal, the Monroe Doctrine, and the Latin American Context.* Baton Rouge: Louisiana State University Press, 1990.

Connell, Evan S. *Son of the Morning Star: Custer and the Little Bighorn.* San Francisco: North Point, 1984.

Cosmas, Graham A. *An Army for Empire: The United States Army and the Spanish-American War.* Columbia: University of Missouri Press, 1971.

Couttie, Bob. *Hang the Dogs: The True History of the Balangiga Massacre.* Quezon City, Philippines: New Day Publishers, 2004.

Crouch, Thomas W. *A Yankee Guerrillero: Frederick Funston and the Cuban Insurrection, 1896–1897.* Memphis: Memphis State University Press, 1975.

DeMontravel, Peter R. *A Hero to His Fighting Men: Nelson A. Miles, 1839–1925.* Kent, OH: Kent State University Press, 1998.

Dewey, George. *Autobiography of George Dewey: Admiral of the Navy.* New York: Scribner, 1913.

Dierks, Jack Cameron. *A Leap to Arms: The Cuban Campaign of 1898.* Philadelphia: Lippincott, 1970.

Dioso, Marconi M. *A Trilogy of Wars: The Philippine Revolutionary Wars of 1896–97, the Spanish-American War in the Philippines in 1898, and the Filipino-American War, 1899–1902.* Pittsburgh: Dorrance, 2004.

Dobson, John M. *Reticent Expansionism: The Foreign Policy of William McKinley.* Pittsburgh: Duquesne University Press, 1988.

Dorwart, Jeffery Michael. *The Office of Naval Intelligence: The Birth of America's First Agency, 1865–1918.* Annapolis, MD: Naval Institute Press, 1979.

Dunlay, Tom W. *Kit Carson and the Indians.* Lincoln: University of Nebraska Press, 2000.

Esherick, Joseph W. *The Origins of the Boxer Uprising.* Berkeley and Los Angeles: University of California Press, 1989.

Foner, Jack D. *The United States Soldier between Two Wars: Army Life and Reforms, 1865–1898.* New York: Humanities, 1970.

Foner, Philip S. *The Spanish-Cuban-American War and the Birth of American Imperialism, 1895–1902.* 2 vols. New York: Monthly Review Press, 1972.

Freidel, Frank Burt. *The Splendid Little War.* Boston: Little, Brown, 1958.

Gauld, Charles A. *America's First General Overseas: The Story of Thomas M. Anderson.* Vancouver, WA: Fort Vancouver Historical Society, 1973.

Gordon-McCutchan, R. C., ed. *Kit Carson: Indian Fighter or Indian Killer?* Niwot: University Press of Colorado, 1996.

Gould, Lewis L. *The Spanish-American War and President McKinley.* Lawrence: University Press of Kansas, 1982.

Guild, Thelma S., and Harvey L. Carter. *Kit Carson: A Pattern for Heroes*. Lincoln: University of Nebraska Press, 1984.

Hagan, Kenneth J. *American Gunboat Diplomacy and the Old Navy, 1877–1889*. Westport, CT: Greenwood, 1973.

Hamilton, Holman. *Zachary Taylor: Soldier of the Republic*. New York: Bobbs-Merrill, 1941.

Harris, Theodore D., ed. *Black Frontiersman: The Memoirs of Henry O. Flipper, First Black Graduate of West Point*. Fort Worth: Texas Christian University Press, 1997.

Harrison, Noel Garraux. *City of Canvas: Camp Russell A. Alger and the Spanish-American War*. Falls Church, VA: Falls Church Historical Commission and Fairfax County History Commission, 1988.

Hatley, Tom. *The Dividing Paths: Cherokees and South Carolinians through the Era of Revolution*. New York: Oxford University Press, 1993.

Healy, David. *Drive to Hegemony: The United States in the Caribbean, 1898–1917*. Madison: University of Wisconsin Press, 1988.

Healy, David. *The United States in Cuba, 1898–1902: Generals, Politicians and the Search for Policy*. Madison: University of Wisconsin Press, 1963.

Healy, David. *U.S. Expansionism: The Imperialist Urge in the 1890s*. Madison: University of Wisconsin Press, 1970.

Heidler, David S., and Jeanne T. Heidler. *Old Hickory's War: Andrew Jackson and the Quest for Empire*. Mechanicsburg, PA: Stackpole, 1996.

Hendrickson, Kenneth E. *The Spanish-American War*. Westport, CT: Greenwood, 2003.

Hernández, José M. *Cuba and the United States: Intervention and Militarism, 1868–1933*. Austin: University of Texas Press, 1993.

Hilton, Sylvia L., and Steve J. S. Ickringill. *European Perceptions of the Spanish-American War of 1898*. New York: Lang, 1999.

Hirshson, Stanley P. *Grenville M. Dodge: Soldier, Politician, Railroad Pioneer*. Bloomington: Indiana University Press, 1967.

Hoagland, Alison K. *Army Architecture in the West: Forts Laramie, Bridger, and D. A. Russell, 1849–1912*. Norman: University of Oklahoma Press, 2004.

Hoganson, Kristin L. *Fighting for American Manhood: How Gender Politics Provoked the Spanish-American and Philippine-American Wars*. New Haven, CT: Yale University Press, 1998.

Hoig, Stan. *Perilous Pursuit: The U.S. Cavalry and the Northern Cheyennes*. Boulder: University Press of Colorado, 2002.

Hurt, R. Douglas. *The Indian Frontier, 1763–1846*. Albuquerque: University of New Mexico Press, 2002.

Hurtado, Albert L. *Indian Survival on the California Frontier*. New Haven, CT: Yale University Press, 1988.

Hutton, Paul Andrew, ed. *The Custer Reader*. Lincoln: University of Nebraska Press, 1992.

Iriye, Akira. *Pacific Estrangement: Japanese and American Expansion, 1897–1911*. Cambridge, MA: Harvard University Press, 1972.

Iverson, Peter. *Diné: A History of the Navajos*. Albuquerque: University of New Mexico Press, 2002.

Jamieson, Perry D. *Crossing the Deadly Ground: United States Army Tactics, 1865–1899*. Tuscaloosa: University of Alabama Press, 1994.

Jeffers, H. Paul. *Colonel Roosevelt: Theodore Roosevelt Goes to War, 1897–1898*. New York: Wiley, 1996.

Josephy, Alvin M., Jr. *The Nez Percé Indians and the Opening of the Northwest*. New Haven, CT: Yale University Press, 1965.

Kaplan, Lawrence S. *Thomas Jefferson: Westward the Course of Empire*. Wilmington, DE: Scholarly Resources, 1999.

Karamanski, Theodore J. *Fur Trade and Exploration: The Far Northwest, 1821–1852*. Norman: University of Oklahoma Press, 1983.

Karnow, Stanley. *In Our Image: America's Empire in the Philippines*. New York: Random House, 1989.

Kenner, Charles L. *Buffalo Soldiers and Officers of the Ninth Cavalry, 1867–1898: Black and White Together*. Norman: University of Oklahoma Press, 1999.

Knaut, Andrew L. *The Pueblo Revolt of 1680: Conquest and Resistance in Seventeenth-Century New Mexico*. Norman: University of Oklahoma Press, 1995.

Knetsch, Joe. *Florida's Seminole Wars, 1817–1858*. Charleston, SC: Arcadia, 2003.

Knight, Oliver. *Following the Indian Wars: The Story of the Newspaper Correspondents among the Indian Campaigners*. Norman: University of Oklahoma Press, 1960.

Bibliography

Kroeber, Clifton B., and Bernard L. Fontana. *Massacre on the Gila: An Account of the Last Major Battle between American Indians, with Reflections on the Origins of War.* Tucson: University of Arizona Press, 1986.

Kroeker, Marvin E. *Great Plains Command: William B. Hazen in the Frontier West.* Norman: University of Oklahoma Press, 1976.

Kukla, Jon. *A Wilderness So Immense: The Louisiana Purchase and the Destiny of America.* New York: Knopf, 2003.

LaFeber, Walter. *The New Empire: An Interpretation of American Expansion, 1860–1898.* Ithaca, NY: Cornell University Press, 1963.

LaFeber, Walter. *The Panama Canal: The Crisis in Historical Perspective.* New York: Oxford University Press, 1978.

Lane, Jack C. *Armed Progressive: General Leonard Wood.* San Rafael, CA: Presidio, 1978.

Langley, Lester D. *The Cuban Policy of the United States: A Brief History.* New York: Wiley, 1968.

Lansing, Ronald B. *Juggernaut: The Whitman Massacre Trial, 1850.* Los Angeles: Ninth Judicial Circuit Historical Society, 1993.

Larson, Robert W. *Red Cloud: Warrior-Statesman of the Lakota Sioux.* Norman: University of Oklahoma Press, 1997.

Laumer, Frank. *Dade's Last Command.* Gainesville: University of Florida Press, 1995.

La Vere, David. *Contrary Neighbors: Southern Plains and Removed Indians in Indian Territory.* Norman: University of Oklahoma, 2000.

Lazarus, Edward. *Black Hills/White Justice: The Sioux Nation versus the United States, 1775 to the Present.* New York: HarperCollins, 1991.

Leckie, William H. *The Buffalo Soldiers: A Narrative of the Negro Cavalry in the West.* Norman: University of Oklahoma Press, 1967.

Leckie, William H., and Shirley A. Leckie. *Unlikely Warriors: General Benjamin H. Grierson and His Family.* Norman: University of Oklahoma Press, 1984.

Leiker, James N. *Racial Borders: Black Soldiers along the Rio Grande.* College Station: Texas A&M University Press, 2002.

Lekson, Stephen H. *Nana's Raid: Apache Warfare in Southern New Mexico, 1881.* El Paso: Texas Western Press/University of Texas, 1987.

Linderman, Gerald F. *The Mirror of War: American Society and the Spanish-American War.* Ann Arbor: University of Michigan Press, 1971.

Linn, Brian McAllister. *The Philippine War, 1899–1902.* Lawrence: University Press of Kansas, 2000.

Linn, Brian McAllister. *The U.S. Army and Counterinsurgency in the Philippine War, 1899–1902.* Chapel Hill: University of North Carolina Press, 1989.

Lodge, Henry Cabot. *The War with Spain.* New York: Harper and Bros., 1899.

Lofaro, Michael A. *Daniel Boone: An American Life.* Lexington: University Press of Kentucky, 2003.

Madsen, Brigham D. *The Shoshoni Frontier and the Bear River Massacre.* Salt Lake City: University of Utah Press, 1985.

Mahon, John K. *History of the Second Seminole War, 1835–1842.* Gainesville: University of Florida Press, 1967.

Mancall, Peter C., and James H. Merrell, eds. *American Encounters: Natives and Newcomers from European Contact to Indian Removal, 1500–1850.* New York: Routledge, 1999.

Mangum, Neil C. *Battle of the Rosebud: Prelude to the Little Bighorn.* El Segundo, CA: Upton and Sons, 1987.

Marks, Frederick W., III. *Velvet on Iron: The Diplomacy of Theodore Roosevelt.* Lincoln: University of Nebraska Press, 1979.

Marolda, Edward J. *Theodore Roosevelt, the U.S. Navy, and the Spanish-American War.* New York: Palgrave, 2001.

Marquis, Thomas B. *Custer, Cavalry, and Crows.* Fort Collins, CO: Old Army Press, 1975.

Marshall, Joseph M., III. *The Journey of Crazy Horse: A Lakota History.* New York: Viking, 2004.

McCormick, Thomas J. *China Market: America's Quest for Informal Empire, 1893–1901.* Chicago: Quadrangle Books, 1967.

McDermott, John D. *Forlorn Hope: The Battle of White Bird Canyon and the Beginning of the Nez Perce War.* Boise: Idaho State Historical Society, 1978.

McGaw, William C. *Savage Scene: The Life and Times of James Kirker, Frontier King.* New York: Hastings House, 1972.

McGinnis, Anthony. *Counting Coup and Cutting Horses: Intertribal Warfare on the Northern Great Plains, 1738–1889.* Evergreen, CO: Cordillera, 1990.

McKee, Delber L. *Chinese Exclusion versus the Open Door Policy, 1900–1906: Clashes over China Policy in the Roosevelt Era.* Detroit: Wayne State University Press, 1977.

McLoughlin, William G. *After the Trail of Tears: The Cherokees' Struggle for Sovereignty, 1839–1880.* Chapel Hill: University of North Carolina Press, 1994.

McNitt, Frank. *Navajo Wars: Military Campaigns, Slave Raids, and Reprisals.* Albuquerque: University of New Mexico Press, 1972.

McPherson, Robert S. *The Northern Navajo Frontier, 1860–1900: Expansion through Adversity.* Albuquerque: University of New Mexico Press, 1988.

Meadows, William C. *Kiowa, Apache, and Comanche Military Societies: Enduring Veterans, 1800 to the Present.* Austin: University of Texas Press, 1999.

Merrell, James H. *The Indians' New World: Catawbas and Their Neighbors from European Contact through the Era of Removal.* Chapel Hill: University of North Carolina Press, 1989.

Milanich, Jerald T. *Florida Indians and the Invasion from Europe.* Gainesville: University Press of Florida, 1995.

Miller, Richard H. *American Imperialism in 1898: The Quest for National Fulfillment.* New York: Wiley, 1970.

Miller, Stuart Creighton. *"Benevolent Assimilation": The American Conquest of the Philippines, 1899–1903.* New Haven, CT: Yale University Press, 1982.

Millis, Walter. *The Martial Spirit: A Study of Our War with Spain.* New York: Houghton Mifflin, 1931.

Montoya, María E. *Translating Property: The Maxwell Land Grant and the Conflict over Land in the American West, 1840–1900.* Berkeley: University of California Press, 2002.

Moore, William Haas. *Chiefs, Agents, and Soldiers: Conflict on the Navajo Frontier, 1868–1882.* Albuquerque: University of New Mexico Press, 1994.

Morgan, H. Wayne. *America's Road to Empire: The War with Spain and Overseas Expansion.* New York: Wiley, 1965.

Morris, Edmund. *The Rise of Theodore Roosevelt.* New York: Coward, McCann, and Geoghegan, 1979.

Morris, Edmund. *Theodore Rex.* New York: Random House, 2001.

Musicant, Ivan. *The Banana Wars: A History of United States Military Intervention in Latin America from the Spanish-American War to the Invasion of Panama.* New York: Macmillan, 1990.

Musicant, Ivan. *Empire by Default: The Spanish-American War and the Dawn of the American Century.* New York: Henry Holt, 1998.

Nester, William R. *The Arikara War: The First Plains Indian War, 1823.* Missoula, MT: Mountain Press, 2001.

Nichols, Roger L. *Black Hawk: A Biography.* Wheeling, IL: Harland Davidson, 2000.

Nichols, Roger L. *Black Hawk and the Warrior's Path.* Arlington Heights, IL: Harland Davidson, 1992.

Nichols, Roger L. *General Henry Atkinson: A Western Military Career.* Norman: University of Oklahoma Press, 1965.

Nichols, Ronald H. *In Custer's Shadow: Major Marcus Reno.* Norman: University of Oklahoma Press, 2000.

Nish, Ian. *The Origins of the Russo-Japanese War.* Edited by Harry Hearder. London: Longman, 1985.

O'Donnell, Terence. *An Arrow in the Earth: General Joel Palmer and the Indians of Oregon.* Portland: Oregon Historical Society Press, 1991.

Offner, John L. *An Unwanted War: The Diplomacy of the United States and Spain over Cuba, 1895–1898.* Chapel Hill: University of North Carolina Press, 1992.

Oliva, Leo E. *Soldiers on the Santa Fe Trail.* Norman: University of Oklahoma Press, 1967.

Ostler, Jeffrey. *The Plains Sioux and U.S. Colonialism from Lewis and Clark to Wounded Knee.* New York: Cambridge University Press, 2004.

O'Toole, G. J. A. *The Spanish War: An American Epic, 1898.* New York: Norton, 1984.

Padelford, Norman J. *The Panama Canal in Peace and War.* New York: Macmillan, 1942.

Parker, Arthur Caswell. *Red Jacket: Seneca Chief.* Lincoln: University of Nebraska Press, 1998.

Patrick, Rembert W. *Aristocrat in Uniform: General Duncan L. Clinch.* Gainesville: University of Florida Press, 1963.

Paul, R. Eli. *Blue Water Creek and the First Sioux War, 1854–1856.* Norman: University of Oklahoma Press, 2004.

Paul, R. Eli, ed. *Autobiography of Red Cloud: War Leader of the Oglalas.* Helena: Montana Historical Society Press, 1997.

Bibliography

Pérez, Louis A., Jr. *Cuba between Empires, 1878–1902.* Pittsburgh: University of Pittsburgh Press, 1983.

Pérez, Louis A., Jr. *The War of 1898: The United States and Cuba in History and Historiography.* Chapel Hill: University of North Carolina Press, 1998.

Perkins, Dexter. *The Monroe Doctrine, 1867–1907.* Baltimore: Johns Hopkins University Press, 1937.

Peterson, John Alton. *Utah's Black Hawk War.* Salt Lake City: University of Utah Press, 1998.

Pierce, John R., and Jim Writer. *Yellow Jack: How Yellow Fever Ravaged America and Walter Reed Discovered Its Deadly Secrets.* Hoboken, NJ: Wiley, 2005.

Pratt, Julius W. *America's Colonial Experiment: How the United States Gained, Governed, and in Part Gave Away a Colonial Empire.* New York: Prentice Hall, 1950.

Pratt, Julius W. *Expansionists of 1898: The Acquisition of Hawaii and the Spanish Islands.* Baltimore: Johns Hopkins University Press, 1936.

Prucha, Francis Paul. *American Indian Policy in the Formative Years: The Indian Trade and Intercourse Acts, 1790–1834.* Cambridge, MA: Harvard University Press, 1962.

Prucha, Francis Paul. *American Indian Treaties: The History of a Political Anomaly.* Berkeley: University of California Press, 1994.

Prucha, Francis Paul. *The Great Father: The United States Government and the American Indians.* 2 vols. Lincoln: University of Nebraska Press, 1984.

Prucha, Francis Paul. *The Sword of the Republic: The United States Army on the Frontier, 1783–1846.* Toronto: Macmillan, 1969.

Rankin, Charles E., ed. *Legacy: New Perspectives on the Battle of the Little Bighorn.* Helena: Montana Historical Society Press, 1996.

Reeves, Carolyn Keller, ed. *The Choctaw before Removal.* Jackson: University Press of Mississippi, 1985.

Remini, Robert V. *Andrew Jackson and His Indian Wars.* New York: Penguin, 2001.

Remini, Robert V. *Andrew Jackson and the Course of American Empire, 1767–1821.* New York: Harper and Row, 1977.

Remini, Robert V. *The Legacy of Andrew Jackson: Essays on Democracy, Indian Removal, and Slavery.* Baton Rouge: Louisiana State University Press, 1988.

Rickover, Hyman G. *How the Battleship* Maine *Was Destroyed.* Washington, DC: Naval History Division, 1976.

Robertson, R. G. *Rotting Face: Smallpox and the American Indian.* Caldwell, ID: Caxton, 2001.

Robinson, Charles M., III. *Bad Hand: A Biography of General Ranald S. Mackenzie.* Austin, TX: State House Press, 1993.

Robinson, Charles M., III. *General Crook and the Western Frontier.* Norman: University of Oklahoma Press, 2001.

Robinson, Charles M., III. *A Good Year to Die: The Story of the Great Sioux War.* New York: Random House, 1995.

Robinson, Charles M., III. *Satanta: The Life and Death of a War Chief.* Austin, TX: State House Press, 1997.

Rogin, Michael Paul. *Fathers and Children: Andrew Jackson and the Subjugation of the American Indian.* New York: Knopf, 1975.

Roosevelt, Theodore. *The Rough Riders.* New York: Scribner, 1899.

Rosebush, Waldo E. *Frontier Steel: The Men and Their Weapons.* Appleton, WI: C. C. Nelson, 1958.

Russell, Carl P. *Guns on the Early Frontiers: A History of Firearms from Colonial Times through the Years of the Western Fur Trade.* Berkeley: University of California Press, 1957.

Russell, Don. *The Lives and Legends of Buffalo Bill.* Norman: University of Oklahoma Press, 1960.

Ruth, Kent. *Great Day in the West: Forts, Posts, and Rendezvous beyond the Mississippi.* Norman: University of Oklahoma Press, 1963.

Ryden, George Herbert. *The Foreign Policy of the United States in Relation to Samoa.* New Haven, CT: Yale University Press, 1933.

Sajna, Mike. *Crazy Horse: The Life behind the Legend.* New York: Wiley, 2000.

Samek, Hana. *The Blackfoot Confederacy, 1880–1920: A Comparative Study of Canadian and U.S. Indian Policy.* Albuquerque: University of New Mexico Press, 1987.

Samuels, Peggy, and Harold Samuels. *Remembering the* Maine. Washington, DC: Smithsonian Institution Press, 1995.

Samuels, Peggy, and Harold Samuels. *Frederic Remington: A Biography.* Garden City, NY: Doubleday, 1982.

Samuels, Peggy, and Harold Samuels. *Teddy Roosevelt at San Juan: The Making of a President.* College Station: Texas A&M University Press, 1997.

Saulo, Alfredo B. *Emilio Aguinaldo: Generalissimo and President of the First Philippine Republic—First Republic in Asia.* Quezon City, Philippines: Phoenix Publishing House, 1983.

Saunt, Claudio. *A New Order of Things: Property, Power, and the Transformation of the Creek Indians, 1733–1816.* New York: Cambridge University Press, 1999.

Schirmer, Daniel B. *Republic or Empire: American Resistance to the Philippine War.* Cambridge, MA: Schenkman, 1972.

Schoonover, Thomas D., and Walter Lafeber. *Uncle Sam's War of 1898 and the Origins of Globalization.* Lexington: University Press of Kentucky, 2003.

Schwartz, E. A. *The Rogue River Indian War and Its Aftermath, 1850–1980.* Norman: University of Oklahoma Press, 1997.

Seager, Robert, II. *Alfred Thayer Mahan: The Man and His Letters.* Annapolis, MD: Naval Institute Press, 1977.

Sexton, William T. *Soldiers in the Sun: An Adventure in Imperialism.* Harrisburg, PA: Military Service Publishing, 1939.

Shulimson, Jack. *The Marine Corps' Search for a Mission, 1880–1898.* Lawrence: University Press of Kansas, 1993.

Silver, James W. *Edmund Pendleton Gaines: Frontier General.* Baton Rouge: Louisiana State University Press, 1949.

Silver, Peter. *Our Savage Neighbors: How Indian War Transformed Early America.* New York: Norton, 2008.

Simmons, Marc. *Massacre on the Lordsburg Road: A Tragedy of the Apache Wars.* College Station: Texas A&M University Press, 1997.

Simmons, Marc, ed. *On the Santa Fe Trail.* Lawrence: University Press of Kansas, 1986.

Simmons, Virginia McConnell. *The Ute Indians of Utah, Colorado, and New Mexico.* Niwot: University Press of Colorado, 2000.

Sklenar, Larry. *To Hell with Honor: Custer and the Little Bighorn.* Norman: University of Oklahoma Press, 2000.

Smith, David Paul. *Frontier Defense in the Civil War: Texas Rangers and Rebels.* College Station: Texas A&M University Press, 1992.

Smith, Elbert B. *The Presidencies of Zachary Taylor and Millard Fillmore.* Lawrence: University Press of Kansas, 1988.

Smith, Winston O. *The Sharps Rifle: Its History, Development, and Operation.* New York: William Morrow, 1943.

Smythe, Donald. *Guerrilla Warrior: The Early Life of John J. Pershing.* New York: Scribner, 1973.

Sonnichsen, C. L., ed. *Geronimo and the End of the Apache Wars.* Lincoln: University of Nebraska Press, 1990.

Spears, John R. *Our Navy in the War with Spain.* New York: Scribner, 1899.

Spector, Ronald H. *Admiral of the New Empire: The Life and Career of George Dewey.* Baton Rouge: Louisiana State University Press, 1974.

Sprague, Marshall. *Massacre: The Tragedy at White River.* Boston: Little, Brown, 1957.

Stephanson, Anders. *Manifest Destiny: American Expansionism and the Empire of Right.* New York: Hill and Wang, 1995.

Sternlicht, Sanford V. *McKinley's Bulldog: The Battleship Oregon.* Chicago: Nelson-Hall, 1977.

Stevens, Sylvester K. *American Expansion in Hawaii, 1842–1898.* Harrisburg: Archives Publishing, 1945.

St. Germain, Jill. *Indian Treaty-Making Policy in the United States and Canada, 1867–1877.* Lincoln: University of Nebraska Press, 2001.

Stockel, Henrietta. *Survival of the Spirit: Chiricahua Apaches in Captivity.* Reno: University of Nevada Press, 1993.

Stout, Joseph A., Jr. *Apache Lightning: The Last Great Battles of the Ojo Calientes.* New York: Oxford University Press, 1974.

Sugden, John. *Blue Jacket: Warrior of the Shawnees.* Lincoln: University of Nebraska Press, 2000.

Sugden, John. *Tecumseh: A Life.* New York: Holt, 1997.

Sugden, John. *Tecumseh's Last Stand.* Norman: University of Oklahoma Press, 1985.

Sully, Langdon. *No Tears for the General: The Life of Alfred Sully, 1821–1879.* Palo Alto, CA: American West Publishing Company, 1974.

Bibliography

Sweeney, Edwin R. *Cochise: Chiricahua Apache Chief.* Norman: University of Oklahoma Press, 1991.

Sweeney, Edwin R. *Mangas Coloradas: Chief of the Chiricahua Apaches.* Norman: University of Oklahoma Press, 1998.

Tate, Michael L. *The Frontier Army in the Settlement of the West.* Norman: University of Oklahoma Press, 1999.

Taylor, Colin F. *Native American Weapons.* Norman: University of Oklahoma Press, 2001.

Thompson, Gerald. *The Army and the Navajo: The Bosque Redondo Reservation Experiment, 1863–1868.* Tucson: University of Arizona Press, 1976.

Thrapp, Daniel L. *Al Sieber: Chief of Scouts.* Norman: University of Oklahoma Press, 1964.

Thrapp, Daniel L. *The Conquest of Apacheria.* Norman: University of Oklahoma Press, 1967.

Tone, John Lawrence. *War and Genocide in Cuba, 1895–1898.* Chapel Hill: University of North Carolina Press, 2006.

Trafzer, Clifford E. *The Kit Carson Campaign: The Last Great Navajo War.* Norman: University of Oklahoma Press, 1990.

Trafzer, Clifford E., and Richard D. Scheuerman. *Renegade Tribe: The Palouse Indians and the Invasion of the Inland Pacific Northwest.* Pullman: Washington State University Press, 1986.

Trask, David. *The War with Spain in 1898.* New York: Macmillan, 1981.

Trask, Kerry A. *Black Hawk: The Battle for the Heart of America.* New York: Henry Holt, 2006.

Travis, Ira Dudley. *The History of the Clayton-Bulwer Treaty.* Ann Arbor: Michigan Political Science Association, 1900.

Traxel, David. *1898: Birth of the American Century.* New York: Knopf, 1998.

Tucker, Spencer C., ed. *Encyclopedia of the Spanish-American and Philippine-American Wars: A Political, Social, and Military History.* 3 vols. Santa Barbara, CA: ABC-CLIO, 2009.

Turk, Richard W. *The Ambiguous Relationship: Theodore Roosevelt and Alfred Thayer Mahan.* Westport, CT: Greenwood, 1987.

Turner, Frederick Jackson. *The Frontier in American History.* New York: Henry Holt, 1920.

Twichell, Heath. *Allen: The Biography of an Army Officer, 1859–1930.* New Brunswick, NJ: Rutgers University Press, 1974.

Utley, Robert M. *Custer: Cavalier in Buckskin.* Rev. ed. Norman: University of Oklahoma Press, 2001.

Utley, Robert M. *Frontier Regulars: The United States Army and the Indian, 1866–1890.* New York: Macmillan, 1973.

Utley, Robert M. *Frontiersmen in Blue: The United States Army and the Indian, 1848–1865.* New York: Macmillan, 1967.

Utley, Robert M. *The Indian Frontier of the American West, 1846–1890.* Albuquerque: University of New Mexico Press, 1984.

Utley, Robert M. *The Lance and the Shield: The Life and Times of Sitting Bull.* New York: Henry Holt, 1993.

Utley, Robert M., and Wilcomb E. Washburn. *The American Heritage History of the Indian Wars.* Edited by Anne Moffat and Richard F. Snow. New York: American Heritage, 1977.

Vorpahl, Ben Merchant. *Frederic Remington and the West: With the Eye of the Mind.* Austin: University of Texas Press, 1978.

Wallace, Anthony F. C. *The Long, Bitter Trail: Andrew Jackson and the Indians.* New York: Hill and Wang, 1993.

Wallace, Anthony F. C., with Sheila C. Steen. *The Death and Rebirth of the Seneca.* New York: Knopf, 1970.

Wallace, Edward S. *General William Jenkins Worth: Monterey's Forgotten Hero.* Dallas, TX: Southern Methodist University Press, 1953.

Warde, Mary Jane. *George Washington Grayson and the Creek Nation, 1843–1920.* Norman: University of Oklahoma Press, 1999.

Ware, Eugene F. *The Indian War of 1864.* New York: St. Martin's, 1960.

Welch, James, and Paul Stekler. *Killing Custer: The Battle of Little Bighorn and the Fate of the Plains Indians.* Baltimore: Johns Hopkins University Press, 1994.

Welch, Richard E., Jr. *Response to Imperialism: The United States and the Philippine-American War, 1899–1902.* Chapel Hill: University of North Carolina Press, 1979.

West, Richard Sedgwick, Jr. *Admirals of American Empire: The Combined Story of George Dewey, Alfred Thayer Mahan, Winfield Scott Schley, and William Thomas Sampson.* Indianapolis: Bobbs-Merrill, 1948.

Westermeier, Clifford P. *Who Rush to Glory—The Cowboy Volunteers of 1898: Grisby's Cowboys, Roosevelt's Rough Riders, Torrey's Rocky Mountain Riders.* Caldwell, ID: Caxton Printers, 1958.

Wheeler, Joseph. *The Santiago Campaign, 1898.* Philadelphia: Drexel Biddel, 1899.

Willert, James. *March of the Columns: A Chronicle of the 1876 Indian War, June 27–September 16.* El Segundo, CA: Upton and Sons, 1994.

Wooster, Robert. *The Military and United States Indian Policy, 1865–1903.* New Haven, CT: Yale University Press, 1988.

Wooster, Robert. *Nelson A. Miles and the Twilight of the Frontier Army.* Lincoln: University of Nebraska Press, 1993.

MATTHEW J. WAYMAN